T5-AAP-371

4-3 Financial resources: provided, $287,500; applied, $158,500.

4-4 *a* Current assets, $635,000; current liabilities, $814,800; retained earnings, $1,935,200.

4-5 *a* Working capital, $920,170; *c* Current ratio, 2.6 to 1.

4-6 *a* Total assets, $7,755,300; total stockholders' equity, $4,827,300.

4-7 *a* (1) Cash balance, $64,250; (3) Net income, $44,200; *b* Total assets, $397,900.

4-8 *a* Unrealized purchasing power gain, $104,000.

5-1 Present value of contract, $934,360.

5-2 (1) $9,079,924; (2) $70,670; (3) $318,895; (4) 3%.

5-3 (1) $5,035; (2) $45,929; (3) $2,056; (4) 1¾%.

5-4 *a* (1) $140,000; (2) $25,619.

5-5 (1) Debit to Accounts Receivable, $25,162; (2) Bonus expense, $32,738; (3) $3,884; (4) 3%.

5-6 (1) 12.6%; (2) $92,278; (3) $46,725; (4) $22,859.

5-7 *a* (1) $10,000; (2) $34,091.

5-8 (1) $62,092; (2) $614,457.

5-9 *a* $26,076; *b* 8%; *c* $24,489.

5-10 *a* $20,000; *b* $10,000; *c* $50,000.

6-1 *a* Cost, $625,000; market value, $708,000; *c* Dividends revenue, $5,400; realized gain, $4,000.

6-2 *a* Correct cash balance, $64,430.58.

6-3 *b* Carrying amount of securities at end of: Year 2, $205,000; Year 3, $125,000; Year 5, $310,000.

6-5 *a* Correct cash balance, $5,373.31.

6-6 *b* Short-term investments (at cost), $143,175; accrued interest receivable, $2,179.

6-7 *a* Correct cash balance, $20,700.

6-8 *a* Correct cash balance, $93,562.59.

6-9 *b* Carrying amount of securities at end of: Year 4, $245,000; Year 7, $207,000.

6-10 *a* Correct cash balance, $281,173.

7-2 *a* Gain on disposal of land, $60,478; *b* Installment notes receivable (net), $240,183.

7-3 *b* Net sales, $749,670; net notes and accounts receivable, $253,000.

7-4 (2) Loss on sale of accounts receivable, $26,000.

7-5 *a* Debit RE, $20,000; *b* Balance of allowance on Dec. 31, Year 5, $24,820.

7-6 Reduce allowance by $2,730.

7-7 (2) Debit gain on disposal of land, $11,529.

7-8 *b* Net accounts receivable, $307,392.

7-9 *b* Required increase in allowance, $12,350.

7-10 *b* Net income for Year 5 on accrual basis of accounting, $52,650.

7-11 *a* Net loss, $6,350; *b* Total assets, $830,350.

7-12 *b* Equity in assigned accounts receivable on May 31, $58,200.

7-13 *a* Cost of goods sold percentage, 65%; gross profit on sales for Year 4, $46,935; *b* Debit Doubtful Accounts Expense, $6,980; *c* 2%.

8-1 *a* $18,000; *b* $15,200; *c* $16,560.

8-2 Inventory, $974,700; accounts payable (net), $616,700; sales, $8,240,000.

8-3 Cost of goods sold: (1) $5,112; (2) $4,622; (3) $4,876.80.

8-4 Inventory, June 30, Year 5: Material J, $27,705; Material K, $100,249.

8-5 *a* Inventory, March 31: (1) $72,000; (2) $42,000; *b* Gross profit on sales for March: (1) $75,500; (2) $66,500.

8-6 *b* Inventory valuation, $45,660.

8-7 Dollar-value lifo inventories: Year 4, $255,500; Year 6, $315,500.

8-8 *a* (1) $8,817; (2) $8,976; (3) $8,992.

8-9 *a* Dollar-value lifo inventories at end of: Year 3, $152,950; Year 5, $108,125.

8-10 *a* Corrected income before income taxes: Year 2, $135,860; Year 3, $110,440; Year 4, $126,300.

8-11 *a* Cost of goods sold during second year: (1) $129,750; (2) $143,750.

8-12 *a* Ending inventories: (1) $6,000; (2) $5,600; (3) $5,870 *b* Ending inventories: (1) $6,000; (2) $4,800; (3) $5,448.

8-13 *a* Inventory cost, $80,635; *b* Net income, $70,200; *c* Total assets, $519,500.

8-14 *a* Index: Year 2, 110%; Year 3, 120%; Year 4, 125%; *b* Dollar-value lifo inventories: Year 3, $100,500; Year 4, $77,200.

9-1 *a* (1) None; (2) Billings in excess of costs, $550,000; *b* (1) $250,000; (2) Billings in excess of costs, $300,000.

9-2 *a* $39,208; *b* $190,000.

9-3 *a* $57,984; *b* $54,220.

9-4 *a* $20,400.

9-5 *a* $37,300; *b* Net income for Sept., $39,360.

9-6 Fire loss, $115,500.

9-7 *a* Fire loss, $194,160; *b* $38,500; *c* Gross profit realized in Year 12, $39,800.

9-8 *a* $87,000; *b* $80,925.

9-9 Fire loss, $52,750.

9-10 Loss before income taxes, $57,500.

9-11 *a* (2) Gross profit realized, $113,375; *b* (1) $34,000; (2) $82,000; *c* (1) $145,375.

9-12 *b* Realized gross profit in Year 2, $47,900; *c* Deferred income taxes payable, $5,280.

10-1 *a* $49,500; *b* $45,000; *c* $19,038.

10-2 *a* Federal income tax, $150,000; state income tax, $25,000.

10-3 *a* Cost of machine, $18,453; *c* Carrying amount of note payable, $13,929.

10-4 *b* Promotional expense, $68,200.

Continued on inside back cover

INTERMEDIATE
ACCOUNTING

495 3881

INTERMEDIATE ACCOUNTING

Fifth Edition

A. N. MOSICH, Ph.D., C.P.A.
William C. Hallett Professor of Accounting
University of Southern California

E. JOHN LARSEN, D.B.A., C.P.A.
Associate Professor of Accounting
University of Southern California

McGRAW-HILL BOOK COMPANY

New York | St. Louis | San Francisco | Auckland | Bogotá | Hamburg
Johannesburg | London | Madrid | Mexico | Montreal | New Delhi
Panama | Paris | São Paulo | Singapore | Sydney | Tokyo | Toronto

INTERMEDIATE ACCOUNTING

 234567890 DODO 898765432

ISBN 0-07-041580-3

This book was set in Helvetica by Progressive Typographers.
The editors were Donald G. Mason, Barbara Brooks, and Peggy Rehberger;
the designer was Nicholas Krenitsky;
the cover photographs were taken by De Marco/Tamaccio;
the production supervisor was Phil Galea.
R. R. Donnelley & Sons Company was printer and binder.

Library of Congress Cataloging in Publication Data

Mosich, A. N.
   Intermediate accounting.

   Fourth ed. by Walter B. Meigs, A. N. Mosich, Charles E.
Johnson, c1978.
   Includes index.
   1. Accounting. I. Larsen, E. John. II. Meigs,
Walter B. Intermediate accounting. III. Title.
HF5635.M8754 1982   657'.044   81-8351
ISBN 0-07-041580-3   AACR2

CONTENTS

V

PART TWO WORKING CAPITAL

PART LONG-TERM
THREE ASSETS AND LIABILITIES

PART FOUR STOCKHOLDERS' EQUITY

PART FIVE MORE COMPLEX ACCOUNTING TOPICS

accounting guidelines for pension plans. AICPA and FASB pronouncements on pension plans. Minimum-maximum range for pension cost. Accounting for the cost of a pension plan illustrated. Actuarial cost methods. Actuarial gains and losses. The Employee Retirement Income Security Act of 1974 (ERISA). Disclosure of pension plans in financial statements. Deferred compensation contracts. Future outlook for pension accounting.

PREFACE

This fifth edition of **Intermediate Accounting** is designed for use in an intermediate-level financial accounting course following the introductory-level financial accounting course. The book may be used in a two-semester or a three-quarter course, or in a single course at the graduate level. The emphasis throughout is on accounting theory and concepts and on analysis of the problems that arise in the application of these underlying concepts to financial accounting. Particular attention is given to the use of accounting information as a basis for decisions by management, stockholders, creditors, and other users of financial statements.

The fifth edition reflects the dramatic changes that have been occurring in the development and application of accounting principles, with special attention to the official pronouncements and the exposure drafts of the Financial Accounting Standards Board (FASB) and the Securities and Exchange Commission (SEC). We have prepared the fifth edition of **Intermediate Accounting** as a companion volume for **Modern Advanced Accounting** (by the same author team), thus creating the only coordinated series for the important intermediate-advanced sequence of courses and providing the foundation for a truly professionally oriented education for accountants.

New features of this edition

Every chapter has been updated to include relevant pronouncements by accounting rule-making bodies. For example, the efforts of the FASB in the development of the Conceptual Framework of Accounting and **FASB Statement No. 33,** "Financial Reporting and Changing Prices," have been incorporated in this new edition. A discussion of the economic consequences of new accounting principles has been added, and the complex and significant topics of leasing and pension plans are covered in separate chapters in this edition. By streamlining the discussion of corporations, we were able to cover stockholders' equity and earnings per share in three chapters instead of four. This enabled us to maintain the length of this edition at 25 chapters.

Instead of developing two groups of roughly parallel problems as in previous editions, we have presented the problem material in an expanded single group. This permitted us to include a wider variety of coverage. In addition, there are more exercises, including many multiple-choice questions of the type used in recent Uniform CPA Examinations.

We have divided the new edition into six cohesive parts or learning units to give clearer focus to the subject matter and provide a psychological benefit for students by making the material appear more digestible. Finally, side captions have been added in the margins to highlight important illustrations.

Organization of subject matter

We hope that the organization of chapters into cohesive and meaningful parts or learning units will prove useful both to instructors and to students. This arrangement should facilitate the planning and presentation of the subject matter and, we hope, make it easier for students to learn and retain the concepts and procedures presented. A brief description of the contents of each of the six parts follows.

Part One: Basic Concepts and Financial Statements (Chapters 1–5). The first part deals with an overview of accounting principles and professional practice, a concise summary of the accounting process, financial statements, and the application of present and future value concepts to financial accounting measurements. Chapter 1 serves to place in perspective for the student the development and application of accounting principles. Increased emphasis is given to the objectives of financial statements, the conceptual framework project of the FASB, and the role of the SEC in stressing disclosure and in protecting investors. The review of basic data-collecting processes in Chapter 2 reinforces the student's understanding of fundamental recording, classifying, and summarizing procedures. This background leads to a consideration, in Chapters 3 and 4, of the basic assumptions and principles on which income measurement and financial position are based. The discussion in these chapters (and throughout the remainder of the book) is not limited to a description of acceptable practices. We believe it is important at this stage in accounting education to encourage students to participate in a critical evaluation of accounting principles and to make them aware of the conflicts and shortcomings that exist in the traditional structure of accounting theory. At the same time, it is important to provide students with an analytical basis for making this evaluation, to help them see that most of the controversial areas of accounting ultimately center on underlying issues to which there are no simple answers. To this end, the critical evaluation of accounting concepts is correlated with the **Statements** of the FASB, the **Opinions** and **Statements** of the APB, and the **Accounting Series Releases** of the SEC.

The first four chapters of the book constitute an overview of the entire accounting process and are designed to provide a gradual transition from the introductory course in financial accounting to the more rigorous level of analysis in the following chapters.

Chapter 5 is devoted to present value concepts. The early introduction of this topic paves the way to using present and future value concepts for receivables and liabilities, for amortization of bond discount and premium, and for leases and pension plans.

Part Two: Working Capital (Chapters 6–10). The second part of the book addresses the accounting for cash and short-term investments, receivables, inventories, current liabilities, and contingencies. In Chapter 6, the sections on bank reconciliations and proof of cash have been modernized and the section on accounting for short-term investments has been expanded to include commercial paper and U.S. Treasury bills. In Chapter 7, the sections dealing with sales discounts, factoring and sale of accounts receivable, and notes issued for other rights or privileges have been extensively rewritten. The two chapters on inventories and the chapter on current liabilities and contingencies have been updated and made more efficient.

Part Three: Long-Term Assets and Liabilities (Chapters 11–15). This part includes the chapters on plant and intangible assets, long-term investments, and long-term debt. The chapter on long-term investments has been placed immediately before long-term debt to permit a natural transition from the accounting procedures for investors in bonds and other long-term debt instruments to the accounting procedures for issuers of long-term debt. **FASB Statement No. 34,** "Capitalization of Interest Cost," is fully discussed and illustrated, the section on impact of depreciation on rate-of-return computations (a managerial accounting topic) has been eliminated, and a new section designed to implement bond refunding decisions has been added.

Part Four: Stockholders' Equity (Chapters 16–18). The coverage of accounting topics unique to corporations has been reduced from four chapters in the previous edition to three chapters in this edition. No important topics have been eliminated, although the discussion of equity (book value) per share has been repositioned to the analysis of financial statements in Chapter 24. Recent disclosure requirements relative to redeemable preferred stock are included, the accounting for stock option plans has been extensively rewritten, and new sections dealing with stock appreciation rights and evaluation of standards for earnings per share have been added.

Part Five: More Complex Accounting Topics (Chapters 19–22). These four chapters are grouped together because they address more specialized and complex subject matter. As stated earlier, separate chapters are devoted to pension plans and lease transactions. The two new chapters include the latest pronouncements of the FASB. Accounting for income taxes has been significantly revised. The final chapter of this section, "Accounting Changes, Errors, and Statements from Incomplete Records," has been streamlined.

Part Six: Analytical Procedures and Statements (Chapters 23–25). The final section consists of three chapters that deal with special financial statements (statement of changes in financial position, constant-dollar and current-cost financial statements as required by **FASB Statement No. 33**) and the analysis and interpretation of financial statements. Special emphasis is given in this final section of the book to the impact of double-digit inflation experienced in the United States in recent years.

Features carried forward from prior editions

A continuing feature of this edition is an **Examination Questions Manual** with test material arranged chapter by chapter. This examination manual contains an abundant number of true or false and multiple-choice questions, as well as numerous short problems for each chapter. It should be a most useful source for instructors who prefer to assemble their own examinations and to emphasize certain chapters or topics.

An especially useful supplement carried forward from the prior edition is a **Study Guide** prepared by the authors and designed to help students measure their progress by immediate feedback. The **Study Guide** contains an outline of the most important points for each chapter, plus a variety of objective questions and short exercises. Answers to the questions and short exercises appear at the end of each chapter of the **Study Guide** to help students evaluate their understanding of the contents of each chapter.

Also continued from the previous edition are the following: (1) two sets of partially filled-in working papers, one set for Chapters 1 through 13 and one set for Chapters 14 through 25, (2) transparencies for problem solutions, (3) checklist of key figures for problems, and (4) an annual **FASB Update** prepared by Professor Lane G. Collins of Baylor University.

Questions, exercises, cases, and problems

An abundance of learning and assignment material is provided at the end of each chapter. This material is divided into four groups: questions, exercises, short cases for analysis and decision, and problems.

The questions are intended for use by students as a self-testing and review device to measure their comprehension of key points in each chapter. Many of the questions are provocative, which makes them suitable for written assignments and engenders lively class discussion.

Each exercise typically covers a specific point or topic and does not require extensive computations. Many instructors will wish to use the exercises to supplement problem assignments, for class discussion, and for examination purposes.

The short cases for analysis and decision require analytical reasoning but involve little or no quantitative data. In these cases, students are required to analyze business situations, to apply accounting principles, and to propose a course of action. However, they are not required to prepare lengthy working papers or otherwise to manipulate accounting data on an extensive scale. The short cases have been class-tested and are an effective means of encouraging students to take positions in the argument of controversial accounting issues. In all but the early chapters of the book, a number of the short cases for analysis have been adapted from Uniform CPA Examinations. The cases and questions are especially recommended if the instructor wishes to develop in students skill in communicating accounting concepts and in weighing the merits of opposing arguments.

Many of the problems are new, and most of the problems carried over from the preceding edition have been updated and revised. Special attention has been given to the inclusion of an adequate number of short problems in each chapter. The problems range in difficulty from easy to strong. Most of the problems in the Accounting Theory and Accounting Practice sections of recent Uniform CPA Examinations that are appropriate to intermediate accounting are included, although many have been considerably modified. In addition, several problems have been designed especially to demonstrate the concepts presented in the theoretical discussion included in the chapter. Probably no more than a third of the total case and problem material would be used in a given course; consequently, ample opportunity exists to vary problem assignments from semester to semester.

Helping students to achieve proficiency in handling professional level problems

A feature of this edition is the inclusion of a large number of short problems closely correlated with the text material. No CPA Examination problems are used in the early chapters of the book. The gradation of problems in difficulty is carefully tailored to aid the student in a smooth progression from introductory accounting to a professional level of achievement.

A Checklist of Key Figures for Problems is provided for most problems. The purpose of the checklist is to aid students in verifying problem solutions and in discovering errors. The checklist appears on the inside front and back covers of the book.

Two sets of partially filled-in working papers are available. One set is designed for problems in Chapters 1 through 13, and one set for problems in Chapter 14 through 25. Partially filled-in working papers thus are provided for all problems. On these working papers, the company names, problem numbers, numerous headings, and some preliminary data (such as trial balances) have been entered to save student time and to facilitate rapid review by the instructor. Many users of previous editions of this book have found that the use of partially filled-in working papers permits assignment of a larger variety of problems and eliminates much student frustration in deciding on a proper solution format.

Transparencies of problem solutions

Transparencies are available for most problems to be used by instructors who wish to display in a classroom complete solutions to problems. For longer more complex problems, the transparencies are considered by many instructors to be a highly effective means of showing desired organization and format of solutions.

Contributions by others

The many instructors and students who used the earlier editions of this book have contributed to the improvements in this edition. Their suggestions for modification of certain problems and expansion or contraction of certain sections of the text material have been most useful. Especially helpful was the advice received from Professors Lane G. Collins, Baylor University; Robert W. Hill, California Polytechnic University at San Luis Obispo; Jerry Arnold, Douglas A. Hester, and John Lacey of the University of Southern California; Don Tang, Portland State University; John R. Twombly, the Wharton School of the University of Pennsylvania; Steven D. Grossman, Texas A&M University; Brian O'Doherty, University of Houston; Fred W. Norwood, the University of Texas; Gregory P. Cermignano, Widener University; and John F. Logan, Thiel College.

We are especially indebted to George W. Saunders, Jr., of the University of California Berkeley, and to Mark Robert Palmer of the University of Southern California, for their careful review of the entire manuscript and to Professor Joseph F. Guy of Georgia State University and Professor Walter A. Parker of Central Connecticut State College for their thorough review of end-of-chapter problem material for accuracy and clarity.

Our sincere appreciation goes to our spouses, Dorothy Mosich and Kathleen Larsen, for their assistance in the preparation of this edition and for their understanding when writing and proofreading took priority over family obligations.

We acknowledge the permission received from the American Institute of Certified Public Accountants to quote from many of its pronouncements and to adapt materials from the Uniform CPA Examinations. All quotations and material from the Uniform CPA Examinations are copyright by the American Institute of Certified Public Accountants.

We also are grateful to the Financial Accounting Standards Board, which granted us permission to quote from FASB *Statements, Discussion Memoranda, Interpretations,* and *Exposure Drafts.* All quotations used are copyrighted by the Financial Accounting Standards Board, High Ridge Park, Stamford, Connecticut 06905, U.S.A., and are reprinted with permission. Copies of the complete documents are available from the FASB.

Our list of acknowledgments must include the three coauthors of earlier editions: Walter B. Meigs, the late Charles E. Johnson, and Thomas F. Keller. Much of their masterful interpretation of complex accounting issues survives in this edition.

A. N. Mosich
E. John Larsen

BASIC
CONCEPTS
AND
FINANCIAL
STATEMENTS

1 DEVELOPMENT OF ACCOUNTING PRINCIPLES AND PROFESSIONAL PRACTICE

THE ENVIRONMENT OF ACCOUNTING

Fair presentation of financial affairs is the essence of accounting theory and practice. With the increasing size and complexity of United States business enterprises and the increasing economic role of government, the responsibility placed on accountants is greater today than ever before. If accountants are to meet this challenge fully, they must have a logical and consistent body of accounting theory to guide them. This theoretical structure must be realistic in terms of the economic environment and must be designed to meet the needs of users of financial statements.

Financial statements prepared by accountants are vital to the successful working of our society. Economists, investors, business executives, labor leaders, bankers, and government officials all rely on these financial statements as fair and meaningful summaries of the multitude of day-to-day business transactions. In addition, these groups are making increased use of accounting information as a basis for forecasting future economic trends. Accountants are being challenged to go beyond the timely reporting and interpretation of past events and to aid in the creation of useful forecasts of future operations. Consequently, accountants and the theoretical principles they use are at the center of our financial and economic activities.

Users of accounting information

The basic assumptions that underlie current accounting practice have evolved over the years in response to the needs of various users of accounting information. The users of accounting information may be divided into two broad groups: *internal users* and *external users.*

Internal users include all the management personnel of a business enterprise who use accounting information either for planning and con-

3

operation = ...

bond

bond holder

Potential

Creditors

numerous

primarily

efficiently

goal

trolling current operations or for formulating long-range plans and making major business decisions. The term *managerial accounting* relates to internal measurements and reporting; it includes the development of detailed current information helpful to all levels of management in decision making designed to achieve the goals of the business enterprise.

External users of accounting information include stockholders, bondholders, potential investors, bankers and other creditors, financial analysts, economists, labor unions, and numerous government agencies. The field of *financial accounting* is directly related to external reporting because it provides investors and other outsiders with the financial information they need for decision making.

In this book we are primarily concerned with financial accounting; therefore, we shall concentrate on the accounting principles and reporting standards that produce timely and informative financial statements. The increasing importance of financial accounting rests upon the premise that the public has a right to know whether large business enterprises are functioning efficiently and in harmony with the broad goals of modern society.

Organizations and laws affecting financial accounting

Certain professional organizations, governmental agencies, and legislative acts have been extremely influential in shaping the development of the existing body of accounting theory. Among the most important of these have been the American Institute of Certified Public Accountants, the Financial Accounting Standards Board, the American Accounting Association, and the Securities and Exchange Commission. Other organizations and laws that have influenced the development of accounting principles are the New York Stock Exchange, the National Association of Accountants, the Financial Executives Institute, the Cost Accounting Standards Board, the Institute of Internal Auditors, the Federal Government Accountants Association, and the whole complex of federal, state, and local income tax laws.

Awareness of the roles of these institutional forces is helpful in gaining an understanding of current accounting principles and practices. Efforts to improve existing principles of accounting will have a better chance of success if they are made with full recognition of the needs and special problems of business executives, financial analysts, investors, government agencies, and others who use accounting information.

American Institute of Certified Public Accountants (AICPA) The American Institute of Certified Public Accountants is the professional organization of practicing certified public accountants. As a professional organization, the "Institute" has been vitally concerned with developing standards of professional practice for its members. The AICPA publishes the *Journal of Accountancy* monthly as a forum for practitioners. Beginning in the early 1930s, the Institute, in concert with the newly created Securities and Exchange Commission, began to develop standards of financial reporting. From 1939 to 1959, the Institute published a series of *Accounting Research Bulletins* dealing with a wide variety of accounting and reporting issues.

Accounting Principles Board (APB) In 1959 the AICPA undertook a more comprehensive program of research into the problems of financial reporting. The Accounting Principles Board was established with the responsibility of formulating financial accounting and reporting principles based on underlying research. The APB consisted of 21 (later 18) part-time members who served without pay.

The APB issued two separate series of publications. The more influential series consisted of the 31 *Opinions of the Accounting Principles Board,* issued between 1959 and 1973. Prior to 1964, pronouncements by the AICPA were not binding on practicing CPAs. However, in 1964, the Institute began requiring that departures from *APB Opinions* be disclosed either in notes to financial statements or in the audit reports of AICPA members in their capacity as independent auditors. Stated bluntly, this pronouncement meant that CPAs could not give their approval to financial statements that deviated from *APB Opinions,* unless they wanted to assume the considerable personal risk and burden of proof of defending the "unauthorized practices." Few business enterprises or auditors were anxious to assume the burden of defending financial statements that differed from *APB Opinions;* thus, this action gave a new strength and authority to Opinions of the APB. Consequently, *APB Opinions* represented authoritative support for generally accepted accounting principles.

Financial Accounting Standards Board (FASB) The Financial Accounting Standards Board was established in 1972 to develop financial accounting standards for business enterprises and nonprofit organizations. This independent body consisted of seven full-time members and a large supporting staff.

Lending support and counsel to the FASB are the Financial Accounting Foundation, which appoints members of the FASB and raises funds for its operations, the Financial Accounting Standards Advisory Council, a Screening Committee on Emerging Problems, and numerous Task Forces consisting of financial executives, accounting educators, lawyers, and CPAs.

CPAs are not the only persons concerned with financial accounting and reporting. Consequently, the articles of incorporation creating the FASB required that only four members shall be CPAs from public accounting practice; the other three members must be highly qualified in financial accounting and reporting but need not be CPAs. An individual appointed to the FASB must sever all connections with other organizations to avoid any suggestion of **conflict of interest.** Briefly stated, the public accounting profession is now engaged in a strenuous effort to improve the quality of financial accounting and reporting through an independent rule-making body that includes representatives from outside the field of public accounting.

The FASB is authorized to issue **Statements of Financial Accounting Standards** as well as **Interpretations** to guide persons and organizations in preparing and auditing financial statements. Before a formal statement is drafted, the FASB frequently issues a **Discussion Memorandum** that identifies and analyzes the issues to be considered. Public hearings then are held on the issues identified in the Discussion Memorandum. Next, an Exposure Draft of the proposed statement is circulated. These steps are designed to encourage the widest participation possible by all interested parties before a new financial accounting standard is issued. As of the middle of 1981, the FASB had issued 47 Statements. Those Statements dealing with the subject matter of Intermediate Accounting have been incorporated in this book to the maximum extent possible.

American Accounting Association (AAA)   The American Accounting Association, an organization of accounting teachers and practitioners, has played an important part in the development of accounting principles. The activities of the AAA have emphasized the development of a logical and theoretical foundation for accounting rather than the application of the theory to practical situations. The AAA encourages accounting research and continuous appraisal of accounting concepts through committee reports and the publication of a quarterly journal, **The Accounting Review.**

Securities and Exchange Commission (SEC)   The Securities and Exchange Commission was established in 1934 by Congress to regulate the sale of securities to the general public, including the securities listed on stock exchanges. The SEC has broad authority to prescribe accounting principles, forms to be filed, and information to be disclosed by business enterprises under the regulatory control of the Commission. Although the SEC has the legal authority to prescribe accounting principles, it generally has relied on the accounting profession to perform this function. However, the Commission has exerted strong influence on the development of accounting principles and reporting practices. SEC actions have included: (1) continual review (and occasional rejection) of financial statements; (2) issuance of **Regulation S-X,** which prescribes detailed accounting and financial reporting requirements; (3) publication of nearly 300 **Accounting Series Releases** (ASRs) and numerous **Staff Accounting Bulletins;** and (4) prodding the private sector (FASB and registrants) to develop or revise certain financial accounting and reporting practices.

A corporation planning to issue securities to the public must prepare a **prospectus** and have it reviewed by the Commission. This prospectus contains detailed information about the corporation's products, competition, and management, as well as financial statements. Corporations that are under the jurisdiction of the SEC must file voluminous documents, including an annual report (Form 10-K) that includes more information than does the annual report to shareholders, and a quarterly report (Form 10-Q). The financial statements included in the annual report filed with the Commission must be audited by independent CPAs; the financial information included in the quarterly reports need not be audited but must be reviewed by independent CPAs.

The primary concern of the SEC is **disclosure** of all relevant and material facts about the financial affairs of publicly owned business enterprises. In recent years, the Commission has become more active in its role as the watchdog for investors. The chief accountants of the SEC have pushed to expand the quality as well as the quantity of information disclosed to the public. The SEC has been primarily responsible for expansion of disclosure into such areas as inventory profits caused by inflation, replacement costs of inventories and plant assets, unusual risks and uncertainties, and replacements of independent auditors. Particular emphasis has been placed by the SEC on the concept of **continuous disclosure** of **relevant** information on a **timely basis** so that the information is of maximum value to investors. Accordingly, the Commission has required independent auditors to review the quarterly financial reports and also has encouraged business enterprises to issue financial forecasts. As further evidence of its deep concern with disclosure, the Commission has accepted several recommendations of an Advisory Committee on Corporate Disclosure for the improvement of the corporate disclosure system in the United States.

Cost Accounting Standards Board (CASB)   Although our interest in this book is focused on financial accounting rather than managerial or cost accounting, our listing of organizations that have contributed importantly to improved accounting practices must include the federal Cost Accounting Standards Board, which was active from 1971 to 1980. The primary goal of the CASB was to issue standards that achieve more uniformity in accounting practices among business enterprises working on government contracts and more consistency in the accounting treatment of costs incurred by these contractors. Because almost every large industrial enterprise has government contracts, the issuance of standards by the CASB had considerable impact on financial statements and measurement of contract costs.

Income Tax Laws   The enactment of the federal income tax law in 1913 and the subsequent amendments and legal interpretations comprising the present tax law have been perhaps the most important forces on the development of applied accounting procedures, as distinguished from accounting theory. As the rate of taxation has increased, managers of business enterprises have attempted to lessen the impact of the tax on the enterprises. The result has been the adoption of accounting procedures that conform to accounting principles and at the same time minimize taxable income.

The Internal Revenue Code has been developed with the interests of the federal government as its focal point, which means that Congress has been more concerned with public policy objectives than with the development of accounting theory. The acceptance of certain tax regulations as the basis for accounting has resulted in the adoption of procedures that have as their primary rationale the fact that they result in accelerating the recognition of expenses or postponing the recognition of revenue. In Chapter 21 we consider some of the reporting problems created by these differences, and throughout this book reference is made to income tax regulations and their specific impact on accounting practice. However, we must keep in mind that this book is concerned with the principles and procedures of financial accounting, not of income taxation.

Attest function of CPAs

A conflict of interest may exist between a business enterprise preparing financial statements and some of the users of those statements. For example, an enterprise applying for a loan from a bank may tend to be overly optimistic in portraying its financial position. Similarly, a corporation attempting to raise funds by issuing capital stock to the public has an incentive to overstate its reported net income. To protect the users of financial statements against a natural bias or outright misrepresentation, it is important to have independent professional accountants (auditors) examine the financial statements (and supporting evidence) prepared by the accounting staff of an enterprise. The auditors then have a basis for expressing their professional opinion on the financial statements. This **attest function** is the primary role of **certified public accountants.** To attest to financial statements means to vouch for their validity. Performance of the attest function requires the existence of an independent public accounting profession.

Because of the public interest in **audited financial statements,** each state recognizes public accounting as a profession and issues the certificate of Certified Public Accountant to those who demonstrate through written examinations and the satisfaction of educational and experience requirements their competence to enter the public accounting profession.

CONCEPTUAL FRAMEWORK
FOR FINANCIAL ACCOUNTING AND REPORTING

One of the initial projects of the FASB was a study designed to identify the "broad qualitative standards for financial reporting." After extensive work on the project, the Board decided to expand the scope of the project to include the entire conceptual framework of financial accounting and reporting, including objectives, qualitative characteristics, and the needs of users of accounting information. The diagram below depicts the elements of a conceptual framework for financial accounting and reporting.[1]

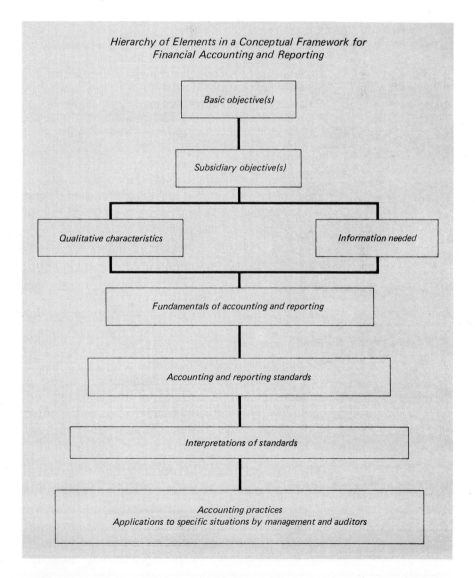

Hierarchy of Elements in a Conceptual Framework for
Financial Accounting and Reporting

Basic objective(s)

Subsidiary objective(s)

Qualitative characteristics

Information needed

Fundamentals of accounting and reporting

Accounting and reporting standards

Interpretations of standards

Accounting practices
Applications to specific situations by management and auditors

[1] *FASB Discussion Memorandum,* "Conceptual Framework for Accounting and Reporting," FASB (Stamford: 1974), p. 15.

The **fundamentals of accounting and reporting** are the basic concepts underlying the measurement and disclosure of business transactions and events. For example, fundamentals might include the definitions of an accounting entity, assets, liabilities, net income, revenue, and expenses. **Accounting and reporting standards** represent general solutions to financial accounting problems, and **interpretations** clarify the accounting and reporting standards as an aid to their application in accounting practices. **Accounting practices** are the means used by managements and independent auditors to achieve the objectives of financial statements and financial reporting.

The expanded conceptual framework project undertaken by the FASB has resulted in the publication of the following relating to business enterprises:

Statement of Financial Accounting Concepts No. 1, "Objectives of Financial Reporting by Business Enterprises"

Statement of Financial Accounting Concepts No. 2, "Qualitative Characteristics of Accounting Information"

Statement of Financial Accounting Concepts No. 3, "Elements of Financial Statements of Business Enterprises"

Other components of the conceptual framework project include the following:

Elements of financial statements and their measurement

Accounting recognition criteria for elements of financial statements

Reporting earnings

Reporting funds flows, liquidity, and financial flexibility

Financial statements and other means of financial reporting

It is expected that **Statements of Financial Accounting Concepts** eventually will be issued on all eight components of the conceptual framework project. **Statements of Financial Accounting Concepts,** unlike **Statements of Financial Accounting Standards,** do not establish generally accepted accounting principles. Instead, they establish the objectives and concepts that the FASB will use to establish financial accounting and reporting standards.

A diagram of the eight components of the conceptual framework project appears on page 11. In the following sections we consider the objectives, qualitative characteristics, and elements components of the conceptual framework project applicable to business enterprises.

Objectives of financial reporting and financial statements

The objectives of financial reporting and financial statements are derived from the needs of the external users of accounting information. Financial statements intended to serve all external users often are called **general-purpose financial statements.** Stating the objectives of financial statements would be simpler if all external users had the same

**Components of FASB
conceptual framework
project**

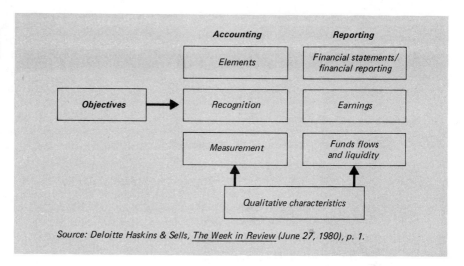

Source: Deloitte Haskins & Sells, The Week in Review (June 27, 1980), p. 1.

needs and interests, but they do not. For example, a banker considering the granting of a 90-day loan is primarily interested in the short-run debt-paying ability of the business enterprise, whereas the long-term investor in common stocks is more concerned with earning capacity, potential growth in earnings per share, and the ability of the enterprise to survive as a going concern.

Because general-purpose financial statements serve a variety of users, the needs of some users receive more emphasis than the needs of others. In present-day practice the needs of the potential investor or creditor are subordinated to those who have already committed resources to the enterprise. This emphasis leads management of the enterprise to stress the uses made of the resources entrusted to it. A deep concern over reporting on management's role as custodian of resources may be one reason for the adherence to historical cost despite substantial changes in the general price level in recent years. This tradition may also explain, in part, the omission from the financial statements of **social costs,** which may be increasingly important to a society becoming more aware of the need for preserving the quality of its environment.

In recent years the environment in which business enterprises operate has been changing at a rapid pace. Changes in the economic, political, and social structure of society cause changes in the informational needs of users of financial statements. Higher standards of measurement and reporting, along with a significant expansion of the amount of information disclosed, have been foremost among the new needs of users of financial statements.

The FASB issued **Statement of Financial Accounting Concepts No. 1,** "Objectives of Financial Reporting by Business Enterprises," to establish the objectives of general-purpose external financial reporting by business enterprises.[2] The objectives established by the FASB were as follows:[3]

1 Financial reporting should provide information that is useful to present and potential investors and creditors and other users in making rational investment, credit, and similar decisions. The information should be comprehensible to those who have a reasonable understanding of business and economic activities and are willing to study the information with reasonable diligence.

2 Financial reporting should provide information to help present and potential investors and creditors and other users in assessing the amounts, timing, and uncertainty of prospective cash receipts from dividends or interest and the proceeds from the sale, redemption, or maturity of securities or loans. The prospects for those cash receipts are affected by an enterprise's ability to generate enough cash to meet its obligations when due and its other cash operating needs, to reinvest in operations, and to pay cash dividends and may also be affected by perceptions of investors and creditors generally about that ability, which affect market prices of the enterprise's securities. . . .

3 Financial reporting should provide information about the economic resources of an enterprise, the claims to those resources, . . . and the effects of transactions, events, and circumstances that change resources and claims to those resources.

4 Financial reporting should provide information about an enterprise's financial performance during a period. Investors and creditors often use information about the past to help in assessing the prospects of an enterprise. . . .

5 The primary focus of financial reporting is information about an enterprise's performance provided by measures of earnings and its components.

6 Financial reporting should provide information about how an enterprise obtains and spends cash, about its borrowing and repayment of borrowing, about its capital transactions, including cash dividends and other distributions of enterprise resources to owners, and about other factors that may affect an enterprise's liquidity or solvency.

7 Financial reporting should provide information about how management of an enterprise has discharged its stewardship responsibility to owners (stockholders) for the use of enterprise resources entrusted to it.

8 Financial reporting should provide information that is useful to managers and directors in making decisions. . . .

Summarizing, the FASB identified eight objectives of financial reporting, all of which focused on providing information needed by current and prospective investors and creditors of a business enterprise in their decision making. The primary emphasis was placed on information regarding the enterprise's earnings.

Qualitative characteristics

The FASB issued **Statement of Financial Accounting Concepts No. 2,** "Qualitative Characteristics of Accounting Information," to examine the

[2] Statement of Financial Accounting Concepts No. 1, "Objectives of Financial Reporting by Business Enterprises," FASB (Stamford: 1978), p. 1.
[3] Statement of Financial Accounting Concepts No. 2, "Qualitative Characteristics of Accounting Information," FASB (Stamford: 1980), pp. 9–10.

characteristics of accounting information that make it useful.[4] Thus, the FASB identified **usefulness for decision making** as the most important qualitative characteristic of accounting information.[5] The Board summarized the qualitative characteristics in the diagram below.[6] The diagram identifies **relevance** and **reliability** as the two primary qualities of useful accounting information, with related ingredients of each primary quality also set forth. **Comparability** (including **consistency**) and **neutrality** are identified as secondary qualities of useful accounting information, and the concepts of **cost-benefit considerations** and **materiality** are recognized as constraints. In the following pages, we discuss the qualities set forth in this diagram.

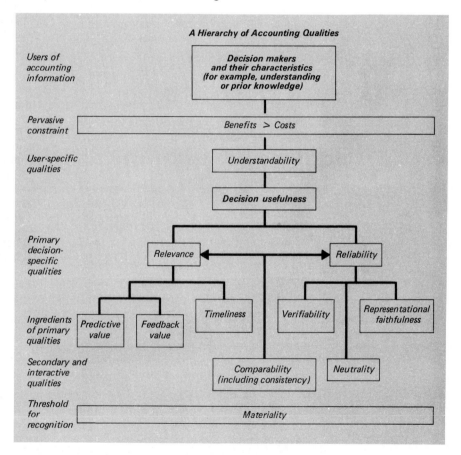

Relevance Relevant accounting information can make a difference in a decision by helping investors, creditors, and other users to evaluate past, present, and future events (**predictive value**) or to confirm or cor-

[4] Ibid., p. 1.
[5] Ibid., pp. 13–14.
[6] Ibid., p. 15.

rect expectations (*feedback value*).[7] For example, information concerning past dividends declared by a corporation enables investors to predict the prospects of dividends in future years. Information on net income of a business enterprise for the first three quarters of its fiscal year enables investors to evaluate a prior estimate of the enterprise's net income for the entire fiscal year.

Accounting information cannot be relevant unless it is *timely,* that is, unless it is available to a decision maker before it becomes too dated to influence the decision.[8] The availability of electronic computers has enabled accountants to make great strides in providing timely information to decision makers.

Reliability Accounting information is reliable if it is reasonably free from error and bias and faithfully represents what it purports to present.[9] To be reliable, information must be *verifiable* and must have *representational faithfulness,* or *validity.*[10] Supporting documents showing the details of "arm's-length" completed transactions provide clear evidence that can be verified. To *verify* means to prove something to be true by examination of evidence of underlying facts. If accounting information is free from bias on the part of the preparer, the same conclusions would be reached by different accountants working independently and following the same measurement techniques. In most cases, actual costs provide the most objective data capable of being independently verified.

However, financial statements are not completely factual; *estimates* on such matters as the economic life of plant assets, the net realizable value of inventories, and the collectibility of accounts receivable are inherent in the accounting process. The reliability quality calls for accountants to adhere as closely as possible to objectively verifiable evidence. The alternative approach would be to establish accounting values through unrestricted use of appraisal reports, estimates of future events, and expressions of opinion. Such an approach to accounting, although often helpful in providing more relevant data, makes it more difficult for CPAs to perform independent verifications of financial statements. Today, accountants recognize that a trade-off exists between *relevance* and *reliability* of data used in the preparation of financial statements. In recent years, the SEC consistently has favored relevance as the more useful criterion. For example, the SEC has encouraged the issuance of financial forecasts and has required the disclosure of replacement cost data (both based on estimates), on the grounds that such information is useful to investors in making decisions to buy, sell, or hold corporate securities.

[7] Ibid., pp. xv, xvi.
[8] Ibid., p. 25.
[9] Ibid., p. xvi.
[10] Ibid., p. 26.

Conservatism Although not a qualitative characteristic of accounting information, conservatism is a concept that may be discussed in connection with reliability. Many accounting determinations do not have a single "correct answer"; a choice must be made among alternative assumptions under conditions of uncertainty. The concept of **conservatism** holds that when reasonable support exists for alternative accounting methods and for different measurement techniques, accountants should select the method or technique with the least favorable effect on net income and financial position in the current accounting period.

Conservatism generally is regarded as a powerful influence stressing caution against the danger of overstating earnings or financial position. However, many business enterprises are not in favor of conservative accounting policies. Enterprises planning to issue securities to the public naturally try to project an image of superior management and rising earnings. An enterprise that reports higher earnings year after year gains the reputation of being a "growth company"; financial analysts refer to its common stock as a "glamor issue"; and the market price of its common stock often rises to a high multiple of earnings per share. Once such a reputation is established, an enterprise finds it easier to raise needed capital through the issuance of additional securities or through bank loans. Attracting management talent also is easier. Executive compensation tends to rise, both in salaries and through stock option and pension plans. All these pleasant consequences of a reputation for rising earnings give enterprise management a powerful incentive to choose accounting policies that **maximize** current income.

On the other hand, enterprises must be alert to the possible adverse consequences of following unconservative accounting policies. The issue we are raising relates to the **quality of reported earnings.** The earnings of an enterprise using unconservative accounting policies are viewed as being of lower quality, and its common stock will tend to sell at a low price-earnings ratio. Small business enterprises that do not seek capital from the public and do not report their earnings to anyone other than income tax authorities have an incentive to choose acceptable accounting policies that hold income to the lowest level that can be justified.

Ideally, accountants should make estimates and select accounting policies which **neither overstate nor understate** the current income and financial position of a business enterprise. The concept of conservatism should not be distorted to the point of deliberate understatement; however, the judicious use of conservatism in accounting may help to prevent the catastrophes which have befallen many investors and employees when enterprises with excessively optimistic accounting policies suddenly reached the limit of credibility and collapsed.

Comparability and Consistency Comparability of the financial statements of a business enterprise from one accounting period to the next is essential if favorable and unfavorable trends in the enterprise are to be identified. If the financial statements for the current accounting period show larger earnings than for the preceding period, the user assumes that operations have been more profitable. However, if a material change in an accounting principle has occurred, the reported increase in earnings **could** have been caused solely by the accounting change, rather than by any improvement in the underlying business activity. Consistent application of accounting principles for a business enterprise from one accounting period to the next is needed in order that the financial statements of successive periods will be comparable.

The consistency principle does not mean that a particular method of accounting once adopted cannot be changed. Accounting principles and methods change in response to changes in the environment of accounting. When an accounting change is desirable, it should be made, **together with disclosure** of the change and its effect in dollar amounts on the reported net income of the accounting period in which the change is made. **APB Opinion No. 20,** "Accounting Changes," stated that:[11]

> The presumption that an entity should not change an accounting principle may be overcome only if the enterprise justifies the use of an alternative acceptable accounting principle on the basis that it is preferable. . . .
> The nature of and justification for a change in accounting principle and its effect on income should be disclosed. . . . The justification for the change should explain why the newly adopted accounting principle is preferable.

Comparability among financial statements of business enterprises in the same industry also is a useful quality. However, differences in the operating policies and procedures among such enterprises result in the adoption of various accounting practices in such areas as valuation of inventories and depreciation of plant assets. Thus, comparability of financial statements of enterprises in the same industry is difficult to achieve.

Neutrality The FASB defined the quality of **neutrality** as the absence in reported information of bias intended to attain a predetermined result or to induce a particular mode of behavior.[12] Because of the many users of general-purpose financial statements, freedom from bias is essential. For example, financial statements designed solely to influence the actions of investors could be damaging to the needs of creditors, another major user group for financial statements.

Cost-Benefit Considerations In recent years, the demands of many users of financial statements and other financial information have appeared insatiable to accountants. There has been an explosive growth in the amount of information disclosed in the annual reports of business en-

---

[11] *APB Opinion No. 20,* "Accounting Changes," AICPA (New York: 1971), p. 391.
[12] *Statement of Financial Accounting Concepts No. 2,* p. xvi.

terprises, and the cost of producing such information is high. The FASB recognized the impact of cost-benefit considerations as follows:[13]

> Before a decision is made to develop a standard, the Board needs to satisfy itself that the matter to be ruled on represents a significant problem and that a standard that is promulgated will not impose costs on the many for the benefit of a few. If the proposal passes that first test, a second test may subsequently be useful. There are usually alternative ways of handling an issue. Is one of them less costly and only slightly less effective? Even if absolute magnitudes cannot be attached to costs and benefits, a comparison between alternatives may yet be possible and useful.

Materiality Disclosure is necessary in financial statements only for *material* matters. The meaning of materiality in an accounting context is a state of *relative importance.* Items that are trifling in amount need not be treated in strict accordance with accounting theory but rather should be handled in the most economical manner. For example, most business enterprises establish a minimum dollar amount in considering whether an expenditure should be recorded as a depreciable asset. In theory, the cost of a new pencil sharpener should be capitalized and depreciated over its economic life. As a practical matter, the expense of making such allocations of cost would exceed the cost of the pencil sharpener and would represent an unjustifiably wasteful accounting policy.

That which is material for one business enterprise may not be for another. For a small enterprise, an uninsured loss, say $50,000, might be considered as material; for a large enterprise it would not be material. In deciding upon the materiality of an item in terms of financial statement disclosure, accountants should consider whether knowledge of the item would be likely to influence the decisions of users of financial statements.

Qualitative standards should be considered in judging the materiality of an item as well as its dollar amount. For example, a transaction between a business enterprise and its president is not at arm's length and suggests a possible conflict of interest. Disclosure of the transaction is appropriate, even though disclosure of such a transaction between independent parties would not be required.

In discussing quantitative measures of materiality, the FASB made the following statement:[14]

> The Board's present position is that no general standards of materiality could be formulated to take into account all the considerations that enter into an experienced human judgment. However, that position is not intended to imply either that the Board may not in the future review that conclusion or that quantitative guidance on materiality of specific items may not appropriately be written into the Board's standards from time to time. That has been done on occasion already (for example, in the Statement on financial reporting by segments of a business enterprise), and the Board recognizes that quantitative materiality guidance is sometimes needed. . . . However, whenever the

[13] Ibid., p. 58.
[14] Ibid., p. 53.

Board or any other authoritative body imposes materiality rules, it is substituting generalized collective judgments for specific individual judgments, and there is no reason to suppose that the collective judgments are always superior.

Elements of financial statements of business enterprises

In *Statement of Financial Accounting Concepts No. 3,* "Elements of Financial Statements of Business Enterprises," the FASB identified ten interrelated elements (building blocks) of financial statements: Assets, liabilities, equity, investments by owners, distributions to owners, comprehensive income, revenues, expenses, gains, and losses. These elements were defined by the Board as follows:[15]

Assets are probable future economic benefits obtained or controlled by a particular entity as a result of past transactions or events.

Liabilities are probable future sacrifices of economic benefits arising from present obligations of a particular entity to transfer assets or provide services to other entities in the future as a result of past transactions or events.

Equity is the residual interest in the assets of an entity that remains after deducting its liabilities. In a business enterprise, the equity is the ownership interest.

Investments by owners are increases in net assets of a particular enterprise resulting from transfers to it from other entities of something of value to obtain or increase ownership interests (or equity) in it. Assets are most commonly received as investments by owners, but that which is received may also include services or satisfaction or conversion of liabilities of the enterprise.

Distributions to owners are decreases in net assets of a particular enterprise resulting from transferring assets, rendering services, or incurring liabilities by the enterprise to owners. Distributions to owners decrease ownership interests (or equity) in an enterprise.

Comprehensive income is the change in equity (net assets) of an entity during a period from transactions and other events and circumstances from nonowner sources. It includes all changes in equity during a period except those resulting from investments by owners and distributions to owners.

Revenues are inflows or other enhancements of assets of an entity or settlements of its liabilities (or a combination of both) during a period from delivering or producing goods, rendering services, or other activities that constitute the entity's ongoing major or central operations.

Expenses are outflows or other using up of assets or incurrences of liabilities (or a combination of both) during a period from delivering or producing goods, rendering services, or carrying out other activities that constitute the entity's ongoing major or central operations.

Gains are increases in equity (net assets) from peripheral or incidental transactions of an entity and from all other transactions and other events and circumstances affecting the entity during a period except those that result from revenues or investments by owners.

Losses are decreases in equity (net assets) from peripheral or incidental transactions of an entity and from all other transactions and other events and circumstances affecting the entity during a period except those that result from expenses or distributions to owners.

[15] *Statement of Financial Accounting Concepts No. 3,* "Elements of Financial Statements of Business Enterprises," FASB (Stamford: 1980), pp. xi–xii.

Except for "comprehensive income," the foregoing elements are similar to the traditional concepts of components of financial statements. The FASB deliberately used the term **comprehensive income** rather than **earnings** to broaden the scope of measurements of the operating results of business enterprises.[16]

To allay fears that the foregoing definitions of elements of financial statements might suggest a radical change in financial reporting, the FASB stated:[17]

> The Board expects most assets and liabilities in present practice to continue to qualify as assets or liabilities under the definitions in this Statement. The Board emphasizes that the definitions neither require nor presage upheavals in present practice, although they may in due time lead to some evolutionary changes in practice or at least in the ways certain items are viewed. They should be especially helpful in understanding the content of financial statements and in analyzing and resolving new financial accounting issues as they arise.

GENERALLY ACCEPTED ACCOUNTING PRINCIPLES (GAAP)

The term **generally accepted accounting principles** has long been used in accounting. This term also is used by CPAs in their audit reports to indicate whether the business enterprise being audited has prepared its financial statements in an acceptable manner, so that they may be compared with the prior year's statements and to some extent with the statements of other enterprises.

Alternative terms for **accounting principles** have included standards, practices, postulates, assumptions, basic concepts, axioms, and conventions. The variety of terms employed indicates the many efforts that have been made to formulate a conceptual framework for financial accounting and reporting. These efforts are still in process, and the goal of a concise and consistent statement of accounting principles has not yet been achieved. The principles of accounting are not rooted in the laws of nature as are the physical sciences. Therefore, **accounting principles must be developed in relation to the stated objectives of financial reporting and financial statements.**

Although a body of generally accepted accounting principles has long been recognized, no complete official list of such accounting principles exists. The most authoritative sources of generally accepted accounting principles in recent years have been the **Statements** issued by the FASB, the **Opinions** issued by the APB, the **Accounting Research Bulletins** issued by the AICPA Committee on Accounting Procedure, and **Accounting Series Releases** issued by the SEC.

In the following sections we discuss a number of fundamental accounting principles and concepts. These principles and concepts are

---

[16] Ibid., p. 28.
[17] Ibid., p. xiii.

broad in nature and have been developed by accountants in an effort to meet the needs of the users of financial statements. In later chapters we shall consider the more detailed application of these broad principles and concepts to specific accounting and reporting issues.

Business entity principle

Because economic activity is carried on by various legal and economic entities, accounting results are summarized in terms of these entities. Accountants deal primarily with three general kinds of business entities: the single proprietorship, the partnership, and the corporation. Regardless of the form of organization, the business affairs of the entity are distinguished from those of its owners. We see the effect of this principle when accounting income is measured as it accrues to the entity, not when it is distributed to owners. Similarly, an obligation of the entity to owners is treated as a liability, despite the fact that the owners owe a portion of the debt to themselves.

Accountants sometimes find it useful to prepare financial statements for economic entities that do not coincide with legal entities. For example, **consolidated financial statements** often are prepared for an economic entity that includes several corporate entities operating under common control exercised through common stock ownership. In contrast, separate financial statements may be prepared for divisions or segments of a large corporation.

Continuity or going-concern principle

The **continuity** or **going-concern principle** means that accountants assume that the business entity will continue to exist indefinitely. In deciding how to report various items in financial statements, accountants often are faced with this issue: "Shall we assume that the business enterprise (entity) will continue to operate, or shall we assume that the enterprise will be terminated in the near future?" The most probable situation for enterprises in general is that they will continue to operate for an indefinite period of time, and this general assumption is one of the most fundamental assumptions underlying financial accounting.

To illustrate the significance of the continuity principle, consider the possibility that if an enterprise ceased operations, certain liabilities would mature immediately and require a payment in excess of their carrying amount. Productive assets such as machinery may have to be sold at a substantial loss. The assumption of continued existence provides the logical basis for recording probable future economic benefits as assets and probable future outlays as liabilities.

The continuity principle implies not permanence of existence but simply that the enterprise will continue in existence long enough to carry out present plans and meet contractual commitments. This principle affects the classification of assets and liabilities in the balance sheet. Because it is assumed that assets will be used and obligations paid in the normal course of operation, no attempt is made to classify assets and liabilities in terms of their ultimate disposition or legal priority in case of liquidation.

There are times when the going-concern principle gives way to evidence that an enterprise has a limited life or intends to terminate operations. In such cases, accountants prepare financial statements under the assumption of a **quitting concern** rather than a going concern.

Monetary principle

The **monetary principle** means that accountants assume money to be a useful **standard measuring unit** for reporting the effects of business transactions. Money is used as the common denominator throughout the accounting process. Some of the information necessary to give a comprehensive picture of a business enterprise is difficult or impossible to quantify and express in money or other units of measurement. Examples are the competence, health, and morale of management and employees, and the effect of the operations of the enterprise on the natural environment. However, if information is to be included in financial statements, it must be expressed in monetary terms. If such measurement is not practicable, a possible alternative method of communication is to use notes that accompany the financial statements.

In the United States the monetary unit is the dollar. To meet the test of being a useful unit of measurement, the dollar ideally should be of unchanging value. For many years the rate of price-level change in the United States was not considered to be significant enough to cast serious doubt on the usefulness of the dollar as a measuring unit. However, in recent years, the continuing and relatively rapid inflation has reduced significantly the "value of a dollar" and has made the monetary principle one of the most controversial elements of generally accepted accounting principles. By the "value of a dollar" we usually mean the **quantity of real goods and services** that the dollar will command. What kind of common denominator will enable us to measure the physical quantities of all the diverse goods and services that the dollar will buy?

The statistical solution to this question is a **price index.** An index number is a somewhat imperfect device for measuring changes in the weighted-average price of a representative collection of goods and services between two points in time. Despite their shortcomings, price indexes covering broad categories of goods and services are useful, if rough, tools for measuring changes in the value of the dollar.

When inflation causes a substantial increase in the price of goods and services, the value of the dollar goes down and the monetary principle becomes the weakest link in the chain of accounting principles. The FASB and the SEC have considered several possible alternatives to the stable-price-level assumption and have implemented some steps to make financial statements more meaningful in an inflationary environment. For example, **FASB Statement No. 33,** "Financial Reporting and Changing Prices," required the reporting of certain effects of price changes in supplementary data to the financial statements of certain large, publicly owned corporations, and **ASR No. 253,** "Adoption of Requirements for Financial Accounting and Reporting Practices for Oil and Gas Producing Activities," called for the development of *reserve recognition accounting*—a technique based on valuations of proved oil and gas reserves. These and other possible solutions to the impact of inflation on financial statements are considered in Chapter 25.

Revenue realization principle

Revenue may be defined as the value of goods and services which a business enterprise transfers to its customers.[18] Thus, revenue is the principal factor responsible for increases in the net assets of a business enterprise apart from investments by owners. For a given accounting period, revenue equals the inflow of cash and receivables from sales made during that period. For a single transaction, revenue equals the value of assets (cash and accounts receivable) received from the customer.

Any definition of revenue immediately raises questions as to timing—the essence of the *revenue realization principle.* At what point or points during the creation of marketable products or services should revenue be recorded? What is the *critical event* that indicates revenue has been realized and justifies recording a change in net assets by replacing the carrying amount of assets such as inventories with a higher valuation representing their current fair value? Ideally, because each step in the process of producing and distributing goods is essential to earning revenue, the accounting recognition of revenue should be continuous rather than being linked to a single critical event. However, as a practical matter, objective evidence is needed to support the recording of revenue, and for most business enterprises that evidence lies in an arm's-length transaction in which title to goods passes to the customer. Thus, the revenue realization principle dictates that assets such as inventories be carried *at cost* until appreciation in value is realized through sale. The reasoning underlying this practice of recording revenue at the point of sale is expanded in Chapter 3.

Cost principle

The *cost principle* is a pervasive concept that affects most aspects of financial accounting. *Cost* (or *historical cost*) is assumed to be the

---

[18] A more formalized definition of *revenues,* developed by the FASB, appears on page 18.

proper basis of accounting for assets acquired, for services received, and for the interests of creditors and owners of a business enterprise. Completed business transactions are the events to be recognized and made part of the accounting records under the cost principle. At the time of a transaction, the exchange price usually represents the current fair value of the goods or services exchanged, as evidenced by the contract between an informed purchaser and seller. With the passage of time, the current fair value of an asset such as land or a building may change, particularly in periods of inflation. However, the cost principle requires that historical cost, rather than a later current fair value, continue to serve as the basis for asset valuations in the accounting records and in the financial statements.

How should cost be measured when assets or services are acquired in noncash transactions? For example, land may be acquired in exchange for a corporation's own shares of capital stock. Cost then is defined as the cash equivalent (current fair value) of the land acquired or the cash equivalent of the capital stock issued, whichever is more clearly evident. If the capital stock is listed on a stock exchange and is widely traded, the market price of the capital stock may be stronger and more objective evidence of the cost of the land than is an appraisal of the land.

The cost principle applies to the measurement of liabilities as well as of assets. The dollar valuation assigned to a liability should be its cash equivalent. For example, if a business enterprise borrows $200,000 and signs a note promising to repay $220,000 a year later, the cash equivalent value of the liability is $200,000, and this is the net amount at which the liability should be included in a balance sheet prepared immediately after the loan is obtained. Thus, the cost principle applies to all types of business transactions.

The implications of the cost principle are considered in more detail in our study of income determination in Chapter 3 and in later chapters of this book.

Matching principle

The **matching principle** means that after the revenue for an accounting period has been determined, the costs associated with this revenue must be deducted to measure net income. The term **matching** refers to the close relationship that exists between certain costs and the revenue realized as a result of incurring those costs. Thus, the use of matching as an accounting principle in income measurement offers another practical reason for the widespread use of the cost principle.

Expenses may be defined as the cost of goods or services used to obtain revenue.[19] The matching of a business enterprise's expenses (or

[19] A more formalized definition of expenses, developed by the FASB, appears on page 18.

expired costs) with its revenue for an accounting period is the primary activity in the measurement of the results of the enterprise's operations for that period. For example, expenditures for advertising attract customers and generate sales. The outlay for the advertising is one of the expenses to be deducted from the revenue of the accounting period. Similarly, the recognition of doubtful accounts expense illustrates the importance of the accounting period in the matching of expenses and revenue. Doubtful accounts expense is caused by selling goods or services on credit to customers who fail to pay their bills. To match this expense with the related revenue, the expense must be recorded and deducted from revenue in the accounting period in which the sales are made, even though the receivables are not determined to be uncollectible until the following period. The use of estimates is necessary in this and in many other cases in order to implement the matching principle.

Disclosure principle

The *disclosure principle* requires that financial statements be complete in the sense of including all information necessary to users of the statements. If the omission of certain information would cause the financial statements to be misleading, disclosure of such information is essential.

Published financial statements include detailed notes that are considered to be an integral part of the statements. However, disclosures in the notes should supplement the information in the body of the financial statements and should not be used to correct improper presentation of information in the body of the statements.

Typical examples of information often disclosed in notes to financial statements include the following: a summary of significant accounting policies, descriptions of stock option and pension plans, status of litigation in which the business enterprise is a party, amount and nature of loss contingencies and commitments, and terms and status of proposed business combinations. The first item listed above (a summary of significant accounting policies) is prescribed by *APB Opinion No. 22,* "Disclosure of Accounting Policies," as essential. Among the policies to be described in this note to financial statements are changes in accounting principles and justification therefor, depreciation methods, and inventory pricing methods.[20]

The concept of disclosure applies not only to transactions and events that have occurred during the accounting period covered by the financial statements, but also to material *subsequent events* that occur after the balance sheet date but before the financial statements are released. For example, the sale of a major segment of the business enterprise, a significant decline in the market price of raw material, and the institu-

[20] *APB Opinion No. 22,* "Disclosures of Accounting Policies," AICPA (New York: 1972), p. 436.

tion or settlement of important litigation are events likely to have a substantial influence on the future earnings and financial position of an enterprise. Such events must be disclosed in notes to the financial statements.

The examples cited indicate that disclosure in notes to financial statements may be lengthy and involved. However, these notes, as well as the financial statements themselves, should be as concise as possible in order to keep financial reporting understandable and not excessively detailed.

CASH FLOWS AND INCOME MEASUREMENT

Accountants assume that a business enterprise has continuous existence. Therefore, they record the prospect of future cash inflows as an increase in assets and as revenue whenever they have objective evidence of the amount of the future cash receipt. Cash inflows often occur before an enterprise has performed its part of a contract. In this case, an increase in assets is recorded, but a liability is recognized instead of revenue. The liability indicates an obligation on the part of the enterprise to perform in accordance with the contract. When performance is completed, the revenue is earned and recorded. We can readily see that cash inflows are closely related to revenue realization; however, the assumptions underlying the timing of revenue realization do not always permit cash inflows and revenue to be recorded in the same accounting period.

Similarly, cash outflows are closely related to expenses of a business enterprise; however, cash outflows and expenses may not be recorded in the same accounting period. For example, enterprises frequently acquire for cash in one period assets that will be productive over several future periods, and assets that are productive only during the current period often are acquired in exchange for a promise to pay cash in a future period.

Information concerning cash flows during an accounting period is valuable in judging the ability of the business enterprise to pay its debts, to maintain regular dividend payments, to finance replacements of productive assets, and to expand the scope of the business operations. However, the net increase or decrease in cash during a period is not useful in evaluating an enterprise's operating performance, because cash receipts and payments are not representative of the economic activities carried on in specific periods.

Accrual basis of accounting

The *accrual basis of accounting* is assumed throughout this book. Revenue is recorded when realized and expenses are recorded when incurred, without regard to the time of cash receipt or payment. The focus of the accrual basis of accounting is on the realization of revenue, the incurrence of costs, and the matching of revenue realized with the costs expired (expenses). Adopting the assumption that revenue is recorded when realization occurs and the related assumption that costs contributing to the realization of this revenue can be traced through the earning process requires the use of an accrual-deferral system of accounting.

The need for frequent measurement of the past performance of a business enterprise as the basis for decisions about the future by management and investors alike has forced accountants to adopt the accrual basis of accounting. Under the accrual basis, the accounting records are adjusted periodically to ensure that all assets and liabilities (and thus revenue and expenses) are correctly stated.

Cash basis of accounting

Under the *cash basis of accounting,* revenue is recorded only when cash is received; expenses are recorded when cash is paid. The determination of income thus rests upon the *collection* of revenue and the *payment* of expenses, rather than upon the *earning* of revenue and the *incurring* of expenses. A business enterprise using the cash basis of accounting is not following the matching principle described earlier in this chapter. Consequently, financial statements prepared on the cash basis of accounting do not present the financial position or operating results of an enterprise in conformity with generally accepted accounting principles.

A strict cash basis of accounting seldom is found in practice, but a *modified cash basis* (really a mixed cash-accrual basis) is allowed for income tax purposes. Under the modified cash basis of accounting, taxpayers who acquire property having an economic life of more than one year cannot deduct the entire cost in the year of purchase. They must treat the cost as an asset to be depreciated over its economic life. Expenses such as rent or advertising paid in advance also are regarded as assets and are deductible only in the year or years to which they apply. Expenses paid after the year in which incurred are deductible only in the year paid. Revenue is reported for income tax purposes in the year received. However, in any business enterprise in which the purchase, production, or sale of merchandise is a significant factor, these transactions must be reported on an accrual basis. For example, when merchandise is sold on credit, the revenue must be recognized immediately. The cost of goods sold must reflect purchases on credit and inventories on hand whether paid for or not. Thus, for a merchandising enterprise the revenue from sales, the cost of goods sold, and the gross profit on sales will be the same under the accrual basis of accounting as under the modified cash basis of accounting.

Illustration   The difference between the cash basis and accrual basis of accounting will be illustrated for Tina Carson, a practicing CPA, who maintains accounting records on a cash basis. During Year 10, Carson collected $150,000 from her clients and paid $80,000 for operating expenses, resulting in a cash-basis net income of $70,000. Carson's fees receivable, accrued liabilities, and short-term prepayments on January 1 and on December 31, Year 10, were as follows:

Accrual-basis items of business enterprise using cash basis of accounting

	Jan. 1, Year 10	Dec. 31, Year 10
Fees receivable.	$18,200	$37,000
Accrued liabilities	6,200	4,000
Short-term prepayments	3,500	2,500

A working paper showing the necessary adjustments to restate Carson's income statement from the cash basis to the accrual basis of accounting is illustrated below:

TINA CARSON, CPA
Working Paper to Restate Income Statement from Cash Basis to Accrual Basis of Accounting
For Year Ended December 31, Year 10

	Cash collected from revenue and paid for expenses	Adjustments to restate to accrual basis of accounting		Income statement on accrual basis of accounting
		Add	Deduct	
Revenue from fees	$150,000			
Add: Fees receivable, Dec. 31, Year 10.		$37,000		
Less: Fees receivable, Jan. 1, Year 10.			$18,200	$168,800
Operating expenses	80,000			
Add: Accrued liabilities, Dec. 31, Year 10		4,000		
Short-term prepayments, Jan. 1, Year 10		3,500		78,800
Less: Accrued liabilities, Jan. 1, Year 10			6,200	
Short-term prepayments, Dec. 31, Year 10.			2,500	
Net income on cash basis of accounting.	$ 70,000			
Net income on accrual basis of accounting				$ 90,000

Because the revenue from fees on the cash basis does not include the fees receivable on December 31, which were earned in Year 10, this amount is added to the cash collected in the restatement of revenue from fees to the accrual basis of accounting. Because fees receivable on January 1 were earned in Year 9 and collected in Year 10, this amount is subtracted from cash collections in the restatement of revenue from fees to the accrual basis of accounting.

The adjustments to restate operating expenses from the cash basis to the accrual basis of accounting are explained below:

1 The amount of accrued liabilities on December 31, Year 10, represents expenses incurred in Year 10 that will be paid in Year 11, and the amount of short-term prepayments on January 1, Year 10, represents services paid for in Year 9 that were consumed in Year 10. Therefore, both amounts are **added** to the amount of cash paid in the restatement of operating expenses for Year 10 to the accrual basis of accounting.

2 The amount of accrued liabilities on January 1, Year 10, represents expenses of Year 9 paid for in Year 10, and the amount of short-term prepayments on December 31, Year 10, represents cash outlays in Year 10 for services that will be consumed in Year 11. Therefore, both amounts are **deducted** from the amount of cash paid in the restatement of operating expenses for Year 10 to the accrual basis of accounting.

REVIEW QUESTIONS

1 Identify the organizations or legislative acts that have been primarily responsible for the development of accounting principles and practices in the United States. What is the relationship between each of these organizations or acts and the practicing certified public accountant?

2 Are generally accepted accounting principles equally applicable to the fields of financial accounting and managerial accounting? Explain.

3 Define **general-purpose financial statements** and point out the limitations of such statements.

4 Briefly describe the FASB's conceptual framework project for financial accounting and reporting.

5 What are three publications of the FASB issued as parts of the conceptual framework project?

6 Briefly describe three objectives of financial reporting identified by the FASB.

7 What is the most important qualitative characteristic of accounting information, according to the FASB?

8 The two primary qualities of accounting information identified by the FASB are **relevance** and **reliability.** Are these qualities as likely to be present in a forecast of future earnings as in an income statement? Explain.

9 Is **conservatism** a qualitative characteristic of accounting information? Explain.

10 Briefly summarize the position of the FASB on *materiality* as an influencing factor on the quality of accounting information.

11 What is *comprehensive income* as defined by the FASB?

12 Identify the following as being governmental organizations or part of the private sector of the economy: Financial Accounting Standards Board, Securities and Exchange Commission, New York Stock Exchange, American Accounting Association.

13 Describe the steps followed by the FASB in the development of a new financial accounting standard.

14 What is meant by the *continuity* or *going-concern principle* of accounting? How does it affect the valuation of assets? When is this principle not applicable?

15 The *monetary principle* of accounting assumes that money is a useful standard measuring unit for reporting the effects of business transactions. State and explain two major criticisms or limitations of this accounting principle.

16 Define the *revenue realization principle* of accounting. How is this principle related to the *cost principle* and the *matching principle?*

17 Wembley Corporation acquired land in exchange for 50,000 shares of its $5 par capital stock. How is the cost principle of accounting applied in recording this transaction?

18 Distinguish between the *cash basis of accounting* and the *accrual basis of accounting.* Will financial statements prepared under either method present the financial position and operating results of a business enterprise in conformity with generally accepted accounting principles?

EXERCISES

Ex. 1-1 Select the best answer for each of the following multiple-choice questions:

1 Generally, revenue is recorded by a business enterprise at a point when:
   a Management decides it is appropriate to do so
   b The product is available for sale to consumers
X **c** An exchange has taken place and the earning process is virtually complete
   d An order for merchandise has been received

2 Why are certain costs capitalized when incurred and then depreciated or amortized over subsequent accounting periods?
   a To reduce the income tax liability
   b To aid management in making business decisions
X **c** To match the costs of production with revenue as earned
   d To adhere to the accounting concept of conservatism

3 What accounting principle or concept justifies the use of accruals and deferrals?
X **a** Going concern
   b Materiality
   c Consistency
   d Stable monetary unit

4 An accrued expense can best be described as an amount:
   a Paid and currently matched with revenue

> **b** Paid and not currently matched with revenue
> , **c** Not paid and not currently matched with revenue
> ✗ **d** Not paid and currently matched with revenue

5 Continuation of a business enterprise in the absence of contrary evidence is an example of the principle or concept of:
   a Business entity
   b Consistency
✗ **c** Going concern
   d Substance over form

Ex. 1-2 Identify each of the following phrases as being associated with the cash basis of accounting or the accrual basis of accounting:

   a Revenue recorded at time of collection
   b Individual income tax returns
   c Business enterprise in which inventories are material in amount
   d Minimum amount of record keeping
   e Generally accepted accounting principles
   f Postponement of recognition of revenue
   g Flexibility in determining timing of expenses
   h Emphasis on consistency and matching in the measurement of net income
   i Sophisticated accounting system
   j Small service enterprise with accounting records limited to information required for income tax purposes

Ex. 1-3 The general-purpose financial statements of Garfield Corporation contain the following item and note to the financial statements:

*Inventories (**Note 3**)* *$1,760,000*

Note 3: *Inventories are valued at the lower of cost or market; cost is determined on the first-in, first-out basis.*

   Discuss the appropriateness of **Note 3** in relation to the disclosure principle of accounting.

Ex. 1-4 Colonial Company uses the accrual basis of accounting. It reported advertising expense for Year 7 of $35,460. Prepaid advertising at the end of Year 7 amounted to $4,820, and cash paid for advertising during Year 7 amounted to $36,680. There was no accrued advertising expense at either the beginning or the end of Year 7.
   Compute the amount, if any, of prepaid advertising at the beginning of Year 7.

Ex. 1-5 The financial statements of Chun Company include the items shown below, along with the related notes to the financial statements.

*Cash (**Note 1**)* . . . . $ 96,500
*Accounts receivable (**Note 2**)*   210,300

Note 1: *The amount reported as cash includes four checking accounts, two petty cash funds, and one change fund.*
Note 2: *Accounts receivable include $48,400, representing the selling price of merchandise shipped on consignment and held for sale by consignees acting as agents. It is anticipated that this merchandise will be sold within six months and that none of it will have to be returned to the warehouse.*

   Discuss the appropriateness of **Note 1** and **Note 2** to Chun Company's financial statements as a means of carrying out the disclosure principle of accounting and the objectives of general-purpose financial statements.

SHORT CASES FOR ANALYSIS AND DECISION

Case 1-1 Generally accepted accounting principles require the use of accruals and deferrals in the determination of net income.

Instructions
a How does the accrual basis of accounting affect the determination of net income? Include a discussion of what constitutes an accrual and a deferral, and give examples of each.
b Contrast the accrual basis of accounting with the cash basis of accounting.

Case 1-2 During the first class meeting in an accounting course, Professor Logan asked three students to explain the nature of revenue and expenses as related to the preparation of financial statements for business enterprises. Carl Lucas stated that revenue and expenses reflect changes in the owners' equity of a business enterprise. Lois Chu stated that Carl was dead wrong and explained that revenue represents inflows of assets and expenses represent outflows of assets. Morris Dean responded as follows: "Revenue and expenses are those things which determine net income." Professor Logan took the position that each student was on the right track, but that none had presented an entirely satisfactory explanation.

Instructions Evaluate Professor Logan's response and describe the nature of revenue and expenses as these terms are used in financial accounting.

Case 1-3 The board of directors of DuPre Corporation is debating whether to adopt straight-line depreciation or an accelerated depreciation method. Some directors are primarily interested in reporting steadily increasing earnings; others argue that the best way to achieve a favorable "accounting image" in the financial community is to adopt conservative accounting policies.

Instructions Explain whether the conservative effect of accelerated depreciation on net income and financial position will be realized for only a few years or whether it will continue indefinitely to result in the reporting of lower earnings and a lower valuation of plant assets.

Case 1-4 A financial newspaper carried an advertisement of a small manufacturing enterprise being offered for sale by its owner. The advertisement emphasized the unusual profitability of the enterprise. Assume that you were interested in purchasing a business of this type and you therefore contacted the owner, Lee Griffin, who stated that Griffin Company in its first year of operations had realized net income of $95,000. You inquired whether the accrual basis of accounting had been used to determine the net income, and Griffin replied as follows:
"We use a mixed cash-accrual basis of accounting, just as many other small companies do. As you probably know, a strict cash basis is not satisfactory, but a modified or mixed cash-accrual basis is acceptable for income tax purposes and meets our other needs. For example, our purchases of merchandise are recorded only when cash payment is made. Our sales are recorded immediately, whether on a cash or credit basis. We do not guess about doubtful accounts receivable in advance, but we do not hesitate to write off any receivable that proves to be uncollectible. We took a physical inventory at year-end and recorded it in the accounting records. We did not record any depreciation on equipment because equipment was acquired by issuance of long-term notes. No journal entry will be made for these transactions until cash payments are made. We find this system gives us better results than a pure cash basis and requires less work than the accrual basis."

Instructions Evaluate point by point the statement made by Griffin. Do you regard Griffin Company's system as conforming to the usual standards of a "modified cash basis" of accounting? Is the determination of net income of $95,000 during the first year of operations a valid measurement? Explain.

Case 1-5 In a discussion of the concept of conservatism as an influence on financial accounting and reporting, Alice Wu argued that conservatism often is used as a means of understating net income of the current accounting period and the financial position at the end of the period. George Case defended conservatism on the ground that accountants frequently had to make choices among alternative assumptions under conditions of uncertainty and that making such choices on a conservative basis would help avoid dangerous overstatements of net income that could injure both investors and certified public accountants.

Wu and Case considered the five following situations but were unable to reach agreement on the proper accounting treatment for any of them.

(1) A business enterprise has expended $125,000 (which is 5% of its annual sales) for research and development in an effort to develop new commercial products. No specific products have emerged from this research, but management believes that the research, if continued, eventually will lead to important new products. Furthermore, management believes that its existing products will lose their market appeal in a few years and that the enterprise must have new products to survive.

Wu favors including the $125,000 in the balance sheet as an intangible asset, Deferred Research and Development Costs. Case favors treating the $125,000 as expense of the current year.

(2) After occupying an old building on leased land for 17 years of a 20-year lease, the lessee constructed a new frame building, because the old building was unsatisfactory and the lessor refused to make repairs. Improvements on the land will revert to the lessor at the end of the lease. There is a possibility, but no assurance, that the lessor will agree to renew the lease.

Wu favors capitalizing the cost of the building. Case favors writing off the cost of the building as expense of the current accounting period.

(3) The products sold by a manufacturer are guaranteed for a period of one year. Wu favors recognizing warranty expense only as claims are presented for repair or replacement of products. Case favors recording warranty expense and crediting a liability for an estimated amount in the period of sale.

(4) The inventory contains a large quantity of item K for which demand has largely disappeared. Wu wants to include item K as an asset in the balance sheet on the grounds that the item is not subject to deterioration and customer demand for it may revive. Case favors writing off the cost of this item.

(5) Credit terms are 30 days. Case favors writing off a large receivable six months past due from a customer who went to Europe for an extended stay and cannot be located. Wu is opposed because the customer has been delinquent before and later paid in full.

Instructions For each of the five situations, state your position on the proposed action and explain the reasoning underlying your position.

Case 1-6 Spivak Corporation owns several office buildings and rents space to tenants. One of these office buildings was acquired at a cost of $750,000 and has been depreciated for five years on a straight-line basis. Residual value is zero. The carrying amount, net of accumulated depreciation, will be $680,000 at the end of the current year.

At the time of acquiring the building, Spivak Corporation had borrowed $750,000 from Curtis Spivak, one of the founders of the company and presently a director and major stockholder. The note payable issued for the loan made no mention of interest but called for repayment of $1,000,000 five years from the date of the note. In a directors' meeting near the end of the current year, Spivak stated that because of rising price levels he considered the office building to be worth more than it had cost. Spivak offered to accept the office building in full settlement of the $1,000,000 promissory note, which was about to mature.

During a discussion of the offer by the board of directors, the following opinions were expressed:

Director Jacobs: "If we give up the building in settlement of the $1,000,000 note payable, we shall increase our earnings this year by $250,000, and we shall have to correct our prior years' earnings by eliminating all depreciation on the building, because this transaction provides objective evidence that the building has not depreciated. My understanding of accounting principles is that our accounting treatment of the transaction must use the objective evidence provided by Spivak's offer."

Director Winton: "In my opinion we could accept the offer and not have to recognize any gain. The corporation will not receive cash, receivables, or any other asset, so there is no gain involved. The revenue realization principle of accounting states that there must be an inflow of cash or receivables in order to have revenue."

Director Toby: "The corporation received only $750,000 when it issued the note payable, and it has not paid or recorded any interest. Now we will give up an asset that cost $750,000 to discharge a recorded liability of the same amount, so this is a perfect example of the matching principle of accounting, and no gain or loss is involved."

Instructions
a Evaluate the opinions expressed by each of the three directors, giving special attention to the references made to accounting principles. Use a separate paragraph or paragraphs for evaluation of each director's position and indicate what accounting principles are involved.
b Explain how the proposed transaction should be accounted for by Spivak Corporation. Indicate the accounting principle or principles you consider to be applicable. Include in your answer whether interest and depreciation should be recognized and the amount of the gain or loss, if any, that would result from acceptance of Curtis Spivak's offer.
c In the financial statements prepared immediately after carrying out the exchange with Curtis Spivak, is it necessary to make any disclosure of this transaction apart from the normal accounting for disposal of a building? Explain.
d Assuming that the corporation accepts Curtis Spivak's offer, prepare a journal entry to record the transaction. Assume that depreciation has been recorded for the current year but that the accounting records have not been closed. No interest expense has ever been recorded on the note payable. Assume also that the journal entry made at the time the note payable was issued consisted of a debit to Cash for $750,000, a debit to Discount on Notes Payable for $250,000, and a credit to Notes Payable for $1,000,000. **Suggestion:** The interest expense applicable to prior years may be debited to Correction of Prior Years' Income (Interest Expense). Assume that the interest expense applicable to the current year is $55,000.

PROBLEMS

1-1 Steele Corporation was organized by Howard Steele and Richard Steele for the purpose of operating a hardware store. Each invested $60,000 cash, and each received 3,000 shares of $1 par common stock. Howard Steele also loaned $50,000 to the corporation and received a two-year, 12% promissory note. The corporation then issued 3,600 shares of its common stock in exchange for land and a building. The land was appraised at a value of $30,000.

Merchandise costing $70,000 was acquired on credit, and a salesman was employed to begin work the following week at a weekly salary of $500. The corporation plans to use the periodic inventory system. Office supplies and office equipment were acquired for $14,000. The office supplies were valued at $1,600 and the office equipment at $12,400.

Instructions

a What cost should be recorded for the land and the building acquired in exchange for Steele Corporation's common stock? Explain the reasoning underlying your answer.

b Prepare journal entries for the foregoing transactions in the accounting records of Steele Corporation.

c After one year of operations, Steele Corporation had a strong working capital position, but retained earnings amounted to only $20,000. Under these circumstances, would it be proper for the corporation to pay the $50,000 note payable to Howard Steele? Explain.

1-2 Carl Will and George Burr formed Wilbur Corporation to operate a charter fishing boat. Each invested $54,000 cash, for which each received 6,000 shares of $1 par capital stock. The corporation also issued 2,400 shares of capital stock to acquire a used boat. Wilma Todd, the former owner of the boat, had pledged it as collateral for a $45,000 bank loan, and this $45,000 liability was assumed by Wilbur Corporation in the contract for acquisition of the boat.

Wilma Todd's accounting records showed that the original cost of the boat was $150,000 and that she had expensed by the straight-line method of depreciation a total of $90,000.

Wilbur Corporation acquired fishing equipment for $12,000 and supplies for $1,500. A crew member was hired to begin work the following week at a weekly salary of $550.

Instructions

a What effect, if any, does the amount of recorded depreciation and the depreciation method used by Wilma Todd have on the depreciation program to be used for the boat by Wilbur Corporation? Explain the reasoning underlying your answer.

b What cost should be recorded for the boat acquired in exchange for 2,400 shares of Wilbur Corporation capital stock? Explain.

c Prepare journal entries to record the transactions completed by Wilbur Corporation.

1-3 Cagle Company is a successful enterprise that is expanding rapidly. On May 1, Year 5, additional manufacturing facilities were acquired from the Towne & Bates Partnership, which was terminating operations because of a dispute between the partners. The property had been advertised for sale at a price of $950,000. Bates asserted that the land alone was worth that much and that the building was insured for $500,000, its cost of construction.

Cagle Company acquired the property by issuing to the partnership 60,000 shares of its $5 par capital stock and agreeing to assume a $250,000 mortgage note payable on the property.

Prior to the acquisition, Cagle Company hired a firm of industrial engineers to appraise the building. The report from this firm set forth a current fair value for the building of $480,000. The capital stock of Cagle Company is listed on a stock exchange and was being traded on May 1, Year 5, at a price of $11 a share.

Shortly after acquiring the property, Cagle Company received a letter from a large corporation offering to buy the property for $1,000,000.

Instructions

a Prepare a journal entry to record the transaction in the accounting records of Cagle Company.

b Explain the reasoning underlying your answer to part a.

comprelation *55-58*

1-4 Kentucky Corporation issues notes payable frequently in borrowing from various sources. Some of the notes provide for payment of interest in advance; others do not. (For the purposes of this problem, you need not challenge the propriety of prepaid interest.) Kentucky uses the accrual basis of accounting. Interest expense on the accrual basis for Year 3 was $19,600. Information relating to prepaid interest and to accrued interest payable at two successive balance sheet dates appears below:

	Dec. 31, Year 2	Dec. 31, Year 3
Prepaid interest	$ 800	$ 400
Accrued interest payable	1,700	2,200

The corporation owns several properties that it rents to lessees. Some lessees pay rent in advance; others do not. The amount of cash collected from lessees during Year 3 was $56,400. The following information relates to rent receivable and unearned rent revenue on two successive balance sheet dates:

	Dec. 31, Year 2	Dec. 31, Year 3
Rent receivable	$6,400	$5,000
Unearned rent revenue	1,600	2,800

Instructions
a Compute the amount of cash paid for interest during Year 3.
b Compute the amount of rent revenue for Year 3, under the accrual basis of accounting.

1-5 Langston Company uses the accrual basis of accounting. The company owns real estate that it rents to various lessees. Rent collected in cash during Year 5 amounted to $108,400. The amounts of rent receivable and of unearned rent revenue on two successive balance sheet dates were as follows:

	Dec. 31, Year 4	Dec. 31, Year 5
Rent receivable	$3,600	$4,900
Unearned rent revenue	4,400	1,640

The company advertises its merchandise through television, radio, and newspapers. Some of the advertising is paid in advance and some is paid on receipt of invoices. Advertising expense on the accrual basis of accounting for Year 5 was $64,200. The amounts of prepaid and accrued advertising expense at the beginning and at the end of Year 5 were as follows:

	Dec. 31, Year 4	Dec. 31, Year 5
Prepaid advertising	$5,360	$6,400
Accrued advertising payable	7,840	2,900

Instructions
a Compute the amount of rent revenue that should appear in the income statement for Year 5, under the accrual basis of accounting.
b Compute the amount of cash paid for advertising during Year 5.

1-6 A summary of operating results for Cantor Company for Year 2 is presented below:

Cash collected from customers	$466,000
Cash paid to merchandise creditors	268,200
Cash paid for operating expenses	79,300

The following data were taken from comparative balance sheets prepared on the accrual basis of accounting:

	Dec. 31, Year 1	Dec. 31, Year 2
Accounts receivable	$52,400	$48,600
Inventories	75,000	72,100
Short-term prepayments	4,100	9,500
Accounts payable (merchandise creditors)	32,000	37,400
Accrued liabilities	2,800	3,200
Accumulated depreciation (no retirements during the year)	50,000	74,000

Instructions   Prepare income statements for Cantor Company for Year 2, under (**a**) the accrual basis of accounting and (**b**) the modified cash basis of accounting whereby operating expenses (other than depreciation) are computed on a strict cash basis. Show supporting computations. Disregard income taxes.

1-7   The information listed below was obtained from the comparative balance sheets of Bogarde Company for Year 4:

	Year 4 Jan. 1	Year 4 Dec. 31
Accounts receivable	$ 77,500	$ 84,200
Inventories	110,000	125,000
Short-term prepayments	6,200	1,700
Accounts payable (merchandise purchases)	49,500	38,000
Accrued operating expenses payable	3,200	900
Accumulated depreciation (no retirement during the year)	66,000	100,000

A summary of cash receipts and payments for Year 4 follows:

Cash collected from customers	$723,500
Cash paid to suppliers for merchandise	440,000
Cash paid for operating expenses	122,800

Instructions   Prepare income statements for Bogarde Company for Year 4, under (**a**) the accrual basis of accounting and (**b**) the modified cash basis of accounting whereby operating expenses (excluding depreciation) are computed on a strict cash basis. Show supporting computations. Disregard income taxes.

2 SUMMARY OF THE ACCOUNTING PROCESS

Accounting has been called the "language of business" because it is the method of communicating business information. Like other languages, it is undergoing continuous change in an attempt to discover better means of communicating.

The **accounting process** consists of three major parts: (1) the recording of transactions during an accounting period, (2) the summarizing of information at the end of the period, and (3) the reporting and interpreting of the summary information.

During an accounting period accountants record transactions as they occur, reflecting the situation as it exists at the time of the transaction. The recording phase of accounting is thus a continuing activity. At the end of each accounting period accountants carry out the functions of summarizing and reporting. After a trial balance is prepared, certain adjusting entries are required to bring the accounting records up to date. Some adjustments must be made to the recorded data for changes that have occurred since the transactions were recorded; other adjustments are needed for events which have not been recorded but which affect the financial position and operating results of the business enterprise. Examples of these unrecorded events are depreciation and other expirations of asset services and the accrual of expenses such as interest and salaries.

When the accounting records have been made as complete, accurate, and up-to-date as possible, accountants prepare financial statements reflecting financial position and the results of operations. An important measure of the success of the accounting process is the responsiveness of financial reporting to the needs of the users of accounting information.

RECORDING FINANCIAL TRANSACTIONS

If the accounting process is to provide the users of accounting information with reliable, timely reports, transactions during the period must be interpreted in conformity with generally accepted accounting principles and recorded promptly and accurately. A **transaction** is an event that causes a change in the assets, liabilities, or owners' equity of a business enterprise. Transactions may be classified into two broad groups: (1) **external transactions,** or those between the business enterprise and another party, and (2) **internal transactions,** such as the expiration or transfer of costs within the enterprise. Examples of this second group include the depreciation of plant assets, the recognition of obsolescence in inventory, and the transfer of production costs from the goods in process inventory to the finished goods inventory.

Supporting documents

A **supporting document** (sometimes called a **business paper** or a **voucher**) is the first record prepared for a transaction. Such documents show the date, amount, and nature of the transaction, and the parties involved. Entries in the various journals are prepared from supporting documents; for example, sales invoices support entries in the sales journal. The original copy of a sales invoice is sent to the customer, who uses it as a basis for recording the purchase; a duplicate copy is retained by the seller as evidence of the sale. Some supporting documents never leave the business enterprise, as, for example, cash register tapes, receiving reports, time reports, journal vouchers, and minutes of directors' meetings.

Any verification of financial statements or accounting records is likely to include tests in which summary amounts are traced to the underlying supporting documents. The practice of identifying each type of document with serial numbers and accounting for all numbers in the series helps prevent the omission of a transaction because of a missing document. Proper design and use of supporting documents is an important element in the system of internal control, regardless of whether the enterprise uses a manual accounting system or an electronic data processing system.

Electronic data processing

The increasing use of computers by business enterprises, government units, and other organizations has greatly modified the methods of recording, summarizing, and classifying accounting information. The computer not only processes data with incredible speed and a high degree of accuracy, but also permits the classification and summarization of data in more forms and at lower cost than has been possible with manual systems.

The input data for the computer are often on punched cards or tapes, created as a by-product when business papers are prepared. The computer output, also on cards or tapes, is read by printers that can produce reports and financial statements of traditional appearance.

In business enterprises that use electronic data processing systems, the recording, classifying, and summarizing steps in creating accounting information may be blended into one. With an **on-line, real-time computer system,** the recording of a business transaction causes instantaneous updating of all relevant files. You have probably encountered these on-line, real-time (OLRT) systems at airline ticket offices and in savings and loan associations. At any branch of a savings and loan association, a teller can update a depositor's account immediately by recording the deposit or withdrawal on a computer terminal. It is not difficult to envision an electronic data processing system that produces daily a set of financial statements or special reports updated to include all transactions to date and also provides the current amounts for such items as interest, depreciation, and labor costs.

Although the traditional forms of journals and ledgers are not essential to the electronic processing of accounting information, the concepts implicit in these records also are used in a computerized system. Furthermore, the output of the computers can be programmed to provide information in a form similar to traditional journals and ledgers.

Because our primary goal in this book is an understanding of accounting principles rather than expertise in accounting systems, we shall rely on manual recording methods as the simplest and clearest means of illustrating the application of accounting principles to business transactions and events.

Double-entry system

The standard accounting model for accumulating data in a business enterprise consists of the **double-entry system** based on the basic accounting equation. As the name implies, the **journal entry** made for each transaction is composed of two parts: one or more debits and one or more credits. All journal entries are made within the framework of the basic accounting equation (assets = liabilities + owners' equity). Each transaction must be analyzed in terms of its effects on the elements of this equation. The advantages of the double-entry system include built-in controls which automatically call attention to many types of errors and offer assurance that once assets are recorded, they will not be forgotten or simply overlooked. Management's responsibility for the custody of resources entrusted to it thus is strengthened by the inherent discipline of the double-entry system. The self-balancing nature of this system facilitates the preparation of a complete set of financial statements as frequently as desired.

The double-entry system is in practically universal use; it takes its name from the fact that equal debit and credit entries are made for every transaction. The terms *debit* and *credit* can be related to the basic accounting equation A = L + OE in the following way:

Changes in balance sheet accounts

Asset accounts	*= Liability + Owners' Equity accounts*
Increases are recorded by debits	*Increases are recorded by credits*
Decreases are recorded by credits	*Decreases are recorded by debits*

Assets and liabilities are the two independent variables in the above equation; the dependent variable, owners' equity, is derived from the valuation assigned to assets and liabilities. One source of change in the owners' equity is the change in the *net assets* (assets minus liabilities) as a result of operations, measured by two classes of accounts—revenue and expenses. Revenue accounts measure the inflow of assets resulting from the production and distribution of goods and services to customers. Expense accounts measure the outflow of assets necessary to produce and distribute these goods and services. The change in the net assets as a result of these two flows is reflected in the owners' equity. Revenue and expense accounts are subject to the rules of debit and credit which were applied to assets, liabilities, and owners' equity accounts. The application of the rules of debit and credit for revenue and expenses is summarized below:

Changes in income statement accounts

Expense accounts	*Revenue accounts*
Increases in expenses are recorded by debits	*Increases in revenue are recorded by credits*
Decreases in expenses are recorded by credits	*Decreases in revenue are recorded by debits*

As the terms *debit* and *credit* are used in accounting, they have no meaning except as a directive for recording data in ledger accounts. Debit refers to the left side of the ledger account, and credit refers to the right side.

The accounting period

The normal accounting period is one year, beginning on any given day and ending 12 months later. A *calendar-year* accounting period ends on December 31; all other 12-month accounting periods are known as *fiscal years.* Business enterprises frequently adopt accounting periods that end when operations are at a low point in order to simplify year-end procedures and facilitate a better measurement of operating results and financial position. Such an accounting period is referred to as a *natural business year* because it conforms to the natural annual cycle of the enterprise.

Reports issued for shorter periods, such as one quarter of the year or one month, are called *interim reports.* These interim reports on the operating results of public corporations are needed to assist investors in reaching decisions to buy, hold, or sell securities. Traditionally, interim reports have not been audited by certified public accountants. At present, however, there is a new awareness of the need for CPAs to review their clients' interim reports to assure consistency with the annual financial statements.[1]

The accounting cycle

The *accounting cycle* is a complete sequence of accounting procedures which are repeated in the same order during each accounting period. The cycle in a traditional manual system (and with modifications in an EDP system) includes:

1 Recording transactions in the journals
2 Classifying data by posting from the journals to the ledger
3 Summarizing data from the ledger in a trial balance
4 Adjusting, correcting, and updating recorded data after consideration of all pertinent facts
5 Summarizing adjusted data in the form of financial statements
6 Closing the accounting records to summarize the activities of the period
7 Reversing certain adjusting entries to facilitate the recording process in subsequent periods[2]

When these steps are completed, the cycle begins again for the next accounting period.

A brief explanation of the journals, the ledger, and the various steps of the operating cycle is presented in the following sections.

The journals

The information shown in business papers is recorded in chronological order in the appropriate journals. Because a journal is organized chronologically by transaction, we may say that the unit of organization for a journal is the individual transaction. Although a small business enterprise conceivably could record all transactions in a single journal, this approach is seldom used. When numerous transactions of the same nature occur (such as transactions involving the receipt of cash), a special journal can be designed as a more efficient means of entering and sum-

---

[1] For a discussion of the special measurement problems relating to interim financial reports, see *APB Opinion No. 28,* "Interim Financial Reporting," AICPA (New York: 1973).
[2] This is an optional step, as explained on pages 55–58.

marizing these transactions. Several types of special journals are illustrated in this chapter.

The journalizing process requires the analysis of transactions in terms of debits and credits to the ledger accounts they affect: (1) assets, (2) liabilities, (3) owners' equity, (4) revenue, and (5) expenses. In this book our interest in journal entries lies in their usefulness as a clear, concise analytical device. To portray a business transaction in a journal entry, we must identify and classify each important element of the transaction.

The ledger

We have indicated how the information contained in business documents is analyzed and expressed in terms of debits and credits by entries in the journals. Next is the step of transferring this information to ledger accounts. This transfer process is called **posting,** which means that each debit and credit amount in the journals is entered in the appropriate account in the ledger.

A ledger consists of a number of accounts. Each ledger account represents stored information about a particular kind of asset, liability, owners' equity, revenue, or expense. As previously indicated, the transaction is the unit of organization for the journal; similarly, the ledger account is the unit of organization for the ledger. When computers are used, accounting information may be stored on magnetic tapes rather than on the pages of a traditional ledger. However, the printed form of ledger page is most convenient for our illustrations and analyses and is still used by many business enterprises.

Ledger accounts often are classified as **nominal** (temporary) and **real** (permanent) accounts. The nominal accounts (revenue and expense accounts) are closed at the end of the period by transferring their balances to other accounts. The real accounts (balance sheet accounts) remain open and normally show a balance after the accounting records are closed. During the accounting period, a balance sheet account or an income statement account may contain both real and nominal portions. Such accounts are known as **mixed accounts.** For example, the account Unexpired Insurance may include both unexpired insurance premiums and expired premiums before the end-of-period adjusting entries are made. When the time arrives for preparation of financial statements, the nominal and real portions of a mixed account are separated by end-of-period adjusting entries. Thus, the nominal portion in the Unexpired Insurance account is transferred to Insurance Expense.

Two forms of the ledger account for Accounts Receivable are illustrated on page 43 for Merchandise Mart, Inc.

"T" form of ledger account

				Accounts Receivable				Account No. (7)
Date	Explanation	Ref.	Amount	Date	Explanation	Ref.	Amount
Year 10				Year 10			
Jan. 1	Balance		12,682	Jan. 24		J10	150
31		S50	42,460	31		CR42	31,780
				31	Balance		23,212
			55,142				55,142
Feb. 1	Balance		23,212				

Running balance form of ledger account

						Accounts Receivable	Account No. (7)
Date	Explanation	Ref.	Debit	Credit	Balance
Year 10					
Jan. 1	Balance		12,682		12,682 dr
24		J10		150	12,532 dr
31		S50	42,460		54,992 dr
31		CR42		31,780	23,212 dr

In many cases greater detail is desired for a particular account included in the general ledger, and a **subsidiary ledger** is set up to contain the details supporting the main or **controlling account.** For example, the controlling account, Accounts Receivable, is adequate for general purposes; however, in order to facilitate the preparation of monthly statements to customers, it is desirable to have each customer's purchases and payments separately classified. In such situations a subsidiary ledger is established to provide the desired information. At all times, the total of the subsidiary ledger should agree with the related controlling account in the general ledger.

In addition to the use of a controlling account and subsidiary ledger for accounts receivable, other common examples of this concept include:

A Vouchers Payable controlling account supported by a voucher register (illustrated later in this chapter)

A Buildings controlling account supported by a subsidiary ledger which shows the individual buildings owned

A Capital Stock controlling account supported by a stockholders' ledger

Separate sudsidiary ledgers not only provide the detailed information needed for certain purposes, but also strengthen internal control by bringing to light most kinds of errors in the recording of business transactions.

Trial balance

At the end of each accounting period a **trial balance** of the general ledger is prepared to determine that the mechanics of the recording and posting operations have been carried out accurately. The trial balance consists of a listing of all ledger accounts and their balances; it provides evidence that an equality of debits and credits exists in the general ledger. The account balances then are used as a basis for preparing the financial statements. The trial balance illustrated below summarizes the account balances in the general ledger of Merchandise Mart, Inc.:

Trial balance at end of first month of fiscal year

MERCHANDISE MART, INC.
Trial Balance
January 31, Year 10

	Debit	Credit
Cash	$ 15,454	
Accounts receivable	23,212	
Allowance for doubtful accounts		$ 850
Inventory, Jan. 1, Year 10	47,860	
Unexpired insurance	200	
Land	45,000	
Building	80,000	
Accumulated depreciation of building		10,000
Equipment	16,000	
Accumulated depreciation of equipment		4,000
Notes payable		15,000
Vouchers payable		17,000
Capital stock, $10 par		75,000
Paid-in capital in excess of par		55,000
Retained earnings, Jan. 1, Year 10		49,207
Sales		45,883
Sales discounts	256	
Purchases	25,680	
Freight-in	980	
Salaries expense	8,220	
Advertising expense	4,620	
Delivery expense	2,180	
Property taxes expense	1,220	
Interest expense	80	
Miscellaneous expenses	978	
Totals	$271,940	$271,940

Trial balances of the subsidiary ledgers also may be prepared to prove that their balances agree with the balances in the related controlling accounts in the general ledger. These trial balances also may be used for other purposes; for example, a copy of the accounts receivable trial balance (see below) may be sent to the credit department for use in following up collections and as a basis for setting future credit policy.

List of claims from customers

MERCHANDISE MART, INC.
Accounts Receivable Trial Balance
January 31, Year 10

D. A. Adams	$ 1,500
R. O. Black	3,410
Other accounts (not listed here to avoid unnecessary detail)	18,302
Balance of Accounts Receivable controlling account (account No. 7) .	$23,212

The number of accounts, type of financial statements, and other aspects of the accounting system should be geared to meet the requirements of a particular business enterprise; the preceding examples simply illustrate the type of accounting system employed by many small and medium-sized enterprises.

Use of journals

A growing business enterprise usually is compelled to modify its accounting system to handle efficiently the increasing volume of transactions. One purpose of the accounting system is to facilitate the summarization of a large volume of transactions into meaningful totals for various uses. The basic accounting problems for large and small business enterprises are quite similar; however, the procedures adopted for accumulating and distributing accounting data may differ. When there is a large volume of transactions, procedures must be developed that permit the data to be handled rapidly.

Every business enterprise, regardless of its size, has certain established routines which are basic to the collection of accounting data. For example, documents are used to initiate transactions or to report their occurrence. As the complexity of the enterprise increases, methods such as the preparation of several copies of these documents may be instituted and various types of billing machines, mechanical registers, and preprinted forms may be used. In this way the time lag between the initiation of a transaction and its ultimate disposition can be shortened. Obviously, as the volume of similar transactions increases, the degree of automation possible in handling the data increases.

The great majority of business transactions are of four types, and for that reason most of the data can be handled by the use of four special multicolumn journals and a general journal. The four special journals are: sales journal, voucher register (or purchases journal), cash receipts journal, and cash payments journal. The primary types of transactions and the journals in which these are recorded are:

Type of transaction	Journal
Sales of merchandise on credit	Sales journal (S)
Purchases of merchandise, supplies, etc., on credit	Voucher register (VR) (or purchases journal PJ)
Receipts of cash	Cash receipts journal (CR)
Payments of cash	Cash payments journal (CP)
Other transactions	General journal (J)

A set of five journals, similar to those listed, can handle the transactions of most small business enterprises. The general journal is necessary, regardless of the special journals involved, to record unusual and nonrepetitive transactions and also to record adjusting and closing entries at the end of the accounting period.

The following forms are presented as an illustration of one possible form for each journal. The columnar headings are dictated by the circumstances of each business enterprise.

Illustration Merchandise Mart, Inc., uses special journals to facilitate the handling of the transactions involving sales, purchases, cash receipts, and cash payments. Subsidiary ledgers are used for accounts receivable and vouchers (accounts) payable.

The procedure for recording sales requires that all credit sales be entered at the gross amount in the sales journal (see page 47) and all cash sales in the cash receipts journal (see page 48). There is no need for a breakdown of sales by item or department, and the accounts receivable ledger is posted from the sales journal. When the individual accounts are posted, a check mark (√) is placed beside the amount in the sales journal. The total of the one money column is posted monthly as a debit to Accounts Receivable (account No. 7) and a credit to Sales (account No. 115). All credit sales have terms of 2/10, n/30.

All cash receipts are recorded in the cash receipts journal (see page 48) from a detailed list of checks received by mail, a report by the internal auditor of daily cash sales and store collections, and a report by the treasurer of other cash sources. If a credit customer takes the cash discount offered, it is recorded at the time cash is received. The customers' accounts are posted daily from the cash receipts journal. The sundry general ledger accounts are posted weekly from the Other Accounts columns, and the column totals are posted monthly, except for the Other Accounts columns for which totals are not posted (NP).

Merchandise Mart, Inc., has found that control over cash payments is improved with the use of a voucher register. The voucher register serves both as a subsidiary ledger for vouchers payable and as a pur-

	Sales Journal			(Page 50)
Date	Customer	Inv. No.	Ref.	Amount
Year 10 Jan. 2	Emily Taylor	1001	√	690
3	R. O. Black	1002	√	850
5	Dan Crane	1003	√	1,020
28	D. A. Adams	1025	√	600
29	Jack Urbanks	1026	√	1,215
				42,460
				(7) (115) Dr, A/R Cr, Sales

chases journal. The system of internal control requires that all checks be supported by a voucher. At the time a voucher is paid, the check number is entered in the appropriate column of the voucher register. Any vouchers entered in the register without check numbers are unpaid and constitute the liability to vendors at that time. Note in the illustrative voucher register on page 48 that voucher No. 1500 has not been paid and that voucher No. 1501 was paid by check No. 1001. The totals of the special columns are posted monthly, and the individual accounts in the Other Accounts columns are posted at least once a month. The total liability represented by unpaid vouchers may include certain vouchers from the preceding month.

The requirement that all checks be supported by a voucher means that only one column is needed in the cash payments journal (see page 49). The total of this one column is posted to the Vouchers Payable account as a debit and to the Cash account as a credit. Recording the payment in the subsidiary ledger for vouchers payable (the voucher register) is done by simply entering the check number in the voucher register. The totals of the cash payments journal are posted monthly.

The general journal (see page 49) is used to record all transactions which do not involve accounts represented in the special journals and for adjusting, closing, and reversing entries. The vast majority of all transactions normally will be recorded in the special journals.

The posting instructions for the illustrated journal entry in the general journal are: (1) Post the debits and credits to the accounts in the general ledger indicated by the account numbers in the ledger page (LP) column (the debit is posted to ledger page No. 8 and the credit is posted to ledger page No. 7) and (2) post the $150 credit to the accounts receivable subsidiary ledger in the account of Sheldon Ausman. The check mark indicates that the posting to the subsidiary ledger has been completed.

Cash Receipts Journal

| | | Debits | | | | | | | Credits | | | |
| | | | | Other accounts | | | Accounts receivable | | | Other accounts | | |
Date	Explanation	Cash	Sales discounts	Account	Ref.	Amount	√	Amount	Sales	Account	Ref.	Amount
Year 10												
Jan. 2	1st Union Bank	10,000								Notes Payable	71	10,000
5	D. A. Adams	833	17				√	850				
6	Cash sales	452							452			
8	Dan Crane	98	2	Notes Receivable	8	920	√	1,020				
31	Cash sales	800							800			
		46,807	256			1,240		31,780	3,423			13,100
		(1)	(117)			(NP)		(7)	(115)			(NP)

Voucher Register

| | | | | | Credit | Debits | | | Other accounts | | |
| | | | Ck. No. | Vou. No. | Vouchers payable | Purchases | Freight-in | Salaries expense | Account | Ref. | Amount |
Date	Payee	Explanation									
Year 10											
Jan. 2	Adams Supply Co.	Merchandise		1500	8,000	8,000					
2	Bross Trucking, Inc.	Freight	1001	1501	50		50				
5	1st Union Bank	Pay note and interest	1002	1502	4,040				Notes Payable	71	4,000
									Interest Expense	170	40
30	Media Services	Advertising		1597	2,000				Advertising Exp.	165	2,000
31	Ace Company	Merchandise		1598	900	900					
					45,720	25,680	980	8,220			10,840
					(70)	(104)	(105)	(72)			(NP)

Cash Payments Journal				(Page 60)
Date	Payee	Vou. No.	Check No.	Amount
Year 10				
Jan. 5	Bross Trucking, Inc.	1501	1001	50
5	1st Union Bank	1502	1002	4,040
31	Dart Brothers	1593	1090	570
				42,690
				(70) (1)
				Dr, V/P
				Cr, Cash

General Journal				(Page 70)
Date	Account titles and explanations	LP	Debit	Credit
Year 10				
Jan. 24	Allowance for Doubtful Accounts	8	150	
	Accounts Receivable—Sheldon Ausman	7/√		150
	To write off uncollectible account.			

ADJUSTING ENTRIES

Financial reporting on an annual, quarterly, or monthly basis requires accountants to summarize the operations of a business enterprise for a specific time period. Basically, the two types of adjusting entries are those (1) to recognize **prepayments** of expenses and revenue and (2) to record **accrued** expenses and revenue. Transactions which were recorded during the accounting period in balance sheet or income statement accounts may affect two or more periods, and an end-of-period adjustment may be needed. Some financial events not recognized on a day-to-day basis must be recorded at the end of the period **to bring the accounting records up to date.** If one should choose to record depreciation daily or to accrue interest expense daily, no adjustment for depreciation or interest expense would be needed at the end of the accounting period, except to correct errors.

Note that every adjusting entry affects both a balance sheet account and an income statement account. This characteristic of adjusting entries reflects their dual purpose: (1) to measure all assets and liabilities accurately, and (2) to measure net income correctly under the accrual basis of accounting.

In illustrating the wide variety of adjusting entries, it is helpful to classify them into the following groups:

Apportionment of recorded costs
Apportionment of recorded revenue
Accrual of unrecorded expenses
Accrual of unrecorded revenue
Valuation of accounts receivable

Apportionment of recorded costs

Costs which will benefit more than one accounting period are frequently incurred. These costs must be apportioned between periods in a manner which approximates the usefulness derived from the goods and services in the production of revenue; this apportionment process is a necessary step to determine net income of each period. Recording periodic depreciation expense is an example of a cost-apportionment adjusting entry, as shown below:

Journal entry for depreciation

Depreciation Expense	12,000	
Accumulated Depreciation of Building		12,000
To record depreciation expense for one year.		

The periodic depreciation expense is considered a cost of production or a period expense to be deducted from revenue, depending on the nature of the asset and the service performed. In the balance sheet, accumulated depreciation is deducted from the cost of plant assets.

Cost apportionment also is involved in accounting for all types of prepayments. However, the adjusting entry will vary depending on the accounting procedure followed in recording the original transaction. To illustrate, assume that office supplies are acquired during the accounting period at a cost of $5,000. At the end of the period a physical inventory reveals that supplies on hand cost $550. At the time the supplies were acquired, the $5,000 may have been debited to an asset account or an expense account. The required adjusting entry for each approach is illustrated below and on page 51.

Prepayment Debited to Asset Account The adjusting entry required is to transfer the **expired** portion of the cost to an **expense** account as illustrated below:

Adjusting entry reduces asset account

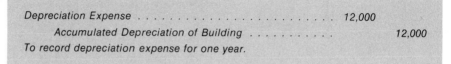

	Inventory of Office Supplies		Office Supplies Expense	
Balance, Dec. 31	5,000			
Adjusting entry		4,450	4,450	

Prepayment Debited to Expense Account The adjusting entry required is to transfer the **unexpired** portion of the cost to an **asset** account as illustrated below:

	Inventory of Office Supplies		Office Supplies Expense	
Adjusting entry establishes asset account				
Balance, Dec. 31			5,000	
Adjusting entry	550			550

Under either original recording, the final result is the same. There is an asset of $550 and an expense of $4,450. In both cases the amount of the unexpired cost was determined; an adjusting entry is necessary to make the account balances agree with the information available.

Apportionment of recorded revenue

Occasionally a business enterprise will receive payment for goods and services before the goods are delivered or the services are performed. A liability exists which will be satisfied when performance takes place. When cash is received, the original transaction may be recorded by a credit to a liability account or a revenue account.

Assume that customers paid $500,000 for magazine subscriptions during the current accounting period; however, $75,000 represented payments for magazines to be delivered in subsequent periods. The adjusting entries for each of the two methods of recording cash receipts are:

Liability Account Credited on Receipt of Cash The required adjusting entry to recognize the **earned** revenue for the period appears below:

	Unearned Subscriptions		Subscriptions Revenue	
Adjusting entry reduces liability account				
Balance, Dec. 31		500,000		
Adjusting entry	425,000			425,000

Revenue Account Credited on Receipt of Cash The required adjusting entry to transfer the **unearned** revenue to a liability account is shown below:

	Unearned Subscriptions		Subscriptions Revenue	
Adjusting entry establishes liability account				
Balance, Dec. 31				500,000
Adjusting entry		75,000	75,000	

Accrual of unrecorded expenses

The incurring of certain expenses is related to the passage of time. These expenses generally are not recorded until payment is made, unless the end of the accounting period comes before the required date of payment. Interest and salaries are typical of the expenses which accrue with the passage of time and are recorded only when paid, except when the end of the accounting period occurs between the time the expense was incurred and the payment is due. In order to measure expenses accurately for an accounting period, an adjusting entry is necessary to record the accrued expense and the corresponding liability.

For example, interest of $18,000 on a $400,000 note payable is paid on March 1 and September 1 of each year. If expenses and liabilities are to be reported properly on December 31, the following year-end adjusting entry is required:

Journal entry to record accrued expense

Interest Expense.	12,000	
Accrued Interest Payable.		12,000
To record the interest owed on a 9%, $400,000 note for four months to Dec. 31.		

Accrual of unrecorded revenue

Revenue which has been earned but not recorded must be recognized at the end of the accounting period. For example, revenue which is earned on assets leased to others or on interest-bearing loans seldom is recorded until the cash is received, except at the end of the accounting period. In order to measure accurately the results of operations and to avoid shifting income between periods, revenue should be recognized in the period earned.

To illustrate, assume that rents totaling $625 which have been earned but not collected for the month of December have not been recorded. The following adjusting entry on December 31 is required for a complete measurement of revenue and assets:

Journal entry to record accrued revenue

Rents Receivable	625	
Rent Revenue		625
To record rents earned during December.		

Valuation of accounts receivable

A policy of making sales on credit almost inevitably results in some accounts receivable which prove uncollectible. To achieve a satisfactory matching of revenue and related expenses, the estimated expense arising from sales on credit should be recorded in the accounting period in which sales occur. This estimate of probable expense from the granting of credit requires an end-of-period adjusting entry to revise the valuation originally assigned to accounts receivable. Once the estimate of the doubtful accounts expense is established, the following adjusting entry is made:

Journal entry to record doubtful accounts expense

Doubtful Accounts Expense.   2,500
*   Allowance for Doubtful Accounts. 2,500*
To record doubtful accounts expense.

The Doubtful Accounts Expense account generally is reported as an operating expense in the income statement. Some accountants prefer to deduct it directly from sales to measure net sales, because no revenue is realized if accounts receivable are not collected. The credit balance of the allowance account is deducted from accounts receivable in the balance sheet to indicate the net collections expected.

CLOSING PROCEDURES

Closing revenue and expense accounts

Revenue and expense accounts are closed at the end of each accounting period by transferring the balances in each such account to a summary account, Income Summary. Revenue and expense accounts are extensions of owners' equity and are used to measure net income for an accounting period. Once this information has been summarized, the revenue and expense accounts have served their purpose, and the net increase or decrease in owners' equity is transferred to an appropriate owners' equity account. Thus, the closing of the revenue and expense accounts keeps separate the operating results of each period.

If we assume that a Subscriptions Revenue account after adjustment has a credit balance of $425,000, the closing entry is:

Journal entry to close revenue account

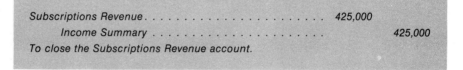

Subscriptions Revenue.   425,000
*   Income Summary 425,000*
To close the Subscriptions Revenue account.

The balance in the Subscriptions Revenue account is now zero. Temporarily, the Income Summary account has a credit balance of $425,000. All other revenue accounts are closed similarly.

To close an expense account, one must transfer its debit balance to the left side of the Income Summary account. The following journal entry to close a Salaries Expense account with a debit balance of $61,625 is illustrative of this phase of the closing process:

Income Summary	61,625	
Salaries Expense		61,625
To close the Salaries Expense account.		

The Salaries Expense account now has a zero balance, and the credit balance in the Income Summary account is reduced by the debit for salaries expense in the amount of $61,625. All other expense accounts are closed similarly. When there are numerous expense accounts, each generally can be closed in one journal entry, with one debit to the Income Summary account and a separate credit to each expense account.

Closing inventory and related ledger accounts

When the periodic inventory system is used, the journal entries to establish the cost of goods sold and the ending inventory balance for the accounting period may be thought of as adjusting entries; however, because there may be little need for a ledger account for cost of goods sold, the adjusting and closing entries may be combined. This procedure is accomplished by closing the beginning inventory, purchases, and all related accounts to the Income Summary. The ending inventory is recorded by a debit to the Inventory account and a credit to the Income Summary account. The balance remaining in the Income Summary account is the cost of goods sold for the period. To illustrate, assume the following: January 1 inventory, $80,000; purchases, $275,000; freight-in, $40,000; purchases returns and allowances, $2,500; December 31 inventory, including applicable freight, $60,000. The journal entries to close the accounts and to record the ending inventory are as follows:

Purchases Returns and Allowances	2,500	
Income Summary	392,500	
Inventory, Jan. 1		80,000
Purchases.		275,000
Freight-in		40,000
To close beginning inventory and net purchases for the period.		
Inventory, Dec. 31	60,000	
Income Summary		60,000
To record ending inventory.		

The debit balance in the Income Summary account after these two closing entries is $332,500, the cost of goods sold for the year. Some accountants prefer to use a separate account, Cost of Goods Sold, to summarize the merchandising accounts when the periodic inventory system is used. The journal entry *reflecting cost of goods sold in a separate account* follows:

Alternative: Record cost of goods sold in ledger account . . .

Purchases Returns and Allowances	*2,500*	
Inventory, Dec. 31	*60,000*	
Cost of Goods Sold	*332,500*	
Inventory, Jan. 1		*80,000*
Purchases		*275,000*
Freight-in		*40,000*
To record cost of goods sold for the period.		

The journal entry to close the Cost of Goods Sold account to the Income Summary account is illustrated below:

. . . and close cost of goods sold

Income Summary	*332,500*	
Cost of Goods Sold		*332,500*
To close Cost of Goods Sold account.		

Closing the Income Summary account

At this point the balance of the Income Summary account indicates the net income or net loss for the year. A credit balance in the Income Summary account indicates a profitable year and an increase in owners' equity; a debit balance indicates a net loss and a decrease in owners' equity. The Income Summary account is closed by transferring its balance to Retained Earnings.

REVERSING ENTRIES

After the accounting records have been adjusted and closed at the end of an accounting period, reversing entries *may be made* on the first day of the next accounting period. The purpose of the reversing entries is to simplify the recording of routine transactions by disposing of the accrued items (assets and liabilities), which were entered in balance sheet accounts through the adjusting entries. A reversing entry, as the name implies, is the exact reverse of an adjusting entry. It consists of the same accounts and dollar amounts as the adjusting entry, but the debits and credits are reversed, and the date is the beginning of the next accounting period.

For example, assume that July 31, Year 1, Clark Company borrowed $200,000 at 12% on a long-term note with interest of $6,000 payable every three months. The first payment of interest was made on October 31, Year 1; the next interest payment is due on January 31, Year 2. The company is on a calendar-year basis. Before the accounting records are closed on December 31, Year 1, an adjusting entry must be made debiting Interest Expense and crediting Accrued Interest Payable for $4,000, the amount of interest applicable to November and December. If no reversing entry is made on January 1, Year 2, the next quarterly interest payment of $6,000 on January 31, Year 2, will be recorded by a debit of $4,000 to Acquired Interest Payable, a debit of $2,000 to Interest Expense, and a credit of $6,000 to Cash. However, assume that on January 1, Year 2, the following reversing entry is made:

Reversing entry for accrued expense

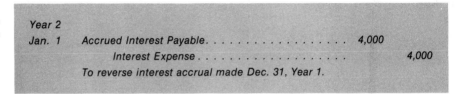

Year 2			
Jan. 1	Accrued Interest Payable.	4,000	
	Interest Expense		4,000
	To reverse interest accrual made Dec. 31, Year 1.		

This reversing entry has eliminated the liability account Acquired Interest Payable and has caused the Interest Expense account to have a $4,000 credit balance. Consequently, the cash payment of three months' interest on January 31 will not need to be apportioned. The January 31 entry will consist of a debit to Interest Expense for $6,000 and a credit to Cash for $6,000. In other words, the interest payment on January 31 (by reason of the reversing entry) can be recorded in exactly the same manner as the three other quarterly interest payments during the year. After the January 31 interest payment has been recorded, the Interest Expense account for the new year will contain a debit of $6,000 and a credit of $4,000, which produce the correct debit balance of $2,000 representing interest expense for the month of January.

An argument for reversing entries is apparent from this example. Employees with limited knowledge of accounting can be instructed to follow a standard procedure for recording all recurring transactions. The reversing entries, as well as the year-end adjusting entries, are recorded in the general journal by an accountant who understands the issues involved.

General guidelines for reversing entries

When a **policy of using reversing entries is adopted,** the following general rules should be followed:

1 When an adjusting journal entry creates an asset or liability account which normally is not used during the accounting period, a reversing entry is required. Thus, adjustments to record revenue and expenses are reversed because asset and liability accounts such as Rents Receivable and Accrued Interest Payable are not used in the normal course of accounting during the period. Similarly, if payments for insurance and supplies during the period are recorded in expense accounts, or if revenue received in advance during the period is recorded in revenue accounts, the adjusting entries would have to be reversed because asset and liability accounts not used during the period would be established by the adjusting entries.

2 When an adjusting entry adjusts an asset or liability account which normally is used to record transactions during the period, no reversing entry is required. Thus, if acquisitions of supplies and other short-term prepayments are recorded during the period in asset accounts, or if revenue received in advance is recorded during the period in liability accounts, the adjusting entries would bring *existing* asset and liability balances up to date, and no reversing entry would be required. For the same reason adjusting entries for depreciation and doubtful accounts expense are not reversed.

Previously, we suggested that reversing certain adjusting entries is an *optional procedure* designed to simplify recording of recurring transactions. Another way of stating this is that reversing entries are never required as long as adjusting entries bring existing asset and liability accounts up to date.

To illustrate three alternative approaches for adjusting and reversing entries, let us go back to the Clark Company example on page 56. Use of any of the three approaches illustrated below results in a balance of $24,000 in Interest Expense and a balance of $4,000 in Accrued Interest Payable at the end of Year 2:

Each alternative approach produces identical results

(1)	(2)	(3)
No reversing entry; $4,000 of first interest payment in Year 2 is debited to Accrued Interest Payable	*Reversing entry (R) is made; all interest payments in Year 2 are recorded in Interest Expense*	*No reversing entry; all interest payments in Year 2 are recorded in Interest Expense*

Interest Expense		Interest Expense		Interest Expense	
(a) 20,000		(a) 24,000	(R) 4,000	(a) 24,000	
(b) 4,000		(b) 4,000			
Bal. 24,000		Bal. 24,000			

Accrued Interest Payable			Accrued Interest Payable			Accrued Interest Payable		
(a) 4,000	Bal. 4,000		(R) 4,000	Bal. 4,000			Bal. 4,000	
	(b) 4,000			(b) 4,000				
	Bal. 4,000			Bal. 4,000				

(a) *Payments of interest in Year 2; Cash account is credited.*
(b) *Adjusting entries on Dec. 31, Year 2.*
(R) *Reversing entry on Jan. 1, Year 2.*

Note that no adjusting entry was required under alternative (3) because the accrued interest payable at the end of Year 2 was the same as it was at the end of Year 1. If the accrued interest at the end of Year 2 was other than $4,000, an adjusting entry would be required to Accrued Interest Payable, with a corresponding debit or credit to Interest Expense.

THE WORK SHEET

Accountants have found the work sheet useful in performing the year-end accounting procedures and in preparing financial statements. The work sheet is especially helpful in avoiding errors in the general journal and the ledger in more complex situations.

Purpose of the work sheet

A *work sheet* is a columnar working paper designed to facilitate the organization and arrangement of accounting data at the end of an accounting period. It is designed to minimize errors by automatically bringing to light many types of discrepancies which otherwise might be entered in the permanent accounting records. Accountants prepare a work sheet as an informal record strictly for their own purposes; it does not replace any financial statement and is never presented as the end result of the accountants' work. The work sheet is a tool which permits the adjusting and closing entries and the financial statements to be prepared informally before any part of this work is formalized.

The work sheet may be thought of as a "testing ground" on which the ledger accounts are adjusted, balanced, and arranged in the general form of financial statements. The satisfactory completion of the work sheet provides considerable assurance that all end-of-period accounting procedures have been brought together properly. The finished work sheet then serves as the source for the preparation of the formal financial statements and the adjusting and closing entries, which are recorded in the general journal and posted to the general ledger.

Illustration of work sheet for a merchandising enterprise

A commonly used form of work sheet with appropriate headings is illustrated on pages 60 and 61 for Village Merchandising Company for Year 4. The work-sheet heading should contain the name of the company, the title (work sheet), and the period covered. The body of this work sheet contains six pairs of money columns, each pair consisting of a debit and credit column. The procedures required in the preparation of the work sheet when the periodic inventory system is used are described below:

1 Enter the ledger account titles and balances on the work sheet, using the first two money columns—the Unadjusted Trial Balance. The accountant often can save time and effort by arranging the accounts in the order in which they will appear on the financial statements. Frequently several adjustments will affect a single account; consequently, several lines should be left blank following this account to facilitate listing the adjustments.

2 Enter the adjustments in the Adjustments columns. Adjusting entries always should be entered on the work sheet before they are journalized. One of the functions of the work sheet is to establish the correctness of the adjusting entries. The information used as the basis for the adjustments illustrated on the work sheet for Village Merchandising Company is stated below:

   (a) The short-term investments consist of government bonds on which accrued interest receivable amounts to $33 on December 31.

   (b) The accounts receivable arising from sales of the current period which are expected to be uncollectible are estimated to be $\frac{1}{2}$% of gross sales.

   (c) Accounts receivable totaling $520 are considered to be uncollectible, and the credit manager has authorized the write-off of these accounts.

   (d) The balances in the Short-Term Prepayments account are as follows:

	Jan. 1	Dec. 31
Unexpired insurance.	$ 750	$ 450
Inventory of supplies.	600	700
Prepaid rent	150	400
Totals.	$1,500	$1,550

All cash payments for these items were recorded in expense accounts. Village Merchandising Company **does not reverse any adjusting entries.**

   (e) The furniture and fixtures are estimated to have an economic life of 10 years, with no residual value at the end of that time.

   (f) Accrued interest payable on the notes payable amounts to $40 on December 31.

   (g) Salaries accrued since the last payday total $818 on December 31.

   (h) The inventory on December 31 totals $28,900, and income taxes expense is estimated at $370.

After adjustments (a) through (h) are entered on the work sheet, the Adjustments columns must be totaled to prove the equality of the debits and credits. Without this proof of arithmetical accuracy, errors are likely to be carried forward in the remaining work.

3 Determine the new account balances and enter these in the Adjusted Trial Balance columns. The purpose of this step is to prove the accuracy of the work of combining the adjustments and the original balances. The Adjusted Trial Balance columns often are omitted from the work sheet if adjustments are few.

4 Extend each balance from the adjusted trial balance (or from the first four columns) to the Income Statement, Retained Earnings Statement, or Balance Sheet columns. Note that the beginning inventory of $28,000 is entered in the Income Statement debit column.

5 Enter the ending inventory in the Income Statement credit column and the Balance Sheet debit column. This procedure in effect deducts the ending inventory from the total goods available for sale to leave the costs comprising the cost of goods sold for the year in the Income Statement columns.

6 Total the Income Statement columns. The balancing figure is the net income or loss for the year. The difference of $1,860 between the credit and debit columns in this illustration represents net income which is entered in the debit column of the Income Statement and in the credit column of the Retained Earnings Statement.

7 Balance the Retained Earnings Statement columns and enter the difference in the debit column of the Retained Earnings Statement and in the credit column of the Balance Sheet. This adjusts the retained earnings balance for changes during the year.

VILLAGE MERCHANDISING COMPANY
Work Sheet
For Year Ended December 31, Year 4

	Unadjusted trial balance		Adjustments		Adjusted trial balance		Income statement		Retained earnings statement		Balance sheet	
	Debit	Credit	Debit	Credit	Debit	Credit	Debit	Credit	Debit	Credit	Debit	Credit
Cash	8,650				8,650						8,650	
Short-term investments	2,000				2,000						2,000	
Accounts receivable	15,700			(c) 520	15,180						15,180	
Allowance for doubtful accounts		800	(c) 520	(b) 875		1,155						1,155
Inventory (periodic system)	28,000				28,000		28,000	28,900			28,900	
Short-term prepayments	1,500		(d) 50		1,550						1,550	
Furniture and fixtures	6,000				6,000						6,000	
Accumulated depreciation		1,800		(e) 600		2,400						2,400
Notes payable		4,000				4,000						4,000
Accounts payable		10,000				10,000						10,000
Capital stock		40,000				40,000						40,000
Retained earnings, Jan. 1, Year 4		3,170				3,170				3,170		
Dividends	1,500				1,500				1,500			
Sales		175,000				175,000		175,000				
Sales returns and allowances	2,500				2,500		2,500					

Account	Trial Balance Dr	Trial Balance Cr	Adjustments Dr	Adjustments Cr	Adjusted Trial Balance Dr	Adjusted Trial Balance Cr	Income Statement Dr	Income Statement Cr	Retained Earnings Dr	Retained Earnings Cr	Balance Sheet Dr	Balance Sheet Cr
Sales discounts	3,150				3,150		3,150					
Purchases	128,000				128,000		128,000					
Purchases returns and allowances		3,000				3,000		3,000				
Salaries expense	22,500		(g) 818		23,318		23,318					
Rent expense	5,050			(d) 250	4,800		4,800					
Advertising expense	9,000				9,000		9,000					
Janitorial expense	1,500				1,500		1,500					
Miscellaneous expenses	2,000			(d) 100	1,900		1,900					
Interest expense	120		(f) 40		160		160					
Property taxes expense	600				600		600					
Accrued interest receivable			(a) 33		33						33	
Interest revenue				(a) 33		33		33				
Doubtful accounts expense			(b) 875		875		875					
Insurance expense			(d) 300		300		300					
Depreciation expense			(e) 600		600		600					
Accrued interest payable				(f) 40		40						40
Accrued salaries payable				(g) 818		818						818
Income taxes expense			(h) 370		370		370					
Income taxes payable				(h) 370		370						370
Net income							1,860			1,860		
Retained earnings, Dec. 31, Year 4									3,530			3,530
Totals	237,770	237,770	3,606	3,606	239,986	239,986	206,933	206,933	3,530	5,030	62,313	62,313

8 Total the Balance Sheet columns. Considerable assurance of the arithmetical accuracy of the year-end procedures is provided if these two columns balance. The Balance Sheet columns prove the equation that assets are equal to the total of liabilities and stockholders' equity.

Although the work sheet proves the mathematical accuracy of what has been done, it does not prove that some adjustments have not been omitted or that the amounts used in making the adjustments were correct.

Work Sheet and Year-End Procedures   The work sheet is the source of the formal adjusting entries. Once the adjusting entries are entered in the work sheet, the identical information is recorded in the general journal and the ledger. The adjusting journal entries for Village Merchandising Company on December 31, Year 4, are illustrated below and on page 63.

Adjusting entries at end of period

	VILLAGE MERCHANDISING COMPANY		
	Adjusting Entries		
	December 31, Year 4		
(a)	Accrued Interest Receivable.	33	
	Interest Revenue.		33
	To accrue interest on short-term prepayments.		
(b)	Doubtful Accounts Expense.	875	
	Allowance for Doubtful Accounts.		875
	To increase allowance for doubtful accounts by ½% of gross sales.		
(c)	Allowance for Doubtful Accounts	520	
	Accounts Receivable		520
	To write off uncollectible accounts.		
(d)	Short-Term Prepayments	50	
	Insurance Expense	300	
	Rent Expense		250
	Miscellaneous Expenses		100
	To adjust Short-Term Prepayments account to year-end balance.		
(e)	Depreciation Expense	600	
	Accumulated Depreciation.		600
	To record depreciation at 10% of cost of furniture and fixtures.		
(f)	Interest Expense	40	
	Accrued Interest Payable.		40
	To accrue interest on notes payable.		

(g) Salaries Expense 818
         Accrued Salaries Payable   818
     To accrue unpaid salaries.

(h) Income Taxes Expense. 370
         Income Taxes Payable   370
     To record estimated income tax liability.

The data in the Income Statement columns of the work sheet also can be used to prepare the closing entries. When the work sheet is prepared, the closing process generally is summarized in a series of closing entries as illustrated below and on page 64 for Village Merchandising Company:

Closing entries at end of period

VILLAGE MERCHANDISING COMPANY
Closing Entries
December 31, Year 4

Income Summary	153,000	
Purchases Returns and Allowances	3,000	
Purchases.		128,000
Inventory, Jan. 1, Year 4		28,000
To close beginning inventory and net purchases.		
Inventory, Dec. 31, Year 4	28,900	
Income Summary		28,900
To record ending inventory.		
Sales.	175,000	
Interest Revenue.	33	
Sales Returns and Allowances		2,500
Sales Discounts		3,150
Salaries Expense.		23,318
Rent Expense.		4,800
Advertising Expense.		9,000
Janitorial Expense.		1,500
Miscellaneous Expenses		1,900
Interest Expense.		160
Property Taxes Expense		600
Doubtful Accounts Expense		875
Insurance Expense		300
Depreciation Expense.		600
Income Taxes Expense		370
Income Summary		125,960
To close revenue and expense accounts.		

Income Summary	*1,860*	
Retained Earnings		*1,860*
To close Income Summary account.		
Retained Earnings	*1,500*	
Dividends		*1,500*
To close Dividends account.		

Illustration of work sheet for a manufacturing enterprise

The procedures for preparing a work sheet for a manufacturing enterprise are similar to those used for a merchandising enterprise. The addition of a pair of columns to summarize the manufacturing operation is the major difference. These columns allow for one more step in the classification of the data. The adjusted trial balance, which is an optional step, is omitted from this illustration.

The following data are the basis for the adjusting entries included in the work sheet for Cole Manufacturing Company for Year 4 on pages 66 and 67.

(a) Doubtful accounts expense is estimated to be $3,000 for Year 4.

(b) A three-year insurance policy was purchased 18 months ago at a cost of $1,800. The insurance expense is allocated to other factory costs and general expense on an 80:20 basis.

(c) The wages accrued since the last pay period are: direct labor, $1,800, and indirect labor, $950. The officers, office staff, and sales staff are paid on the last day of the month.

(d) Interest of $1,125 has accrued on notes payable.

(e) Depreciation for the plant assets is computed by the straight-line method based on the following information:

Asset	Estimated economic life, years	Estimated residual value	Cost allocation, % Factory	Cost allocation, % General
Building	40	$ –0–	80	20
Machinery and equipment .	10	–0–	100	–0–
Furniture and fixtures	20	2,000	10	90

(f) The light bill for December has not been received as of December 31. Based on past experience, the cost applicable to December is estimated to be $1,450. All heat, light, and power costs relate to the factory.

(g) An inventory of factory supplies on December 31 indicates that supplies costing $850 are on hand.

(h) The income taxes expense for Cole Manufacturing Company is assumed to be $3,500.

(*i*) Physical inventories indicate that the cost of inventories on December 31 is as follows:

Finished goods	$41,500
Goods in process	26,350
Raw material	12,650

Work Sheet and Year-End Procedures The journal entries for closing the manufacturing accounts, for adjusting the inventory balances, for closing the revenue and expense accounts, and for closing the Dividends account are illustrated below and on page 68, for Cole Manufacturing Company.

Closing entries for manufacturing enterprise

COLE MANUFACTURING COMPANY
Closing Entries
December 31, Year 4

Cost of Finished Goods Manufactured	434,770	
Raw Material Inventory, Dec. 31, Year 4	12,650	
Goods in Process Inventory, Dec. 31, Year 4	26,350	
Purchases Returns and Allowances	4,000	
Raw Material Inventory, Jan. 1, Year 4		16,000
Goods in Process Inventory, Jan. 1, Year 4		21,000
Raw Material Purchases		125,000
Freight-in		3,500
Direct Labor Costs		194,300
Indirect Labor Costs		73,550
Heat, Light, and Power		13,750
Other Factory Costs		14,630
Depreciation of Buildings		3,000
Depreciation of Machinery and Equipment		13,000
Depreciation of Furniture and Fixtures		40
To record cost of finished goods manufactured and ending inventories of raw material and goods in process.		
Finished Goods Inventory, Dec. 31, Year 4	41,500	
Cost of Goods Sold	441,270	
Cost of Finished Goods Manufactured		434,770
Finished Goods Inventory, Jan. 1, Year 4		48,000
To record ending finished goods inventory and cost of goods sold.		

COLE MANUFACTURING COMPANY
Work Sheet
For Year Ended December 31, Year 4

	Unadjusted trial balance		Adjustments		Manufacturing		Income statement		Retained earnings statement		Balance sheet	
	Debit	Credit	Debit	Credit	Debit	Credit	Debit	Credit	Debit	Credit	Debit	Credit
Cash	32,000										32,000	
Accounts receivable	70,000										70,000	
Allowance for doubtful accounts		1,200		(a) 3,000								4,200
Inventories, Jan. 1, Year 4:												
Finished goods	48,000						48,000	41,500			41,500	
Goods in process	21,000				21,000	26,350					26,350	
Raw material	16,000				16,000	12,650					12,650	
Unexpired insurance	1,500			(b) 600							900	
Land	72,000										72,000	
Buildings	150,000										150,000	
Accum. depr. of buildings		45,000		(e) 3,750								48,750
Machinery and equipment	130,000										130,000	
Accum. depr. of mach. and equip.		52,000		(e) 13,000								65,000
Furniture and fixtures	10,000										10,000	
Accum. depr. of furn. and fixtures		3,000		(e) 400								3,400
Notes payable		75,000										75,000
Accounts payable		41,300		(f) 1,450								42,750
Capital stock, $10 par		100,000										100,000
Paid-in capital in excess of par		100,000										100,000
Retained earnings, Jan. 1, Year 4		88,875								88,875		
Dividends	6,000								6,000			
Sales		633,600						633,600				
Sales returns and allowances	3,600						3,600					

Raw material purchases	125,000				125,000							
Purchases returns and allowances		4,000				4,000						
Freight-in	3,500				3,500							
Direct labor costs	192,500		(c) 1,800		194,300							
Indirect labor costs	72,600		(c) 950		73,550							
Heat, light, and power	12,300		(f) 1,450		13,750							
Other factory costs	15,000		(b) 480	(g) 850	14,630							
Advertising expense	35,000						35,000					
Sales salaries expense	42,000						42,000					
Delivery expense	8,000						8,000					
Administrative salaries expense	50,000						50,000					
Office salaries expense	20,000						20,000					
Telephone and telegraph expense	1,800						1,800					
Other general expenses	2,800		(b) 120				2,920					
Interest expense	3,375		(d) 1,125				4,500					
Doubtful accounts expense			(a) 3,000				3,000					
Accrued wages payable				(c) 2,750								2,750
Accrued interest payable				(d) 1,125								1,125
Depreciation of bldg. (factory)			(e) 3,000		3,000							
Depreciation of bldg. (general)			(e) 750				750					
Depreciation of mach, and equip. (factory)			(e) 13,000		13,000							
Depreciation of furn. and fix. (factory)			(e) 40		40							
Depreciation of furn. and fix. (general)			(e) 360				360					
Inventory of factory supplies			(g) 850								850	
Income taxes expense			(h) 3,500				3,500					
Income taxes payable				(h) 3,500								3,500
Cost of finished goods manufactured						434,770	434,770					
Net income							16,900			16,900		
Retained earnings, Dec. 31, Year 4									99,775			99,775
Totals	1,143,975	1,143,975	30,425	30,425	477,770	477,770	675,100	675,100	105,775	105,775	546,250	546,250

Sales.	633,600	
Cost of Goods Sold		441,270
Sales Returns and Allowances		3,600
Advertising Expense.		35,000
Sales Salaries Expense.		42,000
Delivery Expense		8,000
Administrative Salaries Expense		50,000
Office Salaries Expense.		20,000
Telephone and Telegraph Expense.		1,800
Other General Expenses		2,920
Interest Expense.		4,500
Doubtful Accounts Expense		3,000
Depreciation of Buildings		750
Depreciation of Furniture and Fixtures		360
Income Taxes Expense		3,500
Income Summary		16,900
To close revenue and expense accounts.		
Income Summary	16,900	
Retained Earnings.		16,900
To close Income Summary account.		
Retained Earnings.	6,000	
Dividends		6,000
To close Dividends account.		

Statement of cost of finished goods manufactured

The cost of goods completed during an accounting period is summarized in a statement of cost of finished goods manufactured. The information for this statement, illustrated on page 69 for Cole Manufacturing Company, is taken from the Manufacturing columns of the work sheet.

Using accounting information for business decisions

The ultimate objective of accounting is the *use* of accounting information, through analysis and interpretation, as a basis for business decisions. Information derived from accounting records serves business executives in controlling current operations and in planning future operations. Published financial statements afford outsiders a means of analyzing and interpreting past operations of business enterprises in which they have an interest. These published financial statements tradi-

A statement of
production costs for an
accounting period

COLE MANUFACTURING COMPANY
Statement of Cost of Finished Goods Manufactured
For Year Ended December 31, Year 4

Goods in process inventory, Jan. 1, Year 4.		$ 21,000
Raw material used:		
Raw material inventory, Jan. 1, Year 4	$ 16,000	
Raw material purchases (net).	124,500	
Cost of raw material available for use.	$140,500	
Less: Raw material inventory, Dec. 31, Year 4	12,650	
Cost of raw material used.	$127,850	
Direct labor costs	194,300	
Factory overhead costs (see work sheet for details)	117,970	
Total manufacturing costs		440,120
Total cost of goods in process during Year 4		$461,120
Less: Goods in process inventory, Dec. 31, Year 4		26,350
Cost of finished goods manufactured		$434,770

tionally have been, for the most part, reports of past events. The past is often the key to the future, however, and for this reason accounting information is highly valued by decision makers, both inside and outside the enterprise.

Limitations of accounting information

The objective of this book is to examine the basic accounting principles and their effectiveness as the underlying assumptions of accounting, to explore the rules and conventions, and to consider the possible uses of accounting information once it is accumulated. One must be aware of the fact that accounting is justified only because the information accumulated and presented is useful. At the same time, one must remember that accounting information often is limited because many factors that are not subject to measurement in terms of money have been omitted. Examples are the human resources of a business enterprise and the political and economic environment in which the enterprise exists. Furthermore, in recent years persistent inflation has made the dollar an imperfect tool for measurement of accounting information.

REVIEW QUESTIONS

1 Describe the **accounting cycle** and list the sequence of procedures involved in the accounting cycle.

2 State in concise form the rules of debits and credits for the five basic types of ledger accounts.

3 Describe the function of the *journals.*

4 What is the function of the *ledger*?

5 Explain the advantage of using controlling accounts and subsidiary ledgers.

6 What is the purpose of the *trial balance*? Does it provide proof that there have been no errors in the recording, classifying, and summarizing of business transactions?

7 How are the temporary or nominal ledger accounts (revenue and expense accounts) related to the basic accounting equation, $A = L + OE$?

8 What is the objective of using special journals?

9 With the advent of electronic computers, the cost of data-processing equipment and the complexity of operations increased many times. What economies are available to the user to offset the added costs of converting to and using this type of equipment?

10 What are *adjusting entries,* and why are they necessary?

11 Why is it necessary to prepare adjusting entries to change the carrying amount of the accounts receivable when the journal entries for receivables usually are made only on objective evidence of credit sales and cash collections?

12 Prepare adjusting entries on June 30 indicated by the following information:
  a Accrued wages total $3,000.
  b The estimate of doubtful accounts expense is $2,000, and the allowance for doubtful accounts has a zero balance.

13 What are *closing entries*? Why are they made? What ledger accounts are closed?

14 You are given the following information about the merchandise accounts of Foxx Company and are asked to prepare the necessary journal entries to adjust the Inventory account and close the relevant accounts to cost of goods sold.

Inventory, Jan. 1, Year 10 (ledger balance)	$ 44,000
Purchases	276,400
Purchases returns and allowances	1,700
Purchases discounts	3,800
Freight and transportation-in	4,800
Handling and storage costs	26,800
Inventory, Dec. 31, Year 10 (physical count; valued at net invoice cost plus freight, handling, and storage costs)	46,200

15 What are *reversing entries,* and under what circumstances are they most commonly used?

16 Which of the following adjusting entries might be reversed? For each entry indicate your reasons for reversing or not reversing.

a Unearned Subscriptions 10,000
        Subscriptions Revenue.   10,000

b Inventory of Office Supplies 5,000
        Office Supplies Expense   5,000

c Interest Expense 300
        Accrued Interest Payable   300

d Depreciation Expense 8,000
        Accumulated Depreciation   8,000

17 What is the purpose of the **work sheet,** and what benefits may be derived from using it?

EXERCISES

Ex. 2-1 Total manufacturing costs for Bronze Products, Inc., for Year 3 were $642,700. The cost of finished goods manufactured in Year 3 was $655,500.
    Compute the amount of the goods in process inventory at the end of Year 3, assuming that the goods in process inventory at the beginning of Year 3 was $40,000.

Ex. 2-2 The balance in the Accounts Receivable controlling account on January 1, Year 6, was $146,220. During January, sales on credit were $109,800, and cash collections were $120,000 after sales discounts of $1,800. Accounts receivable of $2,200 were written off as uncollectible on January 22, and a provision of $1,460 for doubtful accounts was included as an expense in the income statement for January.
    Reproduce the ledger account (three-column form) for the Accounts Receivable controlling account for the month of January, Year 6.

Ex. 2-3 All but one of the ledger accounts of Hale Shoe Store, a single proprietorship owned by J. D. Hale, appear in the following list on December 31 of the current year:

Accounts receivable . . . . $ 7,500
Accounts payable 11,000
Accrued liabilities 300
Accumulated depreciation 10,000
Cash 6,000
Inventory 15,000
Notes payable 14,000
Plant assets 31,000
Short-term prepayments 500

    On January 1 of the current year, Hale's equity in the proprietorship amounted to $15,000. During the current year Hale withdrew $5,200 cash and made an additional investment of $3,000 of plant assets which had previously been part of another business enterprise owned by Hale.
    Compute the net income or net loss of Hale Shoe Store for the current year, and show supporting computations.

Ex.2-4 The following transactions were completed in January (the first month of operations) by Lane's Markets:

(1) Sales on credit totaled $13,000. Terms, 2/10, n/60.
(2) Cash sales amounted to $24,000.
(3) Purchases of merchandise totaled $50,000.
(4) Payments of $28,600 were made to creditors in full settlement of purchase invoices totaling $29,000.
(5) Accounts receivable in the amount of $10,000 were collected; one-half of these collections were made before the expiration of the 10-day discount period.
(6) Lane, the owner, withdrew merchandise for personal use. This merchandise had a cost of $3,000 and had been marked to sell for $3,900. Lane also withdrew $500 cash during January.
(7) Inventory on hand at the end of January was determined by physical count to consist of goods which cost $23,000.
(8) Operating expenses for the month totaled $8,500.

Determine the net income or net loss of Lane's Markets for the month of January. Show supporting computations.

Ex. 2-5 The accounting policies of Gina Publications, Inc., provide that subscriptions received from customers be credited to Subscriptions Revenue when received. Purchases of supplies are regularly debited to Supplies Expense at time of purchase. The after-closing trial balance on December 31, Year 5, includes the following accounts:

	Debit	Credit
Accounts receivable	$ 24,000	
Allowance for doubtful accounts		$ 2,200
Inventory of supplies	1,710	
Equipment	135,500	
Accumulated depreciation		48,000
Notes payable		20,000
Accrued interest payable		350
Accrued wages payable		1,230
Unearned subscriptions		2,940

Assuming that Gina Publications, Inc., follows a policy of reversing those adjusting entries that set up new balance sheet accounts, prepare the appropriate reversing entries on January 1, Year 6.

Ex. 2-6 Selected account balances of Lobo Company before and after the December 31 adjusting entries are listed below:

	Before adjustment	After adjustment
a Allowance for doubtful accounts	$ 2,000 credit	$ 5,500 credit
b Accumulated depreciation	14,000 credit	16,000 credit
c Sales salaries expense	24,200 debit	24,650 debit
d Income taxes payable	3,700 credit	6,250 credit

e Interest revenue	6,500 credit	6,585 credit
f Royalty revenue	5,000 credit	5,800 credit

Prepare the adjusting journal entries that were made for each account on December 31.

Ex. 2-7 Rainbow Company's accounting records provide the following information concerning certain account balances and changes in the account balances during the current year:

a Accounts receivable: Jan. 1 balance, $15,000; Dec. 31 balance, $20,500; uncollectible accounts written off during the year, $4,100; accounts receivable collected during the year, $56,000. (Record sales on credit.)

b Allowance for doubtful accounts: Jan. 1 balance, $1,500; Dec. 31 balance, $2,200; adjusting entry increasing allowance on Dec. 31, $4,800. (Record write-off of uncollectible accounts receivable.)

c Inventory of office supplies: Jan. 1 balance, $1,500; Dec. 31 balance, $1,350; office supplies expense for the year, $9,500. (Record purchase of office supplies.)

d Equipment: Jan. 1 balance, $20,500; Dec. 31 balance, $18,000; equipment costing $8,000 was sold during the year. (Record purchase of equipment.)

e Accounts payable: Jan. 1 balance, $9,000; Dec. 31 balance, $11,500; purchases on account for the year, $48,000. (Record cash payments.)

Transaction information is missing from each of the above. Prepare the journal entry to record the missing information for each account.

Ex. 2-8 For Year 5, the gross profit on sales of Madrid Company was $102,000; the cost of finished goods manufactured was $340,000; the beginning inventories of goods in process and finished goods were $28,000 and $45,000, respectively; and the ending inventories of goods in process and finished goods were $38,000 and $52,000, respectively.

Compute the amount of sales for Year 5.

SHORT CASES FOR ANALYSIS AND DECISION

Case 2-1

X

Carmen Garcia began her working career in the accounting department of Mod Company. Although Garcia had never taken a formal course of study in accounting, she gradually developed a thorough knowledge of Mod's accounting policies, and eventually she was promoted to the position of chief accountant.

While attending a regional meeting of accounting executives, Garcia was puzzled by a statement made in a group discussion. The statement was: "Reversing entries are frequently very helpful in accounting for business transactions; however they are seldom, if ever, essential to the record-keeping function." Garcia was concerned because reversing entries had been used regularly by Mod Company, and she had always considered them essential.

Instructions

a Explain why reversing entries are not essential but why they may be helpful. Your answer should include an explanation as to when reversing entries are appropriate and when they should not be used.

b Using the data below, demonstrate with journal entries how reversing entries may be used or ignored. The accounting policy is to debit Supplies Expense for all supplies purchased. The value of supplies on hand on December 31, Year 4, was determined by count to be $1,150. The balance in the asset account, Inventory of Supplies, in the ledger was zero. The following adjusting entry was made:

Inventory of Supplies	1,150	
Supplies Expense		1,150
To record inventory of supplies on Dec. 31, Year 4.		

During Year 5, supplies were purchased at a cost of $17,500 and debited to Supplies Expense. The inventory of supplies on December 31, Year 5, was $850.

Case 2-2 On January 1, Year 5, Paul Falk established a single proprietorship, Falk's Nursery. He signed a three-year lease on a store building at a monthly rental of $300 and made the first monthly payment on January 1, Year 5. Also on that date, Falk purchased store equipment for $10,000 and merchandise for $16,000. The store equipment was expected to have an economic life of 10 years with no residual value. Falk made no other investment in the enterprise.

Both Falk and his wife worked in the enterprise; they had no employees. From time to time the Falks withdrew cash from the enterprise to meet their personal needs. Because the Falks had no prior business experience, they chose to minimize record keeping. The only records maintained were a checkbook, which was reconciled monthly with the bank statement, a file folder of unpaid purchase invoices, and another file folder of uncollected sales invoices for a few select customers.

On December 31, Year 6, Falk carried out the following procedures in an effort to see how the proprietorship stood after two years of operations.

(1) Took a physical inventory and priced the items, using invoice prices of recent purchases. This procedure indicated a total cost for the inventory of $45,000.
(2) Reconciled the December 31 bank statement with the checkbook and found the cash balance to be $7,200.
(3) Added the unpaid purchase invoices in the file, which showed a total liability to suppliers of $22,700.
(4) Added the uncollected sales invoices and found that the total amount receivable from customers was $4,200.
(5) Estimated that withdrawals of cash for personal needs during the two-year period were $20,000.

Instructions

a Prepare a balance sheet for Falk's Nursery (a single proprietorship) on December 31, Year 6. (Disregard income taxes, including the fact that apparently no personal income tax return was prepared to reflect Falk's tax liability for the first year of operations.)
b Explain to Falk the advantages of a double-entry accounting system as compared with his present set of accounting records. Could the same information obtainable from a double-entry system be obtained from his present system?
c Point out to Falk what you can determine about the results of operations for the first two years.

PROBLEMS

2-1 Caliri Manufacturing Company uses the periodic inventory system. Its adjusted trial balance on December 31, Year 2, follows:

CALIRI MANUFACTURING COMPANY
Adjusted Trial Balance
December 31, Year 2

	Debit	Credit
Cash	$ 22,100	
Accounts receivable (net)	62,000	
Inventories, Jan. 1, Year 2:		
Finished goods	40,000	
Goods in process	20,000	
Raw material	25,000	
Short-term prepayments	2,000	
Plant assets (net)	254,400	
Accounts payable		$ 35,500
Income taxes payable		40,000
Capital stock, $1 par		100,000
Paid-in capital in excess of par		150,000
Retained earnings, Jan. 1, Year 2		82,000
Dividends	50,000	
Sales (net)		980,000
Raw material purchases (net)	210,000	
Direct labor costs	220,000	
Factory overhead costs	190,000	
Selling expenses	130,000	
General and administrative expenses	122,000	
Income taxes expense	40,000	
Totals	$1,387,500	$1,387,500

Inventories, Dec. 31, Year 2, are:

Finished goods	$ 45,000
Goods in process	27,500
Raw material	32,500

Instructions
a Prepare closing entries on December 31, Year 2, similar to those illustrated on pages 65 and 68 in the text.
b Prepare a statement of cost of finished goods manufactured for the year ended December 31, Year 2.

2-2 The Income Statement columns in the work sheet for Seal Beach Outlets, Inc., for the year ended September 30, Year 10, are reproduced below:

	Debit	Credit
Inventory (periodic system)	$ 55,800	$ 64,200
Sales		875,000
Sales returns and allowances	10,800	
Sales discounts	12,500	
Purchases	588,000	
Purchases returns and allowances		15,000
Purchases discounts		10,200
Salaries expense	82,500	
Rent expense	24,000	
Advertising and promotion expense	52,100	
Other operating expenses	38,700	
Income taxes expense	26,750	
Net income	73,250	
Totals	$964,400	$964,400

Instructions Prepare closing entries on September 30, Year 10, similar to those illustrated on pages 63–64.

2-3 Agua Dulce Company uses a periodic inventory system. Selected transactions and adjustments for Year 2 are listed below:

(1) Sales on credit totaled $34,290.
(2) A building and a tract of land were acquired at a cost of $300,000. The current fair value of the land was estimated at $90,000. One-fifth of the purchase price was paid in cash, and a 10% mortgage note payable was issued for the balance.
(3) Merchandise costing $24,200 was purchased, subject to a cash discount of 2% if paid within 10 days. (Record invoice at net amount.)
(4) Freight charges of $495 related to merchandise purchased were paid.
(5) Accounts receivable of $515 were written off. Agua Dulce uses an allowance for doubtful accounts and makes provisions for doubtful accounts at the end of each year.
(6) The invoice for the purchase in item (3) was paid in full within the discount period.
(7) Cash collections on customers' accounts totaled $27,400, after sales discounts of $350.
(8) Equipment which cost $4,800, and on which accumulated depreciation amounted to $4,000, was sold for $500 cash.
(9) A cash dividend of $0.25 a share on 100,000 shares of outstanding capital stock was declared and paid. (Prepare separate journal entries for the declaration and the payment.)
(10) 20,000 shares of $10 par capital stock were issued for $14 a share.
(11) Defective merchandise, which was purchased on account for $650 (net amount), was returned for full credit.
(12) A customer's check for $80 received and deposited by Agua Dulce was returned by the bank marked "not sufficient funds."
(13) An expense account was debited when supplies were purchased. The Inventory of Supplies account has an unadjusted balance of $750, but the inventory of supplies at the end of Year 2 was $950.

(14) The building acquired in item (2) was used in operations for nine months during Year 2. The building has an economic life of 25 years and no residual value. Depreciation is computed by the straight-line method.

Instructions Prepare journal entries to record the above transactions and adjustments.

2-4 Home Supply Corporation uses a perpetual inventory system. A selected list of transactions and adjustments for the current accounting period is given below:

(1) Sales on credit totaled $38,800; the cost of the goods was $25,500.
(2) The corporation acquired land and a building at a total cost of $310,000. One-tenth of the purchase price was paid in cash, and a 9% mortgage note payable was issued for the balance. The building had an estimated current fair value of $192,000.
(3) Merchandise costing $29,500 was purchased. The invoice amount is subject to a 2% cash discount if paid within 10 days. Home Supply records purchases invoices at the net amount.
(4) The corporation paid $850 for freight charges on merchandise purchased. Freight charges are recorded in a separate account.
(5) Accounts receivable of $350 were written off as uncollectible. The corporation maintains an allowance for doubtful accounts and makes provision for doubtful accounts expense at the end of each accounting period.
(6) The invoice for the purchase of merchandise in item (3) was paid within the discount period.
(7) Cash collections on customers' accounts amounted to $39,880. No sales discounts were allowed.
(8) Cash of $4,000 was received from disposal of equipment. The cost of the equipment was $20,000, and the accumulated depreciation was $17,500.
(9) A cash dividend of $0.50 a share on 80,000 shares of common stock was declared and paid. (Prepare separate journal entries for the declaration and payment.)
(10) Defective merchandise was returned to a supplier for full credit. The merchandise had been purchased on account for $750 (net).
(11) Home Supply issued 10,000 shares of its $5 par common stock and received cash of $9 a share.
(12) A customer's check for $180, received and deposited by Home Supply, was returned by the bank marked "not sufficient funds."
(13) The building acquired in item (2) was used in operations for 10 months during the current accounting period. The building has an economic life of 40 years and no residual value. Depreciation is computed by the straight-line method.
(14) Accrued property taxes at the end of the current accounting period amounted to $280.

Instructions Prepare journal entries to record the above transactions and adjustments.

2-5 Subsidiary ledgers and related controlling accounts for accounts receivable and accounts payable are maintained by Gracie Company. The following trial balances summarize the two subsidiary ledgers on December 31, Year 9:

Accounts Receivable Trial Balance
December 31, Year 9

Paul Davis	$ 2,000
Ed Fairly	6,000
Ken Iverson (credit balance).	(750)
Dolores Kiley	13,500
Balance in controlling account	$20,750

Accounts Payable Trial Balance
December 31, Year 9

Joann Edwards.	$ 588
John Gates (debit balance)	(570)
Julie Loomis	8,050
David Parks.	2,330
Balance in controlling account	$10,398

Gracie Company offers credit terms of 2/10, n/30 to all its customers and records all sales at gross prices. Purchases of merchandise from suppliers are recorded at net prices because it is the company's policy to take all purchases discounts available.

In any transaction in which Gracie Company fails to take advantage of a discount offered by a supplier, the journal entry to record payment of the supplier's invoice should include a debit to Purchases Discounts Lost.

Gracie Company carried customers' credit balances as an offset against debit balances, and suppliers' debit balances as an offset against credit balances in the ledgers. These balances are reclassified for reporting purposes to reflect customers' credit balances as liabilities and suppliers' debit balances as assets.

Transactions for January, Year 10, are presented below:

(1) Received a check from Kiley for $13,230 in full settlement of her account within the discount period.
(2) Purchases from Edwards totaled $11,224.49, terms 2/10, n/30. (Record at net.)
(3) Payment to Loomis of $8,050 was made within the discount period.
(4) Sales to Iverson were $23,000, terms 2/10, n/30.
(5) Cash of $4,500 was received from Davis, including a $2,500 advance payment.
(6) Payment of $11,600 was made to Edwards in settlement of the account payable. Because of an oversight, the payment was not made until after the discount period had lapsed on the December invoice. Also, Gracie made another purchase from Edwards for $13,200, terms 2/10, n/30.
(7) Cash of $3,920 was received from Fairly in partial payment of his account balance. The discount was allowed on this portion of the account balance, because cash was received within the discount period.
(8) Paid Parks $4,130, which represented payment of the balance due within the discount period and an $1,800 advance on a new order.

Instructions

a Enter the December 31, Year 9, balances and the above transactions directly in the appropriate accounts in both the general ledger and the subsidiary ledgers for accounts receivable and accounts payable. You need not maintain a ledger account for cash. (Because this problem does not include journals or monthly totals, each transaction should be entered individually in a general ledger controlling account as well as in a subsidiary ledger account. The use of three-column, running-balance-account form is recommended.)

  b Prove the accuracy of the accounting records by preparing trial balances of the subsidiary ledgers on January 31, Year 10, and by determining that the totals agree with the respective controlling accounts.

  c Which accounts with customers and suppliers should be reclassified in the balance sheet prepared on January 31, Year 10? Explain how such accounts should be presented in the balance sheet.

2-6 Listed below are the account balances from the ledger of Serena Company on January 31, Year 3, except for retained earnings, which is the January 1 balance. There are no assets or liabilities other than those listed. The Dividends account represents the amount declared and paid during January.

Accounts payable	$120,000
Accounts receivable	96,000
Accumulated depreciation	222,000
Capital stock, $10 par	660,000
Cash	126,000
Dividends	24,000
Inventories	192,000
Plant assets	870,000
Retained earnings, Jan. 1, Year 3	231,000

Instructions

a Compute the net income of Serena Company for January by preparing a balance sheet on January 31 which includes details showing the beginning balance, increases and decreases, and the ending balance of retained earnings.

b What was the amount of total sales for January, assuming that the accounts receivable were $108,000 on January 1 and that $480,000 was received on customers' accounts and from cash sales during January? Show computations.

c Determine the cost of goods sold for January, assuming that inventories at January 1 were $174,000 and that purchases of merchandise totaled $330,000 in January.

d Compute the total of all other expenses for the month. Show computations.

e Determine the total cash outlay for merchandise purchases during January, assuming that the beginning balance of accounts payable was $114,000 and that purchases (all on credit) amounted to $330,000. Show computations.

2-7 Penich Corporation adjusts and closes its accounting records at the end of each calendar year. The information presented below provides the basis for making the adjusting entries needed on December 31, Year 5:

 (1) On July 1, Year 5, Penich received $4,800 of rent revenue covering a one-year period beginning with the date of receipt. Rent Revenue account was credited.

 (2) Unexpired Insurance was debited on September 1, Year 5, when Penich paid a $2,700 premium for a three-year insurance policy effective on that date.

 (3) Penich borrowed $90,000 on March 1, Year 5, by issuing a three-year, 10% mortgage note payable with interest quarterly. Interest payments were made on May 31, August 31, and November 30 of Year 5.

 (4) Bonds in the face amount of $20,000 with an interest rate of 12% were acquired at face amount as an investment on April 1. Interest payment dates are April 1 and October 1.

 (5) The building occupied by Penich has a cost of $96,000. Estimated economic life is 20 years with no expected residual value. Straight-line method of depreciation is used.

 (6) An aging of the accounts receivable on December 31 indicated $4,100 to be a reasonable estimate of doubtful accounts. At this date the allowance for doubtful accounts had a **debit** balance of $460.

(7) Office Supplies Expense was debited on July 1, Year 5, when $2,200 was paid for office supplies. On December 31, Year 5, office supplies of $1,195 were on hand.

Instructions

a Prepare year-end adjusting entries. Include in the explanation portion of each journal entry any calculations used to determine the amount of the adjustment.

b Prepare the appropriate reversing entries on January 1, Year 6, assuming that Penich follows a policy of reversing those adjusting entries that include a balance sheet account normally not used during the accounting period.

2-8 Bargain Retail Company uses the periodic inventory system and maintains its accounting records on a calendar-year basis. The trial balance shown below was prepared from the general ledger on December 31, Year 3, and no adjusting entries have been made.

BARGAIN RETAIL COMPANY
Trial Balance
December 31, Year 3

	Debit	Credit
Cash	$ 8,000	
Accounts receivable	40,000	
Inventory, Dec. 31, Year 2	23,000	
Land	80,000	
Building	200,000	
Accumulated depreciation of building		$ 42,000
Equipment	240,000	
Accumulated depreciation of equipment		59,500
Accounts payable		38,000
Accrued interest payable		-0-
Accrued salaries and wages payable		-0-
Bonds payable, 12%		100,000
Capital stock		200,000
Retained earnings, Dec. 31, Year 2		75,200
Dividends	25,000	
Sales		806,000
Purchases	479,500	
Salaries and wages expense	55,200	
Selling expenses	120,000	
General and administrative expenses	40,000	
Interest expense	10,000	
Totals	$1,320,700	$1,320,700

Reversing entries were made on January 1, Year 3, for the accrued interest payable and the accrued salaries and wages payable which had been recorded by adjusting entries on December 31, Year 2.

Additional data
(1) The company has decided, after an aging and analysis of accounts receivable, to establish an allowance for doubtful accounts of $3,000.
(2) The building is being depreciated on the straight-line basis; economic life is 40 years and the residual value is zero. Estimated economic life for equipment is 15 years and estimated residual value is $15,000.
(3) Interest on the bonds payable is paid on May 1 and November 1.
(4) Salaries and wages earned by employees but unpaid on December 31 amounted to $6,000.
(5) Income taxes are estimated to be $17,000.
(6) The inventory on December 31, Year 3, was determined by physical count to amount to $28,000.

Instructions
a Prepare a 12-column work sheet to adjust the accounts and classify the balances as to income statement, retained earnings statement, and balance sheet. (Include columns for an adjusted trial balance.)
b Use the work sheet as a source for preparation of closing entries. (Adjusting entries are not required; entries to record cost of goods sold are considered closing entries.)
c Prepare reversing entries dated January 1, Year 4, with respect to the accrued salaries and wages payable and to the accrued interest payable, for which adjustments were made on December 31, Year 3.

2-9 The unadjusted trial balance on page 82 was prepared from the ledger of Elite Manufacturing Corporation on December 31, Year 10. The company used reversing entries on January 1 of each year to reverse accrued wages and accrued interest payable.

ELITE MANUFACTURING CORPORATION
Trial Balance
December 31, Year 10

	Debit	Credit
Cash	$ 14,050	
Accounts receivable	80,000	
Allowance for doubtful accounts		$ 200
Inventories, Jan. 1, Year 10:		
Raw material	12,000	
Goods in process	56,000	
Finished goods	80,000	
Short-term prepayments	9,000	
Land	50,000	
Building	457,000	
Accumulated depreciation of building.		54,800
Machinery and equipment.	400,000	
Accumulated depreciation of machinery and equipment		120,000
Accounts payable		70,000
Accrued wages payable		–0–
Accrued interest payable		–0–
Bonds payable, 12%		200,000
Capital stock, $10 par		400,000
Paid-in capital in excess of par		170,000
Retained earnings, Jan. 1, Year 10		56,025
Dividends	15,000	
Sales (net)		992,000
Raw material purchases	310,000	
Direct labor costs	292,900	
Factory overhead costs	120,000	
Selling expenses	95,000	
General and administrative expenses	52,000	
Interest expense	20,075	
Totals	$2,063,025	$2,063,025

Additional data
(1) The allowance for doubtful accounts should be increased to a balance equal to 6% of accounts receivable.
(2) Short-term prepayments at the beginning and end of Year 10 are as follows (insurance is considered an administrative expense):

	Jan. 1	Dec. 31
Unexpired insurance (two years remaining on Jan. 1)	$3,600	$1,800
Factory supplies	5,400	7,000
Totals	$9,000	$8,800

(3) Invoices for raw material included in the ending inventory but not recorded in the accounting records total $12,000.

(4) The straight-line method of depreciation is used to allocate the cost of plant assets. Other relevant data are presented below:

	Estimated economic life, years	Estimated residual value	Percentage allocated to	
			Factory	Administration
Building.	50	$7,000	70	30
Machinery and equipment	10	5%	80	20

(5) Interest payments to bondholders are made semiannually on May 1 and November 1.

(6) The factory power bill for December, $3,200, has not been recorded.

(7) Direct factory wages earned but not paid on December 31 total $1,800.

(8) Income taxes are estimated at $4,700.

(9) The ending inventories on December 31 are: Raw material, $18,000; goods in process, $53,000; and finished goods, $75,000.

Instructions

a Prepare a work sheet to adjust the accounts and classify the data as to manufacturing costs, income statement, retained earnings statement, and balance sheet. Do not include columns for an adjusted trial balance.

b Prepare the journal entries required to adjust the inventory accounts and to record the cost of finished goods manufactured and the cost of goods sold. You need not close any accounts to Income Summary.

c Prepare reversing entries as of January 1, Year 11, relating to the accrued wages payable and accrued interest payable.

2-10 The after-closing trial balance for Westchester, Inc., on June 30, Year 5, is given below:

WESTCHESTER, INC.
After-Closing Trial Balance
June 30, Year 5

	Debit	Credit
Cash	$ 26,200	
Accounts receivable	32,600	
Allowance for doubtful accounts		$ 1,100
Inventory	54,950	
Unexpired insurance	600	
Store fixtures	38,400	
Accumulated depreciation of store fixtures		13,800
Vouchers payable		18,300
Income taxes payable		6,100
Accrued wages payable		1,300
Capital stock, no-par value, 2,000 shares outstanding . . .		70,000
Retained earnings		42,150
Totals	$152,750	$152,750

Transactions recorded in the journals for the month of July, Year 5, are summarized below (to avoid unnecessary detail, all expenses are recorded in a single Operating Expenses account):

Sales Journal (S): *Debit to Accounts Receivable and credit to Sales* . . . $82,100

Cash Receipts Journal (CR):

Debits:	Cash	$88,800
	Sales Discounts	1,200
Credits:	Accounts Receivable	$70,000
	Capital Stock	5,000
	Sales	15,000

Voucher Register (V):

Debits:	Purchases	$45,200
	Freight-in	900
	Operating Expenses	13,800
Credits:	Vouchers Payable	$59,200
	Purchases Discounts	700

Check Register (Ch.R): *Debit to Vouchers Payable and credit to Cash* . . $68,200

General Journal (J):

Debits:	Allowance for Doubtful Accounts	$ 200
	Notes Receivable	5,000
	Accumulated Depreciation of Store Fixtures	150
Credits:	Accounts Receivable	$ 5,200
	Store Fixtures	150

The information needed to adjust the accounting records on July 31, Year 5, follows:

(1) Aging of accounts receivable indicates that an allowance for doubtful accounts of $1,250 is required.
(2) Depreciation for the month of July is computed at $850.
(3) Unexpired insurance amounts to $520.
(4) Accrued wages payable amount to $800.
(5) Accrued interest on notes receivable is $40.
(6) Income taxes expense for July is estimated at $10,000.
(7) A physical inventory indicates that merchandise costing $51,000 is on hand.

Instructions
a Post the June 30 balances and all transactions for July from the journals to general ledger accounts.
b Prepare an unadjusted trial balance on July 31, Year 5, in the first pair of columns of a 12-column work sheet that includes an adjusted trial balance.
c Enter the adjustments in the work sheet and complete the work sheet.
d Record the adjusting and closing entries in the general journal and post these entries to the general ledger.
e Prepare an income statement for the month of July, and a balance sheet on July 31, Year 5.
f Prepare an after-closing trial balance on July 31, Year 5.

3 REVENUE AND EXPENSES; STATEMENTS OF INCOME AND RETAINED EARNINGS

MEASUREMENT OF INCOME: REVENUE REALIZATION

The measurement of periodic income of a business enterprise is perhaps the foremost objective of the accounting process. The word *estimate* is appropriate because income is one of the most elusive concepts in the business world. The art of accounting probably never will progress to the point where "income" can be defined to everyone's satisfaction.

To illustrate the complexity of defining income, let us assume that newly organized Pinecrest Corporation buys a large tract of land for the purpose of developing a residential community. Purchase of the land required only a small down payment (and the assumption of a large mortgage note payable), but even that small payment used up most of the corporation's cash. Some of the land is level, some rolling, and some extremely steep. A golf course, riding stables, tennis courts, and a lake are to be constructed. Colorful sales brochures were prepared showing the attractiveness of the community upon completion.

Residential lots are offered for sale, with a down payment of only 2% of the selling price. Assume that 100 lots are sold with an average down payment of $200 received, along with long-term sales contracts calling for monthly payments of $125 on the balance due. How much, if any, income should be recognized when the first lots are sold?.

As indicated in Chapter 1, income usually is determined by measuring revenue and deducting the related expenses. But how should revenue and expenses be measured by Pinecrest Corporation? Among the questions which arise are: What is the value of a long-term sales contract from buyers making a small down payment on a vacant lot? How many of the 100 buyers actually will make the monthly payments? What will be the costs of developing roads, sewers, the golf course, lake, and other recreational facilities which Pinecrest Corporation has promised to provide? How many lots will be sold, and at what prices and on what terms? How should the total estimated costs be allocated among the level lots, hillside lots, and lakefront lots?

Despite all the effort which has been devoted to the development of accounting principles, it should be clear that a wide range of answers could be given to the question of how much, if any, income is earned from the sale of the first 100 lots. We might even question whether a sale has really occurred, or whether Pinecrest Corporation is a "going concern" reasonably capable of carrying out its commitments and thus warranting application of the going-concern principle.[1] Assuming that Pinecrest Corporation does carry the development project to a successful completion, the income can then be measured as the amount of revenue received from customers minus the costs of the land and the costs of developing and selling it. However, the objective of timeliness in financial reporting requires the making of decisions as to the periodic net income being earned long before the project is completed. This example of a land development company illustrates some of the practical difficulties faced by accountants in the measurment of net income.

In this chapter we first consider the nature of net income and the basic assumptions accountants make in measuring it. Then we turn to the problem of reporting in the income statement the results of these measurement efforts.

The meaning of *net income*

In a very general sense, the objective in measuring net income is to determine by how much a business enterprise has become better off during some period of time as a result of its operations. **Net income** might be described as the maximum amount of resources that could be distributed to the owners during an accounting period and still leave the business enterprise as well off at the end of that period as it was at the beginning. The critical words in this definition are in the phrase "as well off." Anyone who studies the concept of income will soon discover that controversies over the meaning and measurement of periodic income center on the problem of determining what the financial position of an enterprise is at any given time, whether its position has improved or worsened, and by how much.

---

[1] *Accounting Series Release No. 95,* "Accounting for Real Estate Transactions Where Circumstances Indicate that Profits Were Not Earned at the Time the Transactions Were Recorded," issued by the Securities and Exchange Commission, indicated that the circumstances set forth above make it inappropriate to recognize gross profit as realized at the time of the sale. The AICPA took a similar position in *An AICPA Industry Accounting Guide,* "Accounting for Retail Land Sales."

Let us begin with a relatively simple problem in income determination. If we were asked to measure the lifetime net income of a business enterprise at the time it was being liquidated, we could probably agree on the following computation:

Lifetime income of a business enterprise

Total proceeds received on liquidation of the business enterprise.	*$800,000*
Add: Amounts withdrawn by owners during the life of the enterprise . .	*300,000*
Less: Amount of capital invested in the enterprise by its owners.	*(600,000)*
Lifetime net income of the enterprise	*$500,000*

If we ignore the time value of money and assume a stable price level, lifetime net income of a business enterprise is comparatively easy to measure. The reason is that at the beginning and end of the life of any enterprise, the value of its net assets can be established with reasonable accuracy. The original investment of the owners and the proceeds on liquidation usually are definite sums of money or their equivalent.

At any stage prior to final liquidation, however, the **net assets** of an enterprise constitute a complex set of resources, whose collective value depends largely on future earning power. In theory, the only direct way to determine how well off an enterprise is at any point in time is to compute the net present value of all its future cash receipts and disbursements. This is sometimes called the process of **direct valuation.** Estimates of future earning power obviously are subject to a large margin of error.

Accountants readily admit an inability to determine at frequent time intervals the **direct value** of the net assets of an enterprise. For this they can hardly be criticized for undue caution or modesty; they simply are being realistic about their limitations. The role of an economic reporter is perhaps less glamorous than that of the economic forecaster, but it is no less useful. Thus, in measuring how well off an enterprise is at any time in order to measure periodic income, accountants include in the accounting records only those changes in financial position that can be substantiated by reasonably objective evidence.

The meaning of *objective evidence*

Facts form a basis for most business decisions and forecasts of the future. Most of what is contained in accounting records purports to be factual. Like everyone else, however, accountants often have considerable difficulty in deciding what the facts are.

Business enterprises are engaged in the continuing process of transforming one series of economic goods and services (inputs) into another essentially different series of goods and services (outputs), in the expectation that the aggregate output will command a higher selling price in the market than the cost of the input. In reporting periodic progress in this endeavor, accountants seek objective evidence to support the information they present. But what is meant by objective evidence? The important element in the objectivity of any information is **verifiability,** the agreement of competent persons as to what has been observed or experienced. The term **objective evidence,** then, means data that are sufficiently clear-cut that reasonable individuals will vary in their interpretation of it only within narrow limits. Thus, objective evidence is **reliable evidence.**

External Data Purchases of asset services, hiring and paying employees, sales of goods and services, borrowing funds, issuing shares of capital stock—all are examples of market transactions between a business enterprise and outsiders. These transactions stem from express or implied contracts and usually represent an exchange between independent parties at arm's-length prices. In other words, there is **external evidence** to support an accounting record of what has taken place.

At times the evidence is somewhat hazy. For example, if a tract of land originally acquired as a site for plant construction is exchanged directly for a smaller site with a complete operating plant, no explicit market price is established, and accountants are forced to look for evidence of an **implicit price** at which to record the transaction. They try to obtain independent evidence of the current fair value of the operating plant or the current fair value of the land given in exchange. Such independent evidence is needed to estimate the price that would have been established had the plant been acquired and the land sold for cash. A similar problem arises in the "basket purchase" situation, when two or more assets are acquired for a single price. The task is to allocate the total price among the assets acquired, and accountants must seek independent evidence to support this allocation. Despite these troublesome cases, arriving at a reasonable and acceptable basis for recording most transactions between a business enterprise and outsiders causes relatively little difficulty.

Internal Data The second type of economic event in business leaves a much less distinct trail of evidence; consequently, it creates a far more troublesome set of problems for accountants. The amount spent for material, labor, and other services can be measured objectively. The continuous process of transforming these inputs into more valuable outputs, however, is an internal, not an external, affair. In tracing the effect of this productive process and portraying it in terms of dollars, accountants do not have the objective or reliable evidence of actual market transactions as a basis for measurement.

The flow of costs

Ideally, all costs should be associated with some physical product or output. If the entire resources of a business enterprise are devoted to the production and sale of a single product, this assumption might be reasonable. All costs incurred could be accumulated as inventory costs until the sale of the product provides objective evidence of gain or loss.

Even in this single-product case, however, it is apparent that some costs are more directly related to production than others. The costs of direct material, direct labor, and some kinds of variable factory overhead, for example, can be traced to physical production because the relationship between effort and accomplishment is relatively clear. At the other extreme, such costs as sales salaries, advertising, and administrative expenses are productive, but the relationship between effort and accomplishment is far more nebulous. A selling effort today may result in a sale two years hence. The installation of a new cost accounting system may provide better control over operations and produce benefits to the business enterprise for years to come. In either case it is virtually impossible to trace these efforts to the physical product with any degree of precision. When we shift this problem to the more realistic setting of a business enterprise producing not one but many different products or services the difficulty of cost assignment increases immensely, and one can easily see that tracing costs is more an art than a science.

Confronted with this sort of vague evidence, accountants find it necessary to adopt a series of reasonable assumptions. It is hardly surprising that opinions as to what is "reasonable" in any given case will differ. The fact that alternative accounting principles, each of which may produce significantly different results, may be "generally accepted" stems directly from these differences of opinion.

Product and Period Costs   In the measurement of income, certain **product costs** are traced to physical output and are accumulated in inventory accounts until evidence of gain or loss is available. For example, the costs of direct material and labor used to fabricate a product can be identified directly with the cost of producing a unit of inventory.

Other costs, called **period costs,** are considered expenses of the accounting period in which they occur. Period costs, such as advertising and other selling expenses, usually are not related to the flow of production and are deducted from revenue immediately, because the benefits received expire in the same period as the costs are incurred. As pointed out in **APB Statement No. 4,** "Enterprises never acquire expenses per se; they always acquire assets. Costs may be charged to expenses in the period goods or services are acquired . . . if they only benefit the period in which they are acquired. . . ."[2]

[2] *APB Statement No. 4,* "Basic Concepts and Accounting Principles Underlying Financial Statements of Business Enterprises," AICPA (New York: 1970), p. 85.

Making a theoretical distinction between product costs and period costs may be easier than the practical application of the concept. To illustrate this problem, consider the cost of merchandise purchased by a trading enterprise. There are certain costs directly related to the purchase of merchandise, such as the price paid to vendors and the cost of freight-in. There are other indirect costs of buying, handling, storage, and display. The salary of a purchasing agent may be one of these borderline cases. Decisions on the treatment of some costs as product costs or as period costs are likely to differ between enterprises and often may be resolved on the grounds of convenience. If such controversial expenditures are material in amount, different practices may lead to significantly different net income amounts.

In addition to the question of product versus period costs, another issue arises when identical items in inventories have been acquired in different lots and at different prices. As these items are sold, decisions must be made as to which of the different unit costs are to be assigned to the particular items sold. The decision to assume a first-in, first-out, a last-in, first-out, or a weighted-average flow of costs is somewhat arbitrary, but important, because different assumptions may produce materially different amounts of net income.

The Cost of Asset Services   Certain asset services, such as buildings, machinery, or patents, are acquired in advance of their use. In buying machinery, for example, a business enterprise acquires a bundle of productive services. Some portion of the services will be withdrawn from the bundle and used during the current accounting period; other portions will not be withdrawn for several periods. Accountants are faced with the problem of determining whether the cost of expired services is a period or a product cost. In addition, they are confronted with two even more perplexing questions: (1) How much of the total bundle of lifetime services has been used during the current period? (2) What is the cost of the services used? In the case of raw material or merchandise, there is at least a physical flow of goods to indicate the changes that are taking place. Productive assets such as machinery, on the other hand, exhibit little or no change in their physical characteristics as they provide services.

The services of some productive assets expire as a function of time. If a three-year premium is paid for an insurance policy, the service acquired is three years of freedom from a given amount of risk. It seems reasonable to assume that one-third of the cost of acquiring this service is used up in each of the three years.

Suppose, however, that the asset in question is an apartment building. The services acquired are a given amount of building space which can be rented to tenants. The value of the right to occupy a new building is greater than that of an older building. Ignoring the effects of inflation, the rent revenue during the early life of the building tends to be higher than during its later years, and thus the value of the services yielded by the building is higher in early years than in later years. These facts should be considered in the establishment of a cost flow assumption. Objective evidence of the value of services year by year is very difficult to obtain. Furthermore, the economic life of the building is indefinite. Accountants know objectively only that the investment in future building services has been X dollars, that the owners may dispose of the building at some future time, and that if they do not, the building eventually will be worthless and must be torn down. Accountants also know that the business enterprise must recover the cost of expired building services (depreciation) from revenue in order to be as well off in monetary terms at the end of any period as at the time the original investment was made. In the face of these imponderables, it is likely that any solution adopted will prove to be erroneous to some degree. It is not surprising that the measurement of depreciation always has been a controversial issue in accounting.

In subsequent chapters we shall consider these issues in more detail, and examine some of the assumptions and techniques that accountants employ in dealing with internal cost data. Our purpose at this stage is to make the point that the measurement of expired costs (expenses) is, at best, an intelligent estimate of the cost of resources used in operations during an accounting period.

Revenue recognition (realization)

Realization of revenue refers to the timing of its recognition in the accounting records. A practical working rule is needed to signal that an increase in net assets has resulted from the activities of a business enterprise. Discussion of the revenue realization principle in Chapter 1 stressed that each step in the production and distribution of goods and services is essential to earning revenue. Ideally, the recognition of revenue should be continuous rather than occurring at a single critical point in the activities of the enterprise.

If the plans of a business enterprise are achieved, at some time in the productive process (in fact continuously) there is an increase in the value of the products and services (output) produced by the enterprise. Because continuous direct valuation is a practical impossibility, an alternative procedure must be found to measure this increase as objectively as possible in order to measure net income. The basic assumption adopted as a means of dealing with this problem is called the *revenue realization principle.*

When a business enterprise acquires asset services in exchange for money (or promises to pay money), accountants assume an even exchange of values; that is, that no gain or loss occurs at the time of purchase. An arm's-length exchange price is viewed as the best objective evidence of value at the time of acquisition, and a subjective judgment that the buyer has obtained something for nothing or has received the worst of the bargain is not sufficient to overcome such evidence. In tracing the flow of costs internally, the assumption of an "even exchange" continues to control accounting procedures. For example, the allocation of material, direct labor, and factory overhead costs to inventories is limited to the actual costs incurred, and the fact that there may be an increase in value beyond the costs added is ignored.

Somewhere along the line, however, objective evidence will arise that the value of the output is greater (or possibly less) than the cost of the inputs. When such evidence becomes conclusive, accountants stop dealing solely in costs. The value of the output is measured, and revenue emerges. ***The revenue realization principle is the set of rules adopted by accountants to decide when a change in the value of output is recognized in the accounting records.***

When is revenue realized?

The two primary criteria for recording realized revenue are:

1 Sufficient objective evidence exists as to the market value of the output. Usually such evidence is provided by an arm's-length sales transaction.
2 The earnings process (in essence the creation of marketable goods and services) is substantially complete. This means that all necessary costs have been incurred or can be reasonably estimated.

Revenue Recognized at Time of Sale   In the application of these criteria to various practical situations, the most widely accepted evidence of revenue realization is the sale of merchandise. There is little question about the reliability of evidence: a completed transaction with outsiders which transfers possession of, and usually title to, the product in return for money or the promise to pay money at some future date. One may question why accountants choose so late a stage in the production process to record revenue and thus net income. The answer comes in two parts: (1) At any point prior to the sale, the expected selling price of most products and the ability to sell them at a given price are so uncertain that they do not constitute sufficient evidence to justify an upward revaluation of the product, and (2) for most business enterprises the actual sale of the products is the most important step in the earning process. Until a sale is made the future stream of revenue is unearned. It is usually easier to make a good product than to sell it in large volume at a profit.

Even when a sale has been made, the recognition of revenue may be delayed because of unusual terms surrounding the sales transaction. For example, in the record and printed music industry and in the book publishing industry, it is common practice to give retail stores the ***right to return*** products sold to them if they cannot resell these products. When customers have the right to return products, the seller may continue to be exposed to the usual risks of ownership, and sales revenue should be recognized at time of sale only if **all** the following conditions are met:[3]

1 The seller's price to the buyer is substantially fixed or determinable at the date of sale.

2 The buyer has paid the seller, or is obligated to pay the seller and the obligation is not contingent on resale of the product.

3 The buyer's obligation to the seller would not be changed in the event of theft or physical destruction or damage of the product.

4 The buyer acquiring the product for resale has economic substance apart from that provided by the seller.

5 The seller does not have significant obligations for future performance to directly bring about resale of the product by the buyer.

6 The amount of future returns can be reasonably estimated.

If these conditions are met and sales are recognized, provision for any costs or losses which may be expected in connection with any returns is made at the time of sale. The sales and cost of goods sold in the income statement exclude the portion for which returns are expected, and the allowance for estimated returns is deducted from accounts receivable in the balance sheet. Transactions for which revenue recognition is postponed are recorded as sales only when the return privilege expires.

Although the point of sale has been widely accepted as evidence of revenue realization, the preceding discussion clearly points out that **sale** and **revenue realization** are not necessarily synonymous. Under certain circumstances, accountants record realized revenue at three other stages discussed below:

Revenue Recognized during Production   In some business enterprises the product consists of a few major projects which require considerable time to complete. Major construction projects for dams or ships are examples. For such projects, production is the major element of the earning process; the final sale is assured by a binding contract subject only to satisfactory performance by the contractor. The recognition of revenue only at the point of final sale, under these conditions, results in a highly distorted picture of income for various accounting periods. Therefore, as progress on the project is made, a percentage of the ultimate contract price is recorded as realized revenue. Accounting for long-term construction contracts is illustrated in Chapter 9.

[3] *FASB Statement No. 48,* "Revenue Recognition When Right of Return Exists," FASB (Stamford: 1981), pp. 2–3. See also: *FASB Statement No. 49,* "Accounting for Product Financing Arrangements," FASB (Stamford: 1981), pp. 1–5; *Statement of Position 76-1,* "Accounting Practices in the Record and Printed Music Industry," Recommendation to FASB issued by Accounting Standards Division of AICPA (New York: 1976), pp. 9–12.

Revenue Recognized When Production Is Complete   When a business enterprise produces merchandise that is sold in large quantities at prices that can be determined objectively at any time, there is a basis for valuing output as soon as it is produced. Farm products, diamonds, platinum, gold, and silver meet all the conditions requisite to this test of realization. In these cases it is possible to value inventories at selling prices less any direct marketing costs not yet incurred (sometimes called *net realizable value*), resulting in the recognition of revenue at the time production is completed.

Revenue Recognized When Cash Is Received   The two procedures just discussed move the point of realization forward to an earlier stage in the production process, that is, prior to the point of sale. Another possibility is that the recognition of revenue should be delayed beyond the point of sale until additional evidence confirms the sales transaction. Under some conditions a sales transaction may be lacking in substance and therefore may offer inadequate evidence of realization. An example is found in land sale contracts in which the purchasers make only a nominal down payment, have no established credit status, and are free to cancel the contracts at any time without penalty other than the loss of the payments they already have made. In many states the seller has no legal right to take any action on such defaulted contracts other than to repossess the property sold. However, as the number of cash payments by a given customer under a sales contract of this type increases, the evidence of an authentic sale and valid receivable also increases.

An extreme application of this test of revenue realization is the so-called *cash basis of accounting* described in Chapter 1. In its most unrefined state, the cash basis of accounting calls for the recognition of revenue only when cash is received, and recognition of expenses when cash is paid. Another practical application of the view that revenue realization coincides with the receipt of cash is a procedure known as the *installment method of accounting.* This procedure is applied when the sales contract calls for payment in periodic installments. The installment method of accounting delays the recognition of revenue (and thus net income) until collections from customers are received.

The cash basis of accounting and the installment method of accounting are widely used in the computation of taxable income, because their use makes it possible for taxpayers to defer the payment of income taxes. However, the acceptability of these procedures for income tax purposes is not in itself a reason for their use in financial accounting.[4] The income tax rules are based on the belief by government that it must collect income taxes when the taxpayer has available the cash arising

---

[4] The Accounting Principles Board stated that "the installment method of recognizing revenue is not acceptable" unless circumstances are such that there is no reasonable basis for estimating the collectibility of installment receivables (*APB Opinion No. 10,* p. 149).

from a business transaction, rather than on any rational analysis of the timing of revenue realization.

Pressures for speeding up the recognition of revenue

Many enterprises, in an effort to enhance their ability to attract capital from investors and bankers, are impelled to treat revenue as realized at the earliest possible time. In certain industries franchising enterprises **(franchisors)** often have recognized revenue at the time of signing contracts. The contracts typically called for the franchisor to guide the franchisee in locating a site, training a work staff, and commencing operations. In return, the franchisor received promissory notes from the franchisee, but no cash. The collectibility of the notes was dependent on the success of the proposed new business and on a commitment by the franchisor to provide future "consulting services."

The rapidly rising earnings reported by franchising enterprises as they granted new franchises often was attributable to recording these promissory notes as assets and revenue at face amount. In part, this abuse of the revenue realization principle was mitigated by issuance of **APB Opinion No. 21,** which required that long-term notes receivable be valued, not at face amount, but at current fair value, or (if current fair value was not determinable) at a discounted present value computed by use of an imputed interest rate.

Although the discounting of receivables to their present value reduces the opportunities for the so-called "front-ending of income" on long-term contracts, it does not provide a direct answer to the question of when revenue should be recognized on the types of franchising contracts described above.[5] Because of the current widespread use of innovative financing arrangements, accountants face a more difficult problem than ever before in determining when a "sale" is a genuine sales transaction.

Matching costs and revenue

As stated in Chapter 1, the interrelation of the cost and revenue realization principles is often described as a process of **matching costs and revenue.** Accountants associate costs with output and then determine the value of output at the point of revenue realization. Any costs treated as period costs are related to whatever revenue has been recognized during that accounting period.

A simple illustration will make this point clear. A department store sells a dress for $60 to a customer. Look behind this transaction and you will find that the "product" sold in this case is more than a dress. The

[5] The problem was alleviated with the publication of *An AICPA Industry Accounting Guide,* "Accounting for Franchise Fee Revenue," AICPA (New York: 1973). This subject is covered in more detail in Chapter 13.

store has sold some portion of the service potential of the building in which the sale took place. It also has sold the services of a buyer who studied fashion trends and made one or more trips to the designers' showrooms. Freight, insurance, storage, and handling charges also have been sold, as well as advertising and the services of a salesclerk. Our list is not complete, but let us assume that the cost of acquiring the dress and all services necessary to put that dress where the customer would buy it amount to $45. In exchange for this the customer promises to pay $60. An ideal accounting for this transaction would show that the store had invested $45 in an asset (the "product" sold to this customer) and that this asset had been revalued from $45 to $60 (and retitled accounts receivable) at the time of sale, when evidence of an increase in value became available.

Money as a standard measuring unit

We have seen how the cost and realization assumptions affect the accounting measurement of income. Now let us look briefly at an accounting assumption that is equally fundamental—the assumption that money is a **standard measuring unit** for reporting the effect of business transactions.

Assume that a business enterprise invests $80 in Year 1 to manufacture a product which is expected to sell for $120. The cost of producing the identical product has risen to $130 in Year 2, and because demand is strong the enterprise is able to sell the product for $180 in that year. Between Year 1 and Year 2, prices in general throughout the economy have risen 10%. On these facts, the income from this transaction might be computed in three different ways:

Method 1. Nominal-Dollar Income

Conventional way of measuring income	
Revenue realized in Year 2	$180
Less: Actual cost incurred in Year 1	80
Monetary income	$100

Method 2. Mixed-Dollar Income with Price Gain Isolated

Price gain (inventory profit) isolated	
Revenue realized in Year 2	$180
Less: Replacement cost at the date of sale	130
Operating margin	$ 50
Add: Price gain or inventory profit (the difference between current replacement cost of $130 and actual cost of $80)	50
Monetary income	$100

Method 3. Constant-Dollar Income

<table>
<tr><td>**Revenue and cost are stated in dollars of uniform purchasing power**</td><td>*Revenue in constant (Year 2) dollars.* *$180*
Less: Actual cost expressed in dollars of constant (Year 2) purchasing power
   ($80 × 110%). *88*
Net income measured in dollars of constant value. . . . . *$ 92*</td></tr>
</table>

Nominal-dollar income (method 1) reflects the entire difference between dollars of revenue and dollars of cost, without regard to differences in their size. Under method 2, the effect of changes in **specific prices** is isolated, and the fact that one-half of monetary income is attributed to rising replacement costs (or to **inventory profits**) is disclosed. In method 3, the measuring unit has been changed to dollars of constant value, that is, purchasing power. Both costs and revenue are expressed in Year 2 dollars. Net income in Year 2 dollars is only $92, because the enterprise must now recover $88 to be as well off as it was when it invested $80 in the manufacture of the product in Year 1.

During periods when prices in general are rising, a clear understanding of the limitations of the dollar as a unit of measurement is invaluable in the interpretation of financial statements. Supplementary measurement of net income in constant dollars now is required by the FASB. This topic is considered in Chapter 25.

INCOME REPORTING: THE INCOME STATEMENT

We have seen that the problem of measuring net income is formidable. Also important is the related problem of presenting net income in a financial statement. A good income statement is something more than an itemized list of revenue and expenses. Attention must be given to such issues as the system of classification, the amount of detail that is useful, the order of presentation, the relationship between elements of net income, and the titles used to describe the items appearing in an income statement.

A traditional income statement may not be as significant to management as statements showing income by products, departments, or divisions. Managers are obviously interested in detailed accounting and statistical data that shed light on the contribution of the various segments of a business enterprise to its overall success. Such information might also be of great interest to outsiders, but the information appearing in published income statements is usually highly condensed. More detailed income statements often are submitted to credit grantors and others having a special interest in the enterprise.

The income statements for some enterprises are quite complex. For example, if a change in accounting principle was made, if a major industry segment was sold, or if extraordinary items were reported, the lower section of the income statement is expanded. Finally, **earnings per share** must be presented in the income statement of publicly owned corporations, and this can become quite cumbersome for corporations that report both **primary** and **fully diluted** earnings per share. In this section we shall illustrate some relatively simple income statements, to be followed by a discussion and illustrations of more complex situations.

Alternative forms of the income statement

The choice between the **multiple-step** and the **single-step** form of income statement is an unsettled question in income reporting. In the multiple-step form (illustrated on page 99 for Sample Corporation) various intermediate balances, such as gross profit on sales, income from operations, and income before income taxes, are computed and labeled in the statement. The single-step form (illustrated on page 100) presents a grouping of revenue in one category, all expenses in another, and derives a single net income figure. This form is widely used by publicly owned companies in their annual reports.[6]

Those who favor the multiple-step form argue that there are a number of significant subtotals on the road to net income. The **gross profit on sales** indicates the average markup on the merchandise sold which is available to cover operating expenses. The distinction between operating and nonoperating revenue and expenses permits the showing of **income from operations** as a measure of operating results. The **income before income taxes** reflects pre-tax earnings and emphasizes the special nature of income taxes expense.

Proponents of the single-step form maintain that net income emerges as the overall amount by which a business enterprise is better off after taking into account all revenue and all expenses incurred in producing that revenue. They object to the implication of the multiple-step form that there is a priority of cost recovery; that is, that cost of goods sold is recovered first, then operating expenses, then interest expense. The multiple-step form also implies relationships that do not exist. For example, showing interest revenue as other revenue below income from operations implies that interest is realized without cost; yet some general and administrative expenses usually are incurred to produce interest revenue.

The sequence of listing of expenses and the amount of detail shown in published income statements vary considerably. The multiple-step form is more likely to be found in more detailed financial statements prepared for the use of management, bankers, and other creditors; it is particularly appropriate when financial statements are prepared for both internal and external users.

[6] Of the 600 companies included in *Accounting Trends & Techniques,* 34th ed. (1980), 351 used the single-step form and 249 used the multiple-step form.

Multiple-step form of income statement

SAMPLE CORPORATION
Income Statement
For Year Ended December 31, Year 5
(In thousands of dollars)

Gross sales			$18,700
Less: Returns and allowances		$ 324	
Discounts		268	592
Net sales			$18,108
Cost of goods sold:			
Beginning inventories		$ 1,000	
Purchases (net of discounts)	$10,668		
Freight-in	1,266		
Delivered cost of purchases	$11,934		
Less: Purchases returns and allowances	366	11,568	
Cost of goods available for sale		$12,568	
Less: Ending inventories		580	
Cost of goods sold			11,988
Gross profit on sales			$ 6,120
Operating expenses:			
Selling expenses:			
Sales salaries	$ 1,260		
Advertising and promotion	880		
Delivery	180		
Building occupancy (including depreciation of building)	240		
Other selling expenses	80	$ 2,640	
General and administrative expenses:			
Administrative salaries	$ 960		
Property taxes	208		
Depreciation of equipment	80		
Other general and administrative expenses	372	1,620	
Total operating expenses			4,260
Income from operations			$ 1,860
Other revenue and (expenses):			
Investment income from affiliated companies		$ 420	
Gain on disposal of equipment		50	
Interest expense		(230)	240
Income before income taxes			$ 2,100
Income taxes expense			1,043
Net income			$ 1,057
Earnings per share of common stock			$ 1.25

**Single-step form of
income statement**

SAMPLE CORPORATION		
Income Statement		
For Year Ended December 31, Year 5		
(In thousands of dollars)		
Revenue:		
Net sales		$18,108
Investment income		420
Gain on disposal of equipment		50
Total revenue		$18,578
Costs and expenses:		
Cost of goods sold	$11,988	
Selling expenses.	2,640	
General and administrative expenses	1,620	
Interest expense.	230	
Income taxes expense	1,043	
Total costs and expenses		17,521
Net income		$ 1,057
Earnings per share of common stock		$ 1.25

Most published income statements appear in single-step form and almost always are presented in **comparative form,** similar to the one illustrated for Arkansas Oil Company on page 101 (see also page 152).

Financial statements prepared in comparative form highlight trends and changes, and emphasize the fact that financial statements for a single accounting period are only a small part of the continuous history of a business enterprise.

Classification of revenue

For most business enterprises the major source of revenue is the production and sale of goods and services. Examples of secondary sources are dividends, royalties, interest, rents, investment income from affiliated companies, and gains on the disposal of assets. An objective of reporting revenue in an income statement is to disclose the major sources of revenue and to separate primary from miscellaneous sources. For example, some enterprises report revenue from government contracts separately from revenue from nongovernment sources, which enables the user to form some opinion of future prospects in the light of projected governmental expenditures.

Revenue offsets should be distinguished from expenses and should be deducted from gross revenue in the income statement. Such items as sales discounts and sales returns and allowances do not represent expenses, but rather revenue that is never realized.

ARKANSAS OIL COMPANY
Income Statement
For Years Ended December 31,
(In thousands of dollars)

	Year 10	Year 9
Sales.	$444,645	$568,526
Royalties, interest, and other revenue	17,007	15,280
Total revenue	$461,652	$583,806
Cost and expenses:		
Operating, delivery, and other related costs and expenses	$246,652	$260,278
Exploration expenses	13,414	21,295
Selling, general, and administrative expenses	16,130	18,741
Interest expense	13,982	14,424
Income taxes expense	68,250	121,768
Total costs and expenses	$358,428	$436,506
Net income	$103,224	$147,300
Earnings per share of common stock.	$ 3.37	$ 4.83

Classification of expenses

Expenses are classified in the income statement to help users grasp important operating cost relationships. Classification may be according to the ***nature*** of expenses, business ***functions,*** areas of ***responsibility,*** or any other useful basis.

Natural Classification In many published income statements, expenses are reported in single-step form, classified according to the nature of expenses, that is, in categories that reflect the kind of resources used during the accounting period. Examples of such categories include merchandise and supplies, salaries and fringe benefits, purchased services, depreciation, property taxes, interest, and income taxes.

Functional Classification The multiple-step income statement for Sample Corporation on page 99 illustrates a classification of expenses into three categories on a functional basis: (1) cost of goods sold, (2) selling expenses, and (3) general and administrative expenses.

For internal reports, the usefulness of the functional classification system is improved by identifying many more than three functions. For example, material handling, production scheduling, assembly, packing, and crating are manufacturing subfunctions.

Expenses versus Losses *Losses* are nonproductive expenditures or asset expirations that have no observable relation to either current or future revenue. Thus, the cost of mistakes, waste, and unusual casualties or calamities over which there is no control may be distinguished from ordinary operating expenses on the grounds that the former are nonproductive. This distinction, although difficult to draw in many practical situations, can be useful for managerial purposes. For external reporting, minimum standards of disclosure require that unusual losses which are material in amount be disclosed in the income statement.

Cost offsets (savings) are not revenue

Cost offsets or savings should be distinguished from revenue. Revenue arises from realized increases in the value of net assets. Cost offsets are expenditures that a business enterprise is able to avoid. For example, suppose that a machine can be purchased for either $1,000 in cash or $1,200 on a time-payment basis. If the buyer chooses to pay $1,200, it has acquired two types of asset services—the machine for $1,000 and the privilege of deferring payment for $200. If the buyer chooses to pay cash, the $200 is not revenue but a cost saving, and the machine still costs $1,000. Similarly, purchases discounts are cost savings that should not be confused with revenue.

Offsetting revenue and costs

When a plant asset is sold, the price received (revenue) and the carrying amount of the asset (undepreciated cost) are offset, and only the net gain or loss is shown in the income statement. Because the sale of a plant asset is not a part of ordinary operations, the net gain or loss is the significant amount.

In other cases, revenue is reported as a cost reduction. For example, revenue realized through the sale of scrap or by-products often is recorded as a reduction of the cost of the main product. Because the main product and by-products usually emerge jointly from a single raw material (and joint cost allocation is a difficult problem), this procedure has merit. If carried to extremes, offsetting revenue against costs misstates both revenue and costs.

Interim reports of earnings

Interim financial information may include current data on financial position, results of operations, and changes in financial position. However, interim financial reports issued to stockholders seldom include a complete set of financial statements. Although practices differ somewhat, most publicly owned companies issue only highly condensed *interim reports of earnings,* such as the one illustrated on page 103 for Arlington Corporation.

Interim report of earnings

ARLINGTON CORPORATION
Income Statements
(In thousands —except per-share data)

	For three months ended		For nine months ended	
	Sept. 30, Year 2	Sept. 30, Year 1	Sept. 30, Year 2	Sept. 30, Year 1
Total revenue	$1,238,600	$1,184,100	$3,973,900	$3,428,900
Costs and expenses, includ-				
ing interest expense	1,221,300	1,145,500	3,876,200	3,319,200
Income before income taxes	$ 17,300	$ 38,600	$ 97,700	$ 109,700
Income taxes expense	4,100	18,500	39,100	52,800
Net income.	$ 13,200	$ 20,100	$ 58,600	$ 56,900
Earnings per common share:				
Primary.	$ 0.64	$ 1.30	$ 3.25	$ 3.60
Fully diluted.	$ 0.62	$ 1.23	$ 3.20	$ 3.40
Dividends per common share	$ 0.40	$ 0.30	$ 1.20	$ 0.90
Average common shares out-				
standing	17,600	15,800	17,600	15,700

Note: Shares outstanding and per-share data have been restated for the 3 for 1 common stock split in Year 1.

Publicly owned companies are required to issue **quarterly reports** to their shareholders, the SEC, and the stock exchanges which list their stock. Such reports are prepared in accordance with standards set forth in **APB Opinion No. 28,** "Interim Financial Reporting."[7] An audit of interim reports of earnings is not currently required. However, auditors generally perform a **limited review** of interim financial information and convey their findings in a report addressed to the company, its board of directors, or its stockholders. The auditor's report on interim financial information does not include any expressions of assurance concerning the information, and each page of the interim financial information should be clearly marked as "unaudited."[8]

Earnings and objectives of financial reporting

Among the objectives of financial reporting developed by the FASB (previously listed in Chapter 1) are:[9]

[7] APB Opinion No. 28, "Interim Financial Reporting," AICPA (New York: 1973).
[8] Statement on Auditing Standards No. 24, "Review of Interim Financial Information," AICPA (New York: 1979), p. 8.
[9] Statement of Financial Accounting Concepts No. 1, "Objectives of Financial Reporting by Business Enterprises," FASB (Stamford: 1978), p. ix.

1 The primary focus of financial reporting is information about earnings and its components.

2 Information about enterprise earnings based on accrual accounting generally provides a better indication of an enterprise's present and continuing ability to generate favorable cash flows than information limited to the financial effects of cash receipts and payments.

3 Financial reporting is expected to provide information about an enterprise's financial performance during a period and about how management of an enterprise has discharged its stewardship responsibility to owners.

4 Investors, creditors, and others may use reported earnings . . . in various ways to assess the prospects for cash flows. They may wish, for example, to evaluate managements' performance, estimate "earning power," predict future earnings, assess risk, or to confirm, change, or reject earlier predictions or assessments. . . .

The highly condensed income statements issued by most business enterprises are less than adequate to achieve these objectives. Considerable improvements in the reporting of results of operations are needed if income statements are to be of maximum value to users in predicting, comparing, and evaluating the earning power of business enterprises. For example, the earning of income consists of **earnings cycles** which may be **completed, incomplete,** or **prospective;** it may be useful to segregate precisely measured results from estimated results. The basis of estimates might be explained so that sophisticated users would be able to interpret the reported results in line with their own judgment and experience. Also, it may be useful to report the effects of changes in values of assets and liabilities on net income and to segregate expenses between fixed and variable to help users predict cash flows and the possible effects of changes in volume of activity on net income.

In an effort to improve the usefulness of the income statement, the FASB reviewed the form and content of earnings reports. In the opinion of the Board, better information on earnings may help users of financial statements with their main need—the assessment of future earnings and cash flows.[10] A major criticism of the traditional income statement is that it does not provide enough information about past earnings to help users assess future earnings. For example: (1) Effects of some unusual events or transactions are not separately disclosed; (2) economic changes that affect relationships between recurring revenue and expenses are not explained sufficiently; and (3) excessive emphasis may be placed on a single earnings number, such as net income or earnings per share. To alleviate these criticisms, the format of the income statement may have to be changed significantly in the future.

Financial forecasts

One of the objectives of financial statements is to provide information useful for the predictive process. The public accounting profession and

---

[10] *FASB Discussion Memorandum,* "An Analysis of Issues Relating to Reporting Earnings," FASB (Stamford: 1979), p. 1.

the Securities and Exchange Commission have sought to find a satisfactory basis for the preparation and issuance of **financial forecasts,** including the results of future operations. Virtually every large business enterprise prepares forecasts of future operations as a means of defining goals and measuring performance. The problem is how to make such information available to the investing public yet avoid the danger of misleading investors. At one time the SEC proposed to require companies making earnings forecasts to meet detailed reporting standards but eventually withdrew its proposal. The SEC currently encourages companies to file financial forecasts with the Commission, but such filings are not mandatory.

Few companies issue financial forecasts to the public at present. However, many companies issue such forecasts to lenders, underwriters, and prospective investors in connection with obtaining debt or equity financing. In 1975, the Accounting Standards Division of the AICPA issued **Statement of Position 75-4** "as a guide for CPAs in the preparation of financial forecasts for clients."[11] The AICPA suggested that financial forecasts generally should include at least the following information: (1) sales or gross revenue, (2) gross profit, (3) provision for income taxes, (4) net income, (5) gain or loss on disposal of an industry segment, (6) extraordinary items, (7) earnings per share, and (8) significant anticipated changes in financial position.

In 1980, the AICPA issued **Guide for a Review of Financial Forecasts** that provides guidance to accountants for the review of enterprises' financial forecasts. The Guide neither requires nor recommends the preparation or review of financial forecasts.

SPECIAL PROBLEMS IN INCOME REPORTING

Income reporting in recent years has become more complicated as a result of new accounting principles relating to income tax allocation, extraordinary items, discontinued operations of an industry segment, changes in accounting principles, and the reporting of earnings per share data. These topics are discussed in the following sections.

Income tax allocation

Income taxes on corporate income constitute a major expense of doing business. **Taxable income** is a legal concept; it is related to accounting income, but there are significant differences. As a result, a corporation's taxable income for a given year may differ substantially from its pre-tax accounting income as reported in the income statement. Accountants have attempted to deal with this problem by **in-**

[11] *Statement of Position 75-4,* "Presentation and Disclosure of Financial Forecasts," AICPA (New York: 1975).

come tax allocation, which is the subject matter of Chapter 21. At this point only the general nature of income tax allocation is considered, with attention focused on the method of presenting clearly in the income statement the income tax effect of extraordinary items, discontinued operations, and the cumulative effect of changes in accounting principles.

Tax allocation falls into two major types: (1) interperiod tax allocation, and (2) intraperiod tax allocation. *Interperiod tax allocation* means that income taxes expense should be allocated between accounting periods because of *timing* differences in the recognition of income; that is, expenses or revenue appear in the income statement either before or after they appear in the income tax return. By means of interperiod tax allocation, the income taxes expense in the income statement is based on earnings as reported in the income statement rather than on the amount of income taxes actually payable for the current period. Thus, income taxes are allocated between periods as are other expenses. *Intraperiod tax allocation* is the process of allocating income taxes to income from operations, to extraordinary items, and to other sources of income and loss which require separate presentation in the income statement. Similarly, corrections of material errors made in prior periods are recorded in the Retained Earnings account net of any related income tax effect. Such allocation is required, as indicated by the following statement in *APB Opinion No. 11:*[12]

> The income tax expense attributable to income before extraordinary items is computed by determining the income tax expense related to revenue and expense transactions entering into the determination of such income, without giving effect to the tax consequences of the items excluded from the determination of income before extraordinary items. The income tax expense attributable to other items is determined by the tax consequences of transactions involving these items. If an operating loss exists before extraordinary items, the tax consequences of such loss should be associated with the loss.

The important point to keep in mind is that extraordinary items and other unusual components of net income should be reported *net of income taxes in the income statement,* and prior period adjustments should be reported *net of income taxes in the statement of retained earnings.* The application of intraperiod tax allocation in the income statement, including the presentation of earnings per share, is illustrated for Comprehensive Corporation on page 112; the reporting of a prior period adjustment in the statement of retained earnings is illustrated for Sample Corporation on page 115.

Extraordinary items

A troublesome problem in reporting periodic income is the proper treatment of extraordinary gains and losses. General agreement exists

---

[12] *APB Opinion No. 11,* "Accounting for Income Taxes," AICPA (New York: 1967), p. 175.

that unusual gains and losses, if material in amount, should be clearly disclosed in the income statement. They should be distinguished from the ordinary operating revenue and expenses of the period. However, such gains and losses should be reported as extraordinary items in the income statement only when the events or transactions giving rise to the gains and losses are of **unusual nature** and **infrequent occurrence.** This standard is summarized in **APB Opinion No. 30** as follows:[13]

> Extraordinary items are events and transactions that are distinguished by their unusual nature and by the infrequency of their occurrence. Thus, **both** of the following criteria should be met to classify an event or transaction as an extraordinary item:
> **a Unusual nature**—the underlying event or transaction should possess a high degree of abnormality and be of a type clearly unrelated to, or only incidentally related to, the ordinary and typical activities of the entity, taking into account the environment in which the entity operates.
> **b Infrequency of occurrence**—the underlying event or transaction should be of a type that would not reasonably be expected to recur in the foreseeable future, taking into account the environment in which the entity operates.

To be considered unusual in nature, the underlying event or transaction should be abnormal and clearly unrelated to the ordinary and typical activities of the entity. The scope of operations, lines of business, operating policies, and the environment in which an entity operates should be considered in applying this criterion. The environment of an entity includes such factors as the characteristics of the industry in which it operates, the geographic location of its activities, and the degree of government regulation.

If an event or a transaction is not reasonably expected to take place in the foreseeable future, it is considered to occur infrequently. Past experience of the entity is generally a helpful guide in determining the frequency of an event or transaction. Thus, only **unusual** and **infrequent** events and transactions produce extraordinary gains and losses. However, these qualitative standards are difficult to apply in practice, and differences of opinion still exist in identifying extraordinary items. Listed on page 108 are some examples of how certain gains or losses should be classified in the income statement.

[13] *APB Opinion No. 30,* "Reporting the Results of Operations—Reporting the Effects of Disposal of a Segment of a Business, and Extraordinary, Unusual and Infrequently Occurring Events and Transactions," AICPA (New York: 1973), pp. 564–565.

Items which are or are not extraordinary items

Extraordinary Items	*Not Extraordinary Items*
1 *Effects of major casualties (such as earthquakes or severe hailstorms in localities where such events are infrequent)*	**1** *Write-down or write-off of receivables, inventories, plant assets, or intangible assets*
2 *Effects of a prohibition under a newly enacted law or regulation*	**2** *Gains or losses from exchange or translation of foreign currencies (including major devaluations and revaluations)*
3 *Loss from an expropriation of assets by a foreign country*	**3** *Gains or losses on disposal of an industry segment*
4 *Material gain or loss on early extinguishment of debt*	**4** *Other gains or losses from sale or abandonment of plant assets used in the business enterprise*
5 *Realization of income tax benefit in the current accounting period of an earlier-period operating loss carry-forward*	**5** *Effects of a strike and adjustments of accruals on long-term construction contracts*
6 *Gain or loss on sale of **only** holding of stock or land which has been owned for many years*	**6** *Cumulative effect of a change in accounting principle*

Relatively few extraordinary items currently are reported by publicly owned corporations, as a result of the rigid criteria established in **APB Opinion No. 30.** The presentations of extraordinary items, including the separate per-share effect in the income statement, are illustrated below and on page 112.

Extraordinary item in income statement

Income before income taxes and extraordinary item	*$500,000*
Income taxes expense (actual income taxes payable are $80,000 as a	
result of the tax reduction from the extraordinary loss)	*200,000*
Income before extraordinary item	*$300,000*
Extraordinary loss (net of income tax credit of $120,000)	*180,000*
Net income	*$120,000*
Earnings per share:	
Income before extraordinary item	*$ 3.00*
Extraordinary item	*(1.80)*
Net income	*$ 1.20*

The effect of a material event or transaction which is considered either unusual in nature or infrequent in occurrence, **but not both,** should be included in the determination of income before extraordinary items. The nature and effects on net income of each such event or transaction should be disclosed either in the income statement or in notes to the financial statements.

Discontinued operations of an industry segment

An **industry segment** is a component of a business enterprise engaged in providing a product or service for a profit. The assets and operating results of such a segment should be clearly identifiable from the other assets and results of operations of the enterprise. Users of financial statements consider the income statement more useful when the results from the **continuing operations** of an enterprise are reported separately from the results of material and unusual transactions or events. For this reason, the operating results of a **discontinued industry segment** (including any gain or loss on the disposal of the segment) for the current accounting period should be reported separately in the lower section of the income statement. The operating results and the gain or loss on the disposal of an industry segment are reported net of applicable income taxes. The purpose of such separate disclosure is to enable users of financial statements to make better predictive judgments of future earnings of the enterprise.

Thus, the revenue and expenses included in an income statement for the year in which an industry segment is eliminated consist only of the revenue and expenses from continuing operations. The net income or loss from the discontinued segment for the current accounting period is reported separately to arrive at **income before extraordinary items,** and the revenue applicable to the discontinued segment should be disclosed separately in the notes to financial statements. Any gain or loss from disposal of an industry segment should be reported in conjunction with the operations of the segment, not as an extraordinary item.[14] Per-share data relating to discontinued operations "may be included on the face of the income statement or in a related note."[15] These reporting requirements are illustrated for Comprehensive Corporation on page 112.

Accounting changes

We have stated earlier that the consistent use of accounting principles from one accounting period to another increases the usefulness of financial statements by facilitating analysis of comparative accounting data. However, management may justify a change to an alternative ac-

---

[14] Ibid., p. 557.
[15] Ibid., p. 559.

ceptable accounting principle on the ground that it is preferable.[16] Basically, there are two types of accounting changes: (1) change in accounting principle, and (2) change in accounting estimate.

Some **changes in accounting principle** (such as a change in the method of computing depreciation) are recognized by inclusion of the **cumulative effect** of a change to a new accounting principle in net income of the period of change.[17] Such changes require the restatement of assets and liabilities as of the beginning of the current period to the amounts that would have existed if the newly adopted principle had been used in prior years. The related debit or credit reflecting the **cumulative effect** of the change on earnings of prior years is reported in the current year's income statement **between** any extraordinary items and net income. The method of reporting the cumulative effect of the change is essentially the same as for extraordinary items, as illustrated for Comprehensive Corporation on page 112.

Other changes in accounting principle (such as a change from lifo to fifo method of inventory pricing) are reported by a restatement of the financial statements of prior accounting periods.

Another type of accounting change is a **change in estimate,** such as the revision of an original estimate of an 8-year economic life for a jet aircraft to a 12-year life. The new estimate affects only the current and future years' financial statements, and no correcting journal entry is necessary. The carrying amount of the jet aircraft at the date of the change in the estimated economic life is allocated to the remaining years of economic life. Accounting changes are discussed and illustrated in Chapter 22.

Earnings per share

The amount of earnings per share of common stock for an accounting period is computed by dividing the net income available by the weighted-average number of shares of common stock outstanding during the period. The purpose is to show earning power on a per-share basis so that investors can relate the market price of a share of common stock to the income per share. However, when a corporation has outstanding stock options, convertible bonds or preferred stock, and other hybrid securities, we cannot compute a **single** meaningful earnings per share amount. In such cases a **dual presentation** of **primary** and **fully diluted** earnings per share is required. When extraordinary items appear in the income statement, primary and fully diluted earnings per share are presented as illustrated on page 111.

---

[16] *APB Opinion No. 20,* "Accounting Changes," AICPA (New York: 1971), p. 391.
[17] Ibid., pp. 391–392.

Dual presentation of earnings per share

	Year 2	Year 1
Earnings per share of common stock:		
Primary:		
Income before extraordinary item.	$4.00	$3.35
Extraordinary item	(0.50)	1.65
Net income	$3.50	$5.00
Fully diluted:		
Income before extraordinary item.	$3.55	$3.00
Extraordinary item	(0.42)	1.58
Net income	$3.13	$4.58

A more extensive example of presentation of earnings per share data appears on page 112 for Comprehensive Corporation. This topic is covered in Chapter 18.

Comprehensive illustration of income reporting

The presentation of extraordinary items, discontinued operations, cumulative effect of a change in accounting principle, and per-share data in the income statement is illustrated, along with the related notes, on pages 112–113 for Comprehensive Corporation.

Note the extensive detail of the per-share and pro forma amounts in the lower section of the income statement for Comprehensive Corporation, despite the fact that a dual presentation of earnings per share (primary and fully diluted) was not required.

Disclosure requirements

Companies reporting to the public are required to disclose, either in the income statement or in the accompanying notes, certain information which may be helpful to users of financial statements. Although these disclosure requirements are stressed throughout this book, some of the \more important items relating directly to the income statement which call for disclosure, either in reports to the SEC or in the annual report to stockholders, are listed below:

1 Accounting policies, including depreciation methods, amortization of intangible assets, inventory pricing, and revenue recognition procedures

2 Management's discussion and analysis of the summary of operations, including reasons for material changes in specific items

3 The amount of depreciation expense and research and development expense for each accounting period for which an income statement is presented

4 An analysis of the composition of income taxes expense, including a reconciliation of the company's effective income tax rate with the statutory federal income tax rate

Comprehensive illustration of income statement

COMPREHENSIVE CORPORATION*
Income Statement
For Years Ended December 31,
(In thousands of dollars, except per-share data)

	Year 11	Year 10
Net sales and other revenue.	$85,360	$75,750
Costs and expenses (**Note 1**)	65,880	60,390
Income from continuing operations before income taxes	$19,480	$15,360
Income taxes expense	9,350	7,370
Income from continuing operations	$10,130	$ 7,990
Discontinued operations (**Note 2**):		
Income from operations of discontinued Division X (net of		
income tax effect of $383 in Year 11 and $442 in Year 10).	410	470
Loss on disposal of Division X (net of income tax effect of		
$1,880)	(2,040)	
Income before extraordinary item and cumulative effect of		
change in accounting principle	$ 8,500	$ 8,460
Extraordinary item (net of income tax effect of $493) (**Note 3**)		1,224
Cumulative effect (to Dec. 31, Year 10) of change to a dif-		
ferent depreciation method (net of income tax effect of		
$1,150) (**Note 4**).	1,250	
Net income.	$ 9,750	$ 9,684
Earnings per share:		
Income from continuing operations.	$ 2.03	$ 1.60
Income from discontinued Division X.	0.08	0.10
Loss on disposal of Division X	(0.41)	
Income before extraordinary item and cumulative effect		
of change in accounting principle.	$ 1.70	$ 1.70
Extraordinary item (net of income tax effect)		0.24
Cumulative effect (to Dec. 31, Year 10) of change to a dif-		
ferent depreciation method.	0.25	
Net income.	$ 1.95	$ 1.94
Pro forma amounts, assuming the new depreciation method		
is applied retroactively:		
Income from continuing operations.	$10,130	$ 8,125
Per common share	2.03	1.63
Income before extraordinary item	8,500	8,595
Per common share	1.70	1.72
Net income.	8,500	9,819
Per common share	1.70	1.96

* Adapted from Extraordinary Items, Prior Period Adjustments and Changes in Accounting Principles, Accountants International Study Group: 1974, Exhibit 1.

Notes to income statement

Note 1—*Loss on Sale of Plant Facilities*

Other expenses for Year 11 include $675,000 representing the loss incurred on the disposal of obsolete plant facilities. Based on provisions of **APB Opinion No. 30,** *this is not an extraorindary item.*

Note 2—*Discontinued Operations*

In October, Year 11, the company decided to dispose of its retail business which had consisted of 20 outlets in localities adjacent to its principal customers. Two of the outlets were closed in October and the remaining 18 were sold prior to December 31, Year 11. Charges resulting directly from the decision to dispose of this business, principally termination costs on long-term leases, severance pay, and losses on disposal of facilities and equipment related to the retail business, less reduction in income taxes of $1,880,000, are reported separately from the results of the company's continuing operations. The income statement for Year 10 has been reclassified to give effect to this presentation.

Note 3—*Extraordinary Item*

During Year 10, the company received settlement from a state government for condemnation of land which had been held for future expansion of a manufacturing plant. The related gain, less income taxes of $493,000, is reported as an extraordinary item.

Note 4—*Change to a Different Depreciation Method*

Depreciation of plant facilities has been computed by the straight-line method in Year 11. Depreciation of plant facilities in prior years was computed by the sum-of-the-years'-digits method. The new method of depreciation was adopted to recognize . . . (state justification of change of depreciation method) . . . and has been applied retroactively to facilities acquisitions of prior years. The effect of the change in Year 11 was to increase income before extraordinary item by approximately $100,000 (or $0.02 per share). The adjustment of $1,250,000 (after reduction for income taxes of $1,150,000) to apply retroactively the new method is included in net income of Year 11. The pro forma amounts shown in the income statement have been adjusted for the effect of retroactive application of depreciation, the change in provisions for incentive compensation which would have been made had the new method been in effect, and related income taxes.

5 Supplementary constant-dollar and current-cost data required to be disclosed by certain large publicly owned companies

Some of these items of disclosure are illustrated in the financial statements for International Harvester Company in the Appendix at the end of Chapter 4.

STATEMENT OF RETAINED EARNINGS

The statement of retained earnings generally is included with every set of financial statements, although it is not considered to be one of the major financial statements. Changing concepts of financial reporting in recent years have firmly established the all-inclusive income statement, thus tending to shorten and simplify the statement of retained earnings. Also significant has been the trend away from the use of appropriations of retained earnings. Consequently, the typical statement of retained earnings includes the beginning balance of retained earnings, the net income for the accounting period as an addition, and the dividends (both cash and stock) as deductions, and concludes with the ending balance of retained earnings. Cash dividends per share and the total amount declared during the period are disclosed. If operations for the latest period resulted in a loss, the beginning balance of retained earnings is reduced by the amount of the net loss. In addition, the beginning balance may be increased or decreased by a *prior period adjustment* (such as the correction of a material error) or the effect on prior years' operations resulting from certain types of changes in accounting principles.

Prior period adjustments

In contrast to extraordinary items described earlier, *prior period adjustments* are excluded from the determination of net income for the current accounting period and are reported (*net of any related income tax effect*) in the statement of retained earnings. Prior period adjustments originally were defined by the APB in *Opinion No. 9* as:[18]

> . . . those material adjustments which (a) can be specifically identified with and directly related to the business activities of particular prior periods, and (b) are not attributable to economic events occurring subsequent to the date of the financial statements for the prior period, and (c) depend primarily on determinations by persons other than management and (d) were not susceptible to reasonable estimation prior to such determination.

In the view of the SEC, the application of these guidelines proved to be unsatisfactory, particularly in relation to numerous out-of-court settlements of litigation. The amounts of such settlements generally were reported as prior period adjustments, despite the fact that management made a number of significant judgments in reaching the settlements. Consequently, the test that a prior period adjustment must "depend primarily on determinations by persons other than management" was not met. To correct the loose applications of the guidelines established by the APB, the FASB (with urging from the SEC) redefined *prior period adjustments* as follows:[19]

> . . . all items of profit and loss recognized during a period, including accruals of estimated losses from loss contingencies, shall be included in the determination of net income for that period.
>
> Items of profit and loss related to the following shall be accounted for and reported as prior period adjustments and excluded from the determination of net income for the current period:
> *a* Correction of an error in the financial statements of a prior period, and
> *b* Adjustments that result from realization of income tax benefits of pre-acquisition operating loss carryforwards of purchased subsidiaries.

Material errors in the financial statements might include arithmetical

---

[18] *APB Opinion No. 9,* "Reporting the Results of Operations," AICPA (New York: 1966), p. 115.

[19] *FASB Statement No. 16,* "Prior Period Adjustments," FASB (Stamford: 1977), p. 5.

mistakes, the misuse or omissions of information, mistakes in the application of accounting principles or procedures, and failure to interpret properly the accounting aspects of transactions. Another example of a correction of an error is a change from an accounting principle that is not generally accepted to one that is.

In the financial statements for the current accounting period, a prior period adjustment is reported as a correction to the beginning balance in retained earnings (see illustration for Sample Corporation below). When a correction of an error is made as a prior period adjustment, the issuance of comparative financial statements requires the restatement of prior periods' financial statements to reflect the correction.

Alternative forms of statement of retained earnings

The basic format of a statement of retained earnings which includes a prior period adjustment is illustrated below for Sample Corporation. The related income statement (multiple-step form) for Sample Corporation appears on page 99; the related balance sheet and statement of changes in financial position for Sample Corporation are presented in Chapter 4 (pages 146–147 and 151).

Statement of retained earnings with a prior period adjustment

SAMPLE CORPORATION
Statement of Retained Earnings
For Year Ended December 31, Year 5
(In thousands of dollars)

Retained earnings, beginning of year, as originally reported		$2,800
Less: Prior period adjustment—correction of error (net of applicable in-income tax effect of $240,000)		360
Retained earnings, beginning of year, as restated		$2,440
Add: Net income		1,057
Subtotal		$3,497
Less: Dividends on preferred stock ($6.00 a share)	$ 57	
Dividends on common stock ($0.50 a share)	400	457
Retained earnings, end of year		$3,040

As with other financial statements, the statement of retained earnings generally is presented in **comparative** form showing data for two years. The comparative form of retained earnings statement, which also includes an appropriation for general contingencies, is illustrated on page 116 for Blue Company.

Statement of retained
earnings in comparative
form

BLUE COMPANY

Statement of Retained Earnings

For Years Ended June 30,

	1983	1982
Unappropriated, beginning of year.	$240,604	$193,240
Add: Net income.	108,166	80,887
Subtotals.	$348,770	$274,127
Less: Cash dividends:		
Common stock—$1 a share and $0.90 a share, respectively	(32,991)	(29,336)
Preferred stock—$2 a share	(4,187)	(4,187)
Unappropriated, end of year.	$311,592	$240,604
Appropriated for general contingencies	50,000	50,000
Total retained earnings, end of year.	$361,592	$290,604

A significant number of companies combine the income statement with the statement of retained earnings. Such a presentation has the advantage of displaying in one statement any prior period adjustments and extraordinary gains and losses, thus reducing the possibility that any of these items will be overlooked. One minor objection to this form is that the net income or net loss appears in the middle of the statement. Such a *combined statement of income and retained earnings,* showing comparative data for two years, is presented below for Red Company:

Combined statement of
income and retained
earnings

RED COMPANY

Combined Statement of Income and Retained Earnings

For Year Ended December 31,

	Year 2	Year 1
Net sales	$1,295,100	$1,260,300
Less: Costs and expenses	1,014,000	1,021,600
Income before income taxes	$ 281,100	$ 238,700
Income taxes expense	142,100	126,900
Net income.	$ 139,000	$ 111,800
Less: Cash dividends—$1.75 and $1.72 a share, respectively.	87,500	85,800
Addition to retained earnings	$ 51,500	$ 26,000
Retained earnings, Jan. 1	403,800	377,800
Retained earnings, Dec. 31	$ 455,300	$ 403,800
Earnings per share of common stock	$ 2.78	$ 2.24

REVIEW QUESTIONS

1 Ten accountants, if asked to measure the *lifetime net income* of a business enterprise and to assume no change in the purchasing power of the dollar, probably would agree within narrow limits on this long-run income measurement. The same ten accountants might vary over a wide range in their measurement of *periodic net income* for the same enterprise. Why?

2 One of the basic standards recommended as a criterion to be used in evaluating accounting information is *verifiability.* Explain how you would expect this standard to be related to the accountants' search for objective evidence.

3 What is the distinction between *product costs* and *period costs?* Give an example of each type of cost.

4 What is the accounting principle of *revenue realization,* and how does it affect the measurement of periodic income? What are two primary criteria used in the determination of when revenue has been realized?

5 Describe three stages in the earning process, other than the point of sale, at which revenue might be recognized. Give an example of a situation in which use of each of these three stages might be appropriate.

6 The owner of an appliance store has just sold a refrigerator to a customer for $350. An employee recorded cost of goods sold of $240 relating to this sale. What elements probably are included in this cost amount? What elements of cost are probably omitted from the $240?

7 Would you expect a newly organized corporation engaged in the restaurant franchising field, having limited capital and attempting to secure capital from public investors and bankers, to favor accounting policies that would speed up the recognition of revenue or delay it? Explain.

8 Distinguish between a *functional* and a *natural* classification of expenses. What are the advantages of a functional classification for managerial purposes?

9 Distinguish between an *expense* and a *loss,* and between *revenue* and a *cost offset.*

10 Explain the principal differences between the *single-step* and the *multiple-step* forms of income statement. Should earnings per share data be shown with either or both these forms of income statement?

11 What is the usual form of the *interim report of earnings?* Are such reports audited by independent CPAs?

12 What changes would you suggest in the content of income statements so that corporate earnings reports would better meet the objectives of financial statements?

13 In what ways would a *financial forecast* be useful to investors in making investment decisions?

14 Explain the meaning of *intraperiod tax allocation* and *interperiod tax allocation.*

15 Describe the criteria for *extraordinary items* as set forth in *APB Opinion No. 30.*

16 How are the results of a discontinued industry segment reported in the income statement for the accounting period in which the segment is eliminated? Is the loss or gain on the disposal of an industry segment reported as an extraordinary item in the income statement? Explain.

17 Describe two types of *accounting changes* and indicate how each type is reported in the income statement.

18 What is the purpose of reporting *earnings per share* in the income statement? Under what circumstances is a *dual presentation* of earnings per share required in the income statement?

19 Give some examples of supplementary information relating to the income statement that may be disclosed in reports filed with the SEC or in annual reports issued to stockholders.

20 Define *prior period adjustments* and indicate how these are reported in financial statements.

21 What is the major advantage of a combined statement of income and retained earnings? What disadvantage do you see in such a statement?

22 Briefly explain how each of the following material "losses" should be reported in the income statement or in the statement of retained earnings for a corporation:
  a Shutdown expenses incurred during a major strike by employees.
  b A loss incurred upon the abandonment of outmoded equipment.
  c A loss sustained as a result of damage caused by a tornado to the company's main warehouse. Tornadoes are unusual and infrequent in the geographic area in which the company is located.
  d Reduction in the carrying amount of plant assets as a result of a major error in recording the acquisition of these assets two years ago.

EXERCISES

Ex. 3-1 Select the best answer for each of the following multiple-choice questions:

  1 Which of the following is an example of an extraordinary item in the income statement?
    a A loss incurred because of a strike by employees
    b The write-off of equipment believed to have no future benefit
    c A gain resulting from the devaluation of the U.S. dollar
    d A gain resulting from the state exercising its right of eminent domain on a parcel of land used as a parking lot
  2 Which of the following is not a generally accepted method of presenting the income statement?
    a Including prior period adjustments in the determination of net income
    b The single-step income statement
    c The consolidated income statement
    d Including gains and losses from discontinued operations of an industry segment in the determination of net income
  3 The accounting concept of *matching* is best demonstrated by:
    a Not recognizing any expense unless some revenue is realized
    b Associating effort (cost) with accomplishment (revenue)
    c Recognizing rent received in advance as realized revenue
    d Establishing a Reserve for Possible Future Price Decline in Inventories

4 Conventionally accountants measure income:
   a By applying a value-added concept
   b By using a transactions approach
   c As a change in the current fair value of owners' equity
   d As a change in the purchasing power of owners' equity

Ex. 3-2 Given below are selected account balances for Carthage Corporation for the current year:

Beginning inventories	$ 35,600	Selling expenses	$52,800
Ending inventories	27,200	General and administrative	
Sales	374,000	expenses	32,400
Sales returns	6,480	Interest revenue	1,800
Sales discounts	5,360	Dividend revenue	4,000
Purchases	218,200	Interest expense	1,000
Freight-in	25,320	Income taxes expense	22,000
Purchases discounts	4,840	Retained earnings, beginning	80,000
Purchases returns	7,320	Retained earnings, ending	88,000

From the foregoing information, compute the following for the current year:

a Total net revenue
b Total costs and expenses (including cost of goods sold)
c Net income
d Dividends declared

Ex. 3-3 Horizon Corporation had inventories at the beginning and end of its current year as follows:

	Beginning	Ending
Raw material	$22,000	$30,000
Goods in process	40,000	48,000
Finished goods	25,000	18,000
Totals	$87,000	$96,000

During the year the following costs and expenses were incurred:

Raw material purchased	$300,000
Direct labor	120,000
Indirect factory labor	60,000
Property taxes and depreciation of factory building	20,000
Property taxes and depreciation of salesroom and office	15,000
Sales salaries	40,000
Office salaries	24,000
Utilities (60% applicable to factory, 20% to salesroom, and 20% to office)	60,000

Compute the cost of goods sold for the current year.

Ex. 3-4 For each of the following events and transactions, state whether revenue or a gain has been realized. Give reasons in support of your conclusions.

   a Gift certificates, which may be exchanged by the holder for merchandise in a subsequent accounting period, were sold for cash of $200.
   b Land purchased for $45,000 two years ago has a current appraised value of $65,000.

c A new factory building was constructed by a business enterprise's employees at a cost of $190,000. Bids from independent contractors for $205,000 and $210,000 were rejected.

d Short-term investments with a current fair value of $17,650 were received from a customer in settlement of an account receivable for $16,600 which was more than a year past due.

e Merchandise with a cost of $480 was sold under a 24-month installment contract for a 10% down payment of $60. Title to the merchandise remained with the seller until all installment payments have been collected.

f Land held for investment is planted in tomatoes. If the crop is harvested successfully and demand remains strong, cash receipts are expected to exceed expenses by $20,000. The crop growth is halfway to maturity at this time.

g Services are rendered to a customer, and a check drawn on a small out-of-state bank is received from the customer.

Ex. 3-5 Alfredo Company declared and paid cash dividends of $12,500 during Year 5. The company's accounting records show that changes in ledger account balances occurred during Year 5 as follows:

	Increase	*Decrease*
Cash	$40,000	
Accounts receivable (net)		$ 2,000
Inventories	15,000	
Equipment (net)	18,000	
Buildings (net)	30,000	
Notes payable	50,000	
Accounts payable		15,000
Capital stock, $5 par	30,000	
Paid-in capital in excess of par	10,000	
Retained earnings	?	

Assuming that there were no transactions other than the cash dividends affecting retained earnings, compute the net income for Year 5.

Ex. 3-6 For the year ended December 31, Year 2, Canton Noodle Company had general and administrative expenses of 10% of sales (or 20% of cost of goods sold). Selling expenses equaled 20% of sales. Beginning inventories were $100,000, and purchases amounted to 55% of sales. Income before income taxes of 40% was $80,000.

Prepare an income statement for the year ended December 31, Year 2. (Give supporting computations.) **Suggestion:** (1) Compute the cost of goods sold as a percentage of sales by using the information given relating general and administrative expenses to cost of goods sold **and** to sales; (2) prepare an income statement in percentages, including all items from sales to income before income taxes, with sales representing 100%; (3) prepare an income statement in dollars, using the dollar amounts given and deriving the other dollar amounts from the percentage relationships.

Ex. 3-7 Selected information for Dynasty Land Company for the year ended December 31, Year 5, follows:

Total assets	$2,260,000
Total liabilities	600,000
Preferred stock, $10 par	100,000
Common stock, $1 par	300,000
Paid-in capital in excess of par	600,000

> *Prior period adjustment—overstatement of net income in Year 4 as a*
> *result of major accounting error (net of income tax effect)* $100,000
>
> *Net income for Year 5* 175,000
>
> *Dividends on common stock* 60,000
>
> *Dividends on preferred stock* 10,000

Prepare a statement of retained earnings for the year ended December 31, Year 5.

Ex. 3-8 Hansen Company is subject to a 45% tax rate on all sources of income. Information for the current year follows:

> *Income from continuing operations before income taxes* $600,000
>
> *Income taxes payable ($40,000 of current income taxes expense is de-*
> *ferred because depreciation is computed at an accelerated rate for in-*
> *come tax purposes)* 297,500
>
> *Extraordinary gain (before income tax effect)* 100,000
>
> *Prior period adjustment (gain not recognized in prior year as a result of*
> *an accounting error)* 200,000
>
> *Loss from discontinued operations* 150,000
>
> *Dividends declared on capital stock* 165,000

a Prepare a partial income statement for the current year with appropriate allocation of income taxes.

b Reconcile the income taxes included in the income statement and the taxes applicable to the prior period adjustment with the income taxes actually payable for the current year ($297,500).

SHORT CASES FOR ANALYSIS AND DECISION

Case 3-1 Six different enterprises recognized the following items in their accounting records during Year 10:

(1) A gain of $3.9 million was recognized by Soledad Gravel Corporation on early extinguishment of convertible bonds which were selling in the open market at a substantial discount because of the deteriorated financial position of Soledad.

(2) An out-of-court settlement of litigation resulted in a payment by Exeter Corporation of $2 million to plaintiffs. The legal action was initiated two years ago.

(3) A pre-tax loss of $4 million resulted from the disposal of a chemical division operated by a grocery chain. In the year of disposal, the chemical division had sales of $10 million and operating expenses of $12 million. The income tax rate is 45%.

(4) A loss of $6 million was recorded by XY, Inc., from write-offs of receivables and inventories caused by a severe business recession.

(5) A loss of $8 million was recognized from sale of all assets used in the manufacture of sweaters by an apparel manufacturer.

(6) A large diversified company sold a block of common stock from its portfolio of short-term investments. This is the first sale from its portfolio and resulted in a material gain of $4.5 million before applicable income taxes.

Instructions Indicate how each of the items above should be reported in the respective enterprise's financial statements at the end of Year 10. Give a brief explanation for each item.

Case 3-2 The financial statements of Right-on Publishing Company are presented to the board of directors for review upon completion of the annual audit. Karen Young, a director, asks why the income statement is based on the assumption that an equal proportion of the revenue is earned with the publication of every issue of the company's magazine. She feels that the "critical event" in the process of earning revenue in the magazine business is the cash sale of the subscription. She says that she does not understand why—other than for the smoothing of income—most of the revenue cannot be recognized in the period of sale.

Instructions
a List three accepted methods for recognizing revenue and indicate the conditions under which the use of each method would be appropriate. Do not limit your listing to the methods for the recognition of revenue by magazine publishing enterprises.
b Discuss the propriety of timing the recognition of revenue in the Right-on Publishing Company's accounting records with:
(1) The cash sale of the magazine subscription
(2) The publication of the magazine every month
(3) Both events, by recognizing a portion of the revenue with the cash sale of the magazine subscription and a portion of the revenue with the publication of the magazine every month

Case 3-3 Creative Advertising Agency handles advertising for clients under contracts which provide that the agency shall develop advertising copy and layouts and place ads in various media (television, radio, newspapers, etc.), charging clients a commission of 18% of the media cost as its fee. The agency makes advance billings to its clients of estimated media cost plus its 18% commission. Later adjustments of these advance billings usually are minor. Both the billings and receipt of cash from these billings often occur before the period in which the advertising appears in the media.

In devising a system for measuring income, the agency considered the following possible points at which revenue and costs might be recognized and income measured: (1) At the time of the advanced billing; (2) when payment is received from clients; (3) in the month in which the advertising appears in the media; (4) when the bill for advertising is received from the media.

The agency chose (1) above as the point at which it would recognize revenue and income, on the grounds that it has a contract with clients for specified advertising, and thus revenue and income are earned when billed. At the time of billing, the agency establishes accounts receivable with clients and records the estimated liability to the media and its commission earnings. At this time the agency also estimates its expenses and establishes a liability for the estimated expenses related to the client's billing. Adjusting entries are made to establish actual cost and revenue amounts when billings are received from media, when actual expenses are determined, and when final billings invoices are sent to clients.

Instructions Discuss each of the four points at which Creative Advertising Agency might recognize revenue and income, and state your opinion as to the proper basis for accounting for revenue and income in this case. If you disagree with the method followed by the agency, explain the basis for your disagreement and why you support an alternative point for revenue recognition.

Case 3-4 The combined statements of income and retained earnings shown on page 123 was prepared by Modern Fabrics, Inc. The company is in a retail business and makes most of its sales on credit. Accounts receivable are aged at the end of each accounting period, and the allowance for doubtful accounts is adjusted to an amount required to value receivables at estimated net collectible amount (net realizable value).

MODERN FABRICS, INC.
Combined Statements of Income and Retained Earnings
For Years Ended December 31,

	Year 5	Year 4
Revenue:		
Gross sales, including sales taxes collected	$ 876,900	$ 782,500
Less: Returns, allowances, and sales discounts . . .	18,800	16,200
Net sales	$ 858,100	$ 766,300
Dividends, interest, and purchases discounts	30,250	18,300
Recoveries of accounts receivable written off in prior		
years	11,800	3,000
Total revenue	$ 900,150	$ 787,600
Costs and expenses:		
Cost of goods sold, including sales taxes		
collected	$ 415,900	$ 332,200
Salaries and related payroll expenses	60,500	62,100
Rent	19,100	19,100
Freight-in and freight-out	3,400	2,900
Doubtful accounts expense	24,000	26,000
Total costs and expenses	$ 522,900	$ 442,300
Income before extraordinary items	$ 377,250	$ 345,300
Extraordinary items (before income tax effects):		
Loss on discontinued styles (**Note 1**)	$ 124,000	$ 4,800
Loss on sale of short-term investments (**Note 2**) . .	52,050	
Loss on sale of surplus warehouse (**Note 3**)	17,950	
Total extraordinary items	$ 194,000	$ 4,800
Net income	$ 183,250	$ 340,500
Retained earnings, beginning of year	312,700	163,100
Subtotal	$ 495,950	$ 503,600
Less: Income taxes expense	(100,000)	(170,000)
Cash dividends on common stock	(41,900)	(20,900)
Retained earnings, end of year	$ 354,050	$ 312,700
Earnings per share of common stock	$ 1.83	$ 3.41

Note 1: *Rapidly changing customer preferences resulted in a loss on the disposal of discontinued styles and related accessories.*
Note 2: *A short-term investment was sold at a loss, with no income tax effect.*
Note 3: *A surplus warehouse and adjacent land were sold at a loss.*

Instructions Identify and discuss the weaknesses in classification and disclosure in the combined statements of income and retained earnings above. Your discussion should explain why you consider these treatments to be weaknesses and what you consider to be the proper treatment of items. Do not discuss form and terminology, and do not prepare revised statements of income and retained earnings.

Case 3-5 At the beginning of the current year, Robert Hill, owner and operator of a large farm, had no inventories on hand. During the current year, he produced 8,000 bushels of soybeans, 10,000 bushels of barley, and 16,000 bushels of rye. During the year, Hill sold one-half of each of his crops at the following prices: soybeans $6.50 per bushel, barley $3.25 per bushel, rye $2 per bushel. Hill followed the daily price quotations of these commodities very closely, and at the end of the year he noted that the market price for each of these commodities was as follows: soybeans $7 per bushel, barley $3.50 per bushel, and rye $2.20 per bushel.

The expenses incurred in operating the farm during the year totaled $51,550, including depreciation of buildings and equipment. Hill estimates that his cost of selling and delivering these crops is 40 cents per bushel. The selling and delivering expenses applicable to the portion of the crops sold during the year are included in the total operating expenses given above.

Instructions

a Prepare an income statement for Hill for the current year. Explain the concept of revenue realization employed in your measurement of income and, in particular, the basis you used in assigning a valuation to the commodities on hand at the end of the year.

b In measuring income before income taxes for the current year, what consideration did you give to the possibility that the market price of these three commodities might change between the end of the current year and the time Hill finally sells them?

c What is the essential difference between the problem of measuring income for Hill and measuring income for a manufacturer of farm machinery?

PROBLEMS

3-1 Charles Harrison started a single proprietorship early in Year 5 by investing $60,000 cash and plant assets with a current fair value of $100,000. A few days later, Harrison admitted Mike Urban as a partner upon an investment of $120,000 cash. The balance sheet of the partnership at the end of Year 10 follows:

HARRISON & URBAN PARTNERSHIP
Balance Sheet
December 31, Year 10

Assets		*Liabilities & Partners' Capital*	
Cash	$ 16,200	Current liabilities	$ 33,160
Accounts receivable (net). .	57,820	Mortgage note payable . . .	100,000
Inventories	64,200	Harrison, capital	267,060
Plant assets (net)	392,000	Urban, capital	130,000
		Total liabilities &	
Total assets	$530,220	partners' capital	$530,220

On December 31, Year 10, the partners disagreed over business policies and decided to liquidate. Inventories were sold for $50,000 and plant assets for $500,000. Of the accounts receivable, $24,000 were collected, $32,000 were sold (without recourse) for $25,000, and $1,820 were written off as uncollectible. All liabilities were paid, including $400 of interest on the mortgage note payable not accrued at the time of the above balance sheet. During the life of the partnership, Harrison and Urban had withdrawn $360,000 and $85,000, respectively.

Instructions

a Compute the lifetime net income of the Harrison & Urban Partnership on the basis of the above information. Income taxes are to be ignored, because a partnership is not a taxable entity.

b Explain whether there are any areas of uncertainty in your determination of the lifetime net income of the Harrison & Urban Partnership.

3-2 Pushkin Corporation had 100,000 shares of a single class of capital stock outstanding throughout Year 5. During Year 5, the company sold a segment of its business. The results of operations for the year ended December 31, Year 5, are summarized below:

	Continuing operations	Discontinued operations
Sales (net of returns, allowances, and discounts) . .	$8,600,000	$2,800,000
Cost and expenses:		
Cost of goods sold	5,700,000	2,000,000
Operating expenses	1,800,000	500,000
Gain on disposal of discontinued operations (before income tax effect)		200,000
Extraordinary loss from early extinguishment of debt (before income tax effect)	120,000	
Prior period adjustment—correction of material accounting error applicable to Year 3 (debit balance before income tax effect)	777,000	

Income taxes at the rate of 45% apply to all items listed above.

Instructions Prepare an income statement for the year ended December 31, Year 5, including earnings per share data.

3-3 Onegin Company is engaged in the manufacture and sale of ethical drugs. Several years ago it acquired a book publishing business, which has been operated at a loss since it was acquired. In Year 9, the board of directors of Onegin Company sold the book publishing business. The results of operations for the year ended December 31, Year 9, are summarized below:

	Drugs	Books
Net sales	$14,900,000	$3,500,000
Cost of goods sold	9,500,000	2,700,000
Operating expenses	2,900,000	1,200,000
Loss on disposal of book publishing business (before income tax effect)		900,000
Extraordinary loss from earthquake (before income tax effect)	300,000	
Prior period adjustment—correction of material errors (credit balance, net of income tax effect)	1,200,000	

The extraordinary loss is fully deductible for income tax purposes. The income tax rate for the company is 45%. There were 125,000 shares of common stock (the only capital stock issued) outstanding during Year 9.

Instructions Prepare an income statement for the year ended December 31, Year 9, including earnings per share data.

3-4 The information on page 126 was compiled from the accounting records of Tatania Corporation as a basis for preparation of an income statement for the current year.

Beginning inventories	$ 496,300
Ending inventories	542,700
Purchases returns and allowances	65,200
Common stock, $10 par	200,000
Sales	4,231,200
Sales returns and allowances	44,100
Depreciation of plant assets (75% selling; 25% general and administra-	
tive)	220,000
Gain on disposal of equipment	13,500
Rent revenue	18,200
Interest expense	12,840
Purchases	3,100,850
Freight-in	123,400
Selling expenses:	
Salaries and wages	301,010
Purchased services	72,150
Supplies	66,050
General and administrative expenses:	
Salaries and wages	420,200
Purchased services	62,800
Supplies	101,100

Assume that the company's income tax rate is 40% and that any loss can be carried back to obtain a refund of income taxes paid in prior years.

Instructions
a Prepare a multiple-step income statement for the current year. Include earnings or loss per share data in the income statement.
b Prepare a single-step income statement for the current year, using a functional classification of expenses. Include earnings or loss per share data in the income statement.
c Explain which form you prefer, giving reasons for your answer.

3-5   Saleco, Inc., is a merchandising enterprise with $5 par common stock, of which 50,000 shares are outstanding. In addition to its merchandising activities, the company obtains rent revenue of $28,324 a year for a part of its building leased to another business enterprise.

The following information is available concerning the merchandising activities for the current year:

Ending inventories (a decrease of $54,264 during the year)	$ 100,944
Purchases of merchandise (of which $11,224 was returned)	737,696
Freight-in	63,504
Sales (of which $21,696 was returned by customers)	1,584,768
Selling expenses (salaries and wages, $182,340; purchased services,	
$41,248; supplies, $20,224)	243,812
General and administrative expenses (salaries and wages, $120,688;	
purchased services, $38,048; supplies, $14,832)	173,568
Depreciation expense (75% selling; 25% general and administrative) .	67,840

In addition to these operating revenue and expenses, Saleco, Inc., incurred interest expense of $13,568 and declared dividends of $50,000. Income taxes expense was $108,368.

Instructions

a Prepare a multiple-step income statement for the current year. Include earnings per share data in the statement.

b Prepare a single-step income statement for the current year, classifying expenses on a natural basis (for example, merchandise and supplies, salaries and wages, purchased services, depreciation, interest, and income taxes) rather than a functional basis. Include earnings per share data in the statement.

3-6 The following data were taken from the accounting records of Gee Imports Company at the end of Year 5. Income taxes for the current year applicable to ordinary income are $27,600. Income taxes applicable to the extraordinary gain are $10,500. Income tax credit applicable to the extraordinary loss is $28,500. Gee Imports has 10,000 shares of a single class of capital stock outstanding.

Cost of goods sold	$ 820,000
Depreciation expense	30,000
Cash dividends declared	32,000
Extraordinary gain	35,000
Insurance expense	7,000
Sales	1,200,000
Extraordinary loss	60,000
Salaries expense	195,000
Retained earnings, Jan. 1, Year 5	265,500
Other operating expenses	62,400

Instructions

Prepare a combined statement of income and retained earnings for the year ended December 31, Year 5. Use the single-step form for the revenue and expenses part of the statement, and provide earnings per share information in the statement.

3-7 Western Produce Company's capital structure consists solely of common stock, of which 200,000 shares are authorized and 40,000 shares were outstanding throughout Year 2. On December 31, Year 2, an analysis of the accounting records and discussions with management revealed the following information:

Sales	$1,495,200
Sales discounts	22,000
Purchases discounts	21,050
Purchases	901,250
Earthquake loss (before income tax effect)	120,000
Selling expenses	132,400
General and administrative expenses	163,500
Dividend revenue	12,000
Cash dividends declared	60,000
Interest expense	19,000
Inventories, Jan. 1, Year 2	252,500
Inventories Dec. 31, Year 2	225,600
Retained earnings, Jan. 1, Year 2	890,000
Reduction in retained earnings as of Jan. 1, Year 2, resulting from prior period adjustment (no income tax effect)	137,000

The amount of income taxes applicable to ordinary income for Year 2 was $113,200, but the income tax effect of the loss from the earthquake amounted to $50,000, resulting in actual income taxes payable for the year of $63,200.

Instructions Prepare a combined statement of income and retained earnings for the year ended December 31, Year 2. Use the single-step form for the revenue and expense part of the statement, and include earnings per share data.

3-8 The information listed below was available for Rosen Corporation on December 31, Year 8:

Sales	$1,747,500
Extraordinary gain	200,000
Income taxes applicable to extraordinary gain	60,000
Prior period adjustment (debit balance before applicable income tax	
credit of $70,000)	150,000
Dividends declared	200,000
Purchases	1,392,000
Purchases discounts	20,000
Inventories, Jan. 1, Year 8	146,000
Income taxes applicable to ordinary income	65,000
Selling expenses	100,000
General and administrative expenses	96,000
Inventories, Dec. 31, Year 8	152,000
Sales returns and allowances	25,500
Cumulative effect on prior years of change in accounting principle	
(credit balance after income tax effect of $18,000)	30,000

The retained earnings on January 1, Year 8, were originally reported at $932,400. There were 100,000 shares of a single class of capital stock outstanding throughout Year 8.

Instructions
a Prepare a multiple-step income statement, including per-share data, for the year ended December 31, Year 8.
b Prepare a statement of retained earnings for the year ended December 31, Year 8.

3-9 General Carpet Corporation had 50,000 shares of a single class of capital stock outstanding throughout Year 4. Selected information on December 31, Year 4, is presented below and on page 129.

Retained earnings, Jan. 1, Year 4	$1,375,800
Inventories, Jan. 1, Year 4	192,500
Extraordinary gain (before income tax effect of $40,000)	135,000
Purchases (continuing operations)	1,510,000
Sales (continuing operations)	2,195,000
Royalty revenue	24,100
Inventories, Dec. 31, Year 4	208,000
Selling expenses (continuing operations)	120,400
Sales returns, allowances, and discounts	25,100
Purchases returns, allowances, and discounts	23,450
Dividends declared	200,000

Gain on disposal of equipment used in continuing operations	*$ 27,500*
Income taxes applicable to results from continuing operations	*192,500*
General and administrative expenses (continuing operations)	*197,550*
Prior period adjustment: Decrease in retained earnings on Jan. 1, Year 4, as a result of correction of error (net of income tax effect of $85,500)	*110,000*
Loss from disposal of an industry segment. An unprofitable venture in a professional tennis team was sold. The loss is net of income tax credit of $70,000 and includes all revenue and expenses of the tennis team for Year 4.	*80,000*

Instructions

a Prepare an income statement for the year ended December 31, Year 4. The results from continuing operations should be in single-step form. (A number of account balances may be combined to obtain summary amounts to appear in the single-step format for the income statement.) Include earnings per share data in the statement.

b Prepare a statement of retained earnings for the year ended December 31, Year 4.

4 BALANCE SHEET: A STATEMENT OF FINANCIAL POSITION

NATURE OF THE BALANCE SHEET

A *balance sheet* presents the financial position of a business enterprise at a given date. The financial position consists of the assets, liabilities, and owners' equity. An integral part of the balance sheet (or statement of financial position) consists of notes to the financial statements, which disclose contingencies, commitments, and other important matters relevant to the enterprise.

A balance sheet provides a historical summary of the following elements as defined by the Financial Accounting Standards Board:[1]

Assets are probable future economic benefits obtained or controlled by a particular entity as a result of past transactions or events.

Liabilities are probable future sacrifices of economic benefits arising from present obligations of a particular entity to transfer assets or provide services to other entities in the future as a result of past transactions or events.

Equity is the residual interest in the assets of an entity that remains after deducting its liabilities. In a business enterprise, the equity is the ownership interest.

The balance sheet is basically a historical report, because it shows the cumulative effect of past transactions and events. It is often described as a detailed expression of the basic accounting equation:

Assets = Liabilities + Owners' Equity

The theoretical concept of an asset may be related to our discussion of revenue and expenses in Chapter 3. Assets are costs that have not been applied to past revenue; they represent **expected future economic benefits.** However, the rights to assets have been acquired by a business enterprise as a result of past transactions. If no future economic benefit is expected from a cost incurred by the enterprise, it follows that the

---

[1] *Statement of Financial Accounting Concepts No. 3,* "Elements of Financial Statements of Business Enterprises," FASB (Stamford: 1980), p. xi.

cost in question is not an asset and should not be included in the balance sheet.

Liabilities also result from past transactions; they are obligations which require settlement in the future, either by the transfer of assets or by the performance of services.

Implicit in these concepts of the nature of assets and liabilities is the meaning of owners' equity as the **residual interest** in the assets of a business enterprise.

Uses and limitations of the balance sheet

At one time the balance sheet was considered the primary end product of the accounting process. However, experience pounded home the economic lesson that earning power is the prime determinant of the value of a going business concern, and users of financial statements gradually placed more emphasis on the income statement. Today the balance sheet, supported by the statement of changes in financial position, is recapturing much ot the status it once had. Some evidence of this is found in the following excerpt from a leading business publication.[2]

> A quiet, but potentially explosive, revolution is sweeping the U.S. business world as lenders, investors, regulators, accountants, and corporate managers rediscover what should never have been lost: the balance sheet.
>
> Behind the revolution is the inescapable fact that inflation, and all that goes with it, has made a shambles of the traditional income statement that shows only whether a company has made or lost money. Earnings-per-share growth may still captivate naive investors, but more critical observers now realize that it does not tell how much a company owes, or whether it can raise enough money to keep growing, or whether the earnings were real or simply the result of inflation and arcane accounting practices.
>
> Only by studying the balance sheet can a lender or an investor—or a regulator—measure a company's liquidity and its ability to generate profits and pay debts and dividends year after year. . . . It shows whether the company will survive, how profitable it can be, and whether it has a major obstacle to profits, like a pile of debt coming due.
>
> Because the balance sheet tells so much, it is astonishing that it could ever have gotten lost. . . . Then came the go-go years of the late 1960s and early 1970s, when the only thing that seemed to matter was how fast a company could grow, a game that the biggest, most sophisticated institutional investors played as avidly as the rankest amateur in for a fast kill.
>
> But the go-go years ended in the inflation-recession agony of 1974–75, and people are focusing on the balance sheet as they have not in years.

In addition to looking at earnings, investors and creditors are placing more emphasis on a business enterprise's current ratio, debt-to-equity ratio, and rate of return on investment. After recent experiences with the "liquidity crisis" triggered by high levels of interest rates and inflation, enterprises are giving more attention to their balance sheets in order to preserve their ability to borrow or issue shares of capital stock. The accounting profession, cognizant of this growing emphasis on financial position, has taken significant steps to make the balance sheet more rel-

---

[2] *Business Week,* "Focus on Balance Sheet," June 7, 1976, p. 52.

evant and useful for decision makers. These steps have included a movement toward disclosure of the effects of inflation, immediate expensing of most research and development costs, and the mandatory amortization of goodwill.

Balance sheets in **comparative form** provide a great deal of information to creditors, stockholders, management, prospective investors, and the public. Individuals with the ability to interpret comparative balance sheets can learn much as to the short-run solvency of an enterprise, favorable or unfavorable trends in liquidity, commitments that must be met in the future, and the relative positions of creditors and stockholders.

In an ideal balance sheet, the list of assets and liabilities would be all-inclusive, and each would be reported at its current fair value. As a result, the residual equity (assets minus liabilities) would reflect meaningful net worth of the enterprise. The major **limitation** of the traditional balance sheet lies in the inability of accountants to measure the "current fair value" of the entire collection of net resources making up the enterprise.

The inability of accountants (or anyone else) to foresee future economic events forces us to prepare balance sheets on a different basis. It is necessary to use indirect methods of valuation to measure certain assets and liabilities in the balance sheet. Furthermore, we are unable to identify and provide a valuation for many factors that have a material effect on the financial position of a business enterprise. The quality, morale, and character of management and personnel, the market position of the enterprise and the reputation of its products, the growth potential implicit in the nature and diversity of its operations—all these are subjective and intangible factors of great importance in the evaluation of the financial position of the enterprise at any given point in time. None of these factors is reported directly in the dollar and cents framework of the accounting process that leads to a balance sheet.

Some critics, in discussing the merits of various accounting principles and procedures, take the position that because the balance sheet does not reflect "current fair value" it does not matter what amounts appear in it. There is a serious defect in such thinking. To imply that **meaningful** income statements can be prepared as an adjunct to **meaningless** balance sheets shows a failure to understand the relationship between these two financial statements. A consistently applied and meaningful set of assumptions for the measurement of assets and liabilities is a prerequisite to a meaningful measurement of net income.

Accounting principles underlying the balance sheet

A number of important basic principles of accounting impinge on the data appearing in balance sheets. Because all the principles discussed in the preceding chapters are relevant, we shall concentrate here only on their balance sheet implications.

Valuation Principle   Realization, which is a key principle in income measurement, also forms the basis for distinguishing methods of valuation used in the reporting of assets and liabilities in the balance sheet.

A general class of assets called **monetary assets** usually is carried in the balance sheet at amounts closely approximating present value. Examples are cash, certificates of deposit, investments in bonds, and receivables; all these represent current purchasing power. Notes receivable and notes payable which are noninterest-bearing, or which carry an unrealistically low rate of interest, are not to be valued at face amount, but at their present value. **Present value** is determined by discounting all future payments on a note at the current fair rate of interest. This requirement for discounting receivables and payables to their present value applies principally to notes; it is not applicable to receivables and payables arising from transactions with customers or suppliers in the ordinary course of business which are due within one year or less.

Another broad category of assets, termed **productive resources,** is reported in the balance sheet at cost. Inventories and prepayments are examples of short-term productive resources that will be realized (used) at an early date. Buildings, equipment, patents, and investments in affiliated companies are examples of long-term productive resources that will be realized over a number of accounting periods. Until realization occurs, productive resources are measured and reported in the balance sheet at historical costs; after realization, valuations of the monetary assets received in exchange for productive assets generally approximate current fair value. These valuation principles govern the accounting for assets.

Because a liability is an obligation to convey assets or perform services, the appropriate valuation of liabilities in the balance sheet is in terms of the cash (or cash equivalent) necessary to discharge the obligation at the balance sheet date. If payment is to be made later, liabilities should be measured at the present discounted value (determined by use of the current fair rate of interest) of the future payments necessary to discharge the obligation. In the double-entry system of accounting, the present value of a debt at the time it is incurred determines the cash proceeds of the borrowing or the cost of the asset received in exchange. As the maturity of a debt approaches, its present value may increase or decrease, and this change is a part of the computation of the interest expense on the debt. This problem is considered in Chapter 15.

The measurement of assets and liabilities is closely related to the measurement of net income. Revenue arises as the result of increases in assets or decreases in liabilities, and expenses result from increases in liabilities and decreases in assets. Consequently, we can conclude that in the measurement of assets and liabilities we are at the same time engaged in the measurement of net income.

Continuity or Going-Concern Principle   The valuations used in a balance sheet and the classification of items into current and noncurrent groups are based on the continuity or going-concern principle discussed in Chapter 1. This principle, as applied to the balance sheet, requires an assumption that a business enterprise will continue operations long enough for assets to be used or sold according to plan. The going-concern principle is applicable to all cases, except when specific evidence, such as inability to meet the demands of creditors, indicates that the assumption of continued operations is unreasonable.

Monetary Principle   The monetary principle is described in Chapter 1 as an assumption that the dollar is a useful measuring unit, and implications of this principle on income determination are discussed in Chapter 3. The principle is reflected in the balance sheet by valuations expressed in dollars of different time periods, that is, **nominal dollars** having different purchasing power (if there have been changes in the general price level).

If the monetary assumption were changed, and balance sheets were expressed in **constant dollars,** the two categories most affected would be productive assets (plant assets and inventories) and owners' equity. As we have noted, monetary assets and most liabilities are stated at approximately their current fair values, and thus are automatically expressed in constant dollars. However, the accounting valuation of productive assets is a mixture of historical costs. Similarly, paid-in capital and retained earnings in the stockholders' equity section of the balance sheet are expressed in nominal dollars which may have lost much of their significance because of changes in the general price level.

To illustrate this point, consider the case of Inflation Company, which has been in business for 10 years, during which period the general price level has risen steadily. Shown on page 135 is a balance sheet (in highly condensed and somewhat unorthodox form) for this company, expressed in both "nominal dollars" and "constant dollars." Compare the amounts under each approach.

Note the upward revision of productive assets and stockholders' equity when they are expressed in "constant dollars." The decline in retained earnings expressed in constant dollars (from $100,000 to $60,000) occurs because the cost of goods sold, depreciation, and amortization of intangible assets are larger when they are expressed in constant dollars during a period of inflation. The "unrealized purchasing power gain" ($140,000) is more complex. It results from the fact that productive assets were financed in part by debt. Creditors are entitled to a repayment of only a fixed number of dollars. Thus, when productive assets are restated in terms of an increased number of constant dollars, the company gains at the expense of its creditors. Bear in mind that this illustration does not use current fair values for assets, but historical costs adjusted for the change in the general price level.

Financial reporting in terms of constant dollars has been tried in a few countries where price inflation has been extreme. In the United

INFLATION COMPANY
Balance Sheet
At End of Current Year

	Nominal dollars (monetary assumption)	Constant dollars (revised assumption)
Assets		
Monetary assets (cash, investments in debt securities, and receivables)	$200,000	$200,000
Productive resources (inventories, plant assets, and intangible assets)	400,000	700,000
Total assets	$600,000	$900,000
Liabilities & Stockholders' Equity		
Liabilities (stated in fixed number of dollars)	$300,000	$300,000
Stockholders' equity:		
Capital stock $200,000 / $400,000		
Retained earnings 100,000 / 60,000		
Unrealized purchasing power gain –0– / 140,000		
Total stockholders' equity	300,000	600,000
Total liabilities & stockholders' equity	$600,000	$900,000

States, supplementary constant-dollar data in notes to financial statements have attracted considerable attention and now are required by **FASB Statement No. 33** for some of the largest publicly owned corporations. However, it appears unlikely that the monetary principle will be abandoned completely in primary financial statements, barring a greater change in the value of the dollar than we have thus far experienced. The procedures for converting nominal-dollar financial statements to constant dollars are discussed in Chapter 25.

Other Accounting Principles The *disclosure principle* and the closely related concept of *materiality,* which are discussed in Chapter 1, are especially applicable to the balance sheet. The disclosure principle does not require the listing of precise dollar amounts. In the published financial statements of most large companies, all amounts are rounded to the nearest thousand dollars. The largest companies go a step further; they omit digits for units, tens, and hundreds, and place the heading "amounts in thousands" at the top of the balance sheet and other financial statements. For example, if the general ledger has a balance for accounts receivable of $5,278,501.50 and a related allowance for doubtful accounts of $100,000.00, the balance sheet would show among the current assets "Receivables. . . . $5,179." In reading this amount, one must bear in mind that five digits have been omitted. Supplementary information concerning credit operations, including the amount of doubtful accounts expense, might appear in notes to the financial statements.

In order that the balance sheet may provide a fair presentation of the financial position of a business enterprise, it usually is necessary to go considerably further than the listing and classifying of ledger account balances. Additional vital information, such as the existence of loss contingencies and gain contingencies, a summary of accounting policies, changes in accounting principles, and the occurrence of important events subsequent to the balance sheet date are reported in notes to the financial statements.

FORM AND PRESENTATION OF THE BALANCE SHEET

Two objectives are dominant in the presentation of information in a balance sheet. One is clarity and readability; the other is disclosure of significant facts within the framework of the basic assumptions and principles of accounting. Balance sheet classification, terminology, and the general form of presentation should be studied with these objectives in mind.

Balance sheet classification

The classifications, group headings, and number of items on a balance sheet will vary considerably depending on the size of the enterprise, the nature of its operations, and whether the financial statements are intended for wide distribution or for the use of a few owners and creditors. As an example of the diversity encountered in published financial statements, public utility companies usually place plant assets at the top of the balance sheet, followed by current assets. They also may use such fuzzy group headings as "Assets and Other Debits," along with "Liabilities and Other Credits." Financial institutions do not use the current/noncurrent classification for assets and liabilities.

As a generalization subject to many exceptions, the following classification of balance sheet items is suggested as representative. However, other groupings will be used at times in this and following chapters to reflect acceptable alternatives.

Assets:
    Current assets
    Investments (held for control or not readily marketable)
    Plant assets

Intangible assets
Other noncurrent assets (including deferred charges)
Liabilities:
Current liabilities
Long-term debt (including deferred credits)
Stockholders' equity:
Capital stock
Paid-in capital in excess of par or stated value
Retained earnings

This classification reflects the three elements of the basic accounting equation and is theoretically supportable. In practice, it is not unusual to find a fourth category placed between liabilities and stockholders' equity (often with the caption "Reserves" or "Deferred Credits"), to include items such as deferred income taxes, unamortized investment tax credits, reserves for overhaul of leased equipment, and minority interest in subsidiaries. The possibilities for elimination of this separate category are discussed later in this chapter and in Chapter 16.

Working capital

The **working capital** of a business enterprise is defined as the excess of current assets over current liabilities. This amount always has been of considerable interest to credit grantors as an easily interpreted measure of the short-run solvency of the enterprise—the ability to finance current operations and to meet obligations as they fall due. The amounts of current assets and current liabilities, and the relationship between them (the **current ratio**), are widely quoted in financial circles and often are incorporated in contracts between the enterprise and outsiders. A generally accepted and consistent basis is needed for determining which items are included in, and which are excluded from, the current asset and current liability categories.

Current Assets As a practical matter, it is easy to grasp the conceptual difference between a current asset and a noncurrent asset. The boundary between these two categories, however, is hazy, and defining an exact boundary is not an easy task.

Five general types of assets usually are included in the current asset classification:

1 *Cash.* Money in any form—cash and checks awaiting deposit, balances in checking accounts, and expendable cash funds.
2 *Secondary cash resources.* Various short-term investments that are readily marketable. Any such resources whose availability for current use is restricted by contract are excluded.
3 *Short-term receivables.* Accounts receivable and notes receivable with short-term maturities.
4 *Inventories.* Material, supplies, goods in process, finished goods. This category includes items held for sale in the ordinary course of operations, items in process of production, and items that will be consumed in the production

of goods or services. Goods held on consignment from others are not included because title is not held to such goods.

5 *Short-term prepayments.* The cost of various services, such as insurance, taxes, and rent, that have been paid for in advance of use. Short-term prepayments sometimes are referred to as **prepaid expenses.**

There is little question or difficulty about including cash, secondary cash resources, and short-term receivables in the current asset category. As might be expected, the troublesome area is the distinction between short- and long-term investments in productive assets. The test usually applied in distinguishing current from noncurrent productive assets is whether the investment in these assets will be realized within the operating cycle or one year, whichever is the longer period.

The term **operating cycle** refers to the circulation of items within the current asset category. In a typical business enterprise, cash is invested in material, supplies, labor, and overhead costs, and these costs are traced through and assigned to inventories. Inventories eventually are realized by conversion into trade receivables, and trade receivables in turn are collected and become once more available in the form of cash. The average lapse of time between the investment in goods and services and the final conversion back to cash is the length of the operating cycle of an enterprise. In most cases this is a matter of days or months, but in some industries, the operating cycle may extend beyond one year. Thus, the conventional time test for current assets is realization within one year or the operating cycle, whichever is longer.

There are some theoretical flaws in the application of the time test. In a realistic sense, all asset services that will be used to produce revenue during the immediately succeeding operating cycle or accounting period will be realized and converted into liquid assets. Some portion of the investment in plant assets will be realized in the same sense as will be the investment in material. For example, it may be argued that standing timber which will be used to manufacture plywood in the next operating cycle has as good a claim to inclusion among current assets as the inventory of glue that will bind the layers of wood. Thus, the attempt to distinguish between assets that are consumed in definite physical installments and assets that yield services gradually through use has some logical stumbling blocks in its way. These conceptual niceties generally are ignored in the reporting of current assets in the balance sheet.

In any system of classification, there are troublesome items that do not fit neatly into designated niches. For example, if money is borrowed for the express purpose of constructing plant assets, it may be argued that its inclusion in working capital is misleading. If fire insurance is acquired covering a three-year period, a question may be raised about the logical consistency of including the full amount of unexpired insurance as a current asset.

In resolving these difficulties, accountants find themselves at odds with a neat, logical statement of the characteristics that distinguish current assets. They may explain their difficulties as an inevitable conflict between theory and practice, but the result is that the practical distinction between current and noncurrent assets is based more on a rule-of-thumb than on a precise definition.

Current Liabilities The distinction between current and noncurrent is easier to make for liabilities than for assets. Current liabilities may be defined as obligations whose liquidation is expected to require the use of existing current assets or the creation of other current liabilities. Three main classes of current liabilities fall within this definition:

1 Obligations for the acquisition of goods and services which have entered the operating cycle. These include trade payables (including notes and accounts payable to suppliers) and accrued liabilities such as wages, commissions, income taxes, property taxes, etc.
2 Other debts that may be expected to require payment within the operating cycle or one year. This includes short-term notes payable to banks and the currently maturing portions of long-term debt.
3 Collections received in advance of the delivery of goods or the performance of services. These advances often are described as "deferred revenue," but it is the obligation to furnish the goods or services or to refund the payment that puts them in the current liability category.

Some liabilities that will be paid shortly after the balance sheet date are excluded from the current liability category, because of the requirement that a current liability must involve the use of current assets or the issuance of new short-term debt for its extinction. Examples are (1) obligations due at an early date that will be retired by the issuance of new long-term debt, for example, bonds that will be refunded or a loan secured by the cash surrender value of life insurance policies (the amount of cash that would be received if the policies were canceled) that will be renewed, and (2) obligations that will be paid from a fund included among noncurrent assets, for example, a life insurance policy loan that will be liquidated by cancellation against the cash surrender value of the policy, or by deduction from the proceeds of the policy at maturity.

Noncurrent Assets The definition of current assets automatically determines by exclusion the assets that are reported as noncurrent. There are four categories of noncurrent assets:

1 *Long-term or restricted funds, investments, and receivables.* A variety of long-term commitments of funds do not qualify as secondary cash resources. Investments in the capital stock of investees made for the purpose of influence or control are included in this category. Also included are noncurrent receivables (such as long-term advances to affiliated companies), the cash surrender value of life insurance policies, and funds established for such purposes as the payment of pensions, retirement of capital stock, or repayment of long-term debt. Assets such as land held for speculative purposes and future plant sites not presently in use may be included in this category.
2 *Long-term tangible resources used in operations.* The distinguishing characteristics of assets in this category are that they are tangible (have physical substance) and are held for productive use in business operations. Land, natural resources subject to depletion, buildings, equipment, machines, tools, leased

assets under capital leases, leasehold improvements, and plant assets under construction are included. Long-term prepayments for the use of physical assets, such as leaseholds, easements, or rights of way, also may be included in this category, though some accountants group these in the next category.

3 *Long-term intangible resources.* Long-term rights and privileges of an intangible nature may be of greater importance to a business enterprise than its tangible assets. Examples of such assets are patents, goodwill, trademarks, copyrights, organization costs, and franchises. However, under current accounting principles most of these items are recognized as assets only when an expenditure has been made to acquire an intangible right from outsiders. For example, internally developed goodwill is not recognized as an asset; instead, the costs incurred in building such goodwill are recognized currently as expenses. Similarly, all research and development costs, except those which are reimbursable, are recorded as expenses.

4 *Other noncurrent assets.* Most published balance sheets include a category titled "Other Assets," "Other Noncurrent Assets," or "Deferred Charges." Included in this category are items such as plant assets no longer used in operations and held for resale, costs incurred in the issuance of debt, deferred start-up and moving costs, and any other noncurrent asset that cannot be classified readily in one of the first three categories.

Noncurrent Liabilities A noncurrent liability is an obligation that will not require the use of current assets or the issuance of short-term debt within the next year or operating cycle, whichever is longer. There is some question whether there is any useful basis for subclassification within this category. In general practice, a distinction may be drawn between the following two classes:

1 *Long-term debt based on security issues or related contractual arrangements.* Included in this category would be notes and bonds, reported net of any unamortized discount and including any unamortized premium. The distinguishing characteristic is that there is a borrowing transaction supported by a contractual obligation to pay principal and interest.

2 *Other noncurrent liabilities.* As the word "other" implies, this includes all long-term liabilities that do not fit into the first category. An amount received in advance on a long-term commitment to furnish goods or services is an example. Any portion of such advances that will be earned during the current accounting period is reported as a current liability. Other examples are long-term advances from affiliated companies, amounts payable under pension plans, lease obligations under capital leases, deferred revenue, and deferred income taxes.

Contingent Liabilities Liabilities that ***may*** or ***may not*** come into existence as a result of transactions or activities that ***have not yet been finalized*** usually are not reported in dollar amounts in the balance sheet. Not only is the evidence with respect to such liabilities too vague to be called objective, but the events ***(loss contingencies)*** necessary to bring the liabilities into existence have not yet been completed. Such ***contingent liabilities*** should be disclosed. The disclosure usually is made by means of a note to the financial statements. The obligation to reimburse a bank in case of default by the maker of a discounted note receivable, pending lawsuits that may result in an obligation to pay damages, income taxes and other charges that are being contested—all are examples of contingent liabilities.

Management would be imprudent to provide dollar estimates on anticipated unfavorable results from pending lawsuits, because such disclosure might be considered an admission of the merits of the opposing case. If the item is material, disclosure in general terms is essential.

A common error is the failure to distinguish between contingent liabilities and obligations that exist but are not definite either as to amount, due date, or both. These latter are called *estimated liabilities.* There are varying degrees of uncertainty about liabilities; some may be estimated with a high degree of accuracy; others may be subject to no more than an informed guess. The liability for income taxes or the amounts payable to employees under pension plans are examples of estimated liabilities that can be measured with reasonable precision on the basis of tentative tax returns or actuarial data. On the other hand, the cost of making good product guarantees is an existing obligation that can be estimated only within a fairly wide range of probability. When liabilities exist, accountants should estimate them and include them in the balance sheet.

Contingent Assets   Assets, as well as liabilities, may be contingent. A contingent asset is a property right whose existence is conditional on the happening of some future event *(gain contingency).* Generally, it is not appropriate to recognize contingent assets in the accounting records, because to do so would violate the principle of revenue realization. There is a lack of objective evidence that an asset exists or that the earnings process has been completed. However, the disclosure of the existence of contingencies which may result in material gains or assets is useful.[3] An example of such disclosure in a recent annual report follows: ". . . the company has a tax loss carryforward of $15,200,000 which can be deducted from any future taxable income. . . ."

Contra-Asset and -Liability Accounts   Some assets and liabilities are reported in two amounts as a convenient means of disclosing more information about these items than would be afforded by a net valuation. For example, accounts receivable are reported as the difference between the gross amount due from customers and an allowance for accounts estimated to be uncollectible. Similarly, bond discount is shown as a deduction from the face amount of bonds payable. The general criterion for determining whether to display a balance sheet item in one amount or two is the degree of usefulness of the added information. The amount of estimated uncollectibles may provide users of financial statements with information about the expected collection experience on current accounts receivable. Reporting the amount of accumu-

---

[3] *FASB Statement No. 5,* "Accounting for Contingencies," FASB (Stamford: 1975), p. 8.

lated depreciation of plant assets separately from original cost provides information about depreciation policy and the age of plant assets. The disclosure may be made as a separate valuation account in the balance sheet, or by a parenthetical notation of the amount that has been deducted to arrive at a net valuation.

Offsetting Assets and Liabilities The use of contra or valuation accounts should be distinguished from an actual *offsetting* of asset and liability accounts. When valuation accounts are used, the amount deducted from an asset is not a liability, and the amount deducted from a liability is not an asset. Offsetting assets and liabilities is improper, because it implies an association between the two that seldom exists. For example, if a business enterprise accumulates a special fund to pay a debt when it matures, the intention may be revoked before the fund actually is devoted to that purpose. The fund should be reported as an asset and the debt as a liability until payment is made.

There is a sound basis for the rule against offsetting assets and liabilities. A limited amount of offsetting probably would not cause a material distortion in financial statements, but there is no obvious place to draw the line. The issue is *disclosure in a manner that is not misleading,* and there is little doubt that offsetting assets and liabilities is likely to result in misleading information.

One recognized exception to the rule against offsetting occurs when an enterprise acquires securities acceptable for the payment of income taxes in circumstances such that the acquisition is an advance payment of taxes. This may occur as an accommodation to a governmental unit which issues securities specifically designated as acceptable for the payment of taxes.[4]

Owners' equity

The owners' equity in a business enterprise is the residual interest in assets, after liabilities have been deducted. The amount appearing in the owners' equity section of a balance sheet thus is directly dependent on the values assigned to assets and liabilities. When owners invest assets in an enterprise, the valuation placed on assets determines the amount added to owners' equity. When operating results are summarized, the increase in net assets determines the amount of net income added to the owners' equity. This point is worth noting, because accountants sometimes are tempted to reverse this process and assume that if an amount (for example, the par or stated value of capital stock) is associated with an element of ownership, there must be an asset to match.

Because of the legal differences between incorporated and nonincorporated business enterprises, there are variations in the balance sheet presentation of owners' equity for such organizations.

[4] *APB Opinion No. 10,* "Omnibus Opinion—1966" AICPA (New York: 1966), p. 147.

Single Proprietorships and Partnerships   The owners' equity in single proprietorships and partnerships usually is reported in the balance sheet as a single amount for each owner. There is no reason why the amount of capital invested by each owner should not be shown separately from the reinvested earnings, but because there is no legal restriction on the amounts proprietors or partners may withdraw from the enterprise, such information is less significant than in the case of corporations.

The ownership rights of a partner typically are more complex than those of a corporate stockholder. Contractual arrangements among partners governing salaries and interest on capital as a share of net income or net loss, and investments and drawings make it important that the relative rights of each partner are determined accurately and reported in the balance sheet. A statement showing the changes in partners' capital for Year 5 is illustrated below for the Allen & Bates Partnership:

ALLEN & BATES PARTNERSHIP
Statement of Partners' Capital
For Year 5

	Allen	Bates	Combined
Partners' capital, beginning of year.	$25,000	$34,000	$59,000
Add: Net income	12,600	18,200	30,800
Subtotals	$37,600	$52,200	$89,800
Less: Drawings.	15,000	10,000	25,000
Partners' capital, end of year	$22,600	$42,200	$64,800

The combined capital of $64,800 is reported as owners' equity in the balance sheet for the Allen & Bates Partnership.

Corporations   The presentation of stockholders' equity in the balance sheet of a corporation is influenced strongly by legal considerations. As a result there are a number of classifications (particularly within the "invested capital" section) that have no particular accounting significance. Below is an outline of the main sections of corporate owners' equity:

1 Invested capital
a Stated capital. The amount assigned to shares of capital stock outstanding as par or stated value is known as **legal capital** or **stated capital** of a corporation. This amount usually appears under the heading **capital stock.** For each class of stock, the amount of par or stated value per share, the number of shares issued, outstanding, and held in the treasury, and any dividend or liquidating preference should be disclosed.
b Additional paid-in capital. This category includes all amounts assigned to shares of capital stock in excess of par or stated value. The terms **paid-in capital in excess of par** and **paid-in capital in excess of stated value** are used throughout this book. Financial statements of publicly owned corporations show a continuing trend away from the term **surplus,** either

standing alone or in such combinations as *capital surplus* or *paid-in surplus.* Use of the term *surplus* long has been discouraged by the AICPA. This term generally is unsuitable in a stockholders' equity section of the balance sheet, because its popular meaning—something over and above what is necessary—gives a misleading impression to users of financial statements.

Paid-in capital in excess of par or stated value may include both positive and negative amounts. If a corporation receives less than par or stated value for its capital stock, the contra-capital account Discount on Capital Stock belongs in this section of the balance sheet. Positive items include any amount in excess of par or stated value arising from the issuance of capital stock, the reissuance of treasury stock at more than cost, donations of assets to the corporation (donated capital), or transfers from retained earnings through stock dividends. Similarly, the cost of *treasury stock* (a debit balance) is a contra–stockholders' equity item.

2 Increase in stockholders' equity through the retention of earnings
   a Retained earnings. Net income of past accounting periods that has not been distributed to stockholders as dividends falls in this category. The term *retained earnings* is used far more widely than any other to describe this part of stockholders' equity. Alternative terms are *income retained for use in business* and *earnings reinvested in the business.* The term *earned surplus,* although still used by a few companies, is obsolete.
   b Appropriated retained earnings. A corporate board of directors sometimes may wish to indicate that a portion of retained earnings has been appropriated. A formal segregation of retained earnings is a means of disclosing that future dividend payments are restricted to some degree, either because of legal or contractual agreements or by management intent. The use of appropriations of retained earnings as a means of disclosure has almost disappeared; other more effective means of indicating the restriction of retained earnings are available, principally the use of notes to financial statements.

3 Unrealized appreciation in value of productive assets; and unrealized loss in value of long-term investments. In unusual cases a business enterprise may report unrealized appreciation or decline in the value of its assets in the balance sheet to disclose a material discrepancy between carrying amount and current fair value. This procedure is an *exception* to the basic accounting assumption that only realized increases in asset values are recognized in the accounting records. The offsetting increase or decrease in owners' equity is shown separately and designated as "unrealized appraisal capital" or as "unrealized loss in value of long-term investments."

Use of term "reserve"

In the past the term *reserve* has been used by accountants in a number of different and somewhat misleading ways. A reserve, in nonaccounting usage, usually is thought of as something held for a specific purpose, often for emergencies. This connotation leads to misinterpretation when the word "reserve" is included in the title of an asset valuation or estimated liability account. The trend in accounting terminology is to avoid the use of the word "reserve," although some companies continue to use it in the asset or liability sections of the balance sheet.

The term "reserve," when used to describe an appropriation of retained earnings, is considered acceptable, although its use continues to decline. A Reserve for Contingencies is more likely to be misunderstood than Retained Earnings Appropriated for Contingencies. If used at all, the term "reserve" should appear only in the stockholders' equity section of the balance sheet. Because its principal purpose is to indicate a restriction of retained earnings, the nature of the restriction can be set forth more clearly in a note to the financial statements than by an appropriation of retained earnings.

Standards of disclosure

Accountants apply the "adequate disclosure" test as a basis for resolving a number of questions that arise in the preparation of balance sheets.

Account Titles In providing titles for general ledger accounts, considerable leeway is permissible, in deference to convenience and economy of space. The persons involved in the accounting function understand the nature of the item; thus, short account titles are a matter of convenience. However, in the preparation of financial statements, users of the information must be kept in mind, and a clearly worded description of each item is desirable. For example, the title "Accounts Receivable" may be stated in the balance sheet as "Amounts Due from Customers." In the choice between brevity and clarity, the latter should prevail in the preparation of financial statements. Of course, several ledger accounts may be combined into a single financial statement item, such as "inventories."

Basis of Valuation Informed readers of balance sheets are presumed to be familiar with the general assumption governing the accounting valuation of assets and liabilities. However, variations in accounting procedures often produce balance sheet amounts whose significance is difficult to interpret unless the procedure used is disclosed. For example, the choice of "fifo" or "lifo" cost in inventory valuation results in materially different asset amounts during periods of inflation. An acceptable standard of disclosure requires that the basis of valuation be indicated in the caption of all balance sheet items or in a note titled "Summary of Significant Accounting Policies," unless it is obvious (as in the case of cash, for example).

Notes to Financial Statements Explanatory comments and supplementary disclosure are made in "Notes to financial statements." Often a note may be applicable to both the balance sheet and the income statement, and the notes in their entirety may occupy several pages. As explained in Chapter 1 (page 24), a note summarizing significant accounting policies is prescribed as essential by **APB Opinion No. 22,** "Disclosure of Accounting Policies." For such matters as stock option plans, pension plans, leases, and business combinations, the only reasonable way to provide an adequate explanation is by use of notes. A complete set of notes to the financial statements of International Harvester Company appears in the Appendix on pages 157–172.

Supporting Exhibits   If the detail involved in a full picture of a section of the balance sheet interferes with a concise presentation, it may be desirable to summarize the item in the balance sheet and show the detail in a supporting exhibit. For example, inventories may be reported in a single amount, and the detailed amounts of material, goods in process, goods on consignment, and finished goods presented in a separate exhibit. Business enterprises having a large number of bond issues outstanding frequently show long-term debt as a single amount and include a supporting exhibit in which the details are furnished (see **Note 14** on page 162, for example). For users of financial statements who want only "highlight" information, the balance sheet thus gives this in a concise and easily digestible manner; users who want more detailed information will find it in the supporting notes and exhibits.

SAMPLE CORPORATION
Balance Sheet
December 31, Year 5
(In thousands of dollars)

Assets

Current assets:

Cash			$ 485
Short-term investments (at cost, market value $220,000)			210
Notes receivable and accrued interest			125
Accounts receivable		$1,162	
Less: Allowance for doubtful accounts		50	1,112
Inventories (at lower of average cost or market)			580
Short-term prepayments			60
Total current assets			$ 2,572

Investments:

Common stock of affiliated companies (at equity)		$1,250	
Fund for retirement of preferred stock		60	
Land held for future expansion		100	
Cash surrender value of life insurance policies.		50	1,460

Plant assets:

	Cost	Accumulated depreciation	Carrying amount	
Land	$ 3,015	$ –0–	$3,015	
Buildings	10,950	5,992	4,958	
Equipment.	8,430	2,720	5,710	
Totals	$22,395	$8,712		13,683

Intangible assets:

Goodwill (net of amortization)		$1,105	
Patents (net of amortization)		105	1,210
Other noncurrent assets—plant assets held for resale.			45
Total assets.			$18,970

Form of the balance sheet

Fairly standard ways of presenting balance sheet information have been developed, but there is no universal form. The objectives are *clarity* and *adequate disclosure of all pertinent and material facts;* there are various ways of meeting these objectives, and experimentation should be encouraged. The arrangement of the major sections of the balance sheet also may vary. We shall describe the basic features of three forms of the balance sheet: *account form, report form,* and *financial position form.* Within the framework of these three forms a number of variations are possible. In a recent survey of 600 large companies, 363 used the account form, 228 used the report form, and only 9 used the financial position form.[5]

[5] *Accounting Trends & Techniques,* 34th ed., AICPA (New York: 1980), p. 127.

Liabilities & Stockholders' Equity			
Current liabilities:			
Accounts payable —trade			$ 390
Accrued liabilities			130
Income taxes payable			200
Dividends payable			125
Advances from customers			20
Exployees' retirement benefits payable currently			40
Total current liabilities			$ 905
Long-term debt:			
10% bonds payable, due Dec. 31, Year 15		$ 4,000	
Less: Discount on bonds payable		20	
Net bonds payable		$ 3,980	
Employees' retirement benefits payable in future years		250	
Deferred income taxes		300	
Total long-term debt			4,530
Total liabilities			$ 5,435
Stockholders' equity:			
6% cumulative, convertible preferred stock, $100 par (callable at $105 a share, authorized 10,000 shares, issued and outstanding 9,500 shares)			$ 950
Common stock, no par, stated value $5, authorized 1,000,000 shares, issued and outstanding 800,000 shares			4,000
Paid-in capital in excess of par or stated value:			
On preferred stock	$ 95		
On common stock	5,450	5,545	
Total paid-in capital		$10,495	
Retained earnings		3,040	
Total stockholders' equity			13,535
Total liabilities & stockholders' equity			$18,970

Account Form A balance sheet for Sample Corporation in the traditional account form appears on pages 146 and 147. The distinguishing characteristic of this form is that all assets are listed on the left-hand side and liabilities and stockholders' equity are "balanced" against them on the right-hand side. This balance sheet includes typical accounts in each classification and follows current standards of disclosure and terminology. The appropriate degree of condensation within the balance sheet depends on the needs of users. A balance sheet prepared for stockholders is more condensed than one prepared for management. Notes relating to the balance sheet are purposely omitted from this illustration. An example of notes to financial statements is included in the Appendix at the end of this chapter.

Report Form The report form of balance sheet differs from the account form only in that the liabilities and stockholders' equity sections are listed below, rather than to the right of, the asset section.

Financial Position Form Both the account form and the report form of the balance sheet express the basic accounting equation **Assets = Liabilities + Owners' Equity.** However, a few enterprises prefer to use a format which emphasizes working capital; this usually carries the title Statement of Financial Position rather than Balance Sheet. This is a **vertical** format in which current assets are listed and totaled; then current liabilities are listed and deducted from current assets to derive working capital. Other assets then are added and other liabilities are deducted, leaving a residual amount as stockholders' equity.

Comparative balance sheet

The illustrated balance sheet for Sample Corporation on pages 146–147 is for only one point in time, December 31, Year 5. However, comparative amounts for the previous year are presented in almost every published balance sheet. Such a **comparative balance sheet** for International Harvester Company is illustrated on pages 154–155 of the Appendix. Many companies also publish 5- or 10-year summaries which bring out important trends in financial statements.

Statement of stockholders' equity

As stated in Chapter 3, a statement of retained earnings explains the changes which have occurred in retained earnings during an accounting period. However, changes requiring explanation also may occur in the other stockholders' equity accounts. The explanation may take various forms, as suggested at the top of page 150.[6]

---

[6] *APB Opinion No. 12,* "Omnibus Opinion—1967," AICPA (New York: 1967), p. 190.

PUBLIC CORPORATION
Statement of Stockholders' Equity
For Years Ended June 30, Year 2 and Year 3
(In thousands of dollars)

	Preferred stock, $100 par	Common stock, $10 par	Paid-in capital in excess of par	Retained earnings	Stock in treasury (at cost)	Total
Balances, June 30, Year 1	$36,485	$12,177	$137,858	$306,535	$ (208)	$492,847
Net income				68,066		68,066
Cash dividends paid:						
Preferred stock				(1,733)		(1,733)
Common stock				(11,883)		(11,883)
Acquisition of treasury stock					(10,427)	(10,427)
Balances, June 30, Year 2	$36,485	$12,177	$137,858	$360,985	$(10,635)	$536,870
Net income				79,685		79,685
Cash dividends paid:						
Preferred stock				(1,310)		(1,310)
Common stock				(19,227)		(19,227)
Issuance of common stock in acquisition of X Company		936	24,335			25,271
Conversion of preferred stock to common stock	(36,485)	1,173	35,312			
25% stock dividend		3,563		(3,563)		
Balances, June 30, Year 3	$ –0–	$17,849	$197,505	$416,570	$(10,635)	$621,289

When both financial position and results of operations are presented, disclosure of changes in the separate accounts comprising stockholders' equity (in addition to retained earnings) and of the changes in the number of shares of equity securities during at least the most recent annual fiscal period and any subsequent interim period presented is required to make the financial statements sufficiently informative. Disclosure of such changes may take the form of separate statements or may be made in the basic financial statements or notes thereto.

To achieve such disclosure, a number of companies prepare a **statement of stockholders' equity,** such as the one illustrated for Public Corporation on page 149 and for International Harvester Company on page 156.

STATEMENT OF CHANGES IN FINANCIAL POSITION

Along with the income statement and the balance sheet, the **statement of changes in financial position** is included in the annual reports of publicly owned corporations and is covered by the auditors' report. The objectives of the statement of changes in financial position are (1) to summarize the financing and investing activities of a business enterprise during an accounting period, including the extent to which the enterprise obtained funds from operations, and (2) to complete the disclosure of changes in financial position during the accounting period. In this context, the term **funds** may be interpreted to mean **cash and its equivalent,** or it may mean **working capital.**

Most enterprises prepare the statement of changes in financial position on a working capital concept. Under either the cash concept or the working capital concept, the statement includes the impact of financing and investing activities which do not directly affect funds (cash or working capital). For example, the issuance of long-term bonds in exchange for land valued at $1 million should be reported as a $1 million source of funds from issuance of bonds and a $1 million use of funds to acquire land.

A complete discussion of the statement of changes in financial position is found in Chapter 23. At this point we shall illustrate the statement without further explanation. The statement of changes in financial position on a working capital concept for Sample Corporation appears on page 151. The related income statement and statement of retained earnings for Sample Corporation appear on pages 99 and 115 in Chapter 3, and the related balance sheet is presented earlier in this chapter (pages 146–147). Note that the statement of changes in financial position is prepared in two sections—the first section shows the **financial resources** (working capital) **provided and applied,** and the second section shows the **composition of working capital** at the beginning and end of Year 5. A more comprehensive statement of changes in financial position in comparative form for International Harvester Company appears in the Appendix at the end of this chapter (page 153).

SAMPLE CORPORATION
Statement of Changes in Financial Position (Working Capital Concept)
For Year Ended December 31, Year 5
(In thousands of dollars)

Financial resources provided

Operations —net income.		$1,057
Add: Charges not requiring use of working capital:		
Depreciation expense	$186	
Amortization of goodwill, patents, and bond discount	64	
Employee retirement benefits payable in future years	40	
Deferred income taxes.	20	
Less: Investment income from affiliated companies in excess of		
dividends received	(110)	200
Working capital provided from operations		$1,257
Issuance of preferred stock		250
Disposal of investments in exchange for land.		323
Disposal of equipment		100
Total financial resources provided		$1,930

Financial resources applied

Dividends on preferred and common stock	$457	
Increase in fund for retirement of preferred stock.	30	
Acquisition of land in exchange of investments	323	
Increase in cash surrender value of life insurance policies . .	10	
Acquisition of patents.	120	
Total financial resources applied.		940
Increase in financial resources (working capital).		$ 990

	End of Year 5	End of Year 4	Increase or (decrease) in working capital
Composition of working capital			
Current assets:			
Cash.	$ 485	$ 200	$285
Short-term investments	210	150	60
Notes receivable and accrued interest . . .	125	–0–	125
Accounts receivable (net)	1,112	800	312
Inventories	580	1,000	(420)
Short-term prepayments	60	20	40
Total current assets	$2,572	$2,170	
Current liabilities:			
Accounts payable —trade	$ 390	$ 790	400
Accrued liabilities.	130	80	(50)
Income taxes payable	200	350	150
Dividends payable	125	100	(25)
Advances from customers.	20	138	118
Employee ret. benefits pay. currently.	40	35	(5)
Total current liabilities.	$ 905	$1,493	
Working capital	$1,667	$ 677	
Increase in working capital			$990

APPENDIX: FINANCIAL STATEMENTS FOR INTERNATIONAL HARVESTER COMPANY

Statements of Income (Loss)

International Harvester Company and Subsidiaries

(Thousands of dollars, except per-share data) For the Years Ended October 31

	1980	1979
Sales and Other Revenues		
Sales	$6,311,804	$8,392,042
Interest income (Note 7)	28,517	26,666
Other income, less sundry deductions	1,777	7,683
Total sales and other revenues	6,342,098	8,426,391
Costs and Expenses		
Cost of sales (Notes 3 and 9)	5,700,126	6,904,442
Marketing and administrative expenses	811,949	769,260
Provision for losses on receivables	17,622	5,430
Financing charges on receivables sold		
to sales finance subsidiaries	254,282	240,510
Interest expense (Note 2):		
Long-term debt	114,274	77,405
Other	169,664	71,003
Exchange (gain) loss (Note 3)	30,008	(20,878)
Major modernization and expansion program (Note 4) . . .	135,800	—
Total costs and expenses	7,233,725	8,047,172
Income (Loss) of Consolidated Group		
Income (loss) before taxes on income	(891,627)	379,219
Taxes on income (benefit) (Note 6)	(387,311)	116,130
Income (loss) of consolidated group	(504,316)	263,089
Income of Nonconsolidated Companies		
Income before taxes on income	217,600	190,866
Taxes on income (Note 6)	82,912	84,393
Income of nonconsolidated companies	134,688	106,473
Income (Loss) from Continuing Operations	(369,628)	369,562
Wisconsin Steel, net of income		
tax benefit (Notes 5 and 6)	(27,700)	—
Net Income (Loss)	$ (397,328)	$ 369,562
Per Common Share:		
Income (loss):		
Continuing operations	$(12.02)	$12.01
Wisconsin Steel	(.89)	—
Net income (loss)	$(12.91)	$12.01
Dividends paid	$ 2.50	$ 2.35
Average number of common shares outstanding (thousands)	31,224	30,347

See Notes to Financial Statements

Statements of Changes in Financial Position

(Thousands of dollars)
For the Years Ended October 31

International Harvester Company and Subsidiaries

	1980	1979
Working Capital (Used) Provided by Operations		
Income (loss) from continuing operations	$ (369,628)	$ 369,562
Items not affecting working capital:		
Depreciation and amortization	129,646	126,798
Undistributed earnings of nonconsolidated companies	(119,849)	(102,728)
Deferred income taxes	(59,956)	159,021
Other	961	2,033
Working capital (used) provided by continuing operations	(418,826)	554,686
Wisconsin Steel, net (loss)	(27,700)	—
Item not affecting working capital—deferred income taxes	(27,200)	—
Working capital (used) by Wisconsin Steel	(54,900)	—
Total working capital (used) provided by operations	(473,726)	554,686
Other Sources of Working Capital		
Additions to long-term debt	442,858	117,690
Issuance of preferred stock—Series C	150,000	—
Issuance of common stock	32,914	30,726
Property disposals	16,025	8,685
Total other sources of working capital	641,797	157,101
Other Uses of Working Capital		
Capital expenditures	383,763	284,907
Cash dividends	83,141	76,389
Reduction of long-term debt	63,960	102,061
Increase in investments and long-term receivables	67,136	52,060
Other	15,280	13,792
Total other uses of working capital	613,280	529,209
Increase (Decrease) in Working Capital	(445,209)	182,578
Working Capital		
At beginning of the year	1,392,398	1,209,820
At end of the year	$ 947,189	$1,392,398
Changes in Working Capital		
Current assets—increase (decrease):		
Cash	$ 111,901	$ (2,051)
Receivables	(169,548)	113,974
Refundable income taxes	132,762	8,927
Inventories	(11,265)	450,011
Other current assets	97,800	46,197
Current liabilities—decrease (increase):		
Notes payable	(397,550)	(105,932)
Accounts payable	(41,150)	(333,657)
Accrued liabilities	(147,229)	(38,517)
Current maturities of long-term debt	(20,930)	43,626
Increase (Decrease) in Working Capital	$ (445,209)	$ 182,578

See Notes to Financial Statements

Statements of Financial Condition

(Thousands of dollars) October 31

Assets	1980	1979
Current Assets		
Cash and cash equivalents	$ 137,106	$ 25,205
Receivables, net (Note 8)	627,067	796,615
Refundable income taxes	141,689	8,927
Inventories (Note 9)	2,331,676	2,342,941
Other current assets	189,881	92,081
Total current assets	3,427,419	3,265,769
Investments and Long-Term Receivables (Note 10)		
Equity in and advances to nonconsolidated companies	1,014,349	827,096
Long-term receivables and other investments, at cost	82,846	83,114
Total investments and long-term receivables	1,097,195	910,210
Property		
Net of accumulated depreciation and amortization of		
$1,045,033 in 1980 and $1,005,125 in 1979 (Note 11)	1,277,239	1,039,147
Other Assets	41,605	32,349
Total Assets	$5,843,458	$5,247,475

Statements of Financial Condition (cont.)

(Thousands of dollars) October 31

International Harvester Company and Subsidiaries

Liabilities and Stockholders' Equity	1980	1979
Current Liabilities (Note 13)		
Notes payable	$ 808,938	$ 411,388
Accounts payable	984,719	943,569
Accrued liabilities	635,044	487,815
Current maturities of long-term debt	51,529	30,599
Total current liabilities	2,480,230	1,873,371
Long-Term Debt (Note 14)	1,327,068	948,170
Deferred Income Taxes	139,705	226,861
Preferred Stock (Note 16)		
Authorized 5,000,000 shares without par value:		
Redeemable:		
Series A—Issued 500,000 shares, $10 cumulative	50,000	50,000
Convertible:		
Series C—Issued 3,000,000 shares, $5.76 cumulative	150,000	—
Common Stockholders' Equity		
Common stock—authorized 45,000,000 shares of $20 par value:		
issued 32,210,276 shares in 1980 and 31,146,238 shares in 1979	644,206	622,925
Capital in excess of par value	42,405	36,195
Retained earnings (Note 17)	1,024,311	1,504,780
	1,710,922	2,163,900
Less:		
Common stock held in treasury, at cost - 380,016 shares	12,057	12,057
Receivables from sale of common stock (Note 20)	2,410	2,770
Total common stockholders' equity	1,696,455	2,149,073
Total Liabilities and Stockholders' Equity	$5,843,458	$5,247,475

See Notes to Financial Statements

Statements of Common Stockholders' Equity

(Thousands of dollars)
For the Years Ended October 31, 1980 and 1979

International Harvester Company and Subsidiaries

	Common Shares Outstanding	Common Stock	Capital in Excess of Par Value	Retained Earnings	Common Stock Held in Treasury	Receivables from Sale of Common Stock	Total Common Stockholders' Equity
Balance at October 31, 1978	29,953,844	$607,177	$22,010	$1,211,607	$(12,850)	$(1,796)	$1,826,148
Issuance of stock:							
Stock options (Note 19)	69,050	1,381	728	—	—	—	2,109
Sales to:							
Savings and investment program	602,066	12,042	11,151	—	—	—	23,193
Employee stock ownership plan	30,801	616	589	—	—	—	1,205
Automatic dividend and interest							
investment plan	85,461	1,709	1,536	—	—	—	3,245
Officer (Note 20)	25,000	—	181	—	793	(974)	—
Net income		—	—	369,562	—	—	369,562
Dividends:							
Preferred, Series A: $10 per share .		—	—	(5,000)	—	—	(5,000)
Common, $2.35 per share		—	—	(71,389)	—	—	(71,389)
Balance at October 31, 1979	30,766,222	622,925	36,195	1,504,780	(12,057)	(2,770)	2,149,073
Issuance of stock:							
Stock options (Note 19)	20,340	407	165	—	—	—	572
Sales to:							
Savings and investment program	861,235	17,225	9,628	—	—	—	26,853
Employee stock ownership plan	54,136	1,083	487	—	—	—	1,570
Automatic dividend and interest							
investment plan	128,327	2,566	1,353	—	—	—	3,919
Reduction of officer receivable							
(Note 20)	—	—	—	—	360	360
Net income (loss)		—	—	(397,328)	—	—	(397,328)
Issuance cost of preferred stock . . .		—	(5,423)	—	—	—	(5,423)
Dividends:							
Preferred, Series A: $10 per share .		—	—	(5,000)	—	—	(5,000)
Common, $2.50 per share		—	—	(78,141)	—	—	(78,141)
Balance at October 31, 1980	31,830,260	$644,206	$42,405	$1,024,311	$(12,057)	$(2,410)	$1,696,455

See Notes to Financial Statements

Notes to Financial Statements

1. Summary of Accounting Policies
Basis of Consolidation

The consolidated financial statements include the accounts of International Harvester Company and its significant subsidiary companies except for wholly-owned sales finance subsidiaries.

Sales finance subsidiaries (Note 22), other nonconsolidated subsidiaries and corporate joint ventures are included in the consolidated financial statements at the Company's equity in their net assets. Investments in dealerships are carried at cost.

Taxes on Income

The tax effect of each item in the Statements of Income (Loss) is recognized in the current period regardless of when the tax is paid. Taxes on amounts which affect financial and taxable income in different periods are reported as deferred income taxes.

The investment tax credit is taken into income in the year it reduces the Company's tax liability.

Inventory Valuation

Inventory values are stated at lower of cost or market. The cost of substantially all domestic inventories is determined using the last-in, first-out (LIFO) method. Foreign subsidiaries account for cost using either the first-in, first-out (FIFO) or the average cost method. Market is defined as replacement value, which with respect to labor and overhead, is the cost considered attainable under normal operating conditions.

The Company's method of pooling by natural business units makes it impracticable to classify LIFO inventories into finished goods, work in process, and raw material components.

Property

The replacement of significant items of equipment and the expenditures for tooling and pattern equipment required because of increased capacity, new products and changes in existing products or equipment are capitalized. Expenditures for major rebuilding of machine tools are also capitalized. Expenditures for maintenance and repairs and for renewals of relatively minor items are charged to costs and expenses as incurred.

Depreciation and amortization are generally computed on the straight-line basis. The useful lives of the various classes of properties are as follows:

  Building and building equipment - 3 to 50 years
  Land improvements - 3 to 50 years
  Automotive equipment - 3 to 7 years
  Machinery - 4 to 20 years
  Auxiliary equipment - 1 to 13 years
  Furniture and fixtures, etc. - 1 to 20 years
  Tooling and pattern equipment - 1 to 8 years
  Leasehold improvements - lease term or life of asset, whichever is shorter.

Gains and losses on property disposals are included in income.

In fiscal 1980, the Company elected to adopt the provisions of Statement of Financial Accounting Standards (SFAS) No. 34, requiring the capitalization of interest expense related to property constructed for use in the business. Previously all interest cost was charged to expense when incurred.

Retirement Plans

Income is charged with pension costs applicable to current service and the amortization of prior service cost. Prior service costs attributable to benefit levels in effect prior to October 1, 1979 were amortized generally over the period ending in the year 2006 except for selected parent company plans which were amortized over the period ending in the year 1995. Prior service costs attributable to increases in benefit levels becoming effective on or after October 1, 1979 were amortized over a period ending 30 years after the year in which such increases became effective. The costs of supplemental allowance benefits resulting from retirements before age 65 are charged to income as incurred.

Net Income Per Common Share

Net income (loss) per common share is computed by dividing net income (loss), reduced by preferred dividend requirements, by the average of the number of common shares outstanding at the end of each month during the year.

Net income (loss) per common share assuming full dilution is not presented because the convertible preferred stock outstanding at October 31, 1980 did not have a dilutive effect in fiscal 1980.

Notes to Financial Statements (cont.)

2. Capitalization of Interest

The Company elected to adopt in fiscal 1980 the provisions of SFAS No. 34 requiring the capitalization of interest expense related to property constructed for use in the business.

During fiscal 1980, total interest cost incurred was $298.1 million. Of this amount interest capitalized amounted to $14.2 million (net income benefit of $7.5 million or $.24 per share after related tax effect).

3. Foreign Currency Translation

The effect of foreign currency rate changes resulted in a credit or (charge) to net income classified in the Statements of Income (Loss), as follows:

	1980	1979
	(Thousands of dollars)	
Exchange gain or (loss) classified as:		
Exchange gain (loss)	$(30,008)	$ 20,878
Income of nonconsolidated companies	7,162	(8,288)
Taxes on income	4,261	(5,143)
Net income effect of exchange gain or (loss) as defined by SFAS No. 8	$(18,585)	$ 7,447
Effect of foreign currency rate changes included in cost of sales-decrease	$ 27,597	$ 24,899

The effect of foreign currency rate changes included in cost of sales is measured by the difference between foreign currency cost of sales translated at average daily rates and cost of sales included in the Statements of Income (Loss) which include foreign currency costs, primarily inventory, translated at historical rates.

4. Major Modernization and Expansion Program

In connection with the Company's continuing major modernization and expansion program, approved by the Board of Directors, a special provision of $135.8 million ($68.6 million after tax benefit, $2.20 per share) was made against operations in 1980. This provision is to cover the estimated costs of writing down assets, facility rearrangements and other expenses, including the phase-out of industrial wheel tractors marketed by the Construction Equipment Group, and the sport utility vehicles marketed by the Truck Group under the trade name

"Scout". The Company is pursuing possibilities for the sale of the "Scout" division. The program, as approved, is planned to be completed by the end of fiscal 1982.

In the accompanying Statements of Income (Loss), the estimated aggregate cost of $135.8 million is shown as Major Modernization and Expansion Program, and its related tax benefits of $67.2 million is included in Taxes on Income (Benefit) of the Consolidated Group. The provision is based upon presently available information, not definitely ascertainable until the program is completed, and is summarized as follows in thousands of dollars:

Writedown of assets (primarily inventories) to net realizable value	$ 29,700
Operating, administrative and other costs to be incurred	106,100
Total	$135,800

In the October 31, 1980 Statements of Financial Condition, the net realizable value of inventories and property relating to the program approximated $60.6 and $22.3 million, respectively. The remaining accruals for phase-out costs of $54.8 million are included in current liabilities.

5. Wisconsin Steel

On March 27, 1980, the Company assumed ownership of certain iron and coal mining properties of its former Wisconsin Steel Division. These properties were security for $50 million of notes received when EDC Holding Company (EDC) acquired the Wisconsin Steel Division from the Company on July 31, 1977. In addition, the mines also served as security for other indebtedness to the Company and guarantees which the Company provided to third parties on behalf of EDC. The properties include coal mines at Benham, Kentucky, and partnership interests in two iron ore mining and pelletizing operations in Upper Michigan.

On March 31, 1980, EDC and certain of its steel and transportation subsidiaries filed Chapter 11 bankruptcy petitions.

Company management has completed its assessment of the financial effect of the above matters, and as a result, net income was reduced by $27.7 million (after tax benefits of $27.2 million), $.89 per share. The provision represents the estimated losses on receivables from EDC and liabilities to be assumed by the Company under various guarantees reduced by the esti-

Notes to Financial Statements (cont.)

mated value of the mining properties. The liabilities include $9.8 million for estimated vested benefits of participants in various retirement plans for former Wisconsin Steel Division employees over the total of retirement trust assets and the statutory obligations of the Pension Benefit Guaranty Corporation to participants measured as of March 31, 1980.

The value of the mines was based on the Company's assessment of current studies by outside engineers.

The Company has been informed that legal action may be instituted by EDC Holding Company and its related companies who are parties to the bankruptcy proceedings referred to above, in an attempt to have the iron and coal properties (Note 10) returned to EDC ownership. In addition, the Pension Benefit Guaranty Corporation (PBGC) guidelines may result in review and claims by the PBGC against the Company for funding of vested retirement benefits resulting from the terminated Wisconsin Steel pension plans following the Wisconsin Steel sale and bankruptcy proceedings. The Company has been advised by outside counsel that it has strong legal defenses against any such legal actions or claims.

While any such actions are subject to many uncertainties and delays, the Company believes that the resulting liability, if any, should not materially affect its financial condition.

6. Taxes on Income

The provision for taxes on income is analyzed by category and by income statement classification as follows:

	1980	1979
	(Thousands of dollars)	
Current:		
Federal	$(176,846)	$ 53,765
Investment tax credits	17,549	(14,528)
Foreign	19,232	68,164
State and local	(1,715)	2,889
Total current	(141,780)	110,290
Deferred:		
Federal	(155,422)	108,675
Foreign	(24,765)	(32,349)
State and local	(9,632)	13,907
Total deferred	(189,819)	90,233
Total provision (benefit)	$(331,599)	$200,523
Consolidated group	$(387,311)	$116,130
Nonconsolidated companies	82,912	84,393
Wisconsin Steel	(27,200)	—
Total	$(331,599)	$200,523

The deferred income tax provision representing the tax effects of timing differences between financial and taxable income is analyzed as follows:

	1980	1979
	(Thousands of dollars)	
Excess of tax over book depreciation	$ 898	$ 21,569
Inventory writedown including U.K. stock relief	(7,217)	(36,144)
Deferred margins on installment sales	(21,842)	86,587
Gain on installment sale—Wisconsin Steel	(10,057)	—
Unrealized exchange gain (loss), net	(1,097)	47,942
Volume discount	(3,635)	(14,236)
Wisconsin Steel	(21,011)	—
Retirement plan funding	(67,379)	—
Investment tax credits	(18,422)	—
Major modernization and expansion program	(41,712)	—
Other, net	1,655	(15,485)
Total deferred provision (credit)	$(189,819)	$ 90,233

An analysis of the variance from the United States statutory rate follows:

	1980	1979
U.S. statutory rate	(46.0)%	46.3 %
Increases (decreases) resulting from:		
Income (loss) from foreign sources including exchange adjustments	1.3	(2.4)
Domestic international sales company - DISC	(.1)	(1.0)
Investment tax credits	(2.5)	(2.6)
United Kingdom inventory stock relief	(.5)	(8.7)
State and local taxes, net of federal income tax benefit	(.9)	1.6
Carryback of U.S. net operating loss at other than current statutory rate	3.3	—
Other, net	(.1)	2.0
Effective income tax rate	(45.5)%	35.2 %

As a result of changes in the United Kingdom tax law related to "stock relief", 1979 net income was increased by $49.3 million ($1.63 per share). This includes the reversal to income of $41.6 million of deferred taxes recorded in prior years and $7.7 million of 1979 tax benefits from "stock relief", all relating to year-to-year increases in inventory. Of this amount, $43.5 million ($1.43 per share) was subject to payment if United Kingdom inventories decrease during the applicable recapture periods ranging up to six years.

The parent Company's share in undistributed earnings of foreign companies and its DISC subsidiary was $552 million at October 31, 1980. An income tax provision of $.3 million was made on $20.5 million of these earnings which are expected

Notes to Financial Statements (cont.)

to be remitted during 1981. The remaining undistributed earnings are considered to be permanently reinvested.

At October 31, 1980 the Company had $165.8 million of net operating loss carryforwards available to reduce future taxable income in foreign countries. Of this amount, $1.1 million will be available through 1981, $6.2 million through 1982, $41.1 million through 1985, $20.9 million through 1987 and $96.5 million will be available for an indefinite number of years. The tax effect on $78.3 million has been realized for financial purposes. The tax effect on the remaining $87.5 million will be credited to income when realized.

The Company has investment tax credit carryovers of approximately $48.1 million which are available to reduce future federal tax liabilities. Investment tax credits of $18.4 million have been realized for financial purposes. The remaining $29.7 million will be credited to income when realized. Such carryovers expire, if not previously utilized, in fiscal years ending 1984 through 1987.

7. Supplementary Income Statement Data

Interest Income includes interest received from nonconsolidated companies of $3.6 million in both 1980 and 1979.

Costs and Expenses includes the following:

	1980	1979
	(Thousands of dollars)	
Research and development	$255,356	$217,796
Maintenance and repairs	140,479	172,097
Taxes, other than taxes on income:		
Social security, unemployment and		
other social insurance	222,273	153,440
Real estate, personal property, etc	38,266	45,774

8. Receivables

Receivables at October 31 by major classifications are as follows:

	1980	1979
	(Thousands of dollars)	
Trade notes	$ 67,360	$ 71,685
Less unearned finance charges	4,291	3,159
Sub-total	63,069	68,526
Trade accounts	442,895	551,196
Nonconsolidated companies	60,859	121,605
Other	76,010	68,732
Total	642,833	810,059
Less allowance for losses	15,766	13,444
Receivables, net	$627,067	$796,615

Sales finance subsidiaries purchase nearly all notes receivable and some accounts receivable arising from sales by operations in Australia, Canada, Great Britain, New Zealand and the United States and some receivables arising from sales by other affiliated companies.

9. Inventories and Cost of Sales

The cost of substantially all domestic inventories, or approximately 65% of consolidated inventories, is accounted for using the LIFO method.

Had the Company accounted for cost of the inventories on the average cost basis rather than on the LIFO method, inventories would exceed reported amounts by approximately $236.2 million at October 31, 1980 and $113.4 million at October 31, 1979.

During 1980, inventory quantities were reduced. As a result, the 1980 cost of sales includes charges for goods carried at prior years' LIFO values which are less than current replacement costs; the effect was to reduce the 1980 net loss by $7.5 million ($.24 per share).

The inventory used in computing cost of sales was less than the inventory in the Statements of Financial Condition, as the latter includes items such as trade-ins, repossessions and freight on shipments to sales outlets. Inventories used in the computation for the years ended October 31, 1980 and 1979 were as follows, in thousands of dollars:

October 31:	
1980	$2,231,536
1979	2,249,199
1978	1,830,342

10. Investments and Long-Term Receivables

Equity in and Advances to Nonconsolidated Companies consists primarily of the Company's investment in its wholly-owned sales finance subsidiaries at October 31, 1979. At October 31, 1980, Equity in and Advances to Nonconsolidated Companies also includes an $11.9 million investment in coal mining properties (Notes 5 and 22).

Long-Term Receivables and Other Investments consists of investments in the stock of and long-term advances to dealerships and a $54.3 million investment in iron ore properties at October 31, 1980. Included in the October 31, 1979 amount was $50 million of interest bearing notes from the sale of Wisconsin Steel Division in 1977 (Note 5).

Notes to Financial Statements (cont.)

11. Property

At October 31, Property includes the following:

	1980	1979
	(Thousands of dollars)	
Buildings, machinery and equipment, at cost:		
Manufacturing	$1,744,201	$1,521,470
Distribution	239,092	220,058
Other	63,307	57,468
Total	2,046,600	1,798,996
Less accumulated depreciation	928,725	897,952
Net	1,117,875	901,044
Tooling and pattern equipment, at cost, less amortization of $116,308,000 in 1980 and $107,173,000 in 1979	127,008	106,041
Land	32,356	32,062
Property, net	$1,277,239	$1,039,147

Buildings, machinery and equipment include $57.7 million and $54.1 million at October 31, 1980 and 1979, respectively, representing gross amounts of capitalized lease obligations.

12. Leases

The Company has long-term noncancelable leases for use of various assets, primarily distribution facilities and warehouses. Lease terms are generally for 5 to 25 years and, in many cases, provide for renewal options. The Company is generally obligated for the cost of property taxes, insurance and maintenance. In addition, the Company leases office space and equipment.

The amount of total rent expense for all operating leases was $57 million in 1980 and $49 million in 1979. Contingent rentals and sublease rentals were not material.

Future minimum lease payments required under noncancelable operating leases having a lease term in excess of one year, and the future minimum lease payments under capital leases, together with the amount of imputed interest necessary to reduce the minimum capital lease payments to present value as of October 31, 1980 are as follows:

	Capital Leases	Operating Leases
	(Thousands of dollars)	
1981	$ 7,636	$ 27,956
1982	7,275	18,798
1983	6,003	12,508
1984	5,160	8,581
1985	4,557	6,611
Thereafter	59,061	27,618
Total minimum payments	89,692	$102,072
Less imputed interest	45,315	
Present value of minimum lease payments	$44,377	

13. Current Liabilities

The classifications of Current Liabilities at October 31 are as follows:

	1980	1979
	(Thousands of dollars)	
Notes payable:		
Banks	$ 659,667	$ 285,098
Commercial paper	52,110	31,339
Trade	33,200	37,250
Nonconsolidated companies	58,841	54,045
Other	5,120	3,656
Total notes payable	808,938	411,388
Accounts payable:		
Trade	766,628	835,626
Nonconsolidated companies	157,729	30,931
Other	60,362	77,012
Total accounts payable	984,719	943,569
Accrued liabilities:		
Payrolls and commissions	116,407	108,548
Taxes	80,755	102,761
Interest	49,011	23,128
Special compensation	8,762	48,064
Pension, health and welfare	134,729	38,537
Major modernization and expansion program	54,794	—
Other	190,586	166,777
Total accrued liabilities	635,044	487,815
Current maturities of long-term debt	51,529	30,599
Total current liabilities	$2,480,230	$1,873,371

Notes to Financial Statements (cont.)

Information regarding commercial paper and short-term borrowings from lending institutions for the years ended October 31 is as follows:

	1980	1979
	(Thousands of dollars)	
Aggregate borrowings outstanding:		
Daily average	$ 923,000	$446,000
Maximum month-end balance	1,343,000	627,000
Weighted average interest rate:		
On average borrowings*	14.36%	10.97%
At October 31	13.18	11.50

*Calculated by dividing the actual interest expense for the year by the average daily balance outstanding.

The parent Company's unsecured lines of credit with various banks constitute business commitments, not legal obligations of the lender. These lines of credit are subject to the usual terms and conditions applied by banks and are typically reviewed and renewed annually. At October 31, 1980, the Company maintained lines of approximately $1,745 million; $1,230 million of these lines were unused of which $1,077 million were mutually available to both the parent Company and International Harvester Credit Corporation. Under the terms of the most restrictive long-term debt agreement, the Company, at October 31, 1980, is limited to the amount of additional indebtedness it can incur to $630 million.

There are no withdrawal restrictions on any cash balances maintained at the various banks. The parent Company and International Harvester Credit Corporation maintain average compensating balances over a twelve-month period equal to accepted banking industry practice. The compensating balances expected of the parent Company and International Harvester Credit Corporation under informal arrangements at October 31, 1980, including the mutual lines, were approximately $64 million and the estimated collected balances were $118 million. Because the arrangements are based on a twelve-month average balance, none of the cash balances are considered to be restricted as of any specific date.

Lines of credit arrangements of the consolidated subsidiaries are generally in connection with bank overdraft and note facilities for which there are neither material commitment fees nor compensating balance requirements. Unused lines of the consolidated subsidiaries at October 31, 1980 were $254 million.

14. Long-Term Debt

Long-Term Debt at October 31, excluding amounts maturing within one year, is summarized as follows:

	1980	1979
	(Thousands of dollars)	
International Harvester Company:		
Borrowings under revolving credit agreements, interest rates from 10⅛% to 14%, expiring in 1982 thru 1985 .	$ 230,000	$ —
Short-term debt supported by revolving credit agreements	270,000	240,000
8½% loan, repayable $10,000,000 annually, 1983 to 1997	150,000	150,000
3½% loan, repayable $5,000,000 annually to 1982	5,000	10,000
14½% note, due 1983	10,417	18,750
5% debentures, due 1986	11,156	11,497
4⅝% subordinated debentures, due 1988 . .	23,493	28,528
4.80% subordinated debentures, due 1991 .	32,495	34,303
8⅝% sinking fund debentures, due 1995 (face value $91,724,000)	91,630	96,336
6¼% sinking fund debentures, due 1998 . .	41,251	43,880
9% sinking fund debentures, due 2004 (face value $150,000,000)	149,055	149,016
11.9% note, due 1982	50,000	—
7¾% loan, due 1983	16,969	—
Capitalized lease obligations	40,734	50,975
Other	26,626	8,918
Nonconsolidated companies	5,750	—
Subsidiaries:		
Debt payable in United States dollars or United States dollar equivalents of other currencies, interest rates from 3.8% to 26¼% due 2002 or prior:		
Australian dollars	33,427	14,333
French francs	40,198	12,224
German marks	48,640	53,987
U.S. dollars	12,200	13,145
Other	11,597	12,278
Nonconsolidated companies	26,430	—
Total long-term debt	$1,327,068	$948,170

Notes to Financial Statements (cont.)

The weighted average interest rate applicable to long-term debt at October 31, 1980 is 10.2% compared with 8.6% at October 31, 1979.

The aggregate annual maturities and sinking fund requirements of long-term borrowings are as follows for the years ending October 31: 1982, $275 million; 1983, $151 million; 1984, $141 million and 1985, $235 million.

In July, 1980, the Company borrowed $150 million under an amended revolving credit agreement with a consortium of banks, expiring in December, 1981.

During 1979, the Company entered into revolving credit agreements with various banks aggregating $90 million which expire in February, 1984. Payment of a commitment fee of ¼% on the unused portion is required. In July, 1980, the Company borrowed $20 million under these agreements.

During fiscal 1980, the Company entered into revolving credit agreements with various banks aggregating $385 million, expiring in 1985 or prior. Payment of a commitment fee of ¼% on the unused portion is required. In July, 1980, the Company borrowed $60 million under these agreements.

Interest rates on borrowing under the above agreements are a fraction over the London Interbank Offered Rate, Prime Rate or Federal Funds Rate.

At October 31, 1980 and 1979, the Company had classified as long-term debt $270 million and $240 million, respectively, of short-term obligations relating to unused revolving credit agreements in accordance with SFAS No. 6.

15. Commitments and Contingent Liabilities

At October 31, 1980, commitments on appropriations for capital expenditures in progress are approximately $302 million.

The Company is a guarantor of debt at October 31, 1980 of nonconsolidated companies and distributors in the amount of $57 million. In addition, certain subsidiaries were contingently liable for approximately $243 million, primarily for notes receivable discounted and bills of exchange.

16. Preferred Stock

Redeemable:

Series A

The Company may redeem, subject to certain conditions, any number of its Series A preferred shares outstanding at a price of $110 per share until 1981, decreasing annually to $100 per share in 1992. Commencing in 1981, the Company is required to redeem 33,333 shares at $100

per share plus accrued dividends annually. In 1985 and thereafter, the Company may increase the number of shares to be redeemed at $100 per share to a maximum of 100,000.

Convertible:

Series C

Holders of the Series C preferred stock have the right, at their option, to convert shares of the Series C preferred stock into 1⅓ shares of the Company's common stock at any time, at the initial conversion price of $37.50 per share of common stock, subject to adjustments under certain circumstances. The Company may redeem, subject to certain conditions in whole or in part, its Series C preferred shares outstanding. The optional redemption price to 1981 is $55.76 per share, decreasing annually to $50.00 per share after 1990.

17. Retained Earnings

Under the terms of the most restrictive long-term debt agreement as amended, $100 million of retained earnings are available for the payment of cash dividends at October 31, 1980.

Equity in undistributed earnings of nonconsolidated companies of $632 million at October 31, 1980 and $507 million at October 31, 1979 is included in Retained Earnings.

18. Retirement Plans

The parent Company and its domestic and Canadian subsidiaries have pension plans covering substantially all of their employees. Generally, the plans are noncontributory and benefits are related to an employee's length of service and wage rate.

Most foreign subsidiaries have separate retirement plans that are integrated with and supplement the benefits provided by laws of the various countries.

It is the Company's policy to fund accrued pension costs. The plans vary in the extent to which they are funded, but for plan years ended during the current fiscal year, all funding obligations have been fulfilled.

Total pension costs charged to income were $246 million for 1980 and $212 million for 1979. This increase results primarily from an increase in retirement benefit levels under the Company's retirement plans.

At January 1, 1980, unfunded prior service costs approximated $1,613 million and the actuarially computed value of vested benefits was estimated to exceed the total market value of the pension funds by $1,079 million.

Notes to Financial Statements (cont.)

19. Stock Option Plans

The Company's 1968 and 1975 Stock Option Plans provide for the granting of options to key employees for the purchase of shares of common stock at a price equal to the fair market value of the stock on date of grant. Qualified options have a term, from date of grant, of not more than five years and non-qualified options have a term of not more than ten years. Options are not exercisable during the first year. There are 567,325 and 835,680 shares available for grant and 360,445 and 258,910 options exercisable at October 31, 1980 and 1979, respectively. Authority to grant options under the 1968 Plan expired on December 20, 1977.

Stock appreciation rights are granted at the discretion of the Committee on Organization of the Board of Directors. Holders of stock options with stock appreciation rights are entitled to receive cash or cash and shares of common stock, equal in value to the difference between the option price and the current market value of the common stock at the date the option is surrendered. During 1980 and 1979, 160,995 and 146,375 stock appreciation rights were granted, and 298,725 and 145,295 were outstanding at October 31, 1980 and 1979, respectively. There was no charge to income in 1979 or 1980 because the option prices exceeded the current market value of the shares at October 31.

A tax benefit related to stock options of $167 thousand for 1979 is included in capital in excess of par value. There was no comparable benefit in 1980.

The following table summarizes changes in common stock under the option for the years ended October 31, in thousands of dollars except per-share data:

| | Number of Shares | | Option Price | | | Market Value | |
	1980	1979	Per Share	Total 1980	1979	Per Share	Total
Outstanding options at beginning of the year:							
1980	406,205		$26.69 to $42.50	$13,229			
1979		332,785	26.00 to 40.13		$ 9,832		
Options granted:						At date granted:	
1980	290,155		30.81 to 36.94	9,568		$30.81 to $36.94	$ 9,568
1979		148,375	33.81 to 42.50		5,520	33.81 to 42.50	5,520
Options exercised:						At date exercised:	
1980	(20,340)		26.69 to 31.50	(572)		$30.25 to $40.00	$ 703
1979		(69,050)	26.00 to 31.50		(1,942)	32.81 to 43.50	2,643
Options terminated:							
1980	(25,420)		26.69 to 36.81	(811)			
1979		(5,905)	26.00 to 36.81		(181)		
Outstanding options at end of the year:						At date granted:	
1980	650,600		27.25 to 42.50	$21,414		$27.25 to $42.50	$21,414
1979		406,205	26.69 to 42.50		$13,229	26.69 to 42.50	13,229
By year of grant:							
1980	286,795		$30.81 to $36.94	$ 9,457			
1979	139,730	147,295	33.81 to 42.50	5,202	$ 5,481		
1978	131,540	142,440	28.00 to 40.13	3,948	4,268		
1977	63,740	70,635	31.50 to 36.06	2,010	2,227		
1976	28,795	30,735	27.25 to 27.69	797	850		
1975	—	15,100	$26.69	—	403		
	650,600	406,205		$21,414	$13,229		
Options becoming exercisable during year:						At date became exercisable:	
1980	147,295		$33.81 to $42.50	$ 5,481		$25.38 to $36.31	$ 4,832
1979		155,625	28.00 to 40.13		$ 4,655	35.38 to 41.88	5,806

Notes to Financial Statements (cont.)

20. Management Incentive Program

The management incentive programs are administered by the Committee on Organization of the Board of Directors. Members of the Committee are not employees and are not eligible for participation in the following plans. The Committee determines the managerial employees who will be eligible for the respective incentive compensation plans and either the amount to be granted to each individual or criteria to be applied.

The parent Company's Management Performance Assurance Award Plan (MPAAP) and the Sustained Performance Achievement Award Plan (SPAAP) require the establishment of performance goals for selected employees having substantial responsibility in an executive or managerial capacity. Under MPAAP, awards are determined at the end of each fiscal year based on established goals. Performance under SPAAP is measured in five-year cycles and awards are based on achievement of long-term corporate goals. Under these plans, $1 million in 1980 and $11.3 million in 1979 were charged to costs and expenses. Employees participating in these Plans are not eligible to participate in any other group incentive compensation plan of the Company.

As part of the Management Performance Assurance Program, the Key Management Incentive Plan (KMIP) provides awards to managers above a certain level who are not participants in any other Company incentive compensation plan. The amount of the KMIP award is dependent upon the degree to which the Company and groups achieve goals established in the annual business plan as well as an annual achievement evaluation of the participant. During 1980 and 1979, $.4 million and $13.2 million, respectively, were charged to costs and expenses to meet the provisions of this Plan.

The Company loaned Mr. McCardell, Chairman of the Board and Chief Executive Officer, $1,796,250 and Mr. Hayford, President and Chief Operating Officer, $973,438 under their respective compensation agreements, with which they purchased from the Company shares of International Harvester Company common stock at market price on the date of the loans. The loans are evidenced by notes which bear interest at 6% and are due on October 31, 1985.

The compensation agreements provided the basis for Mr. McCardell and Mr. Hayford to earn awards to be applied as reductions of the principal of the notes. The amounts of any such awards are based upon the degree to which the Company exceeded certain financial objectives. No awards were granted for fiscal 1978 performance. During fiscal 1980, the Committee approved loan forgiveness in the amount of $1,796,250 to Mr. McCardell based on the Company's fiscal 1979 performance, of which the Committee directed that $359,250 be applied as immediate reduction of Mr. McCardell's loan and that the note balance be reduced equally in each subsequent fiscal year through 1984, subject to the contingencies of his compensation agreement. The Committee also interpreted Mr. Hayford's loan agreement to require that $243,360 be applied to reduce the note balance in each of the fiscal years 1981 through 1984, determined as a fixed percentage of Mr. McCardell's loan reduction, provided Mr. Hayford meets the contingencies of his compensation agreement at the time of each annual reduction.

The loan balances at October 31, 1980 were $1,437,000 due from Mr. McCardell and $973,438 due from Mr. Hayford.

21. Foreign Operations

Sales by subsidiaries outside the United States accounted for 35% of total sales in 1980 and 27% in 1979.

Net income of consolidated foreign subsidiaries and equity in net income of nonconsolidated foreign companies amounted to $5.5 million in 1980 and $183 million in 1979. Included in 1979 is a tax benefit of $49.3 million from United Kingdom "stock relief" (Note 6).

Net assets of foreign operations at October 31 are analyzed as follows, in millions of dollars:

	1980				1979
	Working Capital	Non-current Assets	Non-current Liabilities	Net Assets	Net Assets
Canada	$102	$129	$ 16	$215	$172
Europe, Africa and Middle East	187	310	110	387	422
Latin America	14	99	5	108	54
Pacific Area	8	125	38	95	138
Total	$311	$663	$169	$805	$786

Notes to Financial Statements (cont.)

22. Nonconsolidated Sales Finance Subsidiaries

The combined accounts of International Harvester Credit Corporation, a domestic subsidiary, and other sales finance subsidiaries in Australia, Bermuda, Canada, Great Britain, Netherlands Antilles, New Zealand and Switzerland are included in the following summaries. Prior to November 1, 1979, International Harvester Overseas Finance Co. N.V. (Netherlands Antilles) was consolidated with International Harvester Company and Subsidiaries. This subsidiary's retained earnings of $5 million at November 1, 1979 has been included in retained earnings - beginning of the year for 1980 in the following summary.

The financial condition at October 31 is as follows:

	1980	1979
	(Thousands of dollars)	
Assets		
Cash	$ 39,321	$ 82,883
Marketable securities, principally at cost which approximates market	—	51,000
Receivables	5,124,532	4,889,648
Less: Allowance for losses	(22,660)	(13,421)
Receivables from affiliated companies	406,001	186,126
Repossessions	25,500	10,574
Other assets	40,709	14,882
Total assets	$5,613,403	$5,221,692
Liabilities and Stockholder's Equity		
Liabilities:		
Short-term notes payable	$2,278,960	$2,360,644
Accounts payable and accrued liabilities	155,124	113,756
Amounts due affiliated companies	78,893	126,834
Long-term debt	2,201,032	1,884,239
Long-term debt due affiliated companies	26,047	25,565
Deferred income taxes	1,972	5,764
Total liabilities	4,742,028	4,516,802
Stockholder's Equity:		
Capital stock	258,452	235,813
Capital in excess of par value	41,405	5,460
Retained earnings	571,518	463,617
Total stockholder's equity	871,375	704,890
Total liabilities and stockholder's equity	$5,613,403	$5,221,692

Income and retained earnings for the fiscal years ended October 31 are as follows:

	1980	1979
	(Thousands of dollars)	
Revenues	$768,089	$617,598
Expenses:		
Interest expense:		
Other than affiliates	495,566	383,550
Affiliated companies	7,215	5,073
Total interest expense	502,781	388,623
Provision for losses on receivables	20,268	7,630
Operating expenses	20,259	17,507
Exchange (gain) loss	(6,737)	4,730
Fees paid to affiliated companies	54,156	43,301
Total expenses	590,727	461,791
Income before taxes on income	177,362	155,807
Taxes on income	(73,055)	(72,355)
Net income	104,307	83,452
Retained earnings - beginning of the year	468,612	380,950
Dividends paid	(1,401)	(785)
Retained earnings - end of the year	$571,518	$463,617

Revenues include approximately $282 million in 1980 and $251 million in 1979 from affiliated companies.

23. Segment Information

The Company operates in both the domestic and foreign markets in four industry segments. The Truck segment encompasses the manufacture and sale of gasoline and diesel powered trucks/tractors, cab and chassis units for medium-sized school buses. The Agricultural Equipment segment manufactures and sells agricultural tractors, grain harvesting equipment, crop production equipment and other implements used in the agricultural industry. The products of the Construction Equipment segment include a wide variety of crawler loaders and dozers, rubber-tired loaders, scrapers, off-highway dump trucks, excavators, utility tractors, forklifts, logging equipment and tow vehicles for aircraft. The Turbo Machinery segment manufactures turbine-driven equipment which it sells to a broad spectrum of industrial markets.

Notes to Financial Statements (cont.)

International Harvester Company and Subsidiaries

23. Segment Information (continued)

Operations by Industry are as follows

(Millions of dollars):

For the years ended October 31:	Trucks			Agricultural Equipment			Construction Equipment			Turbo Machinery			Consolidated		
	1980	1979	1978	1980	1979	1978	1980	1979	1978	1980	1979	1978	1980	1979	1978
Sales	$2,701	$3,966	$3,211	$2,507	$3,069	$2,348	$ 760	$1,000	$ 852	$ 344	$ 357	$ 253	$6,312	$8,392	$6,664
Intersegment sales	21	31	21	69	94	133	33	31	33	—	—	1			
Total sales	$2,722	$3,997	$3,232	$2,576	$3,163	$2,481	$ 793	$1,031	$ 885	$ 344	$ 357	$ 254			
Operating profit (loss)	$ (153)	$ 303	$ 245	$ (1)	$ 442	$ 290	$ (119)	$ 53	$ 55	$ 11	$ 29	$ 20	$ (262)	$ 827	$ 610
General corporate items:															
Expenses													(85)	(72)	(56)
Financing charges on receivables sold to sales finance subsidiaries													(254)	(241)	(149)
Interest expense													(284)	(148)	(126)
Exchange gain (loss)													(8)	12	(85)
Income (loss) before taxes of nonconsolidated companies:															
Identifiable with segments	$ 15	$ 3	$ (5)	$ 4	$ 4	$ —	$ 11	$ 15	$ 8				30	22	3
Financial services													190	169	143
(Taxes on income) benefit of:															
Consolidated group													387	(116)	(85)
Nonconsolidated companies													(83)	(84)	(68)
Income (loss) from continuing operations													(369)	369	187
Wisconsin Steel, net of income tax benefit													(28)	—	—
Net income (loss)													$ (397)	$ 369	$ 187
Depreciation and amortization expense	$ 46	$ 43	$ 40	$ 63	$ 62	$ 51	$ 13	$ 14	$ 13	$ 8	$ 8	$ 7	$ 130	$ 127	$ 111
Capital expenditures	$ 104	$ 102	$ 82	$ 229	$ 136	$ 102	$ 33	$ 31	$ 16	$ 18	$ 16	$ 10	$ 384	$ 285	$ 210
At October 31:															
Identifiable assets	$1,579	$1,745	$1,365	$1,739	$1,548	$1,387	$ 698	$ 646	$ 507	$ 305	$ 288	$ 240	$4,321	$4,227	$3,499
Intersegment receivables	—	—	—	1	1	—	—	—	—	—	—	—			
Total identifiable assets	$1,579	$1,745	$1,365	$1,740	$1,549	$1,387	$ 698	$ 646	$ 507	$ 305	$ 288	$ 240			
Equity in net assets of nonconsolidated companies:															
Identifiable with segments	$ 48	$ 33	$ 22	$ 19	$ 17	$ 12	$ 24	$ 18	$ 21	$ 1	$ —	$ —	92	68	55
Financial services													910	741	607
General corporate items													520	211	155
Total consolidated assets													$5,843	$5,247	$4,316

Sales include both sales as reported in the Company's consolidated statements of income and intercompany sales which are eliminated in consolidation. Intercompany sales (intersegment sales or transfers between geographic areas) are accounted for at prices which the Company believes approximate market.

Operating profit is total revenue less operating expenses. Operating profit excludes general corporate expenses, financing charges on receivables sold to sales finance subsidiaries, interest expense, corporate exchange gain or loss and equity in income of nonconsolidated companies.

Notes to Financial Statements (cont.)

International Harvester Company and Subsidiaries

23. Segment Information (continued)

Operations by Geographic Areas are as follows

(Millions of dollars)

	United States 1980	1979	1978	Canada 1980	1979	1978	Latin America 1980	1979	1978	Europe, Africa and Middle East 1980	1979	1978	Pacific 1980	1979	1978	Consolidated 1980	1979	1978
For the years ended October 31:																		
Sales	$4,125	$6,099	$4,836	$ 603	$ 717	$ 493	$ 68	$ 55	$ 37	$1,140	$1,159	$1,005	$ 376	$ 362	$ 293	$6,312	$8,392	$6,664
Transfers between geographic areas	416	610	390	280	318	252				223	231	103	10	—	—			
Total sales	$4,541	$6,709	$5,226	$ 883	$1,035	$ 745	$ 68	$ 56	$ 37	$1,363	$1,390	$1,108	$ 386	$ 362	$ 293			
Operating profit (loss)	$ (348)	$ 555	$ 430	$ 49	$ 79	$ 41	$ 13	$ 7	$ 3	$ 3	$ 145	$ 118	$ 21	$ 41	$ 18	$ (262)	$ 827	$ 610
General corporate items:																		
Expenses																(85)	(72)	(56)
Financing charges on receivables sold to sales finance subsidiaries																(254)	(241)	(149)
Interest expense																(284)	(148)	(126)
Exchange gain (loss)																(8)	12	(85)
Income (loss) before taxes of non-consolidated companies:																		
Identifiable with segments	$ 4	$ 4	—				$ 2	$ 2		$ 13	$ 2	$ (5)	$ 11	$ 14	$ 8	30	22	3
Financial services																190	169	143
(Taxes on income) benefit of:																		
Consolidated group																387	(116)	(85)
Nonconsolidated companies																(83)	(84)	(68)
Income (loss) from continuing operations																(369)	369	187
Wisconsin Steel, net of income tax benefit																(28)	—	—
Net income (loss)																$ (397)	$ 369	$ 187
At October 31:																		
Identifiable assets	$2,829	$2,795	$2,299	$ 250	$ 269	$ 200	$ 79	$ 58	$ 37	$ 910	$ 861	$ 763	$ 253	$ 244	$ 200	$4,321	$4,227	$3,499
Interarea receivables	45	11	37	12	27		1	1		12	22	27	4	1				
Total identifiable assets	$2,874	$2,806	$2,336	$ 262	$ 296	$ 201	$ 80	$ 59	$ 37	$ 922	$ 883	$ 790	$ 257	$ 245	$ 200			
Equity in net assets of nonconsolidated companies:																		
Identifiable with segments	$ 11	$ 10	$ 7				$ 12	$ 10	$ 2	$ 44	$ 28	$ 31	$ 25	$ 20	$ 15	92	68	55
Financial services																910	741	607
General corporate items																520	211	155
Total consolidated assets																$5,843	$5,247	$4,316

Identifiable assets by industry segments and geographic areas are those assets identified with operations in respective industry segments and geographic areas. Corporate assets primarily consist of cash, non-trade receivables and other items of a general corporate nature.

The Company's equity in income and net assets of its nonconsolidated companies are not included in computing operating profit and the identifiable assets of each industry and geographic segment. Identifiable amounts are displayed under the appropriate industry and geographic area columns.

foreign countries totaled $472 million, $447 million, and $377 million in 1980, 1979, and 1978, respectively.

Fiscal year 1980 operating profit includes a special provision of $52 million in U.S. for the Truck Group, $15 million in U.S. for the Agricultural Equipment Group, and $52 million in U.S. and $16 million in European area for the Construction Equipment Group to cover the estimated cost of writing down assets, facility rearrangements and other expenses attributed to the Company's continuing major modernization and expansion program approved by the Board of Directors. The special provision also covers estimated costs associated with the proposed sale of Truck Group's sport utility vehicles marketed under the trade name "Scout" and

Notes to Financial Statements (cont.)

24. Quarterly Financial Information (Unaudited)

(Millions of dollars except per-share data)

	1st Quarter		2nd Quarter		3rd Quarter		4th Quarter		Fiscal Year	
	1980	1979	1980	1979	1980	1979	1980	1979	1980	1979
Sales	$1,008.0	$1,609.6	$1,160.2	$2,205.4	$1,822.7	$2,082.2	$2,320.9	$2,494.8	$6,311.8	$8,392.0
Gross profit	$ (73.0)	$ 288.1	$ (54.8)	$ 394.3	$ 351.3	$ 361.7	$ 388.2	$ 443.5	$ 611.7	$1,487.6
Income (Loss):										
Continuing operations	$ (222.2)	$ 58.8	$ (229.5)	$ 95.3	$ 61.9	$ 67.9	$ 20.2	$ 147.6	$ (369.6)	$ 369.6
Wisconsin Steel, net of income tax benefit	—	—	(27.7)	—	—	—	—	—	(27.7)	—
Net income (loss)	$ (222.2)	$ 58.8	$ (257.2)	$ 95.3	$ 61.9	$ 67.9	$ 20.2	$ 147.6	$ (397.3)	$ 369.6
Income (loss) per share:										
Continuing operations	$ (7.24)	$ 1.91	$ (7.43)	$ 3.12	$ 2.01	$ 2.19	$ .64	$ 4.79	$ (12.02)	$ 12.01
Wisconsin Steel	—	—	(.89)	—	—	—	—	—	(.89)	—
Net income (loss)	$ (7.24)	$ 1.91	$ (8.32)	$ 3.12	$ 2.01	$ 2.19	$ .64	$ 4.79	$ (12.91)	$ 12.01

The United Auto Workers (UAW) strike, which began November 1, 1979, against most of the Company's United States manufacturing operations, was settled April 20, 1980. The strike severely impacted the first two quarters' sales and earnings.

The 1980 second quarter net income was reduced by $27.7 million (after tax benefits of $27.2 million), ($.89 per share), for the estimated losses on receivables from the sale of the Wisconsin Steel Division and liabilities to be assumed as explained in Note 5.

In connection with the Company's continuing major modernization and expansion program, approved by the Board of Directors, a special provision of $122.9 million ($62.1 million after tax benefit, $2.01 per share) and $12.9 million ($6.5 million after tax benefit, $.19 per share) was made against operations in the second and fourth quarters, respectively. See Note 4.

In the third quarter of fiscal 1980, the Company elected to adopt, retroactive to the beginning of the 1980 fiscal year, the provisions of SFAS No. 34, requiring the capitalization of interest expense related to property constructed for use in the business. The capitalization of interest increased net income by $5 million ($.16 per share) in the third quarter of 1980. The results of the previous quarters of 1980 have not been restated because the amounts involved are not considered material.

The Company uses an estimated annual effective tax rate for interim reporting of income taxes. During the third quarter of fiscal 1980, the estimated consolidated group's annual effective tax rate changed, resulting in the recognition of increased expected tax benefits from the first two quarters' pre-tax losses.

In the fourth quarter of 1980, net income was increased by $7.5 million ($.24 per share) due to reduction in LIFO inventory quantities. See Note 9.

Net income in 1979 was increased by $2.6 million ($.08 per share) and $46.7 million ($1.55 per share) in the third and fourth quarters, respectively, as a result of 1979 changes in the United Kingdom tax law related to "stock relief". See Note 6.

In the opinion of management, the most appropriate measure of the effect of foreign currency rate changes on quarterly financial results represents the total of (a) exchange gains (losses) as determined under SFAS No. 8 less related income taxes and (b) the effect of foreign currency rates changes included in cost of sales as defined in Note 3. This is shown as follows:

Fiscal Quarter	Exchange Gain (Loss) Less Related Income Tax Effects		Foreign Currency Effect Included in Cost of Sales (Increase) Decrease		Total Gain (Loss)			
					Amount		Per Share	
	1980	1979	1980	1979	1980	1979	1980	1979
1st	$(15.1)	$15.2	$ 5.7	$ 4.2	$(9.4)	$19.4	$(.31)	$ .65
2nd	4.7	.2	(7.5)	.6	(2.8)	.8	(.09)	.02
3rd	(11.0)	(10.8)	23.9	9.0	12.9	(1.8)	.42	(.06)
4th	2.8	2.8	5.5	11.1	8.3	13.9	.27	.46
Total	$(18.6)	$ 7.4	$27.6	$24.9	$ 9.0	$32.3	$ .29	$1.07

Notes to Financial Statements (cont.)

25. Supplementary Information on the Effect of Inflation on Selected Financial Data (Unaudited)

Financial statements in the U.S. have traditionally been expressed in terms of historical costs in effect when the transactions occurred. The historical cost concept is in accordance with generally accepted accounting principles and such principles were not designed to measure the effects of inflation. The Financial Accounting Standards Board issued SFAS No. 33, "Financial Reporting and Changing Prices", which requires two supplementary computations of income: one based on the effect of general inflation as measured by the United States Consumer Price Index For All Urban Users (CPI-U), referred to as constant dollar; and the other based on the effect of the change in prices for specific resources used in the operation of the Company, referred to as current costs.

This supplemental information, prepared in accordance with SFAS No. 33, involves a substantial number of judgements and estimating techniques and should be viewed in that context and not as a reliable indicator of the effect of inflation on the Company's financial statements and results.

Statement of Loss Adjusted for
Changing Prices (Stated in Average Fiscal 1980 Dollars)
For the Year Ended October 31, 1980
(Millions of dollars)

	Historical Cost	Adjusted for General Inflation Constant Dollar (a)	Adjusted for Changes in Specific Prices (Current Costs) (b)
Total sales and other revenues ..	$6,342.1	$6,342.1	$6,342.1
Cost of sales (excluding depreciation and amortization)	5,585.9	5,698.0	5,615.1
Depreciation and amortization expense	129.6	189.3	212.7
Marketing and administrative expenses (excluding depreciation and amortization)	796.5	796.5	796.5
Other, net	721.7	721.7	721.7
Total costs and expenses ...	7,233.7	7,405.5	7,346.0
Income (loss) of nonconsolidated companies before taxes on income	217.6	217.6	217.6
Loss from continuing operations before income tax benefit..................	674.0	845.8	786.3
Income tax benefit (c)	304.4	304.4	304.4
Loss from continuing operations (c)	$ 369.6	$ 541.4	$ 481.9
Effective income tax rate (c)	45.2%	36.0%	38.7%
Unrealized gain from decline in purchasing power of net amounts owed (d)		$ 280.6	$ 280.6
Increase in current cost of inventories and property, net, over (under) the increase in general price level (e)			$ (317.8)

Notes to Financial Statements (cont.)

Explanations and Comments

(a) Adjusted for General Inflation - Constant Dollar

In a period of inflation, the purchasing power of the dollar deteriorates. The constant dollar values represent historical costs restated in dollars of the same purchasing power as measured by the average fiscal 1980 CPI-U. Depreciation and amortization expense was calculated by restating the historical cost of depreciable assets to average fiscal 1980 dollars as measured by the CPI-U and by applying to the restated amounts the same useful lives and depreciation methods that were used in the historical cost financial statements. Cost of sales was determined by restating the historical cost of beginning and ending inventories to average fiscal 1980 dollars. All other items have not been restated as they are assumed to have occurred ratably in relation to the change during the year in the CPI-U.

(b) Adjusted for Changes in Specific Prices - Current Costs

In a period of inflation, prices of most goods and services used by the Company increase but not necessarily at the same rate as the CPI-U used in the constant dollar calculations. The current cost accounting method measures inventories and property at the current cost as of the balance sheet date. Cost of sales is based on the current cost of inventories at the date of sale, and depreciation is computed on the average current cost of property during the fiscal year.

The current cost of property was determined by applying appropriate 1980 fiscal year end external indices to the historical costs of the appropriate class of assets. The current cost of depreciation and amortization was calculated using the average current cost of property during the year, and the same useful lives and depreciation methods used in the financial statements. The current cost of property relates to the assets presently owned by the Company rather than to technologically superior assets which may be available. The cost of technologically superior replacement assets may require significantly greater capital outlays than reflected by the current cost of the assets presently owned by the Company. These higher replacement costs could be offset to a certain extent by the operating cost savings that would often result from the use of technologically superior assets.

The Company uses the LIFO method for most inventories in the U.S. and since under the LIFO method the current cost of inventories consumed during the year are charged to cost of sales, no adjustment was required to restate to current cost the cost of sales for U.S. inventories except that required by reduc-

tion of inventory quantities (Note 9). The cost of sales related to other inventories was restated to current cost by assuming such inventories were on the LIFO method.

Current cost amounts for inventories were calculated by first comparing material prices and labor rates in effect at year end to the standard costs of materials and standard rates for labor. The ratios resulting from these comparisons were then applied to the components of inventories at standard cost.

In fiscal year end dollars, at October 31, 1980, the current cost of inventories and property, net of accumulated depreciation was $2,769.8 million and $1,776.9 million, respectively.

(c) Overall Comments on Results

Under both the constant dollar and current cost methods, the net loss is larger than that determined under the historical cost method. This is due primarily to the significant increase in depreciation and amortization expense as the high rates of inflation in recent years have substantially increased the costs to replace fixed assets. Net loss as computed under the current cost method is not necessarily an indication of what the results would be if the existing assets were replaced, because the new assets would be expected to generate operating efficiencies which would partially offset the increased depreciation expense.

Cost of sales did not change significantly due to the LIFO method used for most U.S. domestic inventories.

In accordance with SFAS No. 33, the income tax benefit is not adjusted for the increase in costs, since present tax laws do not allow deductions for inflation adjustments. As a result, the effective tax benefit rate decreases from 45.2% under the historical cost basis to 36.0% and 38.7% under the constant dollar and current cost bases, respectively.

(d) Unrealized Gain From Decline in Purchasing Power of Net Amounts Owed

When prices are increasing the holding of monetary assets (e.g., cash and receivables) results in a loss of general purchasing power. Similarly, liabilities are associated with a gain in general purchasing power because the amount of money required to settle the liabilities represents dollars of diminished purchasing power. The amount has been calculated based on the Company's average net monetary liabilities for the year multiplied by the change in the CPI-U for the year. Such amount does not represent funds available for distribution to shareholders.

Notes to Financial Statements (cont.)

(e) Increase in Current Costs of Inventories and Property, Net, Over (Under) the Increase in General Price Level

The increase in current cost of inventories and property, net, is less than the increase in the general price level because the general rate of inflation per the CPI-U outpaced the specific prices during fiscal 1980. The $317.8 million is comprised of $161.3 million and $156.5 million for inventory and property, net, respectively.

Five Year Comparison of Selected Supplementary Data

Adjusted for Changing Prices

(Millions of dollars, except per share data)

	For Years Ended October 31				
	1980	1979	1978	1977	1976
Total sales and other revenues					
- as reported	$6,342.1	$8,426.4	$6,698.4	$6,004.6	$5,526.4
- in constant dollars	6,342.1	9,573.1	8,420.0	8,094.2	7,912.2
Loss from continuing operations					
- as reported	369.6				
- in constant dollars	541.4				
- in current cost	481.9				
Loss per common share from continuing operations					
- as reported	12.02				
- in constant dollars	17.52				
- in current cost	15.62				
Dividends per common share					
- as reported	2.50	2.35	2.10	1.85	1.70
- in constant dollars	2.50	2.69	2.66	2.51	2.44
Net assets at fiscal year end (b)					
- as reported	1,846.5				
- in constant dollars	2,822.4				
- in current cost	2,677.3				
Unrealized gain from decline in purchasing power of net amounts owed	280.6				
Increase in specific prices of inventory and property over (under) the increase in general price level	(317.8)				
Market price per common share at year end					
- in historical dollars	30.125	36.50	32.625	26.75	28.375
- in constant dollars	28.710	39.20	39.320	35.10	39.640
Average Consumer Price Index for Urban Users (CPI-U)	242.1	213.1	192.6	179.6	169.1

Explanations and Comments

(a) General

All restated amounts are in average 1980 dollars as measured by the CPI-U. Certain data related to years ended on or before October 31, 1979 is omitted as it is not required by SFAS No. 33.

(b) Net Assets

Certain noncurrent nonmonetary assets (i.e., goodwill and equity in nonconsolidated subsidiaries) totaling $1,021.4 million are included in the net assets valuation at historical cost.

26. Reclassification

Certain 1979 amounts have been reclassified to conform with the presentation used in the 1980 financial statements.

Auditors' Opinion

Deloitte
Haskins+Sells

International Harvester Company,	200 East Randolph Drive
its Directors and Stockholders:	Chicago, Illinois 60601

We have examined the statements of financial condition of International Harvester Company and subsidiaries as of October 31, 1980 and 1979 and the related statements of income (loss), changes in financial position, and common stockholders' equity for the years then ended. Our examinations were made in accordance with generally accepted auditing standards and, accordingly, included such tests of the accounting records and such other auditing procedures as we considered necessary in the circumstances.

In our opinion, the accompanying financial statements present fairly the financial position of International Harvester Company and subsidiaries at October 31, 1980 and 1979 and the results of their operations and the changes in their financial position for the years then ended, in conformity with generally accepted accounting principles applied on a consistent basis.

Deloitte Haskins & Sells

December 10, 1980

Statement of Financial Reporting Responsibility

The preceding financial statements of International Harvester Company and Subsidiaries were prepared by and are the responsibility of management. The statements have been prepared in conformity with generally accepted accounting principles appropriate in the circumstances and necessarily include some amounts that are based on management's best estimates and judgments.

The Company maintains systems of internal accounting controls and procedures to provide reasonable assurance that transactions are properly recorded in the books and records, that policies and procedures are adhered to and that assets are protected from unauthorized use. The degree of internal control is determined by the optimum balance between the costs incurred and the benefits derived. The systems of internal accounting controls are supported by written policies and guidelines and are complemented by a staff of internal auditors who conduct extensive internal audits and by the selection, training and development of professional financial managers.

The financial statements have been audited by our independent public accountants, Deloitte Haskins & Sells, whose appointment was ratified by stockholder vote at the annual stockholders' meeting. They conducted a review of internal accounting controls to the extent required by generally accepted auditing standards and performed such tests of transactions and balances as they deemed necessary.

The Audit and Finance Committee of the Board of Directors, composed solely of nonmanagement directors, meets periodically with the independent public accountants, management and the internal auditors to satisfy itself that such persons are properly discharging their responsibilities regarding financial reporting and auditing. Both the independent public accountants and the internal auditors have unrestricted access to this Committee, without management present, to discuss the results of their audit work and their opinions on the adequacy of internal accounting controls and the quality of financial reporting.

REVIEW QUESTIONS

1 What are three major limitations of the balance sheet as a source of information useful to management and investors?

2 In a description of the accounting valuation assumptions, assets may be classified into two groups: monetary assets and productive resources. What is the relationship between the method of valuation applied to these two classes of assets and the measurement of revenue and expenses?

3 Sunrise Corporation issued $100 million of 13% bonds, receiving proceeds of $98 million. The bonds are callable at any time at 103. An argument has arisen over the proper valuation of these bonds in the corporation's balance sheet. One official supports $98 million; another argues for maturity value, $100 million; a third argues that $103 million is the proper amount because the bonds may be called at any time. What basic accounting principle should govern the decision? Which position do you support, and why?

4 A partnership earned $25,000, divided equally between two partners. Each partner will pay income taxes of $3,600 on the partnership income each earned. One partner argues that a liability of $7,200 should appear in the partnership balance sheet, because both partners plan to withdraw from the partnership an amount of cash sufficient to pay their income taxes. What accounting principle is at issue? What is your position, and why?

5 As a supplement to its nominal-dollar balance sheet, a company prepared a **comparative balance sheet** expressed in **constant dollars.** In the supplementary statement the amount of liabilities was the same as in the nominal-dollar balance sheet. One company officer commented, "We know that the general price level has been rising in recent years. Why should our liabilities be the same on these two balance sheets?" Explain.

6 Paul Caruso is a member of the American Institute of Certified Public Accountants. In auditing the financial statements of Elm Company, Caruso found that the company applied an accounting principle with which he agrees but which has not been accepted by the Securities and Exchange Commission or the Financial Accounting Standards Board. Assuming that the difference in treatment has a material effect on the financial statements of the company, what are the alternatives facing Caruso in preparing his audit opinion on the financial statements of Elm Company?

7 What is the distinction between an **estimated liability** and a **loss contingency?** Give an example of each.

8 How is the definition of a **current liability** related to the definition of a **current asset?**

9 What is the basis for the rule against offsetting assets and liabilities?

10 In practice, the term **reserve** has been used to describe a contra-asset account, an estimated liability, and an appropriation of retained earnings. Why are these uses of the term **reserve** in account titles objectionable? In which of the three uses is the term least misleading?

11 The financial statements prepared by a corporation include several items

which, taken together, represent the excess of assets over liabilities. What are these items and what is the term used to describe them as a group?

12 Shea Corporation issued its note payable at 12% interest to obtain a bank loan, but concurrently it issued a three-year note payable to a supplier at an annual interest rate of only 6%. Should both notes payable be recorded at their face amount? Explain.

13 Could the current liability section of a balance sheet properly include an obligation for which no specific creditor could be named and no cash payment will be required? Explain.

14 In the financial statements of a large company, would you expect to find a summary of the **significant accounting policies** followed by the company? Explain.

15 Explain the term **operating cycle** and its significance to the classification of balance sheet items as current or noncurrent.

16 Indicate circumstances under which liabilities payable within a month or two after the date of the balance sheet should be excluded from the current liabilities classification.

17 A balance sheet may be prepared in different forms. List these forms and indicate which one is most widely used.

18 What is the purpose of the **statement of stockholders' equity?**

19 a Briefly state the functions of the **statement of changes in financial position.**
  b What are the two basic approaches that may be used to prepare such a statement?

20 "The statement of changes in financial position is superfluous when a comparative balance sheet is made available to users of financial statements." Comment on the validity of this assertion.

EXERCISES

Ex. 4-1 The balance sheet of Malibu Surfboard Company contains the following group headings:

A Current assets
B Investments and restricted funds
C Plant assets
D Intangible assets
E Other assets (including deferred charges)

F Current liabilities
G Long-term debt
H Deferred credits
I Invested capital
J Retained earnings

For each of the 20 items listed on page 176, indicate the preferable balance sheet classification by using the appropriate letter from the listing above. Place brackets around the letter if the item is **subtracted** from other items in that classification.

1 Accrued interest on bonds payable
2 Convertible preferred stock
3 Mortgage note payable (outstanding for $19\frac{1}{2}$ years; due in six months)
4 Land held for price appreciation
5 Payroll bank account
6 Patents
7 Discount on bonds payable
8 Unexpired insurance
9 Deferred cost of moving home office (including employees) from New York to California
10 Leasehold improvements
11 Allowance for doubtful accounts
12 Cash surrender value of life insurance policies
13 Premium on bonds payable
14 Accumulated depreciation
15 Paid-in capital in excess of par
16 Short-term prepayments
17 Machinery retired from use and held for resale
18 Accrued payroll
19 Investment in Sears, Roebuck and Co. common stock (100 shares at cost)
20 Advance payments from customers

Ex. 4-2 Prepare a skeleton balance sheet for Zeus Company (a hypothetical corporation) in account form, showing only major classifications (approximately ten group headings).

Ex. 4-3 You have been asked to assist the chief accountant of Julie Corporation in the preparation of a balance sheet. The outline presented below represents the various classifications suggested by the chief accountant for the balance sheet; classification "L" has been added for items to be excluded from the balance sheet. (You are not asked to approve or disapprove the various classifications set forth below.)

A Current assets
B Investments and restricted funds
C Plant assets
D Intangible assets
E Other assets (including deferred charges)
F Current liabilities
G Long-term debt (including deferred credits)
H Preferred stock
I Common stock
J Paid-in capital in excess of par
K Retained earnings
L Items excluded from the balance sheet or reported in notes

Using the letters representing the various balance sheet classifications, identify each of the 20 items listed below according to the preferred balance sheet presentation. If an account is an offsetting or valuation account, place brackets around the letter.

1 Dividend payable (on Julie Corporation's preferred stock)
2 Plant assets under construction
3 Goodwill
4 Bond issuance costs
5 Land (held for possible future building site)
6 Merchandise (held by Julie Corporation on consignment)
7 Stock dividend on common stock to be distributed (stated at par)
8 Inventory of office supplies
9 Sinking fund (First National Bank, Trustee)
10 Reserve for retirement of preferred stock
11 Installment accounts receivable (average collection period 18 months)
12 Premium on preferred stock
13 Advances to officers (indefinite repayment date, noninterest-bearing)
14 Unredeemed merchandise coupons issued to customers
15 Shares of preferred stock held in treasury (at par)
16 Small tools used in factory
17 Contingent liability from notes receivable discounted at bank
18 Allowance to reduce inventories to lower of cost or market

19 Capital stock subscriptions receivable (considered currently collectible)

20 Common stock subscribed (Julie Corporation's common stock)

Ex. 4-4   From the following balances, compute **(a)** the amount of working capital and **(b)** the equity (book value) per share of capital stock:

Investment in affiliated companies (at equity)	$100,000
Cash surrender value of life insurance policies	10,000
Organization costs	5,000
Interest receivable	2,000
Other current assets	198,000
Other current liabilities	88,000
Reserve for loss contingencies (recorded by a debit to retained earnings)	50,000
Retained earnings – unappropriated	170,000
Capital stock, $5 par	300,000
Paid-in capital in excess of par	200,000
Deferred income taxes payable	40,000
Construction in progress (for customers)	150,000
Bond sinking fund	80,000
Product warranties outstanding	6,000
Creditors' accounts with debit balances	4,500

Ex. 4-5   The December 31, Year 5, balance sheet and other data for Borg Corporation are presented below. These are the only accounts in Borg's balance sheet. Amounts indicated by a question mark (?) can be computed from the other data given.

BORG CORPORATION
Balance Sheet
December 31, Year 5

Assets

Cash	$ 25,000
Accounts receivable (net)	?
Inventories	?
Plant assets (net)	294,000
Total assets	$432,000

Liabilities & Stockholders' Equity

Accounts payable	$?
Income taxes payable (current)	25,000
Long-term debt	?
Common stock, $1 par	300,000
Retained earnings (deficit)	?
Total liabilities & stockholders' equity	$432,000

The following additional information also is available:

Current ratio at end of Year 5	1.5 to 1
Total liabilities divided by total stockholders' equity at end of Year 5 .	0.8
Turnover of ending inventories (based on sales) for Year 5	15 times
Turnover of ending inventories (based on cost of goods sold) for Year 5	10.5 times
Gross profit on sales for Year 5	$315,000

Instructions   Compute the amount of each of the following on December 31, Year 5:

a Inventories
b Accounts receivable (net)
c Accounts payable
d Retained earnings (deficit)
e Long-term debt

Ex. 4-6   The stockholders' equity of Thomasville Corporation on June 30, Year 2, was as follows:

Capital stock, $10 par	$ 200,000
Paid-in capital in excess of par	225,000
Retained earnings	610,000
Total stockholders' equity	$1,035,000

The transactions affecting stockholders' equity for the year ended June 30, Year 3, are:

(1) An additional 5,000 shares of capital stock were issued at $28 a share.
(2) Dividends declared amounted to $100,000.
(3) Net income amounted to $195,000.

Prepare a statement of stockholders' equity for the year ended June 30, Year 3.

Ex. 4-7   On January 1, Year 10, Gerald Company and Jackson Company each had $100,000 of excess cash. Gerald Company kept the money in a checking account throughout Year 10. In contrast, Jackson Company purchased a parcel of land for $1 million, paying $100,000 down and issuing a note for $900,000 due in three years. The general price level increased from 100 to 120 during Year 10.

Compute the unrealized purchasing power gain or loss in Year 10 for each company. Ignore interest and income taxes.

Ex. 4-8   Listed below are selected account balances of Equity Services, Inc., on December 31, Year 1:

Advances from customers	$ 15,000
Surplus equipment held for resale	25,600
Bond sinking fund	60,000
Bonds payable	750,000
Premium on bonds payable	15,500
Installment notes payable (due $100,000 per year)	600,000
Accrued payroll	72,000
Cash surrender value of life insurance policies	42,100
Unamortized bond issuance costs	21,100
Advance to supplier (12% interest, no due date)	100,000

Prepare the Investments and Long-Term Debt sections of Equity's balance sheet on December 31, Year 1.

SHORT CASES FOR ANALYSIS AND DECISION

Case 4-1   The complete set of financial statements issued by Jamie Corporation for the year ended August 31, Year 5, is presented on page 179.

JAMIE CORPORATION
Statement of Income and Retained Earnings
For Year Ended August 31, Year 5
(in thousands of dollars)

Product sales (net of $850,000 sales returns and allowances)		$10,700
Cost of goods sold		8,700
Gross profit on sales		$ 2,000
Operating expenses:		
Selling expenses	$1,500	
General and administrative expenses	940	2,440
Operating loss		$ (440)
Interest expense		150
Net loss		$ (590)
Retained earnings, Sept. 1, Year 4		1,700
Subtotal		$ 1,110
Dividends:		
Cash — $1 a share	$ 40	
Stock — 6% of shares outstanding	24	64
Retained earnings, Aug. 31, Year 5		$ 1,046
Average market price of capital stock during the year		$ 15

JAMIE CORPORATION
Balance Sheet
August 31, Year 5
(In thousands of dollars)
Assets

Cash		$ 103
Securities, at cost, which approximates market value.		54
Accounts receivable (net of $65,000 allowance)		917
Inventories (at cost)		775
Plant assets	$3,200	
Less: Accumulated depreciation	1,475	1,725
Prepayments and other assets		125
Total assets		$3,699

Liabilities & Stockholders' Equity

Accounts payable		$ 221
Accrued taxes payable		62
Bank loans and long-term debt		1,580
Total liabilities		$1,863
Capital stock, $10 par (authorized 50,000 shares, issued and		
outstanding 42,400 shares)	$ 424	
Paid-in capital in excess of par	366	
Retained earnings	1,046	1,836
Total liabilities & stockholders' equity		$3,699

Instructions List and briefly discuss deficiencies and omissions in Jamie Corporation's financial statements. Consider each deficiency or omission separately, and do not consider the cumulative effect of the deficiencies and omissions. There are no arithmetical errors in the financial statements. Assume that Jamie Corporation is not required to report constant-dollar and current-cost data under *FASB Statement No. 33.*

Case 4-2 Kelvin Chen, a consulting engineer, developed and patented a device for measuring temperatures encountered in space travel. He offered to sell the patent rights to Dymo Company. A contract was signed under which Dymo Company acquired the patent rights and gave Chen in exchange $500,000 cash and a note for $500,000. The note provided for payment only in shares of common stock of Dymo Company, at the rate of 4,000 shares of $25 par common stock a year for each of the next five years.

The accountant for Dymo Company included $100,000 among the current liabilities, labeled Note Payable in Common Stock, and $400,000 among the long-term liabilities similarly labeled. The accountant attached a note to the financial statements explaining the terms of the contract with Chen.

The president of Dymo Company, who was about to present the company's financial statements to a bank in support of a loan application, objected to this treatment, contending that the company's liabilities were overstated. The accountant replied that liabilities were obligations to convey something of value, and that the company's common stock had a par value of $25 a share.

Instructions
a Discuss the appropriate balance sheet treatment of the note payable in common stock, giving reasons for your conclusions.
b Suppose that under the terms of the note, Chen had the option of accepting each year $100,000 cash or 4,000 shares of common stock. Would this change your answer? Why?

Case 4-3 Doris Tang owns a resort located on an excellent fishing lake. Her busy season begins May 15 and extends through mid-fall. During the winter she engaged a contractor to build a boathouse for $50,000. The contract called for completion by May 15, because the resort was completely reserved for the week of May 15 to 22, the opening week of the fishing season. Because the completion date was so important to Tang, she specified in the contract that if the construction were not completed by May 15 the price would be adjusted downward by a penalty of $400 a day, until completed.

The construction was not completed until June 9, at which time Tang paid the contractor $40,000, deducting $400 for each of the 25 days of delay. Tang is convinced that she lost goodwill because her facilities were inadequate and that several of her clients reduced their stay because the facilities were still under construction.

In her balance sheet prepared at September 30, the end of her fiscal year, Tang included the boathouse at $50,000. Included in her revenue was an item "Penalty payments received in lieu of lost revenue, $10,000."

The auditor who examined Tang's balance sheet objected to this treatment and insisted that the boathouse be recorded at its actual cost, $40,000. Tang stated that she could not understand the logic of this position. "Accounting principles are out of tune with reality," she complained. "What if the contract had been 125 days late and the boathouse had cost me nothing; would you record in my balance sheet that I had no asset? I lost at least $400 a day in revenue because of the construction delay."

Instructions At what amount should the boathouse be reported in the balance sheet on September 30? (You may ignore any question of depreciation from June 9 to September 30.) Explain your position in terms of generally accepted accounting principles.

PROBLEMS

4-1   The following information (listed in random order) is available for Sanford Company on December 31, Year 5:

Income taxes payable (current)	$ 36,625
Cash surrender value of life insurance policies	10,800
Accounts receivable (net of $10,000 advances from customers)	92,000
Allowance for doubtful accounts	5,800
Cash on hand	800
Cash in National Bank of Toledo	44,025
Cash in Bank of Trenton	26,000
Short-term prepayments	3,500
Retained earnings	322,300
Current installment of long-term debt	20,000
10% long-term note payable (excluding current installment of $20,000)	230,000
Accounts payable	220,000
Inventories, at fifo cost	332,600
Short-term investments (at cost, market value, $58,500)	51,800
Buildings and equipment	400,000
Accumulated depreciation	109,600
Paid-in capital in excess of par	155,200
Organization costs	16,000
Capital stock, $2 par, authorized 100,000 shares	60,000
Long-term advance to affiliated company	50,000
Patents (net of accumulated amortization of $18,950)	32,000
Land	100,000

Instructions   Use the information given to prepare a balance sheet in report form. Use two money columns with rulings as necessary under subtotals. Notes accompanying the balance sheet are not required.

4-2   The following memorandum contains information concerning the financial position of Swanson Airlines, Inc., on December 31, Year 10:

> Our plant assets consist of aircraft and other flight equipment acquired at a cost of $10,880,000, on which we have recognized depreciation to date of $2,431,200. In addition, we have one other aircraft which has been withdrawn from use and is being held for resale. The carrying amount of this aircraft is $750,000, and we are currently negotiating for its sale at a price of $600,000. The negotiations for this sale soon will be completed.
>
> When we acquired Commerce Parcel Service we paid $550,000 for goodwill, of which $348,000 has been amortized since acquisition.
>
> We have cash in checking accounts amounting to $380,600, and certificates of deposit for $801,600, including accrued interest at 15% a year. The general ledger controlling account for accounts receivable shows a debit balance of $1,660,000, but this total includes a credit balance of $120,000 from a customer who made an advance payment. The allowance for doubtful accounts amounts to $44,400. Our inventories are carried at average cost, and amount to $91,200. Short-term prepayments amount to $42,000. The cash surrender value of life insurance policies, naming the company as beneficiary, amounts to $147,600.

Among our liabilities are $3,000,000 in 8% long-term notes payable, of which $300,000 is due within the coming year. Accounts payable total $780,000, accrued liabilities $100,000, and income taxes payable $385,200.

We have 5 million shares of $1 par capital stock authorized, of which 1,440,000 shares were issued at a price of $5 a share. Our earnings, which we have reinvested in the business, total $864,200.

Instructions Use the above information to prepare a balance sheet in report form. Use two money columns, with rulings as necessary under subtotals. Notes to accompany the balance sheet are not required.

4-3 A condensed income statement prepared by Summit Company for the year ended March 31, Year 2, follows:

SUMMIT COMPANY

Income Statement

For Year Ended March 31, Year 2

Sales (net)		$900,000
Costs and expenses:		
Cost of goods sold	$620,000	
Depreciation	28,000	
Amortization of intangible assets	7,000	
Other operating expenses	112,000	
Income taxes (including deferred income taxes of $10,000)	45,000	812,000
Net income		$ 88,000
Earnings per share		$ 4.40

Additional information for year ended March 31, Year 2
(1) Dividends of $50,000 were declared and paid.
(2) Equipment of $40,000 was acquired in exchange for common stock.
(3) Equipment was sold for $14,500, its carrying amount.
(4) The common stock was split 2 for 1.
(5) Long-term investments were acquired for $60,000 cash.
(6) Treasury stock was acquired for $8,500 cash.
(7) Cash received as proceeds from long-term borrowing was $100,000.
(8) The working capital at the beginning of the year was $425,400; working capital at the end of the year was $554,400.

Instructions Prepare a statement of changes in financial position on a working capital concept for the year ended March 31, Year 2. Use the form illustrated on page 151. Do not list the composition of working capital, because the information for this section of the statement is not available.

4-4 The financial position of Space Laboratories, Inc., on June 30, Year 4, is presented in highly condensed form on page 183.

SPACE LABORATORIES, INC.
Balance Sheet
June 30, Year 4

Assets		Liabilities & Stockholders' Equity	
Current assets	$1,500,000	Current liabilities	$ 560,000
Noncurrent assets (net) . . .	6,860,000	Long-term debt	2,500,000
		Paid-in capital	3,800,000
		Retained earnings	1,500,000
		Total liabilities &	
Total assets	$8,360,000	stockholders' equity. . .	$8,360,000

    Comments taken from an auditor's notes, describing certain components of the balance sheet, are listed below. Some of these comments indicate that the accountant for Space Laboratories has handled certain items improperly.

(1) Included in long-term debt is a loan payable of $250,000 due on April 30, Year 5.

(2) A $125,000 dividend to be distributed in the form of the company's common stock is included in current liabilities.

(3) Included in current liabilities is a loss contingency of $50,000 for possible legal suits which may be filed. This amount was recorded by a debit to Retained Earnings.

(4) Included in current assets is $90,000 in cash surrender value of life insurance on the lives of company officers. Included in long-term debt is an $80,000 loan made against this cash surrender value. The company intends to renew this borrowing annually at the maturity date of the loan.

(5) Discount on long-term debt of $161,500 is included in noncurrent assets.

(6) Included in long-term debt is a $500,000 appropriation of retained earnings for retirement of preferred stock.

(7) The company purchased 11,000 shares of its common stock for $400,000. This amount is equal to the par value of the stock and is included in noncurrent assets.

(8) Rent received in advance, $74,800, is included in retained earnings.

(9) A cash dividend of $80,000 declared on June 15, Year 4, and payable on July 22, Year 4, has not been recorded in the accounting records.

(10) A fully depreciated plant asset was sold for $40,000, and the proceeds were credited to the Equipment account.

(11) Deposits of $25,000 made with suppliers for goods ordered have been netted against the balance in the accounts payable controlling account.

(12) An investment in 18% of the common stock of an affiliated company is included in current assets at a cost of $800,000.

(13) Research and development costs of $417,500, incurred in developing new products, have been debited to expense. The new products are expected to be successful revenue producers for at least three years.

Instructions
a List the dollar amounts of each of the six categories of the company's balance sheet on the first line of a six-column working paper. On separate lines below show the effect of any necessary corrections to the accountant's figures as a result of the information contained in the auditor's notes. Identify each correction with the related number above. Show as an end result the corrected balance sheet data on June 30, Year 4. If the information contained in any of the auditor's notes does not indicate an improper treatment, explain why no adjustment is necessary in each case. Ignore any possible effect on income taxes as a result of your corrections.

b Would your appraisal of the company's financial position be changed as a result of the revised data? Explain.

4-5   The controller of Portillo Corporation must prepare a statement of working capital on June 30, the close of the company's current fiscal year. The purpose of this statement is to demonstrate that the company's working capital exceeds $750,000, the amount Portillo agreed to maintain under the terms of a loan contract, which defined **working capital** as the excess of current assets over current liabilities. The statement below, based on information taken from the accounting records on June 30, was prepared by the assistant to the controller:

PORTILLO CORPORATION

Statement of Working Capital

June 30, Current Year

Current assets:		
Cash on hand and in banks		$ 157,500
Notes and securities		480,000
Receivables		542,500
Inventories and prepayments		562,300
Total current assets		$1,742,300
Current liabilities:		
Notes and accounts payable	$411,530	
Payroll taxes and pensions payable	495,000	
Reserve for loss contingencies	200,000	
Total current liabilities		1,106,530
Working capital, June 30, current year		$ 635,770

The controller, after some investigation, made the following notes relative to the items included in the above statement:

(1) *Notes and securities.* Includes $280,000 of notes receivable, of which $100,000 has been discounted at a bank. Also, $250,000 face amount of U.S. Treasury notes (current market value $236,000) purchased for $216,000, on which $8,500 of interest has accrued since the last interest date. Portillo holds $84,000 in five-year notes receivable from a subsidiary company, on which $5,200 of interest is accrued at June 30 and is payable annually.

(2) *Receivables.* A single controlling account is used for receivables. The balance of the controlling account, $542,500, includes trade accounts receivable of $394,040, a current receivable from a subsidiary company of $40,000, current advances to employees of $28,460, and an installment note receivable of $80,000 received in payment for the sale of a warehouse, due in four installments of $20,000 a year; accrued interest on this note at June 30 was $4,800. Certain customers have credit balances in their accounts, totaling $35,000, because they have made advances prior to the shipment of merchandise ordered. Of the trade accounts receivable, $12,000 are worthless and should be written off; it is estimated that $20,000 of the remainder will prove uncollectible.

(3) *Inventories and prepayments.* The inventory of merchandise on June 30 on a lifo cost basis amounted to $320,750; its current replacement cost is estimated to be $471,000. Included in the $562,300 balance shown in the above statement is $98,000 of equipment that is rented to customers and $19,750 of merchandise on order for delivery in six months, the full cost of which is included in accounts payable. Also included in this balance are short-term prepayments of $94,800 and $29,000 representing a defalcation loss, of which $25,000 is expected to be recovered from an insurance company.

(4) *Current liabilities.* Current accounts payable amount to $261,530, and the company owes $150,000 on a 90-day note payable to the bank, on which unre-

corded interest of $900 has accrued. Amounts withheld from employees for various payroll taxes amount to $70,000; the company's required contribution of $28,700 for such taxes has not been recorded. A provision for employee pensions amounts to $425,000, of which $51,500 will be paid in the coming fiscal year. The reserve for loss contingencies was set up to provide for **possible** losses that may arise from the obsolescence of plant assets. The reserve was established by a debit to Retained Earnings.

Instructions

a On the basis of this information, prepare a corrected statement of working capital of Portillo Corporation on June 30 of the current year. List current assets in detail, followed by a detailed list of current liabilities. Provide supporting computations to show how specific items are determined.

b Is the company complying with the terms of the loan contract as to the maintenance of working capital?

c Compute the current ratio on June 30 of the current year.

4-6 Presented below is an alphabetical list of account balances taken from the ledger of Nogales Corporation on December 31, Year 2:

Accounts payable	$ 743,400
Accounts receivable	1,016,000
Accumulated depreciation of buildings	1,104,000
Accumulated depreciation of leased equipment	220,000
Allowance for doubtful accounts	36,000
Buildings (at cost)	3,951,800
Cash	164,100
Cash surrender value of life insurance policies	115,000
Common stock, $50 par, authorized 100,000 shares	2,500,000
Dividends, common stock	125,000
Dividends, preferred stock	45,500
Goodwill (net)	62,400
Income summary (credit balance)	208,000
Income taxes payable	92,600
Insurance claim receivable (approved by insurance company)	250,000
Inventories (lower of fifo cost or market)	1,146,000
Land	800,000
Leased equipment under capital leases	1,400,000
Note payable, 9%, due Oct. 1, Year 10	1,000,000
Obligation under capital leases (including current portion of $120,000)	1,050,000
Paid-in capital in excess of par, common stock	295,000
Preferred stock, 7%, $100 par, authorized 10,000 shares	650,000
Premium on note payable	30,000
Retained earnings, Jan 1, Year 2	1,344,800
Short-term investments (market value $205,000)	200,000
Unamortized issue costs on note payable	10,000
Unearned rent revenue	12,000

Instructions

a Prepare a classified balance sheet on December 31, Year 2.

b Prepare a statement of retained earnings for the year ended December 31, Year 2.

4-7   On January 2, Year 8, Maria Alamo and Jean Mears organized a partnership known as Executive Assistance. Alamo, who had been in business as a single proprietor for several years, invested data-processing equipment with a current fair value of $50,000. This equipment originally had cost Alamo $60,000 and had been depreciated by $21,000 in her accounting records. Mears invested $40,000 cash, a set of data-compiling forms which she had developed and which the partners agreed were worth $6,000, and land valued at $27,200. The partners agreed to share net income or loss equally.

      The partnership immediately acquired a small computer for $250,000, paying $25,000 down and issuing a 12% note for the balance of $225,000. This balance is payable in installments of $45,000 a year plus interest. The first payment on this note is due on January 2, Year 9.

      During Year 8, the partnership collected $116,500 for computer rentals and had receivables of $32,200 at the end of the year. Mears borrowed $4,000 from the partnership on October 1 to meet emergency medical bills. She agreed to pay this back at the rate of $200 a month, with accured interest at 10% on the unpaid balance of the loan starting on April 1, Year 9.

      The partnership paid operating expenses in the amount of $36,250 during Year 8, including $650 rent paid in advance for January, Year 9. Alamo withdrew $1,000 a month from the partnership, and Mears withdrew $1,250 a month. The new computer is depreciated by the straight-line method (no residual value) at the rate of 10% a year, and the used equipment at the rate of 20% a year. The data-compiling forms developed by Mears were to be amortized over a four-year period.

      The partnership had unpaid bills for operating expenses of $5,500 on December 31, Year 8. No provision for doubtful accounts is required.

Instructions

a   Prepare three separate working papers to compute the (1) cash receipts and cash payments, concluding with the balance of cash on December 31, Year 8; (2) amount of equipment on December 31, Year 8, and depreciation for Year 8; and (3) the amounts of revenue and expenses for Year 8, concluding with the net income for the year ended December 31, Year 8. (Accrue interest on the note issued for the purchase of the computer for a full year.)

b   Prepare a balance sheet on December 31, Year 8, and a statement of partners' capital for the year ended December 31, Year 8. Incorporate the amounts determined in **a** in the appropriate financial statements.

4-8   A condensed balance sheet of Capital Resources Corporation at the end of the current year is shown below:

CAPITAL RESOURCES CORPORATION
Balance Sheet
End of Current Year

Assets		Liabilities & Stockholders' Equity	
Cash	$100,000	Current liabilities	$142,000
Receivables (net)	138,000	Long-term debt	350,000
Inventories	78,000	Capital stock, $1 par	225,000
Plant assets (net)	650,000	Retained earnings	249,000
		Total liabilities &	
Total assets	$966,000	stockholders' equity	$966,000

During a discussion by the board of directors concerning the above balance sheet, Director Clyde Suttle raised a question as to what effect inflation had on the financial position of the company. He pointed out that the general price level had **doubled** since the original issuance of the company's capital stock and that there had been a substantial increase in the general price level after the company had acquired many of its plant assets.

The president felt that an answer to this question would require some study, and therefore asked the controller of the company to restate the company's balance sheet on the basis of constant dollars as of the end of the year, using a general price index to measure the change in the purchasing power of the dollar. After considerable analysis, the controller determined that the carrying amount of plant assets stated in constant dollars would be $910,000 and that the equivalent of $90,000 in constant dollars had been invested in inventories. Realized retained earnings stated in constant dollars were computed by the controller to be $192,000.

Instructions

a Using the information compiled by the controller, restate the balance sheet of Capital Resources Corporation in terms of constant dollars. Prepare a comparative balance sheet showing both nominal-dollar and constant-dollar amounts.

b Write a report to the board of directors explaining the significance of the supplementary data expressed in constant dollars which appear in the comparative balance sheet prepared in *a*.

5 ACCOUNTING APPLICATIONS OF PRESENT AND FUTURE VALUES

Ignoring the effects of inflation, a dollar today is worth more than the assurance of receiving a dollar a year from now. In other words, we would all prefer to receive a given sum of money now rather than at some future date. This preference rests on the **time value of money.** We use the term **interest** to describe the price charged for using money over time. When we make payments for the time value of money, we incur **interest expense.** When we receive payments for the time value of money, we earn **interest revenue.**

Business decisions often involve receiving money or other assets **now** in exchange for a promise to make payments after one or more periods. A common example is a decision to borrow money. Another important group of business decisions involves investing money now in order to receive money, goods, or services in future periods.

Inflows of dollars at various future dates cannot be added together as if they were of equal value. These future dollar inflows must be restated at their **present values** before they are aggregated. The concept of the time value of money tells us that the more distant dollar inflows have a smaller present value than dollar inflows to be received within a shorter time span.

Similar reasoning applies to dollar outflows. Before we can add together dollar outflows at various future dates, we must restate these outflows at their present value. The more distant the date of a dollar outflow, the smaller is its present value.

As a very simple example of this concept of present value, assume that you are trying to sell your car and you receive offers from three prospective buyers. Buyer A offers you a price of $4,000 to be paid immediately. Buyer B offers you a price of $4,100 to be paid to you one year from now. Buyer C offers the highest price, $4,600, but this offer provides that payment will be made after five years. Assuming that the offers by B and C involve absolutely no credit risk, which offer would

188

you accept? You should accept the offer of $4,000 to be received immediately, because the **present value** of both the other offers is less than $4,000. If you were to invest $4,000 today, even at a very modest rate of interest such as 5%, your investment would grow and be worth more than $4,100 in one year and more than $4,600 in five years.

This example suggests that the timing of receipts and payments has an important effect on the economic worth and the accounting values of both assets and liabilities. Consequently, investment and borrowing decisions should be made only after a careful analysis of the relative present values of the prospective cash inflows and outflows.

Accountants find many situations in which an objective measurement of a transaction depends upon the present value of future cash inflows and outflows. For example, the amount received for a bond issue by the issuing enterprise reflects the present value of the issuer's promise to make a series of future interest payments and to repay the principal when the bonds reach maturity. Some other examples of the need for measuring present or future dollar flows are listed below:

1 Measuring and reporting capital leases and pension plans
2 Measuring and reporting notes receivable and notes payable when the interest rate is not specified or differs from the current fair interest rate
3 Measuring and reporting plant assets acquired by issuance of long-term debt when the interest rate is not specified or differs from the current fair interest rate
4 Accumulating sinking funds for retirement of long-term debt or preferred stock
5 Computing periodic depreciation under the sinking fund and the annuity methods of depreciation

Measuring the values implicit in these transactions involves the use of compound interest principles. In this chapter we shall illustrate the basic principles of compound interest in a format which will be useful throughout this book. We shall stress the use of compound interest tables (presented in the Appendix at the end of the book) as a basis for solving a wide range of financial accounting problems.

Simple interest and compound interest

Interest is the growth in a principal sum representing the fee charged for the use of money for a given time period. Because the concept of economic earnings is periodic, we typically think of return on investment in terms of return per year.

Simple interest is the return on a principal sum for one time period. We may also think of simple interest as a return for more than one time period if we assume that the interest itself does not earn a return, but this kind of situation occurs rarely in the business world. Simple interest usually is applicable only to short-term investment and borrowing transactions involving a time span of one year or less.

Compound interest is the return on a principal sum for two or more time periods, assuming that the interest in each time period is added to the principal sum at the end of that period and earns a return in all subsequent periods. Because many important investment and borrowing transactions involve more than one time period, business executives evaluate investment opportunities in terms of periodic returns, each of which is assumed to be reinvested to yield additional returns.

Because interest generally is expressed in terms of the annual rate, the simple interest formula is $I = prt$ (interest = principal × annual rate of interest × number of years or fraction of a year that interest accrues). For example, interest on $10,000 at 8% for one year is expressed as follows:

Simple interest formula

$$I = prt$$

$$I = \$10,000 \times 0.08 \times 1$$

$$I = \$800$$

In contrast, if interest were compounded quarterly for one year, the total interest would be $824.32, determined as follows:

Compounding interest quarterly

Period	Principal	× Rate	× Time =	Compound interest	Accumulated amount
1st quarter	$10,000.00	× 0.08	× $\frac{1}{4}$	$200.00	$10,200.00
2d quarter	10,200.00	× 0.08	× $\frac{1}{4}$	204.00	10,404.00
3d quarter	10,404.00	× 0.08	× $\frac{1}{4}$	208.08	10,612.08
4th quarter	10,612.08	× 0.08	× $\frac{1}{4}$	212.24	10,824.32
Interest on $10,000 at 8% compounded quarterly for one year				$824.32	

In the computation of compound interest, the accumulated amount at the end of each period becomes the principal sum for purposes of computing interest for the following period.

Amount of 1

The accumulated **amount** (small a) of a single sum invested at compound interest can be computed period by period by a series of multiplications, as illustrated above for the $10,000 invested for one year at 8% compounded quarterly. If n is used to represent the number of periods that interest is to be compounded, i is used to represent the interest *per period,* and p is the principal sum invested, the *series of multipli-cations* to compute the accumulated amount a in the example above can be determined as follows:

Long-hand method for amount of 1

$$a = p(1 + i)^n$$

$$a = \$10,000 \, (1 + 0.02)^4$$

$$a = \$10,000 \, (1.02)(1.02)(1.02)(1.02)$$

$$a = \underline{\underline{\$10,824.32}}$$

It is important to observe that i is the *rate of interest for each time period* that interest is *compounded.* For example, the formulas for the compound amount a of 1 at 12%, assuming different compounding patterns, are:

12% interest at different compounding patterns

Interest at 12% per year compounded annually $= a_{\overline{n}|\,i} = (1 + 0.12)^1$

Interest at 12% per year compounded semiannually $= a_{\overline{n}|\,i} = (1 + 0.06)^2$

Interest at 12% per year compounded quarterly $= a_{\overline{n}|\,i} = (1 + 0.03)^4$

Interest at 12% per year compounded monthly $= a_{\overline{n}|\,i} = (1 + 0.01)^{12}$

The symbol $a_{\overline{n}|i}$ is the amount to which 1 will accumulate at i rate of interest per period for n periods. This symbol is read as "small a angle n at i." If annual interest of 8% is compounded quarterly for one year, the rate of interest per time period (one-fourth of a year) would be 2%, and the number of interest periods n would be 4. Thus, the amount of 1 for-mula at 8% compounded quarterly for one year is:

Amount of 1 formula

$$a_{\overline{n}|\,i} = (1 + i)^n \quad \text{or} \quad a_{\overline{4}|\,2\%} = (1 + 0.02)^4$$

Tables are available which give the value of $a_{\overline{n}|\,i}$. Use of these tables involves reference to a line showing the number of periods and a col-umn showing the rate of interest per period. For example, Table 1 in Ap-pendix A in the back of this book shows that $a_{\overline{4}|\,2\%}$ is equal to 1.082432, which means that $10,000 would accumulate to $10,824.32 in one year at 8% compounded quarterly. Compound interest tables generally are prepared for $1 and *the dollar sign is omitted.* This provides a conve-nient means of finding the accumulated amount of any number of dollars by multiplying the amount of 1 at i interest for n periods by the number of dollars involved in a problem.

Summary and Examples The amount of 1 formula, $a_{\overline{n}|\,i}$, is used to compute the future amount a of a principal sum p which earns compound interest at a specified interest rate i per period for n periods. A diagram for the amount of 1 is shown below:

Diagram for amount of 1

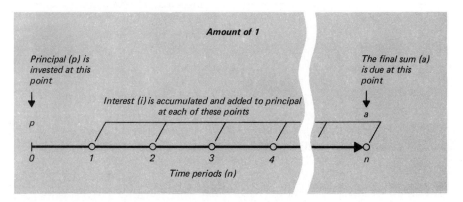

Example 1: Finding the interest rate If $1,000 is deposited at compound interest on January 1, Year 1, and the amount on deposit on December 31, Year 10, is $1,806.11, what was the semiannual interest rate accruing on the deposit?

Answer The amount of 1 for 20 periods at an unstated rate of interest is 1.80611 ($1,806.11 ÷ $1,000 = 1.80611). Reference to Table 1 in the Appendix at the end of the book indicates that 1.806111 is the amount of 1 for 20 periods at 3%. Therefore, the semiannual interest rate was 3%.

Example 2: Amount accumulated when interest rate changes Marie deposited $10,000 in a fund which will earn 8% interest compounded quarterly for four years, and 10% interest compounded semiannually for the next six years. How much will Marie have in the fund at the end of 10 years?

Answer Using Table 1 in the Appendix at the end of the book, we have the following amount at the end of four years at 8% interest compounded quarterly:

$10,000 $\times a_{\overline{16}|\,2\%} =$ $10,000 $(1 + 0.02)^{16}$
$10,000 $\times a_{\overline{16}|\,2\%} =$ $10,000 (1.372786)   or $13,728

And for the next six years at 10% compounded semiannually, we have:

$13,728 $\times$ $a_{\overline{12}|\,5\%}$ = $13,728 $(1\,+\,0.05)^{12}$
$13,728 $\times$ $a_{\overline{12}|\,5\%}$ = $13,728 (1.795856)   or $24,654

In this case the interest rate **per period** changed at the end of four years from 2% to 5%. Therefore, it was first necessary to compute the amount on deposit at the end of four years ($13,728) and then to accumulate compound interest on this sum for six additional years at 10% compounded semiannually.

Present value of 1

In financial accounting many measurement and valuation problems require the computation of the discounted present value of a principal sum to be paid or received at a fixed future date. As the diagram below illustrates, the present value of 1 is closely related to the procedures used to compute the amount of 1:

Diagram for present value of 1

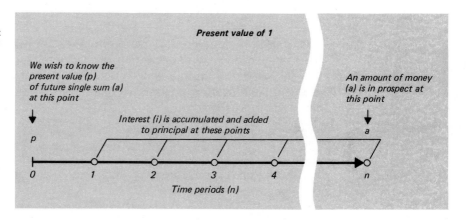

From this diagram we see that finding the present value of a single future sum is a **reversal** of the process of finding the amount to which a present sum will accumulate. For example, we have seen that since $(1\,+\,0.02)^4$ = 1.082432, the principal sum p of $10,000 will accumulate to $10,824.32 in one year if interest is compounded quarterly. To find the principal p that must be invested now at 8% compounded quarterly to give us $10,824.32 in one year, we can proceed as follows: We know that $a = p(1 + i)^n$. If we solve for p by dividing both sides of the equation by $(1 + i)^n$, we have the following:

$$p = \frac{a}{(1 + i)^n}$$

And if we substitute $(1 + 0.02)^4$ for $(1 + i)^n$ and $10,824.32 for a, we have

$$p = \frac{\$10,824.32}{(1 + 0.02)^4} = \frac{\$10,824.32}{1.082432} = \underline{\underline{\$10,000}}$$

It should be clear that we can determine the present value p of any future amount a by dividing the future amount a by $(1 + i)^n$. Thus, the formula for the present value of 1 due in n periods at i rate of interest per period is:

Present value of 1 formula

$$p_{\overline{n}|\,i} = \frac{1}{(1 + i)^n}$$

The symbol $p_{\overline{n}|\,i}$ is read "small p angle n at i." The present value of 1 formula at 8% compounded quarterly for one year is:

$$p_{\overline{4}|\,2\%} = \frac{1}{(1 + 0.02)^4}$$

It should be apparent that a table showing values for $1 \div (1 + i)^n$ at different interest rates i and different number of periods n would be useful. Table 2 in the Appendix at the end of the book provides such values. The value for $p_{\overline{4}|\,2\%}$ in this table is 0.923845; therefore, the present value of $10,824.32 discounted for one year at 8% compounded quarterly also can be computed as follows:

$$\$10,824.32 \times 0.923845 = \underline{\underline{\$10,000}}$$

Summary and Examples The present value of 1 formula, $p_{\overline{n}|\,i}$, is used to compute the discounted present value p of a given sum a due at some future date, discounted at a specified interest rate i per period for n periods.

Example 1: Finding the approximate interest rate by interpolation If the present value of $100,000 discounted at an unstated rate of interest for 20 periods is $64,162.10, what was the approximate interest rate per period used in computing this present value?

Answer From Table 2 in the Appendix at the end of the book, we can obtain the following present values for different interest rates:

Estimating the rate of interest

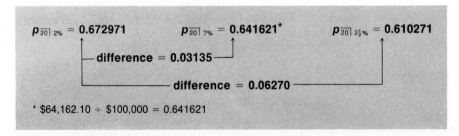

$p_{\overline{20}|\,2\%} = 0.672971 \qquad p_{\overline{20}|\,?\%} = 0.641621^* \qquad p_{\overline{20}|\,2\frac{1}{2}\%} = 0.610271$

difference = 0.03135

difference = 0.06270

* $64,162.10 \div $100,000 = 0.641621

The unknown interest rate is exactly at the midpoint between 2% and $2\frac{1}{2}$%. Therefore, the approximate interest rate per period is computed as follows:

$$2\% + \tfrac{1}{2}\% \left(\frac{0.03135}{0.06270}\right) \quad \text{or} \quad 2\% + (\tfrac{1}{2}\% \times \tfrac{1}{2}) = \underline{\underline{2\tfrac{1}{4}\%}}$$

Example 2: Present value when interest rate changes   Dudley wants to deposit a lump sum in a savings account at the beginning of Year 1 so that he will have $50,000 at the end of Year 6. How much must he deposit at the beginning of Year 1 if the interest rate is 6% compounded semiannually for the first three years and 8% compounded quarterly for the next three years?

Answer   Using Table 2 in the Appendix at the end of the book, we have the following present value at the beginning of Year 4 of the $50,000 required at the end of Year 6:

$$\$50{,}000 \times p_{\overline{12}|\ 2} = \$50{,}000 \times 0.788493 = \$39{,}425$$

And at the beginning of Year 1, we have:

$$\$39{,}425 \times p_{\overline{6}|\ 3\%} = \$39{,}425 \times 0.837484 = \underline{\$33{,}018}$$

Thus, Dudley must deposit $33,018 at the beginning of Year 1 to have $50,000 at the end of Year 6. Because the interest rate per period changed at the beginning of Year 4, it was necessary to prepare the solution in two separate steps.

Relationship of amount of 1 and present value of 1 to *n* and *i*

In dealing with computations of accumulations and present values, it is useful to have some general idea of relationships as a basis for verifying the reasonableness of results. We can reason, for example, that $a_{\overline{n}|\ i}$ should grow **larger** for increasing rates of interest *i* and for an increasing number of periods *n*, because the longer a principal sum accumulates interest the larger it grows, and the higher the rate of interest the larger the future amount. The reverse situation is true of present values. The longer the time period *n* or the higher the rate of interest *i*, the **smaller** is the present value of any future sum. This squares with our intuition that a far-distant prospect is worth less than one in the near future, and that the higher the rate of interest that can be earned on a present-dollar amount, the less valuable is the prospect of receiving an amount of money in the future.

Annuities

Many measurement situations in financial accounting involve periodic deposits, receipts, withdrawals, or payments (called **rents**), with interest at a stated rate compounded at the time that each rent is paid or received. These situations are considered **annuities** if all the following conditions are present:

1 The periodic rents are equal in amount.
2 The time period between rents is constant, such as a year, a quarter of a year, or a month.
3 The interest rate per time period remains constant.
4 The interest is compounded at the end of each time period.

When rents are paid or received at the end of each period and the total amount on deposit is determined at the time the final rent is made, the annuity is an **ordinary annuity** (or **annuity in arrears**). Other types of annuities, that is, an **annuity due** (or **annuity in advance**) and a **deferred annuity,** are defined and illustrated in subsequent sections of this chapter.

Amount of ordinary annuity of 1

The amount of an **ordinary annuity** (or **annuity in arrears**) consists of the sum of the equal periodic rents and compound interest on the rents **immediately after the final rent.** The amount A to which an ordinary annuity of n rents of R dollars each will accumulate in n periods at i rate of interest per period is illustrated below:

Diagram for amount of ordinary annuity

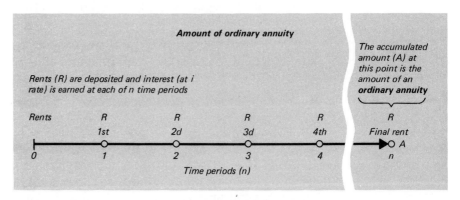

The amount A of an ordinary annuity of n rents of 1 at i interest rate per period is determined **by dividing the compound interest** that accumulates on a single deposit of 1 for n periods at i interest **by i** (the interest rate per period). This is expressed as follows:

Formula for amount of ordinary annuity of 1

$$A_{\overline{n}|\,i} = \frac{(1 + i)^n - 1}{i}$$

For example, the amount of an ordinary annuity of 16 rents of 1 at 2% is determined below:

Solving the formula

$$A_{\overline{16}|\,2\%} = \frac{(1 + 0.02)^{16} - 1}{0.02} = \frac{1.372786 - 1}{0.02} = \frac{0.372786}{0.02} = \underline{\underline{18.6393}}$$

Tables, such as Table 3 in the Appendix at the end of the book, have been prepared to give the amount of ordinary annuities for different numbers of rents at varying interest rates. Note that in Table 3 the value for $A_{\overline{16}|\,2\%}$ is 18.64 (rounded to two decimal places). Table 3 in the Appendix is used to compute the amount of an ordinary annuity for rents of any dollar amount by the process of multiplication. For example, because the amount of an annuity of 16 rents of 1 at 2% is 18.64, the amount of an ordinary annuity of 16 rents of $500 would be $9,320 ($500 × 18.64 = $9,320).

Other applications of amount of an ordinary annuity of 1 formula

In the example above the amount of an ordinary annuity of 16 rents of 1 at 2% (18.64) and the periodic rent ($500) were known. From the information available we were able to compute the amount of the ordinary annuity of 16 rents of $500 at 2% as $9,320. Thus, four variables were involved:

1 The number of rents (16)
2 The interest rate per period (2%)
3 The amount of each periodic rent ($500)
4 The accumulated amount of the ordinary annuity immediately after the last rent ($9,320)

If any three of these variables are known, the fourth one can be determined by using Table 3 in the Appendix at the end of the book, as illustrated below:

1 Question How many quarterly rents of $500 are required to accumulate $9,320 if the amount on deposit earns interest at 8% compounded quarterly?

Answer $9,320 ÷ $500 = 18.64, the amount of an ordinary annuity of 1 at 2% for an unknown number of rents. The 2% column in Table 3 in the Appendix shows that the required number of rents is 16 because the amount of an ordinary annuity of 16 rents at 2% is 18.64 (rounded to two decimal places).

2 Question If an amount of an ordinary annuity of 16 rents of $500 equals $9,320 immediately after the sixteenth rent, what is the interest rate?

Answer $9,320 ÷ $500 = 18.64, the amount of an ordinary annuity of 16 rents of 1 at an unstated interest rate per period. The line for 16 rents in Table 3 in the Appendix shows that the interest rate per period is 2%.

3 Question If the required amount of an ordinary annuity of 16 rents at 2% is $9,320, what periodic rents are required to accumulate this sum?

Answer Table 3 in the Appendix shows that the amount of an ordinary annuity of 16 rents at 2% is 18.64 (rounded). The periodic rents are $500 ($9,320 ÷ 18.64 = $500).

Summary and Example The amount of an ordinary annuity of 1 formula, $A_{\overline{n}|\,i}$, is used to compute the future value A of n equal periodic rents of R dollars which earn compound interest i at a fixed rate per period. The periodic rent is computed by dividing the dollar amount to be accumulated by the amount of an ordinary annuity of 1 at the given interest rate for the number of periods equal to the number of rents (deposits).

Example: Accumulation of a fund to retire debt Dawn Company wants to accumulate $600,000 on December 31, Year 5, to retire a long-term note payable. The company intends to make five equal annual deposits in a fund which will earn interest at 6% compounded annually. The first deposit is made on December 31, Year 1. Compute the amount of the periodic deposits and prepare a fund accumulation table to prove that $600,000 will be available on December 31, Year 5.

Answer The amount of the periodic deposits is $600,000 ÷ 5.637093 (the amount of an ordinary annuity of five rents of 1 at 6% from Table 3 in the Appendix), or $106,438 (rounded). The fund accumulation table appears below:

Example of fund buildup

	Fund Accumulation Table		
End of year	*Annual deposit*	*Interest earned at 6%*	*Fund balance*
1	$106,438	$ –0–	$106,438
2	106,438	6,386	219,262
3	106,438	13,156	338,856
4	106,438	20,331	465,625
5	106,438	27,937*	600,000

* Adjusted for slight rounding error.

Amount of an annuity due

The amount of an **annuity due** (or **annuity in advance**) is the total amount on deposit **one period after the final rent.** This is illustrated below for an annuity due of 16 rents:

Diagram for amount of annuity due

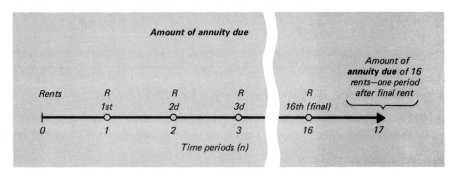

This diagram suggests that there are two ways of computing the amount of an annuity due of 16 rents of 1 at, say, 2% interest per period, as follows:

1 Take the amount of an ordinary annuity of 16 rents of 1 at 2% from Table 3 in the Appendix and accrue interest at 2% for one additional period: 18.639285 × 1.02 = <u>19.01207</u>.

2 Take the amount of an ordinary annuity of 17 rents of 1 at 2% from Table 3 in the Appendix and subtract 1, the rent not made at the end of time period 17: 20.01207 − 1 = <u>19.01207</u>.

The application of the amount of an annuity due is illustrated in the following example.

Example   Greco Corporation needs $200,000 on March 31, Year 5. This amount is to be accumulated by making 16 equal deposits in a fund at the end of each quarter, starting March 31, Year 1, and ending on December 31, Year 4. The fund will earn interest at 8% compounded quarterly. Compute the periodic rents.

Answer   The balance in the fund on March 31, Year 5, represents the amount of an annuity due of 16 rents at 2% per period. Therefore, the periodic rents are: $200,000 ÷ 19.01207 = $10,519.63. This amount can be verified as follows:

Ordinary annuity plus interest for 1 period = amount of annuity due

Amount of **ordinary annuity** of 16 rents of $10,519.63 at 2% on December 31, Year 4: $10,519.63 × 18.639285	$196,078
Add: Interest for first quarter of Year 5: $196,078 × 0.02.	3,922
Balance in fund on March 31, Year 5 (amount of an **annuity due** of 16 rents of $10,519.63 at 2%).	$200,000

Amount of deferred annuity

When the amount of an ordinary annuity remains on deposit for a number of periods beyond the final rent, the arrangement is known as a **deferred annuity.** The diagram on page 199 shows that the amount of an annuity due of 16 rents is also the amount of an ordinary annuity deferred for only one period. Thus, when the amount of an ordinary annuity continues to earn interest for an additional period, we have an annuity due situation; when the amount of an ordinary annuity continues to earn interest for more than one additional period, we have a deferred annuity situation.

The amount of a deferred annuity may be computed by multiplying the amount of the ordinary annuity by the amount of 1 for the period of deferral to accrue compound interest. Alternatively, we can take the amount of an ordinary annuity for all periods (including the period of deferral) and subtract from this the amount of the ordinary annuity for the deferral period when rents **were not made,** but interest continued to accumulate. The diagram below illustrates the relationship of an ordinary annuity of 16 rents, an annuity due of 16 rents, and an ordinary annuity of 16 rents deferred for five periods:

Diagram of three types of annuity amounts

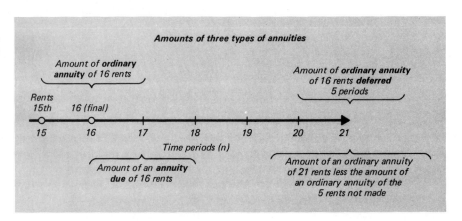

Using the Appendix at the end of the book, and assuming a 2% rate of interest per period, we can compute the amount of an ordinary annuity of 16 rents of 1 deferred for 5 periods (at time period 21) two ways, as follows:

Alternative computations for amount of deferred annuity

$$1 \quad A_{\overline{16}|\,2\%} \times (1 + 0.02)^5 = 18.639285 \times 1.104081 = \underline{\underline{20.57928}}$$

$$2 \quad A_{\overline{21}|\,2\%} - A_{\overline{5}|\,2\%} = 25.783317 - 5.204040 = \underline{\underline{20.57928}}$$

Although deferred annuity situations are relatively rare in the business world, accountants should understand the concepts illustrated here.

Present value of ordinary annuity of 1

Present values of annuities are used more frequently in financial accounting than any of the other concepts discussed to this point. For example, the computation of (1) proceeds on a bond issue, (2) value of assets acquired through capital leases, (3) past service pension costs, (4) amount of debt or receivables under installment contracts, and (5) amount of mortgage debt or investments in mortgage notes all require the application of the present-value-of-annuity concept.

A diagram depicting the present value (*P*) of an **ordinary annuity (annuity in arrears)** of five rents (*R*) is given below:

Diagram of present value of ordinary annuity

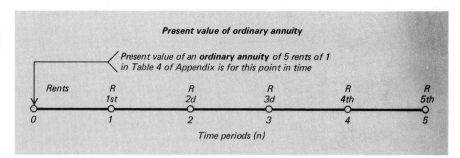

Present value of ordinary annuity

*Present value of an **ordinary annuity** of 5 rents of 1 in Table 4 of Appendix is for this point in time*

The present value of an ordinary annuity of five rents depicted above is the value of the rents, discounted at compound interest, at a point in time **one period before the first rent.** The present value of an ordinary annuity is computed as the sum of the present values of the individual rents, but the use of a table, such as Table 4 in the Appendix, is considerably more efficient.

The present value (*P*) of an ordinary annuity of *n* rents at *i* rate of interest can be computed **by dividing the compound discount** on 1 for *n* periods at *i* rate of interest by *i* (the interest rate per period). This is illustrated below in the computation of the present value of an ordinary annuity of five rents at 8% per period:

Solution for present value of an ordinary annuity

$$P_{\overline{n}|\,i} = \frac{1 - \dfrac{1}{(1+i)^n}}{i} = \frac{1 - \dfrac{1}{(1+0.08)^5}}{0.08} = \frac{1 - 0.680583}{0.08}$$

$$= \frac{0.319417}{0.08} = \underline{3.99271}$$

The present value of 1 at 8% for five periods (0.680583) is taken from Table 2 in the Appendix. Dividing the compound discount of 0.319417 by 8% gives the present value of an ordinary annuity of five rents of 1 at 8%. In Table 4 in the Appendix, the present value of an ordinary annuity of five rents of 1 at 8% is given as 3.992710, thus confirming the computation above.

To illustrate the application of the present value of an ordinary annuity of 1, assume the following: Evans Company has outstanding a $500,000 noninterest-bearing debt, due at the rate of $100,000 per year for five years starting on December 31, Year 1. What is the present value of this debt on January 1, Year 1, for financial accounting purposes if 8% compounded annually is considered a fair rate of interest? The present value of the debt on January 1, Year 1 is equal to the present value of an ordinary annuity of five rents of $100,000 at 8% per period. Therefore, the debt should be reported at $399,271 ($100,000 × 3.99271) in the accounting records on January 1, Year 1. The repayment program for this debt is summarized below:

Repayment program for debt

EVANS COMPANY
Repayment Program for Debt of $399,271 at 8% Interest

Date	Interest expense at 8% per year	Repayment at end of year	Net reduction of debt	Debt balance
Jan. 1, Year 1				$399,271
Dec. 31, Year 1	$31,942	$100,000	$68,058	331,213
Dec. 31, Year 2	26,497	100,000	73,503	257,710
Dec. 31, Year 3	20,617	100,000	79,383	178,327
Dec. 31, Year 4	14,266	100,000	85,734	92,593
Dec. 31, Year 5	7,407	100,000	92,593	–0–

As illustrated in our earlier discussion of the amount of an ordinary annuity, Table 4 in the Appendix can be used to compute other variables in the formula for the present value of an ordinary annuity. For example, if we know that $P_{\overline{5}|\,8\%} = 3.99271$ and the present value of an ordinary annuity of five rents at 8% per period is $399,271, we can compute the periodic rent of $100,000 by dividing $399,271 by 3.99271.

Summary and Example   The present value of an ordinary annuity of 1 formula $P_{\overline{n}|\,i}$, is used to compute the sum P that would settle a debt one period before the first rent of n equal rents of R dollars discounted at compound interest rate i per period. Stated differently, $P_{\overline{n}|\,i}$ is used to compute the value one period before the first rent of a series of equal cash inflows or outflows discounted at a constant interest rate per period.

Example: Proceeds from bonds issued at a discount   Murphy Company issued $5 million face amount of 9%, five-year bonds on June 30, Year 5. The bonds pay interest on June 30 and December 31 and were issued to yield 10% compounded semiannually. Compute the proceeds from this bond issue.

Answer Because the 9% interest rate on the bonds is less than the 10% current fair rate of interest, the bonds were sold at a discount equal in amount to the present value of the semiannual interest **deficiency** (interest that will not be paid to bondholders) of $25,000 [$5,000,000 × (0.050 − 0.045) = $25,000] for 10 semiannual periods discounted at the 5% **current rate of interest per period.** Therefore, the proceeds from the bond issue are determined as follows:

<table>
<tr><td rowspan="4">**Computation of proceeds from bonds payable**</td><td>Face amount of bonds . . . .</td><td>$5,000,000</td></tr>
<tr><td>Less: Present value of ordinary annuity of 10 rents of $25,000 dis-</td><td></td></tr>
<tr><td>counted at 5% per period: $25,000 × 7.721735 . . . .</td><td>193,043</td></tr>
<tr><td>Proceeds from bond issue . . . .</td><td>$4,806,957</td></tr>
</table>

Alternatively, the proceeds from the bond issue may be determined as the sum of (1) the present value of the $5 million to be paid at maturity, discounted at the 5% semiannual current rate of interest for 10 periods, plus (2) the present value of an ordinary annuity of 10 rents of $225,000 semiannual interest payments, also discounted at 5% per period. This approach is illustrated below:

<table>
<tr><td rowspan="5">**Alternative computation of proceeds from bonds payable**</td><td>Present value of $5 million discounted at 5% for 10 six-month periods:</td><td></td></tr>
<tr><td>$5,000,000 × 0.613913 . . . .</td><td>$3,069,565</td></tr>
<tr><td>Add: Present value of ordinary annuity of 10 rents of $225,000 dis-</td><td></td></tr>
<tr><td>counted at 5%: $225,000 × 7.721735 . . . .</td><td>1,737,390</td></tr>
<tr><td>Proceeds from bond issue . . . .</td><td>$4,806,955*</td></tr>
</table>

* $2 discrepancy between this amount and the amount computed above is caused by rounding in present value tables.

The proceeds from the issuance of bonds at a premium (when the interest rate paid on the bonds is larger than the current rate of interest) are computed similarly. This topic is discussed in Chapter 15.

Present value of annuity due

The present value of an ordinary annuity falls one period before the first rent. In contrast, the **present value of an annuity due falls on the date the first rent is deposited or withdrawn.** For this reason an annuity due often is referred to as an **annuity in advance.** The difference between the present value of an ordinary annuity and the present value of an annuity due is illustrated at the top of page 204.

**Diagram of present
values for ordinary an-
nuity and annuity due**

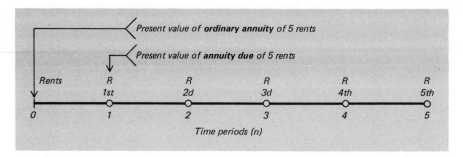

For example, we need the present value of an annuity due of *n* rents of 1 to compute the periodic rent payments on an equipment contract or a lease when the first payment is due at the beginning of each period. The diagram above indicates that the present value at time period 1 of an annuity due of five rents can be computed (1) by adding interest for one period to the present value of an ordinary annuity of five rents, or (2) by obtaining the present value of an ordinary annuity of four rents and then adding 1, representing the "extra" rent at time period 1. These two approaches are illustrated below, using Table 4 in the Appendix, to compute the present value of an annuity due of five rents of 1 at 8% per period.

**Two ways of computing
present value of annuity
due**

> **1** *Present value of ordinary annuity of five rents of 1 at 8%, plus interest at 8% on this present value for one period: 3.99271 × 1.08 = present value of annuity due* *4.312127*
>
> **2** *Present value of ordinary annuity of four rents of 1 at 8%, plus 1, the fifth rent at time period 1: 3.312127 + 1 = present value of annuity due* *4.312127*

To illustrate the application of the present value of an annuity due of 1, assume the following: On January 1, Year 1, Fernando, Inc., acquired a plant asset for $64,682. The company agreed to make five equal annual payments starting on January 1, Year 1, and ending on January 1, Year 5, at 8% compounded annually. The annual payments on the debt are determined below:

$64,682 ÷ 4.312127 = $15,000

The repayment program for this debt is presented on page 205.

Repayment program for debt

	FERNANDO, INC.				
	Repayment Program for Debt of $64,682 at 8% Interest				
Jan. 1, Year	Debt at beginning of year	Payment at beginning of year	Balance accruing interest	Interest at 8%	Debt at end of year
1	$64,682	$15,000	$49,682	$3,975	$53,657
2	53,657	15,000	38,657	3,093	41,750
3	41,750	15,000	26,750	2,140	28,890
4	28,890	15,000	13,890	1,110*	15,000
5	15,000	15,000	–0–	–0–	–0–

* Adjusted for $1 discrepancy due to rounding of computations.

Present value of deferred annuity

When periodic rents are postponed for more than one period, the present value of such an annuity at some date prior to the first rent may be computed by using two different methods as follows: (1) Discount the present value of the ordinary annuity portion at compound interest for the periods the annuity is deferred, or (2) determine the present value of an ordinary annuity equal to the total number of periods involved and subtract from this the present value of the "missing" ordinary annuity for rents equal in number to the number of periods the annuity is deferred. To illustrate, assume that we wish to know the sum at time period 0 which would pay off a debt of five payments of $100,000 each, payments starting at time period 4 and interest compounded at 8% per time period. First it would be helpful to diagram the periodic rents (payments) as follows:

Diagram of present value of deferred annuity

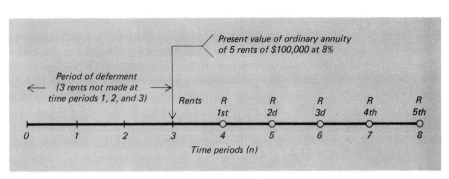

Using Tables 2 and 4 in the Appendix, we can compute the present value of the ordinary annuity of five rents of 1 *deferred for three periods* as follows:

Two ways of
computing present
value of deferred
annuity

1 *Present value of ordinary annuity of five rents of 1 at 8% at time
period 3, discounted at 8% for three periods: 3.992710 × 0.793832 .* 3.169541
2 *Present value of an ordinary annuity of eight rents of 1 at 8% at time
period 0, less the present value of an ordinary annuity of three rents
of 1 (the rents not made) at 8% at time period 0: 5.746639−2.577097* 3.169542*
* *Slight discrepancy due to rounding of present values in the Appendix.*

Thus, cash in the amount of $316,954 ($100,000 × 3.169542 =
$316,954) would be needed at time period 0 to repay the debt dia-
gramed on page 205. The repayment of the debt is summarized below:

Proof that computation
is correct

Repayment Program for Debt of $316,954 at 8% Interest

Time period	Interest expense at 8% per period	Repayments	Net reduction of debt	Debt balance
0	Present value of debt			$316,954
1	$25,356			342,310
2	27,385			369,695
3	29,576			399,271
4	31,942	$100,000	$68,058	331,213
5	26,497	100,000	73,503	257,710
6	20,617	100,000	79,383	178,327
7	14,266	100,000	85,734	92,593
8	7,407	100,000	92,593	−0−

Concluding comments

Many complex situations involving compound interest may be encountered in the business world. An understanding of the concepts
discussed in the preceding pages enables accountants to analyze and
solve problems requiring the application of compound interest principles. Because money can be invested readily to earn a return, there is
a universal service charge (interest) for its use, and any given amount
of money available on a stated date has a different value at all other
points in time. Compound interest procedures are a means of moving
money inflows and outflows forward and backward in time on a basis
that permits a comparison of values in equivalent terms.

For example, if you are given a choice of receiving $20,000 in two
years or $30,000 in eight years, the choice is not obvious. Assuming a
current fair interest rate of 10%, these two sums can be compared
only by measuring their present value or accumulated amount on a
particular date. If we choose *now* (time point zero), the following
present-value analysis shows that the $20,000 in two years is preferable
to receiving $30,000 in eight years:

Comparing present values of future cash flows

$20,000(p_{\overline{2}|\,10\%}) = \$20,000 \times 0.826446 = \underline{\$16,529}$

$30,000(p_{\overline{8}|\,10\%}) = \$30,000 \times 0.466507 = \underline{\$13,995}$

We can reach the same conclusion by comparing **the accumulated amounts** of the two sums eight years from now as follows:

Comparing amounts at a fixed future date

$20,000(a_{\overline{6}|\,10\%}) = \$20,000 \times 1.771561 = \underline{\$35,431}$

$30,000 at the end of eight years is equivalent to $\underline{\$30,000}$

The receipt of $20,000 in two years again is shown to be preferable to the receipt of $30,000 in eight years, because if $20,000 is invested at 10% at the end of the second year, it would accumulate to $35,431 by the end of the eighth year. We could choose any other point in time at any rate of interest and make a similar comparison without changing the validity of the decision in favor of the option calling for the receipt of $20,000 two years from today.

REVIEW QUESTIONS

1 Briefly explain the difference between simple interest and compound interest.

2 a Explain the meaning of $(1 + i)^n$ and define the symbols i and n.
  b Give the formula for each of the following:
      (1) Present value of 1
      (2) Amount of an ordinary annuity of 1
      (3) Present value of an ordinary annuity of 1

3 Define each of the following:
  a Present value of an annuity due
  b Present value of a deferred annuity
  c Amount of an annuity due
  d Amount of a deferred annuity

4 Give the formula, including the numerical value for i and n, for computing the compound amount of $500 invested for five years.
  a At 10% compounded semiannually
  b At 8% compounded quarterly
  c At 12% compounded monthly
  d At 6% compounded annually

5 The following values are taken from compound interest tables for the same number of periods n and at the same rate of interest i:
  a 13.180795
  b 1.790848
  c 0.558395
  d 7.360087
  What does each of the four values represent? Explain.

6 Indicate the compound interest table that would be used in solving each of the following problems:

a Sheila Jones wants to know how much she would have in her saving account at the end of five years if she deposits a single sum and leaves it to accumulate interest.

b Eva Smith owes Olson $5,000 due in two years at no interest. Smith wants to know how much she should pay Olson now if they can agree on a current fair rate of interest.

c Joe Harrison owes money to Andersen which is payable in semiannual installments of $2,000 each. The first installment is due today. Harrison wants to know the lump-sum amount he should pay to Andersen today to eliminate his liability.

d Adam Kirkpatrick wants to know what equal annual deposits he should make at the beginning of each of 10 years so that he will have $20,000 to buy a cabin cruiser at the end of the tenth year. Interest at a fixed rate will be compounded annually on the cumulative amount in Kirkpatrick's "cruiser fund."

EXERCISES

Ex. 5-1   From the compound interest tables in the Appendix at the end of the book, compute the following values at 4%:

a Amount of 1 for 10 periods
b Present value of 1 for 20 periods
c Amount of ordinary annuity of 15 rents of 1
d Amount of annuity due of 15 rents of 1
e Amount of ordinary annuity of 15 rents of 1 deferred for 10 periods
f Present value of ordinary annuity of 25 rents of 1
g Present value of annuity due of 25 rents of 1
h Present value of ordinary annuity of 25 rents of 1 deferred for 5 periods

Ex. 5-2   Celestial Company acquired $10,000 face amount noncallable 10% bonds which have a remaining life of 12 years. The bonds pay interest every six months. The present value of 1 at 4% for 24 periods is 0.390121, and the present value of 1 at 5% for 24 periods is 0.310068. The present value of an ordinary annuity of 1 at 4% for 24 periods is 15.246963, and the present value of an ordinary annuity of 1 at 5% for 24 periods is 13.798642.

Compute the price paid for the bonds if the market rate of interest for bonds of comparable quality is 8% compounded semiannually. Round computations to the nearest dollar.

Ex. 5-3   On December 31, Year 1, Long Beach Development Company issued $10 million of 8% bonds payable. Interest is payable on December 31 of each year. The bonds mature on December 31, Year 11. The bonds were issued to yield an annual rate of 10%. The present value of an ordinary annuity of 10 rents of 1 at 10% is 6.144567; the present value of 1 for 10 periods at 10% is 0.385543.

Compute the amount received from issuance of the bonds. Round computations to the nearest dollar.

Ex. 5-4   Fred Dryer sold a parcel of land for $44,000. He received $12,000 cash on the date of sale and 16 notes of equal amount due serially, one each six months starting six months from the date of sale. It was agreed that the notes will include interest in their face amount at 12% compounded semiannually.

Using the Appendix at the end of the book, compute (to the nearest dollar) the face amount of each note.

Ex. 5-5 Denise deposited $1,000 each quarter starting on June 30, Year 1, in a savings account that earned interest at 8% compounded quarterly. She has already made seven deposits, the last one on December 31, Year 2.

Using the tables in the Appendix, compute the amount Denise has on deposit on each of the following dates (assuming that she made no withdrawals from the savings account):

a December 31, Year 2, including the deposit made on this date
b March 31, Year 3, including the deposit made on this date
c June 30, Year 5, assuming that Denise made the last deposit on March 31, Year 5

Ex. 5-6 On January 2, Year 3, Alameda Manufacturing Company leased equipment from Pico Corporation. This lease was noncancelable and was in substance an installment purchase (a capital lease). The initial term of the lease was 12 years, with title passing to Alameda at the end of the twelfth year at no additional cost. Annual rent to be paid by Alameda is $10,000 at the beginning of each year. The first rent payment was made on January 2, Year 3. The equipment has an estimated economic life of 20 years, with no residual value. The prevailing interest rate for Alameda on similar financing arrangements was 8%. The present value of an **annuity due** of 12 rents of 1 at 8% is 8.138964.

Compute the cost of the equipment for financial accounting purposes.

Ex. 5-7 Given below are the present values of 1 discounted at 8% for one to five periods. Each of the values is based on 8% interest compounded annually from day of deposit to day of withdrawal.

Periods	Present value of 1 discounted at 8% per period
1	0.926
2	0.857
3	0.794
4	0.735
5	0.681

Choose the best answer for each of the following four questions:

1 What amount should you deposit in a bank account today in order to have $5,000 three years from today?
a $5,000 ÷ 0.794
b $5,000 × 0.926 × 3
c ($5,000 × 0.926) + ($5,000 × 0.857) + ($5,000 × 0.794)
d $5,000 × 0.794

2 What amount should you have in your bank account today before withdrawal if you need $5,000 each year for four years, with the first withdrawal to be made today and each subsequent withdrawal at one-year intervals? (You will have exactly a zero balance in your bank account after the fourth withdrawal.)
a $5,000 + ($5,000 × 0.926) + ($5,000 × 0.857) + ($5,000 × 0.794)
b ($5,000 ÷ 0.735) × 4
c ($5,000 × 0.926) + ($5,000 × 0.857) + ($5,000 × 0.794) + ($5,000 × 0.735)
d ($5,000 ÷ 0.926) × 4

3 If you deposit $8,000 in a savings account today, what amount will you have available two years from today?

　a $8,000 × 0.857
　b $8,000 × 0.857 × 2
　c $8,000 ÷ 0.857
　d ($8,000 ÷ 0.926) × 2

4 What is the present value today of $2,000 you will receive six years from today?

　a $2,000 × 0.926 × 6
　b $2,000 × 0.794 × 2
　c $2,000 × 0.681 × 0.926
　d Amount cannot be determined from the information given

Ex. 5-8　Sonar Products, Inc., wants to accumulate a fund of $80,000 at the end of Year 10 to retire a debt. The fund will be accumulated by making 20 equal semiannual deposits starting on June 30, Year 1.

　　　　　If the fund will earn interest at 6% compounded semiannually, compute the amount of each deposit to the nearest dollar. Use the Appendix at the end of the book.

Ex. 5-9　Ken Krueger has a 6% loan with an unpaid balance of $17,169. The principal and interest are payable quarterly at the rate of $1,000. Krueger has 20 more payments to make, having just made the payment due December 31, Year 5. The lender approaches Krueger and offers to reduce the principal of the debt from $17,169 to $16,500 if he would take out a new loan for $16,500 at 10% (the current market rate), payable quarterly for the next five years.

　　　　　Should Krueger refinance the loan? Present computations (to the nearest dollar) in support of your answer. Ignore income tax considerations.

SHORT CASES FOR ANALYSIS AND DECISION

Case 5-1　While on an audit with a CPA firm at the end of Year 5, Ted Tarbet observed the following deferred compensation contract signed by his client:

> "In lieu of any salary and bonus for Year 5, Robert Davis will receive $25,000 at the end of Year 6 and each year thereafter through December 31, Year 11. Robert Davis will not be required to perform any services after December 31, Year 5."

　　　　　The client of the CPA firm recorded this contract as follows:

Executive Salaries Expense ($25,000 × 6 years) . . . .　150,000
　　Notes Payable . . . .　　　　　150,000
To record salary and bonuses payable to Robert Davis.

　　　　　A staff assistant working under Tarbet's supervision stated: "This journal entry is proper; the expense is applicable to Year 5, and the notes meet all the traditional tests of a liability. The salary and bonus payments to Robert Davis had been over $130,000 per year for several years; therefore, the amount of $150,000 debited to Executive Salaries Expense in Year 5 is reasonable."

　　　　　Tarbet pointed out that there is no mention of interest in the contract with Davis and that the client had to pay 8% interest on most of its bank loans in the last quarter of Year 5. He agreed that the notes were genuine liabilities, but also added that an auditor must ascertain not only whether a liability exists but also that the amount of the liability at the balance sheet date is correctly stated.

Instructions Use the appropriate table in the Appendix at the end of the book to arrive at your conclusions.

a Evaluate the positions taken by the staff assistant and by Ted Tarbet.

b What correcting entry, if any, would you recommend on December 31, Year 5. assuming that a Discount on Notes Payable account is used?

c What journal entry should be made on December 31, Year 6, to record the first payment to Robert Davis?

Case 5-2 Vincent Lee's godfather, Linton Chu, decided to make him a gift of $27,000 with an option to receive the cash in any of the following three patterns:

(1) One thousand dollars at the end of each of the first three years, starting one year from now; $3,000 at the end of each of the next three years; and $5,000 at the end of each of the last three years. Chu suggests that this arrangement might be preferable because Lee is young and will need more money as he grows older, not only because he will learn to spend more but also because inflation will increase his cost of living.

(2) Three thousand dollars at the end of each of the next nine years, starting one year from now. Chu pointed out that this option offers Lee the advantage of a steady cash flow.

(3) Five thousand dollars at the end of each of the first three years, starting one year from now; $3,000 at the end of each of the next three years; and $1,000 at the end of each of the last three years. Chu points out that he would not recommend this option to Lee because it would give him an excess of cash flow during the first three years which would be invested at a rate of interest lower than he (Chu) could earn. Lee had told Chu that he would invest all this money in San Francisco at 6% compounded annually; Chu had responded that he invests his money at 10% compounded annually in a Hong Kong bank.

After discussing these alternatives with several philosophy students at Golden Shark University, Lee said to Chu: "All three options are the same; obviously I will get an average of $3,000 at the end of each of the nine years, so it makes no difference." Chu responded, "I am happy to know that you are in school; there is much to learn."

Instructions

a Did Vincent Lee make the right decision? Why?

b What is the present value of each option at 6% interest compounded annually, given the following present values of 1 at 6%?

Periods	Present value of 1	Present value of ordinary annuity of 1
3	0.8396	2.6730
6	0.7050	4.9173
9	0.5919	6.8017

c Briefly evaluate the observations made by Linton Chu relative to each of the three options he presented to Vincent Lee.

Case 5-3 The following letter was mailed by Glibb Finance Company to residents of a large city:

Dear Ms. Reliable:

You are one of a select group of creditworthy individuals in your community who qualify for a unique opportunity. Without additional credit references or time-consuming technicalities, you are guaranteed a "Prestige Loan" of $10,000 now.

Because you are financially responsible, and you've always handled your financial obligations with efficiency, your loan **already has been approved.** The enclosed certificate entitles you to a loan of $10,000 any time you'd like to have it. So please call or come to our office at your earliest convenience.

Sincerely,
Gregory Glibb

The certificate referred to in the letter indicated that the repayment of the loan was to be made in 24 equal monthly payments of $534 each.

Instructions

a What is the total amount a borrower would have to pay to Glibb Finance Company over the two-year period of this installment loan?

b Compute the approximate **annual rate** of interest (as a percentage) compounded monthly, using Table 4 in the Appendix at the end of the book.

c Is the rate of interest computed in *b* attractive for "creditworthy" borrowers if the current bank prime interest rate is 15%? Why?

PROBLEMS

5-1 Homer Base has been a star baseball player for the Rochester Zebras for many years. At age 34, he decided to become a free agent. He offered his services to the highest bidder for four more years, before retiring to operate a restaurant in Chicago. After many weeks of negotiations, he accepted the following offer from the Waco Beanballs:

(1) An annual salary of $300,000 for four years, payable in monthly installments of $25,000, starting one month from today.

(2) A deferred compensation of $240,000, payable in monthly installments of $5,000 for four years, for services rendered during the four years of active service for the Waco Beanballs. These payments will commence one month after the last payment of $25,000 is made.

Headlines in sport pages around the country stated that "Homer Base signed a $1,440,000 contract with the Beanballs."

Instructions Assuming that interest at the rate of $1\frac{1}{2}\%$ per month is charged on personal loans to professional athletes, compute the present value of the contract signed by Homer Base. Round computations to the nearest dollar.

5-2 This problem consists of four separate parts, each relating to the business activities of Oakmount Company. Determine the answer for each part by using the compound interest tables in the Appendix at the end of the book.

(1) On July 1, Year 1, Oakmount issued $10 million of 20-year, 8% bonds, which paid interest semiannually. The bonds were issued to yield 9% compounded semiannually. What were the proceeds from this bond issue?

(2) On April 1, Year 1, Oakmount purchased a plant asset by paying $5,000 down and $5,000 at the beginning of each of the next 19 calendar quarters. What was the cost of the plant asset for financial accounting purposes if the rate of interest agreed on was 16% compounded quarterly?

(3) Oakmount holds a promissory note in the amount of $300,000 issued by Cindy Corporation. The note calls for payment of $100,000 of principal at the end of each year starting in three years, plus interest at the rate of 12% a year on the unpaid balance of the note. Only interest is due at the end of the first two years. Oakmount immediately discounted this note with a finance com-

pany at 10% interest compounded annually. How much did Oakmount receive from the finance company for the note?

(4) Oakmount wishes to accumulate a $5 million fund with Horner Trust for the retirement of bonds in 10 years. The company plans to make 20 equal deposits of $186,078.54, starting in six months, to accumulate the $5 million fund. What semiannual interest rate will be earned by Oakmount on the balance of the fund?

5-3   This problem consists of four independent parts, each related to the business activities of Rosenblum Corporation. Compute the answer (to the nearest dollar) for each by using the compound interest tables in the Appendix at the end of the book.

(1) Rosenblum wants to accumulate $500,000 on December 31, Year 10, to retire preferred stock. The company deposits $125,000 in a savings account on January 1, Year 1, which will earn interest at 6% compounded quarterly. Rosenblum wants to know what additional amount it has to deposit at the end of each quarter for 10 years to have $500,000 available at the end of Year 10. The periodic deposits also will earn interest at 6% compounded quarterly.

(2) Rosenblum wants to make five equal annual deposits beginning June 1, Year 4, in order to be able to withdraw $50,000 at six annual intervals beginning June 1, Year 9. The amount on deposit will earn interest at 5% annually until the savings fund is exhausted. Compute the equal deposits that should be made.

(3) On June 30, Year 1, Rosenblum purchased a machine for $80,000. The down payment was $10,000, and the balance will be paid in 48 equal monthly payments, including interest at 18% compounded monthly. What is the amount of the monthly payment if the first payment is due one month from the date of purchase?

(4) On April 1, Year 2, Rosenblum made a deposit of $100,000 in a fund and left the fund undisturbed for four years to earn compound interest at a rate which did not change during the four-year period. At the end of four years, the fund had accumulated to $132,088.60. If interest was compounded quarterly, what was the rate of interest earned each quarter?

5-4   The management of Dapper Manufacturing Company is evaluating a proposal to purchase a new drill press as a replacement for a less efficient old press which would be sold. The total cost of the new press is $175,000. If the new press is purchased, Dapper will incur costs of $5,000 in removing the old press. The old press has a carrying amount of $100,000 and a remaining economic life of ten years. Because of new technical improvements which have made the old press uneconomical, it presently has a resale value of only $40,000.

Additional information:
(1) Management has provided you with the following comparison of annual production and operating costs:

	Old press	New press
Annual production (units)	400,000	500,000
Annual operating costs:		
Labor	$ 30,000	$ 25,000
Depreciation (10% of asset carrying amount)	10,000	17,500
Other costs	48,000	20,000
Total annual operating costs	$ 88,000	$ 62,500

(2) Management believes that if the old press is not replaced now, the company would have to wait seven years before replacement would be economically justifiable.

(3) Both the old and the new press are expected to have a negligible residual value at the end of ten years.

(4) If the new press is purchased, the management of Dapper will require a 15% return on the investment before income taxes.

(5) The present value of an ordinary annuity of 10 rents of 1 at 15% is 5.018769.

Instructions

a In order to assist the management of Dapper in reaching a decision on the proposal, prepare a working paper showing the computation of the following (ignore any effects of net incremental cash flow from increased sales of units produced by the new machine):

(1) Net initial cash investment, before income taxes.

(2) Net present value of the net initial cash investment, before income taxes. Assume that the annual cash savings before income taxes are realized at the end of each year. Round computations to the nearest dollar.

b Would you recommend the purchase of the new press? Explain.

5-5 In the course of your December 31 audit engagement for Deltona Company, the following situations required you to apply compound interest principles:

(1) A noninterest-bearing note receivable in the face amount of $120,000 and maturing in three years was received on December 31 in partial payment of an account receivable. The accountant for the company credited the customer's account for $120,000, despite a written agreement that the customer was to receive credit for the "present value of the note discounted at 8% for three years, interest compounded semiannually."

(2) The company agreed to pay $10,000 per year for five years to a retiring executive. The payments, which start three years from the end of the current year, were not recorded in the accounting records. The payments were in lieu of a year-end bonus which would have been taxed at a combined federal and state income tax rate of over 60%. The company regularly borrows money at a 9% annual rate of interest.

(3) The company wants to accumulate a fund of $100,000 in six years (from December 31 of the current year) to retire a long-term note. Three years ago, the board of directors had passed a resolution instructing the treasurer to make ten equal annual deposits in a fund earning interest at 8% compounded annually. Because no one knew how to compute the equal deposits, the treasurer decided to deposit $10,000 at the end of each year. The fourth deposit was made on December 31 of the current year. What equal annual deposits should be made during the next six years, starting a year from now, if exactly $100,000 is to be accumulated six years from now?

(4) The company recently purchased a barge for $500,000. The purchase contract calls for 20 payments of $32,629 every three months starting immediately. You have been asked by the president of the company to compute the approximate rate of interest charged on this contract every three months.

Instructions Prepare journal entries, with supporting computations, to correct the accounting records for situations (1) and (2) above, and compute the answers for situations (3) and (4). Round computations to the nearest dollar, and record notes receivable or notes payable at face amount.

5-6   As a summer intern with Finnell and Gagliano, Certified Public Accountants, you are presented with the following situations.

(1) Client A called to inquire whether a proposed transaction made economic sense. The client sold a parcel of land for $51,000 and was given the choice of receiving $51,000 cash or $17,000 per year for four years starting one year from now. The client does not need cash but would like to earn 12% before income taxes annually on idle cash resources; consequently, the client wants to know what interest rate (to the nearest tenth) would be earned if the installment payment option is taken.

(2) Client B wanted to know how much to pay for $100,000 face amount of 8% bonds which mature in five years if interest is payable semiannually and if 10% compounded semiannually is a fair return on this type of investment.

(3) Client C was negotiating to purchase a going concern and was uncertain whether the asking price for goodwill (present value of future superior earnings) was reasonable. The seller asked $50,000 for goodwill, but the client did not want to pay more than the present value of projected superior earnings for the next three years discounted at 15% annually. Superior earnings (to be realized at the end of each year) were estimated as follows:

At end of first year	$25,000
At end of second year	20,000
At end of third year	15,000

(4) On June 1, Year 1, Client D wanted to make the first of four equal annual deposits in a fund that will earn 6% and will amount to $100,000 immediately after the last deposit on June 1, Year 4. The client wanted to know the amount of each deposit and "proof" that $100,000 would be available on June 1, Year 4.

Instructions   Prepare appropriate computations and a working paper that will give each of the four clients the information requested. Round all computations to the nearest dollar.

5-7   Ellen Reed was recently hired as an accountant by Mosebar Corporation. Reed's first assignment was given to her as follows:

"To get your feet wet and to give you some practice with the calculator, I want you to prepare tables summarizing our interest expense or revenue and the liability or asset balance for these two transactions:

(1) Today we purchased a machine for $54,173. We paid $5,000 down and agreed to make six equal payments, including interest at 12% compounded semiannually, every six months starting six months from now.

(2) We will need $200,000 five years from now to reline our furnaces. We want to deposit five equal amounts in a fund starting one year from now so that we will have the money we need in five years. We have arranged to invest the money with Fontana Trust Company at 8% compounded annually."

Instructions
a Compute (1) the amount of the semiannual payments on the contract for the purchase of the machine, and (2) the amount of the annual deposits in the furnace relining fund.
b Prepare (1) a loan amortization table for the installment debt on the purchase of the machine, and (2) a fund accumulation table for the deposits to the furnace relining fund.

5-8 As an accountant for Adriatic Shipyards, Inc., you find the following memorandum on your desk from John Petrovich, controller of the company:

(1) On December 31, Year 1, we will sign a noninterest-bearing note for $100,000 due in five years. The lender wants to earn 10% compounded annually on the amount advanced to us. Please compute the proceeds on this borrowing transaction and prepare a table showing our interest expense and net liability for each of the five years of the loan. Round all computations to the nearest dollar.

(2) Also on December 31, Year 1, the installment sale of the land in Novo will be completed. The buyer will pay us $100,000 per year for ten years starting a year from now. Our contract includes interest at 10% per year in the face amount of the notes. The land is carried in our records at $400,000. I want you to prepare a journal entry to record the sale of the land and to prepare a table which will show interest revenue for each year and the carrying amount of the notes receivable at the end of each year. Round all computations to the nearest dollar, and record the note receivable at face amount.

Instructions Prepare a memo to the controller which includes the information he asked you to assemble. Use the Appendix at the end of the book in making required computations.

5-9 Teakwood, Inc., has a debt for $250,000 maturing on June 30, Year 10. The company wishes to deposit $20,000 in a debt retirement fund on June 30 each year for eight years, starting on June 30, Year 3. In addition, the company wants to deposit a lump sum on June 30, Year 2, which, together with the annual deposits in the debt retirement fund, will be sufficient to repay the debt on June 30, Year 10. The amount in the debt retirement fund earns interest at 7% compounded annually.

Teakwood, Inc., also has made annual deposits of $40,000 in a "contingency fund" at the end of each of the last four years. The balance in the "contingency fund" after the fourth deposit on December 31, Year 4, was $180,244. Interest on the "contingency fund" is compounded annually.

Instructions (Use the Appendix at the end of the book and round computations to the nearest dollar.)

a Compute the lump-sum amount that must be deposited on June 30, Year 2, if $250,000 is to be available on June 30, Year 10, in the debt retirement fund.

b What was the annual rate of interest earned on the "contingency fund" through December 31, Year 4?

c Compute the amount that can be withdrawn from the "contingency fund" at the end of each year for ten years, starting on December 31, Year 5, assuming that the amount on deposit in the "contingency fund" earns interest at 6% annually from January 1, Year 5, through December 31, Year 14.

5-10 This problem consists of three independent parts relating to the business activities of Rollo & Company.

(1) Rollo invested $37,368 with Panorama Insurance Company on January 1, Year 1. The amount on deposit earned interest at 10% a year. Rollo plans to withdraw the amount on deposit in three equal annual installments starting December 31, Year 4.

(2) Rollo wishes to accumulate a fund of $58,666 at Reliance Bank at the end of five years by making five equal annual deposits starting one year from now. The fund will earn interest at 8% compounded annually.

(3) On January 1, Year 1, Rollo invested $199,635 at 8% compounded annually with Annuity Corporation. The amount invested and accrued interest are to be withdrawn in five equal installments starting on December 31, Year 1.

Instructions (Use the Appendix at the end of the book and round computations to the nearest dollar.)

a Compute the three equal amounts that Rollo will receive from Panorama Insurance Company, and prepare a table which shows that the entire amount on deposit will have been withdrawn by December 31, Year 6.

b Compute the annual deposits that Rollo should make with Reliance Bank and prepare a fund accumulation table for the five-year period.

c Compute the amounts Rollo can withdraw each year from Annuity Corporation, and prepare a table which confirms that the amount invested will be exhausted by December 31, Year 5.

WORKING CAPITAL

6 CASH AND SHORT-TERM INVESTMENTS

CASH

Cash is a medium of exchange which a bank will accept for deposit and immediate credit to the depositor's account. Cash includes currency and coin, personal checks, bank drafts, money orders, credit card sales drafts, and cashiers' checks, as well as money on deposit with banks. Items usually under the control of the cashier that sometimes are confused with cash include postage stamps, postdated checks, and IOUs. Postage should be classified as a short-term prepayment; postdated checks and IOUs should be classified as receivables.

Deposits with a trustee, for example, a bond sinking fund which is not under the control of management of a business enterprise, should not be included in cash. As another example, many airline companies have millions of dollars in cash deposits with manufacturers for purchase of flight equipment. Such deposits do not qualify as current assets because they are not available for payment of current liabilities.

Certificates of deposit generally are classified as short-term investments rather than as cash because they are not available for immediate withdrawal. Strictly speaking, savings deposits also may not be withdrawn without prior notice to the bank, but banks very seldom enforce this requirement. Consequently, savings deposits usually are viewed as cash. Petty cash funds and change funds are minor elements of cash under the control of management, even though these funds usually are intended to be used for very specific purposes. The limitations placed on the use of these funds do not remove them from the category of cash but simply aid in the control of cash on hand.

In summary, the criteria generally used to define *cash* are that the item be a medium of exchange, be available immediately for the payment of current debts, and be free from any contractual restriction which would prevent management of the business enterprise from using it to meet any and all obligations.

Management of cash

The management of cash is of major importance in any business enterprise because cash is the means of commanding goods and services. In

221

addition, careful scrutiny of cash transactions is required because this asset may be readily misappropriated.

The management of cash generally is centered around two areas: forecasting and internal controls. The responsibilities of management with respect to cash are: (1) to ensure that there is sufficient cash to carry on the operations, (2) to invest any idle cash, and (3) to prevent loss of cash due to theft or misappropriation. Cash forecasting is necessary for the proper planning of future operations and to assure that cash is available when needed but that cash on hand is not excessive. Internal controls are necessary to provide a basis for the planning function and to assure that the cash is used for proper business purposes and not wasted, misused, or stolen. Management is responsible for controlling and protecting all assets of a business enterprise. Special problems exist in controlling cash, however, because of its liquid nature and universal attractiveness.

Internal controls

The purpose of a system of internal controls is to assure that assets which belong to the business enterprise are received when tendered, are protected while in the custody of the enterprise, and are used only for authorized business purposes. The system of internal controls consists of *administrative controls* and *accounting controls,* which are defined below.[1]

> *Administrative controls* include, but are not limited to, the plan of organization and the procedures and records that are concerned with the decision processes leading to management's authorization of transactions. Such authorization is a management function directly associated with the responsibility for achieving the objectives of the organization and is the starting point for establishing accounting controls for business transactions.
>
> *Accounting controls* comprise the plan of organization and the procedures and records that are concerned with the safeguarding of assets and the reliability of financial records, and consequently are designed to provide reasonable assurance that:
> a Transactions are executed in accordance with management's authorization.
> b Transactions are recorded (1) to permit preparation of financial statements in conformity with generally accepted accounting principles or any other criteria applicable to such statements, and (2) to maintain accountability for assets.
> c Access to assets is permitted only in accordance with management's authorization.
> d The recorded accountability for assets is compared with the existing assets at reasonable intervals and appropriate action is taken with respect to any differences.

Administrative and accounting controls are not designed primarily to detect errors but rather to reduce the opportunity for errors or dishon-

---

[1] *Statement on Auditing Standards No. 1,* "Codification of Auditing Standards and Procedures," AICPA (New York: 1973), p. 20.

esty to occur. In an effective system of internal controls, no one person should handle all phases of a given business transaction from beginning to end. For example, if one person were permitted to order merchandise, receive it, write a check in payment, and record the transaction in the accounting records, there would be no protection against either fraud or errors. In large business enterprises, separate and independent departments are established for such functions as purchasing, receiving, selling, finance, and accounting, to assure that no one department handles all phases of a business transaction.

The system of internal controls frequently can be improved by physical safeguards. Computers help to improve the efficiency and accuracy of the record-keeping function. Cash registers, safes, and prenumbered business forms are very helpful in safeguarding cash and establishing responsibility for it. Any system of internal controls must be supervised with care if it is to function effectively.

If an attempt is made to design a foolproof system, it should be remembered that management's primary responsibility is profitable operation of the business enterprise. The cost of the system of internal controls must be balanced against the benefit to be derived in preventing errors and losses.

Controlling cash receipts and payments

The objective sought in the control of cash receipts is to ensure that all cash which is receivable by the business enterprise is collected and recorded without loss. The system of controlling cash payments should be designed to ensure that no unauthorized payments are made. Control is accomplished by division of responsibility to achieve independent verification of cash transactions without duplication of effort. Cash is safeguarded by keeping it in a safe, depositing it in banks, and through the use of special cash funds.

Imprest cash fund (petty cash fund)

The term *imprest cash fund* refers to a fund of fixed amount used for small expenditures that are most conveniently paid in cash. The imprest fund is restored to its original amount at frequent intervals by the issuance of a check on the general bank account payable to the custodian of the petty cash fund. The replenishment check is equal in amount to the expenditures made from the fund. Imprest cash funds placed in the custody of responsible employees thus serve to maintain control over cash without involved procedures for small payments.

The size of the fund should be sufficient to meet the normal need for small cash payments for a period of two or three weeks. As each cash payment is made, a *voucher* or receipt is placed in the fund in lieu of the cash removed. The vouchers are reviewed and canceled when the fund is replenished.

To illustrate the accounting for petty cash transactions, assume that on December 1, Year 6, Golnar Corporation established a petty cash fund of $250. On December 21, the custodian requested replenishment for bills paid during the intervening period. The following itemized list of payments from petty cash was presented on December 21 for replenishment and on December 31 in connection with the year-end audit:

Summary of activity in petty cash fund for December

GOLNAR CORPORATION
Composition of Petty Cash Fund
December 21 and 31, Year 6

	Dec. 21	Dec. 31
Cash in fund	$ 9	$150
Office supplies expense	171	77
Miscellaneous selling expenses....	65	25
Cash (over) and short.............	5	(2)
Totals	$250	$250

The petty cash fund also should be replenished at the end of the accounting period so that the expenses paid from the fund are recorded in the proper period and the year-end cash balance is stated correctly. The journal entries required to record petty cash transactions for the month of December, Year 6, for Golnar Corporation are as follows:

Journal entries to record petty cash transactions

Year 6

Dec. 1	Petty Cash Fund........................	250	
	Cash		250
	To record establishment of petty cash fund.		
Dec. 21	Office Supplies Expense	171	
	Miscellaneous Selling Expenses	65	
	Cash Over and Short	5	
	Cash		241
	To record expenses incurred since Dec. 1, and to replenish petty cash fund.		
Dec. 31	Office Supplies Expense	77	
	Miscellaneous Selling Expenses	25	
	Cash Over and Short		2
	Cash		100
	To record expenses incurred since Dec. 21, and to replenish petty cash fund.		

The Cash Over and Short account in the foregoing journal entries is classified as revenue when it has a credit balance and as expense when it has a debit balance.

If for any reason the petty cash fund is not replenished at the end of the period, it is still desirable that the expenses be recorded before the accounting records are closed. In this situation the December 31 entry illustrated above would be changed in only one respect: the credit of $100 would be to Petty Cash Fund rather than to Cash. The effect on the financial statements is the same as if the fund actually had been replenished.

Change fund

A *change fund* is an imprest fund used to facilitate the collection of money from customers. The amount of the change fund is deducted from the total cash on hand at the close of business each day to determine the daily cash collections. The cash should be counted and checked against the cash register tape daily. In general, change and petty cash funds are combined with cash on hand and in the bank and are presented as a single amount in the balance sheet.

Reconciliation of bank balances

The cash balance indicated on the monthly bank statement seldom agrees with the cash balance indicated by the depositor's ledger account for cash. These two balances do not agree even though they purport to measure the same quantity, because there is a lag between the time that transactions are recognized by the two parties, the bank and the depositor. For example, the depositor credits the ledger account, Cash, when writing a check in payment of an account payable. The bank does not reduce the depositor's account until the check is presented for payment by the payee. Another common difference between the two balances results when the deposit of cash receipts is made after the bank closes its records for the month. Both of these differences are self-correcting over time; the outstanding checks are presented for payment and the deposit is entered by the bank within a few days.

There are also time lags in transactions initiated by the bank. For example, a depositor generally is not notified of the bank's charges for servicing the account or for collecting a note receivable until the monthly bank statement is received.

In addition to items which involve merely a lag in the recording process, various clerical errors may be made by the depositor or by the bank. The process of reconciling the balances forces a careful review of all transactions involving cash and provides a means of proving the accuracy of the depositor's accounting records. The value of this review stems from the fact that two independent parties have recorded the same transactions and that their records are being compared. When differences arise they must be explained. Those differences which are self-correcting require no further consideration. However, corrections must be made for omissions or other errors in recording transactions in the depositor's accounting records. Errors made by the bank should be called to its attention for correction.

Two forms of bank reconciliation are in common usage: (1) both the bank balance and the balance per depositor's records are reconciled to a correct balance, and (2) the bank balance is reconciled to the balance in the depositor's records. The first form is illustrated on page 227. The second form, which is preferred by practicing accountants, is illustrated on page 229.

Illustration 1:   Bank Balance and Depositor's Balance Reconciled to Correct Balance   The Cash in Bank ledger account for Crossland Company shows a debit balance of $10,592.66 on December 31, Year 5. The bank statement indicates a balance on deposit of $12,269.02 on December 31. Receipts of December 31 in the amount of $1,144.60 were left in the bank's night depository on December 31 but were not included on the bank statement. The December bank statement included a debit memorandum for $13.50 for service charges for December. A credit memorandum included with the statement indicated that a note receivable in the amount of $2,000, left with the bank for collection, had been collected and credited to the Crossland Company account by the bank for $2,030, including interest revenue of $30. Comparison of the paid checks with the check stubs indicated that check no. 821 for $463.90 on December 15, for the purchase of office equipment, had been entered erroneously in the cash payments journal as $436.90. In addition, the following checks written in December, Year 5, had not been paid by the bank:

Checks not paid by the bank in December	
No. 811	$421.96
No. 814	93.00
No. 822	250.00
No. 823	116.50

Also included with the bank statement was a check for $50 drawn by Robert Davis, a customer of Crossland Company. This check was marked NSF (not sufficient funds). Finally, an examination of the accounting records indicated that the bank had collected for Crossland cash of $10,000 on December 31, Year 5, representing the maturity value of a U.S. Treasury bill, but the bank did not credit Crossland's account until January 2, Year 6. The U.S. Treasury bill had been purchased by the bank for Crossland at a discount for $9,652 and had been recorded at cost in the Short-Term Investments account by Crossland.

A reconciliation of both the balance per depositor's records and the balance per bank statement to the correct cash balance on December 31, Year 5, is presented below:

CROSSLAND COMPANY
Bank Reconciliation
December 31, Year 5

Balance per depositor's records		$10,592.66
Add: Note collected by bank	$ 2,000.00	
Interest on note collected by bank	30.00	
Proceeds of U.S. Treasury bill which had been pur-		
chased for $9,652.00 (interest revenue = $348.00)	10,000.00	12,030.00
Subtotal		$22,622.66
Less: Bank service charges for December	$ 13.50	
NSF check drawn by Robert Davis	50.00	
Error in recording check no. 821		
($463.90 − $436.90)	27.00	90.50
Correct cash balance		$22,532.16
Balance per bank statement		$12,269.02
Add: Deposit in transit	$ 1,144.60	
Proceeds of U.S. Treasury bill	10,000.00	11,144.60
Subtotal		$23,413.62
Less: Outstanding checks:		
No. 811	$ 421.96	
814	93.00	
822	250.00	
823	116.50	881.46
Correct cash balance		$22,532.16

The bank reconciliation serves three functions: (1) to arrive at the correct cash balance to be reported in the balance sheet, (2) to uncover errors made in recording cash transactions, either by the bank or by the depositor, and (3) to provide information necessary to bring the accounting records up to date. The journal entry required to adjust the accounting records for errors and omissions is taken from the adjustments to the depositor's records in the bank reconciliation. All the items appearing in the reconciliation as additions to or deductions from the "balance per depositor's records" must be reflected in the journal entry. The journal entry on December 31, Year 5, to adjust the accounting records of Crossland Company appears at the top of page 228.

Cash	11,939.50	
Office Equipment	27.00	
Accounts Receivable: Robert Davis	50.00	
Miscellaneous Expenses	13.50	
Interest Revenue ($30.00 + $348.00)		378.00
Notes Receivable		2,000.00
Short-Term Investments (U.S. Treasury bill)		9,652.00

To adjust Cash account to correct balance as shown in December 31, Year 5, bank reconciliation.

The balance per depositor's records, $10,592.66, plus the debit of $11,939.50 in the journal entry, equal the correct cash balance of $22,532.16.[2] If there had been arithmetic errors in balancing the Cash account, these would be corrected and the balance per depositor's records in the reconciliation also would be changed. Errors of this type seldom are found in bank reconciliation procedures if a trial balance of the general ledger is prepared prior to the preparation of the reconciliation.

The deposit in transit and the outstanding checks will be processed by the bank in the regular course of business during January, Year 6.

Illustration 2: Bank Balance Reconciled to Balance in Depositor's Records
The form of bank reconciliation preferred by practicing accountants reconciles the bank balance to the unadjusted balance of the depositor's Cash account in the general ledger. Then, the required adjusting entry to the Cash account is entered in the bank reconciliation, resulting in the correct Cash balance. This type of bank reconciliation is illustrated on page 229 for Crossland Company on December 31, Year 5.

Comparison of Two Forms of Bank Reconciliation   Each of the two forms of bank reconciliation illustrated in the foregoing sections has advantages and disadvantages. The form which reconciles both the bank balance and the depositor's balance to the correct cash balance has the advantages of being "self-balancing" and clearly identifying items requiring adjustment in the depositor's accounting records. The disadvantage of this form is that it does not **directly** reconcile the bank balance to the unadjusted balance of the Cash account in the depositor's general ledger.

[2] As a general rule, the journal entry resulting from a bank reconciliation is the only example of an adjusting or correcting entry which involves the Cash account.

Reconciliation of bank
balance to unadjusted
Cash account balance

CROSSLAND COMPANY
Bank Reconciliation
December 31, Year 5

Balance per bank statement		$12,269.02
Add: Deposit in transit.	$1,144.60	
Bank service charges for December	13.50	
NSF check drawn by Robert Davis	50.00	
Error in recording check No. 821		
($463.90 − $436.90)	27.00	1,235.10
Subtotal		$13,504.12
Less: Outstanding checks:		
No. 811	$ 421.96	
814	93.00	
822	250.00	
823	116.50	
Total outstanding checks	$ 881.46	
Note collected by bank.	2,000.00	
Interest on note collected by bank	30.00	2,911.46
Balance per depositor's records, unadjusted		$10,592.66
Add: Adjustment to Cash account (see page 228).		11,939.50
Correct cash balance.		$22,532.16

The second form of bank reconciliation has the advantage of reconciling the bank balance to the balance of the Cash account (unadjusted) in the depositor's general ledger. Practicing accountants prefer this form because they are interested in substantiating the balance of the Cash account (unadjusted) in the general ledger of the depositor. They then prepare any required adjusting journal entries for posting to the Cash account. A disadvantage of the second form of bank reconciliation is that it does not present in one place all items requiring adjustment of the Cash account. However, this disadvantage is mitigated by the fact that, generally, **all** reconciling items in a bank reconciliation require adjustment of the Cash account, **other than deposits in transit and outstanding checks.**

A difference in the two forms of bank reconciliation is found in the handling of the $10,000 collected by the bank on behalf of Crossland Company on December 31, Year 5, for the matured U.S. Treasury bill. This item appeared as a reconciling item in both sections of the first form of reconciliation, because neither the bank statement nor the Cash account (unadjusted) reflected the $10,000 item on December 31, Year 5.

Reconciliation of cash receipts and cash payments (proof of cash)

Cash balances per the bank statement and the depositor's ledger are reconciled to establish the accuracy of the cash records. A full reconciliation of cash receipts and payments (known as a *proof of cash*) also may be made to establish the accuracy of the cash balance and the effectiveness of internal controls over cash.

To illustrate a reconciliation of cash receipts and cash payments for Crossland Company, we need, in addition to the information already provided for the month of December, Year 5, the bank reconciliation for November and cash receipts and payments data for December from both the bank's and Crossland's records. This information is provided below and on page 231.

(1) The following bank reconciliation was prepared on November 30, Year 5:

Bank reconciliation on November 30, Year 5

CROSSLAND COMPANY		
Bank Reconciliation		
November 30, Year 5		
Balance per bank statement		$6,947.26
Add: Deposit in transit	$1,055.52	
Bank service charges for November	3.25	
NSF check drawn by James Price	75.00	1,133.77
Subtotal		$8,081.03
Less: Outstanding checks:		
No. 760	$ 244.18	
762	197.50	
763	88.49	
764	151.25	681.42
Balance per depositor's records, unadjusted		$7,399.61
Less: Adjustment to Cash account (see journal entry below)		78.25
Correct cash balance		$7,321.36

(2) The adjusting journal entry on November 30, Year 5, based on the bank reconciliation above, was as follows:

Journal entry to adjust accounting records for items in bank reconciliation

Miscellaneous Expenses	3.25	
Accounts Receivable: James Price	75.00	
Cash		78.25
To adjust Cash account to correct balance as shown in November 30, Year 5, bank reconciliation.		

(3) The cash receipts journal showed total cash received during December of $22,640.50, and the cash payments journal showed cash payments during December of $19,369.20. Thus, the unadjusted cash balance in Crossland's accounting records on December 31, Year 5, was $10,592.66, as follows:

Cash account for December

Cash

Date	Explanation	Debit	Credit	Balance
Year 5				
Nov. 30	Unadjusted balance			7,399.61 dr
30	Adjustment for items in bank reconciliation		78.25	7,321.36 dr
Dec. 31	Cash receipts for December	22,640.50		29,961.86 dr
31	Cash payments for December		19,369.20	10,592.66 dr

(4) The bank statement for December indicated that the total deposits of cash during December were $24,581.42 and that the total checks paid, including bank charges of $13.50, amounted to $19,259.66. This resulted in an unadjusted bank balance on December 31, Year 5, of $12,269.02 ($6,947.26 + $24,581.42 − $19,259.66 = $12,269.02).

The cash receipts, cash payments, and the cash balances reflected in the bank statement and in the ledger of Crossland Company are reconciled to the correct balances for December as follows:

Proof of cash

CROSSLAND COMPANY
Proof of Cash
December 31, Year 5

	Balance, Nov. 30, Year 5	Receipts	Payments	Balance, Dec. 31, Year 5
Balances per bank statement	$6,947.26	$24,581.42	$19,259.66	$12,269.02
Deposits in transit:				
Nov. 30, Year 5.	1,055.52	(1,055.52)		
Dec. 31, Year 5.		1,144.60		1,144.60
Outstanding checks:				
Nov. 30, Year 5.	(681.42)		(681.42)	
Dec. 31, Year 5.			881.46	(881.46)
Other reconciling items:				
Bank service charges for December .			(13.50)	13.50
NSF check drawn by Robert Davis . .			(50.00)	50.00
Error in recording check No. 821 . . .			(27.00)	27.00
Note and interest collected by bank .		(2,030.00)		(2,030.00)
Balances per depositor's records	$7,321.36	$22,640.50	$19,369.20	$10,592.66
Add: Adjustment to Cash account on Dec. 31, Year 5 (see page 228)				11,939.50
Correct cash balance				$22,532.16

The proof of cash for Crossland Company on December 31, Year 5, is explained below:

1 *Reconciliation of cash receipts per bank statement and per depositor's records.* The $1,055.52 deposit in transit on November 30 is deducted from the deposits recorded by the bank in December because it was a receipt of cash in November. The $1,144.60 deposit in transit on December 31 is a receipt of cash in December and should be included in total cash receipts for December. The $2,030.00 proceeds of the note and interest collected by the bank must be deducted from the deposits recorded by the bank because the proceeds had not been entered in the accounting records (before adjustment) on December 31, Year 5.

2 *Reconciliation of cash payments per bank statement and per depositor's records.* The outstanding checks of $681.42 on November 30 are included in the bank debits for December. These do not represent cash payments during December but rather were shown properly as cash payments in November. The outstanding checks of $881.46 on December 31 did not include any checks which were outstanding on November 30; therefore, this total is properly classified as a cash payment by Crossland during December. The bank service charges of $13.50 and the NSF check of $50.00 were included in the bank's debits for December but not in the accounting records (unadjusted). The bank recorded check no. 821 at its correct amount of $463.90; that amount is $27.00 larger than the $436.90 amount recorded in the depositor's cash payments records.

3 *Reconciliation of bank and depositor cash balances.* The last column of the reconciliation is identical to the reconciliation of the bank and depositor balances to the correct cash balance illustrated on page 229. The journal entry required to adjust the accounting records of Crossland Company on December 31, Year 5, is the same as that illustrated on page 228.

Cash overdraft

The issuance of checks in excess of the balance on deposit will create an **overdraft** in the bank account. Banks often (but not always) refuse to pay a check which exceeds the balance of the depositor's account. Such refusal prevents an overdraft from occurring. In the rare situation in which a business enterprise maintains only one bank account and that account is overdrawn at the balance sheet date, the overdraft should be shown as a current liability. However, if an enterprise has other accounts in the same bank with larger positive balances, it is reasonable to present the net balance of cash as a current asset. This treatment is based on the reasoning that users of financial statements are interested primarily in an enterprise's cash position, rather than in the status of its individual bank accounts.

In rare instances, an accountant may encounter a situation in which checks are written (and recorded) in excess of the amount on deposit, but the checks are not issued to creditors. In preparing financial statements, the accountant should eliminate the credit balance in the Cash account by a journal entry debiting Cash and crediting Accounts Payable (or other liability accounts) for the amount of the checks written but not released.

Disclosure of compensating cash balances

The Securities and Exchange Commission requires that companies filing financial statements with the Commission disclose compensating cash balances.[3] A **compensating balance** generally is defined as that portion of any demand deposit maintained by a depositor which constitutes support for existing borrowing arrangements with banks.

Disclosure of compensating-balance arrangements is required because such cash balances are not readily available for discretionary use by management at the balance sheet date. Because the maintenance of compensating cash balances affects liquidity and the effective cost of borrowing from banks, users of financial statements may find such information useful.

An example of disclosure of compensating cash balances, taken from a recent annual report of a publicly owned company, is presented below:

> *Compensating Balances*—Informal lines of credit agreements with several banks require the company to maintain average cash compensating balances equal to 20% of the average outstanding short-term bank loans or 10% of the amount of the credit line, whichever is higher. The agreements require interest on the loans at the prime rate and are subject to review from time to time and can be terminated at the option of either party.
>
> In 19—, the average compensating balance required to be maintained amounted to $4,354,000, and the amount required on December 31, 19—, was $4,008,000 after adjustment for estimated average float. The average amount of outstanding loans amounted to $9,461,000, and the maximum amount outstanding at the end of any month was $16,631,000. The unused available borrowings under the lines of credit agreements amounted to $58,150,000 on December 31, 19—. The weighted average interest rate on the short-term bank loans during the year amounted to 14.65%.

Credit card sales drafts as cash

Merchants making sales to customers who present bank credit cards prepare a **sales draft** to evidence the credit sale. One copy of the sales draft is given to the customer, another copy is retained by the merchant, and a third copy is deposited in the bank which issued the credit card. Usually the deposit of the sales draft must be made no later than three bank business days following the date of sale. Thus, the copy of the sales draft deposited in the bank by the merchant is the equivalent of **cash.** Accordingly, the general journal entry to record a sale to a customer who presents a bank credit card is as follows:

Journal entry to record credit card sale	*Cash* *345*	
	Sales	*345*
	To record sale to customer, sales draft no. 4672.	

[3] *Accounting Series Release No. 148,* SEC (Washington: 1973).

Any undeposited sales drafts at the end of an accounting period should be reflected as undeposited cash (an addition to the bank balance) in the bank reconciliation at that date.

The bank which issued the credit card charges a *discount* on credit card sales drafts deposited by the merchant. The discount, which varies based on average amounts and monthly volume of sales drafts issued by the merchant, is either deducted from the gross amount of each sales draft deposited or subtracted monthly from the merchant's bank balance. In either case, the appropriate general journal entry for the discount is a debit to an account such as Credit Card Discount Expense and a credit to Cash. The credit card discount expense is included with interest expense in the income statement for the merchant.

SHORT-TERM INVESTMENTS

Investment of idle cash

To achieve efficient use of all resources, management of a business enterprise frequently turns unproductive cash balances into productive resources through the purchase of short-term investments. In some cases a business enterprise may follow a policy of holding, more or less continuously, investments that can be converted to cash as needed.

Short-term investments held by a business enterprise for the purpose of earning a return on cash resources are characterized by their salability at a readily determinable price. Stocks and bonds which are not widely held or frequently traded usually do not meet the marketability test; consequently, securities of this latter type are not considered in this discussion.

Investments in securities of other companies purchased as a means of exercising influence or control over the operations of such companies are of a quite different character and should not be considered as short-term investments. If the holding is for the purpose of exercising control, the effective operation of the enterprise may be hampered by the liquidation of the investment. Investments of this nature are discussed in Chapter 14.

In summary, short-term investments which are classified in the balance sheet as current assets must be readily salable and should not be held for purposes of bolstering business relations with the issuing entity. On the other hand, there is no requirement that the investment be held for a limited time only or that management express its intent as to the duration of the holding. The objectives of acquiring short-term investments are twofold: (1) to maximize the return on invested capital, and (2) to minimize the risk of loss from price fluctuations.

When excess cash is available for short periods, the investment media typically used are certificates of deposit, commercial paper, U.S. Treasury bills, and bonds (both government and corporate) with near-term maturities (in order to minimize price fluctuations). *Certificates of deposit* essentially are promissory notes issued by banks for varying periods of time. **Commercial paper** is the term used for short-term unsecured promissory notes issued by corporations and sold at a discount to investors, generally other companies. **U.S. Treasury bills** are issued at a discount by the United States Treasury with maturities of thirteen weeks, twenty-six weeks, and fifty-two weeks. Longer-term bonds and common stocks, although occasionally used as a medium for investing idle cash, do not meet the objective of limited price fluctuation. Long-term bond prices fluctuate with changes in the level of interest rates, as do prices of bonds with short-term maturities; the degree of fluctuation is greater for bonds with longer maturities. On the other hand, common stocks are subject to wide and erratic price movements because of changes in investor sentiment, corporate earnings, and other business and economic factors.

Recording transactions in short-term investments

At acquisition, short-term investments are recorded at cost, the price of the item in the market *plus any costs incident to the acquisition,* such as brokerage commissions and transfer taxes. Bonds acquired between interest dates are traded on the basis of the market price plus the interest accrued since the most recent interest payment. The accrued interest is a separate asset which is purchased with the bonds. The cost of these two assets should be separated to achieve a clear picture of the results of the investment in bonds.

Illustration   On January 31, Year 5, Sawyer Company placed an order with a broker to buy 100, $1,000, 9% Atlantic Railroad bonds which mature on November 30, Year 8, with interest dates May 31 and November 30. The bonds were purchased on the same day at 103, plus accrued interest of $1,500 for two months. The brokerage commission was $500. The total cost of the bonds and the total cash outlay are computed below:

Computation of cost of short-term investment in bonds and total cash outlay	

Market price of bonds ($1,030 × 100)	$103,000
Add: Brokerage commission	500
Total cost of bonds	$103,500
Add: Accrued interest for two months on $100,000, at 9% per year . . .	1,500
Total cash outlay	$105,000

The journal entry required to record the purchase of the bonds is given at the top of page 236.

Short-Term Investments.	103,500
Accrued Interest Receivable	1,500
Cash	105,000

To record purchase of 100 bonds at 103 plus accrued interest
of $1,500 and brokerage commission of $500.

On April 30, Year 5, Sawyer Company sold the Atlantic Railroad bonds at 104¾ plus accrued interest for five months. The cash received from sale of the bonds, after brokerage commission of $500, is computed below:

Market price of bonds ($1,047.50 × 100)	$104,750
Less: Brokerage commission	500
Proceeds on sale of bonds	$104,250
Add: Accrued interest for five months on $100,000, at 9% per year . . .	3,750
Total cash received	$108,000

The following journal entry is required in the accounting records of Sawyer Company on April 30, Year 5, to record the sale of the bonds and to recognize interest revenue:

Cash	108,000	
Short-Term Investments.		103,500
Accrued Interest Receivable		1,500
Interest Revenue		2,250
Gain on Sale of Short-Term Investments.		750

To record sale of Atlantic Railroad bonds at 104¾, less brokerage commission of $500, plus accrued interest of $3,750.

The gain of $750 realized on the sale of the Atlantic Railroad bonds is the result of a change in the market price of the bonds, which may have occurred for any number of reasons. The two most likely causes of such a gain are (1) a decline in the level of interest rates, or (2) a more favorable appraisal of this particular bond issue. If the level of interest rates had risen since January 31, Year 5, these bonds probably would have been sold at a loss.

The $1,500 of accrued interest on the bonds acquired on January 31, Year 5, might at that time have been recorded as a debit to the Interest Revenue account. This procedure would require that the $3,750 of accrued interest received on April 30 be credited to the Interest Revenue account. The net effect would be to show $2,250 as interest revenue for the three months the bonds were owned.

Discount or Premium on Short-Term Investments in Bonds In accounting for short-term investments in bonds, it usually is unnecessary to amortize premiums or to accumulate discounts. Such temporary investments generally have near-term maturities; consequently, any premium or discount is likely to be negligible. The holding period by the investor also is likely to be very short, which means that any change in market price usually is attributable to the two causes mentioned on page 236 rather than to the approach of the maturity date. In theory, the amortization of premium or the accumulation of discount always is proper, but as a practical matter such amortization or accumulation on short-term investments in bonds would add little to the accuracy of financial statements.

Computation of Interest on Investment in Bonds Accrued interest on notes and bonds issued by business enterprises generally is computed on the basis of a 360-day year. Any full month expired, whether it has 31 days, 30 days, or only 28 days, is viewed as one-twelfth of a year. Additional interest is determined on the basis of the number of days elapsed. For example, interest from April 25 to August 10 is computed for three months (May, June, and July) and 15 days (5 days in April and 10 days in August), or 105/360 of a year.

Interest on U.S. government securities is computed on the basis of a 365-day year; thus the **exact number of days** for the interest computation period must be determined. Interest on a U.S. Treasury bond from April 25 to August 10, for example, would be 107/365 of a full year's interest.

Accounting for commercial paper and U.S. Treasury bills

Unlike bonds, commercial paper and U.S. Treasury bills are noninterest-bearing. The interest revenue earned on these investments is measured by the **discount**—the difference between the face amount and the issuance price. The discount is accumulated in the Short-Term Investments account and recorded as interest revenue at the end of each accounting period during the stated term of the commercial paper or U.S. Treasury bills.

To illustrate, assume that Rochester Company on December 1, Year 1, invested $95,000 in Berg Company's four-month commercial paper with a face amount of $100,000. The discount is $5,000 ($100,000 − $95,000 = $5,000) and the discount rate is 15% a year ($100,000 × 15% × $\frac{4}{12}$ = $5,000). Assuming that Rochester's fiscal year ends on December 31, the journal entries relating to the short-term investment in commercial paper are illustrated on page 238.

ROCHESTER COMPANY
Journal Entries

Year 1			
Dec. 1	Short-Term Investments (Commercial Paper). . . .	95,000	
	Cash		95,000
	To record purchase of $100,000 face amount of four-month commercial paper of Berg Company.		
Dec. 31	Short-Term Investments (Commercial Paper). . . .	1,250	
	Interest Revenue		1,250
	To record accrued interest for one month on short-term investment in commercial paper: $5,000 \times \frac{1}{4} = \$1,250.$		
Year 2			
Mar. 31	Short-Term Investments (Commercial Paper). . . .	3,750	
	Interest Revenue		3,750
	To record accrued interest for three months on short-term commercial paper: $5,000 \times \frac{3}{4} = \$3,750.$		
Mar. 31	Cash	100,000	
	Short-Term Investments (Commercial Paper).		100,000
	To record maturity of four-month commercial paper of Berg Company.		

Cost Selection   The cost of securities sold is not always as definite as in the preceding illustrations. If there are several purchases of the same security at different dates and prices, and it is then decided to sell a portion of the holdings, some procedure of cost selection must be employed. Among the methods commonly used are specific identification, first-in, first-out, and average cost. For income tax purposes only the specific identification and the first-in, first-out methods are acceptable.

Stock and bond certificates generally have serial numbers which make it easy to identify the cost of specific investments. By using the specific identification method, management may influence the amount of realized gain or loss by deliberately selecting the certificates to be sold from a high-cost lot or a low-cost lot. As an example, assume that Kane Company buys 100 bonds of Lowe Corporation for $96,000 and a few months later buys another 100 bonds for $99,000. A month later Kane sells 100 Lowe Corporation bonds for $98,000. The sale will show a gain of $2,000 or a loss of $1,000, depending on which bonds are sold.

organizations, mutual life insurance companies, and employee benefit plans. The Statement for the most part does not apply to business enterprises in industries having specialized accounting practices with respect to marketable equity securities. Such industries include investment companies, brokers and dealers in securities, stock life insurance companies, and fire and casualty insurance companies.

Definition of Terms The FASB defined the following terms relating to marketable equity securities:[6]

1 *Equity securities* include instruments representing ownership shares or the right to acquire or dispose of ownership shares at fixed or determinable prices. The following are not equity securities: preferred stock that by its terms either must be redeemed by the issuing enterprise or is redeemable at the option of the investor; treasury stock; and convertible bonds.

2 *Marketable* means that sales prices (or bid and ask prices) are currently available for an equity security on a national securities exchange or in the publicly reported over-the-counter market.

3 *Market price* refers to the price of a single share or unit of a marketable equity security.

4 *Market value* refers to the aggregate of the market price times the number of shares or units of each marketable equity security in the portfolio.

5 *Cost* refers to the original cost of a marketable equity security, unless a new cost basis has been assigned on recognition of an impairment of value that was deemed other than temporary. In such cases, the new cost basis shall be the cost.

6 *Valuation allowance* for a marketable equity securities portfolio represents the net unrealized loss in that portfolio.

7 *Carrying amount* of a marketable equity securities portfolio is the amount at which that portfolio of marketable equity securities is reported in the balance sheet.

8 *Realized gain or loss* represents the difference between the net proceeds from the sale of a marketable equity security and its cost. (Such gain or loss results only upon sale of a security.)

9 *Net unrealized gain or loss* on a marketable equity securities portfolio represents at any date the difference between the aggregate market value and aggregate cost. (Such gain or loss is recognized only at the end of an accounting period and is not a factor in the computation of taxable income.)

Accounting for Current Marketable Equity Securities The FASB stated that the carrying amount of a marketable equity securities portfolio should be the lower of its aggregate cost or market value, as determined at each balance sheet date. The amount, if any, by which the aggregate cost of the portfolio exceeds market value is accounted for by use of a valuation allowance. The treatment of changes in the valuation allowance depends on whether the securities are considered current or noncurrent assets. In the case of a classified balance sheet, marketable equity securities are grouped into separate current and noncurrent portfolios for the purpose of comparing aggregate cost and market

[6] *FASB Statement No. 12,* pp. 3–5.

value. In the case of an unclassified balance sheet, marketable equity securities should be considered as noncurrent assets. Generally, the current marketable equity securities portfolios of all entities included in consolidated financial statements are treated as a single consolidated portfolio; noncurrent portfolios are treated similarly.

Realized gains and losses from sale of current or noncurrent marketable equity securities are included in the determination of net income of the period in which they occur. Changes in the valuation allowance for a marketable equity securities portfolio included in current assets also are included in net income of the period in which they occur. Changes in the valuation allowance result in **unrealized gains and losses.** A recovery in the aggregate market value of securities which had been written down to a market value below cost requires the recognition of an **unrealized gain** which is included in net income. However, increases in the aggregate market value of the current portfolio of marketable equity securities above aggregate cost are not recognized in the accounting records. **Unrealized losses** on securities held in the noncurrent portfolio are not included in net income of the period in which they occur; such losses are reported as direct reductions in stockholders' equity. In the balance sheet, the adjusted valuation allowance is deducted from the cost of marketable equity securities.

If there is a change in the classification of a marketable equity security between current and noncurrent, the security should be transferred between the corresponding portfolios at the lower of its cost or market value at date of transfer. If market value is less than cost, the market value becomes the new cost basis, and the difference is accounted for as a realized loss and is included in net income.

Unrealized gains and losses on marketable equity securities are not taken into account in the determination of taxable income. Such gains and losses result in **timing differences** between taxable income and pretax accounting income reported in the income statement. Interperiod tax allocation procedures, described in Chapter 3 and in Chapter 21, should be applied to determine whether a net unrealized gain or loss should be reduced by the applicable income tax effect. However, a tax effect should be recognized on a net unrealized loss only when there exists **assurance beyond a reasonable doubt** that the benefit will be realized by an offset of the unrealized loss against future unrealized gains.

Illustration To illustrate the application of **FASB Statement No. 12** to a current portfolio of marketable equity securities, assume the following changes in the portfolio of Weber Company from December 31, Year 1, through December 31, Year 3, set forth on page 243.

WEBER COMPANY
Changes in Current Portfolio of Marketable Equity Securities
For Years Ended December 31, Year 1 through Year 3

	Cost	Market value	Unrealized gain (loss)
Dec. 31, Year 1			
Security A.	$100,000	$ 80,000	$(20,000)
Security B.	200,000	160,000	(40,000)
Security C.	50,000	75,000	25,000
Totals	$350,000	$315,000	$(35,000)
Dec. 31, Year 2			
Security A.	$100,000	$ 75,000	$(25,000)
Security B.	100,000*	70,000	(30,000)
Security C.	50,000	60,000	10,000
Totals	$250,000	$205,000	$(45,000)
Dec. 31, Year 3			
Security A.	$100,000	$ 80,000	$(20,000)
Security B.	100,000	90,000	(10,000)
Security C.	50,000	65,000	15,000
Totals	$250,000	$235,000	$(15,000)

* On March 1, Year 2, one-half of the holdings of Security B (cost, $100,000) was sold for
$75,000. There were no other sales of securities in Year 2 or Year 3.

December 31, Year 1, the date of initial application   A valuation allowance of
$35,000 is required for marketable equity securities included in the cur-
rent portfolio to reflect the excess of cost, $350,000, over market value,
$315,000. The unrealized loss of $35,000 is included in the net income
for Year 1. The journal entry to record the unrealized loss and the valuation allowance is:

Journal entry to establish valuation allowance for current portfolio of marketable equity securities	*Unrealized Loss in Value of Marketable Equity Securities. . . . 35,000*	
	Valuation Allowance to Reduce Marketable Equity Se-	
	curities to Market Value.	*35,000*
	To establish valuation allowance for decline in market value of	
	current portfolio of marketable equity securities.	

March 1, Year 2, sale of security at a loss   The sale of one-half of the holdings of Security B for $75,000 resulted in a ***realized loss*** of $25,000. The
loss is included in net income for Year 6. The journal entry to record the
sale is shown at the top of page 244.

Journal entry for sale of
marketable equity secu-
rity at a loss

Cash. 75,000
Realized Loss on Sale of Marketable Equity Securities. 25,000
       Short-Term Investments   100,000
To record sale of Security B at a realized loss.

December 31, Year 2, increase in valuation allowance A valuation allowance of $45,000 is required for marketable equity securities in the current portfolio to reflect the excess of cost, $250,000, over market value, $205,000. Because the balance in the valuation allowance account is $35,000, an increase of $10,000 is required. The journal entry to record the increase in the valuation allowance is:

Unrealized Loss in Value of Marketable Equity Securities. . . . 10,000
     Valuation Allowance to Reduce Marketable Equity Se-
        curities to Market Value.   10,000
To record increase in valuation allowance as a result of further
decline in market value of current portfolio of marketable equity
securities.

December 31, Year 3, recovery in market value of portfolio There has been a market recovery during Year 3, as evidenced by the need to reduce the valuation allowance from $45,000 to $15,000. The difference of $30,000 is an **unrealized gain** and is included in net income for Year 3. The journal entry to record the reduction in the valuation allowance is:

Valuation Allowance to Reduce Marketable Equity Securities to
     Market Value 30,000
        Unrealized Gain in Value of Marketable Equity Securities   30,000
To reduce valuation allowance as a result of recovery in market
value of current portfolio of marketable equity securities.

Note that in Year 2, the amount of the realized loss recognized was based on the actual cost of Security B ($100,000), not the carrying amount at the time of sale ($80,000), and that the **valuation allowance is adjusted only at the end of the accounting period.** It also should be observed that the valuation of the entire current portfolio at lower of cost or market results in the recognition of the unrealized gain on Security C in Year 1, which defers recognition of part of the unrealized loss of $60,000 on Securities A and B. Also, the current versus noncurrent portfolio approaches adopted by the FASB can result in possible manipulative practices to avoid recognition of unrealized losses in the current portfolio. This can be achieved by the transfer of a security with a market value above cost from the noncurrent portfolio to the current portfolio.

Disclosure Requirements   The following information with respect to marketable equity securities included in the current portfolio is disclosed either in the financial statements or in notes to the financial statements:[7]

1 As of the date of each balance sheet presented, aggregate cost and aggregate market value, with identification as to which is the carrying amount.

2 As of the date of the latest balance sheet presented, the gross unrealized gains representing the excess of market value over cost for all marketable equity securities in the portfolio, and the gross unrealized losses representing the excess of cost over market value for all marketable equity securities in the portfolio.

3 For each accounting period for which an income statement is presented:
   a Net realized gain or loss included in the determination of net income.
   b The basis on which cost was determined in the computation of realized gain or loss (that is, average cost or other method used).

4 Financial statements should not be adjusted for realized gains or losses or for changes in market prices when such events occur after the date of the financial statements but prior to their issuance. However, significant net realized and net unrealized gains and losses arising after the date of the financial statements, but prior to their issuance, applicable to securities owned at the date of the most recent balance sheet, should be disclosed.

Balance sheet presentation of cash and short-term investments

Cash is the most liquid asset which a business enterprise owns, in the sense that it is most easily converted into other assets and services. This characteristic justifies its position as the first item in the current asset section of the balance sheet. There seldom is any reason to be concerned about the valuation of cash. There are few sources of possible loss except for theft, which cannot be anticipated. Loss due to bank failure has all but disappeared in recent years with the institution of the Federal Deposit Insurance Corporation. This agency of the United States government insures accounts up to $100,000 in banks which are covered under provisions of its charter. Therefore, cash is reported in the balance sheet at the amount which represents its current fair value.

As stated on page 233, banks often require that borrowers maintain **compensating balances** of cash on deposit as a condition for borrowing money. The net effect of such arrangements is to increase the effective interest rate on loans because the full amount of the loan is not available to the borrower. Compensating-balance agreements with banks should be disclosed in financial statements to give more information about the effective cost of borrowing and the relationship between business enterprises and banks.

[7] Ibid., pp. 7–8.

Short-term investments rank next to cash in liquidity and should be listed below cash in the current asset section of the balance sheet. Whether short-term investments are reported at cost or at the lower of cost or market, disclosure of the current market value is required. The presentation of cash and short-term investments in a balance sheet on December 31, Year 4, is illustrated below:

Balance sheet presentation of cash and short-term investments

Current assets:

Cash (Note 1)		$21,100,000
Short-term investments in corporate and U.S. government obligations, at cost which approximates market value		9,000,000
Marketable equity securities, at cost (Note 2)	$12,000,000	
Less: Valuation allowance to reduce marketable equity securities to market value.	1,500,000	10,500,000

Note 1: The company maintains lines of credit with a group of domestic banks for borrowing funds on a short-term and long-term basis. The company has agreed to maintain an average compensating balance of 10% of the unused lines of credit and 15% of the amounts borrowed. On December 31, Year 4, the aggregate compensating-balance requirement was approximately $11,250,000.

Note 2: The gross unrealized loss on December 31, Year 4, was $4,000,000, and the gross unrealized gain was $2,500,000. On February 15, Year 5, the gross unrealized loss was $3,200,000, and the gross unrealized gain was $2,950,000.

REVIEW QUESTIONS

1 What are the normal components of **cash?**

2 How would you classify the following items in a balance sheet?
  a Travel advances to employees
  b Cash deposited with a trustee for the repayment of bonds
  c Undeposited cash representing receipts of the prior day
  d Customer's check returned by the bank marked NSF (not sufficient funds)
  e A nonreturnable deposit with a real estate broker as an option on a tract of land
  f Deposit in a foreign bank where there are restrictions on currency conversions
  g U.S. Treasury bills temporarily held until cash is needed to make payments on building under construction
  h A petty cash fund composed of the following:

Coin and currency	$110
Vouchers:	
Selling expenses	61
General and administrative expenses.	29

3 What is **management's responsibility** with respect to cash? What techniques are used to aid in carrying out this responsibility?

4 a What is a system of *internal controls?*
  b Differentiate between *internal administrative controls* and *internal accounting controls.*
  c Why is internal control over cash and short-term investments particularly important?

5 Parr Company has a change fund of $100 in its cash register. The cash sales tickets for May 25 total $2,049.60, and cash in the cash register, verified by count, totals $2,154.25. Prepare the journal entry necessary to record sales for May 25.

6 Why are adjusting entries usually not made to reflect outstanding checks as liabilities or deposits in transit as cash on hand?

7 a What are three functions of the bank reconciliation?
  b What function does the reconciliation of cash receipts and cash payments (proof of cash) serve?

8 a Describe two forms of bank reconciliation in common usage.
  b Which form of bank reconciliation is preferred by practicing accountants? Explain.

9 How should a material *cash overdraft* be reported in the balance sheet? Explain.

10 Define *compensating cash balances* and state the reasons for disclosure of such balances in financial statements.

11 Why is management concerned with investing cash, which is only temporarily in excess of actual requirements, in short-term investments? What can be done to eliminate or minimize the risk of loss from temporary fluctuations in the market price of securities held as short-term investments?

12 Can you justify the use of current market value as the basis for valuing all short-term investments? Explain.

13 What two questions relative to marketable equity securities held in the current portfolio did the FASB attempt to answer in *Statement No. 12?*

14 Define the following terms relating to the accounting for marketable equity securities:
  a Equity securities
  b Valuation allowance
  c Carrying amount
  d Realized gain or loss
  e Net unrealized gain or loss

15 Briefly state the accounting treatment of the valuation allowance to reduce marketable equity securities to market value. Include in your answer the treatment of realized gains and losses and changes in market value in subsequent accounting periods.

16 What information with respect to marketable equity securities should be disclosed in the financial statements or in the notes to the financial statements?

17 Should certificates of deposit be included in cash in the balance sheet for a business enterprise? Explain.

EXERCISES

Ex. 6-1 Select the best answer for each of the following multiple-choice questions:

1 Karmin Company's marketable equity securities portfolio, which is appropriately included in current assets, is as follows:

		December 31, Year 2	
	Cost	Market value	Unrealized gain (loss)
Robi, Inc.	$100,000	$100,000	$ –0–
Willson Company	200,000	150,000	(50,000)
Rivas Company	250,000	260,000	10,000
Totals	$550,000	$510,000	$(40,000)

		December 31, Year 1	
	Cost	Market value	Unrealized gain (loss)
Robi, Inc.	$100,000	$120,000	$ 20,000
Willson Company	300,000	260,000	(40,000)
Rivas Company	200,000	240,000	40,000
Totals	$600,000	$620,000	$ 20,000

Disregarding income taxes, what amount should be reported as an unrealized loss in Karmin's Year 2 income statement?
a $0 *b* $10,000 *c* $40,000 *d* $60,000

2 Whalen Company maintains two checking accounts. A special account is used for the weekly payroll only, and the general account is used for all other disbursements. Each week, a check in the amount of the net payroll is drawn on the general account and deposited in the payroll account. The company maintains a $5,000 minimum balance in the payroll account. In a monthly bank reconciliation, the payroll account should:
a Show a zero balance in the bank statement
b Show a $5,000 balance in the bank statement
c Reconcile to $5,000
d Be reconciled jointly with the general account in a single reconciliation

3 Which of the following conditions generally exists before market value can be used as the basis for valuation of current marketable equity securities?
a Market value must approximate historical cost
b Management's intention must be to dispose of the securities within one year
c Market value must be less than cost for each security held in the current marketable equity securities portfolio
d The aggregate valuation of a current marketable equity securities portfolio must be less than the aggregate cost of the portfolio

4 How is the premium or discount on bonds purchased as a short-term investment generally reported in financial statements?
a As an integral part of the cost of the investment and amortized over a period of not less than 60 months
b As an integral part of the cost of the investment until it is sold
c As expense or revenue in the accounting period the bonds are purchased
d As an integral part of the cost of the investment and amortized over the period the bonds are expected to be held

5 A marketable equity security must have a ready market in order to be classified as current, and must:

    a Be available to management for use in current operations

    b Be traded on a recognized national exchange

    c Have a current market value in excess of cost

    d Have been owned less than one year

Ex. 6-2 How should the following reconciling items appear in a four-column proof of cash for the month of November, Year 8? Explain.

    a Outstanding checks on November 30, Year 8

    b Bank service charge for month of October, Year 8

    c Deposit in transit on October 31, Year 8

    d NSF check returned to depositor by the bank on November 17, Year 8; redeposited on November 18, Year 8, with no journal entry in the accounting records

Ex. 6-3 The items required for the September 30, Year 9, bank reconciliation of Coleman Company's demand (checking) account follow:

Balance per bank statement, Sept. 30, Year 9		$12,370.68
Balance per depositor's records, Sept. 30, Year 9		4,977.47
Bank charges for month of September, Year 9.		3.25
Bank error in recording check no. 648:		
Drawn and recorded in depositor's records	$411.42	
Encoded incorrectly and paid by bank	41.42	
Net bank error		$ 370.00
Outstanding checks:		
No. 643	$ 10.00	
651	50.00	
654	750.00	
655	750.00	
671	55.00	
673	750.00	
674	2,000.00	
675	14.00	
676	250.00	
678	5.00	
679	2,390.96	
680	1.50	
Total outstanding checks		$7,026.46

Prepare a bank reconciliation for Coleman Company on September 30, Year 9. Use the total for outstanding checks on September 30, Year 9; do not list individual checks. Reconcile both the bank balance and the depositor's balance to a correct balance.

Ex. 6-4 The petty cash fund for Grant Company is $100. During March, $15.00 was spent on entertainment, $18.10 was spent on office supplies expense, $26.50 was spent on postage expense, $20.00 was spent for merchandise, $16.45 was spent on miscellaneous items, and $3.95 remained on hand.

Prepare a journal entry to record the replenishment of the petty cash fund on March 31.

Ex. 6-5 From the following data, **(a)** compute the cash balance in the accounting records before adjustments are recorded, and **(b)** prepare a journal entry to bring the accounting records up to date:

Balance per bank statement	$15,500
Checks outstanding	6,400
Receipts recorded in the accounting records, not yet deposited	1,920
Bank service charges not recorded in the accounting records	12
Promissory note collected by bank, not recorded in the accounting records (includes interest of $40)	4,040

Ex. 6-6 The following bank reconciliation was prepared for Caleb Company on June 30, Year 6:

CALEB COMPANY

Bank Reconciliation

June 30, Year 6

Balance per bank statement, June 30, Year 6		$ 8,308
Add: Deposit in transit	$ 1,690	
Check incorrectly charged to Caleb Company by bank	250	
Bank service charge	10	
NSF check from customer returned by bank.	120	2,070
Subtotal.		$10,378
Less: Proceeds of bank loan arranged on June 30, Year 6. .	$10,000	
Outstanding checks	2,940	
Error in recording check in payment of vendor's invoice	18	12,958
Balance per accounting records, June 30, Year 6		$ (2,580)

Compute the correct cash balance on June 30, Year 6, and prepare a journal entry to adjust the Cash account to the correct balance. Interest on the bank loan is payable at maturity, and all payments on vendors' invoices are debited to Accounts Payable.

Ex. 6-7 Prepare journal entries to record the following transactions relating to short-term investments of Robards Company:

June 11 Purchased $50,000 face amount 15% bonds issued by Lamar Company. Total purchase price was $52,800, which included accrued interest of $1,250 from April 11.

Oct. 11 Received semiannual interest on Lamar Company bonds, $3,750.

Dec. 11 Sold $20,000 face amount Lamar Company bonds for total consideration of $20,500, which included accrued interest of $500 from Oct. 11.

Dec. 31 Recorded accrued interest for 80 days on remaining Lamar Company bonds.

Ex. 6-8 Presented on page 251 is a condensed version of the bank reconciliation prepared by Edgewood Company on March 31, Year 1.

EDGEWOOD COMPANY
Condensed Bank Reconciliation
March 31, Year 1

Balance per bank statement		$11,120
Add: Deposit in transit	$1,390	
Service charge	8	1,398
Subtotal		$12,518
Less: Outstanding checks		2,008
Balance in Cash account (before adjustment)		$10,510

Cash receipts and payments recorded in the accounting records during the month of April, Year 1, are listed below:

Cash receipts $29,400
Cash payments (including adjusting entry for March bank service charge) 26,950

On April 30, Year 1, checks outstanding amounted to $2,950, and deposits in transit amounted to $1,911. There was no service charge for April, and no errors were made either by the bank or by the company.

Prepare a proof of cash for the month of April, Year 1, similar to the illustration on page 231.

Ex. 6-9 Italia Company began investing idle cash in marketable equity securities in Year 3. The cost and market value of the securities held in its current portfolio at the end of its fiscal years were as follows:

End of Year	Cost	Market
3	$200,000	$210,000
4	310,000	260,000
5	280,000	220,000
6	400,000	425,000

Prepare journal entries at the end of each year to adjust the valuation allowance to reduce current marketable equity securities to market value.

Ex. 6-10 In auditing the accounting records of Skube Company for Year 10, you find the following account:

Short-Term Investment — Lee Industries Common Stock

Purchased 200 shares @ 26¼	5,250	Dividend received	80
		Dividend received	80
		Proceeds on sale of 100 shares	2,940

You also find that a commission of $106 on the purchase of the 200 shares of Lee Industries common stock was debited to the Miscellaneous Expenses account.

Prepare a journal entry on December 31, Year 10, to correct the accounting records.

SHORT CASES FOR ANALYSIS AND DECISION

Case 6-1 Presented below are four unrelated situations involving marketable equity securities:

a A noncurrent portfolio with an aggregate market value in excess of cost includes one security whose market value has declined to less than one-half of the original cost. The decline in value is not considered to be temporary.

b The balance sheet does not classify assets and liabilities as current and noncurrent. The portfolio of marketable equity securities includes securities normally considered current that have an aggregate cost in excess of market value of $2,000. The remainder of the portfolio has an aggregate market value in excess of cost of $5,000.

c A marketable equity security, whose market value currently is less than cost, is classified as noncurrent but is to be reclassified as current.

d The noncurrent portfolio of marketable equity securities consists of the common stock of one company. At the end of the prior year the market value of the security was 50% of original cost, and this effect was reflected properly in a valuation allowance account. However, at the end of the current year the market value of the security had appreciated to twice the original cost. The security still is considered noncurrent at year-end.

Instructions What is the effect on the balance sheet classification, carrying amount, and net income for each of the above situations? Complete your response to each situation before proceeding to the next situation.

Case 6-2 Management of Providence Company foresees a period of three to five years of reduced operations. During this period, management does not expect to replace any plant assets. Management presents the board of directors with a plan (1) to maintain the ratio of dividends to net income at 60%, and (2) to invest all cash which accumulates in excess of normal operating needs in a diversified list of high-quality common stocks. Management also proposes that the stocks be carried in the balance sheet at market value at the balance sheet date. Any change in market value from date of purchase or the most recent valuation for financial statement purposes is to be reflected in the income statement.

Instructions

a What are the advantages of accounting for and reporting of investments in this manner?

b What objections might be made to this method of reporting the investments?

c Should the investments be reported as a current or a noncurrent asset? Why?

Case 6-3 Segura Company is projecting an increased level of operations for the coming year (Year 4), which will require an additional investment in inventories and accounts receivable. The minimum cash balance required is $50,000. After a detailed review of the prospects for the coming year, the controller prepared the following forecast of monthly cash balances (brackets indicate projected cash deficiency):

January	$110,000	July	$395,000
February	50,000	August	450,000
March	(100,000)	September	80,000
April	(230,000)	October	(250,000)
May	(150,000)	November	(290,000)
June	150,000	December	(50,000)

Short-term investment decisions are made and loans are negotiated on the fifteenth day of each month in an amount equal to the projected cash surplus or deficiency for the month. Changes in the short-term investment or loan positions are made in multiples of $5,000.

Assume that surplus cash can be invested in short-term U.S. Treasury notes bearing 10% interest and that borrowed funds cost 15%. The cash balance on January 1 was $50,000.

Instructions

a Prepare a working paper to compute the net cost (interest expense less interest revenue on temporary investments) of short-term borrowing to finance the operations for the year ended December 31, Year 4. Carry computations to nearest dollar.

b If Segura Company is to avoid short-term borrowing, how much long-term debt or equity capital must be raised? Would you recommend that the company attempt to raise the capital or follow a policy of short-term borrowing? Why?

Case 6-4 Since the issuance of **FASB Statement No. 12,** Coldwater Company has intended to follow the practice of valuing its short-term investments in marketable equity securities at the lower of cost or market. On December 31, Year 10, the account Marketable Equity Securities (Current Portfolio) had a balance of $260,000, and the account Valuation Allowance to Reduce Marketable Equity Securities to Market Value had a balance of $40,000. The valuation allowance account had been unchanged during Year 10; the balance of $40,000 was based on the following facts relating to the securities owned on December 31, Year 9:

Security	Cost	Market value	Valuation allowance required
X Company common stock	$150,000	$120,000	$30,000
Y Company common stock	80,000	70,000	10,000
Z Company warrants to purchase			
common stock	30,000	75,000	–0–
Totals	$260,000	$265,000	$40,000

During Year 10, the Y Company common stock was sold for $65,000, the difference between the $65,000 and the cost of $80,000 being debited to the Loss on Sale of Marketable Equity Securities account. The market values of the securities remaining on December 31, Year 10, were: X Company common stock, $90,000; Z Company warrants to purchase common stock, $40,000.

Instructions

a What argument supports the use of the lower-of-cost-or-market rule in the valuation of marketable equity securities?

b Did Coldwater Company apply the lower-of-cost-or-market rule correctly at the end of Year 9? Explain.

c What correcting entries are required on December 31, Year 10, assuming that any error made in Year 9 is corrected as a prior period adjustment? Ignore income taxes.

d Assume that the president of Coldwater Company does not wish to recognize any unrealized loss in the value of marketable equity securities at the end of Year 10. Instead, the president wants to transfer a block of K Company common stock from the noncurrent portfolio to the current portfolio. The stock of K Company is listed on the New York Stock Exchange with a market value of $200,000. K Company is a major customer, and its stock was acquired many years ago at a cost of $100,000 to maintain good business relations between Coldwater Company and K Company. Would you approve the president's proposal? Explain.

PROBLEMS

6-1 Mobile Company owned marketable equity securities on December 31, Year 5, which were appropriately recorded as current assets as follows:

	Carrying amount on Dec. 31, Year 5
Bart Corporation, 500 shares of $200 par 6% cumulative preferred stock, at cost (market value $240,000)	$110,000
Behrend Corp., 1,000 shares of $3 no-par convertible preferred stock, at cost (market value $230,000)	225,000
Bella Company, 10,000 shares of common stock, at cost (market value $250,000)	200,000
Chockey, Inc., 3,000 shares of common stock, at cost (market value $92,000)	90,000
Dempsey Co., 4,000 shares of common stock, at cost (market value $25,000)	24,000
Total marketable equity securities	$649,000

During Year 6 the following transactions occurred:

(1) Bart Corporation could not pay dividends on preferred stock in Year 6 due to adverse business conditions. The market value of the stock was $120,000 at December 31, Year 6.

(2) Behrend Corp. pays cash dividends once a year to stockholders of record on May 31. The cash was received on June 10, Year 6. On June 15, Year 6, Mobile converted 500 shares of Behrend Corp. $3 no-par convertible preferred stock to 1,000 shares of Behrend Corp. common stock which had a market value of $114,000 at the date of the conversion and $116,000 on December 31, Year 6. The market value of the remaining $3 no-par convertible preferred stock was $117,000 on December 31, Year 6.

(3) Bella Company issued a 10% stock dividend in Year 6. The market value of the common stock on December 31, Year 6, was $24 a share.

(4) Chockey, Inc., effected a 2 for 1 stock split in Year 6. The market value of the stock on December 31, Year 6, was $91,000.

(5) Dempsey Co. declared cash dividends to stockholders of record on March 31, Year 6, and June 30, Year 6, of $0.30 a share at each date. The cash was received on April 15, Year 6, and July 15, Year 6, respectively. On July 4, Year 6, Mobile sold all its shares of Dempsey for $7 a share.

Instructions

a Prepare a working paper to compute the aggregate cost and aggregate market value of Mobile Company's current marketable equity securities on December 31, Year 6.

b Prepare a partial balance sheet and related note for Mobile Company's marketable equity securities on December 31, Year 6.

c Compute and list the amounts of the Year 6 marketable equity securities transactions that should appear in Mobile Company's income statement for Year 6.

6-2   The bank statement for Delaware Corporation showed a balance of $70,694.88 on December 31, Year 9. The balance of the Cash account was $65,194.43. In comparing the bank balance with the cash balance in the accounting records, the corporation's accountant discovered the following:

(1) Checks amounting to $18,830 had not cleared the bank.
(2) A check in payment of an account payable was recorded in the accounting records for $857.20; the correct amount of the check was $875.20.
(3) A customer's check for $739.90 was returned marked NSF. No journal entry had been made in the accounting records to record this check.
(4) A deposit of $12,565.70 had not been recorded by the bank.
(5) The bank's charge for printing checks was $5.95.

Instructions
a Prepare a bank reconciliation in the format which is preferred by practicing accountants.
b Prepare a journal entry to bring the accounting records up to date. Record the journal entry's net effect on the cash account in the working paper prepared in *a*.

6-3   Prescott Company was organized early in Year 2. During the next four years it completed the following transactions in the current portfolio of marketable equity securities:

Year 2: Purchased the following marketable equity securities:

Security A $100,000
Security B   50,000
Security C   75,000

Year 3: Sold Security A for $140,000, net of brokerage commission and other charges.
Year 4: Purchased Security D for $80,000.
Year 5: Sold Security B for $37,500, net of brokerage commission and other charges. Purchased Security E at a total cost of $180,000.

The market values of the current portfolio on December 31 of each year were as follows:

	Year 2	Year 3	Year 4	Year 5
Security A	$125,000			
Security B	30,000	$ 45,000	$ 35,000	
Security C	50,000	90,000	70,000	$ 55,000
Security D			85,000	80,000
Security E				175,000
Totals.	$205,000	$135,000	$190,000	$310,000

Instructions
a Prepare journal entries to record the transactions in marketable equity securities listed above for the four-year period, including appropriate adjustments to the valuation allowance account at the end of each year. Ignore income tax considerations.
b Show how the current portfolio of marketable equity securities would be presented in the balance sheet at the end of each of the four years. Supplementary disclosure pursuant to *FASB Statement No. 12* is not required.

6-4   On June 1, Year 2, Katz Corporation adopted a petty cash fund procedure for minor cash payments. Also on June 1, Year 2, the company made an initial investment of idle cash in marketable equity securities. The fiscal year ends on June 30. The operations of the petty cash fund for the last month of the fiscal year and the first month of the following fiscal year, and the purchase of marketable equity securities, are summarized below:

June 1   Petty cash fund was established with a company check for $2,500 payable to the petty cash custodian.

June 1   The company purchased 1,000 shares of Data Processing Associates, Inc., common stock at 40½, plus a commission of $825, as a short-term investment.

June 19   A request for replenishment of the petty cash fund was received by the accounts payable department, supported by appropriate signed vouchers summarized as follows:

Selling expenses	$ 468
Administrative expenses	678
Factory overhead costs	383
Special tools	192
Telephone, telegraph, and postage expenses	48
Miscellaneous expenses	308
Total	$2,077

June 20   A check for $2,077 was drawn payable to the petty cash custodian.

June 30   The company's independent certified public accountant counted the fund in connection with year-end audit work and found the following:

Cash in petty cash fund		$1,010
Employees' checks with July dates (postdated checks)		180
Expense vouchers properly approved as follows:		
Selling expenses	$249	
Administrative expenses	387	
Factory overhead costs	89	
Office supplies expense	96	
Telephone, telegraph, and postage expenses	56	
Miscellaneous expenses	428	1,305
Total		$2,495

The petty cash fund was not replenished on June 30, Year 2.

June 30   The independent certified public accountant also noted that the closing market price of the Data Processing Associates, Inc., stock on June 30 was $35 a share.

July 15   The employees' checks which were held in the petty cash fund on June 30 were cashed, and the proceeds were held in the petty cash fund.

July 31   A request for replenishment of the petty cash fund was received by the accounts payable department, and a check was drawn to restore the fund to its original balance of $2,500. The supporting vouchers for July expenditures are summarized at the top of page 257.

Selling expenses	$ 149	
Administrative expenses	164	
Factory overhead costs	349	
Telephone, telegraph, and postage expenses	35	
Miscellaneous expenses	338	
Total	$1,035	

Instructions

a Prepare journal entries for the foregoing transactions, including any adjustment required at the end of the fiscal year ended June 30, Year 2. Ignore any income tax effects.

b Evaluate Katz Corporation's use of the petty cash fund.

6-5   Martinez, Inc., received the following bank statement for the month of September, Year 6:

MARTINEZ, INC.

In Account with Valley Bank

Waco, Texas

Checks			Deposits	Date	Balance
				Sept. 1	3,658.75
310.00	35.48	130.00	820.00	Sept. 2	4,003.27
60.00	31.15	510.00	72.80	Sept. 5	3,474.92
70.00	515.00		361.00	Sept. 7	3,250.92
90.00			280.00	Sept. 8	3,440.92
13.30	62.50		510.00	Sept. 9	3,875.12
28.00			205.60	Sept. 12	4,052.72
650.00			180.14	Sept. 14	3,582.86
			345.00	Sept. 16	3,927.86
85.00			427.50	Sept. 19	4,270.36
24.10	125.06			Sept. 20	4,121.20
40.00	65.00		90.00	Sept. 21	4,106.20
162.40			360.00	Sept. 23	4,303.80
15.00			625.00	Sept. 26	4,913.80
355.00	270.00	225.00	130.25	Sept. 28	4,194.05
7.50s			280.50	Sept. 30	4,467.05

s = Service charge

The entries in the cash journals for the month of September are shown on page 258.

The cash balance in the depositor's accounting records on August 31 agreed with the balance per bank statement, although a deposit was in transit and two checks were outstanding. The balance in the Cash account on September 30 was $5,380.81.

Cash Receipts Journal			Cash Payments Journal			
Date	Explana-tion	Cash (debit)	Date	Explana-tion	Check no.	Cash (credit)
Sept 1		72.80	Sept 1		65	130.00
3		361.00	1		66	90.00
6		280.00	1		67	35.48
8		510.00	2		68	31.15
10		205.60	4–19		69–78	1,648.86
13		180.14	20		79	24.10
15		345.00	20		80	38.60
17		427.50	20		81	65.00
20		90.00	22		82	162.40
22		360.00	23		83	150.00
24		625.00	26		84	15.00
27		130.25	28		85	270.00
28		280.50	28		86	105.20
29		1,710.10	28		87	225.00
30		315.25	28		88	355.00
		5,893.14	30		89	25.00
			30		90	645.29
			30		91	155.00
						4,171.08

Instructions

a Prepare a bank reconciliation on September 30, Year 6. Use the form preferred by practicing accountants.

b Prepare the necessary journal entry to adjust the Cash account on September 30, Year 6. Record the journal entry's net effect on the Cash account in the
working paper prepared in *a*.

6-6   On February 1, Year 1, Kubec Company had cash in excess of its immediate
needs. Management decided to invest this cash, and any other cash which appeared to be temporarily in excess of current needs, in short-term U.S. government securities. The following transactions occurred during the fiscal year
ended January 31, Year 2:

Year 1
Feb. 2   Purchased for $97,376, including accrued interest of $876, U.S. Treasury 10% bonds, due in two years, $100,000 face amount, with interest
payable June 30 and December 31. (Debit Accrued Interest Receivable
for $876.)
May 31   Sold for $50,834, including accrued interest of $2,084, one-half of the
U.S. Treasury 10% bonds acquired February 2.
June 30 Received interest on U.S. Treasury 10% bonds, $2,500.
Aug. 1   Purchased 40 U.S. Treasury 12%, $1,000 bonds, interest payable April 1
and October 1, at 102 plus accrued interest of $1,600 and a commission
of $125. These bonds mature three years after the next interest date.
Oct. 1   Received interest on U.S. Treasury 12% bonds, $2,400.
Dec. 15 Sold for $49,352, including accrued interest of $2,302, the remainder of
the U.S. Treasury 10% bonds acquired February 2.

Year 2

Jan. 16 Purchased $100,000 face amount U.S. Treasury 14% notes for a net price of $102,250. Interest is paid on these notes on January 16 and July 16.

Jan. 31 Adjusted the accounting records to reflect interest accrued to the end of the fiscal year. Management decided that the premium on bonds and notes purchased will not be amortized. Interest on U.S. Treasury obligations is computed based on the exact number of days elapsed, using a 365-day year. Compute interest on each security to the nearest dollar.

Instructions

a Record the above transactions in general journal form.

b The closing market quotes for the U.S. Treasury 12% bonds and the U.S. Treasury 14% notes on January 31, Year 2, were $101\frac{1}{2}$ and 104, respectively. Prepare a partial balance sheet showing all data for short-term investments. Assume that short-term investments are reported at cost and that market value is shown parenthetically.

6-7 The following data pertaining to the cash transactions and bank account of Chung Company for September, Year 4, are available to you:

(1) *Cash balance per accounting records, Sept. 30, Year 4* $18,104.50

(2) *Cash balance per bank statement, Sept. 30, Year 4* 24,090.80

(3) *Bank service charge for September* 9.00

(4) *Debit memo for printed checks delivered by the bank; the charge has not been recorded in the accounting records* 5.00

(5) *Deposit of Sept. 30 not recorded by bank until Oct. 1* 3,870.00

(6) *Outstanding checks, Sept. 30, Year 4* 8,128.30

(7) *Proceeds of a bank loan on Sept. 30 not recorded in the accounting records (interest payable at maturity)* 2,970.00

(8) *Proceeds from customer's promissory note, principal amount $800, collected by the bank; collection fee of $3 charged by the bank* 810.00

(9) *Check no. 1086 to a supplier entered in the accounting records as $1,879.10; deducted in the bank statement in the correct amount of.* 1,789.10

(10) *Stolen check lacking an authorized signature deducted from Chung's account by the bank in error.* 867.50

(11) *Customer's check returned by the bank marked NSF, indicating that the customer's balance was not adequate to cover the check; no entry has been made in the accounting records to record the returned check* 1,260.50

Instructions

a Prepare a reconciliation of the cash balances to the correct cash balance on September 30, Year 4.

b Prepare a journal entry to adjust the accounting records on September 30, Year 4.

6-8 You are the senior accountant in charge of the March 31, Year 2, audit of Motown Company. Motown's inexperienced accountant has prepared the bank reconciliation on page 260 for your consideration. You have reviewed the dollar amounts in the reconciliation, and have determined that they are accurate.

MOTOWN COMPANY
Bank Reconciliation
March 31, Year 2

Balance per general ledger, Mar. 31, Year 2	$ 84,316.66
Add: Deposit in transit, mailed Mar. 31, Year 2	8,197.66
$9,200 note receivable and $47 interest collected by bank Mar. 31, Year 2, less $1.07 service charge	9,245.93
Bank service charge for March, Year 2	10.88
Check in payment of account payable, drawn and paid by bank as $91.73, recorded in cash payments journal as $917.30 . .	825.57
Subtotal	$102,596.70

Less: Outstanding checks:

No. 413	$ 185.22	
419	216.25	
420	96.44	
421	123.80	
422	314.55	
423	112.01	
Total outstanding checks	$1,048.27	
Check of customer J. K. Lane, deposited Mar. 26, Year 2, returned NSF by bank Mar. 31, Year 2 . . .	814.69	1,862.96
Computed balance per bank statement, Mar. 31, Year 2		$100,733.74
Unlocated difference		(14,320.54)
Balance per bank statement, Mar. 31, Year 2		$ 86,413.20

Instructions
a Prepare a corrected bank reconciliation for Motown Company on March 31, Year 2, in the form preferred by practicing accountants.
b Prepare a correcting journal entry for Motown Company's Cash account on March 31, Year 2. Record the net effect of the journal entry in the reconciliation prepared in *a*.

6-9 The following information pertains to marketable equity securities in the current portfolio of Masters Corporation on December 31, Year 3:

	Cost	Market value
1,000 shares of M Company common stock	$ 50,000	$ 55,000
2,000 shares of N Company common stock	125,000	120,000
500 shares of P Company convertible preferred stock	60,000	62,000

The company was organized on March 4, Year 3, and did not establish a valuation allowance to reduce marketable equity securities to market value at the end of Year 3, because the aggregate market value of the current portfolio exceeded aggregate cost.

During Year 4, the company completed the following transactions in marketable equity securities in its current portfolio:

Feb. 10 Purchased 1,000 shares of Q Company common stock for $32,000.
June 19 Sold 500 shares of P Company convertible preferred stock for $66,000.
Sept. 5 Purchased 800 shares of R Company common stock at a total cost of $47,500.

Market values of the securities held in the current portfolio on December 31, Year 4, were as follows:

1,000 shares of M Company common stock	$ 60,000
2,000 shares of N Company common stock	110,000
1,000 shares of Q Company common stock	25,000
800 shares of R Company common stock	50,000
Total market value	$245,000

On May 1, Year 5, the 800 shares of R Company common stock were sold for $44,000. There were no other purchases or sales through December 31, Year 7. The market values of the equity securities held in the current portfolio on December 31 of each of the succeeding three years were as follows:

	Year 5	Year 6	Year 7
1,000 shares of M Company common stock .	$ 52,000	$ 48,000	$ 65,000
2,000 shares of N Company common stock .	90,000	120,000	125,000
1,000 shares of Q Company common stock .	30,000	24,000	40,000
Totals	$172,000	$192,000	$230,000

Instructions
a Prepare journal entries to record transactions relating to marketable equity securities for the four years (Year 4 through Year 7), including appropriate entries (if any) to the valuation allowance account at the end of each year. Ignore income tax considerations.
b Prepare the balance sheet presentation of current marketable equity securities at the end of each year (Years 4 through 7).

6-10 In connection with an audit of cash of Webb Company as of December 31, Year 15, the following information has been obtained:

(1) Balances per bank statement:

Nov. 30	$ 195,700
Dec. 31	313,674

(2) Balances per accounting records:

Nov. 30	$ 164,826
Dec. 31	287,598

(3) Cash receipts for the month of December:

Per bank statement	$1,670,450
Per accounting records	2,751,445

(4) Outstanding checks:

Nov. 30	$ 63,524
Dec. 31	75,046

(5) Dishonored checks are recorded as a reduction of cash receipts. Dishonored checks which are redeposited then are recorded as a regular cash receipt. Dishonored checks returned by the bank and recorded by Webb amounted to $6,250 during the month of December; according to the accounting records, $5,000 of dishonored checks were redeposited. Dishonored checks recorded in the bank statement but not in the accounting records until the following months amounted to $250 on November 30 and $2,300 on December 31.

(6) On December 31, a $2,323 check on which a stop-payment order was in force was charged to the Webb account by the bank in error.

(7) Proceeds of a promissory note from Capp Company, collected by the bank on December 30, were not entered in the accounting records:

Principal amount of note	$2,000
Interest, $20, less collection charge of $5	15
Net proceeds	$2,015

(8) The company has pledged its accounts receivable with the bank under a contract whereby the bank lends the company 80% on the pledged accounts receivable. Accounting for and collection of the accounts are performed by the company, and adjustments of the loan are made from daily sales reports and daily cash deposits.

The bank credits the Webb account and increases the amount of the loan for 80% of the reported sales. The loan contract states specifically that the sales report must be accepted by the bank before Webb is credited. Sales reports are forwarded by Webb to the bank on the first day following the date of sales. The bank allocates 80% of each deposit to the payment of the loan and 20% to Webb's account. Thus, only 80% of each day's sales and 20% of each collection deposit are entered on the bank statement.

The accountant for Webb records the pledge of new accounts receivable (80% of sales) as a debit to Cash and a credit to Loans Payable to Bank on the date of sales. Of the collections on accounts receivable, 100% is recorded as a cash receipt; 80% of the collections is recorded in the cash payments journal as a payment on the loan. In a review of the loan contract, the following facts were determined:

(a) Included in the deposits in transit is cash from the pledged accounts receivable. Sales were $40,500 on November 30 and $42,250 on December 31. The balance of the deposit in transit on December 31 was made up from collections of $32,110, which were entered in the accounting records in the manner indicated above.

(b) Collections on accounts receivable deposited in December, other than deposits in transit, totaled $1,320,000.

(c) Sales for December totaled $1,600,000.

(9) Cash receipts from other sources which were deposited intact during December totaled $120,835.

(10) Interest on the bank loan for the month of December, charged by the bank but not recorded in the accounting records, amounted to $6,140.

Instructions

a Prepare a four-column reconciliation (proof of cash) of beginning and ending cash balances, cash receipts, and cash payments for December, Year 15.

b Prepare the adjusting journal entry or entries required to correct the Cash account on December 31, Year 15. Record the net effect on the Cash account in the proof of cash prepared in *a*.

7 RECEIVABLES

The term *receivables* includes a variety of claims that generally will provide a future inflow of cash. Receivables come into existence as a result of transactions such as sale of goods or services, loans made, subscriptions obtained from investors for capital stock or bonds, claims for tax refunds, claims for damages to property, and receivables from rents and leases.

Receivables from customers frequently represent a substantial part of a business enterprise's liquid resources. Poor screening of applicants for credit or an inefficient collection policy can result in large losses. Consequently, the accounting methods and internal controls for receivables are important factors in the achievement of profitable operations.

Valuation of receivables

For most receivables the amount of money to be received and the due date can be estimated reasonably. Accountants thus are faced with a relatively certain future inflow of cash, and the problem is to determine the net realizable value of this inflow.

A number of factors must be considered in the valuation of a prospective cash inflow. One factor is the probability that a receivable actually will be collected. For any single receivable, the probability of collection might be difficult to establish; however, for a large group of receivables a reasonably accurate estimate of collectibility can be made.

The uncertainty of collectibility of receivables has been cited by the FASB as an example of a *loss contingency,* because a future event (inability to collect) confirming the loss is *probable* and the amount of the loss can be *reasonably estimated.*[1] If the estimate of possible uncollectible accounts can be made within a range, but no single amount appears to be a better estimate than any other amount within the range, the FASB recommended that the minimum amount in the range be accrued as a contingency loss.[2] In the measurement of the amount of loss or the range of possible loss, the FASB stated:[3]

> Whether the amount of loss can be reasonably estimated . . . will normally depend on, among other things, the experience of the enterprise, information about the ability of individual debtors to pay, and appraisal of the receivables in light of the current economic environment. In the case of an enterprise that has no experience of its own, reference to the experience of other enterprises

[1] *FASB Statement No. 5,* "Accounting for Contingencies," FASB (Stamford: 1975), p. 4.
[2] *FASB Interpretation No. 14,* "Reasonable Estimation of the Amount of a Loss (an interpretation of *FASB Statement No. 5*)," FASB (Stamford: 1976), p. 2.
[3] *FASB Statement No. 5,* pp. 11–12.

in the same business may be appropriate. Inability to make a reasonable estimate of the amount of loss from uncollectible receivables . . . precludes accrual and may, if there is significant uncertainty as to collection, suggest that the installment method, the cost recovery method, or some other method of revenue recognition be used. . . .

Another factor to be considered in the valuation of receivables is the length of time until collection. As stated in Chapter 5, a sum of money due at some future time is not worth as much as the same sum due immediately. The longer the time to maturity, the larger is the difference between the **maturity value** and the **present value** of a receivable. When the time to maturity is long, most contracts between debtors and creditors call for the payment of interest to compensate for the time value of money, and the present value of such a contract may correspond to its face amount. The present value of any noninterest-bearing receivable is less than the amount that will be received at the due date. If the lapse of time to maturity is short, this difference usually is ignored. For example, an ordinary 30-day unsecured account almost always is recorded at its face amount. The difference between present value and face amount of receivables always should be considered, because this difference may be material.

Receivables from sale of goods and services

The most common receivables are those that result from revenue-producing activities, such as the sale of goods and services. The unsecured **open account,** or **trade account,** is the most important of these. Contracts governing open accounts typically are informal and are supported by such documents as sales orders, specifications, invoices, and delivery contracts. Most open accounts are noninterest-bearing. However, in the retail trade the addition of interest or a service charge to revolving charge accounts or installment receivables is a common practice. Manufacturers and wholesalers use disallowed cash discounts as a form of interest charge if payment is made after the discount period.

Trade receivables also are represented by various commercial credit instruments such as promissory notes and security agreements. Such commercial credit instruments have a stronger legal status than open accounts, and because the terms are specified in writing, the holder finds it somewhat easier to borrow against them.

A customer who requests an extension of time on an open account often is asked to sign a promissory note so that the payee can discount the note and receive cash immediately. Most notes and other commercial credit instruments bear interest, because they involve credit for long periods of time. Amounts due from employees and owners of a business enterprise may be included among trade receivables if they result from sales of goods and services and are subject to the usual credit terms.

Receivables from miscellaneous sources

Some receivables result from transactions not directly related to the sale of goods and services. For example, a short-term advance to an affiliated company, to a subcontractor, or to a customer, is in essence a lending transaction made in anticipation of future benefits. A claim against an insurance company and a claim based on a legal suit for damages are other examples of miscellaneous receivables. Prospective refunds of amounts previously paid, such as a claim for refund of prior years' income taxes, represent receivables whenever the collection of the claim is reasonably certain. Sale of capital stock and bonds to subscribers and sales of plant assets also represent sources of miscellaneous receivables. Any type of receivable which is material in amount should be listed separately in the balance sheet. If miscellaneous receivables probably will be collected in one year, they should be classified as current assets; long-term receivables generally are reported as Investments.

Accruals of interest, dividends, rent, and royalties are current receivables that represent a prospective inflow of cash. Rent and interest receivable accrue as a function of time. Dividends usually are not recognized as a receivable prior to the ex-dividend date. Royalties usually accrue as a function of the manufacture or sale of products or the extraction of natural resources.

Occasionally, a receivable arises out of a debit balance in accounts payable when, for one reason or another, overpayment has been made to a supplier. If the purchaser expects a cash refund, the amount involved is clearly a receivable. The rule against offsetting assets and liabilities requires that any sizable debit balance in accounts payable be treated as a receivable rather than as an offset against other accounts payable. Similarly, a large credit balance in customers' accounts should be reported as a current liability. An advance payment on a purchase contract should be reported as a prepayment for goods rather than as a receivable.

Receivables arising from certain types of leasing transactions are discussed in Chapter 20.

TRADE ACCOUNTS RECEIVABLE

A large portion of retail trade in the United States involves credit in some form; at the wholesale and manufacturing level almost all business is transacted on a credit basis. Terms on ordinary open accounts range from the 10 days typically allowed for taking cash discounts to as long as six months or a year in some cases.

Accounting System and Internal Controls Business enterprises with a large volume of credit sales usually adapt their recording procedures to the use of accounting machines or computers. A relatively simple machine system will enable the operator to record the credit sale, post to the controlling account, and post to subsidiary ledger accounts in a single operation. Electronic data-processing equipment makes possible a system that is highly automated. All information pertaining to a credit sale may be recorded on punched cards, magnetic tapes, or magnetic drums. The computer prepares a sales journal, posts to the Accounts Receivable controlling account and to customers' subsidiary ledger accounts, prepares monthly statements, and issues an aged list of receivables at required intervals.

A procedure known as **cycle billing** may be used by department stores and public utilities with a large number of customers. Accounts receivable subsidiary ledgers are divided into a number of groups on the basis of geographical location, type of customer, or alphabetically, with each group having its own subcontrol account. The customers in each subcontrol group are then billed at different times during the month. This procedure has the advantage of spreading the work of preparing customer statements more evenly through the month and assuring a more uniform cash flow from collection of accounts receivable.

It is possible to reduce record keeping by the elimination of subsidiary accounts receivable ledgers altogether. Invoices for credit sales first are sorted by subcontrol groups, and the total amount is entered directly in the controlling account. The individual invoices then are filed according to customer. At the end of the month or cycle billing period, the amount receivable from each customer is summarized in a statement, the duplicate copy of which becomes the subsidiary ledger record for that customer. Invoices are reproduced (to provide a record for the enterprise) and are mailed to each customer along with the statement of his or her account. At the billing date, customers' statements can be reconciled with the amount shown in the appropriate subcontrol account to disclose any discrepancies.

Effective internal controls over the sale of goods and related cash collections is an integral part of the system for handling trade receivables. The responsibility for recording sales and collections of customers' accounts should not be assigned to individuals who handle cash receipts or who prepare bank deposit slips and bank reconciliations. Without such segregation of duties, a dishonest employee could abstract cash collections from customers and conceal the theft by recording the collection as a debit to Sales Returns and Allowances, or by writing off the receivable against the Allowance for Doubtful Accounts.

Recognition of trade receivables

Two important questions faced by accountants in recording trade receivables are:

1 At what point in the stream of business activities between a business enterprise and its customer does a trade account receivable warrant recognition in the accounting records?

2 How should the amount of trade accounts receivable be measured so that this asset and the related revenue and doubtful accounts expense will be recorded accurately?

Trade accounts receivable generally are recorded when the sale is made and title to the goods has passed. Receivables for services should be recognized only as services are performed. Receivables should not be recorded when a customer's order is received, or when goods are produced. Shipments on consignment are not sales, because title to the goods does not pass until sales agents (consignees) sell the consigned goods. On the other hand, receivables should be recognized for work completed on long-term construction contracts or on cost-plus-fixed-fee contracts.[4]

When it is determined that revenue has been earned and recognition of the claim against a customer is warranted, the question of measuring the amount of the receivable (and the revenue) still remains. For example, assume that a parcel of land is sold by a land developer for $5,000. The buyer can pay $5,000 cash, or $1,000 down and $1,100 at the end of each year for five years. If the sale is made on the deferred payment plan, should the receivable be reported at $4,000 ($5,000 cash price less the $1,000 down payment) or at $5,500, the face amount of the five remaining payments of $1,100 each? Is the revenue realized in the current year $5,000, $6,500, or some other amount? One of our objectives in this chapter is to explore these and similar questions.

Valuation of accounts receivable

The valuation of accounts receivable is linked directly with the amount of revenue ultimately realized. There is no way of measuring revenue independently of the value of the claims resulting from revenue transactions.

The problem of valuation of accounts receivable centers on three issues: (1) the amount due, (2) the time of collection, and (3) the estimate of the probability that the receivable will be collected. A number of problems relating to these issues are discussed in the following sections.

Determining the amount due

Trade Discounts In some industries it is customary to bill customers a gross price subject to one or more trade discounts. The gross price is usually the suggested price for resale, and the trade discount represents the difference between gross (list) price and the price to the purchaser before cash discounts. The use of fixed list prices and varying

[4] Accounting for consignment shipments is covered in *Modern Advanced Accounting* of this series; procedures relating to long-term construction contracts are covered in Chapter 9.

trade discounts enables the seller to change prices, or to grant special discounts to large buyers, without reprinting catalogs or price lists. For financial accounting purposes, these discounts should be recognized for what they are—a convenient means of pricing. The amount that a customer will pay is the net price after the trade discount, and this is the amount at which the receivable and the related revenue should be recorded.

Cash (or Sales) Discounts Cash discounts are used to establish a *cash price* when payment is received shortly after delivery of goods, as distinct from a higher *time payment price.* For example, if an invoice for $10,000 provides for terms of 2/10, n/30, the customer is faced with two alternatives: (1) pay $9,800 within 10 days, or (2) wait the full 30 days and pay $10,000. The differential of $200 represents an effective interest rate of 36.7% for the use of the $9,800 for the extra 20-day period, and thus offers a strong incentive for payment within the 10-day discount period.[5]

A theoretical valuation of receivables subject to cash discounts should allow for the probability that discounts will be taken. In the case cited above, for example, if the probability is high that the customer will take the discount, the receivable is worth only $9,800. If the customer is expected to pay the face amount, the receivable is worth $10,000.

In dealing with a large number of receivables, accountants find that past experience usually is a good guide in estimating customer reaction to discounts that are available to be taken. In view of the generous saving inherent in the cash price, the assumption that most customers will take the discounts probably is justified.

Several approaches may be used to account for sales discounts. For example, Accounts Receivable and Sales may be recorded at the face amount of the receivables, and discounts taken by customers are recorded by debits to Sales Discounts. No journal entry is made at the end of the accounting period to anticipate discounts that may be taken by customers on outstanding accounts receivable.

Alternatively, the same procedure may be followed, except that an adjusting entry is made at the end of the accounting period to accrue discounts that may be taken by customers on outstanding accounts receivable. The Sales Discounts account is debited, and the Allowance for Sales Discounts is credited, for the amount of potential discounts that may be taken on outstanding accounts receivable. The Allowance for Sales Discounts is deducted from Accounts Receivable in the balance sheet. Actual discounts taken by customers at the beginning of the following accounting period may be debited to the Allowance for Sales Discounts. If a reversing entry was made to eliminate the allowance account, discounts taken then may be recorded in the usual manner by a debit to Sales Discounts.

[5] There are eighteen 20-day periods in one year; therefore, the annualized rate earned can be computed as follows: ($200 × 18) ÷ $9,800, or 36.7%.

Under the first approach, accounts receivable and net income theoretically are overstated by the amount of estimated sales discounts not accrued. These overstatements are eliminated under the alternative approach, which is consistent with the objective of reporting accounts receivable and revenue at *net realizable values* in the financial statements. However, we should point out that the accrual of sales discounts at the end of an accounting period is not often used in practice, and is not allowed for income tax purposes.

Estimated Collection Expenses Valuation of accounts receivable at the balance sheet date should take into account any direct costs (which are material in amount) of collecting outstanding receivables. For example, if the collection of certain receivables has been placed in the hands of an attorney, the estimated legal costs should be recognized as an expense of the current accounting period, and deducted from accounts receivable as a valuation account in the balance sheet. Observe the following title of the valuation account used by a publicly owned company:

Estimated collection costs deducted from face amount of receivables

Accounts receivable:

Customers' installment accounts, substantially all of which are due within one year	*$58,216,135*
Other	*926,889*
Total face amount of receivables	*$59,143,024*
Less: ***Allowance for returns, losses in collection, and collection costs***	*13,563,641*
Total net accounts receivable	*$45,579,383*

Sales Returns and Allowances The value assigned to accounts receivable also should recognize the probability that some customers will return goods that are unsatisfactory or will make other claims requiring reduction in the net amount receivable. Potential sales returns and allowances reduce the amount that ultimately will be collected from customers and thus reduce the net realizable value of accounts receivable. If the amounts are material, as in the recorded music and catalog sales industries, periodic income measurement is improved by an adjustment for estimated returns and allowances.

To illustrate, assume that experience shows that sales returns average 10% of accounts receivable, and that an average of 60% of the original selling price ultimately is realized from the returned goods. If gross accounts receivable at the end of the accounting period amount to $100,000 and the perpetual inventory system is in use, the appropriate end-of-period adjusting entry is shown on page 270.

Accrual of sales returns

Inventory—Anticipated Sales Returns (net realizable value) . .	*6,000*	
Sales Returns	*10,000*	
Cost of Goods Sold		*6,000*
Allowance for Sales Returns (contra A/R)		*10,000*
To record anticipated sales returns.		

The effect of this journal entry is to reduce current assets and the gross profit on sales by $4,000—the difference between the original selling price and the estimated net realizable value of the goods returned. This adjusting entry may be reversed on the first day of the next accounting period; then, as sales returns are made by customers, the normal journal entry may be made by debiting Sales Returns and Allowances and crediting Accounts Receivable.

The accrual of sales returns at the end of an accounting period is widely used in industries experiencing material amounts of returns.[6] However, the accrual of sales returns (as in the case of accrual of sales discounts) is not allowed for income tax purposes.

Freight Allowances   Occasionally goods are sold on terms "FOB destination" with the understanding that the customer will pay the transportation charges and then deduct that amount from the remittance. In such instances, accounts receivable should be valued at the net amount to be collected. The easiest way to deal with this problem is to record the sale net of the transportation charge. If it is difficult or inconvenient to estimate the actual freight charges that will be incurred, it may be preferable to record the receivable at the gross amount and to set up an estimated allowance for freight. This allowance account is deducted from accounts receivable in the balance sheet, and the offsetting debit balance in Freight Paid by Customers may be deducted from sales or reported as a selling expense in the income statement.

Sales and Excise Taxes   Many government units impose sales and excise taxes on particular products or on the sales transaction itself. Usually, the seller is responsible for the remittance of these taxes to the government. An excise tax imposed on the manufacture of a product is a part of the cost of production, but an excise tax on the sale of the product is imposed on the purchaser and is collected by the seller.

If sales and excise taxes are collected as separately disclosed additions to the selling price, they should not be confused with revenue but should be credited to a liability account. Whether this is done at the time of each sale or as an adjustment at the end of the accounting period is

---

[6] See also discussion on pages 92 and 93 in Chapter 3.

a matter of convenience.[7] Generally, it is preferable to record the tax liability at the time of sale. For example, if a day's sales amount to $20,000 and are subject to a 6% sales tax, the sales tax payable is $1,200, and the journal entry to record sales is:

Recording one day's sales and sales tax payable	Accounts Receivable (or Cash). 21,200	
	Sales Tax Payable.	1,200
	Sales	20,000
	To record sales and sales tax liability.	

Container Deposits Customers may be charged for deposits on containers, with the understanding that the deposit will be refunded when the container is returned. The containers, such as drums, are depreciable plant assets of the business enterprise that owns them. If the container deposit is collected in cash, the only problem is the correct accounting for the refund obligation. When the container is returned, the liability will be canceled by the refund of the deposit. If the container is not returned, the liability no longer exists, and the difference between the amount of the deposit and the cost of the containers not returned represents a gain or loss which, as a matter of convenience, may be combined with the account reporting the depreciation of containers. When no time limit is set for the return, an estimate is made of the number of containers that will not be returned, and adjustment is made periodically on the basis of actual experience.

In some cases, the container fee is debited to customers' accounts. This creates an uncertainty with respect to the amount which will be collected. Until the uncertainty is resolved, accounts receivable should show as a separate item the amount charged to the customer for containers, and a liability is established for the refund obligation.

Time of collection and valuation of receivables

Mention has been made previously of the need to consider the length of the collection period and the need to assign a present value to receivables. The procedure is particularly significant when the collection period is long and interest is not charged to customers. For example, if a receivable of $5,500 is expected to be collected one year hence and the

---

[7] Business enterprises account for sales and excise taxes in a variety of ways: Some do not report such taxes either in sales or in expenses; others include such taxes in gross sales, then deduct them in arriving at net sales; still other enterprises report sales and excise taxes either as part of cost of goods sold or as operating expenses. The amounts of excise taxes can be staggering: For example, some years ago one enterprise reported gross sales of $145 million less excise taxes of $110 million, leaving net sales of only $35 million.

prevailing interest rate is 10%, the receivable and sale are recorded at a net amount of $5,000 ($5,500 ÷ 1.10 = $5,000), and interest revenue of $500 is recognized during the period the receivable is outstanding.

Estimating probability of collection

Thus far we have considered the problem of determining the amount due and the time of collection under the terms of a credit sale. A third major valuation problem is to evaluate the probability that customers will be willing and able to pay their accounts. Because a business enterprise does not make a credit sale unless ultimate collection is reasonably assured, the probability of loss with respect to any given sale is presumably low. Even the best efforts of a capable credit department, however, cannot eliminate all uncollectible accounts. Furthermore, the managerial objective is not to minimize this expense but to maximize net income. Too stringent a credit policy may cause loss of sales volume, which more than offsets the reduction in the doubtful accounts expense.

Receivables that will never be collected have a zero present value, and the corresponding revenue will not be realized. The objective in the estimation of doubtful accounts expense is to prevent an overstatement of assets and revenue in the accounting period in which sales are made.

In the balance sheet, the estimate of doubtful accounts is carried as a credit balance in a valuation account titled Allowance for Doubtful Accounts or Allowance for Uncollectible Accounts. A separate valuation account is used, because it is not known which specific accounts will prove uncollectible, and the Accounts Receivable controlling account should agree with the subsidiary ledger detail. The allowance account is deducted from gross receivables to arrive at the **net realizable value** of accounts receivable. The Allowance for Doubtful Accounts should not be shown among liabilities or elsewhere in the equities side of the balance sheet.[8]

The doubtful accounts expense can be classified several ways in the income statement. Logically, doubtful accounts expense should be classified as an offset against gross sales, on the grounds that it represents revenue which will not be collected. In practice, doubtful accounts expense usually appears among operating expenses. Finally, some consider doubtful accounts expense as a financial management item and report it as "other expense." Because each of these reporting practices produces the same net income, the issue is not a major one.

Two kinds of evidence are used in estimates of doubtful accounts expense: (1) the average relationship between sales and uncollectible accounts in past years, and (2) an analysis of the quality and age of outstanding receivables at the end of an accounting period.

[8] *APB Opinion No. 12,* "Omnibus Opinion—1967," AICPA (New York: 1967), p. 188

Estimate of Doubtful Accounts Expense Based on Sales The average percentage of credit sales not collected in past accounting periods is a logical basis for estimating the portion of current credit sales that will prove uncollectible. This approach, often referred to as the *income statement approach,* is simple to apply and makes possible an estimate of doubtful accounts expense as soon as credit sales are recorded. It results in a sound matching of costs and revenue, and is especially appropriate in the preparation of interim reports. For example, if sales for the first quarter of the current year are $250,000, and doubtful accounts expense is estimated at 2% of sales, the following journal entry is required:

Journal entry to record doubtful accounts expense

Doubtful Accounts Expense	*5,000*
Allowance for Doubtful Accounts	*5,000*
To record estimated doubtful accounts expense at 2% of sales for	
first quarter of year.	

If the ratio of cash sales to credit sales is relatively constant, estimates of doubtful accounts expense as a percentage of *total sales* may produce reasonably accurate results. Strictly speaking, however, the estimate of doubtful accounts expense should be based on *credit sales* only. The estimate may be further refined by analyses of the experience for different classes of customers or in different geographical locations.

Application of the appropriate percentage to the credit sales for an accounting period provides an estimate of the sales of that period which will not be collected. The degree of error in the estimate cannot be determined until the record of collection experience is in. It is useful, therefore, to make periodic tests to determine the adequacy of the provision for doubtful accounts in the light of actual experience.

Estimate of Doubtful Accounts Expense Based on Receivables A good way to test the adequacy of the allowance for doubtful accounts and to recognize the current charge against revenue is to make an analysis of accounts by age group and probability of collection. This procedure is known as the *balance sheet approach* of estimating doubtful accounts expense. Generally, a significant correlation exists between the length of time an account is past due and its collectibility. A summary which classifies the balances of all accounts receivable according to whether the amounts are not yet due, or past due by varying lengths of time, is known as an *aging of accounts receivable.*

The number of different age classes to be used depends on actual experience and the terms of sale. An estimate of the average collection experience for each age class provides a basis for estimating the portion of outstanding accounts receivable that may prove to be uncollectible.

The summary of an accounts receivable aging for Midwest Company is illustrated below:

MIDWEST COMPANY
Aging of Accounts Receivable
June 30, 19__

Credit terms: Net 30 days

Classification by due dates	Balances in each category (sum-marized from analysis of indi-vidual accounts)	Estimated uncollect-ibles, %	Estimated doubtful accounts
Not yet due	$2,400,000 (75.0%)	1	$24,000
Under 30 days past due	416,000 (13.0%)	3	12,480
30–60 days past due.	208,000 (6.5%)	5	10,400
61–120 days past due	96,000 (3.0%)	10	9,600
121–180 days past due	48,000 (1.5%)	30	14,400
Over 180 days past due	32,000 (1.0%)	Individual analysis	25,000
Totals.	$3,200,000 (100.0%)		$95,880

The percentages shown next to each category are useful in detecting an imbalance between current and past-due accounts. When an aging of receivables is used as a basis for the estimate of doubtful accounts expense, the current provision will be an amount sufficient to bring the balance in the Allowance for Doubtful Accounts to the amount indicated by the aging analysis. For example, if the balance in the Allowance for Doubtful Accounts for Midwest Company on June 30 is $75,000 after interim provisions and write-offs, the analysis above calls for the following journal entry to bring the allowance account to the required $95,880:

Doubtful Accounts Expense 20,880
    Allowance for Doubtful Accounts 20,880
To adjust allowance to required balance of $95,880.

A simpler method sometimes followed is to increase the allowance **to a given percentage** of receivables or to increase the allowance **by a given percentage** of receivables. These latter procedures are not recommended because the results they produce are less accurate than those obtained through an aging analysis.

In the process of aging the accounts receivable, management should evaluate current financial statements of major customers to make a better assessment of the probability of collection. The credit department of a business enterprise is assigned responsibility for a continuing analysis of the financial statements of customers and prospective customers so that sales will not be made to those who represent excessive risk of nonpayment.

Estimated uncollectibles and income measurement

It is unlikely that estimated uncollectibles will agree with actual write-offs applicable to each year's revenue. As long as there is a reasonably close correlation between the annual estimate and actual experience, minor discrepancies from year to year may be ignored.

A major adjustment to reduce or increase the Allowance for Doubtful Accounts may involve receivables originating in prior accounting periods. Such adjustments could be included in doubtful accounts expense and explained in a note, or listed as a separate item in the computation of income before extraordinary items. However, such adjustments should not be reported as extraordinary items, as prior period adjustments, or as cumulative effects of changes in accounting principles.

In rare situations, an unusual and infrequent event may take place, such as the destruction of a customer's business by a major and infrequent earthquake, which results in a material write-off of accounts receivable. In such a situation, the effect of the write-off should be included in the computation of the extraordinary item if the write-off was a direct result of the earthquake. However, any portion of the write-off which would have resulted from a valuation of accounts receivable on a going-concern basis should not be included in the determination of the extraordinary item.[9]

A major adjustment to the allowance for doubtful accounts or a revision of the method used to compute doubtful accounts expense is viewed as a *change in accounting estimate* by *APB Opinion No. 20,* which states:

> Future events and their effects cannot be perceived with certainty; estimating, therefore, requires the exercise of judgment. Thus accounting estimates change as new events occur, as more experience is acquired, or as additional information is obtained.[10]

> The Board concludes that the effect of a change in accounting estimate should be accounted for in (a) the period of change if the change affects that period only or (b) the period of change and future periods if the change affects both. A change in an estimate should not be accounted for by restating amounts reported in financial statements of prior periods or by reporting pro forma amounts for prior periods.[11]

---

[9] *APB Opinion No. 30,* "Reporting the Results of Operations- . . .," AICPA (New York: 1973), p. 566.

[10] *APB Opinion No. 20,* "Accounting Changes," AICPA (New York: 1971), p. 338.

[11] Ibid., p. 397. See Chapter 22 for a more complete discussion of changes in accounting estimate.

The effect of a change in an accounting estimate on income before extraordinary items, net income, and earnings per share of the current accounting period should be disclosed *if material* in amount. Estimates made each period in the ordinary course of accounting for doubtful accounts expense need not be disclosed.

In income tax returns, a change in estimate may be treated differently from the method used for financial accounting purposes. Income tax regulations provide that an excessive or inadequate balance in the allowance account may be corrected by adjusting the rate used in estimating doubtful accounts expense in future years—in effect overstating or understating taxable income in future years until the allowance is consistent with actual experience.

Collection of an account receivable previously written off

When the decision is made to write off an uncollectible account, the debit to the allowance account and the credit to Accounts Receivable have no effect on either the carrying amount of accounts receivable or the net income of the accounting period in which the write-off occurs. If an account that has been written off is collected later, a common procedure is to debit Accounts Receivable and credit Allowance for Doubtful Accounts. This reverses the journal entry originally made, and the collection then is recorded in the usual manner. This method has the advantage of providing in the customer's account a complete record of credit experience with that customer.

Direct write-off method of recognizing doubtful accounts expense

Some business enterprises may elect to recognize doubtful accounts expense only as specific accounts become worthless. Although this practice gives the appearance of being more objective, it overstates the net realizable value of receivables and does not properly match doubtful accounts expense with revenue, as required by the accrual basis of accounting. Under the direct write-off method, an account receivable representing a sale in Year 1 may be recorded as an expense in Year 2, and a receivable originating in Year 2 may be written off against revenue of Year 3 or Year 4. In the application of the direct write-off method, subjective judgment still is required to determine when an account receivable becomes worthless.

The direct write-off method is likely to be less objective than it appears at first glance. Uncollectible accounts receivable under this method are written off by a debit to Doubtful Accounts Expense and a credit to Accounts Receivable. Collection of a receivable written off in a previous period is credited to Doubtful Accounts Recovered (a miscellaneous revenue item); recovery of a receivable written off earlier in the current period is recorded as a credit to Doubtful Accounts Expense to eliminate the expense that was recorded prematurely.

Either the allowance or the direct write-off method can be used for income tax purposes, but the method adopted must be followed consistently. The allowance method generally is more advantageous for income tax purposes, because deductible expenses are anticipated, and income taxes are not paid on revenue which never may be collected.

Use of receivables to raise cash

In the normal operating cycle of a business enterprise, cash needed for current operations is provided through the collection of accounts receivable. It is possible to accelerate this process by selling receivables or by borrowing money and pledging accounts receivable as collateral. In some industries, such procedures are quite common; in other industries, this may be done only in times of absolute necessity.

Enterprises making a business of buying receivables are known as *factors,* and the process of selling receivables is called *factoring.* A factor may buy receivables outright, with or without recourse, or may lend money to the owner of the receivables and take the collections on accounts receivable in repayment.[12] In such cases customers generally are notified, and are instructed to make payment directly to the factor.

Factoring goes back to the Roman Empire. Today factoring is a $25 billion business and is an important source of cash for industries such as textiles, apparel, furniture, floor covering, and consumer electronics. If a factor advances money with the expectation of obtaining accounts receivable from the borrower as collateral, interest on the amount advanced and a fee of 1% or more of the receivables factored are charged.

Factoring transactions cause no special accounting problems for the borrower. Accounts receivable are converted to cash, and both the factor's fee and interest are recorded as interest expense. The factor generally advances 90% of net receivables to the borrower, and "reserves" 10% as a margin of protection against sales returns and allowances. This "reserve" is the borrower's equity in the factored receivables and is included, net of the appropriate valuation allowance, in the current assets section of the borrower's balance sheet.

Sale of Receivables without Recourse   The purpose of selling receivables without recourse is to shift to the purchaser of the receivables the risk of credit, the effort of collection, and the waiting period which result from granting credit. Accounts receivable usually are sold *without recourse.* The acceptance of credit cards by retail merchants is a familiar form of sale of accounts receivable without recourse. For example, when a restaurant accepts Visa, American Express, or Diners Club cards, it avoids

---

[12] "With recourse" means that the factor is protected by the seller against loss; "without recourse" means that the factor assumes full risk of failure to collect the accounts purchased.

accounting costs and doubtful accounts expense, and obtains cash almost immediately in return for a 4 to 7% fee (discount). The amount of the fee or discount depends on the volume of business the restaurant generates for the credit card company. The fee or discount may be reported as **interest expense** in the income statement of the restaurant, because the sale of accounts receivable is essentially a financing transaction.

Sale of Receivables with Recourse   When receivables are sold **with recourse,** the seller in effect guarantees the receivables, and the buyer of the receivables is assured of earning a desired rate of return on the funds invested. The sale of receivables on a recourse basis should be viewed as a financing transaction rather than as a sale transaction that gives rise to immediate profit or loss.

Generally, the sale of ordinary receivables on a recourse basis results in receipt of proceeds less than the face amount of receivables sold. Similarly, the sale of installment receivables which bear a lower interest charge than the discount rate used in the "sale" of the receivables produces less than the carrying amount of the receivables. For example, a sale on a recourse basis of accounts receivable with a face amount of $20,000 for $19,000 is recorded as follows:

Sale of accounts receivable

Cash	19,000	
Deferred Finance Charges.	1,000	
Accounts Receivable.		20,000
To record sale of accounts receivable on a recourse basis.		

The Accounting Standards Division of the AICPA recommended that the deferred finance charges (differential) be amortized as interest expense over the period during which the receivables are collected.[13] This **delayed recognition method** also would be applied to the sale of receivables on a recourse basis for more than the carrying amount of receivables. Installment receivables which require the payment of interest by the debtor at a rate higher than the rate used to compute the proceeds on sale would result in an excess of proceeds over the carrying amount of the installment receivables. For example, assume that Dodson Company has the following installment receivables:

[13] *Statement of Position 74-6,* "Recognition of Profit on Sales of Receivables with Recourse," AICPA (New York: 1974), p. 13

Carrying amount of receivables sold

> *Installment receivables, including deferred interest at 1½% per month, payable at the rate of $723 per month for 36 months commencing in one month* $26,028
> *Less: Unearned interest and finance charges*   6,028
> *Carrying amount of receivables* $20,000

If these receivables are sold on a recourse basis at a price to yield a 1% rate of return per month to the purchaser, the proceeds on the sale are determined below:

Proceeds on sale of receivables

> *Present value of ordinary annuity of 36 payments of $723 per month with interest at 1% per month: $723 × 30.107505 (Table 4 in the Appendix)* . $21,768

The sale of these receivables on a **_recourse basis_** would be recorded as follows:

Journal entry to record sale of receivables on recourse basis

> *Cash*   21,768
> *Unearned Interest and Finance Charges*   6,028
> *Installment Receivables*   26,028
> *Unearned Interest Revenue*   1,768
> *To record sale of receivables on a recourse basis. The receivables bear interest at 1½% per month, but were sold to yield 1% per month.*

A sale of receivables on a recourse basis is similar to financing transactions in which funds are borrowed and assets are pledged as collateral for the loan. In our example, the sale of the installment receivables on a recourse basis has not reduced Dodson Company's risk in any way, and the difference of $1,768 represents unrealized revenue from financing activities. The $1,768 is the difference between the present value of future interest receipts on the receivables sold (1½% per month) and the present value of the interest charged by the purchaser of the receivables (1% per month). Consequently, Dodson Company should recognize the $1,768 unearned interest as realized interest revenue as the receivables are collected.[14]

[14] Ibid., p. 24.

Assignment of Receivables   Instead of selling receivables, management may prefer to borrow money using accounts receivable as collateral. This may involve a pledge of accounts receivable under a contract providing that the proceeds from the collection of the receivables must be used to retire the loan. Alternatively, receivables may be **assigned** under a more formal arrangement whereby a business enterprise **(assignor)** pledges the receivable to the lender **(assignee)** and signs a note payable. Assignment gives the lender the same right to bring action to collect the receivables that the assignor possesses. The assignor assumes its own credit risk and collection effort, and promises to make good any receivables that cannot be collected. Debtors generally are not notified of the assignment and make payments directly to the assignor; they may, however, be instructed to make payments to the assignee. The assignor generally has some equity in the assigned receivables because the financing company usually advances less than 100% of the face amount of assigned receivables.

The primary accounting problem raised by assignment of receivables is to measure the assignor's equity in the assigned receivables and the liability to the assignee. Assigned accounts are transferred to a separate ledger account, Assigned Accounts Receivable, and a liability to the assignee is recorded. As collections are received by the assignor, assigned receivables are reduced, and the liability to the assignee is correspondingly reduced as cash is remitted by the assignor. Fees and interest charges are included in the remittance and are recorded as expenses.

To illustrate, assume that on January 2, Year 1, Adams Company assigned accounts receivable of $50,000 to Finco, Inc., and received $45,000, less a fee of 2% on the advance. Interest of 1% of the unpaid balance of the loan is to be paid monthly. The journal entries for Adams Company to record the assignment and subsequent transactions are shown at the top of page 281.

The assignor's equity in assigned receivables may be shown in the current assets section of the assignor's balance sheet by deducting the unpaid balance of notes payable from the amount of the assigned receivables. Offsetting the liability against the asset is appropriate in this situation because collections on assigned receivables are contractually earmarked to liquidate the loan. This treatment is illustrated below for Adams Company on January 31, Year 1:

Balance sheet presentation of assignor's equity in accounts receivable

Current assets:		
Accounts receivable		$200,000
Assigned accounts receivable	$19,850	
Less: Notes payable to Finco, Inc. (assignee).	15,300	
Equity in assigned accounts receivable		4,550
Total accounts receivable		$204,550

Journal
entries for
assign-
ment of
accounts
receivable

Transaction	Journal entries in assignor's accounting records		
Jan. 2: Assigned accounts receivable of $50,000. Finco, Inc., remitted 90% of receivables, less 2% fee ($45,000 × 2% = $900).	Assigned Accounts Receivable. .	50,000	
	Accounts Receivable		50,000
	Cash	44,100	
	Interest Expense	900	
	Notes Payable to Finco, Inc.		45,000
Jan. 31: Collected $30,150 and paid this amount to Finco, Inc., including interest at 1% a month on unpaid balance of loan, $45,000.	Cash	30,150	
	Assigned Accounts		
	Receivable		30,150
	Notes Payable to Finco, Inc. . . .	29,700	
	Interest Expense	450	
	Cash		30,150
Feb. 28: Collected $17,000 and paid balance owed to Finco, Inc., plus interest at 1% a month on unpaid balance of loan, $15,300 ($45,000 − $29,700 = $15,300).	Cash	17,000	
	Assigned Accounts		
	Receivable		17,000
	Notes Payable to Finco, Inc. . . .	15,300	
	Interest Expense	153	
	Cash		15,453
Transferred balance of assigned receivables to Accounts Receivable account.	Accounts Receivable	2,850	
	Assigned Accounts		
	Receivable		2,850

Adequate disclosure should be made of all accounts receivable pledged, assigned, or sold, including any possible loss contingency.

Installment accounts receivable

Many individuals and business enterprises find it convenient to buy certain items on the installment plan. The installment contract, in essence a promissory note providing for payment over an extended period of time, is widely used at the retail level. Most enterprises that sell goods on the installment plan have adequate financial resources to carry their own installment accounts receivable. Other enterprises, however, sell or assign their installment accounts receivable to finance companies.

Installment accounts receivables from the sale of goods or services in the ordinary course of business, including those not coming due for more than one year from the balance sheet date, are included in current assets. In the valuation of installment receivables, the unearned interest and finance charges included in the contract are excluded from net installment receivables and from sales revenue. For example, a recent balance sheet included the presentation of receivables on page 282.

Receivables:
    Customer installment accounts receivable—
        Easy payment accounts *$2,790,500*
        Revolving charge accounts *2,510,100*
    Other accounts (net of $85,000 accounts sold) *72,600*
    Miscellaneous accounts and notes receivable *61,000*
    Less: Unearned interest and finance charges of $205,000, and al-
        lowance for doubtful accounts of $95,000 . . . .   *(300,000)*
    Net receivables *$5,134,200*

Interest and finance charges should be recognized as revenue only when earned and should be disclosed separately. Deferred income taxes related to installment receivables are reported as current liabilities if the gross profit on installment sales is recognized as collections are made for income tax purposes. The accounting for installment sales and the installment method of accounting are included in *Modern Advanced Accounting* of this series.

NOTES RECEIVABLE

The term *notes receivable* is used in accounting to designate several types of credit instruments. The distinguishing characteristic common to all is that they are written contracts containing an unconditional promise to pay a certain sum of money under terms clearly specified in the contract. Most credit instruments used as a basis for business transactions are *negotiable,* which means in essence that a *holder in due course* is free of certain equity defenses that might otherwise be available to prior parties. Negotiability is a valuable characteristic which makes the instrument freely transferable and thus enhances the ability of the holder to sell it, discount it, or borrow against it.

Notes receivable often are used when the goods sold have a high unit or aggregate value and the buyer wants to extend payment beyond the normal 30- to 90-day period of trade credit. In the banking and commercial credit fields, notes are the typical form of credit instrument used to support lending transactions. Notes receivable also may result from sale of plant assets, or from a variety of other business transactions.

Valuation of notes receivable

As in the case of accounts receivable, the proper valuation of notes receivable and similar credit instruments is their current fair value (present value) at the time of acquisition. Accountants can value notes receivable because their terms generally provide sufficient evidence of the rights inherent in them. Except for questions of collectibility, there is little uncertainty with respect to the amounts that will be received and the dates on which the amounts will be received.

Notes receivable, like trade accounts receivable, may prove to be uncollectible. If a business enterprise uses notes as a regular credit medium and has a large volume outstanding, the amounts of probable uncollectible notes may be estimated, and an allowance for such notes established by procedures similar to those discussed for accounts receivable.

Strictly speaking, there is no such thing as a noninterest-bearing note; there are only **notes that contain a stated provision for interest and notes that do not.** The time value of money is present in any case, because the present value of a promise to pay money at some future date is not as large as the amount to be paid at maturity. The so-called noninterest-bearing note has a lower present value than its face amount by an amount equivalent to an interest charge. On the other hand, if a note bears a fair rate of interest, its **face amount** and **present value** are the same at the date of issuance.

This point may be illustrated by an example. Suppose that two notes are received in connection with the sale of goods. In settlement of the first sale, Customer X gives a one-year, 12% note, with a face amount of $25,000. In settlement of the second sale, Customer Y gives a one-year note with a face amount of $28,000, but with no interest provision specified in the note. If accountants look only at face amounts of the notes, they might be tempted to record these notes as follows:

Note from Customer Y is not recorded correctly	*Customer X*			*Customer Y*		
	Notes Receivable. . 25,000			*Notes Receivable . 28,000*		
	Sales	*25,000*		*Sales. . . . .*	*28,000*

A careful examination of the evidence indicates that the two notes are identical, assuming that 12% is a reasonable rate of interest. Both customers have promised to pay $28,000 at the end of one year, and both notes have a present value of $25,000 ($28,000 ÷ 1.12 = $25,000). A logical method of accounting is to record both notes at $25,000, and to record interest of $3,000 as it is earned. Thus, the note received from Customer Y may be recorded at $25,000 (the same as the note from Customer X), or preferably by use of a Discount on Notes Receivable account as illustrated below:

The correct way to record note from Customer Y	*Notes Receivable 28,000*	
	Discount on Notes Receivable	*3,000*
	Sales.	*25,000*
	To record sale in exchange for note receivable.	

The discount on notes receivable is transferred periodically to Interest Revenue, and the balance in the discount account at the end of the accounting period is reported as a deduction from Notes Receivable in the balance sheet.

In practice, noninterest-bearing, short-term notes received from customers often are recorded at the outset at face amount (maturity value). The foregoing analysis shows that this procedure overstates assets and fails to recognize interest revenue. Although *APB Opinion No. 21* requires that notes be recorded at present value, the provisions of this Opinion do not apply to trade receivables with customary trade terms not exceeding one year. When the amount of the unearned implicit interest is substantial, this treatment may result in a significant overstatement of assets, stockholders' equity, and net income in the accounting period that the note is received.

Discounting notes receivable

Negotiable notes receivable may be sold or discounted. The term *sale* is appropriate when a note is indorsed to a bank or finance company on a *nonrecourse* basis; that is, in the event the maker of the note defaults, the bank or finance company has no recourse against the seller of the note. The term *discounted* applies when an enterprise borrows against notes receivable and indorses them on a *recourse* basis, which means that the borrower must pay the note if the maker does not.

The *proceeds* received when a note is discounted are computed by deducting from the maturity value of the note the amount of interest (discount) charged by the bank or other financing source. Banks usually compute the discount on the *maturity value* of the note rather than on the proceeds (amount actually borrowed), which in effect gives the bank a higher *effective rate of interest* than the rate of interest used to discount the note.

To illustrate these points and the accounting involved, assume that Scott Company wishes to discount two notes receivable arising from the sale of merchandise. Both notes have a face amount of $100,000 and are due in one year. Note No. 1 carries no provision for interest; note No. 2 is to be paid with interest at 15%. The bank also charges a 15% discount rate.

If we assume that the notes are discounted immediately upon receipt, the proceeds and the difference between the proceeds and the present value are determined as illustrated at the top of page 285.

The difference between the proceeds and the present value of each note represents additional interest charged by the bank due to the fact that the 15% discount is computed on maturity value rather than on the amount actually borrowed (proceeds). The additional interest should be recognized as expense when the note is discounted. The journal entries

Proceeds and present value of notes discounted

	Note No. 1 (no interest)	Note No. 2 (15% interest)
Face amount of notes.	$100,000	$100,000
Add: Interest to maturity	–0–	15,000
Maturity value of notes	$100,000	$115,000
Less: Bank discount (15% of maturity value for one year)	15,000	17,250
Proceeds on notes.	$ 85,000	$ 97,750
Present value @ 15% (maturity value ÷ 1.15). . .	86,957	100,000
Difference between proceeds and present value .	$ 1,957	$ 2,250

to record the receipt and the discounting of these notes are shown below:[15]

Note No. 1			Note No. 2		
At time of sale:					
Notes Receivable. . .	100,000		Notes Receivable. . .	100,000	
Discount on Notes			Sales		100,000
Receivable. . . .		13,043			
Sales		86,957			
At time notes are discounted:					
Cash	85,000		Cash	97,750	
Discount on Notes			Interest Expense . . .	2,250	
Receivable	13,043		Notes Receivable.		100,000
Interest Expense . . .	1,957				
Notes Receivable .		100,000			

An alternative procedure for recording discounted notes is to credit Notes Receivable Discounted (a contra-asset account) rather than Notes Receivable. In the balance sheet the Notes Receivable Discounted account is deducted from Notes Receivable. When the note is paid at maturity, the Notes Receivable Discounted account is debited and Notes Receivable is credited. Because most discounted notes are paid at maturity, this journal entry can be avoided by crediting the Notes Receivable account at the time notes are discounted.

If Scott Company had held these notes for some time before dis-

[15] An alternative approach is to view the proceeds received from the bank as the "true" present value of the notes. This interpretation calls for the recording of the two notes and related sales at $85,000 and $97,750, respectively; thus, the need to recognize interest expense when the notes are discounted is eliminated.

counting them, interest revenue earned prior to the time the notes were discounted should be recorded. The discounting of the notes then would be recorded in the manner previously illustrated.

If the discounted notes are dishonored, Scott Company would be required to pay the bank. The amount that would be due in such an event, however, is not the present value at the time the note was received but rather the maturity value of the note, plus any fees charged by the bank.

Notice of the dishonor of a discounted note must be given promptly; therefore, the indorser may assume that payment has been made if no notice is received within a few days after maturity date. If notes are dishonored, the total amount paid to the bank should be debited to Accounts Receivable (or Dishonored Notes Receivable). Subsequent collection would be recorded as a credit to this account; failure to collect would require that the receivable from the maker of the note be written off against the Allowance for Doubtful Accounts and Notes.

The party discounting notes receivable is contingently liable on the notes until the maker pays them in full at maturity. The *loss contingency* may be disclosed (1) in a note to the financial statements, (2) parenthetically in the balance sheet, or (3) by use of a Notes Receivable Discounted account deducted from Notes Receivable. Disclosure by means of a note to the financial statements is by far the most common practice. A more detailed discussion of loss contingencies is presented in Chapter 10.

APB Opinion No. 21 and the accounting for notes receivable

APB Opinion No. 21 is applicable if the face amount of a receivable (especially a note) does not reasonably represent the present value of the consideration given in exchange. This situation may arise if no interest is explicitly stated or if the stated rate of interest is not appropriate. Recording the receivable at an amount in excess of its present value would overstate net income in the current accounting period and understate net income (interest revenue) in subsequent periods.

As a highly simplified example, assume that Caine buys a tract of land for $6,000 cash and immediately sells it to Dean for $10,000, with payment consisting solely of a 5-year, noninterest-bearing note for $10,000. It would be improper for Caine to record this transaction as producing a $4,000 gain, because the noninterest-bearing, 5-year note has a present value far less than its $10,000 face amount. (Assuming that 10% is the current fair rate of interest, the note has a present value of approximately $6,209.)

APB Opinion No. 21 applies to secured and unsecured notes, debentures, bonds, mortgage notes, equipment obligations, and some accounts receivable and accounts payable. It is not intended to apply to "receivables and payables arising from transactions with customers or suppliers in the normal course of business which are due in customary trade terms not exceeding approximately one year."[16] A brief summary of **APB Opinion No. 21** as it relates to receivables is presented in the following paragraphs.

Notes Received for Cash Interest on a cash loan generally is equal to the excess of the amount the borrower agrees to repay over the amount of cash received. The stated interest rate may differ from the prevailing rate for similar notes, and the proceeds may differ from the face amount of the note. These differences indicate that the present value of the note at the time of issuance differs from the face amount. The difference between the face amount and the proceeds is recorded as a premium or as a discount to be amortized over the term of the note.

Notes Received in Exchange for Cash and Other Rights or Privileges Instead of issuing a note solely for cash, the parties may agree to exchange other rights or privileges (stated or unstated). These rights and privileges should be given accounting recognition by taking into account any implicit discount or premium on the note. For example, assume that on November 30, Year 1, Lori Company lends $112,000 to a supplier for one year, without interest, although the going rate of interest for this type of loan is 12%. In return, the supplier agrees to sell a quantity of scarce merchandise to Lori during the month of December at a favorable price. Neither of these transactions was made in the normal course of business at the usual trade terms. The merchandise was purchased for $300,000 on December 5 and sold prior to December 25. Lori's fiscal year ends on December 31. Obviously, the note has a present value of $100,000 ($112,000 ÷ 1.12 = $100,000); hence, the logical conclusion is that Lori obtained a property right (lower cost of merchandise) with a value of $12,000. Consequently, the loan to the supplier, the purchase of merchandise, and the accrual of interest on the note receivable are recorded by Lori as illustrated on page 288.

If the loan had been recorded by a debit to Notes Receivable and a credit to cash for $112,000, the following errors would have resulted in Lori's financial statements for the year ended December 31, Year 1:

(1) Purchases and cost of goods sold would have been understated by $12,000.
(2) Interest revenue would have been understated by $1,000.
(3) Income before income taxes would have been overstated by $11,000 ($12,000 − $1,000 = $11,000).
(4) The carrying amount of notes receivable in the current assets section of the balance sheet would have been overstated by $11,000.

[16] *APB Opinion No. 21*, "Interest on Receivables and Payables," AICPA (New York: 1971), p. 418.

LORI CORPORATION
Journal Entries

November 30, Year 1:

Note Receivable	112,000	
Property Right with Supplier	12,000	
Cash		112,000
Discount on Note Receivable		12,000

To record noninterest-bearing one-year loan to supplier.

December 5, Year 1:

Purchases (or Inventories)	312,000	
Accounts Payable (or Cash)		300,000
Property Right with Supplier		12,000

To record purchase of merchandise.

December 31, Year 1:

Discount on Note Receivable	1,000	
Interest Revenue		1,000

To record interest revenue: $100,000 \times 12\% \times \frac{1}{12} = \$1,000$.

In the supplier's accounting records, the loan from Lori Company is recorded as follows:

Parallel journal entry in creditor's accounting records

Cash	112,000	
Discount on Note Payable	12,000	
Note Payable		112,000
Obligation to Customer		12,000

To record noninterest-bearing one-year loan from customer.
Present value of note: $112,000 \div 1.12 = \$100,000$.

When the merchandise is sold to Lori, the supplier debits the Obligation to Customer account and credits the Sales account for $12,000. The Discount on Note Payable account is amortized to Interest Expense over the one-year term of the loan.

When notes are received in exchange for assets or services, and interest either is not stated or is unreasonably low, the notes are recorded at the current fair value of the assets or services or at the market value of the notes, whichever is more clearly determinable. In the absence of exchange prices for the assets or services, or evidence of the market value of the note, the present value of a note must be computed. This computation is made at the time the note is acquired, and any subsequent changes in interest rates are ignored.[17]

[17] Ibid., pp. 421–422.

Determining an Appropriate Interest Rate and Present Value of Note   The appropriate interest rate used in the computation of the present value of a note receivable depends on factors such as the credit standing of the issuer, terms of the note, the quality of collateral offered by the issuer, and the general level of interest rates. The interest rate selected for this purpose should approximate the interest rate at which the debtor could obtain similar financing from other sources.

To illustrate the computation of the present value of a note, assume that on January 1, Year 1, Software Associates presents a $39,930 invoice for services to Z Corporation. The president of Z Corporation protests the amount of the invoice and asks that as a compromise Z be allowed to pay the invoice in three annual installments of $13,310, starting on December 31, Year 1. Software Associates agrees to this compromise, and receives three noninterest-bearing notes for $13,310 each dated January 1, Year 1. How should these notes be recorded in the accounting records of Software Associates if the current fair rate of interest is 10%? First, the present value of the three notes is computed from Table 4 in the Appendix, as follows:

Computation of present value of notes

Amount of annual receipts (notes).	$13,310
Multiply by present value of ordinary annuity of 1 at 10% interest	2.486852
Present value of three annual receipts of $13,310 at 10% interest	$33,100

The journal entries to record the original billing, the receipt of the notes by Software Associates on January 1, Year 1, and three annual collections from Z Corporation are illustrated below and on page 290. We have assumed that the notes are recorded at the face amount of $39,930 and that a Discount on Notes Receivable account is used to record the implicit interest to be earned over the term of the notes.

Journal entries for notes

January 1, Year 1:

Accounts Receivable.	39,930	
Revenue from Services		39,930

To record original billing.

January 1, Year 1:

Notes Receivable.	39,930	
Revenue from Services	6,830	
Discount on Notes Receivable		6,830
Accounts Receivable.		39,930

*To record receipt of noninterest-bearing notes for $39,930 payable in three annual installments. The notes are recorded at their **present value** based on an interest rate of 10% per year.*

(cont.)

December 31, Year 1:

Cash *13,310*		
Discount on Notes Receivable *3,310*		
Notes Receivable		*13,310*
Interest Revenue		*3,310*

To record collection of first note. Interest for first year:
($39,930 − $6,830) × 10% = $3,310.

December 31, Year 2:

Cash *13,310*		
Discount on Notes Receivable *2,310*		
Notes Receivable		*13,310*
Interest Revenue		*2,310*

To record collection of second note. Interest for second year:
($26,620 − $3,520) × 10% = $2,310.

December 31, Year 3:

Cash *13,310*		
Discount on Notes Receivable *1,210*		
Notes Receivable		*13,310*
Interest Revenue		*1,210*

To record collection of third note. Interest for third year:
($13,310 − $1,210) × 10% = $1,210.

In the second journal entry on January 1, Year 1, the discount on the notes, $6,830, is recorded as a reduction in the previously recorded Revenue from Services account. The discount then is recognized as interest revenue over the three-year term of the notes at 10% a year, applied to the carrying amount of the notes receivable **at the beginning of each year.**

Analysis of accounts receivable

Accounts receivable are an important factor in an analysis of financial liquidity and a projection of cash flows. Changes in the length of the average collection period or the number of days' sales in receivables, for example, should be watched carefully, and action should be initiated to correct unfavorable trends. A discussion of several analytical techniques for accounts receivable appears in Chapter 24.

Presentation of receivables in the balance sheet

In the current asset section of the balance sheet, material amounts of the following classes of receivables should be reported separately: (1) notes and other receivables based on written negotiable contracts, (2) ordinary trade receivables, (3) installment accounts receivable, (4) receivables from the U.S. government, and (5) other current claims. Negotiable notes and contracts have a special status because of the ease with which they can be converted to cash through discounting. Users of financial statements may be interested in the percentage relationship between trade receivables and credit sales as an indication of a business enterprise's collection experience.

Any discount or premium relating to notes receivable is reported in the balance sheet as a direct deduction from or as an addition to the face amount of the note. The description of notes receivable should include the effective interest rate.[18]

Receivables that have been pledged should be identified, and any receivables that will not be collected within a year or the operating cycle should be excluded from the current assets category. A credit balance in an individual account receivable, if material, should be reported as a current liability. Receivables from officers, employees, and stockholders generally are classified as noncurrent unless current collection is assured.

The presentation of various types of receivables and related accounts in the balance sheet is illustrated below:

Receivables in the balance sheet

Receivables:	
Trade notes receivable *(net of unearned discounts of $5,000)*	$ 205,000
Trade accounts receivable *(net of allowances of $45,000 for doubtful accounts, returns, and sales discounts)*	620,000
Installment receivables *(net of unearned interest and finance charges)*.	400,000
Current amount receivable from affiliated company, *interest at 11%*	45,000
Miscellaneous *(including $4,000 debit balance in accounts payable)*	10,000
Total receivables.	$1,280,000
Investments:	
Receivable from sale of equipment *(due with interest at 13% in three years)*	$ 150,000
Notes due from officers and employees *(due with interest at 12% in installments over 10 years)*	85,000
Dishonored notes receivable *(net of $6,000 allowance for doubtful notes)*	12,000
Current liabilities:	
Container deposits by customers	$ 17,500
Accounts receivable with credit balances	4,250

[18] Ibid., p. 423.

REVIEW QUESTIONS

1 Briefly discuss the significance of accounts receivable in an analysis of the financial position of a business enterprise.

2 What is meant by *valuation of receivables?* If accountants generally require that assets be recorded at *cost,* why are accounts receivable not recorded at the cost of the merchandise sold?

3 What is the distinction between *trade receivables* and *miscellaneous receivables?* Give two examples of each.

4 At what point should trade receivables be recorded? Are shipments to consignees recorded as receivables?

5 Describe a *cycle billing system* and state its advantages.

6 Describe how the following items affect the valuation of receivables: *trade discounts, sales discounts, sales returns and allowances, freight allowances,* and *sales and excise taxes.*

7 Describe two methods of accounting for cash (sales) discounts.

8 Some accountants classify Doubtful Accounts Expense as an operating expense, while others classify it as a contra-revenue account. Discuss the reasoning behind these alternative positions. What objection, if any, do you have to the account title "Loss from Bad Debts?"

9 What is an *aging of accounts receivable?* Describe how such an analysis may be used to estimate doubtful accounts expense and to analyze the quality of accounts receivable.

10 According to *APB Opinion No. 20,* how should a change in the method for estimating doubtful accounts expense and a major increase or decrease in the allowance for doubtful accounts be reported in the financial statements?

11 Briefly discuss the logic of basing the estimate of doubtful accounts expense on **(a)** total sales, **(b)** credit sales, and **(c)** a fixed percentage of receivables at the end of an accounting period.

12 Discuss the accounting procedures necessary to record recoveries of accounts previously written off **(a)** if an allowance for doubtful accounts is used, or **(b)** if the direct charge-off method is used.

13 Explain the distinction between *factoring* and *assigning* accounts receivable.

14 Explain the *delayed recognition method* of accounting for the excess of proceeds received over the carrying amount of interest-bearing receivables sold on a *recourse basis.*

15 City Equipment Company sells certain merchandise with a sales price of $10,500 on an installment contract covering 24 months. Payments of $500 are to be made by the customer each month. Interest of $1,300 and finance charges of $200 are added to the sales price to arrive at total installment contracts receivable. The company records the sale by a debit to Installment Contracts Receivable and a credit to Sales for $12,000. Evaluate this procedure.

16 What errors result when a noninterest-bearing note receivable due in one year is recorded at its face amount? Explain.

17 Describe various ways that the loss contingency relating to notes receivable discounted can be presented in the balance sheet.

EXERCISES

Ex. 7-1 On September 30, Year 1, the following notes receivable from customers are discounted at the bank. The bank charges a 10% discount rate on the maturity value of the notes. Compute the proceeds of each note, using 360 as the number of days in a year.

  a 90-day, $24,000, 10% note dated September 30, Year 1
  b 90-day, $18,000, noninterest-bearing note dated August 15, Year 1
  c 60-day, $6,000, 8% note dated September 15, Year 1
  d 6-month, $12,000, 15% note dated June 1, Year 1

Ex. 7-2 Wool Corporation started in business in Year 1 and had accounts receivable of $300,000 at the end of the year. In arriving at the valuation of receivables at the end of the year, management wished to recognize the following:

Estimated doubtful accounts	$6,240
Estimated collection costs	1,800
Estimated price adjustments and other allowances on outstanding receiv-	
ables (no returns of merchandise are anticipated)	3,000
Estimated cash (sales) discounts	3,600

  a Prepare an adjusting entry to recognize management's estimate of the net realizable value of accounts receivable at the end of Year 1. No accounts were written off in Year 1.
  b Show how accounts receivable should be reported in the balance sheet at the end of Year 1.

Ex. 7-3 Albert Company acquired merchandise having a cost of $4,000. The merchandise was offered for sale by Albert Company at a list price of $6,500, before a trade discount of 20% and a cash discount of 2% if the invoice is paid within 10 days. Albert Company bills customers net of the trade discount, records accounts receivable and sales at the invoice price, and uses the perpetual inventory system.
    Prepare journal entries to record **(a)** the sale and the cost of the goods sold, and **(b)** the collection of the account within 10 days.

Ex. 7-4 From the following information, compute the doubtful accounts expense for Year 1: Beginning balance in Accounts Receivable was $80,000; beginning balance in Allowance for Doubtful Accounts was $6,000; ending balance in Accounts Receivable was $110,000, of which 4% was estimated to be uncollectible. During the year, $7,490 of accounts receivable were written off as uncollectible.

Ex. 7-5 Certain information relative to the operations of Murphy Company for Year 10 is given at the top of page 294.

Accounts receivable, Jan. 1 . . . . $16,000
Accounts receivable collected 52,000
Cash sales 10,000
Inventories, Jan. 1 24,000
Inventories, Dec. 31 22,000
Purchases 40,000
Gross profit on sales 18,000

Compute the amount of accounts receivable on December 31, Year 10.

Ex. 7-6 Your accounts receivable clerk, who earns a salary of $950 a month, has just purchased a new luxury car. You decide to test the accuracy of the accounts receivable balance of $30,400 as shown in the general ledger. All sales are on credit.

The following information is available for your first year of operation: Collections from customers, $125,000; payments for merchandise purchases, $130,000; ending inventories, $40,000; and ending accounts payable to merchandise suppliers, $30,000. All goods purchased were marked to sell at 40% above cost (sales price equals 140% of cost).

Compute an estimate of any apparent shortage in accounts receivable at the end of the year.

Ex. 7-7 The following accounts appear in the general ledger of Delphine Company at the end of the current year:

Sales $1,200,000
Accounts receivable 500,000
Allowance for doubtful accounts . . . . 2,000 dr

Prepare a journal entry to recognize doubtful accounts expense for each independent assumption below:

a The Allowance for Doubtful Accounts is increased to a balance of $15,000.
b The company recognizes 2% of sales as doubtful accounts expense.
c Through an aging of the accounts, $24,750 of accounts receivable is estimated to be uncollectible.

Ex. 7-8 On March 1, Beckman Company assigned accounts receivable of $60,000 to Rec-Fin, Inc., and received $54,000, less a 2% fee. Interest is charged at the rate of 1% a month of the unpaid balance. Beckman made collections on the assigned accounts and remitted the proceeds at the end of each month to Rec-Fin, Inc. Collections in March were $30,000.

Prepare journal entries in the accounting records of Beckman to record the transactions for March relating to the assignment of accounts receivable.

Ex. 7-9 You are auditing the financial statements of Kelly Corporation at the end of its fiscal year. Your review of accounts receivable and discussions with client personnel disclose that the following items are included in the accounts receivable (both controlling account and subsidiary ledgers):

Customers' accounts with credit balances . . . . $ 2,950
Receivables from officers 12,500
Advances to employees 2,200
Customers' accounts known to be uncollectible 2,880

Prepare a correcting journal entry to reclassify items which are not trade accounts receivable and to write off the uncollectible accounts receivable.

Ex. 7-10 According to *APB Opinion No. 21,* how should you record a low-interest, one-year loan for $250,000 by Company A to a supplier who agreed to sell materials to Company A at a favorable fixed price during the term of the loan?

Explain the approach used in recording this transaction. Prepare a journal entry in Company A's accounting records to record the loan, assuming that the present value of the note receivable is $225,000.

Ex. 7-11 Excelsior Corporation sold a machine with a cost of $20,000 and a carrying amount of $2,000 for $9,000, payable $1,014 down and $2,662 at the end of each of the next three years. No interest was mentioned in the contract, although 10% per year would have been a fair rate of interest for this type of transaction.

Compute (without using compound interest tables) the present value of the $7,986 to be received over the next three years and record the sale of the machine as recommended in *APB Opinion No. 21.* Verify your answer by using Table 4 in the Appendix at the end of the book.

Ex. 7-12 The information below is available for Rocky Corporation:

	Amounts in thousands		
	Year 1	Year 2	Year 3
Credit sales	$ 900	$1,100	$1,000
Cash sales	600	800	700
Total sales	$1,500	$1,900	$1,700
Accounts receivable (end of year)	$ 170	$ 230	$ 220
Allowance for doubtful accounts (end of year). . . .	47	30	56
Accounts receivable written off during the year . . .	2	50	4

Assuming there was no change in the method used to estimate doubtful accounts during the three-year period, compute the balance in the allowance for doubtful accounts at the beginning of Year 1.

SHORT CASES FOR ANALYSIS AND DECISION

Case 7-1 Business transactions often involve the exchange of plant assets, merchandise, or services for promissory notes or similar instruments that may stipulate no interest rate or an interest rate that varies from prevailing rates.

Instructions
a When a promissory note is exchanged for plant assets, merchandise, or services, what value should be placed on the promissory note
   (1) if it bears interest at a reasonable rate and is issued in a bargained transaction entered into at arm's length? Explain.
   (2) if it bears no interest and/or is not issued in a bargained transaction entered into at arm's length? Explain.
b If the recorded value of a promissory note differs from the face amount,
   (1) how should the difference be accounted for? Explain.
   (2) how should the difference be presented in the balance sheet? Explain.

Case 7-2 During the audit of accounts receivable of Daley Company, the president, Roberta Daley, asked why the current year's expense for doubtful accounts is debited because some accounts may become uncollectible next year. She then said that she had read that financial statements should be based on verifiable, objective evidence, and that it seemed to her to be much more objective to wait until specific accounts receivable actually were determined to be uncollectible before an expense is recorded.

Instructions
a Discuss the theoretical justification of the allowance method as contrasted with the direct write-off method of accounting for doubtful accounts.
b Describe the following two methods of estimating doubtful accounts. Include a discussion of how well each accomplishes the objectives of the allowance method of accounting for doubtful accounts.
(1) The percentage-of-sales method
(2) The aging method
c Of what merit is the president's contention that the allowance method lacks the objectivity of the direct write-off method? Discuss in terms of accounting's measurement function.

Case 7-3 As a result of earthquake losses, River Company, one of the oldest and largest customers of Barge Transport, Inc., suddenly and unexpectedly became bankrupt. Approximately 30% of the total sales of Barge Transport, Inc., have been made to River Company during each of the past several years.

The amount due from River Company—which is uncollectible—equals 25% of total accounts receivable, an amount which is considerably in excess of what was determined to be an adequate allowance for doubtful accounts at the end of the preceding year.

Instructions How should Barge Transport, Inc., record the write-off of the River Company receivable, if it uses the allowance method of accounting for doubtful accounts? Justify your suggested treatment.

Case 7-4 The annual report for Year 10 of Systems Corporation, which operates a group of correspondence and resident schools, included the following relating to contracts receivable and sales:

Current assets:

Contracts receivable, less allowance for doubtful contracts of
   $3,228,180 **(Note 2)** . . . . $ 6,599,399

Current liabilities:

Estimated costs to service contracts . . . . $ 264,281
Unearned tuition revenue **(Note 2)**   1,074,226

Income statement:

Sales, net of discounts and allowances of $2,076,911 . . . . $14,350,698
Provision for doubtful contracts receivable   3,863,800

Note 2—Contracts receivable:
Students in home study courses enter into contracts which contain various payment plans, generally for a term of one to three years. Similarly, home study courses generally are completed over a term of one to three years. Revenue on home study courses and estimated costs to service the contracts are recorded when the contract is received.

Many of the contracts receivable are due from resident students and represent advance registrations for classes which will begin subsequent to December 31, Year 10. Tuition revenue on these contracts and a portion of tuition applicable to the classes in progress on December 31, Year 10, net of an allowance for cancellations, have been deferred and will be credited to revenue as earned over the period of attendance.

It is estimated that gross contracts receivable of approximately $1,900,000 on December 31, Year 10, are not expected to be realized within one year. It is not practical, however, for the company to state separately the long-term portion of contracts receivable in the balance sheet, because of the difficulty of determining the allowance for doubtful contracts relating to the long-term contracts receivable.

Instructions Briefly evaluate the accounting practices of Systems Corporation. Your answer should refer to such accounting concepts or principles as revenue realization, matching of costs and revenue, conservatism, objectivity, and classification of contracts receivable as current assets based on the length of the operating cycle.

PROBLEMS

7-1 The accountant for Newport Enterprises was hired at the beginning of the current year. At the end of the year, before making any adjusting entries, the accountant prepared a trial balance which included the following account balances:

	Debit	Credit
Accounts receivable	$300,000	
Notes receivable (received in exchange for accounts receivable)	30,000	
Allowance for doubtful accounts	6,000	
Sales		$1,830,000
Sales returns and allowances	8,850	
Sales discounts	15,540	

Instructions Prepare an appropriate adjusting entry at the end of the current year to provide for estimated doubtful accounts under each of the following independent assumptions. Explain the basis for each journal entry:

a Newport's experience indicates that 80% of all sales are credit sales, and that on the average 3% of gross credit sales prove uncollectible.

b An analysis of the aging of accounts receivable indicates that potential uncollectible accounts (including notes receivable) at the end of the year amount to $25,000.

c Newport's policy is to maintain an allowance for doubtful accounts equal to 5% of outstanding trade receivables, including notes received from customers.

d The allowance for doubtful accounts is increased by $1\frac{1}{2}$% of gross sales, and an allowance for sales discounts of $4,000 on outstanding accounts receivable is established.

7-2 On January 1, Year 1, Salinas Corporation sold to Dan Lee a parcel of land with a carrying amount of $400,000. Lee gave Salinas $100,000 cash and $500,000 non-interest-bearing notes payable in five equal annual installments of $100,000, with a first payment on the notes due on January 1, Year 2. Neither the land nor the notes had readily ascertainable current fair value. The market rate of interest for notes of this type is 12% per year. The present value of an ordinary annuity of 1 for five periods at 12% is 3.604776. The fiscal year for Salinas Corporation ends on December 31.

Instructions

a Prepare journal entries for Salinas Corporation to record the sale of the land in Year 1, the collection on the notes receivable in Year 2, and adjusting entries at the end of Year 1 and Year 2. Use a Discount on Installment Notes Receivable account. Include supporting computations as part of the explanation for each journal entry. Round all computations to the nearest dollar.

b Show how the notes receivable should be presented in the balance sheet for Salinas Corporation on December 31, Year 2.

7-3   The following information is taken from the trial balance for Horizon Evergreens, Inc., on September 30, Year 10, the end of its fiscal year:

	Debit	*Credit*
Notes receivable from customers (due within one year, 9%		
interest)	*$ 60,000*	
Accounts receivable	*220,000*	
Allowance for doubtful accounts and notes	*3,300*	
Allowance for sales discounts		*$ 620*
Allowance for sales returns		*-0-*
Sales—cash		*150,000*
Sales—credit		*630,000*
Sales returns	*6,500*	
Sales discounts	*9,250*	

Accounts receivable written off during the year were debited to the Allowance for Doubtful Accounts and Notes; merchandise returns by customers were recorded in the Sales Returns account; and sales discounts allowed to customers were recorded in the Sales Discounts account. Horizon uses the perpetual inventory system.

Instructions
a Prepare journal entries on September 30, Year 10, to adjust the Allowance for Doubtful Accounts and Notes, the Allowance for Sales Discounts, and the Allowance for Sales Returns accounts based on the following information:
   (1) Aging of accounts and notes receivable indicates that the following balances are required on September 30, Year 10:

   Allowance for doubtful accounts and notes *$11,800*
   Allowance for sales discounts *3,200*

   (2) Based on many years of experience, management estimated that of the $220,000 in accounts receivable on September 30, Year 10, $12,000 sales price of merchandise will be returned. The net realizable value of the returned merchandise was estimated at $7,200. Horizon follows the practice of establishing an inventory account for the merchandise expected to be returned by customers (see pages 269 and 270).

b Assuming that the allowance accounts are adjusted correctly on September 30, Year 10, show how sales, doubtful accounts expense, and receivables should appear in the financial statements for the fiscal year ended September 30, Year 10. Doubtful accounts expense is reported as an operating expense in the income statement.

7-4   In the second half of Year 3, Gill Company required additional cash for its operations and used accounts receivable to raise cash as follows:

   (1) On July 1, Gill assigned $200,000 of accounts receivable to Family Finance Company. Gill received an advance from Family of 85% of the assigned accounts receivable, less a fee of 3% on the advance. Prior to December 31, Year 3, Gill collected $150,000 on the assigned accounts receivable, and remitted $148,000 to Family, $8,000 of which represented interest on the advance.

(2) On November 10, Gill sold $310,000 of accounts receivable for $268,000. The receivables had a carrying amount of $294,000 and were sold outright on a nonrecourse basis.

(3) On December 31, Gill received an advance of $100,000 from Cathay Bank by pledging $120,000 of accounts receivable.

Instructions Prepare journal entries to record the transactions listed above.

7-5 From inception of its operations in Year 1, Koyanagi Company carried no allowance for doubtful accounts. Uncollectible receivables were expensed as written off, and recoveries were credited to income as collected. On March 1, Year 5 (after the Year 4 financial statements were issued), management recognized that Koyanagi's accounting policy with respect to doubtful accounts *was not correct,* and determined that an allowance for doubtful accounts was necessary. A policy was established to maintain an allowance for doubtful accounts based on Koyanagi's historical uncollectible accounts percentage applied to year-end accounts receivable. The historical uncollectible accounts percentage is to be recomputed each year based on all available past years up to a maximum of five years.

Information from Koyanagi's accounting records follows:

Year	Credit sales	Accounts written off	Recoveries
1	$1,500,000	$15,000	$ -0-
2	2,250,000	38,000	2,700
3	2,950,000	52,000	2,500
4	3,300,000	65,000	4,800
5	4,000,000	83,000	5,000

Accounts receivable balances were $1,250,000 and $1,460,000 on December 31, Year 4, and December 31, Year 5, respectively.

Instructions

a Prepare a journal entry, with appropriate explanation, to establish the allowance for doubtful accounts as of January 1, Year 5. Show supporting computations.

b Prepare a working paper to analyze the changes in the Allowance for Doubtful Accounts for the year ended December 31, Year 5. Show supporting computations.

7-6 The Allowance for Doubtful Accounts in the accounting records of DG Corporation for Year 5 is summarized below:

Allowance for Doubtful Accounts

Mar. 31	Write-off, Year 3 accounts	6,650	Jan.	1	Balance	21,100
June 30	Write-off, Year 4 accounts	9,100	Mar. 31		Provision	7,850
Sept. 30	Write-off, Year 4 accounts	6,840	June 30		Provision	9,720
Dec. 31	Write-off, Year 5 accounts	14,190	Sept. 30		Provision	14,200
			Dec. 31		Provision	12,550

The company sells on 30-day credit and has followed a practice of debiting Doubtful Accounts Expense in an amount equal to 4% of sales. The accountant regularly prepares quarterly income statements and makes adjusting entries at the end of each quarter in order to measure the interim net income. At the end of Year 5, the accountant suggested that an aging be made of accounts receivable to test the adequacy of the Allowance for Doubtful Accounts. The aging of accounts receivable on December 31, Year 5, follows:

Classification by due date	Amount
Current accounts, outstanding 30 days or less	$260,000
31–60 days old	85,200
61–120 days old	50,000
121 days–6 months old	31,000
Over 6 months old	16,800
Balance in controlling account, Dec. 31, Year 5	$443,000

After discussion with the credit manager of the company, the accountant estimated that the following percentages represented a reasonable estimate of the doubtful accounts in each category: current, 3%; 31 to 60 days old, 5%; 61 to 120 days old, 10%; 121 days to 6 months old, 15%; over 6 months old, 25%.

Instructions
a On the basis of this information, test the adequacy of the balance in the company's Allowance for Doubtful Accounts on December 31, Year 5.
b Prepare an adjusting journal entry on December 31, Year 5, based on your analysis. The accounting records have not been closed for Year 5. You should adjust the Doubtful Accounts Expense for Year 5 for any required increase or decrease in the Allowance for Doubtful Accounts.

7-7 In auditing the financial statements of Energy Service Corporation for Year 5, you discover the following information:

(1) On April 30, Year 5, the company received a noninterest-bearing note for $30,000 maturing in one year, as payment for a consulting fee. The fee originally was established at $27,600, but, because the client was short of cash, the company agreed to accept the note. The note was recorded at $30,000 by a debit to Notes Receivable and a credit to Fees Revenue. A discount account representing unearned interest revenue is used by the company.
(2) The company sold a parcel of land on June 30, Year 5, for $10,000 cash and a noninterest-bearing note of $40,000 due in three years. The land had a cost of $32,100, and Gain on Disposal of Land was credited for $17,900. You ascertain that the present value of the note on June 30, Year 5, discounted at 12%, was $28,471.
(3) A note receivable of $6,000, on which interest receivable of $340 had been recorded in the Accrued Interest Receivable account, was discounted at a bank at a rate of interest higher than the rate on the note. Proceeds of $6,280 were credited to Notes Receivable. The company does not use a Notes Receivable Discounted account. The note matures early in Year 6.
(4) Accounts receivable in the amount of $3,640 are considered worthless at the end of Year 5. (Debit Doubtful Accounts Expense.)
(5) Interest accrued on investment in bonds at the end of Year 5 amounts to $6,425.
(6) The company has recognized doubtful accounts expense only as specific receivables were deemed to be worthless. You ascertain that an allowance for doubtful accounts of $10,500 is required at the end of Year 5.

Instructions Prepare an adjusting or correcting journal entry on December 31, Year 5, for each item (1) through (6) above. The accounting records are still open for Year 5. Ignore income tax considerations and round all computations to the nearest dollar.

7-8 The following information appeared in the balance sheet for Empire Lumber Company on December 31, Year 4:

Note receivable			$ 24,000
Accrued interest receivable			1,000
Accounts receivable		$280,000	
Less: Allowance for doubtful accounts	$11,200		
Allowance for sales returns	4,000	15,200	264,800
Total notes and accounts receivable			$289,800

The note receivable is a six-month 10% note for $24,000 from R Company dated July 31, Year 4. (A 60-day 12% note for $36,000 from P Company dated Nov. 15, Year 4, had been discounted at Royal Bank on Nov. 30, Year 4.)

A summary of transactions relating to notes and accounts receivable for January of Year 5 follows:

Jan. 11 Received a 90-day, 12% note from a customer, Riki Morimoto, in exchange for an account receivable of $14,400. 12% is a fair rate of interest for the note.

13 Collected from Alice Tapp an account receivable written off in Year 4, $868.

15 Notice was received from Royal Bank that P Company paid the $36,000 note due January 14, together with the interest of $720. The company does not use a Notes Receivable Discounted account.

20 Worthless accounts totaling $4,808 were written off.

30 Received payment on R Company note, including interest of $1,200.

31 Sales on account for the month totaled $688,600.

31 Collections on accounts receivable, excluding Tapp account, were as follows:

(1) From accounts outstanding on December 31, Year 4, after $3,000 in sales discounts, $240,000.

(2) From current month's sales, after $5,400 in sales discounts, $368,000.

31 Recorded accrued interest for 20 days on note from Riki Morimoto.

31 Aging of accounts receivable shows that $18,000 is required in the Allowance for Doubtful Accounts and $7,600 is required in the Allowance for Sales Returns.

Instructions

a Record the transactions and other information given for the month of January in journal entry form. The company does not reverse any adjusting entries.

b Show how the information relating to notes and accounts receivable should appear in the balance sheet on January 31, Year 5.

7-9 In Year 3, Evans Company adopted a policy of providing for doubtful accounts expense at the rate of 3% of credit sales. A record of the company's experience for the past three years appears at the top of page 302.

The company's accountant made no journal entries affecting accounts receivable, other than those necessary to record sales, cash collections from customers, the annual provision for doubtful accounts, and the write-offs of individual accounts against the allowance account.

The company engaged you at the end of Year 5 to make an examination of its financial statements for the purpose of supporting a loan application. You have the foregoing data available as a basis for determining the adequacy of the allowance for doubtful accounts. You propose to adjust the allowance to conform to the actual experience relating to doubtful accounts expense during Years 3 and 4.

	Year 5	Year 4	Year 3
Credit sales	$535,000	$380,000	$320,000
Cash collected on credit sales:			
Year 3			$211,580
Year 4		$318,420	85,000
Year 5	$370,000	47,000	10,000
Accounts written off as uncollectible:			
Year 3			500
Year 4		8,180	8,800
Year 5	2,200	6,400	4,120
Balance in accounts receivable, Dec. 31,			
Year 5	162,800		
Totals.	$535,000	$380,000	$320,000

Instructions

a Set up ledger accounts for Accounts Receivable (controlling account), Doubtful Accounts Expense, and Allowance for Doubtful Accounts, and post all journal entries as the company's accountant made them in Years 3 through 5.

b Prepare in journal entry form, and post to the accounts set up in *a,* any adjusting entries you deem necessary on December 31, Year 5, assuming that the accounting records have not been closed. Explain briefly the reasons for your adjustments and the basis for your determination of the proper allowance for doubtful accounts on December 31, Year 5. The company records corrections of prior years' doubtful accounts expense in the current year's doubtful accounts expense.

7-10 Kahala Company started business on January 4, Year 3, and reported net income of $25,000 in Year 3, $33,000 in Year 4, and $52,420 in Year 5. The accounting records for the year ending December 31, Year 5, are closed.

Kahala did not use accrual accounting for some items. It was agreed that adjustments should be made in the accounting records to report the assets, liabilities, and owners' equity on the accrual basis of accounting.

Accounts receivable at the end of each year consisted of the following:

	Year 3	Year 4	Year 5
Relating to sales made in:			
Year 3	$20,000	$ 6,000	$ 3,000
Year 4		24,000	7,500
Year 5			35,000

Doubtful accounts expense was recorded when accounts receivable were deemed uncollectible. Based on an aging of accounts receivable, an allowance for doubtful accounts should be established at the end of Year 5, and should be recognized as follows: Current-year accounts receivable, 5%; accounts receivable relating to sales of Year 4, 10%; accounts receivable relating to sales of Year 3, 50%. Doubtful accounts expense previously recorded and years of sale are given at the top of page 303.

	Doubtful accounts expense recorded		Doubtful accounts expense recorded for sales made in		
Year	Amount		Year 3	Year 4	Year 5
3	$1,500		$1,500		
4	2,000		1,400	$ 600	
5	5,500		500	2,000	$3,000
Totals	$9,000		$3,400	$2,600	$3,000

Salaries and insurance were recorded as expense when paid. The amounts of accrued salaries and unexpired insurance at the end of each year were as follows:

	Dec. 31,		
	Year 3	Year 4	Year 5
Accrued salaries payable.	$ 800	$ 1,050	$ 1,420
Salaries paid in cash	20,000	25,000	26,500
Unexpired insurance	600	800	650
Insurance premiums paid	2,500	2,000	2,200

Instructions

a Determine the required balance in the Allowance for Doubtful Accounts on December 31, Year 5.

b Compute net income for Year 5, using the accrual basis of accounting. First, prepare a working paper to compute each of the following expenses for Year 5, on the accrual basis of accounting. (Ignore income taxes.)
(1) Doubtful accounts expense
(2) Salaries expense
(3) Insurance expense

c Prepare a journal entry to restate the accounting records to the accrual basis of accounting on December 31, Year 5. Close the net adjustment to net income for the three-year period to the Retained Earnings account.

7-11 General Factors, Inc., was incorporated in December, Year 1. The capital stock of the company consists of 50,000 shares of $10 par, all of which were issued at par. The company was organized for the purpose of factoring (purchasing) accounts receivable.

General Factors charges a fee to its clients of 5% of all accounts receivable factored and assumes all credit risks. In addition to the 5% fee, 10% of gross accounts receivable is withheld on all purchases and is credited to the Payable to Clients account. This account is used for merchandise returns made by customers of the clients for which a credit memo would be due. Payments are made to its clients by General Factors at the end of each month to adjust the Payable to Clients account so that it equals 10% of the uncollected accounts receivable as of the end of the month.

Based on the collection experience of other factoring companies, the management of General Factors decided to make monthly provisions to Allowance for Doubtful Accounts based on 1% of all accounts receivable purchased during the month.

The company also decided to recognize fees revenue only on the factored accounts receivable which have been collected; however, for accounting simplicity all fees originally are credited to Fees Revenue, and an adjusting entry is made to Unearned Fees at the end of each quarter, based on 5% of accounts receivable then outstanding.

Operations of the company during the first quarter of Year 2 resulted in the following:

Accounts receivable factored: January	*$400,000*
February	*500,000*
March	*800,000*

Collections on accounts receivable for the first quarter of Year 2 totaled $950,000. General and administrative expenses paid during the first quarter of Year 2 were as follows:

Salaries expense	*$19,500*
Office rent expense	*9,500*
Advertising expense	*800*
Equipment rent expense	*1,600*
Miscellaneous expenses	*1,450*

On January 31, Year 2, a six-month, 12% bank loan was obtained for $200,000, with interest payable at maturity.

For the first three months of the year, the company rented all its office furniture and equipment; however, on March 31, Year 2, it purchased office furniture and equipment for $20,200, payable within 10 days. This purchase was not entered in the accounting records.

Instructions

a Prepare a six-column (Transactions for Quarter, Income Statement, and Balance Sheet) working paper to summarize the activities of the company for the quarter ended March 31, Year 2. (Disregard all withholding taxes and the company's liability for FICA and income taxes.)

b Prepare a balance sheet for the company on March 31, Year 2.

7-12 Blass Corporation finances some of its current operations by assigning accounts receivable to EZ Finance Company. On May 1 of the current year, it assigned accounts receivable amounting to $300,000. EZ advanced 80% of the accounts receivable assigned, less a fee of 2% of the total accounts receivable assigned. Customers are instructed to make payment directly to EZ. Collections in excess of the loan and the fee will be remitted to Blass. At the time of remittance, the accountant for Blass transfers any balance in Assigned Accounts Receivable to the Accounts Receivable account.

The status of assigned accounts receivable at the end of May and June follows:

May 31 Blass received a statement which showed that EZ had collected $180,000 of the assigned accounts receivable and had made an additional charge for interest of $1\frac{1}{2}$% of assigned accounts receivable outstanding on May 31. This charge is to be deducted from the first remittance of cash by EZ to Blass.

June 30 Blass received a second statement from EZ, together with a check for the amount due. The statement indicated that EZ had collected an additional $66,000 and had made an additional charge for interest of $1\frac{1}{2}$% of assigned accounts receivable outstanding on June 30.

Instructions

a Prepare the journal entries necessary to record the above transactions in the accounting records of Blass Corporation. Debit all financing and interest charges to Interest Expense.

b Show how the information regarding assigned receivables should be presented in the balance sheet of Blass Corporation (1) on May 31 and (2) on June 30.

7-13   Nostalgia Company has not prepared financial statements for three years, since December 31, Year 1. The company has used the accrual basis of accounting and had reported income on a calendar-year basis prior to Year 2. During the past three years (Years 2, 3, and 4), the company has maintained cash records and has entered credit sales in an accounts receivable ledger; however, no general ledger postings have been made and an allowance for doubtful accounts has not been used.

The balances at the beginning and end of the three-year period accumulated as a result of your examination are presented below:

	Dec. 31,	
	Year 4	Year 1
Aging of accounts receivable:		
Less than 1 year old	$14,562	$7,700
1–2 years old	1,900	600
2–3 years old	2,138	
Over 3 years old (known to be uncollectible)	1,100	
Totals.	$19,700	$8,300
Inventories	$ 9,400	$5,800
Accounts payable (merchandise purchases)	6,500	4,305

Other information compiled from the company's accounting records follows:

	Year 4	Year 3	Year 2	Total
Cash received on account, relating to:				
Current year's collections	$103,938	$80,900	$74,400	$259,238
Accounts of the prior year	8,400	7,500	6,700	22,600
Accounts of two years prior	262	200	300	762
Total cash received in Years 2–4 . . .	$112,600	$88,600	$81,400	$282,600
Accounts to be written off in addition to				
the $1,100 which are over 3 years old .	$ 1,062	$ 820	$ 1,988	$ 3,870
Of receivables remaining at end of Year 4,				
estimated uncollectible percentage . .	10%	50%	80%	
Cash sales.	$ 15,600	$13,200	$13,500	$ 42,300
Payments for merchandise purchases . .	$ 86,900	$70,600	$62,500	$220,000

No accounts receivable have been written off as uncollectible during the three-year period. The rate of gross profit has remained relatively constant for many years.

Instructions

a Prepare a statement showing the gross profit on sales for Years 2, 3, and 4. (Hint: First, compute cost of goods sold as a percentage of sales for the three-year period.)

b Prepare adjusting entries at the end of Year 4 to (1) establish an adequate allowance for estimated doubtful accounts, and (2) write off accounts receivable known to be uncollectible. Debit Retained Earnings for the full amount required to establish the allowance for doubtful accounts.

c The company wishes to know what percentage of credit sales would be reasonable as an estimate of yearly doubtful accounts expense in the future, based on the experience of the past three years. Support your recommendation with appropriate computations.

8 INVENTORIES: COST AND COST FLOW ASSUMPTIONS

Nature of inventories

Inventories consist of goods held for sale to customers, partially completed goods, materials, and supplies to be used in production. Inventory items are acquired and sold continuously by a merchandising enterprise; or acquired, placed in production, converted into a finished product, and sold by a manufacturing enterprise. The sale of merchandise or finished products is the primary source of revenue for most business enterprises.

In a retail or merchandising operation, inventories consist principally of products purchased for resale in their existing form. A retail enterprise also may have an inventory of supplies such as wrapping paper, cartons, and stationery. A manufacturing enterprise, on the other hand, has several types of inventories: materials, parts, and factory supplies; goods in process; and finished goods.

Materials and parts are basic commodities or other products obtained directly from natural resources or acquired from others, which will be incorporated physically into the finished product. *Factory supplies* are similar to materials, but their relation to the end product is indirect. For example, in the manufacture of shirts, cloth is inventoried as materials, whereas the cleaning supplies and the oil to lubricate the machinery are classified as factory supplies. *Goods in process* is the title given to the inventory of partially completed product. The goods in process inventory includes the cost of direct materials, direct labor, and factory overhead assigned to the partially completed units. *Finished goods* are items which are complete and ready for sale. The cost of finished goods is composed of the same elements as those found in goods in process, the difference being that all necessary production costs have been incurred and allocated to the finished goods inventory.

Inventory procedures

Two methods may be employed to ascertain the inventory quantities on hand, the periodic system and the perpetual system. Both systems may be employed simultaneously for various inventories, such as materials, finished goods, and goods in process.

The *periodic system* relies on a periodic physical count of the goods on hand as the basis for control, management decisions, and financial accounting. Although this procedure may give accurate results at a given time, there is no continuing record of the inventory. The *perpetual system* requires a continuous record of all receipts and withdrawals of each item of inventory. The perpetual record sometimes is kept in terms of quantities only. This procedure provides a better basis for control than can be obtained under the periodic system. When a perpetual system is used, a physical count of the goods on hand must be made periodically to verify the accuracy of the inventory as reported in the accounting records. Any discrepancies discovered must be corrected so that the perpetual inventory records are in agreement with the physical count.

COST AND QUANTITY ACCUMULATION

Timing errors in the recording of purchases and sales

When the cost of goods available for sale during a particular accounting period is being accumulated, decisions frequently must be made as to whether certain goods become the property of the purchaser in the current period or in the succeeding period. If acquisitions of goods are not recorded in the accounting period in which they become the property of the purchaser, errors in the financial statements will result.

Three common types of timing errors in recording inventory acquisitions may occur. The errors and their effect on financial statements are:

1 A purchase is recorded properly, but goods are not included in the ending inventory. The result is to understate current assets and net income.
2 A purchase is not recorded, but goods are included in the ending inventory. The result is to state the assets properly but to understate current liabilities and to overstate net income.
3 A purchase is not recorded, and goods are not included in the ending inventory. Net income in this case is unaffected, because purchases and ending inventory are understated by the same amount, but both current assets and current liabilities are understated.

The first two errors are most likely to occur when the periodic inventory system is used; the third type may occur under either system, but it is more likely when the perpetual system is used. In most cases, timing errors are corrected automatically in the following accounting period; however, the fact that the errors may be self-correcting does not remove the need for correct presentation of financial position and results of operations for each period.

The valuation of inventories has important effects, both on the balance sheet and on the income statement. The investment in inventories is frequently a major part of a business enterprise's total assets, and the valuation of inventories has a direct effect on the determination of the cost of goods sold. The role of inventory valuation on the balance sheet and on the income statement for a merchandising enterprise which has a single class of inventory is illustrated below:

Valuation of inventory determines the cost of goods sold

Beginning inventory (*current asset in balance sheet at end of Year 9*) .	$200,000
Add: Purchases during Year 10.	700,000
Cost of goods available for sale during Year 10.	$900,000
Less: Ending inventory (*current asset in balance sheet at end of Year 10*)	150,000
Cost of goods sold during Year 10.	$750,000

In this illustration the cost of goods available for sale is $900,000, composed of the beginning inventory and the costs incurred during Year 10. The cost of goods available for sale is allocated between (1) the inventory on hand at the end of the period, $150,000, and (2) the cost of goods which have been sold during the current period, $750,000. The cost of goods sold is the difference between the cost of goods available for sale and the cost of the ending inventory. Any failure to determine accurately either the cost of goods available for sale or the ending inventory can have a material effect on financial statements.

Goods in transit

Orders for goods which have not been filled by the seller present little difficulty for accountants. Those orders which have been filled by the seller but not received by the purchaser are the crucial ones. The problem which must be resolved in these cases is to determine whether the goods in transit are the property of the purchaser or of the seller. The passage of title from the seller to the purchaser marks the time when the legal responsibility for the goods changes from one party to the other.

Contracts for purchases usually specify which party is responsible for the goods and the exact location where the responsibility changes. This point usually is indicated by the letters *"FOB,"* meaning *"free on board,"* followed by the designation of a particular location, for example, "FOB Denver." This means that title is held by the seller until the goods are delivered to a common carrier in Denver who will act as an agent for the purchaser.[1] The following example illustrates this concept:

KC Shirt Shop orders 200 shirts from Denver Fashions to be shipped "FOB Denver," the invoice to be paid within 10 days after shipment.

---

[1] Other important FOB designations are "FOB point of destination" and "FOB point of shipment," meaning that title passes at the purchaser's plant and at the seller's plant, respectively.

When Denver Fashions delivers the goods to a common carrier which acts as an agent of KC Shirt Shop, title to the goods passes to KC Shirt Shop. At this time, KC Shirt Shop would record the purchase if it knew that the goods were shipped. Of course the freight charges in this case must be paid by KC Shirt Shop; however, this liability does not arise until the agent delivers the goods to KC Shirt Shop.

Suppose at the same time KC Shirt Shop also orders 1,000 shirts from Chicago Fabrics to be delivered "FOB Kansas City." In this case the shirts are the property of Chicago Fabrics until they are delivered, and KC Shirt Shop does not recognize an asset or a liability until the shirts are received.

Goods on consignment and installment sales

Goods may be transferred by one party to another without the typical sale and purchase contract. The party receiving the goods, the *consignee,* agrees to accept the goods without any liability beyond that of providing reasonable protection from loss or damage, until the goods are sold to a third party. At this time the consignee must remit to the shipper, the *consignor,* the sales price less a selling commission and costs incurred in connection with the sale. The consignor retains title to the goods until the time of sale to the third party, and the consignee, acting only as an agent, never takes title to the goods. Therefore, until the goods are sold by the consignee, they remain the property of the consignor and must be included in the consignor's inventory at cost, including the handling and shipping costs involved in the transfer to the consignee. The consignee does not own the consigned goods and, therefore, should not include them in its inventory.

When goods are sold on the installment plan, the seller usually retains legal title to the goods until full payment has been received; however, such goods are excluded from inventory of the seller. The expectation is that customers will make payment in the ordinary course of business; therefore, strict adherence to the "passing-of-title" rule is not considered a realistic approach to the recording of installment sales transactions. Problems that arise in the recording of consignments and installment sales are discussed in *Modern Advanced Accounting* of this series.

Inventoriable costs

The two most important functions of accounting for inventories are (1) to determine the quantity of goods to be included in inventories, and (2) to determine the cost of the inventories on hand. The first function involves the *taking of inventory,* the second a *valuation of inventory.*

After the quantity of goods on hand has been determined, the starting point in the valuation process is to ascertain the inventoriable cost elements of goods purchased or products manufactured. For inventory items purchased from outsiders, the net invoice cost generally is considered to be the inventoriable cost. **Net invoice cost** is the invoice price of the item less any cash (purchases) discounts **available** to the purchaser. Cash discounts should not be included in inventory cost, regardless of whether the purchaser takes advantage of the discounts or fails to do so.

In theory, if a given cost is expected to contribute to the production of revenue, that cost should be associated with the goods acquired. Thus, a theoretical justification exists for adding the indirect costs of ordering, freight-in, handling, and storing to the net invoice cost to determine the total cost of goods acquired. However, the work involved in the allocation of these costs to inventories often exceeds the benefits derived from the increased accuracy in the valuation of inventories. Furthermore, the allocation of some indirect costs to goods acquired may be highly subjective.

Although the assignment to inventories of all costs incurred in the preparation of goods for sale is desirable, unrealistic allocations of indirect costs should be avoided to prevent a false implication of precision in the measurement of inventory costs. When costs are incurred which are necessary to the acquisition or production of goods but which are not expected to produce future benefits or are not material in amount, the costs usually are not included in inventories. Instead, such costs are considered period costs to be deducted from revenue of the current accounting period. The foregoing discussion is summarized in the diagram below:

Flow of inventory costs to the financial statements

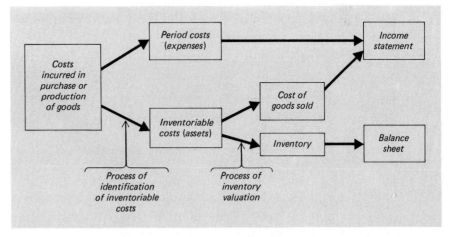

Purchased Inventories All costs incurred in the ordering, securing, handling, and storing of goods are as much a part of the total cost of the goods as the net invoice cost itself. The following example involving the purchase of shirts by KC Shirt Shop described on pages 309–310 illustrates the determination of the cost of goods acquired.

Assume that the invoice from Denver Fashions indicates the price of the 200 shirts to be $10 each, with terms 2/10, n/30. This means that KC Shirt Shop must pay Denver Fashions either $1,960 within 10 days of the date of the invoice or $2,000 within 30 days after the date of the invoice. The net invoice cost is $1,960. If payment is not made within 10 days, the $40 cash discount lost is treated as a financing expense of the period rather than as a cost of inventories.

The cost of deciding to order these particular shirts, the actual cost of ordering them, the transportation cost, and the handling and storage cost incurred after receipt of the shirts, are costs which logically might be added to the net invoice cost of $1,960.

Manufactured Inventories   In many ways the problems of measuring inventory costs are the same for a manufacturing enterprise as they are for a retailing enterprise. This is particularly true of materials and other purchased inventoriable items. The major difference is found in the measurement of the cost of finished goods and goods in process. Tracing the movement of goods and costs through the production process often is difficult, but if done with reasonable care, the resulting information is useful to management and outsiders.

As stated earlier, three classes of inventory usually are found in a manufacturing enterprise: (1) materials, parts, and factory supplies, (2) goods in process, and (3) finished goods. The costs of these inventories emerge as a part of the general process of the measurement of the costs of the three elements (direct materials, direct labor, and factory overhead) that flow through the manufacturing process, and of the tracing of these costs to specific quantities of partially finished and finished products as illustrated below:

Flow of production costs

Direct materials
Direct labor $\Big\}$ → *goods in process* → *finished goods*
Factory overhead*

* Heat, light, and power; indirect materials; indirect labor; rent; depreciation; insurance; supplies; maintenance; property taxes; etc.

There are basically two **cost systems** that are used to accumulate product costs for a manufacturing enterprise: the job order cost system and the process cost system.

A **job order cost system** is used when an enterprise manufactures several distinct products. For example, a job order system is used for a construction or specialty product enterprise. Each product or group of products is distinct in some way, and the production costs are identified with the specific job. **Job order cost sheets** are used to accumulate the cost of direct materials, direct labor, and factory overhead incurred on each job. Costs entered in job order cost sheets make up the goods in process inventory until the jobs are completed. The cost of completed jobs is a part of the finished goods inventory until the title to goods passes to customers.

A **process cost system** is used when large numbers of similar units are produced on an assembly-line operation. The production process typically is divided into **cost centers** or departments, based on logical divisions for the assignment of responsibility. Direct materials, direct labor, and factory overhead costs then are accumulated by cost center, and the goods in process inventory is the sum of all costs incurred on the partially finished units in the various cost centers. The finished goods inventory is composed of all costs incurred to produce the finished goods on hand.

When a process cost system is used, the cost to produce a complete unit of product usually is determined from departmental **cost of production reports.** Such reports show how the total costs incurred were assigned to any **by-products** (or scrap) and to the **main products.** By-products usually are priced at net realizable value; if such value is immaterial, no cost is assigned to by-products.

Accountants frequently encounter situations in which production costs in a given manufacturing process relate to two or more products. The allocation of these **joint costs** is necessary to determine the unit cost of each product and frequently is made on the basis of the **relative sales value** of the **joint products.** Dividing the total costs by the total sales value of the joint products determines the **cost percentage,** which then is applied to the unit selling price of each product to determine the estimated unit cost of each product.

Many enterprises engaged in manufacturing activities use standard costs as an integral part of their cost systems. **Standard costs** are estimates of what costs **should be** under relatively ideal conditions. The basic purpose of standard costs is to aid in measuring the efficiency of an operation, but standard costs also may be used for inventory valuation. The factors that make standard costs a good control tool serve to reduce their usefulness for inventory valuation purposes. To be a good control tool a standard cost of a product should represent what cost **ought to be,** not what it **is** or **has been.** When standard costs are used for inventory valuation, accountants should ascertain that the standard costs are reasonable estimates of costs actually incurred.

COST FLOW ASSUMPTIONS

The term **cost flow** refers to the inflow of costs when goods are purchased or manufactured and to the outflow of costs when goods are sold. The cost remaining in inventories is the difference between the inflow and outflow of costs. During a given accounting period such as a year or a month, identical goods may be purchased or manufactured at different costs. Accountants then face the problem of determining which costs apply to items in inventories and which to items that have been sold. The critical issue in accounting for inventories is summarized below:[2]

> A major objective of accounting for inventories is the proper determination of income through the process of matching appropriate costs against revenues.
>
> Cost for inventory purposes may be determined under any one of several assumptions as to the flow of cost factors (such as, first-in, first-out, average, and last-in, first-out); the major objective in selecting a method should be to choose the one which, under the circumstances, most clearly reflects periodic income.

The **assumed flow of costs** to be used in the assignment of costs to inventories and to goods sold need not conform to the physical flow of goods. **Cost flow assumptions relate to the flow of costs, rather than to the physical flow of goods.** The question of which physical units of identical goods were sold and which remain in inventories is not relevant to the accounting problem of income determination.

All methods of inventory valuation are based on the **cost principle;** no matter which method is selected, the inventory is stated **at cost.** In selecting an inventory valuation method (or cost flow assumption), we are matching costs with revenue, and the ideal choice is the method that "most clearly reflects periodic income." The most widely used methods of inventory valuation are:

1 First-in, first-out method (fifo)
2 Last-in, first-out method (lifo)
3 Weighted-average method
4 Specific identification method

A recent survey of 600 corporate annual reports indicated that fifo was used by 390 companies; lifo was used by 374 companies; average cost was used by 241 companies; and 56 companies applied a variety of other methods to the valuation of inventories. Obviously, many of the companies included in the survey used more than one method.[3]

First-in, first-out method

The first-in, first-out method assumes a flow of costs based on the assumption that the oldest goods on hand are sold first. This assumption about cost flow generally conforms to reality; management usually finds it desirable to keep the oldest goods moving out to customers in order to keep fresh goods on hand. The method is systematic and is easy to

---

[2] *Accounting Research and Terminology Bulletins—Final Edition,* AICPA (New York: 1961), chap. 4, pp. 28–29.
[3] *Accounting Trends & Techniques, 34th ed.,*AICPA (New York: 1980), p. 139.

apply; it adheres to the cost principle; and the cost assigned to inventory is likely to be in close harmony with the current prices being paid for inventory replacements.

To understand the application of the fifo method, assume the following data for the month of January relating to item X in the inventory of West Company:

A total of 2,000 units was
available for
sale . . . and 1,300
units were sold

WEST COMPANY

Record of Purchases of Item X during January

Jan. 1	*Inventory on hand. . . . .*	*200 units @ $ 7*	*$ 1,400*
Jan. 8	*Purchase . . . .*	*1,100 units @ $ 8*	*8,800*
Jan. 25	*Purchase . . . .*	*300 units @ $ 9*	*2,700*
Jan. 30	*Purchase . . . .*	*400 units @ $10*	*4,000*
	Totals	*2,000*	*$16,900*

A physical inventory taken on January 31 shows 700 units on hand. The inventory could be composed of any combination of 700 units on hand at the beginning of January or purchased during January. If we follow the fifo procedure, however, we assume that the inventory on January 31 is composed of the items which were acquired most recently. The computation of the inventory cost on January 31, based on fifo assumption, is illustrated below:

Fifo inventory of 700
units on hand

WEST COMPANY

Inventory of Item X: First-In, First-Out Method

Jan. 30 (last purchase).	*400 units @ $10*	*$4,000*
Jan. 25 (next-to-last purchase)	*300 units @ $ 9*	*2,700*
Totals.	*700*	*$6,700*

The cost of goods sold is $10,200 (total goods available, $16,900, less ending inventory, $6,700, equals $10,200). The cost of goods sold consists of the earliest costs incurred. The fifo method gives the same result whether the periodic or perpetual inventory system is used. Each withdrawal of goods is from the oldest stock. For example, if the perpetual inventory system is used and the cost of units sold is determined on a daily basis, the cost of goods sold is computed as shown at the top of page 316.

Cost of goods sold on fifo basis

WEST COMPANY		
Cost of Goods Sold (Item X): First-In, First-Out Method		
Jan. 6.	100 units @ $7	$ 700
Jan. 9.	200 units { 100 @ $7 { 100 @ $8	1,500
Jan. 15.	400 units @ $8	3,200
Jan. 27.	600 units @ $8	4,800
Totals	1,300	$10,200

The cost of the inventory on the fifo basis under a perpetual inventory system also is $6,700 ($16,900 goods available for sale, less $10,200 cost of goods sold, equals $6,700).

Last-in, first-out method

The last-in first-out method assumes a flow of inventory costs based on the assumption that the most recently acquired goods on hand are sold first, because current costs are incurred to make current sales and to maintain an adequate inventory on hand. Under this view, the latest costs are most closely associated with current revenue, and thus the matching principle of income determination is carried out. In the balance sheet, however, inventory under the lifo method is valued at the earliest costs incurred.

The following data for the month of January relating to item X in the inventory of West Company are the same as those used for the fifo illustration on page 315, except for the addition of the number of units sold and the dates when the sales were made:

Summary of purchases and sales on lifo basis

WEST COMPANY						
Record of Purchases and Sales of Item X during January						
Purchases					Sales	
Date		Units	Price	Total	Date	Units sold
Jan. 1	Inventory on hand . .	200	$ 7	$ 1,400	Jan. 6	100
Jan. 8	Purchase	1,100	8	8,800	Jan. 9	200
Jan. 25	Purchase	300	9	2,700	Jan. 15	400
Jan. 30	Purchase	400	10	4,000	Jan. 27	600
	Totals	2,000		$16,900		1,300

The cost assigned to the ending inventory under lifo depends on whether the periodic or the perpetual inventory system is used.

Periodic Inventory System Based on the information given on page 316, the cost of the 700 units on hand on January 31 is computed under the lifo periodic inventory system as follows:

Lifo inventory of 700 units on hand

WEST COMPANY		
Inventory of Item X: Last-In, First-Out Method (Periodic Inventory System)		
Jan. 1 (beginning inventory)...............	200 units @ $7	$1,400
Jan. 8 (first purchase)...................	500 units @ $8	4,000
Totals	700	$5,400

The lifo inventory on January 31 is composed of two layers: the 200 units on hand on January 1, plus the layer of 500 units added during January. Should sales exceed purchases in any subsequent period, the costs of units comprising the most recently added layer or layers would be removed from inventory and transferred to cost of goods sold. The cost of the original layer would not be reduced until all subsequently added layers had been assigned to cost of goods sold. The cost of goods sold for January is $11,500 ($16,900 cost of goods available for sale, less $5,400 cost of inventory at January 31, equals $11,500), and consists of the most recent costs incurred for purchases.

Perpetual Inventory System Unlike the first-in, first-out method, the last-in, first-out method does not produce the same result when the perpetual inventory system is used. When a perpetual inventory system is used, each withdrawal must come from the most recent purchase; however, this may mean that under certain conditions items will be withdrawn from the beginning inventory or the earliest purchase. If we assume the same record of purchases and sales as for the fifo procedure above, the costs assigned to the goods sold under the lifo perpetual inventory system is $10,600, as computed below:

Lifo method: cost of goods sold . . .

WEST COMPANY		
Cost of Goods Sold (Item X): Last-In, First-Out Method		
(Perpetual Inventory System)		
Jan. 6.	100 units @ $7	$ 700
Jan. 9.	200 units @ $8	1,600
Jan. 15.	400 units @ $8	3,200
Jan. 27.	600 units { 300 @ $9	2,700
	300 @ $8	2,400
Totals	1,300	$10,600

The ending inventory under the lifo perpetual inventory system amounts to $6,300 ($16,900 − $10,600 = $6,300), and consists of the following:

. . . and ending inventory under perpetual inventory system

WEST COMPANY Inventory of Item X: Last-In, First-Out Method (Perpetual Inventory System)		
Jan. 1 (Balance of beginning layer not sold).	100 units @ $7	$ 700
Jan. 8.	200 units @ $8	1,600
Jan. 30	400 units @ $10	4,000
Totals.	700	$6,300

Thus, it is apparent that the results of the lifo method of valuing the inventory under the perpetual inventory system may vary somewhat, depending on the timing of sales and purchases.

Unit-Lifo Method   The practical problems of determining the cost of inventory under the lifo procedure may be overwhelming, especially without the aid of a computer. When there are large numbers of similar items and numerous transactions, the weighted-average unit cost of the items purchased during an accounting period is considered the cost for purposes of calculating additions to inventory for the period. Such a procedure eliminates the need for identifying the cost of particular units. This adaptation is used in conjunction with a periodic inventory system and is called the *unit-lifo method.* Given the data presented on the bottom of page 316 for West Company, the unit-lifo inventory at January 31 is computed below:

Illustration of unit-lifo method

WEST COMPANY Inventory of Item X: Unit-Lifo Method		
Beginning inventory.	200 units @ $7.00	$1,400
Layer added in January.	500 units @ $8.61*	4,305
Totals	700	$5,705

* Computation of weighted-average unit cost for units acquired in January:	
Cost of purchases	$15,500
Total units purchased in January.	1,800
Weighted-average unit cost of purchases: $15,500 ÷ 1,800	$ 8.61

The unit-lifo method is applied only when there is an increase in the inventory during the period. The layer added in January retains its identity in subsequent months as long as the inventory consists of 700 units or more. However, if the inventory decreased to 400 units in February, the inventory on February 28 would consist of 200 units at $7 and only 200 units at $8.61.

Dollar-Value Lifo The **dollar-value lifo** method is another procedure designed to facilitate the calculation of inventory. Under dollar-value lifo, the inventory can be priced at current cost, which eliminates the need for identification of the specific costs of units in inventory. The total current cost of the inventory then is restated, by means of a specific cost index, to the cost prevailing when lifo was adopted. The ending inventory in terms of base-year dollars is compared with the beginning inventory, also priced at base-year dollars, to determine the **physical change** in the inventory on hand. Increases or decreases in the inventory then are assigned costs prevailing **at the end of the accounting period** in which the items were acquired.

The essence of the dollar-value lifo method can be observed in the following simplified example: If the beginning inventory was valued at $10,000 and the ending inventory, at end-of-year prices, was valued at $11,000, there appears to have been a $1,000 increase in inventory. However, if prices have increased by 10% during the year, the $1,000 increase is attributable entirely to price increases. Because lifo values inventory at earliest costs incurred, **if the quantity of goods on hand is unchanged, the lifo inventory valuation stated in dollars also should remain unchanged.** In the valuation of lifo inventory by the dollar-value method, the increase in the physical quantity of the inventory during the year is ascertained, and then an appropriate current cost is assigned to the increase.

Any increase in the inventory quantity is valued at costs prevailing during the current year. In practice, the index of costs as of the **end of the current year** often is used to value the added layer. Although the use of the year-end cost index implies the use of the fifo method, practical limitations of computing several indexes during a year have led to acceptance of the year-end cost index for this purpose. A decrease in the inventory is deducted from the most recent layer added to the inventory at the costs prevailing in the year when that layer was added.

Illustration of Dollar-Value Lifo The data at the top of page 320 concerning ending inventories and the specific cost indexes for the inventories at the end of each year are used to illustrate the application of the dollar-value lifo method for Doval Company.

Computation of dollar-value inventories for Doval Company is summarized on page 321.

DOVAL COMPANY			
Inventories and Cost Indexes			
December 31, Year 1 through Year 5			
Year ended		*Inventories at year-end costs*	*Cost indexes at end of year*
Dec. 31, Year 1		$36,000	100
Dec. 31, Year 2		57,500	125
Dec. 31, Year 3		60,000	150
Dec. 31, Year 4		65,800	140
Dec. 31, Year 5		44,400	148

Explanation of computations:

Year 2: The ending inventory is converted to a valuation of $46,000 at base-year costs by dividing the year-end cost of $57,500 by the year-end cost index of 1.25. The increase in the inventory is $10,000. This increase then is converted to year-end costs by multiplying the increase, stated in base-year costs, by the cost index at the end of the year. Thus, the dollar-value inventory at the end of Year 2 is $48,500, the beginning inventory of $36,000 plus the layer of $12,500 ($10,000 × 1.25 = $12,500) added in Year 2.

Year 3: A decrease in inventory of $6,000 ($46,000 − $40,000 = $6,000) took place in Year 3. This decrease is considered a reduction in the most recent addition to the inventory. The most recent addition was $10,000 (in terms of base-year costs), which took place in Year 2. The decrease of $6,000 from the $10,000 layer leaves only $4,000 of the Year 2 layer in inventory. This $4,000 then is converted to the cost level at the end of Year 2, when this layer was added. Thus, the ending inventory at the end of Year 3 is $41,000, consisting of the base-year layer of $36,000 plus the remaining portion of the Year 2 layer, $5,000.

Year 4 The ending inventory of $47,000 at base-year costs increased by $7,000 ($47,000 − $40,000 = $7,000) during Year 4. This increase is multiplied by 1.40, the cost index at the end of Year 4, to convert it to the year-end cost of $9,800. The increase then is added to the beginning inventory of $41,000 to compute the ending inventory of $50,800.

Year 5 The ending inventory at base-year costs, $30,000, is less than the base-year layer of $36,000 on hand at the end of Year 4. Therefore, the ending inventory consists entirely of base-year costs.

The key feature of the dollar-value lifo method is the conversion of the beginning and ending inventories to base-year costs. The difference between the two converted inventory amounts indicates the increase or decrease in the inventory expressed in terms of base-year costs. The lifo layers then must be valued at costs prevailing when the layers were added to the inventory.

**Dollar-value
method
illustrated**

DOVAL COMPANY
Computation of Dollar-Value Lifo Inventories
Year 1 through Year 5

Year	Inventories at year-end costs	÷	Deflator (cost index at year-end)	=	Inventories at base-year costs	Determination of inventory layers	Dollar-value lifo inventories at year-end
1 (base year)	$36,000	÷	1.00	=	$36,000	$36,000 × 1.00	$36,000
2	$57,500	÷	1.25	=	$46,000	$36,000 × 1.00 10,000 × 1.25 $46,000	$36,000 12,500 $48,500
3	$60,000	÷	1.50	=	$40,000	$36,000 × 1.00 4,000 × 1.25 $40,000	$36,000 5,000 $41,000
4	$65,800	÷	1.40	=	$47,000	$36,000 × 1.00 4,000 × 1.25 7,000 × 1.40 $47,000	$36,000 5,000 9,800 $50,800
5	$44,400	÷	1.48	=	$30,000	$30,000 × 1.00	$30,000

Cost Index Specific cost indexes, such as the index for nonferrous metals or for department store prices, often are used to make inventory cost adjustments to compute dollar-value lifo inventories.

In the absence of an appropriate cost index, the accountant can take a **sample** of the inventory and value this sample both at current-period and at base-period prices. The total cost in terms of the current period's prices then is divided by the total cost in terms of the base period's prices. The cost index thus determined is used to value the entire inventory. In the calculation of this index, discontinued and new products deserve special consideration. The best approach is to eliminate these items from the calculation. They in turn must be valued separately, and in many cases the only feasible way is to refer to particular invoice costs. The cost index for a sample of inventory items can be computed as illustrated at the top of page 322. This computation indicates that current prices have risen on the average by 10% from base-period prices.

		Unit costs		Total costs	
Items	Inventory quantity	End of current period	Base period	End of current period	Base period
A	150	$40.00	$36.00	$6,000	$5,400
B	60	15.00	13.00	900	780
C	200	4.00	4.10	800	820
				$7,700	$7,000

Base Stock Method   The *base stock method* is similar to lifo, but, because it is not acceptable for income tax purposes and has little theoretical support, it seldom is used in practice. This method assumes a continuous existence of a minimum stock of goods, and inventory is considered to be a permanent asset. Any excess over the base stock is considered a temporary increase and is priced at current replacement costs; any decrease in the base stock is considered to be temporary and is assigned to cost of goods sold at current replacement costs.

The base stock method differs from lifo in that it uses *current replacement costs* as an element in the pricing of inventory; on the other hand, lifo relies exclusively on actual costs.

Weighted-average method

The weighted-average method of inventory valuation is based on the assumptions that all goods are commingled and that no particular batch of goods is retained in the inventory. Thus, the inventory is priced on the basis of average prices paid for the goods, weighted according to the quantity purchased at each price. Given the information for West Company, the ending inventory and cost of goods sold are determined under the weighted-average method as follows:

WEST COMPANY
Inventory and Cost of Goods Sold (Item X): Weighted-Average Method
(Periodic Inventory System)

Cost of goods available for sale	$16,900
Total units available for sale	2,000
Unit price = cost ÷ number of units ($16,900 ÷ 2,000)	$ 8.45
Inventory valuation: 700 × $8.45.	$ 5,915
Cost of goods sold ($16,900 − $5,915)	$10,985

This method produces a result, for both inventory valuation and income determination, which lies between the results achieved under fifo and those achieved under lifo. The weighted-average method does not produce an inventory value consistent with the current cost of the items in inventory; by its very nature it lags behind market prices. During a period of rising prices the inventory cost tends to be below replacement cost; and during a period of falling prices it tends to be above replacement cost.

When the perpetual inventory system is used, the weighted-average method gives the result of a *moving weighted average.* Under a perpetual inventory system, a new weighted-average unit cost is computed after each purchase, and for this reason is known as the moving-weighted-average method. Units sold are priced at the latest weighted-average unit cost. Given the information for West Company, the moving-weighted-average method is illustrated below:

Weighted-average method under perpetual inventory system

WEST COMPANY

Inventory of Item X: Moving Weighted Average (Perpetual Inventory System)

	Units	Amount
Jan. 1 inventory	200 @ $ 7.00	$1,400
Less: Jan. 6 issue	(100) @ $ 7.00	(700)
Balance, Jan. 6.	100 @ $ 7.00	$ 700
Add: Jan. 8 purchase	1,100 @ $ 8.00	8,800
Balance, Jan. 8 (new unit cost computed)	1,200 @ $ 7.92	$9,500*
Less: Jan. 9 issue	(200) @ $ 7.92	(1,584)
Balance, Jan. 9.	1,000 @ $ 7.92	$7,916*
Less: Jan. 15 issue	(400) @ $ 7.92	(3,168)
Balance, Jan. 15	600 @ $ 7.92	$4,748*
Add: Jan. 25 purchase.	300 @ $ 9.00	2,700
Balance, Jan. 25 (new unit cost computed).	900 @ $ 8.28	$7,448*
Less: Jan. 27 issue	(600) @ $ 8.28	(4,968)
Balance, Jan. 27.	300 @ $ 8.28	$2,480*
Add: Jan. 30 purchase.	400 @ $10.00	4,000
Balance, Jan. 31 (inventory at new unit cost).	700 @ $ 9.26	$6,480*

* Slight discrepancy due to rounding of average cost to nearest cent.

Specific identification method

At first thought one might argue that each item of inventory should be identified with its cost and that the sum of these amounts should constitute the inventory value. Although such a technique might be possible for a business enterprise handling a small number of items, for example, an automobile dealer, it becomes completely inoperable in a complex manufacturing enterprise when the identity of the individual item is lost. Practical considerations thus make specific identification inappropriate in most cases.

Even when specific identification is a feasible means of valuation, it may be undesirable from a theoretical point of view. The method permits income manipulation when there are identical items acquired at varying prices. By choosing to sell the item which was acquired at a specific cost, management can cause material fluctuations in income. For example, assume that Grain Company acquires 1 million bushels of wheat in four equal lots of 250,000 bushels each, at costs of $3.50, $4, $4.50, and $5 a bushel. Grain Company receives an order to sell 250,000 bushels at $4.75 a bushel. If management is accounting for inventory in accordance with specific identification, it can determine the income reported for the period by selecting the batch of wheat which will produce the desired objective. The results of the transaction could range from a profit of $312,500, if the $3.50 wheat were sold, to a loss of $62,500 if the $5 wheat were sold. If an assumption regarding the flow of goods were adopted (fifo or lifo, for example), the effect of such arbitrary decisions on reported income would be removed.

The total profit or loss derived from the sale of the 1 million bushels of wheat will be the same, ignoring income tax effects, regardless of the order in which the batches are sold. The important consideration here is the potential impact on the financial statements as a result of varying assumptions regarding the flow of goods. Consequently, a systematic cost flow assumption is desirable in the interests of objective financial accounting and reporting.

Summary of inventory valuation methods

The inventory valuation and cost of goods sold for West Company as determined in the preceding illustrations are summarized on page 325. Results from use of the specific identification method are not shown, because we did not identify the compositon of the units in inventory by date of purchase.

In the West Company example in which prices were rising, the costs assigned to inventory range from a high of $6,700 under the fifo method to a low of $5,400 when the lifo method is used in conjunction with the periodic inventory system. The disparity in inventory valuation under the various cost flow assumptions depends on the trend and volatility of prices paid for new purchases and, of course, on the length of time the lifo method has been in use.

Summary of cost flow assumptions

	WEST COMPANY		
Inventory and Cost of Goods Sold (Item X): Various Cost Flow Assumptions			
Cost flow assumption	Goods available for sale	Inventory	Cost of goods sold
First-in, first-out method	$16,900	$6,700	$10,200
Last-in, first-out method:			
Periodic inventory system	16,900	5,400	11,500
Perpetual inventory system . . .	16,900	6,300	10,600
Unit lifo	16,900	5,705	11,195
Weighted-average (periodic			
inventory system)	16,900	5,915	10,985
Moving weighted average			
(perpetual inventory system) . .	16,900	6,480	10,420

INVENTORY VALUATION AND INFLATION

Although both lifo and fifo are accepted inventory valuation methods, they may lead to significant differences in the financial statements during a period of inflation. Neither method achieves an entirely satisfactory reporting of both inventories and cost of goods sold when prices are going up. Therefore, it is not surprising that a controversy has evolved around the relative importance of working capital and net income. In an inflationary period, this controversy is somewhat overshadowed by the managerial and income tax implications of inventory valuation procedures.

Effect on working capital and net income

As illustrated earlier, the fifo method has the effect of assigning the most recently incurred cost to inventories, whereas the lifo assumption assigns the first costs incurred to inventories. During periods of rising price levels, inventories valued on the fifo basis approximate more closely the current cost of the inventories; the cost of items valued on the lifo basis are less than the current cost. The difference between the inventories valued at lifo and at current cost depends on the magnitude of the price level increases. The lifo method produces a seriously distorted inventory valuation when it is used over a long period during which the price level increases steadily or when the price level increases very rapidly.

The understatement of inventories resulting from the use of the lifo method is objectionable because of the effect on working capital, current ratio, and inventories turnover rate. The problem is rather serious when no indication is included in the financial statements of the degree of understatement. The advocates of lifo minimize the importance of this understatement by their insistence that the income statement is more important than the balance sheet. They argue that a more accurate measure of net income may justify a less meaningful balance sheet.

Proponents of the lifo method argue that realized revenue should be matched with the cost of acquiring goods at or near the time the revenue is realized. They contend that during periods of rising prices, for example, two types of profits, **inventory profits** and **operating profits,** may be included in net income, unless diligence is exercised to avoid the inclusion of inventory profits. **Inventory profits** arise as a result of holding inventories during periods of rising inventory costs, and are measured by the difference between the historical cost of the goods sold and their current cost at the time the goods are sold. On the other hand, **operating profits** result from sales of a product at a price above current cost. Because the lifo method matches the most recently incurred costs with realized revenue, it tends to exclude inventory profits from net income. Supporters of lifo favor the exclusion of inventory profits from net income, on the premise that inventories which are sold must be replaced and that inventory profits are fictitious and illusory.

Those supporting the fifo method of inventory valuation agree that there may be two types of profits, but they consider both to be an element of income realized at the time of sale. They argue that if the proponents of lifo are interested in measuring **real** rather than **monetary** income, they should extend their proposal to use current costs to value all assets. The cost of goods sold should not be the most recently incurred costs but rather those costs which will be incurred to replace the items which have been sold. This method has been referred to as the **next-in, first-out (nifo)** method of inventory valuation. At the present time nifo is not acceptable, because it is considered a departure from the cost principle.

The measurement of **real income** poses another problem during a period of general inflation. To illustrate, assume that an inventory item was purchased by a business enterprise for $100 when the general price-level index stood at 120, and was sold for $150 when the general price-level index stood at 132 and when the current cost of the item was $124. The apparent gross profit of $50 ($150 − $100 = $50) on the sale of the item may be allocated between the (1) general price-level adjustment, (2) holding gain, and (3) operating profit as follows:

Analysis of gross profit

General price-level adjustment: ($100 × 132/120) − $100 (original cost). . . $10
Holding gain: $124 (current cost) − $100 (original cost) − $10 (general
  price-level adjustment computed above) 14
Operating profit: $150 (selling price) − $124 (current cost). 26
  Total difference between selling price and original cost ($150 − $100). . . $50

The **holding gain** of $14 is the increase accruing as a result of owning the item while the specific price (current cost) of the item was rising. The holding gain does not include the $10 increase in price of the item caused by general inflation. The total of the price-level adjustment and the holding gain is the **inventory profit** as defined above. Finally, the **operating profit** is the real economic reward to the enterprise for handling and selling the item.

Managerial and income tax implications

The proponents of lifo argue that this method is an invaluable aid to management because it excludes inventory profits from the determination of net income. External factors which are beyond the control of management often create inventory profits. Moreover, inventory profits are reinvested in inventories, which means that disposable income is measured more accurately by the use of lifo.

Fifo advocates agree that management may need information about the current cost of the inventory and its effect on net income; however, they maintain that this information can be compiled without distorting working capital and net income. Moreover, they argue that if the inventory profits are excluded from net income, then similar profits derived from other investments should be excluded. If in fact management decisions regarding dividend declarations, wage negotiations, and prices are based on the concept of disposable income, then a more extensive modification of the determination of net income is needed than that achieved by lifo.

Despite the theoretical arguments in support of lifo, the dominant reason for its popularity appears to be the income tax benefits that result from the use of this method. During periods of rising prices, taxable income and income taxes are reduced through the use of lifo. If prices later fall to the level at the time lifo was adopted, this reduction is simply a deferral of taxes. If prices continue to rise, the reduction will be permanent. In either case, the lifo user gains, because a postponement of taxes has economic value. The federal income tax law requires that lifo must be used for financial accounting if it is used for income tax purposes.

The income tax benefits of lifo are not guaranteed. If prices fall below levels at the time lifo is adopted, or if the quantity of inventories is reduced below the amount on hand at the inception of lifo, it is conceivable that the lifo method could produce a tax disadvantage. Before adopting lifo solely for income tax reasons, management should consider such factors as the expected course of prices, future income tax rates, inventory fluctuations, the enterprise's net income pattern, and the existence of provisions in the income tax law (such as operating loss carrybacks and carryforwards) which even out the tax burden over periods of income and loss. Finally, when lifo is used and prices decline, inventories cannot be valued on the basis of lower of cost or market for income tax purposes.

Disclosure of inventory profits

The Securities and Exchange Commission has urged publicly owned companies to disclose the amount of profit included in the income statement which is not repeatable due to increased replacement costs of inventories caused by inflation. The disclosure may be made in the financial statements, the notes to the financial statements, or in textual material accompanying the financial statements. Included in the Commission's reasons for recommending the disclosure of inventory profits was the following paragraph:[4]

> The most significant and immediate impact of price fluctuations on financial statements is normally felt in cost of goods sold in the income statement. In periods of rising prices, historical cost methods result in the inclusion of "inventory profits" in reported earnings. "Inventory profit" results from holding inventories during a period of rising inventory costs and is measured by the difference between the historical cost of an item and its replacement cost at the time it is sold. Different methods of accounting for inventories can affect the degree to which "inventory profits" are included and identifiable in current income, but no method based upon historical cost eliminates or discloses this "profit" explicitly. Such "profits" do not reflect an increase in the economic earning power of a business and they are not normally repeatable in the absence of continued price-level increase. Accordingly, where such "profits" are material in income statements presented, disclosure of their impact on reported earnings and the trend of reported earnings is important information for investors assessing the quality of earnings.

An example of disclosure of inventory profits by a large oil company a few years ago follows: "Included in the net income of $1,292,-400,000 is an estimated inventory profit of $422,000,000, related to consolidated worldwide inventories."

In 1976, the Securities and Exchange Commission issued **ASR No. 190,** which required disclosure of the estimated current replacement cost of inventories and the approximate amount of cost of goods sold based on replacement cost for the two most recent fiscal years.[5] **ASR No. 190** was withdrawn in 1979 when the FASB issued **Statement No. 33,** which required the disclosure of current cost information (including for inventories) by certain large companies.[6] Requirements of **FASB Statement No. 33** are discussed in Chapter 25.

[4] *Accounting Series Release No. 151,* SEC (Washington: 1974), p. 1.
[5] *Accounting Series Release No. 190,* SEC (Washington: 1976).
[6] *FASB Statement No. 33,* "Financial Reporting and Changing Prices," FASB (Stamford: 1979).

VALUATION OF INVENTORIES AT LOWER OF COST OR MARKET

Pricing an inventory includes tabulating the number of units, determining the unit cost, and computing the total cost. We shall now consider another possibility: that of a decrease in the economic value of inventories below their cost. If some items of inventory are used for display or demonstration, a part of the cost of these units should be absorbed prior to their sale. Whenever an asset contributes to the production of revenue and a part of the usefulness of the asset is consumed, a part of the cost of the asset should be deducted from revenue.

Assume, for example, that the owner of Delphine's Dress Shop wants her store to have a reputation as *the* fashion shop in her area. To accomplish her objective she knows that she must stock the extreme styles in sufficient volume to satisfy a substantial part of her clientele. In many cases she will buy more dresses than she expects to sell in order to maintain her reputation. To obtain a proper measure of income and to value her inventories properly, a part of the cost of the excess supply of dresses will have to be charged against revenue prior to the sale of these dresses. The problem is one of ascertaining the amount of the cost that should be charged off. The loss of economic value is believed to have contributed to the production of revenue, and the selling price of dresses on hand will have to be reduced. The expired costs of dresses still on hand may be added to the cost of goods sold.

Obsolescence of inventories

In other situations part of the cost of inventories must be deducted from revenue even though no benefit has accrued to the business enterprise. Inventory items frequently become unsalable at regular prices because of obsolescence, damage, or deterioration. If items which are to become a part of a manufactured article are damaged or spoiled during the production process, the loss need not be segregated, but may become a part of the cost of the completed product. This procedure is acceptable, provided the damage or loss is expected as a part of the normal operation of the plant. On the other hand, unusual loss or damage should not be included in the cost of finished goods manufactured.

Damaged or obsolete goods frequently are valued at **net realizable value**—estimated selling price less direct costs of completion and disposal. A more severe standard is to write the goods down to replacement cost—the price that the present owners would pay for the goods in their present condition if they were considering buying the goods for resale. In some cases an arbitrary percentage of the cost is written off; this is difficult to defend, but in such cases no more objective basis is available. Finally, when there is doubt about the existence of any net realizable value, the cost of the goods should be reduced to scrap value, or to zero in the absence of scrap value.

Price fluctuations and valuation of inventories

Price changes which result in loss of economic usefulness of inventories should be deducted from revenue in the accounting period in which the loss takes place. Because the cost of the inventories is determined by negotiation between the purchaser and supplier based on the purchaser's expectation of earning a normal gross profit margin on resale, a significant decline in the selling price of inventories requires a reduction in the carrying amount of inventories. The inventory value which is most appropriate in such situations is **replacement cost** (or a "derived market" price), that is, a price which will allow the business enterprise to recover the adjusted cost of the inventories and still earn a normal gross profit margin.

At present, generally accepted accounting principles hold that gains attributable to price increases should not be recognized until inventories are sold. However, losses resulting from decreases in the prices of the inventories should be recognized in the accounting period in which the price decreases occur. The basis for this **lower-of-cost-or-market rule** can be found in the concept of conservatism which has guided accounting policy for a long time.

Lower-of-cost-or-market procedures

The lower-of-cost-or-market (LCM) rule requires that inventories be priced at the lower of these two values (cost price or market price). The benefits attributed to this method of inventory valuation are (1) the loss, if any, is identified with the accounting period in which it occurred, and (2) goods are valued at an amount that measures the expected contribution to revenue of future periods. The following principle supports the lower-of-cost-or-market rule:[7]

> A departure from the cost basis of pricing the inventory is required when the utility of the goods is no longer as great as its cost. Where there is evidence that the utility of goods, in their disposal in the ordinary course of business, will be less than cost, whether due to physical deterioration, obsolescence, changes in price levels, or other causes, the difference should be recognized as a loss of the current period. This is generally accomplished by stating such goods at a lower level commonly designated as **market.**

The measurement of utility is almost impossible, and the adoption of the LCM price is a practical means of approximating the decline in utility of goods in inventories.

What is meant by "market" in the expression "lower of cost or market"? Is it the price the item will bring when it is sold, or is it the price that would be paid to purchase the item? Current practice requires the use of the current purchase price, that is, **replacement cost,** with certain limitations. Replacement cost is a broader term than purchase price

[7] *Accounting Research and Terminology Bulletins—Final Edition,* chap. 4, p. 30.

because it includes incidental acquisition costs. Replacement cost also can be applied to manufactured inventories with reference to the prevailing prices for direct materials, direct labor, and factory overhead. In cases where replacement cost is not reasonably determinable or exceeds the amount expected to be realized by the sale of the items, the **net realizable value** should be used instead of replacement cost. The net realizable value is determined by subtracting from the expected selling price all prospective direct costs of completing and selling the item. The following limits (**ceiling** and **floor**) have been placed on "market."[8]

> As used in the phrase **lower of cost or market** the term **market** means current replacement cost (by purchase or by reproduction, as the case may be) except that:
> **1** Market should not exceed the net realizable value (i.e., estimated selling price in the ordinary course of business less reasonably predictable costs of completion and disposal); and
> **2** Market should not be less than net realizable value reduced by an allowance for an approximately normal profit margin.

Thus, the **ceiling** is equal to the selling price reduced by the estimated costs of completion and sale; and the **floor** is equal to the selling price reduced by the estimated costs of completion and sale, and a normal gross profit. *Replacement cost is used as "market" price if it falls between the ceiling and the floor; the ceiling amount is used as "market" price when replacement cost is above the ceiling; and the floor amount is used as "market" price when replacement cost is below the floor.* This general rule is diagramed below for a unit costing $40, three different assumptions as to replacement cost ($38, $34, and $28), a ceiling limit on market price of $36, and a floor limit on market price of $30.

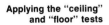

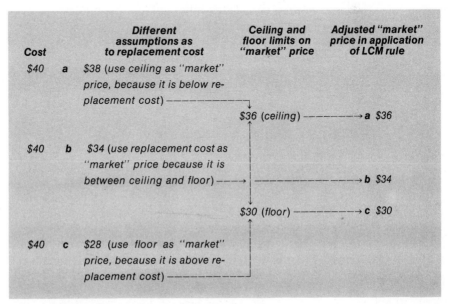

Applying the "ceiling" and "floor" tests	Cost		Different assumptions as to replacement cost	Ceiling and floor limits on "market" price	Adjusted "market" price in application of LCM rule
	$40	a	$38 (use ceiling as "market" price, because it is below replacement cost)		
				$36 (ceiling)	a $36
	$40	b	$34 (use replacement cost as "market" price because it is between ceiling and floor)		b $34
				$30 (floor)	c $30
	$40	c	$28 (use floor as "market" price, because it is above replacement cost)		

[8] Ibid., chap. 4, p. 31.

When the ceiling, replacement cost, and floor amounts are ranked from highest to lowest, the amount in the middle is used as the "market" price. Once the adjusted amount for market price is determined, *the final step is to compare the actual cost of the inventory item with the adjusted market price* to arrive at an LCM valuation. In each of the three assumptions in the diagram, the adjusted market price is less than actual cost, and is the value assigned to inventory under the LCM rule. This adjusted market price is used as the "cost" for future comparisons with market prices.

Although replacement cost is the basic concept of market, it should not be used blindly. Conservatism is the basis for the LCM rule. When the replacement cost of an item is higher than its net realizable value, conservatism requires that the item be written down to its net realizable value. Otherwise, a loss which is already apparent would be deferred. For this reason, net realizable value must be the ceiling. On the other hand, if a business enterprise is required to write down its inventories, it might be tempted to "take a big bath" and write off as much as it can. In the following year, the gross profit on sales would be overstated; thus, investors would have an impression of a strong "turnaround." To prevent this type of manipulation, accountants state that the write-down of inventories cannot be below the floor valuation.

Federal income tax regulations state that "market" means the current bid price prevailing at the date of the inventories for the particular item in the volume in which it usually is purchased by the taxpayer. The "volume" restriction is relevant when prices vary depending on the quantity purchased. As stated earlier, current income tax rules do not permit the use of the LCM rule in the computation of taxable income when cost is determined by the last-in, first-out method. However, write-down of lifo inventories to market is allowed in the financial statements.

Taxpayers using the LCM rule cannot write down excessive inventories below replacement costs, unless such inventories actually have been scrapped, sold, or offered for sale at prices lower than replacement costs. The Internal Revenue Service has defined "excessive inventories" as goods which are (1) held for sale, (2) in excess of any reasonably foreseeable future demand, and (3) not scrapped or sold at reduced prices.

Illustrations of Selection of "Market" and "Lower of Cost or Market" The following additional examples illustrate the application of the LCM rule. The inventory value for each item is in bold face type. Completion and selling costs are $6 for each item, and the normal gross profit margin is 25% of the selling price.

**Application of LCM rule
to five examples**

	Inventory items				
	A	B	C	D	E
Selling price	$20	$20	$28	$36	$36
Cost (determined by specific identification, fifo, average, etc.).	16	15	20	25	20
Selling price less $6 completion and selling costs **(ceiling)**	14	14	22	30	30
Selling price less completion and selling costs and normal gross profit margin of 25% of selling price **(floor)**	9	9	15	21	21
Replacement cost on inventory date	15	16	17	20	19

Explanations

Item A Replacement cost of $15 exceeds the ceiling of $14; ceiling of $14 is the adjusted market price; because cost is $16, the inventory value is $14, the lower of cost or adjusted market price.

Item B Replacement cost of $16 exceeds the ceiling of $14; ceiling of $14 is the adjusted market price; inventory value is $14, although replacement cost of $16 exceeds the cost of $15.

Item C Replacement cost of $17 is between the ceiling-floor limit ($22 to $15); replacement cost is the adjusted market price; inventory value is $17, because it is less than the cost of $20.

Item D Replacement cost of $20 is below the floor of $21; floor is the adjusted market price; the inventory value is $21, because it is less than the cost of $25.

Item E Replacement cost of $19 is below the floor of $21; floor is the adjusted market price; the inventory value is $20, or cost, because cost is lower than adjusted market price. In this case, the normal gross profit margin will be earned when the unit is sold; therefore, no loss in value is recognized.

Application of LCM The LCM rule can be applied to (1) each individual item in inventories, (2) major categories of inventories, or (3) inventories as a whole. Regardless of which of the three methods is adopted, each inventory item should be priced at cost and at market as a first step in the valuation process. The item-by-item method produces the lowest inventory value, and the application of the LCM rule to inventories as a whole produces the highest valuation. For income tax purposes, the item-by-item method must be used. For financial accounting purposes, the authors favor the application of the LCM rule to inventories as a whole. This approach is consistent with the rule established for marketable equity securities in **FASB Statement No. 12.** The illustration on page 334 demonstrates the variation in LCM amounts that result from the application of these three methods.

Applying
LCM to
each item
results in
lowest
inventory
value

Determination of Value of Inventories by Use of the LCM Rule–End of Year 1

Inventory categories	Cost	Market	(1) Item by item	(2) Category of inventories	(3) Inventories as a whole
No. 1: Item A	$ 6,000	$ 9,000	$ 6,000		
Item B	10,000	9,500	9,500		
Subtotals	$16,000	$18,500		$16,000	
No. 2: Item C	$15,000	$17,000	15,000		
Item D	20,000	14,000	14,000		
Subtotals	$35,000	$31,000		31,000	
Totals	$51,000	$49,500			$49,500
Valuation of inventories. . . .			$44,500	$47,000	$49,500

In the valuation of inventories for a manufacturing enterprise, goods in process and finished goods inventories must be adjusted for any decline in the price of direct materials as well as direct labor and factory overhead costs.

Subsequent Valuation Problems Suppose that at the end of Year 2, item D in the illustration above is still on hand and that the market value has risen from $14,000 to $19,000. What valuation should be assigned to item D at the end of Year 2? Generally, accountants have held that, once an inventory item has been written down, this lower value *is considered cost* for future comparisons with "market." Therefore, in the application of the item-by-item method, the value of item D is $14,000 at the end of Year 2 because the item was written down to this amount at the end of Year 1.

For *interim reporting purposes,* this rule was modified by the Accounting Principles Board as follows:[9]

> Inventory losses from market declines should not be deferred beyond the interim period in which the decline occurs. Recoveries of such losses on the same inventory in later interim periods of the same fiscal year through market price recoveries should be recognized as gains in the later interim period. Such gains should not exceed previously recognized losses. Some market declines at interim dates, however, can reasonably be expected to be restored in the fiscal year. Such *temporary* market declines need not be recognized at the interim date since no loss is expected to be incurred in the fiscal year.

Valuation allowance for write-down of inventories

When inventories are written down below cost, the reduction may be credited to an inventory valuation account. This procedure accomplishes the objective of a write-down, and at the same time permits the

[9] *APB Opinion No. 28,* "Interim Financial Reporting," AICPA (New York: 1973), pp. 524–525.

original cost of the inventory to be reported in the balance sheet. Use of the valuation account is especially appropriate with a perpetual inventory system, because it eliminates the necessity of adjusting the detailed inventory records (maintained at actual costs) to lower market prices.

The journal entry to record the reduction of inventories at the end of Year 1 from a cost of $100,000 to a market valuation of $92,000 is illustrated below for Karen Company:

Recording inventory valuation account

Cost of Goods Sold	8,000	
Allowance for Price Decline in Inventories		8,000
To record the reduction in value of inventories caused by declining prices.		

In the balance sheet at the end of Year 1, inventories are listed at cost and are reduced to a lower market by deduction of the allowance for price decline from cost. This procedure is illustrated for Karen Company below:

Balance sheet presentation

Current assets:		
Inventories (at fifo cost)	$100,000	
Less: Allowance for price decline in inventories	8,000	$92,000

If the write-down of inventories is material, it may be shown separately from cost of goods sold in the income statement.

The inventory valuation allowance is not needed after the goods in question are sold. Therefore, at the time the cost of beginning inventories is transferred to Income Summary (or to the Cost of Goods Sold account), the allowance account also should be closed, to reduce the cost of beginning inventories to market value. For example, the following journal entry would be made at the end of Year 2 by Karen Company to close beginning inventories, assuming that the periodic inventory system is used:

Closing journal entry when inventory valuation account is used

Income Summary	92,000	
Allowance for Price Decline in Inventories	8,000	
Inventories (beginning).		100,000
To close beginning inventories to Income Summary.		

If the market value of inventories at the end of Year 2 is below cost, an allowance for inventory price decline again should be established.

An inventory allowance account similar to the one illustrated on page 335 is used by some enterprises to reduce inventory costs to a lifo basis. Such an account is established by a debit to Cost of Goods Sold or Income Summary and a credit to Allowance to Reduce Inventory to Lifo Basis. The valuation allowance, sometimes improperly referred to as a **lifo reserve account,** is used to preserve inventory cost on the fifo or average cost basis for internal purposes while obtaining the advantages of using lifo for income tax purposes.

Valuation of purchase commitments at lower of cost or market

If at the end of an accounting period a business enterprise has a contract to purchase goods at a fixed price that is higher than the current price of the goods, a loss should be recognized. In other words, the outstanding purchase commitment should be valued on a lower-of-cost-or-market basis by recognition of a current loss and the accrual of a current liability. These accounting procedures are described in Chapter 10.

Appraisal of the lower-of-cost-or-market rule

The lower-of-cost-or-market rule originated in an era of emphasis on balance sheet conservatism. It exemplifies an old accounting axiom: "Anticipate no profit and provide for all possible losses." In following this axiom accountants assume that purchase prices and selling prices move in the same direction. Therefore, if prices of inventory items decline, selling prices also will decline. By reducing inventories to market, accountants also reduce net income for the current accounting period; however, presumably the business enterprise is enabled to earn a normal profit in the next period. On the other hand, if the price of the goods rises, generally accepted accounting principles do not permit the value of inventories to be increased. Such action would result in the recognition of income before revenue is realized.

The treatment of damaged and obsolete goods was discussed earlier, in accordance with the principle of valuing inventory at cost less an amount which measures any deterioration in usefulness. Also, the argument has been presented that a decline in prices casts a shadow over a part of the inventory cost because the revenue in future accounting periods may not be adequate to provide a normal margin of profit. Thus, accountants have been led to the conclusion that the goods have lost a part of their economic utility, and that the unrecoverable portion of cost should be deducted from current revenue.

One should not dismiss such an argument lightly; unrecoverable costs are not assets. On the other hand, every price decline does not necessarily mean that the cost of goods on hand will not be recovered. The price system is not so sensitive that it transmits related price movements quickly and uniformly throughout the economy.

The indiscriminate application of the lower-of-cost-or-market rule should never be allowed to replace sound professional judgment in the valuation of inventories. There are cases when recognition of losses prior to sale is justified. However, a careful evaluation of the particular circumstances is necessary before the amount of the loss can be determined. The ceiling and floor limits on "market" serve a useful function in making such an evaluation.

Anticipation of price declines

The lower-of-cost-or-market rule is applicable to price declines which actually have occurred, not to possible future price declines. The AICPA has made the following distinction between inventory losses which can be measured objectively and those which are conjectural in nature:[10]

> It has been argued with respect to inventories that losses which will have to be taken in periods of receding price levels have their origins in periods of rising prices, and that therefore reserves to provide for future price declines should be created in periods of rising prices by charges against the operations of those periods. Reserves of this kind involve assumptions as to what future price levels will be, what inventory quantities will be on hand if and when a major price decline takes place, and finally whether loss to the business will be measured by the amount of the decline in prices. The bases for such assumptions are so uncertain that any conclusions drawn from them would generally seem to be speculative guesses rather than informed judgments.

Only *actual* losses on goods included in inventories which arise from price declines should enter into the determination of net income; *possible* future losses should not be entered in the accounting records.

REVIEW QUESTIONS

1 What features distinguish inventory costs from other costs which are allocated between deferred and expired portions?

2 There are two systems of maintaining inventory records: (a) *periodic inventory system,* and (b) *perpetual inventory system.* What are the basic differences between the two systems, and under what circumstances should each be used?

3 Why is the valuation of inventories critical to financial reporting? What criteria should accountants use in deciding between alternative methods of valuation?

4 At the end of the accounting period, the following purchase invoices dated December 27 are on hand, but the goods have not been received. How would you treat each invoice in the determination of the ending inventories?
  a Invoice amount, $12,670; terms, 2/10, n/30; "FOB shipping point."
  b Invoice amount, $14,860; terms, 1/5, n/30; "FOB destination."

---

[10] *Accounting Research and Terminology Bulletins—Final Edition,* chap. 6, p. 42.

5 Indicate the effects on the financial statements for the current and succeeding years of each of the following types of errors in accounting for inventories. Simply indicate the direction of error—overstatement, understatement, or no effect.

    a An invoice for goods shipped "FOB shipping point" has been received, but no journal entry has been made to record the purchase. The goods have not been received and are not included in the ending inventories.

    b An invoice for goods shipped, but not received, has been recorded correctly to indicate that the goods belong to the purchaser, but the items have not been included in the ending inventories.

    c Goods which have been received, but the purchase of which has not been recorded in the accounting records, are included in the ending inventories.

    d The ending inventories do not include goods shipped on consignment. The transfer of these goods to the consignee has been recorded as a sale, even though they remain in the consignee's possession at the end of both the current year and the succeeding year.

6 What costs should be included in the cost of inventories? What objectives are considered in deciding what costs are to be included in inventories?

7 Midtown Faucet Company is licensed to manufacture and sell a certain product under a patent owned by Alan Bella. A royalty of 10 cents is payable to Bella for each unit sold. For accounting purposes, Midtown Faucet Company treats royalty payments as a selling expense and does not accrue a royalty liability on the unsold faucets in inventory. The property tax assessor claims that 10 cents should be treated as a production cost and included in the valuation of inventory of faucets. Do you agree with the tax assessor? Explain.

8 If two or more **joint products** are produced in a given department, how are the total production costs incurred in the department allocated to the joint products?

9 The **specific identification** method has been supported by some accountants as the ideal method of achieving a matching of costs and revenue. What objections may be raised to the use of this method for the valuation of inventories?

10 Differentiate between the **weighted-average method** and the **moving-weighted-average method** of determining cost of inventories.

11 Frank Caliri tells you that he is considering changing from the fifo to the lifo method of inventory valuation and that he would like your advice on the matter. He admits that his primary objective is to reduce his income tax liability, and his friends tell him this is a good way to do it. What factors would you consider in advising Caliri?

12 In the application of the **dollar-value lifo** method of valuing inventories, it is necessary to convert both the beginning and the ending inventory amounts to base-year prices. Why? Why would a conversion of end-of-year prices to beginning of-year prices not serve equally as well?

13 Under what conditions may a portion of the cost of inventories be written off prior to the actual disposal of the items comprising the inventories?

14 Define the term **market** as used in the inventory valuation procedure referred to as the lower-of-cost-or-market rule.

15 What are the arguments against the use of the lower-of-cost-or-market rule in the valuation of inventories?

16 Is there any difference, insofar as inventory valuation is concerned, between an item having a cost of $50 which regularly sells for $75 but which has been so physically damaged that it can be sold for no more than $55, and the same item which has no physical damage, but the cost of replacing the item has declined to $30?

17 Under what conditions, if any, is it appropriate to recognize anticipated inventory price declines in the accounting records?

18 Under what conditions, if any, should losses arising out of price declines involving future purchase commitments be recognized in the accounting records?

19 The balance sheet for Copek Corporation included the following:

Inventories	$62,062,774
Less: Allowance to reduce inventories to last-in, first out basis.	12,398,448
Net inventories	$49,664,326

Give the probable reason for the use of the inventories valuation account by Copek Corporation.

EXERCISES

Ex. 8-1   The following information relates to commodity M for the month of January:

Inventory, Jan. 1	100 units @ $5
Purchases	500 units @ $6
Inventory, Jan. 31	200 units

a What cost should be assigned to the ending inventory under the first-in, first-out cost flow assumption?
b What is the cost of goods sold for January under the last-in, first-out cost flow assumption?

Ex. 8-2   The following information was available from the inventory records of Gee Company for January:

	Units	Unit cost	Total cost
Balance, Jan. 1	2,000	$ 9.775	$19,550
Purchases:			
Jan. 6	1,500	10.300	15,450
Jan. 26	3,400	10.750	36,550
Sales:			
Jan. 7	(1,800)		
Jan. 31	(3,200)		
Balance, Jan. 31	1,900		

a Assuming that Gee Company maintains perpetual inventory records, compute the inventory on January 31 under the moving-weighted-average method, rounded to the nearest dollar.
b Assuming that Gee Company maintains periodic inventory records, compute the inventory on January 31 under the weighted-average method, rounded to the nearest dollar.

Ex. 8-3 Presented below is the inventory activity for product Z for the month of April:

Date	Transaction	Units	Cost	Total	Units sold
Apr. 1	Inventory	1,200	$8.00	$ 9,600	
4	Purchase	800	8.25	6,600	
7	Sale				600
10	Purchase	400	8.10	3,240	
13	Sale				1,000
16	Purchase	700	7.90	5,530	
19	Sale				900
22	Purchase	300	7.90	2,370	
25	Purchase	600	7.80	4,680	
28	Sale				500
	Totals	4,000		$32,020	3,000

Assuming that a periodic inventory system is used, compute the inventory cost under each of the following cost flow assumptions:

a First-in, first-out
b Last-in, first-out
c Weighted-average

Ex. 8-4 The following information was taken from the financial statements of Nati Company for the year ended April 30, Year 3:

Sales	$600,000
Beginning inventories (lifo basis)	50,000
Net purchases	340,000
Ending inventories (lifo basis)	60,000
Cash	45,000
Accounts receivable (net)	75,000
Short-term investments (at cost, which approximates market value) . .	8,000
Short-term prepayments	2,000
Current liabilities	100,000

The inventories on the first-in, first-out basis were $120,000 on April 30, Year 2, and $132,000 on April 30, Year 3.

a Compute the following amounts or ratios, assuming that inventories are valued on the (1) last-in, first-out basis, and on the (2) first-in, first-out basis:
Current assets
Working capital
Current ratio
Cost of goods sold
Inventories turnover

b Does the use of the first-in, first-out method of inventory valuation give a more meaningful measure of the company's working capital, current ratio, and inventories turnover than the last-in, first-out method? Explain.

Ex. 8-5 The controller of Fleetwood Corporation, a retail enterprise, made three different schedules of gross profit for the first quarter ended March 31, Year 10. These schedules appear below:

	Sales ($10 per unit)	Cost of goods sold	Gross profit
Schedule 1	$280,000	$118,550	$161,450
Schedule 2	280,000	116,900	163,100
Schedule 3	280,000	115,750	164,250

The computation of cost of goods sold in each schedule is based on the following data:

	Units	Cost per unit	Total cost
Beginning inventory, Jan. 1.	10,000	$4.00	$ 40,000
Purchase, Jan. 20.	8,000	4.20	33,600
Purchase, Feb. 12	5,000	4.13	20,650
Purchase, Mar. 14	7,000	4.30	30,100
Purchase, Mar. 27	12,000	4.25	51,000
Totals.	42,000		$175,350

Nancy Rogers, president of the corporation, cannot understand how three different gross profit amounts can be computed from the same data. As controller, you have explained to her that the three schedules are based on three different assumptions concerning the flow of inventory costs; that is, first-in, first-out; last-in, first-out; and weighted average. Schedules 1, 2, and 3 were not necessarily prepared in this sequence of cost flow assumptions.

Prepare a schedule to compute the cost of goods sold and the composition of the ending inventory under each of the three cost flow assumptions.

Ex. 8-6 Dreem Company sells water beds. The perpetual inventory was stated as $19,600 in the accounting records on December 31, Year 4. At the close of the year, a new approach for compiling inventory was used, but apparently a satisfactory cutoff for preparation of financial statements was not made. Some events that occurred near the end of Year 4 are listed below:

(1) Beds shipped to a customer on January 2, Year 5, costing $2,000, were included in inventory on December 31, Year 4. The sale was recorded in Year 5.
(2) Beds costing $9,000 received on December 30, Year 4, were recorded as received on January 2, Year 5.
(3) Beds received costing $1,900 were recorded twice in the perpetual inventory records.
(4) Beds shipped FOB shipping point on December 28, Year 4, which cost $7,000, were not recorded as a sale by Dreem until January 3, Year 5. The beds were included in the ending inventory.
(5) Beds on hand which cost $2,300 were not recorded in the accounting records in Year 4.

Prepare a working paper showing the correct amount of inventory on December 31, Year 4.

Ex. 8-7 Algiers Company manufactures a single product. On December 31, Year 1, Algiers adopted the dollar-value lifo method. The inventory on that date under the dollar-value lifo method was $300,000. Inventory data for succeeding years are as follows:

Year ended Dec. 31,	Inventories at year-end costs	Cost indexes (base = Year 1)
Year 2	$363,000	1.10
Year 3	420,000	1.20
Year 4	430,000	1.25

Compute the inventory amounts on December 31, Year 2, Year 3, and Year 4, under the dollar-value lifo method.

Ex. 8-8 Jensen Corporation uses the dollar-value lifo method of pricing inventories. The inventories valued at end-of-year prices and the cost indexes are given below:

Year	Inventories at year-end costs	Cost indexes at end of year
1	$ 80,000	100
2	90,000	125
3	127,400	130
4	140,000	140
5	101,250	135

Prepare a working paper to show the calculation of the ending inventories under the dollar-value lifo method for Years 1 through 5.

Ex. 8-9 A company acquired goods for $4,000 when the general price-level index was 110. These goods were sold for $7,500 when the current cost of the goods was $5,400 and the general price-level index stood at 121. The gain of $3,500 on the sale of the goods may be attributed to three factors: change in the general price level, holding gain, and operating profit (margin to seller for distributing the goods to customers).
Compute the portion of the total gain caused by each of the three factors.

Ex. 8-10 Given below are three different sets of assumptions (cases) relating to an item in inventory:

	Case 1	Case 2	Case 3
Cost	$12,400	$20,000	$28,000
Selling price	$30,000	$30,000	$30,000
Cost to complete and ship to customers	$ 4,000	$ 4,000	$ 4,000
Normal gross profit on selling price	25%	25%	10%
Replacement cost	$14,000	$18,000	$26,500

Compute the inventory at lower of cost or market for each case.

Ex. 8-11 You are given the following facts about four items included in the inventory of Toro Specialty Shop:

	Item			
	W	**X**	**Y**	**Z**
Cost.	$50	$62	$29	$46
Replacement cost	52	48	25	40
Sales price less selling and completion costs.	53	59	23	42
Sales price less selling and completion costs and less normal profit	47	51	20	38

Indicate which amount would be used in pricing the ending inventory in accordance with the lower-of-cost-or-market rule.

Ex. 8-12 The inventories for Southern Supply Company consist of two major categories listed below:

	Quantities	**Unit cost**	**Market**
Category A:			
Item XP	80	$ 6	$ 5
Item XQ	40	8	9
Item XR	30	10	8
Category B:			
Item YS	100	$ 4	$ 3
Item YT	150	9	8
Item YU	300	12	14

Prepare a summary similar to the one illustrated on page 334 to compute inventory values under the lower-of-cost-or-market rule applied on (1) each item, (2) separate categories, and (3) inventories as a whole.

Ex. 8-13 Valley Development Company buys and sells land. On January 18, Year 1, a tract of land was bought for $500,000. Costs of leveling the land were $125,000. The land was subdivided as follows:

25 Class A lots to sell for $20,000 each

30 Class B lots to sell for $15,000 each

10 Class C lots to sell for $5,000 each

On December 31, Year 1, the unsold lots consisted of 15 Class A lots, 6 Class B lots, and 3 Class C lots.

Compute the cost of unsold lots on December 31, Year 1. Total cost is allocated to the lots on the basis of relative sales value.

Ex. 8-14 Salamanca Corporation uses the first-in, first-out method to determine the cost of its inventory. The physical inventory at the end of the current year is summarized at the top of page 344.

Item number	Unit cost*	Inventory (units)	Freight applicable to inventory
101	$ 2	6,000	$ 915
102	5	9,000	675
103	6	4,500	1,110
104	10	2,400	960

* Before purchases discounts

The company regularly takes a 2% discount on all purchases (excluding freight) and allocates an appropriate portion of freight-in to the ending inventory. Additional information available at the end of the current year is presented below:

Beginning inventory $100,500
Purchases (net of returns and discounts) 535,500
Freight-in 19,500
Sales (net of returns) 721,500
Sales discounts 9,300

a Determine the cost of the inventory at the end of the current year.
b Compute the amount of gross profit on sales for the current year.

SHORT CASES FOR ANALYSIS AND DECISION

Case 8-1 Ota Manufacturing Company purchased 10,000 pounds of material at an invoice cost of $50,000 with terms 3/5, 2/10, n/30. The freight cost applicable to this purchase was $4,500. The total cost of handling and storing the material was $50,000 a year, and the quantity handled each year was about 500,000 pounds. This $50,000 handling and storage cost was not controllable; that is, it was fixed in amount and did not vary in relation to variations in the quantity of material in storage. The quantity of material on hand fluctuated widely during the year. The accountant for Ota is uncertain whether this $50,000 should be treated as an expense or included in the cost of inventory.

Instructions
a Under what circumstances should handling and storage costs be included in inventory? Do these circumstances prevail in Ota Manufacturing Company's case?
b Determine the cost per pound of this purchase of material.
c Would the cost per pound be different if the company did not pay the invoice within the first 15 days? What would the cost per pound be if the invoice were paid between the fifth and tenth day? State the accounting principle underlying your answers.

Case 8-2 In order to effect an approximate matching of current costs with related sales revenue, the last-in, first-out (lifo) method of pricing inventories may be used.

Instructions
a Describe the establishment of and subsequent pricing procedures for each of the following lifo inventory methods:
(1) Lifo applied to units of product when the periodic inventory system is used.
(2) Application of the dollar-value method to a retail lifo inventory or to lifo units of product. (These applications are similar.)

> **b** Discuss the specific advantages and disadvantages of the dollar-value lifo method. Ignore income tax considerations.
>
> **c** Discuss the general advantages and disadvantages claimed for lifo methods. Ignore income tax considerations.

Case 8-3 Paul Dunn, a partner in the law firm of Dunn, Ekker, and Finley, wants to withdraw from the partnership effective April 1, Year 1. Because the partnership maintains its accounting records on the cash basis of accounting, no recognition is given to accounts receivable and work (legal action suits) in process in the preparation of financial statements for the partnership. The partnership contract includes the following provision relative to the withdrawal of a partner:

"A partner who withdraws from the firm shall be entitled to an immediate cash payment equal to that partner's capital account balance, increased by (1) a share of uncollected accounts receivable, and (2) a share of work in process. No diminution in the withdrawing partner's capital will be made for outstanding liabilities."

The senior partner computed the carrying amount of work in process at March 31, Year 1, as follows:

Direct reimbursable costs (travel, outside experts, etc.) chargeable to clients	*$ 4,000*
Salaries paid to staff attorneys working on cases (excluding time of any of the partners).	*29,500*
Total carrying amount of work in process.	*$33,500*

Dunn objected to this procedure on grounds that it does not include the value of partners' time spent on work in process, and the amount "represents a bare minimum value" of the work in process. He feels that the billable value of the work performed for clients to date amounts to at least $100,000, and that this amount represents the current fair value of the work in process.

An accountant who was asked to arbitrate the dispute suggested that the senior partner's amount of $33,500 should be increased by $10,000, representing "general office overhead" applicable to the work in process. The accountant feels that partners' time should not be treated as an inventoriable cost because partners' salaries are not expenses for the partnership.

Instructions Briefly evaluate each of the three approaches to the valuation of work in process and recommend the procedure you consider equitable in this circumstance.

Case 8-4 City Corporation had followed the practice of pricing its year-end inventories at the lower of fifo cost or market for many years. During this period prices had tended to move in a rather general upward trend. For the past three years the general trend of price movement has been very erratic, and management has become concerned with the effect on net income of the lower-of-cost-or-market rule for inventory valuation. You have been requested to analyze the situation and make a recommendation to management supported by computations and accounting logic. The beginning inventories on January 1, Year 1, were valued (both cost and market) at $60,000; additional data are given below:

	Year 3	Year 2	Year 1
Sales	*$425,000*	*$325,000*	*$375,000*
Net purchases.	*300,000*	*225,000*	*260,000*
Year-end inventories:			
At cost	*75,000*	*70,000*	*60,000*
At market	*55,000*	*82,000*	*45,000*

Instructions
a Prepare partial income statements for each of the three years using (1) cost and (2) lower of cost or market to determine cost of goods sold.
b Draft a report to management explaining the effect of their present procedure on net income. Assuming that this pattern of fluctuating net income is expected to continue, which method would you recommend? Why?

Case 8-5 On October 1, Year 10, Basin Oil Company, a wholesale dealer, had an inventory of 100,000 barrels of heating oil valued at $600,000 on a lifo basis. During the remainder of Year 10 the company completed the following transactions:

Date	Purchase for cash	Replacement cost of crude oil	Sales for cash
Oct. 10		$25	80,000 @ $30
Oct. 20	100,000 @ $26	26	
Dec. 5		28	90,000 @ $35

The company sells numerous other products, in addition to heating oil. On December 31, Year 10, the replacement cost of the heating oil is $35 a barrel, and the president of the company is concerned about financing the purchase of approximately 100,000 barrels of heating oil which is needed to meet customer needs during the early months of Year 11. The president knows that the large profit from the liquidation of the inventory valued at lifo will be taxed at a rate of approximately 40%. Furthermore, heating oil is in short supply, and the company is unable to find a supplier who has oil for sale.

Instructions
a Compute the gross profit Basin Oil Company realized on the sale of heating oil in the last quarter of Year 10 on a lifo basis.
b How much of the gross profit computed in a was attributed to "inventory profits?" Show computations.
c Assuming that the general price level throughout the economy had not changed materially since Basin Oil Company started dealing in heating oil, is the gross profit you computed in a fictitious and illusory?
d Assuming that the operating expenses allocated to the sales of heating oil are negligible, and that Basin Oil Company wishes to set aside cash to pay income taxes at the rate of 40% of the profits earned on the sale of heating oil in the last quarter of Year 10, prepare a summary of cash needed and the cash available to purchase the 100,000 barrels of heating oil on December 31, Year 10. Comment on the results.

PROBLEMS

8-1 The following information relating to product Q was taken from the inventory records of Somerset Corporation for the three-month period ending March 31, Year 2:

	Units	Unit cost
Jan. 1, Year 2 (beginning inventory)	800	$ 9.00
Purchases:		
Jan. 5	1,500	10.00
Jan. 25	1,200	10.50
Feb. 16	600	11.00
Mar. 26	900	11.50

The inventory on March 31, Year 2, consists of 1,600 units.

Instructions Compute the cost of the inventory on March 31, Year 2, under each of the following inventory methods (show supporting computations):
a First-in, first-out
b Last-in, first-out
c Weighted average

8-2 Arroyo Company is a wholesale distributor of automotive replacement parts. Initial amounts taken from Arroyo's accounting records are as follows:

Inventory, Dec. 31, Year 2 (based on physical count in Arroyo's warehouse on Dec. 31, Year 2) .... $ 920,000

Accounts payable, December 31, Year 2:

Supplier	Terms	Amount
B Company	2/10, n/30	$ 265,000
C Company	n/30	210,000
D Company	n/30	50,000
E Company	n/30	225,000
F Company	n/30	–0–
G Company	n/30	–0–
Total		$ 750,000

Sales in Year 2 .... $8,200,000

Additional information:

(1) Parts held on consignment from C Company, amounting to $155,000, were included in the physical count in Arroyo's warehouse on December 31, Year 2, and in accounts payable on December 31, Year 2.

(2) $22,000 of parts which were purchased from F Company and paid for in December, Year 2, were sold in the last week of Year 2, and appropriately recorded as sales of $28,000. The parts were included in the physical count in Arroyo's warehouse on December 31, Year 2, because the parts were on the loading dock waiting to be picked up by Arroyo's customers.

(3) Parts in transit on December 31, Year 2, to customers, shipped FOB shipping point on December 28, Year 2, amounted to $34,000. The customers received the parts on January 6, Year 3. Sales of $40,000 to the customers for the parts were recorded by Arroyo on January 2, Year 3.

(4) Retailers were holding $210,000 at cost ($250,000 at retail), of goods on consignment from Arroyo, the consignor, at their stores on December 31, Year 2.

(5) Goods were in transit from G Company to Arroyo on December 31, Year 2. The cost of the goods was $25,000, and the goods were shipped FOB shipping point on December 29, Year 2. The purchase was recorded on January 5, Year 3, when the goods were received.

(6) A quarterly freight bill of $2,000 relating to merchandise purchased in December, Year 2, all of which was still in the inventory on December 31, Year 2, was received on January 3, Year 3. The freight bill was not included either in the inventory or in accounts payable on December 31, Year 2.

(7) All purchases from B Company occurred during the last seven days of the year. These items have been recorded in accounts payable and were included in the physical inventory at cost before cash discounts. Arroyo's policy is to pay invoices in time to take advantage of all cash discounts, to adjust inventory accordingly, and to record accounts payable net of cash discounts.

Instructions Prepare a working paper for adjustments to the initial amounts on December 31, Year 2, using the format shown at the top of page 348. Show the effect, if any, of each of the transactions separately. Identify each adjustment with the number of the related paragraph above.

	Inventory	Accounts payable (net)	Sales
Initial amounts, Dec. 31, Year 2	$920,000	$750,000	$8,200,000
Adjustments—increase (decrease):			
(1)			
(2) etc.			
Adjusted amounts, Dec. 31, Year 2	$_____	$_____	$_____

8-3 Fallbrook Bargain Counter began operations on January 2 with 200 units of item X at a cost of $1,800. The following data pertaining to purchases of item X were taken from the accounting records at the end of the first year's operations:

Lot. no.	Number of units	Total cost
1	24	$ 240
2	84	924
3	126	1,244
4	96	864
5	170	2,040
Totals	500	$5,312

A physical inventory on December 31 revealed that 220 units of item X remained in stock.

Instructions Based on the data provided, compute **(a)** the cost of inventory on December 31, and **(b)** the cost of goods sold during the year, under each of the following cost flow assumptions:
(1) Lifo
(2) Fifo
(3) Weighted average

8-4 In the process of determining the inventory on June 30, Year 5, for Essick Corporation, you are presented with the following summary relating to material J and finished part K.

	Material J (units)	Finished part K (units)
(1) Units on hand in warehouse per physical count. Cost is $4 a unit for material J and $20 a unit for finished part K	6,200	4,600
(2) Units in receiving department, to be refused because of poor quality. Invoice cost is $4.20 a unit	1,000	
(3) Units stored in parking lot considered worthless. Cost is $21 a unit		100
(4) Units in receiving department; no invoice has been received. Price on purchase order is $4.10 a unit .	500	
(5) Units not received, for which invoice marked "FOB shipping point" has been received. Total cost of invoice, including freight, is $855	200	

	Material J (units)	Finished part K (units)
(6) Units shipped on June 30, Year 5; invoice marked "FOB shipping point" has been mailed to customer. Total cost is $6,330		300
(7) Units completed in factory not transferred to warehouse. Cost is $21.50 a unit		150
(8) Units in shipping department; invoice marked "FOB shipping point" has been mailed to customer. Cost is $20 a unit		50
(9) Units in shipping department; invoice has not been mailed to customer. Cost is $20.30 a unit		80
(10) Units in possession of consignees with a total cost of $2,400		120

Instructions Prepare a summary similar to the one above, showing the cost of the various items comprising the inventory of material J and finished part K on June 30, Year 5. Place amounts (in dollars) in the two columns at the right. Give a brief reason for including or excluding each item.

8-5 Blasier Company sells a single product which has been steadily increasing in selling price in recent months. The inventory at January 1, and the purchases and sales for the current year, are presented below:

	Number of units	Unit cost	Average selling price
Jan. 1, Inventory	8,000	$3.50	
Jan. 10, Purchase	3,000	4.50	
Jan. 21, Purchase	5,000	5.00	
Jan. 1–31, Sales for month	10,000		$ 9.00
Feb. 5, Purchase	4,000	6.00	
Feb. 18, Purchase	6,000	7.00	
Feb. 1–28, Sales for month	9,000		11.00
Mar. 5, Purchase	5,000	7.50	
Mar. 22, Purchase	10,000	8.00	
Mar. 1–31, Sales for month	13,000		13.00

The company uses the periodic inventory system. Inventories are valued at the end of each month.

Instructions
a Compute the cost of inventories on hand at the end of each of the first three months of the current year under (1) the first-in, first-out cost flow assumption, and (2) the last-in, first-out cost flow assumption.
b Prepare a comparative statement summarizing the gross profit on sales for each month, assuming that inventories are valued under (1) the first-in, first-out cost flow assumption, and (2) the last-in, first-out cost flow assumption. Use the following form:

	(1) First-in, first-out			(2) Last-in, first out		
	January	February	March	January	February	March
Sales. . . .						

8-6 Salinas Company manufactures and sells four products, the inventories of which are priced at the lower of cost or market. The company considers a gross profit margin of 30% of selling price to be normal for all four products.

The following information was compiled as of December 31:

Product	Units	Original unit cost	Cost to replace	Estimated cost to dispose	Expected selling price
W	500	$35.00	$42.00	$15.00	$ 80.00
X	200	47.50	45.00	20.50	95.00
Y	480	17.50	18.00	4.00	21.00
Z	240	45.00	46.00	26.00	100.00

Instructions

a Why are expected selling prices important in the application of the lower-of-cost-or-market rule?

b Prepare a working paper containing unit values (including "floor" and "ceiling") for determining the lower of cost or market on an individual product basis. Underscore for each product the unit value for the purpose of inventory valuation resulting from the application of the lower-of-cost-or-market rule. The last column of the working paper should contain the value assigned to each product and the total valuation of inventories.

c What effects, if any, do the expected selling prices have on the valuation of the four products under the lower-of-cost-or-market rule?

8-7 On December 31, Year 1, Fairbanks Novelty Store adopted the dollar-value lifo inventory method. The inventory on that date under the dollar-value lifo inventory method was $200,000. Inventory data for the following five years are as follows:

Year	Inventories at respective year-end prices	Price indexes (base = Year 1)
2	$231,000	1.05
3	299,000	1.15
4	300,000	1.20
5	273,000	1.30
6	420,000	1.50

Instructions Compute the inventories on December 31, Years 2 through 6, under the dollar-value lifo method.

8-8 The following data were taken from the inventory records of Handy Tool Company on December 31 of the current year:

Department	Item number	Quantity (units)	Unit cost	Market (per unit)
Garden tools	10	140	$24.00	$25.00
	11	350	12.10	11.70
	12	10	8.00	9.60
Electric tools	20	60	4.00	3.00
	21	14	14.00	13.00
	22	8	36.00	37.00
Miscellaneous.	30	70	2.40	2.00
	31	80	4.90	4.50
	32	110	1.20	1.30

Instructions

a Price the inventories under the lower-of-cost-or-market rule applied to: (1) each individual item, (2) major categories, and (3) inventories as a whole.

b Which value would you recommend for inclusion in the financial statements? Why is the value you recommended preferable to the other two?

8-9 On June 30, Year 1, the end of the fiscal year, Robert Thorell & Co. decided to adopt the dollar-value lifo method of pricing the ending inventories. The data on inventories valued at end-of-year prices and a cost index for the succeeding four years are as follows:

Date June 30,	Inventories at end-of-year costs	Cost indexes at end of year
Year 1 (base year)	$105,000	100
Year 2	140,000	125
Year 3	196,000	140
Year 4	154,560	115
Year 5	129,000	120

Instructions

a Prepare a working paper to present the calculation of the ending inventories at lifo cost for the four years, Year 2 through 5.

b Explain how the dollar-value method facilitates the valuation of inventories at lifo cost.

8-10 Provencial Furniture Company reported income before income taxes as follows:

Year 2	$132,600
Year 3	115,000
Year 4	125,000
Total	$372,600

The company uses the periodic inventory system. An analysis of inventory on December 31, Year 4, indicates the following:

(1) The inventory on December 31, Year 1, was correct.

(2) Furniture costing $340 was received in Year 2 and included in the inventory at the end of Year 2; however, the journal entry to record the purchase was made in January, Year 3, when the invoice was received.

(3) The Year 2 ending inventory includes 1,000 units of item Z, which cost $7.30 a unit, erroneously priced at $3.70 a unit.

(4) Furniture that cost $500 and sold at $700 was shipped to a customer "FOB shipping point" on December 31, Year 3, and was not included in the Year 3 ending inventory; however, the sale was not recorded until January 5, Year 4.

(5) Furniture costing $6,000 shipped "FOB shipping point," was recorded as a purchase in Year 3 when the invoice was received; however, it was not included in the ending inventory because it was not received until January 6, Year 4.

(6) Furniture costing $5,750 was sold in Year 3 for $8,000 and billed on December 31, Year 3. This sale was recorded on December 31, Year 3, but the furniture was included in the ending inventory because it had not been separated from regular stock and was not shipped until January 3, Year 4. (Assume that the sale should have been recorded in Year 4.)

(7) The inventory on December 31, Year 4, is correct.

Instructions

a Calculate the corrected income before income taxes for each of the three years and the total for the three years (Years 2 through 4).

b Prepare a journal entry to correct the accounting records on December 31, Year 4, assuming that the accounting records have not been closed. Any corrections to income of Year 3 (or earlier) should be made to "Correction of Income for Prior Years." Ignore income taxes.

8-11 During the first two years of operations, Matsui Corporation acquired units of a product as follows:

	First year				Second year		
Lot no.	Number of units	Unit price	Total cost	Lot no.	Number of units	Unit price	Total cost
1	13,000	$4.00	$ 52,000	6	12,000	$3.25	$ 39,000
2	4,000	3.75	15,000	7	6,000	3.50	21,000
3	12,000	3.50	42,000	8	4,000	3.50	14,000
4	5,000	3.50	17,500	9	5,000	3.75	18,750
5	8,000	3.00	24,000	10	16,000	4.00	64,000
	42,000		$150,500		43,000		$156,750

The replacement cost of these units at the end of the first year is $4.00 and at the end of the second year is $4.20. There are 16,000 units on hand at the end of the first year and 20,000 on hand at the end of the second year.

Instructions

a Compute the inventory and the cost of goods sold for each year under (1) the fifo method, and (2) the lifo method.

b If 800 units had been stolen during the second year and you wanted to separate the theft loss from the cost of goods sold, how would you determine the amount of the loss?

8-12 The perpetual inventory records of Home Emporium, Inc., indicate that the purchases, sales, and inventory quantities for product KB-80 for the month of March are as follows:

	Purchases		
Date	Units	Unit cost	Sales (units)
Mar. 1 Inventory	800	$ 8	
6			500
10	700	9	
18			800
22	1,000	10	
30			600

Instructions

a Compute the cost of the ending inventory and the cost of goods sold for March, assuming that a perpetual inventory system is used, under each of the following methods for inventory valuation. The following columnar headings are suggested: Date, Transaction, Units, Unit Cost, Inventory Balance.
(1) First-in, first-out
(2) Last-in, first-out
(3) Moving average

    b Assuming that a periodic inventory system is used, compute the inventory cost and cost of goods sold, under each of the following methods:
    (1) First-in, first-out
    (2) Last-in, first-out
    (3) Weighted average

    c Where differences occur between the results in *a* and *b*, explain why they exist. Under what conditions would you recommend use of the perpetual inventory system? The periodic inventory system?

8-13 The trial balance for Eugene Cement Company shown below has been adjusted for all items except ending inventory and income taxes:

EUGENE CEMENT COMPANY

Trial Balance

December 31, Year 2

Cash	$ 21,000	
Accounts receivable (net)	40,000	
Inventory, Dec. 31, Year 1 (at cost)	52,000	
Short-term prepayments	4,000	
Land	125,000	
Buildings	200,000	
Accumulated depreciation of buildings		$ 60,500
Equipment	225,000	
Accumulated depreciation of equipment		105,000
Accounts payable		55,000
Mortgage note payable ($12,000 due in Year 3)		50,000
Capital stock, no par, 50,000 shares issued and out-		
standing		90,000
Retained earnings, Dec. 31, Year 1		266,500
Dividends	50,000	
Sales		505,000
Sales returns and allowances	10,000	
Sales discounts	5,000	
Purchases (including freight charges)	280,000	
Purchases discounts		3,500
Selling expenses	73,000	
General and administrative expenses	50,500	
Totals	$1,135,500	$1,135,500

Additional information

(1) Inventory on December 31, Year 2, consisted of the following:

	Cost	Replacement cost (net of freight and purchases discounts)
Inventory (cost includes freight charges but has not been reduced for 2% purchases discounts)	$87,000	$70,000

The controller for the company wants to recognize the decline in the market value of the inventory by setting up an Allowance for Price Decline in Inventory; the write-down would be included in the cost of goods sold in the income statement. The cost of the inventory should be reduced for purchases discounts that normally are taken. You also ascertain that the cost of ending inventory includes $4,700 of worthless goods and $2,300 of freight charges. Freight charges applicable to the worthless goods amount to $65. Purchases discounts of 2% are offered on the invoice price of all purchases.

(2) Assume that Eugene Cement Corporation pays income taxes at the rate of 35%.

Instructions

a Determine the adjusted cost of the inventory on December 31, Year 2, and prepare a journal entry to record the estimated loss in value of the inventory caused by declining prices. Assume that the ending inventory was recorded in the accounting records by an appropriate closing entry.

b Prepare an income statement for the year ended December 31, Year 2. Include the write-down of inventory to market in cost of goods sold.

c Prepare a balance sheet on December 31, Year 2.

d Prepare a statement of retained earnings for the year ended December 31, Year 2.

8-14 Wendell Wo's Department Store decided in December, Year 1, to adopt the dollar-value lifo method for computation of the ending inventory for Year 2 and each year thereafter. Management believes that the published price indexes are too general for its use; therefore, it intends to compute an index of price changes by sampling the stock of goods. The inventory on December 31, Year 1, was $75,000, and Year 1 is considered the base year for purposes of the dollar-value lifo method.

The following data have been accumulated as the basis for inventory valuation:

	Number of units				Prices at end of year			
Item	Year 2	Year 3	Year 4	Item	Year 1	Year 2	Year 3	Year 4
M	40	80	40	M	$ 10.00	$ 12.00	$ 13.00	$ 13.00
N	80	100	102	N	12.00	13.75	14.40	15.00
O	30	40	43	O	8.00	9.00	10.00	10.00
P	100	120	100	P	14.00	14.50	16.00	17.30
				Total cost at end-of-year prices.	$75,000	$99,000	$117,000	$96,250

Instructions

a Compute the indexes of inventory costs for Wendell Wo's Department Store for Year 2, Year 3, and Year 4.

b Compute the dollar-value lifo inventories at the end of Year 2, Year 3, and Year 4.

9 INVENTORIES: SPECIAL VALUATION METHODS

Inventory valuation methods based on cost flow assumptions and the application of the lower-of-cost-or-market rule are described in Chapter 8. Special inventory valuation methods, such as the *retail* and *gross profit* methods, are discussed in this chapter. In addition, the accounting for long-term construction contracts (which involves the valuation of construction work in process) is included in this chapter.

RETAIL METHOD

The retail method of estimating the cost of inventories is used primarily by retailers. Under periodic inventory procedures, the cost of the ending inventory is subtracted from the total cost of goods available for sale to compute the cost of goods sold. Under the retail method, a record is kept of goods available for sale at selling prices, and sales for the accounting period are deducted from this total to determine the ending inventory at selling prices. The ending inventory valued at selling prices then is reduced to estimated cost by multiplying the inventory at selling prices by the cost percentage computed for the accounting period.

   Some uses of the retail method of estimating the cost of inventories are:

1 To verify the reasonableness of the cost of inventories at the end of the accounting period. By using a different set of data from that used in pricing inventories, accountants can establish that the valuation of inventories is reasonable.

2 To estimate the cost of inventories for interim accounting periods without taking physical inventories.

3 To permit the valuation of inventories when selling prices are the only available data. The use of this method allows management to mark only the selling prices on the merchandise and eliminates the need for referring to specific purchase invoices.

Illustration of retail method

The retail method is illustrated by the following simplified example for Robinson Company:

ROBINSON COMPANY
Estimate of Inventory by Retail Method
End of Current Year

	Cost	Retail
Beginning inventory	$ 40,000	$ 50,000
Net purchases	150,000	200,000
Goods available for sale	$190,000	$250,000
Cost percentage ($190,000 ÷ $250,000) = 76%		
Less: Sales and normal shrinkage		220,000
Ending inventory, at retail		$ 30,000
Ending inventory, at cost ($30,000 × 76%)	$ 22,800	

Although the retail method permits the calculation of inventory without a physical count of the items on hand, the accountant should insist that a physical inventory be taken periodically. Otherwise, shrinkage due to shoplifting, breakage, and other causes might go undetected and might result in an increasingly overstated inventory.

Normal shrinkage in the inventory can be estimated on the basis of the goods which were available for sale. The method frequently used is to develop a percentage from the experience of past years, such as 2% of the retail value of goods available for sale. This percentage is used to determine the estimated shrinkage, which is deducted, along with sales, from goods available for sale at retail prices to compute the estimated inventory at retail prices.[1] The cost of normal shrinkage is included in the cost of goods sold; the cost of abnormal shrinkage (theft, unusual spoilage, etc.) which is material in amount is reported separately in the income statement.

The estimated cost of the inventory is computed by use of a **cost percentage,** that is, the relationship between the cost of goods available for sale and their retail value. The reliability of this procedure rests on the conditions that (1) a uniform relationship exists between selling price and cost for all goods available for sale during the accounting period, or (2) if the markup on individual items stocked differs, the distribution of items in the ending inventory is roughly the same as the "mix" in the

---

[1] When sales are made to employees or selected customers at a special discount price, such discounts are added to sales to arrive at the estimated inventory at retail prices.

total goods available for sale. When one of these conditions is not present, the accuracy of the retail method is improved by applying it to the individual departments of the business enterprise, and adding the resulting departmental inventories to compute the estimated cost of the total inventory.

Retail trade terminology

The following terms are used in the application of the retail method of estimating inventory:

Original selling price   The price at which goods originally are offered for sale.

Markup   The initial margin between the selling price and cost. It also is referred to as **gross margin** or **mark-on.**

Additional markup   An increase above the original selling price.

Markup cancellation   A reduction in the selling price after there has been an additional markup. The reduction does not reduce the selling price below the original selling price. Additional markups less markup cancellations are referred to as **net markups.**

Markdown   A reduction in selling price below the original selling price.

Markdown cancellation   An increase in the selling price, following a markdown, which does not raise the new selling price above the original selling price. Markdowns less markdown cancellations are referred to as **net markdowns.**

To illustrate these terms, assume that an item which cost $20 is priced to sell for $30 a unit. The **markup** is $10 (50% of cost or $33\frac{1}{3}$% of selling price). In response to strong demand for the item an **additional markup** of $3 is added, so that the selling price is increased to $33. As the demand slackens, the price is reduced to $31 by a **markup cancellation** of $2. Subsequently, in order to dispose of the remaining units, the selling price of the item is reduced to $25 by a markup cancellation of $1 and a **markdown** of $5. Finally, if management concludes that the remaining units can be sold at a price of $28, a **markdown cancellation** of $3 is required to increase the selling price from $25 to $28.

Retail method—valuation at average cost

An understanding of the meaning of each term defined above is important in the application of the retail method, because the treatment of net markups and net markdowns affects the estimate of the ending inventory. The data on page 358 for Western Company are used to illustrate the treatment of new markups and net markdowns in the application of the retail method at the end of Year 1.

Data for illustration of
retail method

	Cost	Retail
Beginning inventory.	$15,810	$ 27,000
Net purchases	75,190	110,000
Additional markups		5,000
Markup cancellations		(2,000)
Markdowns		(10,875)
Markdown cancellations		875
Net sales		(90,000)
Ending inventory, at retail		$ 40,000

The inventory for Western Company at the end of Year 1 at **average cost** is computed by the retail method as follows:

Net markdowns are
used to compute cost
percentage for estima-
tion of ending inventory
at average cost

WESTERN COMPANY
Estimate of Inventory by Retail Method—Valuation at Average Cost
End of Year 1

	Cost	Retail
Beginning inventory.	$15,810	$ 27,000
Net purchases	75,190	110,000
Net markups ($5,000 − $2,000)		3,000
Less: Net markdowns ($10,875 − $875)		(10,000)
Goods available for sale	$91,000	$130,000
Cost percentage ($91,000 ÷ $130,000) = 70%		
Less: Net sales.		(90,000)
Ending inventory, at retail		$ 40,000
Ending inventory, at average cost ($40,000 × 70%)	$28,000	

The cost percentage of 70% is determined after net markups are added to, and net markdowns are deducted from, the goods available for sale at retail. This procedure results in valuation of the ending inventory at average cost. The estimated cost of $28,000 for the ending inventory is accurate only if the goods on hand consist of a representative sample of all goods available for sale during Year 1. For example, if the ending inventory does not include any goods that were on hand at the beginning of the year, the cost percentage should be computed without use of the beginning inventory amounts. Similarly, if all goods on which the net markups and net markdowns were made have been sold, both the net markups and the net markdowns should be excluded from the computation of the cost percentage. Under such circumstances, however, the net markups and net markdowns still are used to compute the ending inventory at retail prices.

Retail method—valuation at lower of average cost or market

The retail method can be adapted to produce inventory valuations approximating the lower of cost or market when there have been changes in the costs and selling prices of goods during the accounting period. The crucial factor in the calculation of estimated cost of ending inventory by the retail method is the treatment of net markups and net markdowns in the computation of the cost percentage. The inclusion of net markups and the exclusion of net markdowns in the computation of the cost percentage produce an inventory valued at the *lower of average cost or market.* This is sometimes called the *conventional retail method* and is illustrated for Western Company below:

Net markdowns are not used to compute cost percentage for estimation of ending inventory at lower of average cost or market

WESTERN COMPANY

Estimate of Inventory by Retail Method—Valuation at
Lower of Average Cost or Market
End of Year 1

	Cost	Retail
Beginning inventory.	$15,810	$ 27,000
Net purchases	75,190	110,000
Net markups ($5,000 − $2,000)		3,000
Goods available for sale	$91,000	$140,000
Cost percentage ($91,000 ÷ $140,000) = 65%		
Less: Net sales.		(90,000)
Net markdowns ($10,875 − $875)		(10,000)
Ending inventory, at retail		$ 40,000
Ending inventory, at lower of average cost or market		
($40,000 × 65%).	$26,000	

Net markups and net markdowns change the relationship between the selling price and the cost for goods available for sale, and thus affect the estimate of the ending inventory and the cost of goods sold computed by the retail method.

In the illustration above, the cost percentage is 65%, and the ending inventory at *lower of average cost or market* is $26,000. When both the net markups and the net markdowns were used in the computation of the cost percentage, the percentage was 70%, and the ending inventory at *average cost* was $28,000. The inclusion of net markups in the computation of the cost percentage assumes that the additional markups apply proportionately to items sold and to items on hand at the end of the accounting period; however, net markdowns are assumed to apply only to the goods sold. Because the selling price of goods to which the markdowns apply is less than the original selling price, the net markdowns as well as sales must be deducted from goods available for sale at retail to determine the inventory at retail price. If these assumptions are correct, the exclusion of net markdowns in the computation of the cost percentage values the ending inventory at average cost.

However, in some cases the net markdowns do not apply solely to goods sold; instead, they apply both to goods sold and to goods in the ending inventory. In such cases the exclusion of net markdowns from the computation of the cost percentage does not produce an inventory value in terms of average cost but rather at a value below average cost. Consequently, if net markdowns are excluded from the computation of the cost percentage, the inventory would be estimated at lower of average cost or market.

As stated previously, the retail method is based on an assumption that the ending inventory is composed of the same mix of items as the total pool of goods from which sales were made. If there are markdowns for special sale promotions, this assumption implicit in the retail method may not be valid. Some markdowns may apply to goods available for sale and to goods in ending inventory in equal proportions, but others may apply only to goods which have been sold. In essence, we are saying that there are really two lines of merchandise, "special sale" items and regular items, on which the markup is different. The two lines may not be held in equal proportions in the goods available and in the ending inventory. Attempts to handle the two lines in one computation are likely to prove inadequate as a means of deriving meaningful inventory cost amounts.

Retail method—valuation at last-in, first-out

The preceding discussion illustrated two variations of the retail method which produce an inventory valuation at **average cost** or at the **lower of average cost or market.** If the last-in, first-out method is used to estimate the cost of inventory, the conventional retail method must be modified. The retail method can be adapted to approximate lifo cost of the ending inventory by the computation of a cost percentage for purchases of the current accounting period only. The objective is to estimate the cost of **any increase** in inventory during the period.

Because lifo is a cost (not lower-of-cost-or-market) method of inventory valuation, both net markups and net markdowns are included in the computation of the cost percentage for purchases of the current period, in accordance with the discussion of the average-cost procedure on pages 357 to 358.

The modification of the retail method necessary to value inventory at lifo cost is shown on page 361 for Western Company (using the same data as in previous illustrations). For purposes of this illustration, assume that selling prices have remained unchanged and that net markups and net markdowns apply only to the goods purchased during Year 1.

Exclude beginning
inventory from compu-
tation of the cost per-
centage when retail lifo
method is used

WESTERN COMPANY

Estimate of Inventory by Retail Method—Valuation at Lifo Cost

End of Year 1

	Cost	Retail
Beginning inventory.	$15,810	$ 27,000
Net purchases	75,190	110,000
Net markups ($5,000 − $2,000)		3,000
Less: Net markdowns ($10,875 − $875).		(10,000)
Goods available for sale, at retail.		$130,000
Less: Net sales.		90,000
Ending inventory, at retail		$ 40,000
Cost percentage for net purchases, including net markups and net markdowns ($75,190 ÷ $103,000* = 73%)		
Ending inventory, at lifo cost:		
Beginning inventory layer	$15,810	$ 27,000
Add: Layer added in Year 1 ($13,00 × 73%)	9,490	13,000
Ending inventory, at retail		$ 40,000
Ending inventory, at lifo cost	$25,300	

* $110,000 + $3,000 − $10,000 = $103,000.

The inventory at the end of Year 1 is composed of the cost of the beginning inventory plus the estimated cost of the layer added during Year 1. If in Year 2 the inventory decreased, the decrease would be taken from the layer added in Year 1, $9,490, and then from the layer on hand at the beginning of Year 1, $15,810. For example, if the ending inventory for Western Company totaled $30,000 at retail at the end of Year 2, the inventory at lifo cost would be computed as illustrated below:

Note the cost of layer
added in previous year

	Cost	Retail
Inventory, end of Year 2, at lifo cost:		
Inventory layer, beginning of Year 1	$15,810	$27,000
Layer added in Year 1 ($3,000 × 73%).	2,190	3,000
Ending inventory, at retail		$30,000
Inventory, end of Year 2, at lifo cost	$18,000	

Under retail lifo procedures, computation of a cost percentage for current year's purchases is required **only when an increase in inventory (at retail) occurs during the current year.** The cost percentage is computed for the sole purpose of pricing the incremental layer in inventory. On the other hand, if a decrease in inventory takes place, the ending inventory consists of a fraction of the beginning inventory cost. For example, if the ending inventory at retail for Western Company at the end of Year 2 amounted to only $18,000, or two-thirds of the layer at the beginning of Year 1, the inventory at the end of Year 2 at lifo cost would be determined as follows:

Inventory consists of two-thirds of base layer

$$\$15,810 \times \frac{\$18,000}{\$27,000} = \underline{\$10,540}$$

Retail method—valuation at first-in, first-out

The cost of the inventory on a first-in, first-out basis can be estimated from the data used to determine the lifo cost. For example, the cost of the inventory at the end of Year 1, for Western Company on the first-in, first-out basis would be $29,200 ($40,000 × 73%, the cost percentage applicable to Year 1 purchases). If the cost percentage for Year 2 is assumed to be 68% and the inventory at retail amounted to $30,000, the inventory of fifo cost would be $20,400 ($30,000 × 68% = $20,400).

Changes in price levels and the retail lifo method

Let us now remove the simplifying assumption of the stability of selling prices. In reality, retail prices do change from one accounting period to another, and this is particularly significant for pricing inventories at retail lifo. Because the procedure employed under these circumstances is similar to that used in conjunction with dollar-value lifo described in Chapter 8, it is known as the ***dollar-value retail lifo method.*** The ending inventory at retail must be converted to beginning-of-year prices to ascertain the increase in the inventory at beginning-of-year prices. An appropriate cost index must be used to convert from end-of-year prices to beginning-of-year prices. There are several indexes published regularly by various governmental agencies and trade associations that might be used. For example, the Bureau of Labor Statistics regularly publishes national indexes for 20 major groups of retail departments, as well as for soft goods and durable goods.

The procedure for estimating the lifo cost of the ending inventory, under the retail method and assuming increasing selling prices, is shown on page 363 for Rising Company. The sales price index at the beginning of the current accounting period, ***when lifo was adopted,*** is assumed to be 100, and the index at the end of the current period is assumed to be 110, an increase of 10%.[2] In order not to complicate the

[2] When the base-period index is other than 100, the percentage increase is determined by dividing the index at the end of the current period by the base-period index and subtracting 100. For example, if the base-period index is 125 and the index at the end of the current period is 150, the increase would be 20% [(150/125) − 100].

example, we have assumed that there were no net markups or net markdowns in the current period.

Dollar-value retail lifo method when prices are rising

RISING COMPANY
Dollar-Value Retail Lifo Method
End of Current Period

	Cost	Retail
Beginning inventory (date lifo was adopted)	$18,000	$ 30,000
Purchases during the period (cost percentage = 65%) . . .	65,000	100,000
Goods available for sale during the period, at retail prices		$130,000
Less: Net sales during the period		75,000
Inventory at end of period, at retail prices		$ 55,000
Computation of inventory increase at end-of-period retail prices:		
Inventory, at beginning-of-period retail prices ($55,000 ÷ 1.10)		$ 50,000
Less: Beginning inventory, at retail prices		30,000
Inventory increase, at beginning-of-period retail prices .		$ 20,000
Inventory increase, at end-of-period retail prices, $20,000 × 1.10		$ 22,000
Ending inventory, at dollar-value retail lifo cost:		
Beginning inventory layer	$18,000	
Add: Layer added in current period ($22,000 × 65%) . .	14,300	
Ending inventory, at dollar-value retail lifo cost	$32,300[3]	

GROSS PROFIT METHOD

The gross profit method is useful for several purposes: (1) to control and verify the validity of inventory cost; (2) to estimate interim inventory valuations between physical counts; and (3) to estimate the inventory value when necessary information normally used is lost or unavailable. The procedure involved is one of reducing sales to a cost basis; that is, cost of goods sold is estimated. The estimated cost of goods sold then is subtracted from the cost of goods available for sale to compute the estimated cost of the ending inventory.

---

[3] Failure to recognize the increase in the price level would result in an erroneous ending inventory cost of $34,250, as illustrated below:

	Lifo cost	Selling price
Beginning inventory layer	$18,000	$30,000
Incremental layer [lifo cost = ($55,000 − $30,000) × 65%]	16,250	25,000
Ending inventory	$34,250	$55,000

In the event that both merchandise and inventory records are destroyed by fire, the inventory value also can be estimated by use of the gross profit method. The gross profit and cost of goods sold percentages are obtained from prior years' financial statements, which presumably are available. The beginning inventory for the current year is the ending inventory of the preceding year. Net purchases are estimated from copies of the paid checks retained by the bank and through correspondence with suppliers. Sales are computed by reference to cash deposits and by estimation of the uncollected receivables through direct correspondence with customers.

Gross profit method is really a "cost percentage" method

The crucial factor in the application of the gross profit method is the development of an accurate cost percentage, obtained by deduction of the gross profit rate from 100%. Frequently the best available measure is an average of the cost percentages for recent years, adjusted for any changes which have taken place in the current year.

To illustrate the computation of the cost of inventory by the gross profit method, assume the following data for Marina Sea Store for Year 4:

Cost percentage of 80% means that gross profit is 20%

Beginning inventory, at cost	$ 40,000
Net purchases	200,000
Net sales	225,000
Average cost percentage for past three years	80%

Assuming that the cost percentage for Year 4 remained at 80%, the cost of the inventory at the end of Year 4 is estimated as follows:

The critical step in the gross profit method is the estimate of cost of goods sold

MARINA SEA STORE
Estimate of Cost of Inventory by Gross Profit Method
End of Year 4

Beginning inventory, at cost		$ 40,000
Net purchases		200,000
Goods available for sale		$240,000
Less: Estimated cost of goods sold:		
Net sales	$225,000	
Cost percentage	80%	180,000
Estimated ending inventory, at cost		$ 60,000

The ending inventory computed by the gross profit method is reasonably consistent with the usual method of pricing inventory. This follows from the fact that the gross profit percentage is based on historical records which have reflected the particular method of valuing the inventory. If the inventory is valued at lifo, the estimated inventory will approximate lifo cost; therefore, if the gross profit method is used as a basis for recovering an insured fire loss, the inventory should be restated for insurance purposes to current fair value at the time of the fire.

Sometimes the gross profit percentage is stated as a percentage of cost. In such situations the gross profit percentage must be restated to a percentage of net sales in order to compute the cost percentage for the period. For example, if the gross profit is stated as 25% of cost, the gross profit percentage can be restated to 20% of net sales as follows:

Restatement of gross profit based on cost to percentage based on net sales

(1) 25% $= \frac{1}{4}$ gross profit based on cost

(2) Add numerator of fraction to denominator to make $\frac{1}{5}$

(3) $\frac{1}{5}$ = 20% gross profit based on net sales

When 20% is subtracted from 100%, we have the cost percentage of 80% of net sales. Alternatively, the cost percentage based on net sales can be determined directly as follows:

Direct computation of cost percentage

Let X = cost as percentage of net sales (100%)

$0.25X$ = gross profit percentage

then $X + 0.25X = 100\%$

$1.25X = 100\%$

$X = \dfrac{100\%}{1.25}$

$X = 80\%$ (cost percentage based on net sales)

Applying the gross profit method to departments

If there are several classes of merchandise which have different markup percentages, the gross profit method yields accurate results only if the inventory for each class of merchandise is computed individually. The use of a combined cost percentage would require the unlikely assumption that the various classes of merchandise are sold in the same relative proportions each year. To illustrate this point, assume that the gross profit percentages for Bane Sales Company have averaged 50% for Department A and 30% for Department B in recent years. Thus, the cost percentage is 50% for Department A and 70% for Department B; the combined cost percentage has averaged 65% in recent years. The cost of the combined ending inventory for the current year may be estimated as follows:

Use of recent years' combined cost percentage does not work in this example

BANE SALES COMPANY
Estimate of Cost of Departmental and Combined Inventories
For Current Year by Gross Profit Method

	Dept. A	Dept. B	Combined
Beginning inventory, at cost	$ 20,000	$ 40,000	$ 60,000
Net purchases.	90,000	95,000	185,000
Cost of goods available for sale	$110,000	$135,000	$245,000
Less: Estimated cost of goods sold:			
Net sales.	$150,000	$150,000	$300,000
Average cost percentage, **prior years**. . .	50%	70%	65%
Estimated cost of goods sold	$ 75,000	$105,000	$195,000
Estimated ending inventory, at cost	$ 35,000	$ 30,000	$ 50,000

Use of the combined cost percentage (based on prior years' experience) produces an inventory estimate of $50,000, although the sum of the two departmental ending inventories is estimated at $65,000 ($35,000 + $30,000 = $65,000). The source of the error is clear when we note that the cost percentage for the current year, determined by combining the departmental results, is not 65% but 60%, because a higher-than-usual proportion of total sales in the **current year** was made by Department A, which has a lower cost percentage. The **actual** combined cost percentage (60%) for the current year is determined below:

Actual combined cost percentage is 60%, not 65%

Total sales ($150,000 + $150,000) $300,000
Total estimated cost of goods sold ($75,000 + $105,000) $180,000
Combined cost percentage for current year ($180,000 ÷ $300,000) . . . 60%

If the combined current year's cost percentage of 60% is used, the combined ending inventory would be computed correctly at $65,000 ($245,000 − $180,000 = $65,000). Stated simply, separate departmental cost percentages should be used to estimate inventories by the gross profit method when the cost percentages differ materially among departments.

Gross profit method for interim financial reports

The gross profit method frequently is used in the preparation of interim financial reports. It should be clear that the use of the gross profit method results in an **estimated cost** of inventory. If the reporting enterprise normally values inventory at lower of cost or market for annual reporting purposes, it must follow the same procedure for interim reporting purposes. Thus, the estimated cost obtained by use of the gross profit method must be compared to current replacement costs to determine whether a write-down to a lower "market" is required. The gross profit method may be used for interim financial reports even though annual inventories are determined by use of one of the cost flow assumptions described in Chapter 8. Enterprises that use the gross profit method for interim purposes "should disclose the method used . . . and any significant adjustments that result from reconciliations with the annual physical inventory."[4]

OTHER VALUATION METHODS

Valuation of inventories at replacement costs

The valuation of inventories at replacement costs has been advocated by accountants who believe that the current asset section of the balance sheet should reflect current fair values. The cost methods of inventory pricing frequently understate the value of the inventory, particularly during periods of rising prices. The significance of replacement costs as a measure of inventory value varies considerably depending on the type of inventory involved. In the retail market, the selling prices of staple commodities, such as sugar, copper, cotton, etc., tend to follow cost prices closely. In such situations, replacement costs of inventories are important to management and outsiders.

Replacement-cost valuation of inventories in the preparation of financial statements has not been widely adopted. Perhaps the closest practical approach is the fifo method. Unless prices are rising rapidly, the fifo method of pricing presents inventories in the balance sheet at or near current replacement costs without a departure from the cost principle. The need for disclosure of replacement costs of inventories arises when the lifo method is used for pricing inventories.

The theoretical objection to the use of replacement costs as a method of inventory valuation is implicit in the arguments previously presented. Some of the advantages of inventory valuation at replacement costs can be achieved by the use of notes to disclose current replacement costs of inventories. Many accountants have argued for the adoption of replacement costs as a means of pricing inventories

[4] APB Opinion No. 28, "Interim Financial Reporting," AICPA (New York: 1973), p. 524.

whether replacement costs are above or below actual costs. They base their argument on the fact that the economic utility of inventories is indicated by the current costs of replacement. A valid point made by proponents of replacement costs is that if replacement costs are objective and more useful when they are lower than actual costs, they also possess those attributes when they are higher than actual costs.

The consistent use of replacement costs for the valuation of inventories would require some broadening of the revenue realization principle as presently applied. Under current generally accepted accounting principles, revenue emerges at the time inventories are sold and converted to accounts receivable (or cash), as indicated in the following diagram:

Revenue is realized when inventories are sold

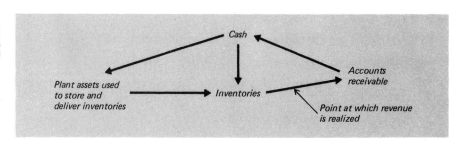

If replacement costs were adopted as the basis of inventory valuation, gains and losses represented by the difference between historical costs and replacement costs would be recognized and included in income prior to the sale of finished products. The information resulting from such a procedure would be useful in periods when prices were changing significantly. The real issue is whether replacement costs can be determined with sufficient accuracy and objectivity to provide a reliable basis for financial reporting. At present, however, valuation of inventories at replacement costs which are **higher** than historical costs is not considered a generally accepted accounting principle.

Restatement of inventory costs to a common measuring unit is another approach to the problem of changing prices. This subject is considered in Chapter 25.

Valuation of inventories at net selling prices

The valuation of inventories at **net selling prices** (sales prices less direct costs of completion and disposal) has some appeal, especially when one considers that economic value is added as the goods are brought to market. For example, in a retail store, goods are more valuable than they were at the wholesaler's warehouse; value is added by the process of bringing the goods nearer the ultimate market. In a manufacturing enterprise, costs are blended together, and a product emerges which is more valuable than the sum of the production costs. However, this method of inventory valuation has not been widely adopted for two reasons: (1) the lack of objectivity in determining the net selling price; and (2) the fact that the selling price has not been realized in cash or cash equivalents. Accountants generally consider revenue to be realized at the time of sale, not at the time of production.

The valuation of inventories at net selling prices is appropriate for some types of business enterprises producing commodities which have readily determinable market prices. When the production of such commodities is complete, revenue may be considered realized. In other enterprises in which selling prices are established by contract, the sale follows production as a matter of course, and completed inventories may be valued at net selling prices.

The use of net selling prices to value inventories moves the point of revenue realization back one step in the earning process. As costs are incurred during the process of bringing an item to market, income is earned in the most fundamental sense. Each activity necessary to advance the goods closer to the customer and ultimately to close the sale transaction adds an element of income—the increase in selling price over the added cost. Therefore, if there are costs still to be incurred, there is still an element of income to be earned. The valuation of inventories at net selling prices means that an element of income may be accrued before it is earned through sale.

VALUATION OF LONG-TERM CONSTRUCTION CONTRACTS

Contracts for construction of ships, bridges, dams, and similar projects often require several years to complete. Such long-term contracts present special problems of inventory valuation and revenue recognition. For business enterprises engaged in long-term construction contracts, two approaches to inventory valuation and revenue recognition are available:

1 The completed-contract method
2 The percentage-of-completion method

Under the **completed-contract method,** inventory of construction in progress is valued at cost; no profit is recognized on the contract until it is completed and the work is accepted by the customer. There may be a year in which no contract is completed; consequently, in that year the contractor would have neither revenue nor profit on construction contracts. In fact, a loss would be reported to the extent of expenses incurred which are not chargeable to the construction inventory. In the year in which a contract is completed, the entire profit earned through several years of production is recognized, even though only a small part of the work may have been performed in the final year of construction.

To avoid such misleading reporting, most contractors employ the **percentage-of-completion method** of accounting. This method requires the accrual of revenue and profit over the term of the contract based on the progress achieved each year. If the work performed in a given year is estimated to represent 40% of the total work required on the contract, then 40% of the total estimated revenue and profit is considered earned. This accrual of profit is accomplished by increasing the carrying amount of the Construction in Progress account, which is an inventory account for a contractor.

Accounting for long-term construction contract illustrated

A bridge is to be constructed by Regal Construction Company beginning in Year 1 at a contract price of $900,000 with estimated construction costs totaling $750,000. The bridge is expected to be completed in Year 3. The construction costs incurred, cost estimates, and other data are presented below in summary form for each of the three years:

Data for illustration

	Year 1	Year 2	Year 3
Construction costs incurred	$125,000	$495,000	$145,000
Estimated cost to complete the contract . . .	625,000	155,000	–0–
Amounts billed to customers	110,000	565,000	225,000
Collections from customers on billings	90,000	520,000	265,000
Operating expenses incurred (selling, general, and administrative)	15,000	30,000	22,500

Completed-Contract Method The journal entries to record the transactions relating to the construction of the bridge under the **completed-contract method** are shown on page 371 for Regal Construction Company.

Direct costs incurred on the contract are accumulated in the Construction in Progress (Inventory) account, and amounts billed to the customer are recorded in the Partial Billings on Contract account. These account titles may vary. When the contract is completed and approved by the customer, the costs applicable to the completed contract are transferred to the Construction Costs Applicable to Realized Revenue (Cost of Sales) account, and partial billings relating to the contract are transferred to the Construction Revenue (Sales) account.

The only closing entries required at the end of Year 1 and Year 2 are to close the Operating Expenses account, because no revenue or profit has been recognized in these years. If operating costs can be identified with particular contracts, inclusion of these in the Construction in Progress (Inventory) account may be appropriate. When a long-term construction contract is expected to result in a loss, the loss is recorded under the completed-contract method as soon as it is determinable by a debit to Loss on Long-Term Construction Contract and a credit to Con-

Illustrative
journal
entries
under
com-
pleted-
contract
method

REGAL CONSTRUCTION COMPANY
Journal Entries—Completed-Contract Method

Accounts and explanations of transactions	Year 1 Debit	Year 1 Credit	Year 2 Debit	Year 2 Credit	Year 3 Debit	Year 3 Credit
(1) Operating Expenses	15,000		30,000		22,500	
Construction in Progress (Inventory)	125,000		495,000		145,000	
Material, Cash, etc.		140,000		525,000		167,500
To record operating expenses and construction costs.						
(2) Accounts Receivable	110,000		565,000		225,000	
Partial Billings on Contract .		110,000		565,000		225,000
To record billings on contract.						
(3) Cash	90,000		520,000		265,000	
Accounts Receivable		90,000		520,000		265,000
To record collections from customer.						
(4) Partial Billings on Contract . . .					900,000	
Construction Costs Applicable to Realized Revenue (Cost of Sales)					765,000	
Construction Revenue (Sales)						900,000
Construction in Progress (Inventory)						765,000
To record realized revenue and applicable construction costs upon final approval of project by customer.						

struction in Progress (Inventory). The credit to Construction in Progress (Inventory) eliminates from inventory the excess of the total estimated cost of the contract over the total contract revenue.

In Year 3, balances in the Operating Expenses account, the Construction Costs Applicable to Realized Revenue (Cost of Sales) account, and the Construction Revenue (Sales) account are closed to the Income Summary account. The income statement for Year 3 for Regal Construction Company includes the following:

Construction revenue (sales)	$900,000
Less: Construction costs applicable to realized revenue (cost of sales) .	765,000
Gross profit on long-term construction contract	$135,000
Operating expenses	22,500
Income before income taxes	$112,500

The balance sheets for Regal Construction Company include the following amounts when the **completed-contract method** is used:

	End of Year 1	End of Year 2	End of Year 3
Current assets:			
Accounts receivable	$20,000	$65,000	$25,000
Inventories:			
Construction in progress . . .	$125,000		
Less: Partial billings on contract	110,000		
Costs of uncompleted contract in excess of billings . .	$15,000		
Current liabilities:			
Partial billings on contract . . .		$675,000	
Less: Construction in progress		620,000	
Billings on uncompleted contract in excess of costs		$55,000	

Under the completed-contract method, the amount billed to customers may exceed the amount of construction costs incurred; therefore, when the Partial Billings on Contract account balance is deducted from the Construction in Progress (Inventory) account balance, a credit balance results. The AICPA offers the following guidelines for reporting this credit balance in the balance sheet:[5]

> When the completed-contract method is used, an excess of accumulated costs over related billings should be shown in the balance sheet as a current asset, and an excess of accumulated billings over related costs should be shown among the liabilities, in most cases as a current liability. If costs exceed billings on some contracts, and billings exceed costs on others, the contracts should ordinarily be segregated so that the figures on the asset side include only those contracts on which costs exceed billings, and those on the liability side include only those on which billings exceed costs. It is suggested that the asset item be described as "costs of uncompleted contracts in excess of related billings" . . ., and that the item on the liability side be described as "billings on uncompleted contracts in excess of related costs."

In our illustration of the bridge construction contract, the $15,000 excess of construction costs over partial billings on contract at the end of Year 1 appears as a current asset in the balance sheet; at the end of Year 2, the $55,000 excess of partial billings on contract over construction costs to date is included with current liabilities. These accounts are considered current because they arise in the normal operating cycle of a contractor. The balance in Accounts Receivable at the end of Year 1,

[5] *Accounting Research and Terminology Bulletins—Final Edition, ARB No. 45,* AICPA (New York: 1961), p. 6.

$20,000, is composed of billings of $110,000, less collections to date of $90,000; at the end of Year 2, the balance in Accounts Receivable is $65,000, consisting of cumulative billings to date of $675,000, less total collections to date of $610,000; and at the end of Year 3, only $25,000 ($900,000 − $875,000 = $25,000) remains to be collected from the customer.

Percentage-of-Completion Method The percentage of completion represented by each year's work may be based on (1) **engineering estimates** of the work performed to date relative to the total work required under the contract, or (2) the **relationship between the cost incurred to date and the total estimated cost to complete the contract.** The percentage of completion determined by either of these two methods is applied to the contract price to determine the amount of revenue and gross profit realized to date under the **percentage-of-completion method** of accounting.

In choosing between these two methods of establishing the percentage of completion, it is well to recognize that performance under some contracts requires that a substantial part of the material to be used for the entire contract must be ordered before any actual construction takes place. These costs incurred for material can constitute a large part of the total costs of the contract, although little or no actual progress has been made toward the completion of the contract. When these conditions exist, a percentage of completion based on engineering and architectural estimates may be superior to that based on relative costs for purposes of recognizing realized contract revenue and gross profit. The AICPA has suggested that during the early stages of a contract, costs of items such as material and subcontracts should be excluded from the total cost incurred in the computation of the percentage of completion.[6] Mere acquisition of material or advances to subcontractors does not result in the realization of revenue.

The AICPA has sanctioned the percentage-of-completion method under the following circumstances:[7]

> It is . . . a generally accepted accounting procedure to accrue revenues under certain types of contracts and thereby recognize profits, on the basis of partial performance, when the circumstances are such that total profit can be estimated with reasonable accuracy and ultimate realization is reasonably assured. Particularly when the performance of a contract requires a substantial period of time from inception to completion, there is ample precedent for prorata recognition of profit as the work progresses, if the total profit and the ratio of the performance to date to the complete performance can be computed reasonably and collection is reasonably assured.

The use of the percentage-of-completion method for financial accounting purposes is preferable if (1) contractors are able to make rea-

---

[6] Ibid., p. 4.
[7] *Accounting Research and Terminology Bulletins—Final Edition,* AICPA (New York: 1961), chap. 11A, p. 95.

sonably accurate estimates of the degree that contracts are completed; (2) contracts include provisions which specify the enforceable rights of parties, the consideration to be exchanged, and the manner and terms of settlement; and (3) contractors and their customers are expected to satisfy their contractual obligations. On the other hand, the use of the completed-contract method is preferable if (1) reasonably dependable estimates of costs remaining to be incurred cannot be made, or (2) if the results of operations would not vary materially from what they would be

Illustrative journal entries under percentage-of-completion method

REGAL CONSTRUCTION COMPANY
Journal Entries—Percentage-of-Completion Method

Accounts and explanations of transactions	Year 1 Debit	Year 1 Credit	Year 2 Debit	Year 2 Credit	Year 3 Debit	Year 3 Credit
(1) Operating Expenses	15,000		30,000		22,500	
Construction in Progress (Inventory)	125,000		495,000		145,000	
Material, Cash, etc.		140,000		525,000		167,500
To record operating expenses and construction costs.						
(2) Accounts Receivable	110,000		565,000		225,000	
Partial Billings on Contract .		110,000		565,000		225,000
To record billings on contract.						
(3) Cash	90,000		520,000		265,000	
Accounts Receivable		90,000		520,000		265,000
To record collections from customer.						
(4) Construction Costs Applicable to Realized Revenue (Cost of Sales)	125,000		495,000		145,000	
Construction in Progress (Inventory)	25,000		75,000		35,000	
Construction Revenue (Sales)		150,000		570,000		180,000
To record realized revenue estimated on the basis of cost incurred to total estimated cost. (Computations appear on p. 375.)						
(5) Partial Billings on Contract . . .					900,000	
Construction in Progress (Inventory)						900,000
To record approval of project by customer.						

under the percentage-of-completion method because the construction period covers a short period of time.[8]

If Regal Construction Company determines the percentage of completion on the basis of cost incurred to date as a fraction of the total estimated cost to be incurred on the contract, the journal entries for the three-year period are as shown on page 374. The computation of realized construction revenue on the contract is presented below:

Computation of realized revenue under percentage-of-completion method

REGAL CONSTRUCTION COMPANY
Computation of Realized Construction Revenue on Contract
Years 1, 2, and 3

Year 1:	Construction costs incurred in Year 1	$125,000	
	Estimated remaining costs to complete contract .	625,000	
	Total estimated costs to complete contract	$750,000	
	Realized construction revenue in Year 1:		
	Contract price, $900,000 × ($125,000/$750,000)		$150,000
Year 2:	Construction costs incurred to date ($125,000 + $495,000)	$620,000	
	Estimated remaining costs to complete contract .	155,000	
	Total estimated costs to complete contract . . .	$775,000	
	Contract price, $900,000 × ($620,000/$775,000) . .	$720,000	
	Less: Realized construction revenue in Year 1	(150,000)	
	Realized construction revenue in Year 2		570,000
Year 3:	Contract price	$900,000	
	Less: Realized construction revenue in Year 1 and Year 2 ($150,000 + $570,000).	720,000	
	Realized construction revenue in Year 3		180,000
	Total realized construction revenue on contract		$900,000

The first three journal entries on page 374 are the same as illustrated on page 371 for the completed-contract method. However, under the percentage-of-completion method, two nominal accounts are used at the end of each of the first two years and when the contract is completed in Year 3—the Construction Costs Applicable to Realized Revenue (Cost of Sales) and the Construction Revenue (Sales) accounts. The excess of realized construction revenue over the related costs represents the gross profit earned on the contract for each year and is debited to the Construction in Progress (Inventory) account. When the contract is completed in Year 3, the Partial Billings on Contract account is debited and the Construction in Progress (Inventory) account is cred-

[8] *Exposure Draft: Proposed Statement of Position,* "Accounting for Performance of Construction-Type and Certain Production-Type Contracts," AICPA (New York: 1979), pp. 10–12.

ited to eliminate the balances in these accounts relating to the completed contract.

Although the percentage-of-completion method allows for the recognition of revenue and gross profit on a contract as work progresses, this same calculation may indicate that a *loss is probable.* In the event that a loss is expected, ***ARB No. 45*** requires that "in most circumstances provision should be made for the ***estimated loss on the entire contract.*** If there is a close relationship between profitable and unprofitable contracts, . . . the group may be treated as a unit in determining the necessity for a provision for loss."[9] When the percentage-of-completion method of accounting for long-term construction contracts is used, the loss on the completed portion of the contract is the difference between construction costs applicable to realized revenue (cost of sales) and the realized construction revenue (sales). The estimated loss applicable to the uncompleted portion of the contract is recorded by a debit to Estimated Loss on Long-Term Construction Contract and a credit to Construction in Progress (Inventory). Thus, both the completed-contract method (see page 370) and the percentage-of-completion method of accounting for a given long-term construction contract produce identical results when it appears that a loss will be incurred on that contract.

The presentation of construction revenue and construction costs applicable to realized revenue in the income statement is illustrated below for Regal Construction Company:

Presentation in income statements: Percentage-of-completion method

	Year 1	Year 2	Year 3
Construction revenue	$150,000	$570,000	$180,000
Less: Construction costs applicable to realized revenue	125,000	495,000	145,000
Gross profit on long-term construction contract	$ 25,000	$ 75,000	$ 35,000

The balance sheets for Regal Construction Company include the amounts shown at the top of page 377 when the ***percentage-of-completion method*** is used.

When the percentage-of-completion method of accounting is used, the balance in the Construction in Progress (Inventory) is shown in the balance sheet as a current asset (the same as under the completed-contract method). The inventory is valued at the cumulative construction costs incurred, plus the gross profit earned to date, less partial billings on the contract to date. The $150,000 balance in the Construction in Progress (Inventory) account at the end of Year 1 consists of construction costs of $125,000 plus the $25,000 gross profit recognized in Year 1.

[9] *Accounting Research and Terminology Bulletins—Final Edition, ARB No. 45,* p. 5.

Presentation in balance sheets: Percentage-of-completion method

	End of Year 1	End of Year 2	End of Year 3
Current assets:			
Accounts receivable	$20,000	$65,000	$25,000
Inventories:			
Construction in progress . . .	$150,000	$720,000	
Less: Partial billings on contract	110,000	675,000	
Costs and profit on uncompleted contract in excess of billings.	$40,000	$45,000	

At the end of Year 2, the balance of $720,000 in the Construction in Progress (Inventory) account consists of construction costs of $620,000 incurred in Years 1 and 2 plus $100,000 gross profit recognized in Years 1 and 2.

Special problems relating to long-term construction contracts

Income tax laws permit the use of either the completed-contract method or the percentage-of-completion method for long-term construction contracts. For income tax purposes, expenses which are not directly related to the project under construction are expenses of the year in which they are incurred. Also, the contractor is required to use one of the two methods consistently. A change in the method of valuing the construction in progress for income tax purposes requires the approval of the Internal Revenue Service.

If the percentage-of-completion method is used for financial accounting purposes and the completed-contract method is used for income tax purposes, deferred income taxes should be recorded to give effect to the timing difference in income recognition. This problem is considered in Chapter 21. A change in the method of accounting for long-term construction contracts for financial accounting purposes requires the retroactive restatement of prior years' financial statments issued currently. The accounting for changes in accounting principles is discussed in Chapter 22.

The Securities and Exchange Commission requires extensive disclosure of accounting policies for long-term construction contracts (extending over a period longer than 12 months). The SEC stated that such disclosure is necessary because long-term contracts "involve inventories and receivables with unique risk and liquidity characteristics."[10] The disclosure required includes the amount of inventoried costs, the

---

[10] *Accounting Series Release No. 164,* SEC (Washington: 1974).

nature of cost elements included in inventories, and the principal assumptions used to determine total contract costs.

Supplies and short-term prepayments

In addition to inventories of merchandise, finished goods, raw material, parts, and goods in process, a business enterprise may have several types of supplies on hand. For example, inventory of supplies may include office supplies, promotional materials, shipping supplies, and factory supplies. The problems of determining cost and valuation of supplies are similar to those for inventories discussed in Chapter 8. Supplies are purchased for use in operations, and any quantities remaining on hand at the end of an accounting period are included among current assets in the balance sheet.

The term **prepaid expenses** is widely used to describe unexpired costs which are expected to be consumed within a relatively short period of time. However, this term is somewhat of a misnomer and should be replaced by a more descriptive title such as **short-term prepayments.** Prepaid expenses are costs of goods and services which have not been consumed in the revenue-earning process. Strictly speaking, both depreciable plant assets and inventories fall within this definition. Plant assets are classified separately because they provide services over relatively long time periods; inventories require separate disclosure because of their materiality and importance. There is a presumption that short-term prepayments will be consumed within one year or within the business enterprise's next operating cycle, and for this reason are included among current assets in the balance sheet.

Inventories and financial reporting standards

The objectives of reporting inventories in the balance sheet are to reveal the type, the relative liquidity, and the basis of valuation of the inventories. In reporting the investment in inventories, as in reporting other assets, accountants are concerned with disclosing all significant information; they are particularly concerned that the investment in inventories has been determined on a basis consistent with that of preceding years. If a change is made in the method of calculating inventory cost, the change should be explained fully as to its effect on the current and prior year's financial statements. The accounting problems of reporting changes in inventory valuation methods are illustrated in Chapter 22.

When a valuation account is used as a means of valuing the inventory at the lower of cost or market or on the last-in, first-out basis, this account is subtracted from inventory cost for presentation in the balance sheet.

Financial accounting standards require that the various categories of inventories be indicated under the general caption "Inventories," and that the basis of valuation and the method of determining costs be disclosed. The FASB also requires disclosure of current cost of inventories by large publicly owned corporations.

Goods on order and advance payments to suppliers are not considered a part of the inventories, unless title to the goods has passed to the purchaser in accordance with the legal tests described in Chapter 8. Inventories which have been pledged as collateral for loans are included in the Inventories section rather than being offset against the loans secured by the inventories. Such financing agreements also are described in notes to the financial statements. Firm purchase commitments also are disclosed in a note to the financial statements.

Most business enterprises report inventories in a single amount, accompanied by an explanatory note. An example from an annual report of a publicly owned company follows:

Inventories in the balance sheet

	Year 10	Year 9
Inventories **(Note 3)**	$75,863,808	$79,407,280

Note 3—*Inventories are valued at the balance sheet dates as follows:*

	Year 10	Year 9
Logs, pulpwood, clips, and sawdust	$14,808,908	$10,337,848
Lumber and other manufactured wood products	9,092,589	9,759,782
Pulp, paper, and converted paper products	33,522,887	41,204,047
Material and supplies	18,439,424	18,105,603
Totals	$75,863,808	$79,407,280
Valued at lower of cost or market:		
First-in, first-out basis	$ 9,525,121	$ 9,423,818
Last-in, first-out basis	17,128,752	16,049,015
Average-cost basis	49,209,935	53,934,447
Totals	$75,863,808	$79,407,280

If the last-in, first-out inventory had been priced at current cost, the values would have been $11,404,000 higher on December 31, Year 10, and $12,637,000 higher on December 31, Year 9. There was no significant liquidation of prior years' lifo layers of inventory during Year 10 or Year 9.

The above inventory balances were used to calculate cost of goods sold. The beginning inventories for Year 9 were $52,484,190.

REVIEW QUESTIONS

1 For what purposes may the **retail method** of inventory valuation be used?

2 Distinguish between **(a) markup** and **additional markup, (b) markup cancellation** and **markdown,** and **(c) markdown cancellation** and **additional markup.**

3 Describe the computation of the cost percentage when inventory is determined at average cost by the retail method.

4 Describe the computation of the cost percentage when inventory is determined at the lower of average cost or market by the retail method.

5 What is the basic assumption as to the composition of the ending inventory when the retail method is applied on the basis of average cost or on the basis of the lower of average cost or market?

6 Describe the application of the retail method when cost is determined on a last-in, first-out basis.

7 Describe the special procedure required to estimate inventory on the **retail lifo** basis after retail prices have increased.

8 List three uses that may be made of the **gross profit method.**

9 **(a)** Distinguish between gross profit as a percentage of net sales and as a percentage of cost. **(b)** Convert the following gross profit percentages based on net sales to gross profit percentages based on cost: $16\frac{2}{3}$%, 25%, and 50%. **(c)** Convert the following gross profit percentages based on cost to gross profit percentages based on net sales: 25%, 50%, and 150%.

10 Explain the possible limitations of the use of an average-cost percentage for prior years to estimate inventories by the gross profit method.

11 There are two accepted procedures of accounting for operations involving long-term construction contracts. What are the two methods? What criteria are used in choosing between the methods? How can you justify a departure from the accepted practice of recognizing revenue only at the time of sale?

12 When a business enterprise adopts the percentage-of-completion method of accounting for long-term construction contracts, there are two generally used methods of estimating the portion completed. What are these two methods, and under what circumstances might each be used?

13 During the early stages of a construction project, some material costs and subcontract costs generally are not included in the total cost incurred for the computation of the percentage of completion. Why are these costs generally not included?

14 Under the percentage-of-completion method of accounting for long-term construction contracts, anticipated profits are recognized as the construction progresses, but anticipated losses are recognized as soon as they reasonably can be ascertained. Why does this inconsistency exist?

15 In view of the variety of procedures available for valuing inventories and the diverse results that are produced by the various methods, how can users of financial statements be assured that comparability exists between financial statements of the same business enterprise over a period of years?

16 What objections can you give to the use of the term **prepaid expenses?** Can you suggest a better term?

17 What objectives do accountants seek to achieve in reporting inventories in the balance sheet?

EXERCISES

Ex. 9-1   Cramer Company uses the gross profit method to estimate monthly inventories. In recent months gross profit has averaged 30% of net sales. The following data are available for the month of January:

Inventories, Jan. 1	$ 26,580
Purchases	120,000
Purchases returns	5,000
Freight-in	6,000
Gross sales	169,000
Sales returns and allowances	10,000

Compute the estimated cost of the inventories on January 31 by the gross profit method.

Ex. 9-2   You computed the cost of your inventory at the close of business on July 20, Year 2, at $20,500. Your fiscal year ends on June 30; therefore you find it necessary to establish an inventory amount on June 30, Year 2. You find that during the period July 1–20 sales were $70,500; sales returns, $1,800; gross purchases, $65,000; purchases returns, $1,200; freight-in, $600.

Compute the estimated cost of the inventory on June 30, Year 2, assuming that goods are sold at prices 25% above cost.

Ex. 9-3   The following information is taken from the accounting records of Bradshaw Company for the current year:

	Cost	Retail
Beginning inventory	$ 25,000	$ 46,200
Purchases (net)	120,000	191,800
Net markups		12,000
Sales (net)		180,000
Net markdowns		3,800

You are to assume that all net markups and net markdowns apply to purchases of the current year, and that it is appropriate to treat the entire inventory as a single department, with no markdowns having occurred during the prior year.

Compute the ending inventory at lower of average cost or market by the retail method.

Ex. 9-4   Using the information given in **Ex. 9-3** for Bradshaw Company, compute the ending inventory by the retail lifo method.

Ex. 9-5   Assuming that sales for Bradshaw Company in the current year were $223,100 instead of $180,000, and that all other facts are identical to those given in **Ex. 9-3,** compute the ending inventory by the retail lifo method.

Ex. 9-6   During the current year the index of selling prices for merchandise handled by Stever Company increased from 90 to 108. From the information on page 382, compute the ending inventory at estimated lifo cost, taking into account the increase in selling prices.

	Cost	Selling price	Cost percentage
Beginning inventory (date lifo was adopted)	$ 40,000	$ 50,000	80%
Purchases	150,000	200,000	75%
Goods available for sale	$190,000	$250,000	
Less: Net sales		178,000	
Ending inventory		$ 72,000	

Ex. 9-7 In Year 1, Tandem Corporation began construction work under a long-term contract. The contract price is $800,000, and the construction is expected to be completed in three years. Tandem uses the percentage-of-completion method for financial accounting purposes. The revenue to be recognized each year is based on the proportion of costs incurred to total estimated costs for completing the contract. The information relating to this contract in the financial statements for the year ended December 31, Year 1, follows:

Balance sheet:
Accounts receivable—construction contract billings $18,000
Construction in progress $200,000
Less: Partial billings on contract 188,000
Costs and profit on uncompleted contract in excess of billings . . . 12,000
Income statement:
Gross profit on long-term construction contract $20,000

a Compute the amount of cash collected on this contract in Year 1.
b Compute the total estimated gross profit on this contract.

Ex. 9-8 Mae Construction Company began operations in Year 3. By year-end, the first project was finished and a second project was partially completed. Information for Year 3 follows:

	Project No. 1	Project No. 2
Costs incurred to date	$ 80,000	$105,000
Portion of estimated total costs incurred to date	100%	60%
Total contract price	$100,000	$200,000
Billings on contracts	$100,000	$115,000
Collections from customers	$ 92,000	$ 75,000

Prepare journal entries for Year 3 (excluding closing entries) to record the transactions relating to the two projects if (1) the completed-contract method of accounting for long-term construction contracts is used, and (2) the percentage-of-completion method of accounting for long-term construction contracts is used.

Ex. 9-9 Refer to **Ex. 9-8.** Show how the account balances relating to long-term construction contracts appear in the balance sheet of Mae Construction Company at the end of Year 3 if (1) the completed-contract method of accounting is used, and (2) the percentage-of-completion method of accounting is used.

Ex. 9-10   In Year 1, Bold Construction Company contracted to construct a building for $400,000. The building was completed in Year 2. Bold uses the percentage-of-completion method of accounting for long-term construction contracts. Data relating to this contract are summarized below:

	Year 1	Year 2
Costs incurred	$ 90,000	$221,400
Estimated costs to complete contract	210,000	–0–
Partial billings	100,000	300,000
Cash collections	80,000	295,000

Prepare journal entries for Year 1 and Year 2 relating to this contract. Journal entries to close nominal accounts are not required.

Ex. 9-11   The following data are available for the month of May for Frank's Store:

	Cost	Retail
Inventory, May 1	$107,600	$160,000
Purchases	346,400	447,200
Purchases returns	6,000	7,200
Sales (net of returns and allowances)		488,000
Markdowns		42,000
Markups		58,000
Markdown cancellations		26,000
Markup cancellations		18,000

Compute the estimated inventory on May 31 at the lower of average cost or market by the retail method.

Ex. 9-12   On July 10, Year 10, a fire destroyed the goods in process inventory of Lowe Company. Inventories of material and finished goods were not damaged. Physical inventories taken after the fire are as follows:

Material	$ 65,000
Finished goods	120,000
Total	$185,000

Inventories on January 1, Year 10, are shown below:

Material	$ 45,000
Goods in process	80,000
Finished goods	150,000
Total	$275,000

The accounting records disclosed the following through July 10, Year 10:

Sales	$380,000
Purchases of material	117,500
Direct labor costs	92,000
Factory overhead costs	58,200

The gross profit in recent years has averaged $33\frac{1}{3}\%$ of cost of finished goods sold.

Compute the estimated cost of the goods in process inventory lost in the fire.

SHORT CASES FOR ANALYSIS AND DECISION

Case 9-1   West Department Store uses the conventional retail method as a means of controlling the investment in inventories at its branch stores. The central accounting office summarizes the recorded activity at each branch and estimates the ending inventories monthly. The estimate is then compared with a normal inventory investment based on expected volume. Store managers are required to explain deviations of 5% or more from the expected normal inventory. The following data have been accumulated for the Avalon Branch on April 30, Year 5:

	Cost	Retail
Net sales		$630,000
Beginning inventory	$150,000	222,000
Net purchases	560,000	823,000
Net markups		20,000
Net markdowns		10,000
Estimated shrinkage		5,000

Instructions
a The normal inventory of the Avalon Branch is $220,000 at cost. Compute the amount of the ending inventory at retail and at cost, and indicate the nature of the explanation to be made by the store manager.
b What effect, if any, would the following factors have on the effectiveness of the retail method as a control device?
   (1) A widely fluctuating shrinkage factor
   (2) A shift in the volume of goods handled at various markups
   (3) Additional markups related to goods sold by the end of the accounting period
   (4) Markdowns included as markup cancellations
   (5) Additional markups included as markdown cancellations

Case 9-2   Edgemar Company has used the gross profit method for estimating the investment in inventories and as a check on the physical inventory at the end of each year. The company has two lines of merchandise which have produced gross profit margins of 25 and 35%, respectively, on selling price over the past several years. The gross profit margin for the company as a whole has averaged 30% of sales.
   The operation data for the current year are as follows:

	Economy line	Quality line	Total
Sales	$100,000	$200,000	$300,000
Beginning inventories.	10,000	25,000	35,000
Purchases.	80,000	130,000	210,000
Gross profit margins on selling price.	25%	35%	30%

A physical inventory of the merchandise totaled $40,000, but the estimate by the gross profit method indicates ending inventory should be $35,000. The manager is of the opinion that the discrepancy is too large to accept without explanation. A test sample is selected and reveals that the gross profit margins on the two lines are unchanged at 25 and 35%.

Instructions
a Show how the manager computed the ending inventory by the gross profit method.

b Compute the ending inventory by the gross profit method in the manner in which it should be used in this situation.

c Explain to the manager why the difference exists between the physical inventory and the estimate of the inventory value under the gross profit method.

Case 9-3 ABA Construction Company has three long-term construction contracts in progress on December 31, Year 1, the data for which are presented below:

Contract No.	Contract price	Estimated total costs	Costs incurred to date (all in current year)	Billings to date	Cash collections to date
1	$ 750,000	$ 600,000	$400,000	$450,000	$405,000
2	1,000,000	1,050,000	525,000	400,000	380,000
3	900,000	675,000	202,500	225,000	202,500

Instructions

a Prepare partial income statements and balance sheets for ABA Construction Company reporting the details of the above contracts under (1) the completed-contract method, and (2) the percentage-of-completion method. Use adjacent columns for (1) and (2). Show total construction revenue and applicable costs in the partial income statement.

b What are the differences between the two sets of financial statements?

c Which set of financial statements do you think presents the more meaningful data about the long-term construction contracts of ABA Construction Company?

Case 9-4 In accounting for long-term construction contracts (those taking longer than one year to complete), the two methods commonly followed are the percentage-of-completion method and the completed-contract method.

Instructions

a Discuss how earnings on long-term construction contracts are recognized and computed under these two methods.

b Under what circumstances is it preferable to use one method instead of the other?

c Why is earnings recognition as measured by interim billings not generally accepted for long-term construction contracts?

d How are job costs and interim billings reported in the balance sheet under the percentage-of-completion method and under the completed-contract method?

PROBLEMS

9-1 Doder Construction Company began operations on March 1, Year 2. During Year 2, Doder entered into a contract with Kral Emblem Corporation to construct a factory. At that time, Doder estimated that it would take four years to complete the factory at a total cost of $4,800,000. The contract price for the construction of the factory was $6,000,000. During Year 2, Doder incurred $1,250,000 in construction costs related to this project, and Kral was billed and paid 30% of the contract price. The remaining costs to complete the contract are estimated at $3,750,000 on December 31, Year 2.

Instructions Prepare working papers to compute (1) the amount of gross profit realized for the year ended December 31, Year 2, and (2) the amount to be shown as "costs of uncompleted contract in excess of related billings" or "billings on uncompleted contract in excess of related costs" on December 31, Year 2, under each of the following accounting methods:

a Completed-contract method
b Percentage-of-completion method

9-2 (This problem consists of two independent parts)

a Valley Store uses the retail method to estimate its inventory. Information relating to the computation of the Inventory on December 31, Year 1, is as follows:

	Cost	Retail
Inventory, Jan. 1, Year 1	$ 55,000	$ 90,000
Sales		620,000
Purchases	355,000	580,000
Freight-in	7,600	
Markups		60,000
Markup cancellations		10,000
Markdowns		25,000
Markdown cancellations		5,000

Estimated normal shrinkage is 2% of sales.

Instructions Compute the estimated cost of the inventory on December 31, Year 1, at the lower of average cost or market. Use the retail method and show supporting computations.

b On June 28, Year 1, a fire at Lum Company's warehouse caused severe damage to its inventory. Lum estimates that the value of the inventory after the fire is $25,000, and that its gross profit rate is 30% of net sales. The following information was available from Lum's accounting records:

Inventory, June 1, Year 1	$250,000
Purchases from June 1, Year 1, to date of fire	350,000
Net sales from June 1, Year 1, to date of fire	550,000

Instructions Compute the estimated cost of the inventory lost in the fire. Use the gross profit method and show supporting computations.

9-3 Information relating to the operations of the sportswear department of Dry Goods, Inc., for the year ended December 31, Year 10, is presented below:

	Cost	Retail
Beginning inventory	$ 49,600	$ 83,600
Purchases	257,800	406,900
Freight-in	10,400	
Purchases returns	4,200	7,000
Additional markups		15,000
Markup cancellations		8,500
Markdowns		8,000
Markdown cancellations		1,600
Gross sales		396,500
Sales returns		6,700
Estimated shrinkage from theft and spoilage		3,200

Instructions

a Compute the ending inventory at the lower of average cost or market by the retail method.

b Compute the ending inventory by the retail lifo method.

9-4 Tampa Bay Company uses the retail inventory method to estimate ending inventories for its monthly financial statements. The following data pertain to a single department for the month of May:

Inventory, May 1:	
At cost	$ 19,000
At retail	30,000
Purchases (exclusive of freight and returns):	
At cost	83,558
At retail	146,495
Freight-in	5,100
Purchases returns:	
At cost	2,100
At retail	2,800
Additional markups	2,500
Markup cancellations	265
Net markdowns	800
Normal spoilage and breakage (at retail)	2,930
Sales (net of sales returns)	138,200

Instructions

a Using the conventional retail method, prepare a working paper to compute estimated lower-of-cost-or-market inventory on May 31.

b A department store which uses the conventional retail inventory method estimates the cost of its ending inventory at $30,600. A physical inventory reveals only $26,000 of inventory at lower of cost or market. List the factors that may have caused the difference between the computed inventory and the physical inventory.

9-5 This problem consists of two independent parts, one for Earnst Company and one for Peet Company.

Earnst Company uses the retail lifo method. Information relating to the computation of the inventory on December 31, Year 5, follows:

	Cost	Retail
Inventory, Jan. 1, Year 5	$ 30,200	$ 45,000
Purchases	120,000	172,000
Freight-in	22,000	
Net sales		190,000
Net markups		40,000
Net markdowns		12,000

Peet Company prepares quarterly financial statements and estimates inventory at the end of each quarter by the gross profit method, because the relationship of selling prices and costs remains relatively stable during the year. The inventory on December 31 is determined by a physical count. The data on page 388 for the first three quarters of the year ended December 31, Year 5, were taken from the accounting records.

	Mar. 31	June 30	Sept. 30
Sales	$993,600	$963,000	$808,500
Sales returns	13,000	20,000	8,000
Sales discounts	600	3,000	500
Purchases	745,000	735,000	665,000
Freight-in.	9,500	9,100	8,210
Purchases returns and allowances	500	2,400	4,630
Operating expenses	102,000	103,000	94,400

The physical inventory for Peet Company on December 31, Year 4, was $105,000.

Instructions

a Assuming that there was no change in the price index during the year, compute the inventory on December 31, Year 5, for Earnst Company by the retail lifo method.

b Assuming that the gross profit rate for the prior fiscal year was 20% of net sales and that this rate is expected to prevail throughout the current year, prepare quarterly income statements for Peet Company for the first three quarters of Year 5. Income taxes expense is estimated at 40% of pre-tax income.

9-6   Industrial Products Corporation is a small manufacturing company producing a highly flammable fluid. On March 31, Year 6, the company had a fire which completely destroyed the factory building and the inventory of goods in process; some of the equipment was saved.

After the fire a physical inventory was taken. The material was valued at $37,500 and the finished goods at $62,000.

The inventories on January 1, Year 6, consisted of:

Material	$ 15,500
Goods in process	60,500
Finished goods	85,000
Total	$161,000

A review of the accounting records disclosed that the sales and gross profit on sales for the last three years were:

	Sales	Gross profit on sales
Year 3	$400,000	$120,000
Year 4	380,000	110,500
Year 5	250,000	88,800

The sales for the first three months of Year 6 were $150,000. Material purchases were $62,500, transportation-in on purchases was $5,000, and direct labor cost for the three months was $50,000. For the past two years factory overhead cost has been 80% of direct labor cost.

Instructions   Compute the cost of inventory of goods in process lost, using the weighted-average gross profit for the last three years.

9-7   This problem consists of three unrelated parts, each for a different company.

Axel Company lost all its inventory by fire on January 1, Year 10. A physical inventory was not taken on December 31, Year 9. The following data are available for the three preceding years:

	Year 9	Year 8	Year 7
Inventory, Jan. 1	$170,160	$168,000	$161,600
Sales	812,000	788,000	724,000
Sales returns	12,000	8,000	12,000
Purchases	720,000	656,000	644,000
Purchases returns	40,000	32,000	36,000
Operating expenses	240,000	221,000	198,000
Accounts receivable, Dec. 31.	60,000	50,000	55,000
Accounts payable, Dec. 31	40,000	35,000	28,000

Bela Company uses the retail method to value its merchandise inventory. The following information is available for Bela Company for Year 10:

	Cost	Retail
Beginning inventory	$ 40,500	$ 65,000
Purchases (net of returns)	290,000	405,000
Freight-in	2,000	
Net markups		5,000
Net markdowns		9,000
Employee discounts		1,000
Net sales		410,000

Carr Company is in the construction business. A long-term contract was entered into in Year 10. The contract price was $700,000, and the company expected to earn a gross profit of $80,000 on the contract. The following information is available through the end of Year 12:

Year ended Dec. 31,	Cumulative costs incurred to date	Estimated costs to complete contract
Year 10	$ 49,600	$570,400
Year 11	172,800	467,200
Year 12	504,000	126,000

Instructions
a Assuming that the gross profit percentage for Year 9 was estimated to be the same as the weighted-average gross profit percentage for the two previous years, compute the estimated cost of Axel Company's inventory destroyed by fire on January 1, Year 10.

b Compute the estimated inventory by the retail method on December 31, Year 10, for Bela Company on the basis of lower of average cost or market.

c Compute the gross profit realized by Carr Company in each year (Years 10–12) under the percentage-of-completion method.

9-8 On January 1, Purdue Company installed the retail method of accounting for its merchandise inventory.

When you undertook the preparation of Purdue Company's interim report of earnings on June 30, Year 2, the data on page 390 were available.

	Cost	Retail
Inventory, Jan. 1	$ 76,200	$120,000
Markdowns		31,500
Additional markups		58,500
Markdown cancellations		19,500
Markup cancellations		13,500
Purchases	265,860	335,400
Sales		366,000
Purchases returns and allowances	4,500	5,400
Sales returns and allowances		18,000

Instructions

a Prepare a working paper to compute Purdue Company's June 30, Year 2, inventory under the retail method of accounting. The inventory is to be valued at lifo cost. Assume that net markups and markdowns apply to purchases.

b Without prejudice to your solution to part *a,* assume that you computed the June 30, Year 2, inventory to be $132,300 at retail and the ratio of cost to retail to be 75%. The general price level has increased from 100 on January 1 to 105 on June 30. Prepare a working paper to compute the June 30 inventory at the June 30 price level, using the dollar-value retail lifo method. Round amounts to nearest dollar and percentage.

9-9 On April 15, Year 5, a fire damaged the office and warehouse of Modern Wall Paper Company. The only accounting record saved was the general ledger, from which the following trial balance was prepared:

MODERN WALL PAPER COMPANY
Trial Balance
March 31, Year 5

	Debit	Credit
Cash	$ 23,800	
Accounts receivable	27,000	
Inventory, Dec. 31, Year 4	36,000	
Land	24,000	
Building and equipment	120,000	
Accumulated depreciation		$ 46,000
Other assets	3,600	
Accounts payable		23,700
Accrued liabilities		7,200
Capital stock, $2.50 par		100,000
Retained earnings		47,700
Sales		135,400
Purchases	103,000	
Operating expenses	22,600	
Totals	$360,000	$360,000

The following information has been gathered:

(1) The fiscal year of the company ends on December 31.
(2) An examination of the April bank statement and paid checks disclosed that checks written during the period April 1 to 15 totaled $11,600: $5,700 paid on accounts payable as of March 31, $2,000 for April purchases, and $3,900 for operating expenses. Deposits during the same period amounted to $10,650, all of which consisted of receipts on account from customers, with the exception of a $450 refund from a vendor for goods returned in April.
(3) Correspondence with suppliers disclosed unrecorded obligations on April 15 of $3,500 for April purchases, including $1,300 for shipments in transit on that date.
(4) Customers acknowledged indebtedness of $26,400 as of April 15. It also was estimated that customers owed another $5,000 which will never be acknowledged or recovered. Of the acknowledged indebtedness, $600 probably will be uncollectible. All sales were on credit.
(5) Assume that the weighted-average gross profit percentage for the past two years was in effect during the current year. The company's audited financial statements disclosed the following:

	Year ended	
	Dec. 31, Year 4	Dec. 31, Year 3
Net sales	$400,000	$300,000
Net purchases	226,000	174,000
Beginning inventory	45,000	35,000
Ending inventory	36,000	45,000

(6) Inventory with a cost of $8,250 was salvaged and sold for $4,500. The balance of the inventory was lost.

Instructions Prepare a working paper to compute the amount of the inventory fire loss, including a supporting computation of the cost of goods sold percentage.

9-10 Ecology Construction Company was incorporated in Year 4. The company constructs water treatment plants for small communities. All its long-term contracts are accounted for by the percentage-of-completion method, except for two contracts which are accounted for by the completed-contract method because of a lack of dependable cost estimates at the time of entering into these contracts.

The following information is available for the year ended December 31, Year 5:

Long-Term Contracts: Percentage-of-Completion Method

Long-term contracts accounted for by the percentage-of-completion method totaled $6,050,000. Costs incurred on these contracts were $1,500,000 in Year 4 and $3,000,000 in Year 5. On December 31, Year 5, it is estimated that additional costs of $1,000,000 are required to complete these contracts. Revenue of $1,750,-000 was recognized in Year 4, and a total of $4,800,000 has been billed, of which $4,600,000 has been collected. No long-term contracts accounted for by the percentage-of-completion method were completed in Year 5.

Long-Term Contracts: Completed-Contract Method

The two long-term contracts accounted for by the completed-contract method were started in Year 4. One is a $5,000,000 contract. Costs incurred were $1,400,000 in Year 4 and $1,600,000 in Year 5. A total of $3,100,000 has been billed, and $2,800,000 collected. Although it is difficult to estimate the additional costs required to complete this contract, indications are that this contract will be profitable.

The second contract is for $4,000,000. Costs incurred were $1,200,000 in Year 4 and $2,600,000 in Year 5. A total of $3,300,000 has been billed, and $2,900,000 collected. Although it is difficult to estimate the additional costs required to complete this contract, indications are that there will be a loss of $100,000.

Other information

Selling and administrative expenses, exclusive of amounts specified earlier, were $200,000 in Year 5. Other revenue, exclusive of amounts specified earlier, was $42,500 in Year 5.

Instructions Prepare an income statement for Ecology Construction Company for the year ended December 31, Year 5, stopping at income (or loss) before income taxes. Show supporting computations. Ignore income tax and deferred tax considerations. Notes to the income statement are not required.

9-11 On-Time Construction Company began business on January 5, Year 10. Construction activities for Year 10 are summarized below.

Project	Total contract price	Contract costs to Dec. 31, Year 10	Estimated additional costs to complete contracts	Cash collections to Dec. 31, Year 10	Billings to Dec. 31, Year 10
100	$ 310,000	$187,500	$ 12,500	$155,000	$160,000
101	415,000	195,000	248,000	210,000	249,000
102	350,000	320,000	–0–	300,000	350,000
103	300,000	16,500	183,500	–0–	10,000
Totals	$1,375,000	$719,000	$444,000	$665,000	$769,000

The president of On-Time has asked you to compute the amounts of revenue for the year ended December 31, Year 10, that would be reported under the completed-contract method and under the percentage-of-completion method of accounting for long-term construction contracts.

The following information is available:

(1) All contracts are with different customers.
(2) Any work remaining to be done on the contracts is expected to be completed in Year 11.
(3) The company's accounting records have been maintained by the completed-contract method.

Instructions

a Prepare a working paper to compute the amount of gross profit realized by project for the year ended December 31, Year 10, under:
  (1) The completed-contract method
  (2) The percentage-of-completion method
b Prepare a working paper under the completed-contract method to compute the amounts that would appear in the company's balance sheet on December 31, Year 10, for:
  (1) Costs in excess of billings
  (2) Billings in excess of costs
c Prepare a working paper under the percentage-of-completion method to compute the amounts that would appear in the company's balance sheet on December 31, Year 10, for:
  (1) Costs and profits in excess of billings
  (2) Billings in excess of costs and profits

9-12 General Dredging Corporation undertakes long-term construction projects. General began operations on October 15, Year 1, with contract No. 1 as its only job during Year 1. A trial balance of the company's general ledger on December 31, Year 2, follows:

GENERAL DREDGING CORPORATION
Trial Balance
December 31, Year 2

	Debit	Credit
Cash on hand and in banks	$ 23,300	
Accounts receivable	136,480	
Construction in progress (inventory)	469,120*	
Plant assets	135,500	
Accumulated depreciation		$ 13,880
Accounts payable		70,820
Deferred income taxes payable		2,400
Partial billings on contracts		459,400
Capital stock, $5 par		235,000
Retained earnings		3,500
Operating expenses	20,600	
Totals	$785,000	$785,000

*Includes $8,000 gross profit recognized on contract No. 1 in Year 1.

The following additional information is available:

(1) The company determines income on the completed-contract basis for income tax purposes and on the percentage-of-completion basis for financial accounting purposes.

(2) During Year 2, there were three contracts in progress, the contract prices of which had been computed as follows:

	Contract No. 1	Contract No. 2	Contract No. 3
Labor and material costs . .	$169,000	$34,500	$265,700
Indirect costs.	30,000	5,500	48,000
Total costs	$199,000	$40,000	$313,700
Add: Gross profit	40,000	3,000	30,300
Total contract price. . . .	$239,000	$43,000	$344,000

During the year, billings are credited to Partial Billings on Contracts; at year-end this account is debited for the amount of revenue applicable to contracts completed during the year. Construction revenue is recorded at year-end by offsetting debits to the Construction in Progress and Construction Costs Applicable to Realized Revenue accounts.

(3) All contract costs are debited to Construction in Progress. Cost estimates, which are derived by engineers, are considered reliable. Data on costs to December 31, Year 2, are given at the top of page 394.

Contract	Original estimate	Cost incurred to date		
		Total	Labor and material costs	Indirect costs
No. 1	$199,000	$115,420	$ 92,620	$22,800
No. 2	40,000	32,000	26,950	5,050
No. 3	313,700	313,700	265,700	48,000
Totals	$552,700	$461,120	$385,270	$75,850

(4) On December 31, Year 1, accumulated costs on contract No. 1 were $39,800, or 20% of the total; no costs had been accumulated on contracts No. 2 and No. 3. All work on contract No. 3 was completed prior to December 31, Year 2, and the full contract price has been billed to the customer.

(5) Assume that the company is subject to an income tax rate of 30%.

Instructions

a Prepare a working paper to compute the percentage of completion of contracts on December 31, Year 2.

b Prepare a working paper to compute construction revenue, related costs, and gross profit to be recognized in Year 2.

c Prepare a working paper to compute estimated income taxes expense and income tax liabilities (including deferred income taxes) on December 31, Year 2.

d Prepare journal entries on December 31, Year 2, to record (1) construction revenue, applicable costs, and realized profit for Year 2; (2) income taxes for Year 2; and (3) approval of contract No. 3 by the customer.

10 CURRENT LIABILITIES AND CONTINGENCIES

A *liability* is an obligation, based on a past transaction, to convey assets or perform services in the future. Liabilities are recorded when obligations are incurred, and are measured at the amounts to be paid or at the present value of these amounts. The distinction between current liabilities and long-term liabilities is important in an evaluation of the financial position of a business enterprise and in forecasting its ability to meet maturing obligations. Some liabilities are definitely determinable, both as to existence and as to amount; other liabilities definitely exist, but the amount of the liability must be estimated. Finally, some contingent obligations may or may not be subject to accrual. Current liabilities and contingencies are discussed in this chapter; long-term liabilities are discussed in subsequent chapters.

The distinction between current liabilities and long-term liabilities

Traditionally, one year marked the accounting boundary between current liabilities and long-term liabilities. The maturity-within-a-year rule was simple and easy to follow, but arbitrary. When strictly applied it sometimes caused a misleading financial picture, particularly when the operating cycle of a business enterprise exceeded one year.

The modern viewpoint is that current liabilities include: (1) all obligations for which payment will require the use of existing current assets or the creation of other current liabilities, and (2) all other obligations that are expected to be paid from current assets within one year. The definition of current liabilities logically is correlated with the definition of current assets. Thus, current liabilities include obligations for items which have entered into the operating cycle, such as payables to suppliers and employees, cash collections received in advance of the delivery of merchandise or performance of services, and accruals for rents, taxes, product warranties, etc. Obligations incurred outside of the operating cycle and not payable within one year are considered long-term liabilities; obligations which will be liquidated by the issuance of additional shares of capital stock are not liabilities and should be included in stockholders' equity.

The importance of current liabilities

Short-term credit is an important source of financing for most business enterprises. In part, its use is involuntary; current obligations such as accounts payable and other accrued liabilities regularly arise from business operations. An important element, however, results from a conscious decision by management to obtain credit from suppliers and to borrow from banks and others to meet cash needs during periods of expanding or peak business activity.

Financial analysts keep a close watch on the amount of current liabilities, the relationship of current assets to current liabilities, and the relationship between cash balances and current liabilities. These relationships are considered by many analysts to be important indicators of financial stability and **solvency** — the ability to pay debts as they mature.

Valuation of current liabilities

A logical measure of any liability at the time it is incurred is the **present value** of the required future outlay of money.[1] In practice, however, current liabilities usually are carried in accounting records at face amount. The difference between the present value of a current liability and the amount that ultimately will be paid at maturity usually is not large because of the short time period involved. Thus, the slight overstatement of liabilities that results from the recording of current obligations at face amount often can be excused as a compromise of accuracy in favor of convenience.

When is a prospective future outlay a liability?

Every business enterprise faces the prospect of a wide variety of future cash outlays in order to continue in operation. An enterprise must, for example, buy material, pay wages, pay for services, replace equipment, and pay taxes. We might take an extreme view and consider the present value of all these future outlays as the total debt of the enterprise at any given time. This would correspond to the concept of assets as the present value of all future cash inflows. However, these theoretical extremes are beyond the accountants' powers of measurement; as a practical matter, we need a basis for establishing some limits on the liability concept.

---

[1] The present value of a liability is the sum of expected future payments discounted to the present date at an appropriate rate of interest. *APB Opinion No. 21* states that presentation of liabilities at their discounted present value is not required for "payables arising from transactions with customers or suppliers in the normal course of business which are due in customary trade terms not exceeding approximately one year." The Opinion also is not intended to apply to estimates of warranty obligations assumed in connection with sales of property, goods, or services.

A logical starting point is to say that the amounts of all legally enforceable debts should appear as liabilities in the balance sheet. But what about legal obligations that are highly uncertain in amount? Because liabilities must be measured, the ability to measure with reasonable accuracy is essential. Then we must consider whether a strict legal test excludes any obligations to convey assets that are significant in an economic sense. The process of measuring periodic income may require that a valuation be placed on highly uncertain future outlays that result from past transactions, because the cost incurred must be deducted from revenue.

These two elements, **measurability** and **relation to past events,** lead us to conclude that liabilities should be defined to include all future outlays that result from transactions or events of the past and that can be measured with reasonable accuracy. Because we are dealing with a **future** payment, the element of uncertainty plays an important role in the problem of accounting for current liabilities. To emphasize the importance of the degree of uncertainty, we shall discuss some of the specific problems relating to current liabilities under the following headings: (1) definitely determinable liabilities, (2) liabilities dependent on operating results, and (3) contingencies.

DEFINITELY DETERMINABLE LIABILITIES

Liabilities in this category are the result of contracts or the operation of legal statutes such that the amount of an obligation and its due date are known with reasonable certainty. The accounting problems are to ascertain that an obligation exists, to measure it as accurately as possible, and to record it in the accounting records.

Trade accounts payable

The accounting procedures for recording and controlling the payments for the purchase of merchandise and services generally are designed so that the existence, amount, and due date of such liabilities are readily determinable. Accountants give particular attention to transactions occurring near the end of one accounting period and at the beginning of the next accounting period to see that the recording of merchandise and services received is consistent with that of the liability. For example, if merchandise is received near the end of the accounting period but an invoice has not arrived, the merchandise may have been counted as part of the ending inventories, but the recording of the liability may have been overlooked.

As stated in Chapter 8, Accounts Payable may be recorded net of purchases discounts and only Purchases Discounts Lost recorded in the accounting records.

Loan obligations and refinancing

In this category are included short-term promissory notes (including **commercial paper**[2]) issued as evidence of borrowing transactions, and any portion of long-term indebtedness that matures currently. If long-term debt currently maturing will be retired from sinking funds, from the proceeds of new long-term indebtedness, or through conversion to common stock, current funds are not required, and the debt is reported as noncurrent, accompanied by a note disclosing the plan for its liquidation.

When a business enterprise expects to **refinance** short-term debt on a long-term basis, a question arises as to the proper classification of such a debt. The FASB has taken the position that a short-term debt must be classified as a current liability unless the enterprise **intends to refinance the debt on a long-term basis** and can demonstrate its **ability to carry out the refinancing.**[3]

Refinancing means replacing short-term debt with either long-term debt or equity securities, or renewing, extending, or replacing the short-term debt with other short-term debt for an uninterrupted period extending beyond one year (or the operating cycle, if applicable) from the date of the balance sheet.[4] **Ability to refinance** on a long-term basis must be demonstrated either by (1) actually having issued long-term debt or equity securities to replace short-term debt after the date of the balance sheet but before it is issued, or by (2) having entered into a firm financing contract that will enable the debtor to refinance short-term debt when it becomes due.[5]

Accountants generally agree that cash earmarked for the retirement of a debt should be excluded from current assets if the debt to be liquidated is reported as a noncurrent liability. Following the issuance of **FASB Statement No. 6,** the FASB was asked to clarify whether a short-term debt should be excluded from current liabilities if it is repaid after the balance sheet date and is then replaced by long-term debt before the balance sheet is issued. Because the repayment of a short-term debt before funds are obtained through a long-term refinancing requires the use of current assets, the Board concluded that:[6]

---

[2] Commercial paper (as defined in Chapter 6) is the term used in the money market for short-term unsecured promissory notes issued by corporations and sold at a discount to investors, generally other companies.

[3] *FASB Statement No. 6,* "Classification of Short-Term Obligations Expected to Be Refinanced. . . ," FASB (Stamford: 1975), p. 4.

[4] Ibid., p. 1.

[5] Ibid., pp. 4–5.

[6] *FASB Interpretation No. 8,* "Classification of a Short-Term Obligation Repaid Prior to Being Replaced by a Long-Term Security (an Interpretation of *FASB Statement No. 6*)," FASB (Stamford: 1976), p. 2.

. . . if a short-term obligation is repaid after the balance sheet date and subsequently a long-term obligation or equity securities are issued whose proceeds are used to replenish current assets before the balance sheet is issued, the short-term obligation shall not be excluded from current liabilities at the balance sheet date.

Dividends payable

Cash dividends are declared by a corporation's board of directors. On the date of declaration, the corporation incurs a legal obligation to pay the amount of the dividend at the specified time, and stockholders gain creditor status to the extent of the declared amount. Because the time between declaration and payment is short, dividends payable in cash are a current liability. Dividends in arrears on cumulative preferred stock are disclosed by a note to the financial statements, because there is no legal obligation to pay dividends on preferred stock until they are declared. Undistributed **stock dividends** are not included among current liabilities, because no cash outlay will be required; the account Stock Dividends to Be Distributed is classified as part of stockholders' equity, preferably as an addition to the common stock outstanding.

Advances from customers

When customers make payment in advance of performance by sellers, a liability is created. The sellers are obligated to perform by delivery of merchandise or services, or to refund the advance if they fail to perform. Generally, the cost of performance will not be as large as the advance, because there is an element of unrealized profit in the price charged. The profit element emerges only with performance by sellers; prior to this time the sellers essentially are trustees of the funds received from customers. As performance is made under the terms of the contract, the amount of the liability diminishes and is transferred to a revenue account. The costs of performance are recorded as expenses, and income (or loss) emerges.

Advances from customers that are expected to be realized as revenue within a year or within the next operating cycle are classified as current liabilities. Examples include deposits on sales orders received, magazine subscriptions received in advance, and billings in excess of costs incurred on long-term construction contracts. Advances from customers that are not expected to be realized as revenue within one year or the operating cycle are classified as noncurrent liabilities. It may be argued that certain short-term unearned revenue, such as rents and interest received in advance, should be classified as noncurrent liabilities because the realization of such revenue is not expected to require current expenditures. Although this position has some merit, it has not been widely accepted, because the amounts involved generally are immaterial and because it may be difficult to estimate the expenditures to be incurred in the process of realizing short-term un-earned revenue items.

Deposits received from customers for containers normally are re-funded when the containers are returned (usually within a short period); therefore, such deposits are classified among current liabilities.

Accrued liabilities

The term **accrued liabilities** (sometimes referred to as **accrued expenses**) is used to designate obligations that come into existence as the result of past contractual commitments or as the result of tax legislation such as payroll, income, property, and sales tax laws. Because of their materiality, income tax liabilities are listed separately among the current liabilities. Most other accruals may be combined under one heading, or, as in the case of accrued interest on current debts, combined with the liability to which they relate. The problems involved in determining some types of accrued liabilities require special attention.

Liabilities relating to payrolls

The employer is by law a tax collector for the federal and state govern-ments with respect to taxes withheld from employees' earnings. An em-ployer may also withhold from salaries and wages amounts for such items as union dues, state disability insurance, group life insurance and pension plans, and for the purchase of savings bonds. Accountants should be familiar with the general terms of payroll tax legislation.

Social Security Taxes (FICA)   The Federal Insurance Contributions Act provides for old age and survivors' benefits for qualified employees and members of their families, and hospitalization insurance (Medicare) provides for medical costs. These payroll taxes usually are referred to as **social security taxes** and are levied against both the employer and the employee at the same rate, based on the employee's gross earnings. Both the rates and base earnings have been increased many times in recent years and are scheduled to change in the future. For purposes of discussion and problems in this chapter, we shall assume that a rate of 7% applies for both the employer and the employee on earnings up to $30,000. FICA taxes apply to employers of one or more persons, with certain exceptions.

Federal Unemployment Tax   The Federal Unemployment Tax Act (FUTA) provides for a system of unemployment insurance established in coop-eration with state governments. Employers of one or more persons, with certain exceptions similar to those under FICA legislation, are subject to the federal unemployment tax. In 1981, the tax applied to the first $6,000 of earnings paid to each employee during the calendar year. The federal tax is levied only on employers at a rate of 3.4%. However, a credit against the federal tax up to 2.7% of taxable earnings is allowed for contributions which an employer makes to a state plan. Thus, the effective federal unemployment tax is 0.7% of earnings up to $6,000 per employee. Employers are required to make quarterly deposits of taxes when the amount payable exceeds $100.

State Unemployment Tax The provisions of the various state laws governing unemployment compensation differ from the federal law, and differ among various states. Most state laws tax only employers, but a few apply taxes on employees as well. An important feature of all state unemployment tax laws is the merit rating provision, under which a reduction in the tax rate levied by the state is granted to employers whose unemployment experience is better than a specified standard. Thus, employers whose employee turnover rate is low may be entitled to a lower state tax rate. To make this type of incentive toward stable employment effective, the federal law provides that an employer who pays less than 2.7% to any state under a merit rating system is still entitled to the full 2.7% credit against the federal tax.

Income Taxes Withheld Employers of one or more persons are required to withhold from employees' earnings an amount approximating the federal income tax due on those earnings. A number of cities and states which levy income taxes also require that income taxes be withheld from employees' earnings. An employer is required to withhold income taxes only if the legal relationship of employer and employee exists; this excludes payments to persons who perform services as independent contractors. Certain other limited classes of wage payments are exempt from withholding.

The amount of income taxes withheld is determined by formula or may be obtained from tables prepared by the government; it varies according to the length of the pay period, the amount of taxable earnings, and the marital status and the number of dependents of the employee. The employer makes payment of income taxes withheld and FICA taxes at regular intervals.

Compensated Absences Vacation, holiday, and illness pay (referred to as *compensated absences*) are today a standard element of most employment contracts. The right to such pay usually depends upon the length of employment, and may increase after an employee completes a specified number of years of service.

When does the liability for compensated absences come into existence for accounting purposes? Does it arise only when employees have met all the conditions, or does it accrue through the employment period? For example, it seems clear that an employee who earns $400 a week and is entitled to a two-week vacation is paid $20,800 for 50 weeks of work, or

$416 a week. This reasoning suggests that the vacation pay accrues at the rate of $16 a week, or 4% of the weekly earnings, during the 50 weeks prior to the vacation. Whether a legal liability exists for the vacation pay depends on the terms of the employment contract. If the paid vacation is contingent on the employee remaining in service until the vacation period, the legal obligation does not arise until this condition has been met. However, an obligation exists that meets the tests of a liability, because the employer estimates the liability for vacation pay on the basis of employee turnover experience. Generally, the probability is high that a future outlay for vacation pay will be made, and the recording of a liability may be warranted.

Liabilities for employees' compensation for future absences are accrued if *all* of the following conditions are met:[7]

1   The employer's obligation to compensate employees for future absences is attributable to services already rendered by employees.
2   The obligation relates to rights that *vest* (are not contingent on an employee's future service) or *accumulate* (may be carried forward to one or more accounting periods subsequent to that in which earned).
3   Payment of the compensation is probable.
4   The amount can be reasonably estimated.

Inability to estimate a liability for compensated absences that meet the first three tests above must be disclosed in a note to the financial statements.

Recording Payroll Liabilites   The liability aspect of the problem of accounting for payroll centers on the amounts due employees, the liabilities associated with withholdings from employees' earnings, and the employer's share of payroll taxes and fringe benefits. There is also a cost side to the problem. The total costs incurred for employee services, including gross earnings, payroll taxes, and other fringe benefit costs, must be allocated to functions or departments to provide useful cost information for management.

To illustrate the recording of a payroll in the accounting records, we have assumed some payroll data for a merchandising enterprise for the month of May. Because this is the fifth month of the year, some employees will have received salaries in excess of the limits subject to payroll taxes, so that the amount subject to payroll taxes will be less than the total amount earned. We also have assumed that the enterprise is entitled to a merit rate of 2% on the state unemployment tax. A summary of total salaries earned and earnings subject to payroll taxes for the month of May are presented at the top of page 403.

---

[7] *FASB Statement No. 43,* "Accounting for Compensated Absences," FASB (Stamford: 1980), pp. 2–3.

Total salaries and earnings subject to payroll taxes

Classification of expense	Total salaries earned	Earnings subject to payroll taxes		
		FICA taxes, 7%	Federal un-employment tax, 0.7%	State un-employment tax, 2%
Sales salaries	$ 60,000	$50,000	$35,000	$42,000
Administrative salaries.	40,000	30,000	25,000	28,000
Total	$100,000	$80,000	$60,000	$70,000

The employer's total payroll costs, including fringe benefits, are summarized below:

Employer's total payroll costs

Payroll costs	Total	Sales Salaries	Adminis-trative salaries
Total salaries earned	$100,000	$60,000	$40,000
FICA taxes ($80,000 × 7%).	5,600	3,500	2,100
Federal unemployment tax ($60,000 × 0.7%) .	420	245	175
State unemployment tax ($70,000 × 2%) . . .	1,400	840	560
Vacation pay ($100,000 × 4%).	4,000	2,400	1,600
Total payroll costs.	$111,420	$66,985	$44,435

The amounts withheld from employees' salaries and the computation of employees' net take-home pay are summarized below:

Amounts withheld and employees' take-home pay

Total salaries earned		$100,000
Withholdings:		
FICA tax	$ 5,600	
Income taxes withheld.	13,200	
Hospital insurance premiums (private plans)	1,500	20,300
Employees' net take-home pay		$ 79,700

Assuming that payroll taxes are combined with gross salaries for accounting purposes, the summary journal entry at the top of page 404 would be prepared to record the payroll for the month of May.

Selling Expense—Salaries	66,985	
Administrative Expense—Salaries	44,435	
FICA Taxes Payable		11,200
Liability for Income Taxes Withheld		13,200
Hospital Insurance Premiums Payable		1,500
Federal Unemployment Tax Payable		420
State Unemployment Tax Payable		1,400
Vacation Pay Payable		4,000
Accrued Payroll		79,700
To record payroll for the month of May.		

Payroll taxes on employers become a legal liability when salaries and wages actually are paid, rather than at a time services are rendered by employees. For example, if salaries and wages accrued at year-end amount to $1,500, payroll taxes would not be levied on these earnings until the following year.

Property taxes

Property taxes, based on the assessed value of real and personal property, usually represent the primary source of revenue for local governmental units. From the viewpoint of the business enterprise owning property, property taxes are a part of the cost of the services of such property. Legally, property taxes arise as of a particular date, usually on the so-called *lien date,* the date established by law on which the taxes become a lien against the property.

The accounting issues relating to property taxes are: (1) When should the liability for property taxes be recorded? (2) To which period does the tax expense relate? The legal liability for property taxes arises on the lien date, and there is thus a clear basis for recognizing the liability at this time. Some accountants argue that the liability accrues throughout the tax year. Because property taxes are expenses associated with the right to use property during the fiscal year of the taxing authority, it seems reasonable to allocate the tax expense against revenue during this period.

The following illustration will help to clarify the issues. Assume that Lee Company has property subject to property taxes by city and county governmental units. The fiscal year of the city and county runs from July 1 to June 30. Property taxes of $36,000 were assessed on March 15, covering the fiscal year starting on July 1. The lien date is July 1, and taxes are payable in two installments of $18,000 each on December 10 and on April 10.

The accounting for property taxes for the period from July 1 to December 31 is shown on page 405 under two alternative methods. Under

Comparison of two methods for recording property taxes expense

Explanation	Liability recorded on lien date	Taxes accrued over fiscal year of taxing body
July 1. Liability for property taxes of $36,000 comes into existence on July 1, the lien date.	Deferred Property Taxes. . . . . 36,000 Property Taxes Payable . 36,000	No journal entry

At the end of July, August, September, October, and November. To record monthly property taxes expense, $3,000.	Property Taxes Expense. 3,000
	  Deferred Property Taxes . 3,000
		Property Taxes Expense. 3,000
		  Property Taxes Payable . 3,000

Dec. 10. Payment of first installment of property tax bill, $18,000.	Property Taxes Payable 18,000
	  Cash. 18,000
		Property Taxes Payable 15,000
		Prepaid Property Taxes 3,000
		  Cash. 18,000

Dec. 31. To record monthly property taxes expense.	Property Taxes Expenses 3,000
	  Deferred Property Taxes . 3,000
		Property Taxes Expense. 3,000
		  Prepaid Property Taxes . 3,000

the first method, the property taxes liability is recorded on the lien date (July 1), and the deferred property taxes (an asset) are amortized monthly throughout the following 12-month period; under the second method, property taxes are accrued monthly during the fiscal year of the taxing body.

Under the first method, deferred property taxes of $18,000 appear as a current asset in the December 31 balance sheet; this amount will be amortized at the rate of $3,000 per month during the first six months of the next calendar year. Under the second method, neither a prepayment nor a liability is reported in the balance sheet on December 31. Because the liability comes into existence on the lien date (July 1), the first method provides a more complete record of Lee Company's financial position. However, the AICPA has taken the position that monthly accrual in the taxpayer's accounting records during the fiscal period of the taxing body for which the taxes are levied generally is the most acceptable method.[8]

Losses on firm purchase commitments

To assure a steady supply of merchandise or material, a business enterprise may enter into contracts for the future delivery of such goods at a fixed price. It is assumed in this discussion that the contract is **not subject to cancellation,** regardless of changes in market price. If the current price of the goods falls below the contract price, the lower-of-cost-or-market rule should be applied to the commitment and the loss recognized in the accounting records. If material in amount, the loss is listed separately in the income statement.

The AICPA also concluded that if a loss is not sustained because of the price decline, the decline need not be recognized. "The utility of such commitments is not impaired, and hence there is no loss, when the amounts to be realized from the disposition of the future inventory items are adequately protected by firm sales contracts or when there are other circumstances which reasonably assure continuing sales without price decline."[9]

A sustained loss should be recognized in the accounting period during which the price decline occurred. The value of the goods to be purchased under the commitment has been reduced just as though these goods were included in inventories currently. The journal entries to record an assumed loss of $15,000 and the subsequent purchase at a fixed price of $100,000 are illustrated on page 407.

[8] *Accounting Research and Terminology Bulletins—Final Edition,* AICPA (New York: 1961). pp. 83–84.
[9] Ibid., p. 35.

<table>
<tr><td>Journal entries for
loss on purchase
commitment</td><td>

Year of price decline:

| Loss on Purchase Commitments Due to Price Decline..... | 15,000 | |
| Liability Arising from Purchase Commitments...... | | 15,000 |

To record loss due to decline in price of merchandise ordered.

Year of purchase:

Inventories (or Purchases)......................	85,000	
Liability Arising from Purchase Commitments..........	15,000	
Accounts Payable......................		100,000

To record purchase of merchandise under contract on which a
loss due to price decline was recognized in an earlier year.

</td></tr>
</table>

The liability recorded in the year of price decline is the estimated amount which the purchaser would be required to pay the seller if the purchaser canceled the contract. When the merchandise is purchased, this estimated liability is transferred to Accounts Payable. If the expectation is that the purchase will be made during the regular operating cycle of the business enterprise, the liability arising from the purchase commitment should be presented as a current liability in the balance sheet.

If contracts to purchase goods at fixed prices are subject to cancellation, no liability is recognized for declines in market prices, because such unfavorable contracts generally would be canceled.

LIABILITIES DEPENDENT ON OPERATING RESULTS

The amount of certain obligations cannot be measured until operating results are known. These include income taxes, bonuses, profit-sharing distributions, royalties, and contributions to employee retirement plans. There is no particular accounting problem in determining such liabilities at the end of a fiscal year, when the operating results are known. For *interim* reporting purposes, difficulties may arise in estimating such obligations in advance of the final determination of annual net income.

Income taxes

The most familiar example of a liability whose amount is dependent on operating results is income taxes. Individual proprietors and members of a partnership are subject to personal income taxes on their share of the net income of the business enterprise. Single proprietorships and partnerships are not taxable entitles, and therefore do not report income tax liabilities in their balance sheets.

Corporations, estates, and trusts are separate taxable entities and are subject to income taxes. Income tax liabilities, therefore, appear in the balance sheets of such entities. In most cases, corporations are required to make payments in advance of the estimated income tax liability. If payments of estimated taxes are not made when due, a penalty is assessed. The remaining tax not covered by the estimated payments is payable on March 15 of the year following the taxable calendar year. Calendar-year corporations may elect to pay the remaining tax in two equal installments (on March 15 and June 15). Frequent changes in tax rates, as well as rules regarding estimated tax payments, are made by Congress.

The estimated tax payments can be recorded in a Prepaid Income Taxes account or as debits to Income Taxes Payable if the accrued tax liability previously had been recorded. A credit balance in Income Taxes Payable is reported as a current liability.

Accounting for Income Taxes in Interim Periods   When interim financial reports are prepared, an estimate of accrued income tax liability must be made before the actual income tax liability for the year is known. If income taxes were assessed at a flat rate, it would be a relatively simple matter to compute the tax on the income to date. However, the progressive feature of the corporate income tax raises the question whether the income to date should be annualized and proportionate income tax accrued for the period to date, or whether the marginal approach should be used so that the first amount of income is taxed at lower rates.

A similar question arises in business enterprises having a seasonal income pattern. For example, high income experienced early in the year may be offset by losses during the latter part of the year. If we follow the marginal approach, the income tax liability (in terms of the actual amount which ultimately will be paid) will be overstated during the early part of the year and must be adjusted downward during the latter part of the year when losses are sustained.

The Accounting Principles Board provided the following answers to these questions:[10]

At the end of each interim period the company should make its best estimate of the effective tax rate expected to be applicable for the full fiscal year. The rate so determined should be used in providing for income taxes on a current year-to-date basis. The effective tax rate should reflect anticipated investment tax credits, foreign tax rates, percentage depletion, capital gains rates, and other available tax planning alternatives. However, in arriving at this effective tax rate no effect should be included for the tax related to significant unusual or extraordinary items that will be separately reported or reported net of their related tax effect in reports for the interim period or for the fiscal year.

The tax effects of losses that arise in the early portion of a fiscal year (in the event carryback of such losses is not possible) should be recognized only when realization is assured beyond any reasonable doubt. . . . An established seasonal pattern of loss in early interim periods offset by income in latter interim periods should constitute evidence that realization is assured

[10] *APB Opinion No. 28,* "Interim Financial Reporting," AICPA (New York: 1973), pp. 527–528.

beyond reasonable doubt, unless other evidence indicates the established seasonal pattern will not prevail. The tax effects of losses incurred in early interim periods may be recognized in a latter interim period of a fiscal year if their realization, although initially uncertain, later becomes assured beyond reasonable doubt. When the tax effects of losses that arise in the early portions of fiscal year are not recognized in that interim period, no tax provision should be made for income that arises in later interim periods until the tax effects of the previous interim losses are utilized. Changes resulting from new tax legislation should be reflected after the effective dates prescribed in the statutes.

Additional discussion of accounting for income taxes in interim periods appears in Chapter 21 and in **Modern Advanced Accounting** of this series.

Interperiod Allocation of Income Taxes As stated in Chapter 3, a problem arises in accounting for income tax obligations because of differences between *taxable income* and *pre-tax accounting income.* As a result of these differences, the amount of income tax liability incurred by a corporation in any given year may differ materially from the amount of income taxes expense reported in the income statement. Many corporations report Prepaid Income Taxes as an asset or Deferred Income Taxes Payable as a liability. These accounts may be current or noncurrent, depending on the reasons for the differences between taxable income and pre-tax accounting income. A complete coverage of this topic is presented in Chapter 21.

Bonus and profit-sharing plans

Contractual agreements covering rents, royalties, or employee compensation sometimes call for conditional payments in an amount dependent on revenue or income for an accounting period. We shall use the term *bonus* to describe conditional payments of this type.

Conditional expenses based on revenue cause little difficulty. For example, if a contract calls for a fixed rent of $500 per month and 1% of all sales over $100,000 per year, the fixed rent accrues at the rate of $500 per month, and when sales reach $100,000 each additional dollar of sales creates an additional rent obligation.

Some bonus plans provide for a bonus based on income. The plans generally are drawn so that the income amount to be used in determining the bonus is clearly defined. For example, the bonus may be based on:

1 Income before income taxes and bonus
2 Income after bonus but before income taxes
3 Net income

To illustrate the calculations involved, assume that Sullivan Company has a bonus plan under which a branch manager receives 20% of the income over $20,000 earned by the branch. Income for a given branch amounted to $80,000 before the bonus and income taxes. Assume for purposes of illustration that income taxes are 40% of pre-tax income.

The bonus under each of the three plans listed above is computed as follows:

Plan 1 Contract provides that bonus is to be computed on income in excess of $20,000 before deduction of income taxes and the bonus:

$$\text{Bonus} = 0.2(\$80,000 - \$20,000) = \underline{\$12,000}$$

Plan 2 Contract provides that the bonus is to be computed on income in excess of $20,000 after deduction of the bonus but before income taxes have been deducted:

$$B = \text{Bonus}$$
$$B = 0.2(\$80,000 - \$20,000 - B)$$
$$B = \$16,000 - \$4,000 - 0.2B$$
$$1.2B = \$12,000$$
$$B = \underline{\$10,000}$$

The computation of the bonus can be proved by taking 20% of the amount by which the income after the bonus exceeds $20,000. Thus, 20% of $50,000 ($80,000 − $10,000 − $20,000 = $50,000) equals the bonus of $10,000.

Plan 3 Contract provides that the bonus is to be computed on *net income* in excess of $20,000 after deduction of the bonus and income taxes:

$$B = \text{Bonus}$$
$$T = \text{Income taxes}$$
$$B = 0.2(\$80,000 - \$20,000 - T - B)$$
$$T = 0.4(\$80,000 - B)$$

Substituting for *T* in the first equation, the bonus is computed as follows:

$$B = 0.2[\$60,000 - 0.4(\$80,000 - B) - B]$$
$$B = \$12,000 - \$6,400 + 0.08B - 0.2B$$
$$1.12B = \$5,600$$
$$B = \underline{\$5,000}$$

The computation of the bonus can be proved by taking 20% of the amount by which the net income after the bonus of $5,000 and income taxes of $30,000 (40% of $75,000) exceeds $20,000. Thus, 20% of $25,000 ($80,000 − $5,000 − $30,000 − $20,000 = $25,000) equals the bonus of $5,000.

The journal entry to record the bonus under Plan 3 is shown below:

Journal entry to record bonus

Bonus Expense.	5,000	
Bonus Payable		5,000
To record liability for bonus to branch manager.		

Bonus Expense is included as an operating expense in the income statement and Bonus Payable as a current liability in the balance sheet. The Securities and Exchange Commission required disclosure of bonus and profit-sharing plans involving only directors, officers, and key employees; but the Commission recently rescinded the requirement.[11]

CONTINGENCIES

Loss contingencies were defined in Chapter 4 as potential losses, the existence of which is conditional upon the happening of some future event. Until the issuance of *FASB Statement No. 5,* the distinction between potential liabilities from loss contingencies and estimated liabilities was not clear to many accountants.[12] Similarly, some confusion existed as to which contingencies required the accrual of a loss or expense, which contingencies simply called for disclosure in the financial statements, and which general risk contingencies inherent in a business enterprise required neither accrual nor disclosure in the financial statements. Some enterprises accrued estimated losses or expenses from certain contingencies prior to the occurrence of the events expected to resolve the uncertainties, and, under similar circumstances, other enterprises recognized such losses or expenses only when the contingent events occurred. The purpose of *FASB Statement No. 5* was to establish more definitive standards of accounting for loss contingencies.

FASB Statement No. 5, "Accounting for Contingencies"

A *contingency* is an existing condition, a situation, or a set of circumstances involving uncertainty as to possible gain *(gain contingency)* or loss *(loss contingency)* to an enterprise that ultimately will be resolved

---

[11] *Accounting Series Release No. 280,* SEC (Washington: 1980).
[12] *FASB Statement No. 5,* "Accounting for Contingencies," FASB (Stamford: 1975).

when a future event or events occurs or fails to occur.[13] (The term **loss** is used by the FASB to include some items that commonly are referred to as **expenses.**) Resolution of the uncertainty surrounding a gain contingency generally results in an acquisition of an asset or the reduction of a liability; resolution of the uncertainty surrounding a loss contingency generally results in reduction of an asset or the incurrence of a liability. The likelihood that the future event or events will confirm the loss may be **probable** (likely to occur), **reasonably possible** (more than remote but less than likely), or **remote** (slight chance of occurring).

The FASB stated that "not all uncertainties inherent in the accounting process give rise to contingencies." The preparation of financial statements requires estimates for many business activities, and the use of estimates does not necessarily mean that a contingency exists. For example, the measurement of depreciation and income taxes expense involves estimates, but neither is a contingency. Neither the expiration of the cost of depreciable assets nor the incurrence of the obligation to pay income taxes is uncertain; however, the periodic amounts recognized in the accounting records require the use of estimates.

Examples of Loss Contingencies The FASB identified the following examples of loss contingencies:

1 Collectibility of receivables
2 Obligations related to product warranties and product defects
3 Risk of loss or damage to property by fire, explosion, or other hazards
4 Threat of expropriation of assets
5 Pending or threatened litigation
6 Actual or possible claims and assessments
7 Risk of loss from catastrophes assumed by property and casualty companies, including reinsurance companies
8 Guarantees of indebtedness of others
9 Obligations of commercial banks under "standby letters of credit"
10 Agreements to repurchase receivables or other assets that have been sold

Accrual of Loss Contingencies According to the FASB, an estimated loss or expense from a loss contingency shall be accrued by a charge to income if **both** of the following conditions are met:[14]

a Information available prior to issuance of the financial statements indicates that it is **probable that an asset had been impaired or a liability had been incurred** at the date of the financial statements. It is implicit in this condition that it must be probable that one or more future events will occur confirming the fact of the loss.
b The amount of the loss can be **reasonably estimated.**

When the range of loss can be reasonably estimated but no single amount within the range appears to be a better estimate than any other

[13] Ibid., p. 1.
[14] Ibid., p. 4.

amount within the range, ***the minimum amount in the range should be accrued.***[15] For example, assume that at the balance sheet date a business enterprise had lost a court case, but the amount of damages remains unresolved. A reasonable estimate is that the judgment will be for not less than $2 million or more than $6 million. No amount between $2 million and $6 million appears to be a better estimate than any other amount. According to the FASB, $2 million is accrued as a loss, and the possibility of an additional loss of $4 million is disclosed in a note to the financial statements. Both accrued and actual contingency losses are included in the determination of income before extraordinary items, unless such losses meet the criteria for classification as extraordinary items.

The important points to keep in mind are: (1) a loss contingency is accrued only when it is probable that an asset has been impaired or a liability incurred; (2) it must be probable that a future event or events will confirm the existence of the loss; and (3) the amount of the loss must be reasonably estimable. The absence of insurance (sometimes improperly referred to as ***self-insurance***) covering property losses, or the possibility that injury claims will be made against a business enterprise, for example, does not indicate that an asset has been impaired or that a liability has been incurred. Mere exposure to risk does not require the accrual of losses.

Included in the category of accruable loss contingencies are estimates of doubtful accounts expense and sales returns when the customers have a right to return merchandise. Both these contingencies are discussed in Chapter 7. The accounting for other accruable contingencies such as product warranty expense, gift certificates, service contracts outstanding, and coupons and trading stamps outstanding are described in a subsequent section of this chapter.

Loss Contingencies Which Are Not Accrued   Certain loss contingencies which do not meet the two criteria for accrual, but which are at least "reasonably possible," should be disclosed in notes to the financial statements. The disclosure should indicate the nature of the contingency and provide an estimate of the possible loss, or state that such an estimate cannot be made. An example of such a contingency is a legal action against a business enterprise in which an unfavorable outcome is quite possible, but a reasonable estimate of loss cannot be made.

Even if the probability of loss from a nonaccruable contingency is remote, the contingency still is disclosed. Such contingencies include guarantees of indebtedness of others, agreements to repurchase receivables, and obligations of commercial banks under "standby letters of credit." Disclosure is not required for a loss contingency involving claims or legal suits not yet filed, unless it appears probable that a claim or legal suit will be filed and that an unfavorable outcome is reasonably

---

[15] *FASB Interpretation No. 14,* "Reasonable Estimation of the Amount of a Loss. . . ." FASB (Stamford: 1976), p. 2.

possible. General or unspecified business risks do not meet the conditions for accrual and need not be disclosed.

Gain Contingencies   Those contingencies that might result in gains should not be recognized until the gains are realized or realizable. This is consistent with the general principles of revenue realization. Although disclosure should be made of contingencies that *might* result in gains, care should be exercised not to give an impression that realization of such gains is *likely.* Examples of gain contingencies include probable favorable outcome of plaintiff litigation and future benefits of operating loss carryforwards for income tax purposes.

Accounting for loss contingencies when liability has been incurred

The accrual of loss contingencies requires a debit to a loss or expense account and a credit to either an asset (or asset valuation) account or an estimated liability account. The term *estimated liability* is used to describe an obligation which definitely exists but which is uncertain as to amount and due date. The primary accounting problem is to obtain objective evidence on which to base a reasonable estimate of the amount of the liability. Estimated liabilities may be current or long term. The accounting for certain contingencies which require the recognition of estimated current liabilities is described in the following sections.

Product Warranties   Estimating the liability that arises in connection with various kinds of product warranties often poses a difficult problem. Warranties to replace or repair a product if it proves unsatisfactory within some specified time period are made by most business enterprises. Such liabilities arise at the time of sale and may be recorded, either at the time of sale or at the end of the accounting period. The following journal entries are made if the liability is recorded at the time of sale:

Journal entries for product warranty liability recorded on date of sale

Product Warranty Expense	XXX	
Estimated Liability under Product Warranty		XXX
To record estimated liability under product warranty.		
Estimated Liability under Product Warranty	XXX	
Cash (or Accounts Payable, Inventories of Parts, etc.)		XXX
To record costs of servicing customer claims.		

The balance in the estimated liability account at the end of the acounting period should be reviewed and adjusted if necessary to make certain that it reflects a reasonable measure of potential customer claims on outstanding product warranties.

An acceptable alternative would be to make no journal entry in the estimated liability account at the time of sale; Product Warranty Expense would be debited as actual costs are incurred in servicing customer claims and at the end of the accounting period to recognize outstanding potential claims.

Income tax regulations allow a deduction for product warranty expense only when the cost has been incurred. In the past, many business enterprises followed the income tax regulations in their accounting records, thus overstating net income and understating current liabilities. When the outstanding liability under a product warranty is significant, neither income tax laws nor the uncertainty of the amount of expense to be incurred is a valid excuse for failure to include the expense and the related current liability in the financial statements. **FASB Statement No. 5** has made that procedure mandatory.

Gift Certificates Some enterprises issue tickets, tokens, or gift certificates which are promises to perform services or to furnish merchandise at some later date. The amount of the liability is equal to the amount advanced by customers. As redemptions are made, the liability account is debited and a revenue account is credited. Examples of this type of transaction are meal tickets issued by restaurants, coupons issued by garages and gasoline stations, tickets and tokens issued by transportation enterprises, and gift certificates issued by retail stores. Because such advances are in small individual amounts and relatively numerous, it is almost certain that some never will be presented for redemption. Estimating the amount of forfeited claims is simplified when there is an agreement that the obligation lapses after a stated time. When the offer is of indefinite duration, it is necessary to estimate the amounts of potential claims that will not be redeemed and to transfer this amount from the liability account to a revenue account.

Service Contracts Enterprises selling or servicing household appliances often sell service contracts to customers under which the enterprises agree to service the appliance for a specified period of time. In this case, the price of service contracts constitutes unearned revenue, which is earned by performance over the period of the contract. To illustrate, assume that an enterprise sells television service contracts for $150 each, agreeing to service customers' sets for one year. If 1,000 such service contracts are sold, the journal entry is:

Journal entry for sale of service contracts

Cash (or Accounts Receivable)	150,000	
Unearned Service Contract Revenue		150,000
To record sale of 1,000 service contracts at $150 per contract.		

During the ensuing 12-month period, the unearned service contract revenue will be converted to realized revenue, and actual costs of servicing the television sets will be debited to expense accounts. On the basis of experience, it is often feasible to establish a pattern of probable service calls as a guide for recognizing revenue. For example, if the bulk of the service calls tend to be made in the first part of the year covered by the service contract, a policy of crediting realized revenue with, say, 30% of the contract price in the first month, 20% in the second month, and 5% in each of the ten subsequent months might be reasonable. The journal entries below are illustrative of this procedure for the first month of the service contract period, if we assume that costs of $30,735 were incurred in servicing the contracts during the first month:

<table>
<tr><td rowspan="7">Journal entries for revenue earned and costs incurred under service contracts</td><td>Unearned Service Contract Revenue . . . .</td><td>45,000</td><td></td></tr>
<tr><td>   Service Contract Revenue. . . . .</td><td></td><td>45,000</td></tr>
<tr><td>To record 30% of unearned service contract revenue as realized revenue for the first month of the contract period ($150,000 × 0.30 = $45,000).</td><td></td><td></td></tr>
<tr><td>Service Contract Expense. . . . .</td><td>30,735</td><td></td></tr>
<tr><td>   Parts Inventory . . . .</td><td></td><td>14,250</td></tr>
<tr><td>   Cash, Accrued Payroll, etc. . . . .</td><td></td><td>16,485</td></tr>
<tr><td>To record costs incurred under service contracts.</td><td></td><td></td></tr>
</table>

At the end of the first month, the balance of $105,000 ($150,000 − $45,000 = $105,000) in the Unearned Service Contract Revenue account is presented as a current liability in the balance sheet.

Coupons and Trading Stamps In an effort to promote the sales of certain products, a business enterprise may issue coupons exchangeable for prizes such as cash or merchandise. In such cases, the enterprise incurs an estimated liability equal to the cost of the prizes which are expected to be claimed by customers.

The estimated liability for prizes to be distributed should be based on the enterprise's past and anticipated experience with redemptions of coupons. For example, assume that in Year 1 Lena Company issues coupons which may be redeemed for prizes costing $2,500 if all the coupons are presented for redemption. If past experience indicates that only 80% of the coupons issued will be presented for redemption, the estimated liability is $2,000 (80% of $2,500, the maximum cost of prizes that are expected to be claimed by customers).

The purchase of prize merchandise to be given away, such as toys or kitchen utensils, is recorded in an inventory account. For example, the journal entry to record the purchase of $2,800 of prize merchandise by Lena Company in Year 1 is illustrated at the top of page 417.

<table>
<tr><td>Journal entry for
purchase of prizes</td><td>

Inventory of Prize Merchandise   2,800
    Cash (or Accounts Payable)   2,800
To record purchase of merchandise to be offered as prizes.

</td></tr>
</table>

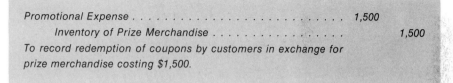

Generally, the cost of the coupons is immaterial in amount and thus is not accounted for separately; if the cost of coupons is material, the cost may also be recorded in an appropriate inventory account. Assuming that customers present coupons during Year 1 in exchange for prizes costing $1,500, the following journal entry would be made by Lena Company:

<table>
<tr><td>Journal entry for
redemption of coupons
for prizes</td><td>

Promotional Expense   1,500
    Inventory of Prize Merchandise   1,500
To record redemption of coupons by customers in exchange for
prize merchandise costing $1,500.

</td></tr>
</table>

At the end of Year 1, an adjusting entry is required to recognize the promotional expense and the estimated liability relating to the coupons outstanding. In our example, the total cost of prizes expected to be claimed by customers was estimated at $2,000, and $1,500 of this amount has been redeemed during Year 1. Thus, an estimated liability of $500 at the end of Year 1 is recorded by Lena Company as follows:

<table>
<tr><td>Adjusting entry for
estimated liability
for unredeemed
coupons</td><td>

Promotional Expense   500
    Estimated Liability for Coupons Outstanding   500
To record estimated liability for coupons outstanding at the end of
Year 1.

</td></tr>
</table>

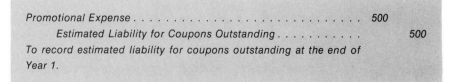

At the end of Year 1, the inventory of prize merchandise is $1,300 ($2,800 − $1,500 = $1,300). This inventory is listed among the current assets in the balance sheet. The liability for coupons outstanding, $500, should be included among current liabilities. The promotional expense for the year, $2,000, is classified as a selling expense in the income statement.

A slightly different situation exists when a retailing enterprise gives its customers **trading stamps** (Blue Chip Stamps, Green Stamps, etc.) to be redeemed by another enterprise engaged in the sale and redemption of trading stamps. The retailer pays a fixed price for the trading stamps, which are recorded in an Inventory of Trading Stamps account. When stamps are issued to customers, an operating expense account is debited, and the Inventory of Trading Stamps account is credited. The obligation to redeem the stamps is assumed by the enterprise which sells and redeems trading stamps. The trading stamp enterprise usually records the proceeds from the sale of stamps in a revenue account and recognizes an estimated liability for the cost of merchandise and related service costs to be incurred when stamps are redeemed. When merchandise is issued for redeemed stamps, the estimated liability is debited and the inventory of merchandise is credited.

Operating Reserves and Discountinued Operations Some enterprises debit an expense account and credit an *operating reserve* account for costs such as repairs or maintenance which have not yet been incurred. Also, estimated disbursements for deferred compensation, restoration of leased properties, plant closing and relocation costs, and provisions for discontinued operations sometimes are included in the current liability section of the balance sheet.

The recording of these estimated costs presumably is an effort to implement accrual accounting by recognition of an expense or loss when an obligation to incur costs in the future can be identified with reasonable certainty. The operating reserve account is debited when such costs are incurred.

There is some evidence that operating reserves have at times been used by management as "income-smoothing" devices. Accountants should analyze the nature of these reserves and determine whether a liability has been incurred (or an asset impaired) or whether the reserves improperly relieve future accounting periods of expenses and losses.

When a cost that is expensed for annual reporting purposes clearly benefits interim periods, each interim period should be charged for an appropriate portion of the expense by the use of accruals and deferrals.[16] Costs and expenses expected to be incurred in carrying out a disposal of an industry segment should be accrued and included in the measurement of the gain or loss on the disposal.[17] For example, a few years ago the balance sheet for the Singer Company included a "Provision for discontinued operations" of $275.7 million in current liabilities. A note to the financial statements stated that Singer Company "decided to withdraw from the manufacture and sale of its Business Machines Division product lines over a period of 12 months." The total provision was for $325.2 million for "estimated expenses and write-downs . . . to be incurred subsequent to the date of the decision to discontinue these operations." Interim reporting and discontinued operations are discussed further in *Modern Advanced Accounting* of this series.

---

[16] *APB Opinion No. 28,* p. 526.
[17] *APB Opinion No. 30,* "Reporting the Results of Operations— . . ," AICPA (New York: 1973), p. 563.

Disclosure of contingencies not accrued

If a loss contingency does not meet the two conditions for accrual described on page 412, and the likelihood of loss is reasonably possible or even, in some cases, remote, the loss contingency should be disclosed in the financial statements. The disclosure should include the nature of the contingency and, if possible, an indication of the amount involved. Adequate disclosure may be accomplished in a number of ways: (1) by a parenthetical comment in the balance sheet, (2) by a note to financial statements, (3) by inclusion of the item among the liabilities with no dollar amount included in the liability total, or (4) by an appropriation of retained earnings authorized by the board of directors. Disclosure by note probably is the most satisfactory procedure and is almost universally used. Some examples are discussed and illustrated in the following sections.

Guarantees of Indebtedness of Others　A contingency may arise from the discounting of notes receivable with recourse, from the assignment of accounts receivable with recourse, and from accommodation indorsements added to the obligations of other parties such as customers, employees, or affiliated business enterprises. In such cases little question exists as to the amount of the obligation or its due date. The central issue is whether the parties primarily liable will pay the liability. If the probability is strong that the original debtor will make payment, the chance of the indorser being required to pay is correspondingly remote. An example of disclosure of this type of contingency is illustrated below:

> In connection with providing for its future bituminous coal supply, the Company . . . has guaranteed capital and other obligations of certain coal suppliers (including five owned and two controlled coal companies) aggregating $131.6 million.

Pending or Threatened Litigation　If an enterprise is the defendant in a lawsuit calling for the payment of damages, a loss contingency exists. The outcome of such litigation seldom can be predicted with any assurance. The decision of the court either may release the enterprise of any obligation, or may establish an enforceable claim against it. However, the possibility of an appeal to a higher court still may exist. Another possible outcome is an out-of-court settlement between the parties, thus ending the litigation.

Even though the evidence available at the balance sheet date does not favor the defendant enterprise, it is hardly reasonable to expect the enterprise to publish in its financial statements a dollar estimate of the probable outcome. Such publicity could influence unfavorably the chances of an out-of-court settlement or encourage the opposing party to intensify its efforts. As a generalization, then, we may say that contingency from pending litigation should be disclosed in notes to the financial statements, but this disclosure will seldom, if ever, reach the point of estimating the dollar amount of a future settlement. To do so would weaken the enterprise's position in the dispute.

In the area of threatened litigation or unasserted claims against a client company, a letter of audit inquiry to the client company's lawyers is the auditors' primary means of obtaining confirmation of the information provided by management. This audit step has been a source of considerable controversy between independent accountants and lawyers. The issue boils down to a struggle between the accountants' quest for adequate disclosure and the lawyers' responsibility to preserve the confidentiality of the lawyer-client privilege. A compromise position was reached between the AICPA and the American Bar Association, which resulted in the issuance of a pronouncement by the Auditing Standards Executive Committee of the AICPA.[18] An example of disclosure of an asserted claim follows:

> In January, 1982, a purported class action was filed in the U.S. District Court for the Southern District of New York against the Corporation, certain of its present and former directors and its independent accountants. Plaintiff alleges that the Corporation's Annual Reports for 1979 and 1980 and other statements and reports failed to make proper disclosures with respect to the Corporation's consolidated financial condition and earnings resulting in violation of Section 10(b) of the Securities Exchange Act of 1934 and Rule 10b-5 thereunder and constituting common law fraud. Plaintiff seeks damages in an unspecified amount on behalf of the alleged class consisting of all persons who purchased the corporation's common stock during the period of the alleged wrongful conduct. Management denies the claims asserted.

Actual or Possible Claims and Assessments   The Internal Revenue Service may disagree with the treatment of items in the computation of taxable income and (within the period of the statute of limitations) may assess additional taxes. Because this contingency is well-recognized and understood, no specific disclosure is required prior to the time that an actual assessment has been made. Except in cases of fraud or failure to file a return, the statute of limitations on federal income tax expense deficiencies is three years; thus, at any given time it is only the income taxes expense of the last three years that may be in doubt as to matters involving an interpretation of the law. A note may be attached to financial statements to indicate that income tax returns have been examined and final determination of income taxes has been made for certain years. The following disclosure of a proposed tax deficiency is given as an example:

> The Internal Revenue Service issued a notice of deficiency of $823,000, plus interest, relating primarily to the allocation of the purchase price to the acquired assets of a subsidiary and the subsequent valuations of its LIFO inventories. The Company has petitioned the United States Tax Court; however,

---

[18] *Statement on Auditing Standards No. 12,* "Inquiry of a Client's Lawyer Concerning Litigation, Claims, and Assessments," AICPA (New York: 1976).

no trial date has been set. In the event any portion of the deficiency is sustained, the adjustments would represent timing differences that should result in tax deductions in future years; consequently, there would be no material adverse effect on the consolidated financial statements.

Future liabilities and commitments

Most business enterprises are continuously planning activities for some time in the future. In many instances, commitments may be made that will result in substantial liabilities in the near future. On any balance sheet date, an enterprise ordinarily will have made certain commitments that are of a recurring nature and normal in amount; these do not require special disclosure. However, when unusual commitments that are large in amount have been made, their nature and amount should be disclosed. Examples are commitments for an unusually large purchase of material, a major expansion of plant assets, acquisitions of natural resources, additional payments to be made contingent on earnings of acquired enterprises, or unusually large commitments for advertising and product development costs. An example of disclosure of commitments appears below:

> The Company has commitments under contracts for the purchase of land and for the construction of buildings. Portions of such contracts not completed at year-end are not reflected in the financial statements. Such unrecorded commitments amounted to approximately $58,575,000 at the end of 1983 as compared to $83,757,000 for 1982.

Presentation of current liabilities in the balance sheet

Two questions arise in connection with the presentation of current liabilities in the balance sheet: (1) the order in which short-term debt is to be listed, and (2) the extent of the detail disclosure necessary for different types of current liabilities. Current liabilities can be reported in the *order of maturity* or according to *amount* (largest to smallest). It is difficult to satisfy both objectives, and the usual compromise is to rank current liabilities in order of size unless differences in maturity dates are significant. However, cash overdrafts and promissory notes maturing shortly after the balance sheet date usually are listed first in deference to their priority of maturity.

In the balance sheet, the discount or premium on notes payable is reported as a direct deduction from or addition to the face amount of the notes. The description of the notes payable includes the effective interest rate and the face amount of the notes is disclosed in the financial statements or in the accompanying notes.[19]

The matter of detail will depend to some extent on the purpose for which the balance sheet is prepared. In a balance sheet prepared in sup-

[19] *APB Opinion No. 21,* "Interest on Receivables and Payables," AICPA (New York: 1971), p. 423.

port of a loan application or for use in forecasting short-term financial requirements, a listing of current liabilities in greater detail is desirable. For financial statements presented in annual reports, the classification illustrated below is recommended:

Current liabilities:

Notes payable to banks (interest rate, 17%)		$ 600,000
Notes payable to trade creditors (effective interest rate, 18%)	$475,000	
Less: Discount on notes payable	30,000	445,000
Accounts payable		325,200
Current maturities of long-term debt (including bonds payable, mortgage notes payable, and equipment contracts payable)		150,500
Income taxes payable		112,500
Other accrued liabilities (payroll, interest, royalties, guarantees, etc.)		29,000
Dividends payable		25,000
Miscellaneous current liabilities (advances from customers, credit balances in customers' accounts, etc.)		21,800
Total current liabilities		$1,709,000

If the due date of any liability can be extended, the details should be disclosed parenthetically or in notes accompanying the financial statements. Any short-term obligation which is expected to be liquidated by the issuance of additional shares of capital stock is reported in the stockholders' equity section of the balance sheet.

REVIEW QUESTIONS

1 Liabilities sometimes are referred to as "equities of outsiders in the assets of a business enterprise." Do you agree with this description of liabilities? Explain.

2 Distinguish between a **liability** and a **commitment.** Should the currently maturing installment of a deferred compensation contract that is to be liquidated by the issuance of capital stock be reported as a liability in the balance sheet? Explain.

3 What is the basis for distinguishing between a **current liability** and a **long-term liability?**

4 Distinguish among the following: **definitely determinable liability, liability dependent on operating results, estimated liability, loss contingency.** Give an example of each.

5 Under what circumstances would it be proper to report a currently maturing debt as a noncurrent liability?

6 When should deferred revenue (or unearned revenue) be reported as a current liability? When should deferred revenue be reported as noncurrent?

7 What are the usual liabilities that arise in connection with payroll?

8 When should the liability for property taxes be recognized in the accounting records? Over what period should property taxes be debited to an expense account? Explain.

9 Where should the liability for current year's income taxes appear in the balance sheet of a partnership? Explain.

10 What recommendations did the APB make in **Opinion No. 28** regarding the accrual of income taxes for interim periods?

11 A company acquired certain patent rights in return for an agreement to pay royalties equal to "10% of the company's income." What difficulties may arise in the interpretation of this agreement?

12 a Define a **contingency** and differentiate between a **gain contingency** and a **loss contingency.**
  b Give some examples of gain contingencies and loss contingencies.
  c What two conditions must be met before a loss contingency is accrued?

13 On December 31, Year 6, Exeter Company had an investment of $2 million in the bonds of Canlis Company, which has filed for bankruptcy. A reasonable estimate of the possible loss is in the range between $600,000 and $900,000. No amount of the estimated loss in this range appears to be a better estimate than any other amount. How should Exeter Company account for this loss contingency in its financial statements for the year ended December 31, Year 6?

14 Briefly describe the accounting for promotional plans involving coupons and prizes, product guarantees, and the sale of service contracts.

15 Todd Company does not carry workers' compensation insurance, but it does have its own plan for payments to disabled employees. Should estimated obligations to employees under this plan be reported as a liability? Are potential losses on "self-insurance" plans properly reported as liabilities? Why?

16 Included among the current liabilities of American Corporation is an item described as "Excess of Checks Outstanding over Balance in Bank Account, $506,041." The current liabilities of Livermore Steel Products, Incorporated, include "Estimated Costs of Closing of Plainfield Plant, $3,480,000." Explain the nature of these two current liabilities.

17 Explain how each of the following items is measured and reported in the balance sheet:
  a Bank overdraft
  b Customers' accounts with credit balances
  c Service guarantee on products sold
  d Bonds maturing in three months, to be paid from a sinking fund
  e Stock dividend to be distributed in the form of common stock of the issuing corporation
  f Dividends in arrears on cumulative preferred stock
  g Interest on notes payable, deducted from the face amount of the note to determine the net proceeds
  h Estimated payments to employees under a three-year union contract
  i Potential payments to stockholders of an acquired company based on future earnings of the acquired company.

18 Describe four ways in which a loss contingency may be disclosed in financial statements.

19 Under what circumstances should commitments for future expenditures be disclosed in financial statements? How should this disclosure be made?

20 List some general guidelines for reporting current liabilities in the balance sheet.

EXERCISES

Ex. 10-1 Select the best answer for each of the following multiple-choice questions:

1 Which of the following is the proper accounting treatment of a gain contingency?
a An accrued amount
b Deferred earnings
c An account receivable with an additional disclosure explaining the nature of the transaction
d Disclosure only

2 Colortone Corporation, a manufacturer of household paints, is preparing annual financial statements on December 31, Year 3. Because of a recently proven health hazard in one of its paints, the United States government has indicated clearly its intention of having Colortone recall all cans of this paint sold in the last six months. The management of Colortone estimates that this recall would cost $1,000,000. What accounting recognition, if any, should be accorded this situation?
a No recognition
b Disclosure in a note to the financial statements
c Operating expense of $1,000,000
d Extraordinary loss of $1,000,000

3 Utica Corporation provides an incentive compensation plan under which its president is to receive a bonus equal to 10% of Utica's income in excess of $100,000 before deduction of income taxes but after deduction of the bonus. If income before income taxes and the bonus is $320,000, the amount of the bonus is:
a $44,000   *b* $32,000   *c* $22,000   *d* $20,000

4 Shoppers' Haven is a retail store operating in a state with a 5% retail sales tax. The state law provides that the retail sales tax collected during the month must be remitted to the state during the following month. If the amount collected is remitted to the state on or before the twentieth day of the following month, the retailer may keep 2% of the sales tax collected. On April 10, Shoppers' Haven remitted $16,905 sales tax to the state tax division for March retail sales. What was the amount of the March retail sales subject to sales tax?
a $331,340   *b* $331,480   *c* $338,100   *d* $345,000

5 Noxious Company was sued for illness caused to local residents as a result of negligence on the company's part in permitting the local residents to be exposed to highly toxic chemicals from its plant. Noxious lost the suit, and its lawyers have concluded that it is probable that Noxious will be liable for a judgment costing Noxious anywhere from $500,000 to $2,500,000. However, the lawyers state that the most probable cost is $1,000,000. As a result of the above facts, Noxious should accrue:
a A loss contingency of $500,000, and disclose an additional contingency of up to $2,000,000

     b A loss contingency of $1,000,000, and disclose an additional contingency of up to 1,500,000

     c A loss contingency of $1,000,000, but not disclose any additional contingency

     d No loss contingency, but disclose a contingency of $500,000 to $2,500,000

Ex. 10-2   In Year 1, Colby Corporation began selling a new line of products that carry a two-year warranty against defects. Based on past experience with other products, the estimated warranty costs related to dollar sales are as follows:

First year of warranty 2%

Second year of warranty 5%

     Sales and actual warranty expenditures for Year 1 and Year 2 are presented below:

	Year 1	*Year 2*
Sales	$500,000	$700,000
Actual warranty expenditures	10,000	30,000

     Compute the estimated warranty liability at the end of Year 2.

Ex. 10-3   Cornucopia Company distributes to consumers coupons which may be presented (on or before a stated expiration date) to grocers for discounts on certain products of Cornucopia. The grocers are reimbursed when they send the coupons to Cornucopia. In Cornucopia's experience, 40% of such coupons are redeemed, and generally one month elapses between the date a grocer receives a coupon from a consumer and the date Cornucopia receives it. During Year 8, Cornucopia issued two separate series of coupons as follows:

Date issued	*Total value*	*Consumer expiration date*	*Amount disbursed as of Dec. 31, Year 8*
Jan. 1, Year 8	$100,000	*June 30, Year 8*	$34,000
July 1, Year 8	120,000	*Dec. 31, Year 8*	42,000

     Compute the liability for unredeemed coupons on December 31, Year 8.

Ex. 10-4   In an effort to increase sales, Retailers Company inaugurated a sales promotional campaign on June 30, Year 5, whereby Retailers placed a coupon in each package of product sold, the coupons being redeemable for a premium. Each premium costs Retailers $2.00, and five coupons must be presented by a customer to receive a premium. Retailers estimated that only 60% of the coupons issued will be redeemed. For the six months ended December 31, Year 5, the following information is available:

Packages of product sold	*Premiums purchased*	*Coupons redeemed*
800,000	*60,000*	*200,000*

     Compute the estimated liability for premium claims outstanding on December 31, Year 5.

Ex. 10-5   On December 31, Year 3, Albertson Company issued a two-year noninterest-bearing promissory note with a face amount of $58,320 for the purchase of scrap metal. The transaction was recorded as follows:

Purchases 58,320

    Note Payable 58,320

a Prepare a correcting journal entry on December 31, Year 3, assuming that a fair rate of interest is 8% per year and that the accounting records for Year 3 are still open. Use the Appendix at the end of the book to determine the present value of the note.

b Prepare an adjusting entry on December 31, Year 4, to record interest expense on the note.

c Show how the note should be presented in the balance sheet on December 31, Year 4.

Ex. 10-6   The following information is taken from the accounting records of Clubb Company for the first three months of its operations:

Month	Total salaries earned	Income taxes withheld	FICA taxes withheld (7%)	Remitted to Internal Revenue Service
January	$ 2,600	$ 290	$182	$ –0–
February	3,400	360	238	654 (1)
March	4,000	410	280	836 (2)
Totals	$10,000	$1,060	$700	$1,490

(1) *Income taxes ($290), FICA taxes withheld from employees' salaries in January ($182), and employer's FICA taxes for January ($182).*
(2) *Income taxes ($360), FICA taxes withheld in February ($238), and employer's FICA taxes for February ($238).*

Journal entries to record the payroll for January and February, including taxes on the employer (FICA, 7%; state unemployment tax, 2.7%; and federal unemployment tax, 0.7%) were recorded properly. Remittances to the Internal Revenue Service were debited to the respective liability accounts. All salaries earned through March are subject to payroll taxes.

a Prepare a compound journal entry to record the payroll for March. Record all payroll taxes on the employer in the Payroll Taxes Expense account.

b Prepare a journal entry at the end of April to record payment of the balance of the amount due for income taxes withheld, FICA taxes, and the full amount of state unemployment tax for the first quarter of the year. Federal unemployment tax is not due until the amount payable exceeds $100.

Ex. 10-7   Lee Bell has a contract with Richards Corporation in which he is to receive a bonus of 20% of any net income over $100,000. Income before the bonus and income taxes for the year is $385,000. Income taxes are 60% of taxable income.

Compute the amount of the bonus, assuming that it is computed on the net income in excess of $100,000 after deduction of both the bonus and income taxes.

Ex. 10-8   Supreme Company offers a coupon with each unit of product sold. A customer who turns in 100 coupons is given a choice of prizes consisting of a football, a basketball, or a baseball glove. These miniaturized prizes cost the company $5.00 each. The Promotional Expense account is debited as redemptions are made during the year and also at the end of the year when an estimate is made of outstanding coupons which will be redeemed. The following five summary transactions listed at the top of page 427 occurred in Year 1:

a Purchased for cash 800 coupon books, each containing 1,000 coupons, for a total cost of $800. (Debit Inventory of Coupons.)

b Issued 500,000 coupons to customers.

c Purchased for cash 2,200 items of prize merchandise (miniaturized footballs, basketballs, and baseball gloves).

d Issued 1,500 prizes to customers.

e Of the coupons issued, it is estimated that an additional 120,000 will be redeemed.

Prepare journal entries to record the five transactions.

Ex. 10-9 Krane Company sold a machine on account early in the current year for $1,200, along with a one-year warranty. Maintenance on each machine during the warranty period averages $100.

Prepare journal entries to record the sale of the machine and the subsequent cash expenditure of $85 to service the machine during the warranty period, assuming that the Product Warranty Expense account is debited at the time of sale.

Ex. 10-10 In October of the current year, Long Company contracted to purchase 7,500 tons of material next year at a fixed price of $100 a ton. The contract is not subject to cancellation. At the end of the current year the replacement cost of the material was $88 a ton.

Prepare the journal entry to record the loss on the purchase commitment at the end of the current year.

Ex. 10-11 Cortez Company had $6 million of short-term commercial paper outstanding on June 30, Year 6, the end of its fiscal year. On that date, the company intended to refinance the commercial paper by issuance of long-term debt. However, because the company had excess cash in July, it retired $2 million of the commercial paper. On August 10, Year 6, the company issued $12 million long-term bonds, and on August 15, it issued financial statements for the year ended June 30. The proceeds of the $12 million long-term bond issue were intended to be used as follows:

(1) To increase working capital, $2 million

(2) To pay balance of commercial paper, $4 million

(3) To finance construction of new warehouse, $6 million

Indicate how the foregoing information should be presented in the balance sheet on June 30, Year 6.

SHORT CASES FOR ANALYSIS AND DECISION

Case 10-1 An unclassified balance sheet of Canfield Corporation on December 31, Year 5, is given at the top of page 428.

CANFIELD CORPORATION
Balance Sheet
December 31, Year 5

Assets

Current assets	$15,000,000
Other assets	25,000,000
Total assets	$40,000,000

Liabilities & Stockholders' Equity

Accounts payable and accrued liabilities	$ 5,000,000
Bank loan payable, 15%, due Feb. 1, Year 6	2,500,000
Note payable, 18%, due July 10, Year 6	1,500,000
Bonds payable, 16%, due Dec. 31, Year 25	12,500,000
Stockholders' equity	18,500,000
Total liabilities & stockholders' equity	$40,000,000

Before the company issued a classified balance sheet on March 1, Year 6, as of December 31, Year 5, you ascertained that the company intends to refinance the bank loan and the note payable on a long-term basis. During December of Year 5, the company negotiated a financing contract with a major bank for a maximum amount of $4 million at any time through December 31, Year 7. The terms of the contract are as follows:

(1) Funds will be made available at the request of Canfield, and any amount borrowed will mature three years from the date of borrowing. Interest at the prevailing bank prime rate will be due quarterly.
(2) An annual commitment fee of 1% will be charged by the bank on the difference between the amount borrowed and $4 million.
(3) The contract is cancelable by the bank only if:
  (i) The borrower's working capital, excluding borrowings under the contract, falls below $6 million.
  (ii) The borrower becomes obligated under a lease contract to pay annual rent in excess of $1 million.
  (iii) The borrower acquires treasury stock without the prior approval of the bank.
  (iv) The borrower guarantees indebtedness of other companies in excess of $200,000.

Instructions
a Is Canfield's intention to refinance sufficiently finalized to permit the classification of the bank loan and the note payable as noncurrent liabilities in a classified balance sheet as of December 31, Year 5?
b Assuming that the bank loan and the note payable are properly excluded from current liabilities in the balance sheet as of December 31, Year 5, prepare an appropriate note relating to the refinancing contract which should accompany the balance sheet.

Case 10-2 Vance Company has a bank loan which is due within three months of the balance sheet date. The loan has been in existence for five years, although it is of short maturity and it is the intent of both the company and the bank to renew the loan indefinitely. The loan is collateralized by the cash surrender value of a life insurance policy.

The company over a period of years has been offering to officers and employees the right to buy the company's 18% bonds, which will be redeemed at the holder's request at any time after two years from the date of issue. In the past, certain bonuses have been paid to employees by the issuance of these bonds. All the bonds presently outstanding have or will have an issued status for two years within one year of the balance sheet date. During the past 10 years, bonds redeemed were less than 10% of bonds outstanding, and evidence indicates that no employee-bondholders intended to redeem their bonds in the coming year.

Instructions State how you would classify the cash surrender value of the life insurance policy, the bank loan, and the bonds payable in the balance sheet of Vance Company at the end of the current year. Give reasons for your answer.

Case 10-3 At the end of the current year, the balance sheet of DeLay Corporation did not include among the current liabilities the following items (all of which are material in amount):

(1) Notes payable to a group of stockholders, the notes to become due and payable on demand of at least eight of the group of twelve stockholders
(2) A note payable due three months after the balance sheet date, in settlement of which the holder accepted 1,000 shares of preferred stock 15 days after the balance sheet date
(3) Rent collected one year in advance
(4) Bonds payable maturing in 90 days

Instructions Assuming that in each case the exclusion from current liabilities was based on logical reasoning, give the arguments in support of the financial statement presentation used by DeLay. If your answer involves assumptions as to facts not given in the case, state your assumptions.

Case 10-4 Promotional Company was organized early this year to sell trading stamps throughout the country to retailers who distribute the stamps gratuitously to their customers. Books for accumulating the stamps and catalogs illustrating the merchandise for which the stamps may be exchanged are given free to retailers for distribution to stamp recipients. Centers with inventories of merchandise have been established for redemption of the stamps. Retailers may not return unused stamps

The analysis below shows the company's expectations as to percentages of a normal month's activity which will be attained. For this purpose, a "normal month's activity" is defined as the level of operations expected when expansion of activities ceases or tapers off to a stable rate. The company expects that this level will be attained in the third year and that sales of stamps will average $2,000,000 per month throughout the third year.

Month	Actual stamp sales, %	Merchandise purchases, %	Stamp redemptions, %
6th	30	40	10
12th	60	60	45
18th	80	80	70
24th	90	90	80
30th	100	100	95

Promotional Company plans to adopt a fiscal year ending with the first 12 months of operations.

Instructions
a Discuss the accounting alternatives that should be considered by Promotional Company for the recognition of its revenue and related expenses.
b For each accounting alternative discussed in **a** above, identify balance sheet accounts that should be used and indicate how each should be classified.

PROBLEMS

10-1   The general manager of Kane Company wants a bonus based on income of the current accounting period, which the general manager estimates will be approximately $495,000 before the bonus and income taxes.

Instructions   If the bonus rate is established at 10% and income taxes amount to 60% of taxable income, compute the estimated amount of the bonus to the general manager under each of the following assumptions. (Round all answers to nearest dollar.)
a Bonus is based on income before income taxes and the bonus.
b Bonus is based on income after the bonus but before income taxes.
c Bonus is based on income after income taxes and the bonus.

10-2   Carthay Company operates in a state which levies a 10% tax on corporate income after federal income taxes. The state income tax for any year is an allowable deduction for the federal income tax for that year, but is not deductible for the state income tax for any year. Federal income tax rates are 40% on all taxable income. During the current year, the corporation had $400,000 of income subject to both state and federal income taxes, before deduction of either state or federal income taxes.

Instructions
a Compute the company's liability for both federal and state income taxes for the current year, and prepare a working paper to prove that the computed amounts are consistent. (Round all amounts to the nearest dollar.)
b Prepare a journal entry to record the income taxes expense for the current year, and compute net income for the current year.

10-3   Wong Company acquired a machine on July 1, Year 1, for $5,000 and an 18-month $15,000 face amount note on which interest was payable at the annual rate of 8% on December 31 and June 30. The current fair rate of interest on a note of comparable quality was 16% compounded semiannually.

Instructions   (Round all computations to the nearest dollar.)
a Compute the cost of the machine and record the acquisition of the machine on July 1, Year 1. Use the Appendix at the end of the book to determine the present value of the note payable.
b Prepare journal entries to record the following:
  (1) Payment of interest on the note and adjustment of the Discount on Note Payable account on December 31, Year 1.
  (2) Payment of interest on the note and adjustment of the Discount on Note Payable account on June 30, Year 2.
  (3) Payment of the note (including interest) and adjustment of the Discount on Note Payable account on December 31, Year 2.
c Show how the note payable should be presented in the balance sheet on December 31, Year 1.

10-4   Beverages Company sells carbonated juice in six-packs, cases, and through vending machines. In order to promote the drink, the company inaugurated in Year 10 a promotional plan called "Win-O." For every 10 bottle caps and 10 cents turned in, customers receive a ball-point pen and become eligible for a grand prize of $100 cash, one of which is awarded for every 15,000 caps turned in. The company estimates that only 40% of the bottle caps will be presented for redemption. A summary of transactions for Year 10 follows:

(1) Sold 3,000,000 bottles of juice for $1,510,600 cash.
(2) Purchased 50,000 ball-point pens for $25,000 cash. (Debit Inventory of Prize Merchandise.)
(3) Expenses paid in cash and attributable to the promotional plan were $4,100.

(4) A total of 39,000 ball-point pens were distributed as prizes to customers, and an appropriate number of grand prizes was awarded.

At the end of each year, the company recognizes a liability equal to the esti-mated cost of potential prizes outstanding. The 10 cents received for each pen is considered sufficient to cover the direct expenses of handling each request; therefore, neither the estimated direct expenses nor the potential remittances from customers are accrued at the end of the year.

Instructions
a Prepare journal entries to record the transactions relating to the promotional plan for Year 10. Expenses of the promotional plan are recorded in a Promo-tional Expense account.
b Compute the balances in all accounts relating to the promotional plan; explain how each account would appear in the financial statements for Year 10.

10-5   While auditing the financial statements of Carioca Company, you found that the following contingencies have not been recorded in the accounting records:

(1) Doubtful accounts are estimated at $14,900 as a result of aging of the ac-counts receivable. The unadjusted balance in the Allowance for Doubtful Ac-counts was a debit balance of $3,200.
(2) In prior years, the company had not accrued estimated claims for injuries to customers as a result of using the company's products because such claims were covered by insurance. In the current year, the company discontinued the insurance. A reasonable estimate of outstanding claims at the end of the current year is $25,000.
(3) A former employee has sued the company for $500,000 because of age dis-crimination. Outside legal counsel does not think the suit has any merit but has suggested that the company pay the former employee an out-of-court settlement of $5,000, because the cost of defending the suit was estimated at $50,000. Carioca agreed, and the former employee signed appropriate settle-ment papers.
(4) The company has lost a breach of contract suit, but the amount of damages has not been determined. The plaintiff is seeking damages of $100,000. Man-agement and legal counsel are of the opinion that the damages the court would find for the plaintiff would be a minimum of $10,000 and a maximum of $50,000. No amount within this range is a better estimate of potential dam-ages than any other amount.
(5) The company is an indorser on notes receivable discounted at a bank in the amount of $150,000, including interest. All but one of the makers of the notes are financially sound companies. The one maker had issued a one-year, 10% promissory note of $20,000 to Carioca. The note matures in 30 days, but the maker's bankruptcy referee has estimated that only 40% of the maturity value of notes will be paid.
(6) A lower court has awarded $200,000 in damages to Carioca in litigation in which the company was the plaintiff. The defendants have appealed the deci-sion to a higher court, which is not expected to issue a decision for a year.
(7) During the current year, the company discontinued collision coverage on its vehicles and assumed the risk for this contingency. Actual losses of $15,000 during the year were debited to Delivery Expense. Because the premiums for collision insurance in past years averaged $45,000, the controller wants to set up a "reserve for self-insurance" by increasing the Delivery Expense ac-count by $30,000.
(8) Management has requested your consent to record a provision for unspeci-fied general business risks for $80,000 by a debit to an expense account.

Instructions   For each contingency described above, prepare a journal entry to record the contingency, or briefly explain why an entry would not be in accord-ance with generally accepted accounting principles.

10-6   Listed below are selected transactions for Hernandez Company relating to current liabilities during the current fiscal year:

Jan. 10 Purchased merchandise for $25,000. A 2% discount is offered by suppliers. Hernandez records purchases and accounts payable net of discounts and uses the periodic inventory system.

19 Paid $16,660 on invoice of January 10. The invoice was billed to Hernandez for $17,000 and was paid within the discount period.

31 Paid balance of January 10 invoice, $8,000, after the discount period.

Apr. 1 Issued one-year promissory note to supplier in settlement of an invoice for $10,000 dated March 31. The invoice was recorded net of 2% purchases discount; that is, $9,800. The face amount of the note was $11,368, including interest at 16% on $9,800 for one year. The note was recorded at face amount.

30 Wages for April were $16,000 before the following withholdings:

Income taxes	$2,380
FICA, 7%	1,120

The company records payroll taxes at the end of each month in a Payroll Taxes Expense account. All wages for April are subject to 2.7% state unemployment tax and 0.7% federal unemployment tax.

May 20 The company declared dividends as follows:

Cash	$18,000
Stock	5%

The dividends are scheduled for distribution to stockholders on June 25. There are 120,000 shares of $5 par capital stock outstanding; the current market price of the stock is $30 a share. (Debit Retained Earnings for total amount of dividends.)

June 25 Paid the cash dividend and distributed the stock dividend declared on May 20.

Dec. 31 The company sells service contracts on its products and credits Deferred Service Contract Revenue when payments from customers are received. For the current year, $7,400 of the service contract revenue is considered realized.

31 Recorded interest expense for the current year on the note issued to supplier on April 1.

Instructions   Prepare journal entries to record the transactions listed above.

10-7   Account balances and other data relating to liabilities, obligations, and commitments of Amber Company on December 31, Year 5, are as follows:

Accounts payable	$ 96,750
Notes payable	70,000
Discount on notes payable	4,100
Accounts receivable (excluding $40,000 which have been sold to a factor on a recourse basis)	171,200
Bonds payable ($100,000 due on June 30 of each year)	800,000
Accrued payroll	4,280
FICA and income taxes withheld and accrued	1,770
Property taxes payable	600
Stock dividend to be distributed (at par value of capital stock)	20,000
Income taxes payable	32,100

Deferred income taxes payable (resulting from use of accelerated depreciation method for income tax purposes) 145,000

Estimated liability for coupons outstanding 7,500

Unearned service contract revenue (contracts are for one year) 6,000

Notes payable to officers (renewed annually) 60,000

The company signed a contract on October 10, Year 5, to purchase merchandise in Year 6 at a fixed price of $60,000. This merchandise has a market value in excess of $62,400 on December 31, Year 5.

Instructions Prepare the current liabilities section of the balance sheet on December 31, Year 5, and list any loss contingencies or commitments which should be disclosed.

10-8 Big Rock Mining Corporation started mining in the current year on certain land leased from Prairie Company. Big Rock previously had paid minimum royalties of $48,000 to Prairie, none of which was earned, during a three-year period prior to the current year. The royalty provisions in the lease contract are as follows:

(1) Minimum annual royalty is $16,000, with a minimum of $4,000 payable quarterly. Unearned minimum royalties may be recovered in any subsequent period from earned royalties in excess of minimum royalties.

(2) Earned royalty shall be 10 cents per ton shipped from the mine plus a per-ton amount equal to 2% of the amount that the market value of the ore at the mine exceeds $4 per ton.

Operations for the current year are summarized below:

Quarter	Tons shipped	Market value at destination, per ton	Freight from mine to destination, per ton
1st	None		
2d	150,000	$11.50	$3.50
3d	300,000	12.50	3.50
4th	None		

Instructions

a Compute the amount of royalty to be paid to Prairie Company for the current year and the amount of unearned minimum royalty at the end of the current year.

b How should the unearned minimum royalty paid be reported in the balance sheet of Big Rock Mining Corporation at the end of the current year? Explain.

10-9 Tabriz Company requests that you make an estimate of the company's product warranty obligation at the end of the first six months of the current year.

The company manufactures television tubes and sells them under a six-month guarantee to replace defective tubes without charge. At the beginning of the year, the company reported a Liability for Product Warranty of $374,800. By June 30, this account had been reduced to $32,920 by debits for the net cost of defective tubes returned which had been sold in the previous year. The net cost of replacing defective tubes sold in the current year (January to May) was recorded in the Product Warranty Expense account.

The company began the current year expecting tube returns to equal 8% of the dollar volume of sales for the year. However, as a result of the introduction of new models during the year, this estimated percentage of returns was increased to 10% on May 1. It is assumed that no tubes sold during a given month are returned in that month. Each tube is stamped with a date at the time of sale so that the warranty may be administered properly. The following table indicates the likely pattern of sales returns during the six-month period of the warranty, starting with the month following the sale of the tubes:

Month following sale	Percentage of total returns expected
First	20
Second	30
Third	20
Fourth – sixth (10% each month)	30

Gross sales of tubes for the first six months of the current year were:

January	$3,600,000	April	$2,850,000
February	3,300,000	May	2,000,000
March	4,100,000	June	1,960,000

The company's warranty also covers payment of the shipping cost on defective tubes returned and on new tubes sent out as replacements. This shipping cost averages approximately 10% of the sales price of the tubes returned. The manufacturing cost of the tubes is roughly 80% of the sales price, and the residual value of returned tubes averages 20% of their sales price. Returned tubes on hand at the beginning of the year were valued in inventories at 20% of their original sales price.

Instructions
a Prepare a working paper to estimate the company's liability under its product warranty on June 30.
b Prepare the necessary adjusting journal entry on June 30. (Income tax considerations may be ignored.)

10-10 Described below are selected transactions of Carterville Company during the current year:

(1) The company is obligated under an operating lease for the payment of monthly rent of $1,000 in advance, plus an additional rent (payable by the tenth day of the following month) equal to 8% of the net income earned by its branch store, after both total rent and a 40% provision for income taxes have been deducted. Operating income of the branch store during January (before rent and income taxes) was $20,000. Income taxes expense is recorded monthly. (Compute rent expense to the nearest dollar and debit Rent Expense for both the rent advance on January 1 and the accrual of rent on January 31.)

(2) The company issues gift certificates in denominations of $5, $10, and $25. These certificates are redeemable in merchandise having an average gross profit of 25% of selling price. During March, the company sold $31,000 of gift certificates and redeemed certificates having a sales value of $27,400. It is estimated that 8% of the certificates issued will not be redeemed. The company uses a periodic inventory system, and thus does not compute the cost of goods sold until the end of the fiscal year. The sales of gift certificates are recorded in an Estimated Liability for Gift Certificates Outstanding account.

(3) Sales during June totaled $310,800, of which $195,000 were on open account. The company operates in a state where there is a 6% sales tax. Included in the sales amount are sales taxes collected from customers on all items except food, which is exempt from sales tax. Food sales amounted to 40% of total sales before the sales tax was added.

(4) Salaries for November were $250,000, of which $80,000 represented amounts paid over $30,000 and $150,000 represented amounts paid over

$6,000 to certain employees. Income taxes withheld totaled $32,000, and FICA tax withholdings were at the rate of 7% (on wages up to $30,000 per year). The company is subject to a state unemployment tax rate of 2.7% and a federal unemployment tax rate of 0.7% (on wages up to $6,000 per year). Payroll taxes on the employer are recorded in separate expense accounts. The accrued payroll and related payroll tax liabilities are recorded in the same journal entry.

Instructions

a Prepare all necessary journal entries to record the transactions described above. An entry to record the accrual of income taxes for January should be made in part (1).

b Prepare a list of all current liability accounts involved in the journal entries in *a.* (Do not give account balances.)

10-11   A summary of financial position of Ventura Company on December 31, Year 8, is presented below:

Cash—includes an overdraft of $1,250 with Suburban Bank, receivables from employees of $300, and checks from customers of $3,500 dated January 10, Year 9, which have been recorded as cash receipts . . . $ 40,300

Customers—includes promissory notes of $20,000 (accrued interest of $800 has not been recorded), open accounts of $77,500 (including an uncollectible account of $1,200 which should be written off), and an allowance for doubtful accounts of $1,300. Aging of accounts indicates that an allowance of $4,200 is required on December 31, Year 8. Customer's promissory note of $12,000 maturing on March 31, Year 9, has been discounted at a bank. 96,200

Inventories—include $2,000 of prize merchandise, $6,800 of worthless goods, and $5,000 of goods held on consignment owned by P. F. Company. 60,000

Prepayments—include tools of $2,000, cash surrender value of life insurance policies of $3,100, long-term utility deposits of $1,000 12,500

Fixtures—net of $34,500 accumulated depreciation 197,000

Total assets $406,000

Current liabilities, recorded in a single account which includes the following:

*Note payable due in three annual installments; interest at
    15% since Sept. 1, Year 8, has not been accrued* $45,000

Accounts payable 46,000

Payable to P. F. Company for consigned goods 5,000

Estimated liability for coupons outstanding . . . . 1,500 $ 97,500

*(The company has been sued for damages of $25,000 but
    does not anticipate that any liability will result.)*

*Capital—125,000 shares of no-par value capital stock issued for $120,000
    (less 1,000 shares of treasury stock reacquired for $2,800) and retained
    earnings of $191,300* 308,500

Total liabilities & stockholders' equity. $406,000

Instructions Prepare a revised balance sheet, including notes. Ignore the income tax effect of any corrections to previously reported net income. A working paper to determine correct account balances is recommended in the following form:

	Unadjusted balances		Adjustments and corrections		Corrected balances	
Accounts	Debit	Credit	Debit	Credit	Debit	Credit

10-12 Selected transactions completed by Tremaine Company during the current year are described below:

(1) On February 20, the company had an opportunity to obtain for $60,000 a special stock of merchandise being closed out by a manufacturer. The company purchased the merchandise on February 23 and paid for it on March 1 by borrowing $60,000 from Commerce Bank, on a promissory note for $63,750, due on March 1 of next year. The company uses a periodic inventory system and records notes payable at face amount. The discount on the note payable is amortized by the straight-line method.

(2) On July 1, property taxes on the company's retail stores for the ensuing 12-month period became a lien against the property. The company treasurer estimated that property taxes for the year in the amount of $13,200 would be paid on November 1. (Do not record the payment of the tax on November 1 because the actual amount of the tax is not yet known.)

(3) On August 2, the company purchased $30,000 of merchandise from Y Company, terms 2/10, n/30; and $10,000 of merchandise from Z Company, terms 2/10, n/e.o.m. The company records accounts payable net of cash discounts offered. The invoice from Y Company was paid on August 10, but the invoice from Z Company was not paid until August 25, and the cash discount was lost.

(4) On December 1, the sales department launched a special one-month promotion of one of the company's products. Included in each product package sold during December was a coupon which, if sent back to the company with $1 enclosed, entitled the customer to receive a toy. The sales manager estimated that 50% of the customers would accept the offer, which would cost the company 80 cents for each toy claimed plus 30 cents in packaging and shipping costs. The company purchased 50,000 toys for cash. During December, 100,000 of the products were sold for $3 each (debit Cash), and 30,000 coupons were presented for redemption. (Credit the Packaging and Shipping Expense account for 30 cents for each coupon redeemed because actual costs incurred in packaging and shipping were recorded in that account.) On December 31, on the basis of experience to date, it was estimated that only 12,000 additional coupons will be presented by customers before the offer expires. Toys which will not be distributed as prizes can be sold for 40 cents each. The inventory of prize merchandise should be written down to net realizable value by a debit to Promotional Expense.

Instructions

a Prepare journal entries to record the transactions described above.

b Assume that no journal entries have been made other than the entries to record the above transactions as they occurred. Prepare any necessary adjusting entries on December 31 relating to each of the four transactions.

c Prepare a list of accounts used in a and b and indicate the financial statement classification, that is, current asset, current liability, cost of goods sold, operating expense, etc., for each account. (Do not give account balances.)

3

LONG-TERM ASSETS AND LIABILITIES

11 PLANT ASSETS: ACQUISITION AND DISPOSAL

Nature of plant assets

The terms *plant assets; plant and equipment; property, plant, and equipment;* or *fixed assets* often are used to describe the entire complex of tangible assets used by a business enterprise in its operations. Active use in operations distinguishes these assets from other tangible assets which are reported as Investments. Land held as a prospective building site, for example, is an investment. When a building is constructed on the land and is in service, the land is reclassified as a plant asset. A characteristic common to all plant assets is that they yield services over many years. Plant assets other than land have a limited economic life; consequently, the cost of plant assets must be allocated as depreciation expense to the accounting periods receiving benefit from their use.

Classification of assets used in operations

Assets used in operations may be divided into tangible and intangible categories as follows:

Tangible Assets   Tangibility is the characteristic of bodily substance, as exemplified by a tract of timber, a bridge, or a machine.

1 Plant assets   Included in this category are properties acquired for use in operations. Examples are land, buildings and structures of all types, machinery, equipment, furniture, tools, orchards, returnable containers, and leasehold improvements. Assets in this category normally are acquired for use rather than for resale. In yielding services over a number of accounting periods, a plant asset does not change in physical characteristic; that is, it does not become physically incorporated in the finished products. For example, a building or machine wears out and eventually loses the ability to perform its function efficiently, but its physical components remain relatively unchanged. In contrast, material is incorporated in the finished products. Plant assets include land and properties having a limited economic life.

a Land   In contrast to the other kinds of tangible property, land has an indefinite economic life. In general it does not deteriorate with the passage of time, and, unlike wasting natural resources, land is

439

not physically exhausted through use. There are, of course, exceptional cases. Agricultural land may suffer a loss of usefulness through erosion or failure to maintain fertility. Building sites may be damaged or destroyed by slides, floods, or earthquakes. Generally, land is treated for accounting purposes as a nondepreciable asset.

b Property having a limited economic life With the exception of land, all other plant assets have limited economic lives. The investment in such assets is allocated through the process of **depreciation** to the goods and services produced.

2 *Natural resources* This term includes **wasting assets** that are subject to exhaustion through extraction. The principal types of wasting assets are mineral deposits, oil and gas deposits, and standing timber. In essence, natural resources are long-term inventories acquired for resale or use in production over a number of years. The cost of acquiring and developing wasting assets is transformed to periodic charges (known as **depletion**) against revenue.

Intangible Assets Intangibility denotes a lack of physical substance. Examples of intangible assets include patents, copyrights, trademarks, franchises, organization costs, and goodwill. The cost of purchased intangible assets is **amortized** over their estimated economic lives, but not in excess of 40 years.[1] Costs incurred in the creation of internally developed intangible assets are recorded as expenses.

Accounting for plant assets

A plant asset is a **bundle of future services.** The cost of acquiring such an asset is a measure of the amount invested in future services that will be provided by the asset. At the time of acquisition, cost is also an objective measure of the exchange value of an asset. The market price represents the simultaneous resolution of two independent opinions (the purchaser's and the seller's) as to the current fair value of the asset changing hands. There are cases where the purchaser pays too high a price because of errors in judgment or excessive construction costs, and it is sometimes possible to acquire plant assets at bargain prices. These, however, are exceptional cases; accountants seldom have objective evidence to support either "unfortunate" or "bargain" acquisitions. Accountants use cost as the basis of recording and reporting plant assets because it is objective and because it is a measure of the investment in future services.

The problem of determining **carrying amount** (often referred to as **carrying value** or **book value**) subsequent to acquisition is also important. As a given plant asset is used in operations, a portion of the original bundle of services is used up. This is illustrated in the diagram on page 441.

---

[1] A more complete discussion of intangible assets appears in Chapter 13.

Bundle of asset services is used up and is called depreciation

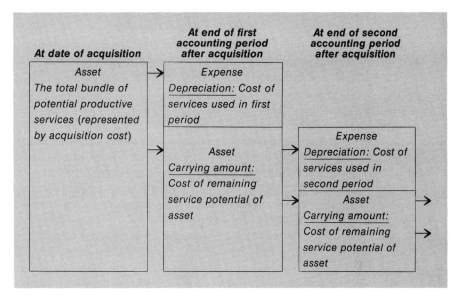

At date of acquisition	At end of first accounting period after acquisition	At end of second accounting period after acquisition
Asset The total bundle of potential productive services (represented by acquisition cost)	*Expense* Depreciation: Cost of services used in first period	
	Asset Carrying amount: Cost of remaining service potential of asset	*Expense* Depreciation: Cost of services used in second period
		Asset Carrying amount: Cost of remaining service potential of asset

The carrying amount of a plant asset thus is reduced by depreciation, because a smaller bundle of potential services remains at the end of each accounting period. The problem of measuring depreciation and the carrying amount of plant assets is discussed in Chapter 12.

Because plant assets generally have long economic lives, it is possible that their current fair value may rise above or fall below carrying amount between the time of acquisition and the time the services are used. When such price movements are material, a question may be raised about the continuing significance of historical cost. This issue is discussed in Chapter 25.

COST OF PLANT ASSETS

The total cost of a plant asset is the cash outlay, or its equivalent, made to acquire the asset and place it in operating condition. This is a clear and simple statement of the principle involved; however, problems arise in the application of this principle to practical situations. In essence, these problems raise three questions: (1) What is included in the cost of plant assets? (2) How is the cost of plant assets measured? and (3) How are costs subsequent to acquisition recorded? Each of these questions is examined in the following sections.

What is included in the cost of plant assets?

Until a plant asset is ready to perform the services for which it was acquired, it is not complete. Some assets, for example a truck or an electronic calculator, are complete and ready to function at acquisition. The cost of such assets may be measured by the total of the invoice price (including sales tax) and transportation costs. Other assets, for example an automobile assembly line or the machinery for a paper mill, must be assembled, installed, and tested. All expenditures connected with the assembling, installing, and testing logically are viewed as a part of cost of the asset.

Capital Expenditures and Revenue Expenditures Initial expenditures that are included in the cost of assets are called *capital expenditures,* and such expenditures are commonly said to be *capitalized;* expenditures treated as expenses of the current accounting period are called *revenue expenditures.* This terminology, while not ideal, is satisfactory and is widely used.

The distinction between capital expenditures and revenue expenditures is important in the measurement of income. If the cost of acquiring plant assets is recorded as a current expense, income of the current accounting period is understated, and income of future periods, when the asset services are used, will be overstated.

The theoretical test to distinguish a capital expenditure from a revenue expenditure is simple: Have the services acquired been consumed entirely within the current accounting period, or will there be a carryover of services to future periods? As we shall see, this test is not always easy to apply. At the outset, however, matters of accounting convenience should be distinguished from questions of principle. Many business enterprises follow an arbitrary procedure of debiting all asset expenditures of relatively small amounts (for example, those under $250) to expense accounts, to minimize accounting effort. Unless these small expenditures are significantly large in the aggregate, such practices, if consistently followed, are reasonable and efficient. They are condoned as a matter of expedience, because they do not materially distort periodic income measurement.

Specific types of capital expenditures and revenue expenditures after acquisition, such as additions, betterments, replacements, and repairs, are covered in a subsequent section of this chapter.

Land Special problems arise in the determination of the initial cost of land. Normally, the acquisition cost of land includes: (1) the purchase price; (2) all costs of closing the transaction and obtaining title, such as real estate commissions, legal fees, escrow fees, title investigations, and title insurance; (3) all costs of surveying, clearing, draining, or filling to make the land suitable for the desired use; and (4) costs of land improvements.

It sometimes is necessary to examine the terms of the purchase contract to determine the price paid for land. Suppose, for example, that a purchaser agrees to pay $80,000 for a parcel of land in addition to delinquent property taxes of $5,000 and past-due mortgage note payments of $1,500. The purchase price of the land in this case includes this additional consideration and is $86,500 ($80,000 + $5,000 + $1,500 = $86,500), not $80,000.

When newly acquired land is not in the condition necessary for the intended use, the purchaser will incur certain costs which should be recorded as part of the cost of the land. For example, costs of clearing trees, or of leveling hills or filling low spots, are included in the cost of the land. Any salvage realized in the process of clearing land should be treated as a reduction in cost.

Land improvement costs are capital expenditures; they are treated as a part of land cost or recorded in a separate Land Improvements account. Improvements, such as landscaping and drainage which have indefinite economic lives, are added to land cost. The cost of improvements such as sidewalks, streets, and sewers may or may not have indefinite economic lives. In many localities, the cost of streets, sewers, and similar improvements are paid by the owners of the benefited property, but the local governmental unit agrees to maintain and replace them if they are built to standard specifications. In such cases the special assessment expenditure is a part of land cost, because it is permanent in nature. If the property owner is responsible for eventual replacement, however, land improvements have a limited economic life and are recorded in a separate account to facilitate depreciation accounting.

Land held as a potential building site or for other investment purposes is not currently used in operations and should be reported under Investments rather than as a part of the plant asset category. The *carrying costs,* such as property taxes and weed control incurred prior to the time that the land is placed in use, are capitalized (added to the cost of the land). When the site is placed in use, the land is reclassified from the investment category to the plant asset category, and future carrying costs are recorded as expenses.

Buildings   The distinction between land and building costs may be of considerable importance because of the potential effect on net income. For example, suppose that a parcel of land is acquired as the site for a new building. On the land is an old building that must be razed before the new structure can be built. Is the cost of tearing down the old building (net of any salvage recovery) a current expense, a part of the cost of the new building, or a part of land cost? If it is a current expense, it is deducted from revenue immediately; if it is a part of the cost of the new building, it will be depreciated over the economic life of the building; if it is a part of land cost, it will not be depreciated. What are the standards to be used in the application of these guidelines?

The primary issue is the nature of the relationship between the expenditure and a particular plant asset. Accountants must ask: What is the asset that has been acquired, and is the cost at issue reasonably related to the acquisition of this particular asset? If land is acquired for a building site, the entire cost of bringing the land into suitable condition as a building site is allocated to the land; on the other hand, excavation costs incurred to construct the foundation for the new building are a part of the cost of the building.

The line of reasoning outlined above can be used to determine the proper accounting treatment of various costs incurred during the construction of a new building. The examples below are illustrative:

Cost incurred	Accounting treatment
1 Cost of temporary structures used for offices or for storing tools and material during construction of a new building.	Record as cost of new building. This is a necessary cost of constructing the *new* building.
2 Cost of tearing down an old building previously used in operations in order to construct a new building.	Record as a loss on retirement of old building. This cost is related to the services of the *old* building.
3 Cost of accident insurance coverage during construction of a new building.	Record as cost of new building. This is an ordinary and necessary cost of constructing the *new* building.

When a building is being constructed, all costs necessary to complete the construction should be included in the cost of the building. These may include architects' fees, building permit, and a variety of overhead costs. When a building is purchased, all costs relating to the purchase (termite inspection fee, for example) and considered applicable to future revenue should be capitalized. Separate ledger accounts may be used for the building shell (foundation, walls, and floors), partitions, air-conditioning units, roof, wiring, and siding.

Costs which will not benefit future accounting periods should not be capitalized. For example, suppose that immediately after the purchase of a used building it is found that extensive repairs will be necessary. The proper treatment of such costs must rest on evidence as to the circumstances of the purchase. If the purchaser recognized the need for these repairs at the time of purchase, the repair costs are a part of the cost of placing the building in serviceable condition and should be capitalized. The reasoning is that paying $100,000 for a rundown building and $50,000 for renovation is equivalent to paying $150,000 for a renovated building. If, on the other hand, a building is purchased for $150,000 under the assumption that it is in condition for occupancy and it is later discovered that there are serious defects requiring an expenditure of $50,000 to correct, any portion of the $50,000 expenditure that does not either result in an improved structure or add to the originally anticipated economic life of the building should be deducted from revenue as incurred.

A similar line of reasoning can be used to reject proposals to treat the carrying amounts of obsolete plant assets replaced as part of the cost of the new plant assets acquired. It is difficult to see how the new assets can have greater value, or how future accounting periods will receive greater service benefit, because of obsolescence of assets no longer in service. Future periods will benefit from the ownership and use of new assets, not from the retirement of the old assets or from the failure to depreciate the old assets fast enough.

Leaseholds and Leasehold Improvements A *leasehold* is a personal property right granting to the *lessee* the use of real property for a specified length of time. The contract under which this right is granted is called a *lease,* and the owner of the property is known as the *lessor.* A lease contract generally requires monthly rent payments. On rare occasions, leases provide for a lump-sum payment of the entire rent in advance.[2] A lease contract gives the lessee the right to use the property in exchange for a contractual obligation to make future rent payments. Thus, it may be appropriate to record both the leased asset and the corresponding obligation to pay rent in the accounting records of the lessee. This topic is discussed in Chapter 20.

Leasehold improvements in the form of buildings or structural alterations sometimes are made on leased property. Accounting for leasehold improvements by the lessee is comparable to accounting for similar owned property, except that economic life should be related to the duration of the lease. A building expected to last 20 years which is built on land leased for 15 years with no renewal option has a 15-year economic life insofar as the lessee is concerned, and a residual value that is determined by the amount, if any, that the lessor agrees to pay to the lessee at the end of the lease term. When the lease contract contains a provision to renew at the option of the lessee, the length of economic life becomes uncertain, except in terms of the present intentions of the lessee. In the above example, if the lease contract contained a renewal option for an additional 5-year period, the economic life for the building would be either 15 or 20 years, depending on the intent of the lessee with respect to renewal.

The lessor generally does not record leasehold improvements made by the lessee. However, if the lessor pays for any of the improvements, the cost should be recorded in a plant asset account by the lessor and depreciated over the economic life of the improvements.

Machinery and Equipment This category may encompass a wide variety of items, including all types of machinery, furniture, fixtures, ships, vehicles of all types, tools, containers, patterns and dies, computers, and other office equipment. Cost of machinery and equipment items is determined and allocated to revenue through the process of depreciation. Several topics relating to the acquisition of machinery, equipment, and buildings are discussed in the following pages.

[2] The lump-sum leasehold is almost extinct, largely because of the income tax law, which requires the lessor to include the entire sum received in taxable income in the year of receipt, without regard to the time period covered by the lease.

Self-Constructed Assets   Occasionally, a building, machine, or equipment may be constructed by a business enterprise that intends to use it, either because this is an economical method of acquisition or because the quality and specifications of the asset can be controlled better if the asset is self-constructed. Determining the cost of the completed asset in this situation raises a number of issues.

Accountants generally agree that all direct costs incurred in construction activities should be capitalized. **Direct costs** are defined as those that can be identified specifically with the construction project in the sense that they would not have been incurred otherwise. Direct costs include the cost of material, labor, design, engineering, etc. Whether any overhead should be included in the cost of the self-constructed asset is a debatable question.

The basic issue is whether overhead costs that will not change as the result of a self-construction project should be included in the cost of the new asset. Some enterprises have engineering and construction departments that regularly engage in new construction. The overhead costs incurred in these departments benefit current revenue-producing activities as well as the new construction. But what about the overhead costs of a regular producing department that occasionally undertakes the construction of a plant asset? It is difficult to imagine a situation in which any significant self-construction project could be undertaken without some increase in overhead. However, there are several fixed costs in overhead which will not increase as a result of construction activities. If these fixed costs are allocated between regular production and self-construction projects, the result may be that the average manufacturing cost for units produced will be reduced during accounting periods in which significant self-construction activities are undertaken. Pre-tax income during the construction period thus would be increased by the amount of the fixed overhead allocated to the self-constructed asset. The three possible approaches to this issue are summarized below:

1 *Allocate no overhead to the self-constructed asset*   This approach has little to recommend it. At least some overhead is the direct result of new construction, and charging this incremental overhead to current operations is a clear case of distortion of income by the failure to recognize a capital expenditure.

2 *Allocate only incremental overhead to self-constructed assets*   This approach may be defended on the grounds that incremental overhead represents the relevant cost which management considered in making the decision to construct the asset. Fixed overhead costs, it is argued, are period costs; because they would have been incurred in any case, there is no relationship between the fixed portion of overhead and the self-constructed project. This approach has been widely used in practice because, its supporters argue, "it does not distort the cost of normal operations."

3 *Allocate a portion of all overhead to the self-constructed asset*   The argument for this approach is that the proper function of cost allocation is to relate all costs incurred in a given accounting period to the output of that period. If an enterprise is able to construct an asset and still carry on its regular activities, it has benefited by putting to use some of its **idle capacity,** and this fact should

be reflected in larger income. To charge the entire overhead to only a portion of the productive activity is to ignore facts and to understate the cost of the self-constructed asset. The authors feel that this line of reasoning is sound and was supported by the Cost Accounting Standards Board as follows:[3]

> Tangible capital assets constructed for a contractor's own use must be capitalized at amounts which include general and administrative expenses when such expenses are identifiable with the constructed asset and are material in amount. When the constructed assets are identical with or similar to the contractor's regular product, such assets must be capitalized at amounts which include a full share of indirect costs.

Profit on Self-Construction Suppose that a business enterprise has asked for bids on a plant asset, and that the lowest bid received is for $50,000. The same asset can be constructed in the enterprise's own plant at a total cost of $40,000, including material, labor, and incremental overhead. If the enterprise chooses to construct the asset, it might be argued that the asset should be recorded at $50,000 and that a profit of $10,000 should be recognized. Although there is some support for this view, the facts do not meet the current accounting test of realization. Profits are generated from asset *use and disposal,* not from asset *acquisition;* the $10,000 is a *saving* which will be realized through lower depreciation expense over the economic life of the asset.

Interest during Construction Period During the time it takes to complete a self-construction project, cash is tied up in material, labor, and other construction costs. Is the interest cost incurred in borrowing funds for this purpose a part of the cost of the constructed asset? This has been a controversial question, both in accounting theory and in accounting practice.

Generally, accountants regard interest as a cost of financing, not as a cost of obtaining asset services. If Company X pays cash for an asset and Company Y borrows cash to acquire an identical asset, there is no logical basis for claiming that Company Y has a more valuable asset simply because it has paid interest on borrowed funds. This reasoning, applied to self-constructed assets, leads to the conclusion that interest on funds borrowed and used in construction should not be capitalized.

The opposing view is that interest during construction is a cost of acquiring future asset services. Funds are immobilized during the construction period. In deciding to construct an asset, management of the business enterprise must have determined that the value created would be sufficient to cover all costs, including interest. Furthermore, interest on investment is included in the price of the asset if it is purchased in finished form. Therefore, it may be argued, the interest on funds employed in construction of an asset prior to the time that the asset is ready to produce revenue should not be expensed. Consequently, many busi-

---

[3] *Standard 404,* "Capitalization of Tangible Assets," CASB (Washington: 1973).

ness enterprises adopted a policy of capitalizing interest paid on loans to finance projects during the construction period.[4] However, the SEC in 1974 placed a moratorium on the adoption or extension of such practices until the FASB developed appropriate standards in this area.

The SEC withdrew the moratorium in 1979 when the FASB issued **Statement No. 34,** which established the current standards of accounting and reporting for capitalized interest costs.[5] The FASB pointed out that the cost of any asset includes all costs "incurred to bring it to the condition and location necessary for its intended uses." When a period of time is needed to bring the asset to that condition and location, the interest costs incurred in these efforts should be included in the cost of the asset. Such a period of time is called the **acquisition period.** The objectives of this accounting treatment of interest costs are (1) to measure more accurately the total investment in the asset, and (2) to charge this investment (interest costs) to future revenue that will benefit from the use of the asset.

Capitalization of interest costs **is permitted** for assets that are constructed for a business enterprise's own use, and for assets intended for sale or lease that are constructed as clearly identifiable projects, such as ships and parcels of real estate. Capitalization of interest costs **is not permitted** for inventories, assets that are either in use or ready for use, and assets that are not intended for use in the activities of the enterprise. For example, interest costs relating to idle land are not capitalized; however, if the land is being developed for a particular purpose, the interest paid on any debt incurred in the acquisition and development of the land is capitalized. Thus, if land is to be used as a parking lot, or sold as developed land, interest is included in the cost of the land. However, if land is to be used to construct buildings for the enterprise's own use or for resale, interest is added to the cost of the buildings.

The amount of interest properly capitalized is that portion of interest cost during the acquisition period that **could have been avoided** if the asset had not been acquired. Needless to say, the application of this concept is not easy. If a project is financed by a specific loan, the interest actually paid on the loan is capitalized. However, if a project is financed from internally generated funds or from general borrowings, the

---

[4] A good justification for capitalizing over $9 million of interest costs was given by Weyerhaeuser Company a few years ago. A note to its financial statements stated:

> The cost of properties includes interest on funds borrowed to finance the acquisition or construction of major facilities. Construction financing is part of the cost of acquiring economic resources which provide benefits beyond the period in which acquired; therefore, deferred expense recognition through association of all property acquisition costs with future revenues through allocation to future periods in a systematic and rational manner is appropriate. A borrowed capital pool rate is applied to construction in progress project balances to compute the amount of interest to be capitalized. Capitalization of interest ceases when the facilities commence operations.

[5] *FASB Statement No. 34,* "Capitalization of Interest Cost," FASB (Stamford: 1979). The remaining discussion in this section is based on pages 2–8 of this *Statement.*

average effective interest rate on all outstanding debt is used to compute the amount of interest capitalized. The total amount of interest capitalized in an accounting period cannot exceed the total amount of interest costs incurred by the business enterprise in that period. The acquisition period begins when the following three conditions are present:

1 Expenditures for a specific asset have been incurred.

2 Activities to prepare the asset for use are in progress.

3 Interest costs are being incurred.

Interest capitalization continues as long as all three of these conditions are present, and ends when the asset is completed and is ready for use. The total interest costs incurred and the total interest costs capitalized in an accounting period must be disclosed.

To illustrate the computation of interest costs capitalized as part of the historical cost of an asset, assume that Clark Steel Company constructed a blast furnace in the current year. The construction activity started on March 1, and the furnace was ready for its intended use on December 1. On March 1, the company borrowed $400,000 at 15% for five years to pay for the parts and material needed, and financed additional costs of $360,000 from the company's general borrowing of approximately $4,000,000, which carried an average interest rate of 12%. The additional costs of $360,000 were incurred at a rate of $40,000 a month from March 1 through December 1. Thus, the average accumulated cost was $180,000 ($360,000 ÷ 2 = $180,000) during the construction period. The total interest included in the cost of the blast furnace is computed below:

	Interest capitalized
Computation of interest capitalized as part of cost of plant asset	
Specific borrowing on Mar. 1: $400,000 × 15% × $\frac{9}{12}$	$45,000
Average accumulated cost from Mar. 1 to Dec. 1:	
$180,000 × 12% × $\frac{9}{12}$	16,200
Total interest included in the cost of the blast furnace	$61,200

The total cost of the blast furnace for financial accounting purposes is $821,000 ($400,000 + $360,000 + $61,200 = $821,200). Note that no interest costs are capitalized after the furnace is placed in use on December 1, even though interest continues to accrue on the $400,000 loan for the purchase of parts and material needed for the construction of the blast furnace.

How is cost of plant assets measured?

We have reviewed some of the problems that arise in the determination of what is included in the cost of plant assets. Now, let us examine the problems that arise in the measurement of the cost of plant assets, when the method of acquisition obscures the purchase price. The objective of cost measurement is to determine the cash outlay or its equivalent necessary to obtain the asset.

Cash Discounts When assets are purchased under terms that allow the deduction of a discount for the payment of cash within a specified period of time, the term "cash equivalent" may be interpreted to mean the invoice price, net of the discount. For example, if M Company purchases a plant asset for $10,000, terms 2/10, n/30, it has the choice of either paying cash (within a 10-day grace period) of $9,800, or deferring payment for an additional 20 days, at an added cost of $200. If payment is made within the 10-day period, the cost of the asset is only $9,800; if payment is deferred for 20 days, the additional $200 paid is a penalty for late payment and is not included in the cost of the asset.

Deferred Payment Contracts In many cases, payment for an asset is delayed for longer time periods. For example, suppose that equipment is purchased under a contract calling for payments of $1,490 at the end of each year for 10 years. To assume that the present value of the liability, and thus the cost of the equipment, is $14,900 ($1,490 × 10), is to ignore the fact that there is an interest charge included in the contract. To arrive at a basis for recording this purchase, accountants must look for evidence of the cash-equivalent price of the equipment. If the equipment can be purchased for $10,000 cash, this amount becomes the measure of cost. If no conclusive evidence of a cash price is available, the rate of interest implicit in the contract price should be determined. The present value of 10 payments of $1,490 each at 8% interest per year is approximately $10,000.[6] Assuming that an 8% rate of interest is reasonable, the purchase and the first two payments are recorded as illustrated on page 451.

When payment is deferred for relatively short time periods, the amount of interest implicit in the purchase price may not be material in amount and can be ignored. However, if the length of time and the amount of interest involved are material, a reasonable estimate of the cash-equivalent purchase price is required.[7]

Property often is acquired by assuming a purchase-money obliga-

---

[6] The computation of this amount requires the use of a present value of ordinary annuity formula, as illustrated in Chapter 5.

[7] See *APB Opinion No. 21,* "Interest on Receivables and Payables," AICPA (New York: 1971).

Journal entries for purchase of plant asset on installment plan

Journal Entries

At acquisition:

Equipment.	10,000	
Discount on Equipment Contract Payable	4,900	
Equipment Contract Payable		14,900

To record purchase of equipment under contract requiring payment of $1,490 at the end of each of 10 years. Present value of equipment contract payable, discounted at 8%, is $10,000.

Payment on contract at end of first year:

Interest Expense	800	
Equipment Contract Payable	1,490	
Cash.		1,490
Discount on Equipment Contract Payable		800

To record interest expense on equipment contract for first year ($10,000 × 8% = $800) and payment of first installment.

Payment on contract at end of second year:

Interest Expense	745	
Equipment Contract Payable.	1,490	
Cash.		1,490
Discount on Equipment Contract Payable		745

To record interest expense on equipment contract for second year [($13,410 − $4,100) × 8% = $745] and payment of second installment.

tion. A **purchase-money mortgage,** for example, is a loan created at the time property is acquired, collateralized by such property, and having priority over any subsequently created lien on the property.

Lump-Sum Acquisitions A single negotiated price may be paid for two or more assets. If the assets have different economic lives, it is necessary to allocate the total lump-sum cost among them to provide a proper basis for the computation of depreciation. The most common example of this situation is the purchase of real property—land and building—for a single price. Because the economic life of land is indefinite and the economic life of a building is limited, an allocation of the total cost is necessary. Assume, for example, that a building and the land on which it is located are acquired for $250,000 (see escrow statement on page 453). How is the accountant to determine how much of the $250,000 applies to the land and how much to the building? An examination of the negotiations that preceded the transaction may show that the price was settled on under the assumption that $200,000 applied to the building and $50,000 to the land. If such evidence is not available or is considered to be unrealistic, the accountant must look elsewhere for more objective evidence of **relative values** as a basis for cost allocation. If, for example, the assessed valuation for property tax purposes is $161,000 for the building and $69,000 for land, the allocation of the total cost of $250,000 would be made as follows:

	Assessed valuation	Relative value	×	Total cost	=	Allocation of cost
Building	$161,000	70%				→$175,000
				$250,000		
Land	69,000	30%				→75,000
Totals	$230,000	100%				$250,000

The Escrow Statement Parties to a real estate transaction generally engage an agent (bank or escrow company) to handle the details of the transaction. When the transaction is closed, each party receives an **escrow statement** which shows the complete details of the transaction. The escrow statement shows (as charges and credits) items such as selling price of the property, mortgage note assumed by the purchaser, transfer taxes, commission charged to the seller, escrow fees, cash received from the purchaser, any amount paid to either party to complete the transaction, etc. The allocation of property taxes, interest on the mortgage note, insurance, rents, and other items also is summarized in the escrow statement. A somewhat condensed escrow statement for the purchaser of the property discussed in the preceding section is given on page 453.

The escrow statement for the purchaser shows that the purchase price of the property was $246,700, a debit in the escrow statement. The purchaser was charged $240 for unexpired insurance, and additional costs of $3,300 ($1,490 + $290 + $20 + $1,500 = $3,300) allocable to the property. Thus, the total cost of the property is $250,000 ($246,700 + $3,300 = $250,000). The purchaser was credited for $104,000, representing the unpaid balance of the mortgage note assumed, $520 of accrued interest on the mortgage note, $2,200 of accrued property taxes, and $143,570 that previously was deposited in escrow to apply on the purchase price. (The cash deposit was recorded in the Escrow Deposit account.) The "check to balance" of $50 is the amount of cash returned to the purchaser to close the escrow on November 1, Year 1.

Escrow statement for purchase of building and land

WESTERN ESCROW COMPANY		
Escrow Statement for Purchaser		

Escrow No. 1-879   **Date: November 1, Year 1**

Items	Charges	Credits
Purchase price of property	$246,700	
Balance of mortgage note.		$104,000
Interest @ 12% from Oct. 16, Year 1, to Nov. 1, Year 1 . .		520
Property taxes prorated, $6,600 per year from July 1, Year 1, to Nov. 1, Year 1		2,200
Fire insurance prorated, $1,440 for three years, Nov. 1, Year 1, to May 1, Year 2.	240	
Deposited in escrow by purchaser.		143,570
Title policy (purchaser agreed to pay full amount)	1,490	
Revenue stamps (tax on transaction)	290	
Recording fee	20	
Escrow fee (purchaser agreed to pay full amount)	1,500	
Check to balance	50	
Totals.	$250,290	$250,290

The escrow statement for the purchaser provides the information needed to record the purchase of the property as illustrated below:

Journal entry to record purchase of property

Cash	50	
Building	175,000	
Land	75,000	
Unexpired Insurance	240	
Accrued Interest Payable		520
Property Taxes Payable		2,200
Mortgage Note Payable		104,000
Escrow Deposit.		143,570

To record purchase of building and land per Escrow No. 1-879. The total cost of $250,000 ($246,700 + $1,490 + $290 + $20 + $1,500 = $250,000) is allocated on the basis of property tax valuation of building and land (see allocation on page 452).

A similar escrow statement prepared for the seller provides the required information to record the sale of the property by the seller.

Securities Issued in Exchange for Assets   When a corporation issues shares of its own capital stock for assets, the proper basis for recording such a transaction is not always clear. The current fair value of the asset acquired is the cash equivalent received by the corporation for its shares of capital stock.[8] On the other hand, the current fair (or market) value of the capital stock given in exchange is a measure of the consideration for the asset. Accountants are thus faced with the problem of obtaining independent evidence of (1) the current fair value of the asset, and (2) the current fair value of the capital stock given in exchange. We should expect these two values to be roughly equivalent; if they are not, a choice between them must be made based on the factors considered by management in making the purchase and on the validity of each valuation.

Shares of capital stock represent an interest in the net assets of a corporation, including the asset being acquired. The market price of the capital stock issued thus is not an entirely independent variable, because it depends to some extent on the value of the asset received in exchange. This reasoning indicates that our first choice should be independent evidence of the current fair value of the asset acquired, determined by appraisal, from previous bid prices, or from other objective sources. For example, if a machine which was appraised at $180,000 is acquired in exchange for 2,000 shares of $50 par capital stock, the exchange is recorded as follows:

Issuance of capital stock for a plant asset	Machinery 180,000	
	Capital Stock, $50 par	100,000
	Paid-in Capital in Excess of Par	80,000
	To record exchange of 2,000 shares of $50 par capital stock for machine appraised at $180,000.	

In some cases, evidence of the market value of shares of capital stock is easier to obtain and more reliable than evidence as to the current fair value of an asset. This is particularly true if the capital stock is listed on a stock exchange and daily quotations of market price are available.

Assets Acquired by Gift   Normally, there is a presumption against the idea that anyone dealing with a business enterprise makes a gift to it. However, a corporation may receive property under conditions which may be interpreted as the receipt of a gift. For example, assume that the City of Stillwater is trying to attract industry to its area. In order to induce Tanner Company to locate a manufacturing plant in its city, the City Council agrees to donate a building site and erect a suitable building for

---

[8] Procedures for recording assets acquired pursuant to business combinations accounted for as **purchases** and as **pooling of interests** are discussed briefly in Chapter 16. A more extensive discussion of this subject is found in **Modern Advanced Accounting** of this series.

the company, in return for which the company promises to operate a plant employing 200 persons for a period of 10 years. The land has a current fair value of $400,000, and the building has a current fair value of $2,000,000.

How should accountants record this transaction? If we adopt the view that the sole responsibility of accountants is to keep track of costs incurred, we might argue that no cost is involved in the receipt of the land and building in this instance, and therefore no journal entry is required. This is, however, too narrow a view of the scope of accounting. A primary justification for recording asset acquisitions at cost is that cost at that time represents more satisfactory evidence of current fair value than any other basis. When cash outlay no longer is a reasonable basis for asset accountability or income measurement, accountants should be prepared to deal with the problem on its merits rather than bury their heads, ostrichlike, in the sands of cost. If a business enterprise receives an asset at no cost, the asset should be recorded at its current fair value, determined on the basis of the best evidence available. Referring to the Tanner Company example, the donation of the land and building results in an increase in the net assets of the company, and is recorded as follows:

Recording a donated asset

Land	400,000	
Building	2,000,000	
Donated Capital		2,400,000
To record at current fair value property donated by City of Stillwater.		

Conditions sometimes are attached to a gift of property so that title is not transferred until the conditions are met (for example, continuing operations for a specified number of years). As long as indications are that the company intends to comply with the conditions, depreciation expense should be recorded in the regular manner, both before and after title is acquired, in order that the services obtained from the use of the asset (whether purchased by or donated to the company) are recorded as expenses in the measurement of net income.

Investment Tax Credit Federal income tax statutes provide for a reduction of income taxes paid by individuals and corporations by an amount known as the **investment tax credit.** The investment tax credit is subject to a number of limitations and has been amended frequently and even suspended. The credit generally has ranged from $3\frac{1}{3}$ to 10% of the cost of depreciable property other than buildings and their structural components. To illustrate, if a corporation purchased equipment with an economic life of seven years or more for $100,000, it would be entitled to a

$10,000 (10% of $100,000), reduction in its federal income tax bill. Despite this tax reduction, the full $100,000 cost may be depreciated for income tax purposes over the economic life of the equipment. Two methods have been used to recognize the effect of the investment tax credit in the accounting records.

1 The *flow-through method,* which reduces income taxes expense by the amount of the investment tax credit in the year the asset is acquired. This method is favored by most business executives on grounds that immediate tax reduction is the intent of the federal income tax law. Because income taxes expense is reduced in the year depreciable assets are acquired, this method allows business enterprises to increase income by acquiring depreciable assets which qualify for the investment tax credit.

2 The *deferral method,* which calls for the amortization of the benefit arising from the investment tax credit over the economic life of the depreciable asset acquired. Under this method the investment tax credit is viewed as a reduction in the effective cost of the asset, although it generally is reported as a deferred credit in the balance sheet and is amortized by periodic reductions of Income Taxes Expense.

The deferral method is favored by most accountants because it avoids an immediate increase in income as a result of purchasing assets, and thus provides a more meaningful measurement of income. However, most individuals and corporations use the flow-through method.[9]

Costs subsequent to acquisition

Expenditures relating to plant assets normally are made throughout the economic life of such assets. Whether these are expenses to be charged against current revenue or whether they should be capitalized often is a difficult question. The general approach for dealing with these expenditures may be stated as follows: Expenditures that result in additional asset services, more valuable asset services, or extension of economic life are capitalized and allocated to future revenue; expenditures to maintain plant assets in good operating condition are recorded as expenses of the accounting period in which they are incurred. This approach is consistent with the principle of matching costs

[9] Because this discussion of the investment tax credit is brief, it should not be concluded that the related federal income tax law is not complex or that the accounting issues are not controversial. The APB in *Opinion No. 2* took the position that the investment tax credit should be reflected in net income over the productive life of assets on which the credit is allowed and not in the year in which the assets are acquired. Because of strong opposition from the business community, and because the SEC permitted either approach, the APB issued *Opinion No. 4,* in which it stated that even though the deferral method was preferable, the alternative method of treating the credit as a reduction in income taxes expense in the year in which the credit arises also was acceptable. Subsequently, the APB issued an exposure draft of an opinion which would have eliminated this alternative treatment by requiring the deferral method. However, strong pressure on Congress by some business groups resulted in a provision in the Internal Revenue Code which permitted taxpayers to choose the method of accounting for the Investment tax credit. The method adopted must be used consistently and must be disclosed.

and revenue and should be applied to any expenditure of significant amount. Future benefit is a characteristic of all capitalized costs relating to plant assets; costs that are applicable to current or past revenue are recorded as expenses or losses.

Although the general approach outlined in the preceding paragraph enables accountants to distinguish between capital expenditures and revenue expenditures incurred subsequent to acquisition, a brief discussion relating to different types of these expenditures should be useful.

Additions   An *addition* is a new and separate asset or an extension of an existing asset. The construction of a new wing on an existing building is an example of an addition to buildings. The installation of two-way communication radios in a fleet of delivery trucks is an example of an addition to equipment. The addition of entirely new units is identical in nature to the acquisition of new assets and raises no accounting problems not discussed previously. When the addition involves an enlargement or extension of an existing asset, the only problem is to determine whether any portion of the service potential of the existing asset has been removed or lost in the process. For example, if in connection with the construction of a building addition, it is necessary to remove the old central heating unit and install one with a larger capacity, the old unit should be retired. The recording of the asset addition should be accompanied by a journal entry to remove the cost of the old heating unit and its related accumulated depreciation from the accounting records and to recognize any resulting loss. The loss is not recorded as part of the cost of the new heating unit.

Improvements, Renewals, and Replacements   Improvements (or betterments), renewals, and replacements are nonrecurring expenditures that add to the service potential of plant assets. The additional value may be the result of extending the economic life, increasing the rate of output, or lowering the cost of operation per unit of output. Therefore, such expenditures are related to future services and should be charged against revenue in the accounting periods in which the services are used. Improvements and renewals may be accomplished through the substitution of better component parts and hence may be labeled as *replacements.* The distinction between these different expenditures is obscure and is not relevant to the basic accounting issues involved. Costs of this type often are referred to as *plant renovation* (or *plant modernization*) *costs.*

To the extent that renovation involves the substitution of a new part for old, the proper accounting is to remove the cost of the old part from the asset account (and the appropriate amount from the related accumulated depreciation account) and to substitute the cost of the new part. If the renovation does not involve a substitution but results only in some modification of the asset, the costs incurred are added to the carrying amount of the asset by a debit to either the asset account or the accumulated depreciation account. These three procedures are explained below:

1 A considerable improvement in accounting for plant assets is possible if property units are defined in terms of major components and separate economic lives are used to depreciate these components. To illustrate, suppose that a glass-lined food storage tank is constructed at a cost of $200,000, of which $40,000 is estimated to be the cost of the glass lining. The estimated economic life of the tank is 20 years; the lining must be replaced approximately every five years. If a single asset account, Storage Tanks, is used, there will be a problem of dealing with the periodic replacement of the lining. A better procedure would be to use two asset accounts, Storage Tanks and Tank Lining, and to depreciate the former over 20 years and the latter over five years. Now, assume that at the beginning of the fifth year the glass lining had to be replaced at a cost of $54,000, but a new material was used that is expected to last six years. The journal entries to record the lining replacement are:

Replacement of a component of a plant asset

Accumulated Depreciation of Tank Lining	32,000	
Loss on Retirement of Tank Lining	8,000	
Tank Lining		40,000

To record removal of old tank lining. Undepreciated cost of tank lining is recorded as a loss.

Tank Lining	54,000	
Cash		54,000

To record replacement of old lining with new material.

Depreciation of the new lining is recorded at $9,000 ($54,000 ÷ 6) in each of the next six years, and the asset account Storage Tanks is undisturbed by these events.

2 An expenditure which does not replace an existing part may enlarge the capacity or improve the efficiency of an asset without prolonging its economic life. Such expenditures should be recorded in the asset account and depreciated over the remaining economic life of the asset. This procedure is similar to the one previously suggested for additions.

3 The cost of asset renovation often is debited directly to Accumulated Depreciation. The rationale for this procedure is that such an expenditure extends the economic life of the asset and thus restores some of the service potential previously written off. A reduction of Accumulated Depreciation means that additional time will be required to depreciate the asset, and it is assumed that this period will correspond to the increased economic life of the asset. This procedure is sound in theory and may be used for income tax purposes, but it should not be followed blindly, particularly when additions and replacements are involved.

Rearrangements and Moving Costs Costs of rearranging machinery and equipment to provide a more efficient plant layout may be recorded in a separate account and amortized over the period of time expected to benefit from the rearrangement (usually a short period because of the possibility of further rearrangements). Costs of moving the entire plant or office may be recorded similarly, unless the moving results from some unusual and infrequent event, in which case the costs of moving are included as part of the related extraordinary loss. However, most business enterprises record moving costs as expenses.

Ordinary Repairs and Maintenance Minor repair and maintenance expenditures usually are required throughout the economic life of a plant asset to keep it in efficient operating condition. The distinguishing characteristic of such expenditures is that they neither add to the value of the asset nor materially prolong its economic life. The usual procedure is to record these costs as current expenses, because maintenance activities are recurring and the costs are related to current revenue. However, any unusual or extraordinary repairs arising from fire or other casualties are recorded as losses if not covered by insurance.

A questionable approach to the problem of dealing with repair costs which vary widely from one accounting period to another and are significant in amount is to anticipate such costs and apportion them over the economic life of the asset. Under this procedure, the total expected repair costs are estimated at the time each asset is acquired, and Repair Expense is debited each accounting period for a portion of the estimated lifetime repair costs. The offsetting credit is to an account titled Allowance for Estimated Repairs. Actual repair expenditures are debited to the allowance account. However, only the actual expenditures are allowed for income tax purposes in the year incurred.

To illustrate, assume that repair costs for an item of equipment are expected to average $250 a year, and that repair costs of $400 are incurred in the second year. The journal entries required during the first two years are given at the top of page 460.

At the end of the second year, the allowance account has a credit balance of $100 ($500 − $400 = $100). Conceivably, a debit balance might appear in the allowance account if major repairs occurred early or if the estimate of repair costs were too low.

A number of criticisms of this method may be raised. Some accountants have argued that it is an income-smoothing device and that it tends to obscure the fact that repair costs may increase as an asset becomes older. Others question whether reliable estimates of repair costs can be made. Finally, the classification of the Allowance for Estimated Repairs poses difficulties. A credit balance in the allowance account cannot be classified as a part of stockholders' equity because it is illogical to debit an expense and increase stockholders' equity. Classification as a liability may be questioned, because no legal obligation

**Journal entries for
accrual of repair costs**

End of Year 1:
    Repair Expense   250
        Allowance for Estimated Repairs   250
    To record estimated repair expense.

During Year 2:
    Allowance for Estimated Repairs.   400
        Cash, Parts, Accrued Payroll, etc..   400
    To record actual repair costs.

End of Year 2:
    Repair Expense   250
        Allowance for Estimated Repairs   250
    To record estimated repair expense.

exists. Recording the allowance as an asset valuation account (to be deducted from or added to the cost of the related asset in the balance sheet) assumes that the "accrued repairs" represent additional depreciation and thus reduce the carrying amount of the asset. This is probably the least objectionable alternative, because it is consistent with the reporting of a debit balance in the allowance account as an asset—in the nature of a prepayment of repair costs.

Anticipation of repair costs does not fit well into the generally accepted measurement concepts of accounting. Year-to-year accrual of estimated repair costs lacks sufficient objectivity and might encourage management to adopt other income-smoothing practices.

RETIREMENTS, DISPOSALS, AND EXCHANGES

Whenever a plant asset is retired, sold, or exchanged, the first step is to bring depreciation expense on the asset up to date. The next step is to remove from the accounting records all ledger accounts relating to the asset. The second step generally requires the recording of any proceeds and gain or loss from the disposal of the asset. Some of the more common situations involving the retirement, disposal, or exchange of plant assets include the following:

1 A fully depreciated plant asset with no residual value is **retired** without receipt of any proceeds; no gain or loss is recognized on such retirement.
2 A partially depreciated plant asset is **retired** without receipt of any proceeds; a loss is recognized on such retirement.
3 A fully or partially depreciated plant asset is **retired** or **sold** with some recovery of residual value; a gain or loss is recognized on such a retirement or sale.

4 A fully or partially depreciated asset is **exchanged** for other assets without any cash being received or paid; the guidelines for the recognition of a gain or loss on such a **nonmonetary exchange transaction** are:

   a If a loss is indicated by the terms of the transaction, the **loss always is recognized.**

   b If a gain is indicated in an **exchange of dissimilar assets** which **results in the completion of the earning process** (such as the exchange of an inventory item which cost $1,000 for a plant asset with a current fair value of $1,500), the **gain is recognized.**

   c If a gain is indicated in an **exchange of similar assets** which **does not complete the earning process** (such as an exchange of an inventory item held for another inventory item or an exchange of a plant asset for a similar plant asset), the **gain is not recognized.**

5 A fully or partially depreciated plant asset may be exchanged for a **similar asset,** with cash being paid or received by the parties to the transaction. The guidelines for the recognition of gains and losses are the same as in *4* above, except that a **partial gain is recognized** on the exchange of similar plant assets **by the party receiving cash.**

The accounting procedures for these situations are described in the following sections.

Retirements and disposals of plant assets

When a fully depreciated plant asset with no residual value is retired, and no proceeds are received, the retirement is recorded by a debit to accumulated depreciation and a credit to the plant asset; when a partially depreciated plant asset is retired and no proceeds are received, a loss is recognized equal to the difference between cost and accumulated depreciation; when a fully or partially depreciated plant asset is retired or sold with some recovery of residual value, a gain or loss is recognized equal to the difference between the carrying amount of the asset and the proceeds received. For example, assume that equipment costing $6,000 with no residual value has been depreciated at an annual rate of 10% for eight years. In the middle of the ninth year the equipment was sold for $1,750 cash (net of any direct costs incurred on the sale). The journal entries to record this sale are shown at the top of page 462.

The proper interpretation of any gain or loss that may arise on the retirement or sale of an asset often is uncertain. To the extent that it stems from errors in estimates of economic life or residual value, the "gain" or "loss" is an adjustment of previously reported income. To the extent that it is due to changes in the current fair value of the asset, the gain or loss is also an element of income for the current year. In most cases a combination of these factors is present. Material gains and losses (or provisions for losses) from the sale or abandonment of plant assets are included in the determination of income before extraordinary items.

Plant assets sometimes are retired from active service and are neither sold nor abandoned but are kept on a **standby status** for use in emergency or to meet peak-load requirements. When this occurs, the assets

Depreciation first is
brought up to date when
a plant asset is sold

Depreciation Expense.	*300*	
Accumulated Depreciation of Equipment		*300*
To record depreciation at 10% for six months on machine costing		
$6,000 with no residual value.		
Cash	*1,750*	
Accumulated Depreciation of Equipment	*5,100*	
Gain on Disposal of Equipment.		*850*
Equipment.		*6,000*
To record sale of equipment.		

should be written down to their standby or residual values. Depreciation of the assets should be discontinued while they remain idle. When the amount of standby equipment is significant, it should be reported separately in the balance sheet.

Exchanges of plant assets

Prior to the issuance of **APB Opinion No. 29,** exchanges of plant assets for similar plant assets were recorded in a variety of ways for financial accounting purposes. Such transactions frequently were recorded following the income tax requirements; that is, the asset acquired was recorded at the carrying amount of the asset given in exchange plus any cash paid or less any cash received, and no gain or loss was recognized. Alternatively, a gain or loss was recognized when the current fair value of the asset given in exchange was used to record the transaction, and the asset acquired generally was recorded at the current fair value of the asset exchanged, plus any cash paid or less any cash received.

Provisions of APB Opinion No. 29   This opinion differentiated **monetary exchanges** involving cash and receivables or payables from **nonmonetary exchanges** involving, for example, inventories, investments in common stocks, and plant assets. An **exchange** was defined as a transfer between business enterprises that results in one enterprise receiving assets or services or satisfying obligations by surrendering other assets or services or incurring other obligations.[10] The portion of the "basic principle" in **APB Opinion No. 29** which relates to exchanges of plant assets appears at the top of page 463.[11]

[10] APB Opinion No. 29, "Accounting for Nonmonetary Transactions," AICPA (New York: 1973), p. 541.
[11] Ibid., p. 547.

The Board concludes that in general accounting for nonmonetary transactions should be based on the fair values of the assets (or services) involved which is the same basis as that used in monetary transactions. Thus, the cost of a nonmonetary asset acquired in exchange for another nonmonetary asset is the fair value of the asset surrendered to obtain it, and a gain or loss should be recognized on the exchange. The fair value of the asset received should be used to measure the cost if it is more clearly evident that the fair value of the asset surrendered.

The APB modified this basic principle in several important respects. First, the accounting for exchanges should not be based on the current fair values of assets unless such values are reasonably determinable. If current fair values are not reasonably determinable, the asset acquired is recorded at the carrying amount of the asset given in exchange plus any cash paid, and no gain or loss is recognized. Second, when an exchange transaction does not result in the completion of the earning process (realization), the asset acquired also should be recorded at the carrying amount of the asset surrendered. An example of such a transaction is an exchange of a plant asset for a similar plant asset. However, if the terms of the transaction indicate that the asset surrendered has a current fair value which is less than the carrying amount, a loss is recognized. Finally, when cash (or other monetary consideration) is received in an exchange of assets, the recipient of the cash is deemed to have realized a gain on the exchange equal in amount to the excess of the cash received over the proportionate share of the carrying amount of the asset given in exchange. A transaction in which a plant asset and cash are received in exchange for another plant asset is viewed as a **sale** to the extent of cash received and an **exchange** to the extent of the current fair value of the plant asset received.

The steps to be followed in recording exchanges of plant assets may be summarized as follows:

1 Compute the indicated gain or loss on the exchange. The gain or loss is equal to the difference between the current fair value of the asset surrendered and its carrying amount.

2 If the computation above results in a loss, the entire indicated loss is recognized for financial accounting purposes, and the asset acquired is recorded at the current fair value of the asset surrendered plus any cash paid (or less any cash received). **A loss always is considered realized.**

3 If the computation in **1** above results in a gain, and the earning process is completed, the full indicated gain is recognized; if the earning process is not completed and cash is paid (or no cash is involved in the exchange), no gain is recognized; if cash is received in the exchange, a portion of the gain is recognized as follows:

Gain is recognized on the cash part of the "sale"

$$\text{Gain} \times \frac{\text{cash received}}{\text{cash received} + \text{current fair value of asset received}} = \text{gain recognized}$$

Illustrations The steps for recording exchanges of plant assets are illustrated in the six examples below. The asset exchanged has a carrying

Examples of exchange transactions	Exchange transaction	Journal entry		
	1 Loss of $2,000 is indicated, no cash is involved. *Current fair value of old asset is $4,000. (Cost of new asset is current fair value of old asset.)*	Plant Asset (new)............	4,000	
		Accum. Depr. (old).........	14,000	
		Loss on Exchange of Plant Asset .	2,000	
		Plant Asset (old)		20,000
	2 Loss of $2,500 is indicated, cash of $1,000 is paid. *Current fair value of old asset is $3,500. (Cost of new asset is current fair value of old asset plus cash paid.)*	Plant Asset (new)............	4,500	
		Accum. Depr. (old).........	14,000	
		Loss on Exchange of Plant Asset .	2,500	
		Cash...............		1,000
		Plant Asset (old)		20,000
	3 Loss of $1,000 is indicated, cash of $200 is received. *Current fair value of old asset is $5,000. (Cost of new asset is current fair value of old asset less cash received.)*	Cash	200	
		Plant Asset (new)...........	4,800	
		Accum. Depr. (old).........	14,000	
		Loss on Exchange of Plant Asset .	1,000	
		Plant Asset (old)		20,000
	4 Gain of $6,500 is indicated, no cash is involved. *Current fair value of old asset is $12,500. (Cost of new asset is carrying amount of old asset.)*	Plant Asset (new)...........	6,000	
		Accum. Depr. (old).........	14,000	
		Plant Asset (old)		20,000
	5 Gain of $6,500 is indicated, cash of $1,000 is paid. *Current fair value of old asset is $12,500. (Cost of new asset is carrying amount of old asset plus cash paid.)*	Plant Asset (new)...........	7,000	
		Accum. Depr. (old).........	14,000	
		Cash..............		1,000
		Plant Asset (old)		20,000
	6 Gain of $4,000 is indicated, cash of $1,000 is received. *Current fair value of old asset is $10,000, indicating a current fair value of new asset of $9,000. The portion of indicated gain recognized is:*	Cash	1,000	
		Plant Asset (new)...........	5,400	
		Accum. Depr. (old).........	14,000	
		Plant Asset (old)		20,000
		Gain on Exchange of Plant Asset		400

For example 6:

$$\$4,000 \times \left(\frac{\$1,000}{\$1,000 + \$9,000}\right) = \$400$$

(Cost of new asset is carrying amount of the old asset, less cash received, plus gain recognized.)

amount of $6,000 (cost of $20,000 less accumulated depreciation of $14,000). Each of the six examples involves similar assets with comparable current fair values, adjusted for any cash paid or received.

The indicated losses in each of the first three examples are recognized for financial accounting purposes. In the next two examples, no gain is recognized because no cash was received in Example 4 and because cash was paid in Example 5. However, in Example 6, 10% of the indicated gain of $4,000 is recognized because 10% of the total consideration received consisted of cash.

If the exchanges in the last three examples involved dissimilar assets, the entire indicated gain would be recognized for financial accounting purposes, because the earning process would be considered completed. Exchanges of plant assets which are material in amount, either individually or in the aggregate, should be disclosed in a note to the financial statements. Such disclosure should include the nature of the exchanges, the basis of accounting for the assets transferred, and the amount of gain or loss recognized.

Involuntary conversions

The services of assets occasionally are lost through condemnation, fire, or other involuntary means. In the accounting for such events, the amount of any loss or gain should be recorded, and all amounts relating to such assets should be removed from the accounting records. For example, assume that certain land and buildings owned by a business enterprise are condemned by the state for the construction of a highway, and that the state sets a price of $140,000 as the condemnation award. Accumulated depreciation of the building is $120,000, and its original cost was $160,000; the cost of the land was $40,000. The journal entry to record this involuntary conversion follows:

Recording involuntary conversion

Cash	140,000	
Accumulated Depreciation of Building	120,000	
Building		160,000
Land		40,000
Gain on Condemnation of Property		60,000
To record disposal of property condemned by state.		

The position of the FASB on involuntary conversions is summarized at the top of page 466.[12]

---

[12] *FASB Interpretation No. 30,* "Accounting for Involuntary Conversions of Nonmonetary Assets to Monetary Assets"—an interpretation of *APB Opinion No. 29,* FASB (Stamford: 1979), p. 1.

Involuntary conversions of nonmonetary assets to monetary assets are monetary transactions for which gain or loss shall be recognized even though an enterprise reinvests or is obligated to reinvest the monetary assets in replacement of nonmonetary assets.

The income tax rule on involuntary conversion is similar to that for exchanges. In most cases no gain is recognized for income tax purposes at the time of disposal if the owner of the property uses the funds received to replace the involuntarily converted asset.

When depreciable assets or merchandise are destroyed by fire or other casualties, accountants often assist in measuring and recording the losses sustained. For example, inventories on hand at the time of fire may have to be estimated by the gross profit method described in Chapter 9.

Insurance on Plant Assets   Most business enterprises insure assets for possible losses resulting from fire, theft, explosion, and other insurable events. A *deductible clause* usually limits recovery to losses in excess of a certain amount, such as $100.

Insurance policies provide for recovery of loss based on the replacement cost (current fair value) of the asset destroyed. The carrying amount of an asset, although irrelevant in determining the amount of recovery from insurance companies, is used to measure the loss (or gain) as a result of the casualty. For example, if $10,000 is collected from an insurance company on complete destruction of an asset with a carrying amount of $7,500, a gain of $2,500 results.

The amount of insurance carried on an asset should never exceed the current fair value of the asset, because the amount recovered cannot exceed the current fair value of the asset. When inadequate insurance is carried on an asset, the insured in effect becomes a "coinsurer" with the insurance company. For example, if an asset worth $5,000 which is insured for only $4,000 is totally destroyed, the insurance company would bear $4,000 of the loss and the owner would absorb the remaining $1,000 of the loss.

Coinsurance Clause in an Insurance Policy   If it were possible to obtain insurance coverage for only a fraction of the current fair value of an asset, the owner could benefit by receiving full reimbursement of most losses with a minimum insurance coverage and cost. However, insurance companies usually include a *coinsurance clause* in the insurance policy to prevent this approach to low-cost insurance protection. A coinsurance clause requires that an asset be insured for a certain minimum amount, usually 80% of current fair value, if a loss is to be absorbed fully by the insurance company. If the insurance purchased is below the stipulated percentage, the owner absorbs a portion of the loss, even though the loss does not exceed the face amount of the insurance policy.

To illustrate the application of a coinsurance clause in a fire insurance policy, assume the following:

Insurance carried (face amount of policy) . . . . $ 60,000
Coinsurance required by policy . . . . 80% of current fair value
Carrying amount of machinery damaged by fire (cost, $140,000) . . . . $ 55,000
Current fair value of machinery on date of fire $100,000
Amount of fire loss (based on current fair value of machinery). . . . . . $ 40,000

The recovery from the insurance company is determined under the coinsurance formula as follows:

$$\frac{\$60{,}000 \text{ (amount of insurance)}}{\$80{,}000 \text{ (coinsurance requirement)}} \times \$40{,}000 \text{ (loss)} = \$30{,}000$$

Several observations may be made at this point. The amount of insurance carried is not dependent on the cost or the carrying amount of the asset. (Cost and carrying amount are irrelevant for purposes of measuring either the amount of insurance that can be carried or the amount of recoverable loss). Recovery on the loss is dependent on the current fair value of the asset, the amount of insurance carried, and the minimum amount of insurance required by the coinsurance clause. If insurance is carried equal to or in excess of the amount required by the coinsurance clause, any loss up to the face amount of the policy is fully recoverable; if less than the required amount of insurance is carried, the loss is absorbed in part by the **insured.** If the amount of insurance carried exceeds the coinsurance requirement, there is no need to apply the coinsurance formula. A careful analysis of the coinsurance formula indicates that the recoverable portion of the loss always is the lower of (1) the amount of the loss adjusted by the coinsurance formula, or (2) the face amount of the policy.

Two or More Insurance Policies When an asset is insured under two or more policies which do not have coinsurance clauses, any loss would be shared by the insurance companies in proportion to the amount of insurance written by each company; the same procedure applies when the insurance policies contain identical coinsurance requirements. If two or more insurance policies cover the same asset, and the policies have **different** coinsurance clauses, the coinsurance formula should be applied to each policy. However, the loss absorbed by any insurance company cannot exceed its proportion of the total insurance carried with all insurance companies. For example, assume that a building with a current fair value of $40,000 is insured under two policies as follows:

Policy A: $15,000 with an 80% coinsurance clause
Policy B: $15,000 with a 70% coinsurance clause

Assuming that a fire causes damage of $24,000 to the building, how much of the loss can be recovered under each policy? If neither policy had a coinsurance clause, each insurance company absorbs 50% of the loss ($12,000) because each policy represents 50% of the total insurance ($30,000). If both policies had a 70% coinsurance requirement, each insurance company absorbs $12,000 of the loss because the total insurance carried ($30,000) exceeds the minimum insurance required by the coinsurance clause ($40,000 × 70% = $28,000). However, because policy A has an 80% coinsurance clause in this case, the recovery under each policy is determined as follows:

Allocation of loss between two insurance companies

Policy A:

$$\frac{\$15{,}000 \text{ (insurance under policy A)}}{\$32{,}000 \text{ (coinsurance requirement for policy A)}} \times \$24{,}000 \text{ (loss)} = \underline{\$11{,}250}$$

Policy B:

$$\frac{\$15{,}000 \text{ (insurance under policy B)}}{\$30{,}000 \text{ (total insurance on building)}} \times \$24{,}000 \text{ (loss)} = \underline{\$12{,}000}$$

The recovery under policy A is $\frac{15}{32}$ of the loss, which is less than the pro rata coverage of $\frac{15}{30}$, because the coinsurance requirement under this policy was not met. On the other hand, the recovery under policy B is $\frac{15}{30}$ of the loss, because the total insurance on the building ($30,000) exceeds the minimum required under policy B ($28,000). Consequently, the coinsurance formula is not applicable to policy B.

Insurance contracts vary in form and complexity. The discussion here is brief and perhaps oversimplified. Although accountants need not be experts in insurance contracts, they should have a basic understanding of insurance to be able to account properly for premiums paid and proceeds received, and to help clients formulate a sound property insurance program.

REVIEW QUESTIONS

1 Define the following terms: **tangible asset, natural resource, intangible asset.** Give a few examples of each.

2 What are the arguments in favor of using historical cost as the basis of accounting for plant assets? Can this be referred to as an asset **valuation procedure?**

3 How is the cost of a plant asset determined for financial accounting purposes? What three issues are involved in accounting for the cost of plant assets?

4 What is meant by the terms *capital expenditure* and *revenue expenditure?* How are they related to the accounting concepts of realization and matching of costs and revenue?

5 Which of the following are capital expenditures? Indicate the proper treatment of items which are not capital expenditures.
   a Cost of grading land prior to construction
   b Cost of installing equipment, including cost of spoiled material during test runs
   c Tax assessment for street paving
   d Delinquent property taxes on land acquired
   e Cost of maintaining equipment in good operating condition
   f Cost of moving and reinstalling equipment in another part of factory
   g Cost of repairs to used equipment; need for repair was discovered immediately after acquisition of the equipment
   h Cost of tearing down an old building in preparation for new construction (old building was used for 24 years and was fully depreciated)
   i Cost of insurance policy covering possible damages that may arise during construction of a new building
   j Excess of operating expenses over revenue during first year of operations
   k Cost of removing soil to build foundation for new building

6 Cathy Company has constructed a special-purpose machine for its own use. Direct labor and material costs were $10,000. Variable overhead is 10% of direct costs, and fixed overhead allocable to the constructed machine is $2,400. Company engineers estimate that an equivalent machine would cost $15,000 if purchased. At what amount should the machine be recorded? Why? Is there a profit on the self-construction? Assuming that the machine could have been acquired for $8,000, at what amount should the machine be recorded?

7 Capitalizing interest costs during construction is an accepted accounting procedure; adding interest on an installment contract to the cost of the asset acquired is not. Explain the distinction between these two situations.

8 What position did the FASB take in *Statement No. 34* on the capitalization of interest costs?

9 Discuss the accounting problem that arises in each of the following situations, and explain the proper accounting procedure:
   a Assets are acquired on a deferred payment plan
   b A group of assets is acquired for a lump-sum price
   c Assets are acquired in exchange for capital stock or bonds issued by the purchaser
   d Assets are acquired by gift

10 What is the *investment tax credit* and how, in your opinion, should it be treated for financial accounting purposes?

11 Briefly describe the accounting procedures appropriate for the following:
   a Additions
   b Improvements, renewals, and replacements
   c Ordinary repair and maintenance costs
   d Extraordinary repairs as a result of fire damage not covered by insurance
   e Gain or loss on involuntary conversion of land to cash

12 The accountant for Ranger Company estimates annual repair costs on equipment and prepares a journal entry each year debiting Repair Expense and crediting Allowance for Repairs, which sometimes shows a credit balance and sometimes a debit balance. What is the appropriate classification of this account in the balance sheet? Why?

13 Holt Company debits the cost of major repairs to Accumulated Depreciation. Evaluate this procedure.

14 How are gains and losses on retirements, disposals, or exchanges of plant assets reported in the income statement?

15 a Describe the basic principle stated in **APB Opinion No. 29** relating to accounting for exchanges of plant assets.
b List three modifications of the basic principle stated in **APB Opinion No. 29.**

16 Describe the conditions in which exchange transactions involving plant assets require the recognition of gains and losses for financial accounting purposes.

17 What is meant by **coinsurance?** Describe the coinsurance formula. Can the destruction of insured property result in a gain for financial accounting purposes? Explain.

EXERCISES

Ex. 11-1   A business enterprise replaced an old machine with a new one having a list price of $10,000, subject to a 2% cash discount if paid promptly. Net cost of removing the old machine to make room for the new one amounted to $800. Installation of the new machine cost $400. Costs of testing the new machine were $250 for operator's time and $125 in wasted material. The cash discount was lost because of late payment of the invoice.
Compute the cost of the new machine for financial accounting purposes.

Ex. 11-2   The costs incurred to acquire land and construct a building are listed below:

Land (*including miscellaneous acquisition costs*)	$150,000
Construction insurance	1,500
Building contract (*excluding excavation*)	220,000
Architect fees	2,000
Street and sidewalk (*maintained by the city*)	4,000
Costs of excavation for foundation	3,100
Property taxes on land (*prior to construction*)	1,600
Advertising costs to attract tenants	1,250
Interest cost during construction period on loan to pay contractor . . .	2,600

Determine the cost of (**a**) land and (**b**) building for financial accounting purposes.

Ex. 11-3   Pandora Company acquired land with a current fair value of $590,000 in exchange for $200,000 face amount of bonds payable and 20,000 shares of its $5 par common stock. The stock was selling at $20½ on the New York Stock Exchange at the time.
Prepare a journal entry to record the acquisition of land. (Record a premium or a discount on bonds payable.)

Ex. 11-4 In Year 2, Peter Saul sold for $55,000 a parcel of land which cost $30,000. The contract required a down payment of $15,000 and a noninterest-bearing promissory note for $40,000 due in four years.

Record the sale of land in Saul's accounting records, assuming that the present value of the note (discounted at compound interest of 12% for four years) was $25,421, and that 12% was a fair rate of interest on this type of note. Assume that the note receivable is recorded at face amount.

Ex. 11-5 On June 30, Year 10, Crane Company acquired equipment at a bankruptcy auction. The purchase price consisted of the following:

Cash down payment	$ 72,150
Four noninterest-bearing promissory notes in the face amount of	
$50,000, payable annually on June 30, commencing in Year 11	200,000
Total purchase price	$272,150

Record the acquisition of the equipment in the accounting records of Crane Company, assuming that a fair rate of interest is 10% compounded annually. Use the appropriate table in the Appendix in back of the book and round computations to the nearest dollar.

Ex. 11-6 Tom Selzer sold land and a building to Mary Beyer. The property had cost Selzer $39,000, including $10,000 allocated to land. Depreciation of $3,500 had been recorded on the building by Selzer. At the close of escrow, the following escrow statements were submitted to Selzer and Beyer:

	Escrow statement to Selzer		Escrow statement to Beyer	
	Charges	**Credits**	**Charges**	**Credits**
Selling price.		$40,300	$40,300	
Cash deposited in escrow.				$10,400
Prorated property taxes	$ 120			120
Prorated interest	70			70
Prorated insurance.		200	200	
Mortgage note assumed by purchaser	30,160			30,160
Commission to broker.	2,370			
Title search fee	150		150	
Escrow fee.	110			
Cash to seller	7,520			
Cash to purchaser			100	
Totals.	$40,500	$40,500	$40,750	$40,750

a Prepare a journal entry to record the sale in Selzer's accounting records.
b Prepare a journal entry to record the purchase in Beyer's accounting records. The value assigned to land is $15,500. Beyer had recorded the cash deposited in escrow, $10,400, in an Escrow Deposit account.

Ex. 11-7 Thelma Lance, a single proprietor, has been doing the accounting for her business enterprise. At the end of Year 3, after the accounting records were adjusted but before they were closed, you were engaged to review the records. The items which require correction are listed at the top of page 472.

(1) Installation costs for fixtures, $1,200, were debited to Maintenance Expense. The fixtures have a five-year economic life, with no residual value, and were installed at the beginning of Year 3. Assume use of the straight-line method of depreciation.

(2) A machine acquired on January 6, Year 1, at a cost of $5,000 has been depreciated on a straight-line basis over a five-year period, with no residual value. The machine was sold on June 20, Year 3. Lance debited Cash and credited Machinery for $2,100, the proceeds on the sale. No depreciation was recorded on this machine in Year 3, but you conclude that one-half year's depreciation should be recorded.

Prepare a correcting journal entry for each of the two items described above.

Ex. 11-8 **a** Salem Corporation acquired machine B by trading in machine A and paying $5,000 cash. Machine A originally cost $90,000 and had accumulated depreciation of $20,000 at the date of exchange. Machine B could have been purchased for $80,000 cash. The machines are similar.

Record the exchange of machine A for machine B.

b Assume the same facts as in **a**, except that instead of paying $5,000 cash, Salem Corporation received $20,000 cash.

Record the exchange of machine A for machine B.

c Assume the same facts as in **a**, except that instead of paying $5,000 cash, Salem Corporation received $5,000 cash. Machine B could have been purchased for $50,000 cash.

Record the exchange of machine A for machine B.

Ex. 11-9 A building has a carrying amount of $11,000 and a current fair value of $20,000. Determine the amount recoverable from the insurance company in each case below, assuming that each insurance policy contains an 80% coinsurance clause:

Case	Insurance coverage	Loss incurred
A	$10,000	$12,000
B	12,000	12,000
C	14,000	12,000
D	16,000	12,000
E	18,000	12,000

Ex. 11-10 Dodson, Inc., purchased three machines at an auction for a lump-sum price of $14,500 and paid $500 to have the machines delivered to its place of business. The current fair values of the three machines are shown below:

Machine X	$ 9,000
Machine Y	6,000
Machine Z	5,000
Total current fair value	$20,000

Determine the cost allocated to each machine, using the relative current fair values of the machines as a basis of allocating the lump-sum price.

SHORT CASES FOR ANALYSIS AND DECISION

Case 11-1 Caliri Pipe Company has just constructed a new building at a cost of $2 million. After reviewing the contracts and cost data, the controller suggests that the company use the following classifications in future accounting for this building: (1) foundation, framing, and sheathing, (2) outside finish, (3) interior finish, (4) roof, (5) electric wiring and fixtures, (6) partitions, (7) acoustical ceiling, (8) furnace and boiler, and (9) plumbing system.

Instructions Discuss the advantages and the disadvantages of following such a system of accounting for the building, particularly its effect on accounting for maintenance, depreciation, and retirement.

Case 11-2 Your client found three suitable sites, each having certain unique advantages, for a new plant facility. In order to investigate thoroughly the advantages and disadvantages of each site, one-year options were purchased for an amount equal to 5% of the contract price of each site. The costs of the options cannot be applied against the contract prices. Before the options expired, one of the sites was purchased at the contract price of $60,000. The option on this site had cost $3,000. The two options not exercised had cost $3,500 each.

Instructions Present arguments in support of recording the cost of the land at each of the following amounts: (1) $60,000; (2) $63,000, (3) $70,000.

Case 11-3 Electro-Age Company manufactures electrical appliances, most of which are used in homes. Company engineers have designed a new type of blender which, through the use of a few attachments, will perform more functions than any blender currently on the market. Demand for the new blender can be projected with reasonable accuracy. In order to make the blenders, Electro-Age needs a specialized machine which is not available from outside sources. Therefore, Electro-Age decided to manufacture the specialized machine in its own plant.

Instructions
a Electro-Age's plant may be operating at capacity or below capacity. Compare and contrast the problems in determining the cost to be assigned to the specialized machine at these different levels of operations.
b Discuss the effect of projected demand in units for the new blenders (which may be steady, decreasing, or increasing) on the determination of a depreciation method to be used for the specialized machine.

Case 11-4 Plant assets generally represent a significant portion of the total assets of most business enterprises. Accounting for the acquisition and use of such assets is, therefore, an important part of financial accounting.

Instructions
a Distinguish between revenue expenditures and capital expenditures and explain why this distinction is important.
b Identify six costs that should be capitalized as the cost of land. For your answer, assume that land with an existing building is acquired for cash and that the existing building is to be removed in order that a new building can be constructed on the site.
c At what amount should a business enterprise record a plant asset acquired on a deferred payment plan?
d In general, at what amount should plant assets received in exchange for other nonmonetary assets be recorded? Specifically, at what amount should a business enterprise record a new machine acquired in exchange for a similar machine and a cash payment?

PROBLEMS

11-1 On December 31, Year 1, the assets included in the plant assets section of Arnold Company's balance sheet had the following balances:

Land	$100,000
Buildings	800,000
Leasehold improvements	500,000
Machinery and equipment	700,000

During Year 2 the following transactions occurred:

(1) Land site No. 20 was purchased for $1,000,000. To acquire the land, Arnold paid a $60,000 commission to a real estate agent. Costs of $15,000 were incurred to clear the land. During the course of clearing the land, timber and gravel were recovered and sold for $5,000.

(2) A second tract of land (site No. 21) with a building was purchased for $300,000. The closing escrow statement indicated that the land value was $200,000 and the building value was $100,000. Shortly after acquisition, the building was demolished at a cost of $30,000. A new building was constructed for $150,000, plus the following costs:

Excavation fees	$11,000
Architectural design fees	8,000
Building permit fee	1,000
Imputed interest on funds used during construction (the company has	
not previously capitalized interest)	8,000

The building was completed and occupied on September 30, Year 2.

(3) A third tract of land (site No. 22) was purchased for $600,000 and was put on the market for resale.

(4) Extensive work was done to a building occupied by Arnold under a lease that expires on December 31, Year 11. The total cost of the work was $125,000, which consisted of the following:

Painting of ceilings (estimated economic life is 1 year)	$ 10,000
Electrical work (estimated economic life is 10 years)	35,000
Construction of extension to the working area (estimated economic	
life is 20 years)	80,000
Total cost	$125,000

The lessor paid one-half the costs incurred in connection with the extension to the working area.

(5) During December, Year 2, costs of $65,000 were incurred to improve leased office space. The related lease will terminate on December 31, Year 4, and is not expected to be renewed.

(6) A group of new machines was purchased under a royalty agreement which provides for payment of royalties based on units of production for the machines. The invoice price (after a 2% cash discount) of the machines was $78,600, freight costs were $2,000, unloading costs were $1,500, and royalty payments for Year 2 were $13,000.

Instructions

a Prepare a detailed analysis of the changes in each of the following balance sheet accounts for the year ended December 31, Year 2:
  Land
  Buildings
  Leasehold improvements
  Machinery and equipment
(Disregard the related accumulated depreciation accounts).

b List the items that were not used to determine the answer to *a* above, and indicate where, or if, these items should be included in Arnold's financial statements.

11-2 Four situations relating to plant assets are described below for Minnesota Corporation. Separate instructions are given for each situation.

a A machine was acquired for $50,000 on May 1, Year 1. At the time of acquisition, the machine was estimated to have an economic life of 10 years and a residual value of $2,000. Monthly depreciation was recorded by the straight-line method. On March 1, Year 10, the machine was sold for $4,200.

Instructions Compute the gain or loss on the disposal of the machine.

b A used delivery truck was traded in for a new truck. Information relating to the trucks follows:

Used truck:

Cost	$ 8,000
Accumulated depreciation	6,000
Estimated current fair value	1,600

New truck:

List price	$10,000
Cash price without trade-in	9,500
Cash paid with trade-in	7,800

Instructions Record the exchange transaction in conformity with generally accepted accounting principles.

c Land, building, and equipment were acquired for $90,000 from a bankrupt company. At the time of acquisition, $6,000 was paid to have the assets appraised. The appraisal indicated the following current fair values of the assets:

Land	$60,000
Building	40,000
Equipment	20,000

Instructions Determine the cost allocated to the land, building, and equipment for financial accounting purposes.

d A building was appraised at $100,000. A fire occurred causing $48,600 damage to the building. The building was insured for $60,000 under a policy which contained an 80% coinsurance clause.

Instructions Compute the amount of the loss that will be recovered under the insurance policy.

11-3   This problem consists of five independent situations relating to plant assets for Kansas Corporation. Each situation contains specific instructions.

a The company has two fire insurance policies. Policy A with Ace Fidelity covers the furniture at a face amount of $108,000 and the office building at a face amount of $360,000. Policy B with Bravo Indemnity covers only the office building at a face amount of $140,000. A fire caused losses to the furniture and the office building. The relevant data are summarized below:

	Furniture	Office building	
Insurance policies	A	A	B
Appraised values before fire	$150,000	$700,000	$700,000
Appraised values after fire	$ 25,000	$406,000	$406,000
Face amounts of insurance policies	$108,000	$360,000	$140,000
Coinsurance requirements	80%	80%	75%

Instructions   Compute the amount to be recovered from each insurance company for the loss on each asset category. Show computations, rounded to the nearest dollar.

b A truck was brought in for inspection when it was noticed that the diesel engine, which normally lasts four years, was in need of an overhaul and that the trailer needed replacement. The engine cost $2,000 new and was two and a half years old. However, with a $500 overhaul, it was expected to last two more years. The old trailer cost $5,000, had a carrying amount of $750, and would be scrapped by the owner. The price of new trailers had increased by $1,000 since the old one was purchased. The company accounts for each truck component separately and computes depreciation by the straight-line method.

Instructions   Prepare journal entries to record the overhaul of the engine and the replacement of the trailer.

c The company exchanged a used business automobile for a new automobile. The used automobile had an original cost of $6,500, a carrying amount of $1,500, and a current fair value of $2,000 when exchanged. In addition, the company paid $7,200 cash for the new automobile. The list price of the new automobile was $9,300, and the cash price was $9,200.

Instructions   Prepare a journal entry to record the exchange of the used automobile for the new automobile.

d The company exchanged 100 shares of treasury stock (its $50 par common stock) for land. The treasury stock had cost $60 a share, and on the exchange date, it had a market price of $82 a share. The company received $1,200 for scrap when an existing building was removed from the land.

Instructions   Compute the cost of the land for financial accounting purposes.

e The company received $20,000 cash and a used computer with a current fair value of $180,000 for the company's old computer with a current fair value of $200,000 and a carrying amount of $150,000.

Instructions   Compute the gain (if any) that the company should recognize on this exchange transaction and the cost basis, for financial accounting purposes, of the used computer.

11-4 Sentinel Products Corporation recently purchased a new machine and retired an old machine which cost $16,000 and had a carrying amount of $4,000 at the time of retirement. The company had received offers from two vendors to sell the new machine as follows:

(1) M Company offered its machine for $18,000 and agreed to allow $1,000 on the old machine as a trade-in.
(2) N Company offered its machine for $17,500, terms 2/10, n/30, but would not accept a trade-in.

Sentinel accepted N's offer and sold its old machine for $700 after incurring $220 in labor costs to remove it from the building. Additional costs incurred in placing the new machine in use were:

Freight (*paid in cash*)	$1,190
Installation:	
Material	250
Labor	440
Travel expenses paid to N Company's engineer, who supervised the instal-	
lation (There was no charge for the engineer's time.)	210
Costs incurred in testing new machine:	
Operator's wages	160
Spoiled material	200

As a result of an error in the treasurer's department, the N Company invoice was not paid until 30 days after invoice date; therefore, the cash discount could not be taken.

During the removal of the old machine, a section of the factory floor was damaged and had to be repaired at a cost of $400 paid to an independent contractor. The damage was caused by extreme carelessness of Sentinel's employees.

Instructions Prepare journal entries, together with supporting computations, to record the retirement of the old machine and the purchase of the new machine. Credit Material Inventory for the cost of material used and Accrued Payroll for labor costs incurred.

11-5 In auditing the financial statements of Belgrade Pottery, Inc., for the fiscal year ended December 31, Year 5, you discover the following:

(1) Machine W with a cash selling price of $18,800 was acquired on April 1, Year 5, in exchange for $20,000 face amount of bonds payable selling at 94 and maturing on April 1, Year 15. The accountant recorded the acquisition by a debit to Machinery and a credit to Bonds Payable for $20,000. Straight-line depreciation was recorded based on a five-year economic life and amounted to $2,400 for nine months. In the computation of depreciation, residual value of $4,000 was used.
(2) Machine X listed at a cash price of $6,400 was purchased on January 2, Year 5. Belgrade paid $1,000 down and $500 a month for 12 months. The last payment was made on December 30, Year 5. Straight-line depreciation, based on a five-year economic life and no residual value, was recorded at $1,400 for the year. Freight of $200 on Machine X was debited to the Freight-in account.
(3) Machine Y was recorded at $5,100, which included the carrying amount of $1,100 for an old machine accepted as a trade-in and cash of $4,000. The cash price of Machine Y was $4,500, and the trade-in allowance was $500. This transaction took place on December 28, Year 5.

(4) Machine Z was acquired on January 10, Year 5, in exchange for past-due accounts receivable of $14,000 on which an allowance of 20% was established at the end of Year 4. The current fair value of the machine on January 10 was estimated at $11,000. The machine was recorded by a debit to Machinery and a credit to Accounts Receivable for $14,000. No depreciation was recorded on Machine Z, because it was not used in operations. In March, Machine Z was exchanged for 100 shares of the company's outstanding capital stock with a market price of $105 a share. The Treasury Stock account was debited for $14,000, the carrying amount of Machine Z.

Instructions Record any correcting journal entries required on December 31, Year 5, for each transaction (1) through (4) above. Assume that revenue and expense accounts have not been closed for Year 5. Amortize bond discount by the straight-line method.

11-6 Dean Company offered Earp Company $200,000 cash for used machinery. Earp replied that the price offered was acceptable but for income tax reasons it did not want an all-cash transaction. Earp then offered to sell the machinery to Dean for a $50,000 cash down payment, the balance payable in five equal annual installments of $30,000 each with interest payable annually at 6% on the unpaid balance. In addition, Dean agreed to sign a contract to purchase merchandise from Earp.

Dean decided that, although Earp's merchandise prices were in excess of current market prices, the 6% interest rate on the promissory note was sufficiently below the 10% that Dean would have to pay to borrow elsewhere to make the contract appealing. Accordingly, on July 1, Year 7, Dean accepted Earp's proposal, made the down payment, signed the 6% note and the contract for the purchase of the merchandise, and accepted delivery of the used machinery.

Instructions
a Record the acquisition of the used machinery in the accounting records of Dean on July 1, Year 7. At that date, the discounted value of the five-year, 6% note, based on an interest rate of 10%, was $135,490.
b Prepare journal entries for Dean's accounting records on December 31, Year 7, to record the following:
  (1) Interest expense for six months. Use the "interest method" of amortization for the discount on the note payable.
  (2) Depreciation for six months. Assume a five-year economic life for the used machinery, no residual value, and the straight-line method of depreciation.
  (3) Any required adjustment to cost of goods sold. Assume that one-half the merchandise contracted for with Earp had been purchased and that the merchandise purchased had been sold by December 31, Year 7.

11-7 Milan Company was incorporated on January 4, Year 10, but was unable to begin manufacturing activities until July 1, Year 10, because its plant was not finished until that date.

On December 31, Year 10, the company's record of the construction and accounting for the plant appears in a Plant account on page 479.

Additional information:
(1) On January 31, the company paid $25,000 cash and issued 3,000 shares of 8% cumulative preferred stock, $100 par, for land and old building. On January 30, a large block of preferred stock had been sold for $105 a share. The preferred stock issued on January 31 was recorded at par.
(2) The demolition company charged $7,400 for removal of the old building. The salvaged material from the old building was sold for $3,000.
(3) Legal fees covered the organization of the company, $1,500; purchase of land, $2,000; and construction contract for the new building, $500.

Plant

Date	Explanation	Debit	Credit	Balance
Year 10				
Jan. 31	Cost of land and old building	325,000		325,000 dr
Feb. 28	Cost of removing old building	7,400		332,400 dr
Mar. 1	Proceeds from sale of salvaged material from old building		3,000	329,400 dr
May 1	Partial payment for new building	175,000		504,400 dr
1	Legal fees	4,000		508,400 dr
June 1	Second payment for new building	175,000		683,400 dr
1	Insurance premium (May 1, Year 10 – Apr. 30, Year 13)	3,600		687,000 dr
1	Special tax assessment	5,000		692,000 dr
30	Expenses	24,000		716,000 dr
July 1	Final payment for new building	175,000		891,000 dr
Dec. 31	Write-up of new building per appraisal	50,000		941,000 dr
31	Depreciation expense for 6 months ($941,000 × 2%)		18,820	922,180 dr

(4) Insurance on the new building was acquired on May 1. The three-year premium was paid on June 1, on receipt of the invoice.

(5) The expenses were for the period from January 2 to June 30 and include president's salary, $12,000; salary of plant superintendent who supervised construction of the new building, $10,000; and office salaries, $2,000.

(6) The special tax assessment covered street improvements.

(7) During the six months' construction period, a new union contract for construction workers was negotiated calling for an increase of 15% in wages, and there were increases in construction material costs. On the basis of these facts, the plant superintendent suggested that the building be written up by $50,000 to recognize the increase in the current cost of the building. The credit was recorded in the Retained Earnings account.

(8) The new building is to be depreciated at the rate of 4% a year, with no residual value. Depreciation of $18,820 for six months was debited to the Depreciation Expense account.

Instructions

a Prepare a working paper to classify the transactions of Milan Company in proper accounts. Provide separate columns for Land and for Building; other accounts should be analyzed in a Miscellaneous column.

b Prepare a single journal entry on December 31, Year 10, to restate the accounting records to an acceptable basis. The accounting records have not been closed for the year ended December 31, Year 10.

11-8 Coal Mining Company completed certain transactions in the current year to simplify its operations, to improve its competitive position, and to resolve several business disputes. Three transactions involved transfers of mining claims to stockholders of Coal Mining Company, and three transactions were with Olson Corporation, a competitor. The transactions are listed below and on page 480.

(1) Claim No. 1, carried in the accounting records at a cost of $5,000, was sold for $12,000 cash.

(2) Claim No. 2, carried in the accounting records at a cost of $3,000, was exchanged for 200 shares of Coal Mining's outstanding common stock. The common stock, which is publicly traded, was selling for $125 a share at the time of the exchange. (Record the common stock acquired in the Treasury Stock account.)

(3) Claim No. 3, carried in the accounting records at a cost of $20,000, was transferred to Betty Strong, a stockholder, in consideration of her withdrawal of a patent infringement suit against Coal Mining. When asked for an estimate of the current fair value of the mining claims, the president of Coal Mining answered that it was "anyone's guess." Further questioning elicited the reluctant response, "Claim No. 1 probably was worth about $15,000 and each of the other two claims was worth about twice that." You have concluded that no more precise estimate of current fair values can be obtained.

(4) Coal Mining exchanged its 5% common stock investment in Belmont Company, carried at cost of $80,000, for a plant site owned by Olson Corporation appraised at $200,000.

(5) Coal Mining traded certain inventory items located in Chicago for similar items held by Olson Corporation in Tulsa. To equalize trading values, Olson also paid $2,000 cash to Coal Mining. The cost of the inventory items given up by Coal Mining was $8,200, and the current fair value was $10,000. Coal Mining uses the perpetual inventory system.

(6) Coal Mining obtained production jigs and dies from Olson Corporation, giving in exchange a used milling machine and cash of $1,700. The milling machine was carried in the accounting records at its original cost of $20,000; accumulated depreciation was $12,000. Olson was willing to pay the $10,500 appraised value of the milling machine in cash, but Coal Mining insisted on making the exchange for the jigs and dies.

Instructions Prepare journal entries for Coal Mining Company to record each of the six transactions described above.

11-9 Melanie Sample maintains her accounting records on a cash basis. On February 28, Year 10, she sold property, purchased 17 years earlier for $110,000, to Denise Douglas for $161,200. The cost allocated to the building was $70,000, and the accumulated depreciation to the date of the sale was $42,500.

The escrow statements on February 28 for the purchaser and the seller are shown below and on page 481.

Purchaser's Escrow Statement (City Escrow Co., Escrow No. 911)

Purchase price of property	$161,200	
Deposit of cash by purchaser on Jan. 30 (recorded in Escrow Deposit account)		$ 83,100
Title fee (one-half)	430	
Drawing and recording deed	15	
Fire insurance, prorated	1,430	
Mortgage note assumed by purchaser		78,460
Property taxes for period Jan. 1 to Feb. 28, Year 10, accrued and unpaid		200
Lease deposits		850
Rent, prorated		340
Interest accrued on mortgage note		185
Cash to purchaser, Denise Douglas	60	
Totals	$163,135	$163,135

Seller's Escrow Statement (City Escrow Co., Escrow No. 911)

Selling price of property		$161,200
Title fee (one-half)	$ 430	
Drawing and recording deed	15	
Property taxes for period Jan. 1 to Feb. 28, Year 10, accrued		
and unpaid	200	
Interest accrued on mortgage note	185	
Lease deposits	850	
Rent, prorated	340	
Mortgage note assumed by purchaser	78,460	
Fire insurance, prorated		1,430
Revenue stamps (tax on real estate transfers)	150	
Real estate broker's commission	10,200	
Cash to seller, Melanie Sample	71,800	
Totals	$162,630	$162,630

Instructions

a Prepare a working paper to show how Melanie Sample should determine the gain or loss on this transaction. Ignore income taxes.

b Prepare a journal entry to record the foregoing transaction in the accounting records of Melanie Sample.

c Prepare a journal entry to record the foregoing transaction in the accounting records of Denise Douglas, assuming that $100,000 of total cost is allocated to land and that items representing future expense or revenue are recorded in nominal accounts.

11-10 Detroit Corporation manufactures auto parts. On August 31, Year 2, the company had a fire which completely destroyed its building, goods in process inventory, and machinery. Additional data follow:

(1) The cost of plant assets destroyed and the related accumulated depreciation accounts on August 31, Year 2, were:

	Cost	Accumulated depreciation
Building	$40,000	$17,500
Machinery	15,000	4,500

At present prices, the cost to replace the destroyed property are: building, $80,000; machinery, $37,500. At the time of the fire it was estimated that the building was 50% depreciated, and the destroyed machinery was one-third depreciated. Insurance companies agreed that the insurable value (current fair value) of the building and machinery was $65,000 on the date of fire.

(2) After the fire, a physical inventory was taken. The raw material and the finished goods had a cost (and current fair value) of $26,000 and $52,000, respectively.

(3) The inventories on December 31, Year 1, were: raw material, $20,000; goods in process, $48,000; and finished goods, $54,000.

(4) The sales of the first eight months of Year 2 were $150,000, and raw material purchases were $55,000. Direct labor for the eight months was $40,000; for the past five years factory overhead has been applied at the rate of 80% of direct labor cost. The gross profit for the last five years has averaged 30% of net sales.

(5) Insurance is carried with two companies, each policy with an 80% coinsurance clause. The amounts of insurance carried with each company are listed below:

	Building and machinery	Inventories
Acme Insurance Company	$42,000	$64,800
Zenith Indemnity Company	20,000	21,600

Instructions

a Compute the estimated cost of the goods in process lost in the fire on August 31, Year 2.

b Compute the expected recovery from each insurance company, assuming that the estimated cost of inventories lost is accepted as a measure of current fair value on the date of the fire.

c Assuming that Detroit Corporation recovers its loss as determined in part b, what is the loss or gain from fire reported in its income statement for the year ended December 31, Year 2? Ignore the income tax effect of the loss or gain.

11-11 On September 20, Year 8, a fire damaged the office and warehouse of Liz Lock, Inc., whose fiscal year ends on December 31. The only accounting record saved was the general ledger, from which the following information was obtained as of August 31, Year 8:

	Debit	Credit
Accounts receivable	$25,000	
Inventory, Dec. 31, Year 7	60,920	
Accounts payable		$ 27,500
Sales through Aug. 31		100,000
Purchases through Aug. 31	80,000	

The following additional data are available:

(1) The September bank statement and paid checks disclosed that checks written during the period September 1 to 20 totaled $15,000: $8,000 for accounts payable as of August 31, $2,000 for September purchases, and $5,000 for other expenses. Deposits during the same period amounted to $11,500, which consisted of receipts from customers, with the exception of a $1,300 refund from a supplier for goods returned in September.

(2) Correspondence with suppliers disclosed unrecorded obligations of $7,200 on September 20, for purchases during September.

(3) Customers confirmed payables of $29,500 to Liz Lock, Inc., as of the close of business on September 20, Year 8.

(4) The following insurance on inventory was in effect at the date of the fire:

	Amount of coverage	Coinsurance requirement
Allied Mutual	$30,000	80%
Blue Regional	20,000	70%
Claim Free	10,000	None

(5) The insurance companies agreed that the fire loss claim should be based on the assumption that the overall gross profit rate of 40% of sales for the past two years was in effect during the current year and that the cost of inventory so determined is a reasonable estimate of the current fair value of the inventory.

(6) Inventory with a cost of $22,400 was recovered and is in good condition. The balance of the inventory was a total loss. The office and the warehouse building were not insured. It cost the company $4,150 to repair the damage to the office, but the warehouse was a total loss. The warehouse (excluding land) cost $50,000 to construct, was fully depreciated, and had a current fair value of $10,000 at the date of the fire.

Instructions

a Prepare a working paper to compute the approximate cost of inventory lost in the fire on September 20, Year 8.

b Prepare a working paper to compute the pro rata claim to be filed with each insurance company.

c Assuming that Liz Lock, Inc., is indemnified as determined in part b, what is the loss or gain from fire included in its income statement for Year 8? Ignore income tax effect of the loss or gain.

12 PLANT ASSETS: DEPRECIATION AND DEPLETION

Meaning of depreciation and depletion

In Chapter 11 we described plant assets as a "bundle of future services," and considered the problem of determining the acquisition cost of the future services embodied in such assets. In this chapter we are concerned with the problem of measuring the cost of asset services "withdrawn from the bundle" and consumed in business operations.

Depreciation is the portion of the cost of plant assets that is deducted from revenue for asset services used in the operations of a business enterprise. In practice, depreciation describes the cost of the expired services of tangible plant assets. Recording the expired service cost of intangible assets, such as patents and goodwill, is called *amortization.* For accounting purposes, *depletion* refers to the estimated cost of natural resources such as oil, gas, timber, and iron ore that have been removed from their source.

DEPRECIATION

The concept of depreciation is linked closely to the concept of business income. Because part of the service potential of depreciable assets is exhausted in the revenue-generating process each accounting period, the cost of these services must be deducted from revenue in the measurement of net income; the expired cost must be recovered before a business enterprise is considered "as well off" as at the beginning of the period. Depreciation is the measurement of this expired cost.

Depreciation is one of the most controversial areas in accounting. In the early history of accounting, it was necessary to convince users of accounting information that depreciation was a cost (expense) of doing business. Business executives tended to view depreciation as a matter of "setting aside something" during profitable years for the replacement of depreciable assets. When earnings were high, large amounts of depreciation might be recorded; when earnings were low or losses were incurred, depreciation was not recorded. Today, it is universally agreed that depreciation is an expense that must be recorded regardless of the level of earnings.

Accounting for depreciation is a process of **cost allocation,** not asset valuation. The acquisition of plant assets means that asset services have been purchased in advance of their use. Between the time of acquisition and the time of use, the value of these services may change materially, because of supply and demand factors or changes in price levels. Therefore, the accountants' measurement of the historical cost of the asset services that are used may differ from the current cost of similar services. This difference is germane to a variety of managerial decisions; however, the question of revaluing depreciable assets (in effect, revaluing the remaining unused services) at some time subsequent to acquisition should not be confused with the cost allocation problem. In this chapter we shall deal only with the allocation of the cost of plant assets. The revaluation of plant assets for financial accounting purposes in response to increases in current costs and the general price level is considered in Chapter 25.

Factors in the estimation of periodic depreciation

The estimate of periodic depreciation is dependent on the following three variables:

1 *Economic life* This involves choosing the unit in which economic life is to be measured and estimating how many units of service are embodied in each asset.

2 *Depreciation base* An asset may be sold by a business enterprise before its service value is completely consumed. The depreciation base is the cost of asset services that will be used; it usually is less than the original investment in the asset because residual value is subtracted from cost to arrive at the depreciation base.

3 *Method of cost allocation* The problem here is to determine the amount of services that has expired in each accounting period. A corollary issue is to decide whether all units of service have an equal cost, or whether some units of service have a larger or smaller cost than others.

Estimate of economic life

The economic life of an asset is the total units of service expected to be derived from that asset. Business managers commonly measure economic life of a plant asset in terms of time units, for example, months or years. Economic life of a plant asset also may be measured in terms of output or activity, expressed in such physical units as tons, miles, gallons, or machine-hours. For example, the estimated economic life of a truck may be described as **four years** or **200,000 miles.** Forces which tend to limit the economic life of an asset should be considered in the determination of the type of **unit of service** to use for a given asset or group of assets. The causes of a decrease in economic life may be divided into two broad classes: (1) physical causes (including casualties), and (2) functional or economic causes.

Physical deterioration results largely from wear and tear due to operating use and the forces of nature. These physical forces terminate the usefulness of plant assets by rendering them incapable of performing the services for which they were intended and thus set the maximum limit on economic life. Unusual events such as accidents, floods, and earthquakes also serve to terminate or reduce the service potential or economic life of plant assets.

Functional or *economic factors* may render an asset in good physical condition no longer useful because it is not economical to keep the asset in service, or because of legal or other limits on the use of the asset. Two primary causes of functional depreciation are obsolescence and inadequacy. *Obsolescence* refers to the effect of innovations and technical improvements on the economic life of plant assets. An inevitable result of research and development activities is the obsolescence of existing plant assets. Jet airliners, for example, made propeller-driven aircraft uneconomical for major airlines to operate. Obsolescence, thus, terminated the economic life of many piston aircraft and sent them to the used-plane market even though they had a physical potential of many more years of service.

Inadequacy refers to the effect of growth and changes in the scale of a business operation in terminating the economic life of assets. A warehouse may be in sound condition, but if more space is required that cannot be provided economically by the addition of a separate building, the old warehouse has become inadequate, and its economic life, from the owner's standpoint, is terminated. In a general sense, any plant asset whose capacity is such that it cannot be operated efficiently or that does not fit the requirements of the enterprise is inadequate.

In a highly developed industrial society, functional causes of depreciation probably have a greater influence on economic lives than physical wear and tear, particularly with respect to special-purpose equipment. Estimates of economic life, therefore, are influenced by these factors.

The choice of an appropriate *unit* of economic life for a plant asset also calls for search for the causes of depreciation. The objective is to choose the unit most closely related to the cause of service exhaustion. When economic life of a plant asset is limited largely by the effect of operating wear and tear, a unit that reflects physical use of the asset is appropriate. For example, hours of service might be chosen as the unit of economic life for an electric motor, or miles of service for a truck. On the other hand, the major physical causes that limit the economic life of buildings probably are related more closely to the passage of time than to actual usage. Thus, an estimated economic life in terms of years is more appropriate for buildings.

No estimate of economic life can be made with high precision. The best procedure is to start with an estimate of physical economic life as a maximum, modify this for the probable effects of obsolescence and inadequacy, and then be prepared to adjust these estimates in the light of actual experience. When the estimated economic life of an asset is revised, the undepreciated cost is allocated to the remaining units of service.

The depreciation base

The depreciation base (or depreciable cost) of a plant asset is the portion of its cost that should be allocated to revenue during its economic life. Because the owner of an asset may sell it before its serviceability is ended, the initial cost of a plant asset, as determined by the guidelines established in Chapter 11, is not necessarily its depreciation base. For example, a car rental company may pay $10,000 for a new car and sell it at the end of three years for $3,000, even though its economic life is much longer. The depreciation base is $7,000, the difference between cost and resale value.

The scrapping or removal of buildings, structures, and heavy equipment may involve substantial costs in the year of retirement. Theoretically, removal costs should be estimated and included in the depreciation base. The inclusion of removal costs in the depreciation base means that the entire cost involved in obtaining services from plant assets will be allocated to the revenue generated by the assets, without regard to the timing of the expenditure. In practice, however, removal costs may be either ignored or netted against the estimated residual value of the assets. The depreciation base for a plant asset thus becomes:

Depreciation base

> **Depreciation base = cost − estimated residual value (net)**

In some instances, net residual value (gross residual value minus estimated removal costs) is likely to be so small or uncertain that it may be ignored in the establishment of the depreciation base. For federal income tax purposes, a net residual value of 10% or less may be ignored.

Depreciation methods—cost allocation

When the economic life of an asset has been estimated, and its depreciation base established, there remains the problem of determining the portion of cost that will expire with each unit of economic life. There are two major variables to be considered in reaching a systematic solution to this problem:

1 The *quantity* of services used may be equal or may vary during each accounting period of economic life.
2 The *cost* of various units of service may be equal or may differ during each accounting period of economic life.

Because of the relatively high degree of uncertainty that surrounds estimates of economic life and service use, the distinction between these two variables may become blurred. We may illustrate by reference to a situation that is familiar—the depreciation of an automobile used for business purposes. Assume that the automobile cost $10,000, has an expected net residual value of $1,000, and is estimated to have an economic life of 100,000 miles. The average depreciation expense per unit of service (1 mile) is 9 cents [($10,000 − $1,000) ÷ 100,000 = $0.09]. However, the miles of service used in each accounting period may vary. If 20,000 miles are driven during the first year and 30,000 miles during the second year, there has been a variation in the **quantity** of service used, and depreciation of $1,800 for the first year and $2,700 for the second recognizes this fact.

On the other hand, even if the automobile is driven 20,000 miles each year for five years, there may be a difference in the **cost** of the miles of service in each of these five accounting periods. The miles of service when the automobile is new and operating efficiently may be more valuable (and thus presumably more costly) than the miles of service during later years. Therefore, the assumption that each mile bears the same depreciation expense may not be reasonable, and we might compute depreciation on the assumption that early miles cost more than later miles. For example, depreciation might be computed at 12 cents a mile for the first 20,000 miles, 10 cents for the next 20,000 miles, etc.

There are a number of depreciation methods that attempt to recognize these factors in varying degrees. They may be classified as follows:

1 Straight-line method (based on expiration of time)
2 Accelerated methods (based on expiration of time)
   a Fixed-percentage-of-declining-balance
   b Sum-of-the-years'-digits
3 Output (or units-of-production) method (based on physical service or production)
4 Retirement and replacement methods
5 Interest methods

Depreciation under the straight-line and accelerated methods is a function of time rather than use. On the other hand, depreciation under the output method is a function of actual usage rather than the passage of time.

Depreciation generally is computed to the nearest month, although other procedures consistently applied may be acceptable. Descriptions of the most widely used depreciation methods follow:

Straight-Line Method   The distinguishing characteristic of the straight-line method of depreciation is that each full year of service absorbs an equal portion of cost. Depreciation per year thus is computed as follows:

$$\text{Depreciation per year} = \frac{\text{cost} - \text{estimated net residual value}}{\text{years of economic life}}$$

To illustrate the straight-line method of depreciation, assume that a machine is acquired at the beginning of Year 1 for $7,000 and that the net residual value of the machine at the end of four years of economic life is estimated at $1,000. The depreciation expense, accumulated depreciation, and **carrying amount** (cost less accumulated depreciation) of the machine over its economic life are presented below:

Carrying amount of machine decreases by $1,500 each year

	Depreciation expense for year	Accumulated depreciation	Carrying amount of machine
Beginning of Year 1			$7,000
End of Year 1	$1,500	$1,500	5,500
End of Year 2	1,500	3,000	4,000
End of Year 3	1,500	4,500	2,500
End of Year 4	1,500	6,000	1,000

At the end of each year, depreciation expense on this machine is recorded as follows:

Journal entry to record depreciation

```
Depreciation Expense. . . . . . . . . . . . . . . . . . . . . . . . . . . . .   1,500
      Accumulated Depreciation of Machinery. . . . . . . . . . . .          1,500
To record depreciation for year.
```

Accelerated Methods The assumption that plant assets yield either a greater quantity of service or more valuable services in early years of economic life has led accountants to devise methods of depreciation that result in larger amounts of depreciation in early years of economic life, and smaller amounts in later years. These are known as **accelerated methods** of depreciation. The two most widely used accelerated methods of depreciation are described below:

1 Fixed-percentage-of-declining-balance method Under this method (frequently called the **declining-balance method**), a percentage depreciation rate is computed which, when applied to the carrying amount of the asset at the beginning of each accounting period, results in reducing the carrying amount of the asset to estimated net residual value at the end of its economic life. Because the rate computed is applied on a constantly declining carrying amount, the depreciation expense decreases each year. The formula for the computation of the required rate per year (when n = years of economic life) is:

Formula to compute fixed percentage

$$\text{Depreciation rate} = 1 - \sqrt[n]{\frac{\text{net residual value}}{\text{cost}}}$$

In the application of this formula a net residual value of at least $1 must be used, because it is impossible to reduce any amount to zero by applying a constant percentage to the successively declining carrying amount. The depreciation rate for an asset which cost $10,000, has a net residual value of $1,296, and has an economic life of four years, is computed below:

Formula solved

$$\text{Depreciation rate} = 1 - \sqrt[4]{\frac{\$1,296}{\$10,000}} = 1 - \frac{6}{10} = \underline{\underline{40\%}}$$

If this formula yields a rate of, say, 39.69%, rounding the rate to 40% would not be objectionable, because measurement of depreciation at best is only a rough estimate.

The tabulation below shows depreciation expense for the four-year period for a fixed percentage of 40% on declining carrying amount of the asset:

Amount of depreciation decreases each year under declining-balance method . . .

Year	Carrying amount at beginning of year	Depreciation expense		Accumulated depreciation
		Amount (40% of carrying amount at beginning of year)	Percentage of total	
1	$10,000	$4,000	46.0	$4,000
2	6,000	2,400	27.6	6,400
3	3,600	1,440	16.5	7,840
4	2,160	864	9.9	8,704
Balance	1,296			
		$8,704	100.0	

It should be noted that the carrying amount at the end of the fourth year is equal to the estimated net residual value, $1,296, and that annual depreciation expense decreases rapidly. (In this example, because the depreciation rate is 40%, the depreciation expense in the second year and each of the succeeding years is only 60% of the expense reported a year earlier.)

Federal income tax laws provide that for certain assets the fixed percentage may be as high as twice the applicable straight-line rate. For example, the straight-line rate for an asset with an estimated economic life of four years is 25%, and the fixed-percentage rate is 50% (25% × 2). This approach is referred to as the **double-declining-balance** (or **200%-declining-balance**) **method.** For some assets, the rate must not exceed 150% of the straight-line rate. Current tax regulations require that net residual value be taken into account only as a limiting factor in the application of these rates; that is, the asset cannot be depreciated below net residual value.

2 Sum-of-the-years'-digits method   Under this method, a decreasing depreciation expense is computed by a simple mathematical procedure relating to arithmetic progressions. The sum of a series of numbers representing the years of economic life becomes the denominator of the depreciation fraction in any year.[1] The numerator of the depreciation fraction for each year is the remaining years of economic life taken from the beginning of the year. Because the denominator remains constant and the numerator declines each year, the result is a decreasing depreciation expense. Furthermore, because the total of the numerators of the depreciation fractions is equal to the denominator, the sum of all the fractions is 1, and 100% of the depreciation base ultimately will be allocated to revenue.

The tabulation on top of page 492 illustrates the application of the sum-of-the years'-digits method to an asset costing $22,000, having a net residual value of $2,000, and an economic life of four years.

Fractional-period depreciation under accelerated methods   Under accelerated methods, depreciation is determined for each full unit of economic life. A question of mechanics arises when assets are acquired during the year and less than a full year's depreciation is to be recorded during the first and last fiscal years of economic life. The logical solution to this problem for each of the accelerated methods of depreciation is:

1 *Double-declining-balance method*   Compute depreciation expense for a fraction of year in the year of acquisition and apply the appropriate percentage to the beginning carrying amount of the asset to compute depreciation for subsequent fiscal years.

---

[1] The formula for determining the sum of any arithmetic progression of n consecutive numbers is $n\left(\dfrac{n+1}{2}\right)$. Thus, the sum of all numbers from 1 to 15 is $15\left(\dfrac{16}{2}\right)$, or 120. Tables are available which provide the decimal equivalent of the depreciation rate for each year of economic life.

. . . and also under the
sum-of-years'-digits
method

Year of asset life	Depreciation fraction	Depreciation base ($22,000 − $2,000)	Depreciation expense	Accumulated depreciation	Carrying amount
					$22,000
1	$\frac{4}{10}$	$20,000	$8,000	$ 8,000	14,000
2	$\frac{3}{10}$	20,000	6,000	14,000	8,000
3	$\frac{2}{10}$	20,000	4,000	18,000	4,000
4	$\frac{1}{10}$	20,000	2,000	20,000	2,000
Sum 10					

2 *Sum-of-the-years'-digits method* Compute the depreciation for each full year of economic life, and then allocate each full year's depreciation between two different fiscal years.

To illustrate, assume the following data for a plant asset:

Data for illustration

Cost of plant asset, Apr. 1, 1984	$8,000
Estimated economic life	5 years
Rate for double-declining-balance method: (100% ÷ 5) × 2	40%
Estimated net residual value	$500

The computation of depreciation for the first partial year (1984) and the next full year (1985) under the two accelerated methods is demonstrated in the tabulation on top of page 493. The depreciation for the remaining $3\frac{1}{4}$ years is determined in a similar manner.

Output Method A more realistic allocation of the cost of some plant assets can be obtained by dividing the depreciation base by the estimated units of use or production (machine-hours, units of product produced, or miles driven) rather than by the years of economic life. For example, a bus company might compute depreciation on its vehicles by a mileage basis. If a bus cost $30,000 and is estimated to have an economic life of 200,000 miles and no residual value, the depreciation rate per mile of operation is 15 cents ($30,000 ÷ 200,000 = $0.15). At the end of each year, the amount of depreciation is determined by multiplying the number of miles the bus was driven during the year by the 15-cent rate.

The estimated economic life of an asset under the output method is measured in terms of potential physical services or units of output, and

Study these computations carefully

Double-declining balance		Sum-of-the-years' digits	
Full year of economic life	*Depreciation*	*Full year of economic life*	*Depreciation*
First year: $8,000 × 40%	*$3,200*	*First year: $7,500 × $\frac{5}{15}$ . . . . .*	*$2,500*
Second year: ($8,000 − $3,200) × 40%. . .	*1,920*	*Second year: $7,500 × $\frac{4}{15}$ . . .*	*2,000*
Depreciation for period from Apr. 1, 1984, to Dec. 31, 1984:			
$3,200 × $\frac{3}{4}$ (9 mo.)	*$2,400*	*$2,500 × $\frac{3}{4}$ (9 mo.) . . . . . .*	*$1,875*
Depreciation for year ended Dec. 31, 1985:			
($8,000 − $2,400 taken in 1984) × 40% . .	*$2,240*	*$2,500 × $\frac{1}{4}$ (3 mo.) . . . .*	*$ 625*
		$2,000 × $\frac{3}{4}$ (9 mo.)	*1,500*
		Total	*$2,125*

periodic depreciation is based on the actual use of the asset. As a result, *total* depreciation expense for a fiscal year varies if use varies, but the *depreciation per unit of output is constant.* The output method of depreciation is particularly appropriate when asset use fluctuates widely from year to year, and depreciation is more closely related to physical use than to functional obsolescence.

Some accountants have suggested that certain assets should be depreciated on the basis of periodic appraisal. This method may result in periodic depreciation charges for certain assets which closely parallel the output method, because the current fair value of an asset depends to a considerable extent on the amount of wear and tear. The *appraisal method* requires a determination of the value of services that *remain in the asset* at the end of each accounting period. Depreciation is estimated by appraising assets on hand at the end of each period, and charging off an amount sufficient to reduce the carrying amount of the asset to its appraised value. The appraisal method of depreciation is appropriate for short-lived plant assets such as small tools, dies, utensils, and containers.

Retirement and Replacement Methods The methods of depreciation discussed thus far represent an attempt to measure the expiration of asset cost as it occurs. An alternative approach, advocated by some public utilities and railroads, is to recognize depreciation only at the time assets reach the end of their economic lives.

The *retirement method* is a system whereby the depreciation base of plant assets is debited to expense in the year in which assets are retired from service. Thus, under the retirement method, the asset accounts include the full cost of all plant assets currently in use. The **replacement method** is a system whereby the original cost of all plant assets is retained in asset accounts, and the cost of all replacements is debited to expense when they are acquired. Thus, under the replacement method, the asset accounts include the cost of the first assets acquired.

There are two objections to these depreciation methods. The first is that no depreciation is recorded until retirement of plant assets occurs. Not only is income overstated in the early years of economic life, but also the original asset cost appears in the balance sheet, despite the fact that a portion of this cost has expired. The second objection is that depreciation expense is determined by the number of assets replaced and the cost of the new assets. The probability that the cost of replacements or retirements in any year will coincide with the cost of asset services used during that year is rather slim. The force of this objection is increased when it is noted that replacement policy of a business enterprise is likely to vary in response to the availability of funds for capital expenditures, the stage of the business cycle, and earnings prospects of the enterprise.

Despite these rather obvious flaws, retirement and replacement methods of depreciation have been used and supported in the public utility industry. This may be explained in part by the fact that utility plants typically are composed of large numbers of interrelated items such as rails, ties, poles, pipe sections, rail cars, transformers, etc., whose individual cost is small. Under these conditions, the economic life of plant assets is difficult to estimate, and the distinction between maintenance and replacement often is difficult to make.

Interest Methods   The **annuity** and **sinking-fund** methods call for application of compound interest concepts in the measurement of periodic depreciation. These methods are illustrated in the Appendix at the end of this chapter.

Composite Depreciation Method   Many business enterprises find it expedient to account for depreciation of certain kinds of plant assets on a **composite** or **group** basis. The Internal Revenue Service allows economic lives to be applied to broad classes of plant assets, rather than to individual assets. Composite or group depreciation is a process of averaging the economic lives of a number of property units and taking depreciation on the entire class of assets as if it were an operating unit. The term **composite** generally refers to a collection of somewhat dissimilar assets; the term **group** usually refers to a collection of similar assets. The procedures for the computation of periodic depreciation is essentially the same in either case.

Several methods may be used to develop a composite or group depreciation rate to be applied to the total cost of a group of assets. The computation of a *straight-line composite depreciation rate* for a group of machines owned by Clarice Company is illustrated below:

Straight-line composite depreciation rate

Machine	Cost	Net residual value	Amount to be depreciated	Economic life (years)	Annual depreciation expense
W	$ 6,000	$ –0–	$ 6,000	5	$1,200
X	10,000	1,200	8,800	8	1,100
Y	15,000	1,000	14,000	10	1,400
Z	19,000	1,000	18,000	12	1,500
Totals	$50,000	$3,200	$46,800		$5,200

CLARICE COMPANY
Computation of Composite Depreciation Rate

Composite depreciation rate based on cost: $5,200 ÷ $50,000 = 10.4%

Composite economic life of machines: $46,800 ÷ $5,200 = 9 years

The composite depreciation rate is 10.4%, and the composite economic life of the assets is 9 years. In other words, the application of the 10.4% composite rate to the cost of $50,000 will reduce the composite net residual value of the assets to $3,200 in exactly 9 years [$50,000 − ($5,200 × 9) = $3,200].

Once the composite depreciation rate is computed, it is continued in use until a material change occurs in the composition of plant assets or in the estimate of their economic lives. The assumptions underlying the use of composite depreciation methods are that (1) plant assets are regularly retired near the end of their economic lives, (2) plant assets are regularly replaced with similar assets, and (3) proceeds on retirement are approximately equal to the net residual value used for the computation of the composite depreciation rate. If assets are not replaced, for example, the use of the 10.4% rate computed above eventually would result in the recording of excessive depreciation.

In the determination of yearly depreciation, the 10.4% rate is applied to the balance in the asset account at the beginning of the year, which balance excludes the original cost of all units retired prior to the beginning of the year. Thus, for each of the first five years, annual depreciation is $5,200; and in the sixth year (assuming machine W was replaced at the end of the fifth year with a similar machine costing $9,000), depreciation is $5,512 [($50,000 − $6,000 + $9,000) × 10.4% = $5,512]. The composite depreciation rate is not revised when assets are replaced with comparable assets, and the asset group should not be depreciated below net residual value at any time.

When composite procedures are employed, a record is not maintained for accumulated depreciation on individual assets. When an asset is retired from use or sold, a journal entry is required to remove the original cost from the asset account, and the difference between original cost and the proceeds received, if any, is debited to Accumulated Depreciation; a gain or loss is not recognized. To illustrate, if machine W were sold at the end of the fourth year for $1,500, the journal entry to record the sale would be:

No gain or loss is recognized

Cash	1,500
Accumulated Depreciation of Machinery	4,500
Machinery	6,000

To record sale of machine W. Composite depreciation method is used; therefore, no gain or loss is recognized.

The primary disadvantage of the composite depreciation method is that the averaging procedure may obscure significant variations from average. The accuracy of the straight-line composite depreciation rate can be verified by recomputing depreciation on the straight-line basis for individual assets. Any significant discrepancies between the two results require a change in the composite depreciation rate.

The advantages claimed for the composite method are simplicity, convenience, and a reduction in the amount of detail involved in property records and depreciation computations. The advent of computers has reduced the force of this argument. In many cases unit property records are now feasible, although composite methods previously were considered a necessity.

The requisites for the successful operation of composite depreciation procedures are that there be a large number of homogeneous assets, of relatively small individual value, with similar economic lives. Telephone and electric transmission poles, underground cables, railroad tracks, and hotel furniture are examples of situations in which composite depreciation may give satisfactory results.

DEPRECIATION METHODS AND MANAGEMENT DECISIONS

In highly industrialized nations, plant assets play a large part in the productive process. It is easy to see that the cost of direct material and direct labor becomes a part of finished product. It is not always so clearly recognized, however, that a business enterprise also sells to its customers the services of the plant assets used to manufacture and market its products.

The importance of depreciation stems from the various management decisions that are affected by it. To the extent that depreciation is a significant part of operating costs, and that operating costs are relevant in business decisions, the relative merits of various depreciation methods are significant in decisions relating to the following areas:

1 Measurement of income and the impact of inflation
2 Computation of income taxes payable
3 Investment of capital

The effect of different depreciation methods in relation to each of these decision areas is discussed briefly in the following sections.

Depreciation, income measurement, and inflation

The purpose of depreciation accounting is to measure the amount that must be recovered from revenue to compensate for the portion of asset cost that has been used up. This idea is embodied in the phrase *maintenance of capital,* which often is used in relation to income measurement.

The widespread use of the straight-line time method of depreciation results from its simplicity and convenience. Two objections may be leveled against the straight-line method, each of which becomes a supporting argument for some other method of depreciation.

1 It does not allow for the fact that productivity of plant assets may decline with age.
2 It does not take into account variations in the rate of asset use.

Some business executives suggest that the decline in productivity of many plant assets is so pronounced that the value (and thus the cost) of asset services in the early stages of economic life is materially greater than in later years. If this is true, accelerated methods of depreciation may achieve a better matching of costs and revenue than the straight-line method. Originally, the declining productivity argument centered on a rising curve of repair and maintenance costs as assets aged. In recent years, greater weight has been given to the effects of obsolescence. Often, the period of high earnings on new plant assets is short because of the inroads of innovation and competition.

The use of the straight-line time depreciation method makes depreciation a fixed period cost by assumption, and thereby fails to allow for the loss of service potential related to wear and tear through usage. If an asset is used twice as much in one year as another, it may be unrealistic to assume that the amount and cost of asset services consumed is the same in both years. This objection to straight-line depreciation becomes an argument for the use of a measure of output as the unit of economic life, which would tend to make depreciation a variable cost rather than a fixed cost.

During an inflationary period, any depreciation method based on historical cost understates the amount of capital consumed (depreciation). Thus, a part of reported net income essentially represents *return of capital.* Users of financial statements should consider this shortcoming in the traditional income measurement model and should make appropriate adjustments to restate depreciation and net income in terms of current cost of plant assets. The impact of inflation on depreciation accounting is considered in Chapter 25.

Depreciation policy and income taxes

Probably the strongest influence on depreciation policy is the income tax law. The direction of the influence is toward accelerated depreciation. Depreciation expense reduces taxable income and income taxes expense. Taxpayers cannot deduct more than the actual cost of a depreciable asset over its economic life, but income taxes can be postponed by acceleration of depreciation deductions, and deferred taxes represent an interest-free loan for the period of the postponement. The only possible tax disadvantage of large initial depreciation deductions is that income tax rates might increase sufficiently during the economic life of the asset to more than offset the implicit interest savings.

Tax factors encourage the use of minimum estimates of economic life and the adoption of accelerated depreciation methods, without regard to issues of accounting theory or economic reality. If such practices applied only to the computation of taxable income, no damage would be done to the validity of financial statements. For many business enterprises, however, the convenience of keeping only one set of depreciation records is such that the accounting records generally are made to conform to the income tax requirements.

If tax depreciation and accounting depreciation substantially are equivalent, there are practical advantages to maintaining the accounting records on a tax basis. Tax deductions, however, are shaped by matters of public policy and the need for revenue by the government, and are not necessarily related to the objectives of financial accounting. Material divergence between income tax and financial accounting data is possible. For example, many business enterprises use accelerated depreciation methods for income tax purposes but use the straight-line method for financial accounting purposes.

Allowing relatively large depreciation deductions for income tax purposes is a means of subsidizing business investment. As a result, proposals for speeding up depreciation allowances as a means of stimulating investment or encouraging certain kinds of investment frequently are made before Congress.[2] The pressure to increase depreciation pro-

---

[2] Despite the numerous steps taken by the U.S. Congress in recent years to liberalize depreciation policies, the United States still lags far behind other industrialized nations in this respect. For example, taxpayers in the United States are permitted to recover on the average less than 70% of the cost of assets over the first seven years of asset life. In contrast, taxpayers in the United Kingdom, France, Italy, Germany, and Switzerland are allowed to deduct 90% or more of the investment in plant assets over the first seven years of asset life.

visions for maximum tax advantage is not likely to wane. Therefore, the continued usefulness of accounting data for managerial and investment purposes may depend on maintaining a healthy state of independence between financial accounting and income tax rules.

Depreciation and capital investment decisions

The two most important questions relating to the role of depreciation in a capital investment decision are: (1) Is depreciation a relevant cost in the decision? (2) How does depreciation affect the cash flows from the investment?

Depreciation Expense May Be Either a Differential Cost or a Sunk Cost   In essence, two kinds of costs are relevant to the decision to invest capital in productive assets: (1) *future costs,* that is, costs that will be incurred as the result of the decision; and (2) *differential costs,* that is, costs that will change as the result of the decision. The expense represented by depreciation on existing assets is attributable to an investment made at some time in the past. Except to the extent that an existing asset can be sold and some portion of the past investment recovered, no present decision can change the amount of cost that has been sunk into that asset. Thus, depreciation often has been referred to as a *sunk cost.*

A decision to invest in productive facilities should be based on an analysis of differential costs and revenue. The carrying amount of existing assets (a sunk cost that cannot be changed in the short run) is an irrelevant factor and should be ignored (except for income tax consideration). Most managerial decisions as to alternative actions such as buying or leasing, buying or making, or accepting or not accepting a special order, depend on an analysis of differential costs and revenue. Depreciation may or may not represent a differential or relevant cost in comparing such alternative courses of action. Depreciation on special equipment that must be purchased specifically for a given activity is always a differential cost to that activity, but depreciation on existing assets is a differential cost only if the use of the assets for the specific activity reduces their economic life.

We have oversimplified the problem in this discussion, but a valid generalization may be drawn. Whether or not depreciation should be regarded as a differential cost depends on whether the limiting factor in asset life is obsolescence or use, and whether the asset in question is being used to capacity. For this reason, depreciation expense computed for purposes of income determination generally is not relevant for decision making.

Effect of Depreciation on Cash Flows   Investment decisions frequently are made on the basis of the expected rate of return on the investment. In the computation of the rate of return, *net cash flow* from the investment generally is a more useful concept than **net income** from the invest-ment. Depreciation expense does not generate cash directly; it is an ex-pense which does not reduce cash, but which is deducted to compute taxable income. Thus, depreciation expense indirectly generates larger cash flows from operations by reducing income taxes. For this reason, depreciation is viewed as a powerful instrument for speeding up cash flows and reducing the **payback period** on new investments in plant assets.

To illustrate the relationships between depreciation and cash flows, assume the following annual results for an asset which is rented to others:

Amount of cash received as rent revenue	*$5,000*
Less: All expenses (except income taxes and depreciation of $2,000)	*1,200*
Net cash received	*$3,800*
Income taxes, 50% of income after depreciation: ($3,800 − $2,000) × 50%	*900*
Net cash flow each year	*$2,900*

The annual net cash flow of $2,900 also may be determined by adding the depreciation expense of $2,000 to the accounting net income of $900. Determination of the net cash flow from an investment is an im-portant step in the evaluation of investment alternatives under **capital budgeting** techniques.

Depreciation procedures and records

Property Records   The typical business enterprise employs many differ-ent kinds of plant assets having varying characteristics and economic lives. Precision in accounting for the use of such assets is facilitated by detailed and complete property records. Property records may be main-tained on ledger cards, tabulating cards, magnetic tapes, or in a com-puter storage.

An ideal system is to maintain a record for each plant asset. The rec-ord should show, for each asset, its original cost, additions, estimated economic life, estimated net residual value, date of installation, loca-tion, basis and amount of periodic depreciation, and any other useful information, such as serial numbers. In addition to providing thorough support for depreciation and retirement journal entries, such property records are useful for maintaining good internal controls for plant assets.

Accumulated Depreciation Account   In theory, depreciation could be recorded as a credit to the asset account, because depreciable assets basically are long-term prepaid costs. The direct write-off procedure often is used for large numbers of small-value assets when periodic inventories are taken to determine the portion of asset cost remaining on hand. For larger assets, the usual practice is to credit a contra-asset account titled Accumulated Depreciation, Allowance for Depreciation, or Reserve for Depreciation.[3] The primary argument for the use of a separate ledger account is to preserve information about the cost of plant assets and the proportion of cost that has expired. Also, in an analysis of account balances, it is convenient to be able to distinguish plant additions and retirements from adjustments in accumulated depreciation.

The Accumulated Depreciation account is frequently, but improperly, referred to as a *valuation account.* The Accumulated Depreciation account represents the portion of the acquisition cost of a plant asset that has been allocated to revenue through the process of depreciation. Its purpose is not to arrive at a valuation of a plant asset in terms of current fair value, but rather to determine the unallocated cost (or carrying amount) of a plant asset at a given date.

Depreciation (Lapsing) Schedules   When the number of individual items within each class of plant assets is not large, a *depreciation schedule* (sometimes known as a *lapsing schedule*) may be used. Lapsing schedules may take many forms and often are prepared by a computer if the number of assets is large. A depreciation schedule is a means of keeping unit property records with a minimum of effort. Its purposes are to facilitate the computation of periodic depreciation, and to provide a continuing record of asset costs and the related accumulated depreciation. An example of a depreciation schedule for the finishing department of General Manufacturing Company appears on pages 502 and 503.

When an asset is acquired, the cost is entered in the first money column of the schedule, and the prospective depreciation charges throughout its economic life are extended in the Depreciation Expense columns. If the asset is retired at the end of its economic life, the original cost is credited to the asset account, and depreciation to date is debited to Accumulated Depreciation. The gain or loss is recorded in the general journal or the cash receipts journal. If an asset is retired prematurely, it is not necessary to erase or change the originally scheduled depreciation amounts. It is more convenient to cancel the future depreciation charges by recording appropriate *deductions* on the line used to record the retirement. This is illustrated for Machine B. It originally was

[3] The 1980 edition of *Accounting Trends & Techniques,* published by the AICPA, reported that of the 600 companies surveyed, 513 companies used the terms *accumulated depreciation* and *accumulated depreciation and amortization* (or *depletion*); 60 companies used the terms *allowance for depreciation* and *allowance for depreciation and amortization* (or *depletion*); and only 27 companies used other captions.

GENERAL MANUFACTURING COMPANY
Depreciation (Lapsing) Schedule—Finishing Department

Date acquired (or retired)	Type of machine	Machinery account Debit (Credit)	Balance	Accumulated Depreciation account Debit (Credit)	Balance
Jan. 3, Year 1	A	$3,100	$ 3,100		
Jan. 4, Year 1	B	6,000	9,100		
July 1, Year 1	C	4,800	13,900		
Depreciation for Year 1				$(2,740)	$(2,740)
April 1, Year 2	D	2,900	16,800		
Aug. 15, Year 2	E	4,000	20,800		
Dec. 29, Year 2 (sold for $2,300)	B	(6,000)	14,800	3,600*	860
Depreciation for Year 2				(3,940)	(3,080)
Depreciation for Year 3				(2,620)	(5,700)

* For two years.

estimated that Machine B had an economic life of three years, but the machine was sold for $2,300 on December 29, Year 2, at the end of only two years of service. The removal of $6,000 from the Machinery account and $3,600 (two years at $1,800 a year) from Accumulated Depreciation is recorded in the schedule. In the Depreciation Expense columns, the $1,800 depreciation originally scheduled for Year 3 is canceled. Journal entries to record annual depreciation and the sale of Machine B are shown on the bottom of page 503.

Disclosure of depreciation in financial statements

Because of the significant effects on financial position and results of operations which stem from depreciation expense and the depreciation methods used, the following disclosures should be made in the financial statements or in the notes accompanying the financial statements:[4]

1 Depreciation expense for the accounting period
2 Balances of major classes of depreciable assets, by nature or function
3 Accumulated depreciation, either by major classes of depreciable assets or in total
4 A general description of the method or methods used in the computation of depreciation with respect to major classes of depreciable assets

[4] APB Opinion No. 12, "Omnibus Opinion—1967," AICPA (New York: 1967), p. 188.

Estimated net residual value	Depre- ciation base	Estimated economic life, years	Depreciation expense (straight-line)		
			Year 1	Year 2	Year 3, etc.
$400	$2,700	5	$ 540	$ 540	$ 540
600	5,400	3	1,800	1,800	1,800
–0–	4,800	6	($\frac{1}{2}$) 400	800	800
			$2,740		
500	2,400	3		($\frac{3}{4}$) 600	800
160	3,840	8		($\frac{5}{12}$) 200	480
					(1,800)†
				$3,940	
					$2,620

† Adjustment for one year.

The 1980 edition of **Accounting Trends & Techniques,** published by the AICPA, showed that 556 of the 600 companies surveyed used the straight-line method, and 168 companies used one or more of the accelerated depreciation methods; only 46 companies used the output

Journal entries from data in lapsing schedule

Year 1

Dec. 31 Depreciation Expense. 2,740
                 Accumulated Depreciation of Machinery   2,740
         To record depreciation for Year 1.

Year 2

Dec. 29 Cash 2,300
         Accumulated Depreciation of Machinery 3,600
         Loss on Sale of Machinery.   100
                 Machinery   6,000
         To record sale of machine B.

Dec. 31 Depreciation Expense. 3,940
                 Accumulated Depreciation of Machinery.   3,940
         To record depreciation for Year 2.

Year 3

Dec. 31 Depreciation Expense. 2,620
                 Accumulated Depreciation of Machinery.   2,620
         To record depreciation for Year 3.

method. If a change in the method of computing depreciation is made, the effect of the change on the current year's net income should be disclosed. Similarly, the effect of any unusual depreciation charges should be disclosed. Accounting for changes in depreciation methods, changes in economic lives of depreciable assets, and corrections of errors in the recording of depreciation are discussed in Chapter 22.

DEPLETION OF NATURAL RESOURCES

Depreciable assets usually retain their physical characteristics as they are used in operations. In contrast, natural resources in essence are long-term inventories of material that will be removed physically from their source. In either case—whether accountants are dealing with a "bundle of services" or a "store of material"—the basic problem is to determine the cost of the units of services or material that are consumed during each accounting period. The portion of the cost (or other valuation) assigned to property containing natural resources that is applicable to the units removed from the property is known as *depletion.*

The depletion base

The *depletion base* of properties containing natural resources is the acquisition cost less the estimated net residual value of the properties after the resources have been removed. The estimated cost of restoring the properties may be taken into account in the determination of the net residual value of the properties, or it may be accrued as the resources are removed from the properties.[5]

Acquisition cost includes expenditures for exploration, drilling, excavation, and construction preparatory to the removal of the natural resources. These costs, known as *development costs,* should be amortized in proportion to the removal of the resources. Structures and equipment used to extract natural resources may have an economic life shorter than the time required to complete the removal, in which case the depreciation of these assets should be recorded over their economic lives.

What if the expenditures made to acquire, explore, and develop natural resources prove unproductive? If each specific property is viewed as a separate venture, the logical interpretation is that no asset exists, and a loss therefore has occurred. On the other hand, from the viewpoint of the enterprise as a whole, particularly if it is seeking constantly to maintain its natural resource base by exploration and acquisition of new deposits, a certain amount of unproductive effort may be viewed as a

[5] Robert E. Field, *Accounting Research Study No. 11,* "Financial Reporting in the Extractive Industries," AICPA (New York: 1969), p. 74.

normal cost of discovering new deposits. If, for example, 10 dry wells are drilled for each producing well brought in, the argument that 11 drillings are necessary to bring in a producing well and that the cost of a producing well includes the cost of 10 unsuccessful efforts has considerable merit. The problem is analogous to that of accounting for spoilage in manufacturing. If a certain amount of spoilage is considered normal, it is treated as a part of the cost of the good units produced; if the amount of spoilage is abnormal, it is reported as a loss.

In the lumber industry, substantial costs are incurred for fire protection, insect and disease control, property taxes, and other maintenance costs applicable to standing timber that will not be harvested for a considerable length of time. These costs, known as *carrying costs,* are capitalized (added to the cost of the property) while the property is being developed. For example, if carrying costs of $40,000 are applicable to a given tract of timber and during the current accounting period 20% of the timber is cut, 80%, or $32,000, is applicable to uncut timber and is capitalized.

Estimate of recoverable units

The estimate of economic lives for plant assets is a relatively simple undertaking compared with the estimate of recoverable units of natural resources. The quantity of ore in a vein and the recoverable deposit in oil-producing property often are difficult to determine, and revisions may be necessary as production takes place and new evidence becomes available. Adding to the problem is the fact that changes in the method of extraction may make it possible to work deposits of natural resources that originally were deemed uneconomical.

Ideally, the recoverable deposit of a natural resource should be measured in units of *desired* product, such as an ounce of silver or a pound of nickel, rather than in units of *mined* product, such as a ton of raw ore. If depletion is based on tons of mined ore, the same charge will be applied to a ton of high-grade ore as to a ton of low-grade ore. This treatment is hardly logical in terms of the way mining property is valued and in terms of efforts by accountants to match costs and revenue.

Cost depletion

Any of the methods of depreciation previously discussed may be applied in a comparable manner to the computation of depletion. The straight-line method, however, is of doubtful applicability because the exhaustion of natural resources is a matter of physical output rather than the passage of time. Accelerated methods have not been commonly used to measure depletion, despite the fact that the productivity of wasting assets may decline rapidly when the cost of recovery per unit increases as production moves from richer to poorer deposits.

By far the most common method of depletion for financial accounting purposes is the output method, which produces a constant depletion charge per unit of the natural resource removed. To illustrate, assume that Komoda Company acquired mining property for $720,000. It is estimated that there are 1.2 million recoverable units of the natural resource, and that the land will have a net residual value (after restoration costs) of $60,000 when the resource is exhausted. The depletion per unit of output is computed as follows:

Formula to compute depletion per unit

$$\text{Depletion} = \frac{\text{cost} - \text{net residual value}}{\text{total recoverable units}}$$

$$= \frac{\$720,000 - \$60,000}{1,200,000 \text{ units}} = \$0.55 \text{ per unit}$$

The amount of cost depletion is included in the cost of the inventory of the natural resource and is recognized as an expense only when the inventory is sold. For example, assume that in the current year Komoda Company removed 300,000 units of the natural resource from the ground and that 200,000 of these units were sold; the cost of goods sold for the current year would be determined as follows:

Depletion is included in total cost and unit cost

	Total	Unit cost
Cost of goods sold:		
Depletion (300,000 units × $0.55).	$165,000	$0.55
Material, labor, and overhead (other than depreciation)	237,000	0.79
Depreciation of equipment.	15,000	0.05
Total cost of production (300,000 units).	$417,000	$1.39
Less: Ending inventory (100,000 units @ $1.39)	139,000	
Cost of goods sold (200,000 units @ $1.39).	$278,000	

When additional costs are incurred in the development of mining properties or estimates of recoverable units are revised, the depletion rate should be redetermined. Depletion previously recorded should not be revised. The new depletion rate is computed by dividing the unamortized cost of the mining property (including any additional development costs) by the new estimate of recoverable units. Changes in accounting estimates are discussed in Chapter 22.

Percentage depletion for income tax purposes

For income tax purposes, a special depletion method known as *percentage* or *statutory depletion* can be used by taxpayers engaged in most mining activities. Under this procedure the depletion deduction may be computed as a percentage of the gross income received, without regard to the cost of the property or the number of units produced. Some examples of percentage depletion (subject to change by Congress at any time) follow:

Gold, silver, oil shale, copper, and iron ore	*15%*
China clay, rock asphalt, borax, and bauxite	*14%*
Coal and sodium chloride.	*10%*
Gravel, peat, sand, and magnesium chloride	*5%*

Some statutory depletion rates

Some years ago, the 22% depletion allowance for major oil and gas producers was discontinued. However, the allowance was retained in limited form for small producers and royalty recipients. The 22% depletion continued in effect for small producers through 1980, and gradually was reduced to 15% in 1984 and beyond.

Taxpayers have the option of using either cost depletion or percentage depletion, whichever is more advantageous. The only limitation on percentage depletion is that it cannot exceed 50% of the taxable income from the property before depletion. To illustrate, assume the following for Arizona Copper Company for the current year:

Information for current year

Sale of copper ore (200,000 tons)	*$15,000,000*
Expenses (excluding depletion)	*$ 6,500,000*
Depletion base (cost) of ore-bearing property	*$ 4,000,000*
Estimated tons of ore recoverable from property	*1,000,000*
Cost depletion per ton of ore ($4,000,000 ÷ 1,000,000).	*$ 4*
Income tax rate	*40%*

The taxable income and net income for financial accounting purposes for Arizona Copper Company are determined on top of page 508.

In the computation of taxable income for the current year, percentage depletion is $2,250,000 (15% of $15,000,000), because this amount exceeds cost depletion of $800,000 and is less than 50% of the $8,500,000 income before depletion. However, if expenses excluding depletion amounted to $12,000,000, percentage depletion would be limited to $1,500,000 (50% of $3,000,000, the income before depletion). For those properties to which the percentage method applies, depletion

	Taxable income	Financial accounting income
Sale of copper ore.	$15,000,000	$15,000,000
Expenses (excluding depletion).	(6,500,000)	(6,500,000)
Income before depletion	$ 8,500,000	
Depletion:		
Percentage basis for income tax purposes:		
$15,000,000 × 15%.	(2,250,000)	
Cost basis for financial accounting purposes:		
200,000 tons of ore @ $4 per ton		(800,000)
Taxable income	$ 6,250,000	
Income taxes, $6,250,000 × 40%		(2,500,000)
Net income		$ 5,200,000

should be computed under both the cost method and the percentage method, and the larger deduction taken for income tax purposes.

The primary advantage of percentage depletion arises not because it may be larger than cost depletion in any given year, but because the cumulative amount of depletion deductions is not limited by the depletion base. There is no cost base for percentage depletion, and taxpayers may deduct depletion on their income tax returns many times in excess of the cost of the property. **Percentage depletion is not recorded in the accounting records;** it represents a special income tax benefit granted to certain natural resource industries as a matter of public policy.

APPENDIX: INTEREST METHODS OF DEPRECIATION

For many years the **annuity** and **sinking-fund** methods of depreciation have received attention from accounting theorists because of their focus on cost recovery and rate of return on the investment in depreciable assets. A depreciable asset represents a bundle of future services to be received periodically over the economic life of the asset. The cost of such an asset logically may be viewed as the present value of the approximately equal periodic rents (services) discounted at a rate of interest consistent with the risk factors surrounding the investment in the asset.

Annuity Method   The annuity method of depreciation is appropriate when the periodic cost (depreciation) of using a long-lived asset is considered to be equal to the total of the expired cost of the asset and the interest on the unrecovered investment in the asset. Depreciation Expense is debited and Accumulated Depreciation and Interest Revenue are credited periodically, as explained in the example below.

Assume that a computer with an economic life of five years and a net residual value of $67,388 at the end of the fifth year is acquired for $800,000. If the fair rate of interest for this type of investment is 10% compounded annually, annual depreciation is computed as illustrated below:

$$\text{Depreciation} = \frac{\text{cost of asset less present value of net residual value}}{\text{present value of ordinary annuity of 5 rents of 1 at 10\%}}$$

$$\text{Depreciation} = \frac{\$800,000 - (\$67,388 \times 0.620921^*)}{3.790787\dagger}$$

$$\text{Depreciation} = \frac{\$800,000 - \$41,843}{3.790787}$$

$$\text{Depreciation} = \underline{\$200,000}$$

* Present value of 1 for five periods at 10% (Table 2 in the Appendix in back of the book).
† See Table 4 in the Appendix in back of the book.

A summary of the results of the annuity method of depreciation, and the journal entries to record depreciation for the first two years, are presented on page 510.

The summary on page 510 shows that: (1) Depreciation computed by the annuity method is debited for $200,000 each year; (2) interest revenue is credited each year with 10% of the unrecovered investment (carrying amount of the computer); (3) the difference between annual depreciation expense and interest revenue is credited to Accumulated Depreciation; and (4) the carrying amount of the computer at the end of Year 5 is $67,388, the net residual value at the end of its economic life. The total depreciation expense over the economic life of the computer exceeds its depreciable cost by $267,388 ($1,000,000 − $732,612 = $267,388), an amount equal to the interest revenue recorded during the economic life of the computer. The net charge to revenue over the five-year period is equal to the depreciation base of the computer and *increases* each year. The annuity method of depreciation thus tends to produce a more constant rate of return on investment than, say, the straight-line method of depreciation. Consequently, the use of the annuity method of depreciation for assets acquired under capital leases has been advocated by some accountants in recent years.

		Annuity Method of Depreciation			
Year	Depre-ciation expense	Interest revenue (10% of carrying amount)	Credit to Accu-mulated Depre-ciation account	Balance in Accu-mulated Depre-ciation account	Carrying amount of com-puter
0					$800,000
1	$ 200,000	$ 80,000	$120,000	$120,000	680,000
2	200,000	68,000	132,000	252,000	548,000
3	200,000	54,800	145,200	397,200	402,800
4	200,000	40,280	159,720	556,920	243,080
5	200,000	24,308	175,692	732,612	67,388
	$1,000,000	$267,388	$732,612		

Journal entries:	Year 1	Year 2
Depreciation Expense	200,000	200,000
Interest Revenue	80,000	68,000
Accumulated Depreciation .	120,000	132,000

To record depreciation by annuity method.

Sinking-Fund Method   The sinking fund method of depreciation might be used when a fund is to be accumulated to replace an asset at the end of its economic life. Under the sinking-fund method, the amount of annual depreciation is equal to the increase in the asset replacement fund. The increase in the fund consists of the equal periodic deposits (rents) plus the interest revenue at the assumed rate on the sinking-fund balance.

We shall illustrate the sinking-fund method of depreciation with the same example as we used to illustrate the annuity method, that is, a computer purchased for $800,000 with an economic life of five years and a net residual value of $67,388 at the end of five years. If we again assume a 10% annual compound rate of interest, the annual deposits to the sinking fund may be determined as follows:

$$\text{Sinking-fund deposits} = \frac{\text{cost of asset less net residual value}}{\text{amount of ordinary annuity of 5 rents of 1 at 10\%}}$$

$$\text{Sinking-fund deposits} = \frac{\$800,000 - \$67,388}{6.1051^{*}}$$

$$\text{Sinking-fund deposits} = \underline{\$120,000}$$

* See Table 3 in the Appendix in back of the book.

A summary of the results of the sinking-fund method of depreciation, and the journal entries for the first two years, are as follows:

	Sinking-Fund Method of Depreciation						
	Sinking fund				Depreciation and carrying amount		
Year	Annual deposit	Interest revenue (10% of fund balance)	Total fund increase	Fund balance	Depreciation expense	Balance in Accumulated Depreciation account	Carrying amount of computer
0							$800,000
1	$120,000	$ –0–	$120,000	$120,000	$120,000	$120,000	680,000
2	120,000	12,000	132,000	252,000	132,000	252,000	548,000
3	120,000	25,200	145,200	397,200	145,200	397,200	402,800
4	120,000	39,720	159,720	556,920	159,720	556,920	243,080
5	120,000	55,692	175,692	732,612	175,692	732,612	67,388
	$600,000	$132,612	$732,612		$732,612		

Journal entries:	Year 1	Year 2
Sinking Fund	120,000	132,000
Depreciation Expense	120,000	132,000
Cash	120,000	120,000
Interest Revenue	–0–	12,000
Accumulated Depreciation	120,000	132,000
To record depreciation by sinking-fund method		

The summary and entries show that: (1) Depreciation computed by the sinking-fund method is debited each year for *increasing* amounts equal to the total increase in the sinking fund; (2) interest revenue is credited each year with earnings at 10% on the fund balance; (3) the net charges to revenue (depreciation less interest earned) each year remain constant at $120,000; and (4) the carrying amount of the computer at the end of Year 5 is $67,388, the net residual value at that date.

The sinking-fund method of depreciation may be used without the accumulation of a sinking fund. However, depreciation still would be recorded equal to the hypothetical fund increases, as illustrated above. The sinking-fund method of depreciation actually is used by some utility companies.

REVIEW QUESTIONS

1 Some enterprises, particularly those owning improved real estate, report an intermediate amount in their income statement and refer to it as "income before depreciation." Comment on this practice.

2 Distinguish among the terms **depreciation, amortization,** and **depletion.** How is depreciation accounting related to the replacement of an asset at the end of its economic life?

3 What are the three variables used in the computation of periodic depreciation? Is depreciation a valuation procedure or a cost allocation procedure?

4 The manager of an electric utility stated, "Our transmission lines are kept in good operating condition by regular repairs and maintenance, and their efficiency is relatively constant—they just don't depreciate!" Do you agree with this statement? Explain.

5 What is meant by the term **estimated economic life** of a plant asset, and how is it measured?

6 What are the major causes of a decrease in the economic life of a plant asset? How reliably can the causes be estimated?

7 Jordan Company buys delivery trucks for $18,000. These trucks have an economic life of six years based on physical deterioration and a residual value of $3,000. The company typically sells a truck for $7,000 after operating it 100,000 miles. What is the depreciation base for this delivery truck? What is its estimated economic life to Jordan Company?

8 Both the quantity of asset services used each accounting period and the relative value of the asset services are factors in the choice of a method of depreciation. Explain.

9 *a* List the methods that may be used to compute depreciation.
   b State two basic objections to the straight-line (time) method of depreciation.
   c List some advantages of the straight-line (time) method of depreciation.

10 Many depreciable assets exhibit a declining productivity with advancing age. Explain how this fact may be used both as an argument for and as an argument against the straight-line method of depreciation.

11 During the current year a strike halted manufacturing operations of Arcadia, Inc., for four months. Depreciation of its spinning and weaving machines for the full year under the straight-line method is $216,000. Its operations for the current year resulted in a loss of $132,000 (after deduction of depreciation expense). The president suggests that the depreciation expense should be reduced because of the low volume of operations. Do you agree?

12 Describe a situation in which the use of the **output method** of depreciation is appropriate.

13 What is meant by **composite** or **group depreciation method?** What are the advantages and limitations of this method?

14 Explain why the use of accelerated depreciation methods is advantageous for income tax purposes, even though total depreciation for income tax purposes cannot exceed cost of an asset, reduced by its net residual value.

15 What principle should be applied to determine whether depreciation is a fixed or a variable expense? Why is depreciation called a "noncash expense"?

16 What disclosures relating to depreciation and depreciation methods should be made in the financial statements or in the accompanying notes?

17 Bronze Corporation purchased for $800,000 land from which it expects to extract 1 million tons of Grade A ore and 2 million tons of Grade B ore. Grade A ore is three times as valuable as Grade B ore. Compute depletion per ton of each grade of ore extracted. Explain the term **percentage depletion.**

18 Plant assets or natural resources donated to a business enterprise generally are recorded in the accounting records, and depreciation or depletion on such assets is allocated to revenue. Justify this practice.

EXERCISES

Ex. 12-1   Southern Company leased a building and immediately purchased equipment for $430,000 and spent $35,000 to have special platforms and supporting encasements built. The lease contract provides that when the lease expires Southern must remove the equipment, tear up the platforms and encasements, and restore the property to its original condition, an operation that is expected to cost $20,000.

Compute the depreciation base of the equipment, including platforms and encasements.

Ex. 12-2   An asset cost $58,000, has an economic life of seven years, and an estimated net residual value of $2,000.

a Compute depreciation for the first year of asset life under the sum-of-the-years'-digits method of depreciation.
b Assume that this asset was acquired on April 1, Year 1. Compute depreciation for the full year beginning on January 1, Year 2, under the sum-of-the-years'-digits method of depreciation.

Ex. 12-3   A machine with an estimated life of five years, or 100,000 units of output, was acquired on October 4, Year 1. The cash price of the machine is $9,000, and it will be paid for as follows:

Old machine accepted as trade-in (carrying amount is equal to current fair	
value)	$ 500
Cash	1,500
Four installments payable at the rate of $2,000 every six months (includes	
$1,000 of interest and financing charges)	8,000
Total	$10,000

Compute depreciation for the three months in Year 1 and for Year 2, assuming that the net residual value of the machine is $1,500, under each of the following methods:

a Straight-line
b Sum-of-the-years'-digits
c Double-declining-balance
d Output (8,000 units were produced in Year 1 and 30,000 units in Year 2)

Ex. 12-4　Clemente Company purchased a plant asset at the beginning of Year 1 for $16,000. The asset has an economic life of four years and an estimated net residual value of $1,000.

Compute the depreciation on the asset for Year 1, under each of the following methods:

a　Straight-line
b　Sum-of-the-years'-digits
c　Fixed-percentage-of-declining-balance (Compute the theoretically correct rate and prove that it yields a net residual value of $1,000 at the end of four years.)

Ex. 12-5　On January 3, Year 1, Flinn Company acquired equipment that had an estimated economic life of 10 years and a net residual value of $10,000. The depreciation expense for Year 5 was $6,000 under the sum-of-the-years'-digits method.

Compute the cost of the equipment.

Ex. 12-6　The controller of Technitronics Company, an electronics manufacturer, maintains records of plant assets on the composite basis. A list of assets acquired on January 2, Year 1, follows:

Assets	Cost	Estimated net residual value	Estimated economic life (years)
A-101	$4,000	$400	3
A-102	1,500	300	4
A-103	7,000	750	5

a　Compute the composite depreciation rate based on cost.
b　If at the end of Year 3, the A-101 assets are sold for $1,500, prepare a journal entry to record the sale.

Ex. 12-7　At the beginning of Year 1, Leo Company acquired 20 similar machines for $4,000 each and developed a composite depreciation rate of 30% based on the following expectations:

	Year 2	Year 3	Year 4
Number of machines to be retired at end of year . . .	5	10	5
Net residual value of machines to be retired	$6,000	$4,000	$-0-

The retirements and proceeds realized were exactly as expected. You may assume that the 30% rate is correct.

Record all transactions for the four-year period in T accounts and explain the balance in the Accumulated Depreciation account at the end of Year 4.

Ex. 12-8　Salt Lake Ore Company acquired mining property for $1.2 million. The property was expected to yield 600,000 tons of ore, after which the property would have a net residual value of $200,000. During the first year, 60,000 tons of ore were mined and sold for $800,000. Operating costs, other than cost depletion, amounted to $350,000. The ore mined is eligible for a 15% percentage depletion for income tax purposes. Income taxes are 45% of taxable income.

Compute the amount of (a) cost depletion on the mining property, (b) income taxes expense, and (c) net income for financial accounting purposes.

Ex. 12-9 An analysis of the Machinery account of Brigham Corporation for the current year appears below:

Jan. 2	Acquired four machines with an economic life of five years . . .	$12,000
Jan. 6	Installation costs	400
	Total debits	$12,400
Dec. 28	Less: Credit representing proceeds on disposal of one machine	
	(debit was recorded in the Cash account)	2,100
Dec. 31	Balance in Machinery account	$10,300

a Prepare a journal entry to record depreciation expense for the current year on the four machines. The estimated net residual value of each machine is $350. Use the straight-line method of depreciation.
b Prepare a journal entry to correct the accounting records on December 31, including the recognition of the gain or loss (which was not recorded on December 28) on the disposal of the one machine. Assume that the accounting records have not been closed for the current year.

Ex. 12-10 Volcan Company acquired land containing an extractable natural resource. The company is required by its purchase contract to restore the land to a condition suitable for recreational use after it extracts the natural resource. Geological surveys indicate that recoverable reserves will be 3 million tons, and that the land will have a value of $600,000 after restoration. Relevant cost information follows:

Land	$6,000,000
Restoration of land	900,000
Geological surveys	300,000

Assuming that the company maintains no inventories of extracted material, compute the depletion per ton of material extracted.

SHORT CASES FOR ANALYSIS AND DECISION

Case 12-1 The controller of Donnie Manufacturing Co. is preparing accounting policies for the company in its first month of operations. The company has a variety of plant assets, including a significant investment in highly specialized equipment. You have been asked to assist the controller with this project.

Instructions
a Define **depreciation** as the term is used in accounting.
b Identify the factors that are relevant in the measurement of annual depreciation on plant assets and explain whether these factors are determined objectively or whether they are based on judgment.
c Explain why depreciation usually is shown in the "Financial Resources Provided from Operations" section of the statement of changes in financial position.

Case 12-2 Kool Steel Corporation computes depreciation based on the level of the company's activity. In the third quarter of the current fiscal year, the company, according to a financial news story, "returned to profit a sum equal to $0.25 a share that had been written off as depreciation in the previous six months but that it determined had not been needed."

Instructions

a Evaluate the company's depreciation policy.

b Do you believe that Kool is smoothing its net income by means of its depreciation policy or simply trying to match the service potential (cost) of its assets with the economic benefits derived (tons of steel produced)?

Case 12-3 Karen Company owned an old factory building that had a carrying amount of $200,000. Machinery and equipment in the building had a carrying amount of $300,000. In Year 5, the company built a new building at a cost of $1.2 million and installed new equipment costing $650,000. Some of the equipment in the old building was replaced, and both plants were operated at near capacity from Year 5 to Year 10. Depreciation was recorded on a straight-line basis.

In Year 10, the company shut down the old plant because of a decline in sales. The president of the company proposes to stop recording depreciation on the old building and machinery, stating that while the old plant is useful, it is not wearing out; furthermore, depreciating the old plant increases costs, overstates inventories, and places the company in a poor position to bid for new business, because its costs are high.

Instructions   Discuss the president's position and evaluate these arguments. What recommendation would you make to the company?

Case 12-4 An article in a financial magazine stated that the net income for Tinsley Oil Company has decreased from $5 million a year ago to only $2 million in the current year, largely because of increases in depletion and depreciation. These increases were necessary because an independent engineering firm prepared revised estimates of oil and gas reserves which were substantially lower than the company's previous estimates. The article further stated that the revised estimates do not affect the company's revenue or cash flow, and that revisions in estimates of oil and gas reserves are not unusual in the oil and gas industry. The president of the company was quoted as saying, "Because we are a relatively small company, these revisions affect us more seriously than they do large companies."

Instructions

a How do you suppose the revised depletion and depreciation amount was determined? Should understatements of depletion and depreciation in prior years result in understatements of income in subsequent years?

b How can independent auditors verify the estimates of deposits of natural resources?

c Explain why an increase in depletion and depreciation does not affect Tinsley Oil Company's revenue or cash flow.

d Why do revisions in estimates of oil and gas reserves affect a small company "more seriously" than they do large companies? Do such revisions affect the percentage depletion allowed for income tax purposes?

PROBLEMS

12-1 Malibu Corporation made a study of its five-year experience with a group of trucks. The appraised values of the trucks at the end of each year and average miles driven each year for each truck during a typical five-year period are given on page 517.

Year	Miles driven	Appraised value (% of cost)
1	40,000	80
2	60,000	55
3	40,000	40
4	30,000	30
5	30,000	25

Instructions On the basis of this information, compute the depreciation each year during the five-year economic life of a truck which cost $18,000 and is expected to have a net residual value of $4,500, under each of the following depreciation methods (round all computations to the nearest dollar):

a Appraisal
b Straight-line
c Output
d Sum-of-the-years'-digits
e Fixed-percentage-of-declining-balance. Use a 40% rate and ignore any limitation imposed by income tax regulations.

12-2 On January 2, Year 2, Tang Company, a machine-tool manufacturer, acquired new equipment for $1,000,000. The equipment was eligible for the investment tax credit, and Tang took full advantage of the credit, accounting for the amount by the flow-through method. The equipment had an estimated economic life of five years, and the net residual value was estimated to be $100,000. Tang estimated that the equipment can produce 10,000 units in its first year. Production was estimated to decline by 1,000 units a year over the remaining economic life of the equipment.

The following depreciation methods may be used:

(1) Double-declining-balance
(2) Straight-line
(3) Sum-of-the-years'-digits
(4) Output

For income tax purposes the Internal Revenue Code permits a taxpayer to ignore net residual value of a plant asset which does not exceed 10% of cost of the asset.

Instructions
a Which depreciation method would result in the maximization of net income for financial accounting purposes for the three-year period ended December 31, Year 4? Prepare a working paper to show the amount of accumulated depreciation on December 31, Year 4, under the method selected. Show supporting computations. Ignore present value, income tax, and deferred income tax considerations in your answer.
b Which depreciation method would result in the minimization of taxable income for the three-year period ended December 31, Year 4? Prepare a working paper to show the amount of accumulated depreciation for income tax purposes on December 31, Year 4, under the method selected. Show supporting computations. Ignore present value considerations in your answer.

12-3 The cash price of a machine acquired by Questor Manufacturing Corporation on September 30, Year 1, was $62,400, including sales taxes; it was paid for as follows:

Cash down payment	$ 7,800
Capital stock, 600 shares with a current market price of $42	
a share	25,200
Promissory note payable in 24 equal monthly installments, including in-	
terest	36,000
Total (paid or payable)	$69,000

The following additional costs were incurred before the machine was ready for use:

Installation costs	$2,600
Direct costs of trial runs	1,000

The machine was expected to produce 100,000 units during its economic life. It was placed in service on October 4, Year 1.

Instructions

a Determine the cost of the machine for financial accounting purposes. Assume that the discount on the promissory note is equal to the difference between the total payments to be made and the cash price of the machine.

b Assuming that the estimated net residual value of the machine is $6,000 and that the economic life is estimated to be five years, compute depreciation for Year 1 (3 months) and Year 2 under:
(1) Straight-line method
(2) Sum-of-the-years'-digits method
(3) Rate of 40% applied to declining carrying amount of the machine
(4) Output method (the machine produced 15,000 units in Year 1 and 24,000 units in Year 2)

12-4 Selected accounts included in the plant assets section of Seahawk Corporation's balance sheet on December 31, Year 8, had the following balances:

Land	$175,000
Land improvements	90,000
Buildings	900,000
Machinery and equipment	850,000

During Year 9, the following transactions were completed:

(1) Land was acquired for $125,000 as a potential future building site.
(2) A facility consisting of land and buildings was acquired from Quon Company in exchange for 10,000 shares of Seahawk's unissued common stock. On the exchange date, Seahawk common stock had a closing market price of $45 a share on a national stock exchange. The facility was carried in Quon's accounting records on the exchange date at $89,000 for land and $130,000 for buildings. Appraised value on the exchange date for property tax purposes was $120,000 for land and $240,000 for buildings.
(3) Machinery and equipment were purchased at a cost of $300,000. Additional costs were incurred as follows:

Freight and unloading	$ 5,000
Sales and use taxes	12,000
Installation	25,000

(4) Expenditures totaling $75,000 were made for new parking lots, streets, and sidewalks at the corporation's various plant locations. These expenditures had an estimated economic life of 15 years.

(5) A machine which was acquired for $50,000 on January 2, Year 1, was scrapped on June 30, Year 9. Double-declining-balance depreciation based on a 10-year economic life has been recorded.

(6) A machine was sold for $20,000 on July 1, Year 9. The cost of the machine was $36,000 on January 2, Year 6, and it was depreciated on the straight-line basis over an estimated economic life of seven years and a net residual value of $1,000.

Instructions

a Prepare a detailed analysis of the changes in each of the following balance sheet accounts for Year 9:

Land
Land improvements
Buildings
Machinery and equipment

(Disregard the related accumulated depreciation accounts.)

b List and compute the items in the fact situation which were not used to determine the answer to *a* above, showing the pertinent amounts and supporting computations for each item. In addition, indicate where, or if, these items should be included in the financial statements.

12-5 In auditing the financial statements of Zany Corporation, you observe the following journal entries in the Machinery account:

Debits:

Jan. 3, Year 3	Purchased Machine A	$22,000	
Jan. 10, Year 3	Installation of Machine A	2,000	
Sept. 28, Year 3	Purchased Machine B	30,000	
Mar. 31, Year 4	Purchased Machine C	16,000	
July 1, Year 5	Repairs as a result of flooding	4,500	$74,500

Credits:

Dec. 31, Year 3	Depreciation for year	$10,800	
Dec. 31, Year 4	Depreciation for year	11,840	
April 1, Year 5	Proceeds on sale of Machine A	8,560	
Dec. 31, Year 5	Depreciation for year	7,460	38,660

Balance, Dec. 31, Year 5 . . . . $35,840

Depreciation was recorded at the end of each year at 20% of the balance in the Machinery account. The estimated economic life of the machines is five years, and the net residual value is estimated at 10% of invoice cost.

Instructions

a Prepare a depreciation (lapsing) schedule through December 31, Year 5, for machinery, under the straight-line method of depreciation. Use the form illustrated on pages 502 and 503.

b Using the information from the lapsing schedule, prepare a single journal entry to restate the accounting records of Zany Corporation to conform with generally accepted accounting principles on December 31, Year 5. The revenue and expense accounts for Year 5 are still open. Record the correction of any errors in depreciation expense for Years 3 and 4 in the Retained Earnings account as a prior period adjustment.

12-6 The following amounts appear in an improperly established Property account in the accounting records of Eagle Western Company at the end of Year 1:

Debit entries:

Feb. 1 Amount paid to acquire building site	$ 45,000
12 Cost of removing old building from site	10,000
15 Contract price for new building which was completed on Apr. 5	160,000
Apr. 1 Insurance and other costs directly connected with construction of new building	8,000
Total debits	$223,000

Credit entries:

Feb. 12 Proceeds from sale of material obtained from dismantling of old building . . . . $ 6,000	
Dec. 31 Depreciation expense for Year 1—5% of balance in Property account, $217,000 (Debit was recorded in the Depreciation Expense account) . 10,850	
Total credits	16,850
Dec. 31 Balance	$206,150

Instructions

a Prepare a correcting journal entry on December 31, Year 1, assuming that the estimated economic life of the new building is 20 years and that depreciation under the straight-line method is to be recorded for nine months in Year 1. The accounting records have not been closed for Year 1.

b Compute depreciation on the building for Year 1, Year 2, and Year 3 under the following methods: (1) straight-line, (2) double-declining-balance, and (3) sum-of-the-years'-digits.

12-7 Platinum Products Company acquired 15 used machines on January 2, Year 1, for $60,000. The machines are not identical but perform similar functions. The machines have an average economic life of four years, and the residual value for each machine will approximately equal the removal costs. A composite depreciation method (straight-line) is used to allocate the cost of the machines to revenue. Depreciation on assets retired or sold is computed for a full year.

Machines retired or sold and the proceeds on sale are summarized below:

End of	Machines retired or sold	Proceeds on sale
Year 3	3	$ 700
Year 4	10	1,200
Year 5	2	100

New machines of this type were not acquired as replacements.

Instructions

a Prepare a cost allocation working paper under the composite depreciation method for the five-year period during which the assets are used. Use the working paper headings given on top of page 521.

End of year	Depreciation expense	Machinery account		Accumulated Depreciation account		Carrying amount
		Debit (Credit)	Balance	Debit (Credit)	Balance	

b Prepare a similar working paper, but assume (1) that nothing is received on the sale of the machines, and (2) that two machines were retired at the end of Year 3, eleven machines were retired at the end of Year 4, and two machines were retired at the end of Year 5.

c Comment on differences between the results obtained in **a** and **b**.

12-8 Montana Mining Company paid $1,850,000 for land containing valuable ore and spent $450,000 in developing the property during Year 1, preparatory to beginning mining activities on January 2, Year 2. Company geologists estimated that the mineral deposit would produce 8 million tons of ore over a 15-year period, and it is assumed that the land will have a net residual value of $300,000 after the ore deposit is exhausted.

A record of capital investments during the last half of Year 1, exclusive of the development costs previously mentioned, follows:

Asset	Estimated economic life, years	Cost
Mine buildings	30	$200,000
Railroad and hoisting equipment	20	600,000
Miscellaneous mine equipment	10	250,000

The buildings, railroad, and hoisting equipment cannot be removed economically from the mine location, but the miscellaneous mine equipment is movable and has alternative uses.

Operations during Year 2 are summarized below:

Tons of ore mined	1,000,000
Tons of ore sold at $5.10 a ton (FOB at the mine)	950,000
Mining labor and other operating costs (exclusive of depreciation and depletion)	$2,400,000
Selling and administrative expenses	$ 625,750

Income taxes expense for the year (based on percentage depletion) was $523,000.

Instructions

a Prepare an income statement for Montana Mining for Year 2, showing the computation of depletion and depreciation per ton of ore mined in supporting working papers. Use straight-line depreciation, with no residual value, for the miscellaneous mine equipment. The company had 200,000 shares of common stock outstanding during Year 2.

b Early in Year 3, Montana Mining received an offer from a Japanese company to purchase 500,000 tons of ore at a price of $3.90 a ton delivered in Japan. The company estimates that it will cost $1.40 a ton to ship the ore to Japan, and believes that accepting this offer will not affect the domestic price. It is estimated that the cost of acquiring and developing additional ore property has not increased. One-fourth of the company's "mining labor and other operating costs" are fixed as long as at least 600,000 tons of ore are produced annually. Would you recommend that the company accept the offer from the Japanese company? Present data to support your conclusion.

12-9 Rapid Transport Company purchased a fleet of 100 fully equipped trucks on January 2, Year 1, for $600,000. The controller of the company decided to use the composite depreciation method for these trucks, and estimated the composite rate at 21% ($126,000 ÷ $600,000 = 0.21) as follows:

Year	Number of trucks to be retired	Cost	Estimated net residual value	Amount to be depreciated	Estimated economic life, years	Annual depreciation expense
1	5	$ 30,000	$ 21,000	$ 9,000	1	$ 9,000
2	20	120,000	72,000	48,000	2	24,000
3	30	180,000	59,400	120,600	3	40,200
4	30	180,000	36,000	144,000	4	36,000
5	15	90,000	6,000	84,000	5	16,800
	100	$600,000	$194,400	$405,600		$126,000

At the end of Year 7, when the last truck had been retired, the controller prepared the following summary of the company's actual experience:

Year	Actual number of trucks retired	Actual proceeds received on retirement
1	4	$ 17,200
2	11	32,800
3	28	74,700
4	42	49,600
5	8	5,000
6	5	1,800
7	2	800
	100	$181,900

The company had followed composite depreciation procedures and recorded no gain or loss when the trucks were retired.

Instructions
a Reconstruct the Trucks and Accumulated Depreciation accounts as they would have appeared had the controller's estimates been realized, and the computed rate of 21% had been used as a basis for recording depreciation. Would the controller's rate have produced accurate results if the assumptions had been correct? Why?
b On the basis of hindsight, that is, the actual record of experience with this fleet of trucks, compute the composite depreciation rate that should have been used. Also determine the composite economic life of the trucks.
c Using the rate computed in **b**, reconstruct the Trucks and Accumulated Depreciation accounts. Explain any balance in the Accumulated Depreciation account at the end of Year 7 and state why this balance, if any, differs from the balance in Accumulated Depreciation obtained in **a**.

12-10 Rock Corporation, a manufacturer of steel products, began operations on October 1, Year 2. Rock's accounting department has begun the depreciation schedule given below:

ROCK CORPORATION

Depreciation Schedule

For Years Ended September 30, Years 3 and 4

Assets	Acquisition date	Cost	Net residual value	Depre- ciation method	Esti- mated life, years	Depreciation for year ended Sept. 30, Year 3	Year 4
Land L	Oct. 1, Year 2	$ (a)	*	*	*	*	*
Building B . . .	Oct. 1, Year 2	(b)	$64,060	Straight-line	(c)	$14,000	$ (d)
Land LL	Oct. 2, Year 2	(e)	*	*	*	*	*
Building BB . .	(Under con-struction)	210,000 to date	none	Straight-line	30	none	(f)
Donated equipment. .	Oct. 2, Year 2	(g)	2,000	150% de-clining-balance	10	(h)	(i)
Machinery M .	Oct. 2, Year 2	(j)	5,500	Sum-of-the-years'-digits	10	(k)	(l)
Machinery MM	Oct. 1, Year 3	(m)	none	Straight-line	12	none	(n)

* Not applicable

You have been asked to assist in completing this schedule. In addition to ascertaining that the data already in the schedule are correct, you have obtained the following information from Rock's accounting records:

(1) Depreciation is computed from the first of the month of acquisition to the first of the month of disposal.
(2) Land L and Building B were acquired from a predecessor corporation. Rock paid a total of $830,500 for the land and building. At the time of acquisition, the land had an appraised value of $72,000 and the building had an appraised value of $828,000.
(3) Land LL was acquired on October 2, Year 2, in exchange for 3,000 shares of Rock's unissued common stock. On the date of acquisition, the stock had a par value of $5 a share and a current fair value of $25 a share. During October, Year 2, Rock paid $10,400 to demolish an existing building on this land in order to construct a new building (Building BB).
(4) Construction of Building BB began on October 1, Year 3. By September 30, Year 4, Rock had paid $210,000 of the estimated total construction costs of $300,000. Estimated completion and occupancy date is July, Year 5.

(5) Equipment was donated to the corporation by the city of Pineridge. An independent appraisal of the equipment at the date of donation placed the current fair value at $16,000 and the net residual value at $2,000.

(6) The total cost of $110,000 for Machinery M includes installation costs of $550 and normal repairs and maintenance of $11,000 incurred through January 31, Year 4. Machinery M was sold on February 1, Year 4.

(7) On October 1, Year 3, Machinery MM was acquired under a contract requiring a down payment of $3,760 and ten annual installments of $4,000 each beginning October 1, Year 4. The prevailing interest rate was 8%. The following data are available from present value tables:

Present value of 1 at 8%

10 periods	0.463
11 periods	0.429
15 periods	0.315

Present value of ordinary annuity of 1 at 8%

10 rents	6.710
11 rents	7.139
15 rents	8.559

Instructions   For each lettered item in the schedule on page 523, supply the correct amount. Round each amount to the nearest dollar. Do not recopy the schedule, but show supporting computations.

13 INTANGIBLE ASSETS

Nature of intangible assets

The basic characteristic that distinguishes intangible assets from tangible assets is that the former are not physical in nature. In legal terminology this distinction is maintained consistently, the term **intangibles** being applied to all nonphysical properties, including cash, accounts and notes receivable, and investments in corporate securities. However, in accounting terminology intangible assets do not include current assets. Intangible assets for accounting purposes include patents, copyrights, trademarks, trade names, secret formulas, organization costs, franchises, licenses, and goodwill (the excess of cost of an acquired business enterprise over the current fair value of identifiable net assets acquired). Some examples of intangibles included in balance sheets of corporations in recent years are presented below:

<table>
<tr><td>Examples of intangible assets</td><td colspan="2">Combined Communications Corporation
Intangibles representing broadcast licenses, network affiliations and goodwill (excess of purchase price over value ascribed to identifiable net assets):</td></tr>
<tr><td></td><td>Not subject to amortization</td><td>$ 8,849,000</td></tr>
<tr><td></td><td>Subject to amortization (over 40 years)</td><td>31,600,000</td></tr>
<tr><td></td><td>Other intangibles (amortized over 5–20 years)</td><td>172,000</td></tr>
<tr><td></td><td>Total intangibles</td><td>$40,621,000</td></tr>
<tr><td></td><td colspan="2">Oxford Industries</td></tr>
<tr><td></td><td>Patents and non-complete agreements, at cost, less amortization</td><td>$ 1,723,000</td></tr>
<tr><td></td><td colspan="2">Twentieth Century–Fox Film Corporation</td></tr>
<tr><td></td><td>Television stations' licenses, contracts and network affiliation agreements</td><td>$11,251,000</td></tr>
<tr><td></td><td>Excess of cost over net assets of acquired companies</td><td>26,169,000</td></tr>
</table>

Some of these companies list other intangible assets in their balance sheets. Generally, a note explaining the nature of the intangible assets and the amortization policy is included with the financial statements.

One reason for distinguishing between tangible and intangible assets is that it often is difficult to identify intangible assets. Because you can "stub your toe" on a tangible asset, it is relatively easy to know when you have one. Evidence of the existence of intangible assets may be vague, and the relationship between an expenditure and the emergence

525

of an asset may be difficult to establish objectively. The economic value of both tangible and intangible assets is dependent on their ability to generate future revenue and earnings, and this often is as difficult to measure for tangible assets as it is for intangibles. However, mere physical existence (obsolete machinery, for example) is no guarantee of economic value, nor does the absence of physical existence (the Listerine formula, for example) preclude economic value. For some business enterprises, the value of intangible assets may exceed the value of the tangible assets.

Cost of intangible assets

A business enterprise may acquire intangible assets from others, or it may develop internally certain types of intangible assets. The general objectives in accounting for intangible assets are comparable to those for tangible assets; the initial cost is determined and charged against the revenue which these assets help to generate. A significant and permanent decline in the value of an intangible asset is debited to expense in the year the decline occurs. Generally, such write-offs are not reported as extraordinary losses in the income statement.

When an intangible asset is **purchased,** its cost can be measured with little difficulty. It may be necessary to estimate the value of nonmonetary assets given in exchange for intangible assets, or to allocate the total cost among various assets acquired as a group. The principles used in dealing with these problems, as previously described in relation to plant assets, are equally applicable to intangible assets. Accounting for intangible assets **developed** by business enterprises is no longer a problem for accountants, because all costs incurred in the "in house" development of intangible assets are recorded as expenses. In 1970 the Accounting Principles Board took the following position relative to the recording of intangible assets:[1]

> The Board concludes that a company should record as assets the costs of intangible assets acquired from other enterprises or individuals. Costs of developing, maintaining, or restoring intangible assets which are not specifically identifiable, have indeterminate lives, or are inherent in a continuing business and related to an enterprise as a whole—such as goodwill—should be deducted from income when incurred.

> Intangible assets acquired singly should be recorded at cost at date of acquisition. Cost is measured by the amount of cash disbursed, the fair value of other assets distributed, the present value of amounts to be paid for liabilities incurred, or the fair value of consideration received for stock issued. . . .

> Intangible assets acquired as part of a group of assets or as part of an acquired company should also be recorded at cost at date of acquisition. Cost is measured differently for specifically identifiable intangible assets and those lacking specific identification. The cost of identifiable intangible assets is an assigned part of the total cost of the group of assets or enterprise acquired, normally based on the fair values of the individual assets. The cost of uniden-

[1] *APB Opinion No. 17,* "Intangible Assets," AICPA (New York: 1970), p. 339.

tifiable intangible assets is measured by the difference between the cost of the group of assets or enterprise acquired and the sum of the assigned costs of individual tangible and identifiable intangible assets acquired less liabilities assumed. Cost should be assigned to all specifically identifiable intangible assets; cost of identifiable assets should not be included in goodwill.

The Accounting Principles Board classified all intangible assets into two categories: (1) those that are specifically **identifiable,** and (2) those that are **unidentifiable.** The costs of developing, maintaining, or restoring intangible assets which are not specifically identifiable (such as goodwill) should be deducted from revenue as incurred. Four years later, the Financial Accounting Standards Board wrestled with one of the most difficult problems related to intangible assets, namely, research and development costs, and reached the conclusion that "all research and development costs . . . shall be charged to expense when incurred."[2]

Amortization of intangible assets

The process of systematically writing off the cost of intangible assets is called **amortization.** For many years, accountants approached the question of amortization by classifying intangible assets into two categories: (1) those having a **limited** term of existence, and (2) those with an **indefinite** or **unlimited** term of existence. Those with a limited economic life were amortized; those with an indefinite or unlimited economic life were maintained intact until they became worthless, at which time they were written off. This gave management considerable leeway in accounting for intangible assets. However, in **Opinion No. 17** the Accounting Principles Board established the following amortization policy for intangible assets acquired after October 31, 1970:[3]

> The Board believes that the value of intangible assets at any one date eventually disappears and that the recorded costs of intangible assets should be amortized by systematic charges to income over the periods estimated to be benefited.

According to the APB, then, all intangible assets acquired after October 31, 1970, and those with a limited term of existence acquired before October 31, 1970, must be amortized. Factors that should be considered in estimating the economic life of an intangible asset include:[4]

1 Legal, regulatory, or contractual provisions when they place a limit on the maximum economic life.
2 Provisions for renewal or extension of rights or privileges covered by specific intangible assets.
3 Effects of obsolescence, customer demand, competition, rate of technological change, and other economic factors.

[2] *FASB Statement No. 2* "Accounting for Research and Development Costs," FASB (Stamford: 1974), p. 6
[3] *APB Opinion No. 17,* pp. 339–340.
[4] Ibid., p. 340.

4 Possibility that economic life of intangible assets may be related to life expectancies of certain groups of employees.

5 Expected actions of competitors, regulatory bodies, and others.

6 An apparently unlimited economic life of an intangible asset may in fact be only indefinite, and future benefits cannot be reasonably projected.

7 An intangible asset may be a composite of many individual factors with diverse economic lives.

The period of amortization for intangible assets is determined after a careful review of all relevant factors. This review enables management to make a reasonable estimate of the economic life of most intangible assets. According to *Opinion No. 17,* the period of amortization for any intangible asset *should not exceed 40 years,* and if a longer economic life is expected, the amortization period should be no less than 40 years.

In the opinion of the authors, the maximum period of amortization of 40 years is much too long for most intangible assets. During the current era of rapid technological innovations and changes in consumer tastes, few intangible assets can be expected to retain their usefulness for 40 years. Consequently, many business enterprises probably overstate their net income by amortizing unidentifiable intangible assets over the maximum period allowed. On the other hand, mandatory amortization of some types of intangible assets which tend to increase in value over time (such as licenses to operate radio or television stations) may be unrealistic. Amortization of these intangible assets (even over a 40-year period) may result in an understatement of assets, stockholders' equity, and net income.

The accounting procedures for the amortization of intangible assets are comparable to those employed for depreciable assets. The cost of intangible assets should be amortized in a systematic manner over their estimated economic lives. A *straight-line* method of amortization usually is employed, unless management presents a convincing case that some other systematic method is more appropriate. For example, if there is evidence that the value of services expiring in early periods is significantly higher, an accelerated method of amortization may be used.

The amortization of intangible assets may be credited directly to the asset account, leaving a balance representing the unamortized cost. This is a matter of custom rather than accounting logic. For example, the journal entry to record the amortization of patents in the amount of $4,200 is illustrated below:

Recording periodic amortization

Amortization of Patents. 4,200
       Patents (or Accumulated Amortization of Patents). *4,200*
To record amortization of patents.

The amortization of intangible assets may be either a factory overhead cost or an operating expense, depending on the nature and use of the assets. For example, the expired cost of a patent on a manufacturing process logically is a part of factory overhead, and the amortization of a trademark used to promote products is a selling expense.

Disclosure of the method of amortization and the estimated economic lives of intangible assets, as well as the amount of amortization for the accounting period, is required in the financial statements. The period used to amortize intangible assets is reviewed continually to determine whether changing circumstances call for a change in the estimate of economic life. When a change is made in the estimated economic life of an intangible asset, the unamortized cost is allocated over the **remaining economic life** of the asset. The remaining economic life may be longer or shorter than the original estimate. The revised economic life, however, cannot exceed 40 years from the date the intangible asset was acquired. A review of the amortization policy also may indicate that a material amount of unamortized cost should be written off. However, a single loss year or even several loss years does not necessarily justify a write-off of all or a large part of the unamortized cost of an intangible asset.

IDENTIFIABLE INTANGIBLE ASSETS

Certain intangible assets, such as patents, copyrights, and franchises, can be identified as distinct and separable property rights; others, such as goodwill, are difficult to identify. The more common identifiable intangible assets are discussed in the following sections.

Patents

A patent is a grant by the federal government giving the owner the exclusive right to manufacture and sell a particular invention for a period of 17 years. Patent rights may be assigned in part or in their entirety. Frequently, contracts require payments of royalties to the owner of a patent for the right to use or manufacture a patented product. Legally, patents cannot be renewed, but in practice their effective life often is extended by obtaining patents on slight variations and improvements near the end of the legal life of the original patent.

A patent has economic value only if the protection it affords against competition results in increased earnings through an ability to operate at a lower cost, to manufacture and sell a product, or to obtain a higher price for goods and services. The economic life of a patent generally is much shorter than its legal life; therefore, amortization over the period of usefulness usually is necessary.

If a patent is purchased, its cost is measured by the purchase price plus any incidental costs. The purchase of a patent from another party is recorded as follows:

Journal entry to record acquisition of an intangible asset

Patents   60,000
    Cash.   60,000
To record purchase of patent.

A patent does not include automatic protection against infringement; owners must prosecute those who attempt to infringe their patents and defend against infringement suits brought by owners of similar patents. The cost of successfully establishing the legal validity of a patent should be capitalized, because such cost will benefit revenue over the remaining economic life of the patent. However, a patent infringement suit may take years to resolve, and the accounting treatment of legal costs during this period must recognize the uncertainties involved by expensing such costs. If the legal decision is favorable, legal costs may be paid by the losing party; if the legal decision is adverse, both the cost of the infringement suit and the unamortized cost of the patent should be written off, because no further economic benefits are expected to result from the patent.

The right to use a patent owned by others under a licensing contract is not recorded as an intangible asset, unless a lump-sum payment is made at the outset of such a contract. The periodic royalty payments are recorded as factory overhead or as operating expense, depending on the use made of the patent.

If a patent is developed as a result of a business enterprise's research and development efforts, the cost assigned to the patent includes only the direct legal costs and fees incurred in obtaining the patent. No research and development costs incurred internally are assigned to the patent, because all such costs must be expensed as incurred. Accounting for research and development costs is covered in another section of this chapter.

Copyrights

A copyright is a grant by the federal government giving an author, creator, or artist the exclusive right to publish, sell, or otherwise control literary or artistic products for the life of the author plus 50 years. The rights granted under copyrights may be acquired by paying royalties, by purchase, or by obtaining a copyright on a product developed by a business enterprise. The problems that arise in measuring the cost of copyrights are comparable to those already discussed in connection with patents.

Although a copyright has a long legal life, its economic life is limited to the period of time for which a commercial market exists for the publication. In order to achieve a proper matching of costs and revenue, copyright costs are amortized against the total revenue that is anticipated from the copyright. Because of the difficulty encountered in estimating copyright revenue and because experience indicates that such revenue generally results over only a few years, copyrights typically are amortized over relatively short periods of time. On occasion, copyrights thought to be valueless may bounce back to life with renewed vigor. An outstanding example is old movies: Their production and copyright costs previously had been fully amortized, but these films suddenly became extremely valuable with the development of television and the apparent incidence of insomnia among television viewers. However, this increase in the value of copyrights was not reflected in the balance sheets of motion picture producers.

Licenses and contracts

Many business enterprises invest considerable sums of capital to obtain licenses to engage in certain types of business activities or to acquire rights to use copyrighted materials owned by others. For example, Federal Communications Commission (FCC) licenses, network-affiliation contracts, and film rights probably are the most valuable assets of an enterprise engaged in the broadcasting industry. Without an FCC license, it would be impossible for a broadcaster to earn revenue; a network-affiliated station is more valuable than an independent station because of network-supplied programming; the rights to show old movies are an important source of revenue for television broadcasters.

The cost of a license or a contract is recorded in the accounting records and is amortized over the accounting periods expected to benefit. An FCC license generally is amortized over a period of 40 years; a network-affiliation contract is amortized over the period specified in the contract; and film rights purchased by a television station generally are amortized on an accelerated basis, because first showings generate more advertising revenue than reruns.[5] If a license or a contract is canceled or for any reason becomes worthless, any unamortized cost should be written off.

Trademarks, trade names, and secret formulas

Trademarks, trade names, secret formulas, and various distinctive labels are important means of building and holding customer acceptance for certain products. The value of such product identification

---

[5] *Statement of Position 75-5,* "Accounting Practices in the Broadcasting Industry," AICPA (New York: 1975), p. 8.

and differentiation stems from the ability of the business enterprise to sell products in large volume and at prices higher than those for un-branded products.

Trademarks, trade names, secret formulas, and labels are property rights that can be leased, assigned, or sold. Their economic lives continue as long as they are used, and their cost is amortized over their estimated economic lives or 40 years, whichever is shorter.

The value of trademarks, trade names, or secret formulas often is enhanced as the enterprise succeeds in building consumer confidence in the quality of products distributed under a particular brand name. Presumably this growth in value is not without cost, because enterprises spend large sums for advertising and otherwise promoting trade names. The relationship between promotional expenditures and the increase in the value of trade names is nebulous; therefore, accountants do not assign a cost to this intangible asset, except when it is acquired by purchase.

Organization costs

The organization of a corporate business enterprise usually requires a considerable amount of time, effort, and cost. Compensation must be paid to those who conceive, investigate, and promote the idea; legal fees relating to drafting of corporate charter and bylaws, accounting fees, and incorporation fees are incurred; and costs may be incurred in conducting initial meetings of stockholders and directors. All these expenditures are made with the expectation that they will contribute to future revenue. It is clear, therefore, that the cost of organizing a corporate enterprise logically should be treated as an asset and not as an expense. On the other hand, items such as losses incurred in the early years of a corporate enterprise, bond discount and issuance costs, large initial advertising expenditures, or discount on capital stock, are not included in organization costs. Expenditures incurred in connection with the issuance of shares of capital stock, such as professional fees and printing costs, generally are deducted from the proceeds received for the stock. Similar expenditures relating to the issuance of bonds or mortgage notes payable are deferred and amortized over the term of the debt.

Theoretically, the costs of organization have an economic life as long as the corporate enterprise remains a going concern. Because the life of most corporate enterprises is unlimited, organization costs may be viewed as a permanent asset that will continue in existence until the enterprise goes out of business. Despite the logic of this position, organization costs generally are amortized over a five-year period, because the federal income tax law permits amortization over a period of "not less than five years." However, amortization over a maximum period of 40 years is permitted by generally accepted accounting principles.

Franchises

A *franchise* is a right or privilege received by a business enterprise for the exclusive right to engage in business in a certain geographic area. The franchise may be acquired from a governmental unit or from another enterprise. For example, public utilities generally receive a franchise from state or federal agencies and are subject to specific regulations; a retailer may obtain an exclusive right from a manufacturer to sell certain products in a specified territory; an operator of a restaurant may obtain the right to utilize trade names and recipes developed by another enterprise.

Some franchises granted by manufacturers or retail chains *(franchisors)* may cost substantial amounts. The amount paid for such a franchise is recorded by the *franchisee* as an intangible asset and amortized over its expected economic life. The proceeds received by franchisors are recorded as revenue when the contractual commitments to franchisees are fulfilled.[6] If the right to operate under a franchise is limited to 10 years, for example, the amortization period should not exceed 10 years. Although some franchises prove to be worthless within a short period of time, others may increase substantially in value if the location and product prove successful.

An *operating right* issued by the Interstate Commerce Commission or a similar state agency to a motor carrier (trucker) to transport goods with limited competition over specified routes is a form of a franchise. Many trucking enterprises acquired such rights to transport goods interstate and paid large sums of money for them. The Motor Carrier Act of 1980 deregulated the interstate trucking industry, thus reducing or eliminating the value of these intangible assets. Consequently, the FASB required that "Unamortized costs of interstate operating rights subject to the provisions of the Act shall be charged to income and, if material, reported as an extraordinary item . . . in the income statement.[7]"

Leasehold costs

The purchase of an existing lease right and a lump-sum payment to acquire rights to explore for oil and minerals on land are valuable property rights which frequently are included under intangible assets in the bal-

---

[6] For a complete discussion on this topic, see *FASB Statement No. 45,* "Accounting for Franchise Fee Revenue," FASB (Stamford: 1981).

[7] *FASB Statement No. 44,* "Accounting for Intangible Assets of Motor Carriers," FASB (Stanford: 1980), p. 2.

ance sheet. However, because such assets represent rights to use tangible assets, they may be included under plant assets.[8]

UNIDENTIFIABLE INTANGIBLE ASSETS: GOODWILL

Thus far we have discussed the major types of identifiable intangible assets. However, the earning power of most prosperous business enterprises is attributable to a variety of factors which cannot be specifically identified, either as tangible assets or as intangible assets. Accountants, business executives, and lawyers often refer to these factors collectively as goodwill.

In ordinary usage the term **goodwill** is associated with a kindly feeling or benevolence. However, in business and law goodwill has a different meaning. The most acceptable evidence of goodwill is the ability of a business enterprise to earn a rate of return on net assets (owners' investment) in excess of a normal rate for the industry in which the business enterprise operates. **Goodwill is the difference between the value of a business enterprise as a whole and the sum of the current fair values of its identifiable tangible and intangible net assets.** Goodwill is in essence a "master valuation account"—the missing link that reconciles the current fair value of an enterprise as a going concern with the current fair value of the sum of its parts.

Nature of goodwill

The first obstacle in the path toward an understanding of goodwill is the problem of estimating the current fair value of a business enterprise as a going concern. The current fair value of the enterprise may be greater than the amount of identifiable tangible and intangible assets, because of the presence of unidentifiable intangible assets. A simple example may help to clarify this point. Assume that Parke Company is offered for sale and that the condensed balance sheet below is used as a basis for negotiating a fair price:

Net assets (stockholders' equity) is $400,000

PARKE COMPANY
Balance Sheet
December 31, Year 10

Cash and receivables	$130,000	Liabilities	$100,000
Inventories	90,000	Capital stock, $1 par	250,000
Plant assets (net)	280,000	Retained earnings	150,000
		Total liabilities & stockholders' equity	
Total assets	$500,000		$500,000

[8] (See p. 535).

We shall assume that Parke Company is expected to earn an average of $60,000 a year indefinitely in the future. Because the current fair value of net assets depends directly on their earning power, we can value Parke Company as a going concern, without reference to its balance sheet, by determining the present value of future earnings of $60,000 a year. A logical way of appraising this is in terms of the rate of return on alternative investment opportunities of comparable risk. We shall assume this rate to be 10%. If it is possible to earn a 10% return on similar investments, the current value of the prospect of receiving $60,000 a year *in perpetuity* may be computed by determining the amount which must be invested at 10% to earn an annual return of $60,000. This procedure is called **capitalization of income,** and the result in this case is a value for the net assets of Parke Company of $600,000 ($60,000 ÷ 0.10 = $600,000), compared with a carrying amount of only $400,000 ($250,000 + $150,000 = $400,000).

If the net assets of Parke Company are worth $600,000, why are they shown in the balance sheet at only $400,000? One possibility is that Parke Company's accounting records do not reflect the current fair value of identifiable net assets. Inventories and plant assets, for example, might be worth considerably more than carrying amount, and liabilities might be overstated. If these discrepancies are brought to light during the negotiations, appropriate adjustments should be made.

It is possible, however, that the carrying amount of each asset and liability included in the balance sheet closely approximates its current fair value, but still Parke Company's net assets are worth $200,000 more than carrying amount. Is this an accounting exception to the principle that the whole must equal the sum of its parts, or is it simply the case that some of the parts are not included in the balance sheet? The latter is the more likely explanation, and it is apparent that the missing parts are those characteristics of the company that enable it to earn $60,000 a year (10% of $600,000) rather than $40,000 a year (10% of $400,000). The company apparently has intangible assets that are not included in its balance sheet. Any of the identifiable intangible assets previously discussed in this chapter are possible sources of the unexplained $200,000 in the current fair value of Parke Company as a going concern.

For purposes of this illustration, we shall assume that Parke Company has a patent worth $50,000 which is not included in the balance sheet, because it was developed internally or because it has been fully amortized. After all identifiable assets, both tangible and intangible, have been appraised, only $150,000 ($200,000 − $50,000) remains un-

[8] For example: United Brands Company recently showed the cost of a leasehold acquired for $3,117,000 under an intangible caption "Trademarks and Leaseholds"; Texasgulf Inc., included the costs of contract rights, unproved properties, and exploration projects under "Property, Plant and Equipment"; Union Oil Company capitalized leasehold costs of exploratory acreage and intangible drilling expenditures and included them under "Property."

explained, and we have isolated the *imputed value* of all unidentifiable intangible assets, that is, goodwill. Goodwill exists as an asset only because it is impossible to identify separately all sources of the prospective earning power of a business enterprise. This analysis may be summarized as follows for Parke Company:

Current fair value of total assets		$700,000*
Less: Current fair value of tangible assets	$400,000	
Current fair value of patent not included in the accounting records	50,000	
Liabilities	100,000	550,000
Unidentifiable intangible assets (goodwill)		$150,000

* $600,000 net assets + $100,000 liabilities = $700,000

If patents of $50,000 and goodwill of $150,000 were added to the assets of Parke Company, the carrying amount of its *net assets* would be $600,000 (assets of $700,000, less liabilities of $100,000). Therefore, if the company earned $60,000, its earnings no longer would be large in relation to the carrying amount of its net assets. Thus, the ability to earn a *superior* rate of return on net assets which *do not include* goodwill is evidence that goodwill exists; the ability to earn a normal rate of return on assets which *include* the goodwill and all identifiable intangible assets is evidence of the existence of goodwill in the amount computed.

Negative goodwill

Goodwill, as we have defined it, can be either positive or negative in amount. Suppose, for example, that the prospective earnings of Parke Company had been estimated at only $36,000 a year indefinitely into the future and that its identifiable net assets are fairly stated at $400,000. On a 10% yield basis, the capitalized value of these earnings is $360,000 ($36,000 ÷ 0.10 = $360,000), and it is evident that the carrying amount of the net assets exceeds the current fair value of the company as a whole by $40,000. This $40,000 is referred to as *negative goodwill.*

When the earning potential of a business enterprise is such that the enterprise as a whole is worth less than its net assets, the owners would be better off to dispose of the assets piecemeal, pay the liabilities, and terminate the enterprise. In reality this may not be done because of concern for the welfare of employees, willingness of the owners to continue operating an unprofitable business, optimism about future prospects, or other considerations. Because the presence of negative goodwill suggests that liquidation is the best course of action, positive goodwill is more likely to be found in going concerns than negative goodwill. Although negative goodwill exists in many unsuccessful enterprises, it is not isolated and reported in the balance sheet; the only evidence of its existence is a *low rate of return* on the net assets of that enterprise.

If an enterprise with negative goodwill is sold as a going concern, the value assigned to the net assets acquired by the purchaser should not exceed the *cost actually paid.* The total current fair value of identifiable assets acquired less the liabilities assumed occasionally may exceed the price paid for the acquired enterprise. According to *APB Opinion No. 16,* such an excess over cost should be allocated to reduce the carrying amounts assigned to noncurrent assets (other than long-term investments in marketable securities). If this allocation reduces noncurrent assets to zero, any remaining excess is classified as a deferred credit and amortized over a period not exceeding 40 years.[9]

Recording of goodwill (excess of cost over net assets acquired)

The high degree of certainty about the future assumed in the measurement of goodwill of Parke Company, in the example above, does not exist in the real world. Assessing the earnings potential of a business enterprise is an uncertain process, and any resulting estimate of goodwill is a matter of judgment and opinion.

In the face of this uncertainty, accountants have adopted a rule of caution with respect to goodwill. It is generally accepted that goodwill should be recorded in the accounting records only when its amount is substantiated by an arm's-length transaction. Because goodwill cannot be either sold or acquired separately, accounting recognition of goodwill is restricted to those occasions in which the entire net assets of a business enterprise, or a substantial interest in the net assets representing a clearly defined segment of a business enterprise, are purchased, and goodwill can be established with reasonable objectivity.[10] In such cases goodwill frequently is labeled as *Excess of Cost over Net Assets Acquired.*

Limiting the recording of goodwill to *purchased goodwill* is admittedly not a perfect solution to the problem. Internally developed goodwill actually may exist in a business enterprise and not be recorded; on the other hand, goodwill acquired in the past may appear in the accounting records when there is no current evidence (in terms of earning power) that it actually exists. The financial statements of business enterprises which have changed ownership will appear to be inconsistent

---

[9] *APB Opinion No. 16,* "Business Combinations," AICPA (New York: 1970), p. 321.

[10] Cases in which goodwill is recorded in connection with the transfer of partnership interests and in the preparation of consolidated financial statements are presented in *Modern Advanced Accounting* of this series. Our discussion at this point is limited to goodwill arising out of the *purchase* of the entire business enterprise for cash. When a going business enterprise is acquired in exchange for shares of capital stock, the transaction may be accounted for as a *pooling of interests.* Goodwill may be recognized in a purchase-type transaction, but not in a pooling of interests.

with those of enterprises which have had a continuing existence. For example, assume that Parke Company, which was discussed earlier, has identifiable net assets of $450,000 and that a new company is formed to purchase its net assets for $600,000 cash. The opening balance sheet of the new company would include goodwill of $150,000. Is there any justification for a rule that prohibits the recording of $150,000 goodwill in the accounting records of Parke Company but permits the inclusion of this amount in the balance sheet of the new company?

On balance, an affirmative answer is warranted. Specific assets represent resources in which the capital of a busines enterprise is invested, to the extent that it has been possible to determine them. The periodic adjustment of these asset valuations by a variable amount labeled "goodwill" to a level consistent with the present value of future earnings not only would be a highly subjective undertaking but also would obscure the significant relationship between actual investment and earning power. If $150,000 of goodwill had been recorded in the accounting records of Parke Company, not only would there be a serious question as to the validity of this amount, but also the high level of earnings on investment that Parke Company had been able to attain would be concealed. The investment of the new owners, on the other hand, was not $450,000, but $600,000. The new owners paid $150,000 for anticipated earnings in excess of normal, and if only $150,000 of excess earnings should materialize, this amount will not represent income to the new owners but a recovery of their investment. The position that goodwill should be recognized in the accounting records only when it is evidenced by a purchase transaction appears to be consistent with the cost principle and the basic assumptions underlying the measurement of net income.

Estimate of goodwill

The price to be paid for a business enterprise is established as the result of bargaining between independent parties. The bargaining process includes the possible existence of goodwill. The amount of goodwill **to be recorded,** however, is determined after the terms of the contract are set by deducting the current fair value of all identifiable net assets from the total purchase price. Accountants are interested in the process of estimating goodwill because they often are called upon to aid in establishing the current fair value of an enterprise, at the time of negotiations for the purchase or sale of an enterprise, and in litigation.

Steps generally required to estimate the current fair value of a business enterprise, and thus the amount of goodwill, are listed on page 539.

1 Estimate the current fair value of all identifiable tangible and intangible assets of the enterprise, and deduct from this total the amount of all liabilities. This gives the current fair value of the identifiable net assets of the enterprise.

2 Forecast the average annual earnings that the enterprise expects in future years with the use of its present facilities.

3 Choose an appropriate rate (or rates) of return to estimate the normal annual earnings the enterprise **should earn** on its identifiable net assets.

4 Compute the amount of expected annual superior earnings, if any.

5 Capitalize the expected annual superior earnings, if any, at an appropriate rate (or rates) of return to estimate the present value of such earnings. The present capitalized value of any expected annual superior earnings is the estimated value of goodwill for the enterprise.

In the following sections, an estimate of goodwill is developed for Reed Company (which is for sale) to serve as a basis for a discussion of the problems that arise in connection with each of the five steps listed above.

Estimate of the Current Fair Value of Identifiable Net Assets Because carrying amounts and current fair values of assets seldom correspond, an appraisal of identifiable assets is necessary to establish the current fair value of the business enterprise (excluding goodwill) and to identify the assets which generate the earnings of the enterprise.

The fair value of current assets, such as cash and accounts receivable, usually will approximate carrying amount. Inventories, if verified by a physical inventory and priced on a fifo or average-cost basis, also may be reasonably stated. Lifo inventories, however, probably are stated in terms of costs incurred many years earlier and should be adjusted to current fair value. The carrying amounts of plant assets are not likely to approximate current fair values. Various methods of indirect valuation may be employed to appraise such assets on a going-concern basis. The current fair value of all identifiable intangible assets should be estimated, even if these assets do not appear in the accounting records. The liabilities of the business enterprise should be reviewed, and any unrecorded liabilities should be estimated and recorded. Liabilities which will not be assumed by the new owners should be ignored, unless payment from present assets is contemplated before the enterprise changes ownership. Assets at current fair values, less liabilities to be assumed by the new owners, gives the adjusted amount (estimated current fair value) of net assets for purposes of estimating the value of goodwill.

The assumed data on top of page 540 for Reed Company illustrate the process of estimating the current fair value of identifiable net assets of a business enterprise.

REED COMPANY
Carrying Amount and Current Fair Value of Net Assets
December 31, Year 10

Items	Carrying amount	Adjust-ments	Estimated current fair value
Cash, receivables, and short-term prepay-ments	$142,000	$ (2,000)	$140,000
Inventories (lifo)	178,000	42,000	220,000
Plant assets (net).	480,000	120,000	600,000
Patents and secret formulas	–0–	30,000	30,000
Total assets	$800,000	$190,000	$990,000
Less: Liabilities	160,000	10,000	170,000
Net assets	$640,000	$180,000	$820,000

Forecast of Expected Average Annual Earnings The aggregate value of any business enterprise depends on its future earnings, not on its past earnings. Thus, the key step in any estimate of the current fair value of an enterprise is a forecast of its future earnings, a process which, unfortunately, can never be more than an intelligent guess. Because the immediate past history of an enterprise ordinarily provides the best available evidence and is most relevant, the usual procedure is to compute the average annual earnings of an enterprise during the past three to six years and to project them into the future, adjusting for any changing conditions that can be foreseen. The estimate of future conditions and earnings generally is made by the parties to the transaction and not by accountants. A single year's performance clearly is not a sufficient basis for judgment; on the other hand, little may be gained by reaching too far into the past, because both the internal and the external conditions influencing business operations may have changed radically.

In the compilation of the past earnings record suitable for estimating future earnings, two points should be kept in mind:

1 We are not interested in establishing what past earnings were, but in learning what past experience can tell us about probable future earnings.

2 Our objective is to obtain an estimate of future earnings that is consistent with the adjusted current fair values of specific identifiable tangible and intangible assets.

It seldom is possible to obtain satisfactory data by simply computing an average of past reported earnings. A more reasonable approach is to work from actual revenue and expense amounts, because changes in revenue and expenses are likely to be related to projected economic and operating conditions. The effect on earnings of a 10% increase in revenue and a 15% increase in operating expenses, for example, may need to be determined. Past data should be adjusted for changes in the value of assets. For example, if inventories and equipment have been understated in terms of current fair values, adjustments of past cost of goods sold and depreciation expense must be made. Extraordinary items generally should be omitted from past earnings. In view of the subjectivity of estimates and income measurement, minor adjustments can be ignored.

In the evaluation of an average of past data, particular attention must be given to **significant trends.** For example, two enterprises may have the same five-year average sales, but if the sales of one enterprise have increased in each of the past five years, while the sales of the other have declined steadily, the average sales amounts should be interpreted differently.

An important point, often overlooked in the adjustment of past earnings in the light of future expectations, is that improvements in earnings expected as a result of the efforts of new owners and management should be distinguished carefully from prospective improvements that can be traced to existing conditions. If the purchaser of a business enterprise expects to make changes in management, production methods, products, and marketing techniques which will increase earnings in the future, these changes should not be considered in the valuation of the enterprise because they will flow from the efforts of the new owners. Of course, the final price paid for goodwill in any transaction is a matter of bargaining between the purchaser and the seller.

The working paper on page 542 is a continuation of the Reed Company example. It represents an assumed computation on December 31, Year 10, of estimated future earnings, based upon an average of the results experienced over the past five years. This estimate might be interpreted by the prospective purchaser to indicate a probable range of future annual earnings for Reed Company of, say, between $90,000 and $120,000 a year. However, for illustrative purposes, we shall use the amount of $106,000.

Normal Rate of Return   The rate of return used to capitalize future earnings and to separate superior earnings from ordinary earnings is determined on the basis of the risks and alternatives involved. The objective is to approximate the rate necessary to attract capital to the business enterprise under review, given the existing risk conditions. The cost of capital, as other costs, varies in relation to a variety of factors. The primary cause of differences in the rate of return necessary to attract capital to different kinds of investment at any given time is the amount of risk involved.

Data on average earnings rates for enterprises in particular industries are available in financial services, trade association studies, and government publications. Care should be exercised in the use of such data to be sure that they are applied to comparable situations; for example,

Working paper for
computation
of estimated average
future earnings

REED COMPANY
Estimate of Average Future Earnings
December 31, Year 10

Revenue:

Average annual revenue for past five years, which is expected to be typical of future years (extraordinary gains and losses have been excluded)		$920,000
Expenses:		
Average cost of goods sold and operating expenses for past five years, excluding depreciation and income taxes	$635,600	
Add: Anticipated annual increase in wages and fringe benefits as a result of a new union contract	45,800	
Less: Average of the five-year increase in inventory valuation not included in the lifo basis of pricing inventories ($42,000 ÷ 5).	(8,400)	
Depreciation and amortization:		
Average depreciation of carrying amounts of assets. . . .	24,000	
Add: Increase in depreciation on the basis of current fair value (25% increase in value)	6,000	
Amortization of patents and secret formulas, not previously carried in the accounting records ($30,000 divided by the economic life of 6 years).	5,000	708,000
Expected average future earnings before income taxes		$212,000
Less: Estimated federal and state income taxes (50%).		106,000
Estimated average future earnings		$106,000

that the earnings rate consistently is assumed to be either before or after income taxes. We shall assume for purposes of illustration that a reasonable normal rate of return for Reed Company is 10% *after income taxes.*

Estimate of Future Superior Earnings   The amount of estimated future superior earnings may be defined as the amount of earnings expected in excess of normal earnings on the current fair value of identifiable tangible and intangible net assets.

All variables necessary to compute the estimated future superior earnings of Reed Company have been discussed and now can be illustrated. The current fair value of Reed Company's identifiable net assets is $820,000 (see data on page 540), and its average future earnings are estimated at $106,000. Because a 10% after-tax rate of return is sufficient to attract an investment in this company, estimated future superior earnings may be determined as illustrated on top of page 543.

Superior earnings: the ultimate source of goodwill	*Estimated average future earnings. . . . .*	*$106,000*
	Less: 10% return on current fair value of identifiable net assets,	
	$820,000 × 10%	*82,000*
	Estimated future superior earnings	*$ 24,000*

This computation shows that $82,000 ($820,000 × 10% = $82,000) a year is necessary to support a valuation of $820,000 for the identifiable net assets of Reed Company. Because the company's prospects are for earnings in excess of $82,000, the source of this excess earning power must be the unidentifiable intangible assets (goodwill) that enable the company to earn a higher-than-normal rate of return.

Estimate of Present Value of Superior Earnings—The Final Step A number of different methods may be used to value the estimated future superior earnings, and thus arrive at an estimate of goodwill. Four widely used methods are illustrated below:

Method 1 *Estimated future superior earnings are capitalized at the normal rate of return.* One assumption is that the superior earnings of $24,000 a year, as determined above, will continue unimpaired into the future and that this prospect is attributable entirely to the existing resources of Reed Company. The annual superior earnings are **capitalized** to answer the following question: How much capital should be invested if the annual return on the investment is $24,000 in perpetuity, and the desired rate of return is 10% a year? Under this approach, goodwill is estimated at $240,000 as follows:

What objection do you see in this approach?	*Value of estimated annual average earnings of $106,000 capitalized at*	
	10% in perpetuity: $106,000 ÷ 0.10	*$1,060,000*
	Less: Estimated current fair value of identifiable net assets.	*820,000*
	Estimated amount of goodwill	*$ 240,000*
	Alternative computation:	
	Value of estimated future superior earnings capitalized at 10% in	
	perpetuity (goodwill): $24,000 ÷ 0.10.	*$ 240,000*

There are serious flaws in the assumptions on which this method rests. It may be reasonable to forecast that a business enterprise will earn a 10% return on its net assets over a very long period of time, but the assumption that superior earning power will persist in perpetuity in the face of competitive pressures and the hazards of free enterprise is optimistic, to say the least. Furthermore, even if superior earnings do continue, it seldom is possible to trace their origin to conditions that existed at the time of acquisition. The forces that erode superior earnings are such that a persistent ability to earn a higher-than-normal rate of return ultimately will be due to some additional propellant in the form of research, innovations, efficiency, and strategy on the part of the new owners and management.

Method 2 *Estimated future superior earnings are discounted for a limited number of years to determine the present value of such earnings.* The estimate of goodwill may be modified in several ways to allow for the uncertain nature of superior earnings. One approach is to assume that any estimated future superior earnings will continue for a **limited period,** say, three, five, or ten years. The **present value** of a given series of superior earnings at a given rate of return can be computed by the use of present value concepts described in Chapter 5. In the Reed Company example, if estimated future superior earnings of $24,000 a year will continue for a five-year period, the present value of this prospect on a 10% basis is approximately $91,000, determined as follows:

<table>
<tr><td>**A conceptually sound approach for estimating goodwill**</td><td>Estimated future superior earnings (assume receipt at end of each year) . . . .</td><td>$24,000</td></tr>
<tr><td></td><td>Present value of ordinary annuity of five payments of 1 each, discounted at 10% . . . .</td><td>× 3.790787</td></tr>
<tr><td></td><td>Present value of estimated future superior earnings (goodwill) . . . .</td><td>$90,979</td></tr>
</table>

Method 3 *Estimated future superior earnings are capitalized at a higher-than-normal rate of return.* A variation of method 1 is to capitalize estimated future superior earnings at a higher discount rate than is used to capitalize normal earnings. For example, if the normal rate of return is considered to be 10%, a rate of, say, 20% or 30% may be used to capitalize superior earnings. The higher assumed rates of return allow for higher risk, because the prospect that superior earnings will continue unimpaired into the future is **much more uncertain** than the prospect of continued normal earnings. Referring once more to the Reed Company illustration, if superior earnings of $24,000 a year are capitalized at 30%, for example, goodwill is estimated at $80,000 as follows:

<table>
<tr><td>**Higher capitalization rate recognizes that superior earnings are subject to erosion**</td><td>Estimated future superior earnings . . . .</td><td>$24,000</td></tr>
<tr><td></td><td>Capitalization rate . . . .</td><td>30%</td></tr>
<tr><td></td><td>Capitalized value of estimated future superior earnings discounted at 30% in perpetuity (goodwill): $24,000 ÷ 0.30 . . . .</td><td>$80,000</td></tr>
</table>

Under this approach, the earnings prospects of Reed Company have been divided into two layers—$82,000 of normal earnings, and $24,000 of superior earnings—and a different discount rate has been used to value each layer. Any number of different layers and any number of different discount rates might be used to estimate goodwill.

Method 4 *Estimated future superior earnings for a given number of years are purchased.* Another approach to the estimate of goodwill is to multiply estimated future superior earnings by a number of years and to refer to the result as a "number of years of estimated future superior earnings purchased." For example, a goodwill estimate of $120,000 may be described as "the purchase of five years of estimated future superior earnings of $24,000 a year." Loose statements of this kind may obscure the real issues involved. As noted previously, the present value of five years of estimated future superior earnings of $24,000 discounted at 10% is approximately $91,000, not $120,000. Therefore, no reason exists for paying $120,000 for superior earnings of $120,000 to be received over a five-year period if money is worth 10% compounded annually.

Summary of methods Uncertainty and subjectivity surround each of the variables involved in an estimate of goodwill. The probable amount of future earnings, the part that represents superior earnings, the length of time, and the appropriate rate of return to be used in the valuation of superior earnings—all are variables not subject to objective verification. They can be estimated only within a reasonable range of probability. The illustrated methods indicate the following possible range (from highest to lowest) in the estimated value of goodwill for Reed Company:

Results of preceding four approaches compared	*Estimated future superior earnings of $24,000 are capitalized at 10% in perpetuity* $240,000
	Estimated future superior earnings of $24,000 for five years are purchased 120,000
	Estimated future superior earnings of $24,000 for five years are discounted at 10% (rounded) 91,000
	Estimated future superior earnings of $24,000 are capitalized at 30% (to recognize a higher risk factor) in perpetuity 80,000

In a transaction involving the purchase of Reed Company, the value established for goodwill probably would be somewhere between $240,000 and $80,000, depending on the relative bargaining power of the purchaser and the seller. Inability to agree on a specific value for goodwill frequently results in an agreement to pay a minimum amount for goodwill, to be supplemented by additional payments **contingent** on future superior earnings of the acquired enterprise. Such agreements may raise numerous accounting questions. For example, (1) How should the future payments be recorded? (2) How should the earnings on which the contingent payments are based be measured? (3) How should future contingent payments be disclosed by the enterprise that may be required to pay them?

It sometimes is suggested that the market value of the shares of capital stock outstanding provides a basis for estimating the current fair value of a corporation. Thus, if Reed Company, whose net assets have a current fair value of $820,000, has 200,000 shares of capital stock outstanding, quoted on the market at $6 a share, this suggests that the company is worth $1,200,000, and that goodwill is $380,000 ($1,200,000 − $820,000 = $380,000). This conclusion would have some merit if the market price of $6 a share applied to the entire issue of 200,000 shares, or to a block representing a substantial and controlling interest in the company. However, only a small fraction of the total shares outstanding normally is offered for sale on the market at any given time. The market prices of this small **floating supply** of capital stock can fluctuate widely, and are influenced by short-run factors that may be unrelated to the long-run prospects of the company. Furthermore, there is no quoted market price for the capital stock of the majority of small corporations. Stock prices may be useful as evidence of **relative** values in the negotiation of a business combination involving an exchange of capital stock, and they also may substantiate or cast doubt on estimates of goodwill reached independently. However, stock prices seldom are useful in the direct valuation of goodwill.

Non-compete agreements

When a going business enterprise is purchased, the purchaser may pay an amount in excess of the current fair value of the identifiable net assets acquired. Typically, the excess is recorded as goodwill. There are situations, however, in which a part of the purchase price may be attributable to a restriction placed on the seller not to engage in a competing enterprise for a specified period of time. The purchaser of a retail store or a restaurant, for example, would not want the former owner to open a competing enterprise in the same geographic area.

A **non-compete agreement** is incorporated in the contract for the purchase of the business enterprise, as for example, "the seller agrees not to engage in the restaurant business in the City of Ames for a period of five years." Such an agreement obviously has value to the purchaser, and a reasonable portion of the purchase price should be assigned to it. Although the value of a non-compete agreement is difficult to determine, the purchaser and seller should be able to agree on a fair price. The value assigned to goodwill does not include the value assigned to the non-compete agreement, because the latter represents an **identifiable** intangible asset. For example, if a business enterprise with net assets of $100,000 at current fair value is purchased for $150,000, it appears that the purchaser paid $50,000 for goodwill. If, however, the parties agree to place a value of $30,000 on a non-compete agreement for five years, the purchase of the enterprise is recorded as follows:

<table>
<tr><td>A non-compete agree-
ment can be amortized
for income tax purposes</td><td>Net Assets.</td><td>100,000</td><td></td></tr>
<tr><td></td><td>Non-Compete Agreement</td><td>30,000</td><td></td></tr>
<tr><td></td><td>Goodwill.</td><td>20,000</td><td></td></tr>
<tr><td></td><td>Cash</td><td></td><td>150,000</td></tr>
<tr><td></td><td colspan="3">To record the purchase of a business enterprise with non-
compete agreement and goodwill valued separately.</td></tr>
</table>

The advantage of reducing the recorded value of goodwill is that the non-compete agreement is amortized at the rate of $6,000 a year over its economic life of 5 years, and this amortization is a deductible expense for income tax purposes; amortization of goodwill is not a deductible expense in the computation of taxable income.

Controversy over amortization of goodwill

Whether goodwill arising out of the purchase of a business enterprise should be amortized has been a controversial issue for many years. Even after the issuance of **Opinion No. 17,** which required the amortization of goodwill acquired after October 31, 1970, many business executives and accountants have continued to question the amortization of purchased goodwill.

It has been argued that goodwill has an indefinite economic life and, therefore, should not be amortized until there is evidence that it no longer exists. Supporters of this view maintain that as long as earnings are sufficient to indicate that goodwill is unimpaired, it is a permanent asset. To amortize goodwill in the absence of a decline in earnings, it is argued, would obliterate the superior earnings which required the recording of the goodwill in the first place.

The argument against the amortization of purchased goodwill is particularly strong when earnings continue at a level which indicates that goodwill continues to exist. It is doubtful that continuing goodwill stems solely from conditions existing at the time of purchase. A more likely situation is that goodwill is maintained through the successful efforts of the new owners and management to stay ahead of competition. It is unlikely that the exact amount of original goodwill which has dissipated will be replaced by a new layer of internally developed goodwill. Retaining purchased goodwill intact in the accounting records would be an attempt to compensate for the accounting inconsistency of recording purchased goodwill and not recording internally developed goodwill. Expenditures for research and development and advertising necessary to maintain superior earning power are recorded as expenses. If purchased goodwill is amortized, there would be a duplication of expenses —the current expenditures incurred to build and maintain goodwill, and the periodic amortization of purchased goodwill.

The opposing view is that the amount paid for goodwill represents the purchase of a group of unidentifiable intangible assets and superior earnings for a limited number of years. It is argued that goodwill does not last forever and that the realization of superior earnings is not income to the new owners but rather a recovery of capital. Amortization of purchased goodwill is supported on practical grounds, because the value of goodwill is likely to become zero at some future date. Thus, the investment in goodwill should be accounted for on the same basis as any other productive asset having a limited economic life. If expectations were realized, that is, if earnings continued unchanged for the period of years used to estimate and amortize purchased goodwill, the result of amortization might be the reporting of less-than-normal earnings on the investment of the new owners during the amortization period. This squares with reality, because the payment for superior earnings makes their ultimate emergence a *return of invested capital,* not income.

Both sides in this controversy agree that goodwill should be written down in the face of clear evidence that it is overstated. If superior earnings are eroded by competitive pressures and other economic conditions, the gradual disappearance of goodwill should be recognized as an expense.

ACCOUNTING FOR RESEARCH AND DEVELOPMENT (R&D) COSTS

Many business enterprises spend large sums of money on research aimed at the discovery and development of improved processes and products. Some research expenditures result in patentable discoveries and some produce nonpatentable benefits of a general nature in the form of better production methods and techniques. However, significant amounts of R&D costs produce no measurable benefits to future revenue.

Corporate managements had almost complete discretion to defer or to expense R&D costs until 1970, when the Accounting Principles Board stated that "a company should record as expenses the costs to develop intangible assets which are not specifically identifiable."[11] However, this accounting principle was vague and did not prevent the accumulation of vast sums of R&D costs in the balance sheets of many enterprises. In some instances such costs could not be related to specific

---

[11] *APB Opinion No. 17,* p. 334.

future revenue and were often written off in a "year of the big bath," because of deterioration in demand for the company's products.

The AICPA recognized the need to develop sharper accounting standards for R&D costs, and in 1973 published **Accounting Research Study No. 14,** "Accounting for Research and Development Expenditures." **ARS No. 14** recommended, among other things, that costs incurred in continuing research programs should be recorded as expenses immediately, and that costs of any substantial development projects should be deferred and amortized over the future accounting periods that they are intended to benefit.[12] This study provided background material for the Financial Accounting Standards Board in the development of **FASB Statement No. 2,** the current accounting standard for R&D costs.

FASB Statement No. 2, "Accounting for Research and Development Costs"

FASB Statement No. 2 was issued in an effort to reduce the diversity of accounting practices and to establish standards of disclosure for R&D costs. The **Statement** specified the activities and costs that should be identified as R&D for financial accounting purposes.

The main conclusion of **FASB Statement No. 2** was that all R&D costs, other than fully reimbursable costs incurred for others under contract, **shall be recorded as expenses when incurred.**[13] R&D costs previously deferred were required to be written off as a prior period adjustment. When financial statements were presented for accounting periods preceding the write-off of R&D costs, the financial statements and summaries based on such statements were **restated retroactively to reflect the prior period adjustment.** The nature of the restatement and its effect on net income and earnings per share for each period presented were disclosed in the period of change. The FASB also required disclosure of total R&D costs expensed in each accounting period for which an income statement is presented.

The FASB defined research and development as follows: **Research** is aimed at discovery of new knowledge with the hope that such knowledge will be useful in developing new products (including services) or processes, or in bringing about improvements in existing products or processes. **Development** is the translation of research findings into a plan or design for new or improved products or processes; it includes the conceptual formulation, design, and testing of product alternatives, construction of prototypes, and operation of pilot plants; it does not include routine or periodic alterations to existing products and processes

[12] Oscar S. Gellein and Maurice S. Newman, *Accounting Research Study No. 14,* "Accounting for Research and Development Expenditures," AICPA (New York: 1973), pp. 6–8.
[13] *FASB Statement No. 2,* "Accounting for Research and Development Costs," FASB (Stamford: 1974), p. 6.

or market research and market testing activities. Activities typically *included* in R&D are listed below:[14]

1 Laboratory research aimed at discovery of new knowledge
2 Searching for applications of new research findings
3 Conceptual formulation and design of possible new products or processes
4 Testing in search for or evaluation of new products or processes
5 Modification of the formulation or design of products or processes
6 Design, construction, and testing of preproduction prototypes and models
7 Design of tools, jigs, molds, and dies involving new technology
8 Design, construction, and operation of a pilot plant that is not of a scale economically feasible to the enterprise for commercial production
9 Engineering activity required to advance the design of a product to the point that it meets predetermined specifications and is ready for manufacture

Activities typically *excluded* from R&D are: (1) engineering follow-through, quality control, and troubleshooting during production; (2) routine efforts to improve products and adapt to changing customer needs; (3) routine design (or changes in design) of tools, jigs, molds, and dies; and (4) legal work in connection with patent applications or litigation, and the sale or licensing of patents. Costs incurred in these activities normally are expensed, except legal costs incurred in connection with patent applications or litigation which are expected to benefit future revenue.

Costs that are classified as R&D costs for financial accounting purposes are:[15]

1 Material consumed in R&D activities and depreciation and amortization on assets used in R&D activities. Material and assets acquired for a particular R&D project that have no alternative uses should be treated as R&D costs as incurred.
2 Salaries, wages, and other related costs of personnel engaged in R&D activities.
3 Contract services performed by others in connection with R&D activities. Intangibles purchased from others which have alternative future uses should be capitalized and amortized over a period of 40 years or less.
4 A reasonable allocation of indirect costs; general and administrative costs which are not clearly related to R&D activities should not be included with R&D costs.

The main provision of *FASB Statement No. 2,* that is, "all research and development costs . . . shall be charged to expense when incurred," was a compromise solution to a very difficult financial accounting problem. Those who opposed the deferral of R&D naturally were pleased with the position of the FASB. On the other hand, some accountants and corporate executives questioned the logic of immediate write-offs of those R&D costs which have a high probability of contributing to future revenue.

[14] Ibid., p. 4.
[15] Ibid., pp. 5–6.

Admittedly, there is a considerable degree of uncertainty as to the future benefits of individual R&D projects. "Estimates of the rate of success of R&D projects vary markedly—depending in part on how narrowly one defines a 'project' and how one defines 'success'—but all such estimates indicate a high failure rate."[16] Because a direct relationship between R&D costs and specific future revenue generally is difficult to establish, the recording of such costs as expenses is a conservative application of the matching principle. For income tax purposes, all R&D costs can be expensed as incurred, and most business enterprises regularly expense such costs in their income tax returns. Thus, **FASB Statement No. 2** eliminated a major difference between financial accounting and income tax rules.

Deferred charges

The term **deferred charges** frequently is used to describe long-term prepayments subject to amortization. For example, the costs of issuing bonds produce benefits by providing funds for use in business; however, the funds provided contribute to revenue over the entire term of the bonds. Similarly, the cost of machinery rearrangements presumably results in a more efficient and valuable plant and, therefore, should be allocated to revenue over an appropriate number of years. Other examples of items sometimes classified in the balance sheet as deferred charges include the following: noncurrent prepaid income taxes, preoperating (or start-up) costs, and certain pension costs.

The use of the term **deferred charges** may be criticized, because all assets other than cash, receivables, investments, and land are forms of deferred charges to revenue. Most deferred charges can be classified either as plant assets (machinery rearrangement) or as intangible assets (oil exploration costs). If a deferrable cost cannot be classified under plant assets or intangible assets, it should be included under Other Noncurrent Assets in the balance sheet to avoid a separate category for deferred charges.

The deferral of an expenditure can be justified only if an asset with future service potential has resulted. If the future service potential of any expenditure is obscure, it should be recorded as an expense.

Accounting for development-stage enterprises

In the 1970s, a special category of deferred charges received considerable attention. Costs incurred by enterprises in the development stage were designated as **preoperating** or **start-up costs.** Such costs generally were deferred and amortized over a relatively short period after the enterprise emerged from the development stage and started gen-

---

[16] Ibid., p. 15.

erating revenue. Preoperating costs which were applicable to abandoned projects and other costs which were not expected to contribute to revenue in future accounting periods were written off in the accounting period in which the loss of service potential became apparent.

Accounting practices for enterprises in the development stage varied considerably. Consequently, the FASB issued **Statement No. 7,** which specified guidelines for identifying enterprises in the development stage and the standards of accounting and reporting applicable to such enterprises. An enterprise is considered to be in a development stage if it is devoting most of its efforts to establishing a new business and planned principal operations have not begun, or, if they have begun, no significant revenue has been realized. A development-stage enterprise typically devotes most of its efforts to financial planning, raising capital, exploring for and developing natural resources, research and development, establishing sources of supply, acquiring plant assets, and gearing up for production.[17] A summary of the accounting and disclosure requirements of **FASB Statement No. 7** follows:[18]

1 Financial statements issued by development-stage enterprises should present financial position, changes in financial position, and results of operations in conformity with generally accepted accounting principles that apply to established operating enterprises.

2 In issuing the same basic financial statements as an established operating enterprise, development-stage enterprises also should disclose the following information:
  a A balance sheet, including any cumulative net losses reported with a descriptive caption such as "deficit accumulated during the development stage" in the owners' equity section.
  b An income statement, showing amounts of revenue and expenses for each accounting period covered by the income statement and, in addition, cumulative amounts from the enterprise's inception.
  c A statement of changes in financial position, showing the sources and uses of financial resources for each accounting period for which an income statement is presented and, in addition, cumulative amounts from the enterprise's inception.

3 A statement of owners' equity, showing for a corporation, for example, each issuance of securities from the company's inception: (a) the date and number of shares of capital stock, warrants, rights, or other securities issued for cash and for other consideration; (b) the dollar amounts assigned to the consideration received; and (c) the nature of the noncash consideration and the basis for assigning current fair values to the noncash consideration.

In addition, the financial statements must be identified as those of a development-stage enterprise and must include a description of the nature of the development-stage activities. The financial statements for the first fiscal year in which an enterprise no longer is considered to be in the development stage should disclose that in prior years it had been in the development stage.

[17] *FASB Statement No. 7,* "Accounting and Reporting by Development Stage Enterprises," FASB (Stamford: 1975), pp. 3–4.
[18] Ibid., pp. 5–6.

Plant and intangible assets in the balance sheet

There is a noticeable trend in corporate financial reporting toward including all noncurrent assets (other than investments) under a single major heading labeled "plant assets," "plant and equipment," "property, plant and equipment," or "fixed assets." Tangible and intangible assets are reported separately, and plant assets held for resale are included under Other Noncurrent Assets. The methods of depreciation and amortization used, as well as the amounts of depreciation and amortization for the latest accounting period, should be disclosed.

In a recent survey of 600 industrial companies, 416 reported intangible assets being amortized and 172 reported intangible assets (presumably acquired before October 31, 1970) not being amortized.[19] The most common types of intangible assets reported were goodwill (excess of cost over net assets acquired in business combinations), patents, trademarks, brand names, copyrights, licenses and contracts, and franchises. The following example illustrates the presentation of plant assets and intangible assets in the balance sheet:

Presentation of plant assets and intangible assets in the balance sheet

Plant assets:

Land, at cost	$ 350,000	
Buildings (cost $1,640,000, less accumulated depreciation of $185,000)	1,455,000	
Equipment (cost $870,000, less accumulated depreciation of $150,000)	720,000	
Tools and patterns (at unamortized cost)	25,000	
Total plant assets (net)		$2,550,000

Intangible assets:

Patents (amortized over 12 years)	$ 85,000	
Trademarks and trade names (amortized over 20 years)	100,000	
Organization costs (amortized over 40 years)	15,000	
Goodwill (amortized over 40 years)	180,000	
Total intangible assets (net)		380,000

Note: Depreciation and amortization of intangible assets amounted to $310,000 for the latest accounting period. The straight-line method is used to compute depreciation and amortization for both financial accounting and income tax purposes.

REVIEW QUESTIONS

1 Accountants use the term *intangible assets* in a more limited sense than the legal meaning of this term. Explain. What are two categories of intangible assets?

[19] *Accounting Trends & Techniques,* 34th ed., AICPA(New York: 1980), p. 179.

2 Why is it more difficult to identify and determine the cost of intangible assets than the cost of tangible assets? What are some similarities between tangible assets and intangible assets?

3 Michigan Corporation has just been organized. The costs of forming the corporation and issuing its capital stock amounted to $85,000. One officer of the company suggests that this amount be charged immediately against the amount paid in by stockholders in excess of the par value of capital stock. Another officer suggests that the amount be amortized over a period of five years as debits to retained earnings. Evaluate these two proposals.

4 In the computation of the equity (book value) per share of common stock, security analysts generally eliminate intangible assets. Can you defend this practice?

5 Lyle Company applied for and received a patent on a manufacturing process. The legal fees and patent application fees totaled $10,000. Research expenditures leading to the patent were estimated at $60,000. Shortly after the patent was issued, the company spent $25,000 in legal fees in a successful defense against a suit in which it was claimed that Lyle's patent infringed on the patent rights of a competitor.

a At what amount should the patent be recorded in Lyle's accounting records?

b What is the legal life of this patent?

c What factors should be considered in the determination of the patent's economic life?

6 What amortization policy should be followed for **copyrights, trademarks, secret formulas,** and **licenses and contracts?**

7 It has been argued, on the grounds of conservatism, that all intangible assets should be written off immediately upon acquisition. Give arguments against this treatment.

8 What expenditures generally are included in **organization costs?**

9 What is meant by the term **goodwill?** What are the tests of the existence of goodwill? What is meant by the term **negative goodwill?** Is negative goodwill reported in the balance sheet?

10 In negotiations for the sale of a going business enterprise, an intangible factor called **goodwill** sometimes is estimated by capitalizing average superior earnings, that is, by dividing average superior earnings by an assumed earnings-rate factor. Explain how the average superior earnings are determined, and justify the capitalization of superior earnings in the estimation of the amount of goodwill.

11 What is the distinction between **capitalizing** estimated future earnings and **measuring the present value** of estimated future earnings?

12 "If all the individual assets and liabilities of a business enterprise are identified and valued properly, goodwill will not exist." Do you agree with this quotation?

13 Purchased goodwill usually is recorded and included in the balance sheet; internally developed goodwill is not. Explain the basis for this apparent inconsistency.

14 Outline five steps usually followed to estimate the amount of goodwill of an existing business enterprise. Can the aggregate market value of capital stock be used to estimate the amount of goodwill of a publicly owned corporation?

15 Endo Company has identifiable net assets with an estimated current fair value of $1 million. The company has an indicated ability to earn $160,000 a year, and the normal earnings rate in its industry is 10%. Describe three methods which might be used to estimate the amount of goodwill of Endo Company.

16 What are two major provisions of **FASB Statement No. 2,** "Accounting for Research and Development Costs"?

17 Iowa Company conducts research on the development of new products, improvement of existing products, and improvement of its manufacturing process. How should these research costs be recorded for financial accounting purposes?

18 a Define **development-stage enterprises.**
   b Briefly summarize the accounting and disclosure requirements for development-stage enterprises, as required by **FASB Statement No. 7.**

EXERCISES

Ex. 13-1 In January, Year 1, Lexor Company purchased for $85,000 a patent for a new consumer product. At the time of purchase, the legal life of the patent was 17 years. Because of the competitive nature of the product, the patent was estimated to have an economic life of 10 years. During Year 5, the product was removed from the market under governmental order because of a potential health hazard present in the product.

Compute the amount that Lexor should debit to expense in Year 5, assuming amortization is recorded at the end of each year.

Ex. 13-2 Wolfgang Corporation incurred research and development (R&D) costs in Year 10 as follows:

Material used in R&D projects	$160,000
Equipment acquired which will be used in future R&D projects	800,000
Depreciation for Year 10 on above equipment	200,000
Labor costs of employees involved in R&D projects	400,000
Consulting fees paid to outsiders for R&D projects	40,000
Indirect costs reasonably allocable to R&D projects	80,000
Fully reimbursable R&D costs	77,200

Compute the amount of R&D costs that should be reported as an expense in the income statement for Year 10.

Ex. 13-3 Early in Year 2, Adam Corporation acquired a patent with a remaining legal life of 15 years and an estimated economic life of 8 years. The cost of the patent was $12,400. Early in Year 6, the company paid $4,800 to Ted Dale, who claimed that the patent acquired in Year 2 infringed on one of his inventions.

Prepare journal entries to record the acquisition of the patent, the payment on the patent infringement suit, and the amortization for Year 6. Amortization is recorded as a credit in the Patents account.

Ex. 13-4   From the following list of accounts, prepare the intangible assets section of Rosario Company's balance sheet:

Deposits with advertising agency which will be used to promote goodwill	$ 4,500
Organization costs	5,000
Discount on bonds payable	15,500
Excess of cost over net assets of purchased subsidiary	40,000
Patents	24,400
Franchise to operate in state of Oklahoma	10,000
Marketing costs of introducing new products	15,000
Research and development costs expected to benefit future accounting periods	42,000

Ex. 13-5   On April 1, Year 10, Barry Corporation purchased the assets and assumed the liabilities of Acme Bricks, a single proprietorship, for $400,000 cash. The balance sheet of Acme Bricks on the date of purchase is shown below:

ACME BRICKS
Balance Sheet
April 1, Year 10

Assets	$480,000	Liabilities	$150,000
		Sam Summa, capital	330,000
Total assets	$480,000	Total liabilities & capital	$480,000

     Barry Corporation valued the tangible assets of Acme Bricks at $525,000, and restated the liabilities at $162,500. Included in the purchase contract is a provision that Summa cannot operate a competing business enterprise for three years; the purchase price of $400,000 included $25,000 for this provision.
     Record the purchase of Acme Bricks in the accounting records of Barry Corporation.

Ex. 13-6   The income before income taxes of Camm Company for Year 1 was $300,000, and included the following:

Extraordinary gains	$80,000
Extraordinary losses	35,000
Profit-sharing payments to employees	25,000
Amortization of goodwill	15,000
Amortization of identifiable intangible assets	17,500
Depreciation of building	44,000

     The building is worth three times as much as carrying amount, and the remaining economic life will be increased by 100% by the new owner of Camm Company. The new owner will continue the profit-sharing payments to employees. These payments are based on income before depreciation and amortization.
     Compute the normal earnings for Year 1 for purposes of measuring the possible existence of superior earnings and goodwill.

Ex. 13-7 Net income and stockholders' equity of Dover Restaurant for a three-year period are shown below:

Year	Net income	Stockholders' equity at end of year
1	$62,000	$180,000
2	75,000	200,000
3	91,000	250,000

At the end of Year 3, James Earp purchased Dover Restaurant on the following basis:

(1) 20% is considered a normal return on restaurant investments.
(2) Payment for goodwill is to be determined by capitalizing at 40% the average annual net income that is in excess of 20% of average stockholders' equity for the past three years.
(3) Net assets, which do not include any goodwill, will be recorded by Earp at the carrying amounts reported by Dover Restaurant.

Prepare a journal entry in the accounting records of Earp to record the purchase of the restaurant at the end of Year 3.

Ex. 13-8 X Company is planning to purchase Y Company. The past earnings of Y Company have averaged $20,000 a year. It is estimated that Y Company's earnings will be 20% higher in the future. Normal earnings for Y Company are $19,000 a year.
Compute the amount which X Company should pay for goodwill, assuming that:
a Goodwill is equal to the sum of superior earnings for five years.
b Goodwill is estimated by capitalization of superior earnings at 25%.

Ex. 13-9 Able Company has just acquired the net assets of Baker Company for $100,000. In acquiring Baker, the owners of Able felt that Baker had unrecorded goodwill. They decided to capitalize the estimated annual superior earnings of Baker at 20% to determine the amount of goodwill. This computation resulted in an estimate of goodwill at $10,000. A rate of 10% on net assets before recognition of goodwill was used to determine normal annual earnings of Baker, because it is the rate that is earned on net assets in the industry in which Baker operates. All other assets of Baker were recorded properly.
Compute the estimated annual earnings of Baker Company.

Ex. 13-10 On January 1, Year 1, Salina Company sold to Cruz Company a patent that had a net carrying amount in Salina's accounting records of $20,000. Cruz gave Salina an $80,000 noninterest-bearing note payable in five equal annual installments of $16,000, with the first payment due and paid on January 1, Year 2. There was no established exchange price for the patent, and the note payable has no ready market. The prevailing rate of interest for a note of this type on January 1, Year 1, was 12%. Information on present value and future amount factors is given on top of page 558.
Compute the income or loss before income taxes (rounded to the nearest dollar) that Salina should record for the years ended December 31, Year 1, and Year 2, as a result of the foregoing information. Show supporting computations.

	Periods				
	1	2	3	4	5
Present value of 1 at 12%	0.893	0.797	0.712	0.636	0.567
Present value of an ordinary annuity of 1 at 12%.	0.893	1.690	2.402	3.037	3.605
Future amount of 1 at 12%	1.120	1.254	1.405	1.574	1.762
Future amount of an ordinary annuity of 1 at 12%.	1.000	2.120	3.374	4.779	6.353

SHORT CASES FOR ANALYSIS AND DECISION

Case 13-1 On June 30, Year 1, your client, Rados Corporation, was granted two patents covering plastic cartons that it has been producing and marketing profitably for the past three years. One patent covers the manufacturing process, and the other covers the related products.

Executives of Rados inform you that the patents represent the most significant breakthrough in the industry in the past 30 years. The products have been marketed under the following registered trademarks: Safetainer, Duratainer, and Sealrite. Licenses under the patents already have been granted by your client to other manufacturers in the United States and abroad and are producing substantial royalties.

On July 1, Rados commenced patent infringement suits against several companies whose names you recognize as those of substantial and prominent competitors. Management of Rados is optimistic that these suits will result in a permanent injunction against the manufacture and sale of the infringing products, and in the collection of damages for lost profits caused by the alleged infringements.

The financial vice president of Rados has suggested that the patents be recorded at the discounted value of expected net royalty receipts.

Instructions
a Explain the meaning of *intangible assets* and *discounted value of expected net royalty receipts.* How is discounted value of royalty receipts computed?
b What basis of valuation for Rados Corporation's patents would be in accordance with generally accepted accounting principles? Give supporting reasons for this basis.
c Assuming no practical problems of implementation and ignoring generally accepted accounting principles, what is the preferable basis of valuation and amortization for patents?
d What recognition, if any, should be made of the infringement suits in the financial statements of Rados for the year ended September 30, Year 1?

Case 13-2 Happy Piston Corporation, a retail fuel distributor, has increased its annual sales volume to a level three times the annual sales of the dealership it purchased in Year 1 to begin operations.

In Year 6, the board of directors of Happy Piston Corporation received an offer to negotiate the sale of the corporation. The majority of the board wants to increase the carrying amount of goodwill in the balance sheet to reflect the larger sales volume developed through intensive promotion and the favorable market price of fuel. However, some board members prefer to eliminate goodwill from the balance sheet "to prevent possible misinterpretations." Goodwill was recorded in Year 1 in conformity with generally accepted accounting principles.

Instructions

a Define *goodwill* and list the techniques used to estimate its tentative value in negotiations to purchase a going concern. To what extent does the value of goodwill depend on sales volume?

b Why are the carrying amount and current fair value for goodwill of Happy Piston Corporation different?

c Discuss the propriety of increasing or eliminating the carrying amount of goodwill prior to negotiations for the sale of a going concern.

Case 13-3 Some years ago the annual report of Combined Communications Corporation (CCC) included the following message to stockholders:

> Because amortization of intangible assets as required by the **Accounting Principles Board Opinion No. 17** is significant to CCC's earnings and because management of CCC does not agree with the amortization requirement of **APB Opinion No. 17,** we wish to make our views known in the hopes you will then be in a better position to analyze our financial statements and the performance of the company.
>
> Intangibles represent the difference between the total amount paid in a purchase acquisition and the fair market value of the tangible assets acquired (also commonly referred to as goodwill). In the broadcasting industry, the amount paid for intangibles includes, among other things, the station's Federal Communications Commission broadcast license, its network affiliation contract, an established audience, established program format, and established advertising clients. In the newspaper industry, the amount paid for intangibles includes, among other things, the paper's established circulation lists, editorial reference library, established news development resources, community loyalty developed through editorial policies and support of local activities, and established advertising clients. The Accounting Principles Board, in issuing **APB Opinion No. 17** requiring the amortization of intangibles acquired after October 31, 1970, apparently made the assumption that purchased goodwill gradually loses its value over a period of years and established an arbitrary maximum life of 40 years.
>
> Management is in absolute disagreement with the required amortization of the intangibles related to broadcast stations and newspapers where the intangibles are clearly marketable assets which retain their value and, in many instances, increase in value over the years. We believe there is a sufficient number of sale and purchase transactions each year in the broadcast and newspaper fields to clearly demonstrate this fact. We simply cannot accept a conclusion that one rule for the amortization of purchased intangibles fits all businesses.
>
> It is management's opinion that intangibles should not be charged off (in whole or in part) until such time as it becomes apparent that there has been or will become a measurable diminution in their value. Should it become apparent in years subsequent to the acquisition that a downward adjustment is necessary, it should be the responsibility of management to determine the amount of the adjustment and the period or periods to which such adjustment should be applied. Such a determination should, of course, be subject to the approval of the certifying public accountants.

Instructions Do you agree with the management of Combined Communications Corporation? Explain your position.

Case 13-4 Canton Company is in the process of developing Novo, a revolutionary new product. A new division of the company was formed to develop, manufacture, and market Novo. As of December 31, Year 7, Novo has not been manufactured for resale; however, a prototype unit of Novo was built and is in operation.

Throughout Year 7 the new division incurred certain costs. These costs included design and engineering studies, prototype manufacturing costs, administrative expenses (including salaries of administrative personnel), and market research costs. In addition, approximately $500,000 in equipment (estimated economic life of 10 years) was purchased for use in developing and manufacturing Novo. Approximately $200,000 of this equipment was built specifically for the design development of Novo. The remaining $300,000 of equipment was used to manufacture the preproduction prototype, and will be used to manufacture Novo once it is in commercial production.

Instructions

a What are the definitions of **research** and of **development,** according to **FASB Statement No. 2?**

b Briefly indicate the practical and conceptual reasons for the conclusion reached by the Financial Accounting Standards Board on accounting and reporting practices for research and development costs.

c In accordance with **FASB Statement No. 2,** how should the various costs of Canton Company described above be reported in the financial statements for the year ended December 31, Year 7?

PROBLEMS

13-1   Alpine Street Company has provided information on intangible assets as follows:

(1) A patent was purchased from Jack Lee & Co. for $1,500,000 on January 2, Year 7. Alpine estimated the remaining economic life of the patent to be ten years. The patent was carried in the accounting records of Jack Lee & Co. at a carrying amount of $1,250,000 when it was sold to Alpine. On January 3, Year 8, Alpine, based on developments in the industry, estimated that the remaining economic life of the patent purchased on January 2, Year 7, was only six years from January 1, Year 8.

(2) In Year 8, a franchise was purchased from Gee Company for $600,000. In addition, 3% of revenue from the franchise must be paid to Gee as a royalty. Revenue from the franchise for Year 8 was $2,000,000. Alpine estimated the economic life of the franchise to be eight years, and decided to take a full year's amortization in the year of purchase.

(3) Alpine incurred research and development costs in Year 8 as follows:

Material	$ 80,000
Personnel	140,000
Indirect costs	60,000
Total research and development costs	$280,000

Alpine estimated that these costs would be recouped by December 31, Year 11.

Instructions   Prepare a working paper for the computation of the dollar amount of (1) intangible assets to be included in the balance sheet on December 31, Year 8, and (2) all expenses related to research and development and intangible assets to be included in the income statement for the year ended December 31, Year 8. Assume that amortization is recorded as a credit to each intangible asset account.

13-2 The following information was obtained from the accounting records of Marie Company and Chor Company on January 2, Year 6, in connection with a proposed merger of the two companies:

	Marie Company	Chor Company
Assets other than goodwill	$2,625,000	$1,593,000
Liabilities	975,000	720,000
Average income before income taxes for Years 1 through 5	408,000	281,400

The current fair values of assets, including goodwill, are to be determined as follows: 20% is considered a reasonable pre-tax return on net assets, excluding goodwill; average pre-tax income for Years 1 through 5 in excess of 20% on such net assets on January 2, Year 6, is to be capitalized at 25% to determine goodwill. The following adjustments to average pre-tax income are required before determination of the going-concern value of each company:

(1) Equipment of Marie Company has a current fair value which is $150,000 in excess of its carrying amount; the equipment has a remaining economic life of 10 years.
(2) At the beginning of Year 1, Chor Company debited the cost of a franchise to expense. The franchise cost $54,000 and had an estimated economic life of 10 years. The current fair value of the franchise on January 2, Year 6, was $27,000.
(3) Included in the net income of Chor Company for Years 1 through 5 are extraordinary gains of $46,500 and extraordinary losses of $99,000.

Instructions Prepare a working paper showing for each company the valuation of:
a Net assets other than goodwill
b Goodwill
c The enterprise as a whole

13-3 Research Corporation performs subcontracting work for several major aircraft manufacturers. Early in Year 3, the company purchased from Zeon Labs, Inc., an unused patent for a new type of navigational instrument. The economic life of the patent is equal to its legal life, which expires on January 1, Year 18. The company intended to incorporate the technology covered by this patent in one of its major projects after addition of several new features to the patent.

In January of Year 4, while auditing the financial statements of Research Corporation for Year 3, you find the ledger account on page 562 that summarizes costs incurred in the development of the new and improved patent for the navigational instrument.

The improved patent was ready for use on July 5, Year 3, but the new navigational instrument was not sold to aircraft manufacturers until Year 4.

Instructions
a Prepare a summary of the costs that should be included in the Patents account in accordance with generally accepted accounting principles.
b Prepare a single journal entry to eliminate the Navigational Instrument Project account and to record the items in this account in conformity with generally accepted accounting principles. Assume that the nominal accounts have not been closed for Year 3.
c Prepare a journal entry, if required, to record the amortization of the patent for Year 3. If no entry is required, explain why.

Navigational Instrument Project

Date	Explanation	Debit	Credit	Balance
Year 3				
Jan. 10	Cost of patent purchased from Zeon Labs, Inc.	60,000		60,000 dr
30	Legal costs incurred in connection with purchase of patent from Zeon Labs, Inc.	4,000		64,000 dr
June 30	Costs of improving patent:			
	Blueprints for improvements	300		64,300 dr
	Assembly and testing of proto-types and models	25,400		89,700 dr
	Other R&D costs incurred	19,300		109,000 dr
July 5	Cost of settlement of a threatened infringement suit on patent pur-chased from Zeon Labs, Inc.	5,000		114,000 dr
Dec. 31	Proceeds on sale of R&D data de-veloped in Year 3		7,500	106,500 dr
31	Royalty received on license granted to competitor to use a design for a navigational instrument		3,100	103,400 dr

13-4 Sun Belt Video operates two television stations. On August 31, Year 10, the company contracted with a film distributor for a series of films. The contract gave the company an option to run the films as follows:

40 initial weekly telecasts starting on September 1, Year 10

12 reruns of the best films during the summer of Year 11

50 more reruns during the period from September of Year 11 to August of Year 12

The company plans to run the original series during prime viewing hours, the summer reruns as a late show, and second-year reruns as a late-late show. The expected revenue from advertisers on both stations is estimated by the manager as follows:

Revenue from original 40 weeks $420,000

Revenue from 12 summer reruns. 108,000

Revenue from 50 second-year reruns (late-late shows). 72,000

The cost of the film rental rights is $240,000, which Sun Belt Video can pay in installments over a two-year period at the rate of $18,000 a month during the first year (starting on September 30, Year 10) and $3,745 a month during the second year. These payments include interest at 1% a month on the carrying amount of the outstanding liability.

Instructions

a Prepare a journal entry to record the film rental contract on August 31, Year 10, assuming that the company elects to make payments on the installment basis. Use a Discount on Contract Payable account.

b Prepare a working paper showing how you would amortize the film rental rights for each telecast over the two-year period.

    c Prepare journal entries to record:
      (1) The first payment on the contract on September 30, Year 10
      (2) Amortization of the film rental rights for the year ended December 31, Year 10 (after 17 telecasts have been run)
    d If Sun Belt Video decided in August of Year 11 not to rerun the films during the second year, what journal entry should be made at that time to write off the unamortized film rental rights?

13-5 Demand Development Company is being audited at the end of Year 1, its first year of operations. The accountant for the company recorded numerous transactions in the Intangible Assets account. You have been assigned to audit this account, which includes the following journal entries for Year 1:

Debit entries in Intangible Assets account:

Jan.	2	Incorporation fees	$ 6,500
Jan.	2	Cost of capital stock certificates (engraving, etc.)	2,100
Jan.	10	Legal fees in connection with organization of company	5,000
Mar.	1	Costs of advertising campaign during Year 1	20,000
July	1	Operating loss for first six months of Year 1	22,200
July	7	Research and development costs on abandoned projects	45,000
Aug.	1	Goodwill recorded by credit to Retained Earnings based on estimate of future earnings	50,000
Sept.	25	R&D costs of computer program for payroll system	8,000
Oct.	10	General research and development costs	40,400
Nov.	1	Purchase of patent (remaining economic life of five years from Nov. 1, Year 1)	25,200
Dec.	30	Bonus to design supervisor for "creative contribution to the product lines for Year 1"	4,800
		Total debits	$229,200

Credit entries in Intangible Assets account:

Jan.	15	Proceeds on issuance of capital stock in excess of par		$80,500
Oct.	1	Proceeds from sale of potentially patentable design of new product. The costs of developing this design were debited to R&D expense in Year 1 and exceeded $15,000	6,000	86,500
Dec.	31	Balance		$142,700

Instructions
a Prepare journal entries to correct the accounts, assuming that the nominal accounts have not been closed for Year 1. Any amount allocated to organization costs should be amortized over five years.
b Prepare the intangible assets section of the balance sheet on December 31, Year 1.

13-6 Oil Field Service Corporation is considering the acquisition of Houston Partners, Inc., on March 31, Year 4. Relevant data for Houston Partners, Inc., follow:

Net assets (stockholders' equity)	$ 749,000
Total assets in latest balance sheet	1,200,000
Pre-tax earnings for prior three fiscal years ($141,000 + $140,000 + $115,000)	396,000
Cash dividends paid during last three years	150,000

Houston Partners, Inc., has a valuable patent that had been fully amortized and will be transferred to Oil Field Service Corporation at a valuation of $126,000. Other assets have a value equal to carrying amount. The estimated remaining economic life of the patent is five years. The earnings of Houston Partners, Inc., during the next four years are expected to average 20% more than the average earnings of the past three fiscal years (before patent amortization).

Instructions Estimate the amount of goodwill under each of the following independent assumptions:

a Average estimated future pre-tax earnings are capitalized at 15% to compute the total value of Houston's net assets.

b Pre-tax earnings at the rate of 14%, based on identifiable net assets at current fair value, are considered minimal for Houston's type of business. Goodwill is estimated to be equal to average superior earnings capitalized at 20%.

c Minimum pre-tax earnings rate on identifiable net assets at current fair value is considered to be $12\frac{1}{2}\%$, and goodwill is estimated at an amount equal to estimated superior earnings for three years.

d Pre-tax earnings of $120,700 are considered normal. Goodwill is estimated to be equal to the present value of average superior earnings (before income taxes) for four years, discounted at 20%. The present value of an ordinary annuity of four $100 payments, discounted at 20%, is $258.87. (See if you can compute the amount of goodwill without knowing the present value of the four payments of $100 each.)

13-7 Pebble Manufacturing Company, a family-owned business enterprise, has not issued financial statements to the public since it was incorporated in 1970. You have been engaged to audit the financial statements of the company for the year ended December 31, 1984. Management of the company wishes to present financial statements to an investment banker in conjunction with a preliminary discussion of the possibility of issuing capital stock to the public. Management would like to report the maximum net income for 1984 permitted by generally accepted accounting principles.

This problem relates solely to your audit of the Intangible Assets account summarized below:

Debit entries in Intangible Assets account:

2/1/70 Organization costs	$ 8,000
3/1/70 Goodwill—purchased a going concern	40,000
12/31/70 Net loss incurred in development stage	55,500
7/1/74 Patent—estimated remaining economic life of 15 years	25,200
12/31/78 Goodwill—purchased a going concern	66,000
12/31/79 Non-compete agreement covering six-year period	12,000
12/31/80 Research and development costs resulting in new and improved products and processes	32,500
12/31/81 Financing costs related to five-year loan of $2 million from Rainbow Insurance Company, arranged on 12/31/81	33,000
12/31/83 Research and development costs—new products	45,000
12/31/84 Research and development costs—new processes	85,000
12/31/84 Balance	$402,200

No credit entries have been made in the Intangible Assets account since the company was organized, and no amortization has been recorded for any of the items included in the account. You ascertain that the dollar amounts for all debits to the Intangible Assets account were determined correctly. Management agreed with your suggestion that the organization costs should have been amortized over a five-year period, and that there has been no decline in the economic value of any goodwill acquired.

Instructions   (Ignore income tax considerations)

a Observing management's desire to report the maximum net income for 1984 in conformity with generally accepted accounting principles, prepare a working paper analysis of the Intangible Assets account. Any unamortized balance of an intangible asset as of December 31, 1984, should be recorded in a separate account. Use the following format (disposition of organization costs is given as an example):

Description of item	Amount recorded in Intangible Assets account	Prior period adjustment (debit)	Expense (or factory overhead) for 1984	Other accounts debited	
				Amounts	Accounts
Organization costs— should have been fully amortized prior to 1984	$8,000	$8,000			

b Prepare a single journal entry to eliminate the Intangible Assets account and to reflect properly the accounting records on December 31, 1984. The accounting records have not been closed for 1984.

13-8 Axel Aranson is investigating the possibility of buying Katie Center, a single proprietorship owned by Katie Carr. The balance sheet of Katie Center on December 31, Year 5, follows:

KATIE CENTER
Balance Sheet
December 31, Year 5

Assets		Liabilities & Proprietor's Capital	
Current assets	$191,500	Current liabilities	$160,000
Land	115,000	12% mortgage note payable	400,000
Buildings	540,000	Total liabilities	$560,000
Less: Accumulated depreciation	(50,000)		
Equipment	186,000		
Less: Accumulated depreciation	(42,500)	Katie Carr, capital	380,000
		Total liabilities & proprietor's capital	
Total assets	$940,000		$940,000

Aranson examined the foregoing balance sheet and determined that all assets are fairly stated, except that land is worth at least $195,000. An independent accountant had examined the income statements of Katie Center the last five years and reported that income, before interest on the mortgage note and income taxes, amounted to $100,000 for Year 5. The average unpaid balance of the mortgage note payable during the next four years will be $370,000. Because of an expected increase in volume, the income before interest and income taxes for each of the next four years is expected to increase at a compound rate of 10% a year. Katie Center's present facilities are sufficient to handle the expected increase in volume. Katie Carr is asking $525,000 cash for her business enterprise. Aranson considers 15% a normal rate of return (before income taxes) for an enterprise of this type.

Instructions

a Prepare an estimate of the goodwill of Katie Center on December 31, Year 5, under each of the following methods. Round estimates of expected average income before income taxes and goodwill to the ***nearest hundred dollars.***

   (1) Capitalization of the average expected superior income before income taxes over the next four years at 15%.

   (2) Purchase of expected superior income before income taxes for the next four years.

   (3) The present value of average superior income before income taxes expected over the next four years, discounted at 15%. (The present value of an ordinary annuity of four rents of 1 at 15% a year is 2.855.)

   (4) Capitalization of the first $5,000 of expected average superior income before income taxes at $12\frac{1}{2}\%$, the next $5,000 at 20%, and the balance at 25%.

b Should Aranson pay the price Katie Carr is asking? Explain.

c Suppose that Aranson's investigation indicates that Katie Center will earn an average income before income taxes of $72,000 a year for an indefinite period. What maximum price should Aranson be willing to pay for Katie Center? Prepare a journal entry to record the purchase in Aranson's accounting records (assume a single proprietorship), under the assumption that he purchased Katie Center for the maximum price you computed.

14 LONG-TERM INVESTMENTS

In Chapter 6 we discussed short-term investments, such as investments in shares of General Motors common stock or in American Telephone bonds. Such investments can be converted quickly to cash and are classified as current assets. Many business enterprises (termed *investors*) also make long-term investments in corporate securities to create close business ties with other companies (termed *investees*). These long-term investments are not current assets, because they do not represent resources available to meet working capital needs.

The basis of distinction between the asset categories of short-term investments (Chapter 6) and long-term investments lies in the nature and purpose of the investment. Investments that are readily marketable and which can be sold without disrupting business relationships or impairing the operating efficiency of the business enterprise are classified as current assets. Investments made to foster operational relationships with other enterprises are classified as long-term investments. Also, investments that do not meet the test of ready marketability are considered long-term, even if these investments do not promote business relationships. Long-term investments usually are listed below the current asset section of the balance sheet.

Objectives of long-term investments

A business enterprise may make long-term investments in the securities of other corporations for many reasons. For example, these investments may be used to create close ties to major suppliers or to retail outlets. The rights of ownership inherent in common stock investments give an investor in such securities a degree of influence or control over the management of the investee company. Thus, many enterprises use investments in common stock as a means of gaining control of a competitor, acquiring ownership of a company with a strong cash position, or diversifying by acquiring an ownership interest in investees in other industries.

Consolidated financial statements

A company that acquires a controlling interest in the common stock of another company is termed the *parent company,* and the controlled company the *subsidiary.* The investment in the common stock of the subsidiary is a long-term investment for the parent company. In addition to the separate financial statements prepared by the parent company and by the subsidiary, **consolidated financial statements** also are prepared. Consolidated financial statements ignore the legal concept that each enterprise is a separate entity and treat the parent company and its subsidiaries as a single economic entity.

Viewing both enterprises as a single economic entity is an alternative to treating the subsidiary as an investment owned by the parent company. The circumstances in which consolidated financial statements are appropriate and the manner in which they are prepared are topics discussed in **Modern Advanced Accounting** of this series.

Cost at acquisition

The cost of an investment in securities includes the purchase price plus brokerage fees, transfer taxes, and any other expenditures incurred in the transaction. If assets other than cash are given in payment for the securities and the current fair value of such noncash assets is unknown, the current market price of the securities may be used to establish the cost of the securities and the value of the noncash assets given in exchange. When neither a market price for the securities nor the current fair value of the assets given in exchange is known, accountants must rely on independent appraisals to establish values for recording the transaction.

If two or more securities are acquired for a lump sum, the total cost should be allocated among the various securities. If the various securities purchased are publicly traded, the existing market prices serve as the basis for apportionment of the total cost. This type of cost apportionment is termed **relative sales value allocation.**

Assume, for example, that X Company acquires from Y Company 100 units, of five common shares and one preferred share each, at a price of $240 a unit, when the common stock is selling for $30 and the preferred stock for $100 a share. The portion of the cost allocated to the common stock is $24,000 × 150/250, or $14,400, and the portion allocated to the preferred stock is $24,000 × 100/250, or $9,600. If only one class of the stock is publicly traded, that class usually will be recorded at its market price, and the remaining portion of the cost is considered the cost of the other class. When neither class of stock has an established market, the apportionment of the cost may have to be delayed until current fair values of the securities can be established.

ACCOUNTING FOR INVESTMENTS IN STOCKS

Measuring return on investment

What is the "return" on an investment in common stock? One point of view is that the investor's return consists of the stream of dividends received from the investment. A second point of view is that the investor's return consists of a proportionate share of the net income (minus preferred dividends, if any) of the investee, without regard to whether this income is distributed during the accounting period in the form of dividends. Supporting this second viewpoint is the fact that the earnings of the investee that are not distributed as dividends are retained by the investee, with a resultant increase in stockholders' equity. A third interpretation of the investor's return consists of the dividends received plus (or minus) the change in the market value of the investment.

Three different accounting methods exist, depending on which return an investor wishes to measure. These methods are:

1 *Cost method.* Investment income consists only of dividends received.
2 *Equity method.* Investment income consists of the investor's proportionate share of the investee's net income.
3 *Market value method.* Investment income includes dividends received and changes in the market value of the investment.

The market value method (as an alternative to the cost method) is illustrated for short-term investments in Chapter 6. However, the market value method is much less appropriate for long-term investments. By definition, long-term investments are not held to take advantage of short-term fluctuations in market prices. When an investor intends to hold an investment in securities for long periods of time, the daily changes in market price lose significance. Therefore, the cost and equity methods generally are used to account for long-term investments in common stock.

Accounting for dividends received

When an investor owns only a small portion (for example, less than 20%) of the total outstanding common stock of an investee, the investor has little or no control over the investee. In this case, the investor cannot influence the investee's dividend policy, and the only portion of the investee's income which reaches the investor is the dividends declared and paid by the investee. Thus, when the investor has little or no control over the investee, the dividends received represent the only return realized by the investor. Under these circumstances, the cost method of accounting for the investment is appropriate.

The payment of dividends on common stock is a discretionary act, requiring that the board of directors first declare the dividend. For this reason, investors should not accrue dividend revenue over a period of time as they do interest revenue on a bond. There are three acceptable alternatives for timing the recognition of dividend revenue: (1) when the dividend is declared (declaration date), (2) when the dividend "accrues" to the current stockholder even if the stock is subsequently sold (ex-dividend date), or (3) when the dividend is received (payment date). For the purpose of consistency, all illustrations in this chapter recognize dividend revenue on the date the dividend is received.

Not all dividends received represent revenue to the investor. Sometimes corporations may pay dividends in excess of net income. In such cases the amount by which the cash distribution exceeds total earnings to date is considered a return of capital, termed a *liquidating dividend,* rather than dividend revenue.

Some accountants have suggested that, from the viewpoint of any given stockholder, a liquidating dividend may be deemed to have occurred if dividends received exceed total net income earned subsequent to the date the investment was acquired. Practical application of such a concept would be difficult, because corporations do not measure net income on a daily basis, whereas the acquisition of shares of common stock by individual investors occurs throughout the year. Moreover, some large investors make a series of acquisitions of an investee's common stock without disrupting the market price of the stock. Only in very special circumstances would an investor be able to determine that a dividend received represented net income earned prior to the date of a specific acquisition of common stock.

For income tax purposes, liquidating dividends are defined with respect to the investee paying the dividend, rather than with respect to individual investors. Tax laws recognize liquidating dividends only to the extent that total dividends paid exceed total net income *over the life of the investee* paying the dividend.

Applying the cost method of accounting

When the cost method of accounting is used, the investment account is maintained in terms of the cost of the common stock acquired. Revenue is recognized only to the extent of dividends received which do not exceed the cumulative earnings from the date the common stock was acquired. Changes in the net assets of the investee are ignored unless a *significant* and *permanent* impairment of value of the investment occurs. Finally, long-term investments in marketable equity securities may be written down to a lower of cost or market as required by *FASB Statement No. 12.* The three events which may cause a departure from the cost basis are discussed below.

Liquidating Dividends   When the cost method is used, ordinary dividends received from an investee are recorded the same as dividends on any other investment. Ordinary net income and losses of the investee are recorded by the investor only when and to the extent that dividends are distributed or when realized as a gain or loss at the time the stock is sold. However, any liquidating dividends received are recorded by credits to the investment account.

To illustrate the accounting for a liquidating dividend, assume that Dunn Company acquired 15% of the common stock of Blue Company early in Year 1. During Year 1, Blue Company reported net income of

$100,000 and declared and paid a cash dividend of $150,000. Because the dividend exceeded the net income of Blue Company for the period Dunn owned Blue's common stock, Dunn should record the dividend as follows:

Journal entry for liquidating dividend

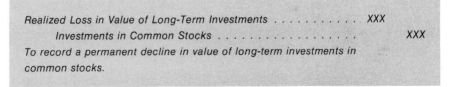

Cash ($150,000 × 15%)   22,500
*   Dividend Revenue ($100,000 × 15%) 15,000*
*   Investment in Blue Company Common Stock 7,500*
To record receipt of dividend, including a distribution of $7,500
in excess of net income since the investment was acquired.

Permanent Decline in Value of Investment Operating losses of the investee that reduce the investee's net assets substantially and seriously impair its future prospects are recorded as losses by the investor. A portion of the long-term investment has been lost, and this fact is recorded by reducing the carrying amount of the investment. The following excerpt from *FASB Statement No. 12* supports this approach:[1]

> If the decline is judged to be other than temporary, the cost basis of the individual security shall be written down to a new cost basis and the amount of the write-down shall be accounted for as a realized loss. The new cost basis shall not be changed for subsequent recoveries in market value.

The journal entry to record such a loss is:

Journal entry for permanent decline in value of long-term investments

Realized Loss in Value of Long-Term Investments   XXX
*   Investments in Common Stocks . . . .   XXX*
To record a permanent decline in value of long-term investments in
common stocks.

The realized loss is included in the computation of income before extraordinary items in the income statement.

Although *FASB Statement No. 12* gave little guidance for the determination of the existence of a permanent decline in the value of long-term investments, consideration should be given to the following:

1 The length of time the security has been owned
2 The length of time the market value of the security has been below cost and the extent of the decline
3 The financial condition and prospects of the investee
4 The financial condition of the investor
5 The materiality of the decline in value of the investment in relation to the net income and stockholders' equity of the investor

[1] *FASB Statement No. 12,* "Accounting for Certain Marketable Securities," FASB (Stamford: 1975), p. 11.

Valuation at Lower of Cost or Market Special accounting procedures are required when the aggregate market value of a noncurrent portfolio of marketable equity securities, accounted for by the **cost method,** is below cost. Such a portfolio should be valued at the lower of cost or market. However, in contrast to the valuation of the current portfolio of marketable equity securities discussed in Chapter 6, the unrealized loss in value of a noncurrent portfolio of marketable equity securities **is not included in net income.** Instead, the unrealized loss is reported as a **reduction of stockholders' equity.**[2]

To illustrate the accounting for long-term investments in marketable equity securities at lower of cost or market, assume the following: Early in Year 1, Investor Company made long-term investments of $200,000 in the common stock of publicly owned corporations. The market value of the investments was $160,000 at the end of Year 1 and $184,000 at the end of Year 2. The journal entries to value the long-term investments in marketable equity securities at lower of cost or market at the end of Year 1 and at the end of Year 2 are:

Journal entries to value long-term investments in marketable equity securities

End of Year 1

Unrealized Loss in Value of Long-Term Investments in Marketable Equity Securities	40,000	
Valuation Allowance to Reduce Long-Term Investments in Marketable Equity Securities to Market Value		40,000

To establish valuation allowance for decline in market value of long-term investments in marketable equity securities ($200,000 − $160,000 = $40,000).

End of Year 2

Valuation Allowance to Reduce Long-Term Investments in Marketable Equity Securities to Market Value	24,000	
Unrealized Loss in Value of Long-Term Investments in Marketable Equity Securities		24,000

To reduce the valuation allowance to a balance of $16,000 ($40,000 − $24,000 = $16,000) required at the end of Year 2.

When a long-term investment in marketable equity securities is sold at a price below original cost, a **realized loss** is recorded; however, no journal entry is made in the unrealized loss and valuation accounts until the end of the accounting period. For example, assume that on July 10, Year 3, Investor Company sold long-term investments which cost $100,000 for $75,000, and that at the end of Year 3 the market value of

[2] Ibid., p. 7.

the investments on hand is $90,000. The journal entry for the sale and the adjusting entry at the end of Year 3 are illustrated below:

<table>
<tr><td>Journal entries to record sale of investments and to adjust allowance at end of Year 3</td><td colspan="3">

July 10, Year 3

Cash   75,000

Realized Loss on Sale of Long-Term Investments in Market-

   able Equity Securities   25,000

       Long-Term Investments in Marketable Equity Securities   100,000

To record sale of long-term investments in marketable equity securities.

End of Year 3

Valuation Allowance to Reduce Long-Term Investments in

   Marketable Equity Securities to Market Value   6,000

      Unrealized Loss in Value of Long-Term Investments in

         Marketable Equity Securities   6,000

To reduce the valuation allowance from a balance of $16,000 to a balance of $10,000 ($100,000 − $90,000 = $10,000) required at the end of Year 3.

</td></tr>
</table>

The balance sheets of Investor Company at the end of each year include the following information:

<table>
<tr><td>Balance sheet presentation of long-term investments in marketable equity securities</td><td></td><td>Year 1</td><td>Year 2</td><td>Year 3</td></tr>
<tr><td></td><td>*Investments:*</td><td></td><td></td><td></td></tr>
<tr><td></td><td>*Long-term investments in marketable equity securities, at cost.* . . . .</td><td>$ 200,000</td><td>$ 200,000</td><td>$ 100,000</td></tr>
<tr><td></td><td>*Less: Valuation allowance to reduce long-term investments in marketable equity securities to market value.* . . .</td><td>40,000</td><td>16,000</td><td>10,000</td></tr>
<tr><td></td><td>*Long-term investments in marketable equity securities, at lower of cost or market* . . . .</td><td>$ 160,000</td><td>$ 184,000</td><td>$ 90,000</td></tr>
<tr><td></td><td>*Stockholders' equity:*</td><td></td><td></td><td></td></tr>
<tr><td></td><td>*Total paid-in capital and retained earnings* . . . .</td><td>$XXX,XXX</td><td>$XXX,XXX</td><td>$XXX,XXX</td></tr>
<tr><td></td><td>*Less: Unrealized loss in value of long-term investments in marketable equity securities.* . . . .</td><td>(40,000)</td><td>(16,000)</td><td>(10,000)</td></tr>
<tr><td></td><td>*Total stockholders' equity* . . . .</td><td>$XXX,XXX</td><td>$XXX,XXX</td><td>$XXX,XXX</td></tr>
</table>

Applying the equity method of accounting

When the investor owns enough common stock of the investee to exercise significant influence over the investee's management, the dividends paid by the investee no longer may be a good measure of the return on the investment. This is because the investor may influence the investee's dividend policy. In such a case, dividends paid by the investee may reflect the *investor's* income tax considerations and cash needs, rather than the profitability of the investment.

For example, assume that an investor owns 100% of the common stock of an investee. For two years the investee is very profitable but pays no dividends, because the investor has no need for additional cash. In the third year, the investee has a net loss but pays a large cash dividend. It would be misleading for the investor to report no investment income while the investee was operating profitably, and then to show large investment income in a year when the investee operated at a loss.

The investee need not be fully owned for the investor to have a significant degree of influence. When the common stock of the investee is widely held, an investor with much less than 50% of the common stock may have effective influence over the investee, because it is doubtful that the remaining outstanding shares will vote as an organized block.

When the investor has a significant degree of influence over the investee, the equity method of accounting more fairly presents the benefits accruing to the investor than does the cost method. When the investor has little or no influence over the investee, the benefits received by the investor may be limited to the dividends received, indicating the cost method of accounting to be more appropriate. The key criterion in selecting between the methods is the *degree of influence* the investor is able to exercise over the investee.

To achieve a degree of uniformity in accounting practice, the Accounting Principles Board took the position in *Opinion No. 18* that "an investment (direct or indirect) of 20% or more of the voting stock of an investee should lead to a presumption that in absence of evidence to the contrary an investor has the ability to exercise significant influence over an investee."[3] Thus, investments representing 20% or more of the voting stock usually are accounted for by the equity method of accounting. However, if the investor owns 20% or more of the voting stock but is unable to exercise significant influence over the investee, use of the cost method would be required. Investments of less than 20% usually are accounted for by the cost method of accounting, unless clear-cut ability to influence the operating and financial policies of the investee can be demonstrated. Investments in preferred

---

[3] *APB Opinion No. 18*, "The Equity Method of Accounting for Investments in Common Stock," AICPA (New York: 1971), p. 355. See also *FASB Statement No. 35*, "Criteria for Applying the Equity Method . . .," FASB (Stamford: 1981).

stock should be accounted for by the cost method, because preferred stockholders usually do not have either voting rights or a residual equity in net income.

When the equity method of accounting is used, an investment in common stock initially is recorded at the cost of the stock acquired, but is adjusted for changes in the net assets of the investee subsequent to acquisition. The investor's proportionate share of the investee's net income is recorded as investment income, causing an increase in the investment account. If the investee's net income includes extraordinary items, the investor should record its share of such items as extraordinary (if material in amount to the investor), rather than as ordinary investment income. Dividends paid by the investee are recorded by the investor as a conversion of the investment to cash, causing the investment account to decrease.

Illustration of Equity Method of Accounting   To illustrate the equity method of accounting, assume that Investor Company purchased 40% of the common stock of Lee Company for $300,000, which corresponded to the underlying carrying amounts of Lee's net assets. During the subsequent accounting period, Lee reported net income of $70,000 (including a $10,000 extraordinary gain) and paid dividends of $30,000. Investor Company accounts for its investment in Lee Company as follows:

Investment in Lee Company Common Stock	*300,000*	
Cash		*300,000*
To record acquisition of 40% of the common stock of Lee Company at carrying amount.		
Investment in Lee Company Common Stock	*28,000*	
Investment Income (ordinary)		*24,000*
Investment Income (extraordinary)		*4,000*
To record 40% of net income of Lee Company ($60,000 × 40% = $24,000; $10,000 × 40% = $4,000).		
Cash	*12,000*	
Investment in Lee Company Common Stock		*12,000*
To record dividends received from Lee Company ($30,000 × 40% = $12,000).		

Journal entries for equity method of accounting

Note that the net effect of Investor's accounting for Lee's net income and dividends was to increase the investment account by $16,000. This corresponds to 40% of the increase in Lee's net assets during the period [($70,000 − $30,000) × 40% = $16,000].

Special Problems in the Application of Equity Method   Two problems often arise in the application of the equity method of accounting. First, intercompany profits and losses resulting from transactions between the investor and the investee must be eliminated until realized by a transaction with an unaffiliated entity. This special problem is discussed in **Modern Advanced Accounting** of this series. Second, when the acquisition cost of an investment differs from the carrying amount of the underlying net assets, adjustments may have to be made to the investment income recorded by the investor.

Cost in Excess of Equity Acquired   Often an investor will pay more than the underlying equity of an investment because current fair values of the investee's assets may be larger than their carrying amounts, or because the investee has unrecorded goodwill. In either case, this excess of cost over the underlying equity will benefit the investor only over the economic lives of the undervalued (or unrecorded) assets.

To the extent that the excess of cost over the underlying equity was paid to acquire an interest in specific undervalued assets, this amount should be amortized over the economic lives of those assets. The journal entry to reflect the amortization is as follows:

Journal entry for amortization of excess of cost over equity acquired

Investment Income (ordinary) XXX
*   Investment in Investee Company Common Stock . . . .   XXX*
To adjust investment income for amortization of excess of cost over
underlying equity of Investee's net assets.

To the extent that the excess cost was incurred because of implied goodwill, the amount should be amortized over the estimated economic life of the goodwill. The Accounting Principles Board took the position that amounts paid for goodwill should be amortized over a period of not more than 40 years.[4] If the excess of the cost over the underlying equity is small, it usually is amortized as goodwill, rather than allocated to specific assets.

Cost Less than Equity Acquired   In some cases, an investor may acquire an investment in common stock at a cost less than the underlying equity. In this event, it should be assumed that specific assets of the investee are overvalued. If these assets have limited economic lives, the investor allocates the excess of the underlying equity over cost to investment income over the economic lives of the assets. The journal entry to record this amortization is given on top of page 577.

[4] *APB Opinion No. 17,* "Intangible Assets," AICPA (New York: 1970), p. 340.

Investment in Investee Company Common Stock XXX
    Investment Income (ordinary) XXX
To adjust investment income for amortization of excess of underlying
equity of Investee's net assets over cost.

Note that this adjustment **increases** investment income. The rationale for this action is that the investee's reported net income is understated, because the investee has recorded depreciation or amortization based on overstated asset values.

Summary of Procedures under the Equity Method of Accounting   Accounting procedures under the equity method may be summarized as follows:

1 The investment initially is recorded at cost.

2 The investor subsequently records its proportionate share of the investee's net income (after elimination of intercompany profits) by a debit to the investment account and a credit to Investment Income. In event of a loss, Investment Loss is debited and the investment account is credited.

3 The investor views its share of dividends paid by the investee as a conversion of the investment to cash. Thus, the investor debits Cash and credits the investment account.

4 The investor adjusts the recorded amount of investment income or loss by the amortization of any excess of cost over the underlying equity associated with depreciable assets or goodwill. This adjustment consists of a debit to Investment Income (or Loss) and a credit to the investment account.

5 The investor adjusts the recorded amount of investment income or loss by the amortization of any excess of the underlying equity over cost by a debit to the investment account and a credit to Investment Income (or Loss).

Comparative illustration of the cost and equity methods of accounting

To illustrate the differences in the cost and equity methods, assume that on January 2 of the current year Investor Company acquired 4,000 shares (20%) of the common stock of Investee Company for $1,000,000. At the date of acquisition, the carrying amount of Investee Company's net assets was $4,550,000. Investor was willing to pay more than the underlying equity for the investment because it was estimated that Investee owned land worth $100,000 more than its carrying amount, depreciable plant assets worth $150,000 more than their carrying amount, and enough goodwill to make a 20% interest in Investee Company worth the $1,000,000 cost.

The excess of the cost of the investment over the underlying equity is analyzed on top of page 578.

Cost of investment	$1,000,000
Underlying equity ($4,550,000 × 20%).	910,000
Excess of cost over underlying equity acquired	$ 90,000
Composition of excess:	
20% interest in undervalued land ($100,000 × 20%)	$ 20,000
20% interest in undervalued depreciable plant assets ($150,000 × 20%)	30,000
Implied goodwill ($90,000 − $20,000 − $30,000)	40,000
Excess of cost over underlying equity acquired	$ 90,000

The undervalued depreciable plant assets have an average remaining economic life of 10 years, and Investor Company's policy with respect to goodwill is to amortize it over 40 years.

During the current year, Investee Company reported net income of $430,000, after an extraordinary loss of $50,000, and declared and paid dividends of $200,000 at year-end. Investor's accounting for its investment in Investee during the year is illustrated on page 579 under the cost and equity methods of accounting.

Note that no adjustment is made under either the cost or the equity method for the $20,000 excess of cost over the underlying equity representing Investor's 20% interest in Investee's undervalued land. This is because land is not depreciated. The results for the current year are illustrated below for both methods of accounting:

	Cost method of accounting	Equity method of accounting
Investment in common stock of Investee Company (ending balance).	$1,000,000	$1,042,000
Investment income (loss) recognized by Investor Company:		
Ordinary income	$ 40,000	$ 92,000
Extraordinary loss		$ (10,000)

ACCOUNTING FOR INVESTMENTS IN BONDS

A bond contract represents a promise to pay a sum of money at maturity and a series of interest payments during the term of the contract. Investors acquire corporate bonds to earn a return on investment. The effective rate of return (yield) on bonds to investors is determined by the price investors pay for the securities (because the terms of the contract are fixed. The yield on the bonds to investors may differ from the effective interest cost to the borrower because the bonds may have been issued at an earlier date at a different price.

INVESTOR COMPANY
Comparison of Cost and Equity Methods of Accounting
For Current Year

Date	Explanation	Cost Method (Investor assumed to have no influence over Investee)	Equity Method (Investor assumed to have influence over Investee)

Jan. 2	To record acquisition of 4,000 shares of Investee Company's common stock	Investment in Common Stock of Investee Company ... 1,000,000
		  Cash ... 1,000,000
			Investment in Common stock of Investee Company ... 1,000,000
			  Cash ... 1,000,000

Dec. 31	To record receipt of dividend of $40,000 from Investee Company ($200,000 × 20% = $40,000).	Cash ... 40,000
		  Dividend Revenue ... 40,000
			Cash ... 40,000
			  Investment in Common Stock of Investee Company ... 40,000

31	To record $86,000 share of Investee Company's net income ($430,000 × 20% = $86,000) including $10,000 share of extraordinary loss ($50,000 × 20% = $10,000).	(No journal entry)	Investment Loss (extraordinary) ... 10,000 Investment in Common Stock of Investee Company ... 86,000 Investment Income (ordinary) ... 96,000
31	To amortize a portion of the excess of investment cost over the underlying equity, as follows: Depreciable plant assets: $30,000 ÷ 10 years ... $3,000 Goodwill: $40,000 ÷ 40 years ... 1,000 Total amortization ... $4,000	(No journal entry)	Investment Income (ordinary) ... 4,000 Investment in Common Stock of Investee Company ... 4,000

Computation of purchase price of bonds

The cost of an investment in bonds is the present value of the future money receipts promised in the bond contract, measured in terms of the market rate of interest prevailing at the time of investment. The stated (coupon) rate of interest in the bond contract measures the cash to be received semiannually by the investor. If the rate of return demanded by investors is exactly equal to the coupon rate, the bond can be acquired at the face amount. If the market rate of interest exceeds the coupon rate, the bond can be acquired at a *discount,* because the investor is demanding a higher return than the bond contract offers; therefore, to equate the yield on the bond with the market rate of interest, the bond is acquired at a price below face amount. If the market rate of interest is *below* the coupon rate, the investor will be willing to pay a *premium* for the bond, that is, a price above face amount.

To illustrate the computation of the purchase price of bonds, assume that $200,000 of 7% bonds maturing in 15 years are purchased by Kane Company to yield 8% compounded semiannually. The bonds pay interest semiannually starting six months from date of purchase. Because the market rate of interest exceeds the coupon rate, the bonds are purchased at a discount, as shown below (using the Appendix at the end of the book):

Computation of purchase price of bonds issued at a *discount*

Present value of $200,000 discounted at 4% for 30 six-month periods:
$200,000 × 0.308319 . . . . $ 61,664
Add: Present value of ordinary annuity of 30 rents of $7,000 (semi-annual interest payments) discounted at 4%: $7,000 × 17.292033   121,044
Purchase price of bonds (discount of $17,292). $182,708*

* Alternative computation: $200,000 − ($1,000 semiannual interest "deficiency" × 17.292033) = $182,708.

If the market rate of interest was only 6% compounded semiannually, the bonds paying semiannual interest at 7% a year would be purchased at a premium, as shown below:

Computation of purchase price of bonds issued at a *premium*

Present value of $200,000 discounted at 3% for 30 six-month periods:
$200,000 × 0.411987 . . . . $ 82,397
Add: Present value of ordinary annuity of 30 rents of $7,000 discounted at 3%: $7,000 × 19.600441   137,203
Purchase price of bonds (premium of $19,600) $219,600*

* Alternative computation: $200,000 + ($1,000 semiannual "extra" interest × 19.600441) = $219,600.

Acquisition between interest dates

Interest on a bond contract accrues with the passage of time in accordance with the provisions of the contract. The issuing corporation pays the contractual rate of interest on the stated day to the investor owning the bond on that day. The investor who acquires a bond between interest dates must pay the owner the market price of the bond plus the interest accrued since the last interest payment. The investor is paying the owner of the bond the interest applicable to the first portion of the interest period and will in turn collect that portion plus the additional interest earned by holding the bond to the next interest payment date.

Illustration On July 1, an investor acquired 10 bonds of Ray Company, which had been issued several years ago. The bond contract provides for interest at 8% a year, payable semiannually on April 1 and October 1. The market rate of interest is higher than 8% at the present time, and the bonds are currently quoted at $97\frac{3}{4}$ plus accrued interest for three months. The journal entry for the investor to record the acquisition of the 10 bonds is:

<table>
<tr><td>Investor's journal entry to record acquisition of bonds between interest dates</td><td>Investment in Ray Company Bonds. . . . .</td><td>9,775</td><td></td></tr>
<tr><td></td><td>Accrued Interest Receivable ($10,000 × 8% × $\frac{3}{12}$) . . . .</td><td>200</td><td></td></tr>
<tr><td></td><td>   Cash . . . .</td><td></td><td>9,975</td></tr>
<tr><td></td><td colspan="3">To record acquisition of 10 bonds plus accrued interest of $200 for three months.</td></tr>
</table>

Discount and premium on investments in bonds

On the date of acquisition of bonds, the investment account usually is debited for the cost of acquiring the bonds, including brokerage and other fees, but excluding the accrued interest. The use of a separate discount or premium account as a valuation account is acceptable procedure; however, it seldom is used. The subsequent treatment of the investment might conceivably be handled in one of three ways: (1) The investment might be carried at cost, ignoring the **accumulation** of discount or **amortization** of premium; (2) the investment account might be revalued periodically to reflect market value changes; or (3) the discount or premium might be accumulated or amortized to reflect the change in the carrying amount of the bonds based on the effective rate of interest prevailing at the time of acquisition.

    The first alternative (the cost basis) is used primarily in accounting for short-term bond investments, as discussed in Chapter 6, for convertible bonds, and for other bonds for which the discount or premium is insignificant. The discount or premium on convertible bonds seldom is related to the level of interest rates, but rather reflects the effect of the price of the security to which the bond is convertible. These securities are subject to wide price movements related to changes in the market price of common stocks; therefore, the amortization of premium or accumulation of discount does not seem appropriate.

The second alternative (valuation at market) is not in accord with the present interpretation of the realization principle or the concept of conservatism, especially during periods of rising bond prices. Changes in market prices of bonds held as long-term investments may be of less significance to the investor than changes in prices of short-term investments, because the long-term investments frequently are held to maturity, at which time market price and face amount of the bonds are equal. When the investment in bonds is in jeopardy because of serious cash shortages of the issuing corporation, it generally is acceptable to write the investment down to its expected net realizable value and to recognize a loss.

The third alternative (the systematic accumulation and amortization) is the preferred treatment for long-term investments in bonds. This approach recognizes that the interest revenue represented by the discount, or the reduction in interest revenue represented by the premium, does not come into being at maturity of the bonds, but accrues over the term of the bonds. The interest revenue should be consistent with the yield on the bonds at the date of acquisition. This method is consistent with the principle that requires assets to be recorded at cost.

Interest revenue

The periodic interest payments provided for in a bond contract represent the total interest revenue to an investor holding a bond to maturity only if the investor acquired the bond at its face amount. If an investor acquires a bond at a premium, the amount received on maturity of the bond will be less than the amount of the initial investment, thus reducing the cumulative interest revenue by the amount of the premium. Similarly, if the bond is acquired at a discount, the amount received at maturity will be larger than the initial investment, thereby increasing the cumulative interest revenue by the amount of the discount.

When an investor intends to hold bonds to maturity, there is little logic in treating the discount or premium as a gain or loss occurring on the maturity date. Rather, the increase in the carrying amount of the bonds as a discount disappears should be viewed as part of the revenue accruing to the investor over the entire period the bonds are owned. Similarly, the decrease in value when a premium disappears is a cost the investor is willing to incur over the entire holding period to receive periodic interest payments higher than the market rate prevailing when the bonds were acquired. Thus, the amount of the discount or premium is viewed as an integral part of the periodic interest revenue earned by the investor. The accumulation of a discount increases periodic interest revenue, and the amortization of a premium decreases periodic interest revenue.

An extreme illustration of this concept has occurred for certain government savings bonds which provided no periodic interest payments at all. Instead, these bonds were issued at a large discount, and the gradual growth in the redemption value of the bonds toward their maturity value (accumulation of the discount) was the investor's only return. Although the investor received no cash proceeds until the bonds matured, interest revenue was being earned. To measure the periodic interest revenue, the accumulation of the discount had to be recognized as interest revenue over the term of the bonds.

Methods of discount accumulation or premium amortization

The methods of amortization for bond discount and bond premium by the issuer are discussed in Chapter 15. These methods present precisely the same problem for the investor as for the issuer. The purpose of accumulating the discount or amortizing the premium is to reflect accurately the interest revenue derived from the investment in bonds.

Interest Method   The *interest method* produces a constant rate of return on the investment in bonds. That is, the periodic interest revenue always represents the same percentage return on the carrying amount of the investment. Thus, when a discount is being accumulated and the investment account is increasing, the interest revenue recognized each interest period also increases. This is accomplished by accumulating an ever-increasing portion of the discount each period. To apply the method, the interest revenue is computed for each interest period by multiplying the balance of the investment account by the effective interest rate at the time the investment was made. The accumulation of the discount (or amortization of the premium) thus is the difference between the periodic cash receipt and the interest revenue for the period computed by the effective rate of interest.

Straight-Line Method   Under the *straight-line method,* the discount or premium is spread uniformly over the term of the bonds. Although the bonds may be sold by the investor or redeemed by the issuer prior to maturity, the accumulation or amortization always *is based on the years remaining to maturity.* The straight-line method is simple to apply and avoids the necessity for determining the yield rate. The primary objection to the straight-line method is that it produces a constant amount of interest revenue each accounting period, which results in an uneven rate of return on the investment.

Illustration   The computation of periodic discount to be accumulated or premium to be amortized and the related journal entries will be illus-

trated with the examples for Kane Company given on page 580. The
Kane Company examples involved (1) the acquisition of $200,000 face
amount of 7% bonds maturing in 15 years (or 30 semiannual periods) to
yield 8% compounded semiannually, and (2) the acquisition of the same
bonds to yield 6% compounded semiannually. The journal entries to
record the investment, receipt of interest for the first year, and the related accumulation or amortization under the interest method and the
straight-line method are presented below and on page 585. (All computations are rounded to the nearest dollar.)

Journal entries
for acquisition
of bonds and
accumulation of
discount or amortization
of premium

KANE COMPANY
Journal Entries

	Interest method		Straight-line method	
(1) *Bonds acquired to yield 8% compounded semiannually:*				
Investment in 7% Bonds	182,708		182,708	
Cash		182,708		182,708
To record acquisition of bonds at a discount of $17,292 to be accumulated over 30 six-month periods.				
Cash	7,000		7,000	
Investment in 7% Bonds	308		576	
Interest Revenue		7,308		7,576
To record receipt of interest at the end of the first six-month period: $200,000 \times 7\% \times \frac{1}{2} = \$7,000.$ *Accumulation of discount:* *Interest method:* ($182,708 \times 4\%) - \$7,000 = \$308.$ *Straight-line method:* $17,292 \div 30 = \$576.$				
Cash	7,000		7,000	
Investment in 7% Bonds	321		576	
Interest Revenue		7,321		7,576
To record receipt of interest at the end of the second six-month period: $200,000 \times 7\% + \frac{1}{2} = \$7,000.$ *Accumulation of discount:* *Interest method:* [($182,708 + \$308) \times 4\%] - \$7,000 = \$321.$ *Straight-line method:* $17,292 \div 30 = \$576.$				

(cont.)

KANE COMPANY
Journal Entries (concluded)

	Interest method		Straight-line method	
(2) Bonds acquired to yield 6% compounded semiannually:				
Investment in 7% Bonds	219,600		219,600	
Cash		219,600		219,600
To record acquisition of bonds at a premium of $19,600 to be amortized over 30 six-month periods.				
Cash	7,000		7,000	
Investment in 7% Bonds		412		653
Interest Revenue		6,588		6,347
To record receipt of interest at the end of the first six-month period: $200,000 × 7% × ½ = $7,000.				
Amortization of premium:				
Interest method: $7,000 − ($219,600 × 3%) = $412.				
Straight-line method: $19,600 ÷ 30 = $653.				
Cash	7,000		7,000	
Investment in 7% Bonds		424		653
Interest Revenue		6,576		6,347
To record receipt of interest at the end of the second six-month period: $200,000 × 7% × ½ = $7,000.				
Amortization of premium:				
Interest method: $7,000 − [($219,600 − $412) × 3%] = $424.				
Straight-line method: $19,600 ÷ 30 = $653.				

When the bonds are acquired at a discount and the interest method of accumulation is used, the investment account is increased to $183,016 at the end of the first six-month period; therefore, interest revenue for the second six-month period is $7,321 ($183,016 × 4% = $7,321), which required $321 of the discount to be accumulated.

When the bonds are acquired at a premium and the interest method of amortization is used, the investment account is reduced to $219,188 at the end of the first six-month period; therefore, interest revenue for the second six-month period is $6,576 ($219,188 × 3% = $6,576), which required $424 of the premium to be amortized.

Interest revenue on bond investments, just as interest revenue on any other investment, is accrued only at significant dates. The significant dates are: (1) interest payment dates, (2) the end of the investor's accounting period, and (3) the time of any transaction involving the particular investment which does not coincide with a regular interest payment date. The interest revenue on bond investments must be accrued, therefore, at the end of the accounting period and before the bonds are sold. The discount also should be accumulated or the premium amortized in accordance with whatever method of accumulation or amortization is used.

SPECIAL PROBLEMS IN ACCOUNTING FOR INVESTMENTS IN SECURITIES

Cost identification

Investments in securities may pose a problem as to which costs should be offset against revenue in the period of sale. For example, assume that an investor acquires 1,000 shares of Z Company common stock at a price of $80 a share, and 1,000 shares at $90 a share. Several years later, the investor sells 1,000 shares of Z Company common stock for $84 a share. Should the investor recognize a $4,000 gain or a $6,000 loss?

The answer to this question requires making a **cost flow assumption,** as with inventories. Because securities usually are identified by a certificate number, it would be possible to use specific identification of stock certificates to establish the cost of the 1,000 shares sold. However, an alternative cost flow assumption might be adopted. The alternative methods of cost flow include: (1) fifo—the first shares acquired are assumed to be the first ones sold; (2) lifo—the last shares acquired are assumed to be the first ones sold; and (3) weighted-average cost—each share is assigned the same cost basis.

Income tax rules require the use of either the specific identification method or the fifo method to measure **taxable gain or loss.** Neither lifo nor weighted-average cost is an acceptable method for income tax purposes. The specific identification method usually is more advantageous for income tax purposes, because it allows the investor to select for sale those securities which will lead to the most desirable tax consequences. For financial accounting purposes, most investors use the same method of cost selection used for income tax purposes, to simplify record keeping. From a theoretical viewpoint, however, weighted average is the only cost flow assumption that recognizes the economic equivalence of identical securities. In our illustration of successive purchases of the common stock of Z Company at different prices, it is undeniable that each share of Z Company common stock owned has exactly the same economic value regardless of the price paid to acquire it. The weighted-average cost flow asumption recognizes the economic reality that, except for income tax purposes, it makes no difference which 1,000-share certificate is sold and which is retained.

Accounting for stock dividends and stock splits

Stock dividends and stock splits do not result in revenue to investors. The income tax regulations are in agreement with financial accounting procedures on this point.[5]

> Since a shareholder's interest in the corporation remains unchanged by a stock dividend or split-up except as to the number of share units constituting such interest, the cost of the shares previously held should be allocated equitably to the total shares held after receipt of the stock dividend or split-up. When any shares are later disposed of, a gain or loss should be determined on the basis of the adjusted cost per share.

The accounting procedure of the investor to record receipt of additional shares from a stock dividend or stock split usually is confined to a memorandum entry which indicates the number of shares of stock received and the new cost per share.

Property dividends

When a corporation distributes a dividend in the form of merchandise, securities of other corporations, or other noncash assets, the investor records the property received at its current fair value. Income tax regulations also require the use of current fair value for property dividends received.

Stock purchase warrants and stock rights

A **stock warrant** is a certificate issued by a corporation conveying to the holder **rights** to purchase shares of its stock at a specified price within a specified time period. A single right attaches to each share of outstanding stock, and several rights usually are required to purchase one new share at the stipulated price. For example, when rights are issued, the owner of 100 shares of common stock will receive a warrant representing 100 rights and specifying the number of rights required to purchase one new share of stock. The term of these rights usually is limited to a few weeks. The rights must be exercised or sold before the expiration date or they become worthless.

Accounting for Stock Warrants Acquired by Purchase The accounting problems involved when an investor buys warrants are similar to those relating to the acquisition of any security. The purchase price, plus brokerage fees and other acquisition costs, is debited to Investment in Warrants, and the credit is to Cash. When warrants are acquired as a part of a package, the total cost must be allocated to the various securities included in the package, based on relative market values.

When the warrants are used to acquire stock, the initial cost of the

---

[5] *Accounting Research and Terminology Bulletins—Final Edition,* AICPA (New York: 1961), chap. 7b, p. 51.

warrants used plus the cash paid is the cost of the stock. The Investment in Stock account is debited; Cash and Investment in Warrants are credited. If the market price of the stock differs from this combined cost, this fact is ignored until the stock is sold, at which time a gain or loss is recorded.

Accounting for Stock Rights   Stock rights are distributed to the stockholders of a corporation in proportion to their holdings. The receipt of stock rights can be compared to the receipt of a stock dividend. The corporation has not distributed any assets; instead, the way has been opened for an additional investment by the present stockholders. Until the stockholders elect to exercise or sell their rights, their investment in the corporation is represented by (1) shares of stock that have been purchased, and (2) the right to acquire additional shares of stock at a price below the current market price. The cost of the original investment consists of the cost of the shares and the rights; therefore, the cost of the original investment is apportioned between these two parts of the investment on the basis of relative market values. The stock will trade in the market on a "rights-on" basis until the ex-rights date, at which time the stock sells "ex-rights," and the warrants for the rights have a market of their own. Relative market value allocation may be used to apportion the cost between the shares of stock and the stock rights as follows:

Allocation of cost of stock investment to stock rights

$$\begin{pmatrix} \text{Cost assigned} \\ \text{to stock rights} \end{pmatrix} = \begin{pmatrix} \text{cost of original} \\ \text{investment in stock} \end{pmatrix} \times \left(\frac{\text{market value of one right}}{\begin{array}{c} \text{market value} \quad \text{market} \\ \text{of one share of} + \text{value of} \\ \text{stock ex-rights} \quad \text{one right} \end{array}} \right)$$

Convertible securities

An investor may invest in bonds or preferred stocks that are convertible to the common stock of the investee at the option of the investor. The characteristics of convertible securities are discussed in Chapters 15 and 17. At this point, we shall consider the action to be taken by investors who exercise the conversion option and receive common stock in exchange for convertible bonds or convertible preferred stock.

The market value of the common stock received may differ materially from the carrying amount of the converted securities. However, it is virtually universal practice to assign the carrying amount of the convertible security to the common stock acquired in exchange. Thus, *no gain or loss is recognized at the time of conversion.* This treatment is supported by the theoretical argument that investors contemplate conversion when they acquire a convertible security. Thus, no gain or loss is recognized until the common stock acquired by conversion is sold.

The following journal entry illustrates the conversion of an investment in Quincy Company bonds with a carrying amount of $96,720 to Quincy's common stock with a current market value of $120,000:

<table>
<tr><td style="vertical-align: top">Journal entry
for conversion
of bonds to
common stock</td><td>Investment in Quincy Company Common Stock 96,720
    Investment in Quincy Company Convertible Bonds. . . .   96,720
To record conversion of bonds to common stock.</td></tr>
</table>

OTHER LONG-TERM INVESTMENTS

Investments in special-purpose funds

Occasionally, a corporation accumulates a fund of cash, usually invested temporarily in securities, for a special purpose. The creation of the fund may be by voluntary action on the part of the management, or it may be required by contract. Funds generally are created to pay a liability or to acquire specific assets. In general, funds are treated as long-term investments only when they are established by contract, and the money invested is not available to management for general operating needs. A fund is classified as a current asset if it is created voluntarily and can be used for operating purposes.

Accounting for funds

The transactions which must be accounted for in connection with fund accumulation and administration are: (1) the transfer of assets to the fund, (2) the investment of the assets in internally managed funds, (3) the collection of revenue and payment of expenses if the fund is managed internally, and (4) the use of fund resources for the intended purpose.

There are two methods of handling funds: (1) The fund may be established and operated internally; or (2) the assets may be deposited with a trustee who is charged with receiving the deposit, investing the assets, collecting the revenue, paying the expenses, and accounting to the responsible officials for cash receipts and payments.

Typically, the funds which are created voluntarily are operated internally, whereas those created by contract are handled by a trustee. The periodic deposit to the fund generally is set in advance. It may be related to the level of operations, or it may be set either as a stated amount each period or as a stated amount less earnings on fund assets for the period. The method of determining the amount and time for the deposit generally can be found by referring to the document authorizing the establishment of the fund. In cases when the fund is committed irrevocably for the purpose designated, and cash actually is deposited with a trustee, the fund itself may not appear among the assets of the business enterprise, and the liability which is to be paid from fund assets may be excluded from the liabilities. This procedure is used most often when the liability does not exceed the fund balance, which means that the enterprise has no liability other than that for the periodic deposits stipulated in the contract. Most employee pension and benefit plans are of this type.

Bond sinking funds usually are included under long-term investments, and bonds outstanding are shown as a long-term liability. The sinking fund should not be offset against the bond liability. A sinking fund and other similar funds usually are included in the balance sheet as an asset even though they are held by trustees.

One of the most common methods of accumulating a sinking fund is to deposit fixed amounts at periodic intervals. The periodic deposit is computed by use of an amount of annuity formula described in Chapter 5.

The transactions relating to the purchase and sale of securities, and the accrual and collection of revenue for the sinking fund, are accounted for in the same manner in which transactions in the general Investments account are recorded.

Cash surrender value of life insurance policies

When a business enterprise is dependent on certain officers for direction and management, life insurance policies may be purchased on the lives of these officers with the enterprise named as the beneficiary. Certain types of insurance policies combine a savings program and an insurance plan. When these are purchased, the savings portion of the insurance premium is reported in the balance sheet as an investment.

The savings part of a life insurance policy is referred to as the *cash surrender value* of the policy. This is the amount the enterprise would receive in the event that the policy were canceled; this same amount also can be used as collateral for a loan.

The following data represent the first four years' experience of White Company, which has a $100,000 life insurance policy on one of its officers:

	Year	Gross premium	Cash value increase	Insurance expense
Breakdown of gross life insurance premium	1	$3,040	$ 30	$3,010
	2	3,040	250	2,790
	3	3,040	250	2,790
	4	3,040	260	2,780

From these limited data, we can readily see the increase in the asset and the decreasing annual cost of life insurance. The journal entries for the first two years are as follows:

Journal entries
for payment
of life insurance
premiums for first
two years

Year 1	Insurance Expense....................	3,010	
	Cash Surrender Value of Life Insurance Policy.....	30	
	Cash.............................		3,040
	To record the payment of life insurance premium.		
Year 2	Insurance Expense....................	2,790	
	Cash Surrender Value of Life Insurance Policy.....	250	
	Cash.............................		3,040
	To record the payment of life insurance premium.		

In the event of death of the insured officer, White Company would collect the face amount of the insurance policy. The journal entry to record this event, assuming death occurred early in the third year, would be as follows:

Journal entry for receipt
of proceeds of life
insurance policy

Year 3	Cash 100,000	
	Gain on Settlement of Life Insurance Policy..	99,720
	Cash Surrender Value of Life Insurance Policy.	280
	To record collection of life insurance proceeds.	

For financial accounting purposes, the gain is included in income before extraordinary items in the income statement. For income tax purposes, the premiums paid on life insurance policies in which the business enterprise is the beneficiary are not deductible. Similarly, the gain on the settlement upon the death of the insured party is not taxable income.

Presentation in financial statements

Long-term investments that cannot be sold without impairing business relationships are classified as noncurrent assets, immediately following current assets.

Dividends and interest revenue normally are listed under the caption Other Revenue and are included in the determination of income before extraordinary items. When the equity method of accounting is used, ordinary investment income (or loss) also is included in Other Revenue, but the investor's share of any material extraordinary item of the investee retains its extraordinary nature and is classified as an extraordinary item by the investor. Because of the nature of long-term investments, gains and losses from sales occur relatively infrequently. A business enterprise with numerous long-term investments can expect occasional gains and losses from sales of these investments and generally should include such gains and losses in income before extraordinary items, under the caption of Other Revenue.

REVIEW QUESTIONS

1 Distinguish between the asset categories of short-term investments and long-term investments. Could the same securities constitute short-term investments for one business enterprise and long-term investments to another? Explain.

2 What is the **cost** of a security acquired for cash? Acquired in exchange for assets for which current fair value is not readily determinable? Acquired as part of a group purchase?

3 Explain three concepts of the "return on investment" to an investor in common stock and identify the appropriate accounting method for each concept.

4 Why should dividend revenue not be accrued by an investor as is interest revenue? What are the alternatives for the timing of dividend revenue?

5 An investor acquired 1,000 shares of E Company capital stock on May 15 for $75 a share when the carrying amount of E Company stock was composed of the following:

Capital stock, $10 par	$1,000,000
Paid-in capital in excess of par	2,000,000
Retained earnings	4,500,000
Total stockholders' equity	$7,500,000

On May 16, E Company declared a dividend of $3 a share. What was the nature of this distribution from the point of view of the investor? Of E Company? What was the legal interpretation of this distribution to the investor?

6 Distinguish between the **cost** and **equity** methods of accounting for a long-term investment in common stock. When is each appropriate?

7 Identify three events that necessitate a write-down of a long-term investment under the cost method of accounting.

8 How can the acquisition price of an investment affect subsequent investment income under the equity method of accounting?

9 Why does the effective yield of an investment in bonds often differ from the interest rate stated in the bond contract? Explain the effect of interest rate fluctuations on bond prices.

10 Why is the discount or premium on bond investments treated as an adjustment of interest revenue rather than as a gain or loss on sale, redemption, or maturity?

11 Distinguish between the *interest* and the *straight-line* methods of accumulating a discount and amortizing a premium on an investment in bonds.

12 What is the theoretical support for the use of weighted average as a basis for determining cost when units of the same security are acquired at different dates and prices? What methods are allowed for income tax purposes?

13 From the investors' point of view, is there any significant difference between a stock dividend and a stock split? Does either represent revenue to investors?

14 What are *stock rights?* How should they be accounted for by an investor?

15 When a convertible bond is converted to common stock, what journal entry should the investor make? Would your answer be different if the market price of the common stock were known? If the market price were not known? Explain.

16 Why is the *cash surrender value* of an insurance policy on the life of an official of a business enterprise carried as a long-term investment in the balance sheet of the enterprise?

EXERCISES

Ex. 14-1 Select the best answer for each of the following multiple-choice questions:

1 A net unrealized loss on a long-term portfolio of marketable equity securities is reported in the financial statements as:
   a An extraordinary item shown as a direct reduction from retained earnings
   b A current loss resulting from holding marketable equity securities
   c A footnote or parenthetical disclosure only
   d A valuation allowance and included in the stockholders' equity section of the balance sheet

2 In its December 31, Year 4, balance sheet, Colbert Company reported the following as investments in long-term marketable equity securities:

Investments in long-term marketable equity securities, at cost $300,000
Less: Allowance to reduce investments in long-term marketable equity
   securities to market value.   28,000
Net amount $272,000

On December 31, Year 5, the market value of the investments was $298,000. What should Colbert report in its Year 5 income statement as a result of the increase in the market value of the investments in Year 5?
   a $0
   b Unrealized loss of $2,000
   c Realized gain of $26,000
   d Unrealized gain of $26,000

3 On January 2, Year 1, Investor Company paid $400,000 for 10,000 shares of Investee Company's common stock, which represents a 10% investment in Investee. Investor received dividends of $1 a share from Investee in Year 1. Investee reported net income of $150,000 for the year ended December 31, Year 1. The market price of Investee's common stock on December 31, Year 1, was $42 a share. Ignoring income taxes, the amount of investment income (or

dividend revenue) reported in Investor's income statement for Year 1 as a result of its investment in Investee was:

a $10,000 *b* $15,000 *c* $30,000 *d* $35,000

Questions 4 and **5** are based on the following information:

On January 2, Year 7, Investor Company acquired 30% of the outstanding common stock of Investee Company for $129,000. Investor is accounting for this investment by the equity method of accounting. On the date of acquisition, the current fair value of Investee's net assets was $310,000. Investor has determined that the excess of the cost of the investment over its equity in Investee's net assets has an indeterminate economic life. Investee's net income for the year ended December 31, Year 7, was $90,000. During Year 7, Investee declared and paid cash dividends of $10,000. There were no other transactions between the two companies.

4 On January 2, Year 7, the investment in Investee Company should have been recorded as:

a $93,000 *b* $120,000 *c* $129,000 *d* $165,000

5 Ignoring income taxes, Investor's income statement for the year ended December 31, Year 7, should include investment income in the amount of:

a $17,000 *b* $26,100 *c* $27,000 *d* $27,900

Ex. 14-2   Prepare a compound journal entry for Covington Company on December 31, Year 4, to correct the following ledger account. Include supporting computations in the explanation for the journal entry. The accounting records have not been closed for Year 4. (**Note:** Credits to the account represent **net cash** received.)

Investment in Cairo Company Common Stock (Long-term)

Date	Explanation	Debit	Credit	Balance
Year 4				
Jan. 18	Acquired 200 shares	24,000		24,000 dr
Mar. 6	Sold 40 shares received as a 20%			
	stock dividend on this date		3,800	20,200 dr
July 26	Received cash dividend		300	19,900 dr
Aug. 21	Sold 200 rights received on this			
	date (3% of adjusted cost is al-			
	locable to rights)		700	19,200 dr
Dec. 20	Sold 100 shares after a 2 for 1 stock			
	split effective Oct. 10, Year 4		5,350	13,850 dr

Ex. 14-3   On January 2, Year 7, Astor Company acquired 40% of the 300,000 shares of common stock of Beaumont Company for $1,800,000, when 40% of the underlying equity of Beaumont was $1,400,000. The excess of cost over the underlying equity is assigned to goodwill. Astor amortizes goodwill over a 40-year period, with a full year's amortization taken in the year of acquisition. As a result of this transaction, Astor has the ability to exercise significant influence over the operating and financial policies of Beaumont. Beaumont's net income for the year ended December 31, Year 7, was $600,000. During Year 7, Beaumont declared and paid $325,000 in dividends to its shareholders.

Compute the investment income to be reported by Astor for its investment in Beaumont for the year ended December 31, Year 7.

Ex. 14-4   On July 1, Year 8, Krystal Company acquired 500 of the $1,000 face amount, 14% bonds of Langdorf Company for $460,481, at a yield rate of 16% a year. The bonds, which mature on January 1, Year 15, pay interest semiannually on January 1 and July 1. Krystal recorded the bonds as a long-term investment and adopted the interest method for accumulating the discount on the bonds.

Compute the carrying amount, rounded to the nearest dollar, of the Langdorf 14% bonds in Krystal's balance sheet on December 31, Year 8.

Ex. 14-5 On January 1, Year 5, Sultana Company purchased at carrying amount 200,000 shares (25%) of common stock of Timmons Company for $2,500,000, including, direct costs associated with the purchase of $60,000. On December 1, Year 5, the board of directors of Timmons declared a dividend of $1.50 a share payable to stockholders of record on December 20, Year 5. The net income of Timmons for the year ended December 31, Year 5, was $2,200,000.

Compute the balance in Sultana's Investment in Common Stock of Timmons Company account on December 31, Year 5.

Ex. 14-6 Ireson Company owns 300 shares of the outstanding common stock of Jeffers Corporation, which has several hundred thousand shares publicly traded. The 300 shares were acquired by Ireson in Year 3 for $105 a share. On June 20, Year 5, Jeffers distributed stock rights to its stockholders to buy one new share of Jeffers common stock for $120 cash and three rights. On June 20, Year 5, each share of stock had a market value of $134 ex-rights, and each right had a market value of $6.

What cost should be recorded for each new share that Ireson acquired by exercising the rights?

Ex. 14-7 The following transactions relate to Holloway Company's long-term investment in Gordon Company:

Apr. 10 Acquired 500 shares of common stock at $22 a share, plus brokerage commission and transfer costs of $400.
June 15 Acquired 1,000 shares of common stock at $29 a share, plus brokerage commission and transfer costs of $712.
Aug. 31 Gordon distributed a 20% stock dividend.

a Prepare journal entries for Holloway Company to record the foregoing transactions.
b Compute the basis per share of the investment in Gordon, assuming (1) the two acquisitions are treated as separate lots (to permit the use of fifo), and (2) a weighted average is computed for the investment as a whole.
c Prepare a journal entry to record the sale of 800 shares at $21 a share, assuming the cost of the shares sold is determined by (1) fifo, and (2) weighted average.

Ex. 14-8 At the beginning of the current year, Rhesus Company acquired 20% of the 100,000 outstanding shares of Solo Company capital stock. During the year, Solo reported net income of $140,000.

Compute the equity per share of Solo's capital stock and the carrying amount per share of Rhesus' investment at the end of the current year under each of the following independent assumptions:
a Rhesus acquired the shares at the underlying equity of $12 a share, and accounted for the investment by the cost method of accounting. Solo declared and paid dividends of $80,000 during the year.
b Same facts as case *a*, except that Solo declared and paid dividends of $160,000 during the year.
c Same facts as case *a*, except that Rhesus used the equity method of accounting to account for the investment.
d Same facts as case *c*, except that Rhesus acquired the shares at a price of $15 a share, although the underlying equity was only $12 a share. The excess of cost over equity was paid because a patent with a remaining economic life of 12 years was undervalued in Solo's accounting records.

Ex. 14-9 Using the information in **Ex. 14-8,** prepare all journal entries in Rhesus Company's accounting records relating to the investment in Solo Company during the current year, under each of the four assumptions. (Omit closing entries and entries to record the initial acquisition of stock.)

Ex. 14-10 Prepare journal entries in the accounting records of Tichnor Company to record the following transactions for long-term investments:

Feb. 10 Tichnor Company acquired 1,000 shares of Uvalde Company common stock at $88 a share.
Mar. 31 Uvalde issued a 10% stock dividend to common stockholders.
June 30 Uvalde issued rights to common stockholders, enabling the acquisition of one additional share at $90 for every five shares held. The common stock was trading ex-rights at $114 a share, and the rights had a market value of $6 each.
July 18 Tichnor exercised 1,000 rights to acquire new shares.
July 20 The remaining 100 rights were sold for $5.50 each.
Oct. 12 Tichnor sold 400 shares of Uvalde common stock for $44,000. The shares sold were specifically identified as being from those acquired on February 10.

Ex. 14-11 The following data (rounded to the nearest dollar) are the beginning of an amortization table prepared by Wayne Company to account for its investment in $80,000 face amount bonds of Clovis Company, maturing in 17 years, which pay interest annually:

Year	Payment received	Interest revenue	Accumulation of discount	Carrying amount of investment
				$61,132
1	$4,000	$4,585	$585	61,717
2	4,000	4,629	629	62,346
3				

a Is the discount being accumulated by the straight-line method or the interest method? Explain.
b What is the coupon rate of interest on the bonds?
c What is the effective yield on the investment?
d Prepare a journal entry to reflect Wayne's interest revenue in Year 2.
e Compute the amounts to be entered in each column of the table for Year 3.
f What would be the interest revenue recognized each year if the discount were accumulated by the straight-line method?
g Compute the percentage return (to the nearest tenth of one percent) on the carrying amount of the investment in Years 1 and 3, assuming that the discount was accumulated by the straight-line method.

SHORT CASES FOR ANALYSIS AND DECISION

Case 14-1 During your examination of the financial statements of Wilbert Company, which has never before been audited, you discover that the cash surrender value of a $250,000 life insurance policy on the president, for which Wilbert was the beneficiary, had not been recorded in the accounting records. The president stated that the total premium on the policy was debited to the Insurance Expense account each year because the company had no intention to "cash in" the policy or to use the cash surrender value as collateral for a loan from the insurance company or a bank. Therefore, asserted the president, it would be misleading for the company to record as an asset an amount never expected to be realized or used by the company.

Instructions Evaluate the position of the president of Wilbert Company.

Case 14-2 For the past five years Cashion Company has maintained an investment (accounted for and reported correctly) in Davila Company amounting to a 10% interest in the common stock of Davila. The cost of the investment was $700,000, and the underlying net equity in Davila at the date of acquisition was $620,000. On January 2 of the current year, Cashion acquired an additional 15% of the common stock of Davila for $1,200,000; the underlying equity of the additional investment on January 2 was $1,000,000. Davila has been profitable and has paid dividends annually since Cashion's initial acquisition.

Instructions Discuss how this increase in ownership affects the accounting for and reporting of the investment in Davila. Include in your discussion adjustments, if any, to the amount shown prior to the increase in investment to bring the amount into conformity with generally accepted accounting principles. Also indicate how the investment should be reported in the financial statements for the current and subsequent accounting periods.

Case 14-3 Colonita Company acquired 2,000 of the 50,000 outstanding shares of DuVall Company common stock on March 15 at $40 a share.
   On April 1, DuVall declared a cash dividend of $0.75 a share payable April 20 to stockholders of record April 12. The operations of DuVall were unsuccessful during the first three quarters of the year, and operating losses exceeded the accumulated retained earnings. On November 20, DuVall declared a liquidation dividend of $0.50 a share payable December 20 to stockholders of record December 10.

Instructions
a Record these two dividend distributions by DuVall in the accounting records of Colonita, following the legal assumption (cost method of accounting).
b From the viewpoint of Colonita, do you favor the legal or the economic (equity method of accounting) treatment of these dividends? Give your reasons.

Case 14-4 Chen Company, a chemical processor, has been operating profitably for many years. On March 1, Year 4, Chen acquired 50,000 shares of Kelvin Company common stock for $2,000,000. The 50,000 shares represented 25% of Kelvin's outstanding common stock. Both Chen and Kelvin operate on a fiscal year ending August 31.
   For the year ended August 31, Year 4, Kelvin reported net income of $800,000, earned ratably throughout the year. During November, Year 3, and February, May, and August, Year 4, Kelvin paid its regular quarterly cash dividend of $125,000.

Instructions
a What criteria should Chen consider in determining whether its investment in Kelvin should be classified as (1) a current asset, or (2) a noncurrent asset in Chen's August 31, Year 4, balance sheet? Confine your discussion to the decision criteria for determining the balance sheet classification of the investment.
b Assume that the investment is classified as a long-term investment in Chen's balance sheet. The cost of the investment equaled Chen's equity in Kelvin's net assets; carrying amounts were not materially different from current fair values (individually or collectively). How much investment income should Chen report as a result of its investment in Kelvin for the year ended August 31, Year 4? Explain.

Case 14-5 Willowbrook Company acquired 45,000 of 150,000 outstanding shares of common stock of Carew Company on January 2, Year 6, at $30 a share. The carrying amount of Carew common stock as of December 31, Year 5, was $22.75 a share. During the year following the acquisition of the stock by Willowbrook, Carew earned $325,000 and paid dividends of $1.10 a share. The management of Willowbrook is concerned about the appropriate method of presenting the investment in Carew in the financial statements. The controller argues that Willowbrook had earned 30% of Carew's net income, because it owns 30% of Carew common stock. The financial vice president argues that the investment must be carried at cost as are all other assets, and that the net income of Willowbrook should include only the dividends received from Carew.

Instructions
a Attempt to resolve this debate by pointing out the relevant issues on both sides of the argument.
b The vice president counters your points in favor of the controller's position with the statement that, "What you say makes sense until you try to explain what the dollar amount of the investment represents. It is not market value of the stock, because the current market value is $29 a share, and it most certainly is not cost." Present your answer to the vice president.

Case 14-6 On April 1, Year 9, Century Company acquired 6% convertible bonds with face amount of $1,500,000 for $1,818,000 plus accrued interest for two months. The bonds pay interest semiannually on February 1 and August 1 and mature in 8 years and 10 months from date of acquisition. Each $1,000 bond is convertible on any interest date to 40 shares of common stock.

On August 1, Year 9, 500 bonds were converted to common stock. On the date of conversion the common stock was selling for $40 a share. On September 1, Year 9, a 10% stock dividend was declared on the common stock, to be distributed on October 10 to stockholders of record on September 20. On December 1, Year 9, 5,500 common shares were sold for $35 a share.

Instructions
a Record the above transactions, including receipt of interest on August 1 and the accrual of interest on December 31, in journal entries, assuming that the conversion of the bonds is recorded at carrying amount.
b Justify your reason for amortizing or not amortizing the premium on the investment in convertible bonds.

PROBLEMS

14-1 On October 1, Year 7, Rasmussen Company acquired for cash 200,000 shares representing 45% of the outstanding common stock of Murphy Company. As a result of the acquisition, Rasmussen had the ability to exercise significant influence over the operating and financial policies of Murphy. Goodwill of $500,000 was appropriately computed by Rasmussen at the date of the acquisition.

On January 3, Year 8, Rasmussen also acquired 300,000 shares representing 30% of the outstanding common stock of O'Brien Company. The amount of cash paid for the stock was $2,500,000. The stockholders' equity section of O'Brien's balance sheet at the date of acquisition was as follows:

Common stock, $2 par	$2,000,000
Paid-in capital in excess of par	1,000,000
Retained earnings	3,500,000
Total stockholders' equity	$6,500,000

Furthermore, at the date of acquisition, the current fair value of O'Brien's net plant assets was $4,000,000, and the carrying amount was $3,500,000. For all the other assets and liabilities of O'Brien, the current fair value and carrying amount were equal. As a result of the acquisition, Rasmussen has the ability to exercise significant influence over the operating and financial policies of O'Brien.

Assume that Rasmussen amortizes goodwill to the nearest month over the maximum period allowed by generally accepted accounting principles.

Instructions   Prepare a working paper for computation of the amount of goodwill and accumulated amortization for Rasmussen Company on December 31, Year 8, and the goodwill amortization for the year ended December 31, Year 8. Show supporting computations.

14-2   Womack Company has supplied you with information regarding two investments which were made during the current year as follows:

(1) On January 1, Womack acquired 40% of the 500,000 shares of voting common stock of Xavier Company for $2,400,000, equal to 40% of the net assets of Xavier. Xavier's net income for the current year was $750,000. Xavier declared and paid dividends of $0.50 a share in the current year. The market price of Xavier's common stock was $14 a share on December 31 of the current year. Womack exercised significant influence over the operating and financial policies of Xavier.

(2) On July 1, Womack acquired 15,000 shares, representing 5% of the voting common stock of Yang Company for $450,000. Yang's net income for the six months ended December 31 of the current year was $350,000; for the year ended December 31, net income was $600,000. Yang declared and paid dividends of $0.30 a share each quarter during the current year to stockholders of record on the last day of each quarter. The market price of Yang's common stock was $32 a share on January 1 and $34 a share on December 31.

Instructions

a   As a result of these two investments, what should be the balance in Womack's Investments account on December 31 of the current year? Show supporting computations. Disregard income taxes and deferred tax considerations.

b   As a result of these two investments, what should be the investment income reported by Womack for the year ended December 31 of the current year? Show supporting computations. Disregard income taxes and deferred tax considerations.

14-3   In Year 5, Lange Corporation acquired 1% of the common stock of Markham Company as a long-term investment. The accountant for Lange was inexperienced and made the following errors in recording the transactions relating to the investment in the common stock of Markham: (1) Shares received as a 10% stock dividend were valued at the market price and recorded by a debit to the investment account and a credit to Dividend Revenue; (2) the net cash proceeds on the sale of shares of stock and stock rights were credited to the investment account; and (3) a cash dividend was credited to the investment account.

On June 27, Year 5, the common stock of Markham Company was selling ex-rights at $98, and the rights were selling at $2.

The activity in the investment account during Year 5 is presented on top of page 600.

Investment in Markham Company Common Stock (Long-term)

Date	Explanation	Debit	Credit	Balance
Year 5				
Jan. 18	Acquired 4,000 shares	374,000		374,000 dr
Feb. 28	Received 400 shares as 10% stock			
	dividend	40,000		414,000 dr
Mar. 6	Sold 400 shares received Feb. 28		38,000	376,000 dr
May 25	Received cash dividend		4,400	371,600 dr
June 27	Sold 4,000 rights received June 9		7,850	363,750 dr
Dec. 20	Sold 3,200 shares (20%) after a 4			
	for 1 split effective Oct. 10		88,800	274,950 dr

Instructions

a Prepare a working paper to summarize the transactions in the Investment in Markham Company Common Stock account as the transactions should have been recorded. Use the following column headings:

Date	Transactions	Number of shares	Cost	Proceeds on sale	Gain or (loss)
Year 5					
Jan. 18					

b Prepare a single journal entry to correct the accounting records as of December 31, Year 5. Assume that the accounting records have not been closed for Year 5.

14-4 At the beginning of Year 1, Mahout Company acquired 10,000 shares of Nasser Company common stock for $300,000 as a long-term investment. At the end of Year 1, the market value of the investment was $258,000. Late in Year 2, Mahout sold 2,000 shares of Nasser common stock for $55,000. At the end of Year 2, the market value of the remaining 8,000 shares of Nasser common stock was $225,000.

Instructions

a Prepare journal entries to record realized and unrealized losses relating to the investment in Nasser common stock in the accounting records of Mahout.

b Show how the investment in Nasser common stock and the unrealized loss should be presented in the balance sheet of Mahout at the end of Year 1 and Year 2. Disregard footnote disclosure.

14-5 The following transactions and adjustments relate to long-term investments of Cantor Company:

Apr. 30 Acquired $60,000 face amount 16% bonds issued by Wing Company at a cost of $63,760 plus accrued interest. Bonds pay interest semiannually on March 1 and September 1, and mature 94 months from the date of acquisition.

July 10 Acquired for the lump sum of $155,000 a package of 500 shares of 6%, $100 par, preferred stock and 1,000 shares of common stock of Stanky Company. The preferred and common stock were trading at $80 a share and $120 a share, respectively.

Sept. 1 Received semiannual interest payment on the Wing Company bonds. Premium is amortized by the straight-line method when interest is received and at the end of the fiscal year.

Oct. 15 Received the quarterly dividend on the Stanky preferred stock.

Oct. 25 Received new shares from a 2 for 1 stock split of the Stanky common stock.

Dec. 31 Adjusting entries (including amortization of premium) were made for the end of the fiscal year.

Instructions Prepare journal entries to record the foregoing transactions and adjustments.

14-6   On July 1 of the current year, Campbell Company acquired 25% of the outstanding shares of common stock of McDowd Company at a total cost of $720,000. The underlying equity of the stock acquired by Campbell was only $600,000.

Campbell was willing to pay more than the underlying equity for the McDowd stock for the following reasons:

(1) McDowd owned depreciable plant assets (10-year remaining economic life) with a current fair value $60,000 more than their carrying amount.

(2) McDowd owned land with a current fair value $300,000 more than its carrying amount.

(3) Campbell believed that McDowd possessed enough goodwill to justify the remainder of the cost. Campbell's accounting policy with respect to goodwill is to amortize it over 40 years.

McDowd Company earned net income of $540,000 uniformly over the current year ended December 31. On December 31, McDowd declared and paid a cash dividend of $360,000. Both companies close their accounting records on December 31.

Instructions

a Compute the total amount of goodwill of McDowd Company, based on the price paid by Campbell for McDowd's common stock.

b Prepare all journal entries in Campbell's accounting records relating to the investment for the year ended December 31, under the cost method of accounting.

c Prepare all journal entries in Campbell's accounting records relating to the investment for the year ended December 31, under the equity method of accounting.

14-7   Ganesha Company acquired $500,000 of Nimitz Company bonds on September 30. The bonds carry a 14% coupon rate with interest payable semiannually on March 31 and September 30. The remaining term of the bonds is ten years, and the bonds have an effective yield to maturity of 16% compounded semiannually.

Instructions   (Round all computations to the nearest dollar.)

a Using the tables in the Appendix in back of the book, compute the amount that Ganesha paid for the Nimitz Company bonds.

b Prepare tables for the first two years to show the accumulation of the discount and interest revenue, under both the interest method and the straight-line method.

c Prepare the journal entries required to record the first year's transactions, excluding the acquisition of the bonds and closing entries, under both the interest method and the straight-line method. Ganesha's fiscal year ends on September 30.

14-8   On June 30, Year 2, Davado Company acquired 20% of the 100,000 outstanding shares of capital stock of Eagan Company. The net assets of Eagan on the date of acquisition were as follows:

Common stock, $10 par	$1,000,000
Paid-in capital in excess of par	1,750,000
Retained earnings	2,350,000
Total stockholders' equity	$5,100,000

Davado paid $1,410,000 cash for the common stock of Eagan. The excess of the cost over the underlying equity was paid because (1) the land owned by Eagan had a current fair value $550,000 more than its carrying amount; (2) the depreciable plant assets of Eagan were worth $450,000 more than their carrying amount; and (3) Eagan had at least the amount of goodwill imputed by the cost of Davado's 20% interest. The accounting policy of Davado with respect to goodwill is to amortize over 40 years. The depreciable plant assets have a remaining economic life of 12 years.

During the last six months of Year 2, Eagan earned net income of $270,000, after an extraordinary loss of $45,000, and declared and paid dividends of $1 a share. In Year 3, Eagan reported a net loss of $90,000 and declared and paid dividends of $2 a share. Both companies end their fiscal year on December 31.

Instructions

a Compute the total imputed amount of Eagan Company's goodwill based on the cost of Davado's 20% interest in Eagan.

b Prepare all journal entries for Year 2 and Year 3 in Davado's accounting records relating to the investment in Eagan, under the cost method of accounting. Assume that all end-of-period adjustments are made and that dividends are received at the end of each year.

c Prepare all journal entries for Year 2 and Year 3 in Davado's accounting records relating to the investment in Eagan, under the equity method of accounting.

d On January 2, Year 4, Davado decided that Eagan's goodwill no longer had any value and that the investment account should be reduced by Davado's portion of unamortized goodwill. Prepare a journal entry to reflect this revaluation, assuming that the equity method of accounting has been in use.

14-9   Nancy Company acquired three lots of Arles Company common stock as follows:

Lot No.	Number of shares	Cost of each share	Brokerage and other costs
1	2,000	$28	$600
2	800	36	300
3	1,200	30	400

Arles issued a 10% stock dividend on May 10 and stock rights on August 15 entitling common stockholders to purchase at $40 one new share for every 10 shares held. Shortly after the rights were issued, the common stock was trading ex-rights at $49 a share, and the rights at $1 a right. Nancy sold 1,000 rights at $1.125 a right, less brokerage and other costs of $45. The remaining rights were exercised. Arles has 5,000,000 shares of common stock outstanding.

Instructions

a Compute the gain or loss on the sale of rights under (1) fifo, (2) lifo, and (3) average cost of the common stock to determine the cost of the rights sold. Round cost of each right to the nearest tenth of a cent.

b Prepare a working paper to show the number of shares in each lot, the total cost of each lot, and the unit cost of each lot (to the nearest cent), assuming the use of fifo in part *a* and considering the shares bought through the exercise of rights as lot no. 4.

14-10 Charter Company issued at face amount $500,000 of 15%, 10-year bonds, interest to be payable annually. A sinking fund was established to accumulate the $500,000 at the end of 10 years. Charter will make payments of $28,492 to the fund at the end of each year. The fund balance will be invested to earn 12% a year.

In addition to the sinking fund, Charter acquired a $100,000 life insurance policy on Carl Charter, the company's president. The terms of the insurance policy were as follows:

Year	Gross premium	Cash surrender value at end of year
1	$7,770	$ 1,340
2	7,770	7,460
3	7,700	13,770
4	7,770	20,290
5	7,770	27,030
6	7,770	34,020
7	7,770	41,290
8	7,770	48,880
9	7,770	56,830
10	7,770	65,200

Instructions
a Prepare a fund accumulation table for the sinking fund for the first three years. Round all computations to the nearest dollar.
b Prepare a table to determine the effect on net income of the life insurance policy for each of the first three years.
c Prepare journal entries for all transactions involving the bonds, the sinking fund, and the life insurance policy for each of the first three years.

14-11 The following transactions relate to the long-term investments of Fortuna Company for the year ended December 31, Year 2:

Jan. 2 Acquired 30,000 of 100,000 outstanding shares of Garth Company common stock for $15 a share. Underlying equity was $12 a share; Fortuna attributed the excess of cost over equity acquired to goodwill, to be amortized over 30 years. The acquisition gave Fortuna a significant degree of influence over Garth.

Jan. 6 Acquired $100,000 of Haggis Company first mortgage 18% bonds at face amount plus accrued interest for 36 days. Interest is payable semiannually on December 1 and June 1, with maturity on December 1, Year 11. The bonds are callable at 106.

Feb. 15 Acquired 1,000 shares of Ingle Company $10 par common stock for $65,280.

May 5 Received cash dividend of 65 cents a share on Ingle Company common stock.

June 1 Received semiannual interest on Haggis Company bonds.

Aug. 5 Received cash dividend of 65 cents a share and a 2% stock dividend on Ingle Company common stock.

Sept. 30 Sold the shares of Ingle Company common received as a stock dividend for $70 a share and acquired 50, $1,000 16% subordinated debenture bonds of James Company at 94 (94% of face amount), with interest payable semiannually on March 31 and September 30, and with maturity 10 years from date of acquisition. The bonds are callable at 102.

Oct.   1 Received a cash dividend of 75 cents a share from Garth Company. (The dividend was paid from earnings.)

Nov.   5 Received cash dividend of 70 cents a share on Ingle Company common stock.

Dec.   1 Received semiannual interest on Haggis Company bonds and surrendered to Haggis 60 of the $1,000 bonds at the call price, in accordance with the provisions of the bond indenture.

Dec. 31 Garth Company reported net income of $164,000 for Year 2, including an extraordinary gain of $24,000.

Instructions

a Prepare journal entries for the above transactions and record any adjustments required on December 31, Year 2. Accumulate the discount on the bonds of James Company to the nearest month, under the straight-line method. The market value of Ingle Company common stock on December 31, Year 2, was $75,000.

b Prepare a listing of investments as they would appear in the balance sheet on December 31, Year 2.

14-12 During the course of your examination of the financial statements of Cole Corporation for the year ended December 31, Year 4, you found a new account, "Investments." Your examination disclosed that during Year 4, Cole began a program of investments, and all investment-related transactions were entered in this account. Your analysis of this account for Year 4 follows:

COLE CORPORATION

Analysis of Investments Account

For Year Ended December 31, Year 4

Date Year 4		Debit	Credit
	Demos Company Common Stock		
Mar. 15	Acquired 1,000 shares @ $25 a share.	25,000	
June 28	Received 50 shares of Edwards Company common stock as a dividend on Demos Company common stock (Memorandum entry in general ledger).		
Sept. 30	Sold 50 shares of Edwards Company common stock @ $14 a share		700
Oct. 31	Awarded 500 shares of Demos Company common stock to selected members of Cole management as an incentive award accounted for as employee compensation.		12,500

Farber Company Common and Preferred Stock

Mar. 15 Acquired 600 units of common and preferred
stock @ $36 a unit. Each unit consists of one
share of preferred stock and two shares of common stock. 21,600

Apr. 30 Sold 300 shares of common stock @ $13 a share. 3,900

June 28 Received 900 common stock rights. Each right entitles the holder to acquire one share of common stock for $12 (Memorandum entry in gen-
eral ledger).

Sept. 30 Exercised 450 common stock rights to acquire 450
shares of common stock @ $12 a share. 5,400

30 Sold remaining 450 common stock rights @ $4 a
right. 1,800

Gobel Company Common Stock

Mar. 15 Acquired 10,000 shares @ $17 a share. 170,000

Oct. 31 Received dividend of $0.75 a share. 7,500

Hammer Company Convertible Bonds
(Due September 30, Year 13, with Interest at
7% Payable March 31 and September 30)

Apr. 30 Acquired 40 bonds @ 100 plus accrued interest.. 40,233

Sept. 30 Received interest for 6 months 1,400

30 Converted 10 bonds to 200 shares of common
stock. 10,000

30 Received 200 shares of common stock on conversion of 10 bonds. 10,000

Oct. 31 Sold the remaining 30 bonds @ 102 plus interest
for one month. (The interest was credited to Interest Revenue.). 30,600

Ilika Company Common Stock

Mar. 15 Acquired 4,000 shares @ $28 a share. 112,000

Apr. 30 Acquired 2,000 shares @ $30 a share. 60,000

June 28 Received dividend of $0.40 a share. 2,400

Other Investment

Oct. 31 Reacquired 1,600 shares of Cole Corporation outstanding common stock @ $14 a share and retired
the stock.. 22,400

Additional information is as follows:

(1) The market values for each security on the Year 4 date of each transaction follow:

Security	Mar. 15	Apr. 30	June 28	Sept. 30	Oct. 31
Demos Company common stock.	25				42
Edwards Company common stock. . . .			8	14	
Farber Company preferred stock.	20				
Farber Company common stock	10	13	15*	16	
Farber Company common stock rights .			3	4	
Gobel Company common stock	17				
Hammer Company bonds		100		100	102
Hammer Company common stock. . . .				65	
Ilika Company common stock	28	30			
Cole Corporation common stock.					14

* Ex-rights

(2) In accordance with Cole's practice, no gain was recognized on conversion of the Hammer convertible bonds to Hammer common stock.

(3) Gobel Company has only one class of stock authorized, and there were 30,000 shares of its common stock outstanding throughout Year 4. Cole's cost of its investment in Gobel was not materially different from its equity in Gobel's net assets; carrying amounts were not materially different from current fair values (individually or collectively). Gobel's net income from the date of acquisition of Cole's investment to December 31, Year 4, was $336,000. There were no intercompany transactions requiring elimination.

(4) Ilika Company has only one class of stock authorized, and there were 40,000 shares of its common stock outstanding throughout Year 4. Cole's cost of its investment in Ilika was not materially different from its equity in Ilika's net assets; carrying amounts were not materially different from current fair values (individually or collectively). Ilika's net income from the date of acquisition of Cole's investment to December 31, Year 4, was $120,000. There were no intercompany transactions requiring elimination.

(5) All other investments of Cole are widely held, and Cole's percentage of ownership in each is nominal (5% or less).

(6) On December 31, Year 4, Cole had 98,400 shares of its $10 par common stock outstanding. The balance in the Paid-in Capital in Excess of Par: Common Stock account was $100,000.

Instructions   Prepare necessary adjusting journal entries, classified by each of the securities analyzed above, to adjust the Investments account. Identify each security by type (preferred stock, common stock, rights, etc.) as well as by company. Supporting computations should be either included as part of the journal entry explanation or cross-referenced to the appropriate journal entry. Disregard brokers' fees, transfer taxes, and income taxes.

15 LONG-TERM DEBT

Liabilities that do not require the use of funds within one year (or the next operating cycle, whichever is longer) for their liquidation are designated **long-term liabilities.** Examples of long-term liabilities are: bonds, notes, equipment purchase obligations, permanent customer deposits, some obligations under pension and deferred compensation plans, certain types of lease obligations, deferred income taxes, and some deferred revenue items.

Long-term debt may be collateralized by liens on business property of various kinds, for example, equipment (equipment notes), real property (mortgages), or securities (collateral trust bonds). Many companies issue **debenture bonds** which are backed only by the general credit standing of the issuing company. The title of a long-term debt obligation, such as First Mortgage Bonds Payable, may indicate the collateral for the debt.

As noted in Chapter 10, some current liabilities involve no specific mention of interest payments. Because money has a time value, some amount of interest probably is included in the face amount of such liabilities, but it often is ignored because of the relatively small amounts involved. The interest factor in long-term debt, however, is significant and should be given accounting consideration. Accounting for bonds and mortgage notes payable is covered in this chapter; pensions and leases are discussed in Chapters 19 and 20, respectively; and deferred income taxes are covered in Chapter 21.

Types of bonds issued by corporations

Bonds are a means of dividing long-term debt into a number of small units. Usually, bonds are issued in $1,000 denominations, or in multiples of $1,000. Occasionally, additional denominations of $100 or $500 are used. In this way, a sum of money larger than that which could be obtained from a single credit source may be borrowed from a large number of investors. The terms of the borrowing are contained in a contract between the corporation and the bondholders, which is known as the **bond indenture.** This contract usually is held by a **trustee** who acts as an independent third party to protect the interests of both the borrower and the bondholders.

Bonds may be issued by corporations, by nations, by state and local governments, and by governmental agencies. They may be **registered bonds** or **coupon bonds.** Interest on registered bonds is paid only to the owner of record, but interest on coupon bonds is paid to persons presenting the periodic interest coupons. Some bond issues, known as **serial bonds,** mature in installments; **term bonds** mature on a single fixed maturity date.

A bond issue may rank behind previously issued **senior bonds** and may be described as **subordinated debentures** or **second mortgage bonds.** Most bonds are **callable**[1] at the option of the issuing company. Bond issues in some cases are **convertible** to common stock of the issuer at the option of the bondholder. **Revenue bonds** (issued by municipalities, turnpikes, bridge authorities, etc.) pay interest only from specific revenue sources. Occasionally, bonds are **guaranteed** by a company other than the issuer.

Bonds may be privately placed with a single institution or sold to investment bankers, who in turn retail the bonds in smaller lots to individual investors. Investment bankers may **underwrite** the bond issue, in which case they guarantee a certain price to the issuer and take the risk in selling the issue to the public. If a bond issue is underwritten, the entire issue is recorded in the accounting records at the time of the sale to underwriters. When an entire bond issue is not sold at one time, both the amount of the bonds authorized and the amount issued should be disclosed in the balance sheet. Unissued bonds represent potential indebtedness which may be incurred without further authorization from the board of directors or additional pledge of properties. Authorized and unissued bonds may be reported in the balance sheet by parenthetical comment or in a note to the financial statements.

Financial management considerations

When financial managers decide to borrow money by issuing bonds, they must resolve a number of questions before they issue the bonds. First, they must relate the need for funds to the amount of long-term debt which can be undertaken safely, by studying the financial position and earning prospects of the company. They must forecast the ability of the company to meet bond sinking fund requirements or periodic maturities of bonds. A decision must be made regarding the features of the bonds, such as collateral to be offered, call provisions, convertibility, etc. It is apparent that a great deal of advance preparation precedes the actual offering of bonds to investors. The requirements of the Securities and Exchange Commission with respect to interstate issuances of bonds to the public are discussed in **Modern Advanced Accounting** of this series.

---

[1] The call provision protects the issuing company, which may wish to retire the debt in advance, particularly when interest rates have fallen and it can secure more favorable financing. Bondholders who are repaid at this time must reinvest their funds at a lower rate of interest, and therefore insist on a call premium as compensation for the reduced interest rate. Call premiums generally are established on a decreasing scale as the bonds move closer to maturity.

ACCOUNTING FOR TERM BONDS

Issuance of bonds

In a typical bond contract, the issuing corporation promises two essentially different kinds of future payments: (1) the payment of a fixed sum (*face amount* or *principal*) at a specified date; and (2) the periodic payment of interest, usually at six-month intervals, in an amount expressed as a percentage of the face amount of the bond. In the light of expectations as to what interest rate is necessary to attract the required funds, a rate of interest is set. It is important to note that the interest expense actually incurred on the bonds is determined by the price at which the bonds are sold; thus, the *effective interest rate* (sometimes called the *yield rate*) is set by the money market. Interest on bonds expressed as a percentage of the face amount is referred to as the *nominal* or *coupon rate.* If the effective interest (yield) rate is identical to the coupon rate, the bonds will sell at face amount. If the effective interest rate is higher than the coupon rate, the bonds will sell at a *discount.* Conversely, if the effective interest rate is less than the coupon rate, the bonds will sell at a *premium.* Differences between the coupon rate and the yield rate thus are adjusted by changes in the price at which the bonds are sold, without the necessity of amendments to the bond contract.

   To illustrate this point, assume that $100,000 of five-year, 7% bonds are offered for sale.[2] The bond contract, which promises $100,000 at the end of five years and $7,000 annual interest, then is offered to investment bankers, or *underwriting syndicates.* The prices bid by these underwriters will depend on their expectations as to the effective rate of interest for this type of bonds. Under two different assumptions as to the effective annual interest rate, the proceeds are determined as follows, using the appropriate present value tables in the Appendix in back of the book:

Computation of proceeds of 7% bonds issued at a *discount* (8% effective rate) and at a *premium* (6% effective rate)	*Amount bid for 7% bonds, assuming an effective rate of 8%:* *Present value of $100,000 due in 5 years @ 8%, with interest paid annually ($100,000 × 0.680583)* . . . $68,058 *Present value of $7,000 every year for 5 years @ 8% ($7,000 × 3.992710)* . . . . 27,949 *Proceeds of bond issue* . . . $96,007	*Amount bid for 7% bonds, assuming an effective rate of 6%:* *Present value of $100,000 due in 5 years @ 6%, with interest paid annually ($100,000 × 0.747258)* . . . $ 74,726 *Present value of $7,000 every year for 5 years @ 6% ($7,000 × 4.212364)* . . . . 29,487 *Proceeds of bond issue* . . . $104,213

[2] Although bonds issued in amounts as small as $100,000, paying interest annually and maturing in five years, are not found in real life, these amounts are used to facilitate the illustration.

The underwriters would expect to resell these bonds to the public at a higher price and thus a lower effective interest rate, to give them a margin to cover their costs and earn a profit. The yield rate to the issuing corporation, however, is determined by the price it receives from the underwriters. The journal entries to record the issuance of 7% bonds at a discount and at a premium are given below:

<table>
<tr><td>Issued at effective rate of 8%:</td><td colspan="2"></td><td>Issued at effective rate of 6%:</td><td colspan="2"></td></tr>
<tr><td>Cash . . . .</td><td>96,007</td><td></td><td>Cash . . . .</td><td>104,213</td><td></td></tr>
<tr><td>Discount on Bonds</td><td></td><td></td><td>Premium</td><td></td><td></td></tr>
<tr><td>Payable . . . . . .</td><td>3,993</td><td></td><td>on Bonds</td><td></td><td></td></tr>
<tr><td>Bonds Pay-</td><td></td><td></td><td>Payable. . .</td><td></td><td>4,213</td></tr>
<tr><td>able . . . .</td><td></td><td>100,000</td><td>Bonds Pay-</td><td></td><td></td></tr>
<tr><td>To record issuance of</td><td></td><td></td><td>able . . . . .</td><td></td><td>100,000</td></tr>
<tr><td>bonds at a discount.</td><td></td><td></td><td>To record issuance</td><td></td><td></td></tr>
<tr><td></td><td></td><td></td><td>of bonds at a prem-</td><td></td><td></td></tr>
<tr><td></td><td></td><td></td><td>ium.</td><td></td><td></td></tr>
</table>

Journal entries to record the issuance of 7% bonds at a discount (8% effective rate) and at a premium (6% effective rate)

Bonds paying 7% sold to yield 7% would sell at face amount, determined as follows:

Computation of proceeds of 7% bonds issued at a 7% effective rate

Present value of $100,000 due in 5 years @ 7%, with interest paid annually ($100,000 × 0.712986).	$ 71,299
Present value of $7,000 every year for 5 years @ 7% ($7,000 × 4.100197)	28,701
Proceeds of bond issue when yield rate equals coupon rate	$100,000

Bond interest expense

Because differences between the effective rate and the coupon rate of interest are reflected in bond prices, the amount of premium or discount affects the periodic interest expense to the issuer. This is illustrated by a comparison of the five-year interest expense under each of the two assumptions in the preceding section as to effective interest rates:

Comparison of five-year interest expense on bonds issued at a discount (8% effective rate) and at a premium (6% effective rate)

Assuming an effective rate of 8%:		Assuming an effective rate of 6%:	
Coupon interest ($7,000 × 5 annual payments).	$35,000	Coupon interest ($7,000 × 5 annual payments).	$35,000
Add: Discount ($100,000 − $96,007).	3,993	Less: Premium ($104,213 − $100,000).	4,213
Five-year interest expense . .	$38,993	Five-year interest expense . .	$30,787

If the bonds are issued to yield 8%, the discount of $3,993 represents an additional amount of interest which will be paid in a lump sum at maturity. Similarly, if the bonds are issued to yield 6%, the premium of $4,213 represents an advance paid by bondholders for the right to receive larger annual interest checks and should be viewed as a reduction in the effective interest expense. The premium in effect is "returned" to bondholders periodically in the form of larger interest payments.

Interest method of amortization

In theory, the recorded interest expense each accounting period should equal the effective interest expense, that is, the effective rate of interest applied to the *carrying amount* of the debt at the beginning of that period. This approach to the computation of interest expense is known as the *interest method of amortization.* The interest method generally should be used to amortize the discount or premium on bonds payable. However, the straight-line method may be used as a matter of expediency if the difference in results between the two methods is not material. The Accounting Principles Board stated that "the interest method of amortization is theoretically sound and an acceptable method."[3] Subsequently, the Board took a more explicit stand in relation to the amortization of discount or premium on notes receivable and payable, but equally applicable to bonds payable, as follows:[4]

> . . . the difference between the present value and the face amount should be treated as discount or premium and amortized as interest expense or income over the life of the note in such a way as to result in a constant rate of interest when applied to the amount outstanding at the beginning of any given period. This is the "interest" method. . . . However, other methods of amortization may be used if the results obtained are not materially different from those which would result from the "interest" method.

Bonds Issued at Discount When bonds are issued at a discount, the carrying amount of the debt increases as the bonds approach maturity; thus, the dollar amount of the effective interest expense increases in each period. Annual "effective" interest expense over the term of the bonds and journal entries to record interest expense for the first two years are given on page 612.

Bonds Issued at Premium When bonds are issued at a premium, the carrying amount of the debt decreases as the bonds approach maturity, and the amount of periodic interest expense decreases over the term of the bonds. Annual "effective" interest expense and journal entries to record interest expense for the first two years are illustrated on page 613.

[3] *APB Opinion No. 12,* "Omnibus Opinion—1967," AICPA (New York: 1967), p. 194.
[4] *APB Opinion No. 21,* "Interest on Receivables and Payables," AICPA (New York: 1971), p. 423.

	(A) Interest paid (7% of face amount)	(B) "Effective" interest expense (8% of bonds' carrying amount)	(C) Discount amorti- zation (B − A)	(D) Bond discount balance (D − C)	(E) Carrying amount of bonds, end of year ($100,000 − D)
Bonds Issued at a Discount					
Interest Expense Determined by Interest Method of Amortization					
($100,000, 5-year bonds, interest at 7% payable annually,					
issued for $96,007, to yield 8% compounded annually)					
Year					
At time of issuance				$3,993	$ 96,007
1	$7,000	$7,681	$681	3,312	96,688
2	7,000	7,735	735	2,577	97,423
3	7,000	7,794	794	1,783	98,217
4	7,000	7,857	857	926	99,074
5	7,000	7,926	926	−0−	100,000

Journal entries:

	Year 1	Year 2
Bond Interest Expense.	7,681	7,735
Cash.	7,000	7,000
Discount on Bonds Payable.	681	735

To record interest expense, including amortization of discount.

Straight-line method of amortization

The additional interest expense (discount) or reduction of interest expense (premium) may be allocated evenly over the term of the bonds. This method, known as the **straight-line method of amortization,** results in a uniform periodic interest expense. Although this method does not give the accurate results obtained by use of the interest method of amortization, it frequently is encountered in practice. As previously stated, the use of the straight-line method may not be objectionable if it is applied to immaterial amounts of discount or premium.

Bonds Issued at Discount When bonds are issued at a discount, the carrying amount of the debt increases as the bonds approach maturity, and periodic interest expense remains constant over the term of the bonds. Annual "average" interest expense over the term of the bonds and journal entries to record interest expense for the first two years appear on page 614.

Bonds Issued at Premium When bonds are issued at a premium, the carrying amount of the debt decreases as the bonds approach maturity,

Premium amortization
table—interest method

Bonds Issued at a Premium
Interest Expense Determined by Interest Method of Amoritization
($100,000, 5-year bonds, interest at 7% payable annually,
issued for $104,213, to yield 6% compounded annually)

Year	(A) Interest paid (7% of face amount)	(B) "Effective" interest expense (6% of bonds' carrying amount)	(C) Premium amor- tization (A − B)	(D) Bond premium balance (D − C)	(E) Carrying amount of bonds, end of year ($100,000 + D)
At time of issuance				$4,213	$104,213
1	$7,000	$6,253	$747	3,466	103,466
2	7,000	6,208	792	2,674	102,674
3	7,000	6,160	840	1,834	101,834
4	7,000	6,110	890	944	100,944
5	7,000	6,056*	944	−0−	100,000

* Adjusted $1 for rounding.

Journal entries:

	Year 1	Year 2
Bond Interest Expense.	6,253	6,208
Premium on Bonds Payable	747	792
Cash.	7,000	7,000

To record interest expense, including amortization of premium.

and periodic interest expense remains constant over the term of the bonds. Annual "average" interest expense and journal entries to record interest expense for the first two years appear on page 615.

A comparison of periodic interest expense under the interest method shown on page 612 and above with the straight-line method shown on pages 614 and 615 reveals the extent of the error involved in the use of a simple average. For example, if the bonds were issued at a discount, the effective interest expense for each year ranges from $7,681 to $7,926; the use of the straight-line method results in a constant annual interest expense of $7,799. In the first year, for example, interest expense on a $100 million bond issue would be approximately $118,000 more under the straight-line method. In choosing the method to use, accountants should balance the simplicity of the straight-line method against the materiality of the error involved. The longer the term of the bond issue and the larger the discount or premium relative to the face amount of the bonds, the larger will be the difference between straight-line "average" interest expense and the "effective" interest expense determined by the interest method of amortization.

Bonds Issued at a Discount

Interest Expense Determined by Straight-Line Method of Amortization

($100,000, 5-year bonds, interest at 7% payable annually,

issued for $96,007 to yield 8% compounded annually)

Year	(A) Interest paid (7% of face amount)	(B) Discount amorti- zation ($\frac{1}{5}$ of $3,993)	(C) "Average" interest expense (A + B)	(D) Bond discount balance (D − B)	(E) Carrying amount of bonds, end of year ($100,000 − D)
At time of issuance				$3,993	$ 96,007
1	$7,000	$799	$7,799	3,194	96,806
2	7,000	799	7,799	2,395	97,605
3	7,000	799	7,799	1,596	98,404
4	7,000	799	7,799	797	99,203
5	7,000	797*	7,797*	−0−	100,000

* $2 adjustment to compensate for rounding average interest expense to the nearest dollar.

Journal entries:

	Year 1	Year 2
Bond Interest Expense.	7,799	7,799
Cash.	7,000	7,000
Discount on Bonds Payable.	799	799

To record interest expense, including amortization of discount.

When interest is paid semiannually or when interest payment dates
do not coincide with the end of the fiscal year, a policy of amortizing the
discount or the premium only at the end of the fiscal year can be
adopted to minimize the routine work involved when the straight-line
method of amortization is used.

Bond discount and premium in the balance sheet

At the time of issue, the carrying amount of bonds payable is equal to
the proceeds received, because these proceeds are computed as the
present value of all future payments at the yield rate set by the market.
Bond discount and bond premium are valuation accounts relating to
bonds payable. This is stated in **APB Opinion No. 21** in relation to notes
(but is equally applicable to bonds) as follows:[5]

[5] Ibid.

Premium amortization table—straight-line method

Bonds Issued at a Premium
Interest Expense Determined by Straight-Line Method of Amortization
($100,000, 5-year bonds, interest at 7% payable annually, issued for $104,213, to yield 6% compounded annually)

Year	(A) Interest paid (7% of face amount)	(B) Premium amortization ($\frac{1}{5}$ of $4,213)	(C) "Average" interest expense (A − B)	(D) Bond premium balance (D − B)	(E) Carrying amount of bonds, end of year ($100,000 + D)
At time of issuance				$4,213	$104,213
1	$7,000	$843	$6,157	3,370	103,370
2	7,000	843	6,157	2,527	102,527
3	7,000	843	6,157	1,684	101,684
4	7,000	843	6,157	841	100,841
5	7,000	841*	6,159*	–0–	100,000

* $2 adjustment to compensate for rounding average interest expense to the nearest dollar.

Journal entries

	Year 1	Year 2
Bond Interest Expense.	6,157	6,157
Premium on Bonds Payable	843	843
Cash.	7,000	7,000

To record interest expense, including amortization of premium.

. . . the discount or premium should be reported in the balance sheet as a direct addition to or deduction from the face amount of the note. It should not be classified as a deferred charge or deferred credit. The description of the note should disclose the effective interest rate; . . . Issue costs should be reported in the balance sheet as deferred charges.

Using the amounts from the previous illustration, bonds payable on the date of issue are reported in the balance sheet as follows:

Balance sheet presentation of bonds payable

Bonds issued at a discount:
Long-term debt:
  7% bonds payable, due in
    5 years (face amount) . $100,000
  Less: Discount 3,993
  Net liability (carrying
    amount). . . . . $ 96,007

Bonds issued at a premium:
Long-term debt:
  7% bonds payable, due in
    5 years (face amount) . $100,000
  Add: Premium 4,213
  Net liability (carrying
    amount). $104,213

At issue date these bonds have a present value below or above face amount because the market rate of interest is higher or lower than the periodic interest payments provided for in the bond contract. Therefore, the process of amortizing the bond discount or premium is a means of recording the increase or decrease *in the carrying amount of the debt obligation as it approaches maturity.* In the bond discount case, the increase in the carrying amount of the debt is caused indirectly through the decrease in bond discount. Similarly, in the bond premium case, the decrease in the carrying amount of the debt is caused directly through the decrease in bond premium. In either case, the carrying amount of bonds payable will be $100,000 at maturity.

Bond issue costs

A number of costs are incurred in connection with a bond issue: fees paid to accountants, attorneys, and other experts in connection with the preparation of the bond contract and prospectus; printing and engraving costs; fees of the Securities and Exchange Commission; and costs incurred in advertising the issue. These are costs for the use of the funds borrowed and are allocated to the years that the bonds are outstanding. Amortization of bond issue costs is recorded by a debit to Bond Issue Expense, as illustrated in the Electronics Devices, Inc., example on page 618.

Bond issue costs are classified as an asset and are amortized on a straight-line basis over the term of the bonds because revenue benefits from the use of the bond proceeds over this period. An alternative procedure advocated by some accountants is to add bond issue costs to the amount of discount or deduct them from bond premium. The latter treatment implies that the amount of funds made available to the borrower is equal to the net proceeds of the bond issue after deduction of all costs of completing the financing transaction. Under this procedure, bond issue costs increase the effective interest expense during the term of the bonds.

Bonds issued between interest dates

Bond interest payments usually are made semiannually on dates specified in the bond contract. When bonds are issued on a date other than an interest payment date, an adjustment for this factor may be made by reducing the amount of the interest payment for the first "short" interest period. However, it is more convenient to add to the price of bonds the amount of interest that has accrued since the last interest payment date. Investors, in effect, reimburse the borrower for the portion of the full six-month interest payment to which they are not entitled. Thus, investors will receive the full six-month interest payment on the next semiannual interest payment date.

Assume that Electronic Devices, Inc., issued $100,000 of 10-year, 12% bonds, with interest payable semiannually on April 1 and October 1 of each year. The bonds were issued on June 1, Year 1, for $107,080 plus accrued interest of $2,000 for two months. The bonds were dated April 1, Year 1, and various issue costs amounted to $2,360. Note that this borrowing actually runs for 9 years and 10 months, or 118 months, and the accounting for the debt and related issue costs should reflect this fact. Assuming that the straight-line method of amortization is used, the average interest expense monthly is determined below:

Computation of average interest expense for each month for bonds issued at a premium	

Actual interest paid to investors over 10-year period ($12,000 × 10) . .	*$120,000*
Less: Premium received on issuance of bonds	*(7,080)*
Accrued interest received from investors (Apr. 1–June 1)	*(2,000)*
Total interest expense (9 years and 10 months)	*$110,920*
Average monthly interest expense ($110,920 ÷ 118 months)	*$ 940*

Because the monthly interest accrual is $1,000 ($12,000 ÷ 12 months = $1,000) and the average interest expense is $940, the monthly premium amortization is the difference, or $60 ($7,080 ÷ 118 months). Issue costs are amortized at the rate of $20 a month ($2,360 ÷ 118 months = $20). Assuming that amortization of the issue costs and the premium is recorded only at the end of the year, the journal entries relating to the bond issue during Year 1 are shown on page 618.

It would be possible to credit Bond Interest Expense (rather than Accrued Bond Interest Payable) on June 1 for $2,000, the amount of the accrued interest for two months purchased by bondholders. On October 1, Bond Interest Expense would be debited for $6,000, thus leaving a balance of $4,000 in Bond Interest Expense representing interest incurred from June 1 to October 1. It also would be possible to amortize the premium and bond issue costs at the time interest is paid, as well as at the end of the fiscal year, but there is little point in following such an inefficient procedure when the straight-line method of amortization is used for the premium.

Early extinguishment of debt

Bonds payable may be redeemed by the issuing corporation prior to their maturity. Such bonds may be held in the treasury or may be retired. The acquisition of bonds prior to maturity completes the "transaction cycle" relating to the borrowing and should be viewed as an *early extinguishment of debt.* The Accounting Principles Board defined early extinguishment of debt as follows:[6]

[6] *APB Opinion No. 26,* "Early Extinguishment of Debt," AICPA (New York: 1972), p. 495.

ELECTRONIC DEVICES, INC.
Journal Entries for Bonds Issued between Interest Dates

Year 1

June 1 Deferred Bond Issue Costs.   2,360
          Cash   2,360
      To record costs of issuing bonds.

June 1 Cash   109,080
          Bonds Payable   100,000
          Accrued Bond Interest Payable   2,000
          Premium on Bonds Payable   7,080
      To record issuance of bonds and accrued interest
      for 2 months.

Oct. 1 Accrued Bond Interest Payable   2,000
      Bond Interest Expense   4,000
          Cash   6,000
      To record interest payment for first 6 months.

Dec. 31 Bond Interest Expense   2,580
      Premium on Bonds Payable   420
      Bond Issue Expense.   140
          Deferred Bond Issue Costs.   140
          Accrued Bond Interest Payable   3,000
      To accrue interest expense for 3 months and record
      amortization of deferred bond issue costs and pre-
      mium for 7 months. Amounts determined as follows:
        Accrued interest: $100,000 \times 12\% \times \frac{3}{12}$. $3,000
        Less: Amortization of premium:
          $7,080 \times 7/118$ 420
        Bond interest expense (net). $2,580
        Amortization of deferred bond issue
          costs: $2,360 \times 7/118$ . . . . $ 140

Early extinguishment is the reacquisition of any form of debt security or instrument before its scheduled maturity except through conversion by the
holder, regardless of whether the debt is viewed as terminated or is held as
so-called "treasury bonds." All open-market or mandatory reacquisitions of
debt securities to meet sinking fund requirements are early extinguishments.

A gain or loss on the early extinguishment of bonds is recognized
equal to the difference between the amount paid to retire the bonds and
their carrying amount less unamortized bond issue costs. The amortization of any bond discount or premium and bond issue costs should be
adjusted to the date of early extinguishment **before** the journal entry to
record the early extinguishment is prepared. To illustrate, assume that

$20,000 (20%) of the Electronic Devices, Inc., bonds described in the previous example are retired on December 1, Year 2, or 18 months after the bonds were issued. If the bonds are redeemed at $102\frac{1}{2}$, plus accrued interest of $400 for two months, the following two journal entries would be required:

ELECTRONIC DEVICES, INC.

Journal Entries to Record Early Extinguishment of Debt

Year 2

Dec. 1   Premium on Bonds Payable   132

        Bond Issue Expense.   44

            Bond Interest Expense   132

            Deferred Bond Issue Costs   44

To bring amortization up to date on $20,000 (or 20%) of bonds for period Jan. 1 to Dec. 1, Year 2.

    Amortization of premium:

      $7,080 × 20% × 11/118 = $132.

    Amortization of deferred bond issue costs:

      $2,360 × 20% × 11/118 = $44.

Dec. 1   Bonds Payable   20,000

        Premium on Bonds Payable ($1,416 − $216)   1,200

        Bond Interest Expense   400

            Cash   20,900

            Deferred Bond Issue Costs ($472 − $72)   400

            Gain on Early Extinguishment of Bonds   300

To record early extinguishment of bonds at $102\frac{1}{2}$ plus accrued interest of $400 for 2 months. The gain is determined as follows:

    Original proceeds, $107,080 × 20% $21,416

    Less: Original portion of bond issue costs,

      $2,360 × 20%.   472

    Carrying amount at issuance date $20,944

    Amortization for 18 months:

      Premium, $60 × 20% × 18 months . . .   (216)

      Bond issue costs, $20 × 20% × 18

      months.   72

    Carrying amount of bonds at date of early

    extinguishment, Dec. 1, Year 2. . . . . . . $20,800

    Amount paid to extinguish bonds.   20,500

    Gain on early extinguishment of bonds . $ 300

Gains and losses on early extinguishment of debt reflect the changes in interest rates since the bonds were issued. Material gains and losses on the early extinguishment of bonds (net of income tax effect) are reported as extraordinary items. On this point **FASB Statement No. 4** stated:[7]

> Gains and losses from extinguishment of debt that are included in the determination of net income shall be aggregated and, if material, classified as an extraordinary item, net of related income tax effect. . . . The conclusion does not apply, however, to gains and losses from cash purchases of debt made to satisfy current or future sinking-fund requirements. Those gains and losses shall be aggregated and the amount shall be identified as a separate item.

When bonds are retired at maturity, no gain or loss results, because the carrying amount of the bonds equals their face amount. Gains on early bond extinguishments represent taxable income; losses are deductible for income tax purposes.

When an entire bond issue is **called for redemption,** the entire unamortized premium or discount and deferred bond issue costs are written off. Losses generally result on such transactions because the sliding call prices ordinarily are in excess of bond carrying amounts on corresponding dates.

If bonds are acquired but not formally retired, a Treasury Bonds account may be debited for the face amount of the **treasury bonds** held, but a gain or loss still should be recognized as illustrated above. The Treasury Bonds account is not an asset; it is deducted from Bonds Payable in the balance sheet. Interest is not paid on reacquired bonds unless they are held as an investment by a company-sponsored fund, such as an employee pension fund.

ACCOUNTING FOR SERIAL BONDS

Nature of serial bonds

Thus far we have considered bonds having a single fixed maturity date. An alternative type of debt contract, known as a **serial bond,** provides for payment of the principal in periodic installments. Serial bonds have the obvious advantage of gearing debt repayment to the periodic cash inflow from operations.

As in the case of term bonds, serial bonds may be issued at a premium or a discount in response to differences between coupon and effective interest rates. The proceeds of a serial bond issue are somewhat more difficult to compute because of the varying maturities, but the approach is the same: The present value of the series of principal payments plus the present value of the interest payments, all at the effective rate of interest, equals the proceeds received for the bonds.

At this point the question arises: Is there any single interest rate applicable to a serial bond issue? We often refer loosely to **the rate** of in-

---

[7] *FASB Statement No. 4,* "Reporting Gains and Losses from Extinguishment of Debt, . . ." FASB (Stamford: 1975), pp. 3–4.

terest, when in fact in the market at any given time there are a number of interest rates, depending on the terms, nature, and length of the contract offered. In a given serial bond issue, the terms of all bonds in the issue are the same except for the differences in maturity. However, because short-term interest rates often differ from long-term rates, it is likely that each maturity will sell at a different yield rate, so that there will be a different discount or premium relating to each maturity.

In accounting for an issue of serial bonds under these conditions, each maturity should be treated as a separate bond issue. Thus, if $500,000 in five-year, 10% serial bonds are issued, to be repaid in the amount of $100,000 each year, and each maturity sells at a price reflecting a different yield rate, the problem would be treated as a summarized accounting for five separate bond issues of $100,000 each, maturing in one, two, three, four, and five years, respectively. Each maturity would have a related discount or premium, and interest expense on each maturity would be computed as previously illustrated for term bonds.

In many cases, however, this degree of precision in accounting for serial bond issues is not possible because the yield rate for each maturity is not known. Underwriters may bid on an entire serial bond issue on the basis of an average yield rate and may not disclose the particular yield rate for each maturity that was used to arrive at the bid price. In this situation we may have to assume that the same yield rate applies to all maturities in the issue, and proceed accordingly.

If the interest method is to be used in accounting for interest expense, the procedure is similar to that illustrated in connection with term bonds. The interest expense for each accounting period is an amount equal to the effective interest rate applied to the carrying amount of the bonds outstanding during that period, and the difference between this amount of interest expense and the actual interest payments represents the amortization of the bond discount or premium. The result is a constant rate of interest expense in relation to the carrying amount of the serial bonds outstanding.

A variation of the straight-line method, known as the **bonds outstanding method,** results in a decreasing amount of premium or discount amortization each accounting period proportionate to the decrease in the amount of outstanding debt.

Accounting for serial bonds illustrated

To illustrate the variation in the pattern of interest expense under each of these methods, assume that James Company issues $100,000 in five-year, 5% serial bonds, to be repaid in the amount of $20,000 each year. To simplify the illustration, assume that interest payments are made annually. If the bonds are issued to yield 6% a year, the proceeds total $97,375, as determined on top of page 622 from the 6% column in Table 2 of the Appendix in back of the book.

Computation of pro-
ceeds (present value) of
serial bonds issued at a
single effective rate of
interest

Principal and interest due at end of Year 1:

 ($20,000 + $5,000) × 0.943396 . . . . $23,585

Principal and interest due at end of Year 2:

 ($20,000 + $4,000) × 0.889996 21,360

Principal and interest due at end of Year 3:

 ($20,000 + $3,000) × 0.839619 19,311

Principal and interest due at end of Year 4:

 ($20,000 + $2,000) × 0.792094 17,426

Principal and interest due at end of Year 5:

 ($20,000 + $1,000) × 0.747258 15,693

    Present value (proceeds) of serial bonds at 6% yield basis $97,375

The accounting problem is to determine how the discount of $2,625 should be amortized over the term of the serial bond issue. Tables to determine periodic discount amortization and interest expense under the **interest** and **bonds outstanding** methods are illustrated below and on top of page 623.

Amortization of Discount on Serial Bonds by Interest Method

Year	(A) Carrying amount of bonds ($100,000 −E − F)	(B) "Effective" interest expense (6% of A)	(C) Interest payment	(D) Discount amortization (B − C)	(E) Bond discount balance (E − D)	(F) Cumulative principal payment
Issue	$97,375				$2,625	
1	78,217	$ 5,842	$ 5,000	$ 842	1,783	$ 20,000
2	58,910	4,693	4,000	693	1,090	40,000
3	39,444	3,534	3,000	534	556	60,000
4	19,811	2,367	2,000	367	189	80,000
5	–0–	1,189	1,000	189	–0–	100,000
Totals		$17,625	$15,000	$2,625		

The bonds outstanding method in this case produces results that are a close approximation of the effective interest expense because of the short term of the issue and the relatively small discount. The longer the term of the bonds and the larger the discount or premium, the larger would be the discrepancy between the two methods.

Under the straight-line method, discount amortization is $525 a year ($2,625 ÷ 5 = $525). The bonds outstanding method is essentially a straight-line method because it results in a constant periodic amortization of discount or premium **per $1,000 face amount of bonds outstanding.** In this example, the amount of annual discount amortization

Discount amortization
table for serial bonds—
bonds outstanding
method

Amortization of Discount on Serial Bonds by Bonds Outstanding Method

Year	Bonds out-standing (face amount)	Fraction of total of bonds out-standing	(A) Amortization of discount ($2,625 × fraction)	(B) Interest payments (5% of bonds out-standing)	Interest expense (A + B)
1	$100,000	10/30	$ 875	$ 5,000	$ 5,875
2	80,000	8/30	700	4,000	4,700
3	60,000	6/30	525	3,000	3,525
4	40,000	4/30	350	2,000	2,350
5	20,000	2/30	175	1,000	1,175
Totals	$300,000	30/30	$2,625	$15,000	$17,625

for each $1,000 bond outstanding is computed by dividing the total discount by the sum of the bonds outstanding over the term of the issue: ($2,625 ÷ $300,000 = $8.75 per $1,000 bond). If the discount amortization for each $1,000 bond is determined at the time of the issuance, it is a simple process to compute the appropriate amount of discount applicable to any amount of bonds in any given year throughout the term of a serial bond issue. Thus, in the fourth year, when $40,000 of bonds were outstanding, the discount to be amortized is computed as follows: $40,000 of bonds times $8.75 per $1,000 face amount equals $350.

Early extinguishment of serial bonds

When serial bonds mature, Bonds Payable is debited and Cash is credited. Because the carrying amount of the bonds in this case is equal to the amount paid, no gain or loss is recognized. If serial bonds are acquired prior to the regularly scheduled maturity date, a price different from carrying amount generally would be paid, and a gain or loss would result. The carrying amount of serial bonds is equal to the face amount plus the related unamortized premium (or less the related unamortized discount) and less any unamortized bond issue costs. All these account balances are canceled at the time of early extinguishment.

To illustrate the early extinguishment of serial bonds, assume that $10,000 of James Company bonds described in the preceding example are retired at the end of Year 2, two years prior to the scheduled retirement date. The bonds are retired at 101, and interest has been paid for Year 2. The discount applicable to the $10,000 of bonds being retired is determined by the bonds outstanding method on top of page 624.

Computation of discount applicable to bonds retired early

Discount applicable to Year 3: $\frac{10,000}{60,000} \times \$525^*$ . . . . $\$\ 87.50$

Discount applicable to Year 4: $\frac{10,000}{40,000} \times \$350^*$ 87.50

Total discount applicable to retired bonds . . . . $\$175.00\dagger$

* From Column A in table on top of page 623.
† Because the discount amortization amounts to $8.75 per $1,000 per year, this amount can be determined as follows: $8.75 × 10 × 2 = $175. Similar procedures can be used to compute amortization of discount on serial bonds when the "bond year" and the fiscal year of the issuer do not coincide.

The journal entry to record the early extinguishment appears below:

Journal entry for early extinguishment of serial bonds

Bonds Payable 10,000
Loss on Early Extinguishment of Bonds 275
    Discount on Bonds Payable. 175
    Cash. 10,100
To record early extinguishment of serial bonds, two years prior
to scheduled maturity date.

OTHER TOPICS RELATING TO LONG-TERM DEBT

Refunding a bond issue

Refunding is the process of retiring one bond issue with the proceeds of a new bond issue. When refunding occurs at the time the old debt matures, the carrying amount of such bonds is equal to face amount; no gain or loss arises from the retirement of the old bonds, and the new bonds are recorded in the usual manner.

A problem arises when refunding occurs prior to the maturity of the old bonds. This usually happens when interest rates have declined and the borrowing company can reduce its interest expense by canceling the old bond contract (paying the required penalty in the form of a call premium) and entering into a new one. If the two transactions (canceling old bonds and issuing new ones) are viewed as separate and unrelated events, no issues are raised that have not already been discussed. Retiring the old bonds results in a realized gain or loss equal to the difference between carrying amount and call price; the new bonds are recorded in the usual manner. However, some accountants have argued that the recognition of loss on the refunding prior to maturity should be postponed and amortized over part of, or the entire, term of the new bond issue.

For example, assume that Cleve Corporation has outstanding $1,000,000 of 12% bonds having 10 years to maturity and a carrying amount of $960,000 (face amount of $1,000,000, less unamortized discount of $40,000). Cleve calls the bonds at 105, using for this purpose the proceeds of a new 20-year issue of 10% bonds (which we will assume can be sold at face amount). Debt having a carrying amount of $960,000 thus is being refunded at a cost of $1,050,000, and a question arises as to the treatment of the $90,000 difference. Three solutions have been proposed:

1 Write off $90,000 (net of income tax effects) immediately as a loss.

2 Record the $90,000 (net of income tax effects) as a deferred charge and amortize it over the remaining term of the retired bonds (in this case 10 years).

3 Record the $90,000 (net of income tax effects) as a deferred charge and amortize it over the term of the new bonds (in this case 20 years).

The first alternative has the weight of logic in its favor. The amount of unamortized bond discount at any time measures the liability for additional interest that will accrue during the remaining term of bonds to compensate for the fact that the coupon rate of interest is less than the effective rate of interest. In order to be relieved of the old bond contract, the issuer is required to pay this $40,000 of interest now rather than at maturity date, and, in addition, to pay a $50,000 call premium. These costs of terminating an unfavorable bond contract are **related** to past periods but are **caused** by current economic factors (decline in the market rate of interest) and by management action (the decision to refund). To defer these costs would penalize future accounting periods, because the new 10% bonds could have been sold even if the 12% bonds had not been outstanding.

The Accounting Principles Board did not make a distinction between refunding and a nonrefunding retirement; it required that losses or gains on refunding, net of the income tax effects "should be recognized currently in income of the period of extinguishment. . . ."[8]

Arguments for the amortization over the remaining term of old bonds are based on the principle that when a cost is incurred, the benefits of which are expected to be realized over a period of years, the cost should be allocated as an expense over those years. It may be argued that the unamortized bond discount and the call premium paid to refund the bonds are costs incurred to obtain the benefit of lower interest expense during the remaining term of the refunded bonds. The payment of a call premium necessary to cancel an unfavorable bond contract and the write-off of unamortized discount on the contract may be viewed as events relating to the old bond contract and not as benefits to be derived from the new bond contract. Had a larger coupon rate of interest been set on the old bonds, they would have sold originally at face

[8] *APB Opinion No. 26*, pp. 501–502.

amount, and there would be no unamortized discount on the refunding date.

The third method rests on the premise that because the new bonds are a continuation of the old, the costs of both the old and new borrowings should be prorated over the term of the new bonds. The term of the new bonds generally is longer than the unexpired term of the refunded bonds. It was suggested that deferral of the "loss" was appropriate when the refunding takes place because of currently lower interest rates or anticipated higher interest rates in the future. This position assumes that the key reason for the refunding is to obtain a lower interest cost over the term of the new bonds.

Although students should be familiar with the alternatives discussed above, we must emphasize that only the first method (immediate recognition of losses or gains) is sanctioned by generally accepted accounting principles.

Deciding When to Refund a Bond Issue A decline in interest rates is not in itself a sufficient basis for a decision to refund a bond issue. The out-of-pocket costs of refunding must be compared with the present value of future interest savings. In addition, the income tax impact of refunding and bond indenture features on both the old and new bonds must be considered. Unamortized discount and bond issue costs applicable to the old bonds may be deducted for income tax purposes in the year of refunding. The call premium also is deductible for income tax purposes, but the issue costs of the new bonds must be amortized over their term. Future interest rates also should be considered, because a further decline in rates may mean that refunding can be made under even more favorable conditions at a later date.

To illustrate the type of analysis required for a bond refunding decision, assume the following for Piper Company on December 31, Year 10:

Data for analysis of bond refunding decision

10% bonds now outstanding, due Dec. 31, Year 20, callable currently at 105, interest payable June 30 and Dec. 31	$10,000,000
Unamortized discount and issue costs on 10% bonds now outstanding	300,000
New 8% bonds to be issued at 100, due Dec. 31, Year 20, callable at any time at 103, interest payable June 30 and Dec. 31	10,000,000
Estimated out-of-pocket costs of issuing new 8% bonds.	250,000
Effective combined federal and state income tax rate	50%

Because the term of the new 8% bonds is the same as the remaining term of the 10% bonds, and $10 million will have to be paid to bondholders at the end of Year 20 in either case, the decision whether or not to refund rests on a comparison between the net cost (after income taxes) of refunding and the present value of 20 rents representing the semiannual after-tax interest saving. Assuming straight-line amortization for income tax purposes, the analysis of the bond refunding is presented below:

<table>
<tr><td style="font-weight:bold">Computations of net after-tax cost of refunding and net semiannual after-tax interest saving from refunding</td><td colspan="3">Net after-tax cost of refunding:</td></tr>
</table>

Net after-tax cost of refunding:			
Call premium on 10% bonds, $500,000, and costs of issuing 8% bonds, $250,000, to be paid in cash			$750,000
Less: Tax saving from loss on call of 10% bonds, $800,000 × 50% (call premium, $500,000, and unamortized bond discount and issue costs on 10% bonds, $300,000).			400,000
Net after-tax cost of refunding.			$350,000
Net after-tax cash outlay for semiannual interest expense:			
On 10% bonds:			
Semiannual after-tax interest paid in cash ($10,000,000 × 10% × ½) × 50%		$250,000	
Less: Tax saving from amortization of bond discount and issue costs (300,000 × 1/20) × 50%		7,500	
Net after-tax cash outlay			$242,500
On 8% bonds:			
Semiannual after-tax interest paid in cash ($10,000,000 × 8% × ½) × 50%		$200,000	
Less: Tax savings from amortization of bond issue costs ($250,000 × 1/20) × 50%		6,250	
Net after-tax cash outlay			193,750
Net semiannual after-tax interest saving if refunding is carried out			$ 48,750

If we assume that the after-tax cost of capital is 4% (50% of interest rate on 8% bonds) compounded semiannually, the refunding would be advantageous. The net present value of the advantage from the refunding is computed as follows:

Net advantage from refunding	*Present value on Dec. 31, Year 10, of ordinary annuity of 20 rents of $48,750 at 2%: $48,750 × 16.351433 (from Table 4 of the Appendix)* $797,132
	Less: Net after-tax cost of refunding on Dec. 31, Year 10 (see above) 350,000
	Net present value on Dec. 31, Year 10, of advantage from refunding . . $447,132

In our example the 8% bonds had a term of 10 years, a period exactly equal to the remaining term of the 10% bonds. If the 8% bonds had a term of, say, 25 years, a question would arise whether there is any interest saving during the 15 years beyond the term of the 10% bonds. If we assumed that Piper Company could borrow at 8% when the 10% bonds mature in 10 years, the same analysis would apply, Piper would be in approximately the same position at the end of Year 20 whether the 10% bonds are refunded or not.

Convertible bonds

Current Practice A convertible bond may be exchanged for a stipulated number of shares of common stock. The conversion feature of a convertible bond enables the holders of such a security to enjoy the status of a creditor and at the same time participate in the price appreciation of the common stock. According to **APB Opinion No. 14,** "no portion of the proceeds from the issuance of . . . convertible debt securities . . . should be accounted for as attributable to the conversion feature."[9] Based on this principle, the accounting for the issuance and conversion of bonds is illustrated in the example below.

Assume that Brazos Company issued at face amount $10 million of 10-year, 6% convertible bonds. Interest on the bonds is paid semiannually. Each $1,000 bond is convertible to 30 shares of the company's $20 par common stock. The journal entries to record the issuance and subsequent conversion of the bonds are illustrated below:

Journal entries for issuance and conversion of bonds

Cash.	10,000,000	
6% Convertible Bonds Payable		10,000,000
To record issuance of 10-year, 6% convertible bonds at face amount.		
6% Convertible Bonds Payable	10,000,000	
Common Stock, $20 par		6,000,000
Paid-in Capital in Excess of Par		4,000,000
To record conversion of 10-year, 6% convertible bonds to 300,000 shares of $20 par common stock.		

When common stock is issued in exchange for convertible bonds, the carrying amount of the bonds is assigned to the common stock. Thus, no gain or loss is recognized on a conversion of bonds to common stock. Additional discussion of convertible bonds appears in Chapters 16 and 17.

[9] *APB Opinion No. 14,* "Accounting for Convertible Debt and Debt Issued with Stock Purchase Warrants," AICPA (New York: 1969), p. 207.

Evaluation of Current Practice Current practice for recording the issuance of convertible bonds does not, in the opinion of the authors, portray the economic substance of such transactions. When convertible bonds are issued, a portion of the proceeds logically should be attributable to the conversion feature, a factor that is reflected in a lower coupon rate of interest. Because the bondholder receives a "call" on the common stock, a portion of the proceeds assignable to the conversion feature theoretically should be recorded as paid-in capital, and a bond discount (or a reduced bond premium) should be recorded. The discount (or reduced premium) is equal to the difference between the amount at which the bonds were issued and the estimated amount for which they would have been issued in the absence of the conversion feature.

To illustrate, assume that the $10 million of 10-year, 6% convertible bonds were issued by Brazos Company (see page 628) when similar nonconvertible bonds were yielding 8% compounded semiannually. Present value tables indicate that 6% nonconvertible bonds would be issued for approximately $8,640,967 to yield 8% compounded semiannually. The journal entry to record the issuance of the bonds by Brazos Company, *if a value is assigned to the conversion feature,* follows:

Journal entry for issuance of convertible bonds, *assuming a value is assigned to the conversion feature*

Cash.	10,000,000	
Discount on Convertible Bonds Payable	1,359,033	
6% Convertible Bonds Payable		10,000,000
Paid-in Capital in Excess of Par		1,359,033
To record issuance of 10-year, 6% convertible bonds valued at $8,640,967 (excluding value of conversion feature).		

The discount would be amortized over the term of the bonds, thus increasing the amount of interest expense. If the bonds were converted prior to maturity, the carrying amount of the bonds would be transferred to the Common Stock and to Paid-in Capital in Excess of Par accounts.

In *Opinion No. 10,* the Accounting Principles Board required the assignment of a value to the conversion feature of convertible bonds as illustrated above, but a few years later, in *Opinion No. 14,* it reversed its position. The opposition expressed by corporate managements and investment bankers to the separate accounting for the debt and the conversion feature probably was responsible for the reversal of position by the APB. In the opinion of the authors, the position finally taken by the Board is difficult to support from a theoretical standpoint. However, the student is reminded that the earlier illustration on page 628 is in accord with current generally accepted accounting principles.

Early Extinguishment of Convertible Bonds   Should a gain or loss be recorded on the retirement of convertible bonds before maturity or conversion? A convertible bond is a hybrid security; thus, a simple answer to this question is not easy to give. When convertible bonds sell at a large premium because of their conversion feature, and management decides to retire the entire issue of bonds, it can call the bonds to force bondholders to convert. However, if management plans to retire only a portion of the issue, it could not exercise the call privilege and would have to pay the going market price for the bonds.

Because convertible bonds which are selling at a large premium are, in effect, an equity security, sound accounting theory suggests that the difference between the carrying amount of the bonds and the amount paid to retire them should be debited to paid-in capital, and not recorded as a loss. Under these circumstances the early retirement of the convertible bonds may be viewed as equivalent to a purchase of common stock for retirement. When convertible bonds sell at a substantial discount, not because of high market rates of interest but because the common stock is selling at a very low price, retirement of such bonds may be viewed as giving rise to paid-in capital. This line of reasoning is based on the fact that the intent of issuing convertible bonds is to raise equity capital, and the low price of the bonds is caused by the fact that the value of the bonds as an equity security has decreased. Despite arguments along these lines, the Accounting Principles Board in *Opinion No. 26* stated:[10]

> The extinguishment of convertible debt before maturity does not change the character of the security as between debt and equity at that time. Therefore, a difference between the cash acquisition price of the debt and its net carrying amount should be recognized currently in income in the period of extinguishment as losses or gains.

In the opinion of the authors, this principle in some cases may result in material gains or losses being reported in the income statement which are more in the nature of increases or decreases in paid-in capital.

Bonds issued with warrants attached

When bonds are issued that are not convertible to common stock but, instead, include **detachable warrants** giving the bondholder the right to purchase a certain number of shares of common stock at a fixed price, a separate value should be assigned to the warrants, based on the relative market values of the two securities. If only one security has a market value, such value is assigned to the one security, and the remainder of the proceeds is assigned to the other security. Thus, if $10 million of bonds, with warrants attached which have a market value of $500,000, are issued for $10 million, the issuance would be recorded as follows:

[10] *APB Opinion No. 26,* p. 502.

Cash	*10,000,000*	
Discount on Bonds Payable	*500,000*	
Bonds Payable		*10,000,000*
Paid-in Capital—Stock Purchase Warrants		*500,000*
To record issuance of bonds with common stock		
purchase warrants attached.		

Journal entry for issuance of bonds with warrants attached (margin caption)

Because the warrants are valued at $500,000, the bonds in effect were issued at 95. The APB supported this approach in *Opinion No. 14* as follows:[11]

> The Board is of the opinion that the portion of the proceeds of debt securities issued with detachable stock purchase warrants which is allocable to the warrants should be accounted for as paid-in capital. The allocation should be based on the relative fair values of the two securities at the time of issuance. Any resulting discount or premium on the debt securities should be accounted for as such. . . . However, when stock purchase warrants are not detachable from the debt and the debt security must be surrendered in order to exercise the warrant, the two securities taken together are substantially equivalent to convertible debt. . . .

When the warrants are exercised, the value assigned to the warrants is viewed as additional proceeds from the issuance of common stock. This topic is discussed in more detail in Chapter 17.

Bond sinking fund and appropriation of retained earnings

Some bond indentures require that a sinking fund be established for the retirement of the bonds. Ordinarily, a bond sinking fund would not be created in connection with the issuance of serial bonds; such bonds are retired periodically in lieu of making sinking fund deposits. A disadvantage inherent in bond sinking funds is that a portion of the money borrowed for business purposes is not being used in this manner if cash is deposited in a sinking fund.

A formal restriction on the payment of dividends, which is typical in bond indentures, does not require the appropriation of retained earnings; however, restrictions on retained earnings should be disclosed in the financial statements or accompanying notes. The appropriation of retained earnings for this purpose was never an efficient means of disclosure and is no longer in common use.

[11] *APB Opinion No. 14*, p. 209.

Miscellaneous long-term liabilities

Other long-term liabilities such as notes payable to banks, equipment contracts payable, purchase-money obligations, and mortgage notes payable, frequently are found in financial statements of business enterprises. The essential accounting problems related to these liabilities are similar to those applicable to bonds. The important point is that all long-term liabilities initially should be recorded at the present value of the amounts to be paid. This is particularly important when debts are incurred in connection with acquisition of noncash assets or are assumed by the combinor (acquiring company) in a business combination. In the acquisition of a going business enterprise, if liabilities are not fairly valued, the amount of unidentifiable intangibles (goodwill) and the periodic amortization of such intangibles will be misstated.

As pointed out in earlier chapters, a variety of other "deferred credit" or "quasi-liability" items sometimes are included under long-term liabilities in condensed balance sheets. These may range from unearned revenue items to items such as "excess of equity in net assets of subsidiary over cost," deferred investment tax credits, and deferred income taxes.

Distinguishing between liabilities and stockholders' equity

Because interest is deductible for income tax purposes and a payment designated as dividends is not, it is inevitable that creative financial managers will devise liability contracts which bestow on the securities as many of the characteristics of enterprise ownership as possible without destroying their income tax status as debt. As a result, the dividing line between debt and stockholders' equity often is blurred. An extreme example on the liability side is *subordinated income bonds.* These bonds are secured only by the general credit standing of the issuer, and the bond contract provides that interest will be paid only when and if earnings are sufficient. Interest payments on such a bond usually are cumulative, but failure to pay interest does not give bondholders the right to interfere in corporate affairs. It is clear that a substantial amount of risk, comparable to that borne by stockholders, attaches to such bonds. The basic characteristic distinguishing subordinated income bonds from preferred stock is that the bonds have a maturity date. The absence of a maturity provision would give the Internal Revenue Service grounds for holding that subordinated income bonds are equivalent to preferred stock.

On the stockholders' equity side of the dividing line, some forms of preferred stock are similar to debt. A preferred stock issue which has no voting rights, carries a stated cumulative dividend, and requires redemption at specified dates represents only a very limited form of ownership equity. Such preferred stock, in effect, represents "a liability masquerading as stockholders' equity," and requires special reporting in the balance sheet. This type of preferred stock is discussed in Chapter 16.

The question arises, in dealing with such cases, whether the distinction can be drawn with sufficient clarity to make a clear-cut division in accounting between liabilities and stockholders' equity. Some accountants have argued that the entire right side of the balance sheet should be labeled "equities," and that the distinction between liabilities and stockholders' equity may not be important.

Accounting for restructured debt

Business enterprises that encounter financial difficulties sometimes are able to negotiate more favorable terms with creditors for currently existing debt. The result of such an arrangement in a troubled loan situation is referred to as a **restructuring of debt** and may include the following provisions:

1 Extension of the due date of principal and interest payments

2 Reduction in the rate of interest on existing debt

3 Forgiveness by creditors of a portion of principal or accrued interest

In considering the appropriate accounting for a restructured debt, the FASB initially suggested that a gain or loss should be recognized by the debtor "in an amount equal to the difference between (1) the net carrying amount of the debt before the restructuring, and (2) the present value of the cash payments (both principal and interest) required to be made by the debtor after the restructuring discounted at the effective pre-restructuring rate of interest."[12]

Most debt restructurings would have resulted in a gain to debtors and a loss to creditors if the foregoing suggestion had been implemented by the FASB. As a result, creditors (particularly banks) opposed this proposed standard, and the Financial Accounting Standards Board issued **Statement No. 15,** which suggested that no gain or loss be recognized by debtors when **only a modification of terms is involved,** unless the carrying amount of the debt exceeds the total future cash payments specified by the new terms.[13] If the carrying amount of the debt exceeds future cash payments, the debtor reduces the carrying amount of the debt, and all cash payments are recorded as reductions in the debt. Thus, the debtor recognizes a gain equal to the reduction in the carrying amount of the debt, and no interest expense is recorded between the date of restructuring and the maturity date of the debt.

[12] *Proposed Statement of Financial Accounting Standards,* "Restructuring of Debt in a Troubled Loan Situation," FASB (Stamford: 1975), p. 3.

[13] *FASB Statement No. 15,* "Accounting by Debtors and Creditors for Troubled Debt Restructurings," FASB (Stamford: 1977), p. 7.

To illustrate the accounting for a debt restructuring as a result of a modification of terms, assume that Paul Corporation has the following debt on December 31, Year 10:

Composition of debt on Dec. 31, Year 10, prior to restructuring

Loan payable, 12%, due Dec. 31, Year 11.	$5,000,000
Accrued interest payable	600,000

On December 31, Year 10, the loan was restructured as follows: (1) $500,000 of the note principal and the $600,000 of accrued interest were forgiven by creditors, (2) the maturity date was extended to December 31, Year 15, and (3) the interest rate was reduced from 12% to 8% a year. Because the total future cash payments under the new terms amount to $6,300,000 (principal of $4,500,000 and interest of $1,800,000 for five years at 8%), which exceeds the $5,600,000 carrying amount of the debt prior to the restructuring, no gain or loss is recognized. The excess of the total payments over the carrying amount of the debt, $700,000 ($6,300,000 − $5,600,000 = $700,000), is recognized as interest expense at a computed effective interest rate on the restructured amount of the debt, that is, $4,500,000.

However, if the interest rate had been reduced from 12% to 4%, the total future cash payments under the new terms would be $5,400,000 (principal of $4,500,000 and interest of $900,000 for five years at 4%), which is $200,000 less than the $5,600,000 pre-restructuring carrying amount of the debt. In this case, the debtor would record the debt restructuring and the subsequent payments as follows:

Journal entries for restructured debt involving a gain on restructuring

Loan Payable.	5,000,000	
Accrued Interest Payable.	600,000	
Restructured Loan Payable (including interest of		
$900,000 for five years).		5,400,000
Gain on Restructuring of Debt		200,000
To record restructuring of debt on Dec. 31, Year 10, including reduction in interest rate from 12% to 4%.		
Restructured Loan Payable	900,000	
Cash		900,000
To record payments of interest at the rate of $180,000 **each year for five years** (Dec. 31, Years 11–15).		
Restructured Loan Payable	4,500,000	
Cash		4,500,000
To record payment of principal on Dec. 31, Year 15.		

Debt restructurings may take many forms and involve complex accounting issues. The example above was designed to illustrate a relatively simple modification of terms without any cash transactions included in the debt restructuring.

Long-term debt in the balance sheet

All long-term debt should be described in the balance sheet or accompanying notes. Business enterprises having large amounts of long-term debt in the form of numerous issues often show only one amount in the balance sheet and support this with a note which presents the details of maturity dates, interest rates, call provisions, conversion features, assets pledged as collateral, and limitations on dividends or other restrictions imposed on the borrower. (For example, see *Note 14* on page 162.)

The FASB requires disclosure of the combined aggregate amount of maturities and sinking fund requirements of all long-term borrowings for each of the five years following the balance sheet date.[14]

Any portion of long-term debt which matures within one year should be listed as a current liability, unless the retirement of the debt will not require the use of current assets. If, during the ensuing year, long-term debt will be converted to common stock, refunded, or repaid from a sinking fund already established, there is no reason to change its classification to a current liability as long as the expected method of retirement is disclosed. Long-term unrecorded purchase obligations also should be disclosed in a note.

REVIEW QUESTIONS

1 Define the following: *debenture bonds, term bonds, serial bonds, convertible bonds, bond indenture, nominal (coupon) rate, effective (yield) rate,* and *call premium.*

2 A bond carrying a coupon rate of interest of 10% is sold to yield 12%. Will the bond sell at a premium or a discount? Explain.

3 A $1 million bond issue is sold for $960,000. A few months later the bonds are selling at 102. Give possible reasons for the increase in the market value of the bonds and explain the significance of the increase to the issuer.

4 Viking Company plans to issue $1 million 12%, 10-year bonds. What will be the average annual interest expense if the bonds are issued at 104? At 97?

5 If bonds are issued at a premium and the *interest method* is used to amortize the premium, will the annual interest expense increase or decline over the term of the bonds? Explain.

6 Canton Company has just issued $100 million of 15-year debenture bonds at a discount. At an annual stockholders' meeting, a stockholder asks the con-

---

[14] *FASB Statement No. 47,* "Disclosure of Long-Term Obligations," FASB (Stamford: 1981), pp. 4–5.

troller to explain the nature of bond discount and issue costs, which are included among the company's assets at $4,829,000. The controller answers, "This represents prepaid interest of $4.7 million and deferred bond issue costs of $129,000 on our bonds, which are being amortized over the term of the debt." Evaluate the controller's answer.

7 Explain how the interest accrued on bonds can be accounted for when bonds are issued between interest dates.

8 How should unamortized discount and premium on bonds payable be classified in the balance sheet? How should deferred bond issue costs be classified?

9 Describe the preferred treatment of the difference between the carrying amount of bonds payable and the amount paid to retire the bonds. How is the difference handled in the accounting records and in the financial statements when bonds are refunded?

10 List some factors that management should consider in deciding when to refund a bond issue.

11 What are the advantages to a growing corporation of issuing convertible bonds?

12 What is the generally accepted practice in regard to the assignment of a value to the conversion feature of convertible bonds? Present an argument in favor of assigning to the conversion feature a part of the proceeds received on the issuance of convertible bonds.

13 Briefly describe the accounting for bonds which include detachable warrants to purchase common stock.

14 An executive of a railroad was quoted as saying, "Debt management is a continuous process that is essential to good operations. I shall never take on debt without a sinking fund." Comment on the executive's position.

15 Pardee Company has outstanding an issue of **10% subordinated debentures** and an issue of **10% cumulative preferred stock,** callable at par. What is the basic distinction between these two securities that determines their balance sheet classification?

16 How should the restructuring of debt through a modification of terms be accounted for by the debtor if the carrying amount of the restructured debt exceeds the total payments to be made on the debt?

EXERCISES

Ex. 15-1   Select the best answer for each of the following multiple-choice questions:

1 When the interest payment dates of a bond issue are May 1 and November 1, and a bond issue is sold on June 1, the amount of cash received by the issuer is:
a Decreased by accrued interest from June 1 to November 1
b Decreased by accured interest from May 1 to June 1

    c Increased by accrued interest from June 1 to November 1
    d Increased by accrued interest from May 1 to June 1

2 On January 2, Year 3, Boston Company issued $600,000 of 12%, 10-year bonds at 103. The bonds are callable at 104. Boston has recorded amortization of the bond premium by the straight-line method (which was not materially different from the interest method). Bond issue costs may be disregarded.

    On December 31, Year 7, Boston reacquired $300,000 of the bonds in the open market at 97. Boston has recorded interest and amortization for Year 7. Disregarding income taxes and assuming that the gain is material, Boston should report this reacquisition as:
    a A gain of 13,500
    b An extraordinary gain of $13,500
    c A gain of $21,000
    d An extraordinary gain of $21,000

3 In theory (disregarding any other market variables), the proceeds from the issuance of bonds will be equal to:
    a The face amount of the bonds
    b The present value of the principal amount due at the end of the term of the bonds plus the present value of the interest payments made during the term of the bonds, each discounted at the market rate of interest at the date of issuance
    c The face amount of the bonds plus the present value of the interest payments made during the term of the bonds discounted at the market rate of interest at the date of issuance
    d The sum of the face amount of the bonds and the periodic interest payments

4 On March 1, Year 7, Coffey Company issued $500,000 of 12%, 20-year nonconvertible bonds at 103. In addition, each $1,000 bond was issued with 30 detachable stock warrants, each of which entitled the bondholder to acquire for $50 one share of Coffey's common stock. Bond issue costs may be disregarded.

    On March 1, Year 7, the current fair value of Coffey's common stock was $40 a share and the current fair value of the warrants was $4. What amount should Coffey record on March 1, Year 7, as paid-in capital from stock purchase warrants?
    a $15,000   *b* $60,000   *c* $375,000   *d* $750,000

Ex. 15-2 On December 1, Year 6, Dover Company issued its 13%, $2,000,000 face amount bonds for $2,200,000, plus accrued interest. Interest is payable on February 1 and August 1. Bond issue costs may be disregarded. On December 31, Year 8, the carrying amount of the bonds, inclusive of the unamortized premium, was $2,100,000. On July 1, Year 9, Dover reacquired the bonds at 98, plus accrued interest. Dover appropriately uses the straight-line method for the amortization of bond premium because the results do not differ materially from the interest method.

    Compute the gain or loss on this early extinguishment of debt. Show supporting computations.

Ex. 15-3 Bostich Company plans to issue $5 million, 12% bonds, due 20 years from date of issue. Interest is payable semiannually.

    Compute the probable proceeds of the bond issue if the market rate of interest compounded semiannually is *(a)* 10%, and *(b)* 14%. Use the present value tables in the Appendix in back of the book.

Ex. 15-4 Cleaves Company issued $2,000,000 of 10%, 10-year convertible bonds on June 1, Year 1, for $1,941,000 plus accrued interest. The bonds were dated April 1, Year 1, with interest payable April 1 and October 1. Bond discount is amortized semiannually on a straight-line basis. Bond issue costs may be disregarded.

On April 1, Year 2, $500,000 of these bonds were converted to 20,000 shares of $20 par common stock. Accrued interest was paid at the time of conversion.

a If the Accrued Bond Interest Payable account was credited when the bonds were issued, prepare a journal entry to record the first interest payment and to amortize the discount on October 1, Year 1. Round computations to the nearest dollar.

b Prepare a journal entry to record the conversion of bonds on April 1, Year 2. Assume that amortization of bond discount and payment of interest have been recorded. Round computations to the nearest dollar.

Ex. 15-5 On January 2, Year 5, Forney Company issued 12% bonds with a face amount of $1,000,000. The bonds mature in 10 years, and interest is paid semiannually on June 30 and December 31. The bonds were issued for $894,060 to yield 14% compounded semiannually.

Using the interest method, compute the amount that should be debited to Bond Interest Expense in Year 5. Round all amounts to the nearest dollar.

Ex. 15-6 On October 1, Year 8, Searle Company issued $6 million serial bonds requiring the payment of $1.2 million principal each year, beginning October 1, Year 9.

a Explain how a $270,000 discount on this bond issue would be amortized if the bonds outstanding method were used.

b How much of the discount would be amortized in the fiscal year ended December 31, Year 10 by the bonds outstanding method?

Ex. 15-7 Suppose that the bonds issued in **Ex. 15–6** required the payment of $1.2 million at the end of each of five years, starting at the end of the third year after issue date.

Prepare a schedule of discount amortization computed by the bonds outstanding method.

Ex. 15-8 On December 31, Year 12, Oxnard Company had outstanding 10 million of 12%, 20-year bonds due in seven years and nine months. The unamortized premium on the bonds on October 1, Year 12, was $840,000.

Prepare journal entries **(a)** to record the accrual of interest and amortization of the premium for the three months ended December 31, Year 12, and **(b)** to record the call of $1 million of these bonds on January 2, Year 13, at 102 plus accrued interest for three months, assuming that premium is amortized on a straight-line basis and that reversing entries are not used. Disregard bond issue costs.

Ex. 15-9 The balance sheet of Kinsey Company included the following items on December 31, Year 4:

10% convertible bonds payable (due Dec. 31, Year 20) $2,000,000
Premium on convertible bonds payable 40,000

No value was assigned to the conversion feature when the bonds were issued. Each $1,000 bond is convertible to 35 shares of $5 par common stock.

Using the theoretically preferable method, record the conversion of all bonds to common stock on January 2, Year 5, assuming a market price of the common stock of $40 a share.

Ex. 15-10 Johnovich Company issued $1 million face amount 9% bonds with detachable warrants attached. The bonds were issued for $1,015,000. Immediately after issuance, the bonds were quoted at 96, and the warrants had a total market value of $90,000.

Prepare a journal entry to record the issuance of the bonds, assuming that no accrued interest was charged to purchasers of the bonds and that total proceeds were allocated on the basis of the relative market values of the bonds and warrants. Disregard bond issue costs.

Ex. 15-11 Lorraine Company plans to finance the purchase of plant assets by issuing 10% bonds. Management projects earnings, **before** deduction of bond interest expense and income taxes expense, at $4,664,000 a year. Lorraine's income tax rate is 40%. Management wants its net earnings **after** deduction of bond interest and income taxes to be ten times the bond interest expense.

Assuming that the bonds can be issued to yield 10%, compute the face amount of bonds which should be issued.

Ex. 15-12 Irvington Company has a $10,000,000 loan payable outstanding on June 30, Year 8, which is due in one year. Interest at 10% a year has been paid through June 30, Year 8. The fiscal year of the company ends on June 30. Because of Irvington's poor financial condition, creditors have agreed to restructure the loan on June 30, Year 8, as follows: The maturity date of the loan is extended to June 30, Year 10; $1,500,000 of the principal is forgiven; and the interest rate is reduced to 5% a year on the reduced amount of principal.

Compute the gain on the restructuring of the debt and prepare journal entries in the accounting records of Irvington Company to record the restructuring of the debt and all payments on the loan through June 30, Year 10.

SHORT CASES FOR ANALYSIS AND DECISION

Case 15-1 a The appropriate method of amortizing a premium or discount on the issuance of bonds is the interest method.

Instructions
(1) What is the interest method of amortization, and how is it different from and similar to the straight-line method of amortization?
(2) How is amortization computed by the interest method, and why and how do amounts obtained by the interest method differ from amounts computed by the straight-line method?

b Gains or losses from the early extinguishment of debt that is refunded can be accounted for in three ways:
   Amortized over the remaining term of the old debt
   Amortized over the term of the new debt
   Recognized in the accounting period of the refunding

Instructions
(1) Discuss the supporting arguments for each of the three methods of accounting for gains and losses from the early extinguishment of debt that is refunded.
(2) Which of the above methods is generally accepted, and how should the appropriate amount of gain or loss be shown in the financial statements?

Case 15-2 The balance sheet for Garvey Company at the end of Year 5 follows:

GARVEY COMPANY
Balance Sheet
End of Year 5
(in thousands of dollars)
Assets

Current assets:

Cash	$ 5,000
Short-term investments (at cost, market value $15.2 million)	15,000
Accounts receivable (net)	10,000
Inventories	24,000
Short-term prepayments	1,000
Total current assets	$ 55,000
Plant assets (net)	40,000
Other noncurrent assets	5,000
Total assets	$100,000

Liabilities & Stockholders' Equity

Current liabilities	$ 35,000
12% bonds payable, callable at 105, each $1,000 bond convertible into 25	
shares of capital stock	40,000
Total liabilities	$ 75,000
Stockholders' equity:	
Capital stock, no par, 2,000,000 shares authorized, 1,000,000	
shares issued and outstanding . . . . $ 5,000	
Retained earnings 20,000	
Total stockholders' equity	25,000
Total liabilities & stockholders' equity	$100,000

The president of Garvey Company thinks that the company is facing a serious financing problem, which she outlines for you as follows:

"We must raise approximately $50 million dollars over the next two years in order to finance the expansion of our product lines and sales territories. My banker friends tell me that our balance sheet is not in good shape. They have pointed out repeatedly that our current ratio (current assets divided by current liabilities) is significantly below the industry standard of 2 to 1 and that approximately 75% of our assets are financed by borrowed capital. They feel this is much too high, considering the type of industry we are in. We don't want to issue more capital stock to the public, and apparently we can't issue additional bonds unless our balance sheet can be cleaned up. I wish we had paid more attention to the management of our assets: We have $15 million invested in low-yielding securities, our accounts receivable and inventories are twice as large as they ought to be, and we have been paying out too much in dividends. Our profits have been growing steadily, and we pay a dividend of $3 a share on our stock. As a result, our stock is selling at $55 a share and our bonds are currently trading close to 140 on the open market. I would appreciate your advice on this matter."

Instructions Briefly outline a course of action the president should follow in "cleaning up" the balance sheet and raising the $50 million needed for expansion. Ignore the effect of income taxes in your answer.

Case 15-3 Largo Company was organized two years ago by two experienced business executives and several members of the faculty at a local university. The main product line of the company consists of medium-size computers and software for all types of data-processing and information-gathering systems. The company's assets total $15 million and the liabilities amount to $10.5 million, consisting of $3 million of short-term debt and $7.5 million of notes payable to an insurance company. There are 100,000 shares of common stock issued and outstanding. In order to expand its activities, the company needs $5 million in long-term capital. Members of the board of directors have discussed various proposals for raising the capital and have asked for your advice regarding the following alternatives:

(1) Issue bonds bearing interest at 13% with a sinking-fund provision.
(2) Issue 10% bonds at face amount. The bonds would be convertible to 40,000 shares of the company's common stock at $125 a share. The current market price of the common stock is $96 a share.
(3) Issue 9% preferred stock at a par of $100. The preferred stock would be callable at $105 and convertible to three-fourths of one share of common stock.
(4) Issue 60,000 shares of common stock at $85 a share through a rights offering. Stockholders would be given rights to buy one additional share of common stock for every 10 shares held.

Instructions Evaluate the advantages and disadvantages of each of the four alternatives.

Case 15-4 The directors of Lomita Company are contemplating the issuance of $15 million of bonds. The company does not need the money immediately, but Director Alan, a former banker, has convinced the board that the bonds should be issued "while interest rates are relatively low and money is readily available."

Banker Krueger, representative of a leading investment banking firm, also recommended that bonds should be issued because interest rates are beginning to turn up and a coupon rate of 12% probably would command a modest premium. Krueger believes that the board is making a mistake in not considering the issuance of convertible debentures instead of regular bonds for the following reasons:

(1) It would be cheaper for the company (a rate of about 9% would probably be sufficient).
(2) The company's stockholders' equity will need "beefing up" as it continues to expand its activities.
(3) It is a means of selling common stock at about 20% above the current market price.

Director Barney, vice president of finance, suggested that a 13% rate be assigned to nonconvertible bonds, stating, "A large premium is a sign of financial strength of our company; if interest rates continue to advance, 12% bonds will sell at a discount, and I don't want people thinking that our credit is so poor that we have to give a discount in order to sell our bonds."

Director Carla, a public relations executive, disagreed with Director Barney. She stated that investors are "bargain hunters" who would be more willing to buy bonds at a discount than at a premium. She would assign an 11% coupon rate to the bonds, stating "discount on bonds payable is prepaid interest, and it will not hurt us to have a jump on our interest payments to bondholders."

Instructions Evaluate each of the four views expressed in this case.

Case 15-5 Ross Company recently issued $1 million face amount, 14%, 30-year subordinated debentures at 97. The debentures are redeemable at 103 on demand by the issuer at any date upon 30 days notice 10 years after issue. The debentures are convertible to $10 par common stock of the company at the conversion price of $12.50 a share for each $500 (or multiple thereof) of the face amount of the debentures. Debenture issue costs may be disregarded.

Instructions

a Explain how the conversion feature of convertible debt has a value to the
(1) Issuer
(2) Investor

b Management has suggested that in recording the issuance of the debentures a portion of the proceeds should be assigned to the conversion feature.
(1) What are the arguments for according separate accounting recognition to the conversion feature of the debentures?
(2) What are the arguments supporting accounting for the convertible debentures as a single element?

c Assume that no value was assigned to the conversion feature on issuance of the debentures. Assume further that five years after issuance, debentures in the face amount of $100,000 and carrying amount of $97,500 were presented for conversion on an interest payment date when the market price of the debentures was 104, the common stock was selling at $14 a share, and the company recorded the conversion as follows:

Bonds Payable	*100,000*	
Discount on Bonds Payable		*2,500*
Common Stock, $10 par		*80,000*
Paid-in Capital in Excess of Par		*17,500*
To record conversion of bonds to common stock.		

Discuss the propriety of the above accounting treatment.

PROBLEMS

15-1 On January 2, Year 4, Bogart Company issued $1,000,000 in five year, 9% serial bonds to be repaid in the amount of $200,000 on January 2 of Year 5 through Year 9. Interest is payable at the end of each year. The bonds were issued to yield an annual rate of 10%.

Instructions

a Prepare a working paper to compute the total amount received from the issuance of the serial bonds. Show supporting computations, rounded to the nearest dollar.

b Prepare a working paper for the amortization of the bond discount for the first two years after issuance, under the interest method. Show supporting computations, rounded to the nearest dollar.

15-2 On December 1, Year 5, Robards Company issued 10-year bonds of $2 million at 102. Interest is payable on June 1 and December 1 at the rate of 9%. On April 1, Year 7, Robards extinguished (retired) 600 of these bonds at 96, plus accrued interest. The accounting period for Robards ends on December 31. Bond issue costs may be disregarded.

Instructions Prepare journal entries to record the following. (Round all amounts to the nearest dollar.)

a The issuance of the bonds on December 1, Year 5.

b Interest payments and amortization in Year 6. Amortization is recorded by the straight-line method at the time of interest payments and at the end of the year. The company does not follow the policy of preparing reversing entries for the accrual of bond interest at the end of the year.

c The early extinguishment of $600,000 of bonds on April 1, Year 7. (Hint: First amortize premium for three months on the bonds retired, with a credit to Bond Interest Expense.)

15-3 On July 1, Year 1, Magnus Company issued bonds with a face amount of $1,000,000 maturing in ten years. The coupon interest rate was 9%, payable semiannually on June 30 and December 31. The bonds were issued to yield 10% compounded semiannually. There were no bond issue costs.

On June 30, Year 2, Magnus issued $500,000 of bonds with warrants attached. These bonds had a coupon interest rate of 8%, payable semiannually, and were issued at 105. One detachable warrant to purchase common stock was attached to each $1,000 bond. The current fair value of each bond without the warrant was $966. There were no bond issue costs.

Instructions
a Using the Appendix in back of the book, compute the proceeds received for the 9% bonds issued on July 1, Year 1.
b Prepare journal entries to record the following:
(1) Issuance of bonds on July 1, Year 1
(2) Payment of interest and amortization (by the interest method) on December 31, Year 1
(3) Payment of interest and amortization (by the interest method) on June 30, Year 2
c Prepare a journal entry to record the issuance of the 8% bonds on June 30. Year 2.

15-4 The balance sheet of Moreno Company on June 30, Year 5, included the following accounts:

12% first mortgage bonds payable, maturing on June 30, Year 20 .	*$20,000,000*
Discount on bonds payable	*600,000*
Deferred bond issue costs.	*132,000*

Instructions
a Compute the annual interest expense, including amortization of bond issue costs. Straight-line amortization is used.
b Prepare a journal entry to record the retirement of $4 million of bonds at 105 on July 1, Year 10. The company's fiscal year ends on June 30.
c Show how the accounts relating to bonds payable would appear in the balance sheet on June 30, Year 15.

15-5 On July 1, Year 5, Yashiro Company issued $5 million of 9%, 20-year bonds with interest payable on March 1 and September 1. Yashiro received proceeds of $5,120,500, including accrued interest from March 1, Year 5. Bond issue costs may be disregarded. The bonds mature on March 1, Year 25.

Instructions Prepare journal entries required on each of the following dates:
a July 1, Year 5 (issuance of bonds)
b September 1, Year 5 (payment of interest and amortization of discount for two months by the straight-line method)
c December 31, Year 5 (accrual of interest and amortization of discount from September 1 to December 31)

15-6 In July, Year 1, the board of directors of Millburn Company authorized the issuance of $50 million of 10%, 20-year bonds payable, dated September 1, Year 1. Interest on these bonds is payable semiannually on March 1 and September 1. The bonds were issued to underwriters on September 1, Year 1. Millburn amortizes discount and premium by the interest method at each interest payment date and at the end of the accounting period. Bond issue costs may be disregarded.

Instructions Prepare journal entries to record the issuance of the bonds, the adjusting entry on December 31, Year 1 (the close of Millburn's fiscal year), the journal entries to record the first two semiannual interest payments, and the adjusting entry on December 31, Year 2, assuming that:

a The bonds were issued to the underwriters to yield 9%. (Round all computations to the nearest dollar.)

b The bonds were issued to the underwriters to yield 11%. (Round all computations to the nearest dollar.)

15-7 Kingston Company was authorized to issue $10 million of 10-year, 12% convertible bonds due December 31, Year 15. Each $1,000 bond is convertible to 40 shares of $10 par common stock, and the bond indenture contained an antidilution provision. The bonds were issued to underwriters on March 1, Year 6, for net proceeds of $10,129,200, including accrued interest. Interest is payable semiannually on June 30 and December 31. Discount is amortized by the straight-line method. Bond issue costs may be disregarded.

Late in Year 6, the company declared a 10% stock dividend on the common stock, and in Year 7 the common stock was split 2 for 1. The interest payments and the amortization of discount by the straight-line method were recorded to January 1, Year 8. On May 1, Year 8, bonds with a face amount of $1,000,000 were converted, and the accrued interest on these bonds was paid.

Instructions

a Prepare a journal entry to record the issuance of bonds. No value was assigned to the conversion feature.

b Prepare a journal entry to record, for the first four months of Year 8, the payment of interest and the amortization of discount on the bonds converted.

c Prepare a journal entry to record the conversion of $1,000,000 face amount of bonds on May 1, Year 8. (An antidilution provision calls for a proportionate adjustment in the number of shares to which each bond can be converted if the common stock is split or if stock dividends are distributed.)

15-8 Chou Company issued $2 million of 11% serial bonds for $2,072,000 on January 2, Year 1. The bonds mature at the rate of $400,000 a year starting on December 31, Year 1. Interest is payable on June 30 and December 31. Bond issue costs may be disregarded.

Instructions

a Prepare a working paper showing the amortization of the premium and total interest expense for each year through Year 5. Amortization is computed by the bonds outstanding method.

b On July 1, Year 2, $200,000 of the bonds, which were scheduled to be retired on December 31, Year 4, were retired at 102. Prepare a journal entry to record the retirement, assuming that the amortization of the premium was recorded through June 30, Year 2, when the semiannual interest was paid.

15-9 Ratkovich Company issued $4 million face amount of three-year, 9% bonds. Interest is payable semiannually on June 30 and December 31. The bonds were issued on January 1, Year 1, at a price which gave the company an effective interest cost of 5% semiannually. Bond issue costs may be disregarded.

Instructions

a Compute the proceeds of the bond issue and prepare an amortization table, similar to that illustrated on page 612, showing the interest expense for each six-month period by the interest method. (Round all computations to the nearest dollar.)

b Using the data in the amortization table prepared in *a,* prepare journal entries to record the issuance of the bonds, the interest payments at the end of the first six months and at the end of the last six months of the bond issue, and the extinguishment of the bonds at maturity on December 31, Year 3.

15-10 Commans Company issued $10 million of 10-year, 12% convertible bonds on September 30, Year 1, for $9,064,000, plus interest for three months. Bond issue costs of $23,400 were incurred and recorded in a separate account. No value was assigned to the conversion feature. Interest is payable semiannually on June 30 and December 31. The bonds were callable after June 30, Year 6, and until June 30, Year 8, at 104, thereafter until maturity, at 102; and were convertible to $2.50 par common stock as follows:

(1) Until June 30, Year 6, at the rate of six shares for each $1,000 bond
(2) From July 1, Year 6, to June.30, Year 9, at the rate of five shares for each $1,000 bond
(3) After June 30, Year 9, at the rate of four shares for each $1,000 bond

The bonds mature on June 30, Year 11. The company prepares adjusting entries monthly and closes its accounting records yearly on December 31. Bond discount and bond issue costs are amortized on a straight-line basis.

The following transactions occurred in connection with the bonds:

July 1, Year 7: $2 million of bonds were converted to common stock.
Jan. 1, Year 9: $1 million of bonds were purchased on the open market at 98 and were retired.
June 30, Year 9: The remaining $7 million of bonds were called for redemption. In order to obtain the necessary funds for redemption and business expansion, Commans issued $10 million of 10% bonds at face amount. These bonds were dated June 30, Year 9, and were due on June 30, Year 29.

Instructions Prepare journal entries to record the above transactions, including monthly adjustments where appropriate, as of each of the following dates. (Do not prepare closing entries, and include supporting computations as part of journal entry explanations.)
a Sept. 30, Year 1. (Record bond issue costs in a separate journal entry.)
b Dec. 31, Year 1. (Record one month's interest and amortization in a separate entry before recording the payment of interest.)
c July 1, Year 7.
d Jan. 1, Year 9.
e June 30, Year 9. (Record the accrual of interest and related amortization of discount and issue costs, the payment of interest, the redemption of $7 million of 12% convertible bonds, and the issuance of $10 million of 10% bonds in separate journal entries.)

4 STOCKHOLDERS' EQUITY

16
CORPORATIONS: PAID-IN CAPITAL,
RETAINED EARNINGS, AND DIVIDENDS

17
CORPORATIONS: STOCK RIGHTS, WARRANTS,
OPTIONS, AND CONVERTIBLE SECURITIES

18
CORPORATIONS: TREASURY
STOCK AND EARNINGS PER SHARE

16 CORPORATIONS: PAID-IN CAPITAL, RETAINED EARNINGS, AND DIVIDENDS

One of the striking features of our economy is the dominant role played by corporations. Corporations are responsible for the bulk of our national output of goods and services; they also are the principal source of employment, a major medium for the investment of capital, and a leading factor in the research and development activities which are so vital in keeping our economy growing and competitive in the world markets.

Efficiency of production and distribution in many industries require more capital than can be obtained by a single proprietor or a partnership. The large amounts of capital needed for successful entry into many fields of business are most easily acquired by selling shares of capital stock to the public. Corporations have reached their dominant role largely because of their efficiency for the concentration of capital. Because most corporations have numerous stockholders who do not participate directly in management, complete accounting and internal control systems are of critical importance as a means of protecting the interests of absentee owners of corporate securities.

Several specific advantages of the corporate form of organization help explain why corporations are so successful in attracting capital. Among these advantages are the following:

1 *Limited liability.* A stockholder has no personal liability for debts of the corporation. Creditors can look for payment only to the corporation itself and not to the personal resources of the owners. Freedom from personal liability is an important factor in encouraging investors to acquire stock in corporations.

2 *Liquidity of investments in corporate securities.* The owners of corporate securities (especially securities listed on stock exchanges) can sell all or part of their investment for cash at any time. The liquidity of corporate securities is a major reason for their popularity.

649

3 *Continuity of existence.* The corporation is a separate legal entity with unlimited life, whereas a partnership may be terminated by the death or retirement of any partner.

4 *Separation of the functions of management and ownership.* By attracting capital from a large number of investors and selecting management on a basis of executive ability, the corporation achieves expert direction of large amounts of economic and human resources.

Structure of the corporation

To form a corporation, one or more incorporators submit an application to the corporation commissioner or other designated official of a state government. The application identifies the incorporators, states the nature of the business, and describes the capital stock to be issued. After payment of an incorporation fee and approval of the application, ***articles of incorporation*** are approved by the state as evidence of the legal existence of the corporation. The incorporators, who must be ***subscribers*** to shares of the corporation's capital stock, elect a ***board of directors*** and approve ***bylaws*** to serve as general guides for the operation of the corporation. The board of directors appoints ***officers*** to serve as active managers of the corporation. Corporate officers usually include a president, one or more vice-presidents, a treasurer, a controller, and a secretary. The organization process is completed by the issuance of shares of capital stock to the subscribers as evidence of their ownership of the corporation.

The corporate form of organization is not limited to companies organized for profit. The term ***public corporation*** is applied to government-owned units (such as the Federal Deposit Insurance Corporation), whereas the terms ***private corporation*** and ***business corporation*** include all companies which are owned by investors. Within the meaning of ***private corporation*** are both the ***nonstock*** corporations (churches, universities, and hospitals which are not organized for profit) and ***stock*** corporations which operate to earn net income and which issue shares of capital stock to investors. Our attention is focused on the stock corporation. Within this group, one can also recognize subgroups such as ***close corporations*** with stock held by a small number of owners (perhaps a family), and ***publicly owned corporations*** with capital stock available for purchase by the public. The capital stock of publicly owned corporations may be ***listed*** (traded on organized stock exchanges) or ***over-the-counter*** (an unlisted market in which dealers buy from and sell to the public).

Although the laws governing the formation and operation of a stock corporation vary among the states, these state laws all emphasize certain basic concepts. Every state recognizes the corporation as a separate entity and provides for the issuance of shares of capital stock as units of ownership.

Ownership equity of the corporation

In the balance sheet of a single proprietorship, the owner's equity is shown as a single amount. For a partnership, the owner's equity of each partner is presented as a single amount, without any distinction between paid-in capital and accumulated earnings. However, in the balance sheet of a corporation, a basic objective in reporting the stockholders' equity is to distinguish clearly between paid-in capital and retained earnings.

Why should the stockholders' equity be subdivided? One reason is that stockholders and creditors need to know whether a corporation which pays dividends is distributing earnings or is returning invested capital. The owners of single proprietorships and partnerships may withdraw capital in any amounts they choose, even though such withdrawals may exceed earnings. In a corporation, however, only the accumulated earnings ordinarily are regarded as available for dividends. This view reflects corporate policy and desire for continuity of existence as well as legal considerations. Consequently, accountants keep a clear distinction between paid-in capital and retained earnings. The maintenance of these two separate categories of capital also is desirable because stockholders are absentee owners who do not participate directly in management. They may regard the active management of the corporation as custodians of the paid-in capital and may judge the efficiency of management to some extent by the amount of earnings accumulated by the corporation.

Therefore, from the standpoint of accounting theory, it is necessary to distinguish total paid-in capital from retained earnings. Any further classification of stockholders' equity usually rests on legal requirements rather than on accounting principles. The framers of corporation laws have attempted to protect creditors by creating the concept of *legal capital*—an amount of stockholders' equity not subject to withdrawal. In recognition of these legal requirements, accountants customarily make a further classification of stockholders' equity by subdividing paid-in capital between legal capital (capital stock) and paid-in capital in excess of par or stated value of capital stock (additional paid-in capital). Legal capital generally is not subject to withdrawal; in some states, however, additional paid-in capital legally is available for dividends, provided that stockholders are notified of the source of the dividends. In a few states, dividends may be paid from paid-in capital without notice to stockholders. Although dividends can be declared in some states even when a deficit exists, corporate financial policy is usually far more cautious, and dividends from any source other than retained earnings are rare.

Components of stockholders' equity

The following components of stockholders' equity generally are used in the balance sheet:

1 Capital stock (legal capital)
2 Paid-in capital in excess of par or stated value
3 Retained earnings (or deficit)
4 Unrealized loss in value of long-term investments in marketable equity securities (discussed in Chapter 14)

A subtotal entitled "total paid-in capital" may be inserted in the stockholders' equity section of the balance sheet to show the aggregate of the capital stock and paid-in capital in excess of par or stated value.

The question of "appraisal capital" has little practical importance, because corporations generally have adhered to the cost principle of asset valuation. If any appreciation in the value of assets is included in the stockholders' equity, it should be shown separately and given a title such as **unrealized appreciation from revaluation of assets** or simply **appraisal capital.**

Paid-in Capital in Excess of Par or Stated Value   Paid-in capital in excess of par or stated value comes principally from the following sources:

1 Excess of issuance proceeds over the par or stated value of capital stock
2 Conversion of convertible bonds or preferred stock to common stock
3 Excess of proceeds from reissuance of treasury stock over the cost of the treasury stock
4 Reduction of par or stated value of capital stock
5 Donations of assets to the corporation by stockholders or governmental units

Although capital from all these sources may be combined into the single balance sheet item of Paid-in Capital in Excess of Par or Stated Value, a separate ledger account is needed for each in order to carry out the principle of classifying stockholders' equity by source. If any part of paid-in capital is distributed as a dividend, management must inform the stockholders that the dividend is a **return of capital** and not a distribution of earnings.

Neither operating losses nor extraordinary losses should be debited to paid-in capital accounts. Examples of improper debits to paid-in capital accounts include the following:

1 Write-off of purchased goodwill
2 Write-down of plant assets that have lost usefulness because of obsolescence or unexpectedly rapid deterioration
3 Write-off of bond discount at the time of issuance of the bonds
4 Loss on sale of investments

The impropriety in all these situations is that paid-in capital is being used to absorb losses which should have been included in the income statement as deductions from revenue. If paid-in capital were to be debited for such losses, net income and retained earnings would be over-stated.

Although acceptable debits to paid-in capital accounts are infrequent, they are warranted in such situations as the following:

1 Declaration of a liquidating dividend.
2 Redemption of capital stock, originally issued for more than par, at a price in excess of par. For example, X Corporation redeemed at a call price of $104 a portion of its $100 par preferred stock originally issued at a price of $105. The $4 a share **redemption premium** may be debited to paid-in capital in excess of par.
3 Absorption of a deficit as part of a quasi-reorganization.
4 Out-of-pocket costs of issuing capital stock, such as accountants' fees, legal fees, underwriting discounts and commissions, and printing costs.

Retained Earnings Retained earnings represents the accumulated net income of a corporation, minus amounts distributed to stockholders and amounts transferred to paid-in capital accounts as a result of stock dividends. Extraordinary gains and losses, cumulative effect of a change in accounting principle, and operating revenue and expenses are included in the determination of net income, which is transferred to the Retained Earnings account. A negative amount (debit balance) in the Retained Earnings account is termed a **deficit.**

PAID-IN CAPITAL

Rights associated with ownership of capital stock

If a corporation has only one class of capital stock, stockholders usually have certain basic rights to be exercised in proportion to the number of shares of capital stock they own. These rights include: (1) right to vote for directors and thus to be represented by management, (2) right to receive dividends declared by the board of directors, (3) preemptive right to purchase additional shares of capital stock in proportion to present holdings in the event that the corporation increases the amount of stock outstanding, and (4) right to share in the distribution of cash or other assets if the corporation is liquidated. Variations in these rights are encountered in individual cases. For example, the preemptive right attached to existing shares of capital stock may prove inconvenient to a corporation interested in acquiring other companies by issuance of additional shares of capital stock. Consequently, this preemptive right has been eliminated (with the approval of stockholders) by some corporations.

Common stock and preferred stock

When only one type of capital stock is issued, it has the basic rights described above and is called **common stock.** However, many corporations, in an effort to appeal to all types of investors, offer two or more classes of capital stock with different rights or priorities attached to each class. Stock that carries certain preferences over the common stock, such as a prior claim on dividends, is called **preferred stock.** Often a preferred stock has no voting rights, or only limited voting rights. The characteristics of preferred stocks vary widely among corporations; it is unwise, therefore, to assume that a preferred stock has any particular rights or priorities without positive determination of its status. The special rights of a particular preferred stock are set forth in the articles of incorporation and in the stock certificates issued by the corporation.

When only one class of stock is issued by a corporation, it is frequently labeled as "Capital Stock" in the ledger and in the balance sheet.

Class A and Class B stock

Corporations that issue more than one class of capital stock may designate the various issues by letter, such as Class A stock and Class B stock. In such cases one of the issues is common stock and the other issue has some preference or restriction of basic rights. To determine the significant characteristics of capital stock, it is necessary to examine the stock certificates.

Characteristics of preferred stock

The following features are associated with most preferred stock issues:

1 Preference as to dividends at a stated rate or amount
2 Preference as to assets in event of liquidation of the corporation
3 Callable at the option of the corporation
4 Absence of voting rights

A preference as to dividends does not give assurance that dividends will be paid; it signifies only that the stated dividend rate applicable to the preferred stock must be paid before any dividends can be paid on the common stock. Unlike interest on bonds and notes payable, dividends do not accrue. A liability to pay a dividend arises only when the board of directors declares a dividend. Any dividend action by the board must take into consideration (1) whether the corporation legally can pay a dividend, and (2) whether the present cash position and future corporate plans make it expedient to pay a dividend.

Many preferred stocks have a par value, and this feature permits the dividend rate to be stated either as a percentage of par value or as a fixed dollar amount. For example, Georgia-Pacific Corporation has issued a $5\frac{1}{2}$%, $100 par, preferred stock. On the other hand, Sperry Rand Corporation has a $4.50 preferred stock with a par value of $25 but with a prior claim of $100 in the event of redemption or liquidation. The annual dividend on no-par preferred stock is stated at a fixed dollar amount, such as "$4.50 Cumulative Preferred Stock."

Cumulative and Noncumulative Preferred Stock   Most preferred stocks have a cumulative provision as to dividends. If all or any part of the stated dividend on a cumulative preferred stock is not paid in a given year, the unpaid portion accumulates and must be paid in a subsequent year *before any dividend can be paid on the common stock.*

A dividend is said to have been *passed* if the directors fail to declare a dividend on the established date for dividend action. Any omitted dividends on cumulative preferred stock constitute *dividends in arrears.* The amount of preferred dividends in arrears is not a liability of the corporation, because no liability exists until the board of directors declares a dividend. However, no dividends can be declared on common stock until any dividends in arrears on preferred stock, as well as the current period's preferred dividend, have been paid. Thus, the amount of any dividends in arrears on preferred stock is important to investors and always should be disclosed. The disclosure usually is made in a note to the financial statements.

In the case of noncumulative preferred stocks, a dividend omitted or passed in one year is lost forever to shareholders. Because most investors refuse to buy noncumulative preferred stocks, they seldom are issued.

As an illustration of the significance of dividends in arrears and the inherent weakness of a noncumulative preferred stock, assume that Leticia Corporation has three classes of capital stock as follows:

Three classes of capital stock issued by a corporation	*6% cumulative preferred stock, $10 par, issued and outstanding 200,000 shares* . . . . $2,000,000 *7% noncumulative second preferred stock, $25 par, issued and outstanding 80,000 shares* . . . . 2,000,000 *Common stock, $10 par, issued and outstanding 200,000 shares* . . . 2,000,000

Assume also that operations of Leticia Corporation were unprofitable in Years 1, 2, and 3 and no dividends were paid during those three years. In Year 4, however, a large net income was earned, and the corporation decided on December 31, Year 4, that $900,000 should be distributed as dividends. Despite the equal amounts of capital represented by the three capital stock issues, the dividend payments favor the cumulative preferred stock and the common stock. The holders of the noncumulative second preferred stock receive relatively little, as illustrated on top of page 656.

Distribution of dividends totaling $900,000 to three classes of capital stock

	6% cumulative preferred stock	7% noncumulative second preferred stock	Common stock
Dividends in arrears. . .	$360,000 (1)		
Preferred dividends, current year	120,000 (2)	$140,000 (3)	
Remainder, to common stock.	–0–	–0–	$280,000 (4)
Total dividends paid .	$480,000	$140,000	$280,000

(1) ($2,000,000 × 6%) × 3 = $360,000
(2) $2,000,000 × 6% = $120,000
(3) $2,000,000 × 7% = 140,000
(4) $900,000 − ($480,000 + $140,000) = $280,000

Participating and Nonparticipating Preferred Stock   A preferred stock is *nonparticipating* unless the stock certificate specifically provides for participation. Participating preferred stocks are rare. A *fully participating* preferred stock shares equally with the common stock in any dividends paid after the common stock has received a dividend at a rate equal to the preference rate on the preferred stock. For example, assume that in the current year Chow Corporation paid the usual 5% dividend on its fully participating $100 par preferred stock and also paid a dividend of $5 on the $100 par common stock. If any additional dividend is paid on the common stock, a corresponding additional amount must be paid on the preferred stock. A *partially participating* preferred stock is one with a ceiling established limiting the extent to which it participates with the common stock.

Convertible Preferred Stock   Many corporations make their preferred stock attractive to investors by including a *conversion option* that entitles the stockholders to exchange their preferred stock for common stock in a stipulated ratio. The holders of convertible preferred stock have the advantage of a preferred claim on dividends and also the option of switching to common stock, which enjoys unlimited participation in dividends.

Preferred stock usually will be converted to common if the dividend rate on the common stock is increased. As long as the conversion option is open, the preferred stockholder gains the benefit of any increase in market price of the common stock without actual conversion, because market price of the preferred increases in proportion to any increase in the price of the common stock. It is sometimes said that the market prices of a common stock and the related convertible preferred stock are "in gear." The primary determinant of when to convert is the relative yields of the common and preferred stock at the prevailing market prices. In addition, consideration may be given to the greater assurance of continued dividend payments on the preferred stock. For some preferred stocks the conversion option expires after a specified number of years; for others the conversion period is unlimited; and in some cases the conversion terms are subject to change at specified future dates.

Callable Preferred Stock Most preferred stocks can be called at the option of the corporation. The call feature is advantageous to the corporation because the capital obtained through issuance of callable preferred stock is available as long as needed and can be repaid whenever the corporation desires. The *call price* is specified in the preferred stock contract and usually is set a few points above the issuance price. The existence of the call price tends to set a ceiling on the market price of nonconvertible preferred stock. Any dividends in arrears must be paid when a cumulative preferred stock is called.

If a convertible preferred stock is called, the holders of the stock have the option of converting to common stock rather than surrendering their investment in the corporation. As a result, the market price of outstanding convertible preferred stocks tends to move with the price of the common stock even though this amount is well above the call price.

Redeemable Preferred Stock Some preferred stocks are subject to mandatory redemption by the corporation on a specific date and at a specific price. Other preferred stocks are redeemable solely at the option of the stockholders. Another category of preferred stocks is redeemable from future earnings of the corporation, or in some other manner not controlled by the corporation. Preferred stocks having these characteristics are referred to collectively as *redeemable preferred stocks.* The corporation does not control the timing of the redemption of redeemable preferred stocks. In contrast, callable preferred stocks are subject to retirement *at the option of the corporation.*

In *Accounting Series Release No. 268,* the SEC required corporations having outstanding redeemable preferred stock to disclose the following in a note to the financial statements:[1]

1 Redemption terms of the preferred stock
2 Amounts of the preferred stock which must be redeemed during each of the five years subsequent to the balance sheet date
3 Changes in the amounts of redeemable preferred stock outstanding during the accounting period

In addition, the Release prohibited both the use of the conventional "Stockholders' Equity" caption by corporations having redeemable preferred stock and the presentation of a combined total for redeemable preferred stock, other preferred stock, and common stock.[2]

---

[1] *Accounting Series Release No. 268,* "Presentation in Financial Statements of 'Redeemable Preferred Stocks,'" SEC (Washington: 1979). See also, *FASB Statement No. 47,* "Disclosure of Long-Term Obligations," FASB (Stamford: 1981), pp. 4–5.
[2] Ibid.

Liquidation Preference Most preferred stocks have preference over common stock as to assets in the event of liquidation of the corporation. The claims of creditors take preference over both preferred and common stock. The preference of a cumulative preferred stock as to assets usually includes any dividends in arrears in addition to the stated liquidation value. Not every preferred stock has a prior claim on assets; the status of the stock in the event of liquidation depends on the specific provisions of the preferred stock contract.

The preference that a preferred stock has in the event of liquidation should be disclosed in the financial statements. In **Opinion No. 10,** the Accounting Principles Board stated:[3]

> Companies at times issue preferred (or other senior) stock which has a preference in involuntary liquidation considerably in excess of the par or stated value of the shares. The relationship between this preference in liquidation and the par or stated value of the shares may be of major significance to the users of the financial statements. . . . Accordingly, the Board recommends that, in these cases, the liquidation preference of the stock be disclosed in the equity section of the balance sheet in the aggregate, . . . rather than on a per share basis or by disclosure in notes.

Is Preferred Stock Debt or Equity? The preferred stockholder is in some respects more a creditor than an owner. Typically, the preferred shareholder provides capital to the corporation for an agreed rate of return and has no voice in management. If the corporation prospers, it probably will increase the dividend rate on its common stock, but it cannot consider increasing the dividend on preferred stock. Unless it is redeemable, preferred stock generally has no maturity date, but the preferred stockholder's relationship with the corporation may be terminated if the corporation chooses to call the preferred stock.

The uncertain status of preferred stock is emphasized by the SEC's prohibition against the inclusion of redeemable preferred stock in the stockholders' equity section of the balance sheet. However, the SEC did not require the inclusion of redeemable preferred stock among the liabilities of the corporation. Thus, the balance sheet status of redeemable preferred stock—as well as preferred stock in general—is not definite.

Par value and no-par value stock

In the early history of American corporations, all capital stock was required to have a par value, but now most state laws permit corporations to choose between par and no-par value stock. A corporation which chooses to issue par value capital stock can set the par at any amount desired, such as $1, $5, or $100 a share. If a corporation subsequently splits its stock, the par value of each share is reduced accordingly. For example, General Motors common stock, which originally had a par value of $100, has been split many times and now has a par value of $1.66⅔ a share.

[3] *APB Opinion No. 10,* "Omnibus Opinion—1966," AICPA (New York: 1966), p. 148.

The par value of capital stock is the amount per share to be entered in the Capital Stock account. This portion of the value of assets originally invested in the corporation must be kept permanently in the enterprise. The par value of the capital stock issued thus signifies a "cushion" of ownership equity for the protection of creditors.

The par value device originally was introduced for the protection of creditors but proved less effective than anticipated, because the intent of the law could be circumvented by the issuance of capital stock in exchange for assets other than cash. In the era before rigorous security laws, large amounts of capital stock sometimes were issued for mining claims, patents, goodwill, and other assets of unproved value. These assets usually were recorded at the par value of the stock issued in exchange, with the result of gross overvaluation of assets and overstatement of stockholders' equity.

To avoid this abuse of the par value concept, most states enacted legislation permitting corporations to issue capital stock without par value. It was argued that many investors had incorrectly assumed that any capital stock was worth as much as its par value, and that the use of no-par stock would force investors to consider more fundamental factors such as earnings, dividends, and current fair value of assets owned by the corporation.

The trend for corporations to set par values at quite low amounts, such as $0.10 or $1 a share, has lessened the effectiveness of the arguments for no-par stock and has reduced some of the significance attached to the term *par value.* Further, recent revisions in the California Corporations Code, which essentially did away with the concept of par value for capital stock, may presage comparable revisions of the corporation laws of other states.

Accounting for capital stock transactions

A clear understanding of the following terms is necessary in accounting for capital stock transactions:

1 *Authorized capital stock* is the number of shares of capital stock which the state has authorized a corporation to issue. Typically, a corporation will obtain authorization for a much larger number of shares than it plans to issue in the foreseeable future. The securing of authority to issue shares of stock does not bring an asset into existence, nor does it give the corporation any capital. Authorization simply affords a legal opportunity to obtain assets through the issuance of stock. Consequently, authorization of capital stock does not constitute a transaction to be recorded in the accounting records. A notation of the event in the general journal and in the ledger account for capital stock is appropriate.

2 *Issued capital stock* is the number of shares of authorized capital stock that have been issued to date. Issued capital stock includes treasury stock, as defined in **5** on page 660.

3 *Unissued capital stock* describes the authorized shares of capital stock that have not been issued to investors.

4 *Outstanding capital stock* is the number of shares of authorized capital stock that have been issued and presently are held by stockholders.

5 *Treasury stock* is the corporation's own capital stock which had been issued, fully paid, and reacquired by the corporation but not canceled. Treasury stock is included in issued capital stock as defined in **2** on page 659, but is not part of outstanding capital stock.

6 *Subscriptions to capital stock* represent an asset, in the form of a receivable from investors who have promised to pay the subscription price at a future date.

7 *Subscribed capital stock* refers to authorized but unissued shares of capital stock which are earmarked for issuance under existing contracts with subscribers. The subscribed capital stock is issued when a subscription contract is collected in full. If financial statements are prepared between the date of obtaining capital stock subscriptions and the date of issuing the stock, the subscribed stock is included in the stockholders' equity section of the balance sheet.

Ledger accounts for paid-in capital

Investments of capital by stockholders usualy require the use of two types of stockholders' equity accounts: (1) capital stock accounts, and (2) accounts for paid-in capital in excess of par or stated value.

Capital Stock Accounts A separate ledger account is used for each class of capital stock. The number of shares authorized may be recorded by a memorandum entry in the general journal and also may be indicated in the ledger accounts as shown below:

Capital stock accounts illustrated

8% Cumulative Preferred Stock, $100 par

Date	Explanation	Debit	Credit	Balance
Year 7 Oct. 1	(Authorized 10,000 shares, callable at $105 a share)			

Common Stock, no-par, stated value $5

Date	Explanation	Debit	Credit	Balance
Year 7 Oct. 1	(Authorized 1,000,000 shares)			

Accounts for Paid-in Capital in Excess of Par or Stated Value Capital stock often is issued at a price above the par or stated value. This additional paid-in capital is credited to an account with a descriptive title indicating its source, such as Paid-in Capital in Excess of Par: Preferred Stock or Paid-in Capital in Excess of Stated Value: Common Stock. In the preparation of financial statements, it is not necessary to use the exact titles of the ledger accounts as long as the sources of capital are disclosed. For example, the paid-in capital indicated by the preceding account titles might appear in the balance sheet as follows (amounts are assumed):

Paid-in capital in the balance sheet

> *Stockholders' equity:*
>
> 8% cumulative preferred stock, $100 par (callable at $105 a share),
>   authorized 10,000 shares, issued and outstanding 9,000 shares . $ 900,000
> Common stock, no-par, stated value $5, authorized 1 million shares,
>   issued and outstanding 600,000 shares 3,000,000
> Paid-in capital in excess of par or stated value:
>   On preferred stock . . . . $ 18,000
>   On common stock. 6,000,000 6,018,000
>   Total paid-in capital. $9,918,000

Some accountants prefer to list the paid-in capital applicable to the preferred stock with the listing of preferred stock, and to place the paid-in capital applicable to the common stock with the listing of common stock. Other accountants combine the various sources of paid-in capital under a single caption such as Paid-in Capital in Excess of Par (or Additional Paid-in Capital). Other sources of paid-in capital in excess of par (such as from treasury stock transactions) are discussed elsewhere in this chapter and in Chapters 17 and 18.

Journal Entries for Issuance of Capital Stock for Cash The following journal entries illustrate issuance of the capital stocks summarized in the foregoing balance sheet:

Journal entries for issuance of preferred and common stock

> Cash 918,000
>   8% Cumulative Preferred Stock 900,000
>   Paid-in Capital in Excess of Par: Preferred Stock . 18,000
> To record issuance of 9,000 shares of $100 par cumulative
> preferred stock for $102 a share.
>
> Cash 9,000,000
>   Common Stock. 3,000,000
>   Paid-in Capital in Excess of Stated Value: Common
>   Stock 6,000,000
> To record issuance of 600,000 shares of no-par common
> stock, stated value $5 a share, for $15 a share.

Discount on capital stock

Many states now prohibit the issuance of capital stock at less than par value. In planning a capital stock issue, a corporation can set the par value as low as it pleases. Because par value usually is set at an amount considerably below the issuance price, the question of discount on capital stock is no longer of much practical importance. The topic deserves brief consideration, however, because of its theoretical implications.

If capital stock is issued at a price below par, the amount of the discount is debited to an account entitled Discount on Capital Stock, which appeared as a deduction (or negative element of paid-in capital) in the stockholders' equity section of the balance sheet. The discount on capital stock is carried in the accounting records as long as the related stock issue is outstanding, so that an accurate record of the original investment by stockholders is maintained.

Assessments on capital stock

Although most states require that capital stock offered to the public be nonassessable, occasionally a corporation may make an assessment against its stockholders. If the capital stock originally was issued at a discount, the amount received by assessment is credited to the Discount on Capital Stock account. If the debit balance in the discount account thus is eliminated, any remaining portion of the assessment is credited to a separate stockholders' equity account such as Paid-in Capital from Assessment of Stockholders. This account is credited with the entire amount of the assessment if the capital stock originally was issued at a price equal to or in excess of par value.

Issuance price and subsequent market price of capital stock

The preceding discussion of the issuance of capital stock at prices above and below par raises a question as to how a corporation decides on the issuance price. For a new issue of capital stock, the corporation usually sets an issuance price based on factors such as the (1) expected future earnings and dividends, (2) financial condition and reputation of the corporation, and (3) current conditions in the security markets.

After capital stock has been issued, the subsequent market price at which it is traded among investors tends to reflect the progress and prospects of the corporation and factors such as the state of investor confidence and the general trend of the economy. The current market prices of capital stock often bear no discernible relationship to par value or to original issuance price.

Subscriptions for capital stock

The preceding sections have illustrated the issuance of capital stock for cash. Often, stock is issued under a subscription contract requiring payment by subscribers at a later date. Generally, the stock certificates are not issued until the subscription price is collected in full.

The increase in assets caused by obtaining a stock subscription receivable is offset by an increase in stockholders' equity. The ledger accounts to be credited (in the case of par value common stock) are Common Stock Subscribed and Paid-in Capital in Excess of Par. At a later date when the stock is issued, the Common Stock Subscribed account is debited and the Common Stock account is credited. If financial statements are prepared between the obtaining of subscriptions and the issuance of the capital stock, the Common Stock Subscribed account appears in the stockholders' equity section of the balance sheet.

Journal Entries   Assume that subscriptions are received for 10,000 shares of $10 par common stock at a price of $50 a share. The journal entry to record the subscriptions follows:

Journal entry to record subscriptions for common stock

Subscriptions Receivable: Common Stock	500,000	
Common Stock Subscribed.		100,000
Paid-in Capital in Excess of Par		400,000
To record subscriptions for 10,000 shares of $10 par common stock at $50 a share.		

All subscribers paid one-half of the amounts due on their subscriptions. The journal entry to record the collection of the subscriptions is:

Collection of subscriptions

Cash	250,000	
Subscriptions Receivable: Common Stock		250,000
To record collection of one-half of subscriptions receivable.		

Subscribers paid the balance due on their subscriptions with the exception of one subscriber who had subscribed for 100 shares. The journal entries to record the collection of the subscriptions and the issuance of common stock are illustrated on top of page 664.

<table>
<tr><td>Collection of
subscriptions
and issuance of
common stock</td><td>

Cash *247,500*

    Subscriptions Receivable: Common Stock *247,500*

To record balance due on subscriptions for 9,900 shares.

Common Stock Subscribed *99,000*

    Common Stock, $10 par *99,000*

To record issuance of 9,900 shares after collection of sub-scriptions in full.
</td></tr>
</table>

Defaults by Subscribers   If subscribers fail to pay all or part of their subscriptions, the disposition of the subscription contracts and of any amounts paid in by the subscribers depends on the laws of the state and the policy of the corporation. If no payment has been made by the subscribers and nothing can be collected from them, the corporation should reverse the journal entries which recorded the subscriptions. If the subscribers have made one or more partial payments prior to default, the entire amount paid in prior to default may be refunded. As an alternative, the amount refunded may be the amount paid in minus any expenses or losses in reselling the subscribed stock. Another possible alternative calls for amending the subscription contracts to permit the issuance of a reduced number of shares corresponding to the cash collected. Still another alternative under some state laws calls for forfeiture by the subscribers of the amount paid prior to the default.

Default by a subscriber requires the writing off of the uncollectible subscription receivable; the journal entry also includes a debit to the account for Common Stock Subscribed and usually a debit to the Paid-in Capital in Excess of Par account. If the corporation retains any amounts paid in on defaulted subscriptions without issuing capital stock, this increase in paid-in capital may be credited to a separate account with a title such as Paid-in Capital from Defaults on Stock Subscriptions. For example, if the $2,500 paid by the defaulting subscriber for 100 shares in the example above is forfeited, the journal entry to record the forfeiture would be:

<table>
<tr><td>Journal entry to
record forfeiture
by defaulting
subscriber</td><td>

Common Stock Subscribed *1,000*

Paid-in Capital in Excess of Par. *4,000*

    Subscriptions Receivable: Common Stock *2,500*

    Paid-in Capital from Defaults on Stock Subscription *2,500*

To record forfeiture of $2,500 paid by subscriber for 100 shares of common stock.
</td></tr>
</table>

Nature of Stock Subscriptions Receivable   From the corporation's viewpoint, a stock subscription contract generally is regarded as an asset (a special type of receivable), and is recorded by a debit to Subscriptions Receivable: Common Stock or to Subscriptions Receivable: Preferred Stock. When there are several subscribers, the subscriptions receivable accounts may be controlling accounts supported by subsidiary ledgers containing an individual account with each subscriber. In the balance sheet, the subscriptions receivable accounts are included among the current assets, provided that early collection is anticipated.

Some accountants argue that stock subscriptions do not represent assets, and that they should be shown as contra items in the stockholders' equity section of the balance sheet. Under this view, a stock subscription receivable is contrasted with the ordinary trade receivable; and it is argued that a stock subscription is a dubious claim against the subscribers because the corporation has not delivered merchandise or rendered services to them. As a practical matter, stock subscriptions constitute valid legal claims and usually are collected in full.

Stockholders' ledger, stock transfer journal, and stock certificate book

In addition to maintaining a general ledger account for each class of capital stock, a corporation must maintain detailed subsidiary records showing the identity of stockholders. A **stockholders' ledger** contains a separate account for each stockholder showing the number of shares owned. The stockholders' ledger is maintained in number of shares of stock rather than in dollars. When a stockholder sells capital stock to another investor, an entry must be made in the **stock transfer journal** and posted to the stockholders' ledger to decrease the number of shares of capital stock held by the first stockholder and to set up an account for the new stockholder. No entry would be necessary in the general journal, because the amount of stock outstanding remains unchanged.

A **stock certificate book** also is needed to control the amount of capital stock outstanding. When a stock certificate is issued, the name of the owner and number of shares are listed on the certificate stub. When a stockholder sells capital stock, the original certificate is canceled and attached to the stub, and a new certificate is issued to the new stockholder. The open stubs in the stock certificate book indicate the number of shares of capital stock outstanding. Most large corporations retain an independent **stock registrar** and **transfer agent** to control stock certificates and to maintain stock transfer journals and stockholder ledgers. Such records are maintained by computers when the volume of transactions is large.

Issuance of two types of securities as a unit

Corporations sometimes offer preferred and common stock as a unit, with no indication of the issuance price of either security considered separately. Such unit offerings raise a question as to how the proceeds should be allocated between the two securities. The same question arises when a corporation issues two or more kinds of securities to acquire another business enterprise. The aggregate par value of preferred and common stock issued as a unit usually is less than the proceeds received. How should the proceeds received be allocated to the two securities? If either security is issued concurrently for cash, the market price of that security can be used as evidence of its value; the remainder of the proceeds is applicable to the other security.

Capital stock issued for assets or services

When capital stock is issued for assets other than cash, the current fair value of the assets or the current market value of the stock, whichever is more clearly evident, is used to record the assets received and the related amount of paid-in capital. In the absence of an arm's-length sale of assets for cash, opinions may differ as to the current fair value of the assets received. Consequently, it is appropriate to consider how much the capital stock would have sold for if offered for cash. The underlying reasoning is that the exchange of capital stock for assets essentially is the equivalent of issuing the stock for cash and using the cash to buy the assets. The two transactions are in effect a single exchange transaction.

If the corporation's capital stock is actively traded, the price of the stock on the date of the exchange constitutes objective evidence as to the values exchanged. However, if stock sales are infrequent and small in amount, there is no assurance that the corporation could have issued a large block of stock for cash without forcing the price down.

Either treasury stock or previously unissued stock may be exchanged for assets. However, the cost of treasury stock used for this purpose does not constitute a proper basis of valuation for the exchange unless by chance the cost is equal to the current fair value of the stock.

The establishing of valuations for assets acquired in exchange for capital stock is the responsibility of the corporation's board of directors. The decisions of the board and the use of appraisals or other valuation techniques should be set forth in the corporate minutes. Under no circumstances should the par or stated value of the capital stock issued in exchange for assets be regarded as the decisive factor in establishing the current fair value of the assets acquired by a corporation.

The valuation problem when a corporation exchanges capital stock for personal services parallels that previously described in Chapter 11 for the exchange of capital stock for plant assets. The current fair value of the services received is a proper basis of valuation, but the market value of the stock often is more readily determinable and also is acceptable for establishing the accounting basis for the transaction.

Watered stock and secret reserves

A corporation's capital stock is said to be **watered** if the stockholders' equity is overstated because of a corresponding overvaluation of assets. The expression "watered stock" stems from the era when cattle ranchers sometimes gave their herds quantities of salt and then all the water they could drink just before they were delivered to the markets. The "watered stock" weighed more and brought a higher total price.

In a corporation, watered stock usually relates to inflated asset values, although capital stock also can be watered through understatement of liabilities. This factor is less common, however, because most liabilities are listed at contractual amounts or at the present value of future payments.

The most direct approach to eliminating "water" from a corporation's capital structure is through writing down the overvalued assets. The reduction in carrying amount of the assets may be accompanied by a reduction of retained earnings, or of the par value of the capital stock outstanding. Because such a write-down affects each stockholder proportionally, no real loss is involved; the proportionate equity of each stockholder in the net assets of the corporation is unchanged.

The existence of **secret reserves** in a corporation's balance sheet means that stockholders' equity is understated. An understatement of stockholders' equity may be achieved by using high depreciation rates, by excessive provision for doubtful accounts, by using lifo inventory procedures in periods of rising price levels, by debiting capital expenditures to expense, or by any other action which understates assets or overstates liabilities. The deliberate creation of secret reserves is inconsistent with the maintenance of integrity in financial accounting.

Stock splits

When the price of a corporation's capital stock reaches a high trading range such as $100 a share or more, the corporation may decide to split the stock. A stock split of, say, 3 for 1 of a stock selling for $150 a share causes the number of shares held by each stockholder to triple and should cause the market price to drop to approximately $50 a share.

A stock split causes no change in the total dollar amount of stockholders' equity and no change in paid-in capital, retained earnings, or other components. The par or stated value per share of capital stock is reduced in proportion to the increase in number of shares. For example, in a 4 for 1 split of $10 par capital stock, the new stock has a par value of $2.50.

When capital stock is split, the old stock certificates usually are not called in or exchanged for new certificates. The corporation issues to stockholders certificates for a sufficient number of new shares to bring their total holdings up to the number indicated by the split. A stockholder who owned 100 shares prior to the previously mentioned 4 for 1 split of $10 par capital stock would receive 300 new shares of $2.50 par value. The stockholder would continue to hold the original certificate for 100 shares of $10 par capital stock. The par value of all the shares is now $2.50, but it is not necessary for any exchange of certificates to be made. Eventually, the old $10 par certificates will disappear from circulation; whenever such a certificate is sold, the new certificate issued to the new owner shows the current par value of $2.50.

Because the only ledger account affected by a stock split is the Capital Stock account, the stock split may be recorded in a memorandum entry. Alternatively, a journal entry such as the following may be made to record the change in par value and number of outstanding shares:

Journal entry for a stock split

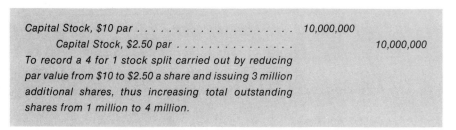

Capital Stock, $10 par *10,000,000*
      Capital Stock, $2.50 par *10,000,000*
To record a 4 for 1 stock split carried out by reducing
par value from $10 to $2.50 a share and issuing 3 million
additional shares, thus increasing total outstanding
shares from 1 million to 4 million.

A *reverse stock split,* as the name suggests, is the opposite of a stock split. The number of outstanding shares of capital stock is reduced proportionately for all stockholders. For example, the outstanding capital stock might be reduced from 3 million shares to 300,000 shares in a 1 for 10 reverse stock split. All stockholders would surrender their stock certificates in exchange for one-tenth as many new shares. A reverse stock split does not affect the assets or liabilities of the corporation and, therefore, does not change the total amount of stockholders' equity. Such transactions are rare; they usually are considered only by corporations with capital stock which has dropped in market price to an extremely low level. A reverse split tends to increase the market price per share in inverse proportion to the reduction in number of shares outstanding.

RETAINED EARNINGS

The illustration below indicates the debits and credits entered in the Retained Earnings account:

Composition of typical Retained Earnings account

Retained Earnings	
1. Net loss	1. Net income
2. Dividends declared	2. Prior period adjustments (to correct material error made in prior periods)
3. Prior period adjustments (to correct material error made in prior periods)	

As explained in Chapter 3, current practice requires that extraordinary gains and losses be included in the determination of net income rather than being entered directly in retained earnings. ***Prior period adjustments*** are entered directly in the Retained Earnings account and are not included in the determination of net income of the current accounting period. The following items are prior period adjustments and are excluded from net income for the current period.[4]

a Correction of an error in the financial statements of a prior period

b Adjustments that result from realization of income tax benefits of preacquisition operating loss carryforwards of purchased subsidiaries

Prior period adjustments do not include normal recurring corrections and adjustments arising from the use of estimates in the accounting process. Thus, changes in depreciation rates because of revised estimates of economic lives of plant assets are not prior period adjustments; they are reflected in operations of the current accounting period.

After listing the principal components of retained earnings, it may be useful to mention a few items which ***do not*** belong in retained earnings. These are:

1 Treasury stock transactions which result in a "gain" or a "loss"

2 Donations of assets (such as the gift of a plant site to a corporation by a city seeking to attract new industries)

3 Increases in stockholders' equity resulting from write-ups of plant assets to current fair values in excess of carrying amounts

Let us consider briefly why each of these items does not belong in retained earnings. The reissuance of treasury stock at an amount in excess of cost increases paid-in capital, and the reissuance of treasury stock at an amount below cost decreases paid-in capital. The receipt of donated assets is not a source of earnings and is recorded in a separate paid-in capital account, Capital from Donation of Plant Site. Increases in the carrying amounts of plant assets, if recorded at all, produce unrealized increases in stockholders' equity and require separate classification. To include such increases in retained earnings would suggest that they are realized and available for dividends.

Restrictions on retained earnings

The board of directors of a corporation may restrict or appropriate a portion of the retained earnings by transfer to a separate account. For example, appropriations of retained earnings (sometimes called ***reserves***) may be made for expansion of plant, retirements of bonds, redemption of preferred stock, and general business contingencies. Although the practice of appropriating retained earnings is not widely followed, the FASB sanctioned such practice as follows:[5]

---

[4] *FASB Statement No. 16,* "Prior Period Adjustments," FASB (Stamford: 1977), p. 5.

[5] *FASB Statement No. 5,* "Accounting for Contingencies," FASB (Stamford: 1975), p. 7.

Some enterprises have classified a portion of retained earnings as "appropriated" for loss contingencies. In some cases, the appropriation has been shown outside the stockholders' equity section of the balance sheet. Appropriation of retained earnings is not prohibited by this Statement provided that it is shown within the stockholders' equity section of the balance sheet and is clearly identified as an appropriation of retained earnings. Costs or losses shall not be charged to an appropriation of retained earnings, and no part of the appropriation shall be transferred to income.

A portion of retained earnings may be restricted and thus not available as a basis for dividend declaration for a variety of legal, contractual, or discretionary reasons. The almost universal practice is to disclose such a restriction in a note to financial statements, rather than to establish an appropriation of retained earnings. An example of such disclosure follows:

> The company's articles of incorporation and credit agreements with commercial banks contain restrictions limiting the payment of cash dividends. Retained earnings of $30 million dollars on December 31, 19—, are free of such restrictions.

DIVIDENDS

Cash dividends

The usual meaning of **dividend** is a distribution of assets to stockholders in proportion to the number of shares of capital stock owned. The term **dividend,** when used by itself, generally means a cash dividend; this usage is followed throughout this book. Corporations frequently distribute additional shares of their common stock to stockholders and call such distributions **stock dividends.** Strictly speaking, a stock dividend is not a dividend at all because no assets are distributed to stockholders. However, stock dividends are of considerable practical importance and pose some challenging accounting questions that are discussed later in this chapter.

No obligation to pay a dividend exists until the board of directors formally declares a dividend. Dividend action by the board consists of a resolution specifying the following information:

1 Date of declaration
2 Date of record
3 Date of payment
4 Amount per share

On the **date of declaration** of a cash dividend, the appropriate journal entry is a debit to Dividends and a credit to Dividends Payable, a current liability. The Dividends account is closed into Retained Earnings at the end of the accounting period. If the corporation has both common and preferred stock, a separate Dividends account is used for each (for example, Dividends: Common Stock, and Dividends: Preferred Stock).

The **date of record** is specified in the dividend declaration and usually follows the date of declaration by a few weeks. To qualify for the dividend, a person must be listed as a stockholder in the corporation's stockholders' ledger on the date of record.

The capital stocks of corporations listed on the stock exchanges sell "ex-dividend" five business days before the date of record, thus facilitating compilation of the list of owners on the record date. An investor who acquires capital stock before the ex-dividend date is entitled to receive the dividend; conversely, a stockholder who sells capital stock before the ex-dividend date is selling the right to receive the dividend that has been declared as well as the shares of stock.

The **date of payment** of a dividend usually is set for a few weeks after the date of record. Payment is recorded by a debit to Dividends Payable and a credit to Cash.

In an accounting textbook emphasizing principles rather than mechanics, it is convenient to speak of dividends being recorded as a debit to Retained Earnings, rather than indicating that the Dividends account is debited and then later closed to Retained Earnings. Consequently, we shall as a matter of convenience sometimes illustrate the declaration of a dividend by showing a debit directly to the Retained Earnings account.

As indicated in the preceding discussion, general requirements for declaration and payment of a cash dividend include (1) existence of retained earnings, (2) an adequate cash position, and (3) action by the board of directors. State laws governing corporations place various other restrictions on the declaration of dividends. These restrictions are designed to protect creditors against unwarranted distributions of corporate assets to stockholders.

Dividends paid in the form of nonmonetary assets

Most dividends are in cash, but occasionally a corporation may declare a dividend in the form of merchandise or other nonmonetary assets, such as securities of another corporation. When such **nonmonetary** dividends are declared, the current fair value (not the carrying amount) of the nonmonetary asset distributed is the appropriate amount to be recorded as a dividend. Similarly, stockholders record the receipt of the nonmonetary dividend at the current fair value of the asset received.

APB Opinion No. 29 established the following principle of accounting for nonmonetary dividends:[6]

> A transfer of a nonmonetary asset to a stockholder or to another entity in a nonreciprocal transfer should be recorded at the fair value of the asset transferred, and a gain or loss should be recognized on the disposition of the asset.

[6] *APB Opinion No. 29,* "Accounting for Nonmonetary Transactions," AICPA (New York: 1973), pp. 547–548.

If the current fair value of the nonmonetary asset distributed is not objectively measurable at the time of the distribution, the only feasible alternative may be to record the dividend at the carrying amount of the nonmonetary asset.

To illustrate the accounting for a dividend paid in the form of a nonmonetary asset, assume that Mayo Corporation owns 10% of the capital stock of Bliss Company with a carrying amount of $400,000 in the accounting records of Mayo. At the end of Year 10, the current fair value of this investment is $750,000. At this time the board of directors of Mayo authorizes the distribution of the Bliss stock as a dividend to the shareholders of Mayo. The journal entries for Mayo to record the declaration and distribution of this nonmonetary dividend are as follows:

Journal entries for nonmonetary dividend

Dividends (or Retained Earnings)...............	750,000	
Dividend Payable in Capital Stock of Bliss Company .		750,000
To record declaration of nonmonetary dividend.		
Dividend Payable in Capital Stock of Bliss Company	750,000	
Investments......................		400,000
Gain on Disposal of Investments		350,000
To record payment of nonmonetary dividend.		

It would be possible for Mayo to record the unrealized gain on the investment in capital stock of Bliss before the declaration of the nonmonetary dividend is recorded. This procedure might be followed to avoid recording a liability in excess of the carrying amount of the asset that will be used to liquidate the dividend liability. If a balance sheet is prepared for Mayo after the declaration but before the payment of the nonmonetary dividend, the asset to be distributed is classified as a current asset because the dividend payable is a current liability.

Liquidating dividends

The term *liquidating dividend* may be used in the following situations:

1 A pro rata distribution of assets to stockholders which reduces paid-in capital rather than retained earnings

2 A pro rata distribution to stockholders by a corporation having wasting assets such as mineral deposits or timberlands, representing a return of invested capital

3 A pro rata distribution to stockholders when a corporation is liquidated

A liquidating dividend may be recorded as a debit to a specific paid-in capital account or to a separate account such as Liquidating Dividend Distributed. Any balance in this account is deducted from total paid-in capital in the balance sheet.

Corporations must inform their stockholders when a dividend, or a portion of a dividend, represents a return of invested capital. Liquidating dividends are recorded by stockholders as reductions in the cost of their investment rather than as revenue. This procedure generally is applicable for both financial accounting and income taxes.

A spin-off is closely related to a liquidating dividend, except that a spin-off may involve a reduction in retained earnings. A **spin-off** is a transfer by a corporation of selected assets to a new corporation in exchange for its capital stock, which then is distributed pro rata to stockholders of the first corporation.

Generally, a gain is not recognized on a distribution of a liquidating dividend or on a transfer of assets to a new corporation in a spin-off, but a loss should be recognized. This point is covered in **APB Opinion No. 29** as follows:[7]

> Accounting for the distribution of nonmonetary assets to owners of an enterprise in a spin-off or other form of reorganization or liquidation or in a plan that is in substance the rescission of a prior business combination should be based on the recorded amount (after reduction, if appropriate, for an indicated impairment of value) of the nonmonetary assets distributed. A pro rata distribution to owners of an enterprise of shares of a subsidiary or other investee company that has been or is being consolidated or that has been or is being accounted for under the equity method is to be considered to be equivalent to a spin-off.

Stock dividends

Many corporations distribute stock dividends to their stockholders. A **stock dividend** is a distribution of additional shares of capital stock, called **dividend shares,** to stockholders in proportion to their existing holdings. "Common on common" is the usual type of stock dividend; such a distribution is known as an **ordinary stock dividend.** When a stock dividend is declared, Retained Earnings (or Stock Dividends) is debited and one or more paid-in capital accounts are credited.

Distribution of a stock dividend causes no change in the assets or liabilities of a corporation; the only effect is a transfer between stockholders' equity accounts. Because there is no decrease in the net assets of the corporation, a stock dividend does not give stockholders anything they did not have before. The number of shares of capital stock held by each stockholder is increased, but each share represents a smaller part of ownership in the corporation.

The principal argument for stock dividends is that they enable a "growth company" to retain accumulated earnings, yet provide the stockholders with additional shares of capital stock as evidence of the growth in the net assets of the corporation. Most stockholders view stock dividends as distributions of corporate earnings in an amount equal to the market value of the shares received. Such a view is strengthened by

[7] Ibid., p. 549.

the fact that small stock dividends often do not cause a decline in the market price of the stock, and the total market value of the original capital stock often remains unchanged.

Securities that are convertible to common stock (such as convertible bonds and convertible preferred stock) contain an **antidilution clause** that requires **adjustment of the conversion ratio** to compensate for the "reduced size" of a share of common stock after a stock dividend or a stock split. If, for example, a preferred stock is convertible into three shares of common stock, the conversion ratio is increased to 3.3 shares after a 10% stock dividend on the common stock, and to 6.6 shares after a 10% stock dividend followed by a 2 for 1 split.

Accounting for stock dividends

What amount of retained earnings should be transferred to the paid-in capital accounts for each share of capital stock issued as a stock dividend? Although the legal requirement in most states is the par or stated value of the dividend shares, generally accepted accounting principles for small stock dividends require the transfer of an amount equal to the **market price per share** prior to the dividend. Both the SEC and the AICPA support the use of market price as a measure of the amount of retained earnings transferred to paid-in capital for all stock dividends that increase the number of outstanding shares of capital stock by less than 20 or 25%. For large stock dividends, only the par or stated value per share is transferred from retained earnings to paid-in capital accounts. The reasons underlying this difference in treatment of small and large stock dividends is explained in the following sections.

Small Stock Dividends   The AICPA has suggested 20 or 25% as a dividing line between large and small stock dividends. Above this amount it may be assumed that the purpose of the stock distribution is to reduce the market price of the stock, as in the case of a stock split. Below this level it may be assumed that the dividend shares will be regarded by most stockholders as a distribution of retained earnings.

Large Stock Dividends   A large stock dividend, such as one increasing the number of outstanding shares by more than 25%, may be expected to cause a material decrease in the market price per share of capital stock. Such dividends are in the nature of stock splits. In other words, the amount of retained earnings transferred to paid-in capital pursuant to a large stock dividend is an amount equal to the par or stated value of the dividend shares. Let us use a somewhat extreme example to illustrate the probable reaction to a large stock dividend by a shareholder. Assume that Stockholder A owns 10 shares of $5 par capital stock of Oscar Company, with a current market price of $150 a share.

A 100% stock dividend is distributed, and the market price promptly drops to $75 a share. Stockholder A no doubt will recognize that the so-called "stock dividend" is not a distribution of earnings but is similar to a 2 for 1 split.

Corporations should avoid the use of the word "dividend" in notices relating to large stock dividends which reduce materially the market price per share. If legal considerations require use of the word "dividend," the transaction might be described as a ***split-up effected in the form of a stock dividend.***

Illustrative Journal Entries for Stock Dividends   Assume that Oscar Company has 1 million authorized shares of $5 par common stock, of which 500,000 shares are outstanding. The market price is $80 a share, and a quarterly cash dividend of 50 cents has been paid for several years. Current earnings are large and rising, but the company wishes to conserve cash for expansion of plant. Consequently, the board of directors decides to issue a 2% stock dividend rather than to increase the established cash dividend. A journal entry summarizing both the declaration and the distribution of the 2% stock dividend is presented below to emphasize the end results of the stock dividend:

Condensed journal entry for declaration and distribution of small stock dividend		

Retained Earnings.	800,000	
Common Stock, $5 par		50,000
Paid-in Capital from Stock Dividends.		750,000
To record the declaration and distribution of a 2% stock dividend consisting of 10,000 shares of $5 par common stock with a market price of $80 a share on the date of declaration.		

The preceding illustration of a journal entry for a small stock dividend could appear as three separate journal entries. The first entry would record declaration of the stock dividend by a debit to Stock Dividends for the market value of the shares to be issued, a credit to Stock Dividends to Be Distributed for the par value of the dividend shares, and a credit to Paid-in Capital from Stock Dividends for the excess of the market value over the par value of the shares to be issued. The second journal entry would record issuance of the shares by a debit to Stock Dividends to Be Distributed and a credit to Common Stock. At the end of the year, the Stock Dividends account is close to Retained Earnings. If a balance sheet is prepared between the date of declaration of the stock dividend and the date of distribution, the account Stock Dividends to Be Distributed is included in stockholders' equity below common stock.

If Oscar Company had declared and distributed a large stock dividend, say 50%, the journal entry on top of page 676 would be required.

Condensed journal entry for declaration and distribution of large stock dividend

Retained Earnings. 1,250,000
    Common Stock, $5 par   1,250,000
To record the declaration and distribution of a 50% stock
dividend consisting of 250,000 shares of $5 par common
stock (250,000 × $5 = $1,250,000).

Fractional Shares When a small stock dividend is declared, stockholders owning only a few shares of capital stock are entitled to receive only a fraction of a share. For example, in the preceding illustration of a 2% stock dividend declared by Oscar Company, the holder of less than 50 shares of common stock is entitled to only a fraction of a share. To avoid the inconvenience of issuing fractional shares, most corporations offer stockholders the alternative of receiving in cash the market value of the fraction of a share due, or of paying sufficient cash to qualify for a full share of stock.

Business combinations—purchase versus pooling of interests

In recent years many corporations have been combined to obtain the economies of large-scale operation and the financial strength arising from diversification in various industries. Business combinations are discussed at length in the *Modern Advanced Accounting* text of this series. Our purpose at this point is to call attention to the difference in impact on retained earnings of the *purchase method* and the *pooling-of-interests method* of accounting for business combinations. In a *purchase,* the capital stock of the acquired corporation usually is paid for in cash or through issuance of debt securities; in a *pooling,* the capital stock of another corporation is acquired by issuance of common stock.

When a business combination is accounted for as a *purchase,* the acquiring corporation records its investment at the cost established by cash paid or current fair value of securities issued in exchange for capital stock of the acquired corporation. *The retained earnings of the corporation acquired do not become part of combined retained earnings.* Net incomes of the two corporations are combined only from the date of the business combination.

On the other hand, when a business combination is accounted for as a *pooling of interests,* the assets of the two corporations are combined at their carrying amounts. The current fair values of the capital stock issued and of assets acquired are ignored. The pooling-of-interests method of accounting rests on an assumption of continuity of ownership, and the *retained earnings accounts of the two corporations are added together to measure the amount of retained earnings of the combined enterprise.* The net income of the combined enterprise includes the earnings of both corporations for the entire year in which the business combination occurred.

Quasi-reorganizations

A *quasi-reorganization* occurs when a corporation in financial difficulties modifies its capital structure without being forced to do so by creditors and without coming under the supervision of a bankruptcy court.[8]

Typically, a quasi-reorganization involves writing off a deficit against paid-in capital; sometimes there is a reduction in the par or stated value of capital stock and a write-down of overvalued assets. Following a quasi-reorganization, the corporation is considered from an accounting standpoint to have a *fresh start,* and the way is cleared for reporting net income and declaring dividends in future years. Although the write-down of asset values and the elimination of a deficit obscure historically significant data, the procedure is generally accepted because it results in more relevant assets amounts. Furthermore, a quasi-reorganization may help a corporation to regain its place as a profitable business enterprise without the stigma that attaches to a large deficit, continuous operating losses, and inability to declare cash dividends.

Sequence of Steps in a Quasi-Reorganization   A quasi-reorganization typically involves the following steps:

1 After stockholders approve the quasi-reorganization, assets that are considered to be overstated are written down to current fair value by a debit to retained earnings. If the current fair value of any asset exceeds carrying amount, increasing the carrying amount of such an asset generally is discouraged.

2 The deficit in retained earnings following the asset write-downs is eliminated against paid-in capital. Gains or losses realized subsequent to the quasi-reorganization which are attributable to the period prior to the quasi-reorganization are recorded as increases or decreases in paid-in capital in excess of par or stated value.

3 If paid-in capital in excess of par or stated value at the time of the quasi-reorganization is insufficient to absorb the deficit, the par or stated value of capital stock is reduced to establish a paid-in capital account which can be used to absorb the deficit.

4 Retained earnings following a quasi-reorganization must be identified (dated), generally for a period not exceeding 10 years, as accruing since the effective date of the quasi-reorganization. In subsequent balance sheets, this disclosure, called *dating the retained earnings,* may appear as follows:

"Dating retained earnings" subsequent to a quasi-reorganization

Retained earnings accumulated since June 30, Year 8, when a deficit of $4,202,000 was written off against paid-in capital as a part of quasi-reorganization $1,917,400

Illustration of a Quasi-Reorganization   To illustrate the accounting for a quasi-reorganization, assume that Quasar Corporation acquired plant

[8] The word *quasi* means resembling or seemingly, but not actually. Thus, a quasi-reorganization resembles, but is not, a formal type of a corporate reorganization.

assets and goodwill at high prices, and that several years of unprofitable operations resulted in the following balance sheet:

QUASAR CORPORATION
Balance Sheet
December 31, Year 15

Assets

Current assets		$ 6,200,000
Plant assets	$12,500,000	
Less: Accumulated depreciation	5,700,000	6,800,000
Goodwill		1,000,000
Total assets		$14,000,000

Liabilities & Stockholders' Equity

Liabilities:		
Current liabilities		$ 3,900,000
Long-term debt		500,000
Total liabilities		$ 4,400,000
Stockholders' equity:		
Capital stock, $10 stated value	$10,000,000	
Paid-in capital in excess of stated value	1,200,000	
Total paid-in capital	$11,200,000	
Retained earnings (deficit)	(1,600,000)	9,600,000
Total liabilities & stockholders' equity		$14,000,000

The existence of the $1,600,000 deficit and the high historical cost of plant assets and goodwill make it impossible for Quasar Corporation to report earnings or to pay dividends. To overcome these obstacles, let us assume that management proposes to effect a quasi-reorganization on December 31, Year 15, as follows:

1 The carrying amount of plant assets is reduced by $2,100,000, consisting of a $4,000,000 reduction in cost and a $1,900,000 reduction in accumulated depreciation; in addition, the entire goodwill of $1,000,000 is written off, thus increasing the deficit from $1,600,000 to $4,700,000.

2 The stated value of capital stock is reduced from $10 a share to $5 a share, thus increasing the paid-in capital in excess of stated value from $1,200,000 to $6,200,000.

3 The deficit of $4,700,000 is written off against paid-in capital in excess of stated value, resulting in a zero balance in the Retained Earnings account and a $1,500,000 balance in the Paid-in Capital in Excess of Stated Value account.

The journal entries to record the quasi-reorganization of Quasar Corporation are given on page 679.

Journal entries for quasi-reorganization

Retained Earnings	3,100,000	
Accumulated Depreciation	1,900,000	
Plant Assets		4,000,000
Goodwill		1,000,000
To write down carrying amount of plant assets as part of quasi-reorganization.		
Capital Stock, $10 stated value	10,000,000	
Capital Stock, $5 stated value		5,000,000
Paid-in Capital in Excess of Stated Value		5,000,000
To reduce the stated value of capital stock from $10 to $5 a share as part of quasi-reorganization.		
Paid-in Capital in Excess of Stated Value	4,700,000	
Retained Earnings		4,700,000
To eliminate accumulated deficit as part of quasi-reorganization.		

Any retained earnings accumulated after December 31, Year 15, are available as a basis for dividend declaration and are dated in balance sheets following the quasi-reorganization. For example, assume that Quasar Corporation reported net income of $375,000 and declared cash dividends of $125,000 in Year 16; the stockholders' equity section of the balance sheet on December 31, Year 16, would be as follows:

Stockholders' equity one year after quasi-reorganization

Stockholders' equity:	
Capital stock, $5 stated value	$5,000,000
Paid-in capital in excess of stated value	1,500,000
Total paid-in capital	$6,500,000
Retained earnings, accumulated since Dec. 31, Year 15, at which time a deficit of $4,700,000 was written off against paid-in capital in excess of stated value as part of quasi-reorganization.	250,000
Total stockholders' equity	$6,750,000

Because replacement costs of plant assets have been increasing steadily in recent years, quasi-reorganizations seldom are encountered in practice. Corporations experiencing severe financial difficulties are more likely to undergo a restructuring of debt or a formal reorganization under the supervision of a bankruptcy court.

REVIEW QUESTIONS

1 Why do corporations often issue two or more types of capital stock?

2 What are the basic rights inherent in the ownership of capital stock? What modification of these basic rights usually is found in preferred stock?

3 If a corporation with cumulative preferred stock outstanding fails to pay any dividend during a given year, what disclosure is made in the financial statements?

4 What is **redeemable preferred stock?**

5 Distinguish between a **conversion provision** in a preferred stock and a **call provision.** Can a preferred stock be both convertible and callable? If so, can both provisions be exercised?

6 In what respects does the position of preferred stockholders resemble that of bondholders rather than common stockholders? How does preferred stock differ from bonds payable?

7 For what purpose was the par value concept originally required for capital stock?

8 State briefly the accounting principle to be followed in recording the issuance of capital stock in exchange for assets or services.

9 Are most preferred stocks:
 a Voting or nonvoting?
 b Cumulative or noncumulative?
 c Participating or nonparticipating?
 d Callable or redeemable?

10 Can a corporation have both **watered stock** and **secret reserves?** Explain.

11 How should a **nonmonetary dividend** be recorded by the issuing corporation?

12 Distinguish between a **stock split** and a **stock dividend.**

13 Reese Corporation distributes a 3% stock dividend each year, in addition to paying an annual cash dividend of $2 a share. How should the amount of the debit to retained earnings for the stock dividend be determined?

14 Stock splits and stock dividends can be used by a corporation to increase the number of shares of its capital stock outstanding.
 a What is meant by a **split-up effected in the form of a stock dividend?**
 b How is a stock dividend that has been declared but not issued classified in a balance sheet? Why?

15 In what ways might a corporation offer bondholders protection against excessive cash dividend payments to stockholders?

16 To eliminate a deficit of $700,000, Wade Corporation obtained approval from its stockholders for a "reverse split." One new share of $5 par capital stock was issued for each two old shares of $10 par capital stock. The entire issue of 100,000 old shares was retired. Prepare the journal entries to record the exchange of shares and the elimination of the deficit.

17 Under what circumstances should the retained earnings be "dated?" Does dating of retained earnings refer to an item in the balance sheet or to a ledger account?

EXERCISES

Ex. 16-1 The stockholders' equity of Cable Company on July 31, Year 6, is presented below:

Common stock, $20 par, authorized 400,000 shares; issued and outstanding 150,000 shares	$3,000,000
Paid-in capital in excess of par	140,000
Retained earnings	390,000
Total stockholders' equity.	$3,530,000

On August 1, Year 6, the board of directors of Cable declared a 4% stock dividend on common stock, to be distributed on September 15. The market price of Cable's common stock was $35 a share on August 1, Year 6, and $40 a share on September 15, Year 6.

Compute the amount of the debit to retained earnings as a result of the declaration and distribution of the stock dividend.

Ex. 16-2 Engel Company had net income for Year 4 of $10,600,000 and earnings per share on common stock of $5.00. Included in the computation of net income was $1,000,000 of bond interest expense on Engel's long-term debt. The income tax rate for Year 4 was 50%. Dividends paid on preferred stock were $600,000. Forty percent of the net income available for common stock was paid as dividends.

Compute the dividends paid on common stock for Year 4.

Ex. 16-3 Portland Corporation was incorporated on January 2, Year 8, with the following authorized capitalization:

5,000 shares of 5% cumulative preferred stock, $10 par

20,000 shares of no-par common stock, stated value $40 a share

During Year 8, Portland issued 12,000 shares of common stock for a total of $600,000 and 3,000 shares of preferred stock at $16 a share. In addition, on December 20, Year 8, subscriptions for 1,000 shares of preferred stock were received at a price of $17 a share. The subscribed shares were paid for on January 2, Year 9.

Compute the amount that Portland should report as total paid-in capital in its December 31, Year 8, balance sheet.

Ex. 16-4 Langley Corporation received authorization to issue an additional 100,000 shares of no-par common stock with a stated value of $10 a share. The stock was offered to subscribers at a subscription price of $50 a share. Subscriptions were recorded by a debit to Subscriptions Receivable and a credit to Common Stock Subscribed and a paid-in capital account. A short time later, subscribers who had contracted to purchase 100 shares defaulted on their contracts after paying 40% of the subscription price.

The method used by Langley to record the default depends on the contractual and legal rights of the defaulting subscribers and especially on the statutes of the state of incorporation.

Identify four methods of accounting at the time of the default for the amount paid in by subscribers prior to the default. Prepare a journal entry for each method to show how the default would be recorded. Omit explanations for the journal entries.

Ex. 16-5 Osmond Company was organized on January 2, Year 5, and issued the following capital stock:

> 50,000 shares of $10 par, fully participating, 10% cumulative preferred stock, at $25 a share (authorized 150,000 shares)
>
> 200,000 shares of $5 par common stock at $12 a share (authorized 500,000 shares)

The net income for Year 5 was $420,000, and cash dividends of $240,000 were declared and paid in Year 5.

Compute the dividends paid on the preferred stock and common stock during Year 5.

Ex. 16-6 Gate Company declared and distributed dividends as follows:

(1) The entire investment in the common stock of Hare Company, a wholly owned subsidiary accounted for by the equity method of accounting, was distributed to Gate Company's stockholders. The carrying amount of this investment on the date of distribution was $725,000; the distribution was made instead of accepting a cash offer of $2,000,000 for the common stock of Hare from an investor.

(2) The company's 5% common stock interest in Pola Company was distributed to stockholders. The investment in Pola was carried at a cost of $62,000; the current fair value of this investment was $90,000.

Prepare journal entries in the accounting records of Gate Company to record the declaration and distribution of the two dividends described above.

Ex. 16-7 The stockholders' equity section of the balance sheet of Comstock Company at the beginning of the year contained the following items:

Convertible preferred stock, $100 par, authorized, issued, and outstanding 10,000 shares **(Note A)**	$1,000,000
Common stock, $5 par, authorized 1 million shares, issued and outstanding 400,000 shares	2,000,000
Retained earnings	6,000,000
Total stockholders' equity	$9,000,000

Note A: The preferred stock is convertible at any time to common stock at a conversion ratio of four common shares for each preferred share, with the conversion ratio subject to adjustment for any dilution of the common stock.

On January 10, a 5% common stock dividend was declared, to be distributed January 30 to stockholders of record January 15. On March 1 all the preferred stock was converted to common stock. Market price a share for the common stock was as follows: January 10, $40; January 15, $42; January 30, $43; March 1, $45.

Post the transactions described above in appropriate ledger accounts and determine the balances of the following accounts after giving consideration to all the listed transactions: **(a)** Common Stock, **(b)** Paid-in Capital in Excess of Par, and **(c)** Retained Earnings. Also compute the total stockholders' equity after giving effect to these transactions.

Ex. 16-8 Obsolescence has become a major problem in the inventories of Shasta Company. Lack of attention to inventory turnover rates, combined with a change in product design to permit use of lighter-weight materials, has caused much of the existing inventories to become obsolete. An analysis of the inventories on December 31 of the current year indicated that the carrying amount of inventories should be reduced by $1,100,000 because of obsolescence.

The income of the current year before the obsolescence loss was estimated at $210,000. The stockholders' equity accounts before year-end adjusting entries had the following balances:

Capital stock, $1 par	$1,000,000
Paid-in capital in excess of par	600,000
Retained earnings	400,000
Total stockholders' equity	$2,000,000

The board of directors informs you that it regards obsolescence as an extraordinary item and that a tentative decision has been made to write down inventories by the full amount of the obsolescence loss; to debit $400,000 to retained earnings, $600,000 to paid-in capital in excess of par, and $100,000 to a loss of the current year.

Evaluate the proposed treatment of the obsolescence loss in the light of generally accepted accounting principles. Disregard income tax considerations. Compute the amount of income or loss before income taxes for the current year and explain how the obsolescence loss should be reported. Disregard other adjustments that may be required in the computation of income before income taxes.

Ex. 16-9 From the following information, prepare the stockholders' equity section of the balance sheet of Moore Corporation on October 31, Year 6:

Subscriptions receivable: common stock	$ 55,000
Paid-in capital in excess of par: preferred stock	50,000
Common stock, $5 par, authorized 40,000 shares, issued and outstanding 20,000 shares	100,000
Paid-in capital in excess of par: common stock	150,000
Retained earnings, unappropriated	327,000
Retained earnings appropriated for general business contingencies . .	125,000
Common stock subscribed	25,000
7% cumulative preferred stock, $50 par, authorized 20,000 shares, issued and outstanding 10,000 shares	500,000
Paid-in capital from donation of plant site by city of Prado	40,000

SHORT CASES FOR ANALYSIS AND DECISION

Case 16-1 You are engaged in an audit of the financial statements of Rotherwood Company on March 31, Year 1, the end of its first year of operations. During your examination of the stockholders' equity accounts, you discover that Rotherwood issued capital stock to three cutomers at a price substantially below the current fair value of the stock on the dates of issuance. (Your determination of current fair value was based on market prices of Rotherwood's capital stock on the dates of issuance to the three customers.)

Rotherwood's controller proposes to present the difference between current fair value of the capital stock and the proceeds received from the customers as an extraordinary loss in Rotherwood's income statement for the year ended

March 31, Year 1. The controller points out that all other capital stock issuances were for proceeds equal to current fair value, and that the "discount" allowed to the customers who acquired Rotherwood's capital stock was for the purpose of encouraging future purchases of merchandise by those customers. The controller acknowledged, however, that the customers purchasing Rotherwood's capital stock at a discount had no long-term contractual commitment to make purchases from Rotherwood.

Instructions   Do you concur with the controller's proposal for the accounting for the discount on capital stock? Explain.

Case 16-2   The independent auditor of Crestview Company explained to the president of the company that the use of the lifo inventory method during an extended period of rising prices and the expensing of all human resource costs (training and development) are among the accepted accounting practices which help create **secret reserves.** The auditor also pointed out that **watered stock** is the opposite of secret reserves.

Instructions
a What are **secret reserves**? How can secret reserves be created or enlarged?
b What is the basis for the statement that the two specific practices cited above tend to create secret reserves?
c Is it possible to create secret reserves in connection with accounting for liabilities? If so, explain or give an example.
d What are the objections to the creation of secret reserves?
e What is **watered stock**?
f Describe the general circumstances in which watered stock can arise.
g What steps can be taken to eliminate "water" from a balance sheet?

Case 16-3   After the cancellation of some of its government contracts, Colbert Company began production under a new long-term government contract. During the period of operating losses the company had suspended dividend payments on all four capital stock issues. These four issues consisted of a $7 cumulative, $100 par, first preferred stock; a $2.50 noncumulative, convertible, $50 par, preferred stock; an 8%, $100 par, noncumulative preferred stock; and a Class A common stock without any dividend preference. 10,000 shares were outstanding of each issue of capital stock. All dividends had been paid through Year 3, but the company had been unable to pay any dividends in Year 4 or Year 5. During Year 6, the company's financial position improved, and at a director's meeting near the end of Year 6, a proposal was made to pay a dividend of $2.25 a share on the Class A common stock to stockholders of record December 31, Year 6.

Edward Cobb, who owned 100 shares of the $2.50 noncumulative, convertible, $50 par, preferred stock, had been considering converting those 100 shares to Class A common stock at the existing conversion ratio of four shares of common stock for each share of the convertible preferred stock. The conversion ratio was scheduled to drop to $3\frac{1}{2}$ to one at the end of Year 6. Observing that the price of the common stock was rising rapidly, Cobb explained that he was "torn between a desire to retain his preferred stock until the dividend of $2.25 a share was received and a desire to convert promptly before the price of the common stock went higher and the conversion ratio was reduced."

Instructions
a Determine the amount of cash needed for dividend payments if the proposal to pay a $2.25 dividend on the Class A common stock is adopted. (Assume that there is no conversion of preferred stock.)
b Advise Cobb on the merits of converting the preferred stock at this time as opposed to converting after the dividends have been paid and the conversion ratio decreased. Explain fully the issues involved.

Case 16-4 A few months after the organization of Haig Corporation, one of the principal stockholders, Hoyt, offered to transfer a factory to the company in exchange for 11,000 shares of Haig's $10 par capital stock. Under the terms of the offer, an existing mortgage note payable of $28,000 on the factory was to be assumed by Haig.

The board of directors of Haig determined that the factory was well-suited to the company's needs. The board was informed by the secretary of the company that 15,000 authorized but unissued shares of capital stock were available.

One member of the board, Sperry, opposed the idea of assuming the mortgage note, on the grounds that long-term debt could prove burdensome for a new company without established earning power, and suggested making a counteroffer of 13,800 shares with the understanding that Hoyt pay the mortgage note in full on the date title to the factory was received.

A second director, Brown, argued against further issuance of capital stock, pointing out that the company had just obtained $325,000 cash from issuance of 26,000 shares of capital stock and that this cash should be used to acquire plant assets. Brown proposed that the company offer Hoyt $110,000 cash, assume the mortgage note, and pay it in full immediately.

A third director, Benson, urged prompt acceptance of Hoyt's offer without modification. Benson produced documents showing that the factory had been purchased by Hoyt 10 years previously at a total price of $206,000 and that Hoyt's accounting records indicated depreciation to date of $36,000. In conclusion, Benson stated that these facts showed that the company would be saving $32,000 by accepting Hoyt's offer.

Instructions
a Comment on the logic and reasonableness of the views expressed by each of the three directors. Explain how each arrived at the amounts mentioned.
b Indicate which deal you believe would be most advantageous to Haig Corporation, assuming that it was acceptable to Hoyt.
c Assuming that Haig Corporation accepted the original offer by Hoyt, prepare the journal entry to record the transaction, and explain the principles underlying the entry. Assume that land is worth 25% as much as the factory building.

Case 16-5 After receiving a stock certificate for three shares, Ruth Ross, a stockholder of Karras Corporation, expressed this reaction:

"Karras Corporation has just declared another stock dividend despite that letter of protest I wrote to the president last year. I wrote that I hate to see a company declare a stock dividend because it causes a transfer of retained earnings to paid-in capital. Such a transfer obviously reduces the amount available for cash dividends."

"You are absolutely right," said Wilma Wade. "When I bought Karras stock I was hoping for an increase in cash dividends over a period of time, but the declaration of stock dividends certainly reduces my expectations for cash dividends. Let's write the president another letter."

Instructions Evaluate the opinions expressed by Ross and Wade from the standpoint of accounting principles, and also in the light of customary dividend practices. Identify any elements of truth in the statements and any lack of logic in the conclusions reached by Ross and Wade.

Case 16-6 Fred Gabel, CPA, was asked by the president of a client corporation for an explanation of a "quasi-reorganization." The president was unfamiliar with the procedure and was concerned that a competitor might have an advantage since it carried out a quasi-reorganization.

Instructions Prepare the report Gabel should provide to the president explaining a quasi-reorganization. The report should include the following points:

a Definition and accounting features of a quasi-reorganization.

b Purpose of a quasi-reorganization. Under what conditions should a quasi-reorganization be considered?

c Authorization necessary to carry out a quasi-reorganization.

d Disclosure required in the financial statements following a quasi-reorganization.

e Possible advantage to the competitor that carried out a quasi-reorganization.

PROBLEMS

16-1 Kasmir Company began operations in January, Year 1, and had the following net income or (loss) for each of its first five years of operations:

Year 1	*$ (150,000)*
2	*(130,000)*
3	*(120,000)*
4	*250,000*
5	*1,022,000*

On December 31, Year 5, Kasmir's capital stock accounts were as follows:

12% nonparticipating, noncumulative preferred stock, $100 par; authorized, issued, and outstanding 1,000 shares	*$ 100,000*
8% fully participating, cumulative preferred stock, $100 par; authorized, issued, and outstanding 10,000 shares	*1,000,000*
Common stock, $10 par; authorized 100,000 shares; issued and outstanding 50,000 shares	*500,000*

Kasmir has never paid a cash dividend or issued a stock dividend. There has been no change in the capital stock accounts since Kasmir began operations. The appropriate state law permits dividends only from retained earnings.

Instructions Prepare a working paper to show the maximum amount available for cash dividends on December 31, Year 5, and how it would be distributed to the holders of the common stock and each of the preferred stocks. Show supporting computations.

16-2 On January 4, Year 1, Palmer Company was organized and received authority from the state to issue capital stock as follows:

$5 preferred stock, $100 par, 250,000 shares

Common stock, no-par, stated value $5 a share, 1,000,000 shares

After this authorization to issue capital stock, the following transactions affecting stockholders' equity occurred during the first quarter of Year 1:

Jan. 15 Received subscriptions for 25,000 shares of preferred stock at $105 a share. A payment of 40% of the subscription price accompanied each subscription; the balance was to be paid on March 15. (Record the full amount subscribed and then, in a separate journal entry, record the cash collection for 40% of this amount.)

Jan. 17 Received subscriptions for 125,000 shares of common stock at $20 a share, payable March 1.

Jan. 30 Issued 1,000 shares of common stock in payment for legal and accounting services valued at $20,000 relating to the organization of the company.

Mar. 1 Received payment in full of the amount due on common stock subscriptions.

Mar. 15 Received payment in full of the balance due on preferred stock subscriptions.

Mar. 30 Issued 5,000 shares of preferred stock for $520,000.

Mar. 30 Issued 6,000 shares of common stock and 2,500 shares of preferred stock in exchange for assets for which the board of directors established the following current fair values:

Land	$154,000
Building	190,000
Delivery equipment	20,000
Inventories	15,000

Mar. 31 Net income earned to March 31 amounted to $136,000. No dividends had been declared.

Instructions

a Prepare journal entries to record the foregoing transactions.

b Prepare the stockholders' equity section of the balance sheet on March 31, Year 1.

16-3 The board of directors of Yeats Corporation declared a 6% stock dividend on October 1, Year 8, to be distributed on October 25 to stockholders of record October 15. The market price of the company's capital stock was as follows on these dates: October 1, $63; October 15, $66; and October 25, $70. The accounting records of Yeats Corporation are maintained on the basis of a fiscal year ended September 30.

On October 28, Year 8, the board of directors declared a cash dividend of $0.80 a share on the capital stock. The dividend was payable December 1 to stockholders of record November 18.

The stockholders' equity section of the balance sheet on September 30, Year 8, is shown below. During October, the net income was $41,750.

Stockholders' equity:

Capital stock, $15 par, authorized 200,000 shares, issued and outstanding 60,000 shares	$ 900,000
Paid-in capital in excess of par	1,250,000
Total paid-in capital	$2,150,000
Retained earnings	2,380,000
Total stockholders' equity	$4,530,000

Instructions

a Prepare journal entries for the declaration and the distribution of the dividends which would be required during the month of October, Year 8. Debit Retained Earnings for dividend declarations. Also prepare a journal entry to record the net income for October (debit Income Summary).

b Prepare the stockholders' equity section of the balance sheet on October 31, Year 8.

16-4 Kotai Corporation was organized on September 5, Year 2, with authorization to issue 600,000 shares of $5 par common stock and 22,500 shares of $50 par, 8% cumulative preferred stock. On September 15, a single proprietorship was acquired in exchange for 12,000 shares of preferred stock, plus the assumption of a mortgage note payable of $276,000. The assets acquired in this manner were valued by a firm of independent appraisers at $900,000. On September 20, subscriptions were obtained for 30,000 common shares at a price of $15 a share.

All subscriptions were collected and recorded on October 5, except for a subscription by Caines for 300 shares. Caines paid $1,500 but defaulted on the balance of the contract. On October 10, the 300 shares were resold for cash by the corporation at a price of $13 a share. In accordance with statutes of the state, Kotai refunded the amount paid by Caines after deducting the loss incurred on the resale of the 300 shares.

No dividends were declared on the common stock. A quarterly dividend of $1 a share on the preferred stock was declared on November 9, payable on December 15, to stockholders of record on December 1. Operations for the period ended December 31, Year 2, resulted in net income of $68,744.

Instructions
a Prepare journal entries for the capital stock transactions and the dividend declaration and payment.
b Prepare the stockholders' equity section of the balance sheet on December 31, Year 2.

16-5 De Sai Corporation maintains its accounting records on the basis of a fiscal year ending March 31. The stockholders' equity section of the balance sheet on March 31, Year 6, appears below:

Stockholders' equity:

Capital stock, $10 par, authorized 250,000 shares, issued and outstanding 100,000 shares	$1,000,000
Paid-in capital in excess of par	2,675,000
Total paid-in capital	$3,675,000
Retained earnings	2,420,000
Total stockholders' equity	$6,095,000

On April 1, Year 6, the board of directors of De Sai declared a cash dividend of $1 a share payable on April 29 to stockholders of record April 15.

On April 10, Year 6, the board of directors of De Sai also declared a 3% stock dividend distributable on May 31 to stockholders of record May 15. The market price of the capital stock on April 10 was $60 a share. The net income for April amounted to $78,500.

Instructions
a Prepare journal entries for the declaration and the distribution of the dividends and to record net income for April. Debit the declarations of dividends directly to the Retained Earnings account, and debit Income Summary to record the net income.
b Prepare the stockholders' equity section of the balance sheet on April 30, Year 6, and a statement of retained earnings similar in format to the one on page 115.

16-6 The market price of Porter Corporation's capital stock on June 30, Year 1, was $52 a share. The stockholders' equity at this date included substantial retained earnings, in addition to 250,000 shares of $2 par capital stock, which had been issued at a price of $12 a share. A total of 500,000 shares was authorized to be issued.

A nonmonetary dividend of $1.10 a share was declared on March 10, Year 2, payable April 25, Year 2, to stockholders of record March 31, Year 2. The carrying amount of the marketable securities (short-term investments) distributed as a nonmonetary dividend was $180,000.

A cash dividend of $1.50 a share was declared on June 1, Year 2, payable July 20, Year 2, to stockholders of record July 1, Year 2; a 5% stock dividend was declared at the same time and with the same dates of record and distribution. The cash dividend was not applicable to the shares issued as a stock dividend. The market price of the capital stock was $55 on June 1, Year 2, and $58 on June 30, Year 2.

During the fiscal year ended June 30, Year 2, net income amounted to $1,643,700 (including the effect, if any, of the nonmonetary dividend), which represented an earnings rate of 10% on total stockholders' equity as of the beginning of the year.

Instructions
a Record the transactions affecting stockholders' equity during Year 2 in the general journal. Debit Retained Earnings for declarations of dividends, and debit Income Summary to record the net income for Year 2
b Prepare a statement of retained earnings for the year ended June 30, Year 2, similar in format to the one on page 115.
c Prepare the stockholders' equity section of the balance sheet on June 30, Year 2.

16-7   Current conditions require that Crake Company carry out a quasi-reorganization on December 31, Year 6. Selected balance sheet items prior to the quasi-reorganization were as follows:

(1) Inventories were carried in the accounting records on December 31, Year 6, at market value of $3,000,000. The cost of the inventories was $3,250,000.
(2) Plant assets were recorded in the accounting records on December 31, Year 6, at $6,000,000, net of accumulated depreciation. Plant assets had a current fair value of $4,000,000.
(3) Stockholders' equity on December 31, Year 6, consisted of the following:

Common stock, $10 par; authorized, issued, and outstanding	
350,000 shares	$3,500,000
Paid-in capital in excess of par	800,000
Retained earnings (deficit)	(450,000)
Total stockholders' equity.	$3,850,000

The par value of the common stock is to be reduced from $10 a share to $5 a share.

Instructions   Prepare the stockholders' equity section of Crake Company's balance sheet on December 31, Year 6, after the quasi-reorganization has been effected. Show supporting computations. Ignore income tax and deferred tax considerations.

16-8   Pittston Corporation was authorized to issue 500,000 shares of $25 par, 8% cumulative preferred stock, and 1,500,000 shares of no-par common stock with stated value of $2.50 a share.

Early operations of the company were profitable, but a prolonged strike caused a net loss of $920,000 for the fiscal year ended June 30, Year 6. Because of the loss, the company paid no dividends on its common stock during the year ended June 30, Year 6. Dividends on preferred stock were paid in the amount of $120,000, but dividends were in arrears on the preferred stock on June 30, Year 6, in the amount of $360,000.

A trial balance of the general ledger on May 31, Year 6, included the following:

8% cumulative preferred stock, $25 par	$6,000,000
Common stock, no-par, $2.50 stated value	1,000,000
Subscriptions receivable: preferred stock	618,000
Retained earnings (June 30, Year 5)	1,476,000
Paid-in capital in excess of par: preferred stock	198,000
Preferred stock subscribed	600,000
Paid-in capital in excess of stated value: common stock	1,375,000
Subscriptions receivable: common stock	525,000
Common stock subscribed	250,000
Dividends: preferred stock	120,000

Transactions during June, Year 6, relating to capital stock included the issuance on June 5 of 4,200 shares of common stock in exchange for a patent. An additional 30,000 shares of common stock were issued for cash on June 11 at a price of $6 a share. Cash was collected on June 21 representing payment in full for common stock subscriptions covering 20,000 shares. These subscriptions had been received and recorded prior to May 31. All common stock offerings by the company prior to May 31 had been at the same price.

Instructions

a Compute the average price at which the preferred stock was issued by the company.

b Compute the price at which the common stock was offered by the company prior to June, Year 6.

c Prepare journal entries to record the transactions (including closing entries for the net loss and dividends) during June which affected the stockholders' equity accounts.

d Prepare the stockholders' equity section of the balance sheet on June 30, Year 6, including any notes to the balance sheet.

16-9 The stockholders of Bragg Corporation have voted approval for the corporation to carry out a quasi-reorganization effective October 1, Year 3. The balance sheet on September 30, Year 3, follows:

BRAGG CORPORATION
Balance Sheet
September 30, Year 3

Assets

Current assets		$1,080,000
Plant assets	$800,000	
Less: Accumulated depreciation	395,000	405,000
Goodwill		1,520,000
Total assets		$3,005,000

Liabilities & Stockholders' Equity

Liabilities:		
Current liabilities		$ 305,000
12% bonds payable		250,000
Total liabilities		$ 555,000

(cont.)

Stockholders' equity:

10.5% preferred stock, $100 par (dividends in arrears,		
$42,000).	$ 200,000	
Common stock, $10 par	2,200,000	
Retained earnings	50,000	2,450,000
Total liabilities & stockholders' equity		$3,005,000

The company is engaged in the manufacture of space exploration equipment and has acquired numerous small business enterprises at amounts in excess of the current fair value of their identifiable net assets. The purchase prices included, among other things, payment for research work and for the services of technically trained personnel. The value assigned to the acquired assets was based on the par value of capital stock issued in the business combinations. The market value of Bragg's capital stock was approximately equal to its par value.

In recent months, several major research projects were abandoned, and some key employees left the company. As a result, many contracts were lost, and the goodwill was deemed to be worthless. In order to get a "fresh start" for financial accounting purposes, the following actions were taken to carry out a quasi-reorganization effective October 1, Year 3, approved by stockholders:

(1) Inventories and net receivables were written down by $150,000 and $10,000, respectively.
(2) The carrying amount of plant assets was reduced to $250,000 by an increase in accumulated depreciation.
(3) The goodwill was written off.
(4) The par value of common stock was reduced to $1 a share.
(5) The dividends in arrears on the preferred stock were paid in cash, and 80,000 shares of $1 par common stock were issued to the preferred stockholders in exchange for their stock.
(6) Following the asset write-offs, the deficit was eliminated against paid-in capital in excess of par.
(7) During the last quarter of Year 3, Bragg earned net income of $85,000, and as a result, current assets increased by $120,000, current liabilities increased by $10,000, and accumulated depreciation increased by $25,000. Current liabilities also increased by $7,000 as a result of additional income taxes assessed for Year 1 because of an error in the computation of income taxes payable.

Instructions
a Prepare journal entries to record the quasi-reorganization and to summarize the activities for the last quarter of Year 3.
b Compute the balance of retained earnings on December 31, Year 3.

16-10 At the beginning of Year 9, the stockholders' equity of Questor Company was as follows:

$6 convertible preferred stock, $100 par, authorized 10,000 shares, issued and outstanding 5,000 shares (**Note 1**)	$ 500,000
Common stock, $2 par, authorized 1,000,000 shares, issued and outstanding 350,000 shares	700,000
Common stock subscribed, 8,000 shares	16,000
Paid-in capital in excess of par: common stock	3,500,000
Total paid-in capital	$4,716,000
Retained earnings	5,262,600
Total stockholders' equity	$9,978,600

Note 1: Preferred stock was issued at par, is callable at $105, and is convertible to common stock at a rate of 3 for 1, subject to an antidilution provision.

During the first quarter of Year 9, the following transactions were completed:

Jan.   7 Collected $310,000 representing payment in full for all outstanding common stock subscriptions; issued the stock.

Jan. 31 Declared the regular quarterly dividend on the preferred stock to be paid March 3 to stockholders of record February 19.

Feb.   1 Declared a 10% common stock dividend to be distributed March 4 to common stockholders of record February 20.

Mar.   3 Paid quarterly dividend on the preferred stock.

Mar.   4 Distributed the 10% common stock dividend.

Mar. 15 Issued 11,000 shares of common stock for cash at $43 a share.

Mar. 30 All preferred stock was converted to common stock.

Mar. 31 Issued 100,000 shares of common stock in exchange for the net assets of Raye Corporation appraised at $4.5 million.

Mar. 31 Net income for the first quarter of Year 9 was $877,700. (Debit the Income Summary account.)

Market price of Questor Company's common stock was as follows: January 7, $40; February 1, $38; February 20, $40; March 4, $42; March 15, $43; March 31, $45.

Instructions

a Prepare journal entries for the transactions described above. Debit Retained Earnings for declarations of dividends.

b Prepare a statement of stockholders' equity (including retained earnings) for the first quarter of Year 9, similar in format to the one on page 149.

16-11 On December 31, Year 1, the end of its first year of operations, Sumiko Company prepared a balance sheet containing the following items, among others:

Subscriptions receivable: preferred stock		$ 208,000
Subscriptions receivable: common stock		720,000
8% cumulative preferred stock, $100 par, authorized		
200,000 shares, issued and outstanding 44,000 shares	$4,400,000	
8% preferred stock subscribed 4,000 shares	400,000	4,800,000
Common stock, $10 par, authorized 400,000 shares, is-		
sued and outstanding 48,000 shares	$ 480,000	
Common stock subscribed 48,000 shares	480,000	960,000
Paid-in capital in excess of par:		
On preferred stock		32,000
On common stock		1,952,000

The corporation had been organized on January 2, Year 1, and had immediately received subscriptions for 40,000 shares of preferred stock. Subscriptions for common stock were received on the same date. (The number of common shares subscribed and the subscription price can be determined from information given in the problem.) On May 5 subscriptions were received for an additional 8,000 shares of preferred stock at a price of $104 a share.

Cash payments were received from subscribers at frequent intervals for several months after subscription. The company followed a policy of issuing stock certificates only when subscribers had paid in full. On December 22, Year 1, Sumiko issued 16,000 shares of its common stock in exchange for a tract of land with a current fair value of $512,000. (Subscriptions were not used in this transaction.)

Instructions

a Prepare journal entries for all the transactions completed during Year 1 by Sumiko Company as indicated by the December 31, Year 1, account balances. Assume that collections on the preferred stock subscriptions were made on a fifo basis.

b Compute the amount of paid-in capital for each class of stock on December 31, Year 1. Also determine the amount of stated capital applicable to the common stock.

17 CORPORATIONS: STOCK RIGHTS, WARRANTS, OPTIONS, AND CONVERTIBLE SECURITIES

STOCK RIGHTS AND WARRANTS

As explained in Chapter 14, a **warrant** is a certificate issued by a corporation conveying to the holder rights to purchase shares of the corporation's common stock at a specified price. The term **stock right** means the privilege attaching to each outstanding share of common stock to buy a fractional share or a specified number of shares of common stock. For example, the owner of 100 shares of common stock might receive a warrant for 100 rights, which would permit the owner to purchase a specified number of new shares at a price below the current market price.

The use of rights is not limited to the acquisition of additional shares of common stock. Some corporations in recent years have issued rights to their common stockholders entitling them to acquire convertible bonds at a stipulated price. The use of rights in the acquisition of bonds is considered later in this chapter. At this point we are concerned only with rights that entitle the owner to purchase common stock at a specified price.

When warrants for stock rights are outstanding, the corporation's balance sheet should disclose the number of shares of common stock held in reserve to meet the contractual commitments to issue additional shares of stock. This disclosure may be made in the stockholders' equity section of the balance sheet or in a note to the financial statements.

Rights granted to existing stockholders

When rights are granted to existing stockholders as a preliminary step to raise capital through the issuance of additional shares of common stock, the corporation receives nothing in exchange for the rights when they are *issued.* Only when the rights are *exercised* does the corporation receive funds.

Stock rights granted to existing stockholders as a preliminary step to raising capital through the issuance of additional common stock usually expire within a few weeks. The corporation thus can complete rapidly its program of raising capital through the issuance of additional common stock to present stockholders before offering stock to other investors. Stock rights of this type are transferable, and some investors acquire rights by purchase from other investors. When investors who have purchased rights from other investors exercise the rights, the cost of the rights is combined with the amount paid to the corporation to determine the total cost of their investment in shares of common stock.

The purchase price specified in stock rights granted to existing stockholders is less than current market price. In the following illustration of a subscription warrant for common stock issued by Pacific Gas and Electric Company some years ago, 15 rights were needed for each share of common stock to be purchased at the subscription price (not shown) of $25.65. The market price of the common stock at the time the rights were issued was $27.62. The term of the rights was short—they were issued March 6 and expired on March 27. Through use of these rights the company sold over 4 million shares of stock and raised capital in excess of $102 million within the three-week term of the rights. The rights were traded on the New York Stock Exchange throughout their brief term, with the price per right varying between $0.125 and $0.50.

The issuance of rights to stockholders does not require debits or credits to any accounts of the issuing corporation, although a memorandum entry stating the number of rights issued and the terms involved

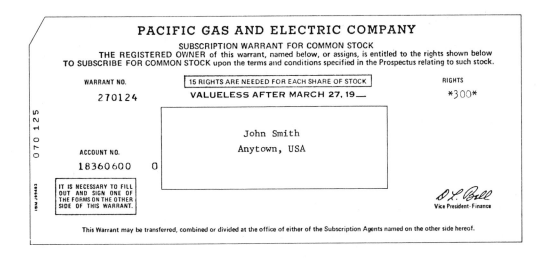

normally is used. When the rights are exercised by the owner, the corporation issues shares of common stock at the stipulated price. This transaction requires the usual journal entry for issuances of capital stock.

Rights to purchase convertible bonds

The preemptive right of common stockholders to purchase additional shares of common stock in proportion to their present holdings in the event that the corporation increases the amount of stock outstanding is discussed in Chapter 16. This preemptive right logically applies also to any new issues of convertible bonds or convertible preferred stock because these securities eventually may be converted to common stock.

During periods of high stock prices, convertible bonds are a popular form of financing. Rights may be issued to common stockholders entitling them to acquire convertible bonds at a specified price, and usually with the provision that the rights will expire if not exercised within a month or two. For example, some years ago National Cash Register issued to its common stockholders warrants for rights to purchase convertible bonds maturing in 1992. Ten rights and $100 cash were required to purchase $100 face amount of bonds. The rights traded for several weeks on the New York Stock Exchange at prices varying between $1 and $2 a right; concurrently, the convertible bonds were trading on a **when-issued** basis at prices ranging from $108 to $116 for each $100 face amount. (Sales of securities on a "when-issued" basis do not require delivery until after the scheduled date of issuance.)

The accounting procedures for rights to purchase convertible bonds are similar to the procedures described for rights to purchase common stock. The corporation makes no journal entry in its accounting records when the rights are issued but must maintain memorandum records of the number of rights issued, exercised, and outstanding. When the rights are exercised, the journal entry usually required is a debit to Cash and a credit to the liability account for the convertible bonds. Usually, the price stipulated by the right is face amount; thus, no discount or premium is involved when the convertible bonds are issued.

Warrants issued in combination with bonds or preferred stock

A corporation may add to the attractiveness of its bonds or preferred stock by attaching a warrant to acquire its common stock at a specified price.[1] The longer the term of the warrant, the greater its speculative ap-

---

[1] Warrants to purchase common stock sometimes have been offered in combination with the public issuance of common stock or in business combinations. For example, some years ago Tenneco, Inc., offered 5.5 million shares of common stock with detachable warrants entitling the owner to purchase additional shares of common stock.

peal; warrants often run for several years, and some have no expiration date.

When bonds are issued with detachable warrants, the interest rate on the bonds usually is less than if the bonds were offered alone. Similarly, preferred stock accompanied by detachable warrants for the purchase of common stock can attract investors even though the dividend rate on the preferred stock is lower than would otherwise be necessary. In other words, a part of the proceeds to the corporation from issuing bonds or preferred stock with warrants attached represents payment by investors for the warrants. Therefore, the accounting for these "combination packages" of securities *requires that part of the proceeds be recorded as attributable to the warrants.*

Accounting for bonds payable issued with detachable warrants is illustrated in Chapter 15. In this chapter, our discussion is focused on the issuance of warrants in combination with preferred stock.

Warrants giving the owner the right to purchase common stock at a specified price at any time during a span of years have an economic value regardless of whether the specified exercise price is higher than, lower than, or equal to the market price of the stock when the warrants are issued. Because the detachable warrants often are traded separately from the preferred stock or bond with which they were originally issued, objective evidence is available for the allocation of the proceeds between the two types of securities.

In *APB Opinion No. 14,* the Accounting Principles Board stated that "the portion of the proceeds of debt securities issued with detachable stock warrants which is allocable to the warrants should be accounted for as paid-in capital. The allocation should be based on the relative fair values of the two securities at time of issuance."[2] Although this discussion related specifically to bonds issued with detachable stock warrants, the reasoning also appears applicable to warrants issued with preferred stock.

Assume, for example, that Gulf, Inc., issues 1 million shares of $25 par preferred stock at 26\frac{1}{2}$ and gives with each share a warrant to purchase one share of common stock at $30 at any time during the next 10 years. The common stock has a par of $5 and a current market price of $26. The warrants have a value because of the likelihood that the market price of the common stock will rise above $30 a share during the next 10 years. Assume also that immediately after issuance the warrants have a market price of $1 each. The journal entry to record the proceeds of the stock offering appears on top of page 698.

---

[2] *APB Opinion No. 14,* "Accounting for Convertible Debt and Debt Issued with Stock Purchase Warrants," AICPA (New York: 1969), p. 209.

Journal entry to record issuance of preferred stock and stock purchase warrants

Cash. 26,500,000		
Preferred Stock		25,000,000
Paid-in Capital in Excess of Par: Preferred Stock .		500,000
Paid-in Capital: Stock Purchase Warrants		1,000,000

To record issuance of 1 million shares of $25 par preferred stock at $25½ and 1 million warrants with a market price of $1 each.

The Paid-in Capital: Stock Purchase Warrants account is classified in the stockholders' equity section of the balance sheet with other types of paid-in capital. If the warrants are exercised and the common stock issued at $30 a share, the journal entry would be as follows:

Journal entry for exercise of warrants for common stock

Cash. 30,000,000		
Paid-in Capital: Stock Purchase Warrants 1,000,000		
Common Stock		5,000,000
Paid-in Capital in Excess of Par: Common Stock		26,000,000

To record issuance of 1 million shares of $5 par common stock in exchange for 1 million warrants and cash of $30 a share.

If a part of stock purchase warrants is not exercised and expires, the balance of the Paid-in Capital: Stock Purchase Warants account remains a part of the corporation's total paid-in capital.

STOCK OPTION CONTRACTS

Stock option contracts with officers and key employees represent an important element of executive compensation in many corporations. A **stock option contract** gives officers and key employees the right to purchase the corporation's common stock at a specified price. The option price usually is 100% of the current fair (or market) value of the stock on the date the option is granted, and the term of the option often is five years. For example, assume that you, as an executive of X Corporation, receive today a five-year option to acquire 1,000 shares of the corporation's common stock at today's market price of $20 a share. If, during the next five years, the market price of the stock rises to, say, $70 a share, you can purchase $70,000 worth of common stock for $20,000. The option is in essence a **call** on the common stock at a fixed price over a period of years with no risk to the owner of the option. The opportunity for gain is unlimited; the chance of loss is zero. In the event of a stock split or stock dividend, the option price is reduced, and the number of shares of common stock under option is increased proportionately to avoid dilution of the options. By means of stock option contracts, corporate employees are rewarded by increases in the price of the corporation's common stock.

In recent years, a modification of stock option contracts known as stock appreciation rights has become popular. **Stock appreciation rights** are awards entitling employees to receive cash, stock, or a combination of cash and stock in an amount equivalent to any excess of the market value of a stated number of shares of the employer company's common stock over a stated price.[3] Although stock appreciation rights may be granted separately, they typically are granted in conjunction with stock option contracts.

Income tax treatment of stock option contracts

The Internal Revenue Code has long provided capital gains treatment for gains on stock option contracts meeting specified conditions. Originally, such contracts were termed **restricted stock options.** From 1964 to 1981, **qualified stock options,** which had to meet more stringent requirements than those of restricted stock options, were accorded capital gains privileges. The final date for exercising qualified stock options was May 21, 1981; thus, they no longer are permitted. Restricted stock options and qualified stock options typically were granted by a corporation to its officers and key employees.

Employee Stock Purchase Plans Presently, the Internal Revenue Code provides special income tax treatment for stock option contracts granted under an employee stock purchase plan. An **employee stock purchase plan** must meet the following criteria:

1 The plan must be approved by the corporation's shareholders.
2 All employees must be covered by the plan, except the following: employees owning more than 5% of the corporation's voting common stock, officers, supervisors, employees with less than two years service, high-salaried employees, and part-time employees.
3 No employee may purchase more than $25,000 of capital stock of the corporation in any year.
4 The recipient of the option must be employed by the corporation from the date the option is granted **(grant date)** until at least three months before the option is exercised **(exercise date)**.
5 The option price must not be less than the smaller of 85% of the current fair value of the corporation's capital stock on either (1) the grant date, or (2) the exercise date.
6 Options meeting the price criteria in **5** above must be exercised within five years of the grant date; all other options must be exercised within 27 months of the grant date.

[3] *FASB Interpretation No. 28,* ''Accounting for Stock Appreciation Rights and Other Variable Stock Option or Award Plans,'' FASB (Stamford: 1978), p. 7.

An employee who realizes a gain on the disposal of capital stock acquired under an employee stock purchase plan more than two years after the grant date and more than nine months after the exercise date is taxed on the gain as follows: (1) At ordinary income rates on the excess of the current fair value of the capital stock on the grant date over the option price of the stock, and (2) at long-term capital gain rates on the excess of the disposal price of the stock over its current fair value on the grant date.

An excess of the option price over the disposal price of the capital stock is treated as a long-term capital loss. If capital stock acquired under option is sold prior to the two-year or nine-month holding period limitations, the employee is taxed at ordinary income rates on the difference between the current fair value of the stock on the exercise date and the option price.

Nonqualified Stock Options Stock option contracts that do not meet the requirements for employee stock purchase plans generally are termed *nonqualified stock options.* Among the income tax consequences resulting from a nonqualified stock option contract are the following:

1 The value of an option is treated as ordinary income to employees when it is granted if it has a readily ascertainable market value at the time of grant. If the option has no readily ascertainable market value on the date of grant, the difference between the option price and the market value of the stock acquired is taxed as ordinary income when employees exercise the option.

2 Options can be set at any price, can be effective for ten years, and there is no limit on the length of time over which the options can be granted to employees.

3 The amount of compensation taxable to employees generally is allowed as a tax-deductible expense to the corporation granting the options.

Theoretical issues

From a theoretical viewpoint, the valuation of stock options is a difficult and challenging problem. In current practice, however, the problem of valuation of stock options generally is ignored, and the accounting procedures for the options are designed to comply with income tax rules. Present income tax rules state that the receipt of stock options under an employee stock purchase plan does not constitute income to the recipient, and that no compensation expense can be deducted by the corporation when the option price is equal to or above the market price of the common stock. Thus, the difficult problem of determining the current fair value of stock options generally is avoided *by assuming that the options have no value.*

Although this treatment of stock options may be convenient for administration of the income tax laws, the current practice clearly has little theoretical support. Because stock options generally represent an important part of the total compensation cost of a corporation, it has been suggested that the options be valued at the amount for which options could be sold to the public at the time similar options are granted to employees. However, the accounting profession has not found this line of reasoning persuasive because stock options are designed to give employees additional compensation and are not available for public sale.

In the opinion of the authors, the current practice of not recording compensation expense for many stock option plans results in an understatement of compensation expense and paid-in capital, and a corresponding overstatement of retained earnings. The basic accounting principle of matching costs with related revenue suggests that the compensation expense implicit in stock option contracts should be accrued throughout the term of the option. Such accruals would require the use of estimates (perhaps based on market prices of common stock from year to year). Thus, the two major accounting problems relating to stock option contracts may be identified as (1) the measurement of any compensation cost implicit in the stock option contract, and (2) the allocation of such compensation cost among accounting periods. The current generally accepted accounting principles addressing these two problems are found in **APB Opinion No. 25.**[4]

APB Opinion No. 25, "Accounting for Stock Issued to Employees"

APB Opinion No. 25 provided a historical summary of the problems encountered in accounting for stock options and set forth the current accounting and disclosure requirements for stock option plans. Generally, such accounting and disclosure requirements depend essentially on whether the stock option contracts are viewed as noncompensatory or compensatory.

Noncompensatory Plan A stock option plan that is designed to raise capital or induce widespread ownership of the corporation's capital stock among officers and employees is classified for financial accounting purposes as a **noncompensatory plan.** Essential characteristics of a noncompensatory plan are (1) participation of all full-time employees; (2) offering of capital stock on an equal basis or as a uniform percentage of salary to all employees; (3) a limited time for exercise of the option; and (4) a discount from market price no greater than would be reasonable in an offering to capital stock to existing stockholders. In such noncompensatory plans, no compensation is presumed to be involved. Consequently, the corporation records no compensation expense in its accounting records and claims no deduction for income tax purposes.

The exercise of noncompensatory stock options is recorded as an issuance of capital stock, as illustrated on top of page 702.

---

[4] *APB Opinion No. 25,* "Accounting for Stock Issued to Employees," AICPA (New York: 1972).

Journal entry for exercise of noncompensatory stock options

Cash	40,000	
Common Stock, $5 par		5,000
Paid-in Capital in Excess of Par: Common Stock		35,000

To record issuance of 1,000 shares of common stock at $40 a share pursuant to exercise of noncompensatory stock options by employees.

The noncompensatory type of stock option plan apparently was summarized in **APB Opinion No. 25** principally to clear the way for consideration of the more controversial issues of accounting for compensatory stock option plans.

Compensatory Plan Any stock option plan not possessing the four specified characteristics of a noncompensatory plan is classified as a **compensatory plan.** The features of a compensatory plan may vary in an almost endless number of respects. For example, the **grantee** (employee granted the option) may be obligated to continue in the employment of the corporation or of its subsidiaries. The number of shares specified in the stock option plan may be acquired at one time or only in a limited number during each year of the plan's term. The consideration received by a corporation for capital stock issued under a compensatory stock option plan may include cash, notes receivable, or other assets, as well as services from the employee. In all compensatory plans, services from the grantee represent part of the consideration for the capital stock issued.

A key provision of **APB Opinion No. 25** is that compensation for services received as consideration for the stock options granted must be measured by the **quoted market price of the stock at the measurement date less the amount, if any, that the employee is required to pay.** In the application of this policy, determination of the measurement date for determining compensation cost touches the theoretical core of the problem. The **measurement date** is stated to be the first date on which are known both the number of shares of capital stock to be received by each individual grantee and the option price. On the measurement date the corporation and the employees presumably reach agreement as to the amount of total compensation to be paid, and the corporation forgoes any alternative uses of the capital stock reserved for the exercise of the options. In most stock option plans, the measurement date is the date that the options are granted.

APB Opinion No. 25 then concludes that a corporation should recognize compensation cost under compensatory stock option plans when the option price is less than the market price of the stock on the measurement date. Because the option price in many stock option plans is set at or above the market price of the capital stock on the date of grant, no compensation cost is recorded for most such plans. When compensation cost is recorded, it should be allocated to the accounting periods that are deemed to have received benefit from the services provided by the grantees. The following guidelines for accruing compensation cost under compensatory stock option plans are presented in *APB Opinion No. 25:*[5]

> Compensation cost in stock option, purchase, and award plans should be recognized as an expense of one or more periods in which an employee performs services and also as part or all of the consideration received for stock issued to the employee through a plan. The grant or award may specify the period or periods during which the employee performs services, or the period or periods may be inferred from the terms or from the past pattern of grants or awards. . . .
>
> An employee may perform services in several periods before an employer corporation issues stock . . . for those services. The employer corporation should accrue compensation expense in each period in which the services are performed. If the measurement date is later than the date of grant or award, an employer corporation should record the compensation expense each period from date of grant or award to date of measurement based on the quoted market price of the stock at the end of each period.
>
> If stock is issued in a plan before some or all of the services are performed, part of the consideration recorded for the stock issued is unearned compensation and should be shown as a separate reduction of stockholder's equity. The unearned compensation should be accounted for as expense of the period or periods in which the employee performs service.
>
> Accruing compensation expense may require estimates, and adjustment of those estimates in later periods may be necessary. . . . For example, if a stock option is not exercised (or awarded stock is returned to the corporation) because an employee fails to fulfill an obligation, the estimate of compensation expense recorded in previous periods should be adjusted by decreasing compensation expense in the period of forfeiture.

The reporting of unearned (deferred) compensation cost as a reduction of stockholders' equity may be justified on grounds that the full recorded consideration relating to issuance of capital stock has not been received. When the services are performed, the debit balance in the Deferred Compensation Cost Account is transferred to compensation expense.

Illustration of Compensatory Stock Option Plan: Measurement Date Is Grant Date To illustrate the accounting for a compensatory stock option plan when the measurement date is the grant date, assume the following facts: On January 2, Year 1, Clark Corporation granted to key employees options to purchase 10,000 shares of its $10 par common stock at $20 a share in exchange for services to be performed over the next three years. The market price of the stock on that date was $23 a share. The options were exercised on December 31, Year 3, when the market price of the stock was $31 a share. The journal entries for each year are given on page 704.

[5] Ibid., pp. 474–475.

Year 1

Jan. 2   Deferred Compensation Cost   30,000

*   Common Stock Options. 30,000*

*To record compensatory stock options on grant date
to purchase 10,000 shares of common stock at $20
a share. Market price of stock is $23 a share. De-
ferred compensation cost: 10,000 × ($23 − $20) =
$30,000.*

Dec. 31   Compensation Expense.   10,000

*   Deferred Compensation Cost 10,000*

*To record compensation expense for Year 1:
$30,000 ÷ 3 = $10,000.*

Year 2

Dec. 31   Same journal entry as on Dec. 31, Year 1.

Year 3

Dec. 31   Same journal entry as on Dec. 31, Year 1.

Dec. 31   Cash   200,000

*   Common Stock Options 30,000*

*   Common Stock, $10 par 100,000*

*   Paid-in Capital in Excess of Par: Common*

*   Stock 130,000*

*To record issuance of 10,000 shares of common
stock at $20 a share pursuant to compensatory
stock option plan.*

The common stock options and deferred compensation cost are included in the paid-in capital section of the balance sheet on December 31, Year 1, as follows:

Common stock options $30,000

Less: Deferred compensation cost 20,000 $10,000

Illustration of Compensatory Stock Option Plan: Measurement Date Is Two Years after Grant Date   To illustrate the accounting for a compensatory stock option plan when the measurement date is **subsequent** to the grant date (because the option price and the number of shares of capital stock that can be acquired have not been irrevocably determined), assume the following facts: On January 2, Year 1, Dome Corporation adopted a compensatory stock option plan for key employees to purchase an estimated 20,000 shares of $1 par common stock at a price estimated at $20 a share. Both the number of shares to be issued and the option price are to be determined on December 31, Year 2, the measurement date. The options were granted on January 2; Year 1, in consideration for services to be performed during Years 1 and 2, and can be exercised at any time starting in Year 3. The number of shares covered by the plan, the option price, and the market price of the common stock on the relevant dates are as follows:

Data regarding compensatory stock option plan

	January 2, Year 1	December 31, Year 1	December 31, Year 2
Number of shares optioned . .	20,000 *(est.)*	20,000 *(est.)*	21,000 *(final)*
Option price	$20 *(est.)*	$20 *(est.)*	$22 *(final)*
Market price of common stock	$19	$25	$33

No journal entry is required on January 2, Year 1, because the estimated option price exceeded the market price of the common stock and because the measurement date is December 31, Year 2. On December 31, Year 1, estimated compensation expense is recorded as illustrated below:

Journal entry for compensatory stock option plan prior to measurement date (which is later than grant date)

```
Year 1
Dec. 31   Compensation Expense. . . . . . . . . . . . . . . .   100,000
               Common Stock Options. . . . . . . . . . . .              100,000
          To record estimated compensation expense for
          Year 1 based on market price of common stock,
          estimated number of shares optioned, and esti-
          mated option price:   20,000 × ($25 − $20) =
          $100,000.
```

On the measurement date, December 31, Year 2, the journal entry on top of page 706 is required. At the time the options are exercised, a journal entry similar to the last entry illustrated on page 704 is required.

When compensation expense is reported by the corporation in an accounting period other than that in which the expense is deductible for income tax purposes, a **timing difference** results that requires the application of interperiod income tax allocation procedures. This topic is covered in Chapter 21.

Journal entry for compensatory stock option plan on measurement date (which is later than grant date)

Year 2

Dec. 31 Compensation Expense.   131,000
              Common Stock Options.   131,000
         To record compensation expense for Year 2 on the
         measurement date, determined as follows:
             Total compensation cost: 21,000 ×
                 ($33 − $22) $231,000
             Less: Estimated compensation ex-
                 pense recorded in Year 1   100,000
             Compensation expense for Year 2 . . $131,000

Accounting for stock appreciation rights

Stock option plans that include stock appreciation rights typically provide that the stock options expire if the stock appreciation rights are exercised, and vice versa. The following discussion of such plans is adapted from **FASB Interpretation No. 28,** "Accounting for Stock Appreciation Rights . . ."

Compensation expense for a stock option plan that includes stock appreciation rights usually is measured under the presumption that the grantee will exercise the stock appreciation rights, which require no cash payment, rather than the stock option, which requires a cash payment. The compensation element of stock appreciation rights is measured by the excess of the market price of the capital stock under option over the option price. Changes in the market price of the capital stock during the period from the grant date to the measurement date of the stock option contract require changes in the measurement of compensation expense. (Generally, the measurement date for stock appreciation rights is the date the related stock option becomes exercisable.) The compensation expense is accrued proportionately for each accounting period during which the option grantee performs services required by the stock option contract. If no service period is specified, the vesting period is the basis for recording of compensation expense. Typically, the **vesting period** runs from the grant date to the date the stock options or stock appreciation rights become exercisable.

Compensation expense accrued in one accounting period is adjusted in subsequent periods for market price changes, but it is never reduced below zero. If the grantee elects to exercise the stock option rather than the stock appreciation rights, the compensation expense previously recorded for the stock appreciation rights becomes part of the paid-in capital for the capital stock issued.

Illustration of Accounting for Stock Appreciation Rights Under a stock option plan which had been approved by its stockholders, Winfield Corporation granted stock options with stock appreciation rights to its employees on January 2, Year 1. The options expire on December 31, Year 10, cover 10,000 shares of Winfield's $1 par common stock and are exercisable beginning January 2, Year 4. No service period was specified for the grantees. The option price was $15 a share, which was equal to the market price of Winfield's common stock on January 2, Year 1.

The market price of the common stock was $18 a share on December 31, Year 1; $21 a share on December 31, Year 2; and $20 a share on December 31, Year 3, and January 2, Year 4. On January 2, Year 4, grantees exercised stock appreciation rights for 6,000 shares of common stock covered by the stock option plan, as follows:

Grantees of options for 4,000 shares elected to receive cash.

Grantees of options for 2,000 shares elected to receive 500 shares of Winfield's common stock in lieu of cash.

The journal entries below and on page 708 are required for Winfield Corporation's stock option plan, under the assumptions that grantees will elect the stock appreciation rights alternative and that the vesting period is three years (January 2, Year 1, to January 2, Year 4):

WINFIELD CORPORATION
General Journal

Year 1

Dec. 31 Compensation Expense   10,000

           Accrued Compensation Payable   10,000

To record compensation expense under stock option plan for Year 1, determined as follows:

Total compensation cost: 10,000 × ($18 − $15)	$30,000
Portion vested on Dec. 31, Year 1	$\frac{1}{3}$
Compensation expense for Year 1	$10,000

Year 2

Dec. 31 Compensation Expense   30,000

           Accrued Compensation Payable   30,000

To record compensation expense under stock option plan for Year 2, determined as follows:

Total compensation cost: 10,000 × ($21 − $15)	$60,000
Portion vested on Dec. 31, Year 2	$\frac{2}{3}$
Accrued compensation cost on Dec. 31, Year 2	$40,000
Less: Accrued compensation cost on Dec. 31, Year 1	10,000
Compensation expense for Year 2	$30,000

Year 3

Dec. 31	Compensation Expense	10,000
	Accrued Compensation Payable	10,000

To record compensation expense under stock option
plan for Year 3, determined as follows:

Total compensation cost: 10,000 × ($20 − $15)	$50,000
Portion vested on Dec. 31, Year 3	$3/3$
Accrued compensation cost on Dec. 31, Year 3	$50,000
Less: Accrued compensation cost on Dec. 31, Year 2	40,000
Compensation expense for Year 3	$10,000

Year 4

Jan. 2	Accrued Compensation Payable ($50,000 × 0.60) . .	30,000
	Cash	20,000
	Common Stock (500 shares × $1)	500
	Paid-in Capital in Excess of Par (500 shares × $19)	9,500

To record exercise of stock appreciation rights as
follows:

Cash: 4,000 × ($20 − $15)	$20,000
Common stock: $\dfrac{2,000 \times (\$20 - \$15)}{\$20}$ . . .	500 sh

For Year 4 through Year 10, Winfield Corporation must debit or credit the Accrued Compensation Payable account for the effects of annual changes in the market price of Winfield's common stock, because the stock appreciation rights were fully vested on January 2, Year 4. The offsetting credit or debits is to the Compensation Expense Account. However, total compensation expense is not reduced below zero. Accrued compensation applicable to any options that expire on December 31, Year 10, would be written off by an offsetting credit to the Compensation Expense account.

Accounting for employee stock ownership plans (ESOP)

Closely related to stock option plans described in the preceding pages are employee stock ownership plans (ESOP). Such plans may be established under the provisions of the Employee Retirement Income Security Act (ERISA) of 1974. An employee stock ownership plan is a **qualified** stock bonus plan designed to invest primarily in the capital stock of the corporation sponsoring such a plan for its employees.[6] An ESOP acquires capital stock of the employer corporation either directly from the employer (as periodic contributions) or by using borrowed funds. The debt of an ESOP usually is collateralized by a pledge of the capital stock owned by the plan and by either a guarantee of the employer corporation or a commitment by the employer to make periodic contributions to the fund. The periodic contributions are treated as deductible expenses in the computation of the employer's taxable income.

In the accounting records of the employer corporation, the periodic contributions to ESOP are recorded as compensation expense, and any debt of the plan guaranteed by the employer corporation is reported as a liability in the balance sheet of the employer. However, assets held by the ESOP are not included in the balance sheet of the employer because such assets are owned by employees, not by the employer. When the liability for the guarantee of the debt of the plan is recorded by the employer, the offsetting debit is recorded in an unearned (deferred) compensation cost account. This account is reported as a deduction from stockholders' equity (similar to the treatment of deferred compensation cost recognized under stock option plans). When the ESOP reduces the debt guaranteed by the employer (presumably from contributions from the employer), both the liability and the deferred compensation cost are reduced. The AICPA summarized these accounting requirements as follows:[7]

> . . . the offsetting debit to the liability recorded by the employer should be accounted for as a reduction of shareholders' equity. Therefore, when new shares are issued to the ESOP by the employer, an increase in shareholders' equity should be reported only as the debt that financed that increase is reduced. . . . When outstanding shares, as opposed to unissued shares, are acquired by the ESOP, shareholders' equity should similarly be reduced by the offsetting debit until the debt is repaid. . . . The liability is initially recorded because the guarantee or commitment is in substance the employer's debt. Therefore, it should not be reduced until payments are actually made. Similarly, the amount reported as a reduction of shareholders' equity should be reduced only when the ESOP makes payment on the debt. These two accounts should move symmetrically.

The amount debited to expense by the employer corporation is the amount (cash or current fair value of capital stock) contributed to the stock ownership plan. In the computation of earnings per share, the employer corporation treats all shares of its capital stock held by the ESOP as issued and outstanding.[8]

---

[6] *Employee Retirement Income Security Act of 1974,* Title II, Subtitle B, Sec. 2003.
[7] *Statement of Position No. 76-3,* "Accounting Practices for Certain Employee Stock Ownership Plans," AICPA (New York: 1976), pp. 3–4.
[8] Ibid., p. 5.

Disclosure requirements for stock option plans

Although differences of opinion exist as to the best method of measuring the amount of compensation expense implicit in stock option plans, there is general agreement as to the necessity of disclosing the significant information contained in such plans. In each set of annual financial statements, information should be given in notes to the statements as to the number of shares under option at a given option price and the time periods within which these options may be exercised. Often this disclosure will show that the corporation has stock options outstanding granted at various dates and at varying prices. The number of shares of common stock reserved for the exercise of stock options also is disclosed. (See **Note 19** on page 164.)

In past years, the notes describing stock option plans have been elaborate and detailed, primarily because the SEC required such detail in financial statements filed with the Commission. However, recently the SEC repealed its disclosure requirements for stock option plans.[9]

CONVERTIBLE SECURITIES

Characteristics of convertible preferred stock

Many preferred stocks are convertible to common stock at the option of the preferred stockholders. The appeal of convertible preferred stock lies in the fact that it combines certain attributes of both common stock and preferred stock in a single security. Because convertible preferred stock can be exchanged for common stock in a fixed ratio (the **conversion ratio**), it has the same appreciation potential as the related common stock. The status of convertible preferred stock as a **senior security** with a stated annual dividend rate gives it the same reduced risk inherent in nonconvertible preferred stock.

The conversion ratio is set when the convertible preferred stock is issued, but the ratio is subject to adjustment in the event a stock split or a stock dividend is distributed on the common stock. For example, each share of American Home Products Corporation's $2 cumulative convertible preferred stock was convertible to $1\frac{1}{2}$ shares of its common stock. When the common stock was split 3 for 1, the conversion ratio increased to $4\frac{1}{2}$ shares of common stock for each share of the convertible preferred stock.

Conversion of preferred stock to common stock

When preferred stock conversions are recorded, any paid-in capital in excess of par applicable to the preferred stock is eliminated by transfer to the paid-in capital accounts representing the common stock being

[9] *ASR No. 280,* SEC (Washington: 1980).

issued. Assume, for example, a $100 par preferred stock convertible at the option of the preferred stockholders to four shares of $10 par common stock. All the preferred stock had been issued at a price of $105 a share, and the account balances relating to the preferred stock were as follows:

Account balances related to convertible preferred stock

Preferred stock	$1,000,000
Paid-in capital in excess of par: preferred stock	50,000

If 100 shares of preferred stock are presented for conversion, the journal entry is as follows:

Journal entry to record conversion of preferred stock

Preferred Stock.	10,000	
Paid-in Capital in Excess of Par: Preferred Stock	500	
Common Stock		4,000
Paid-in Capital in Excess of Par: Common Stock.		6,500
To record issuance of 400 shares of $10 par common stock in exchange for 100 shares of $100 par convertible preferred stock.		

In the rare situation in which the par or stated value of the common stock in a conversion transaction exceeds the par or stated value of the preferred stock being converted, a debit to retained earnings would be necessary. Note, however, that retained earnings cannot be increased by a conversion of preferred stock to common stock.

Investors who purchase convertible preferred stock are influenced by the possibility that conversion would be advantageous on some future date. The paid-in capital received by the issuing corporation for convertible preferred stock, therefore, may be regarded as the appropriate amount of paid-in capital applicable to the common stock that investors receive on exercise of their conversion option.

Conversion of bonds to common stock

Bond contracts that allow investors to exchange their bonds for common stock are known as **convertible bonds,** and this feature is called a **conversion option.** Inclusion of the conversion option makes bonds more attractive to investors and may enable the issuing corporation to obtain funds at an interest rate well below that which would otherwise have to be paid on long-term borrowings. The conversion option also may have the effect of providing for a gradual retirement of debt as the bondholders elect to exchange their bonds for common stock. Thus, by issuing convertible bonds, the corporation in effect issues common stock at a price substantially above the market price prevailing at the time the bonds are issued.

Investors favor the conversion option because they stand to gain if the corporation is successful; at the same time they limit their risk by retaining preferential status as creditors if the corporation is unsuccessful.

If a convertible bond (or convertible preferred stock) is called by the issuing corporation before the scheduled maturity date, the bondholders are given a limited period, such as 30 or 60 days, in which to exchange their convertible bonds for common stock at the predetermined conversion ratio. Consequently, the investor who holds a convertible bond (or preferred stock) with a market price larger than its face amount need not fear a loss caused by the issuing corporation deciding to call the convertible security at or near its face amount (or par value). When a corporation calls a convertible security which has a market price larger than par, the effect is to force investors to convert to common stock. Convertible securities seldom are called until they are selling well above the call price.

The issuing corporation sometimes arranges a sliding scale of conversion prices so that the bondholder is encouraged to convert before a date when the conversion ratio is reduced. For example, a 10-year bond may be convertible during the first five years at the rate of 20 shares of common stock for each $1,000 bond, and during the last five years at a ratio of 18 shares of stock for each $1,000 bond.

In the *indenture* (contract) for convertible bonds, it is standard practice to include a guarantee against dilution through common stock splits or stock dividends. Any increase in the number of common stock shares from splits or stock dividends causes a corresponding adjustment in the conversion ratio.

When bonds are converted, the retirement of the debt and the issuance of additional stock must be recorded. To illustrate, assume that Skagg Corporation has outstanding $10,000,000 of 12% convertible bonds, carried in its accounting records at $10,400,000, the $400,000 representing unamortized bond premium. The bonds are convertible to $25 par common stock with a market price of $125 a share, at a conversion ratio of 10 shares of common stock for each $1,000 bond. Assume that the corporation calls the bonds and that all bondholders present their bonds for conversion.

The corporation has exchanged common stock with a total market value of $12,500,000 (10,000 × 10 × $125 = $12,500,000) for bonded debt with a carrying amount of $10,400,000. However, the market value of the common stock and of the bonds is ignored. The conversion is recorded by assigning the carrying amount of the bonds to paid-in capital, as shown by the journal entry on top of page 713.

Journal entry to record conversion of bonds

12% Convertible Bonds Payable. 10,000,000	
Premium on Bonds Payable 400,000	
Common Stock, $25 par.	2,500,000
Paid-in Capital in Excess of Par: Common Stock	7,900,000
To record conversion of bonds to 100,000 shares of common stock.	

On the original issuance date of the convertible bonds, the price received reflected the prospect that the bonds might be exchanged for common stock at some later time. Thus, the original proceeds represented the market value of the bonds **and** the conversion option. When conversion takes place, *the carrying amount of the bonds measures the increase in paid-in capital from the issuance of additional common stock.*

The issuance of convertible bonds raises a question as to whether the amount received by the issuing corporation should be recorded entirely as debt or whether it should be divided between debt and an element of stockholders' equity representing the portion of the proceeds attributable to the conversion option of the bonds. Accounting Principles Board **Opinions Nos. 10** and **14** cover this issue. The rationale underlying these Opinions is discussed and evaluated in the sections on convertible bonds in Chapter 15.

Presentation of stockholders' equity in the balance sheet

An acceptable balance sheet presentation of stockholders' equity is shown on page 714 for Laborador Company. Note that this illustration discloses the following information:

1 The par value or stated value of each class of capital stock
2 Dividend preference, conversion privilege, and call price of the cumulative preferred stock
3 Number of shares authorized, issued, and outstanding for each class of capital stock
4 Number of shares of common stock reserved for possible issuance on conversion of preferred stock and exercise of stock options
5 Paid-in capital in excess of par applicable to each class of capital stock
6 Total amount of paid-in capital and the total amount of stockholders' equity

In balance sheets of large corporations, the need for concise presentation may require some of the information concerning paid-in capital to be disclosed in the notes to the financial statements rather than in the body of the balance sheet. For example, the information concerning stock options, conversion ratios, and sources of additional paid-in capital, may be disclosed in the notes.

LABORADOR COMPANY
Partial Balance Sheet
December 31, 19—

Stockholders' equity:

$4 convertible and cumulative preferred stock, $100 par, callable at
   $106 a share; authorized, issued, and outstanding 100,000 shares $10,000,000
Common stock, $2.50 par, authorized 2,000,000 shares; issued and
   outstanding 1,000,000 shares (**Notes 1** and **2**)   2,500,000
Paid-in capital in excess of par:
   On preferred stock.   400,000
   On common stock   5,000,000
      Total paid-in capital. $17,900,000
Retained earnings   4,100,000
     Total stockholders' equity $22,000,000

Note 1. On December 31, 19__, 500,000 shares of common stock were reserved for conversion of the $4 convertible preferred stock on the basis of five shares of common stock for each share of preferred stock.
Note 2. Stock options. (See page 710 for a discussion of disclosure of stock options.)

Pro forma financial statements

When significant new financial changes are in prospect, accountants may be asked to prepare financial statements that give effect to the planned transactions. Such statements are called **pro forma financial statements.** For example, when two or more corporations are planning a business combination, the stockholders and management of each corporation will want pro forma financial statements for the combined enterprise to facilitate study of the relative position of each corporation in the combined enterprise.

Another use for pro forma financial statements arises after a business combination of two companies occurs **during** the current fiscal year. A pro forma income statement for a full year may be prepared to show the operating results which **would have** resulted for the entire year **if** the combination had taken place at the beginning of the current fiscal year. Such a pro forma income statement is given on page 715.

Pro forma financial statements also are useful in situations other than business combinations. For example, a corporation might be considering the issuance of preferred stock to obtain funds with which to call bonds outstanding. In weighing the merits of this action, management will need a pro forma balance sheet to show the financial position of the corporation as it will appear if these transactions are carried out. Because the substitution of preferred stock for bonds will eliminate interest expense and have a bearing on taxable income, it also is desirable to prepare a pro forma income statement showing how the operating results of the past year would have been modified if the changes in the capital structure had been in effect.

KING WONG CORPORATION
Unaudited Combined Pro Forma Income Statement

The following pro forma income statement for the twelve-month period ended August 31, Year 2, which has not been examined by certified public accountants, includes the operations of King Corporation, combined with Wong Company, acquired July 1, Year 2, as if Wong Company had been acquired at the beginning of the fiscal year ended August 31, Year 2:

Combined historical:

Sales (net)	$50,501,830
Cost of goods sold	47,712,775
Gross profit on sales	$ 2,789,055
Selling and administrative expenses	1,216,841
Operating income	$ 1,572,214
Other revenue (expense):	
Interest expense	$ (207,032)
Miscellaneous revenue (net)	48,937
Excess of other expense over other revenue	$ (158,095)
Income before income taxes	$ 1,414,119
Income taxes expense	729,162
Combined **historical** net income	$ 684,957
Less: Pro forma adjustment for annualized interest expense (net of income taxes) for debt incurred in connection with acquisition of Wong Company	11,750
Combined **pro forma** net income	$ 673,207
Combined **pro forma** earnings per share of common stock (based on 600,000 shares outstanding)	$ 1.12

Pro forma financial statements may be prepared on a working paper which includes existing account balances as a starting point and adjustments to reflect the planned transactions. The headings of pro forma financial statements summarizing planned transactions should indicate clearly their hypothetical nature, and the character or purpose of the planned transactions to which the statements give effect. The balance sheet heading in the illustration below meets this requirement:

PANORAMA CORPORATION
Pro Forma Balance Sheet on September 30, Year 4
(Giving Effect to Proposed Issuance of
150,000 Shares of Common Stock in
Exchange for Net Assets of Virdon Company)

REVIEW QUESTIONS

1 Foley Corporation issued warrants for rights to the holders of its 600,000 shares of common stock on November 30, 1984, entitling them to acquire one convertible $1,000 bond at face amount for each 100 shares of common stock owned. The rights expired on January 28, 1985. On December 31, 1984, bonds in the face amount of $2,500,000 had been issued through the exercise of rights. What disclosure should be made of these events in the balance sheet on December 31, 1984?

2 Is the **preemptive right** which is inherent in common stock ownership logically applicable only to additional issuance of common stock, or should it also apply to additional issuances of convertible bonds and convertible preferred stocks? Explain.

3 How should outstanding common stock warrants be presented in the balance sheet of a corporation?

4 If common stock warrants are assigned a value at the time of issuance, what action is necessary if the warrants are not exercised and expire?

5 What are the two major accounting problems relating to stock option plans?

6 Como Corporation issued five-year stock options to its key executives on May 21, Year 6, at 100% of the market price of the common stock on that date. State arguments for and against recording compensation expense corresponding to the estimated current fair value of these options.

7 In discussing the establishment of a nonqualified stock option plan for Romaine Corporation, one director advocated a five-year plan with the grantees permitted to exercise only 20% of the option in any one year. What advantage and/or disadvantage can you see in such a provision?

8 What are the major differences between a **compensatory** stock option plan and a **noncompensatory** plan? Does the corporation record compensation expense applicable to either?

9 What date does **APB Opinion No. 25,** "Accounting for Stock Issued to Employees," stipulate for use in the measurement of compensation for services relating to stock option plans? How is the amount of compensation cost measured, and how does this apply to nonqualified stock option plans?

10 What are **stock appreciation rights?** How are they related to stock option plans?

11 List three criteria which must be met in order for an employee stock purchase plan to be subject to special income tax treatment.

12 What is the **vesting period** for stock appreciation rights?

13 Define an **employee stock ownership plan** (ESOP) and briefly describe the significant accounting requirements for the employer corporation relating to such a plan.

14 How are owners of convertible preferred stocks or convertible bonds protected from the dilutive effects of stock dividends and stock splits on the corporation's common stock?

15 What recognition is given to the current fair value of common stock issued in exchange for convertible bonds? Explain.

16 Define *pro forma financial statements* and give some examples of circumstances in which they may be prepared.

EXERCISES

Ex. 17-1 On July 1, Year 7, Wilder Corporation issued for $525,000 a total of 5,000 shares of $100 par, 10% noncumulative preferred stock, together with one detachable warrant for each share of preferred stock issued. Each warrant contains a right to purchase one share of Wilder's $10 par common stock for $15 a share. The market price of the rights on July 1, Year 7, was $2.25 a right. On October 31, Year 7, when the market price of the common stock was $19 a share and the market price of the rights was $3.00 a right, 4,000 rights were exercised.

Prepare a journal entry to record the exercise of the rights and the issuance of the common stock.

Ex. 17-2 In Year 3, Tober Corporation issued for $105 a share, 8,000 shares of $100 par 12% convertible preferred stock. One share of preferred stock can be exchanged for three shares of Tober's $25 par common stock at the option of the preferred shareholder. In August, Year 4, all the preferred stock was converted to common stock. The market price of the common stock on the date of the conversion was $30 a share.

Compute the total amount which should be credited to paid-in capital in excess of par for common stock as a result of the issuance of the preferred stock and its subsequent conversion to common stock.

Ex. 17-3 On July 18, Year 4, Davis Corporation granted stock options to certain of its key employees as additional compensation. The options permitted the purchase of 10,000 shares of Davis common stock at $30 a share. On the grant date, the market price of the common stock was $38 a share. The options were exercisable beginning January 2, Year 5, and expire on December 31, Year 6. On February 3, Year 5, when the common stock was trading at $45 a share, all the options were exercised.

Compute the amount of compensation that Davis should record for the issuance of the stock options.

Ex. 17-4 Hirai Corporation issued for $8,175,000, 150,000 shares of $50 par preferred stock, together with separate stock warrants entitling the holders to purchase one share of common stock for each share of preferred stock on presentation of a warrant and $25 cash. At the time of issuance, the common stock was selling on the stock exchange at $23 a share. The warrants began trading on the stock exchange at a price of $3.50 each, and the preferred stock began trading at $51 a share. The warrants expire in five years.

Prepare a journal entry to record the issuance of the preferred stock with warrants attached.

Ex. 17-5 Hastings Corporation had two issues of securities outstanding: common stock and a 9% convertible bond issue with a face amount of $10,000,000. Interest payment dates of the bond issue are June 30 and December 31. The conversion option in the bond indenture entitles the bondholders to receive 40 shares of $20 par common stock in exchange for each $1,000 bond. On June 30, Year 9, the holders of $900,000 face amount of bonds exercised the conversion option. The market price of the bonds on that date was $1,100 a bond, and the market price of the common stock was $35 a share. The total unamortized bond discount on the date of conversion was $500,000.

Compute the amount which Hastings should credit to the Paid-in Capital in Excess of Par account as a result of the conversion.

Ex. 17-6 Bart Corporation has outstanding three issues of securities: convertible bonds, convertible preferred stock, and common stock. All three securities are actively traded on the New York Stock Exchange. Assume that you bought 100 shares of the 8%, $100 par convertible preferred stock at $103 a share when it was originally issued by the corporation. The preferred stock is convertible to four shares of $10 par common stock at any time. When you made your investment in the convertible preferred stock, the common stock had a market price of $22 a share. Now, several years later, the common stock has a market price of $90 a share, and you decide to convert your preferred stock to common stock.

Prepare a journal entry for Bart Corporation to record the conversion.

Ex. 17-7 The $10 par common stock of Obler Corporation is listed on a major stock exchange and presently is quoted at $30 a share. The corporation has 10 million authorized shares of common stock, of which 4 million are issued and outstanding. Because of a need for additional capital, the corporation issued to its common stockholders stock rights permitting the purchase of one new share of common stock in exchange for five rights and $28 cash. The rights expire 21 days after the date of issuance.

a Prepare the journal entry, if any, to record the issuance of the stock rights.

b Assuming that all the stock rights were exercised, prepare the journal entry to record the exercise of the stock rights.

c Assuming that only 90% of the stock rights were exercised before the expiration date, prepare the required journal entry or entries.

Ex. 17-8 Cobo Corporation established an employee stock ownership plan (ESOP) in Year 1. Selected transactions relating to the plan during Year 1 were as follows:

(1) Cobo contributed $20,000 cash and 2,000 shares of the corporation's $5 par common stock to the plan. The market price of the common stock at this time was $22 a share.

(2) The plan borrowed $500,000 from East River National Bank and purchased an additional 20,000 shares of Cobo's common stock at $23 a share. One-half of these shares were purchased in the open market and the other half directly from the corporation. Cobo guaranteed the loan from the bank.

(3) The plan repaid $25,000 of the loan from East River National Bank and also paid $10,000 interest accrued on the loan.

Prepare any journal entries required in the accounting records of Cobo Corporation as a result of the transactions described above.

Ex. 17-9 On July 1, Year 7, the beginning of a fiscal year, Hooper Corporation granted stock option contracts with stock appreciation rights to officers and key managers of the corporation. The options covered 25,000 shares of Hooper's $5 par common stock, and are exercisable beginning on July 1, Year 9, if the grantees remain employed by Hooper for the entire two-year period ending on that date. The option price was $20 a share. Market prices of a share of Hooper's common stock were as follows:

July 1, Year 7	$20
June 30, Year 8	24
June 30, Year 9	32

Prepare journal entries for Hooper's stock option plan on June 30, Year 8, and on June 30, Year 9.

SHORT CASES FOR ANALYSIS AND DECISION

Case 17-1 A corporation has a noncompensatory stock purchase plan for all of its employees and a compensatory stock option plan for its officers.

Instructions
a Compare and contrast the accounting on the date the common stock is issued for the noncompensatory stock purchase plan and the compensatory stock option plan.
b What journal entry should be made for the compensatory stock option plan at the grant date?

Case 17-2 Largo Corporation uses stock options as a form of compensation for its key employees. Because the options provide a call on common stock at a fixed price over a period of years with no risk to the grantee, the opportunity for gain is unlimited, and the chance of loss is zero. Despite the obvious value of such stock options and their importance in attracting and retaining competent employees, accountants have had difficulty in deciding on the most appropriate method of determining a dollar valuation, if any, to be assigned to stock options. Among the methods which have been proposed for determining the value of stock options granted to employees are the following:

(1) The probable current fair value of the option to the grantees at the grant date
(2) The cash value of the services to be received from employees and for which they are being compensated by the stock option plan
(3) The excess of the market price of the common stock over the option price at the grant date
(4) The excess of the market price of the common stock over the option price at the date the options become exercisable; for example, after the grantees have completed the required period of employment
(5) The excess of the market price of the common stock over the option price at the exercise date

Instructions Discuss the conceptual merits of each of the five methods listed above for determining the value of stock options granted to key employees.

Case 17-3 A corporation granted 10-year stock options to five executives. The options for 50,000 shares of $5 par common stock stipulated an option price of $25 a share. The current market price of the stock on the grant date was $28. Each of the five officers who were granted 10,000-share options under the plan was given the right to exercise the options at any time within a 10-year period and could sell the stock acquired at any time. The corporation's common stock is listed on a stock exchange and is actively traded.

In a discussion of the plan after its adoption by the stockholders, one executive suggested that the difference between the market price and the option price be debited to the Retained Earnings account because the cost to the corporation was attributable in large part to the past services of the five executives. Another executive expressed the view that there was no cost to the corporation because no payment of cash or other assets would be required of the corporation.

Instructions
a In the light of *APB Opinion No. 25,* is there a cost to the corporation which should be recorded? If so, should it be recognized at the time the options are granted, when they are exercised, or at some other time?
b Prepare the journal entry, if any, which you think is required to record issuance of the stock options, and the journal entry required to record the exercise of the options for 50,000 shares of common stock. The market price at the date the options were exercised was $40. Observe the concepts set forth in *APB Opinion No. 25* in your solution.

Case 17-4 On January 2, Year 10, Riesbord Corporation adopted a stock option plan to grant selected executives options for 500,000 shares of its $1 par common stock. The options were granted on May 1, Year 10, at $25 a share, the market price of the common stock on that date. All options were exercisable one year later and for four years thereafter, providing that the grantee was employed by the corporation on the exercise date.

The market price of Riesbord's common stock was $40 a share on May 1, Year 11. All options were exercised before December 31, Year 11, at dates when the market price was between $40 and $50 a share.

Instructions It has been said that the exercise of a stock option would dilute the equity of existing stockholders.
a How could this happen? Discuss.
b What condition could prevent a dilution of existing equities from taking place with regard to Riesbord Corporation's stock option plan? Explain.

PROBLEMS

17-1   On January 2, Year 6, when its $30 par common stock was selling for $80 a share, Westphal Corporation issued $10,000,000 of 8% convertible bonds due in ten years. The conversion option allowed the holder of each $1,000 bond to convert the bond to five shares of the corporation's common stock. The bonds were issued for $11,000,000. The present value of the bond payments at the time of issuance was $8,500,000, and the corporation believed the difference between the present value and the cash received was attributable to the conversion option.

On January 2, Year 7, the corporation's common stock was split 3 for 1. On January 2, Year 8, when the corporation's common stock was selling for $90 a share, holders of 40% of the convertible bonds exercised their conversion option. The corporation uses the straight-line method of amortization for bond discount or premium.

Instructions
a Prepare a journal entry to record the original issuance of the convertible bonds.
b Prepare a journal entry to record the conversion of the bonds to common stock. Show supporting computations.

17-2   On August 31, Year 10, the stockholders' equity section of Crosby Corporation appeared as follows:

CROSBY CORPORATION
Partial Balance Sheet
August 31, Year 10

Stockholders' equity:

Common stock, $2.50 par; authorized 5,000,000 shares, issued and	
outstanding 3,000,000 shares	*$ 7,500,000*
Paid-in capital in excess of par: common stock	*38,400,000*
Retained earnings	*16,600,000*
Total stockholders' equity	*$62,500,000*

On August 31, Year 10, Crosby completed arrangements for a public offering of 200,000 shares of $3 preferred stock with a par of $50 a share. Accompanying each preferred share was a detachable stock warrant entitling the holder to purchase one share of common stock at $40 a share at any time within the next 10 years. The common stock traded on the stock exchange at a price of $36 a share. As soon as the terms of the preferred stock and rights offering were announced, the warrants began trading separately on the stock exchange at a price of $3.50 each on a "when-issued" basis.

The entire issue of 200,000 shares of preferred stock with warrants attached was issued on September 1 at a price of $55 a share. During the next few months the price of the common stock increased rapidly, and on December 1 it traded at $66 a share. On that date, 40,000 warrants were exercised, and Crosby Corporation issued 40,000 shares of common stock.

Instructions
a Prepare journal entries to record the issuance of the preferred stock and detachable stock warrants on September 1, and the issuance of common stock on December 1. (Journal entries are not required for dividend actions.)
b Prepare the stockholders' equity section of the balance sheet on December 31, Year 10, assuming that net income since August 31 was $3,500,000 and that on December 1 a quarterly dividend of 75 cents a share was declared on the preferred stock, payable January 15 to stockholders of record on December 15. Dividends of $120,400 were declared on the common stock during Year 10.
c Prepare any appropriate note or notes to the financial statements based on the information provided.

17-3 The fiscal year for Cardinale, Inc., ends on December 31. On March 1, Year 10, the corporation established a compensatory stock option plan for its key executives who have been employed a minimum of five years. The number of shares of common stock initially included in the plan was approximately 100,000, at an estimated option price of $40 a share. The final determination of the number of shares to be offered and the option price were to be made on December 31, Year 11, based on a predetermined formula. The formula was designed to adjust the number of shares to be optioned and the final option price by taking into account the earnings of the corporation and the market price of the common stock during Years 10 and 11.

Options were granted for services to be performed through the end of Year 11, and were exercisable at any time after January 2, Year 12. The estimated number of shares of common stock to be included in the stock option plan, the estimated option price, and the market price of the common stock on March 1, Year 10, and on December 31, Year 10, were as follows:

	Mar. 1, Year 10	Dec. 31, Year 10
Estimated number of shares of common stock to be included in stock option plan.	100,000	100,000
Estimated option price	$40	$40
Market price of common stock	$38	$45

The final contractual provisions of the stock option plan were determined on December 31, Year 11, as follows:

Number of shares of common stock included in stock option plan	95,000
Option price	$42

The market price of the common stock on December 31, Year 11, was $52 a share.

On April 20, Year 12, grantees exercised options for 30,000 shares of common stock. The corporation had 3,500,000 shares of $5 par common stock outstanding on December 31, Year 11.

Instructions
a What is the measurement date for this stock option plan?
b Compute the total compensation cost that should be recognized by Cardinale, Inc., as a result of this stock option plan. How should the compensation cost be allocated among accounting periods? Show supporting computations.
c Prepare journal entries to record all transactions relating to the stock option plan for Year 10 through Year 12.

17-4 D'Amico Corporation had the following amounts in the stockholders' equity section of its balance sheet on May 31, Year 3:

D'AMICO CORPORATION
Partial Balance Sheet
May 31, Year 3

Stockholders' equity:

Common stock, $10 par; authorized 6,000,000 shares, issued and outstanding 2,500,000 shares	$25,000,000
Paid-in capital in excess of par: common stock	12,500,000
Retained earnings	15,775,000
Total stockholders' equity	$53,275,000

The corporation's operations had been profitable, but management had decided that additional capital was needed. Therefore, authorization was obtained for the issuance of 250,000 shares of $4 preferred stock with a par of $50 a share. To help assure success of this financing, D'Amico offered with each share of preferred stock a detachable stock warrant which entitled the holder to purchase one share of common stock at $40 a share at any time within the next 10 years. The common stock was selling at a price of $35 a share. As soon as the terms of the offering were announced, the warrants began trading at a price of $6 each.

The issuance of 250,000 shares of the $4 preferred stock with warrants attached was completed on June 1 at a price of $60 a share (including the stock warrant). The price of the common stock increased during the next several months. On December 1, when the common stock was selling at $65 a share, 25,000 warrants were exercised, and D'Amico issued 25,000 shares of common stock.

Instructions
a Prepare journal entries to record the issuance of the preferred stock and the detachable common stock warrants on June 1, and the issuance of common stock on December 1 when 25,000 warrants were exercised. (Journal entries are not required for dividends on the preferred stock.)
b Prepare the stockholders' equity section of the balance sheet on December 31, Year 3, assuming that net income since May 31 was $8,400,000, and that dividend action on the preferred stock since that date has been as follows:

Sept. 1 Declared quarterly dividend of $1 a share on preferred stock.
Oct. 1 Paid quarterly dividend on preferred stock.
Dec. 1 Declared quarterly dividend of $1 a share on preferred stock, payable January 10 to stockholders of record December 15.

c Prepare any appropriate note or notes to the financial statements based on the information available in the problem.

17-5 Cantor Corporation had outstanding two issues of securities: (1) $5 par common stock, and (2) 9% convertible bonds in the face amount of $20,000,000. Interest payment dates of the bond issue are April 1 and October 1. The conversion option in the bond indenture entitles the bondholders to receive 30 shares of common stock in exchange for each $1,000 bond.

On March 15, Year 4, the annual dividend rate on the common stock was increased from $1.50 to $2 a share. On April 1, Year 4, the holders of $2 million face amount of bonds exercised the conversion option. The market price of the bonds on that date was quoted at $122 for each $100 face amount; the market price of common stock was $39. The ledger account balances pertaining to the convertible bonds and the common stock were as follows on April 1, Year 4, prior to the conversion:

9% convertible bonds payable (maturing in 10 years)	$20,000,000
Discount on 9% convertible bonds payable (amortized by straight-line method)	800,000
Common stock, $5 par; authorized 1 million shares, issued and outstanding 750,000 shares	3,750,000
Paid-in capital in excess of par	11,830,500

Instructions
a Prepare a journal entry to record the conversion of bonds on April 1, Year 4.
b Evaluate the effects of the conversion on Cantor Corporation with respect to:
(1) Income before income taxes. (Consider amortization of bond discount.)
(2) The amounts of income taxes expense and net income. (Assume an income tax rate of 48%.)
(3) The total annual amount of payments to security holders.
c What effect would the conversion have on the annual cash receipts of an investor who converted 10 bonds to common stock on April 1, Year 4?

17-6 Ward Carle, president of Olav Corporation, commented during the course of a directors' meeting that the corporation had achieved increases in both sales and net income during each of the last seven years. Also, the market price of both the common stock and the convertible preferred stock had been in a definite uptrend. Carle also stated:

"We have 50,000 shares of 12%, $100 par, convertible preferred stock outstanding, which was originally issued for $5,100,000. This stock is callable at $106 and convertible at any time to our $5 par common stock in the ratio of three shares of common for each share of preferred. We have been paying $1 a year dividend on our common stock and do not plan any increase in the near future. Although our earnings have been increasing, we need to reinvest these earnings to take advantage of opportunities for growth. Our common stock is now selling for $70 a share, so apparently our stockholders are more interested in earnings than in dividends."

After these comments, Carle invited questions or suggestions from the directors. Director Anne Asche offered the following suggestion:

"Our convertible preferred stock is too small an issue for a corporation of our size. I propose that we call it all in at once and get rid of it. If everyone is forced to convert to common stock, the additional common dividend will increase by only $150,000 a year, and we can save $600,000 a year in preferred dividends. Also, we can transfer the $100,000 of paid-in capital in excess of par on preferred stock now in our balance sheet to our retained earnings or include it as an extraordinary gain in this year's income statement. If any preferred stockholders fail to convert, we will have a larger gain on those shares equal to the excess of the present market price over the call price. And if we want convertible preferred stock in the future we will be able to issue it at less than the 12% rate we're now paying. Consequently, calling the preferred stock will give us several benefits and cost us nothing."

Instructions

a Evaluate point by point the proposal by Director Asche. For each point indicate (and explain) your agreement or disagreement.

b What is the probable market price of the convertible preferred stock? Explain.

c Prepare the journal entry (or entries) that would be necessary if Asche's plan to call the preferred stock is carried out.

17-7 Luna Corporation recently announced the issuance to preferred stockholders of warrants for two rights for each share of preferred stock outstanding, and the issuance to common stockholders of warrants for one right for each share of common stock outstanding. The preferred stock is cumulative, but is neither convertible nor participating. The announcement stated that 10 rights and $100 cash would be required to purchase $100 face amount of 9% convertible bonds, and that the rights would expire in 60 days.

Some stockholders sold their rights immediately, and trading in the rights began at $3 a right. The convertible bonds, although not yet issued, traded on a "when-issued" basis, meaning that delivery would not be required until after the scheduled issuance date. All the 2 million rights issued were exercised before the expiration date, and the convertible bonds were issued.

Instructions

a Was the distribution of warrants for rights by Luna Corporation typical of current practice? Explain.

b What was the approximate trading price of the convertible bonds on a "when-issued" basis?

c Would a common stockholder, who sold the rights instead of exercising them, own a smaller share of the net assets of the corporation than before the rights were issued? Explain.

d Prepare a journal entry to record the exercise of 2 million rights and the issuance of the convertible bonds.

17-8 On December 31, Year 5, under a stock option plan which had been approved by stockholders in November, Year 5, Morgana Corporation granted stock options for 40,000 shares of $10 par common stock at a price of $16 a share to officers and key employees. The plan included stock appreciation rights that were exercisable only if the stock options were forfeited; exercise of the stock options required forfeiture of the stock appreciation rights. The options are exercisable in full beginning on December 31, Year 9. No service period was specified for the grantees.

Market prices of Morgana's common stock were as follows:

Dec. 31, Year 5	*$16*
Dec. 31, Year 6	20
Dec. 31, Year 7	24
Dec. 31, Year 8	22
Dec. 31, Year 9	28

On December 31, Year 9, grantees exercised their stock appreciation rights and stock options as follows:

Stock appreciation rights exercised:

Grantees of options for 20,000 shares elected to receive cash.

Grantees of options for 15,000 shares elected to receive shares of Morgana's common stock, with cash in lieu of fractional shares.

Stock options exercised: 5,000 shares of Morgana's common stock

Instructions Prepare all journal entries for Morgana Corporation's stock option plan for Year 6 through Year 9. Show supporting computations in explanations for the journal entries. Round computations to nearest dollar.

18 CORPORATIONS: TREASURY STOCK AND EARNINGS PER SHARE

Additional topics dealing with stockholders' equity that were not discussed in the preceding two chapters are (1) the acquisition and retirement or reissuance by a corporation of its capital stock, (2) the preparation of statements of retained earnings and stockholders' equity, and (3) the computation of earnings per share of common stock. A corporation's acquisition of its capital stock reduces its stockholders' equity and affects the computation of earnings per share. Earnings per share is the amount of net income earned on each share of common stock and is considered by many investors as probably the most important financial measurement. These topics present some challenging problems for accountants and are discussed in this chapter.

TREASURY STOCK

Treasury stock is the capital stock of a corporation that has been issued, fully paid for, and subsequently acquired by the corporation but not retired. When a corporation acquires shares of its own capital stock, certain stockholders surrender their ownership interest in the corporation. Thus, the acquisition of treasury stock by a corporation may be viewed as a partial liquidation of the corporation, and no gain or loss results from such transactions.

Treasury stock may be acquired by corporations for a variety of reasons, including the following: (1) to buy out a particular stockholder, (2) for use in connection with stock option and purchase plans or for business combinations, (3) to settle claims against debtors who are also stockholders, (4) to increase earnings per share by reducing the number of shares of capital stock outstanding, and (5) to support the market price

725

of the capital stock.[1] There is no justification for a corporation to attempt to influence the market price of its capital stock through the acquisition and reissuance of treasury stock; such efforts necessarily create a conflict of interest between the corporation and its stockholders and may be illegal in some circumstances. The laws of some states prohibit or severely restrict a corporation's acquisition of its capital stock, as described in the following section.

Treasury stock and stated (or legal) capital

Stated (or *legal*) capital, as explained in Chapter 16, is a statutory definition of the amount of capital to be retained in the corporation for protection of creditors; it is not available for withdrawal by stockholders. Legal capital generally consists of the total par or stated value of capital stock issued. The acquisition of treasury stock is not regarded as a reduction in legal capital; however, such an acquisition involves an outflow of assets to stockholders, and therefore certain legal restrictions are necessary to protect the corporation's creditors. Generally, a corporation is not permitted to acquire treasury stock if the acquisition would cause total stockholders' equity to be reduced below legal capital. Furthermore, a portion of retained earnings is restricted and unavailable for dividends equal to the amount paid for treasury stock.

It should be emphasized that the retirement of capital stock reduces legal capital, but the acquisition of treasury stock does not. In terms of economic significance, the retirement of capital stock and the acquisition of treasury stock are similar, because both transactions consist of a return of corporate assets to stockholders and a corresponding reduction in the amount of capital invested in the corporation.

Treasury stock is not an asset

A corporation cannot own a portion of itself; for this reason, treasury stock should not be viewed as an asset. The ownership of treasury stock does not give the corporation the right to receive cash dividends, to vote, to exercise preemptive rights as a stockholder, or to receive assets when the corporation is liquidated. Corporations can, and sometimes do, formally cancel treasury stock; this action would never be taken if such cancellation actually meant the destruction of assets. If a corporation were to dissolve, any treasury stock owned by the corporation would contribute nothing in the process of converting assets to cash for distribution to shareholders.

The view that treasury stock is not an asset is strengthened by recognition that treasury stock essentially is the same as unissued capital

---

[1] In the 34th edition of *Accounting Trends & Techniques* issued by the AICPA in 1980, 417 of the 600 companies included in the survey reported treasury stock, either common or preferred, in their balance sheets.

stock, and no one advocates that unissued capital stock be classified as an asset in the balance sheet.

The policy of classifying treasury stock as an asset, if justified at all, must rest on expediency rather than on accounting principles. Treasury stock of a large publicly owned corporation sometimes is acquired for subsequent reissuance under an employee stock purchase plan.[2] The corporation may have a liability to employees participating in the stock purchase plan. To meet this liability the corporation expends cash to acquire treasury stock and soon thereafter discharges the liability by delivery of the treasury stock to employees. If shares of treasury stock are few in number as compared with outstanding shares of capital stock, they may be treated much the same as an investment in securities of any other corporation. The Accounting Principles Board has given recognition to this situation as follows:[3]

> When a corporation's stock is acquired for purposes other than retirement (formal or constructive), or when ultimate disposition has not yet been decided, the cost of acquired stock may be shown separately as a deduction from the total of capital stock, capital surplus, and retained earnings, or may be accorded the accounting treatment appropriate for retired stock, or in some circumstances may be shown as an asset. . . .

The reasons for refusing to recognize treasury stock as an asset are many and generally are recognized as valid, yet the issue is kept alive by the policy of a few corporations that persist in listing treasury stock as an asset.

Alternative accounting methods for treasury stock

The two alternative accounting methods for treasury stock are (1) the **cost method,** and (2) the **par** or **stated value method.** Although the par or stated value method still receives some theoretical support in accounting literature, large corporations have turned increasingly to the cost method in recent years.[4] Both methods are sanctioned by generally accepted accounting principles.

Under the cost method, the acquisition of treasury stock is regarded as a first step in a financial move which is completed by the reissuance of the treasury stock. Treasury stock thus is viewed as a "suspense" item of stockholders' equity, with the corporation acting as an interme-

---

[2] At the end of 1980, for example, General Motors Corporation reported as an asset approximately 2 million shares of its common stock, $126 million, as "Common Stock Held for the Incentive Program."

[3] *APB Opinion No. 6,* "Status of Accounting Research Bulletins," AICPA (New York: 1965), p. 40.

[4] In the 34th edition of *Accounting Trends & Techniques* issued by the AICPA in 1980, common stock held in treasury was carried at cost by 351 companies and at par or stated value by 39 companies; preferred stock held in treasury was carried at cost by 21 companies and at par or stated value by 5 companies.

diary between the former stockholders and new stockholders. When the cost method is used, the Treasury Stock account is debited for the cost of the capital stock acquired; this account is reported in the balance sheet as a deduction from the *total* stockholders' equity. With this arrangement of the stockholders' equity section of the balance sheet, there is no reduction in the legal or stated capital. Because the laws of most states indicate that the acquisition of treasury stock does not constitute a reduction in legal capital, this balance sheet presentation may be regarded as reflecting the prevailing legal concept of treasury stock.

Under the par or stated value method, the possibility of reissuance of the treasury stock is not given much weight. The relationship between the corporation and the former owners of shares of capital stock now held in the treasury has ended; therefore, the account showing paid-in capital in excess of par relating to the treasury stock is reduced. If the corporation decides to retire the capital stock, the Capital Stock account also is reduced; the reissuance of treasury stock is recorded as an original issuance of capital stock.

Illustration of Accounting for Treasury Stock—Cost Method To illustrate the cost method of accounting for treasury stock transactions, assume that the balance sheet for Rae Corporation includes the following stockholders' equity section:

Balance sheet stockholders' equity section for treasury stock illustration

RAE CORPORATION
Partial Balance Sheet

Stockholders' equity:
Capital stock, $100 par; authorized, issued, and outstanding 10,000 shares	$1,000,000
Paid-in capital in excess of par	200,000
Total paid-in capital	$1,200,000
Retained earnings	500,000
Total stockholders' equity	$1,700,000

At this time Rae Corporation acquired 300 shares of treasury stock at $115 a share. The acquisition of treasury stock was recorded at cost as illustrated below:

Journal entry for acquisition of treasury stock—cost method

Treasury Stock	34,500	
Cash		34,500
To record acquisition of 300 shares of treasury stock at $115 a share.		

The stockholders' equity section of the balance sheet of Rae Corporation appears as follows when treasury stock was recorded at cost:

Balance sheet stockholders' equity section showing acquisition of treasury stock—cost method

RAE CORPORATION
Partial Balance Sheet

Stockholders' equity:

Capital stock, $100 par; authorized and issued 10,000 shares, of which 300 shares are in treasury	$1,000,000
Paid-in capital in excess of par	200,000
Total paid-in capital	$1,200,000
Retained earnings (see **Note**)	500,000
Total paid-in capital and retained earnings	$1,700,000
Less: Cost of 300 shares of treasury stock	34,500
Total stockholders' equity	$1,665,500

Note: The declaration of dividends and the acquisition of treasury stock are restricted to $465,500, the amount of the retained earnings reduced by the cost of treasury stock.

The presentation of stockholders' equity when treasury stock is recorded at cost does not show the net amount of capital invested by stockholders; thus, it does not achieve one of the more important objectives in the classification of corporate capital. However, the cost approach to treasury stock does have the merit of showing as capital stock an amount equal to the legal capital of the corporation.

Let us assume that Rae Corporation **canceled** the 300 shares of treasury stock recorded at cost. This action caused a reduction in legal capital and in paid-in capital in excess of par by the amount paid for treasury stock. The journal entry to record the cancellation of the treasury stock is as follows:

Journal entry for cancellation of treasury stock—cost method

Capital Stock	30,000	
Paid-in Capital in Excess of Par	4,500	
Treasury Stock		34,500
To record cancellation of 300 shares of treasury stock carried at cost.		

The 300 shares of treasury stock were issued originally at $120 each ($1,200,000 ÷ 10,000 = $120), or for a total of $36,000. The shares were acquired at a cost of $34,500, or $1,500 **less** than the paid-in capital relating to these shares. Therefore, the cancellation of the 300 shares of treasury stock requires a reduction of only $34,500 in the paid-in capital accounts; the excess of the amount originally paid in by stockholders over the cost of the treasury stock, $1,500 ($36,000 − $34,500 = $1,500), remains in the Paid-in Capital in Excess of Par account.

If, instead of canceling the 300 shares of treasury stock as previously illustrated, Rae Corporation had reissued these shares at a price of $108 a share, or $2,100 **below cost,** the journal entry would have been as follows:

Journal entry for reissuance of treasury stock at a price below cost—cost method

Cash	32,400	
Paid-in Capital in Excess of Par	2,100	
Treasury Stock		34,500
To record reissuance of 300 shares of treasury stock at $108 a share, or $2,100 below cost.		

Under the cost method, the Treasury Stock account is credited for the cost of the shares of treasury stock which are reissued. Cost may be computed on an average basis, on a first-in, first-out basis, or by specific identification. When the reissuance price is less than cost, as in the illustration above, the excess of cost over the proceeds from reissuance is debited to Paid-in Capital in Excess of Par. This account was credited at the time the capital stock originally was issued; however, if such paid-in capital is insufficient, paid-in capital from previous treasury stock transactions or Retained Earnings is debited for the excess of the cost over the proceeds from reissuance.

When treasury stock is reissued at a price **above cost,** the excess of the proceeds over cost of the treasury stock is credited to Paid-in Capital in Excess of Par, as illustrated below:

Journal entry for reissuance of treasury stock at a price above cost—cost method

Cash	37,500	
Treasury Stock		34,500
Paid-in Capital in Excess of Par		3,000
To record reissuance of 300 shares of treasury stock at $125 a share, or $3,000 above cost.		

Illustration of Accounting for Treasury Stock—Par or Stated Value Method
To facilitate a comparison between the cost method and the par or stated value method of accounting for treasury stock, we shall use the same transactions illustrated above for Rae Corporation. Under the par value method, the journal entry to record the acquisition of treasury stock by Rae Corporation is shown on top of page 731.

In this journal entry, the reduction in the stockholders' equity amounts to $34,500, or $1,500 less than the $36,000 originally paid by stockholders. In other words, $1,500 of the capital originally invested by

<table>
<tr><td>**Journal entry for acquisition of treasury stock—par value method**</td><td></td></tr>
</table>

Journal entry for acquisition of treasury stock—par value method

Treasury Stock	30,000	
Paid-in Capital in Excess of Par	4,500	
Cash.		34,500
To record acquisition of 300 shares of treasury stock at $115 a share.		

those stockholders who have sold their stock to the corporation remains in the corporation.[5]

After the acquisition of treasury stock, the stockholders' equity section of Rae Corporation's balance sheet appears as follows:

Balance sheet stockholders' equity section showing acquisition of treasury stock—par value method

RAE CORPORATION
Partial Balance Sheet

Stockholders' equity:

Capital stock, $100 par; authorized and issued 10,000 shares	$1,000,000	
Less: Treasury stock, 300 shares at par	30,000	$ 970,000
Paid-in capital in excess of par		195,500
Total paid-in capital		$1,165,500
Retained earnings (see **Note**).		500,000
Total stockholders' equity		$1,665,500

Note: The declaration of dividends and the acquisition of treasury stock are restricted to the amount of the retained earnings reduced by the cost of treasury stock, or $465,500.

[5] If the amount paid for treasury stock is more than the amount originally invested by stockholders, the excess is recorded as a reduction of retained earnings. For example, if Rae Corporation paid $40,000 to acquire 300 shares of its capital stock originally issued for $36,000, the transaction would be recorded under the par value method as follows:

Treasury Stock	30,000	
Paid-in Capital in Excess of Par	6,000	
Retained Earnings	4,000	
Cash		40,000

If treasury stock is acquired at a price below par value, the excess of par value over cost of treasury stock is credited to Paid-in Capital in Excess of Par. For example, if Rae Corporation paid only $25,000 for the 300 shares of capital stock, the journal entry to record the acquisition would be as follows:

Treasury Stock	30,000	
Paid-in Capital in Excess of Par		5,000
Cash		25,000

This form for reporting the stockholders' equity section has the merit of showing the net amount for paid-in capital after the treasury stock acquisitions. However, it may be criticized on grounds that the net amount shown for capital stock ($970,000) may be interpreted erroneously as the legal capital; the legal capital of $1,000,000 was not reduced by the acquisition of treasury stock.

If Rae Corporation should *cancel* all 300 shares of treasury stock, the cancellation is recorded by a debit to Capital Stock and a credit to Treasury Stock for $30,000. After cancellation of the treasury stock, the stockholders' equity section would not include treasury stock and there would be no restriction on retained earnings. The cancellation, in effect, has reduced legal capital permanently to $970,000.

If Rae Corporation, instead of canceling the 300 shares of treasury stock, reissued the shares at a price *above par,* say $108 each, the journal entry is as follows:

Journal entry for reissuance of treasury stock at a price above carrying amount—par value method

Cash	32,400	
Treasury Stock		30,000
Paid-in Capital in Excess of Par		2,400
To record reissuance of 300 shares of treasury stock at $108 a share, or $2,400 above carrying amount (par).		

Note that the foregoing journal entry for reissuance of treasury stock is similar to an entry for original issuance of capital stock. The difference between the issuance price of the treasury stock and the par of the treasury stock, as recorded in the Treasury Stock account, is credited to the Paid-in Capital in Excess of Par account. Under the par value approach, the acquisition of treasury stock is viewed as a temporary retirement of the stock; thus, the reissuance of treasury stock logically should be recorded in the same manner as an original issuance of capital stock.

In the event that the treasury stock were reissued at *less than par,* it would not be appropriate to debit a Discount on Capital Stock account because no "discount liability" attaches to treasury stock reissued below par. Instead, the deficiency is recorded by a debit to Paid-in Capital in Excess of Par if such paid-in capital is available. In the absence of sufficient paid-in capital in excess of par to absorb the deficiency, it should be debited to Retained Earnings.

Points of emphasis in accounting for treasury stock

Certain key points stand out from the procedures and alternative methods used in accounting for treasury stock:

1 Treasury stock is not an asset and is not entitled to receive cash dividends, to vote, or to receive assets on liquidation of the corporation.

2 No gain or loss is recognized on treasury stock transactions, either for financial accounting or for income tax accounting.

3 Retained earnings can never be increased by treasury stock transactions; however, retained earnings may be decreased by such transactions.

4 The total stockholders' equity is the same, regardless of the method used to account for treasury stock; however, there may be variations in the relative amounts of paid-in capital and retained earnings, depending on the method used.

5 Retained earnings in an amount equal to the cost of treasury stock is unavailable for declaration of cash dividends.

Redemption of preferred stock

Most corporations that issue preferred stock include in the contract a provision that all or any part of the preferred stock may be called for redemption (retirement) at any time desired by the corporation. The call price usually is above the issuance price; it may be an unchanging amount or it may be a series of amounts on a sliding scale relating to specified time periods and eventually dropping to par. When preferred stock is called for redemption, the stock is canceled and hence is not available for reissuance. Redemption may be effected by a call of the stock pursuant to the call provision, by purchase in the open market, or by a special offer to preferred stcokholders to **tender** their stock to the corporation at a price above the current market price of the stock.

The redemption of preferred stock should not be confused with the acquisition of treasury stock, because **redemption** signifies both acquisition and cancellation (retirement) of the stock. Preferred stock also can be acquired for subsequent reissuance and held in treasury. However, acquisitions of preferred stock generally are made for the purpose of retiring the stock.

To illustrate the redemption of preferred stock, assume that Lerner Corporation had issued 10,000 shares of $100 par preferred stock at $102. The call price was $105 a share. If Lerner called the entire issue at the call price of $105 a share, the journal entry to record the redemption is as follows:

Journal entry for redemption of preferred stock at a premium

Preferred Stock, $100 par	*1,000,000*	
Paid-in Capital in Excess of Par: Preferred Stock	*20,000*	
Retained Earnings.	*30,000*	
Cash		*1,050,000*
To record redemption of 10,000 shares of preferred stock		
for $30,000 in excess of the original issuance price.		

This journal entry eliminates both the Preferred Stock and the Paid-in Capital in Excess of Par: Preferred Stock accounts, because the capital invested by the preferred stockholders has been returned in full, and these investors no longer have any ownership equity in the corporation. The $30,000 paid to the preferred stockholders in excess of their original investment, referred to as **premium paid on retirement of preferred stock,** is debited to Retained Earnings and not to any paid-in capital accounts applicable to other classes of capital stock.

When the preferred stock is selling at a market price below call price, a corporation may redeem a portion of the stock by purchase in the open market. Returning to the previous example, assume that Lerner Corporation acquired 1,000 shares of preferred stock in the open market at $90 a share. The journal entry to record the redemption is shown below:

Journal entry for redemption of preferred stock at a discount

Preferred Stock, $100 par	100,000	
Paid-in Capital in Excess of Par: Preferred Stock	2,000	
Cash		90,000
Paid-in Capital from Redemption of Preferred Stock . .		12,000
To record redemption of 1,000 shares of preferred stock at a cost $12,000 below the original issuance price.		

By a payment of $90,000, the corporation has eliminated 1,000 shares of preferred stock representing $102,000 of paid-in capital. Recording the $12,000 excess of the original investment by preferred stockholders over the amount paid to redeem the 1,000 shares of preferred stock in the manner illustrated above results in an increase in the equity of the common stockholders. However, this increase should not be regarded as a gain to be reported in the income statement. It also is improper to credit to retained earnings the $12,000 difference between the carrying amount of redeemed stock and the redemption price. The $12,000 originally was recorded as paid-in capital, and it continues in that category with a descriptive title indicating the effect of the redemption of the preferred stock at a price below the original issuance price.

The two preceding examples illustrate the following general rules for interpreting the redemption of preferred stock:

1 When preferred stock is redeemed at a cost in excess of the original issuance price, the excess payment is recorded as a reduction of retained earnings. The excess should **not** be recorded as an extraordinary loss or as a debit to any paid-in capital relating to shares of any other class of capital stock.

2 When preferred stock is redeemed for an amount less than the issuance price, the difference is recorded as a paid-in capital item and **not** as an extraordinary gain or as an increase in retained earnings.

The disclosure requirements for redeemable preferred stock are described in Chapter 16.

STATEMENTS OF RETAINED EARNINGS AND STOCKHOLDERS' EQUITY

Because users of financial statements are interested in all changes in stockholders' equity, a complete set of financial statements includes:

1 A statement of retained earnings accompanied by a statement of paid-in capital, or alternatively,

2 A statement of stockholders' equity

Statement of retained earnings

As explained in Chapter 3, a **statement of retained earnings** shows the changes in retained earnings during an accounting period, thus reconciling the beginning and ending balances of retained earnings.

The content and relative importance of the statement of retained earnings in portraying the financial developments during an accounting period have been reduced by the movement to the all-inclusive concept of income measurement. **FASB Statement No. 16** requires that all items of profit and loss recognized during a period be included in the determination of net income, except for **prior period adjustments.** Currently, very few transactions and events meet the rigorous requirements for classification as prior period adjustments to be recorded in the Retained Earnings account. Thus, the statement of retained earnings is relatively short and consists of the following:

1 The beginning balance of retained earnings (adjusted for any prior period adjustments)

2 An addition of net income (or deduction of net loss) for the accounting period

3 A deduction for any dividends declared

4 The ending balance of retained earnings

	Year 10	Year 9
ATLANTIC LINES, INC.		
Statement of Retained Earnings		
For Years Ended June 30, Year 10 and Year 9		
Retained earnings, beginning of year, as originally reported		$850,000
Less: Prior period adjustment—correction of error, net of income tax effect of $250,000		280,000
Retained earnings, beginning of year (as restated for Year 9)	$675,000	$570,000
Add (or deduct): Net income (or loss)	(85,000)	205,000
Subtotals	$590,000	$775,000
Less: Dividends declared, $0.25 and $1.00 a share.	25,000	100,000
Retained earnings, end of year	$565,000	$675,000

A comparative statement of retained earnings for Atlantic Lines, Inc., that includes a prior period adjustment, appears on page 735.

Instead of a separate statement of retained earnings, many corporations prepare a **combined statement of earnings and retained earnings** such as the one for Handley Corporation below:

HANDLEY CORPORATION
Combined Statement of Earnings and Retained Earnings
For Years Ended December 31, Year 10 and Year 9
(dollars in thousands except per-share amounts)

	Year 10	Year 9
Revenue:		
Sales	$1,317,683	$1,140,485
Other revenue	18,886	15,753
Total revenue	$1,336,569	$1,156,238
Costs and expenses:		
Cost of goods sold	$ 650,275	$ 567,206
Selling and administrative expenses	416,699	362,968
Depreciation and amortization	41,597	35,862
Income taxes expense	103,339	83,747
Other expenses	3,953	4,634
Total costs and expenses	$1,215,863	$1,054,417
Net earnings (per share: Year 10, $2.15; Year 9, $1.82)	$ 120,706	$ 101,821
Retained earnings, beginning of year	469,647	391,850
Cash dividends declared ($0.45 and $0.43 a share)	(25,136)	(24,024)
Retained earnings, end of year	$ 565,217	$ 469,647

Reporting changes in paid-in capital or stockholders' equity

Reporting changes in capital stock and paid-in capital in excess of par is required by **APB Opinion No. 12.** The Accounting Principles Board stated.[6]

> When both financial position and results of operations are presented, disclosure of changes in the separate accounts comprising stockholders' equity (in addition to retained earnings) and of the changes in the number of shares of equity securities during at least the most recent annual fiscal period and any subsequent interim period presented is required to make the financial statements sufficiently informative. Disclosure of such changes may take the form of separate statements or may be made in the basic financial statements or notes thereto.

One approach for compliance with **APB Opinion No. 12** is to prepare a statement of paid-in capital in addition to the statement of retained earnings. A more popular approach is to prepare a statement of stockholders' equity, as illustrated for Lin Corporation on page 737. In this

[6] *APB Opinion No. 12,* "Omnibus Opinion—1967," AICPA (New York: 1967), p. 190.

LIN CORPORATION
Statement of Stockholders' Equity
For Years Ended December 31, Year 4 and Year 5

	Capital stock	Paid-in capital in excess of par	Retained earnings
Balances, Dec. 31, Year 3	$ 5,966,000	$21,419,000	$16,161,000
Net income.			9,938,000
Cash dividends on common stock ($0.10 a share)			(1,229,000)
Transfer to common stock of amount equal to par of common stock issued as a 100% stock dividend	6,266,000		(6,266,000)
Exercise of common stock options and warrants	355,000	4,891,000	
Conversion of subordinated debt	144,000	3,667,000	
Business combination with Butler Company (preferred stock, $13,527,000; common stock, $1,465,000)	14,992,000	35,723,000	
Balances, Dec. 31, Year 4	$27,723,000	$65,700,000	$18,604,000
Net income.			19,518,000
Cash dividends:			
Preferred ($1.50 a share)			(676,000)
Common ($0.12 a share)			(1,741,000)
Exercise of common stock options and warrants	525,000	5,171,000	
Conversion of subordinated debt and preferred stock	1,260,000	27,558,000	
Balances, Dec. 31, Year 5	$29,508,000	$98,429,000	$35,705,000

Note: Stockholders' Equity: The authorized capital stock of the company consists of 25 million shares of common stock and 2 million shares of preferred stock. The preferred stock outstanding on December 31, Year 5, is convertible to 315,561 shares of common stock and has liquidation preference of $13,524,000.

On December 31, Year 5, the company had reserved 710,000 shares of its common stock for issuance under outstanding common stock purchase warrants. The warrants are exercisable prior to May 31, Year 6, at $12.10 a share. The company also had reserved 525,000 shares of common stock for issuance on conversion of the 6% subordinated notes and the convertible preferred stock, and 640,000 shares for issuance under stock option plans.

Common shares issued on exercise of stock options during Year 4 and Year 5 amounted to 99,939 and 109,846, respectively. There were options outstanding on December 31, Year 4 and Year 5, for 280,561 and 383,053 shares of common stock, respectively, and the aggregate purchase price of all outstanding stock options was $6,037,000 and $6,067,000, respectively.

Retained earnings of approximately $15,500,000 are available on December 31, Year 5, for payment of cash dividends under the most restrictive provisions of the company's indebtedness agreements.

example, the amounts for preferred stock and common stock are combined into one column headed "capital stock," and an accompanying note describes in more detail the events of the year presented in the statement of stockholders' equity.

EARNINGS PER SHARE

Because of the complexities of business activities and the need for a small number of comparative measurements to highlight financial analysis, earnings per share has become perhaps the most important computation for many investors. Probably no financial statistic is cited more widely than earnings per share. In the opinion of many investors, market prices of common stocks are closely related to earnings per share.

Earnings per share is the amount of net income earned on each share of common stock during an accounting period. Earnings per share is meaningful only with respect to common stock; it should not be computed for preferred stock because the participation in earnings by preferred stockholders is limited by contract. Assuming that *only one class of capital stock is outstanding* and that there was no change in the number of shares of capital stock outstanding during the accounting period, earnings per share is computed as follows:

$$\frac{\text{Net income}}{\text{Number of shares of capital stock outstanding}} = \text{earnings per share}$$

When cumulative preferred stock also is outstanding, the current dividend requirement on the preferred stock (whether or not declared by the board of directors) is deducted from net income to determine the amount of net income available for the common stock.

Investors in common stocks make extensive use of earnings per share data in the evaluation of the profitability of corporations. By computing the *price-earnings ratio* (market price of a share of common stock divided by earnings per share), investors also attempt to determine whether the market price of the stock is reasonable or whether it might be too high or too low. However, financial statements are only one part of the total information that can be used to evaluate a corporation's past earnings and to predict its future earnings performance, and the earnings per share amount is a small piece of the total information available in financial statements. Excessive reliance on earnings per share data may result in failure to consider the totality of a corporation's operations, including a wide range of nonfinancial data which may be far more important to investors.

Historical perspective

The inclusion of earnings per share in the income statement became a generally accepted accounting principle with the issuance of **APB Opinion No. 9** in 1966.[7] Three years later, the APB issued **Opinion No. 15,** "Earnings per Share," to: (1) recognize the importance of the increasingly complex capital structures of many corporations in which the distinctions between common stockholders' equity and other forms of corporate capital were not clearly apparent; (2) provide guidelines and procedures for the computation of earnings per share in a consistent manner which would be meaningful to investors; and (3) specify procedures for reporting the potential dilution in earnings per share.[8] The APB recognized that it is difficult to identify all conditions that may be encountered in the computation of earnings per share.[9]

In 1978, the FASB suspended earnings per share disclosure requirements for nonpublic enterprises. A **nonpublic enterprise** was defined as an enterprise (1) whose equity and debt securities are not publicly traded on a stock exchange or over the counter, or (2) that is not required to file financial statements with the SEC. The FASB took this action pending completion of a study to consider whether certain types of business enterprises should be exempt from some disclosure requirements required by generally accepted accounting principles.[10]

Computation of weighted-average number of shares of common stock outstanding; stock splits and stock dividends

The first step in the computation of earnings per share is to determine the number of shares of common stock outstanding in each accounting period for which earnings data are to be presented. Earnings per share should be based on the **weighted-average** number of shares of common stock outstanding during each period. (At this point of our discussion we are not concerned with common stock equivalents or other complexities discussed later in this chapter.)

Computation of Weighted-Average Number of Shares Outstanding The weighted-average number of shares of common stock outstanding is determined by relating the portion of time within an accounting period

---

[7] *APB Opinion No. 9,* "Reporting the Results of Operations," AICPA (New York: 1966).
[8] *APB Opinion No. 15,* "Earnings per Share," AICPA (New York: 1969).
[9] Shortly after the issuance of *APB Opinion No. 15,* the AICPA published a 189-page monograph by J. T. Ball, "Computing Earnings per Share—Unofficial Accounting Interpretations of APB Opinion No. 15" (New York: 1970). *APB Opinion No. 15* has been criticized on grounds that it deals with financial analysis rather than accounting principles, that it contains some illogical assumptions, and that it is overly complex. However, *APB Opinion No. 15* has played an important role in standardizing the computation of earnings per share.
[10] *FASB Statement No. 21,* "Suspension of the Reporting of Earnings per Share . . . by Nonpublic Enterprises," FASB (Stamford: 1978).

that a given number of shares of common stock was outstanding to the length of that period. For example, if 1,000 shares of common stock were outstanding during the first nine months of Year 1 and 1,400 shares were outstanding during the last three months of Year 1, as a result of the issuance for cash of 400 additional shares of common stock, the weighted-average number of shares of common stock outstanding during Year 1 is 1,100, determined as follows:

<table>
<tr><td>**Computation of weighted-average number of shares of common stock outstanding**</td><td>*1,000 shares $\times \frac{3}{4}$ of a year* . . . .</td><td align="right">*750*</td></tr>
<tr><td></td><td>*1,400 shares $\times \frac{1}{4}$ of a year* . . . .</td><td align="right">*350*</td></tr>
<tr><td></td><td>*Weighted-average number of shares of common stock outstanding during*
Year 1. . . . .</td><td align="right">*1,100*</td></tr>
</table>

The use of the weighted-average number of shares outstanding is necessary when additional shares of common stock are issued for cash or other assets, in order to compute a more meaningful earnings per share amount. Assuming that 400 shares of common stock were issued for cash on September 30, Year 1 (in the example above) the proceeds on the issuance were available to generate earnings only during the last three months of Year 1. These 400 shares would be outstanding for one-fourth of a year, or an equivalent of 100 shares outstanding for a full year. In other words, the weighted-average number of shares of common stock outstanding consists of 1,000 shares outstanding during the entire year plus 100 full-year-equivalent shares issued on September 30, Year 1.

Effect of Stock Split or Stock Dividend When the number of shares of common stock outstanding changes as a result of a stock split, stock dividend, or reverse split, the computation of the weighted-average number of shares common stock outstanding should be adjusted ***retroactively.*** This is necessary to report earnings per share which are fully comparable in terms of the latest capital structure. If a stock split, stock dividend, or reverse split is to become effective after the close of the latest accounting period but before financial statements are issued, the per-share computations should be made on the basis of the ***new capitalization.*** When earnings per share data are computed on this basis, the method of computation should be disclosed in a note to the financial statements.

The computation of the weighted-average number of shares of common stock outstanding, showing retroactive adjustment for a stock dividend and a stock split, is illustrated on page 741 for Weymouth Corporation.

WEYMOUTH CORPORATION
Computation of Weighted-Average Number of Shares of Common Stock Outstanding

	Year ended Dec. 31,		
	Year 3	Year 2	Year 1
Analysis of actual changes in the number of shares of			
common stock outstanding:			
Year 1			
Jan. 1 Number of shares outstanding, beginning of			
year	840,000	700,000	500,000
Apr. 1 Issuance for cash			200,000
Year 2			
Aug. 5 20% stock dividend		140,000	
Year 3			
Mar. 16 3 for 1 stock split (200% increase)	1,680,000		
Dec. 31 Number of shares outstanding, end of year . .	2,520,000	840,000	700,000
Computation of weighted-average number of shares of			
common stock outstanding (giving retroactive recog-			
nition to stock dividend and stock split:			
Year 1			
Jan. 1 Number of shares outstanding, beginning of			
year	840,000	700,000	500,000
Apr. 1 Issuance for cash (200,000 shares × ¾ yr) . . .			150,000
Subtotals	840,000	700,000	650,000
Year 2			
Aug. 5 20% stock dividend (applied retroactively) . . .		140,000	130,000
Subtotals	840,000	840,000	780,000
Year 3			
Mar. 16 3 for 1 stock split (applied retroactively)	1,680,000	1,680,000	1,560,000
Weighted-average number of shares out-			
standing	2,520,000	2,520,000	2,340,000

In the computation of the retroactive weighted-average number of shares of common stock outstanding in Year 1 for Weymouth Corporation, the 20% stock dividend declared in Year 2 was applied to the 650,000 weighted-average number of shares of common stock outstanding in Year 1; and the 3 for 1 split in Year 3 was applied to the 780,000 weighted-average number of shares of common stock after adjustment for the 20% stock dividend.

To continue the example, assume that the net income of Weymouth Corporation for Year 3 was $5,040,000, and that net income and earnings per share were *originally reported* for Year 2 and Year 1 as shown on page 742.

WEYMOUTH CORPORATION
Earnings per Share (as Originally Reported)
For Years Ended December 31, Year 2 and Year 1

	From income statement for Year 2	From income statement for Year 1
Net income	$3,780,000	$2,574,000
Earnings per share of common stock:		
Year 1: $2,574,000 ÷ 650,000 (weighted-average number of shares outstanding in Year 1, before retroactive adjustment for 20% stock dividend and 3 for 1 stock split)		$ 3.96
Year 2: $3,780,000 ÷ 840,000 (weighted-average number of shares outstanding in Year 2, before retroactive adjustment for 3 for 1 stock split)	$ 4.50	

A comparative income statement at the end of Year 2 would show earnings per share for Year 1 of $3.30 ($2,574,000 ÷ 780,000 shares outstanding after giving effect to the 20% stock dividend in Year 2 = $3.30). The comparative net income and earnings per share amounts for Weymouth Corporation, giving effect to the 20% stock dividend in Year 2 and the 3 for 1 stock split in Year 3, are presented *at the end of Year 3* as follows:

WEYMOUTH CORPORATION
Earnings per Share (Reflecting Retroactive Application of Stock Dividend and Stock Split)
For Years Ended December 31, Year 3, Year 2, and Year 1

	Year 3	Year 2	Year 1
Net income.	$5,040,000	$3,780,000	$2,574,000
Earnings per share of common stock:			
Year 1: $2,574,000 ÷ 2,340,000 shares (adjusted)			$ 1.10
Year 2: $3,780,000 ÷ 2,520,000 shares (adjusted)		$ 1.50	
Year 3: $5,040,000 ÷ 2,520,000 shares (adjusted)	$ 2.00		

Earnings per share data thus are reported on a fully comparable basis in terms of the capital structure at the end of Year 3. For example, because one share of common stock outstanding in Year 1 is equal to 3.6 shares at the end of Year 3 as a result of the 20% stock dividend and the 3 for 1 split, the earnings for Year 1 are restated retroactively at $1.10 per share ($3.96, as originally reported in the income statement for Year 1, divided by 3.6 = $1.10).

The difficulties encountered in the computation of earnings per share do not end with the computation of the weighted-average number of shares of common stock outstanding. For example: How are earnings per share computed for a corporation which has preferred stock (convertible or nonconvertible) or convertible bonds outstanding? How do outstanding stock options and warrants affect the computation of earnings per share? To answer these questions, our discussion focuses on two types of corporate capital structure as follows:

1 For corporations that have a *simple capital structure*
2 For corporations that have a *complex capital structure*
   a *Primary* earnings per share, which takes into account the potential dilutive effect of common stock equivalents outstanding
   b *Fully diluted* earnings per share, which takes into account the maximum potential dilutive effect of convertible securities, stock options, and stock warrants outstanding

Simple capital structure

The capital structure of a corporation may consist only of common stock; or the capital structure may include nonconvertible preferred stock, few or no potentially dilutive convertible securities, and small amounts of stock options and warrants. In such cases the corporation is said to have a *simple capital structure.* The potential reduction in earnings per share that would occur if convertible securities were converted or if outstanding options and warrants were exercised is called *dilution.* If the potential dilution in earnings per share is less than 3%, potentially dilutive securities and options or warrants need not be considered in the computation of earnings per share. In such cases, a *single presentation* of earnings per share in the income statement is appropriate. This single presentation may include an extraordinary item, as illustrated on page 744 for Simplex Corporation.

The example for Simplex Corporation shows that the earnings per share before the extraordinary loss decreased in Year 2, despite the fact that the same number of shares of common stock was outstanding at the end of each year (400,000 shares) and that the income before the extraordinary loss actually increased in Year 2. This is attributed to the increase in the *weighted-average* number of shares outstanding; the 100,000 shares issued on July 1, Year 1, were outstanding for only six months in Year 1, but for all 12 months in Year 2. In the absence of ex-

SIMPLEX CORPORATION
Earnings per Share Data and Computations
For Years Ended December 31, Year 2 and Year 1

	Year 2	Year 1
Data required to compute earnings per share of common stock:		
Income before extraordinary loss.	$810,000	$750,000
Extraordinary loss (net of income taxes)	$140,000	
Dividend requirement on cumulative nonconvertible preferred stock	$ 50,000	$ 50,000
Shares of common stock outstanding:		
Beginning of year.	400,000	300,000
Issued for cash, July 1, Year 1	–0–	100,000
End of year.	400,000	400,000
Shares of common stock reserved for employee stock options (1)	10,000	10,000
Weighted-average number of shares of common stock outstanding.	400,000	350,000 (2)
Presentation in the income statement:		
Earnings per share of common stock:		
Income before extraordinary loss	$ 1.90 (3)	$ 2.00 (4)
Extraordinary loss (net of income taxes)	(0.35) (5)	–0–
Net income.	$ 1.55	$ 2.00

(1) *Excluded from weighted-average number of shares of common stock because options represent less than 3% of weighted-average number of shares. This is below the limitations established by* **APB Opinion No. 15.**
(2) *300,000 shares for the full year, plus 100,000 shares for one-half year (equivalent to 50,000 for a full year) = 350,000 shares.*
(3) *($810,000 – $50,000) ÷ 400,000 weighted-average number of shares = $1.90.*
(4) *($750,000 – $50,000) ÷ 350,000 weighted-average number of shares = $2.00.*
(5) *140,000 ÷ 400,000 weighted-average number of shares = $0.35.*

traordinary items, only a single earnings per share amount appears in the income statement for a corporation with a simple capital structure. When the income statement includes extraordinary items, results of discontinued operations, and the cumulative effect of a change in accounting principle, the presentation of earnings per share is more detailed (see page 112 in Chapter 3).

Complex capital structure

When a corporation has convertible securities, stock options, warrants, or other potentially dilutive securities outstanding, its capital structure is classified as **complex** for purposes of earnings per share computations. The APB took the position that earnings per share should reflect potential dilution when securities which in substance are equivalent to common stock are outstanding. As a result, companies with a complex capital structure must report with equal prominence in the income statement **primary** earnings per share (which include the dilutive effect of common stock equivalents) and **fully diluted** earnings per share (which include the maximum potential dilutive effect of all convertible securities, stock options, and warrants outstanding); this is referred to as a **dual presentation** of earnings per share. (See page 753 for an example.) These reporting requirements for earnings per share do not change the legal rights of the various security holders or the presentation of other data in the financial statements. The computation of primary earnings per share is explained below; the explanation of fully diluted earnings per share begins on page 751.

Primary Earnings per Share and Common Stock Equivalents **Primary earnings per share** is the amount of earnings applicable to each share of common stock; the number of shares of common stock consists of a weighted-average number of common shares actually outstanding plus any common stock equivalents. A **common stock equivalent** is a security which contains contractual provisions enabling its owner to exchange the security for common stock.[11] Such a security is considered equivalent to common stock because its holders have a right to participate in the appreciation of the value of the common stock. This participation is essentially the same as that of a common stockholder, except that the security generally carries a specified dividend or interest rate. The market price of a security which is a common stock equivalent is dependent to a considerable degree on the market price of the common stock. Neither actual conversion nor the assumption that conversion is likely to take place is necessary before a security is classified as a common stock equivalent. **Common stock equivalency is determined at the time the security is issued** and does not change as long as the security remains outstanding.[12]

In a complex capital structure case, potentially dilutive securities may or may not qualify as common stock equivalents for the computation of primary earnings per share. However, common stock equivalents are not used to compute primary earnings per share if they would be **antidilutive,** that is, they would have the effect of **increasing earnings per share** or **reducing a loss per share.** Common stock equivalents generally include convertible bonds, convertible preferred stock, and stock options and warrants.

Convertible Securities A bond or preferred stock which at the time of issuance is substantially equivalent to common stock is treated as a com-

---

[11] *APB Opinion No. 15*, p. 225.
[12] *Ibid.*, p. 227.

mon stock equivalent. Convertible stocks or bonds are considered common stock equivalents if at the time of issuance the cash yield, based on the market price, is less than $66\frac{2}{3}\%$ of the then current bank prime interest rate.[13] The **bank prime interest rate** is the rate banks charge on short-term loans to borrowers with the highest credit standing. If convertible **senior securities** (bonds payable and preferred stock) do not meet the test of common stock equivalency at the time of issuance, they are not a factor in the computation of primary earnings per share, but are used (if dilutive) in the computation of fully diluted earnings per share.

A convertible security which is a common stock equivalent is then assumed to have been converted to common stock at the beginning of the earliest period for which earnings per share data are reported or at the time of issuance, whichever is the more recent date. For example, if convertible preferred stock were issued on April 1, Year 1, the equivalent number of shares of common stock for Year 1 is considered to be outstanding for nine months of Year 1 even though some of the preferred stock was converted to common stock late in Year 1.

In the computation of primary earnings per share, net income is adjusted (increased) by the amount of interest (net of income taxes) on convertible bonds which are dilutive common stock equivalents. In the determination of net income available for common stock, net income is not reduced by the amount of the dividend requirement on convertible preferred stock which is a dilutive common stock equivalent. These adjustments are necessary because it is assumed that both the convertible bonds and the preferred stock are converted to common stock.

Example 1: Convertible preferred stock is a common stock equivalent   At the beginning of Year 1, Carrenga Corporation issued at $100 a share, 50,000 shares of $6 convertible preferred stock. At the time the preferred stock was issued, the bank prime interest rate was 12%. Each share of preferred stock is convertible to two shares of common stock; no shares have yet been converted. If Carrenga Corporation has net income of $1,900,000 in Year 2 and 400,000 shares of common stock outstanding during Year 2, compute the primary earnings per share for Year 2.

Solution: The convertible preferred stock qualifies as a common stock equivalent because its cash yield of 6% ($6 ÷ $100) is less than 8% ($66\frac{2}{3}\%$ of the 12% bank prime interest rate at the date the convertible preferred stock was issued). A convertible preferred stock is dilutive if the dividend per share paid on the stock (computed on the basis of the number of shares of common stock which would be issued on conversion) is less than the earnings per share of common stock before conversion is considered. In this case the convertible preferred stock is dilutive, because the equivalent converted dividend on the preferred

---

[13] *Ibid.*, p. 229.

stock is $3 ($6 ÷ 2 shares of common stock), which is less than the earnings per share of common stock before conversion is assumed, $4 ($1,900,000 net income − $300,000 preferred dividend ÷ 400,000 shares of common stock outstanding). The amount of primary earnings per share for Year 2 is computed below:

<table>
<tr>
<td>Computation of primary
earnings per share:
Convertible preferred
stock is a common
stock equivalent</td>
<td>

$$\frac{\text{Net income (before preferred dividends)}}{\text{Common stock outstanding}}$$
+ dilutive common stock equivalents outstanding

$$= \frac{\$1,900,000}{400,000 + 100,000} = \underline{\underline{\$3.80}}$$

</td>
</tr>
</table>

The conversion of a common stock equivalent, if dilutive, also is assumed for the computation of fully diluted earnings per share; this is illustrated in Example 6 on pages 751–753.

Example 2: Common stock equivalent is antidilutive Assume the same facts as in Example 1 for Carrenga Corporation, except that net income for Year 2 is only $700,000. Compute primary earnings per share for Year 2.

Solution: Although the convertible preferred stock is a common stock equivalent, conversion is not assumed for the computation of primary earnings per share because the effect would be antidilutive. This is illustrated below:

<table>
<tr>
<td>Conversion of
antidilutive convertible
preferred stock
is not assumed</td>
<td>

Earnings per share of common stock:
  Conversion not assumed: $700,000 net income − $300,000 preferred
    dividends = $400,000 ÷ 400,000 shares $1.00
  Conversion assumed: $700,000 net income ÷ 500,000 shares $1.40

</td>
</tr>
</table>

Because earnings per share would be increased if the common stock equivalent were used in the computation, primary earnings per share is reported at $1.00 per share, not $1.40 per share. The assumed conversion of the preferred stock is antidilutive (increases earnings per share); therefore, conversion also is not assumed in the computation of fully diluted earnings per share.

Example 3: Convertible bonds are not common stock equivalents On December 31, Year 1, Mossman Corporation issued at face amount $1 million of 12% convertible bonds when the bank prime rate of interest was 15%. Each $1,000 bond is convertible to 25 shares of the corporation's common stock. In Year 2, Mossman earned $450,000 net income. The income tax rate is 40% of pre-tax income. During Year 2, no bonds had been converted, and 75,000 shares of common stock were outstanding. Compute the primary earnings per share for Year 2.

Solution: The cash yield of 12% ($120 ÷ $1,000) on the convertible bonds exceeded 10% (66⅔% of 15% bank prime interest rate on the date the bonds were issued); therefore, the convertible bonds are not common stock equivalents for the computation of primary earnings per share for Year 2. Primary earnings per share is $6 ($450,000 ÷ 75,000 shares = $6). However, conversion of the bonds is assumed for the computation of fully diluted earnings per share, unless such an assumption would be antidilutive.

Example 4: Convertible bonds are common stock equivalents Assume the same facts as in Example 3 for Mossman Corporation, except that the interest rate on the convertible bonds is 9% rather than 12%. Compute primary earnings per share for Year 2 if net income is $450,000.

Solution: In this case, the convertible bonds are common stock equivalents because the cash yield of 9% ($90 ÷ $1,000) was *less* than 10% (66⅔% of 15% bank prime interest rate at the date the bonds were issued). The computation of primary earnings per share of $5.04 is shown below:

MOSSMAN CORPORATION
Computation of Primary Earnings per Share
(Convertible Bonds Are a Dilutive Common Stock Equivalent)
For Year 2

Earnings to be used in computation of primary earnings per share:

Net income as reported		$450,000
Add: Interest on convertible bonds, net of income taxes:		
Interest: $1,000,000 × 9%	$90,000	
Less: Income taxes: $90,000 × 0.40	36,000	54,000
Earnings to be used in computation of primary earnings per share		$504,000
Number of shares of common stock to be used in computation of primary earnings per share:		
Number of shares of common stock outstanding throughout Year 2		75,000
Number of shares of common stock to be issued, assuming conversion of bonds: 1,000 × 25		25,000
Number of shares of common stock to be used in computation of primary earnings per share		100,000
Primary earnings per share of common stock: $504,000 ÷ 100,000 shares		$ 5.04

If conversion of the bonds were not assumed, the earnings per share would be reported improperly at $6 per share ($450,000 ÷ 75,000 shares). Conversion also is assumed (if dilutive) in the computation of fully diluted earnings per share.

Options or Warrants to Purchase Common Stock   A corporation may issue stock options (including stock appreciation rights) or warrants which give grantees the right to acquire common stock at a stated price. Such options or warrants should be regarded as common stock equivalents **at all times;**[14] however, dilution is disregarded if it is less than 3%. Therefore, primary earnings per share should reflect the impact of the exercise of stock options or warrants, including the possible **use of the proceeds** which would be received on the exercise of the options or warrants. In the computation of primary earnings per share, exercise of the stock options or warrants is assumed **only** if such exercise would result in a dilution of earnings per share.

When the exercise of stock options or warrants is assumed, any proceeds that would be received are assumed to be used to acquire treasury stock at the average market price during the accounting period. This is known as the **treasury stock method.** For example, if options to purchase 10,000 shares of common stock at $5 a share are outstanding, and the average market price during the accounting period was $20 a share, the $50,000 that would be received by the corporation from exercise of the options and the issuance of 10,000 additional shares of common stock would be sufficient to acquire 2,500 shares of common stock ($50,000 ÷ $20 = 2,500). Thus, 7,500 (10,000 − 2,500 = 7,500) shares are added to the number of shares of common stock already outstanding to compute primary earnings per share. The exercise of the options or warrants is assumed to have taken place at the **beginning of the accounting period** or **at the time** the options or warrants were issued, whichever is the more recent date.

The APB recommended that the exercise of stock options or warrants should not be assumed until the common stock sells in excess of the exercise price for "substantially all of three consecutive months ending with the last month of the period to which earnings per share data relate."[15] Under the treasury stock method, options or warrants have a dilutive effect on earnings per share only when the average market price of the common stock exceeds the exercise price of the options or warrants. The computation of primary earnings per share under the treasury stock method is illustrated in the example below. For simplicity, we shall illustrate the computation for a **fiscal year;** in practice, the computation is required for **each quarter** of the year.[16]

Example 5: Options to purchase common stock are outstanding   Dowling Corporation has 200,000 shares of common stock and options to purchase 30,000 shares of common stock at $10 a share outstanding

[14] *Ibid.*, p. 230.
[15] *Ibid.*, pp. 230–231.
[16] J. T. Ball, *Computing Earnings per Share: Unofficial Accounting Interpretations of APB Opinion No. 15, AICPA* (New York: 1970) pp. 50, 56–57.

throughout Year 2. The options were granted to employees several years ago. The average market price of the common stock during Year 2 was $30 a share. Compute primary earnings per share for Year 2 if the net income for Year 2 is $550,000.

Solution: The amount of primary earnings per share for Dowling Corporation for Year 2 is $2.50 a share, as computed below:

DOWLING CORPORATION
Computation of Primary Earnings per Share
(Stock Options Are Dilutive)
For Year 2

Computation of number of shares of common stock to be used in determination of primary earnings per share:

Number of shares of common stock outstanding throughout Year 2 . .		200,000
Add: Number of shares of common stock to be issued on exercise of stock options		30,000
Less: Assumed purchase of common stock with the proceeds received on exercise of stock options: [(30,000 × $10) ÷ $30]	10,000	20,000
Number of shares of common stock to be used in computation of primary earnings per share		220,000
Primary earnings per share of common stock: $550,000 ÷ 220,000 shares		$ 2.50

A departure from the procedure illustrated above is required when the number of shares of common stock assumed to be acquired exceeds 20% of the number of shares of common stock actually outstanding at the end of the accounting period. In such cases, it should be assumed that **all** options and warrants were exercised and the proceeds first were used to purchase 20% of the outstanding common stock, with the balance used to retire outstanding debt. However, if all debt is thus eliminated, it is assumed that the remaining proceeds are used to purchase short-term investments. Appropriate recognition should be given to the income tax effects of the assumed use of the potential proceeds from the exercise of stock options and warrants.

Computation of fully diluted earnings per share when options to purchase common stock are outstanding is illustrated in Example 6 beginning on page 751.

The reader should realize that it is virtually impossible to cover all situations which may arise in the computation of primary earnings per share; our objective has been to describe the basic issues involved. We now turn our attention to the second part of the **dual presentation** of earnings per share—the computation of fully diluted earnings per share.

Fully Diluted Earnings per Share It is apparent from the foregoing discussion that primary earnings per share may include some potential dilution and that certain potentially dilutive securities are not considered common stock equivalents. However, in the computation of fully diluted earnings per share, *all* convertible securities, options, and warrants are assumed to have been converted or exercised in order to reflect the maximum potential dilution. As in the computation of primary earnings per share, conversion of securities or the exercise of options or warrants *should not* be assumed if the effect is antidilutive (would have the effect of increasing earnings per share or reducing a loss per share).

The computation of fully diluted earnings per share differs from the computation of primary earnings per share in the following two respects:

1 All convertible securities, whether or not they qualify as common stock equivalents, which individually would decrease earnings per share if conversion had taken place, are included in the computation of fully diluted earnings per share. All such conversions are assumed to have taken place at the beginning of the accounting period (or at the time of issuance of the convertible security, if later).

2 To recognize the maximum potential dilution, the market price of the common stock at the end of the accounting period, *if it exceeds* the average market price during the period, is used to determine the number of shares of common stock which could be acquired with the proceeds received on the exercise of stock options or warrants. This procedure reduces the number of shares of common stock which could be acquired with the proceeds, and thus has the effect of increasing the number of outstanding shares of common stock on a pro forma basis.

The computation of primary and fully diluted earnings per share is illustrated in Example 6 below:

Example 6: Stock options and convertible preferred stock are outstanding Primary and fully diluted earnings per share for Year 10 are computed on page 752 from the information presented below for Dual Corporation:

Information for computation of primary and fully diluted earnings per share		
Net income for Year 10		$330,000
Number of shares of common stock outstanding throughout Year 10 . .		95,000
Number of shares of $4 convertible preferred stock outstanding throughout Year 10; each share of preferred stock is convertible to three shares of common stock; the preferred stock is **not** a common stock equivalent, but is dilutive		3,000
Outstanding options (issued in Year 6) to purchase common stock at $20 a share; average market price of common stock during Year 10 was $40 a share, and the market price at the end of Year 10 was $50 a share		10,000

DUAL CORPORATION
Computation of Primary and Fully Diluted Earnings per Share
For Year 10

	Number of shares	
	Primary	**Fully diluted**
Computation of number of shares of common stock outstanding to be used in computation of earnings per share for Year 10:		
Number of shares of common stock outstanding throughout Year 10	95,000	95,000
For computation of primary earnings per share:		
Shares of common stock to be issued on exercise of stock options at $20 a share 10,000		
Less: Assumed purchase of common stock at average market price during Year 10 with proceeds received from exercise of stock options [(10,000 × $20) ÷ $40] 5,000 (1)	5,000	
For computation of fully diluted earnings per share:		
Shares of common stock to be issued on exercise of stock options at $20 a share 10,000		
Less: Assumed purchase of common stock at market price at end of Year 10 with proceeds received from exercise of stock options [(10,000 × $20) ÷ $50] 4,000 (1)		6,000
Assume conversion of 3,000 shares of preferred stock to common stock (3 for 1)		9,000
Number of shares of common stock outstanding to be used in computation of earnings per share for Year 10	100,000	110,000
Earnings per share of common stock for Year 10:		
Primary: $318,000 ÷ 100,000 shares (2)	$ 3.18	
Fully diluted: $330,000 ÷ 110,000 shares		$ 3.00

(1) Less than 20% of shares outstanding at end of Year 10 (95,000 × 20% = 19,000).
(2) Net income of $330,000 less preferred dividend requirement of $12,000 = $318,000.

In the computation of fully diluted earnings per share for Dual Corporation, the proceeds of $200,000 from the issuance of 10,000 additional shares of common stock on the assumed exercise of stock options is assumed to be used to acquire common stock at $50 a share, the market price of the common stock at the end of Year 10. Because only 4,000 shares ($200,000 ÷ $50 = 4,000) can be acquired with the proceeds of $200,000, the number of shares of common stock to be used in the computation of fully diluted earnings per share is increased by 6,000

(10,000 − 4,000 = 6,000). In addition, the 3,000 shares of convertible preferred stock which are not common stock equivalents for the computation of primary earnings per share are assumed to be converted to 9,000 shares of common stock. These adjustments recognize the maximum potential dilution in earnings per share.

It should be pointed out that in the computation of primary earnings per share, the amount of the dividend requirement on the convertible preferred stock ($12,000) was deducted from net income to arrive at the income available for common stock. However, when fully diluted earnings per share were computed, net income was **not** reduced by the preferred dividend requirement because the preferred stock was assumed to have been eliminated through conversion to common stock.

Summary of earnings per share computations

The foregoing discussion of the computation of earnings per share is summarized on page 754.

Presentation of earnings per share in the income statement

Shown below is an actual presentation of earnings per share (including the accompanying note) by a publicly owned company with a complex capital structure:

	Year ended December 31,	
	1982	*1981*
Net income.	$342,936,000	$314,149,000
Less: Dividends on preferred stock	29,387,000	35,549,000
Net income available for common stock	$313,549,000	$278,600,000
Earnings per share of common stock **(Note 1):**		
Primary.	$ 4.15	$ 3.98
Fully diluted	$ 3.63	$ 3.35

Note 1: Earnings per share of common stock are based on the average number of shares of common stock outstanding during each year. Such average shares outstanding were 75,608,800 and 70,079,891 shares for 1982 and 1981, respectively. Earnings per share computations, assuming full dilution, include the average common shares issuable for convertible or exchangeable securities and stock options and warrants during each year and the elimination of the related dividend and interest requirements, less applicable income taxes. Such average shares, assuming full dilution, were 92,583,448 and 91,964,825 shares for 1982 and 1981, respectively.

Additional examples of presentation of earnings per share appear in Chapter 3. The presentation of earnings per share following a change in accounting principle is illustrated in Chapter 22.

Summary of
earnings per
share computations

Capital structure	Earnings per share in income statement	Explanation
1 Simple	Single presentation	Divide net income by the weighted-average number of shares of common stock outstanding during the accounting period. Dilutive common stock equivalents are ignored when the potential dilution in the aggregate is less than 3% of earnings.
2 Complex	Dual presentation: **a** Primary	Divide net income (increased by the after-tax effect of assumed conversion of bonds, if any) by the weighted-average number of shares of common stock and common stock equivalents outstanding during the accounting period. Convertible securities may or may not be common stock equivalents on date of issue; stock options and warrants always are common stock equivalents. In no case are common stock equivalents used to determine primary earnings per share if inclusion is antidilutive. Potential earnings dilution of less than 3% (in the aggregate) is ignored.
	b Fully diluted	Essentially the same procedure as above, except that all convertible securities are assumed to have been converted (at the beginning of the accounting period or issue date, if later) if the effect of the assumed conversion is dilutive. The proceeds from the assumed exercise of stock options and warrants are applied to purchase common stock at end-of-period market price if such price is higher than the average market price during the period covered. Potential earnings dilution of less than 3% (in the aggregate) is ignored.

Evaluation of standards for earnings per share

The establishment of uniform standards for the computation and presentation of earnings per share in the income statement of publicly owned corporations has achieved a degree of reliability for this important financial ratio. However, many accountants have reservations about the computational techniques established in **APB Opinion No. 15** for earnings per share data, and other aspects of earnings per share. Among these reservations are the following:

1 The primary earnings per share computation supposedly is based on historical data, in contrast to the fully diluted amount, which is a pro forma computation. However, the computation of primary earnings per share involves pro forma assumptions such as those underlying the treasury stock method for dilutive stock options and warrants.

2 The decision as to whether a convertible security is a common stock equivalent is made only at the issuance date of the security. This method disregards subsequent changes in the market price of the convertible security and of the related common stock which might affect the probability of conversion. Thus, the **permanent status** assigned to a convertible security at its issuance date may be criticized.

3 Accountants acknowledge that accounting is an art, not an exact science. The determination of net income involves numerous assumptions and estimates. The inclusion of net income in the computation of earnings per share brings the same imprecision to earnings per share data that is present in net income.

4 A corporation can affect its earnings per share amounts by the acquisition and reissuance of treasury stock. Because treasury stock is not outstanding, it is excluded from the weighted-average number of shares of common stock outstanding in the denominator of the earnings per share computation. The SEC took note of this problem in **Staff Accounting Bulletin No. 29,** which set forth the view that material changes in earnings per share which result from treasury stock transactions must be included in management's discussion and analysis of earnings in the annual reports of publicly owned corporations.[17]

In view of the foregoing discussion, it is appropriate to stress once again that many factors other than earnings per share should be considered in the appraisal of a business corporation.

REVIEW QUESTIONS

1 Define **treasury stock** and indicate how it is shown in the balance sheet.

2 For what reasons do corporations acquire their own capital stock?

3 The president of Peabody Corporation stated, "We seek to purchase 8.4% of our common stock in order to secure a safe investment for excess cash." Comment on this quotation.

4 Does the acquisition and resale of its own capital stock by a corporation result in a gain or a loss to the corporation?

[17] *Staff Accounting Bulletin No. 29,* SEC (Washington: 1979).

5 In reviewing the Miscellaneous Revenue account of Magdalen Corporation, you find a credit for $200 representing a dividend of $1 a share on 200 shares of treasury stock. You determine that the dividend declaration covered the entire 10,000 shares of capital stock originally issued, that the Retained Earnings account was debited for $10,000, and that $9,800 of cash was paid to stockholders. Discuss the propriety of this accounting procedure.

6 a Discuss the propriety of declaring stock dividends on treasury stock.
  b Should treasury stock be split?
  c How is the issuance of treasury stock (carried at cost) pursuant to a 2% stock dividend recorded?

7 The Treasury Stock account of a corporation had a debit balance of $54,000, representing the cost of 6,000 shares of capital stock reacquired by the corporation. Later, the corporation exchanged the treasury stock for land which is listed in its balance sheet as "Land, at cost . . . $54,000." Do you approve of this treatment? Explain.

8 Most states place some restriction on the reacquisition by a corporation of its capital stock. What is the usual nature of such a restriction? What is the purpose of such a restriction?

9 The majority stockholder in a closely held corporation had an option to acquire all the capital stock of a minority stockholder at carrying amount at any time during the first 10 years of operation. After four years, the method of inventory valuation was changed from fifo to lifo. At the end of the tenth year, the majority stockholder exercised the option. The minority stockholder objected, arguing that "the change in inventory valuation reduced the option price by thousands of dollars." Discuss.

10 What is the appropriate accounting treatment of the difference between original issuance price and the price paid to retire preferred stock?

11 Define *earnings per share* and indicate how this statistic is used by investors.

12 a How is the weighted-average number of shares of common stock outstanding for a given year computed?
  b What effect do stock dividends and stock splits have on the presentation of earnings per share of common stock for two or more years?

13 Differentiate between the following:
  a *Simple* and *complex* capital structure
  b *Primary* and *fully diluted* earnings per share
  c *Single* and *dual* presentation of earnings per share

14 Discuss the reasons why securities other than common stock may be considered *common stock equivalents* for the computation of primary earnings per share.

15 Explain how convertible securities are determined to be common stock equivalents and how convertible senior securities which are not common stock equivalents enter into the computation of earnings per share data.

16 Explain the *treasury stock method* as it applies to stock options and warrants in the computation of primary earnings per share data.

17 For the first six months of the current year, Robb Corporation reported primary earnings per share of $4.50 and fully diluted earnings per share of $2.

What factors may cause such a large difference between the two earnings per share amounts? If the common stock of Robb Corporation sells for $36 per share, what is the price-earnings ratio?

18 In an article in the *Financial Analysts' Journal,* an executive of a large bank observed that "any evaluation of corporate policies in terms of their impact on earnings per share (EPS) is fraught with danger. . . . If the leverage idea is sound, management can increase EPS without making any investment whatever, merely by borrowing to retire common shares." Do you agree with this observation? Explain.

19 What are some shortcomings of earnings per share computations as required by *APB Opinion No. 15?*

EXERCISES

Ex. 18-1   Select the best answer for each of the following multiple-choice questions:

1 The stockholders' equity section of Eames Corporation's balance sheet on December 31, Year 6, was as follows:

Common stock, $20 par; authorized 150,000 shares, issued and outstanding 100,000 shares	$2,000,000
Paid-in capital in excess of par	400,000
Retained earnings	200,000
Total stockholders' equity	$2,600,000

On March 1, Year 7, Eames reacquired 10,000 shares of its common stock for $240,000. The following additional treasury stock transactions were completed in Year 7:

June 1—Reissued 3,000 shares for $84,000.
August 1—Reissued 2,000 shares for $42,000.
September 1—Retired remaining 5,000 shares.

Eames accounts for treasury stock by the cost method. As a result of these transactions:
a Stockholders' equity reamined unchanged.
b Common stock decreased $100,000 and retained earnings decreased $14,000.
c Common stock decreased $100,000 and paid-in capital in excess of par decreased $14,000.
d Common stock decreased $126,000.

2 With respect to the computation of earnings per share, which of the following is most indicative of a simple capital structure?
a Common stock, preferred stock, and convertible bonds outstanding in lots of even thousands
b Earnings derived from one primary product line
c Ownership equity consisting entirely of common stock
d Ownership equity consisting substantially of liquid assets

3 The par-value method of accounting for treasury stock differs from the cost method in that:
a No gains or losses are recognized on the reissuance of treasury stock under the par-value method.

 b Any gain is recognized upon reacquisition of common stock, but a loss is treated as an adjustment of retained earnings.

 c It reverses the original journal entry for the issuance of the common stock, with any difference between carrying amount and cost adjusted through paid-in capital (or retained earnings), and treats a subsequent reissuance as a new issuance of common stock.

 d It reverses the original journal entry for the issuance of the common stock, with any difference reported as a gain or loss, and does not recognize any gain or loss on a subsequent reissuance of the treasury stock.

4 The computation of earnings per share in accordance with generally accepted accounting principles may involve the consideration of securities deemed common stock equivalents. Common stock equivalents are an example of:

 a Form over substance

 b Substance over form

 c Form over accounting principle

 d Substance over accounting principle

5 Winfield Corporation has 80,000 shares of $50 par common stock authorized, issued, and outstanding. All 80,000 shares were issued at $55 a share. Retained earnings of the corporation amounts to $160,000. If 1,000 shares of common stock are reacquired by Winfield at $62 a share and the par value method of accounting for treasury stock is used, stockholders' equity is decreased by:

 a $0   *b* $50,000   *c* $55,000   *d* $62,000

6 Dilutive common stock equivalents must be used in the computation of:

 a Fully diluted earnings per share only

 b Primary earnings per share only

 c Fully diluted earnings per share and primary earnings per share

 d Other potentially dilutive securities only

Ex. 18-2   On December 31, Year 6, Farlow Corporation had 400,000 shares of common stock outstanding. On October 1, Year 7, an additional 100,000 shares of common stock were issued. In addition, Farlow had $10,000,000 of 8% convertible bonds outstanding on December 31, Year 6. The bonds were convertible to 225,000 shares of common stock. The bonds were dilutive common stock equivalents at the time of their issuance. No bonds were converted to common stock in Year 7. The net income of Farlow for the year ended December 31, Year 7, was $3,500,000. The income tax rate was 50%.

 Compute the primary earnings per share of Farlow Corporation for the year ended December 31, Year 7.

Ex. 18-3   The stockholders' equity accounts of Winslow Corporation on January 1, Year 4, are listed below:

Common stock, $20 par; authorized 100,000 shares, issued and out-

standing 60,000 shares $1,200,000

Paid-in capital in excess of par   180,000

Retained earnings   760,000

Winslow uses the cost method of accounting for treasury stock, and during Year 4 completed the following transactions:

(1) Acquired 1,000 shares of its common stock for $35,000.

(2) Reissued 600 shares of treasury stock at $38 a share.

(3) Retired the remaining 400 shares of treasury stock.

Winslow had no other stockholders' equity transactions during Year 4.

 Compute the amount that Winslow should report on December 31, Year 4, as paid-in capital in excess of par.

Ex. 18-4 On the retirement of a key employee, the board of directors of Custer Corporation authorized the presentation to the employee of a certificate for 100 shares of the corporation's $50 par common stock "in appreciation of loyal services." The shares were part of the corporation's holding of treasury stock, acquired and carried at cost of $80 a share. Equity (book value) per share of common stock was $140 and market value was $125 a share.

Prepare a journal entry for the foregoing transaction.

Ex. 18-5 Information relating to the capital structure of Partridge Corporation is as follows:

	December 31,	
	Year 8	**Year 9**
Outstanding shares of:		
Common stock	*90,000*	*90,000*
Convertible preferred stock.	*10,000*	*10,000*
9% convertible bonds	*$1,000,000*	*$1,000,000*

During Year 9, Partridge paid dividends of $2.50 a share on its preferred stock. The preferred stock is convertible to 20,000 shares of common stock and is a common stock equivalent. The 9% convertible bonds are convertible to 30,000 shares of common stock, but are not common stock equivalents. The net income of Partridge for the year ended December 31, Year 9, was $485,000. The income tax rate is 50%.

Compute primary earnings per share and fully diluted earnings per share for Partridge Corporation for Year 9.

Ex. 18-6 The stockholders' equity section of Walden Corporation's balance sheet on December 31, Year 2, appears below:

Stockholders' equity:

Common stock, $10 par; authorized 500,000 shares, issued 90,000 shares, of which 1,210 shares are in treasury	$	900,000
Paid-in capital in excess of par		20,250
Total paid-in capital	$	920,250
Retained earnings		424,680
Total paid-in capital and retained earnings		$1,344,930
Less: Cost of 1,210 shares of common stock in treasury		36,300
Total stockholders' equity		$1,308,630

On January 5, Year 3, 650 shares of treasury stock were reissued, and on January 20, Year 3, a 5% stock dividend was declared. The dividend shares were issued on March 10. The market price of the common stock was $21 a share on January 20.

Prepare separate journal entries to record the declaration (debit Retained Earnings) and distribution of the 5% stock dividend.

Ex. 18-7 Dodd Corporation decided that because it had idle cash and its $100 par 10% cumulative preferred stock (which originally was issued at $98 a share) was selling in the stock market at $85 a share, it should retire as many shares of the preferred stock as possible in an effort to improve earnings per share of common stock. On March 2, the corporation acquired 5,000 shares of the preferred stock at $84 a share and immediately retired the shares.

Prepare a journal entry to record the retirement of the 5,000 shares of preferred stock.

Ex. 18-8   Warrants exercisable at $20 each to purchase 12,000 shares of Tagg Corporation's common stock were outstanding during an accounting period when the average market price of the common stock was $25 and the ending market price was $30.

Determine the **increase** in the weighted-average number of shares of outstanding common stock resulting from application of the "treasury stock method" for the assumed exercise of the warrants for the computation of **(a)** primary earnings per share, and **(b)** fully diluted earnings per share.

Ex. 18-9   The stockholders' equity section of Kasper Corporation's balance sheet on December 31, Year 5, was as follows:

Stockholders' equity:

Capital stock, $100 par; authorized 50,000 shares, issued and outstanding 10,000 shares	$1,000,000
Paid-in capital in excess of par	500,000
Total paid-in capital	$1,500,000
Retained earnings	800,000
Total stockholders' equity	$2,300,000

Early in Year 6, the corporation reacquired 400 shares of its capital stock for $50,000. During the year it reissued 100 shares of the treasury stock at $140 a share, reissued 100 shares at $120 a share, and retired the remaining 200 shares of treasury stock. The corporation records treasury stock at cost.

Prepare journal entries to record the reacquisition, the reissuance, and the retirement of the treasury stock.

Ex. 18-10   Winstead Corporation began operations on January 2, Year 1, by issuing 2,000 shares of common stock for various assets. On July 1, Year 2, an additional 1,000 shares of common stock were issued for cash. On April 1, Year 3, a 10% common stock dividend was issued. On July 1, Year 4, the common stock was split 3 for 1.

Earnings and dividends per share of common stock for each of the first four years of operations are to be reported on a comparable basis in the annual report to stockholders for Year 4.

Compute the current equivalent number of shares outstanding at the end of each of the four years, to be used in the computation of earnings per share of common stock.

Ex. 18-11   Ching Corporation had 5,000,000 shares of common stock outstanding on December 31, Year 6. An additional 1,000,000 shares of common stock were issued on April 1, Year 7, and 500,000 more on July 1, Year 7. On October 1, Year 7, Ching issued 10,000, $1,000 face amount, 10% convertible bonds. Each bond is convertible to 40 shares of common stock. The bonds were not common stock equivalents at the time of their issuance, and no bonds were converted to common stock in Year 7.

Compute the weighted-average number of shares of common stock to be used in the computation of primary earnings per share and fully diluted earnings per share, respectively, for Year 7. Assume that the convertible bonds are dilutive.

SHORT CASES FOR ANALYSIS AND DECISION

Case 18-1   For various reasons a corporation may reacquire shares of its $5 par capital stock. When a corporation reacquires treasury stock, it has two options as to accounting for the stock: (1) cost method, and (2) par value method.

Instructions Compare and contrast the cost method with the par value method for each of the following:

a Reacquisition of treasury stock at a price less than par value.

b Reacquisition of treasury stock at a price more than par value.

c Subsequent reissuance of treasury stock at a price less than cost but more than par value.

d Subsequent reissuance of treasury stock at a price more than either cost or par value.

e Effect on net income.

Case 18-2 The earnings per share data required for a public corporation depend on the nature of its capital structure. A corporation may have a simple capital structure and compute only "earnings per common share," or it may have a complex capital structure and compute both "primary earnings per share" and "fully diluted earnings per share."

Instructions

a Define the term **common stock equivalent** and describe what securities are considered to be common stock equivalents in the computation of earnings per share.

b Define the term **complex capital structure** and discuss the disclosures (both financial and explanatory) necessary for earnings per share when a corporation has a complex capital structure.

Case 18-3 Novack Corporation acquired $180,000 of equipment for $120,000 cash and a promise to deliver an indeterminate number of treasury shares of its $10 par common stock, with a market value of $15,000, on January 2 of each year for the next five years. Hence, $75,000 in "market value" of treasury shares will be required to discharge the $60,000 balance due on the equipment contract payable.

The corporation immediately reacquired 3,000 shares of its common stock for $48,000 with the expectation that the market value of the stock would increase substantially before the delivery dates. A total of 2,500 shares of the reacquired stock subsequently was issued in payment of the $60,000 balance due on the equipment contract payable.

Instructions

a Discuss the propriety of recording the equipment at each of the following amounts:

(1) $120,000 (the cash payment)

(2) $180,000 (the cash price of the equipment)

(3) $195,000 (the $120,000 cash payment plus the $75,000 market value of the treasury stock that must be transferred to the vendor to settle the obligation in accordance with the terms of the contract)

(4) $160,000 (the $120,000 cash payment plus the $40,000 cost of the 2,500 shares of treasury stock reissued in payment for the equipment)

b Discuss the arguments for treating the balance due on the equipment contract as

(1) A liability

(2) Treasury stock subscribed

c Assuming that legal requirements do not affect the decision, discuss the arguments for treating the corporation's treasury stock as

(1) An asset awaiting ultimate disposition

(2) An element of stockholders' equity awaiting ultimate disposition

Case 18-4 Publicly owned corporations are required to present earnings per share data in their income statements.

Instructions Compare and contrast primary earnings per share with fully diluted earnings per share for each of the following:

a The effect of common stock equivalents on the number of shares used in the computation of earnings per share data.

b The effect of convertible securities which are not common stock equivalents on the number of shares used in the computation of earnings per share data.

c The effect of antidilutive securities.

Case 18-5 Castor Corporation had the following account titles in its December 31, Year 4, trial balance:

12% cumulative convertible preferred stock, $100 par
Paid-in capital in excess of par: preferred stock
Common stock, $1 stated value
Paid-in capital in excess of stated value: common stock
Retained earnings

The following additional information about Castor Corporation was available for the year ended December 31, Year 4:

(1) There were 2,000,000 shares of preferred stock authorized, of which 1,000,000 were outstanding. All 1,000,000 shares outstanding were issued on January 2, Year 1, for $120 a share. The bank prime interest rate was 17% on January 2, Year 1, and was 20% on December 31, Year 4. The preferred stock is convertible to common stock on a 1 for 1 basis until December 31, Year 10; thereafter, the preferred stock ceases to be convertible and is callable at $100 by the corporation. No preferred stock has been converted to common stock, and there were no dividends in arrears on December 31, Year 4.

(2) The common stock has been issued at amounts above stated value a share since incorporation. Of the 5,000,000 shares authorized, there were 3,500,000 shares outstanding on January 1, Year 4. The market price of the outstanding common stock has increased consistently for the last four years.

(3) The corporation has an employee stock option plan under which certain employees and officers may purchase shares of common stock at 100% of the market price at the grant date. All options are exercisable in installments of one-third each year, commencing one year after the grant date and expire if not exercised within four years of the grant date. On January 1, Year 4, options for 70,000 shares were outstanding at prices ranging from $47 to $83 a share. Options for 20,000 shares were exercised at $47 to $79 a share during Year 4. No options expired during Year 4, and additional options for 15,000 shares were granted at $86 a share during the year. The 65,000 options outstanding on December 31, Year 4, had option prices ranging from $54 to $86 a share; of these, 30,000 were exercisable at that date at prices ranging from $54 to $79 a share.

(4) The corporation also has an employee stock purchase plan under which the corporation pays one-half and the employee pays one-half of the market price of the common stock on the date of the subscription. During Year 4, employees subscribed to 60,000 shares of common stock at an average price of $87 a share. All 60,000 shares were paid for and issued in September, Year 4.

(5) On December 31, Year 4, there was a total of 355,000 shares of common stock set aside for the granting of future stock options and for future purchases under the employee stock purchase plan. The only changes in the stockholders' equity for Year 4 were those described above, net income, and cash dividends declared.

Instructions

a Prepare the stockholders' equity section of the balance sheet of Castor Corporation on December 31, Year 4; substitute, where appropriate, Xs for unknown dollar amounts. Also prepare appropriate notes to the corporation's financial statements.

b Explain how the amount of the denominator should be determined to compute primary earnings per share for presentation in the income statement. Be specific as to the handling of each item. If additional information is needed to determine whether an item should be included or excluded, or the extent to which an item should be included, identify the information needed and how the item would be handled if the information were known. Assume that Castor had substantial net income for the year ended December 31, Year 4.

PROBLEMS

18-1 The stockholders' equity section of DeVos Corporation's balance sheet on December 31, Year 7, is shown below:

Stockholders' equity:

10% preferred stock, $100 par, callable at $104; authorized 50,000	
shares, issued and outstanding 20,000 shares	$2,000,000
Common stock, $5 par; authorized 500,000 shares, issued and out-	
standing 300,000 shares	1,500,000
Paid-in capital in excess of par: preferred stock	70,000
Paid-in capital in excess of par: common stock	1,500,000
Total paid-in capital	$5,070,000
Retained earnings	4,200,000
Total stockholders' equity	$9,270,000

Early in Year 8, the corporation reacquired and retired 3,000 shares of its preferred stock at $99 a share. These shares had been owned by the estate of a deceased stockholder. Shortly thereafter, the remaining 17,000 shares of preferred stock were called for redemption and retired at the established call price. Net income for Year 8 was $863,000; cash dividends of $2 a share were paid on the common stock in Year 8.

Instructions
a Prepare journal entries to record the reacquisition and redemption of the preferred stock.
b Prepare the stockholders' equity section of the balance sheet on December 31, Year 8.

18-2 In Year 8, Solex Corporation issued all shares of its outstanding capital stock at a price of $25 a share. On December 31, Year 11, the balance sheet included the following stockholders' equity section:

Stockholders' equity:

Capital stock, $10 par; authorized 500,000 shares, issued and out-	
standing 200,000 shares	$2,000,000
Paid-in capital in excess of par	3,000,000
Total paid-in capital	$5,000,000
Retained earnings	1,950,000
Total stockholders' equity	$6,950,000

On February 15, Year 12, the corporation reacquired 10,000 shares of its capital stock at $49 a share. On December 9, Year 12, the corporation reissued 5,000 shares of treasury stock for $284,000.

Instructions

a Prepare journal entries to record the two transactions, assuming that treasury stock is recorded at cost.

b Prepare journal entries to record the two transactions, assuming that treasury stock is recorded at par.

18-3 A comparative summary of the stockholders' equity for Moro Corporation, together with certain additional information, is given below:

	Dec. 31, Year 5		**Jan. 1, Year 5**
Stockholders' equity:			
Capital stock, authorized 250,000 shares; issued:			
On Dec. 31, Year 5, 70,000 shares, $8 par (1,000 in treasury)	$560,000		
On Jan. 1, Year 5, 40,000 shares, $10 par			$ 400,000
Stock dividend to be distributed (6,900 shares)	55,200	$ 615,200	
Paid-in capital in excess of par:			
From issuance of capital stock (including $8,000 on Dec. 31, Year 5, from treasury stock transactions)	$808,700		200,000
From issuance of stock dividend	276,000	1,084,700	
Total paid-in capital		$1,699,900	$ 600,000
Retained earnings		1,379,340	1,420,200
Total paid-in capital and retained earnings		$3,079,240	$2,020,000
Less: Treasury stock, 1,000 shares (at cost)		37,000	
Total stockholders' equity		$3,042,240	$2,020,200

In February, Year 5, the board of directors approved a 5 for 4 stock split which reduced the par of the capital stock from $10 to $8 a share. The split was approved by stockholders on March 1 and distributed on March 25. A memorandum entry was used to record the stock split.

On April 1, Year 5, the corporation reacquired 2,000 shares of its capital stock at $37 a share.

On June 30, Year 5, 1,000 shares of treasury stock were reissued at $45 a share.

On July 1, Year 5, 20,000 shares of $8 par capital stock were issued in exchange for the net assets of Holland Company. The market value of the 20,000 shares issued was $760,700.

A cash dividend of $2 a share was declared on December 2, Year 5, payable on December 29, to stockholders of record on December 15; a 10% stock dividend was declared on December 20, to be distributed on January 25, Year 6. The market price of the stock on December 20 was $48 a share. (Debit Retained Earnings to record the cash and stock dividends.)

The net income for Year 5 was $428,340, which included an extraordinary gain of $124,490, net of income tax effect.

Instructions

a Prepare journal entries to record the transactions relating to stockholders' equity that took place during the year ended December 31, Year 5. (Debit Income Summary and Credit Retained Earnings to record net income for Year 5.

b Prepare the lower section of the income statement for the year ended December 31, Year 5, showing operating income and the extraordinary gain. Include earnings per share (rounded to nearest cent) in the income statement, showing supporting computations.

c Prepare a statement of retained earnings for the year ended December 31, Year 5.

18-4 Richmond Corporation is a publicly owned corporation whose shares of common stock are traded on a national stock exchange. On December 31, Year 7, Richmond had 25,000,000 shares of $10 par common stock authorized, of which 15,000,000 shares were issued and 14,000,000 shares were outstanding.

The stockholders' equity accounts on December 31, Year 7, had the following balances:

Common stock, $10 par.	$150,000,000
Paid-in capital in excess of par	80,000,000
Retained earnings	50,000,000
Treasury stock	18,000,000

During Year 8, Richmond completed the following transactions:

(1) On February 1, Year 8, a distribution of 2,000,000 shares of common stock was completed. The stock was issued to the public at $18 a share, net of issuance costs.

(2) On February 15, Year 8, Richmond issued at $110 a share, 100,000 shares of $100 par, 8% cumulative preferred stock with 100,000 detachable stock warrants. Each warrant contained one right which with $20 could be exchanged for one share of Richmond's common stock. On February 15, Year 8, the market price for one warrant was $1.

(3) On March 1, Year 8, Richmond reacquired 20,000 shares of its common stock for $18.50 a share. Richmond uses the cost method to account for treasury stock.

(4) On March 15, Year 8, when the common stock was trading for $21 a share, a major stockholder donated 10,000 shares of common stock, which appropriately was recorded as treasury stock.

(5) On March 31, Year 8, Richmond declared a cash dividend on common stock of $0.10 a share, payable on April 30, Year 8, to stockholders of record on April 10, Year 8. The applicable state law prohibits cash dividends on treasury stock.

(6) On April 15, Year 8, when the market price of the stock warrants was $2 each and the market price of the common stock was $22 a share, 30,000 warrants were exercised. Richmond used unissued shares of common stock to settle the transaction.

(7) On April 30, Year 8, employees exercised 100,000 options that were granted in Year 6 under a noncompensatory stock option plan. Each option entitled the employee to purchase one share of common stock for $20 a share. On April 30, Year 8, the market price of the common stock was $23 a share. Richmond used unissued shares of common stock to settle the transaction.

(8) On May 31, Year 8, when the market price of the common stock was $20 a share, Richmond declared a 5% stock dividend, distributable on July 1, Year 8, to stockholders of record on June 1, Year 8. The applicable state law pro-

hibits stock dividends on treasury stock. (Credit Common Stock account at date of declaration of the stock dividend.)
(9) On June 30, Year 8, Richmond reissued the 20,000 shares of treasury stock reacquired on March 1, Year 8, and an additional 280,000 treasury shares costing $5,600,000 that were on hand at the beginning of the year. The reissuance price was $25 a share.
(10) On September 30, Year 8, Richmond declared a cash dividend on common stock of $0.10 a share and the yearly dividend on preferred stock, both payable on October 30, Year 8, to stockholders of record on October 10, Year 8. The applicable state law prohibits cash dividends on treasury stock.
(11) On December 31, Year 8, the remaining outstanding stock warrants expired.
(12) Net income for Year 8 was $25,000,000.

Instructions   Prepare a working paper to summarize, for each transaction, the changes in Richmond's stockholders' equity accounts for Year 8. The columns of the working paper should have the following headings:

Date
Common Stock—Number of Shares
Common Stock—Amount
Preferred Stock—Number of Shares
Preferred Stock—Amount
Common Stock Warrants—Number of Rights
Common Stock Warrants—Amount
Paid-in Capital in Excess of Par
Retained Earnings
Treasury Stock—Number of Shares
Treasury Stock—Amount

Show supporting computations.

18-5   Selected data summarizing the earnings performance of Jacoby Corporation for a five-year period are presented below (all amounts are in thousands):

	Year 5	Year 4	Year 3	Year 2	Year 1
Operating income.	$64,120	$38,680	$84,480	$69,940	$47,200
Bond interest expense.	5,200	5,200	9,100	10,400	10,400
Income before income taxes . .	$58,920	$33,480	$75,380	$59,540	$36,800
Income taxes expense	24,400	15,000	37,040	28,940	15,140
Net income	$34,520	$18,480	$38,340	$30,600	$21,660
Number of shares of common stock outstanding at end of year.	13,000	18,000	15,000	12,500	6,250
12%, $100 par preferred stock; number of shares outstanding at end of year.	60	70	80	90	100

Late in December of each of the five years, the corporation called 10,000 shares of its preferred stock, paying the call price of 102 plus the final quarter's dividends. During Year 2 the corporation split its common stock 2 for 1, and in Year 4 it issued a 20% common stock dividend. On October 1, Year 3, $2\frac{1}{2}$ million shares of common stock were issued for cash. On July 1, Year 5, the corporation reacquired 5 million shares of common stock from a major stockholder who was unhappy with corporate earnings. The corporation plans to use the treasury stock for business combinations. There were no common stock equivalents outstanding during the five-year period.

Instructions Earnings per share of common stock for the five-year period are to be reported on a comparable basis in the corporation's annual report for Year 5. Compute the earnings per share data which should be reported in the Year 5 annual report for each of the five years, rounded to the nearest cent.

18-6 Beaconsfield, Inc., was organized in May, Year 7, with 3,000,000 authorized shares of $10 par common stock, and 300,000 shares of its common stock were issued for $3,300,000 on May 15, Year 7. Net income through December 31, Year 7, was $125,000.

On July 3, Year 8, Beaconsfield issued 500,000 shares of common stock for $6,250,000. A 5% common stock dividend was declared on October 2, Year 8, and issued on November 6, Year 8, to stockholders of record on October 23, Year 8. The market price of the common stock was $11 a share on the declaration date. Beaconsfield's net income for the year ended December 31, Year 8, was $350,000.

During Year 9, Beaconsfield completed the following transactions:

(1) In February, Beaconsfield reacquired 30,000 shares of its common stock for $9 a share. Beaconsfield uses the cost method to account for treasury stock.

(2) In June, Beaconsfield reissued 15,000 shares of treasury stock for $12 a share.

(3) In September, each common stockholder was issued warrants (for each share owned) for one stock right to purchase two additional shares of common stock for $13 a share. The rights expire on December 31, Year 9.

(4) In October, warrants for 250,000 stock rights were exercised when the market price of the common stock was $14 a share.

(5) In November, warrants for 400,000 stock rights were exercised when the market price of the common stock was $15 a share.

(6) On December 15, Year 9, Beaconsfield declared its first cash dividend, $0.20 a share, payable on January 10, Year 10, to common stockholders of record on December 31, Year 9.

(7) On December 21, Year 9, in accordance with the applicable state law, Beaconsfield retired 10,000 shares of treasury stock and restored it to the status of unissued common stock. The market price of the common stock was $16 a share on this date.

Net income for Year 9 was $750,000.

Instructions Prepare a working paper to summarize all transactions affecting the Common Stock (shares and dollar amounts), Paid-in Capital in Excess of Par, Retained Earnings, and Treasury Stock (shares and dollar amounts) accounts, and the amounts that would be included in Beaconsfield's balance sheet on December 31, Year 9, as a result of the foregoing information. Show supporting computations.

18-7 On February 1, Year 6, the financial vice president of Achica Corporation requested you to compute comparative earnings per share data for the two years ended December 31, Year 4 and Year 5, for inclusion in the corporation's annual report for Year 5. Your working papers include the following information:

(1) Income statements show net income as follows: Year 4, $5,760,000; Year 5, $4,800,000.

(2) On January 1, Year 4, there were outstanding 200,000 shares of $5 par common stock and 20,000 shares of 12% $100 par convertible preferred stock. The preferred stock had been issued at par. Each share of preferred stock is

initially convertible to 2.5 shares of common stock, to be adjusted for any stock dividends and splits. The market price of common stock has ranged from $45 to $60 a share during the past two years. The bank prime interest rate was 11% at the time the preferred stock was issued.

(3) On December 31, Year 4, a 20% stock dividend was distributed to common stockholders. On this date, the market price of the common stock was $50 a share.

(4) In June, Year 5, the common stock was split 2 for 1.

(5) Cash dividends are paid on the preferred stock on June 30 and December 31. Preferred stock dividends were paid in each year; none of the preferred stock has been converted to common stock.

Instructions

a (1) Prepare a working paper to compute the number of shares of common stock outstanding on December 31, Year 4 and Year 5.

(2) Prepare a working paper to compute the equivalent number of shares of common stock outstanding for each year for the computation of primary earnings per share. *Equivalent shares* means the number of shares outstanding in Year 4 and Year 5 in terms of the present capital structure.

(3) Prepare a working paper to compute the equivalent number of shares of common stock outstanding for each year for the computation of fully diluted earnings per share.

b Prepare the lower section of the income statement, showing primary and fully diluted earnings per share for Year 4 and Year 5.

18-8 The controller of Osaka Corporation has requested your assistance in the determination of net income, primary earnings per share, and fully diluted earnings per share for presentation in the corporation's income statement for the year ended September 30, Year 5. As currently determined, the corporation's net income is $2,100,000 for the year ended September 30, Year 5. The controller has indicated that the net income amount might be adjusted for the following transactions which were recorded by debits or credits directly to the Retained Earnings account. (The amounts are net of applicable income taxes.)

(1) The sum of $1,875,000, applicable to a breached Year 1 contract, was received as a result of a lawsuit. Prior to the award, legal counsel was uncertain as to the outcome of the suit.

(2) A gain of $1,500,000 was realized on the sale of the corporation's only subsidiary.

(3) A special inventory write-off of $750,000 was made, of which $625,000 applied to goods manufactured prior to October 1, Year 4.

Your working papers include the following data for the year ended September 30, Year 5:

(1) Common stock (on October 1, Year 4, stated value $10, authorized 300,000 shares; effective December 1, Year 4, stated value $5, authorized 600,000 shares):

Balance, Oct. 1, Year 4—issued and outstanding, 60,000 shares.
Dec. 1, Year 4—60,000 shares issued in a 2 for 1 stock split.
Dec. 1, Year 4—280,000 shares (stated value $5) issued for cash at $39 a share.

(2) Treasury stock—common:

Mar. 1, Year 5—acquired 40,000 shares at $38 a share.
Apr. 1, Year 5—reissued 40,000 shares at $40 a share.

(3) Series A warrants (each warrant was exchangeable at any time with $60 for one share of common stock; effective December 1, Year 4, when the stock was split 2 for 1, each warrant became exchangeable for two shares of common stock at $30 a share):

Oct. 1, Year 4—25,000 warrants issued at $6 each.

(4) Series B warrants (each warrant is exchangeable with $40 for one share of common stock):

Apr. 1, Year 5—20,000 warrants authorized and issued at $10 each.

(5) First mortgage bonds, 11%, due Year 20 (nonconvertible; priced to yield 10% when issued):

Balance Oct. 1, Year 4—authorized, issued and outstanding, face amount of $1,400,000.

(6) Convertible debentures, 13.6%, issued in Year 4 and due in Year 24 (each $1,000 debenture was convertible at any time until maturity to 15 shares of common stock; effective December 1, Year 4, the conversion ratio became 30 shares of common stock for each debenture as a result of the 2 for 1 stock split):

Oct. 1, Year 4—authorized and issued at face amount of $12,000,000.

The following table shows market prices for the corporation's securities and the bank prime interest rate for selected dates:

	Price (or rate) on			Average for year ended Sept. 30, Year 5
	Oct. 1, Year 4	Apr. 1, Year 5	Sept. 30, Year 5	
Common stock.	60	40*	$36\frac{1}{4}$*	$37\frac{1}{2}$*
First mortgage bonds, 11%	$88\frac{1}{2}$	87	86	87
Convertible debentures, 13.6% . . .	100	120	119	115
Series A warrants	6	22	$19\frac{1}{2}$	15
Series B warrants	0	10	9	$9\frac{1}{2}$
Bank prime interest rate	16%	$15\frac{1}{2}$%	15%	$15\frac{1}{2}$%

* After 2 for 1 stock split.

Instructions

a Show how net income should be presented in Osaka Corporation's income statement for the year ended September 30, Year 5.

b Assuming that net income of Osaka Corporation for the year was $2,800,000 and that that there were no extraordinary items, prepare a working paper to compute (1), the primary earnings per share and (2) the fully diluted earnings per share which should be presented in Osaka's income statement for the year ended September 30, Year 5. A supporting working paper showing the numbers of shares to be used in these computations also should be prepared. (Because of the relative stability of the market price of the common stock, the annual average market price may be used where appropriate in your computations. Assume an income tax rate of 50%. Round earnings per share amounts to the nearest cent.)

18-9 The stockholders' equity section of Tishomingo Corporation's balance sheet on December 31, Year 5, is presented on page 770.

Stockholders' equity:

$2 cumulative convertible preferred stock ($25 par; authorized 1,600,000 shares, issued 1,400,000, converted to common 750,000, and outstanding 650,000 shares. Involuntary liquidation value, $30 a share, aggregating $19,500,000)	$16,250,000
Common stock ($0.25 par; authorized 15,000,000 shares, issued and outstanding 8,800,000 shares)	2,200,000
Paid-in capital in excess of par	32,750,000
Total paid-in capital	$51,200,000
Retained earnings.	40,595,000
Total stockholders' equity	$91,795,000

Included among the liabilities of Tishomingo were 11% convertible debentures issued at the face amount of $20,000,000 in Year 4. The debentures are due in Year 24, and until then are convertible to the common stock of Tishomingo at the rate of 50 shares of common stock for each $1,000 debenture. To date, none of the debentures has been converted.

On April 2, Year 5, Tishomingo issued 1,400,000 shares of convertible preferred stock at $40 a share. Quarterly dividends to December 31, Year 5, were paid on the preferred stock. The preferred stock is convertible to common stock at the rate of two shares of common for each share of preferred. On October 1, Year 5, 150,000 shares and on November 1, Year 5, 600,000 shares of the preferred stock were converted to common stock.

On July 2, Year 4, Tishomingo granted options to its officers and key employees to acquire 500,000 shares of the corporation's common stock at a price of $20 a share.

During Year 5, dividend payments and average market prices of Tishomingo Corporation's common stock were as follows:

	Dividends a share	Average market price a share	Closing market price at end of quarter
First quarter	$0.10	$28	$30
Second quarter	0.15	24	27
Third quarter	0.10	22	23
Fourth quarter	0.15	26	25
Average for the year		25	

Assume that the bank prime interest rate was 14% throughout Year 4 and Year 5, that Tishomingo Corporation's net income for the year ended December 31, Year 5, was $48,500,000, and that the income tax rate was 50%.

Instructions

a Prepare a working paper to show the common stock equivalency status of the (1) convertible debentures, (2) convertible preferred stock, and (3) stock options.

b Prepare a working paper to show for Year 5 the computation of:
   (1) The weighted-average number of shares of common stock for the computation of primary earnings per share
   (2) The weighted-average number of shares of common stock for the computation of fully diluted earnings per share

c Prepare a working paper to show for Year 5 the computation to the nearest cent of:
   (1) Primary earnings per share
   (2) Fully diluted earnings per share

18-10 Slick, Inc., was formed on July 3, Year 4. It was authorized to issue 500,000 shares of $5 par common stock and 100,000 shares of 10%, $10 par, cumulative and nonparticipating preferred stock. Slick adopted a July 1–June 30 fiscal year.

The following information relates to the stockholders' equity accounts of Slick.

30,000 shares of preferred stock were issued at $10 a share on June 30, Year 5.

Prior to the year ended June 30, Year 7, Slick had 160,000 shares of outstanding common stock, issued as follows:

(1) 145,000 shares were issued for cash on July 5, Year 4, at $20 a share.
(2) 10,000 shares were exchanged on August 1, Year 4, for land which had cost the seller $70,000 in Year 1 and which had an estimated current fair value of $130,000 on August 1, Year 4.
(3) 5,000 shares were issued on March 1, Year 6; the shares had been subscribed at $32 a share on October 31, Year 5.

During the year ended June 30, Year 7, the following transactions involving common stock were completed:

October 1, Year 6 Subscriptions were received for 10,000 shares at $40 a share. Cash of $80,000 was received in full payment for 2,000 shares, and stock certificates were issued. The remaining subscriptions for 8,000 shares were to be paid in full by September 30, Year 7, at which time the certificates were to be issued.

December 1, Year 6 Slick purchased 5,000 shares of its common stock on the open market at $38 a share. Slick uses the cost method of accounting for treasury stock.

December 15, Year 6 Slick declared a 5% stock dividend for stockholders of record on January 10, Year 7, to be issued on January 31, Year 7. Slick's common stock was selling at $45 a share on December 15, Year 6.

June 24, Year 7 Slick reissued for $108,000, one-half (2,500 shares) of the treasury stock which it had acquired on December 1, Year 6.

Slick has followed a program of declaring cash dividends in June and December, with payments being made to stockholders of record in the following month. The cash dividends which have been declared since formation of the corporation are summarized below:

Declaration date	Preferred stock	Common stock
Dec. 15, Year 5	$0.50 a share	$0.10 a share
June 15, Year 6	0.50 a share	0.10 a share
Dec. 15, Year 6	0.50 a share	None
June 15, Year 7	0.50 a share	None

On June 30, Year 6, Slick's Retained Earnings account had a credit balance of $1,260,000. For the year ended June 30, Year 7, Slick reported net income of $62,000.

Instructions

a Prepare journal entries to record all transactions affecting stockholders' equity completed during the year ended June 30, Year 7, except for payment of cash dividends. (Record all dividends by a debit to the Retained Earnings account.)

b Prepare the stockholders' equity section of the balance sheet on June 30, Year 7. Show supporting computations.

MORE COMPLEX ACCOUNTING TOPICS

19 ACCOUNTING FOR PENSION PLANS

Pension plans are a prominent feature of employment contracts between most business enterprises and their employees. Amounts accumulated in *private* (nongovernmental) pension funds in the United States are almost staggering. A knowledge of the accounting and disclosure requirements relating to pension plans is essential to students of accounting.

Nature of pension plans

Most medium and large business enterprises incur continuing obligations under employee pension plans. A *pension plan* is a contract between the enterprise and its employees whereby the enterprise agrees to pay benefits to employees after their retirement. In some cases employees contribute to a pension fund; however, most enterprises bear the full cost of a pension plan. Ordinarily, pension benefits consist of monthly payments to employees after retirement and additional payments on death or disability. Pension plans generally are formal; an enterprise's practice of paying retirement benefits to selected employees in amounts determined on a case-by-case basis does not constitute a pension plan.[1]

Pension plans are an integral part of a business enterprise's employment contract with employees, and may be established for one or more of the following reasons:

1 To meet requests from employees and labor unions
2 To increase employee morale and productivity, and to reduce employee turnover
3 To fulfill one of the social responsibilities of business enterprises

Pension plans generally are designed to meet federal income tax requirements of a "qualified plan." A *qualified plan* has the following tax features: (1) The employer's contributions to the pension fund (within certain limits) are deductible for federal income tax purposes; (2) earnings on pension fund assets are not subject to federal income tax; and (3) only the benefits received by retired employees generally represent taxable income to them.

[1] *APB Opinion No. 8,* "Accounting for the Cost of Pension Plans," AICPA (New York: 1966), p. 68.

Assets of all private and public pension funds amounted to nearly $700 billion at the end of 1978 and are expected to continue growing at a fast rate. Assets of private pension funds have been growing much faster than total assets of corporations, and pension expense has been rising much faster than corporate earnings. As a result, accounting for pension costs has become one of the most important topics in financial accounting.

Funded and unfunded pension plans

A **funded pension plan** requires the business enterprise to make periodic payments to a funding agency (a designated trustee or an outside agency such as an insurance company). The process of making payments to the funding agency is known as **funding.** Funding may be accomplished through an **insured plan** with a life insurance company or through a **trust fund plan.** Under an insured plan, individual policies providing death and retirement benefits may be purchased for each employee. Alternatively, a group annuity contract may be purchased by the business enterprise. Under a trust fund plan, the enterprise makes periodic contributions to a trustee that invests the fund assets and pays benefits to employees. If a pension plan is not administered by a funding agency, or if assets are informally set aside for the payment of pensions, the plan is designated as **unfunded.** Most pension plans of business enterprises in the United States are either fully or partially funded.

Prior to the Pension Reform Act of 1974 (ERISA), an enterprise could assume the obligation for pension benefits without establishing a pension fund. However, under ERISA, all current pension costs must be funded. For pension plans which existed on January 1, 1974, past service pension costs must be fully funded in 40 years or less, and past service pension costs that arise after that date must be funded in 30 years or less.

Basic accounting for pension plans

To illustrate the basic accounting for pension plans, assume that (1) the pension expense for Napier Corporation for the current year amounts to $200,000, (2) Napier pays $200,000 to the funding agency (funded plan only), and (3) retired employees are paid $50,000. Journal entries required to record this information appear on page 777.

The periodic contributions to the pension fund (or funding agency) made by an enterprise may not equal the amount currently recorded as pension expense. If the contribution to the pension fund is less than the amount debited to pension expense, the difference is recorded as a liability; if the contribution exceeds the amount debited to pension expense, the difference may be debited to a previously recorded liability or

Journal entries to record pension expense and payments for funded plan and unfunded plan

Transactions	Funded plan	Unfunded plan

Recognition of pension expense for current year.	Pension Expense 200,000
	    Cash 200,000
		Pension Expense . 200,000
		    Liability un-
		    der Pen-
		    sion Plan 200,000

Payment of benefits to retired employees during current year.	None (Funding agency makes payment directly to retired employees)	Liability under Pension Plan . . 50,000 Cash 50,000

to a deferred pension cost account. On this point, **APB Opinion No. 8** stated:[2]

> The difference between the amount which has been charged against income and the amount which has been paid [to a fund or funding agency] should be shown in the balance sheet as accrued or prepaid pension cost. If the company has a legal obligation for pension cost in excess of amounts paid or accrued, the excess should be shown in the balance sheet as both a liability and a deferred charge.

General accounting guidelines for pension plans

Accountants are faced with three significant issues relating to pension plans. These are listed below:

1 **Timing** the recognition of pension costs **as expenses** in measuring periodic net income, particularly when pension plans cover employees who have already worked a number of years for the business enterprise at the time the plans are adopted

2 **Measuring the amount** of pension expense and any related deferred pension cost or accrued pension liability that should be included in the balance sheet

3 **Presenting** significant information relating to pension plans in the financial statements and in notes to the financial statements

The measurement of pension costs involves numerous complexities, including the application of compound interest concepts, estimation of the life expectancy of employees, determination of the age of employees at retirement, future level of interest rates, probable employee turnover, gains and losses on pension fund investments, future salary levels of employees, pension benefits to be paid, and vesting provisions under the pension plan. These complexities, combined with the long-range nature of pension plans, cause significant uncertainties as to the amount of pension benefits ultimately to be paid and the amount of periodic pension expense to be recorded currently.

[2] Ibid., p. 74.

Pension costs and the related costs of administering a pension plan should be allocated to expense under the accrual basis of accounting. The amount of periodic expense should not be left to the whims of management. Ideally, the total pension cost relating to a particular employee should be recorded as expense during the working years of the employee. All employees who may reasonably be expected to receive benefits under a pension plan should be included in the computation of the periodic pension expense, with appropriate recognition of employee turnover rates.

The computation of periodic pension cost is more complex for a defined benefit pension plan than for a defined contribution pension plan. Under a **defined benefit pension plan,** the basis for computation of pension benefits for retired employees usually involves employee compensation and years of service. Under a **defined contribution pension plan,** the annual contribution of the employer is identified, typically as a percentage of employer earnings or employees' salaries, and pension cost usually is measured by the amount of the annual contribution.

AICPA and FASB pronouncements on pension plans

In 1965 the Accounting Principles Board of the AICPA published **Accounting Research Study No. 8,** "Accounting for the Cost of Pension Plans."[3] A year later, **APB Opinion No. 8** was issued to provide guidelines for the measurement of periodic pension costs and for reporting relevant pension plan information in financial statements.

The enactment of ERISA led to the issuance of **FASB Interpretation No. 3,** "Accounting for the Cost of Pension Plans Subject to the Employee Retirement Income Security Act of 1974." Later, concerned about increased uncertainties in the pension environment caused by high interest rates, persistent inflation, and the aging United States population, the FASB undertook a study of accounting for defined benefit pension plans themselves and accounting by employers for pensions. **FASB Statement No. 35,** "Accounting and Reporting by Defined Benefit Pension Plans," and **FASB Statement No. 36,** "Disclosure of Pension Information," were issued in 1980 as a result of the FASB's study. In the remainder of this chapter, we consider the principal provisions of **APB Opinion No. 8, FASB Interpretation No. 3,** and **FASB Statement No. 36.** The key contents of **FASB Statement No. 35** are presented in the Appendix at the end of this chapter.

Minimum-maximum range for pension cost

APB Opinion No. 8 recognized that different viewpoints exist as to the composition of pension cost, especially the extent to which the current

---

[3] Ernest L. Hicks, *Accounting Research Study No. 8,* "Accounting for the Cost of Pension Plans," AICPA (New York: 1965).

period's pension expense should include the cost of employees' services prior to the adoption of a pension plan. The Opinion specified that the entire cost of benefit payments ultimately to be made should be debited to expense *subsequent* to the adoption or amendment of a plan and that no portion of such cost should be debited directly against retained earnings as a prior period adjustment.[4] The annual provision for pension cost to be included in pension expense should be determined in a consistent manner, and the amount of the provision should be within the following prescribed range:[5]

> *Minimum.* The annual provision for pension cost should not be less than the total of (1) normal cost, (2) an amount equivalent to interest on any unfunded prior service cost, and (3) if indicated [under circumstances discussed below] . . . a provision for vested benefits. . . .

> *Maximum.* The annual provision for pension cost should not exceed the total of (1) normal cost, (2) 10% of the past service cost (until fully amortized), (3) 10% of the amounts of any increases or decreases in prior service cost arising on amendments of the plan (until fully amortized), and (4) interest equivalents . . . on the difference between provisions and amounts funded. The 10% limitation is considered necessary to prevent unreasonably large charges against income during a short period of years.

The APB expressed a preference for a method of measuring periodic pension cost that would include an appropriate portion of past service cost and prior service cost increments. However, any "rational and systematic" method that is applied consistently and that provides for periodic pension expense between the minimum and maximum range was considered acceptable.

The terminology used in the measurement of periodic pension cost within the minimum-maximum range is explained below:

> *Normal cost* The cost of prospective retirement benefits accrued (on the basis of current service credits) during any year is known as *normal cost* (or *current service cost*) of the pension plan. Normal cost generally is determined by actuaries using an acceptable actuarial cost method (see pages 785–787) for each year subsequent to the inception of the pension plan.

> *Past service and prior service costs* The estimated cost of prospective retirement benefits considered to have accrued in the years prior to the adoption of a pension plan is known as *past service cost;* the estimated cost of employee services for years prior to the date of a particular actuarial valuation (including the past service cost) is known as *prior service cost.* Increases or decreases in prior service cost as a result of changes in the contractual provisions of the pension plan are referred to as *prior service cost increments.* (In the summary of components of the provision for pension expense shown on page 781, you can see that the minimum provision for pension expense includes only the interest charge on any unfunded prior service cost; the maximum provision may include 10% (based on the 10-year minimum amortization period allowed for income tax purposes) of the prior service cost. Once the prior service cost is fully amortized, no further consideration is given to such cost in the application of the minimum-maximum guidelines.)

> *Vested benefits* Earned pension benefits that are not contingent on the employee remaining in the service of the employer are known as *vested benefits.*

---

[4] *APB Opinion No. 8,* p. 73.
[5] Ibid., pp. 73–74.

Under some pension plans, the payment of vested benefits begins only when an employee reaches a stated retirement age; in other cases the payment of vested benefits begins when an employee retires. The actuarially computed value of vested benefits on a given date consists of the present value of the sum of (1) the expected benefits to be paid to employees who have retired or who were terminated with vested rights, and (2) the benefits already earned and expected to become payable to active employees. A provision for vested benefits is required only when the pension expense (consisting of normal cost and interest on unfunded prior service cost) does not make a reasonable provision for vested benefits.

Interest equivalents   The purpose of a pension fund is to accumulate amounts needed to pay retirement benefits. The fund generally is accumulated through the (1) periodic contributions by the employer, and (2) the earnings (rent, interest, dividends, etc.—collectively called "interest") on pension fund assets. If the employer's contributions exceed the actuarially determined pension expense, the earnings on the pension fund assets will be greater than required and the employer's future contributions should be correspondingly reduced; however, if the contributions are less than required by actuarial computations, the earnings that otherwise would have been realized on the pension fund assets must be made up in future years.

Under the minimim-maximum guidelines, the annual provision for pension expense should be adjusted by an amount equal to the interest on any difference between pension expense previously recorded and the amounts actually funded. (See amortization and funding tables on pages 783 and 784.)

In the computation of the **minimum** annual pension expense, provision must be made for interest on any unfunded prior service cost (or, in certain cases, on the difference between accounting provisions for normal pension costs and the amounts of normal costs actually funded). In the computation of the **maximum** annual pension expense, provision is made for interest on the unfunded prior service cost under the 10% limitation for such cost; in addition, a provision for interest must be made on the difference, if any, between the cumulative provisions for normal pension costs and the amounts of normal pension costs actually funded.

A summary of the components of the minimum and maximum annual provisions for pension expense appears on top of page 781.

The AICPA's annual surveys of the published annual reports of 600 publicly owned corporations show that a majority of the corporations use the maximum limit to compute annual pension expense.[6] Consequently, we use the maximum limit to illustrate accounting for the cost of a pension plan in the following section.

Accounting for the cost of a pension plan illustrated

Once a pension plan is adopted, actuaries are engaged to determine the present value of past service cost (if any) and to compute the normal cost for the current accounting period using an acceptable actuarial

---

[6] *Accounting Trends & Techniques,* 34th ed., AICPA (New York: 1980), p. 267.

Components of mini-
mum and maximum
annual provisions for
pension expense

Component of annual provision for pension expense	Minimum annual provision for pension expense	Maximum annual provision for pension expense
1 Normal cost	Full amount included	Full amount included
2 Prior service cost (which includes past service cost and prior service cost increments)	Only interest provision on unfunded portion is included	Include no more than 10% until fully amortized
3 Vested benefits	Must be included in certain cases	Not applicable
4 Interest equivalents on the difference be- tween provisions and amounts actually funded	Include (or deduct) in certain cases in con- nection with **3** above	Include (or deduct)

cost method.[7] Management then formulates a policy for the amortization and funding of the past service cost. At this point, it is necessary to
ascertain that the computed amount of pension expense falls between
the minimum-maximum range established by **APB Opinion No. 8.**

To illustrate the journal entries required to record annual pension expense, we shall assume that Penn Company adopted a pension plan at
the beginning of Year 1. Penn plans to fund fully the normal (current)
pension cost, which is estimated at $60,000 a year. A number of em-
ployees have been working for Penn for many years, and independent
actuaries have determined the present value of the liability for past
services of those employees at $210,620. This present value of the past
service cost was determined by the actuaries by the estimation of a
6% annual interest rate.

Example 1. Past Service Cost Amortized and Funded Over Same Period If
management of Penn Company elects to amortize and fund the past service cost of $210,620 over a 15-year period by recognizing the pension
expense and making equal payments to the funding agency **at the end
of each year,** the annual amortization of past service cost and the annual payment to the funding agency are determined as follows:

Pension expense com-
puted by maximum
method: Funding and
past service cost amor-
tization over same
number of years

$$\frac{\text{Present value of past service cost}}{\text{Present value of ordinary annuity of 15 payments of 1 at 6\%}}$$

$$= \frac{\$210,620}{9.712249^*} = \$21,686$$

* See Table 4 in the Appendix in back of the book.

[7] Actuarial cost methods are described on pages 785–787.

The journal entry at the end of each year to record the normal cost of $60,000, the amortization of the past service cost of $21,686, and the payment to the funding agency follows:

Journal entry for pension expense computed by maximum method: Funding and amortization of past service cost over same number of years

Pension Expense (Normal Cost and Past Service Cost) 81,686	
Cash.	81,686
To record annual pension expense (including normal cost of $60,000 and past service cost of $21,686) and payment to funding agency.	

The pension expense of $81,686 is at the maximum of the range permitted by **APB Opinion No. 8,** because no interest equivalent is required when the provision for pension expense is fully funded. Pension expense appears as an additional payroll expense in the income statement. The balance sheet does not include any deferred pension cost or accrued pension liability because the entire current provisions for pension expense are funded at the end of each year. After the past service cost is fully amortized and funded at the end of the fifteenth year, only the normal cost is included in the pension expense recorded and funded each year, as long as there are no actuarial valuations resulting in prior service cost.

Example 2. Past Service Cost Amortized over Period Longer than Funding Period   Although management may elect to *fund* the past service cost over any number of years, the *amortization* of such cost cannot be less than 10 years, or longer than 40 years. In order to minimize the computations in the table on page 783, we assume in this example that Penn Company amortizes the past service cost over a period of eight years and funds past service cost by making five equal payments to the funding agency at the end of each of the first five years. Normal cost of $60,000 is funded in full each year. The annual amortization and funding payments for past service costs are computed below and on top of page 783.

Pension expense computed by maximum method: Amortization of past service cost over longer period than funding of that cost

Amortization:

$$\frac{\text{Present value of past service cost}}{\text{Present value of ordinary annuity of 8 payments of 1 at 6\%}}$$

$$= \frac{\$210,620}{6.209794^*} = \$33,917$$

(cont.)

Payments:

$$\frac{\text{Present value of past service cost}}{\text{Present value of ordinary annuity of 5 payments of 1 at 6\%}}$$

$$= \frac{\$210,620}{4.212364^*} = \underline{\$50,000}$$

See Table 4 in the Appendix in back of the book.

A table showing the computation of the annual past service pension expense (column C) and the deferred pension cost balance (column F) is presented below:

PENN COMPANY

Past Service Cost—Amortization over 8 Years and Funding over 5 Years

Year	Amortization (8 years)			Funding (5 years)	Deferred pension cost	
	(A) Computed annual amount at 6% interest	(B) Interest (6% of previous balance in F)	(C) Debit to Pension Expense (A − B)	(D) Credit to Cash	(E) Increase or (decrease) (D − C)	(F) Asset balance (previous balance ±E)
1	$33,917	$ −0−	$33,917	$50,000	$16,083	$16,083
2	33,917	965	32,952	50,000	17,048	33,131
3	33,917	1,988	31,929	50,000	18,071	51,202
4	33,917	3,072	30,845	50,000	19,155	70,357
5	33,917	4,221	29,696	50,000	20,304	90,661
6	33,917	5,440	28,477	−0−	(28,477)	62,184
7	33,917	3,731	30,186	−0−	(30,186)	31,998
8	33,917	1,919*	31,998	−0−	(31,998)	−0−

Adjusted for $1 discrepancy due to rounding of computations.

Because the payments to the funding agency during the first five years exceed the amount debited to expense, an asset (Deferred Pension Cost) is accumulated and reported in the balance sheet. Starting in Year 2, interest (column B) on the deferred pension cost balance (column F) *reduces* the annual debit to Pension Expense (column C).

Journal entries to record the amortization and funding of the past service cost and the normal cost of $60,000 for Year 1 and for Year 8 are illustrated on page 784.

Year 1	Pension Expense (Normal Cost and Past Service Cost)	93,917	
	Deferred Pension Cost..................	16,083	
	Cash ($60,000 + $50,000).............		110,000
	To record pension expense (including normal cost of $60,000 and past service cost of $33,917) and payment to funding agency.		
Year 8	Pension Expense (Normal Cost and Past Service Cost)	91,998	
	Deferred Pension Cost...............		31,998
	Cash........................		60,000
	To record pension expense (including normal cost of $60,000 and past service cost of $33,917, less interest of $1,919) and payment to funding agency.		

Pension expense for each year (Year 1 through Year 8) is at the maximum permitted by **APB Opinion No. 8.** Keep in mind that **APB Opinion No. 8** does not permit the amortization of past service cost over a period less than 10 years; we have used eight years to minimize the computations in the example.

Example 3. Past Service Cost Amortized over a Period Shorter than Funding Period If the past service cost is amortized over a period shorter than the funding period, a pension liability (column F in the table below) is accumulated during the amortization period; this liability is eliminated

PENN COMPANY						
Past Service Cost—Amortization over 3 Years and Funding over 5 Years						
	Amortization (3 years)			Funding (5 years)	Accrued pension liability	
Year	(A) Computed annual amount at 6% interest	(B) Interest (6% of previous balance in F)	(C) Debit to Pension Expense (A + B)	(D) Credit to Cash	(E) Increase or (decrease) (C − D)	(F) Liability balance (previous balance ±E)
1	$78,795*	$ −0−	$78,795	$50,000†	$28,795	$28,795
2	78,795	1,728	80,523	50,000	30,523	59,318
3	78,795	3,559	82,354	50,000	32,354	91,672
4	−0−	5,500	5,500	50,000	(44,500)	47,172
5	−0−	2,828‡	2,828	50,000	(47,172)	−0−

* $210,620 ÷ 2.673012 (present value of ordinary annuity of 3 payments of 1 at 6% from Table 4 in the Appendix in back of the book) = $78,795.
† Same as in example on page 783.
‡ Adjusted for $2 discrepancy due to rounding of computations.

as payments are made to the funding agency in the years following the past service cost amortization period. Because the funding lags behind the recognition of the expense, interest on the fund deficiency (accrued pension liability) is **added** to determine the annual pension expense. A table illustrating the amortization of the past service cost over a three-year period and the funding of this cost over a five-year period by Penn Company is shown on page 784. Normal cost of $60,000 is funded annually.

Journal entries to record the amortization and funding of the past service cost and the normal cost of $60,000 for Year 1 and for Year 5 are illustrated below:

Journal entries for pension expense computed by maximum method: Amortization of past service cost over shorter period than funding of that cost

Year 1   Pension Expense (Normal Cost and Past Service Cost).   138,795
                    Cash ($60,000 + $50,000).   110,000
                    Liability under Pension Plan   28,795
        To record pension expense (including normal cost of $60,000 and past service cost of $78,795) and payment to funding agency.

Year 5   Pension Expense (Normal Cost and Past Service Cost).   62,828
        Liability under Pension Plan.   47,172
                    Cash   110,000
        To record pension expense (including normal cost of $60,000 and interest of $2,828) and payment to funding agency.

Pension expense for each year (Year 1 through Year 5) is at the maximum permitted by **APB Opinion No. 8.** Again, we should emphasize that the short amortization period was used only to minimize the computations. Attention should be focused on the basic principles involved and not on the amortization period used. In practice, the amortization period for past service cost must equal or exceed 10 years; generally a period of 15 to 30 years is used.

Actuarial cost methods

The annual amount of pension expense is based on one of the acceptable **actuarial cost methods.** The factors used in tentatively resolving uncertainties concerning future events affecting pension expense, such as mortality rates, employee turnover, compensation levels, and earnings (interest) on pension fund assets, are referred to as **actuarial assumptions.** An **actuarial valuation** of a pension plan is made by actuaries using these assumptions to determine the amounts an employer is to contribute to a pension fund. The first step in making an actuarial valuation is to determine on the valuation date the present value of future pension benefits to be paid to employees. An actuarial cost method then is applied to the present value of the future pension benefits to determine the current contributions to be made by the employer.

Although actuarial techniques are used primarily to determine the periodic payments to be made to the pension fund (or funding agency), the same techniques are used to measure periodic pension expense. The amount of the pension expense recorded currently is the present value of future pension benefits that are estimated to have accrued during the current accounting period. Acceptable actuarial cost methods include the **accrued benefit cost method** and several **projected benefit cost methods.**

Accrued Benefit Cost Method   Under the accrued benefit cost method (sometimes called the **unit-credit method**), the amount of pension expense of the current accounting period usually is equal to the present value of the increase in the employees' retirement benefits resulting from the services performed in the current period. Thus, the normal annual pension expense under this method is the present value of the **units** of future pension benefits credited to employees for current services.

Projected Benefit Cost Methods   Under the various projected benefit cost methods, the amount of pension expense of the current accounting period usually represents a level amount that will provide for the total projected retirement benefits over the periods of active service of employees. Four projected benefit cost methods (entry-age-normal method, individual-level-premium method, aggregate method, and attained-age-normal method) may be used. A description of these methods is beyond the scope of this discussion.

In contrast to the two types of actuarial cost methods listed above, the terminal funding and the pay-as-you-go methods are not acceptable. Under the **terminal funding method,** provision (funding and recognition of pension expense) for future pension benefits is made only at the end of an employee's period of active service; under the **pay-as-you-go method,** pension expense is recognized only when pension benefits actually are paid to retired employees. The conclusions in **APB Opinion No. 8** relative to actuarial cost methods are summarized below:[8]

> To be acceptable for determining cost for accounting purposes, an actuarial cost method should be rational and systematic and should be consistently applied so that it results in a reasonable measure of pension cost from year to year. . . . Each of the actuarial cost methods . . . , except terminal funding, is considered acceptable when the actuarial assumptions are reasonable and when the method is applied in conformity with the other conclusions of this

[8] *APB Opinion No. 8*, p. 77.

Opinion. The terminal funding method is not acceptable because it does not recognize pension cost prior to retirement of employees. For the same reason, the pay-as-you-go method (which is not an actuarial cost method) is not acceptable.

Actuarial gains and losses

We have seen that in the measurement of periodic pension expense it is necessary to make numerous assumptions based on estimates of future events. Actual events seldom coincide with previous estimates, and the assumptions concerning the future may become invalid. As a result, periodic adjustments may be required to reflect actual experience and to revise the assumptions to be used in the future. These adjustments are known as *actuarial gains and losses.* Actuaries generally compute the amount of the actuarial gains and losses, and management determines the period of time to be used for recording such gains and losses in the accounting records. Prior to the issuance of *APB Opinion No. 8,* three methods were used: (1) immediate recognition, (2) spreading over the current and future accounting periods, and (3) averaging. *APB Opinion No. 8* considered only the *spreading* and *averaging* methods acceptable:[9]

> The Board believes that actuarial gains and losses, including realized investment gains and losses, should be given effect in the provision for pension cost in a consistent manner that reflects the long-range nature of pension cost. Accordingly, . . . actuarial gains and losses should be spread over the current year and future years or recognized on the basis of an average. . . . Where spreading is accomplished by separate adjustments, the Board considers a period of from 10 to 20 years to be reasonable.

> Actuarial gains and losses should be recognized immediately if they arise from a single occurrence not directly related to the operation of the pension plan and not in the ordinary course of the employer's business. An example of such occurrences is a plant closing, in which case the actuarial gain or loss should be treated as an adjustment of the net gain or loss from that occurrence and not as an adjustment of pension cost for the year.

Illustration of Spreading of Actuarial Gains and Losses On January 2, Year 1, Lambert Corporation initiated a defined benefit pension plan approved by the corporation's stockholders. The actuarial gains and losses computed by Lambert's actuaries at the end of each of the first four years of the pension plan were as follows: Year 1—$10,000 loss; Year 2—$14,000 loss; Year 3—$6,000 gain; Year 4—$9,000 loss. Lambert adopted a policy of spreading actuarial gains and losses over 10 years.

The working paper on top of page 788 shows the amount of actuarial gains and losses to be included in the computation of normal cost for pension expense in each of the four years ended December 31, Year 4.

[9] Ibid., pp. 79–80.

LAMBERT CORPORATION

Spreading of Actuarial Gains and Loses

For Four Years Ended December 31, Year 4

Year ended Dec. 31,	Actuarial (gain) loss	Amount included in normal cost	Amount deferred to future years
Year 1	$10,000	$1,000 (1)	$ 9,000 (2)
Year 2	14,000	2,400 (3)	20,600 (4)
Year 3	(6,000)	1,800 (5)	12,800 (6)
Year 4	9,000	2,700 (7)	19,100 (8)
Totals	$27,000	$7,900	

(1) $10,000 ÷ 10 = $1,000
(2) $10,000 − $1,000 = $9,000
(3) ($10,000 + $14,000) ÷ 10 = $2,400
(4) $9,000 + $14,000 − $2,400 = $20,600
(5) ($10,000 + $14,000 − $6,000) ÷ 10 = $1,800
(6) ($20,600 − $6,000) − $1,800 = $12,800
(7) $27,000 ÷ 10 = $2,700
(8) $27,000 − $7,900 = $19,100

Illustration of Averaging of Actuarial Gains and Losses Assume the same data as in the preceding illustration, except that Lambert Corporation adopted a three-year moving-average method for averaging actuarial gains and losses. Because the *actual* actuarial gains and losses for the first three years are unknown on January 2, Year 1, Lambert must **esti-**

LAMBERT CORPORATION

Averaging of Actuarial Gains and Losses

For Four Years Ended December 31, Year 4

Year ended Dec. 31,	Actuarial (gain) loss	Three-year total	Amount included in normal cost	Amount deferred to future years
Year 1	$10,000	$21,000 (est.)	$ 7,000 (1)	$ 3,000 (2)
Year 2	14,000	21,000 (est.)	7,000 (1)	10,000 (3)
Year 3	(6,000)	18,000 (4)	6,000 (5)	(2,000) (6)
Year 4	9,000	17,000 (7)	5,667 (8)	1,333 (9)
Totals	$27,000		$25,667	

(1) $21,000 ÷ 3 = $7,000
(2) $10,000 − $7,000 = $3,000
(3) ($10,000 + $14,000) − ($7,000 + $7,000) = $10,000
(4) $10,000 + $14,000 − $6,000 = $18,000
(5) $18,000 ÷ 3 = $6,000
(6) $18,000 − ($7,000 + $7,000 + $6,000) = ($2,000)
(7) $14,000 − $6,000 + $9,000 = $17,000
(8) $17,000 ÷ 3 = $5,667
(9) $27,000 − $25,667 = $1,333

mate the total. If Lambert estimated a total actuarial loss of $21,000 for Years 1 through 3, the moving-average method is applied as shown on the bottom of page 788.

Note that as of the end of Year 3, Lambert Corporation abandons the *estimated* three-year total actuarial loss of $21,000 in favor of the *actual* three-year actuarial loss of $18,000. Thereafter, actual three-year total actuarial gains and losses are used.

The Employee Retirement Income Security Act of 1974 (ERISA)

Until 1974, the statutes governing the creation and management of private pension plans and pension fund assets were somewhat vague and ineffective. An administrator theoretically could operate a private pension fund by relying on judgment and intuition rather than on established standards. In order to give more protection to employees covered by private pension plans and to eliminate abuses in the management of such plans, Congress enacted the Employee Retirement Income Security Act of 1974 (ERISA), also known as the Pension Reform Act of 1974. The Act essentially attempted to protect employee pension rights through rigid minimum requirements for funding pension benefits, participation in the plan by employees, vesting of pension benefits, and detailed disclosure of pension plan activities. Under the Pension Reform Act of 1974, administrators of private pension plans are required to file with the Department of Labor annual reports that include a description of the plan, financial statements, and supplementary schedules. Some examples of the type of information that must be included in the annual report filed with the Department of Labor by a pension plan are given below:

1 Statements of plan assets and liabilities and changes in net assets available for the payment of benefits
2 Schedules of (a) plan investments, (b) transactions involving "parties in interest" such as officers and plan fiduciaries, (c) loans in default or exceeding 3% of the value of plan assets, and (d) transactions involving amounts exceeding 3% of the value of plan assets
3 A statement of the assets and liabilities of the trustee, if pension fund assets are held in trust by a bank or an insurance company
4 Statements of salaries, fees, and commissions paid by the plan
5 The number of employees covered by the plan, a periodic actuarial report, and an explanation of any changes of trustee, actuary, independent accountant, administrator, investment advisor, custodian, or insurance company

Shortly after the enactment of the Pension Reform Act of 1974, the FASB issued *FASB Interpretation No. 3,* in which it stated the following conclusions:[10]

[10] *FASB Interpretation No. 3,* "Accounting for the Cost of Pension Plans Subject to the Employee Retirement Income Security Act of 1974 (an interpretation of *APB Opinion No. 8*)," FASB (Stamford: 1974), pp. 1–2.

A fundamental concept of **APB Opinion No. 8** is that the annual pension cost to be charged to expense for financial accounting purposes is not necessarily determined by the funding of a pension plan. Therefore, no change in the minimum and maximum limits for the annual provision for pension cost . . . is required as a result of the Act. Compliance with the Act's participation, vesting, or funding requirements may result, however, in a change in the amount of pension cost to be charged to expense periodically for financial accounting purposes even though no change in accounting methods is made. . . . **APB Opinion No. 8** requires that "the entire cost of benefit payments ultimately to be made should be charged against income subsequent to the adoption or amendment of a plan." Consistent with that requirement and within the minimum and maximum limits . . . of **APB Opinion No. 8,** any change in pension cost resulting from compliance with the Act shall enter into the determination of periodic provisions for pension expense **subsequent** to the date a plan becomes subject to the Act's participation, vesting, and funding requirements. That date will be determined either by the effective dates prescribed by the Act or by an election of earlier compliance with the requirements of the Act.

The FASB also concluded that the Act did not create a legal liability for unfunded pension costs. However, if the employer does not fund the minimum amount required by the Act and does not receive a waiver from the U.S. Secretary of the Treasury, the amount currently required to be funded must be recorded as a liability, with a related debit to pension expense or deferred pension cost. Also, in the event of the termination of a pension plan, any excess of the estimated legal liability over pension fund assets had to be accrued.[11]

Disclosure of pension plans in financial statements

The reporting guidelines for pension plans established by **APB Opinion No. 8** were quite limited in scope, which led some critics to suggest that reporting of pension costs and pension funds in most cases tended to be inadequate, casual, and even misleading. The FASB reacted to this criticism by issuing **FASB Statement No. 36,** "Disclosure of Pension Information," which established the following standards:[12]

The Board believes that pension plans are of sufficient importance to an understanding of financial position and results of operations that the disclosures set forth in this paragraph and (the following) paragraph . . . shall be made in financial statements or the notes thereto:
a A statement that pension plans exist, identifying or describing the employee groups covered
b A statement of the company's accounting and funding policies
c The provision for pension cost for the period
d Nature and effect of significant matters affecting comparability for all periods presented, such as changes in accounting methods (actuarial cost method, amortization of past and prior service cost, treatment of actuarial gains and losses, etc.), changes in circumstances (actuarial assumptions, etc.), or adoption or amendment of a plan

[11] Ibid., pp. 2–3.
[12] *FASB Statement No. 36,* "Disclosure of Pension Information," FASB (Stamford: 1980), pp. 3–4.

For its defined benefit pension plans, an employer shall disclose for each complete set of financial statements the following data determined . . . as of the most recent benefit information date for which the data are available:

a The actuarial present value of vested accumulated plan benefits

b The actuarial present value of nonvested accumulated plan benefits

c The plans' net assets available for benefits

d The assumed rates of return used in determining the actuarial present values of vested and nonvested accumulated plan benefits

e The date as of which the benefit information was determined

The data may be reported in total for all plans, separately for each plan, or in such subaggregations as are considered most useful. For plans for which the above data are not available, the employer shall continue to comply with the disclosure requirements originally contained in **Opinion 8,** namely, the excess, if any, of the actuarially computed value of vested benefits over the total of the pension fund and any balance sheet pension accruals, less any pension prepayments or deferred charges. The reasons why the information required by **a** through **e** above is not provided for those plans shall be disclosed.

Much of the data to be disclosed for defined benefit plans were to be obtained from the reports and financial statements prepared for the plans. The Appendix at the end of this chapter summarizes the reporting requirements for defined benefit plans.

The following illustration of pension plan disclosure is adapted from **FASB Statement No. 36:**[13]

The company and its subsidiaries have several pension plans covering substantially all employees, including certain employees in foreign countries. The total pension expense for Year 1 and Year 2 was $XXX and $XXX, respectively, which includes, as to certain defined benefit plans, amortization of past service cost over XX years. The company makes annual contributions to the plans equal to the amounts accrued for pension expense. A change during Year 2 in the actuarial cost method used in the computation of pension cost had the effect of reducing net income for Year 2 by $XXX. A comparison of accumulated plan benefits and plan net assets for the company's domestic defined benefit plans is presented below:

	Dec. 31, Year 1	Dec. 31, Year 2
Actuarial present value of accumulated plan benefits:		
Vested	$XXX	$XXX
Nonvested	XXX	XXX
Totals	$XXX	$XXX
Net assets available for benefits	$XXX	$XXX

The weighted average assumed rate of return used to determine the actuarial present value of accumulated plan benefits was X% for both Year 1 and Year 2. The company's foreign pension plans are not required to report to certain governmental agencies pursuant to ERISA and do not otherwise determine the actuarial value of accumulated benefits or net assets available for benefits as calculated and disclosed above. For those plans, the actuarially computed value of vested benefits on December 31, Year 1, and on December 31, Year 2, exceeded the total of those plans' pension funds and balance sheet accruals less pension prepayments and deferred charges by approximately $XXX and $XXX, respectively.

[13] Ibid., pp. 7–8.

Deferred compensation contracts

The accrual basis of accounting applicable to pension plans also is applicable to other deferred compensation contracts. Such contracts generally stipulate that employees eligible for benefits must be employed for a specified period and that they should be available for consultation after retirement. The principle for the accrual of deferred compensation expense was formulated by the APB as follows:[14]

> The estimated amounts to be paid under each contract should be accrued in a systematic and rational manner over the period of active employment from the time the contract is entered into, unless it is evident that future services expected to be received by the employer are commensurate with the payments or a portion of the payments to be made. If elements of both current and future services are present, only the portion applicable to the current services should be accrued.

Future outlook for pension accounting

The FASB has on its agenda a consideration of the financial accounting and reporting by employers for pension plans and other postemployment benefits. We may assume that some of the accounting principles for pension plans established by *APB Opinion No. 8* may be modified or superseded. For example, two concerns of the FASB are whether unfunded amounts of past service and prior service costs are long-term liabilities and whether actuarial gains and losses should be expensed immediately rather than being spread or averaged.[15] Guidelines for the determination of liabilities, to be developed as part of the FASB's conceptual framework project (see Chapter 1), should assist in resolving this problem.

In addition, the FASB is concerned with the impact of inflation on accounting for defined benefit pension plans. The FASB found that several major U.S. corporations had increased the benefits paid to retired employees in recent years to offset the impact of inflation.[16] The question to be resolved is whether the cost of such increased benefits should be allocated to prior, current, or future accounting periods. After dealing with these and other problems of *single-employer* plans, the FASB plans to consider the issues involved in *multiple-employer* plans, in which a number of companies whose employees belong to a single union enter into a pension contract with that union.[17]

---

[14] *APB Opinion No. 12,* "Omnibus Opinion—1967," AICPA (New York: 1967), p. 189.

[15] *FASB Discussion Memorandum: An Analysis of Issues Related to Employers' Accounting for Pension and Other Postemployment Benefits,* FASB (Stamford: 1981), pp. i–ii.

[16] Ibid., p. 22. See also, *Forbes,* "Can You Measure the Unknowable?" (March 17, 1980, p. 160).

[17] Ibid., p. 5. See also, *Forbes,* "More Hidden Liabilities," (March 2, 1981, pp. 66–67).

APPENDIX: ACCOUNTING PRINCIPLES FOR DEFINED BENEFIT PENSION PLANS

Accounting principles for defined benefit pension plans were established by **FASB Statement No. 35,** "Accounting and Reporting by Defined Benefit Pension Plans." The following discussion summarizes the principal provisions of **FASB Statement No. 35.**[18]

The providing of financial information useful for assessing a pension plan's present and future ability to pay pension benefits when due is the primary objective of the financial statements of the plan. To that end, generally accepted accounting principles are appropriate for pension plans, in addition to accounting standards specified for the plans in **FASB Statement No. 35.** The annual financial statements of a pension plan include the following:

1 Statement of net assets available for benefits
2 Statement of changes in net assets available for benefits
3 Statement of accumulated plan benefits
4 Statement of changes in accumulated plan benefits

The information presented in the first and third financial statements above may be combined in a single statement of accumulated plan benefits and net assets available for plan benefits. Similarly, a single statement of changes in accumulated plan benefits and net assets available for plan benefits may present all the information included in the second and fourth financial statements above.

Statement of net assets available for benefits

The accrual basis of accounting is appropriate for the statement of net assets available for benefits. Typical assets of a pension plan are investments in equity and debt securities and real estate, carried at current fair value; receivables for employees' contributions, investments sold, and accrued interest and dividends; operating assets such as buildings and equipment; and cash.

A unique asset of a pension plan is a contract with an insurance company. Such a contract may be allocated or unallocated. Under an **allocated contract,** the pension plan's payments to the insurance company are used to purchase immediate or deferred annuities for plan participants (current and former employees and others for whom benefits have accumulated under the plan). Under an **unallocated contract,** the payments to the insurance company are accumulated in a fund used to pay benefits or to purchase annuities when employees retire.

In the statement of net assets available for benefits, contracts with insurance companies are presented in the same manner as they are re-

---

[18] *FASB Statement No. 35,* "Accounting and Reporting by Defined Benefit Pension Plans." FASB (Stamford: 1980).

ported to governmental agencies under the Pension Reform Act of 1974, even though the pension plan is not subject to those reporting requirements. Under that Act, unallocated contracts may be measured either at current fair value or at **contract value,** an amount determined by the insurance company.

The accounts payable and accrued liabilities of a pension plan are deducted from the total plan assets to determine the net assets available for benefits. Thus, the statement of net assets available for benefits does not have an ownership equity section.

Statement of changes in net assets available for benefits

In the statement of changes in net assets available for benefits, the net assets available for plan benefits at the beginning of the year are increased by the total of the following:

Investment income (including net appreciation in current fair value of investments), net of investment expenses

Contributions from employer and employees, and state subsidies or federal grants

Deductions in this statement include benefits paid directly to participants, payments to insurance companies for purchases of annuity contracts, and administrative expenses. The resultant balance represents the net assets available for benefits at the end of the year.

Statement of accumulated plan benefits

The statement of accumulated plan benefits presents the total actuarial present value of the following plan benefits:

Vested benefits of participants currently receiving payments
Other vested benefits
Nonvested benefits

Because determination of end-of-year plan benefits cannot always be accomplished by a plan's actuaries on a timely basis, the information in the statement of plan benefits may be presented at the beginning of the plan year. If beginning-of-year amounts are presented, the statements of net assets and changes in net assets must be expanded to include both beginning-of-year and end-of-year amounts.

Statement of changes in accumulated plan benefits

The statement of changes in accumulated plan benefits reconciles the actuarial present value of plan benefits at the beginning and at the end of the plan year. Minimum disclosure in this statement includes significant effects of items such as the following:

Amendments to the pension plan

Changes in the nature of the pension plan

Changes in actuarial assumptions

Benefits accumulated

Increase in interest due to a decrease in the discount period assumed by actuaries

Benefits paid

Additional disclosures in financial statements or notes

FASB Statement No. 35 specified a number of additional disclosures in the financial statements of a pension plan or in the accompanying notes. Among these disclosures, included in the significant accounting policies of the plan, are the actuarial assumptions used to determine the actuarial present value of accumulated plan benefits.

REVIEW QUESTIONS

1 Define a *pension plan* and explain the difference between a *funded plan* and an *unfunded plan.*

2 What funding requirements for pension costs were introduced in the Pension Reform Act of 1974?

3 What are the three main issues relating to the accounting for pension plans?

4 The total cost of contributions that must be paid ultimately to provide pensions for the present participants in a plan cannot be determined precisely in advance; however, reasonably accurate estimates can be made by the use of actuarial techniques. List some of the factors entering into the determination of the ultimate cost of a funded pension plan.

5 Differentiate between a *defined benefit pension plan* and a *defined contribution pension plan.*

6 What is the purpose of the *minimum* and *maximum* limits established by the Accounting Principles Board to measure the annual provision for pension expense?

7 Define each of the following in relation to the measurement of annual pension expense:
a Normal cost
b Past service cost, including amortization policy
c Vested benefits
d Interest equivalents

8 Under what circumstances is a Deferred Pension Cost account used in the accounting for a pension plan?

9 What purpose is served by *actuarial cost methods* in the measurement of pension expense? List two categories of actuarial cost methods that are considered acceptable for financial accounting purposes.

10 Define **terminal funding** and **pay-as-you-go** methods of meeting an enterprise's pension obligations. Why are these methods not considered acceptable?

11 Explain what is meant by **actuarial gains and losses** and describe the treatment of such gains and losses in the measurement of the annual provision for pension expense.

12 What were the major objectives of the Pension Reform Act of 1974 (ERISA)?

13 List some examples of the type of information required to be disclosed in the annual report of a pension plan under the Pension Reform Act of 1974 (ERISA).

14 What information about an enterprise's pension plans should be disclosed in its financial statements, according to **FASB Statement No. 36?**

EXERCISES

Ex. 19-1   Select the best answer for each of the following multiple-choice questions:

1 Which of the following costs is not a part of the defined maximum for pension cost determination?
  a Normal cost
  b Provision for vested benefits
  c Interest on overfunding
  d 10% of prior service costs

2 Cottle Corporation was established in Year 1. In Year 2, it adopted a pension plan for its employees. On January 2, Year 2, the past service cost was determined to be $500,000. Cottle had elected to amortize past service cost over 10 years and to fund past service cost over 15 years. The past service cost of $500,000 on January 2, Year 2, should be accounted for as a debit to:
  a Prior accounting periods as a prior period adjustment
  b Expense in Year 2
  c Expense ratably from Year 2 through Year 11
  d Expense ratably from Year 2 through Year 16

3 In which of the following instances must the accrual of a pension plan's past service cost be reduced for interest presumed earned?
  a When past service cost has been fully accrued prior to funding
  b When pension expense exceeds the maximum allowable accrual
  c When past service cost has been fully funded prior to accrual
  d When interest presumed earned on previously accrued past service cost exceeds interest presumed earned on unaccrued past service cost

4 The vested benefits of an employee in a pension plan represent:
  a Benefits to be paid to the retired employee in the current year
  b Benefits to be paid to the retired employee in subsequent years
  c Benefits accumulated in the hands of an independent trustee
  d Benefits that are not contingent on the employee's continuing in the service of the employer

5 The past service cost in a pension plan:
  a Is debited to expense in the year of the inception of the pension plan
  b Is funded in the year of the inception of the pension plan
  c Represents the pension cost assigned to years prior to the current balance sheet date
  d Represents the pension cost assigned to years prior to the inception of the pension plan

6 *APB Opinion No. 8* set minimum and maximum limits on the annual provision for pension cost. An amount that is always included in the computation of both the minimum and the maximum limit is:

a Amortization of past service cost

b Normal cost

c Interest on unfunded past and prior service costs

d Retirement benefits paid

7 In accounting for the cost of pension plans, an acceptable actuarial cost method for financial accounting purposes is:

a Pay-as-you-go

b Terminal funding

c Entry-age-normal

d Turnover

8 The maximum annual provision for pension cost permitted is normal cost, plus:

a 10% of past service cost (until fully amortized)

b A provision for vested benefits

c 10% of past service cost (until fully amortized), plus 10% of any increases or decreases in prior service cost arising on amendments of the plan, plus interest equivalents on the difference between provisions and amounts funded

d Interest equivalents on any unfunded prior service cost, plus a provision for the excess of the actuarially computed value of vested benefits over the total of the pension fund if such excess is not at least 5% less than the comparable excess at the beginning of the year

Ex. 19-2 Crosby Corporation adopted a pension plan in Year 1 on a funded basis. Crosby elected to amortize past service costs over 12 years and to fund past service costs over 10 years. Normal costs were to be funded each year as incurred. The following data reflect both amortization and funding of past service cost for Year 1 and Year 2:

	Year 1	*Year 2*
12-year amortization	$100,000	$100,000
Reduction for interest	–0–	835
Past service cost	100,000	99,165
10-year funding	113,909	113,909
Balance sheet —deferred charge:		
Balance at end of year	13,909	28,653
Increase during year	13,909	14,744

a Assuming normal cost for Year 1 was $70,000, compute pension expense for Year 1.

b Assuming normal cost for year 2 was $75,000, prepare a journal entry to record pension expense and funding for Year 2.

Ex. 19-3 On May 1, Year 1 (the beginning of a fiscal year), Portland Company instituted a defined benefit pension plan. Portland adopted a policy of spreading actuarial gains and losses over 10 years. For the first three years of the pension plan, Portland's actuarial gains and losses were as follows:

Year ended April 30,	*Actuarial (gain) loss*
Year 2	$18,000
Year 3	22,000
Year 4	(11,000)

Prepare a working paper to compute the amount of actuarial gains and losses to be included in Portland's normal cost for pension expense in each of the three years ended April 30, Year 4. Show supporting computations.

Ex. 19-4 Early in Year 10, Narva Company adopted a pension plan for its employees that was to be administered by a funding agency. Unfunded past service cost was determined to be $3 million; this amount was to be paid to the funding agency in 10 annual payments of $400,000, starting on December 31, Year 10. The past service cost was to be amortized over a 20-year period; the amortization for Year 10 was computed at $265,000. Normal cost of the pension plan for Year 10 of $222,500 was remitted to the funding agency on December 31, Year 10.

Prepare a journal entry to record the foregoing information at the end of Year 10.

Ex. 19-5 Wilkes Company has a contributory pension plan for all its employees. In Year 5, a total of $150,000 was withheld from employees' salaries and deposited in a pension fund administered by an outside trustee. In addition, Wilkes deposited $200,000 cash in the fund in Year 5. Based on the report of outside actuaries that was received in December, Year 5, the actuarial cost of the pension plan for Year 5 was $333,000. As a result of this report, Wilkes deposited $60,000 cash in the fund on January 12, Year 6.

Compute the amount of pension expense to be included in Wilkes Company's income statement for Year 5.

Ex. 19-6 The information given below relates to the past service cost of Allen Company at the beginning of Year 1, when a pension plan was adopted:

Past service cost to be amortized over 10 years and funded over 20

    years $1,104,015

Annual payments at 6% sufficient to pay a debt of $1,104,015 over 10

    years   150,000

Annual payments at 6% sufficient to pay a debt of $1,104,015 over 20

    years   96,253

Prepare a partial table (similar to the one illustrated on page 784) summarizing the amortization and funding of the past service cost for the first two years of the pension plan.

Ex. 19-7 Using the data in the partial table prepared in **Exercise 19-6,** prepare journal entries for Years 1 and 2 and indicate the information that would appear in the balance sheet at the end of Year 2 relative to the past service cost.

SHORT CASES FOR ANALYSIS AND DECISION

Case 19-1 The board of directors of Strong Steel Corporation is meeting to discuss the possibility of closing the corporation's outmoded plant in Clay City and concentrating production in modern facilities in Bryanville. In a discussion of losses and expenses to be incurred in such a shutdown, a director asked the controller how pension plan unamortized prior service cost attributable to employees terminated as a result of the plant closing would be reflected in Strong's financial statements for the year of the plant closing. The controller replied that the unamortized prior service cost could be amortized and funded over the time periods originally established for such costs, because the same pension plan covered employees at both the Clay City and the Bryanville plants. The director commented that generally accepted accounting principles should not be so flexible that undepreciated cost of the abandoned Clay City plant assets would have to be written off as a loss, while the unamortized prior service cost for terminated employees could be expensed over future years.

Instructions Do you agree with the controller of Strong Steel Corporation? Alternatively, do you believe that unamortized prior service costs attributable to employees terminated as a result of the plant closing should be written off as a loss? Explain.

Case 19-2 Cleary Products, Inc., established a defined benefit pension plan on January 2, Year 1, to provide retirement benefits for all employees. The plan is noncontributory and is funded through a trustee, First National Bank, which invests all funds and pays all benefits as they become due. Vesting occurs when the employee retires at age 70. Past service cost of $110,000 is being amortized over 15 years and funded over 10 years on a present value basis at 5%. Cleary also funds an amount equal to current normal cost, net of actuarial gains and losses. There have been no amendments to the plan since inception.

The independent actuary's report on June 30, Year 4, follows:

CLEARY PRODUCTS, INC.
Defined Benefit Pension Plan
Actuary's Report
June 30, Year 4

Current year's funding and pension cost

Normal cost (before adjustment for actuarial gains) computed by the entry-age-normal method		$ 34,150
Actuarial gains:		
Investment gains (losses):		
Excess of expected dividend revenue over actual dividend revenue		$ (350)
Gain on sale of investments		4,050
Gains in actuarial assumptions for:		
Mortality		3,400
Employee turnover		5,050
Reduction in pension cost from closing of plant		8,000
Net actuarial gains		$ 20,150
Normal cost (funded currently)	$14,000	$ 14,000
Past service cost:		
Funding	14,245	
Amortization		10,597
Total funded	$28,245	
Total pension expense in income statement		$ 24,597

Fund assets

Cash		$ 4,200
Dividends receivable		1,525
Investment in common stocks, at current fair value		162,750
Total fund assets		$168,475

(cont.)

Actuarial liability

Number of employees	46
Number of employees retired	0
Yearly earnings of employees	$598,000
Actuarial liability	$145,000

Actuarial assumptions

Interest	5%
Mortality (Year 1 Group Annuity Tables)	
Retirement	Age 70

Instructions On the basis of requirements for accounting for the cost of pension plans, evaluate the (1) treatment of actuarial gains and losses, and (2) computation of pension expense for income statement purposes. Ignore income tax considerations and requirements of ERISA.

Case 19-3 Generally accepted accounting principles require that pension costs be measured by the accrual basis of accounting. The various components of pension expense include (but are not limited to) **normal cost, past service cost, prior service cost,** and **interest.**

Instructions Define each of the four terms designated above, and discuss how each of the costs is accounted for under generally accepted accounting principles.

Case 19-4 On January 2, Year 8, the board of directors of Columbus Company approved the establishment of a pension plan for all employees. The pension is payable to employees when they reach age 70 if they have had three or more years of continuous service with the company. All current employees are eligible; thus, past service cost must be amortized over an appropriate number of years, starting in Year 8. Columbus was organized early in Year 1.

A summary of the employees on January 2, Year 8, who are eligible to participate in the pension plan is presented below:

Number of employees	Years of service as of Jan. 2, Year 8
20	7
18	6
32	5
25	4
40	3
45	2
20	1
200	

A partial list of benefits to be paid to retired employees on the basis of average annual earnings and the number of years of employment appears below:

Average annual earnings	Monthly pension benefits based on years of employment		
	3 years	10 years	25 years
$21,000	$ 60	$240	$ 720
24,000	80	320	960
27,000	100	400	1,200
32,000	120	480	1,440

Columbus plans to amortize and fund any past service cost over a 10-year period.

Instructions

a List some assumptions that would have to be made by Columbus Company to compute the liability for past service cost on January 2, Year 8.

b List some additional facts that would be required by Columbus Company to compute the liability for past service cost on January 2, Year 8.

c In reference to the 200 employees on January 2, Year 8, what factors might cause normal cost of Columbus Company's pension plan for Year 13 to increase over the normal cost for Year 8? What factors might cause the normal pension cost in Year 13 to be less than the normal pension cost in Year 8?

PROBLEMS

19-1 Rogers, Inc., a calendar-year corporation, adopted a funded pension plan at the beginning of Year 4. The independent actuaries for Rogers used an appropriate actuarial cost method to determine its normal annual pension cost for Year 4 and Year 5 as $15,000 and $16,000, respectively, which amounts were paid in the same years.

The actuarially determined past service cost was funded on December 31, Year 4, at an amount computed correctly at $106,000. The past service cost was to be amortized at the maximum amount permitted by generally accepted accounting principles. The interest factor assumed by the actuaries was 6%.

Instructions Prepare journal entries to record the funding of the past service cost on December 31, Year 4, and the pension expense for Years 4 and 5. Round all amounts to the nearest dollar.

19-2 Cranston Corporation initiated a defined benefit pension plan on January 2, Year 1. During the first five years of the plan, actuarial gains and losses were computed by Cranston's actuaries as follows: Year 1—$24,000 gain; Year 2—$12,000 loss; Year 3—$16,000 gain; Year 4—$32,000 gain; Year 5—$8,000 loss.

Instructions

a Assume that Cranston adopted a policy of spreading actuarial gains and losses over 10 years. Prepare a working paper to show the amount of actuarial gains and losses to be included in the computation of normal cost for Cranston's pension expense in each of the five years ended December 31, Year 5.

b Assume that Cranston adopted a four-year moving average method for averaging actuarial gains and losses, and that Cranston estimated total actuarial gains of $52,000 for Years 1 through 4. Prepare a working paper to show the amount of actuarial gains and losses to be included in the computation of normal cost for Cranston's pension expense in each of the five years ended December 31, Year 5.

19-3 Wheeler Chemicals, Inc., fully funds the normal cost portion of its pension expense. When the company started its pension plan early in Year 1, it adopted a 10-year amortization period and a 12-year funding period for the past service cost of $400,000. The data on top of page 802 relate to the pension plan for Years 1–3.

	Year 1	Year 2	Year 3
Normal cost	$102,000	$104,900	$118,100
Past service cost:			
Amortization on 10-year basis	65,098	65,098	65,098
Interest at 10% on accrued pension liability	–0–	639	1,343
Annual payments to funding agency	58,705	58,705	58,705

Instructions

a Prepare journal entries to record the pension expense for the three-year period. Record normal and past service costs in a single Pension Expense account.

b Compute the amount of the accrued pension liability on December 31, Year 3.

19-4 Atlas, Incorporated, adopted a pension plan early in Year 4 and has regularly funded the full amount of its normal cost. At the time the pension plan was adopted, the past service cost amounted to $1,472,020. The company has been amortizing the past service cost over a 15-year period and depositing $200,000 annually with a funding agency. The annual deposits are intended to provide an amount, plus interest at 6%, at the end of 10 years to enable the funding agency to pay the accrued past service pension liability when employees retire. Pertinent pension plan data for Year 6 and Year 7 are presented below:

	Year 6	Year 7
Normal cost	$376,200	$424,500
Past service cost:		
Amortization on 15-year basis	151,564	151,564
Interest at 6% of deferred pension cost	5,987	9,252
Annual payments to funding agency	200,000	200,000

Instructions

a Prepare journal entries to record the pension expense for Year 6 and Year 7. Record normal and past service costs in a single Pension Expense account.

b Compute the balance in the Deferred Pension Cost account at the end of Year 7. (Hint: Remember that the plan was adopted in Year 4.)

19-5 Regis Company adopted a pension plan effective January 2, Year 5. Actuaries had determined that the past service cost applicable to employees who were included in the pension plan was approximately $1,869,330. The company arranged to fund the past service cost by making 10 equal payments to a funding agency at the end of each year, starting December 31, Year 5. The fund earns interest at 5% a year, and past service cost is amortized over a 20-year period.

Instructions

a Compute the annual amortization amounts and the annual payments to the funding agency. The present value of an ordinary annuity of 20 annual payments of 1 at 5% is 12.462210; the present value of an ordinary annuity of 10 annual payments of 1 at 5% is 7.721735. Round computations to the nearest dollar.

b Prepare a partial amortization and funding table (similar to the table illustrated on page 783) for the first four years of the pension plan.

c Prepare journal entries for Year 5 and Year 6 to record the amortization and funding of the past service cost.

19-6 Colby Corporation adopted a pension plan early in Year 5. The plan was to be administered by an insurance company and stipulated that the payments by Colby to the insurance company would consist of three parts as follows:

(1) Annual payments of $10,000 beginning on January 2, Year 5, and ending on January 2, Year 14, covering the past service cost for qualified employees. These payments are to be adjusted periodically by mutual agreement because of changes in pension benefits to be paid to employees or because of termination of employees whose rights are forfeited. An interest rate of 6% a year was used to compute the amount of the annual payments.

(2) Payments for normal cost based on the number of employees, their birth dates, and the earnings rate that the insurance company is able to earn on the pension fund investments. These payments will be based on payroll data for the latest year and will be paid in two installments as follows: $23,000 on June 30 of each year and the balance (as determined on December 31 of each year) on January 5 of the following year.

(3) Payments for supplemental adjustments agreed upon by the insurance company and Colby.

The payments made to the insurance company during the first three years of the pension plan are listed below:

	Past service cost	Normal cost	
Year	Jan. 2	Jan. 5	June 30
5	$10,000	$ −0−	$23,000
6	10,000	27,010	23,000
7	10,000	29,460	23,000

Payments by the insurance company to retired employees for the first three years were: Year 5, $7,390; Year 6, $9,177; and Year 7, $12,380.

The management of Colby Corporation considers the past service cost to be a legal obligation and wishes to follow the requirement of **APB Opinion No. 8** regarding the accounting for this cost, that is, "If the company has a legal obligation for pension cost in excess of amounts paid or accrued, the excess should be shown in the balance sheet as both a liability and a deferred charge." Normal cost is accrued only at the end of the fiscal year, which is the calendar year.

Instructions

a Prepare a partial amortization and funding table for the past service cost for Year 5 and Year 6. Assume that the present value of the 10 annual payments of $10,000 each, beginning on January 2, Year 5, and earning interest at 6% a year, is $78,017. Colby records $10,000 in the Pension Expense account each year.

b Prepare journal entries for Colby relating to the pension plan for Year 5 and Year 6.

c How should the information relating to the pension plan appear in the balance sheet of Colby on December 31, Year 6?

19-7 Actuaries have estimated the past service cost on the date Loomis Corporation adopted its pension plan at $1,578,846. The actuaries estimated that 6% is a reasonable earnings rate on fund investments. Loomis plans to amortize the past service cost over 20 years, and to fund it over the next 30 years. The equal annual payment that will amortize $1,578,846 over 20 years at 6% is $137,650 ($1,578,846 ÷ 11.470, present value of 1 a year for 20 years at 6%); over 30 years it is $114,700 ($1,578,846 ÷ 13.765, present value of 1 a year for 30 years at 6%). The partial table on top of page 804 has been prepared.

Year	(A) 20-year amorti-zation at 6%	(B) Interest (6% of previous balance in E)	(C) Debit to Pension Expense (A + B)	(D) 30-year funding	(E) Accrued Pension Liability account*
1	$137,650	$ –0–	$137,650	$114,700	$ 22,950
2	137,650	1,377	139,027	114,700	47,277
20	137,650	46,461	184,111	114,700	844,203
21	–0–	50,652	50,652	114,700	780,155
29	–0–	12,617	12,617	114,700	108,208
30	–0–	6,492	6,492	114,700	–0–

* The previous year's balance in the Accrued Pension Liability account plus the difference between the pension expense and the payment to the funding agency for the current year.

Instructions

a Prepare journal entries to record the amortization and the funding of past service cost for Years 1, 2, 21, and 30.

b Assuming the same liability for past service cost ($1,578,846), amortization over 30 years, and funding over 20 years, the following partial table has been prepared:

Year	(A) 30-year amorti-zation at 6%	(B) Interest (6% of previous balance in E)	(C) Debit to Pension Expense (A − B)	(D) 20-year funding	(E) Deferred Pension Cost account*
1	$114,700	$ –0–	$114,700	$137,650	$ 22,950
2	114,700	1,377	113,323	137,650	47,277
20	114,700	46,461	68,239	137,650	844,203
21	114,700	50,652	64,048	–0–	780,155
29	114,700	12,617	102,083	–0–	108,208
30	114,700	6,492	108,208	–0–	–0–

* The previous year's balance in the Deferred Pension Cost account plus the difference between the payment to the funding agency and the pension expense for the current year.

Prepare journal entries to record the amortization and the funding of past service cost for Years 1, 2, 21, and 30.

c Explain the balance of $844,203 in the Deferred Pension Cost account at the end of Year 20 as presented in part b of the problem. (Hint: The present value of an ordinary annuity of 10 rents of 1 at 6% = 7.3601.)

(Adapted from Deloitte Haskins & Sells CPA Preparation Course)

20 ACCOUNTING FOR LEASES

The accounting for leasing transactions has been a challenging problem for accountants for many years. Leasing as a means of acquiring the use of plant assets has grown in popularity and complexity as a result of capital shortages and income tax considerations.

Plant assets may be acquired by outright purchase or by rental of the assets under a lease contract. Lease contracts are an important means of obtaining the use or financing the acquisition of almost any kind of property, ranging from office machines to factory buildings.

In some cases, a business enterprise constructs or buys property, sells it to an investor, and simultaneously leases the property from the investor in a **sale-leaseback transaction.** In other cases, an enterprise leases existing property or property constructed to its specifications. An enterprise that leases property for use in its operations may agree to pay certain **executory costs** (such as property taxes, insurance, and maintenance) incident to use of the property.

Numerous standards were developed by the APB to help accountants identify leases of similar economic substance so that they may be reported in a consistent and meaningful manner.[1] The FASB issued **Statement No. 13,** "Accounting for Leases," which superseded all previous official pronouncements for lease accounting. Subsequently, the FASB amended **Statement No. 13** in seven additional Statements and issued six interpretations of **Statement No. 13.** All these pronouncements then were integrated in **Accounting for Leases: FASB Statement No. 13 as Amended and Interpreted through May 1980.**[2]

Nature of leases

A **lease** is a contract conveying the right to use property, usually for a stated period of time. The owner of the property for which the right is transferred is known as the **lessor,** and the party to whom the right is transferred is known as the **lessee.** A further transfer of the right to use an asset from a lessee to another party during the term of the lease is known as a **sublease.**

---

[1] See *APB Opinion No. 5*, "Reporting of Leases in Financial Statements of Lessee," AICPA (New York: 1964); *APB Opinion No. 7*, "Accounting for Leases in Financial Statements of Lessors," AICPA (New York: 1966); *APB Opinion No. 27*, "Accounting for Lease Transactions by Manufacturer or Dealer Lessors," AICPA (New York: 1972); *APB Opinion No. 31*, "Disclosure of Lease Commitments by Lessees," AICPA (New York: 1973).
[2] *Accounting for Leases: FASB Statement No. 13 as Amended and Interpreted through May 1980*, FASB (Stamford: 1980).

Thus, the problem of accounting for leases is twofold—accounting by lessors and accounting by lessees. Lessors must report the transfer of rights to use property which they own, and lessees must account for and disclose the fact that they are paying for rights to use property that they do not own. If all lease contracts were identical, the accounting for and disclosure of leases would be simple. However, the accounting is complicated by the fact that contracts which are in essence sales transactions may be structured as leases; other contracts provide for the lease to be converted to a sale transaction at a later date, usually at the option of the lessee. Although a simple model does not exist which can be used to identify a given transaction as a lease or a sale, a set of guidelines has been developed that can be used to analyze each transaction and to determine the appropriate accounting for it. The remainder of this chapter is devoted to a discussion and illustration of these guidelines.

Terminology for leases

As do many other specialized areas, leasing has its own language. This short summary of the terminology used for leases should be useful in understanding the accounting and reporting issues involved in leasing transactions:[3]

1 *Bargain purchase option*   A provision giving the lessee a right to purchase leased property at a price so favorable that exercise of the option appears virtually assured at the inception of the lease.

2 *Bargain renewal option*   A provision giving the lessee a right to renew a lease at a rental so favorable that exercise of the option appears assured at the inception of the lease.

3 *Contingent rentals*   Increases or decreases in lease payments after the inception of a lease and resulting from changes in factors on which lease payments are based.

4 *Estimated economic life of leased property*   The estimated remaining period during which the leased property is expected to be usable for the purpose for which it was designed, with normal repairs and maintenance, without being limited by the lease term.

5 *Estimated residual value of leased property*   The estimated fair value of the leased property at the end of the lease term. The portion of the estimated residual value that is not guaranteed by the lessee or by a third party unrelated to the lessor is known as the **unguaranteed residual value.**

6 *Fair value of leased property*   In a sales-type lease, the fair value is the normal selling price of the leased property adjusted for any unusual market conditions. In a direct financing-type lease, the cost or carrying amount of the property and the fair value should be the same at the inception of a lease, unless substantial time has passed since the lessor acquired the property.

7 *Inception of lease*   Date of the lease contract or commitment, if earlier.

8 *Incremental borrowing rate*   The rate that, at the inception of the lease, the lessee would have incurred to borrow the funds necessary to purchase a leased asset.

[3] Adapted from *Accounting for Leases,* pp. 219–226.

9 *Initial direct costs* Those costs (such as commissions, legal fees, and costs of processing documents) incurred by a lessor that are directly associated with negotiating and completing a lease contract.

10 *Interest rate implicit in the lease (lessor's implicit interest rate)* The discount rate (applied to the minimum lease payments and any unguaranteed residual value) that causes the aggregate present value to be equal to the fair value of leased property to the lessor, minus any investment tax credit retained by the lessor.

11 *Lease term* The fixed noncancelable term of a lease plus (1) any periods covered by bargain renewal options, (2) any periods for which failure to renew a lease places a heavy penalty on the lessee, (3) any periods covered by renewal options during which a guarantee by the lessee of the lessor's debt related to leased property is expected to be in effect, (4) any periods covered by renewal options which precede the exercise date of a bargain purchase option, and (5) any periods during which the lessor has a right to renew or extend a lease. However, in no case shall the lease term extend beyond the date a bargain purchase option becomes exercisable.

12 *Minimum lease payments* The payments that the lessee is obligated to make or can be required to make; such payments include (1) the minimum periodic rentals up to the date of a bargain purchase option, (2) any guarantee by the lessee of residual value, (3) any payment on failure to renew or extend a lease, and (4) the payment required by a bargain purchase option. Executory costs (such as insurance, maintenance, and property taxes in connection with the leased property) are excluded from minimum lease payments.

13 *Renewal or extension of lease* The continuation of a lease contract beyond the original lease term, including a new lease for the same property with the same lessee.

ACCOUNTING BY LESSEES

Leases are classified for accounting purposes by lessees as either capital leases or operating leases. **Capital leases** are those possessing characteristics of a purchase, and **operating leases** are those covering the use of an asset for a portion of its economic life. The concept of the capital lease is derived from the view that a lease that transfers to the lessee most of the risks and benefits of property ownership should be accounted for by the lessee as the acquisition of an asset and the incurrence of an obligation.[4] In other words, the substance of the leasing transaction is given greater weight than its form.

Criteria for capital lease

If a lease meets any *one* of the following criteria at its inception, it must be capitalized by the lessee:[5]

1 The lease transfers ownership of the leased property to the lessee by the end of the lease term.

2 The lease contains a bargain purchase option.

[4] *Accounting for Leases,* p. 67.
[5] Ibid., pp. 10–11.

3 The lease term is equal to 75% or more of the estimated economic life of the leased property.

4 The present value of the minimum lease payments is at least 90% of the fair value of the leased property.

If the beginning of the lease term falls within the last 25% of the total estimated economic life of the leased property, the last two criteria are not used. To compute the present value of the minimum lease payments, the lessee enterprise uses its incremental borrowing rate, unless **(a)** the lessee can learn the lessor's implicit interest rate, and **(b)** the lessor's implicit interest rate is less than the lessee's incremental borrowing rate. If both these conditions are met, the lessee uses the lessor's implicit interest rate.

Computation of amount capitalized by lessee

The lessee records a capital lease as both an asset and an obligation in the amount equal to the present value of the minimum lease payments during the lease term. However, if the computed present value exceeds the fair value of the leased asset at the inception of the lease, the **amount capitalized is the fair value of the asset.**[6] A leased asset should never be capitalized at an amount in excess of its fair value at the inception of the lease. The lease payments capitalized exclude any executory costs to be paid by the lessor. If the capital lease transfers ownership of the asset to the lessee or if the lease contains a bargain purchase option, the asset is depreciated over its economic life in the same manner as other assets owned by the lessee. Other capital leases are treated similarly, but the depreciation period for the lessee is the period covered by the lease. At the end of the lease term, an amount equal to any residual value to the lessee remains in the leased asset account.

Periodic payments other than contingent rentals made by the lessee are allocated between a reduction of the lease obligation and interest expense. This allocation produces a constant periodic rate of interest on the carrying amount of the lease obligation. Contingent rentals are included in the lessee's expenses as they accrue. Assets and obligations recorded under capital leases are reported as separate items in the lessee's balance sheet, and the obligation is segregated between current and noncurrent amounts.

Illustration of lessee's accounting for a capital lease

Data for Illustration On January 2, Year 1, Lee Company, the lessee, entered into an equipment lease with Lore Corporation having the following provisions:

[6] Ibid., pp. 12–13.

(1) The lease has a fixed noncancelable term of 30 months, with rent of $270 payable at the beginning of each month, starting January 2, Year 1. There are no contingent rental provisions.

(2) The lessee guarantees a residual value of $4,000 at the end of 30 months, when Lore Corporation takes possession of the equipment.

(3) The lessee pays executory costs separately to the lessor, and is to receive any excess of selling price of the equipment over the guaranteed residual value at the end of the lease term.

(4) The lease is renewable periodically based on a schedule of rentals and guarantees of the residual values, which decrease over time.

Other relevant information is as follows:

(1) Lore Corporation's interest rate implicit in the lease is 12% a year (1% a month); Lore has informed Lee Company of this rate. Lee's incremental borrowing rate is 15% a year ($1\frac{1}{4}$% a month).

(2) The lessor's cost of the leased equipment is $10,006; this is also the lessor's fair value at the inception of the lease, January 2, Year 1.

(3) The estimated economic life of the equipment is 60 months; the lessee depreciates owned equipment on a straight-line basis.

(4) The residual value at the end of the lease term is estimated to be $4,000, the amount guaranteed by the lessee.

(5) On July 2, Year 3, the end of the lease term, the equipment is sold by the lessor for $4,200 to a third party.

(6) The fiscal years for the lessee and the lessor end on December 31.

Computations and Classification of the Lease   The minimum lease payments for the lessee are computed as follows:

Minimum rental payments over the lease term ($270 × 30 months). . . .	$ 8,100
Add: Lessee's guarantee of the residual value at the end of the lease term	4,000
Total minimum lease payments	$12,100

Minimum lease payments by lessee

The lease does not meet the first three criteria on pages 807–808. The lease does not transfer ownership to the lessee by the end of the lease term; the lease does not contain a bargain purchase option; and the lease term (30 months) is not equal to 75% or more of the estimated economic life of the equipment (60 months). However, the fourth criterion on page 808 **is met.**

The present value of the minimum lease payments, computed with the lessor's implicit interest rate (because it is less than the lessee's incremental borrowing rate and is known to the lessee), exceeds 90% of the fair value of the equipment at the inception of the lease. Thus, the **lessee classifies the lease as a capital lease.** The present value computations, using the lessor's implicit interest rate of 1% a month, are presented below:

Monthly lease rentals: $270 × present value of annuity due of 30 rents of 1 at 1%: $270 × 26.065785*	*$ 7,038*
Add: Residual value guarantee by lessee: $4,000 × present value of 1 discounted for 30 periods at 1%: $4,000 × 0.741923*	*2,968*
Total present value of minimum lease payments	*$10,006*
Fair value of equipment at inception of lease	*$10,006*
Present value of minimum lease payments as a percentage of fair value of equipment	*100%*

* See Appendix in back of the book.

Journal Entries The journal entries in the accounting records of the lessee for the first two monthly payments, depreciation at the end of the first year, and the disposal of the equipment at the end of the lease term (July 2, Year 3) are illustrated below and on page 811. The related ledger accounts (except Cash), showing all journal entries for the lease during Year 1, appear on pages 811–812. (The lessor accounts for this lease as a direct financing lease, which is discussed on pages 822–823.)

LEE COMPANY (lessee)
Journal Entries

Year 1			
Jan. 2	*Leased Equipment—Capital Lease*	*10,006*	
	Obligation under Capital Lease (net)		*10,006*
	To record capital lease at inception of lease.		
2	*Obligation under Capital Lease (net)*	*270*	
	Cash.		*270*
	To record lease payment for first month.		
Feb. 2	*Interest Expense [($10,006 − $270) × 0.01]*	*97*	
	Obligation under Capital Lease (net) ($270 − $97) .	*173*	
	Cash.		*270*
	To record lease payment for second month.		
Dec. 31	*Depreciation Expense [($10,006 − $4,000) × $\frac{12}{30}$(1)]* .	*2,402*	
	Leased Equipment—Capital Lease		*2,402*
	To record depreciation expense (straight-line method)		
	for first year of lease.		

(1) 30-month term of lease is used for depreciation because the lease does not transfer ownership of the equipment to the lessee and does not contain a bargain purchase option.

Dec. 31 *Interest Expense ($7,739 × 0.01)*. *77*
                 Accrued Interest Payable *77*
         To record accrued interest on lease obligation on Dec.
         31, Year 1. (See below for computation of $7,739 bal-
         ance in Obligation under Capital Lease account.)

Year 3
July 2 *Cash* *200*
         Obligation under Capital Lease (net) *4,000*
                 Leased Equipment—Capital Lease *4,000*
                 Gain on Disposal of Leased Equipment. *200*
         To record lessor's sale of leased equipment at amount
         $200 in excess of guaranteed residual value and
         liquidation of obligation under capital lease.

Lessee's ledger accounts for capital lease

Leased Equipment—Capital Lease

Date	Explanation	Debit	Credit	Balance
Year 1				
Jan. 2	Capital lease at inception	10,006		10,006 dr
Dec. 31	Depreciation for Year 1		2,402	7,604 dr

Obligation under Capital Lease (net)

Date	Explanation	Debit	Credit	Balance
Year 1				
Jan. 2	Capital lease at inception		10,006	10,006 cr
2	First lease payment	270		9,736 cr
Feb. 2	($270 − $97 interest)	173		9,563 cr
Mar. 2	($270 − $96 interest)	174		9,389 cr
Apr. 2	($270 − $94 interest)	176		9,213 cr
May 2	($270 − $92 interest)	178		9,035 cr
June 2	($270 − $90 interest)	180		8,855 cr
July 2	($270 − $89 interest)	181		8,674 cr
Aug. 2	($270 − $87 interest)	183		8,491 cr
Sept. 2	($270 − $85 interest)	185		8,306 cr
Oct. 2	($270 − $83 interest)	187		8,119 cr
Nov. 2	($270 − $81 interest)	189		7,930 cr
Dec. 2	($270 − $79 interest)	191		7,739 cr

(cont.)

Accrued Interest Payable

Date	Explanation	Debit	Credit	Balance
Year 1 Dec. 31	Accrued interest for Dec.		77	77 cr

Depreciation Expense

Date	Explanation	Debit	Credit	Balance
Year 1 Dec. 31	[($10,006 − $4,000) × $\frac{12}{30}$]	2,402		2,402 dr

Interest Expense

Date	Explanation	Debit	Credit	Balance
Year 1				
Feb. 2	($9,736 × 0.01)	97		97 dr
Mar. 2	($9,563 × 0.01)	96		193 dr
Apr. 2	($9,389 × 0.01)	94		287 dr
May 2	($9,213 × 0.01)	92		379 dr
June 2	($9,035 × 0.01)	90		469 dr
July 2	($8,855 × 0.01)	89		558 dr
Aug. 2	($8,674 × 0.01)	87		645 dr
Sept. 2	($8,491 × 0.01)	85		730 dr
Oct. 2	($8,306 × 0.01)	83		813 dr
Nov. 2	($8,119 × 0.01)	81		894 dr
Dec. 2	($7,930 × 0.01)	79		973 dr
31	($7,739 × 0.01)	77		1,050 dr

In the January 2, Year 1, journal entry to record the lease, the Obligation under Capital Lease account was credited with the **present value** of the minimum lease payments during the lease term. This **net method** of accounting by lessees was illustrated in **FASB Statement No. 13.**[7] As an alternative, the Obligation under Capital Lease account might be credited for the $12,100 total of the minimum lease payments, as follows:

Lessee's journal entry to record capital lease obligation at *gross* amount

Year 1		
Jan. 2	Leased Equipment—Capital Lease 10,006	
	Deferred Interest on Capital Lease 2,094	
	Obligation under Capital Lease (gross).	12,100
	To record capital lease at inception of lease.	

[7] Ibid., p. 84.

This **gross method** is consistent with the accounting for deferred payment contracts illustrated in Chapter 11 (page 451). If the lease obligation were recorded in this manner, the journal entry for the **second month's** lease payment would be:

(page 451)

Lessee's journal entry to record lease payment under the gross method

Year 1			
Feb. 2	Interest Expense.	97	
	Obligation under Capital Lease (gross)	270	
	Deferred Interest on Capital Lease		97
	Cash		270
	To record lease payment for second month.		

The credit to the Leased Equipment—Capital Lease account in the December 31, Year 1, journal entry for depreciation is in accordance with the illustration in **FASB Statement No. 13.** Alternatively, an Accumulated Depreciation account might be used, as for owned equipment.

Had the lessee elected on July 2, Year 3, to renew the lease, the renewal would be treated as a new lease extending to the date of the next renewal option. The lessee would compare the present value of the minimum lease payments (rent and guarantee of any residual value) over the renewal period with the $4,000 fair value of the equipment to the lessor at the inception of the new lease. Although the fair value of the equipment at July 2, Year 3, is $4,200, the proceeds from sale of the equipment, the value accruing to the lessor is limited to $4,000, the amount guaranteed by the lessee.

Lessee's accounting for operating leases

Leases that do not qualify as capital leases are accounted for as **operating leases** by the lessee; that is, the lease is **not capitalized,** and periodic lease payments usually are recorded by debits to the Rent Expense account. If an operating lease requires rent to be paid other than in equal periodic amounts, the Rent Expense account should be debited on a straight-line basis unless another method would be more representative of the benefits derived from use of the leased property.[8]

Sale-leaseback transactions

In certain cases an owner of an asset sells it and immediately leases it back from the purchaser. Such **sale-leaseback transactions** give lessees use of assets without a large investment of capital and provide lessors with profitable investments. In addition, both lessors and lessees may derive significant income tax advantages from sale-leaseback transactions.

[8] Ibid., p. 17.

Because the sale of the asset and the leaseback represent in effect a single transaction, neither the selling price of the asset nor the periodic rental payments can be evaluated separately from the other. Consequently, the FASB suggested the following standard to be used in accounting for most sale-leaseback transactions:[9]

> If the lease meets one of the criteria for treatment as a capital lease . . . , the seller-lessee shall account for the lease as a capital lease; otherwise, as an operating lease. Any profit or loss on the sale shall be deferred and amortized in proportion to the amortization of the leased asset, if a capital lease, or in proportion to the related gross rental charged to expense over the lease term, if an operating lease, ...

To illustrate the accounting for a sale-leaseback transaction, assume that on May 1, Year 1, Cree Company sold land and a building for $1,540,000, and immediately leased the property from its owner on a 10-year operating lease for monthly rent of $15,000, beginning May 1, Year 1. On that date, the carrying amounts of the land and building in Cree's accounting records were $400,000 and $900,000, respectively, and the building had a remaining economic life of 15 years. Accumulated depreciation on the building totaled $300,000 on May 1, Year 1.

Journal entries in the accounting records of Cree Company for the sale-leaseback transaction are as follows for the first two months:

Lessee's journal entries for sale-leaseback transaction (operating lease)

CREE COMPANY
Journal Entries

Year 1

May 1	Cash	1,540,000	
	Accumulated Depreciation of Building	300,000	
	Land		400,000
	Building		1,200,000
	Deferred Gain on Disposal of Plant Assets		240,000

To record sale of land and building, and deferral of gain for amortization over life of related operating lease. Deferred gain is computed as follows:

Proceeds on sale		$1,540,000
Less: Carrying amount of land and building ($400,000 + $900,000)		1,300,000
Deferred gain		$ 240,000

1	Rent Expense ($15,000 − $2,000)	13,000	
	Deferred Gain on Disposal of Plant Assets ($240,000 ÷ 120)	2,000	
	Cash		15,000

> To record payment of first month's rent of land
> and building under operating lease, and amorti-
> zation of deferred gain over the lease term.

June 1	Rent Expense	13,000	
	Deferred Gain on Disposal of Plant Assets . . .	2,000	
	Cash		15,000

> To record payment of second month's rent of
> land and building under operating lease, and
> amortization of deferred gain over the lease
> term.

As a result of the deferral of the gain and its amortization over the lease term, total rent expense over the 10-year lease term is $1,560,000, computed as follows:

Total rent expense over the lease term

Gross rent payments over the lease term ($15,000 × 120)	$1,800,000
Less: Deferred gain amortized over the lease term	240,000
Total rent expense over the lease term	$1,560,000

Disclosure of leases in financial statements of lessee

The following information with respect to leases is disclosed in the lessee's financial statements or notes to the financial statements:[10]

1 For capital leases:
  a The gross amount of assets recorded under capital leases as of the date of each balance sheet presented by major classes. This information may be combined with the comparable information for owned assets.
  b Future minimum lease payments as of the latest balance sheet date, in the aggregate and for each of the five succeeding fiscal years, with separate deductions from the total for the amount representing executory costs, including any profit thereon, included in the minimum lease payments and for the amount of the imputed interest necessary to reduce the net minimum lease payments to present value.
  c The total of minimum sublease rentals to be received in the future under noncancelable subleases as of the latest balance sheet date.
  d Total contingent rentals actually incurred for each accounting period for which an income statement is presented.
  e Assets recorded under capital leases and the accumulated depreciation thereon shall be separately identified in the lessee's balance sheet or in notes thereto. Similarly, the related obligations shall be separately identified in the balance sheet as "obligations under capital leases" and shall be subject to the same considerations as other obligations in classifying them with current and noncurrent liabilities. The amount of depreciation on assets recorded under capital leases should be disclosed.

[10] Adapted from *Accounting for Leases,* pp. 17–18.

2 For operating leases having initial or remaining noncancelable terms in excess of one year:

   a Future minimum rental payments required as of the latest balance sheet date, in the aggregate and for each of the five succeeding fiscal years.

   b The total of minimum rentals to be received in the future under noncancelable subleases as of the latest balance sheet date.

3 For all operating leases, rental expense for each period for which an income statement is presented, with separate amounts for minimum rentals, contingent rentals, and sublease rentals. Rental payments under leases with terms of a month or less that were not renewed need not be included.

4 A general description of lease contracts, including, but not limited to, the following:

   a The basis on which contingent rental payments are determined.

   b The existence and terms of renewal or purchase options and rental escalation clauses.

   c Restrictions imposed by the lease contracts, such as those concerning dividends, additional debt, and further leasing.

A note to the financial statements adapted from the annual report of a large railroad company provides an illustration of disclosure of leases by the lessee:

Note: Leases

Leased properties under capital leases presented in the accompanying balance sheet on December 31, Year 11, represent the present value of future rental payments at the inception of the leases of $48.5 million, less accumulated depreciation of $19.6 million computed on a straight-line basis over the terms of the related leases. Obligations under capital leases of $34.7 million represent the present value of future rental payments after deduction of $3.1 million classified as a current liability.

A summary of capital lease arrangements and the aggregate future lease payments on December 31, Year 11, follows:

Year of lease	Term, years	Units leased	Future lease payments (in millions)		
			Present value	Imputed interest	Total
Year 1	15	90 locomotives	$ 8.2	$ 2.0	$10.2
Year 6	18	54 locomotives	17.1	9.7	26.8
Years 9–10	8	900 trailers	5.7	1.6	7.3
Various other capital leases			6.8	4.0	10.8
Totals			$37.8	$17.3	$55.1

Required payments under capital leases during the next five years (Year 12 through Year 16) are $5.3 million; $6.9 million; $6.9 million; $6.9 million; and $5.8 million, respectively.

Total rental expense for all operating leases was $28.4 million in Year 11 and $21.1 million in Year 10.

ACCOUNTING BY LESSORS

Leases are classified for accounting purposes by lessors as **sales-type leases, direct financing leases, leveraged leases,** or **operating leases.** Normally, sales-type leases arise when manufacturers or dealers use leasing as a means of marketing their products. Such leases give rise to a profit (or loss) to the lessor at the inception of the lease. A sales-type lease must meet **one or more** of the criteria for a capital lease (see pages 807 and 808 under accounting by lessees) **as well as the following two additional criteria:** (1) the collectibility of the lease payments is reasonably predictable, and (2) no important uncertainties surround the amount of unreimbursable costs yet to be incurred by the lessor under the lease. Important uncertainties might include commitments by the lessor to protect the lessee from obsolescence of the leased property.[11]

Leases that do not give rise to a profit (or loss) to the lessor at the inception of the lease, but otherwise qualify as sales-type leases, are treated as **direct financing leases** by lessors. Such leases are typically financing arrangements by lessor enterprises that normally are not involved in the direct sale of the assets leased. In direct financing leases, the carrying amount and the fair value of the leased property generally are the same at the inception of the lease.

A **leveraged lease** is an arrangement whereby a long-term creditor provides nonrecourse financing to the lessor for a leasing transaction between the lessee and lessor. A leveraged lease generally is designed to provide maximum income tax benefits to the three parties (lessor, lessee, and long-term creditor) involved in the transaction.

Leases that are not sales-type, direct financing, or leveraged leases are accounted for by lessors as **operating leases.**

Sales-type leases

The accounting for sales-type leases by lessors may be illustrated as follows:[12]

Principal accounting components of sales-type lease

Gross investment in the lease	$XXX
Less: Unearned interest revenue	XXX
Net investment in the lease	$XXX

The **gross investment** in the lease consists of the total of the minimum lease payments (net of any executory costs) and any **unguaranteed** residual value accruing to the lessor at the end of the lease term.

[11] Ibid., p. 11.
[12] Ibid., pp. 18–20.

The **net investment** in the lease is equal to the sum of the present values (at the lessor's implicit interest rate) of the minimum lease payments and any **unguaranteed** residual value. The difference between the gross investment and the net investment represents **unearned interest revenue,** which is **recognized as interest revenue** over the lease term by the interest method. In the balance sheet, the net investment is divided between the current and noncurrent asset categories.

A sales-type lease is recorded in the accounting records of the lessor as follows: (1) The gross investment in the lease is recorded as a debit to Lease Receivables, (2) the present value of the **minimum lease payments** is recorded as a credit to Sales, (3) the difference between the gross investment and the net investment is credited to Unearned Interest Revenue, (4) the cost (or carrying amount) of the leased property, plus any initial direct costs, less the present value of any unguaranteed residual value, is debited to Cost of Goods Sold, and (5) the cost (or carrying amount) of the leased property is credited to Inventories. Periodic cash receipts from the lease are recorded as credits to Lease Receivables, and Interest Revenue is credited in each accounting period as the unearned interest revenue becomes earned.

Any estimated unguaranteed residual value should be reviewed periodically. If the estimate is determined to be excessive, the accounting for the transaction is revised and the resulting reduction in the net investment is recognized as a loss. An upward adjustment of estimated residual value is not made. In leases in which the lessee guarantees a minimum residual value of the property at the end of the lease term, or in which there is a penalty for failure to renew, the minimum lease receivables at the end of the lease term will be equal to the amount of the guarantee or penalty at that date. At the termination of the existing term of a lease being renewed, the net investment in the lease is adjusted to the fair value of the leased property to the lessor at that date, and the net adjustment is debited or credited to Unearned Interest Revenue.

Accounting for a sales-type lease illustrated

To illustrate the accounting for a sales-type lease, assume that on December 31, Year 1, Orr Company leased equipment (which had a cost of $11,500 and a fair value of $14,000) to LSE, Inc., for four years on the following terms:

(1) LSE, Inc., agreed to make four annual rental payments of $4,000 starting on December 31, Year 1.[13] The estimated economic life of the equipment is six years with no residual value; LSE, Inc., planned to use the straight-line method of depreciation.

[13] Lease payments generally are made monthly; we have assumed annual payments to minimize computations in the illustration.

(2) LSE, Inc., agreed to absorb all maintenance costs, insurance, and property taxes; no initial direct costs were incurred by either party.

(3) LSE, Inc., was given an option to buy the equipment for $78 at the end of the lease term, December 31, Year 5. The $78 amount is considered a bargain.

(4) Orr Company's implicit interest rate on December 31, Year 1, for this transaction was 10% a year. LSE, Inc., had an incremental borrowing rate of 12% a year on December 31, Year 1, and could not learn Orr's implicit interest rate.

Orr Company'a ability to collect the minimum lease payments is reasonably predictable, and there are no important uncertainties surrounding the amount of any additional costs to be incurred by Orr.

Because the fair value of the equipment ($14,000) exceeds its cost ($11,500), and because of the bargain purchase option in the lease contract and the conditions described in the foregoing paragraph, Orr Company (the lessor) treats the lease as a sales-type lease. LSE, Inc. (the lessee), treats the lease as a capital lease because of the bargain purchase option.

Computation of Lessor's Net Investment in the Lease Orr Company's net investment in the lease may be computed as shown below. The gross investment in the lease is $16,078 [($4,000 × 4) + $78 = $16,078].

The present value on December 31, Year 1, of the four rental payments and the purchase option consists of the total of (1) $4,000 due on December 31, Year 1, (2) the present value of an ordinary annuity of three additional payments of $4,000 at 10% a year, and (3) the present value of $78 due on December 31, Year 5, at 10% a year, as follows:

Computation of lessor's net investment in sales-type lease	*Payment due on Dec. 31, Year 1* .... $ 4,000
	Add: Present value of ordinary annuity of 3 payments of $4,000 at 10% a
	year on Dec. 31, Year 2–Year 4: $4,000 × 2.486852* 9,947
	Present value of 4 payments of $4,000 at 10% a year $13,947
	Add: Present value of purchase option of $78 on Dec. 31, Year 5, at 10% a
	year: $78 × 0.683013* 53
	Net investment in the lease $14,000
	* See Appendix in back of the book.

In this case, the net investment in the lease is the same as the amount to be credited to Sales (and as the fair value of the equipment) **because there is no unguaranteed residual value.**

Computation of Amount to Be Capitalized by Lessee Because the lessee cannot learn the lessor's implicit interest rate, the lessee uses its incremental borrowing rate, 12% a year, to compute the present value of the minimum lease payments, as follows:

Computation of lessee's
recent value of
minimum lease
payments

Payment due on Dec. 31, Year 1.	$ 4,000
Add: Present value of ordinary annuity of 3 payments of $4,000 at 12% a year on Dec. 31, Year 2–Year 4: $4,000 × 2.401831*.	9,607
Present value of 4 payments of $4,000 at 12% a year	$13,607
Add: Present value of purchase option of $78 on Dec. 31, Year 5, at 12% a year: $78 × 0.635518*.	50
Present value of minimum lease payments (amount to be capitalized by lessee)	$13,657

* See Appendix in back of the book.

Journal Entries   The journal entries for both the lessor and the lessee for Years 1 and 2 are presented on page 821. The lessee's journal entries are shown for comparative purposes.

Termination of Sales-Type Lease   If a sales-type lease is terminated before the end of the lease term by mutual consent without penalty, the lessee recognizes a gain or loss.[14] For example, assume that the lease in the foregoing illustration is terminated on December 31, Year 3, prior to the payment due on that date. The journal entry to record the termination in the accounting records of LSE, Inc. (the lessee), is as follows:

Lessee's journal entry
for termination of
capital lease

Interest Expense [($13,657 − $6,841) × 0.12].	818	
Obligation under Capital Lease (net) ($13,657 − $6,841)	6,816	
Depreciation Expense.	2,276	
Loss on Termination of Capital Lease	1,471	
Leased Equipment—Capital Lease ($13,657 − $2,276) . . .		11,381
To record termination of capital lease through mutual consent and depreciation and interest expense for second year of lease.		

On termination of the lease, the lessor records the equipment at the **lowest** of its original cost, present fair value, or present carrying amount, and recognizes any loss. The lessor does not recognize a gain on an early termination of a lease.[15]

[14] Ibid., p. 15.
[15] Ibid., p. 22.

ORR COMPANY (lessor)
Journal Entries (sales-type lease)

Year 1

Dec. 31

Lease Receivables	16,078	
Unearned Interest Revenue		2,078
Sales		14,000

To record sales-type lease at inception.

31

Cost of Goods Sold	11,500	
Inventories		11,500

To record cost of leased equipment.

31

Cash	4,000	
Lease Receivables		4,000

To record receipt of first lease payment

Year 2

Dec. 31

Cash	4,000	
Unearned Interest Revenue	1,000	
Lease Receivables		4,000
Interest Revenue		1,000

To record receipt of second lease payment, and interest earned during Year 2: ($14,000 − $4,000) × 0.10 = $1,000.

LSE, INC. (lessee)
Journal Entries (capital lease)

Year 1

Dec. 31

Leased Equipment—Capital Lease	13,657	
Obligation under Capital Lease (net)		13,657

To record capital lease at inception. (See page 820 for computations.)

31

No entry.

31

Obligation under Capital Lease (net)	4,000	
Cash		4,000

To record lease payment for first year.

Year 2

Dec. 31

Interest Expense [($13,657 − $4,000) × 0.12]	1,159	
Obligation under Capital Lease (net) ($4,000 − $1,159)	2,841	
Cash		4,000

To record lease payment for second year.

Depreciation Expense ($13,657 ÷ 6)	2,276	
Leased Equipment—Capital Lease		2,276

To record depreciation expense (straight-line method) for first year of lease. Six-year economic life of the equipment is used because the lease contains a bargain purchase option.

Direct financing leases

In direct financing leases, the gross investment in the lease is computed in the same way as for sales-type leases, and the net investment in the lease equals the difference between the gross investment in the lease and the unearned interest revenue.[16] Unearned interest revenue is the difference between the gross investment in the lease and the cost or carrying amount of the leased property. **Any initial direct costs are debited to expense accounts as incurred, and an equal portion of the unearned interest revenue is recognized as interest revenue in the same accounting period.** The net investment in the lease currently recoverable is classified as a current asset, and any contingent rentals are recorded as revenue when such rentals become receivable.

In leases containing a residual value guarantee or a penalty for failure to renew, the lessor follows the same procedure described for sales-type leases. Similarly, any estimated unguaranteed residual value should be reviewed periodically and, if necessary, adjusted as described for sales-type leases.

Illustration of Accounting for a Direct Financing Lease with Initial Direct Costs To illustrate the accounting for a direct financing lease with initial direct costs, assume that on July 31, Year 1, Lessor Corporation leased equipment to Lessee Company with a cost and fair value of $11,127. The initial direct costs incurred by the lessor were $200. The lease was for seven years at an annual rent of $2,000 payable at the beginning of each year. The estimated economic life of the equipment was nine years, and the estimated **unguaranteed** residual value at the end of seven years was $1,200. Lessee Company uses the straight-line method of depreciation. Lease payments were determined at an amount that will give Lessor a 10% annual rate of return on its net investment in the lease. The present value of the lease payments for the lessor, including the unguaranteed residual value, was $11,327, computed as follows:

Computation of lessor's present value of direct financing lease

Present value of annuity due of 7 rents of $2,000 at 10% (present value of minimum lease payments for lessee): $2,000 × 5.355261*	$10,711
Add: Present value of unguaranteed residual value ($1,200 discounted at 10% for 7 years): $1,200 × 0.513158*	616
Present value of lease	$11,327

See Appendix in back of the book.

Lessee Company knows Lessor's implicit interest rate, which is less than Lessee's incremental borrowing rate. Lessee agreed to pay all executory costs; the collectibility of the lease payments was reasonably

[16] Ibid., p. 23.

predictable, and no additional costs were expected to be incurred by Lessor. The lessor uses an Equipment Held for Lease ledger account.

This lease meets the criteria for classification as a sales-type lease, but because there is no element of profit at the inception of the lease, it is recorded as a direct financing lease by Lessor Corporation and a capital lease by Lessee Company. This accounting treatment is appropriate because (1) the lease term exceeds 75% of the economic life of the equipment; (2) the present value of the minimum lease payments is more than 90% of the fair value of the equipment at the inception of the lease; (3) the collectibility of the lease payments is reasonably assured, and no additional costs were expected to be incurred by the lessor; and (4) there is no element of realized profit at the inception of the lease.

The gross investment in the lease, unearned interest revenue, and the net investment in the lease are computed as follows:

Computation of gross investment, unearned interest, and net investment	Gross investment in lease: ($2,000 minimum lease payments × 7) + $1,200 unguaranteed residual value $15,200
	Unearned interest revenue: $15,200 gross investment in lease − $11,127 cost of leased equipment. . . . . $ 4,073
	Net investment in lease: $15,200 gross investment in lease − $4,073 unearned interest revenue. $11,127

Because the lessee does not obtain rights to the equipment at the end of the lease term and the residual value of the equipment is not guaranteed, only the present value of the minimum lease payments is recorded by the lessee. The journal entries to record this lease in the accounting records of the lessee and lessor for the first two years are given on page 824 (both Lessor and Lessee have a July 31 fiscal year).

Note that the initial direct costs of $200 are recorded as operating expenses and that an equal amount of interest revenue is recognized in the same accounting period. This procedure is explicitly required by **FASB Statement No. 13.** After the $200 reduction of the unearned interest revenue, the $3,873 balance, when subtracted from the $15,200 gross investment in the lease, yields the $11,327 present value of the lease for the lessor.

Leveraged leases

From the standpoint of the lessee, leveraged leases are classified and accounted for the same as nonleveraged leases. From the standpoint of the lessor, leveraged leases are treated as direct financing leases; sales-type leases cannot be classified as leveraged leases, according to **FASB**

	LESSOR CORPORATION Journal Entries (direct financing lease)			LESSEE COMPANY Journal Entries (capital lease)		
Year 1 July 31	Lease Receivables [($2,000 × 7) + $1,200] . . .	15,200		Leased Equipment—Capital Lease	10,711	
	Unearned Interest Revenue ($4,073 −			Obligation under Capital Lease (net)		10,711
	$200)		3,873	To record capital lease at inception. (See computa-		
	Equipment Held for Lease		11,127	tion on page 822.)		
	Interest Revenue		200			
	To record direct financing lease at incep- tion, and to record interest revenue equal to initial direct costs of lease.					
31	Cash	2,000		Obligation under Capital Lease (net)	2,000	
	Lease Receivables		2,000	Cash		2,000
	To record receipt of first lease payment.			To record lease payment for first year.		
31	Operating Expenses	200		No entry.		
	Cash		200			
	To record payment of initial direct costs of lease.					
Year 2 July 31	Cash	2,000		Interest Expense [($10,711 − $2,000) × 0.10]	871	
	Unearned Interest Revenue	933		Obligation under Capital Lease (net) ($2,000 − $871)	1,129	
	Lease Receivables		2,000	Cash		2,000
	Interest Revenue		933	To record lease payment for second year.		
	To record receipt of second lease payment, and interest earned during Fiscal Year 2: ($11,327 − $2,000) × 0.10 = $933.			Depreciation Expense ($10,711 ÷ 7)	1,530	
				Leased Equipment—Capital Lease		1,530
				To record depreciation expense (straight-line method) for first year of lease. Seven-year term of lease is used for depreciation because the lease does not transfer ownership of the equipment to the lessee and does not contain a bargain purchase option.		

Statement No. 13.[17] The lessor records the investment in a leveraged lease *net of the nonrecourse debt.* The amount recorded generally consists of (1) rent receivable (net of portion applicable to principal and interest on the nonrecourse debt), (2) the amount of the investment tax credit to be realized in the transaction, (3) any estimated residual value of the leased asset, and (4) a reduction for any unearned revenue items. Because the lease receivables are recorded net of the nonrecourse debt, interest revenue is not earned by the lessor. Instead, a Revenue from Leveraged Leases account is credited for net positive cash flows not allocated to the recovery of the lessor's net investment in the lease.

Accounting procedures for the various aspects of leveraged leases in the accounting records of the lessor are quite complex and therefore are not illustrated in this general discussion of leasing.[18] An illustration of a leveraged lease appears in the Appendix at the end of this chapter.

Operating leases

Rent is reported as revenue by lessors over the lease term of an operating lease as it becomes receivable according to the provisions in the lease. However, if the rent payments are not received in level amounts, rent revenue should be recognized on a straight-line basis, unless another basis is considered more appropriate. An example of a basis which may be more appropriate than straight-line is hours of usage for a machine. Any initial direct costs, if material in amount, relating to an operating lease are deferred and allocated over the lease term in the same manner as rent revenue is accrued.

Leased property under operating leases is included by the lessor with or near plant assets in the balance sheet.[19] The leased property is depreciated in accordance with the lessor's normal depreciation policy, and in the balance sheet the accumulated depreciation is deducted from the investment in the leased property.

Disclosure of leases in financial statements of lessor

When leasing (except leveraged leasing) is a significant part of the lessor's business activities in terms of revenue, net income, or assets, the information on page 826 with respect to leases is disclosed in the financial statements or notes to the financial statements.[20]

---

[17] Ibid., p. 41.
[18] Appendix E of *FASB Statement No. 13* (as amended) contains extensive illustrations of accounting and financial statement presentation for leveraged leases.
[19] *Accounting for Leases,* p. 24.
[20] Adapted from *Accounting for Leases,* p. 24.

1 For sales-type and direct financing leases:

   a The components of the net investment in sales-type and direct financing leases as of the date of each balance sheet presented. The components include (1) future minimum lease payments to be received, with separate deductions for amounts representing executory costs included in the minimum lease payments, and the allowance for doubtful lease payments receivable; (2) the unguaranteed residual values accruing to the lessor; and (3) the unearned interest revenue.

   b Future minimum lease payments to be received for each of the five succeeding fiscal years as of the latest balance sheet date.

   c The amount of unearned interest revenue included in income to offset initial direct costs charged against income for each accounting period for which an income statement is presented. (For direct financing leases only.)

   d Total contingent rentals included in income for each accounting period for which an income statement is presented.

2 For operating leases:

   a The cost and carrying amount, if different, of property on lease or held for leasing by major classes of property, and the total amount of accumulated depreciation as of the latest balance sheet date.

   b Minimum future rentals on noncancelable leases as of the latest balance sheet date, in the aggregate and for each of the five succeeding fiscal years.

   c Total contingent rentals included in income for each accounting period for which an income statement is presented.

3 A general description of lease contracts.

A note to the financial statements adapted from the annual report of a computer company provides an illustration of disclosure of leases by the lessor:

Note: Leasing Arrangements with Company as Lessor —The Company leases computer equipment under various agreements with terms ranging from one to seven years. Substantially all leases are accounted for under the operating method or as leases equivalent to sales in accordance with **FASB Statement Nos. 13** and **17.** The impact of these statements on prior years' net income or retained earnings for leases entered into prior to January 1, Year 1, was not significant and, accordingly, prior years' financial statements have not been restated.

The Company's cost of equipment under operating leases on December 31, Year 2, was $476,540,000 less accumulated depreciation of $269,851,000.

The net investment in sales-type leases on December 31, Year 2, was as follows:

	(Dollars in thousands)
Total minimum lease payments receivable	$44,909
Estimated residual value of equipment	50
Less: Unearned interest revenue	(5,775)
Net investment in sales-type leases	$39,184

Minimum lease payments, including amounts representing executory costs and any related profit, to be received in each of the next five years under the above lease agreements are as follows:

	Sales-type leases	Operating leases
	(Dollars in thousands)	
Year 3	$17,848	$223,483
Year 4	12,701	163,643
Year 5	9,589	107,877
Year 6	3,107	62,073
Year 7	1,183	23,226
Later years	481	–0–
Totals	$44,909	$580,302

The Company retains title to all of its leased computer equipment, pays taxes, licenses and insurance on such equipment and provides for its general maintenance. At the end of the lease term, the equipment normally is returned to the Company.

OTHER ASPECTS OF ACCOUNTING FOR LEASES

In the preceding pages we have discussed and illustrated the principal aspects of lease accounting. In this section, we shall consider the following topics: leases involving real estate, leases between related parties, computation of the lessor's implicit interest rate, and determination of the current portion of lease obligations and receivables.

Leases involving real estate

Leases involving land only are accounted for as capital leases by the lessee if the lease contract includes either of the first two criteria on page 807. Otherwise, a lease for land is accounted for as an operating lease. Normally, the amount capitalized in the Leased Land—Capital Lease account is not depreciated.

The accounting for leases involving both land and buildings depends on (1) which of the criteria on pages 807 and 808 are met by the lease, and (2) the ratio of the fair values of the land and buildings. *Accounting for Leases* specifies the conditions under which the land and building elements are accounted for as a single unit or as separate units, and whether the leases are treated as capital leases or operating leases by lessees and as sales-type leases, direct financing leases, or operating leases by lessors.[21]

If only part of a building is leased, the accounting procedures for both the lessee and the lessor depend on whether the cost and the fair value of the leased part of the building can be determined objectively.

[21] Ibid., pp. 28–30.

Leases between related parties

Leases in which the lessor and the lessee are related parties are accounted for according to the economic substance rather than their legal form if the terms of the lease contract are affected significantly by the relationship. **Related parties** include the following:[22]

A parent company and its subsidiaries

An owner enterprise and its partnerships or joint ventures

An investor and its influenced investees

Two or more entities subject to significant influence of a parent company, owner enterprise, or investor

The nature and extent of leasing transactions between related parties are disclosed in notes to the financial statements of both the lessor and the lessee.

Computation of lessor's implicit interest rate

We have simplified our illustrations of accounting for leases by providing the interest rate implicit in the lease. In practice, this rate must be computed by a process of iteration ("trial and error") involving computers, electronic calculators, or present value tables. Simplification of this process has been a research objective of several accountants.[23]

Determination of current portion of lease obligations and receivables

The current portion of lease obligations is included in the current liabilities section of the lessee's balance sheet, and the current portion of lease receivables appears in the current asset section of the lessor's balance sheet. Without the assistance of a computer, electronic calculator, or present value tables, determination of the current portion of a lease with monthly payments requires separate computations of the principal portion of the next 12 lease payments or receipts.

A short-cut approximation of the current portion is possible by use of the "Rule of 78." (The sum of the digits for 12 consecutive months is 78.) This technique recognizes that the principal portion of each successive monthly fixed lease payment or receipt increases by a nearly uniform amount. For example, the Obligation under Capital Lease ledger account of Lee Company on page 811 indicates that almost every monthly principal payment after the first one (which was not affected by interest) was $2 larger than the previous month's payment. Thus, if we multiply this $2 increment by 78 and add the product to 12 times the $191 princi-

---

[22] Ibid., p. 2.

[23] See Erich Obersteiner and Paul J. Jalics, "Determining Implicit Interest," and Michael Masoner and Jackson A. White, "Implicit Interest Rate Table," *Journal of Accountancy* (May 1980), pp. 34–44.

pal portion of the December 2, Year 1, lease payment, we have an approximation of the current portion of the lease obligation on December 31, Year 1, as follows:

<table>
<tr><td style="text-align:right">Computation of current
portion of lease
obligation
by "Rule of 78"</td><td>$2 × 78 . . . .</td><td>$ 156</td></tr>
<tr><td></td><td>$191 × 12 . . . .</td><td>2,292</td></tr>
<tr><td></td><td>Estimated current portion of lease obligation on Dec. 31, Year 1 . . . . . .</td><td>$2,448</td></tr>
</table>

This estimate is a reasonably close approximation of the actual current portion of the principal payments (applicable to Year 2), which is $2,442.

Appraisal of current accounting standards for leases

Prior to the issuance of **FASB Statement No. 13,** lessees were required to capitalize only leases that were considered the equivalent to a purchase of property. Leases often were designed to enable the lessor to record the lease as a sale but at the same time allow the lessee to account for the lease as an operating lease. Thus, billions of dollars of leased assets were not included in the balance sheet of either the lessee or the lessor. Many lessees viewed leasing as an attractive source of "off-balance-sheet financing," because the lease obligation appeared in notes to the financial statements rather than in the liabilities section of the balance sheet. However, users of financial statements and the Securities and Exchange Commission considered such accounting practices unsatisfactory. **FASB Statement No. 13** changed all this. Under current accounting standards, financial statements are more consistent with the conceptual framework of accounting, more informative, and more comparable between business enterprises that lease and those that purchase assets outright.

However, **FASB Statement No. 13** and related pronouncements may be faulted in some respects. The fact that to date the FASB has issued eight statements and six interpretations on lease accounting indicates that the Board's accounting standards for leases had flaws requiring correction. Further, in view of the Board's emphasis on the economic substance of capital leases (an acquisition of plant assets) over their legal form (a rental of property), the requirement for separate classifications of assets held under capital leases and the related obligations in the lessee's balance sheet (see page 815) is questionable. If a capital lease is in fact an acquisition of a plant asset and an incurring of a liability, such separate classifications appear unwarranted. Finally, the FASB's use of the **net method** of accounting by lessees for obligations under capital leases, but the **gross method** of accounting by lessors for lease receivables, appears inconsistent.

APPENDIX: ILLUSTRATION OF A LEVERAGED LEASE

The following illustration of a leveraged lease is adapted from **Accounting for Leases** (pages 90–105):

On January 2, Year 1, Lessor, Inc., acquired equipment for leasing at a cost of $1,000,000. To pay for the equipment, Lessor used $400,000 of its cash and the proceeds of a $600,000, 9%, nonrecourse bank loan payable in 15 annual installments of $74,435 [$600,000 ÷ 8.060688* = $74,435], beginning on December 31, Year 1. Also on January 2, Year 1, Lessor leased the equipment to Lessee Corporation on a 15-year lease requiring Lessee to pay $90,000 annually, beginning on December 31, Year 1. The unguaranteed residual value of the equipment was estimated at $200,000, to be realized on December 31, Year 16 (one year after the termination of the lease). For depreciation of the equipment, Lessor adopted the following:

Seven-year economic life

Double-declining-balance method for first two years; sum-of-the-years'-digits method for remaining five years, with $100,000 residual value

Lessor's combined federal and state income tax rate is 50.4%, and lessor is entitled to a $100,000 investment tax credit (realizable on December 31, Year 1). There were no initial direct costs of the lease.

Journal entries on January 2, Year 1

The journal entries for the leveraged lease on January 2, Year 1, are given on page 831.

Journal entries on December 31, Year 1

On December 31, Year 1 (and on subsequent year-ends), Lessor prepares journal entries for the leveraged lease as follows:

1 Collection of lease payment ($90,000) for first year

2 Payment on nonrecourse note ($74,435) for first year

3 Apportionment of realized portion of unearned and deferred revenue to Revenue from Leveraged Leases account

4 Income tax effects of timing difference between financial accounting and income tax accounting for the leveraged lease

Journal entries **1** and **2** involve only the Cash and Lease Receivables accounts, because the amount originally recorded in the latter account is net of the total payments required on the nonrecourse note payable. Determination of the amounts for journal entries **3** and **4** requires a detailed analysis of the cash flows for each of the 15 years of the lease and a "trial and error" computation of the lessor's implicit interest rate. Because of the complexity of these computations, they are not illustrated in this Appendix.

* Present value of ordinary annuity of 15 rents of 1 at 9%.

LESSOR, INC.
Journal Entries (leveraged lease)
January 2, Year 1

Equipment Held for Lease	1,000,000	
Cash		400,000
Notes Payable to Bank		600,000

To record acquisition of equipment for cash and 9%, 15-year note, payable $74,435 annually, beginning on Dec. 31, Year 1.

Lease Receivables [($90,000 × 15) − ($74,435 × 15)] . . .	233,475	
Notes Payable to Bank	600,000	
Income Taxes Payable	100,000	
Equipment Held for Lease ($1,000,000 − $200,000) .		800,000
Unearned and Deferred Revenue		133,475

To record lease of equipment on a 15-year lease with annual rent of $90,000 payable beginning on Dec. 31, Year 1. Gross lease receivable of $1,350,000 ($90,000 × 15 = $1,350,000) is reduced by total principal and interest payments of $1,116,525 ($74,435 × 15 = $1,116,525) on related nonrecourse debt. Income taxes liability is reduced by amount of investment tax credit to be realized on the leased equipment. Equipment Held for Lease account is reduced to amount of unguaranteed residual value.

REVIEW QUESTIONS

1 Define each of the following terms:
   a Lease
   b Sublease
   c Sale-leaseback transaction
   d Operating lease
   e Leveraged lease

2 Listed below are some terms used in accounting for leases. Give a short definition of each.
   a Inception of lease
   b Bargain purchase option
   c Unguaranteed residual value
   d Lessor's implicit interest rate
   e Initial direct costs

3 What are the components of the **minimum lease payments** of a typical capital lease of the lessee?

4 To be classified as a **capital lease** by the lessee, the lease must meet one of four criteria. List these four criteria.

5 Briefly describe the accounting procedures which are followed by the lessor and by the lessee for an **operating lease.**

6 Summarize the procedures followed by the lessee to account for a capital lease.

7 A **sales-type lease** (from the standpoint of the lessor) must meet one or more of the criteria of a capital lease as well as two additional criteria. What are these two additional criteria?

8 Differentiate between the accounting procedures used by lessors to account for a **sales-type lease** and for a **direct financing lease.**

9 What disclosures are required for various types of leases in the financial statements of lessees?

10 What disclosures are required for various types of leases in the financial statements of lessors?

11 Dodd Company leased a computer for three years at $25,000 a month, with an option to renew the lease for five years at $1,500 a month or to purchase the computer for $20,000 after the initial lease term of three years. How should this transaction be recorded in the accounting records of Dodd Company? Explain.

12 Wu Corporation leased an asset under a lease calling for the payment of $24,000 a year in rent. At the end of the current year, when the lease had a remaining term of 10 years, Wu subleased the asset for rent of $36,000 a year for 10 years. When will the gain from this transaction be reported by Wu Corporation? Explain.

13 Lessee's incremental borrowing rate is 18% a year. Unknown to lessee, lessor's implicit interest rate is 15%. How do these facts affect lessee's accounting for a capital lease? Explain.

14 The economic life of leased equipment under a capital lease is 10 years, and the lease term is eight years. How do these facts affect the depreciation of the leased equipment in the accounting records of the lessee? Explain.

15 How does the lessor account for contingent rentals under a direct financing lease?

16 What major reforms in lease accounting were made by the FASB in **FASB Statement No. 13** and related pronouncements?

EXERCISES

Ex. 20-1   Select the best answer for each of the following multiple-choice questions:

1 The appropriate valuation of an operating lease in the balance sheet of the lessee is:
   a Zero
   b The sum of the lease payments
   c The present value of the sum of the lease payments
   d The fair value of the leased asset at the inception of the lease

2 What are the three types of period costs that a lessee experiences with capital leases?

a Lease expense, interest expense, depreciation

b Interest expense, depreciation, executory costs

c Depreciation, executory costs, lease expense

d Executory costs, interest expense, lease expense

3 Lessee Company leased equipment from Lessor Company on July 1, Year 8, for an eight-year period expiring June 30, Year 16. Equal annual payments under the lease of $500,000 are due on July 1 of each year. The first payment was made on July 1, Year 8. The lessor's implicit interest rate is 10%. The cash selling price of the equipment is $2,934,000, and the cost of the equipment in Lessor's accounting records is $2,500,000. Assuming that the lease is appropriately recorded as a sales-type lease by Lessor, what is the amount of profit on the sale and the interest revenue that Lessor should record for the year ended December 31, Year 8?

a $0 and $0

b $0 and $121,700

c $434,000 and $121,700

d $434,000 and $133,250

4 Based solely on the four sets of circumstances indicated below, which set gives rise to a sales-type lease or direct financing lease of a lessor?

	Transfers ownership by end of lease?	Contains bargain purchase provision?	Collectibility of lease payments assured?	Any important uncertainties?
a	No	Yes	Yes	No
b	Yes	No	No	No
c	Yes	No	No	Yes
d	No	Yes	Yes	Yes

5 In a lease that is appropriately recorded as a direct financing lease by the lessor, unearned revenue:

a Is recognized as interest revenue over the term of the lease by the interest method

b Is recognized as interest revenue over the term of the lease by the straight-line method

c Does not arise

d Is recognized as interest revenue at the expiration of the lease

6 Rent collected in advance by the lessor for an operating lease is a (an):

a Accrued liability

b Deferred asset

c Accrued revenue

d Deferred revenue

Ex. 20-2 On January 2, Year 7, Lessee Corporation signed a 10-year noncancelable lease for machinery. The terms of the lease called for Lessee to make annual payments of $30,000 for 10 years beginning January 2, Year 7, with title to the machinery to pass to Lessee at the end of this period. The machinery has an estimated economic life of 15 years and no residual value. Lessee uses the straight-line method of depreciation for all its plant assets. Lessee appropriately accounted for the lease transaction as a capital lease, using its incremental borrowing rate of 10% a year.

Compute the following for Lessee Corporation for Year 7:

a Present value of minimum lease payments on January 2, Year 7

b Interest expense

c Depreciation expense

Ex. 20-3 On June 30, Year 4, Rea Corporation sold production equipment for $550,000. The equipment had a carrying amount of $500,000 and a remaining economic life of 10 years. That same day, Rea leased back the equipment at $1,500 a month for five years, with no option to renew the lease or repurchase the equipment.

Compute Rea's rent expense for this equipment for the year ended December 31, Year 4.

Ex. 20-4 Lessor Company leased equipment to Lessee Company on May 1, Year 6. At that time the collectibility of the minimum lease payments was not reasonably predictable. The lease expires on May 1, Year 8. Lessee could have bought the equipment from Lessor for $900,000 instead of leasing it. Lessor's accounting records showed a carrying amount of $800,000 for the equipment on May 1, Year 6. Lessor's depreciation on the equipment in Year 6 was $200,000. During Year 6, Lessee paid $240,000 rent to Lessor. Lessor incurred maintenance and other related costs of $18,000 under the terms of the lease in Year 6. After the lease with Lessee expires, Lessor will lease the equipment to another party for two years.
a Compute Lessor Company's pre-tax income derived from its lease with Lessee Company during Year 6.
b Compute Lessee Company's pre-tax expense incurred from its lease with Lessor Company during Year 6.

Ex. 20-5 Lessor Company, a dealer in machinery and equipment, leased equipment to Lessee, Inc., on July 1, Year 6. The lease is appropriately accounted for as a sales-type lease by Lessor and as a capital lease by Lessee. The lease is for a 10-year term (the economic life of the equipment) expiring June 30, Year 16. The first of 10 equal annual payments of $500,000 was made on July 1, Year 6. Lessor had purchased the equipment for $2,675,000 on January 2, Year 6, and established a list selling price of $3,375,000 for the equipment. Assume that the present value at July 1, Year 6, of the rent payments over the lease term discounted at 12% (the appropriate interest rate) was $3,165,000.
a Compute the amount of (1) gross profit and (2) interest revenue that Lessor Company should record for the year ended December 31, Year 6.
b Compute the amount of (1) depreciation expense (straight-line method, no residual value) and (2) interest expense that Lessee, Inc., should record for the year ended December 31, Year 6.

Ex. 20-6 On January 2, Year 1, El Company (lessor) received a payment of $4,804 from Em Company (lessee) representing an amount equivalent to the present value of three year-end rental payments of $2,000 discounted at 12% a year. The lease was classified as an operating lease.
a Prepare journal entries to record the receipt of the $4,804 in the accounting records of El Company on January 2, Year 1, and to record realized rent revenue and interest expense for the year ended December 31, Year 1. Record unearned rent revenue at present value. Round all amounts to the nearest dollar.
b Prepare journal entries to record the payment of the $4,804 in the accounting records of Em Company on January 2, Year 1, and to record rent expense and interest revenue for the year ended December 31, Year 1. Record prepaid lease rent at present value. Round all amounts to the nearest dollar.

Ex. 20-7 The following information is available for a lease of a machine which is classified as a sales-type lease by the lessor and a capital lease by the lessee:

Cost of machine to lessor	$31,000
Initial payment by lessee at inception of lease	1,000
Present value of remaining 47 monthly payments of $1,000 each discounted at 1% a month	37,354

a Record the lease (including the initial receipt of $1,000) and the receipt of the second installment of $1,000 in the accounting records of the lessor. The lessor records unearned interest revenue in a separate account. Round computations to the nearest dollar.

b Record the lease (including the initial payment of $1,000) and the payment of the second installment of $1,000 in the accounting records of the lessee. The lessee records the lease obligation at present value (net method). Round computations to the nearest dollar.

Ex. 20-8 Lessor Corporation leased a heavy crane to Karen Doherty on July 1, Year 10, on the following terms:

(1) 48 lease payments of $1,500 at the end of each month were to be paid by Doherty.

(2) The cost of the crane to Lessor Corporation was $51,064.

Lessor Corporation accounted for this lease as a direct financing lease; the difference between total rent receipts, $72,000 ($1,500 × 48 = $72,000), and the cost of the crane, $51,064, was computed to yield a return of $1\frac{1}{2}$% a month over the lease term.

Prepare journal entries in the accounting records of Lessor Corporation to record the lease contract and the receipt of the first lease rent on July 31, Year 10. Record unearned interest revenue of $20,936 and round computations to the nearest dollar.

Ex. 20-9 On the first day of its fiscal year, Ray, Inc., leased a new property to Kay Company at an annual rent of $100,000 receivable at the beginning of each year for 10 years. The first payment was received immediately. The leased property cost $650,000 and has an estimated economic life of 13 years and no residual value. The interest rate implicit in the lease is 12%. The present value of an annuity of 1 payable at the beginning of the year at 12% for 10 years is 6.328. Ray had no other costs associated with this lease. Ray should have accounted for this lease as a sales-type lease but mistakenly accounted for it as an operating lease.

Compute the effect on income before income taxes during the first year of the lease as a result of Ray's classification of this lease as an operating lease rather than as a sales-type lease.

Ex. 20-10 Lowe Company retired a machine from active use on January 2, Year 5, for the purpose of leasing it. The machine had a carrying amount of $900,000 after 15 years of use and is expected to have four more years of economic life. The machine is depreciated on a straight-line basis. On March 1, Year 5, Lowe leased the machine to Yee Company for $330,000 a year for a four-year period ending February 28, Year 9. Lowe incurred total maintenance and other related costs under the lease contract of $35,000 relating to the year ended December 31, Year 5. Yee paid $330,000 to Lowe on March 1, Year 5. The lease was classified properly as an operating lease by both Lowe and Yee.

a Compute the income before income taxes derived by Lowe Company from this lease for the year ended December 31, Year 5.

b Compute the amount of rent expense incurred by Yee Company from this lease for the year ended December 31, Year 5.

Ex. 20-11 On January 2, Year 4, La Sore Company leased machinery to Lessee, Inc., for $1,000 a year for 10 years. The first payment is due on January 2, Year 4. The machinery was manufactured by La Sore at a cost of $4,500 and has a list price of $6,500. La Sore consistently uses an interest rate of 12% in establishing lease payment amounts. The estimated residual value of the machinery at the end of its 10 years of economic life is $1,000. The lease is not renewable, but Lessee has an option to purchase the machinery at the end of the lease term for $1. The present value of 1 for 10 periods at 12% a period is 0.3220. The present value of an annuity due of 10 rents of 1 at 12% a period is 6.328.

Assume that this lease is classified as a sales-type lease by La Sore. Ignoring income taxes, compute the amount of gross profit that La Sore should recognize at the date the lease contract is signed.

SHORT CASES FOR ANALYSIS AND DECISION

Case 20-1 Corman Corporation entered into a lease contract with Leman Leasing Corporation for a machine. Leman's primary business is leasing, and it is not a manufacturer or dealer. Corman will lease the machine for a period of three years, which is 50% of the machine's economic life. Leman will take possession of the machine at the end of the initial three-year lease and lease it to an unrelated enterprise that does not need a current version of the machine. Corman does not guarantee any residual value for the machine and will not purchase the machine at the end of the lease term.

Corman's incremental borrowing rate is 10%, and the implicit interest rate in the lease is $8\frac{1}{2}\%$. Corman has no way of knowing the implicit interest rate used by Leman. With either rate, the present value of the minimum lease payments is between 90 and 100% of the fair value of the machine at the date of the lease contract.

Corman has agreed to pay all executory costs directly, and no allowance for these costs is included in the lease payments.

Leman is reasonably certain that Corman will pay all lease payments, and, because Corman has agreed to pay all executory costs, there are no important uncertainties regarding costs to be incurred by Leman.

Instructions

a With respect to Corman (the lessee), answer the following questions:
  (1) What type of lease has been entered into? Explain.
  (2) How does Corman compute the amount to be recorded for the lease or asset acquired?
  (3) What accounts are created or affected by this transaction and how are the lease costs related to the transaction matched with revenue?
  (4) What disclosures must Corman make regarding this lease or asset?

b With respect to Leman (the lessor), answer the following questions:
  (1) What type of lease has been entered into? Explain.
  (2) How is this lease recorded by Leman, and how are the amounts determined?
  (3) How does Leman determine the appropriate amount of revenue to be recognized from each lease payment?
  (4) What disclosures must Leman make regarding this lease?

Case 20-2 *a* Capital leases and operating leases are the two classifications of leases described in FASB pronouncements, from the standpoint of the lessee.

Instructions

  (1) Describe how a capital lease is accounted for by the lessee, both at the inception of the lease and during the first year of the lease, assuming that the lease transfers ownership of the property to the lessee by the end of the lease term, and that equal monthly payments are made by the lessee at the beginning of each month.
  (2) Describe how an operating lease is accounted for by the lessee, both at the inception of the lease and during the first year of the lease, assuming that equal monthly payments are made by the lessee at the beginning of each

month. Describe the change in accounting, if any, when rent payments are not made on a straight-line basis.

Do not discuss the criteria for distinguishing between capital leases and operating leases.

b Sales-type leases and direct financing leases are two of the classifications of leases described in FASB pronouncements, from the standpoint of the lessor.

Instructions Compare and contrast a sales-type lease with a direct financing lease as follows:

(1) Gross investment in the lease
(2) Recognition of unearned interest revenue as interest revenue
(3) Manufacturer's or dealer's profit

Do not discuss the criteria for distinguishing between the leases described above and operating leases.

Case 20-3 Wolfe Aircraft Company manufactures small single- and multiple-engine aircraft primarily for sale to individuals, flying clubs, and corporations. Wolfe is one of the pioneers in the industry and has developed a reputation as a leader in small-craft engineering and marketing innovations.

During the last few years, Wolfe has leased profitably an increasing number of aircraft to flying clubs. The leasing activity currently represents a significant portion of Wolfe's annual volume. Details of a typical lease contract with flying clubs follow:

(1) The flying club signs a long-term lease with Wolfe for the aircraft.
(2) The lease has a noncancelable term of 6 to 18 years, depending on the aircraft's economic life. The lease term is set to be three-fourths of the normal economic life of the aircraft leased.
(3) The club is required to deposit with Wolfe an amount equal to 10% of the total lease rent for the term of the lease. The deposit is not refundable, but it is used in lieu of rent during the last one-tenth of the lease term.
(4) A bank lends Wolfe an amount equal to the remaining 90% of the total lease rent after deducting a discount of 14% a year. The net discounted amount is paid immediately to Wolfe. The bank-loan contract requires Wolfe to use the lease rent payments from the flying club to repay the loan to the bank.
(5) As a condition for the loan, the bank requires Wolfe to insure the leased aircraft for an amount equal to the loan.
(6) The flying club signs Wolfe's bank-loan contract as a surety, thus obligating itself if Wolfe should default on the loan.
(7) When the bank loan is paid in full at the end of the lease term, the flying club may purchase the aircraft and receive title to it by paying Wolfe $100.

Instructions Discuss the criteria and other aspects of Wolfe's leasing activities that it should consider in determining whether to account for its flying club leases as operating leases or as sales-type leases. In your discussion, identify criteria which are clearly met from the facts presented. For criteria which are not clearly met, indicate what additional information is needed to reach a conclusion with respect to each criterion.

Case 20-4 Kosti Airlines recently purchased eight jetliners for a total cost of $180 million. It plans to depreciate the jets by the sum-of-the-years'-digits method over a 12-year period. It is estimated that the jets will have a resale value of $24 million at the end of 12 years. To finance the acquisition of the jets, Kosti borrowed $180 million, payable at the rate of $20 million a year plus interest at 8% on the unpaid balance. The first payment is due one year after the loan is arranged.

Icarus Airlines leased eight jetliners of the same type purchased by Kosti for a 12-year term. Icarus does not have an option to buy the jets at the end of the lease term, and it classified the lease as an operating lease. Lease rent is $22 million a year, payable at the end of each year. The lease rent does not include property taxes, insurance, and maintenance of the jetliners; Icarus pays all such expenses. The annual rent was computed to give the lessor slightly less than 8% return on investment, taking into account the $24 million resale value of the jets at the end of the 12-year lease term. The lease is noncancelable.

Instructions

a Prepare a working paper to compute annual expenses (depreciation and interest) for Kosti Airlines in connection with the ownership of the eight jetliners. How do annual expenses for Kosti compare with the annual lease rental incurred by Icarus Airlines? What is the significance of the difference?

b Show the amounts relating to the jets and the related loan that appear in the balance sheet of Kosti Airlines at the end of the first year. In what respect is the balance sheet for Icarus Airlines different?

c Do you believe that the classification of the lease as an operating lease by Icarus Airlines was in conformity with the provisions of *Accounting for Leases* issued by the FASB? State reasons for your conclusion.

PROBLEMS

20-1   On July 1, Year 4, Listor Corporation leased equipment to Lassie Company. The equipment had been carried by Listor in the Inventories account at a cost of $220,000. Both companies have a June 30 fiscal year. There were no other significant costs associated with the lease and no residual value guarantee by the lessee. The lease is for a noncancelable term of eight years, with $50,000 rent payable at the beginning of each fiscal year; title passes to Lassie at the end of the lease term. Lassie made the first lease payment on July 1, Year 4. The lessor's implicit interest rate, which is known to Lassie and is smaller than Lassie's incremental borrowing rate of 13%, is 10%, and the present value of an annuity due of eight rents of 1 at 10% is 5.868419. The equipment is expected to have an economic life of 11 years with no residual value, and will be depreciated on a straight-line basis.

Instructions   (Round all computations to nearest dollar.)

a Prepare the journal entry for Listor Corporation (lessor) on July 1, Year 4, to record the lease transaction as a sales-type lease. Include the first lease payment in the journal entry.

b Prepare the journal entry for Listor Corporation (lessor) on June 30 Year 5, to record interest revenue for one year.

c Prepare the journal entry for Listor Corporation (lessor) on July 1, Year 4, to record the lease transaction, but for this part of the problem *assume that the transaction was classified as an operating lease.*

d Compute the expenses relative to the lease for Lassie Company (lessee) for the fiscal year ended June 30, Year 5, assuming that it classified the lease (1) as an operating lease, or (2) as a capital lease.

20-2   Techno, Inc., was incorporated in Year 1 with a fiscal year ending August 31. Techno's primary product is a sophisticated on-line inventory control system. Its customers pay a fixed fee plus a usage charge for using the system.

Techno has leased a large, BIG-I computer system from the manufacturer. The lease calls for monthly rent of $31,000 for the 144 months (12 years) of the lease term. The estimated economic life of the computer is 15 years.

Each monthly rent payment includes $6,000 for the full-service maintenance on the computer to be performed by the manufacturer. Rent is payable on the first day of the month beginning on August 1, Year 2, the date the computer was installed and the lease contract was signed.

The lease is noncancelable for its 12-year term, and it is collateralized only by the manufacturer's security interest in the BIG-I system. On August 1, Year 14, Techno acquires title to the BIG-I system under the lease contract.

This lease is to be accounted for as a capital lease by Techno, and the computer will be depreciated by the straight-line method with no residual value. Borrowed funds for this type of transaction would cost Techno 12% a year (1% a month). The lessor's implicit interest rate is unknown to Techno. Following is a schedule of the present value of 1 for selected periods discounted at 1% a period when payments are made at the beginning of each period:

Periods (months)	Present value of 1 each period discounted at 1% a period
1	1.000
2	1.990
3	2.970
143	76.658
144	76.899

Instructions   Prepare journal entries for Techno, Inc., for the month of August, Year 2, relating to this lease. Show supporting computations in the explanation for each entry. Remember, August 31, Year 2, is the end of Techno's fiscal year. Do not prepare closing entries.

20-3   On January 2, Year 1, Racers, Inc., leased a racing car from Daytona Leasing Company. The fixed noncancelable term of the lease was 24 months, with an option to renew month by month based on a schedule of rents and guarantees of the residual value which decrease over time. The cost, fair value, and estimated economic life of the racing car are listed below:

Lessor's cost of racing car (carried in Racing Equipment account of lessor)	$116,070
Fair value of racing car at inception of lease (Jan. 2, Year 1)	$116,070
Estimated economic life	36 months

The lease specified that Racers, Inc., will pay $4,125 on the first day of each month and that it will guarantee a residual value of $35,000 to Daytona Leasing Company at the end of 24 months (December 31, Year 2).

The lessee is to receive any excess over the guaranteed amount at the end of the lease term. Collectibility of lease rent was reasonably predictable, and no unreimbursable costs were expected to be incurred by the lessor. There were no initial direct costs of the lease. The rent was deemed to be fair, and the residual value guarantee was expected to approximate actual realizable value. Racers depreciates other racing cars it owns by the straight-line method, and its incremental borrowing rate generally is 1% a month, which is also the interest rate implicit in the lease. At the end of the lease term, December 31, Year 2, the racing car was sold by Daytona for $40,000. The excess of proceeds received over the guaranteed residual value was paid to Racers, Inc.

Instructions

a How should this lease be classified by the lessor and the lessee? Explain in terms of criteria required by **Accounting for Leases.** Use the Appendix in back of the book to compute the present value of minimum lease payments.

b Prepare journal entries required at the inception of the lease in the accounting records of (1) the lessor, and (2) the lessee. Prepare separate entries to record the lease and the first lease payment.

c Prepare journal entry or entries required at the end of the lease term in the accounting records of (1) the lessor, and (2) the lessee. Assume that entries to record depreciation, interest revenue, or interest expense have been recorded on December 31, Year 2.

20-4 Rosemont Ballroom entered into a lease on April 1, Year 1, for a sound system from Sound Equipment Leasing Co. The fixed noncancelable term of the lease is four years with an option to renew at terms which represent expected fair value at the option date. The following information is available:

Cost of sound system to Sound Equipment Leasing Co. (carried in Equip-
ment Held for Lease account) $19,996
Fair value of sound system at inception of lease $19,996
Estimated economic life of sound system . . . . 4 years

The lease contract specifies that Rosemont will pay $489 on the first day of each month, and that it guarantees a residual value of $2,000 to Sound Equipment Leasing Co. at the end of 48 months. Rosemont is to receive any excess over the $2,000 guarantee at the end of the lease term.

The collectibility of the lease rentals is reasonably predictable, and no unreimbursable costs are to be incurred. There were no initial direct costs of the lease. The rent is deemed to be fair, and the residual value guarantee is expected to approximate the sound system's realizable value at the end of the lease term. Rosemont depreciates its other plant assets on a straight-line basis and has an incremental borrowing rate of 15% compounded monthly. The interest rate implicit in the lease is 1% a month and is known to Rosemont.

At the end of the lease term, the sound system was sold by Sound Equipment Leasing Co. for $1,800, and the excess of the residual value guarantee over the sales proceeds was paid by Rosemont to Sound Equipment Leasing Co.

Instructions

a How should this lease be classified by the lessor and the lessee? Explain your conclusion in terms of the classification criteria required by **Accounting for Leases.** Use the Appendix in back of the book to compute the present value of minimum lease payments.

b Prepare the journal entries required at the inception of the lease in the accounting records of (1) Sound Equipment Leasing Co., and (2) Rosemont Ballroom. Include the first lease rent payment in the entry to record the lease.

c Prepare the journal entry or entries required at the termination of the lease in the accounting records of (1) Sound Equipment Leasing Co., and (2) Rosemont Ballroom. Assume that entries to record depreciation, interest revenue, or interest expense have been recorded on March 31, Year 5.

20-5 Koontz Company leased equipment with an estimated economic life of 12 years to Gage Company on January 2, Year 1, for a period of 10 years. The normal selling price of the equipment was $288,258, and the unguaranteed residual value at the end of the lease term was estimated to be $20,000. Gage agreed to pay annual rent of $40,000 at the beginning of each year and was responsible for all maintenance, insurance, and property taxes. Koontz incurred costs of $200,000 in manufacturing the equipment and $5,000 in negotiating and closing the lease. The collectibility of the lease payments was reasonably predictable, and no additional costs were expected to be incurred by Koontz. The implicit interest rate for Koontz was 9% a year and was known to Gage, which had an incremental borrowing rate of 12%.

Instructions (Use the Appendix in back of the book to obtain present values of 1 at 9%.)

a How should this lease be classified by Koontz Company? Explain.

b Assuming that Koontz Company classified this lease as a sales-type lease, compute the following at the inception of the lease:

(1) Gross investment in lease

(2) Net investment in lease

(3) Unearned interest revenue

(4) Selling price of equipment

(5) Cost of goods sold (cost of equipment plus initial direct costs less present value of the unguaranteed residual value)

c Prepare a working paper summarizing the amortization of the net investment in the lease and the recognition of interest revenue over the lease term for Koontz Company.

d Prepare the journal entries for the first year of the lease in the accounting records of Koontz Company. Include receipt of first rent payment in the entry to record the lease at its inception.

20-6 On December 31, Year 1, Offshore Company leased equipment to Breakwater Company. The equipment had a cost and fair value of $278,158. The term of the lease was for seven years, with a $50,000 payment due each December 31 starting in Year 1. The unguaranteed residual value was estimated at $30,000 at the end of the lease term, and the estimated economic life of the equipment was nine years. The terms were designed to give Offshore a 10% annual rate of return on its net investment (including initial direct costs), which had a present value of $283,158.

The lessee agreed to pay all property taxes, insurance, and maintenance; the lessor paid a commission of $5,000 to a broker for arranging the lease. Collectibility of the lease payments was reasonably predictable, and there were no additional costs to be incurred by the lessor.

Instructions (Use the Appendix in back of the book to obtain any present values of 1 at 10% which you may need to complete the following requirements.)

a How should this lease be classified by Offshore Company? Explain.

b Assuming that Offshore Company classified this lease as a direct financing lease, compute the following at the inception of the lease:

(1) Gross investment in lease

(2) Unearned interest revenue

(3) Net investment in lease

c Prepare a working paper summarizing the amortization of the $283,158 present value of the lease and the recognition of interest revenue over the lease term for Offshore Company.

d Prepare the journal entries in the accounting records of Offshore Company on December 31, Year 1, and on December 31, Year 2, relating to this lease.

20-7 In Year 1, Freighter Company negotiated and closed a long-term lease contract for newly constructed truck terminals. The terminals were constructed to the company's specifications on land owned by the company. On January 2, Year 2, Freighter took possession of the truck terminals.

Although the truck terminals have a composite economic life of 40 years, the noncancelable lease runs for 20 years from January 2, Year 2, with a favorable purchase option available on the expiration of the lease. You have determined that the truck terminals and related obligation should be accounted for as a capital lease by Freighter.

The 20-year lease is effective for the period January 2, Year 2, through December 31, Year 21. Rent payments of $1,000,000 are payable to the lessor on January 2 of each of the first 10 years of the lease term. Rent payments of $300,000 are due on January 2 for each of the last 10 years of the lease. The company has an option to purchase the truck terminals for $1,000 on December 31, Year 21. It also must make annual payments to the lessor of $95,000 for property taxes and $155,000 for insurance; these payments also are due on January 2. The lease was negotiated to assure the lessor a 10% rate of return, which is known to Freighter. The incremental borrowing rate of Freighter is 12%.

Instructions   (Use the Appendix in back of the book and round all computations to the nearest dollar.)

a Prepare a working paper to compute for Freighter Company (lessee) the present value of the minimum lease payments on January 2, Year 2.

b Prepare journal entries for Freighter Company (lessee) to record the:
   (1) Lease transaction and the payment to the lessor on January 2, Year 2 (separate entries). Record executory costs in expense accounts.
   (2) Depreciation of the truck terminals for Year 2, using the straight-line method and assuming a zero residual value.
   (3) Interest expense for the year ended December 31, Year 2.
   (4) Payment to the lessor on January 2, Year 3.

20-8   On April 1, Year 5, Louie Corporation signed a five-year, noncancelable equipment lease with Lenore Corporation. Annual rent of $10,000 is payable in advance, starting on April 1, Year 5. The lease contract gave the lessee an option to purchase the equipment on March 31, Year 10, for $1,000, and the lease is classified appropriately as a sales-type lease by the lessor and as a capital lease by the lessee.

The estimated economic life of the equipment is 10 years, and management of Louie estimated that the residual value of the equipment at the end of its economic life will approximate the dismantling and removal costs. The straight-line method of depreciation is used by Louie, and its fiscal year ends on March 31.

The incremental borrowing rate for Louie on April 1, Year 5, is 10% a year. The present value of an annuity due of five annual payments of 1 at 10% is 4.169865, and the present value at 10% of 1 due March 31, Year 10, is 0.620921. The lessor's implicit interest rate also is 10%.

Instructions

a Prepare a summary of lease payments and lessee's interest expense for each of the five years of the lease.

b Prepare journal entries for Louie Corporation (lessee) relating to the lease for the fiscal year ended March 31, Year 6.

c Assuming that the equipment is carried in the accounting records of Lenore Corporation in the Inventory of Equipment account at $37,000 and that there were no initial direct costs, prepare a journal entry to record the lease in the accounting records of Lenore Corporation. Include the receipt of the initial rent as part of the journal entry.

21 ACCOUNTING FOR INCOME TAXES

One of the more challenging areas of accounting is the reporting problem created when pre-tax accounting income in a corporation's income statement differs materially from taxable income reported in its income tax return. Our discussion in this chapter relates entirely to corporations, because other business enterprises (such as single proprietorships and partnerships) are not taxable entities. We have discussed in previous chapters a number of situations which produce such differences. In the preparation of an income statement, accountants are concerned primarily with the measurement of operating results in accordance with generally accepted accounting principles. Taxable income, on the other hand, is a legal concept. In designing federal tax laws, Congress is interested not only in meeting the revenue needs of government but also in achieving other economic and social objectives. Because the rules for the measurement of pre-tax accounting income and taxable income were developed with different objectives in mind, it is not surprising that the results are sometimes materially different. In this chapter we shall discuss some of those differences. The investment tax credit is considered in Chapter 11.

The nature of tax allocation

Why do differences between pre-tax accounting income and taxable income produce a financial reporting problem? To answer this question, consider the following highly condensed comparative income statements for American Company:

AMERICAN COMPANY Condensed Comparative Income Statement For Years 1 and 2		
	Year 2	Year 1
Sales and other revenue	$9,000,000	$9,000,000
Less:		
Cost of goods sold	(5,400,000)	(5,400,000)
Operating expenses	(2,600,000)	(2,600,000)
Income before income taxes	$1,000,000	$1,000,000
Income taxes expense	600,000	300,000
Net income	$ 400,000	$ 700,000

In the examination of this comparative income statement, the user would want to know why the same pre-tax accounting income resulted in such a large difference in net income for the two years. Corporate income tax rates are changed frequently, but in recent years the rates have been such that corporations with a pre-tax income of $1 million would pay about half of this amount in federal and state income taxes. Knowing this, the user would expect American Company to pay about $500,000 of income taxes each year, and would want to know why income taxes were so much smaller than that in Year 1, and so much larger in Year 2. It is apparent that American's taxable income in each of the two years differed materially from its pre-tax accounting income. By analyzing the source of the differences between pre-tax accounting income as determined from the accounting records and taxable income, we could determine whether income taxes expense was reported in accordance with generally accepted accounting principles.

Another possible distortion between pre-tax accounting income and income taxes expense may result if extraordinary items are included in the income statement and if income taxes are not properly allocated. To illustrate this point, consider the partial income statement for Extra-Ord Corporation below:

EXTRA-ORD CORPORATION
Partial Income Statement
For Year 1

Income before income taxes.	$100,000
Income taxes expense ($400,000 × 0.45, including tax on extraordinary gain of $300,000).	180,000
Operating loss before extraordinary gain	$ (80,000)
Extraordinary gain (before income tax effect).	300,000
Net income	$220,000

The picture presented in the income statement for Extra-Ord Corporation obviously is distorted. The operating income absorbs a charge for income taxes at the rate of 180%, but the extraordinary gain is reported at the full pre-tax amount of $300,000. An allocation of income taxes between pre-tax accounting income and the extraordinary gain at the effective tax rate of 45% would be more consistent with the matching principle and would correct the distorted relationship between pre-tax accounting income and income taxes expense.

Terminology used in accounting for income taxes

A brief definition of terms used in accounting for income taxes is necessary at this point.[1]

1 *Income taxes* Taxes based on income as determined under provisions of federal, state, and, in certain cases, foreign tax laws. This term also is used to describe the amount of income taxes (income taxes expense) allocated to an accounting period.

2 *Pre-tax accounting income* Income for an accounting period before deduction of income taxes. **Accounting income** and **income before income taxes** are alternative terms for pre-tax accounting income.

3 *Taxable income* (or *loss*) The excess of taxable revenue over deductible expenses (or the excess of deductible expenses over taxable revenue) for an accounting period. For purposes of this definition, deductible expenses do not include operating loss carrybacks or carryforwards.

4 *Timing differences* Differences between pre-tax accounting income and taxable income for an accounting period caused by reporting items of revenue or expense in one period for accounting purposes and in an earlier or later period for income tax purposes. Timing differences originate in one accounting period and "reverse" in future periods. Most timing differences reduce income taxes which otherwise would be payable currently, but a few timing differences increase the amount of income taxes payable currently.

5 *Permanent differences* Differences between pre-tax accounting income and taxable income arising from transactions which, under applicable tax laws and regulations, will not be offset by corresponding differences or reversals in future periods.

6 *Tax effects* Differences between actual income taxes payable currently and income taxes expense for an accounting period which are attributable to **(a)** revenue or expense transactions which enter into the determination of pre-tax accounting income in one accounting period and into the determination of taxable income in another period, **(b)** deductions or credits which may be carried backward or forward for income tax purposes, and **(c)** prior period adjustments. A permanent difference between pre-tax accounting income and taxable income does not result in a tax effect.

7 *Deferred taxes* Tax effects which are postponed for allocation (either as increases or decreases) to income taxes expense in future accounting periods.

8 *Interperiod tax allocation* The process of apportioning income taxes expense among accounting periods.

9 *Interim-period tax computation* The computation of income taxes expense for periods, such as fiscal quarters, within a year.

10 *Tax allocation within an accounting period* (*intraperiod tax allocation*) The process of apportioning income taxes expense applicable to an accounting period among income before extraordinary items, extraordinary items, and prior period adjustments.[2]

[1] Adapted with some modifications from *APB Opinion No. 11,* "Accounting for Income Taxes," AICPA (New York: 1967), pp. 158–160.

[2] Tax allocation within a period also applies to "income or loss from discontinued operations" and "cumulative effect on prior years of a change in accounting principle." Tax allocation treatment of these items parallels that accorded to extraordinary items.

Assumptions underlying interperiod tax allocation

Tax allocation procedures are based on the assumption that income taxes represent an expense of doing business and that income taxes will continue in the future. Income measurement on a going-concern assumption requires the application of the accrual basis of accounting. The accrual basis of accounting calls for the matching of realized revenue with expired costs for each accounting period. Accordingly, income taxes applicable to income recognized currently in the income statement should be estimated and accrued currently without regard to the time of payment. Income taxes which must be paid currently but which are applicable to income to be reported in the income statement in future accounting periods should be deferred and recognized as an expense when the related income is reported. Income taxes (or tax reductions) applicable to extraordinary items are offset against the pre-tax amounts of such items so that they are reported in the income statement *net of income taxes.*

Sources of differences between pre-tax accounting income and taxable income

The major sources of differences between pre-tax accounting income and taxable income fall in one of the following three categories:

1 *Timing differences in the recognition of revenue and expenses*   A number of provisions in the income tax law allow (or sometimes require) taxpayers to recognize revenue and expenses at different times than is appropriate under generally accepted accounting principles. When a corporation has an option, it is likely to choose accounting methods for income tax purposes that delay the recognition of revenue and accelerate the recognition of expenses.

2 *Differences due to carryback and carryforward of operating losses for income tax purposes*   The federal income tax law provides that an operating loss in one year may be offset against taxable income of specified previous and future tax years.[3] As a result, an **operating loss** in a given year may result in either a refund of income taxes previously paid or a potential reduction of income taxes in future years. For income tax purposes, **capital losses** incurred by corporations may be deducted only from capital gains, and capital losses in excess of capital gains in one year may be carried back and offset against net capital gains of the preceding three years. Any unused net capital loss may be carried forward and deducted against net capital gains in the succeeding five years.

3 *Permanent differences caused by legal provisions*   Some types of revenue and expense are recognized for accounting purposes but not for income tax purposes; some are recognized in the computation of taxable income but are not included in pre-tax accounting income.

---

[3] The current income tax law provides that an *operating loss* may be carried back to the third year before the loss and applied until exhausted against taxable income in successive years through the seventh year after the loss. The three-year carryback may be waived by the taxpayer and the entire loss carried forward. As in the case of taxable income, there are certain differences between the definition of an operating loss for income tax purposes and the accounting concept of such a loss.

In the following sections we shall consider the financial accounting implications of each of these three categories. In all illustrations we shall assume an effective corporate income tax rate of 45% on ordinary income and 30% on net long-term capital gains to simplify the computations.

Timing differences

In some cases the accounting period in which an item of revenue is taxable or an expense is deductible for income tax purposes differs from the period in which the revenue or expense is recognized in pre-tax accounting income. When pre-tax accounting income in any period differs from taxable income as a result of *timing differences,* the divergence will be counterbalanced in future periods by opposite variations between pre-tax accounting income and taxable income. When pre-tax accounting income is *larger* than taxable income, a deferred income tax liability results; when pre-tax accounting income is *smaller* than taxable income, a prepayment of income taxes results. Deferred income tax liabilities and prepaid income taxes are recognized through interperiod income tax allocation.

Pre-Tax Accounting Income Exceeds Taxable Income: Deferred Income Tax Liability Most timing differences produce pre-tax accounting income which is larger than taxable income. The two reasons for such differences are described below:

Revenue or gain is recognized in the accounting records in the current accounting period but is not taxed until later periods An example of this situation occurs when a corporation sells merchandise on the installment plan and recognizes accounting income on the accrual basis when sales are made, but elects to compute taxable income on the basis of cash collections. Another example involves long-term construction contracts when pre-tax accounting income is measured on the basis of construction in progress (the percentage-of-completion method described in Chapter 9), but taxable income is reported only when the contracts are completed (the completed-contract method described in Chapter 9). Finally, the use of the equity method of accounting for investments in common stock generally results in timing differences between taxable income and pre-tax accounting income.[4]

Expense or loss is deducted for income tax purposes in the current accounting period but is not recognized in the accounting records until later periods An example of this situation occurs when a corporation chooses an accelerated method to depreciate plant assets for income tax purposes but uses the straight-line method for financial accounting purposes.

[4] See Chapter 14 and *APB Opinions No. 23 and No. 24,* AICPA (New York: 1972).

To illustrate the accounting for a deferred income tax liability, assume that on January 2, Year 1, Slow Company acquired for $1 million a machine with an economic life of four years and no residual value. The company uses the sum-of-the-years'-digits method of depreciation for income tax purposes and the straight-line method for financial accounting purposes. Assuming that the company earns $800,000 each year (before depreciation expense and income taxes), the effect of these procedures on pre-tax accounting income and taxable income is shown below:

Effects of depreciation timing differences on pre-tax accounting income and taxable income

Year	Accounting income before depreciation and income taxes	Accounting depreciation	Tax return depreciation	Pre-tax accounting income	Taxable income
1	$ 800,000	$ 250,000	$ 400,000	$ 550,000	$ 400,000
2	800,000	250,000	300,000	550,000	500,000
3	800,000	250,000	200,000	550,000	600,000
4	800,000	250,000	100,000	550,000	700,000
Totals	$3,200,000	$1,000,000	$1,000,000	$2,200,000	$2,200,000

Note that the total pre-tax accounting income and taxable income are identical over the four-year period. The journal entries (explanations omitted) to record income taxes at 45% are presented below:

Journal entries for deferred income tax liability arising from depreciation timing differences

Year 1 Income Taxes Expense ($550,000 × 45%).   247,500
        Income Taxes Payable ($400,000 × 45%) . . .   180,000
        Deferred Income Tax Liability   67,500

Year 2 Income Taxes Expense ($550,000 × 45%).   247,500
        Income Taxes Payable ($500,000 × 45%) . . .   225,000
        Deferred Income Tax Liability   22,500

Year 3 Income Taxes Expense ($550,000 × 45%).   247,500
        Deferred Income Tax Liability   22,500
        Income Taxes Payable ($600,000 × 45%) . . .   270,000

Year 4 Income Taxes Expense ($550,000 × 45%).   247,500
        Deferred Income Tax Liability   67,500
        Income Taxes Payable ($700,000 × 45%) . . .   315,000

A deferred tax liability of $90,000 ($67,500 + $22,500 = $90,000) arises during the first two years when pre-tax accounting income exceeds taxable income and is extinguished during the last two years when the reverse is true. In the income statement for each year, income taxes expense should be divided between the amount currently payable and the amount deferred, as illustrated below for Year 1:

SLOW COMPANY		
Partial Income Statement		
For Year 1		
Income before income taxes (operating income).		$550,000
Income taxes expense:		
Payable currently.	$180,000	
Deferred.	67,500	247,500
Net income		$302,500

Taxable Income Exceeds Pre-Tax Accounting Income: Prepaid Income Taxes
The two reasons why taxable income may exceed pre-tax accounting income are explained below:

Revenue or gain is taxed in the current accounting period but is not recognized in the accounting records until later periods   Congress is conscious of the fact that taxpaying ability arises when taxpayers have cash with which to pay the tax. Therefore, the income tax law tends to make collection of income the general test of tax timing. The accounting test of income recognition depends both on realization and on whether the business enterprise has earned the income. Revenue received in advance is not included in pre-tax accounting income until the earning process is complete, but it usually must be reported for income tax purposes in the period received. For example, suppose that a corporation leases property for five years at $30,000 a year and receives the first and last (fifth) year's rent in advance. For income tax purposes the entire $60,000 must be included in income in the year of receipt; for financial accounting purposes the $30,000 rent for the fifth year is carried as deferred revenue in the balance sheet until the fifth year, when it will be included in pre-tax accounting income but will not be subject to income taxes because it was included in taxable income in the first year.

Expense or loss is recognized in the accounting records in the current accounting period but is not deducted for income tax purposes until later periods   In general, an expense or a loss is recorded when evidence that it has been incurred is reasonably clear. For income tax purposes, more definite evidence sometimes is required. As stated in Chapter 10, corporations often guarantee their products against defects for a number of years. On the basis of experience, a corporation knows that, despite its best efforts, a certain portion of the products sold will prove defective, and it must accrue an estimated liability under the product warranty in order to match the estimated expense with revenue in the year the sale was made. For income tax purposes, however, this estimated expense is not deductible until it actually has been incurred. Pre-tax accounting income therefore is smaller than taxable income in the year the estimated expense is recorded, and the reversal will take place in the year in which customers make claims under the product warranty.

To illustrate the accounting for prepaid income taxes, assume that Fast Company sells products which require servicing over a five-year product warranty period. The company estimates warranty expenses as a percentage of the sales in each year. However, for income tax purposes the warranty expenses are deductible only *as incurred.* During the first three years of operations the estimated warranty expenses and actual servicing costs were as follows:

Effects of warranty expense timing differences on pre-tax accounting income and taxable income

Year	Accounting income before warranty expenses	Estimated warranty expenses	Pre-tax accounting income	Actual servicing costs	Taxable income
1	$ 600,000	$100,000	$ 500,000	$ 20,000	$ 580,000
2	600,000	100,000	500,000	150,000	450,000
3	600,000	100,000	500,000	70,000	530,000
Totals	$1,800,000	$300,000	$1,500,000	$240,000	$1,560,000

Under interperiod tax allocation procedures, Fast Company accrues income taxes expense each year on the basis of pre-tax accounting income and records the difference between the current income tax liability and the income taxes expense as prepaid income taxes. Journal entries (explanations omitted) to record income taxes at the rate of 45% for the three years are shown below:

Journal entries for prepaid income taxes arising from warranty timing differences

Year 1	Income Taxes Expense ($500,000 × 45%).	225,000	
	Prepaid Income Taxes	36,000	
	Income Taxes Payable ($580,000 × 45%) . . .		261,000
Year 2	Income Taxes Expense ($500,000 × 45%).	225,000	
	Prepaid Income Taxes.		22,500
	Income Taxes Payable ($450,000 × 45%) . . .		202,500
Year 3	Income Taxes Expense ($500,000 × 45%).	225,000	
	Prepaid Income Taxes	13,500	
	Income Taxes Payable ($530,000 × 45%) . . .		238,500

In this illustration, pre-tax accounting income and taxable income are not identical over the three-year period, but there is a presumption that the $60,000 excess of estimated warranty expenses over actual servicing costs will counterbalance in future years. The debit balance of $27,000 ($36,000 − $22,500 + $13,500 = $27,000) in the Prepaid Income Taxes account at the end of Year 3 represents the future income tax benefits that will arise when the servicing costs actually are incurred and, although not reported as an expense for financial accounting purposes, are deducted in the computation of taxable income.

In the income statement for Year 1, Fast Company reports $225,000 of income taxes expense. To meet the standards of sound financial reporting, however, the amount of income taxes currently payable and prepaid income taxes applicable to future periods are shown separately as follows:

FAST COMPANY
Partial Income Statement
For Year 1

Income before income taxes (operating income)		$500,000
Income tax expense:		
Payable currently.	$261,000	
Less: Prepaid income taxes	36,000	225,000
Net income		$275,000

Alternative Approaches to Interperiod Tax Allocation Three approaches to the accounting for timing differences have been suggested. These are summarized below:

1 *Deferred method* Under this income statement approach, the income tax effects of current timing differences are computed with **tax rates in effect when the deferral of taxes takes place.** No adjustments are made to the Deferred Income Tax Liability account or to the Prepaid Income Taxes account for subsequent changes in income tax rates. The deferred taxes are allocated to income taxes expense when the timing differences reverse. The treatment of timing difference reversals is illustrated on page 848 in the Slow Company example (Years 3 and 4) and on page 850 in the Fast Company example (Year 2).

2 *Liability method* This is essentially a balance sheet approach to interperiod tax allocation. Its main objective is the correct measurement of the deferred income tax liability. If the income tax rates in the year the deferral takes place are different from the expected tax rates in the year in which the payment of income taxes is anticipated, the latter rates are used to measure the deferred income tax liability. Furthermore, subsequent changes in income tax rates require adjustment of the deferred income tax liability to reflect the new tax rates.

3 *Net-of-tax method* Interperiod tax allocation under the net-of-tax method views the income tax effects of timing differences as **valuation accounts** associated with the related assets and liabilities. The tax effects are applied to reduce specific assets or liabilities. For example, the deferred income tax "liability" arising from the use of an accelerated depreciation method for income tax purposes would be deducted from plant assets in the balance sheet; similarly, the deferred income tax "liability" arising from the use of the installment method of accounting for income tax purposes would be deducted from installment receivables.

APB Opinion No. 11 required the use of the deferred method; the Opinion stated:[5]

> The Board has concluded that the deferred method of tax allocation should be followed since it provides the most useful and practical approach to interperiod tax allocation and the presentation of income taxes in financial statements.

Computational Techniques for Interperiod Tax Allocation   The following provisions of **APB Opinion No. 11** provided guidelines for the computation of tax effects in interperiod tax allocation:[6]

> The tax effect of a timing difference should be measured by the differential between income taxes computed **with** and **without** inclusion of the transaction creating the difference between taxable income and pre-tax accounting income. The resulting income tax expense for the period includes the tax effects of transactions entering into the determination of results of operations for the period. The resulting deferred tax amounts reflect the tax effects which will reverse in future periods. The measurement of income tax expense becomes thereby a consistent and integral part of the process of matching revenues and expenses in the determination of results of operations. (Emphasis added)

The "with" and "without" technique described in the foregoing quotation is illustrated in the examples for Slow Company and Fast Company on pages 848 and 850. The debits to Income Taxes Expense are based on pre-tax accounting income, **without** the timing differences. The credits to Income Taxes Payable are based on taxable income, **with** the timing differences. The Slow Company and Fast Company examples are simple because each company has only one timing difference between pre-tax accounting income and taxable income. The "with" and "without" technique is complicated by numerous types of timing differences.

If income tax rates change, a corporation may select either the gross-change method or the net-change method to compute the tax effects of timing differences. Under the **gross-change method,** the tax effects of timing differences arising in the current accounting period are determined at the current income tax rates. The tax effects of timing differences which arose in prior periods and reverse in the current period are determined at the income tax rates applicable at the time the timing differences arose. Under the **net-change method,** the tax effects of the net change in the original and "reversing" timing differences are determined at the current income tax rates.

---

[5] *APB Opinion No. 11,* p. 169.
[6] Ibid.

Illustration of Gross-Change and Net-Change Methods   To illustrate the gross-change and net-change methods, let us return to the Slow Company example on page 848 and assume that on January 2, Year 3, the company acquired for $1,200,000 another machine with an economic life of four years and no residual value. The sum-of-the-years'-digits method of depreciation was adopted for income tax purposes, and the straight-line method was adopted for financial accounting purposes. The income tax rate decreased to 40% for Year 3 from the 45% rate in effect for Years 1 and 2. Accounting depreciation for the new machine for Year 3 is $300,000 ($1,200,000 × $\frac{1}{4}$ = $300,000); tax-return depreciation for Year 3 is $480,000 ($1,200,000 × $\frac{4}{10}$ = $480,000). Thus, revised pretax accounting income for Year 3 is $250,000 ($550,000 − $300,000 = $250,000), and taxable income is $120,000 ($600,000 − $480,000 = $120,000). The Year 3 journal entry for income taxes under the gross-change method is as follows:

<table>
<tr><td rowspan="8">**Journal entry for income taxes under the gross-change method**</td><td colspan="2">Income Taxes Expense . . . .</td><td>97,500</td><td></td></tr>
<tr><td colspan="2">   Income Taxes Payable . . . .</td><td></td><td>48,000</td></tr>
<tr><td colspan="2">   Deferred Income Tax Liability . . . .</td><td></td><td>49,500</td></tr>
<tr><td colspan="4">To provide for income taxes for Year 3 as follows:</td></tr>
<tr><td colspan="2"> Income taxes payable currently ($120,000 × 0.40)</td><td colspan="2">$ 48,000</td></tr>
<tr><td colspan="2"> Add: Income tax effects of timing differences aris-
    in Year 3 [($480,000 − $300,000) × 0.40] . . . .</td><td colspan="2">72,000</td></tr>
<tr><td colspan="2">   Subtotal . . . .</td><td colspan="2">$120,000</td></tr>
<tr><td colspan="2"> Less: Income tax effects of timing difference re-
    versing in Year 3 [($250,000 − $200,000) × 0.45]</td><td colspan="2">22,500</td></tr>
</table>

Income taxes expense for Year 3 . . . . $ 97,500

Under the net-change method, Slow Company's Year 3 journal entry for income taxes is as follows:

<table>
<tr><td rowspan="4">**Journal entry for income taxes under the net-change method**</td><td colspan="2">Income Taxes Expense ($250,000 × 0.40) . . . .</td><td>100,000</td><td></td></tr>
<tr><td colspan="2">   Income Taxes Payable ($120,000 × 0.40) . . . .</td><td></td><td>48,000</td></tr>
<tr><td colspan="2">   Deferred Income Tax Liability . . . .</td><td></td><td>52,000</td></tr>
<tr><td colspan="4">To record income taxes expense for Year 3.</td></tr>
</table>

The $2,500 difference ($100,000 − $97,500 = $2,500) between income taxes expense computed under the gross-change method and income taxes expense computed under the net-change method is verified on top of page 854.

Reversing timing difference in Year 3.	*$50,000*
Difference between income tax rates for Years 1 and 2 (45%) and Year 3 (40%).	*0.05*
Difference between income taxes expense computed under gross-change method (which reflects tax rate changes) and net-change method (which does not reflect tax rate changes)	*$ 2,500*

Carryback and carryforward of operating losses

To help lighten the income tax burden of corporations that experience losses, the current federal income tax law provides that operating losses may be carried back against the taxable income of the three preceding years and then forward against taxable income earned in the seven years following the loss. The effect of this provision is to create a receivable for a tax refund or potential future tax savings when an operating loss occurs. When an operating loss is carried back or carried forward, pre-tax accounting income and taxable income (after the operating loss is deducted) differ for the year to which the loss is applied. Thus, *operating losses create special kinds of tax timing differences.*

Operating Loss Carryback When an operating loss occurs following a period of profitable operations, a corporation has a claim for a refund of past income taxes which should be recognized in the accounting records in the year in which the loss occurs. On this point, *APB Opinion No. 11* stated:[7]

> The tax effects of any realizable loss *carrybacks* should be recognized in the determination of net income (loss) of the loss periods. The tax loss gives rise to a refund (or claim for refund) of past taxes, which is both measurable and currently realizable; therefore the tax effect of the loss is properly recognizable in the determination of net income (loss) for the loss period.

To illustrate the accounting for an operating loss carryback, assume that Hargis Company reports an operating loss of $100,000 for the current year. Because of certain technical adjustments required by tax laws, the company is able to carry back only $90,000 of this loss and offset it against taxable income of a prior year, thus claiming a tax refund of $40,500 (assuming a 45% income tax rate). The journal entry on top of page 855 recognizes the effect of the loss carryback.

[7] Ibid., p. 172.

Journal entry for operating loss carryback

Income Tax Refund Receivable 40,500

    Income Tax Benefit of Operating Loss Carryback 40,500

To record claim for income taxes previously paid: $90,000 ×
45% = $40,500.

The lower section of the company's income statement for the year in which the operating loss is incurred appears as follows:

Income statement presentation of operating loss carryback

HARGIS COMPANY
Partial Income Statement
For Current Year

Operating loss before income tax effect of operating loss carryback .	$(100,000)
Less: Income tax benefit of operating loss carryback	40,500
Net loss.	$ (59,500)

Operating Loss Carryforward If a corporation must depend on future earnings to use a current year's operating loss as a tax deduction, the accounting for income taxes presents a more difficult problem. For example, suppose that Meagher Corporation had a $200,000 loss in the first year of operations. A question arises as to whether the probability of future income tax benefit is sufficiently high to permit an accounting treatment which *anticipates* the income tax benefit of the operating loss carryforward. On this point, the APB took the following position:[8]

> The tax effects of loss *carryforwards* also relate to the determination of net income (loss) of the loss periods. However, a significant question generally exists as to realization of the tax effects of the *carryforwards,* since realization is dependent upon future taxable income. Accordingly, the Board has concluded that the tax benefits of loss *carryforwards* should not be recognized until they are actually realized, except in unusual circumstances when realization is *assured beyond any reasonable doubt* at the time the loss *carryforwards* arise. When the tax benefits of loss *carryforwards* are not recognized until realized in full or in part in subsequent periods, the tax benefits should be reported in the results of operations of those periods as extraordinary items.

In its first year of operations, then, Meagher Corporation reports the full loss of $200,000 in its income statement without adjustment for the possible income tax benefits in future years. Assuming that Meagher had pre-tax accounting income of $240,000 in the second year and that the income tax rate was 45%, the journal entry to record income taxes expense and the income tax benefit of the operating loss carryforward is given on top of page 856.

[8] Ibid., p. 173.

Income Taxes Expense....................	108,000	
Income Taxes Payable...................		18,000
Extraordinary Item: Income Tax Benefit of Operating		
Loss Carryforward....................		90,000

To record income taxes expense and effect of operating loss carryforward. Amounts are determined below:

Income taxes expense: $240,000 \times 45\% = $108,000.

Income taxes payable: ($240,000 − $200,000) \times 45\% = $18,000.

Income tax benefit of operating loss carryforward: $200,000 \times 45\% = $90,000.

The lower section of the comparative income statements for Meagher Corporation issued at the end of the second year are presented below:

MEAGHER CORPORATION
Partial Comparative Income Statements
For Years 1 and 2

	Year 2	Year 1
Income (loss) before income taxes	$240,000	$(200,000)
Less: Income taxes expense (only $18,000 is actually payable after deduction of $90,000 income tax benefit of operating loss carryforward)................	108,000	–0–
Income before extraordinary item	$132,000	$(200,000)
Extraordinary item: Income tax benefit of operating loss carryforward........................	90,000	–0–
Net income (loss).....................	$222,000	$(200,000)

If the realization of a potential income tax benefit of an operating loss carryforward is "assured beyond any reasonable doubt," the income tax benefit should be recognized in the accounting period of the loss by recording an asset (potential income tax benefit) and reducing the pre-tax loss by the same amount. Because the prospect of future income is always uncertain, the recognition of a potential income tax benefit of an operating loss carryforward in the loss period should be considered an exceptional approach. It might apply, for example, in the case of a well-established company with a history of steadily increasing earnings and good future prospects, which incurs a substantial loss because of an unprofitable venture that is not expected to recur. Under these circumstances the probability that the loss will produce a future income tax benefit may be sufficiently high to permit recognition of the carryforward income tax benefit as an asset.[9]

The amount of the potential income tax benefit recognized in the loss period should be computed with the income tax rate expected to be in effect at the time of realization. The asset (potential income tax benefit of operating loss carryforward) is reduced by a debit to income taxes expense in the computation of net income of future profitable periods.

As an example, assume that Oriole Corporation had pre-tax income of $50,000 in Year 1 (a year in which its income was taxed at only a 20% rate), $200,000 in Year 2, and $400,000 in Year 3, but incurred a $50,000 pre-tax loss in Year 4 because of a labor strike. The strike was settled late in Year 4, and Oriole's management was confident that taxable income for Year 5 would exceed $500,000. Because carryforward of the operating loss to the next year would create tax savings of $22,500 (applying the 45% rate expected in Year 5 to the $50,000 loss) while a carryback would create a refund of only $10,000 (based on the 20% rate that had applied in Year 1), Oriole elected to wave the carryback option and to apply the operating loss to future years.[10] The journal entry to record the potential income tax benefit of the operating loss carryforward in Year 4 is:

Journal entry to record potential income tax benefit of operating loss carryforward	*Current Asset: Potential Income Tax Benefit of Operating Loss Carryforward* *22,500*	
	Income Tax Benefit of Operating Loss Carryforward (reduction of loss)	*22,500*
	To record effect on income taxes of operating loss carried forward to Year 5, based on anticipated income tax rate of 45% for Year 5: $50,000 × 45% = $22,500.	

Assuming that taxable income in Year 5 was $500,000, the income taxes expense for that year is recorded as shown on top of page 858.

---

[9] The SEC (*Staff Accounting Bulletin No. 8*) has stated that an operating loss carryforward should not be recorded as an asset unless the company has a very strong earnings history, the loss was not caused by a general economic or industry decline, the company has reasonable alternative tax strategies available, and a forecast based on reasonable assumptions indicates more than enough future income to offset the operating loss carryforward.
[10] Operating loss carrybacks must be applied first to the earliest year of the allowable carryback period—in this case to Year 1. However, the Tax Reform Act of 1976 added a provision allowing corporations to relinquish irrevocably the entire carryback period with respect to a given loss year.

**Journal entry to record
subsequent realization
of potential income tax
benefit of operating loss
carryforward**

Income Taxes Expense	*225,000*	
Current Asset: Potential Income Tax Benefit of Oper-		
ating Loss Carryforward		*22,500*
Income Taxes Payable.		*202,500*

*To record income taxes expense: $500,000 × 45% = $225,000.
The amount currently payable is reduced by the operating
loss carryforward: ($500,000 − $50,000) × 45% = $202,500.*

Permanent differences between taxable income and pre-tax accounting income

Pre-tax accounting income may differ from taxable income because certain revenue is exempt from taxation or because allowable tax deductions differ from expenses recognized for financial accounting purposes. These differences are permanent in the sense that they arise not from differences in the timing of revenue and expense but because Congress has used the income tax law to accomplish certain public policy objectives. Some illustrations are given below:

Nontaxable Revenue   Examples of accounting revenue which is not subject to federal income taxation are: interest received on state or municipal bonds and life insurance proceeds received by a corporation on death of its officers.

Nondeductible Expenses   Examples of business expenses which are not deductible for federal income tax purposes are: amortization of acquired goodwill, premiums paid on life insurance policies for which the corporation is the beneficiary, certain penalties, and illegal payments, such as those made for the purpose of influencing legislation or to obtain foreign business.

Tax Deductions that Are Not Expenses   The federal income tax law allows some deductions for income tax purposes which do not represent actual business expenses. The special deductions (usually 85%) for certain dividends received by corporations and the excess of percentage (statutory) depletion over cost depletion allowed on certain natural resources are prominent examples. A corporation which has tax-free revenue, nondeductible expenses, or percentage depletion in excess of cost depletion is taxed at an "average" income tax rate that differs from the "normal" tax rate applicable to corporations. This is an economic and political fact which should be reflected in the measurement of net income. Because permanent differences between taxable and pre-tax accounting income do not affect other accounting periods, interperiod tax allocation is not appropriate for such differences. A material permanent difference should be explained in a note to the financial statements.

Evaluation of interperiod tax allocation

We have seen that differences between pre-tax accounting income and taxable income arise from several sources. No allocation problem arises from permanent differences between pre-tax accounting income and taxable income. The *intraperiod* allocation of income taxes to extraordinary items and to prior period adjustments (discussed on pages 862–865) and the recognition of the income tax benefits of operating loss carryforwards as extraordinary gains are widely accepted. Few accountants question the desirability of recognizing the income tax effect of operating loss carryforwards when the tax benefits are virtually certain. Therefore, the controversy over income tax allocation centers on *interperiod* tax allocation.

Arguments in Favor of Interperiod Tax Allocation The two major arguments in favor of interperiod tax allocation may be stated as follows:

1 Income taxes result from the earning of income. The tax expense to be applied in the measurement of periodic income is the tax caused by each period's earnings, independent of the time of payment. Failure to match income taxes against income when it is included in the income statement causes misleading fluctuations in net income.

2 Timing differences are temporary and create liabilities or assets. A tax saving attributable to a timing difference is only a postponement of the income tax, and a highly probable future cash outlay based on a past event is created. Similarly, a tax payment based on income which will be recognized in the accounting records at some later date makes it highly probable that a corporation will earn tax-free income in future years, creating an expected future economic benefit. Consequently, these highly probable future outlays and benefits meet the accounting definitions of liabilities and assets. For these future outlays and benefits to be highly probable, it must be assumed that future income tax rates will remain at similar levels and that a corporation will earn taxable income in future years. Experience in past years has tended to support the assumption as to income tax rates; the assumption as to profitable continuity has proved applicable to most major corporations, especially with liberal operating loss carryback and carryforward provisions in the income tax law.

Arguments against Interperiod Tax Allocation Opposition to interperiod tax allocation is based primarily on the nature of income taxes and the possibility that timing differences may not be temporary. These arguments are summarized below:

1 Income taxes by their nature differ from most expenses. First, income taxes expense emerges only if income is earned; secondly, income taxes expense is based on taxable income, which differs from accounting income in a number of respects. This line of reasoning leads to the conclusion that income taxes are not an expense but an involuntary payment to government units. Furthermore, critics of interperiod tax allocation argue that the income taxes expense for an accounting period should be the legal tax liability for that period because income taxes are based on the legal concept of taxable income rather than on accounting income.

2 When we view the taxable income of a corporation as a whole, the shifting of income taxes in time (particularly the postponement of taxes) tends to be a

permanent rather than a temporary shift, because when one deferral is reversed another arises to take its place. This argument is raised most frequently with respect to one area of timing differences—the case in which a corporation adopts accelerated depreciation methods for income tax purposes, but not for accounting purposes. For example, a corporation acquiring about the same amount of plant assets each year realizes a tax postponement in the year in which accelerated depreciation is adopted, and this postponement is never offset in future years as long as the assets are replaced at a steady rate. If a corporation acquires a larger amount of plant assets each year, the total difference between tax depreciation and depreciation recorded in the accounting records continues to increase.

Evaluation of the Arguments   Neither argument against interperiod tax allocation is without significant logical flaws. Consider the following: Companies AD and SL acquire identical plant assets. Both use straight-line depreciation and the same economic lives for financial accounting purposes, but Company AD uses accelerated depreciation and Company SL uses straight-line depreciation for income tax purposes. Barring unusual circumstances, Company AD is clearly "better off" than Company SL because Company AD owes less income taxes **now** and will enjoy interest-free use of the funds arising from this tax saving until the timing differences reverse. This advantage exists regardless of whether the assets are replaced or whether the total investment in plant assets increases. Yet present income tax allocation requirements produce identical net incomes for both companies, and Company AD's relative economic gain is ignored.

However, this problem is not resolved by failure to allocate income taxes. Nonallocation shows the entire deferral as a net income advantage to Company AD. However, in future years Company SL is able to deduct more depreciation than Company AD from its taxable income with respect to these assets. To the extent that these future deductions have economic value, Company SL is "better off" than Company AD, yet without income tax allocation this relative advantage would be ignored.

There is no easy solution. Clearly in this tax deferral example, Company AD has gained an advantage of using "tax dollars" without paying interest. A reasonable measure of Company AD's economic gain would at first seem to be the difference between the gross income tax deferral and its **discounted value.** This would be consistent with viewing the tax deferral as a long-term liability. But if the tax deferral is a liability, it is indeed a most unusual one. The "liability" is paid only if future taxable income is earned; it may be renewed indefinitely through the acquisition of more depreciable assets, or it may increase or decrease as Congress changes income tax rates. As a result, both the estimate of the amount to be paid and the selection of an appropriate interest rate for discounting this type of liability might be viewed as highly speculative.

From a standpoint of traditional financial accounting, whereby net income is viewed as the critical measure of management performance, discounting the deferred tax items might achieve greater "fairness" than do present interperiod tax allocation procedures. However, from a standpoint of stock market evaluation of earnings potential, there is increasing evidence that the crucial elements are the *timeliness* and *completeness* of financial statement disclosures. Thus, the present interperiod tax allocation procedures may represent the best practical solution from the standpoint of investors. Such procedures appear to be simpler and more objective than discounting.

Partial Allocation versus Comprehensive Allocation In an effort to find a compromise position in the arguments for and against interperiod tax allocation, some accountants recommended *partial allocation* of timing differences. Supporters of partial interperiod tax allocation argued that when recurring differences between pre-tax accounting income and taxable income appear to cause an indefinite postponement of income tax payments, tax allocation is not required for such differences. For example, assume that a corporation with a growing investment in plant assets uses straight-line depreciation for financial accounting purposes and accelerated depreciation for income tax purposes. Under the partial allocation approach, the income taxes expense for the corporation would be the income tax actually payable for the accounting period.

Advocates of partial allocation thus make a general presumption that income taxes expense for financial accounting purposes should be the income tax payable for the accounting period, except for cases in which nonrecurring timing differences between taxable income and pre-tax accounting income cause material misstatement of income taxes expense and net income. Such an exception is illustrated by the installment sale of an asset at a gain, which is reported in accounting income of the current accounting period but is not taxable until future periods.

The more widely accepted position is that all timing differences between pre-tax accounting income and taxable income require *comprehensive allocation* of income taxes. Under comprehensive allocation, income taxes expense for an accounting period includes all accruals, deferrals, and estimates necessary to adjust the income taxes actually payable for the period in order to recognize the tax effects of transactions included in pre-tax accounting income for that period. Tax effects of initial timing differences are recognized and allocated to those periods in which the initial differences *reverse.* Comprehensive allocation thus associates tax effects with related transactions as they are reported in the income statement.

The APB resolved the issue of partial versus comprehensive tax allocation as follows:[11]

> The Board has considered the various concepts of accounting for income taxes and has concluded that comprehensive interperiod tax allocation is an integral part of the determination of income tax expense. Therefore, income tax expense should include the tax effects of revenue and expense transac-

[11] *APB Opinion No. 11*, p. 169.

tions included in the determination of pre-tax accounting income. The tax effects of those transactions which enter into the determination of pre-tax accounting income either earlier or later than they become determinants of taxable income should be recognized in the periods in which the differences between pre-tax accounting income and taxable income arise and in the periods in which the differences reverse.

Although **APB Opinion No. 11** established workable standards for interperiod tax allocation, it by no means eliminated the conceptual controversies associated with this subject. Many accountants and business executives continue to favor the liability method, partial allocation of income taxes, and the net-of-tax method for balance sheet presentation of deferred income tax accounts. Interperiod tax allocation probably will continue to be a controversial topic as long as taxes on corporate income continue to be levied at high rates.

Tax allocation within a period (intraperiod tax allocation)

The need for tax allocation within an accounting period (also known as **intraperiod tax allocation**) arises, for example, when extraordinary items are included in net income or a prior period adjustment is recorded in the current period. If extraordinary items and prior period adjustments are taxable or are deductible for income tax purposes, income taxes (or tax refunds) are apportioned between income before extraordinary items, extraordinary items, and prior period adjustments. Income taxes applicable to income before extraordinary items are based on the difference between revenue and expenses before giving effect to the income tax consequences of extraordinary items. Extraordinary items and prior period adjustments are reported **net** of the income tax effect in the income statement and the statement of retained earnings, respectively.

Extraordinary Gain and Prior Period Adjustment To illustrate a situation involving an extraordinary gain and a prior period adjustment, assume that Marvin Company reported the following for Year 4:

Data for illustration

Income before income taxes (fully taxable at 45%).	$300,000
Extraordinary long-term capital gain (taxable at 30%)	800,000
Prior period adjustment—increase in earnings for Year 1 as a result of	
an error (fully taxable at 45%)	200,000

The presentation of these items in the income statement and the statement of retained earnings with and without intraperiod tax allocation is shown on top of page 863.

Presentation of extraordinary gain and prior period adjustment with and without intraperiod tax allocation

	With tax allocation	Without tax allocation
Income statement:		
Income before income taxes.	$300,000	$ 300,000
Income taxes expense	135,000	465,000*
Income (loss) before extraordinary gain	$165,000	$(165,000)
Extraordinary gain:		
With tax allocation: $800,000 − ($800,000 ×		
30%).	560,000	
Without tax allocation		800,000
Net income	$725,000	$ 635,000
Statement of retained earnings:		
Prior period adjustment: Increase in beginning balance of retained earnings	$110,000	$ 200,000

* Income taxes expense: $300,000 × 45%	$135,000
Tax on long-term capital gain: $800,000 × 30%	240,000
Tax on prior period adjustment: $200,000 × 45% . . .	90,000
Total income taxes currently payable	$465,000

Failure to apply intraperiod tax allocation procedures in this case distorts the income statement and also understates net income by $90,000, the income tax applicable to the prior period adjustment.

Assuming that the extraordinary gain and the prior period adjustment already had been recorded (before recognition of the income tax effects), income taxes for Year 4, with intraperiod tax allocation, should be recorded by Marvin Company as illustrated below:

Journal entry for intraperiod tax allocation to extraordinary gain and to prior period adjustment

Income Taxes Expense	135,000	
Extraordinary Gain (Income tax effect)	240,000	
Prior Period Adjustment (Income tax effect)	90,000	
Income Taxes Payable.		465,000
To record income tax effects on operating income, extraordinary gain, and prior period adjustment (correction of error).		

Extraordinary Loss   To illustrate a situation involving an extraordinary loss, assume that in Year 5 Marvin Company reported pre-tax accounting income of $600,000 and incurred a fully deductible extraordinary loss of $500,000. The tax rate is 45%, and the company's liability for income taxes is $45,000 (45% of taxable income of $100,000). The comparative summary below shows how Marvin's income statement appears with and without intraperiod tax allocation:

	With tax allocation	*Without tax allocation*
Income before income taxes	*$600,000*	*$600,000*
Income taxes expense.	*270,000*	*45,000*
Income before extraordinary loss	*$330,000*	*$555,000*
Extraordinary loss:		
With tax allocation: $500,000 − ($500,000 ×		
45%)	*275,000*	
Without tax allocation.		*500,000*
Net income	*$ 55,000*	*$ 55,000*

The greater clarity obtained with intraperiod tax allocation is apparent. This presentation shows the after-tax effect of the extraordinary loss and the normal impact of income taxes on income before income taxes. If tax allocation is not used, the user of the income statement will question the relationship between the pre-tax income of $600,000 and the disproportionately low income taxes expense of $45,000. Without tax allocation, both the amount of income before extraordinary loss and the amount of the extraordinary loss are overstated by $225,000 ($500,000 × 45% = $225,000), the tax effect of the extraordinary loss. With intraperiod tax allocation, income taxes are recorded as follows:

Income Taxes Expense ($600,000 × 45%).	*270,000*	
Extraordinary Loss (Income tax effect).		*225,000*
Income Taxes Payable.		*45,000*
To record income tax effects on pre-tax income and extraordinary loss.		

Note that the income tax effect is recorded as an offset to the Extraordinary Loss account, which we have assumed had already been recorded at $500,000; it would be possible to record the income tax effect in a separate ledger account. In either case, the extraordinary loss is reported in the income statement net of income taxes, that is, at $275,000, with appropriate disclosure of the current income tax liability and the income tax effect of the loss.

Because extraordinary items and prior period adjustments create certain income tax consequences, intraperiod tax allocation is an effort to match income taxes (or tax credits) with these special items. In this way, extraordinary items and prior period adjustments are reported net of income taxes; that is, at amounts representing the net *economic impact* of such items.

Other situations requiring intraperiod income tax allocation include recognition of the cumulative effect of a change in an accounting principle and reporting gain or loss on disposal of a segment of a business. Treatment of these items is similar to the treatment of extraordinary items and is discussed in Chapters 3 and 22.

Presentation of income tax accounts in financial statements

Thus far we have assumed that income tax allocation which stems from differences in the timing of revenue and expense results in either a liability, Deferred Income Tax Liability, or an asset, Prepaid Income Taxes. Whether these accounts meet the definition of liabilities and assets is an issue worth considering.

A deferred income tax liability arises when a corporation recognizes income for financial accounting purposes before it is taxed. There is no existing debt to the government for taxes on future earnings which may or may not materialize. However, we previously have defined liabilities to include future outlays which result from current or past events and which can be measured with reasonable accuracy. Assuming continuing profitability, it is reasonable to include in this definition the increased taxes which will follow from having recognized income before it is taxed. Even though the deferred income tax liability may not be paid for many years, the APB stated that "deferred taxes should not be accounted for on a discounted basis."[12]

The classification of prepaid income taxes as an asset rests on the assumption that there will be a future income tax benefit to the corporation. At some later time the corporation will realize revenue which will not be subject to income tax, or it will have a tax deduction which will not be reported as an accounting expense. The asset represents the amount of tax that has already been paid on income to be reported in the income statement in future accounting periods.

The APB and the FASB emphasized the "deferred" characteristics of the tax accounts resulting from interperiod tax allocation procedures when they established the following guidelines for presentation of such accounts in the balance sheet:

> Deferred charges and deferred credits relating to timing differences represent the cumulative recognition given to their tax effects and as such do not represent receivables or payables in the usual sense. They should be classified in two categories—one for the net current amount and the other for the net noncurrent amount. This presentation is consistent with the customary distinc-

---

[12] *APB Opinion No. 10*, "Omnibus Opinion—1966," AICPA (New York: 1966), p. 145. This Opinion was issued prior to the adoption of discounting for long-term receivables and payables under *APB Opinion No. 21* (1971). Subsequent reluctance to require discounting for deferred tax items may be explained in part by the difficulty of specifying an appropriate interest rate. Also, see discussion on pages 860–861.

tion between current and noncurrent categories and also recognizes the close relationship among the various deferred tax accounts, all of which bear on the determination of income tax expense.[13]

A deferred charge or credit is related to an asset or liability if reduction of the asset or liability causes the timing difference to reverse. A deferred charge or credit that is related to an asset or liability shall be classified as current or noncurrent based on the classification of the related asset or liability. A deferred charge or credit that is not related to an asset or liability because **(a)** there is no associated asset or liability or **(b)** reduction of an associated asset or liability will not cause the timing difference to reverse shall be classified based on the expected reversal date of the specific timing difference. Such classification disregards any additional timing differences that may arise and is based on the criteria used for classifying other assets and liabilities.[14]

Claims for refunds of taxes previously paid or offsets to future taxes arising from the recognition of the tax effects of operating loss carrybacks or carryforwards should be classified either as current or as noncurrent, depending on the expected period of realization.

The requirements for reporting income tax accounts in the balance sheet are summarized below:

Current assets:

1 *Prepaid income taxes (related to current liabilities such as estimated product warranties outstanding which will be satisfied within one year or the next operating cycle of the corporation)*
2 *Claim for refund of income taxes previously paid*
3 *Potential income tax benefit of operating loss carryforward (if current benefits are assured beyond any reasonable doubt)*

Current liabilities:

1 *Deferred income tax liability (related to current assets such as receivables from installment sales or construction contracts in progress)*
2 *Current income tax liability (balance of tax due on income taxable currently)*

Noncurrent assets:

1 *Prepaid income taxes (related to noncurrent liabilities such as long-term product warranties outstanding)*
2 *Potential income tax benefit of operating loss carryforward (if benefits are assured beyond any reasonable doubt)*

Noncurrent liabilities:

1 *Deferred income tax liability (related to timing differences, such as those caused by use of an accelerated depreciation method for income tax purposes)*

[13] APB Opinion No. 11, p. 178.
[14] *FASB Statement No. 37,* "Balance Sheet Classification of Deferred Income Taxes," FASB (Stamford: 1980), p. 2.

The items listed first under each of the two current categories are offset and reported as a single amount. Similarly, the items listed first under each of the two noncurrent categories are offset and reported as a single amount.

The income taxes currently payable, the tax effects of timing differences, and the tax effects of operating loss carrybacks and carryforwards are disclosed in the income statement or in notes to the financial statements. These amounts are allocated to income before extraordinary items and to extraordinary items. The income tax benefit of an operating loss carryforward not previously recorded is reported as an extraordinary item in the accounting period in which it is realized. In addition, notes to the financial statements include disclosure of unused operating loss carryforwards (along with expiration dates), reasons for significant variations in the customary relationships between income taxes expense and pre-tax accounting income, and any other factors relating to income taxes that users of financial statements would find helpful in evaluating current and future earnings of the corporation.

For companies subject to its jurisdiction, the Securities and Exchange Commission requires more detailed disclosure of income taxes data. Additional SEC requirements include (1) breakdown of pre-tax income into its U.S. and foreign components, and (2) reconciliation of any difference between reported total income taxes expense and the expense that would result from application of the normal federal income tax rate to pre-tax accounting income.[15]

Allocation of income taxes expense to interim periods

Most publicly owned corporations issue earnings reports on a quarterly basis. Determination of income taxes expense for such interim accounting periods involves two classes of problems—estimation of appropriate income tax rates and the treatment of losses.

Estimation of appropriate tax rates includes (1) consideration of the effect of rate differentials, permanent differences between pre-tax accounting income and taxable income, expected investment tax credits, and other items; (2) selection of rates to be applied to ordinary income, extraordinary items, etc.; and (3) adjustment of these rates on the basis of legislation enacted during the fiscal year.[16]

For example, assume that Reynaldo Company is subject to income taxes at 20% on the first $50,000 of taxable income and at 50% on taxable income in excess of $50,000. Capital expenditures yielding $10,000 in investment tax credits are planned for the current fiscal year. Income before income taxes for the first quarter was $20,000, and at the time the

---

[15] *Regulation S-X*, Rule 4-08(g), SEC (Washington: 1980).

[16] *FASB Interpretation No. 18*, "Accounting for Income Taxes in Interim Periods." FASB (Stamford: 1977), pp. 4–5; *APB Opinion No. 28*, "Interim Financial Reporting," AICPA (New York: 1973), pp. 527–528.

income statement for the first quarter was being prepared, income before income taxes for the entire fiscal year was expected to be $100,000. There were no extraordinary items or timing differences. Income taxes expense for the first quarter is computed below:

Computation of income taxes expense for first quarter of fiscal year

Estimated income taxes expense for the year:	
($50,000 × 20%) + ($50,000 × 50%)	*$35,000*
Less: Anticipated investment tax credits	*10,000*
Net estimated income taxes expense for the year	*$25,000*
Estimated effective income tax rate for the year:	
$25,000 ÷ $100,000 = 25%	
Income taxes expense for the first quarter ($20,000 × 25%)	*$ 5,000*

For subsequent quarters the year-to-date income taxes expense is computed with a current estimate of the effective tax rate. The income taxes expense for the quarter is the difference between the new year-to-date income taxes expense and the tax previously recognized up to the beginning of the quarter. If Reynaldo Company had income before income taxes of $30,000 for the second quarter and now expected income before income taxes for the year of $110,000 instead of $100,000, and investment tax credits of $9,200 instead of $10,000, the income taxes expense for the second quarter is computed as follows:

Computation of income taxes expense for second quarter of fiscal year

Estimated income taxes expense for the year:	
($50,000 × 20%) + ($60,000 × 50%)	*$40,000*
Less: Anticipated investment tax credits	*9,200*
Net estimated income taxes expense for the year	*$30,800*
Estimated effective income tax rate for the year:	
$30,800 ÷ $110,000 = 28%	
Income taxes expense for the second quarter:	
Year-to-date income before income taxes ($20,000 + $30,000)	*$50,000*
Estimated effective income tax rate	*0.28*
Year-to-date income taxes expense.	*$14,000*
Less: Income taxes expense accrued for the first quarter	*5,000*
Income taxes expense for the second quarter	*$ 9,000*

Extraordinary items and other items not included in income before income taxes are treated as marginal items for purposes of interim income tax allocation. Income taxes expense is computed both with and without the extraordinary item, and the difference is the tax applicable to the extraordinary item. If the income tax rates are changed during a year, the effects on previous interim periods of new tax legislation should be reflected in the first interim period ending after the new legislation becomes effective; previously issued interim financial reports are not restated to reflect the new legislation.[17]

Treatment of situations involving losses in interim periods is similar to the treatment of operating loss carrybacks and carryforwards in annual reporting. A circumstance unique to interim reporting, however, is when seasonal earnings patterns establish the value of an operating loss carryforward beyond any reasonable doubt. When a seasonal loss is carried forward to a subsequent interim period in the same year, the tax benefits are **not reported as extraordinary items** as is the case in annual financial statements.

REVIEW QUESTIONS

1 What are the objectives of generally accepted accounting principles in their application to the income statement? What are the objectives of income tax laws?

2 Define **interperiod tax allocation, intraperiod tax allocation,** and **interim-period tax computation.**

3 What fundamental assumptions are necessary in the implementation of income tax allocation?

4 What are three sources of differences between pre-tax accounting income and taxable income?

5 Describe two situations which result, under interperiod tax allocation procedures, in a deferred income tax liability.

6 Describe two situations which result, under interperiod tax allocation procedures, in prepaid income taxes.

7 Explain the following interperiod tax allocation approaches:
  a Deferred method
  b Liability method
  c Net-of-tax method

8 Describe the **gross-change method** and the **net-change method** of accounting for timing differences between pre-tax accounting income and taxable income.

9 What is meant by an **operating loss carryback** and an **operating loss carryforward?**

10 Explain the different accounting problems that arise in accounting for an operating loss carryback and an operating loss carryforward.

11 Describe three situations which produce a permanent difference between taxable income and pre-tax accounting income. Give an example of each.

[17] *FASB Interpretation No. 18,* p. 10.

12 Explain how each of the following ledger accounts is classified (for example, current asset or current liability) in the balance sheet:
   a Deferred Income Tax Liability
   b Prepaid Income Taxes
   c Receivable—Refund of Income Taxes Previously Paid
   d Potential Income Tax Benefit of Operating Loss Carryforward

13 What information regarding income taxes should be included in notes to the financial statements?

14 Identify and briefly explain some of the problems involved in the determination of income taxes expense for interim accounting periods.

15 Briefly summarize the arguments for and against interperiod tax allocation.

EXERCISES

Ex. 21-1   Select the best answer for each of the following multiple-choice questions:

1 Wong Corporation had interest revenue on municipal obligations of $150,000 in Year 7. For financial accounting purposes Wong included the $150,000 in its income statement. For income tax reporting, the $150,000 was exempt income. Assuming an income tax rate of 50%, what should be reported in the provision for deferred income taxes relative to the interest revenue in Wong's income statement for the year ended December 31, Year 7?
   a $0   b $75,000 credit   c $75,000 debit   d $150,000 debit

2 Which of the following requires intraperiod tax allocation?
   a The portion of dividends reduced by the dividends received deduction available to corporations under federal income tax law
   b The excess of accelerated depreciation used for income tax purposes over straight-line depreciation used for financial accounting purposes
   c Extraordinary gains or losses as defined by the APB or the FASB
   d All differences between taxable income and pre-tax accounting income

3 Interperiod tax allocation is justified by the theory that income taxes should be treated as:
   a An expense
   b A distribution of earnings
   c A distribution of earnings for the current portion and an expense for the deferred portion
   d An expense for the current portion and a distribution of earnings for the deferred portion

4 The amount of income taxes applicable to transactions that are reported with intraperiod tax allocation is computed:
   a By multiplying the item by the effective income tax rate
   b As the difference between the income taxes computed based on taxable income excluding the item and the taxes computed based on taxable income including the item
   c As the difference between the income taxes computed on the item based on the amount used for financial accounting and the amount used in the computation of taxable income.
   d By multiplying the item by the difference between the effective income tax rate and the statutory income tax rate

5 Which of the following interperiod tax allocation methods uses the income tax rates in effect at the origination of the timing differences and does not adjust for subsequent changes in tax rates?

    a Deferred method
    b Liability method
    c Net-of-tax method
    d Net-present-value method

6 An example of an item requiring intraperiod tax allocation is:
    a Interest revenue on municipal obligations
    b Estimated expenses for major repairs accrued for financial accounting purposes in one year, but deducted for income tax purposes when paid in a subsequent year
    c Rent revenue included in income for income tax purposes when collected, but deferred for financial accounting until earned in a subsequent year
    d Reporting a prior period adjustment in the statement of retained earnings

Ex. 21-2 Wollmer Corporation purchased a machine on January 2, Year 8, for $5,500,000. The machine has an estimated economic life of 10 years with no residual value. The machine is being depreciated by the sum-of-the-years'-digits method for income tax reporting and by the straight-line method for financial accounting. The income tax rate is 45%.

    Compute Wollmer's provision for deferred income taxes for Year 8, labeled "debit" or "credit."

Ex. 21-3 Meserve Corporation reported the following operating results for the two years ended December 31, Year 8, and Year 7, respectively:

	December 31,	
	Year 8	**Year 7**
Pre-tax accounting income	*$1,200,000*	*$800,000*
Taxable income	*1,600,000*	*120,000*

The disparity between pre-tax accounting income and taxable income is attributable to timing differences. The income tax rate is 40%.

    Compute Meserve's income taxes expense for Year 8, divided between current and deferred portions.

Ex. 21-4 Nowack Corporation's accounting records for the year ended December 31, Year 9, showed pre-tax accounting income of $180,000. In the computation of taxable income, the following timing differences were taken into account:

Depreciation deducted for income tax purposes in excess of depreciation recorded in the accounting records	*$8,000*
Income from installment sale reportable for income tax purposes in excess of income recognized for financial accounting	*$6,000*

The federal income tax rate is 40%.

    Compute Nowack's current federal income tax liability on December 31, Year 9.

Ex. 21-5 In Year 5, Wylie Corporation reported $300,000 of pre-tax accounting income, but only $40,000 in its income tax return. In Year 6, pre-tax accounting income was $350,000 and taxable income was $400,000.

    Prepare the journal entry to record income taxes expense and income taxes payable for Year 6, assuming that timing differences were responsible for the disparity between pre-tax accounting income and taxable income. (Assume a 45% tax rate.)

Ex. 21-6 The pre-tax accounting income and taxable income for Abner Corporation for a three-year period are given on top of page 872.

Year	Pre-tax accounting income	Taxable income
1	$70,000	$60,000
2	70,000	70,000
3	70,000	80,000

The differences between pre-tax accounting income and taxable income were due solely to the use of the sum-of-the-years'-digits method of depreciation for income tax purposes and the straight-line method of depreciation for accounting purposes on a machine costing $70,000 and having a $10,000 residual value at the end of its three-year economic life. Income tax rates are 30% on the first $50,000 and 40% on income in excess of $50,000.

Prepare the journal entries required for each year to allocate income taxes resulting from timing differences in accounting for depreciation expense.

Ex. 21-7   The pre-tax accounting income and taxable income for Selkirk Corporation over a three-year period are presented below:

Year	Pre-tax accounting income	Taxable income
1	$100,000	$134,000
2	100,000	98,000
3	100,000	98,000

The differences between pre-tax accounting income and taxable income are explained as follows:

(1) Taxable income in Year 1 includes $36,000 of rent revenue that, for financial accounting purposes, was recorded as earned at the rate of $12,000 a year.
(2) Amortization of goodwill at the rate of $10,000 a year is recorded for financial accounting purposes but is not deductible in the computation of taxable income. (Amortization of goodwill does not give rise to a timing difference for tax allocation purposes.)

Prepare journal entries for Years 1, 2, and 3 to allocate income taxes. Assume that income taxes are 40% of taxable income.

Ex. 21-8   Income statements for Virgil Corporation show the following results for the first three years of its operations:

Year 1: Operating loss (before income taxes) . . . . $(100,000)
Year 2: Operating income (before income taxes)   240,000
Year 3: Operating loss (before income taxes) . . . .   (200,000)

The corporation operates in a cyclical and highly competitive industry.

Prepare the journal entries for each year to record the tax effects of operating loss carryforwards or carrybacks. Assume that operating losses as reported are allowable for income tax purposes and that the income tax rate is 40%.

Ex. 21-9   Carle Corporation reported pre-tax accounting income of $300,000 and an extraordinary gain of $1.2 million for the year ended March 31, Year 4.

Prepare a journal entry to record the tax effect on the pre-tax accounting income and of the extraordinary gain. (Record the tax effect of the extraordinary gain as a debit to the gain account.) Show how the foregoing information should be presented in the income statement for the year ended March 31, Year 4. (The income tax rates are 40% on income before income taxes and 30% on the extraordinary gain.)

Ex. 21-10   Webb Corporation issues financial statements on a quarterly basis. During Year 1, its actual quarterly results and its expectations were as follows:

	Pre-tax accounting income		*Expected for year*	
	Quarter	*Year to date*	*Pre-tax accounting income*	*Investment tax credit*
End of 1st quarter . . .	$20,000	$ 20,000	$ 80,000	$5,000
End of 2d quarter . . .	10,000	30,000	60,000	3,000
End of 3d quarter	40,000	70,000	90,000	6,600
End of year	30,000	100,000	100,000	6,000

Assuming that the income tax rate is 20% on the first $50,000 of taxable income and 50% thereafter, and that taxable income is the same as pre-tax accounting income, compute the **(a)** estimated effective income tax rate for each quarter, **(b)** year-to-date income taxes expense at the end of each quarter, and **(c)** income taxes expense for each quarter.

SHORT CASES FOR ANALYSIS AND DECISION

Case 21-1   Rimpau Corporation, organized on January 2, Year 1, adopted the accrual basis of accounting for financial accounting. For income tax purposes, the corporation elected the cash basis of accounting because accounts receivable were expected to exceed accounts payable by a significant amount each year. Thus, the corporation could defer the payment of income taxes through the use of the cash basis of accounting for income tax purposes.

You were appointed to examine the financial statements of Rimpau Corporation for the year ended December 31, Year 1. In a discussion of interperiod tax allocation procedures with you, Wiley Borden, Rimpau's controller, objected to the use of comprehensive tax allocation for all differences between Rimpau's pre-tax accounting income and taxable income. He stressed that forecasts of Rimpau's future operations indicated an ever-increasing deferred income tax liability from comprehensive tax allocation because of the growth of accounts receivable in relation to accounts payable.

Instructions   How would you respond to the controller's objections? Explain.

Case 21-2   A partial income statement and the related note for Crosby Corporation for the current year are given below and on page 874.

Income before provision in lieu of income taxes	$7,277,326
Provision in lieu of income taxes	3,490,000
Income before extraordinary gain	$3,787,326
Extraordinary gain arising from use of operating loss carryforward .	3,490,000
Net income	$7,277,326

Note—Income Taxes:

No income taxes are payable because of an available operating loss carryforward from prior years. However, in the income statement, a provision in lieu of income taxes which would have been required in the absence of the operating loss carryforward has been deducted to determine income before extraordinary gain, and the gain arising from use of the operating loss carryforward has been reflected as an extraordinary item.

Instructions

a Give an argument in support of the procedure used to account for the tax effect of the operating loss carryforward.

b Prepare a journal entry to reflect the tax effect of the operating loss carryforward. Use the account titles as they appear in the income statement.

c Assume that Crosby had recognized the full potential income tax benefit of the operating loss in prior years. How would the income statement differ for the current year?

Case 21-3 Womack Construction Corporation was organized early in Year 1 after Oscar Womack was awarded a contract to build a major section of a highway in Alaska. The completion of the contract will take four years, and the company does not plan to bid on additional contracts. All costs incurred by the company are chargeable to the highway contract; in other words, the company will not record any selling and administrative expenses. Income tax rates are 21% on the first $50,000 and 48% on any excess.

The pre-tax profit on the contract is estimated at $200,000. Under the percentage-of-completion method of accounting, $50,000 of the profit will be recognized in each of the four years. Income taxes of $10,500 ($50,000 × 21% = $10,500) will be paid on March 15 of each year starting in Year 2 if the percentage-of-completion method is adopted for income tax purposes. If the completed-contract method is adopted for income tax purposes, income taxes in the amount of $82,500 [($200,000 × 48%) − $13,500 = $82,500] will be paid on March 15, Year 5.

Instructions

a Assume that the company considers 8% a fair rate of return after income taxes. Prepare a working paper to show whether the company should use the completed-contract method or the percentage-of-completion method of accounting for income tax purposes. Compute the net advantage of the method you recommend, in terms of dollar savings as of March 15, Year 5. (The amount of an ordinary annuity of four rents of 1 at 8% is 4.5061.)

b Assume that the company had a large amount of income each year from other sources and that the entire profit on the long-term construction contract is taxed at the marginal rate of 48%. What method of accounting do you recommend for income tax purposes? What is the net advantage as of March 15, Year 5, if money is worth 8%?

Case 21-4 Mossback Mining, Inc., received $50,000 in Year 10 as a rent advance on one of its mining properties. The advance is subject to income taxes in Year 10, although the company did not report the advance as revenue in its accounting records until Year 11.

In Year 10, the company reported taxable income of $250,000, paying income taxes of $106,500 (21% on the first $50,000 of taxable income and 48% on the $200,000 remainder). The controller reported $200,000 as the company's pre-tax accounting income for Year 10 and showed the amount of income taxes applicable to the rental advance (48% of $50,000) as an asset entitled "Prepaid income taxes."

In Year 11, the company suffered a decline in income as a result of a bear market in world metal prices, and its operations resulted in pre-tax accounting income of only $50,000, including revenue from the rental advance received in Year 10. When the controller presented the company's Year 11 income statement to the president, the latter commented, "I thought you said the effect of interperiod tax allocation was to show in each year a tax expense that bore a normal relationship to pre-tax accounting income. You report pre-tax accounting income of $50,000 and show income taxes of $24,000. If we had taxable income of only $50,000 we would pay only $10,500 in income taxes. I realize we broke even for income tax purposes this year and won't actually pay any income tax, but I think your tax allocation procedures are off someplace."

Instructions
a Prepare a partial comparative income statement for Year 10 and Year 11, starting with income before income taxes and following the controller's approach.
b What is the issue implicit in the president's question? How would you reply if you were the controller?

PROBLEMS

21-1   Pre-tax accounting income of Cahuenga Corporation, after all adjustments and corrections, was $280,000 for Year 1, $212,000 for Year 2, and $252,000 for Year 3. The income tax rate was 45% in each of the three years. Depreciation expense, rent revenue, and interest revenue have been included in pre-tax accounting income and taxable income for Years 1, 2, and 3, as follows:

	Pre-tax accounting income	*Taxable income*
Depreciation expense:		
Year 1	$50,000	$70,000
Year 2	54,000	71,000
Year 3	58,000	68,000
Rent revenue:		
Year 1	9,000	9,500
Year 2	9,000	8,500
Interest revenue (tax-free municipal bonds):		
Year 1	8,000	–0–
Year 2	4,000	–0–
Year 3	3,800	–0–

Instructions   Prepare a working paper for Cahuenga Corporation to compute:
a Income taxes payable on December 31, Years 1, 2, and 3
b Income taxes expense for Years 1, 2, and 3

21-2   Kingsley Corporation had pre-tax accounting income of $200,000 for the current year and is subject to income taxes of 40%. The following items are treated in one way in arriving at the $200,000 pre-tax accounting income but are treated differently in the computation of taxable income:

(1) Kingsley recorded $35,000 in product warranty expense; for income tax purposes only $22,000 of warranty costs actually incurred are deductible. The warranty liability account is classified as current.
(2) $40,000 of construction profits have been included in pre-tax accounting income on a percentage-of-completion basis. Only one-fourth of this amount is taxable in the current year; the balance will be taxed next year when the remaining long-term construction contracts are completed.

(3) A lease deposit of $20,000 was received and credited to a long-term liability account. It is subject to income taxes in the current year but will not be earned until the fifth year of the lease.

(4) Kingsley has recorded $65,000 depreciation expense in its accounting records by the straight-line method. Accelerated depreciation of $75,000 was taken in the income tax return.

Instructions

a Compute the income taxes expense to be shown in Kingsley's income statement, and the amount of income taxes currently payable.

b Prepare a journal entry to record Kingsley's income taxes expense and related liabilities and prepayments. Separate the deferred income tax items into current and noncurrent components.

c Prepare a partial income statement for Kingsley for the current year beginning with income before income taxes.

d Indicate the amount and classification of any income tax items in the balance sheet at the end of the current year. Deferred charges and credits should be classified in two categories—one for the **net current amount** and the other for the **net noncurrent amount.**

21-3 Jacobs Corporation pays income taxes at 60% of taxable income and has made estimated income tax payments of $400,000 during the current year. No computation of taxable income has been made, but the pre-tax accounting income is stated correctly at $800,000. The following items require consideration in the reconciliation of pre-tax accounting income and taxable income:

(1) Jacobs acquired another business enterprise in a prior year and recorded $80,000 of goodwill; this is being amortized over the maximum allowable period of 40 years.

(2) Gross profit on installment sales has been recognized in the amount of $200,000 in the accounting records. For income tax purposes only $150,000 gross profit is reportable in the current year. All installment contracts receivable are current.

(3) Pension expense accrued during the current year amounted to $40,000; only the $30,000 cash deposited with the pension trustee is deductible in the current income tax return. The related pension plan liability will be paid in the next year.

(4) Interest expense for the year of $120,000 includes $1,800 amortization of bond premium. Jacobs does not amortize bond premium for income tax purposes.

(5) Straight-line depreciation for the year of $200,000 has been recorded in the accounting records; for income tax purposes $220,000 in declining-balance depreciation will be deducted.

Instructions

a Compute the additional income taxes to be paid by Jacobs Corporation for the current year.

b Prepare a journal entry to record the remaining income taxes expense for the year, assuming that the estimated tax payments were debited to the Income Taxes Expense account during the year. Separate the deferred income tax items into appropriate current and noncurrent accounts.

c Prepare a partial income statement for Jacobs Corporation for the current year. Start with the $800,000 income before income taxes.

d Show the balance sheet presentation of all income tax items at the end of the current year. Show deferred charges and credits as one **net current amount** and another **net noncurrent amount.**

21-4 Quick Freight, Inc., began business in Year 1. Anticipating a growth in traffic, the company has developed plans for the purchase of trucks during the next six years. The controller of the company is studying the question of depreciation policies, and feels that the sum-of-the-years'-digits method should be used for income tax purposes but that the straight-line method is preferable for financial accounting purposes. The controller has prepared the data below, using a five-year economic life for the trucks.

	Year 1	Year 2	Year 3	Year 4	Year 5	Year 6
Cost of new trucks acquired	$100,000	$220,000	$300,000	$ 50,000	$ 10,000	$ 25,000
Residual value	10,000	25,000	30,000	5,000	1,000	2,500
Sum-of-the-years'-digits depreciation .	30,000	89,000	160,000	138,000	101,000	67,900
Straight-line depreciation	18,000	57,000	111,000	120,000	121,800	108,300
Excess of income tax depreciation over depreciation recorded in the accounting records	12,000	32,000	49,000	18,000	(20,800)	(40,400)

Instructions

a Verify the $49,000 excess of income tax depreciation over recorded depreciation for Year 3 in the data above. Assume that a full year's depreciation is taken in the year of acquisition.

b Determine the balance of the Deferred Income Tax Liability account at the end of Year 6 if an income tax rate of 40% is applicable. State how this amount is classified in the balance sheet.

c Assuming that Quick Freight's accounting records show pre-tax accounting income of $150,000 in Year 1 and $190,000 in Year 6, prepare partial income statements (starting with income before income taxes) for these two years. In the statements or notes show the taxes currently payable, the tax effects of timing differences, and the reason for the timing differences.

d Compare the net income for Year 1 and for Year 6 as determined above with the net income that would result if income tax allocation procedures were not followed.

21-5 Roy Keith is president and sole shareholder of After Hours, Inc., a successful restaurant. During Year 8, confident in the competence and integrity of the assistant manager, Keith left for a six-month archaeological expedition in Africa. On returning he found that the assistant had been stealing from the restaurant to cover gambling losses and that the quality (and patronage) of the restaurant had suffered seriously; as a result, operations in Year 8 yielded a pre-tax operating loss of $200,000. On the basis of prior success, Keith was confident that under his personal direction the restaurant could be restored to profitability immediately.

Instructions

a Prepare a journal entry to record the effects of income taxes for Year 8. Assume that (1) of the $200,000 operating loss for Year 8, only $140,000 can be carried back to preceding years; (2) no recognition is given to the potential income tax benefit of the $60,000 ($200,000 − $140,000 = $60,000) operating loss carryforward in the financial statements for Year 8; and (3) the income tax rate is 45% for all years involved.

b Prepare partial comparative income statements for Year 8 and Year 9. Pre-tax accounting income was $80,000 in Year 9.

c Using the assumptions in *a* and *b*, **except** that you are to assume that the potential income tax benefit of the $60,000 operating loss carryforward was recognized in the financial statements for Year 8, prepare partial comparative income statements for Year 8 and Year 9.

21-6 The following comparative income statement was presented to Jean Walsh, president of Walsh Corporation:

WALSH CORPORATION
Comparative Income Statements
For Years Ended December 31, Year 6 and Year 5

	Year 6	Year 5
Net sales	$1,090,000	$1,000,000
Cost of goods sold	690,000	630,000
Gross profit on sales	$ 400,000	$ 370,000
Operating expenses	250,000	280,000
Income before income taxes	$ 150,000	$ 90,000
Income taxes expense	90,600	10,500
Net income	$ 59,400	$ 79,500

After examining the statement, Walsh frowned, "When I send this statement to my father, who owns 30% of the common stock, he will never understand why net income fell in the face of a substantial increase in income before income taxes."

"There are two reasons," commented the controller. "You will remember that last year we took a $40,000 fully deductible earthquake loss on the East Bend warehouse, and this year we had a capital gain of $107,000 (taxed at 30%) when we sold our Cable Company capital stock, our only investment, and used the proceeds to build a new warehouse. Both these transactions were reported in the statement of retained earnings, but their tax effects were included in income taxes expense."

"I'll have trouble getting that across to my father," Walsh replied. "He knows we're subject to federal taxes of 48% on all income over $50,000 and 21% on the first $50,000. A ninefold increase in income taxes in the income statement is going to be confusing. Can't you revise the income statement so that the reasons for these odd tax figures will be apparent?"

Instructions Prepare a revised comparative income statement which will, in your opinion, meet the objections raised by Jean Walsh. Assume that both the loss and the gain are extraordinary items.

21-7 Lyle Beale, the controller of Maxi Corporation, has summarized the following data with respect to Maxi's operations for Year 3:

Sales	$1,400,000
Extraordinary gain resulting from a successful antitrust suit for treble	
damages (taxable at ordinary income tax rates)	100,000
Cost of goods sold	1,000,000
Operating expenses (includes $5,000 amortization of goodwill)	285,000
Correction of error resulting from double-counting items in inventories	
at the end of Year 2	30,000

Because Beale is busy with problems arising in connection with a newly installed computer system, he has asked you, an independent consultant, to assist in preparing the income statement for Year 3. There were no timing differences in Year 3.

Instructions

a Compute the income taxes for Year 3 applicable to current operations, to the extraordinary gain, and to the prior period adjustment. The income tax rate for Year 3 is 45%; for Year 2 it was 40%.

b Prepare an income statement for Year 3.

c Prepare a condensed statement of retained earnings for Year 3. The balance reported at the end of Year 2 (without correction for the error in inventories) was $420,000, and cash dividends of $50,000 were declared in Year 3.

21-8 Alice Ames, the controller of Walchek Company, handed an assistant a sheet of paper on which appeared the information shown below, saying, "Here's the story on our accounting and taxable income for the current year; I'd like you to put these amounts together in an income statement and a statement of retained earnings."

WALCHEK COMPANY

Computation of Pre-Tax Accounting Income

For Year Ended March 31, Year 8

	Debit	Credit
Sales (net)		$869,000
Interest revenue on municipal bonds (nontaxable)		10,000
Prior period adjustment—refund of income taxes as a result of error discovered by Internal Revenue agents . .		30,000
Cost of goods sold	$519,000	
Operating expenses	128,000	
Earthquake loss (not covered by insurance), before income tax effect	142,000	
Gain on early extinguishment of debt, before income tax effect		90,000
Subtotals	$789,000	$999,000
Prior period adjustment (see above)	30,000	
Income taxes payable (see below)	51,750	
Net income	128,250	
Totals	$999,000	$999,000

WALCHEK COMPANY

Computation of Income Taxes Payable

For Year Ended March 31, Year 8

Sales (net)	$869,000
Gain on early extinguishment of debt (fully taxable)	90,000
Total revenue	$959,000
	(cont.)

Less: Cost of goods sold	$519,000	
Operating expenses	128,000	
Earthquake loss (fully deductible)	142,000	
Excess of accelerated depreciation over straight-line depreciation used for financial accounting	55,000	844,000
Taxable income		$115,000
Income tax rate		0.45
Income taxes payable		$ 51,750

The amount of income taxes payable for the year ended March 31, Year 8, was computed correctly.

Instructions

a Prepare a journal entry to record income taxes expense, deferred income tax liability, and intraperiod allocation of taxes. Assume that the earthquake loss and the gain on early extinguishment of debt qualify as extraordinary items for financial accounting.

b On the basis of this information, and assuming an income tax rate of 45%, prepare an income statement and a statement of retained earnings for the year ended March 31, Year 8. Walchek Company reported a retained earnings balance of $1,917,200 on March 31, Year 7, and declared cash dividends of $75,000 during the year ended March 31, Year 8.

21-9 In Year 5, Caesar, Inc., had sales of $800,000 and pre-tax accounting income of $300,000. Straight-line depreciation expense of $80,000 was recorded for financial accounting purposes, but accelerated depreciation for income tax purposes amounted to $124,000. Cost depletion of $100,000 was deducted to determine pre-tax accounting income, but a deduction for depletion equal to 22% of sales was allowed in the income tax return.

Pre-tax accounting income did not include a gain of $440,000 from the sale of land on the installment basis, which was reported as an extraordinary item. The gain from the sale of the land was reported as an extraordinary item because it resulted from sale of the only surplus parcel of land the company owned and because it was held for more than 30 years. Only one-fourth of the selling price was collected in Year 5; therefore, only $110,000 of the gain was taxable at 30% in Year 5.

Pre-tax accounting income was taxed at 21% of the first $50,000 and 48% of the balance. An operating loss of $50,000 and a capital loss of $8,000 were carried forward from Year 4, and are available to reduce the income taxes liability for Year 5; the capital loss carryforward is to be offset against the gain from the sale of land in Year 5.

Instructions

a Prepare a journal entry to record income taxes for Year 5. An asset has not been established for the loss carryforwards. Deferred taxes are recognized for the timing differences between pre-tax accounting income and taxable income.

b Prepare an income statement for Year 5.

c Show how the deferred income tax liability appears in the balance sheet at the end of Year 5. Assume that at the beginning of the year the Deferred Income Tax Liability—Noncurrent account showed a balance of $220,000 (there was no current balance) and that one-fourth of the selling price of the land will be collected in Year 6.

21-10 Earl Craig, controller of Southby Corporation, was injured in a plane crash shortly after the end of Year 5. In his absence, the general ledger accountant prepared the following income statement for use in connection with the year-end audit:

SOUTHBY CORPORATION

Income Statement

For Year 5

Sales	$2,000,000
Rent revenue (an additional $5,000 advance rent was received and is	
taxable in Year 5 but will not be earned until Year 6)	45,000
Interest revenue (including $6,000 tax-free municipal bond interest)	14,000
Total revenue	$2,059,000
Cost of goods sold	$1,400,000
Operating expenses (including straight-line depreciation of $45,000;	
accelerated depreciation for income tax purposes is $60,000) . . .	500,000
Loss from seizure of shipment of goods by foreign terrorists (fully de-	
ductible for income tax purposes)	250,000
Additional depreciation expense recognized this year attributable to	
errors in computation of depreciation for Years 3 and 4	49,000
Total costs and expenses	$2,199,000
Loss before income tax effect	$ (140,000)

The income tax rate in effect for Years 1 through 5 is 45%; taxable income has amounted to more than $200,000 each year in Years 2, 3, and 4.

Instructions
a Compute all essential income tax amounts in connection with the income statement shown above.
b Prepare the journal entry to record income taxes at the end of Year 5. Assume that the operating loss for Year 5 is carried back to Year 2, and that amended income tax returns are filed for Years 3 and 4.
c Prepare a combined statement of income and retained earnings for Year 5. The retained earnings balance as previously reported at the end of Year 4 was $843,000; cash dividends of $40,000 were declared during Year 5.

22 ACCOUNTING CHANGES, ERRORS, AND STATEMENTS FROM INCOMPLETE RECORDS

As generally accepted accounting principles change in response to changes in the economic and social environment, accountants must find ways to implement the new principles in financial reporting. Putting new principles and new accounting estimates into the stream of financial statements may make current statements inconsistent with those of prior accounting periods. However, new and improved principles and estimates cannot be ignored simply to maintain consistency with the financial reporting of the past. In this chapter we shall explore some approaches to the adoption of new accounting principles and estimates with the goal of maintaining the maximum degree of comparability and, at the same time, gaining the advantages inherent in a change to improved or preferable accounting principles and estimates.

Also in this chapter we shall discuss methods of correcting and reporting errors which are discovered in previously issued financial statements. Finally, we shall consider ways in which accountants may develop financial statements from incomplete accounting records.

ACCOUNTING CHANGES

In the past, questions often were raised as to how certain accounting changes should be reported in the financial statements while at the same time preserving the consistency and comparability of the statements. By changing accounting practices, a business enterprise might affect significantly the presentation of its financial position and results of operations. The change also might distort the earnings trend reported in income statements for a number of years.

882

For example, suppose that Hester Company purchased equipment early in Year 1 for $500,000. The equipment had an economic life of eight years and a residual value of $50,000. For two years the equipment was depreciated by the straight-line method. Early in Year 3, Hester revised its original estimates and concluded that the equipment had a remaining economic life of 10 years and a revised residual value of $100,000. During Year 3, Hester also changed from the straight-line method of depreciation to an accelerated method of depreciation and merged with Poole Company in a business combination accounted for as a pooling of interests. It is evident that the financial statements prepared by Hester at the end of Year 3 would not be comparable with the financial statements issued in Years 1 and 2, unless the changes that took place are reported in a manner designed to preserve comparability.

In the illustration above we have examples of a *change in accounting estimate* (the revisions of estimated economic life and residual value of the equipment), a *change in accounting principle* (the change from the straight-line method to an accelerated method of depreciation), and a *change in reporting entity* (the inclusion of Poole Company in the financial statements for Year 3). Thus, accountants must find appropriate methods of communicating these accounting changes to users of financial statements so that the statements are not misleading and so that a meaningful comparison of earnings for the three-year period can be made.

For many years, the disclosures of accounting changes often were incomplete and obscure and resulted in suggestions by some critics that such changes were used by management to manipulate earnings. Many users of financial statements not only misunderstood the reasons for accounting changes but also failed to grasp their full impact. In an effort to establish explicit guidelines for reporting the effects of accounting changes on financial statements, the Accounting Principles Board defined the different types of accounting changes and established guidelines for reporting such changes in financial statements.[1]

Types of accounting changes

In *Opinion No. 20,* the APB was concerned with two issues: (1) the reporting of accounting changes, and (2) the accounting for corrections of errors in previously issued financial statements. The Board classified accounting changes in three categories: (1) changes in accounting principle, (2) changes in accounting estimate, and (3) changes in reporting entity.

A *change in accounting principle* can occur in two ways. The first results from the adoption of a generally accepted accounting principle different from one used previously for financial accounting. For exam-

[1] *APB Opinion No. 20,* "Accounting Changes," AICPA (New York: 1971).

ple, the issuance of a new accounting principle by the FASB is sufficient support for a change in accounting principle. The term "accounting principle" also includes the various "methods" that may be used in the application of accounting principles. Examples of changes in accounting principle include a change in the method of computing depreciation, such as a change to an accelerated depreciation method from a straight-line method; and a change in the method of valuing inventory, such as a change from lifo to fifo.

A **change in accounting estimate** may be required as new events occur and as better information becomes available about the probable outcome of future events. Examples of changes in accounting estimates include: An increase in the percentage used to estimate doubtful accounts expense from 2 to 5% of sales; a major write-down of inventories because of obsolescence; a change in the estimated economic life of plant assets; a change in the estimated recoverable units of natural resources; and a revision in the amount of estimated liability for outstanding product warranties.

A **change in reporting entity** takes place when the group of companies comprising the reporting entity changes. For example, if one company combines with another company in a pooling of interests, the financial statements (which combine the revenue, expenses, assets, liabilities, and stockholders' equity of the combining companies) of the current year are not comparable with those of previous years without adequate disclosure of the change in reporting entity and the impact on the financial statements caused by the change.

A **correction of an error** is not considered an accounting change and is required when errors are discovered in previously issued financial statements. Errors may result from mathematical computations, mistakes in the application of accounting principles, or oversight or misuse of facts that existed at the time the financial statements were prepared. Examples of corrections of errors include the discovery that material amounts of depreciation were not recorded in prior accounting periods, and a change from an accounting principle that is not generally accepted to one that is generally accepted.

Change in accounting principle

At first glance, a change in accounting principle seems to violate the assumption that financial statements are prepared "in conformity with generally accepted accounting principles applied on a basis consistent with that of the preceding year." In the preparation of financial statements there is a presumption that accounting principles once adopted should not be changed, so that meaningful comparisons of successive financial statements can be made. Consequently, a change in accounting principle is appropriate only when a business enterprise adopts an *alternative* generally accepted accounting principle which clearly is preferable. A change from an unacceptable accounting principle to an accepted accounting principle is considered a correction of an error rather than a change in accounting principle.

As stated earlier, a change in accounting principle generally is considered appropriate in two situations. The first is a change to a different method of applying a generally accepted accounting principle. For example, a change from the fifo method to the lifo method of inventory valuation would qualify. However, a business enterprise is permitted to change to a new method only if it can demonstrate that the new method is preferable in that it *more fairly presents* the enterprise's financial position and results of operations. The second situation in which a change in accounting principle is appropriate is the issuance of a pronouncement by the FASB or the SEC which creates a new accounting principle, expresses a preference for an accounting principle, or rejects a specific accounting principle.

The reason for the change in accounting principle and the effect of the change on net income are disclosed in the financial statements of the accounting period in which the change is made.

In *Opinion No. 20,* the APB specifically excluded two events from being considered a change in accounting principle. These are: (1) the initial adoption of an accounting principle to report transactions occurring for the first time, and (2) the adoption of a principle to report transactions which are substantially different from those previously occurring.

How should a change to a preferable accounting principle (or the selection of a different method of applying an accounting principle) be implemented in order to preserve the comparability between future financial statements and those issued in the past? The answer to this question depends on the type of change in accounting principle and the magnitude of its effect. A change which has a material effect on net income should be reported more completely than a change which has little effect on net income. Also, the effects of certain types of changes on financial statements of prior accounting periods may be more difficult to analyze than the effects caused by other types of changes. For this reason, the APB stated that those changes which have a material effect on net income should be classified into one of the following categories: (1) those for which the *cumulative effect* of the change applicable to prior accounting periods is included in the income statement for the period in which the change is made, and (2) those which require the *restatement* of the financial statements previously issued.

Cumulative Effect of Change Reported in Current Accounting Period The APB concluded that "most changes in accounting should be recognized by including the cumulative effect, based on a retroactive computation, of changing to a new accounting principle in net income of the period of the change. . . ."[2] The possibility that public confidence in financial statements would be reduced if financial statements of prior periods were restated retroactively was a major factor in the APB's conclusion. Examples of changes in accounting principle in this category are: A change in the method of computing depreciation expense on previously recorded assets (for example, a change from the sum-of-the-years'-digits method to the straight-line method),[3] and a change from the fifo to the lifo method of inventory valuation. The following guidelines should be followed for those changes in accounting principle which require recognition of the cumulative effect of the change:

1 Financial statements for prior accounting periods included for comparative purposes are presented as previously reported.

2 The **cumulative effect** of the change on the retained earnings balance at the beginning of the accounting period in which the change is made is included in the net income of the period of the change. The amount of the cumulative effect is the difference between **(a)** the **actual** amount of retained earnings at the beginning of the period of the change, and **(b)** the amount of retained earnings which **would have been reported** at that date if the new accounting principle had been applied retroactively for **all** prior periods. In the computation of the cumulative effect, appropriate consideration should be given to income taxes. The total and per-share amount of the cumulative effect is shown in the income statement below any extraordinary items.

3 The total and per-share effects of the change on the income before extraordinary items and on the net income of the accounting period of the change are disclosed.

4 Income before extraordinary items and net income computed on a **pro forma basis**[4] are shown in the income statement for all prior accounting periods presented as if the newly adopted accounting principle had been used in prior periods. If an income statement is presented for the current period only, the actual and pro forma amounts (including earnings per share) for the immediately preceding period should be disclosed.

Let us now examine how a change in depreciation method would be reported. Suppose that Shift Company, which owns and operates office buildings, decided to change from the straight-line method to an accelerated method of depreciation. The accelerated method, which has been used for income tax purposes, now was considered preferable for financial accounting for the following reasons: (1) The revenue-producing capability of the office buildings tended to decline as the buildings

---

[2] Ibid., pp. 391–392.

[3] A change to the straight-line method at a specified point in the economic life of an asset may be planned at the time the accelerated depreciation method is adopted to depreciate the cost fully over the economic life of the asset. Consistent application of such a policy is not a change in accounting principle under *APB Opinion No. 20.*

[4] **Pro forma** means "on the assumption that certain transactions are completed or that different accounting principles are used." In connection with our discussion of accounting changes, **pro forma** means that net income and earnings per share of earlier accounting periods are restated retroactively to conform to the newly adopted accounting principle.

became older, and (2) because most competitors used the accelerated method of depreciation, the change would make the operating results of Shift Company more comparable with other companies in the office rental business.

If the accelerated method of depreciation had been used by Shift Company in past years for financial accounting, total depreciation would have been $600,000 more. Therefore, income before income taxes would have been $600,000 less. Assuming an income tax rate of 45%, the journal entry to record the change in accounting principle is:

Journal entry to record change in depreciation method

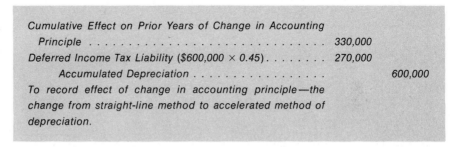

Cumulative Effect on Prior Years of Change in Accounting
   Principle *330,000*
Deferred Income Tax Liability ($600,000 × 0.45) *270,000*
      Accumulated Depreciation *600,000*
To record effect of change in accounting principle—the change from straight-line method to accelerated method of depreciation.

The debit of $270,000 to the Deferred Income Tax Liability account represents the amount of income taxes Shift Company deferred in the past as a result of using the straight-line method of depreciation for financial accounting while using an accelerated method for income tax purposes. The cumulative effect of the change in accounting principle, $330,000, is the net amount by which Retained Earnings would have been **decreased** had the accelerated method of depreciation also been used for financial accounting. The cumulative effect is reported in the income statement after income from operations (or after extraordinary items, if any) as illustrated on page 888.

In the income statement for Shift Company the pro forma income before extraordinary item for Year 4 was decreased by $140,000 ($2,600,000 − $2,460,000 = $140,000), or $0.14 a share. Thus, the pro forma amounts for Years 4 and 5 are fully comparable because they are stated in terms of the newly adopted depreciation method.

In some situations, the determination of the cumulative effect of a change in accounting principle may be impossible. An example of this type of change is a change in inventory pricing method from the fifo method to the lifo method. In such situations, the disclosure is limited to showing the effect of the change on the net income and earnings per share of the accounting period in which the change is made. The reason for not showing the cumulative effect of the change in accounting principle also should be stated.

Cumulative Effect in Interim Periods   In **Opinion No. 28,** the APB stated that a cumulative-effect-type change in accounting principle adopted in

SHIFT COMPANY
Partial Income Statements
For Years Ended December 31, Year 5 and Year 4

	Year 5	Year 4
Income before extraordinary item and cumulative effect on prior years of change in accounting principle (income from operations)	$3,000,000	$2,600,000
Add: Extraordinary item—income tax benefit of operating loss carryforward.	–0–	60,000
Less: Cumulative effect on prior years (to end of Year 4) of change in accounting principle (**Note**)	(330,000)	
Net income	$2,670,000	$2,660,000
Earnings per share of common stock (1 million shares outstanding):		
Income before extraordinary item and cumulative effect on prior years of change in accounting principle	$ 3.00	$ 2.60
Add: Extraordinary item—income tax benefit of operating loss carryforward		0.06
Less: Cumulative effect on prior years (to end of Year 4) of change in accounting principle (**Note**)	(0.33)	
Earnings per share	$ 2.67	$ 2.66
Pro forma amounts, assuming the change in accounting principle is applied retroactively (**Note**):		
Income before extraordinary item	$3,000,000	$2,460,000
Earnings per share before extraordinary item	$ 3.00	$ 2.46
Net income	$3,000,000	$2,520,000
Earnings per share	$ 3.00	$ 2.52

Note: During the year ended December 31, Year 5, the company changed its accounting for depreciation from the straight-line method to an accelerated method. The new method is a generally accepted method used in the industry, and it is believed the new method will cause the company's operating results to be more comparable with other companies in the industry. The effect of the change for the year ended December 31, Year 5, was to decrease income before extraordinary item by $120,000 (or $0.12 per share). The adjustment of $330,000 (after reduction of $270,000 for deferred income taxes) to apply retroactively the new method is included in net income of Year 5. The pro forma amounts for Year 4 have been adjusted for the effect of retroactive application of the change of depreciation expense and related income taxes. The effect of the change for the year ended December 31, Year 4, was to decrease income before extraordinary item by $140,000 (or $0.14 per share).

an interim period "should be reported in the interim period in a manner similar to that to be followed in the annual report."[5] Subsequently, the FASB amended this rather general guideline in two important respects as follows:[6]

1 When a cumulative-effect-type accounting change is made during the **first** interim period of a fiscal year, the cumulative effect of the change on retained earnings at the **beginning of that fiscal year** is included in net income of the first interim period.

2 When a cumulative-effect-type accounting change is made in **other than the first** interim period of a fiscal year, **no** cumulative effect of the change is included in net income of the period of change. Instead, financial information for the pre-change interim periods of the fiscal year in which the change is made is restated by application of the newly adopted accounting principle to the pre-change interim periods. The cumulative effect of the change on retained earnings at the **beginning of that fiscal year** is included in restated net income of the first interim period of the fiscal year in which the change is made. Whenever financial information which includes those pre-change interim periods is presented, it must be presented on the restated basis.

The FASB also required extensive disclosure of a cumulative-effect-type accounting change in interim financial reports, including the nature and justification for the change and the effect of the change on net income and related per-share amounts for all interim periods presented.

Change Requiring Restatement of Prior Periods' Financial Statements Few changes in accounting principles are reported through restatement of the financial statements of prior periods. Examples of accounting changes which require the restatement of financial statements of prior periods include the following:

1 A change from the lifo method of inventory pricing to another method of inventory pricing

2 A change in the method of accounting for long-term construction contracts

3 A change in accounting for development costs in extractive industries

4 A change in reporting entity

5 A change from an acceptable accounting principle to another acceptable accounting principle for a closely held corporation issuing financial statements to the public for the first time

Why did the APB provide for these exceptions? Although a number of reasons might be cited, the main reason for the restatement of prior periods' financial statements is that the amount of the cumulative effect of the accounting change might be so large as to render the income statement potentially misleading. Imagine the effect on a business enterprise changing from the lifo to the fifo method of inventory valuation in, say, 1982. If the enterprise had been in business for 30 years and had valued inventories at the original base layer, the beginning inventory in 1982

---

[5] *APB Opinion No. 28,* "Interim Financial Reporting," AICPA (New York: 1973), p. 530.
[6] *FASB Statement No. 3,* "Reporting Accounting Changes in Interim Financial Statements . . .," FASB (Stamford: 1974), p. 4.

would approximate 1952 prices. Thus, a change from the lifo method to the fifo method of inventory valuation could have such a material effect on net income that the cumulative-effect approach would distort the earnings picture of the enterprise in 1982.

When financial statements are restated, the nature of the change in accounting principle, as well as the justification for the change, are disclosed for the accounting period in which the change is made. Disclosure of the effect of the accounting change on income before extraordinary item, net income, and the related per-share amounts should be made for all periods presented. This disclosure may be in the income statement or in the notes to the financial statements, and need not be repeated in subsequent periods.[7]

To illustrate the restatement of an income statement for a prior period as a result of a change in accounting principle, assume the following: Retro Company adopted the completed-contract method of accounting for long-term construction contracts when it was incorporated in Year 1. The company reported net income of $137,500 in Year 1 and $330,000 in Year 2. In Year 3, the company decided to change to the percentage-of-completion method for long-term construction contracts. The effect of this change in accounting principle, assuming an income tax rate of 45%, is summarized below:

Effect of change from completed-contract method to percentage-of-completion method of accounting for long-term construction contracts

Year	Operating income under		Differences		
	Completed-contract method	Percentage-of-completion method	Before income tax effect	Income tax effect, 45%	Increase in net income
1	$250,000	$550,000	$300,000	$135,000	$165,000
2	600,000	700,000	100,000	45,000	55,000
3	700,000	850,000	150,000	67,500	82,500

The partial comparative income statement at the end of Year 3, giving retroactive effect to the change in accounting principle, appears on top of page 891.

To illustrate the effect of the change in the presentation of retained earnings, the comparative statement of retained earnings for Retro Company is illustrated on bottom of page 891. In this illustration we have assumed that Retro Company has not declared any dividends since it was organized in Year 1.

[7] APB Opinion No. 20, p. 396.

Reporting the effect of retroactive change in the income statement

RETRO COMPANY
Partial Income Statements
For Year 3 and Year 2

	Year 3	Year 2 (restated —see Note)
Operating income.	$850,000	$700,000
Income taxes expense	382,500	315,000
Net income	$467,500	$385,000
Earnings per share (100,000 shares outstanding) . .	$ 4.68	$ 3.85

Note: The company accounted for long-term construction contracts by the percentage-of-completion method in Year 3, whereas in all prior years the completed-contract method was used. The new method of accounting was adopted to report the results of operations in a manner which more closely portrays the economic activity of the company. Financial statements of prior years have been restated to apply the new method of accounting retroactively. For income tax purposes, the completed-contract method will be continued. The effects of the accounting change on net income and earnings per share of Year 3, and on net income and earnings per share previously reported for Year 2, follow:

	Year 3	Year 2
Increase in:		
Net income	$82,500	$55,000
Earnings per share	$ 0.83	$ 0.55

The balances of retained earnings for Year 2 and Year 3 have been adjusted for the effect (net of income taxes) of retroactive restatement of the new method of accounting.

Statement of retained earnings with restatement of beginning balance

RETRO COMPANY
Statements of Retained Earnings
For Year 3 and Year 2

	Year 3	Year 2
Retained earnings at beginning of year, as previously reported	$ 467,500	$137,500
Add: Cumulative effect on prior years of retroactive restatement of new method of accounting for long-term construction contracts	220,000	165,000
Retained earnings at beginning of year, as restated . . .	$ 687,500	$302,500
Net income.	467,500	385,000
Retained earnings at end of year, as restated	$1,155,000	$687,500

In some situations, the pro forma effect on the net income of individual prior accounting periods cannot be computed or reasonably estimated, although the cumulative effect on retained earnings at the beginning of the period of change can be determined. The cumulative effect in such cases should be reported in the income statement of the period of change and the reason for not restating prior periods' results should be given.[8]

Change in accounting estimate

Much of accountants' work involves the use of subjective judgment. That is, accountants often are relied on to estimate such things as the economic life and residual value of plant assets, the amount of probable uncollectible accounts receivable, and inventory obsolescence, and to make other decisions which require the estimate of the effects of future events. As time passes, new events and better information may require that the original estimate of economic life or residual value of plant assets, for example, be revised to reflect these new developments.

For example, assume that management had estimated the economic life of a plant asset at 10 years, with no residual value at the end of that period. The cost of the asset, $20,000, has been depreciated at the rate of $2,000 a year for seven years. At the beginning of the eighth year, management determined that the asset had a remaining economic life of five years and that its residual value would be $500 at the end of 12 years of use. The revised annual depreciation expense over the remaining economic life of the asset is determined as follows:

Computation of revised annual depreciation for plant asset with changed estimates of economic life and residual value	Cost of plant asset $20,000
	Less: Depreciation for Years 1–7 at $2,000 a year 14,000
	Undepreciated cost at beginning of Year 8 (carrying amount) . . . . $ 6,000
	Less: Estimated residual value at end of Year 12 500
	Amount to be depreciated in Years 8–12 (5 years) . . . . $ 5,500
	Revised annual depreciation for Years 8–12: $5,500 ÷ 5 years of remaining economic life . . . . $ 1,100

The change in estimated economic life and residual value affects only the remaining years of economic life (Years 8 through 12); no correction of the previously reported earnings for Years 1 through 7 is required. Because accounting measurements based on estimates are imperfect, and some disparity between past and subsequent estimates cannot be avoided, retroactive restatements of previously reported earnings as a result of changes in accounting estimates may cast suspicion on both the original and the revised earnings amounts. The information used to revise the service potential of the plant asset could not have been anticipated at the time the asset was acquired. Revised estimates are based on present economic facts and management decisions. For this reason,

[8] Ibid., p. 395.

it is logical to allocate the unexpired service potential over the remaining economic life based on the latest information.

A change in an accounting estimate occurs because new or better information has come to light in the current accounting period. Thus, it is logical that the resulting change should affect the computation of net income for the accounting period in which the change is made; if the change has a continuing effect, it should be consistently applied to the periods following the period of the change. A change in accounting estimate **does not** require (as does a change in accounting principle) the recognition of the cumulative effect of the change in the current accounting period **or** the retroactive restatement of financial statements for prior periods. Although disclosure of the effects on prior financial statement amounts is not necessary for estimates which are made in the ordinary course of accounting for items such as doubtful accounts expense or inventory obsolescence, any change in estimate which has a significant effect on net income and earnings per share is disclosed in notes to the financial statements.

A revision of the estimated economic life or residual value of a plant asset, as described above, is a change in accounting estimate. A change in the method of computing depreciation on a previously recorded asset is a change in accounting principle. But what if a business enterprise acquired a new plant asset and decided that the output method of depreciation is the most appropriate method for the asset? As long as it continued to depreciate its previously recorded assets under the same method as before, there is no need for a cumulative adjustment in the income statement because there was no change in accounting principle for those assets. However, the effect of the new method of depreciation for newly acquired assets on the net income of the accounting period of change is disclosed.

In certain instances, a change in accounting principle may be accompanied by a change in accounting estimate. In such cases it is difficult to separate the effect of the change in principle from the effect of the change in estimate. For example, a business enterprise which has been deferring and amortizing certain costs might decide to change to a method of recording the costs as expenses because the future benefits of the costs have become doubtful. This type of change often is related to the process of obtaining additional information which calls for a revision of the original judgment that the costs would have future benefits. Because the new accounting method was adopted in partial or complete recognition of the change in estimated future benefits, such a change is accounted for as a change in accounting estimate.[9]

9 Ibid., p. 388.

Change in reporting entity and initial public issuance of financial statements

Certain events, such as a business combination of two or more corporations accounted for as a pooling of interests, result in financial statements which are in effect the statements for a **different reporting entity.** A change in reporting entity is viewed as a special type of change in accounting principle which requires the restatement of the financial statements of all prior periods as though the new entity had existed all along.

As pointed out earlier, most changes from one acceptable accounting principle to another acceptable principle do not require the restatement of financial statements of prior accounting periods. An exception is made for a closely held company **issuing securities to the public for the first time.** Potential investors in the securities of a company "going public" are better served by earnings summaries for a period of years prepared on the basis of the newly adopted accounting principle. Comparisons of operating results are more meaningful because the newly adopted accounting principle also will be used in future periods. Therefore, the financial statements issued in connection with the initial public offering of securities are restated retroactively for all periods for which financial statements are presented.[10]

CORRECTION OF ERRORS

In previous chapters we have noted the difficulties inherent in any attempt to determine the periodic income of a business enterprise. At best, accountants can only measure the impact of past transactions and events and make informed estimates of the present effect of probable future events. In addition, **errors** in financial statements may result from mathematical mistakes, mistakes in the application of accounting principles, or the oversight or misuse of facts that existed at the time the financial statements were prepared. An example of a correction of an error is a change from an accounting principle which is **not** generally accepted to one which **is** generally accepted.

Correction of an error in previously issued financial statements

When a material error is discovered in previously issued financial statements, the correction of the error is reported as a **prior period adjustment.**[11] The nature of the error and the effect of its correction on net income and earnings per share are disclosed in the accounting period in which the error is corrected. An example of such disclosure, generally presented in a note to the financial statements, is given on page 895.

---

[10] Ibid., pp. 396–397.
[11] *FASB Statement No. 16,* "Prior Period Adjustments," FASB (Stamford: 1977), p. 5.

Illustration of note describing correction of error

> *Note—Correction of error:* A major revision of labor standards in February, Year 3, resulted in a charge to Year 2 earnings of $2,500,000 because of reduced labor and factory overhead costs included in the inventory on December 31, Year 2. In connection with the pricing of the December 31, Year 2, inventory in February, Year 3, it was determined that **an error** had been made in the application of factory overhead to the December 31, Year 1, inventory. The correction resulted in a reduction of the December 31, Year 1, inventory by $450,000. Earnings before income taxes for Year 1 were reduced from $1,500,000 to $1,050,000; net income was reduced from $816,000 to $600,000; and earnings were reduced from $0.41 to $0.30 a share.

If the error has a material effect on previously issued financial statements, retroactive revision of the statements for prior periods may be required. Whenever users of financial statements make a serious analysis of the financial affairs of a business enterprise, they want to see comparative income statement data for a number of years. When such comparative income statements are prepared, it always is desirable to revise prior years' income statements to correct material errors discovered after the original financial statements were issued. The Auditing Standards Division of AICPA has made the following recommendation on this point:[12]

> If the effect on the financial statements or auditor's report of the subsequently discovered information can promptly be determined, disclosure should consist of issuing, as soon as practicable, revised financial statements and auditor's report. . . . Generally, only the most recently issued audited financial statements would need to be revised, even though the revision resulted from events that had occurred in prior years.

Anyone who attempts to assess probable future earnings and financial position of a business enterprise relies on past information. An error that causes a material misstatement of net income for any recent period results in a misleading picture of the earnings pattern of the enterprise. This kind of distortion can affect the decisions of those who rely on financial statements for investment information.

Correction of financial statements illustrated

To illustrate the correction of a material error, assume that Errata Corporation purchased a machine early in Year 1 for $100,000. The machine had an economic life of 10 years with no residual value, and was being depreciated by the straight-line method. The accountant incorrectly recorded annual depreciation expense for Year 1 through Year 4 at $1,000 a year rather than at the correct amount of $10,000 a year because of a computational error. Thus, depreciation expense was understated by $9,000 a year, or $36,000 for the four-year period. The error was discovered early in Year 5, after the condensed financial statements shown on top of page 896 were prepared.

[12] *Statement on Auditing Standards No. 1,* "Codification of Auditing Standards and Procedures," AICPA (New York: 1973), p. 129.

ERRATA CORPORATION
Comparative Income Statements (Before Correction)
For Year 4 and Year 3

	Year 4	Year 3
Sales	$300,000	$280,000
Costs and expenses	270,000	260,000
Net income	$ 30,000	$ 20,000
Earnings per share	$ 3.00	$ 2.00

ERRATA CORPORATION
Comparative Balance Sheets (Before Correction)
End of Year 4 and Year 3

	Year 4	Year 3
Assets		
Assets, excluding machinery	$260,000	$225,000
Machinery	320,000	290,000
Less: Accumulated depreciation	(80,000)	(65,000)
Total assets	$500,000	$450,000
Liabilities & Stockholders' Equity		
Liabilities	$170,000	$150,000
Capital stock, $10 par	100,000	100,000
Retained earnings	230,000	200,000
Total liabilities & stockholders' equity	$500,000	$450,000

Ignoring the income tax effect of the error, the following correcting journal entry is required in Year 5:

Journal entry to correct computational error of prior period

Prior Period Adjustment: Error in Computation of Depreciation	36,000	
Accumulated Depreciation		36,000

To correct error in computation of depreciation for Years 1 through 4.

If corrected financial statements for prior periods are not issued in Year 5, the account Prior Period Adjustment: Error in Computation of Depreciation would be closed to the Retained Earnings account; in the statement of retained earnings for Year 5, the prior period adjustment of $36,000 would be shown as a correction to retained earnings at the beginning of Year 5. When corrected financial statements are prepared in Year 5, the prior period adjustment similarly is closed to the Retained Earnings account, but the ending balances for retained earnings are corrected retroactively for each prior year for which corrected financial statements are presented.

As an example, the corrected comparative financial statements of Errata Corporation for Year 4 and Year 3 are presented below:

ERRATA CORPORATION
Comparative Income Statements (After Correction)
For Year 4 and Year 3

	Year 4	Year 3
Sales	$300,000	$280,000
Costs and expenses	279,000	269,000
Net income.	$ 21,000	$ 11,000
Earnings per share	$ 2.10	$ 1.10

ERRATA CORPORATION
Comparative Balance Sheets (After Correction)
End of Year 4 and Year 3

	Year 4	Year 3
Assets		
Assets, excluding machinery	$260,000	$225,000
Machinery.	320,000	290,000
Less: Accumulated depreciation	(116,000)	(92,000)
Total assets	$464,000	$423,000
Liabilities & Stockholders' Equity		
Liabilities	$170,000	$150,000
Capital stock, $10 par.	100,000	100,000
Retained earnings.	194,000	173,000
Total liabilities & stockholders' equity.	$464,000	$423,000

In the corrected income statement, "costs and expenses" are increased retroactively by the $9,000 understatement in annual depreciation expense. Thus, net income for each year is decreased by $9,000.

The two balance sheet items requiring correction at the end of Year 4 and Year 3 are accumulated depreciation and retained earnings. Because depreciation was understated by $9,000 a year, the cumulative effect is $36,000 at the end of Year 4 and $27,000 at the end of Year 3. The corrected balance in accumulated depreciation at the end of Year 4 is

$116,000 ($80,000 as originally reported plus $36,000 correction = $116,000) and at the end of Year 3 it is $92,000 ($65,000 as originally reported plus $27,000 correction = $92,000). The amount of retained earnings is restated to $194,000 ($230,000 − $36,000 = $194,000) at the end of Year 4, and to $173,000 ($200,000 − $27,000 = $173,000) at the end of Year 3.

Types of errors

Many accounting errors are automatically brought to light by the controls in the double-entry accounting system. Independent auditors, internal auditors, and Internal Revenue agents may uncover errors during an examination of the accounting records. The installation of an improved accounting system may cause the discovery of material errors resulting from the inadequacies of the previous system. Thus, the necessity of correcting errors is more likely to occur in a small business enterprise than in a large publicly owned corporation.

The problem of dealing with errors of the same type can be generalized to some extent. Once the nature of the distortion created by a given class or error is understood, it is possible to determine the effect of similar errors.

Errors Affecting Only Balance Sheet Accounts An error which affects only balance sheet accounts may arise because (1) journal entries were made to the wrong ledger account, (2) transactions were omitted from the journal, or (3) the amounts of certain journal entries were wrong. For example, if Accounts Payable is debited instead of Accounts Receivable, total assets are understated and total liabilities are understated by the same amount. When the error is discovered, only balance sheet accounts require correction.

Errors Affecting Only Income Statement Accounts An error which is confined to income statement accounts has no effect on the amount of periodic net income. Such errors may arise through misclassification; for example, an expense or revenue may be debited or credited to the wrong ledger account.

Errors Affecting Both Balance Sheet and Income Statement Accounts Errors which affect both the balance sheet and the income statement fall into two categories: (1) Those which will be counterbalanced in the next accounting period, and (2) those which will not be counterbalanced in the next accounting period.

Some errors, if not discovered, ***will be counterbalanced*** in the course of the next period's accounting. The typical counterbalancing error causes a misstatement of the net income of one accounting period and the balance sheet at the end of that period, which is offset by a misstatement of income in the opposite direction in the following period. The balance sheet at the end of the second period and the net income of subsequent periods are not affected by the error, which has in a sense "corrected itself" over two accounting periods.

An example of a counterbalancing error is the failure to record accrued wages at the end of an accounting period. The liability, wages payable, is understated at the end of the period, and because wage expense is understated, net income is overstated in the period the error is made. In the following period, the payment of the unrecorded accrued wages is debited to expense; thus, the expenses for the second period are overstated. As a result, net income in the second period is understated by an amount equal to the overstatement of the previous period. If proper wage accruals are made at the end of the second period, the liability account in the balance sheet at that date is correct. Retained earnings also is properly stated at the end of the second period.

Other errors affect both balance sheet and income statement accounts, but **are not counterbalanced** in the next accounting period. For example, suppose an acquisition of equipment is debited to expense by mistake. Because an expense is overstated in the period the error is made, net income for that period is understated. Net income also is overstated in subsequent periods by the amount of unrecorded depreciation on the equipment while it is in service. Equipment in the balance sheet is understated throughout its economic life.

Analyzing the effect of errors

When an error is discovered, the accountant must analyze the effect of the error on financial data for prior, current, and subsequent accounting periods. Because it is not feasible to discuss every possible error which might occur, we shall illustrate the reasoning used in the determination of the effect of errors. The illustrations are designed to show corrections required to produce revised income statements of prior periods, and do not purport to illustrate the application of any APB or FASB pronouncement. In other words, we are concerned primarily with omissions and other errors which may occur in a **small business enterprise which does not issue financial statements to the public.**

As an example, let us trace the effect of an error in the determination of the amount of inventories at the end of an accounting period. Assume that we discover that the inventories on December 31, Year 4, are overstated by $3,400, and that the periodic inventory system is used. We can analyze the effect of this error (ignoring income taxes) as illustrated on top of page 900.

Analysis of effect of
overstatement of inven-
tories at end of Year 4

Income Statement

Year 4	Year 5	Year 6
Net income is overstated by $3,400. (Cost of goods sold is understated, because ending inventories were overstated.)	Net income is understated by $3,400 (Cost of goods sold is overstated, because beginning inventories were overstated.)	Error has fully counter-balanced; no correction is required.

Balance Sheet

Assets are overstated by $3,400. (Ending invento-ries are overstated.) Re-tained earnings is over-stated by $3,400. (Net in-come was overstated.)	Balance sheet items are properly stated, because Dec. 31, Year 5, inventories are correct, and overstate-ment of retained earnings in Year 4 has been offset by understatement of net in-come in Year 5.	No correction is re-quired.

The action to be taken on discovery of this error depends on when the error is discovered and the extent of the revision of financial state-ments which is desired.

Discovery in Year 4   If the error is discovered in Year 4 before the ac-counts are closed, a separate correcting journal entry is not neces-sary. The ending inventories under the periodic inventory system are re-corded in the accounting records at the time closing entries are made, and it is a simple matter to use the revised inventories amount in the closing entries. The ending inventories in the income statement for Year 4 are decreased by $3,400, and net income is decreased by this amount.

Discovery in Year 5   If the error is discovered at any time prior to the clos-ing of the accounts for Year 5, the correcting entry is:

Journal entry to correct
error in ending inven-
tories of prior period

Prior Period Adjustment (Net Income, Year 4)	3,400	
Inventories, Dec. 31, Year 4		3,400
To correct overstatement in beginning inventories.		

The purpose of this entry is to correct the financial statements for Year 5. Both the income for Year 5 and the balance sheet at the end of Year 5 are properly stated after the prior period adjustment is closed to the Retained Earnings account. In the statement of retained earnings for Year 5, the prior period adjustment is reported as a correction of beginning retained earnings.

Discovery in Year 6   If the error in the inventories at the end of Year 4 were not discovered until Year 6, no correcting entry would be required, because the error has been fully counterbalanced. If the Year 4 and Year 5 financial statements were to be corrected retroactively, this could be accomplished by changing the inventories and retained earnings amounts in these statements or by the use of a working paper. As of the beginning of Year 6, however, all balance sheet accounts are free of this error.

Working paper for analysis of errors

The first step in the correction of errors is to analyze the effect of the errors on financial data. The next step is to prepare the necessary correcting journal entries. In the course of an audit or when an accountant is called upon to correct accounting records which had not been maintained properly, a substantial number of errors, affecting several accounting periods, may be discovered. In such cases it may be helpful to use a working paper to analyze the errors and their effect on financial statements. The working paper also serves as the underlying support for a single correcting journal entry to bring the accounting records up to date. There is no standard form of working paper; one form which has proved useful for this purpose is illustrated in the following example:

Illustration   An audit of the accounting records of Small Trading Company early in Year 8 disclosed the following errors affecting the financial statements for Year 6 and Year 7:

(1) Unexpired insurance was omitted from the accounting records; insurance premiums were debited to expense as paid. The correct amount of unexpired insurance at the end of Year 6 was $550; at the end of Year 7, $980.

(2) No journal entry had been made to accrue interest on notes payable at the end of the year. Interest was debited to expense at the time of payment. Accrued interest payable at the end of Year 6 was $1,700; at the end of Year 7, $480.

(3) Interest on notes receivable was credited to Interest Revenue when received. At the end of Year 6, accrued interest receivable amounted to $450; at the end of Year 7, $840.

(4) The company rented land, receiving rent in advance; receipts were credited to Rent Revenue. Unearned rent revenue at the end of Year 6 was $1,800; at the end of Year 7, $740.

(5) The company is subject to state and federal income taxes at a rate of 20% of taxable income. There are no differences between taxable income and pretax accounting income. It is assumed that Year 6 income tax returns will be revised to reflect the foregoing errors, and that the company will claim a refund for excess income taxes paid in Year 6, or will pay any tax deficiency.

SMALL TRADING COMPANY
Working Paper for Analysis of Errors
December 31, Year 7

Explanation	Net income for Year 6 (Dr) Cr*	Net income for Year 7 (Dr) Cr*	Balance sheet accounts requiring correction, Dec. 31, Year 7 (Dr) Cr*	Account title
(1) Unexpired insurance omitted:				
Dec. 31, Year 6	$ 550	$ (550)		
Dec. 31, Year 7		980	$(980)	Unexpired Insurance
(2) Accrued interest on notes payable omitted:				
Dec. 31, Year 6	(1,700)	1,700		
Dec. 31, Year 7		(480)	480	Accrued Interest Payable
(3) Accrued interest on notes receivable omitted:				
Dec. 31, Year 6	450	(450)		
Dec. 31, Year 7		840	(840)	Accrued Interest Receivable
(4) Unearned rent revenue omitted:				
Dec. 31, Year 6	(1,800)	1,800		
Dec. 31, Year 7		(740)	740	Unearned Rent Revenue
Increase (or decrease) in income before income taxes	$ (2,500)	$ 3,100		
(5) Revision of income taxes (20%):				
Year 6 income taxes overstated	500		(500)	Income Tax Refund Receivable
Year 7 income taxes understated		(620)	620	Income Taxes Payable
Increase (or decrease) in net income	$ (2,000)	$ 2,480	480	Prior Period Adjustment
Net income as originally reported	20,000	16,000		
Corrected net income	$18,000	$18,480		

* Separate columns for debit and credit amounts may be used.

Small Trading Company reported net income of $20,000 in Year 6, and $16,000 in Year 7. We wish to determine the extent of the errors in the net income for Year 6 and Year 7, and to correct the accounting records on December 31, Year 7. The working paper on page 902 illustrates a widely used procedure that may be followed.

Let us assume that the accounts **have been closed** at the end of Year 7. On the basis of our working paper analysis, the following journal entry corrects the ledger accounts on December 31, Year 7:

Journal entry to correct accounts for errors *after* accounts are closed		

Unexpired Insurance 980
Accrued Interest Receivable 840
Income Tax Refund Receivable 500
     Prior Period Adjustment (Net Income, Years 6 and 7) 480
     Accrued Interest Payable 480
     Unearned Rent Revenue 740
     Income Taxes Payable 620
To correct errors revealed by audit in Year 8 after the accounts had been closed for Year 7.

Trace the amounts in this correcting entry to the working paper and you will see that all the data necessary for the correcting entry were developed in the working paper. To prepare a corrected income statement for Year 7, it is necessary to revise the individual expense and revenue accounts to reflect the total increase of $2,480 in Year 7 net income. If the accounts **had not been closed** at the time the correcting entry was made, it would be necessary to expand the correcting entry to include corrections to revenue and expense accounts for Year 7, as follows:

Journal entry to correct accounts for errors *before* accounts are closed		

Unexpired Insurance 980
Accrued Interest Receivable 840
Income Tax Refund Receivable 500
Prior Period Adjustment (Net Income, Year 6) 2,000
Income Taxes Expense, Year 7 620   ⎫
     Insurance Expense ($980 − $550) . .   430   ⎬ *Correction of revenue and*
     Interest Expense ($1,700 − $480) . .   1,220   *expense accounts*
     Interest Revenue ($840 − $450) . . .   390   *to reflect $2,480*
     Rent Revenue ($1,800 − $740) . . . . 1,060 ⎭ *increase in net income for Year 7*
     Accrued Interest Payable   480
     Unearned Rent Revenue   740
     Income Taxes Payable   620
To correct errors revealed by audit in Year 8.
Accounts not closed on Dec. 31, Year 7.

The analysis of errors in the working paper indicates that net income for Year 7 was understated by $2,480. If Year 7 revenue and expense accounts are to be corrected, it is necessary to look at the details in the column headed "Net income for Year 7" and determine the individual revenue and expense accounts that require adjustment. All the necessary amounts appear in this column, but the working paper does not show the accounts involved. It is possible to add a column or two to the working paper and enter the account titles at the time the working paper is prepared. However, it usually is easier to determine the appropriate revenue or expense account by noting the description of the error in the explanation column. For example, when we see that unexpired insurance was omitted at the end of both Year 6 and Year 7, it is apparent that the correction involves insurance expense. Unexpired insurance increased from $550 to $980 during Year 7; therefore, it is clear that insurance expense was overstated by the $430, because an increase in assets in this amount was debited to expense in error. This reasoning is used to determine the credit of $430 to Insurance Expense in the correcting entry.

The working paper for analysis of errors illustrated on page 902 is helpful in tracing the effect of errors on net income for several years and in providing the basis for the necessary journal entry or entries to correct ledger account balances at the end of the current year. Once the necessary journal entries have been recorded, the balance sheet and income statement for the current year can be prepared in the usual way.

If comparative financial statements are to be prepared, there remains the problem of revising the financial statements of prior years to reflect the correction of errors. A correcting entry always revises balance sheet accounts to their corrected balances at the end of the current year, but it does not correct account balances at any prior date. Similarly, once the revenue and expense accounts for a year have been closed, a journal entry to correct errors has no effect on the particular revenue and expense items for that year.

If there are few errors affecting data for prior years, it is usually a simple matter to make the necessary changes in amounts appearing in financial statements for prior years. However, when there are numerous errors, or when the correcting entries are complex, it may be desirable to use a working paper to correct the financial statements for prior years. A working paper which provides two columns for the original balances, two columns for the correcting entries, and two columns each for the income statement and balance sheet amounts serves the purpose, and also serves as a permanent record for the accounting files.

STATEMENTS FROM INCOMPLETE ACCOUNTING RECORDS

The heart of the double-entry accounting system is the analysis of the effect of each transaction on the basic accounting equation: Assets = liabilities + owners' equity. Many small business enterprises operate with varying degrees of success with only minimal accounting records and without the benefit of a complete accounting system. A system (or lack of system) in which transactions are not analyzed and recorded in the double-entry framework sometimes is called a **single-entry** system. The accounting records of social clubs, civic organizations, and small business enterprises often are maintained on a single-entry basis.

At some time after the data have been well muddled, an accountant is likely to be called on to sift through the accounting records and gather enough information to complete an income tax return and to prepare financial statements. Thus, the process of recasting single-entry information into the double-entry framework is a practical analytical exercise.

Balance sheet from incomplete accounting records

A business enterprise having no formal accounting system still must record certain basic information. For example, a record of cash received and checks written and a record of amounts receivable from customers and amounts payable to creditors is essential. It is possible to prepare a balance sheet at any given date for such an enterprise from various sources of information. Cash can be determined by count and by examination of bank statements. Amounts receivable from customers can be summarized from unpaid sales invoices. Inventory on hand can be counted and its cost determined from suppliers' invoices. The cost of plant assets owned similarly can be established. Amounts payable to creditors can be determined from invoices and monthly statements. Ownership equity is the difference between the amount assigned to assets and the amount of liabilities.

Computation of net income from single-entry accounting records

One way to determine net income from single-entry accounting records is to analyze the change in owners' equity during an accounting period. We know that owners' equity is the residual interest in the net assets of a business enterprise and that it is increased by net income and additional investments, and decreased by losses and withdrawals by owners. By the process of elimination, if we know the beginning and ending balance of owners' equity and the amount of any additional investments or withdrawals by owners, we can compute the change in owners' equity attributable to the net income or loss from operations during the accounting period as shown on top of page 906.

Computation of net income or loss by analysis of changes in owners' equity	Example I (net income)	Example II (net loss)
Owners' equity at end of accounting period	$22,000	$20,000
Owners' equity at beginning of period	18,500	25,000
Total increase or (decrease) in owners' equity.	$ 3,500	$ (5,000)
Add: Amounts withdrawn by owners	4,800	2,600
Less: Additional investment by owners	(1,000)	(500)
Net income or (loss) for the period	$ 7,300	$ (2,900)

For most purposes a more complete picture of operations is needed than that conveyed by the net income amount. The Internal Revenue Service requires detail of revenue and expenses. For even the most elementary budgeting and managerial control purposes, information is required as to how net income was determined. The objective then is to develop revenue and expenses from single-entry accounting records. Because cash transactions are of major importance in any business enterprise, a detailed record of cash receipts and payments is a valuable source of information. This is demonstrated below:

From a detailed list of cash receipts we can determine:	From a detailed list of cash payments we can determine:
Cash receipts from sales and other revenue	Cash paid for purchases of merchandise and operating expenses
Collections on customers' accounts	Payments to creditors
Proceeds from sale of plant assets	Cash paid to acquire plant assets
Amounts borrowed	Payments on loans
Cash investments by owners	Cash withdrawals by owners

If, in addition to cash receipts and payments data, we have (1) a list of assets at the beginning and end of the accounting period and (2) a list of liabilities at the beginning and end of the period, we can determine the owners' equity at the beginning and end of the period, and prepare comparative balance sheets. From this information, plus some help from miscellaneous sources, we can reconstruct the major components of the income statement. In the sections that follow are some examples to illustrate how the various revenue and expense items can be derived from information available in single-entry accounting records.

Illustration: Income Statement from Incomplete Accounting Records To illustrate the preparation of an income statement, we shall assume a relatively simple situation. The balance sheet at the end of Year 1, summary of operations for Year 2, account balances at the end of Year 2, and additional information for Joe's Place, a single proprietorship, presented below and on page 908, serve as a basis for our illustration.

JOE'S PLACE
Balance Sheet
End of Year 1
(Prepared from Incomplete Records)

Assets		Liabilities & Capital	
Cash	$ 4,680	Accounts payable	$ 9,400
Notes receivable from suppliers	12,000	Accrued salaries payable . .	1,100
Accounts receivable . . . . . : .	4,000	Unearned rent revenue . . .	600
Accrued interest receivable . . .	320	Total liabilities	$11,100
Inventory	18,000		
Unexpired insurance	500	Joe Palermo, capital	55,900
Building and equipment	40,000		
Less: Accumulated depreciation	(12,500)		
Total assets	$67,000	Total liabilities & capital	$67,000

JOE'S PLACE
Summary of Operations
For Year 2
(from cash and supplementary records)

Cash receipts:		
Collections on accounts receivable	$35,000	
Sales for cash	42,000	
Interest revenue	540	
Rent revenue	3,600	$81,140
Cash payments:		
Accounts payable for merchandise (including freight)	$53,400	
Insurance premiums	940	
Salaries	10,700	
Other operating expenses	3,000	
Drawings by owner	6,000	74,040
Sales returns and allowances		1,800
Cash discounts taken by customers (sales discounts)		600
Accounts receivable written off as uncollectible during Year 2		300
Cash discounts taken on purchases (purchases discounts)		1,100
Purchases returns and allowances		970

JOE'S PLACE	
Account Balances	
End of Year 2	
(from supplementary analysis)	
Cash (verified through count and bank reconciliations).	$?
Notes receivable (no change during the year).	12,000
Accounts receivable	7,600
Accrued interest receivable.	530
Inventory.	25,000
Unexpired insurance	700
Accounts payable.	8,500
Accrued salaries payable	1,900
Unearned rent revenue	450

Additional information

(1) No acquisitions or disposals of building or equipment took place during Year 2.

(2) Depreciation is computed at $2,800 for Year 2.

(3) Payroll taxes and income tax withholdings are ignored in order not to complicate the example.

(4) The direct write-off method is used to recognize doubtful accounts expense.

Computation of Gross Sales   Sales arise from two sources, cash receipts from customers and gross increases in accounts receivable. Because beginning receivables reflect revenue realized in prior years, cash collections of these receivables during the current year have no connection with the revenue of the current year. Therefore, the beginning balance of receivables must be deducted from the total cash collections to compute sales for the current year that were realized in cash. On the other hand, receivables at the end of the current year represent sales which are not included in cash receipts and which must be added to cash receipts to compute the sales for the year. Receivables included in this computation should include only accounts and notes receivable arising from the sale of goods and services.

Sales returns and allowances, sales discounts, and accounts receivable written off during the current year represent sales during the year that were not realized in cash and are not included in receivables at the end of the year. However, these amounts should be included in the computation of gross sales. Applying this reasoning, the computation of gross sales for Joe's Place for Year 2 is illustrated at the top of page 909.

JOE'S PLACE
Computation of Gross Sales
For Year 2

Sales on credit for Year 2:		
Collections on accounts receivable.	$35,000	
Accounts receivable written off as uncollectible	300	
Sales returns and allowances	1,800	
Cash discounts taken by customers	600	
Accounts receivable at end of Year 2	7,600	
Less: Accounts receivable at beginning of Year 2	(4,000)	$41,300
Sales for cash		42,000
Gross sales for Year 2.		$83,300

Computation of Other Revenue The amount of other revenue items, such as interest revenue and rent revenue, may be determined from comparative balance sheet and cash data as illustrated below for Joe's Place:

JOE'S PLACE
Computation of Other Revenue
For Year 2

	Interest revenue	Rent revenue
Revenue received in cash in Year 2.	$540	$3,600
Less: Revenue received in cash but not earned in Year 2:		
Unearned rent revenue at end of Year 2		450
Accrued interest receivable at beginning of Year 2	320	
Cash receipts representing revenue for Year 2	$220	$3,150
Add: Revenue earned in Year 2 but not included in cash receipts:		
Unearned rent revenue at beginning of Year 2		600
Accrued interest receivable at end of Year 2	530	
Revenue for Year 2.	$750	$3,750

Computation of Cost of Goods Sold The cost of goods sold is derived from information about purchases and inventories. The ending inventory can be determined by a physical count. Presumably, the beginning inventory also was determined by physical count; if not, an estimated amount must be used.

The amount of purchases may be computed from cash payments and accounts payable at the beginning and end of the year. The balance of accounts payable at the beginning of the year includes purchases during prior years which are not a part of the operating results of the current year. Therefore, from total cash payments to suppliers we must deduct the beginning balance of accounts payable to compute the cash outlays for purchases applicable to the current year. Accounts payable at the end of the year represent credit purchases during the current year which must be added to compute an estimate of the total amount of purchases for the year. An analysis of invoices provides information as to the cash discounts taken and the credits received for purchases returns and allowances.

The following illustration for Joe's Place demonstrates how reasoning and a systematic organization of the available data are used to compute the cost of goods sold. The first step is to compute the amount of gross purchases for Year 2, as shown below:

JOE'S PLACE
Computation of Gross Purchases
For Year 2

Payments on accounts payable during Year 2 (including freight)	$53,400
Add: Cash discounts taken on purchases	1,100
Purchases returns and allowances	970
Accounts payable at end of Year 2	8,500
Less: Accounts payable at beginning of Year 2	(9,400)
Gross purchases for Year 2	$54,570

In the computation of gross purchases, only liabilities relating to merchandise purchases should be included. This analysis, together with the inventory amounts taken from comparative balance sheets, provides the information necessary to compute cost of goods sold as shown below:

JOE'S PLACE
Computation of Cost of Goods Sold
For Year 2

Beginning inventory			$18,000
Gross purchases (see above)		$54,570	
Less: Cash discounts taken on purchases	$1,100		
Purchases returns and allowances	970	(2,070)	
Net purchases			52,500
Cost of goods available for sale			$70,500
Less: Ending inventory			25,000
Cost of goods sold for Year 2			$45,500

Computation of Operating Expenses Expenses arise from cash payments, from purchases of goods and services on credit, and from the consumption of assets. Because cash payments during an accounting period may involve the acquisition of assets or the payment of liabilities that relate to expenses of prior periods, computation of expenses of the current period requires an analysis of both asset and liability accounts as well as of cash payments.

The balance of any asset account which is subject to amortization increases as a result of the acquisition of additional assets, and decreases as the asset is used up. The normal process for the determination of the ending balance of the asset is: Beginning asset balance, plus acquisitions, less assets consumed, equals the ending balance. In the computation of expenses, we usually are able to determine the beginning and ending balance of the related asset and the cost of new acquisitions during the accounting period (through an analysis of cash payments and credit transactions). We can convert this information into the amount of expense for the period as follows:

<table>
<tr><td>**Reconstruction of expense through analysis of related asset account**</td><td>Assets acquired during accounting period ....</td><td>$ XX</td></tr>
<tr><td></td><td>Less: Asset balance at end of period ....</td><td>(XX)</td></tr>
<tr><td></td><td>Add: Asset balance at beginning of period ....</td><td>XX</td></tr>
<tr><td></td><td>Expense for period ....</td><td>$XXX</td></tr>
</table>

The computation of expenses by analysis of accrued liability balances and related cash payments is a similar process. The beginning balance of the accrued liability is deducted from the total cash payments during the current period to compute the cash payments relating to the current period's expense. Adding to this amount the accrued liability at the end of the period produces the expense for the current period.

Computation of operating expenses for Joe's Place is illustrated on page 912.

Working Paper for Preparation of Financial Statements from Incomplete Records The foregoing computations and other information derived from incomplete records can be used to prepare financial statements. Many accountants prefer to summarize the information in working paper form, as illustrated on page 913 for Joe's Place. Financial statements can be prepared from the information in the last four columns of the working paper. Alternative forms of the working paper may be used; for example, a pair of columns for a trial balance at the end of Year 2 may be added following the "Transactions for Year 2" columns in the working paper illustrated on page 913 for Joe's Place.

JOE'S PLACE
Computation of Operating Expenses
For Year 2

	Insurance expense	Salary expense	Other operating expenses	Depreciation expense
Cash payments during Year 2 . .	$940	$10,700	$3,000	
Less: Amounts included in cash payments but not expenses of Year 2:				
Prepayments at end of Year 2	(700)			
Accrued liability at beginning of Year 2		(1,100)		
Add: Amounts not included in cash payments but allocable to operations of Year 2:				
Prepayments at beginning of Year 2	500			
Accrued liability at end of Year 2		1,900		
Depreciation expense (as computed)				$2,800
Operating expenses for Year 2 . .	$740	$11,500	$3,000	$2,800

The income statement and the balance sheet prepared for Joe's Place from the working paper on page 913 have no unusual features and are not illustrated here; the statement of changes in proprietor's capital for Year 2 follows:

JOE'S PLACE
Statement of Proprietor's Capital
For Year 2

Proprietor's capital, beginning of year	$55,900
Add: Net income	21,560
Subtotal	$77,460
Less: Drawings	6,000
Proprietor's capital, end of year	$71,460

JOE'S PLACE

Working Paper for Preparation of Financial Statements

from Incomplete Accounting Records

For Year 2

Accounts	Balances, beg. of Year 2 Debit	Balances, beg. of Year 2 Credit	Transactions for Year 2 Debit		Transactions for Year 2 Credit		Income statement for Year 2 Debit	Income statement for Year 2 Credit	Balance sheet, end of Year 2 Debit	Balance sheet, end of Year 2 Credit
Cash	4,680		(1)	42,000	(5)	53,400			11,780	
			(2)	35,000	(6)	14,640				
			(3)	4,140	(8)	6,000				
Notes receivable	12,000								12,000	
Accounts receivable	4,000		(1)	41,300	(2)	37,700			7,600	
Accrued int. receivable	320		(3)	210					530	
Beginning inventory	18,000						18,000			
Unexpired insurance	500		(6)	200					700	
Bldg. and equipment	40,000								40,000	
Accum. depreciation		12,500			(7)	2,800				15,300
Accounts payable		9,400	(5)	55,470	(4)	54,570				8,500
Accrued sal. payable		1,100			(6)	800				1,900
Unearned rent revenue		600	(3)	150						450
J. Palermo, capital		55,900								55,900
J. Palermo, drawings			(8)	6,000					6,000	
Sales					(1)	83,300		83,300		
Sales ret. and allow.			(2)	1,800			1,800			
Sales discounts			(2)	600			600			
Doubtful accts. expense			(2)	300			300			
Interest revenue					(3)	750		750		
Rent revenue					(3)	3,750		3,750		
Purchases			(4)	54,570			54,570			
Purchases ret. and allow.					(5)	970		970		
Purchases discounts					(5)	1,100		1,100		
Insurance expense			(6)	740			740			
Salary expense			(6)	11,500			11,500			
Other operating expenses			(6)	3,000			3,000			
Depreciation expense			(7)	2,800			2,800			
Ending inventory								25,000	25,000	
Subtotals							93,310	114,870	103,610	82,050
Net income							21,560			21,560
Totals	79,500	79,500		259,780		259,780	114,870	114,870	103,610	103,610

Explanation of transactions for Year 2:

(1) Gross sales, $42,000 in cash and $41,300 on credit

(2) Collections on accounts receivable; sales returns and allowances, sales discounts, and doubtful accounts expense

(3) Collection of interest and rent revenue; adjustment of interest receivable and unearned rent revenue

(4) Gross purchases

(5) Payments on accounts payable; purchases returns and allowances and purchases discounts

(6) Payments for expenses; adjustment of unexpired insurance and accrued salaries payable

(7) Depreciation expense

(8) Owner's drawings

REVIEW QUESTIONS

1 Briefly describe the purpose of **Opinion No. 20** issued by the Accounting Principles Board.

2 What are two types of **accounting changes?** Briefly describe each type.

3 Describe a situation in which a **change in accounting principle** is considered appropriate.

4 How is the **cumulative effect** of a change in accounting principle determined and reported in the income statement for the accounting period in which the change is made?

5 List five examples of changes in accounting principle which require the retroactive restatement of financial statements for prior periods.

6 Mayberry Company wrote down its plant assets by $15 million in Year 2. The reasons given were: "To reduce excess capacity by closing inefficient plants and to recognize obsolescence attributed to new technological developments and a shift in the demand for the company's products."
How should the write-down be reported in the financial statements?

7 Maritime Corporation debited $87.9 million to operating expense as a result of a write-down of its tanker fleet. Included in this amount was $65 million "for possible losses in the future." Evaluate the accounting treatment of this write-down.

8 How is a material error in previously issued financial statements reported in the accounting period the error is discovered?

9 What is the basis for distinguishing between an error in the measurement of the net income of a prior period that should be treated as a prior period adjustment, and an error whose correction should be considered a part of the determination of net income in the accounting period in which it is discovered?

10 Which of the following errors should be treated as a prior period adjustment?
  a A depreciable asset which was estimated to have an economic life of four years is now estimated to have an economic life of six years.
  b A substantial deficiency in income taxes relating to the income of two years ago is assessed by the Internal Revenue Service as a result of an error in the interpretation of tax laws.
  c An analysis of credit experience indicates that actual doubtful accounts expense over the past three years has exceeded the provision for such expense made at the rate of 1% of sales.
  d A substantial amount of merchandise in transit at the close of the previous year was included in purchases but was not included in the ending inventory.
  e An audit reveals that a substantial purchase of a depreciable asset was inadvertently debited to expense last year.

11 Errors affecting both the balance sheet and the income statement may be classified into two major types. State and define each type.

12 Why is it important to correct material errors even after they have counterbalanced?

13 Explain what is meant by the term **single-entry accounting system.**

14 Briefly describe two general approaches that may be followed to compute the amounts required to prepare financial statements from incomplete accounting records.

EXERCISES

Ex. 22-1   Select the best answer for each of the following multiple-choice questions:

1 Which of the following describes a change in reporting entity?
  a A corporation acquires a subsidiary in a business combination accounted for as a purchase
  b A manufacturing company expands its market from regional to nationwide
  c A corporation acquires additional shares of common stock of an investee and changes from the equity method of accounting to consolidation of the subsidiary
  d A business combination is accounted for as a pooling of interests

2 Which of the following is (are) the proper time period(s) to record a change in accounting estimate?
  a Current accounting period and prospectively
  b Current accounting period and retroactively
  c Retroactively only
  d Current accounting period only

3 Robaire Corporation acquired machinery on January 2, Year 3. At the date of acquisition, the machinery had an estimated economic life of 10 years with no residual value. The machinery was depreciated by the double-declining-balance method for both financial accounting and income tax purposes. On January 2, Year 8, Robaire changed to the straight-line method for depreciation of the machinery for financial accounting but not for income tax purposes.
    The accumulated depreciation from January 2, Year 3, through December 31, Year 7, under the double-declining-balance method was $200,000. If the straight-line method had been used, the accumulated depreciation from January 2, Year 3, through December 31, Year 7, would have been $140,000. Assuming that the income tax rate for Year 3 through Year 8 is 50%, the amount shown in the Year 8 income statement for the cumulative effect of changing from the double-declining-balance method to the straight-line method is:
  a $0 *b* $30,000 credit *c* $60,000 credit *d* $60,000 debit

    Questions *4* and *5* are based on the following information:
    Pacer Company acquired a machine on January 2, Year 5, for $3,000,000. At the date of acquisition, the machine had an estimated economic life of six years with no residual value. The machine was depreciated by the straight-line method. On January 2, Year 8, Pacer determined, as a result of additional information, that the machine had an estimated economic life of eight years from the date of acquisition with no residual value. An accounting change was made in Year 8 to reflect this additional information.

4 Assuming that the direct effects of this change are limited to the effect on depreciation and the related income tax provision, and that the income tax rate was 50% in Years 5 through 8, what should be reported in Pacer's income statement for the year ended December 31, Year 8, as the cumulative effect on prior years of the change in the estimated economic life of the machine?
  a $0 *b* $187,500 *c* $250,000 *d* $375,000

5 What is the amount of depreciation expense on this machine that should be included in Pacer's income statement for the year ended December 31, Year 8?
  a $100,000 *b* $300,000 *c* $375,000 *d* $500,000

Ex. 22-2   Corrigan Company was formed on January 2, Year 5, and used an accelerated method of depreciation for its machinery until January 2, Year 7. At that time, Corrigan adopted the straight-line method of depreciation for the machinery previously acquired as well as for any new machinery acquired in Year 7.

Information concerning depreciation expense under each method follows:

Year	Accelerated method	Straight-line method
5	$300,000	$200,000
6	400,000	250,000
7	450,000	280,000

Assume that the direct effects of this change are limited to the effect on depreciation and the related income tax provisions, and that the income tax rate was 40% in each of these years.

Compute the amount to be reported in Corrigan's income statement for Year 7 as the cumulative effect of the change in the method of depreciation.

Ex. 22-3   Castleridge Company began operations on January 2, Year 6, and uses the fifo method to value its inventories. Management is contemplating a change to the lifo method in Year 7 and is interested in determining what effect such a change will have on net income. Accordingly, the following information has been accumulated:

	Year 6	Year 7
Ending inventories:		
Fifo method	$240,000	$270,000
Lifo method	200,000	210,000
Net income (computed under the fifo method	120,000	170,000

Compute net income for Year 7, assuming that the change to the lifo method of inventory valuation was effected in Year 7. The income tax rate is 40% in both Year 6 and Year 7.

Ex. 22-4   Cordoba Company included the following items in its balance sheet at the end of Year 5:

Equipment	$3,780,000	
Less: Accumulated depreciation	1,260,000	$2,520,000
Goodwill		1,225,000

Both assets were acquired early in Year 1. The equipment has been depreciated over an estimated economic life of 15 years with no residual value, and the goodwill has been amortized over a period of 20 years. Late in Year 6, the company decided that the total economic life of the equipment should be reduced to 12 years and that goodwill should be amortized over a period of 30 years from the date of acquisition.

Compute the annual depreciation expense on the equipment and the amortization of goodwill for Year 6, assuming that the residual value of the equipment is estimated at $210,000.

Ex. 22-5   At the end of Year 1, Camm Company's accountant recorded the cost of patents acquired from Roman Company, intending to amortize the cost over five years. At the end of Year 3, it was discovered that the sales manager's Year 1 salary of $25,000 had been recorded in the Patents account at the end of Year 1. The company is subject to a 40% income tax rate and intends to file amended income tax returns for Years 1 and 2.

Prepare a journal entry to correct this error at the end of Year 3, after normal adjusting entries have been made but before the accounts have been closed for Year 3.

Ex. 22-6 The following errors in the accounting records of Craig & Dawson, a partnership, were discovered early in Year 4:

	Ending inventories overstated	Depreciation understated	Accrued rent revenue not recorded	Accrued interest expense not recorded
Year 1	$10,000	$-0-	$3,000	$-0-
Year 2	-0-	2,500	11,000	-0-
Year 3	14,000	-0-	-0-	500

The partners share net income and losses equally.
a Prepare a correcting entry in Year 4, assuming that the accounts were closed for Year 3.
b Prepare a correcting entry in Year 4, assuming that the accounts are still open for Year 3.

Ex. 22-7 The cash records of Cantor Corporation show that $28,400 was collected in July from credit customers and $12,400 was received from cash sales. The amount due from credit customers increased from $7,300 at the beginning of July to $9,150 at the end of July. In July the credit manager had written off $790 of accounts receivable as uncollectible.
From this information, determine the gross sales for July.

Ex. 22-8 Ullrich Company sells television cable services to customers, who may choose to pay $25 per month for the service or may pay in advance a yearly charge of $250 for 12 months of service. During Year 8, the company collected $160,700 from customers. Additional information for Year 8 follows:

	Beginning of Year 8	End of Year 8
Advance payments by customers	$3,500	$5,700
Accounts receivable from customers	6,820	6,930

From the information given, compute the total cable revenue earned during Year 8.

Ex. 22-9 The inventories of Ralph Company increased by $18,500 during Year 4, and the accounts payable to merchandise suppliers increased by $9,600. During Year 4, the company paid $130,200 to suppliers and $7,200 in transportation charges on merchandise. The company also purchased $5,100 of merchandise for cash.
Determine the cost of goods sold for Year 4.

Ex. 22-10 The following information was taken from the accounting records of Kaspar Company for Year 1:

	Jan. 1	Dec. 31
Stockholders' equity (no capital stock issued or retired) . .	$98,000	$117,000
Cash	6,000	12,400
Inventories	20,000	14,000
Payables to merchandise suppliers	8,000	8,500
Accounts receivable	14,200	18,200
Cash paid to merchandise suppliers		70,000

(cont.)

	Jan. 1	Dec. 31
Operating expenses and income taxes paid (including $800 prepaid at end of year)		$32,000
Current year's sales written off as uncollectible (an additional allowance of $750 is required on Dec. 31).		500
Dividends declared and paid		20,000
Depreciation expense		6,200
Other assets	$77,800	82,350
Other liabilities	12,000	22,000

Prepare an income statement for Year 1 on the accrual basis of accounting. Show supporting computations for sales, cost of goods sold, and total operating expenses and income taxes. (Hint: First compute net income and work back to sales.)

Ex. 22-11 Long Company's year-end financial statements contained the following errors:

	Dec. 31, Year 3	Dec. 31, Year 4
Ending inventories (periodic system) .	$2,000 understated	$1,800 overstated
Depreciation expense	400 understated	No error

Net income as determined by the company was $25,000 in Year 3 and $30,000 in Year 4. An insurance premium of $1,500 was prepaid in Year 3 covering Year 3, Year 4, and Year 5. The entire amount was debited to expense in Year 3. In addition, on December 31, Year 4, a fully depreciated machine was sold for $3,200, but the sale was not recorded until January 5, Year 5. There were no other errors during Year 3 or Year 4, and no corrections have been made for any of the errors. Ignore income tax considerations.

  a Compute the corrected amount of net income on the accrual basis of accounting for Year 4.
  b Compute the total effect of the errors on the amount of Long Company's working capital on December 31, Year 4.
  c Prepare a single journal entry to correct the accounting records on January 15, Year 5. Assume that the accounts have been closed for Year 4. (Remember that the gain on the sale of the fully depreciated machine **was recorded,** but in the wrong year.)

SHORT CASES FOR ANALYSIS AND DECISION

Case 22-1 A business enterprise may change its method of accounting for certain items. The change may be classified as a change in accounting principle, a change in accounting estimate, or a change in reporting entity.
    Listed below are two independent sets of facts relating to accounting changes:

  a Ord Company determined that the economic lives of its plant assets were too long to match fairly the cost of the plant assets with the revenue produced. The company decided at the beginning of the current year to reduce the economic lives of all of its existing plant assets by five years.
  b Rill Company decided in January, Year 4, to adopt the straight-line method of depreciation for plant assets. The straight-line method will be used for new acquisitions as well as for previously acquired plant assets for which depreciation had been computed by an accelerated method.

Instructions For each of the situations described above, provide the information indicated on page 919. Complete your discussion of the first situation before going on to the second situation.

(1) Type of accounting change
(2) Manner of reporting the change under generally accepted accounting principles, including a discussion, where applicable, of how amounts are computed
(3) Effect of the change on the balance sheet and on the income statement
(4) Additional disclosure required in notes to the financial statements

Case 22-2 Various types of accounting changes can affect the second reporting standard of generally accepted auditing standards. This auditing standard reads, "The report shall state whether (accounting) principles have been consistently observed in the current period in relation to the preceding period."

Assume that the following list describes changes which have a material effect on a corporation's financial statements for the current year.

(1) A change from the completed-contract method to the percentage-of-completion method of accounting for long-term construction contracts.
(2) A change in the estimated economic life of previously recorded plant assets based on newly acquired information.
(3) Correction of an error in inventory pricing made in a prior period.
(4) A change from prime costing to full absorption costing for inventory valuation.
(5) A change from presentation of financial statements of individual corporations to presentation of consolidated financial statements for all affiliated corporations.
(6) A change from deferring and amortizing preproduction costs to recording such costs as an expense when incurred because future benefits of the costs have become doubtful. The new accounting method was adopted in recognition of the change in estimated future benefits.
(7) A change to including the employer's share of FICA taxes with "retirement benefits" in the income statement from including it with "other taxes."
(8) A change from the fifo method to the lifo method of inventory valuation.
(9) A change from the lifo method to the fifo method of inventory valuation.

Instructions Identify the type of change which is described in each item above and state whether the prior year's financial statements should be restated when presented in comparative form with the current year's statements.

Case 22-3 Deane Corporation, which is closely held, plans to issue additional shares of common stock to the public to finance an expansion program. The corporation has been in operation for five years and has never had an audit. To meet the requirements of the Securities and Exchange Commission, the corporation has hired a firm of CPAs to audit its financial statements for the end of Year 10.

In its financial statements for the past five years, Deane has reported the following earnings and stockholders' equity:

	Net income	Earnings per share of common stock	Stockholders' equity
Year 6	$368,000	$1.84	$4,945,000
Year 7	390,000	1.95	5,195,000
Year 8	435,000	2.18	5,350,000
Year 9	470,000	2.35	5,620,000
Year 10	510,000	2.55	5,870,000

The auditors discovered in the course of their examination that the corporation consistently had omitted from its ending inventories in each of the five years merchandise in a warehouse in Ohio. This warehouse operation had not proved successful and had been discontinued in Year 10; therefore, the inventories at the end of Year 10 were not affected by the error. Warehouse records show that the inventory of merchandise in the warehouse at the end of each year, stated at lower of average cost or market, was as follows: Year 6, $190,000; Year 7, $90,000; Year 8, $220,000; Year 9, $115,000. The auditors also discovered that because the sales report from the warehouse was late in arriving at the end of Year 7, $80,000 of sales applicable to Year 7 operations were not recorded as revenue until Year 8.

When the auditors insisted that these errors be corrected retroactively in the presentation of income data for the five-year period in the SEC registration statement, Deane's controller objected. "The warehouse has been discontinued. There is no inventory there now. All these errors you have dug up have washed themselves out in the accounting records, and there is no point in going back and raking over the dead coals of past history. There's nothing wrong with our balance sheet at the end of Year 10 or our income statement for Year 10, and that's what the people who acquire our common stock are interested in."

Instructions Determine the effect of the errors discovered by the auditors on the financial statements of Deane Corporation. You may ignore income taxes. What position would you take with respect to the controller's objection?

PROBLEMS

22-1 During the year ended December 31, Year 3, Compton Company changed its method of accounting for property taxes during construction of plant assets from expensing property taxes to capitalizing them as building costs. The company was organized in Year 1. The data below were taken from the accounting records:

	Year 3	Year 2	Year 1
Income before cumulative effect of accounting change in Year 3.	$400,000	$270,000	$150,000
Property taxes during construction	125,000	75,000	24,500
Depreciation of buildings—based on expensing all property taxes	50,000	35,000	30,000
Depreciation of buildings—based on capitalizing all property taxes	59,000	39,000	30,980
Earnings per share as reported, before cumulative effect of accounting change in Year 3	$ 2.00	$ 1.35	$ 0.75

The income for Year 3 was determined under the newly adopted accounting principle. The number of shares of a single class of capital stock outstanding during the three-year period was 200,000.

Instructions
a Compute the cumulative effect of the change in accounting principle to be included in the income statement for Year 3. Assume a 60% income tax rate.
b What was the effect of the change in accounting principle on earnings per share for each of the three years?
c Prepare a partial comparative income statement for Years 2 and 3. The income statement should include the cumulative effect on prior years of the change in accounting principle, the earnings per share, and pro forma amounts for Year 2, as illustrated on page 988.

22-2 The following fragmentary information relates to the affairs of Will's Shop, a single proprietorship, during Year 6:

	Jan. 1, Year 6	Dec. 31, Year 6
Owner's equity (Will Day, capital)	$81,900	$97,800
Inventory	15,800	27,320
Payable to suppliers	40,000	25,000
Short-term prepayments	1,800	2,400
Accrued liabilities	3,150	2,850

A summary of checks written shows that $200,000 was paid to suppliers during Year 6, $67,000 was paid for operating expenses, and $17,400 was withdrawn in cash by Will Day. Estimated depreciation expense for the year is $8,400, and a reasonable provision for doubtful accounts expense is 2% of gross sales.

Instructions On the basis of the above information, prepare an income statement for Will's Shop for Year 6. Show all supporting computations. (Deduct the provision for doubtful accounts expense from gross sales in the income statement.)

22-3 Builders, Inc., has used the completed-contract method of accounting for long-term construction contracts for 10 years. In Year 11, the company decided to change to the percentage-of-completion method in order to achieve a better matching of construction effort and realized construction revenue reported in its income statement. The company recently added an expert in cost estimation, and management believes that it is possible to make reasonably accurate estimates of costs to be used in the determination of the percentage of completion on each contract. In addition, management thinks that it would be unfair to stockholders to report a decrease in earnings for Year 11, which can be attributed to two significant factors as follows:

(1) Several major contracts were completed in Year 10, which resulted in an unusually high net income for that year.
(2) Few contracts were completed in Year 11, although the company had 40% more work under construction in Year 11 than it did in Year 10, and had 30% more employees on the payroll.

A summary of results for the last two years under the completed-contract method follows:

	Year 11	Year 10
Contract revenue realized	$6,000,000	$18,600,000
Construction costs applicable to contract revenue realized	4,500,000	14,700,000
Operating expenses	1,050,000	900,000
Income taxes expense, 40%	180,000	1,200,000
Net income	247,500	1,650,000

Application of the percentage-of-completion method to the operations of the last two years would have given the following results:

	Year 11	Year 10
Contract revenue realized	$17,400,000	$9,300,000
Construction costs applicable to contract revenue realized	14,100,000	7,500,000

Operating expenses under the percentage-of-completion method are the same as reported under the completed-contract method. The completed-contract method will continue to be used for income tax purposes. Income tax allocation procedures for timing differences will be used in the preparation of revised financial statements giving retroactive effect to the change in accounting principle. Assume that income taxes are 40% of taxable income.

Instructions   Restate the comparative income statement for Year 10 and Year 11, giving retroactive recognition to the change in accounting principle. Assume that 300,000 shares of a single class of capital stock were outstanding during the two-year period. Prepare a note to the financial statements which explains the reason for the change in accounting principle and the effect of the change on net income and earnings per share. (See illustrative note on page 891 describing this type of accounting change.)

22-4   Condensed statements of income and retained earnings of Gregg Corporation for the years ended December 31, Year 4, and December 31, Year 3, are presented below:

GREGG CORPORATION
Condensed Statements of Income and Retained Earnings
For Years Ended December 31, Year 4 and Year 3

	Year 4	Year 3
Sales	$3,000,000	$2,400,000
Less: Cost of goods sold	1,300,000	1,150,000
Gross profit on sales	$1,700,000	$1,250,000
Operating expenses	$ 450,000	$ 500,000
Income taxes expense, 60%	750,000	450,000
Total expenses	$1,200,000	$ 950,000
Income before extraordinary item	$ 500,000	$ 300,000
Extraordinary item, less income tax effect of $600,000	(400,000)	-0-
Net income	$ 100,000	$ 300,000
Retained earnings, Jan. 1	750,000	450,000
Retained earnings, Dec. 31	$ 850,000	$ 750,000

Following are three **unrelated** situations involving accounting changes and classification of certain items as ordinary or extraordinary. Each situation is based on the condensed statements of income and retained earnings of Gregg Corporation shown above and requires revisions to these statements.

Situation A   On January 2, Year 2, Gregg acquired machinery at a cost of $150,000. The company adopted the double-declining-balance method of depreciation for this machinery for both financial accounting and income taxes, and had been recording depreciation over an estimated economic life of 10 years, with no residual value. At the beginning of Year 4, a decision was made to adopt the straight-line method of depreciation for this machinery for both financial accounting and income taxes. Due to an oversight, however, the double-declining-balance method was used for Year 4. For financial accounting depreciation is included in operating expenses.

The extraordinary item in the condensed statement of income and retained earnings for Year 4 relates to shutdown expenses incurred during a major labor strike during Year 4.

Situation B At the end of Year 4, Gregg's management decided that the estimated rate of doubtful accounts receivable was too low. The rate used for Years 3 and 4 was 1% of total sales, and due to an increase in the write-off of uncollectible accounts, the rate has been raised to 3% of total sales. The amount recorded in doubtful accounts expense (included in operating expenses) was $30,000 for Year 4 and $24,000 for Year 3.

The extraordinary item in the condensed statement of income and retained earnings for Year 4 relates to a loss incurred in the abandonment of obsolete equipment.

Situation C The extraordinary item in the condensed statement of income and retained earnings for Year 4 represents a correction of a material error (after income taxes) in the computation of cost of goods sold. Of the total amount, $340,000 related to Years 1 and 2 and $60,000 related to Year 3.

Instructions For each of the three *unrelated* situations, prepare revised condensed statements of income and retained earnings of Gregg Corporation for the years ended December 31, Year 4, and December 31, Year 3. Each answer should recognize the appropriate accounting changes and other items outlined in the situation. Ignore earnings per share computations.

22-5 Alice Meadows started a single proprietorship, Alice's Boutique, on July 10, Year 1, by investing $75,000 in cash and merchandise. Net income for the remainder of Year 1 was $30,000, and for Year 2 it was $56,250. Meadows has made no additional investments and has not made any withdrawals since July 10, Year 1. A comparative balance sheet prepared by Meadows is shown below:

ALICE'S BOUTIQUE

Balance Sheets

December 31, Year 2 and Year 1

Assets

	Year 2	Year 1
Cash	$ 22,650	$ 16,650
Accounts receivable	67,500	48,750
Inventory of merchandise	60,000	42,600
Equipment	45,000	45,000
Total assets	$195,150	$153,000

Liabilities and Owner's Equity

	Year 2	Year 1
Accounts payable	$ 33,900	$ 33,000
Note payable to bank	–0–	15,000
Alice Meadows, capital	161,250	105,000
Total liabilities & owner's equity	$195,150	$153,000

The following errors were discovered by the auditor who was engaged in January of Year 3 to examine the financial statements of the proprietorship:

(1) Inventory was overstated by $4,500 at the end of Year 1.
(2) Accrued liabilities of $1,800 were not recorded at the end of Year 1.
(3) Inventory of supplies of $1,050 was not recorded as an asset at the end of Year 1, and inventory of supplies of $450 at the end of Year 2 was debited to an expense account.
(4) Accrued revenue of $1,200 at the end of Year 2 was not recorded as a receivable.

(5) An allowance for doubtful accounts equal to 6% of accounts receivable should be established at the end of each year. No accounts receivable were written off during the two years.

(6) Depreciation of $1,500 was not recorded in Year 1 and depreciation of $3,000 was not recorded in Year 2.

Instructions

a Prepare a working paper for analysis of errors to correct the net income for Year 1 and for Year 2.

b Prepare a correcting journal entry early in Year 3, assuming that the accounts are closed for Year 2.

c Prepare a corrected comparative balance sheet for Year 1 and Year 2. (**Note to student:** Be sure that capital for Meadows at the end of Year 1 is equal to the original investment plus the corrected net income for Year 1. Similarly, the capital for Meadows at the end of Year 2 should equal the original investment plus the total corrected net income for Years 1 and 2.)

22-6 The office manager of Kyle Corporation, a closely held corporation, prepared the following balance sheet at the end of Year 3:

KYLE CORPORATION

Balance Sheet

December 31, Year 3

Assets		Liabilities & Stockholders' Equity	
Cash	$ 9,800	Accounts payable	$ 25,600
Accounts receivable (net) .	37,000	Income taxes payable	2,700
Inventory	45,000	Capital stock, $1 par	40,000
Furniture and equipment		Retained earnings	61,500
(net)	38,000	Total liabilities & stock-	
Total assets	$129,800	holders' equity	$129,800

The corporation began operations early in Year 1, and income statements prepared by the office manager have shown the following net income for the three-year period: Year 1, $26,000; Year 2, $19,200; Year 3, $16,300.

Carl Kyle, the president, is concerned about this income trend, and asked a CPA firm to examine the corporation's financial statements. This review disclosed that the following errors and omissions had not been corrected during the applicable years:

End of	Inventory overstated	Inventory understated	Prepaid rent omitted	Unearned revenue omitted	Accrued expenses (misc. payables) omitted	Accrued revenue (misc. receivables) omitted
Year 1	$8,700		$ 950		$1,400	
Year 2	6,500		1,100	$ 800	1,200	$ 400
Year 3		$4,900	1,300	1,250	900	2,700

Combined federal and state income taxes are 40% of pre-tax accounting income. The corporation will file amended income tax returns for Years 1 and 2; the income tax return for Year 3 had not been filed at the time the above errors were discovered. No dividends have been declared by Kyle Corporation in the first three years of its operations.

Instructions

a Prepare a working paper for analysis of errors to correct the net income for Years 1, 2, and 3.

b Assuming that the accounts have been closed at the end of Year 3, prepare a journal entry to correct the accounting records at the end of Year 3.

c Prepare a corrected balance sheet at the end of Year 3.

d If you were presented with revised income statements for Kyle Corporation for the past three years, would your conclusions regarding its earnings trend be changed substantially? Comment.

22-7 Wade Earle started King Company, a single proprietorship, several years ago. For a number of years his wife maintained the accounting records, but early in the current year she became seriously ill. Earle consulted a bookkeeping service whose manager told him, "You keep a record of your cash receipts and payments, and a list of your assets and liabilities at the beginning and end of the year, and I'll prepare financial statements for you at the end of the year."

At the close of Year 5, Earle presented the following data to the manager of the bookkeeping service:

Analysis of Cash Receipts and Cash Payments for Year 5

Cash receipts:		Cash payments:	
Jan. 1, cash balance	$ 18,460	Accounts payable (net of	
Proceeds of bank loan	40,000	$6,480 cash discounts)	$225,650
Cash sales	87,300	Equipment	25,000
Interest received	1,590	Operating expenses	47,610
Notes receivable	13,000	Insurance policy premium	980
Equipment rental	7,000	Freight-in on purchases	12,400
Customers (net of $4,130		Bank notes (including inter-	
cash discounts)	177,690	est of $600)	15,600
		Dec. 31, cash balance	17,800
Total cash receipts	$345,040	Total cash payments	$345,040

List of Assets and Liabilities on January 1 and December 31, Year 5

	Jan. 1	Dec. 31
Cash	$ 18,460	$ 17,800
Notes receivable	15,000	2,000
Accrued interest receivable	900	500
Accounts receivable	43,560	64,320
Inventory	38,900	43,400
Unexpired insurance	1,900	1,500
Equipment (net of accumulated depreciation)	124,000	136,000
Total assets	$242,720	$265,520
Notes payable	$ 10,000	$ 35,000
Accrued interest payable	500	1,750
Accounts payable	47,500	52,300
Other accrued liabilities	3,400	6,300
Unearned rent revenue	1,200	1,800
Total liabilities	$ 62,600	$ 97,150

Earle reported that all accounts and notes receivable arose from merchandise sales and that $1,400 of accounts receivable had been written off during Year 5, of which $850 arose prior to Year 5. Earle estimated that $1,420 of the December 31 receivables will prove uncollectible. Only purchases of merchandise are recorded in accounts payable.

Instructions

a On the basis of the above information, prepare an income statement for King Company for Year 5. Show supporting computations. It is the company's policy to deduct doubtful accounts expense and cash discounts allowed from gross sales in the income statement.

b Prepare a statement of changes in proprietor's capital for Year 5.

22-8 Quinlan Corporation was organized on July 1, Year 1, with authorized stock of 200,000 shares of $5 par common stock and 10,000 shares of $100 par, 12% preferred stock. Carl Quinlan was given 200 shares of preferred and 2,000 shares of common for his work and expenses in organizing and promoting the corporation. Attorneys' fees of $1,800, incurred in connection with the formation of the corporation, have not been paid as of September 30, Year 1.

Additional information

(1) On July 15, Year 1, Carl Quinlan transferred assets from his single proprietorship to the corporation in exchange for 6,000 shares of preferred stock. The current fair values of the assets were as follows: notes receivable, $360,000; inventories $60,000; equipment, $180,000. The corporation did not begin operation until August 1, Year 1, but interest of $900 accrued on the notes receivable between the time they were turned over to the corporation and July 31, Year 1. This amount was recorded as Accrued Interest Receivable on July 31.

(2) On July 31, Year 1, 160,000 shares of common stock were issued at par for cash, of which $150,000 was used to buy land and $600,000 was applied to the cost of a building. The building cost $1,340,000; the balance was represented by a 15% mortgage note payable due in 10 years. Interest on the mortgage note payable did not begin accruing until August 1 and is payable monthly.

(3) On September 30, Year 1, the accountant for the corporation prepared a summary of all transactions completed by the corporation during August and September in the form of "net" debit and credit **changes in ledger accounts.** This information, which includes all adjusting entries, except for ending inventories (periodic inventory system) and income taxes, is shown below:

	Net changes in ledger accounts, Aug. 1–Sept. 30, Year 1	
	Debits	*Credits*
Cash		$ 28,300
Accounts receivable	$ 76,285	
Allowance for doubtful accounts		1,250
Accrued interest receivable	3,600	
Accumulated depreciation of building		8,375
Accumulated depreciation of equipment		6,500
Organization costs		1,060
Accounts payable		18,500
Sales		164,800
Purchases	110,000	
		(cont.)

	Debits	Credits
Operating expenses (including depreciation, amortiza-	$ 24,000	
tion or organization costs, and doubtful accounts ex-	18,500	
pense)		$ 3,600
Interest expense	$232,385	$232,385
Interest revenue (does not include $900 earned in		
July)		
Totals		

The organization costs are being amortized over 60 months, starting August 1, Year 1. The inventories on September 30, Year 1, amounted to $68,200.

Instructions

a Prepare the balance sheet of Quinlan Corporation on July 31, Year 1. Income taxes should be accrued at the rate of 40% on the interest earned in July. This was the only item of revenue or expense through July 31, Year 1.

b Prepare an income statement for Quinlan Corporation, summarizing its activities for the two months ended September 30, Year 1. Assume that income taxes are 40% of pre-tax accounting income. Do not compute earnings per share.

c Prepare a balance sheet for Quinlan Corporation on September 30, Year 1.

d Prepare an analysis of cash receipts and cash payments to reconcile the decrease of $28,300 in the Cash account during the two-month period ended September 30, Year 1.

22-9 Kopack Corporation has decided that in the preparation of its Year 3 financial statements two changes will be made from the methods used in prior years:

(1) **Depreciation** Kopack always has used the declining-balance method for income tax and financial accounting purposes but has decided to change during Year 3 to the straight-line method for financial accounting only. The excess of accelerated depreciation over straight-line depreciation is summarized below:

Prior to Year 2	$1,300,000
Year 2	101,000
Year 3	99,000
Total	$1,500,000

Depreciation is allocated to cost of goods sold and to selling and administrative expenses in the ratio of 75% and 25%, respectively.

(2) **Doubtful accounts expense** In the past Kopack has recognized doubtful accounts expense equal to 1.5% of net sales. After careful review, Kopack decided that a rate of 2% is more appropriate for Year 3. Doubtful accounts expense is included in selling and administrative expenses.

The information on page 928 is taken from preliminary financial statements, prepared before giving effect to the two accounting changes.

KOPACK CORPORATION
Balance Sheets
December 31, Year 3 and Year 2

Assets	Year 3	Year 2
Current assets	$43,561,000	$43,900,000
Plant assets, at cost	45,792,000	43,974,000
Less: Accumulated depreciation............	(23,761,000)	(22,946,000)
Total assets	$65,592,000	$64,928,000

Liabilities & Stockholders' Equity		
Current liabilities	$21,124,000	$23,650,000
Long-term debt	15,154,000	14,097,000
Capital stock	11,620,000	11,620,000
Retained earnings	17,694,000	15,561,000
Total liabilities & stockholders' equity	$65,592,000	$64,928,000

KOPACK CORPORATION
Income Statements
For Years Ended December 31, Year 3 and Year 2

	Year 3	Year 2
Net sales	$80,520,000	$78,920,000
Cost of goods sold	54,847,000	53,074,000
Gross profit on sales	$25,673,000	$25,846,000
Selling and administrative expenses	19,540,000	18,411,000
Income from operations	$ 6,133,000	$ 7,435,000
Other revenue (expense), net	(1,198,000)	(1,079,000)
Income before income taxes	$ 4,935,000	$ 6,356,000
Income taxes expense	2,368,800	3,050,880
Net income	$ 2,566,200	$ 3,305,120

There have been no timing differences between pre-tax accounting income and taxable income prior to the above changes. The income tax rate is 48%.

Instructions Compute for the items listed below the amounts which would appear in the Year 3 and Year 2 financial statements of Kopack Corporation after adjustment for the two accounting changes. Show amounts for both Year 3 and Year 2, and prepare supporting computations as necessary.

a Accumulated depreciation
b Deferred income tax liability
c Selling and administrative expenses
d Current portion of income taxes expense
e Deferred portion of income taxes expense
f Retained earnings
g Pro forma net income

22-10 You have been engaged to examine the financial statements of Haley Corporation for the year ended December 31, Year 6. In the course of your examination you have ascertained the following information:

(1) A check for $1,500 representing the repayment of an employee expense advance was received on December 29, Year 6, but was not recorded until January 2, Year 7.

(2) Haley uses the allowance method of accounting for doubtful accounts receivable. The allowance is based on 3% of past-due accounts (over 120 days) and 1% of current accounts at the close of each month. Because of a changing economic climate, the amount of past-due accounts has increased significantly, and management has decided to increase the percentage based on past-due accounts to 5%. The following balances are available:

	Nov. 30, Year 6 Dr. (Cr.)	Dec. 31, Year 6 Dr. (Cr.)
Accounts receivable	$390,000	$430,000
Past-due accounts (included in accounts receivable)	12,000	30,000
Allowance for doubtful accounts.	(28,000)	9,000

(3) The merchandise inventory on December 31, Year 5 did not include merchandise having a cost of $7,000 which was stored in a public warehouse. Merchandise having a cost of $3,000 was erroneously counted twice and included twice in the merchandise inventory on December 31, Year 6. Haley uses the periodic inventory system.

(4) On January 2, Year 6, Haley had a new machine delivered and installed in its main factory. The cost of the machine was $97,000, and the machine is being depreciated by the straight-line method over an estimated economic life of 10 years, with no residual value. When the new machine was installed, Haley paid for the following items, that were not included in the cost of the machine, but were debited to the Repairs and Maintenance Expense account:

Delivery costs	$ 2,500
Installation costs	8,000
Rearrangement of related equipment	4,000
Total	$14,500

(5) On January 2, Year 5, Haley leased a building for 10 years at a monthly rent of $12,000. On that date, Haley paid the lessor the following amounts:

Rent deposit	$ 6,000
First month's rent	12,000
Last month's rent	12,000
Installation of new walls and offices	80,000
Total	$110,000

The entire amount was debited to the Rent Expense account in Year 5.

(6) In January, Year 5, Haley issued $200,000 of 8%, 10-year bonds at 97. The discount was debited to the Interest Expense account in Year 5. Interest on the bonds is payable on December 31 of each year. Haley has recorded interest expense of $22,000 for Year 5 and $16,000 for Year 6. Haley plans to amortize the discount on bonds payable by the straight-line method.

(7) On May 3, Year 6, Haley exchanged 500 shares of treasury stock (its $50 par common stock) for land to be used as a site for a new factory. The treasury stock had cost $70 a share when it was acquired, and on May 3, Year 6, it had a current fair value of $80 a share. Haley received $2,000 when an existing building on the land was sold for scrap. The land was recorded at $40,000, the $2,000 received for scrap was credited to Other Revenue, and Haley recorded a gain of $5,000 on the reissuance of its treasury stock.

(8) The Advertising and Promotion Expense account included an amount of $75,000 which represented the cost of printing sales catalogs for a special promotional campaign in January, Year 7.

(9) Haley adopted a pension plan on January 2, Year 6, for eligible employees to be administered by a trustee. Based on actuarial computations, the annual normal pension cost was $70,000, and the present value of past service cost on January 2, Year 6, was $900,000. The company decided to use the maximum provision for pension expense and to fund past service cost. On December 31, Year 6, Haley remitted $970,000 to the trustee and debited this amount to the Pension Expense account.

(10) Haley is a defendant in a lawsuit by a former customer. Haley's legal counsel has advised management that Haley has a good defense. Haley's counsel does not anticipate any impairment of Haley's assets or that any significant liabilities will be incurred as a result of the litigation. Management, however, wishes to be conservative and, therefore, has established a loss contingency of $100,000 by a debit to an expense account.

Instructions Prepare a working paper to show the effect of errors on Haley's financial statements for Year 6. The items in the working paper should be presented in the same order as the facts are given with corresponding numbers (1) through (10). Use the following columnar headings for the working paper:

No.	Explanation	Income statement		Balance sheet, Dec. 31, Year 6		
		Dr.	(Cr.)	Dr.	(Cr.)	Account title
(1)						

ANALYTICAL PROCEDURES AND STATEMENTS

23 STATEMENT OF CHANGES IN FINANCIAL POSITION

For many years the basic financial statements of business enterprises were the balance sheet and the income statement. Many enterprises also prepared a third financial statement, called a **statement of source and application of funds,** or simply a **funds statement.** This statement originally was developed as a means of explaining to creditors why net income was not accompanied by a corresponding increase in cash or working capital. The inclusion of such a financial statement in annual reports was an optional matter for many years, and even among those enterprises that prepared funds statements, the content and terminology varied considerably.

APB Opinion No. 3 encouraged but did not require the presentation of a funds statement with financial statements issued to the public.[1] It was recognized that the term **funds** sometimes was used to mean cash or cash equivalents. A funds statement based on this narrow definition of funds was a statement of cash receipts and payments. However, most publicly owned companies defined funds more broadly as **working capital.** A funds statement prepared on the working capital concept usually included only those transactions which directly affected current assets and current liabilities.

The all-financial-resources concept of "funds"

After considering the different prevailing concepts of funds and the varying forms of funds statements, the Accounting Principles Board in **Opinion No. 3** recommended that the concept of funds be broadened to include **all financial resources.** Under this concept, a funds statement is not limited to transactions affecting cash or working capital but includes the financial aspects of **exchange transactions** such as the issuance of capital stock for plant assets and the conversion of bonds payable to common stock.

[1] *APB Opinion No. 3,* "The Statement of Source and Application of Funds," AICPA (New York: 1963), p. 16.

933

APB Opinion No. 19, issued in 1971, required the inclusion of a funds statement in annual reports and recommended that it be given the new title of Statement of Changes in Financial Position.[2] This title better describes the broader concept of "all financial resources." *APB Opinion No. 19* required business enterprises to disclose all important aspects of their financing and investing activities, regardless of whether cash or other elements of working capital are affected directly. For example, the issuance of 10,000 shares of capital stock with a market price of $60 a share in exchange for patents is reported in the statement of changes in financial position as follows:

Exchange transaction:
issuance of capital
stock for patents

Financial resources provided

   Issuance of capital stock in exchange for patents $600,000

Financial resources applied

   Acquisition of patents in exchange for capital stock. $600,000

Similarly, the conversion of $5,000,000 of bonds payable to capital stock is reported in the statement of changes in financial position as follows:

Exchange transaction:
conversion of bonds
payable

Financial resources provided

   Issuance of capital stock pursuant to conversion of bonds payable $5,000,000

Financial resources applied

   Extinguishment of bonds payable through conversion to capital

   stock. $5,000,000

Other examples of exchange transactions are: refunding of bonds payable, exchanges of property, contracts for capital leases by lessees, and donation of plant assets to a business enterprise. In contrast, stock dividends, write-offs of noncurrent assets, and appropriations of retained earnings are not exchange transactions, and their effect on noncurrent accounts is not included in the statement of changes in financial position.

Objectives of statement of changes in financial position

To summarize the impact of the developments described above, we can identify the basic objectives of a statement of changes in financial position for a business enterprise as follows:

[2] *APB Opinion No. 19,* "Reporting Changes in Financial Position," AICPA (New York: 1971), p. 374.

1 To provide information on all financing and investing activities during an accounting period

2 To show the financial resources (funds) provided from operations and other sources during an accounting period

3 To show the uses or applications of financial resources during an accounting period

4 To disclose the amounts and causes of all other material changes in financial position during an accounting period

The statement of changes in financial position is not intended to supplant the income statement or the balance sheet, but is intended to provide information that these statements either do not provide or provide only indirectly. The information included in a statement of changes in financial position is relevant to users of financial statements in making business decisions. Therefore, the format of the statement and the definition of funds adopted should take into consideration the needs of those who use the information to make decisions. For example, the statement may be prepared on a cash concept for internal use and also for external use when cash flow is considered to be of primary importance to creditors and investors. When a broader concept of liquid resources (funds) is considered to be more useful, the statement may be prepared on a working capital concept.

FASB study of funds flows, liquidity, and financial flexibility

As a part of the effort to develop a conceptual framework for financial accounting and reporting, the FASB issued in December 1980 a *Discussion Memorandum,* "Reporting Funds Flows, Liquidity, and Financial Flexibility."[3] Among the reasons given for undertaking this project were the following: (1) Information about liquidity and financial flexibility is needed for making assessments of future cash flows; and (2) current practice with respect to the reporting of funds flow information is not entirely satisfactory.

Many users of financial statements consider current practice of reporting funds flows as confusing because too much information is compressed in the statement of changes in financial position, and because no single definition of *funds* has been established. The FASB identified the following possible uses of funds flows information:

1 A basis for assessing future cash flows

2 A basis for identifying the relationship between net income and net cash flows

3 A basis for making comparisons with earlier assessments of cash flows

4 A basis for assessing the "quality of earnings"

5 An improved basis for comparing information in financial statements

6 A basis for assessing performance of business enterprises

[3] *FASB Discussion Memorandum,* "Reporting Funds Flow, Liquidity, and Financial Flexibility," FASB (Stamford: 1980).

The project is expected to result in the issuance of a Statement of Financial Accounting Standards that will give a sharper definition of "funds," more precise guidelines for the content and form of the funds flows statement, and possibly will require the reporting of several summary indicators of liquidity such as funds flow from operations per share of common stock.

Format and content of the statement of changes in financial position

The statement of changes in financial position may differ in form, content, and terminology to meet its objectives. For example, the working capital format generally would not be relevant to a business enterprise that does not classify assets and liabilities as current and noncurrent. An enterprise should adopt the format that is considered most informative in its circumstances.

The ability of a business enterprise to generate working capital or cash from operations is an important factor in its financing and investing activities. The statement of changes in financial position, therefore, should disclose working capital or cash provided from or applied in operations for the period, and the effects of any extraordinary items should be reported separately from the effects of normal operations. Additional guidelines for the preparation of the statement were offered by the Accounting Principles Board as follows:[4]

> The Statement for the period should begin with income or loss before extraordinary items, if any, and add back (or deduct) items recognized in determining that income or loss which did not use (or provide) working capital or cash during the period. Items added and deducted in accordance with this procedure are not sources or uses of working capital or cash, and the related captions should make this clear, e.g., "Add—Expenses not requiring outlay of working capital in the current period." An acceptable alternative procedure, which gives the same result, is to begin with total revenue that provided working capital or cash during the period and deduct operating costs and expenses that required the outlay of working capital or cash during the period. In either case the resulting amount of working capital or cash should be appropriately described, e.g., "Working capital provided from [used in] operations for the period, exclusive of extraordinary items." This total should be immediately followed by working capital or cash provided or used by income or loss from extraordinary items, if any; extraordinary income or loss should be similarly adjusted for items recognized that did not provide or use working capital or cash during the period.

> Provided that these guides are met, the Statement may take whatever form gives the most useful portrayal of the financing and investing activities and the changes in financial position of the reporting entity. The Statement may be in balanced form or in a form expressing the changes in financial position in terms of cash, of cash and temporary investments combined, of all quick assets, or of working capital. The Statement should disclose all important changes in financial position for the period covered; accordingly, types of transactions reported may vary substantially in relative importance from one period to another.

[4] *APB Opinion No. 19*, pp. 374–375.

The Board also stated that net changes in each element of working capital should be disclosed for at least the current accounting period, either in the statement or in a supporting exhibit. This disclosure applies whether working capital or cash flows are presented in the statement. Thus, when the statement is prepared on the cash concept, changes in working capital accounts constitute sources and uses of cash and should be disclosed. The effects of other financing and investing activities should be presented individually; however, immaterial items may be combined.[5]

The statement of changes in financial position appears in a variety of forms in annual reports issued by publicly owned companies. In a recent survey of 600 annual reports, 402 used a form in which the increase or decrease in working capital is highlighted; 65 companies "balanced" the statement by reporting the increase in working capital as a use of funds (or a decrease in working capital as a source of funds); 51 companies used "cash and cash equivalents" as the definition of "funds," and 82 companies arrived at the ending balance of working capital.[6]

Because the statement of changes in financial position may be prepared either on the working capital concept or on the cash concept, it is appropriate that we now consider these two approaches in greater detail.

Funds defined as *working capital*

One of the primary financial responsibilities of management is seeing that the business enterprise it operates has sufficient liquid financial resources to meet obligations as they mature and to take advantage of favorable investment opportunities as they arise. Managers and those outsiders who evaluate managerial performance keep a sharp eye on the inflow and outflow of liquid financial resources, and the prospective balance between liquid resources available and liquid resources required.

The **working capital** of a business enterprise is the amount by which current assets exceed current liabilities. The amount of working capital is a measure of the safety factor that exists for the protection of short-term creditors. Working capital also may be viewed as funds available for investment in noncurrent assets or to liquidate noncurrent liabilities. Increases in working capital occur when noncurrent assets are decreased (sold) and when noncurrent liabilities and stockholders' equity are increased (as by additional financing activities). Decreases in working capital occur when noncurrent assets are increased (acquired) and when noncurrent liabilities and stockholders' equity are decreased (as by extinguishment of long-term debt or by declaration of cash dividends). The major sources and uses of working capital for a corporation are summarized on top of page 938.

[5] Ibid., p. 376.
[6] *Accounting Trends & Techniques,* 34th ed., AICPA (New York: 1980), pp. 353–354.

Summary of sources
and uses of working
capital

Sources	Uses
1 Profitable operations	**1** Acquisition of noncurrent assets
2 Disposal of noncurrent assets	**2** Extinguishment of long-term debt, or its reclassification as current debt
3 Long-term borrowing	
4 Issuance of equity securities	**3** Distributions to stockholders, including cash dividends, acquisition of treasury stock, and redemption of preferred stock

Both managers and outsiders are interested in the flows of working capital, because an adequate supply of working capital is essential to the health of any business enterprise. The ability of an enterprise to generate working capital internally is an important factor in forecasting cash flows and in estimating ability to pay liabilities at maturity. In the typical operating cycle of an enterprise, the first step is the purchase of inventories (usually on short-term credit); the inventories then are converted to a larger amount of accounts receivable; these receivables are collected, and the inflow of cash is used to retire current payables. The operating cycle then begins anew. The statement of changes in financial position depicts these dynamics of the operating cycle, as well as the inflow and outflow of other financial resources.

The revenue and expenses included in the income statement do not run parallel to the flow of working capital. Consequently, the income statement alone does not call attention to the development of a shortage or an excess of liquid assets. In the preparation of forecasts and planning for future growth, management must coordinate the expected flow of internally generated liquid assets with the inflow of funds obtained from external sources, such as through borrowing or issuance of capital stock. Financial statements showing past and projected flows of working capital thus become basic tools of financial planning and analysis.

Working Capital Provided from Operations   As stated on page 936, special problems arise in the determination of the amount of working capital provided from operations. In the first item listed under **sources** above, revenue and operating expenses generally are combined, and a **net amount** is reported as **working capital provided from operations.** However, deductions from revenue which do not reduce working capital are added to net income (or loss), and revenue items and offsets to expenses which do not provide working capital are subtracted from net income (or loss) in the computation of the amount of working capital provided from operations during an accounting period. Examples of such items are given in the table on page 939.

Depreciation expense, an increase in the deferred income tax liability, the amortization of intangible assets and deferred charges, and the

Adjustments to net income to compute working capital provided from operations

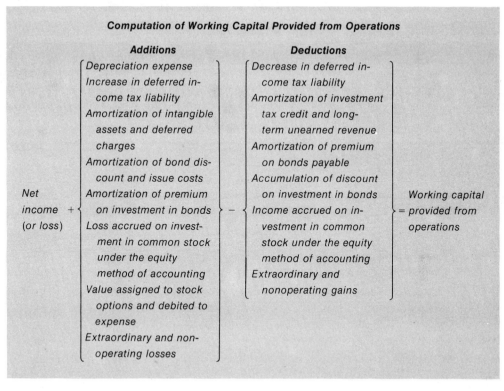

Computation of Working Capital Provided from Operations

Additions	Deductions
Depreciation expense	Decrease in deferred income tax liability
Increase in deferred income tax liability	Amortization of investment tax credit and long-term unearned revenue
Amortization of intangible assets and deferred charges	Amortization of premium on bonds payable
Amortization of bond discount and issue costs	Accumulation of discount on investment in bonds
Amortization of premium on investment in bonds	Income accrued on investment in common stock under the equity method of accounting
Loss accrued on investment in common stock under the equity method of accounting	Extraordinary and nonoperating gains
Value assigned to stock options and debited to expense	
Extraordinary and nonoperating losses	

Net income (or loss) + { Additions } − { Deductions } = Working capital provided from operations

amortization of bond discount and issue costs all reduce net income without reducing working capital and, therefore, are added to net income. Similarly, the amortization of a premium on investment in bonds and a loss on investment in common stock under the equity method of accounting reduce long-term investments and net income but have no effect on working capital; therefore, these items also are added to net income to measure the working capital provided from operations. The value assigned to compensatory stock options is debited to expense and credited to a stockholders' equity account; hence, this is a nonfund expense and is added to net income.

A decrease in the deferred income tax liability, the amortization of investment tax credit or long-term unearned revenue, and the amortization of premium on bonds payable all represent increases in net income and decreases in long-term liability accounts. Because these items increase net income but are not sources of working capital, they are deducted from net income. The accumulation of discount on investment in bonds and the income accrued on investments in common stock under the equity method of accounting represent increases in long-term investments and net income but do not affect working capital; therefore, these items also are deducted from net income to measure the working capital provided from operations.

According to **APB Opinion No. 19,** the working capital or cash provided from (or applied to) extraordinary items should be shown immediately below the amount of working capital provided from (or used in) operations. However, in the opinion of the authors, it is preferable to eliminate extraordinary items, as well as other nonoperating gains and losses, from net income and report separately the full effect on working capital of all extraordinary items and nonoperating gains and losses which are material in amount.

Funds defined as *cash*

As stated previously, the statement of changes in financial position may be prepared with emphasis on cash and cash equivalents rather than on working capital. When funds are viewed as cash and cash equivalents, the statement of changes in financial position is **more than a cash flow statement,** that is, a listing of cash receipts and payments, because financing and investing activities which do not involve cash also are listed as financial resources provided and applied. The all-financial-resources concept of the statement is equally applicable whether funds are defined as working capital or as cash and cash equivalents.

Adoption of cash and cash equivalents as the definition of funds can be justified on grounds that a statement of changes in financial position on a cash concept provides useful **predictive information** for decision makers. Management and outside users of financial statements are concerned with the ability of a business enterprise to meet maturing obligations and remain solvent. A statement of cash inflows and outflows which includes other significant financing and investing activities is viewed by many users of financial statements as a barometer of a business enterprise's financial strength.

Cash Provided from Operations   In the computation of the amount of cash provided from operations, the same additions and deductions to net income (or loss) illustrated on page 939 for computing the amount of working capital provided from operations are made. However, changes also must be considered in current accounts (except cash, short-term investments, loans receivable from others than customers, loans payable to others than suppliers, and dividends payable). The reason for this is apparent in the purchase of merchandise for cash, for example. In this transaction cash is reduced, but working capital is not. Thus, the computation of cash provided from operations for an accounting period is summarized on top of page 941.

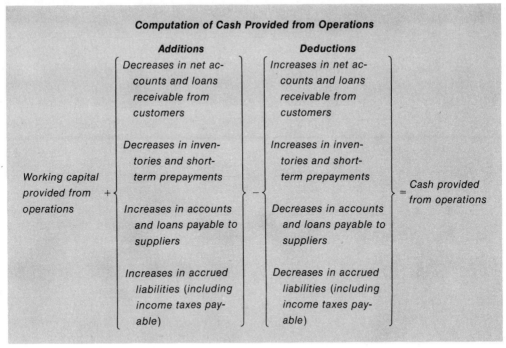

Adjustments to working capital provided from operations to obtain cash provided from operations

Computation of Cash Provided from Operations

Additions	Deductions
Decreases in net accounts and loans receivable from customers	Increases in net accounts and loans receivable from customers
Decreases in inventories and short-term prepayments	Increases in inventories and short-term prepayments
Increases in accounts and loans payable to suppliers	Decreases in accounts and loans payable to suppliers
Increases in accrued liabilities (including income taxes payable)	Decreases in accrued liabilities (including income taxes payable)

Working capital provided from operations + { Additions } − { Deductions } = Cash provided from operations

Decreases in net accounts and loans receivable from customers during an accounting period indicate that more cash was collected from customers than was reported as revenue in the income statement; increases in these accounts indicate that less cash was collected from customers than was reported as revenue in the income statement.

Decreases in inventories and short-term prepayments indicate that a portion of the cost of goods sold and expenses resulted from the use of assets previously paid for and not from current cash outlays; increases in inventories and short-term prepayments indicate that cash was used to accumulate these liquid assets.

Increases in acounts and loans payable to suppliers and accrued liabilities indicate that portions of cost of goods sold and expenses included in the income statement were not paid; decreases in accounts and loans payable to suppliers and accrued liabilities indicate that more cash was paid for these items than was included as expenses in the income statement.

The amount of cash provided from operations should not be viewed as a substitute for net income. Cash flow from operations is essentially the amount of net income on a cash basis of accounting; it is not a summary of revenue realized and expenses incurred. The profitability of a business enterprise is measured by comparing expired costs with realized revenue, not by computing net income on a cash basis of accounting.

Reporting a Cash Flow per Share   Reference often has been made by financial analysts to "cash flow per share," determined by adding depreciation and amortization charges to net income and dividing the result (income before noncash expenses) by the number of shares of common stock outstanding. Accounting authorities generally have discouraged computations of this sort; for example, **APB Opinion No. 19** made the following recommendation:[7]

> Terms referring to "cash" should not be used to describe amounts provided from operations unless all non-cash items have been appropriately adjusted. The adjusted amount should be described accurately, in conformity with the nature of the adjustments, e.g., "Cash provided from operations for the period." . . . The Board strongly recommends that isolated statistics of working capital or cash provided from operations, especially per-share amounts, not be presented in annual reports to stockholders. If any per-share data relating to flow of working capital or cash are presented, they should as a minimum include amounts for inflow from operations, inflow from other sources, and total outflow, and each per-share amount should be clearly identified with the corresponding total amount shown in the Statement.

The Securities and Exchange Commission also has discouraged the inclusion of cash flow per share data in statements filed with the Commission and in annual reports to shareholders. The SEC stated that cash-flow-per-share statistics "appear designed to decrease the credibility of conventional statements as a measure of business activity."[8] The Commission viewed the reporting of cash flow per share (whether based on the amount of cash provided from operations or the amount of net income before depreciation and amortization) to be both **misleading** and **irrelevant.** Accordingly, it urged that per-share data other than those relating to net income, net assets, and dividends should be avoided in reporting financial results. The position of the SEC is summarized below:[9]

> If accounting net income computed in conformity with generally accepted accounting principles is not an accurate reflection of economic performance for a company or an industry, it is not an appropriate solution to have each company independently decide what the best measure of its performance should be and present that figure to its shareholders as Truth. This would result in many different concepts and numbers which could not be used meaningfully by investors to compare different candidates for their investment dollars.

> Where the measurement of economic performance is an industry-wide problem, representatives of the industry and the accounting profession should present the problem and suggested solutions to the Financial Accounting Standards Board which is the body charged with responsibility for researching and defining principles to financial measurement.

---

[7] *APB Opinion No. 19,* pp. 377–378.
[8] *Accounting Series Release No. 142,* "Reporting Cash Flow and Other Related Data," SEC (Washington: 1973).
[9] Ibid.

Simple illustration of statement of changes in financial position

The income statement, the statement of retained earnings, and the comparative balance sheet provide the basic information for preparing a statement of changes in financial position. With this information, the major movements of working capital or cash can be identified for the accounting period under consideration.

When the working capital concept is adopted, the noncurrent assets of a business enterprise represent the financial resources in which working capital has been invested; the noncurrent liabilities and the stockholders' equity represent the financial sources from which working capital was provided. The first clue to an inflow or outflow of working capital, therefore, is changes in noncurrent accounts during the accounting period. The income statement and the statement of retained earnings help to explain the change in financial position that resulted from operations and from distributions to stockholders. The difference between the inflow and outflow of financial resources during the accounting period *must equal* the increase or decrease in working capital between the beginning and end of the accounting period.

When the cash concept is adopted, changes in *all* balance sheet accounts represent potential inflow and outflow of cash. Balance sheet accounts are analyzed to obtain specific amounts of cash inflows and outflows, resulting in a reconciliation of the beginning balance with the ending balance reported in the Cash account.

The data below and on pages 944 and 945 for Elwood Supply Company will be used to illustrate the preparation of a statement of changes

ELWOOD SUPPLY COMPANY
Income Statement
For Year Ended December 31, Year 2

Sales (net)		$107,000
Cost of goods sold:		
Beginning inventories	$40,000	
Purchases (net)	50,000	
Cost of goods available for sale	$90,000	
Less: Ending inventories	30,000	
Cost of goods sold		60,000
Gross profit on sales		$ 47,000
Expenses:		
Operating (excluding depreciation)	$10,000	
Depreciation	7,500	
Interest	1,500	19,000
Income before incomes taxes		$ 28,000
Income taxes expense		7,000
Net income		$ 21,000
Earnings per share (average of 10,500 shares outstanding)		$ 2.00

ELWOOD SUPPLY COMPANY
Statement of Retained Earnings
For Year Ended December 31, Year 2

Balance, beginning of year	$30,000
Add: Net income	21,000
Subtotal	$51,000
Less: Dividends declared	5,000
Balance, end of year	$46,000

ELWOOD SUPPLY COMPANY
Comparative Balance Sheets
December 31,

	Year 2	Year 1	Net change Debit (Credit)
Assets			
Cash.	$ 29,900	$ 14,000	$ 15,900
Accounts receivable (net)	33,000	27,000	6,000
Inventories	30,000	40,000	(10,000)
Short-term prepayments	1,600	1,000	600
Equipment	130,000	100,000	30,000
Less: Accumulated depreciation	(19,500)	(12,000)	(7,500)
Total assets	$205,000	$170,000	$ 35,000
Liabilities & Stockholders' Equity			
Accounts payable	$ 15,500	$ 23,400	$ 7,900
Accrued interest payable.	1,500	–0–	(1,500)
Income taxes payable	7,000	6,600	(400)
Dividends payable.	5,000	–0–	(5,000)
Long-term notes payable, due Year 5 .	8,000	–0–	(8,000)
Capital stock, $10 par	110,000	100,000	(10,000)
Paid-in capital in excess of par	12,000	10,000	(2,000)
Retained earnings.	46,000	30,000	(16,000)
Total liabilities & stockholders' equity	$205,000	$170,000	$(35,000)

in financial position, first on a working capital basis and then on a cash basis, without the use of working papers. The use of working papers is illustrated in the comprehensive illustration starting on page 953.

Additional information for Year 2

(1) Equipment was acquired for $18,000 cash. Additional equipment with a current fair value of $12,000 was acquired on July 1 in exchange for 1,000 shares of capital stock.

(2) Cash of $8,000 was borrowed on a long-term basis (a note due in Year 5).

(3) Cash dividends of $5,000 were declared (but not paid) at the end of Year 2.

Statement of Changes in Financial Position on a Working Capital Concept
When the statement of changes in financial position is prepared on a working capital concept, it explains fully the reasons for an increase or decrease in working capital during an accounting period. Referring to the comparative balance sheet for Elwood Supply Company on page 944, the increase in working capital during Year 2 can be determined as illustrated below:

Computation of increase in working capital

ELWOOD SUPPLY COMPANY Change in Working Capital For Year Ended December 31, Year 2			
	End of Year 2	End of Year 1	Increase (decrease) in working capital
Current assets:			
Cash.	$29,900	$14,000	$15,900
Accounts receivable (net)	33,000	27,000	6,000
Inventories	30,000	40,000	(10,000)
Short-term prepayments	1,600	1,000	600
Total current assets	$94,500	$82,000	
Current liabilities:			
Accounts payable	$15,500	$23,400	7,900
Accrued interest payable	1,500	–0–	(1,500)
Income taxes payable	7,000	6,600	(400)
Dividends payable	5,000	–0–	(5,000)
Total current liabilities.	$29,000	$30,000	
Working capital	$65,500	$52,000	
Increase in working capital			$13,500

The increase in working capital for Elwood Supply Company can be viewed as a *result* which is to be explained by analyzing the changes in non-working capital accounts. In other words, the *causes* of the increase in working capital can be found only in the changes that took place in the noncurrent accounts. However, not all changes in noncurrent accounts cause changes in working capital. For example, distributions of stock dividends and exchange transactions cause changes in noncurrent accounts but do not change working capital. Exchange transactions, such as the issuance of capital stock for equipment by Elwood Supply Company, are financial resources provided and applied.

A statement of changes in financial position on a working capital concept for Elwood Supply Company is illustrated below. This form highlights the increase in working capital. As stated earlier, some companies prepare the statement in "balancing form," showing an increase in working capital as a financial resource provided. Finally, some companies add the financial resources provided to the beginning balance of working capital and deduct the financial resources applied to determine

Funds statement illustrated: working capital flows

ELWOOD SUPPLY COMPANY
Statement of Changes in Financial Position (Working Capital Concept)
For Year Ended December 31, Year 2

Financial resources provided

Operations—net income	$21,000
Add: Expense which did not reduce working capital—depreciation	7,500
Working capital provided from operations	$28,500
Borrowing on long-term notes	8,000
Issuance of capital stock in exchange for equipment	12,000
Total financial resources provided	$48,500

Financial resources applied

Acquisition of equipment for cash	$18,000	
Acquisition of equipment in exchange for capital stock	12,000	
Declaration of cash dividends	5,000	
Total financial resources applied		35,000
Increase in financial resources (working capital)		$13,500

	End of Year 2	End of Year 1	Increase (decrease) in working capital
Composition of working capital			
Current assets:			
Cash	$29,900	$14,000	$15,900
Accounts receivable (net)	33,000	27,000	6,000
Inventories	30,000	40,000	(10,000)
Short-term prepayments	1,600	1,000	600
Total current assets	$94,500	$82,000	
Current liabilities:			
Accounts payable	$15,500	$23,400	7,900
Accrued interest payable	1,500	–0–	(1,500)
Income taxes payable	7,000	6,600	(400)
Dividends payable	5,000	–0–	(5,000)
Total current liabilities	$29,000	$30,000	
Working capital	$65,500	$52,000	
Increase in working capital			$13,500

the ending balance of working capital as the final amount in the statement.

Statement of Changes in Financial Position on a Cash Concept When the statement of changes in financial position is prepared on a cash concept, it contains a summary of all cash receipts and payments, as well as the effect of exchange transactions. This form is a useful analytical tool for management and other users of financial statements because it provides answers to questions such as the following: How much cash was generated by recurring operations last period? What use was made of cash receipts? How much cash was received from nonrecurring sources? Why is the company short of cash? Can the current level of cash dividend payments be maintained? The statement of changes in financial position on a cash concept for Elwood Supply Company is illustrated below:

Funds statement on cash concept

ELWOOD SUPPLY COMPANY
Statement of Changes in Financial Position (Cash Concept)
For Year Ended December 31, Year 2

Financial resources provided			
Operations—net income			$21,000
Add: Depreciation expense			7,500
Decrease in inventories			10,000
Increase in accrued interest payable			1,500
Increase in income taxes payable			400
Less: Increase in net accounts receivable		$ 6,000	
Increase in short-term prepayments		600	
Decrease in accounts payable		7,900	(14,500)
Cash provided from operations			$25,900
Borrowing on long-term notes			8,000
Issuance of capital stock in exchange for equipment			12,000
Total financial resources provided			$45,900
Financial resources applied			
Acquisition of equipment for cash		$18,000	
Acquisition of equipment in exchange for capital stock		12,000	
Total financial resources applied			30,000
Increase in financial resources (cash)			$15,900

(Composition of working capital, as presented on page 946, generally is included in the cash-concept statement or in a separate exhibit.)

The declaration of dividends is not shown in the cash-concept statement for Elwood Supply Company, because the dividends were not paid in Year 2. If the presentation of cash provided from operations is quite detailed, it may be presented in a separate exhibit.

Alternative Approach: Cash-Basis Net Income Instead of reporting the cash provided from operations as shown on page 947, the income statement may be converted from the accrual basis of accounting to the cash basis of accounting to show actual cash receipts and payments from operations (see Chapter 1). Receipts from customers, payment to suppliers, and payments for specific expenses thus are reported with other financial resources provided and applied in the statement of changes in financial position on a cash concept. This approach is illustrated below and on page 949 for Elwood Supply Company.

Net income on cash basis of accounting

ELWOOD SUPPLY COMPANY

Conversion of Income Statement from Accrual to Cash Basis of Accounting

For Year Ended December 31, Year 2

	Income statement (accrual basis)	Add (deduct)	Cash basis
Sales	$107,000		
Less: Increase in net accounts receivable . .		$ (6,000)	$101,000
Cost of goods sold.	60,000		
Add: Decrease in accounts payable.		7,900	
Less: Decrease in inventories		(10,000)	57,900
Gross profit on sales	$ 47,000		$ 43,100
Expenses:			
Operating expenses (excluding depreciation)	$ 10,000		
Add: Increase in short-term prepayments .		600	$ 10,600
Depreciation expense.	7,500	(7,500)	–0–
Interest expense	1,500	(1,500)	–0–
Income taxes expense	7,000		
Less: Increase in income taxes payable . .		(400)	6,600
Total expenses	$ 26,000		$ 17,200
Net income—accrual basis	$ 21,000		
Net income—cash basis (cash provided from operations as reported on page 947)			$ 25,900

Neither depreciation expense nor interest expense required the payment of cash in Year 2; therefore, both amounts are eliminated in the conversion of the income statement to the cash basis.

Special problems

When a statement of changes in financial position is prepared from the detailed accounting records, all the necessary information may be obtained from ledger account balances or from computer printouts. The

Funds statement on cash concept

> **ELWOOD SUPPLY COMPANY**
> **Statement of Changes in Financial Position (Cash Concept)**
> **For Year Ended December 31, Year 2**
>
> **Financial resources provided**
> Collections on accounts receivable. $101,000
> Borrowing on long-term notes. 8,000
> Issuance of capital stock in exchange for equipment 12,000
> Total financial resources provided $121,000
> **Financial resources applied**
> Merchandise purchases. $57,900
> Operating expenses 10,600
> Income taxes expense. 6,600
> Acquisition of equipment for cash 18,000
> Acquisition of equipment in exchange for capital stock . . 12,000
> Total financial resources applied 105,100
> Increase in financial resources (cash). . . . . $ 15,900
> *(Composition of working capital generally is included here.)*

task is more difficult when the statement must be prepared from the comparative balance sheets, the income statement, the statement of retained earnings, and other miscellaneous information. Some special problems involved in the preparation of the statement of changes in financial position **on a working capital concept** are described in the following sections.

Doubtful Accounts Expense Neither the recognition of doubtful accounts expense nor the actual write-off of uncollectible **current** accounts receivable requires any action in the preparation of a statement of changes in financial position on a working capital concept. The recognition of doubtful accounts expense reduces net current accounts receivable and is reflected as a deduction from revenue in the measurement of working capital provided from operations. A write-off of a current account receivable does not reduce net current accounts receivable and thus has no effect on working capital.

In contrast, the recognition of doubtful accounts expense on **noncurrent** accounts receivable does not reduce working capital; therefore, such expense is added to net income in the computation of working capital provided from operations.

Gain or Loss on Sale (or Write-Down) of Short-Term Investments When marketable securities, for example, which are classified as current assets are sold at a gain, working capital is increased by the amount of the gain; if such securities are sold at a loss, working capital is reduced by the amount of the loss. Unrealized gains and losses recognized on marketable equity securities (pursuant to **FASB Statement No. 12**), and included in the determination of net income, also have an effect on working capital. However, because marketable securities generally are acquired to obtain a return on cash not currently needed in operations, such gains and losses normally are included in net income in the computation of working capital provided from or used in operations.

Acquisition of a Going Concern   When a going concern is acquired, the effect of the acquisition on financial resources requires careful analysis. For example, assume the following transaction:

Journal entry to record acquisition of a going concern

Current Assets	*200,000*
Noncurrent Assets	*500,000*
Current Liabilities	*50,000*
Cash	*150,000*
Capital Stock, no-par value	*500,000*
To record acquisition of a going concern.	

The acquisition of current assets in the amount of $200,000 in this example does not affect working capital, because current liabilities in the amount of $50,000 were increased and cash in the amount of $150,000 was paid. The net effect was to increase both the current assets and the current liabilities by $50,000. The exchange of capital stock for noncurrent assets is reported as financial resources provided and applied, both in the amount of $500,000.

Reclassification of Current and Noncurrent Items   When a long-term obligation matures within a year, it is reclassified as a current liability. For example, serial bonds and mortgage notes payable which mature within one year generally are reclassified from long-term debt to the current liabilities category. This reclassification decreases the amount of working capital and thus represents a financial resource applied. Similarly, a long-term receivable which matures within one year from the end of the current accounting period is reclassified as a current asset, thus increasing working capital (a financial resource provided).

A reclassification of a current asset to the noncurrent category (such as an extension of maturity dates on receivables) reduces the amount of working capital; a reclassification of a current liability to long-term debt (through a debt restructuring, for example) increases the amount of working capital. Consequently, such reclassifications are reported as financial resources applied and provided in the statement of changes in financial position prepared on a working capital concept.

Analysis of Changes in Plant Asset Accounts When numerous transactions were recorded in plant asset accounts, it is helpful to analyze these accounts before isolating the effect on working capital. For example, assume that the following information relating to equipment is available from comparative financial statements:

	End of current year	End of previous year
Effect of transactions relating to equipment		
Equipment.	$540,000	$620,000
Accumulated depreciation	230,000	195,000
Depreciation expense	60,000	
Loss on sale of equipment	40,000	

Equipment with a cost of $130,000 and a carrying amount of $105,000 was sold for $65,000 cash and equipment was acquired for $50,000 cash during the current year. The analyses of the Equipment and Accumulated Depreciation accounts shown below identify the transactions that caused the changes in these two accounts and affected working capital. The journal entries prepared at the time of each transaction, and the corresponding effect on the statement of changes in financial position prepared on a working capital concept, are summarized on top of page 952.

	Equipment account dr (cr)	Accumulated Depreciation account dr (cr)
More detailed analysis of changes in plant asset accounts . . .		
Balance, beginning of current year	$ 620,000	$(195,000)
Sale of equipment for $65,000 cash	(130,000)	25,000
Acquisition of equipment for cash	50,000	
Depreciation expense		(60,000)
Balance, end of current year	$ 540,000	$(230,000)

The analyses on page 952 fully explain the changes in the Equipment and Accumulated Depreciation accounts. They provide the support for an increase in net income of $100,000 to cancel the effects of nonfund charges (loss on sale of equipment of $40,000 and depreciation expense of $60,000), and the amounts to be reported as financial resources provided and applied in the statement of changes in financial position prepared on a working capital concept.

. . . and journal entries
causing changes in
plant asset accounts

Journal entries at time of transaction		Effect on statement of changes in financial position (working capital concept)
Cash . . . .　65,000		*Financial resources provided: Sale of equipment, $65,000.*
Accumulated Depreciation . . . . .　25,000		
Loss on Sale of Equipment . . . .　40,000		
Equipment.	130,000	*The loss on sale of equipment, $40,000, is added to net income to measure the amount of working capital provided from operations.*
To record sale of equipment.		
Equipment . . . .　50,000		*Financial resources applied: Acquisition of equipment, $50,000.*
Cash	50,000	
To record acquisition of equipment.		
Depreciation Expense. . . . .　60,000		*Depreciation of $60,000 is added to net income to measure the amount of working capital provided from operations.*
Accumulated Depreciation .	60,000	
To record depreciation expense.		

Capital Leases A lease contract which meets the criteria for a capital lease is recorded by the lessee as a debit to a noncurrent asset and a credit to a liability account, a portion of which is currently due. To illustrate, assume that Lessee Company recorded a capital lease in Year 1 as follows:

Journal entry to record
capital lease by lessee

Leased Equipment under Capital Lease . . . .　100,000		
Obligation under Capital Lease (net) ($15,000 due within		
one year)	100,000	
To record capital lease by lessee.		

In a statement of changes in financial position on a working capital concept for Year 1, the lease contract is reported by Lessee Company as follows:

What part of the
foregoing journal entry
is an "exchange"?

Financial resources provided
　Long-term borrowing under capital lease . . . . $ 85,000
Financial resources applied
　Acquisition of equipment under capital lease $100,000

In a statement of changes in financial position on a cash concept for Year 1, the lease contract is reported as a financial resource provided and applied, both in the amount of $100,000.

COMPREHENSIVE ILLUSTRATION OF STATEMENT OF CHANGES IN FINANCIAL POSITION

The following illustration for Rose Corporation is designed to show how the reasoning discussed thus far can be applied to an analysis of *working capital flows* in a more complex situation. The data on which the analysis is based are contained in the comparative after-closing trial balances below, the income statement for Year 5 on page 954, the statement of retained earnings for Year 5 on page 955, and the additional information listed below and on pages 954 and 955.

Additional information for Year 5
(1) Land was acquired for $150,000 cash.

ROSE CORPORATION
Comparative After-Closing Trial Balances.
December 31, Year 5 and Year 4

	Year 5 Debit	Year 5 Credit	Year 4 Debit	Year 4 Credit
Cash	$ 27,100		$ 52,800	
Notes receivable from customers	50,000		30,000	
Accounts receivable (net).	36,900		50,400	
Inventories.	96,050		57,300	
Short-term prepayments	12,600		9,600	
Land	150,000		–0–	
Buildings and equipment	554,000		826,000	
Accumulated depreciation		$185,000		$ 355,000
Investment in common stock of Z Company (equity method)	53,250		40,000	
Accounts payable		22,150		31,300
Accrued liabilities		17,600		16,300
Income taxes payable		42,800		17,000
Dividends payable		42,000		–0–
8% bonds payable, due Jan. 1, Year 15 . .		150,000		200,000
Premium on bonds payable		6,750		10,000
Deferred income tax liability		45,000		80,000
Capital stock, $10 par		150,000		100,000
Paid-in capital in excess of par		106,200		58,000
Retained earnings		229,900		198,500
Treasury stock, 1,000 shares	17,500		–0–	
Totals	$997,400	$997,400	$1,066,100	$1,066,100

ROSE CORPORATION

Income Statement

For Year Ended December 31, Year 5

Sales		$313,600
Cost of goods sold		158,000
Gross profit on sales		$155,600
Operating expenses:		
Depreciation	$30,000	
Other	28,000	58,000
Income from operations		$ 97,600
Nonoperating revenue and expense:		
Investment income from Z Company	$13,250	
Less: Interest expense	11,250	2,000
Income before income taxes		$ 99,600
Income taxes expense (including $10,000 deferred)		48,300
Income before extraordinary items		$ 51,300
Extraordinary gain on condemnation of building (net of income taxes of $22,500)		27,500
Net income		$ 78,800

(2) An analysis of the changes in the Buildings and Equipment account and the Accumulated Depreciation account during Year 5 is given below:

Changes in plant asset accounts

	Buildings and Equipment account	Accumulated Depreciation account
Balances, Dec. 31, Year 4	$826,000	$355,000
Condemnation of building	(400,000)*	(200,000)
Acquisition of equipment	128,000†	
Depreciation expense		30,000
Balances, Dec. 31, Year 5	$554,000	$185,000

* The condemnation of the building in Year 5 was recorded as follows:

Cash	250,000	
Accumulated Depreciation	200,000	
Deferred Income Tax Liability	45,000	
Buildings and Equipment		400,000
Extraordinary Gain (net of income taxes of $22,500)		27,500
Income Taxes Payable		67,500

To record proceeds received from condemnation of building on leased land.

† Acquired in an exchange transaction through issuance of 4,640 shares of capital stock with a current fair value of $92,800 and $35,200 cash, a total of $128,000.

ROSE CORPORATION
Statement of Retained Earnings
For Year Ended December 31, Year 5

Retained earnings, beginning of year.		$198,500
Add: Net income		78,800
Subtotal		$277,300
Less: Stock dividend (360 shares @ $15 a share).	$ 5,400	
Cash dividends.	42,000	47,400
Retained earnings, end of year.		$229,900

(3) During Year 5, Rose Corporation recorded $13,250 as its share of net income reported by Z Company. Rose Corporation owns 25% of the common stock of Z Company and uses the equity method of accounting for the investment in the common stock of Z Company.

(4) At the beginning of Year 5, $50,000 of bonds payable were retired at 105. Unamortized premium of $2,500 ($10,000 × ¼) on bonds payable was written off, resulting in neither a gain nor a loss. The balance in the Premium on Bonds Payable account, $7,500, is being amortized under the straight-line method over a 10-year period, or $750 a year.

(5) During Year 5, Rose Corporation reacquired 1,000 shares of its capital stock for $17,500. At a time when 9,000 shares of capital stock were outstanding and the market price was $15 a share, the company declared a 4% stock dividend. The board of directors of Rose Corporation authorized a transfer of $5,400 (360 shares × $15) from retained earnings to paid-in capital to record the stock dividend. Later in the year, 4,640 shares of capital stock, with a market price of $20 a share, were issued in exchange for equipment. On December 10, Year 5, a cash dividend of $3 a share was declared on the 14,000 (9,000 + 360 + 4,640 = 14,000) shares of capital stock outstanding at the end of Year 5, payable January 15, Year 6.

Computation of change in working capital

The first step in the preparation of a statement of changes in financial position on a working capital concept for Rose Corporation is to determine its working capital at the beginning and at the end of Year 5, and the increase or decrease in working capital during the year. The composition of working capital is shown in the lower section of the statement of changes in financial position which appears on page 962.

Working paper for statement of changes in financial position

After the composition of working capital is prepared, the beginning working capital, $135,500, is entered in the first column of a working paper. (The use of a working paper to analyze changes in noncurrent accounts and to identify the financial resources provided and applied is not necessary for relatively simple problems; however, for more complex problems the use of a working paper is helpful.) Similarly, the beginning balances in all other noncurrent accounts are recorded in the first column of the working paper. Transactions for Year 5 then are analyzed, and the sources and uses of working capital are determined as described earlier in this chapter. The working paper for the statement of changes in financial position on a working capital concept for Rose Corporation is shown on page 957.

Analysis of Transactions in the Working Paper By studying the changes in the noncurrent accounts, we are able to find the specific reasons for the $37,400 decrease in working capital during Year 5. As previously stated, only changes in the noncurrent accounts represent sources and uses of working capital. The analysis of the transactions completed by Rose Corporation during Year 5 are explained below. (The numbers correspond to the numbers used in the working paper.)

(1) The net income of $78,800 is closed to the Retained Earnings account and is shown under "Financial Resources Provided: Operations." Net income represents an increase in stockholders' equity and is one of the major sources of working capital for most enterprises. However, net income is only the starting point in the computation of the increase in working capital from operations because not all revenue and expense items represent sources and uses of working capital. Furthermore, any extraordinary items are eliminated from net income because the transactions giving rise to such items are *reported separately.*

(2) Because depreciation expense does not reduce a current asset or increase a current liability, it has no effect on working capital. Therefore, the depreciation expense of $30,000 for Year 5 is added to net income and is credited to Accumulated Depreciation. In other words, because depreciation is a nonfund expense, the working capital provided from operations (assuming no other nonfund items) is equal to the amount of net income plus depreciation.

(3) Depreciation was not the only expense which did not reduce working capital. The income taxes expense of $48,300 includes $10,000 payable in future years, which appears as an increase in the Deferred Income Tax Liability account. This portion of income taxes expense is added to net income because it did not reduce working capital during Year 5.

A working paper is
useful to analyze
funds flows

ROSE CORPORATION
Working Paper for Statement of Changes in Financial Position (Working Capital Concept)
For Year Ended December 31, Year 5

	Balances, Dec. 31, Year 4	Transactions for Year 5 Debit	Transactions for Year 5 Credit	Balances, Dec. 31, Year 5
Working capital	135,500		(x) 37,400	98,100
Land	–0–	(4) 150,000		150,000
Buildings and equipment	826,000	(9) 128,000	(5) 400,000	554,000
Investment in common stock of Z				
Company (equity method)	40,000	(8) 13,250		53,250
Treasury stock, 1,000 shares	–0–	(10) 17,500		17,500
Totals	1,001,500			872,850
Accumulated depreciation	355,000	(5) 200,000	(2) 30,000	185,000
8% bonds payable	200,000	(6) 50,000		150,000
Premium on bonds payable.	10,000	(6) 2,500 (7) 750		6,750
Deferred income tax liability	80,000	(5) 45,000	(3) 10,000	45,000
Capital stock, $10 par	100,000		(9) 46,400 (12) 3,600	150,000
Paid-in capital in excess of par . .	58,000		(9) 46,400 (12) 1,800	106,200
Retained earnings	198,500	(11) 42,000 (12) 5,400	(1) 78,800	229,900
Totals	1,001,500	654,400	654,400	872,850
Financial resources provided				
Operations—net income		(1) 78,800		
Add: Depreciation expense. . . .		(2) 30,000		Working capital provided from operations, $77,300
Increase in deferred income tax liability		(3) 10,000		
Less: Amortization of premium on bonds payable			(7) 750	
Investment income from Z Company			(8) 13,250	
Extraordinary gain			(5) 27,500	
Proceeds on condemnation of building (net of income taxes)		(5) 182,500		
Issuance of capital stock in exchange for equipment		(9) 92,800		
Financial resources applied				
Extinguishment of bonds payable			(6) 52,500	
Acquisition of land.			(4) 150,000	
Acquisition of equipment for cash			(9) 35,200	
Acquisition of equipment in exchange for capital stock			(9) 92,800	
Acquisition of treasury stock. . .			(10) 17,500	
Declaration of cash dividends . .			(11) 42,000	
Total financial resources provided and applied		394,100	431,500	
Decrease in working capital		(x) 37,400		
Totals		431,500	431,500	

Explanations of transactions for Year 5 start on page 956.

(4) Land was acquired for $150,000 cash in Year 5. This is a reduction in working capital and is listed in the working paper as a financial resource applied.

(5) The journal entry to record the condemnation of the building on leased land in Year 5 appears on page 954. In the working paper, the condemnation is recorded as a source of working capital of $182,500 because cash increased $250,000 and current income taxes payable increased $67,500. The accumulated depreciation applicable to the building, $200,000, is debited to the Accumulated Depreciation account, and the deferred tax of $45,000 relating to the building is debited to the Deferred Income Tax Liability account. The extraordinary gain of $27,500 is deducted from net income so that the net proceeds (net of income taxes of $22,500) can be listed intact as a source of working capital. The original cost of the building, $400,000, is credited to the Buildings and Equipment account to complete the transaction in the working paper. Note that when the increase of $30,000 for depreciation expense and the decrease of $200,000 on the condemnation of the building are combined with the beginning balance of $355,000, the ending balance of $185,000 in the Accumulated Depreciation account is obtained.

(6) At the beginning of Year 5, bonds payable were retired at 105, as illustrated in the journal entry below:

Journal entry to record retirement of bonds payable

8% Bonds Payable	50,000	
Premium on Bonds Payable	2,500	
Cash		52,500

This transaction is recorded in the working paper by a debit of $50,000 to 8% Bonds Payable, a debit of $2,500 to Premium on Bonds Payable, and a credit of $52,500 to Financial Resources Applied: Extinguishment of Bonds Payable. At this point we have accounted for the decrease in the 8% Bonds Payable account from $200,000 to $150,000.

(7) The amortization of the premium on bonds payable was recorded at the end of Year 5 as follows:

Journal entry to amortize premium on bonds payable

Premium on Bonds Payable	750	
Interest Expense		750

The working paper analysis of this adjusting entry is to debit the Premium on Bonds Payable account and to record a reduction in working capital provided from operations, because the credit to Interest Expense increased net income without increasing working capital. The amount of bond interest paid in Year 5 was $12,000 ($150,000 × 8% = $12,000), not $11,250 reported as interest expense in the income statement. The debit of $750 to the Premium on Bonds Payable account, combined with the debit of $2,500 in transaction (6), explains the decrease in this account from a balance of $10,000 at the beginning of Year 5 to a balance of $6,750 at the end of Year 5.

(8) The net income for Year 5 includes $13,250 of income on the investment in the common stock of Z Company. The investment income was recorded by the equity method of accounting as follows:

Journal entry to record investment income

Investment in Common Stock of Z Company	13,250	
Investment Income from Z Company		13,250

In the working paper, this journal entry is recorded as a debit to the investment account and a credit (reduction) to "operations," because the investment income did not generate working capital. After this journal entry is entered in the working paper, the ending balance of $53,250 in the Investment in Common Stock of Z Company account is determined by adding $13,250 to the balance of $40,000 at the beginning of Year 5.

(9) The acquisition of equipment for cash and the issuance of 4,640 shares of capital stock were recorded as follows:

Journal entry to record acquisition of plant assets . . .

Buildings and Equipment	128,000	
Cash		35,200
Capital Stock, $10 par		46,400
Paid-in Capital in Excess of Par		46,400

Although this transaction actually reduced working capital by only $35,200, the total cost of the equipment acquired is reported as a financial resource applied. The reason for this is that the issuance of capital stock valued at $92,800 is viewed both as a financial resource provided and as a financial resource applied. The working paper analysis of this transaction is presented on top of page 960.

. . . and working paper
analysis of same
transaction

Buildings and Equipment	*128,000*	
Issuance of Capital Stock in Exchange for Equipment	*92,800*	
Acquisition of Equipment for Cash.		*35,200*
Acquisition of Equipment in Exchange for Capital Stock		*92,800*
Capital Stock, $10 par		*46,400*
Paid-in Capital in Excess of Par.		*46,400*

This analysis recognizes the changes in the non-working capital accounts in the upper part of the working paper, and the financial resources provided and applied in the lower part. The debit of $128,000 in the Buildings and Equipment account, less the credit of $400,000 in transaction (5), explains the net decrease in this account in Year 5 from $826,000 to $554,000.

(10) The acquisition of treasury stock for $17,500 is recorded in the working paper as a debit to the Treasury Stock account, thus establishing the ending balance in this account, and as a credit to Financial Resources Applied: Acquisition of Treasury Stock.

(11) The declaration of the cash dividend, $42,000, is entered in the working paper as a debit to Retained Earnings and a credit to Financial Resources Applied: Declaration of Cash Dividends. The declaration of the cash dividend created a current liability and thus reduced working capital.

(12) The declaration of a stock dividend required a transfer from Retained Earnings to paid-in capital accounts. A stock dividend has no effect on working capital and is not considered as a financing and investing transaction under the all-financial-resources concept of funds. The working paper entry for the 4% stock dividend (360 shares valued at $15 per share) requires a debit to Retained Earnings for $5,400, a credit to Capital Stock for $3,600, and a credit of $1,800 to Paid-in Capital in Excess of Par. After this transaction is entered in the working paper, the ending balances in the Capital Stock, Paid-in Capital in Excess of Par, and Retained Earnings accounts can be determined.

(X) After all changes in noncurrent accounts are analyzed in the working paper, the total ($394,100) of the financial resources provided column and the total ($431,500) of the financial resources applied column are obtained. At this point, the decrease in working capital during the year, $37,400, is entered as a credit to "Working Capital" in the first line of the third column in the working paper, and also as a balancing amount on the next to the last line of the second column in the working paper. The account balances at the end of Year 5 now can be determined in the last column of the working paper (including the ending working capital of $98,100), and the subtotals ($654,400) obtained for the "Debit" and "Credit" columns. If the totals ($872,850) for account balances at the end of Year 5 agree, it is reasonable to conclude that all transactions in noncurrent accounts have been analyzed and that the decrease in working capital has been explained.

Summary of Working Paper Procedures The procedures illustrated for Rose Corporation to develop the information needed to prepare a statement of changes in financial position on a working capital concept are summarized below:

1 Determine the amount of working capital at the beginning and at the end of the accounting period under consideration.

2 Enter the amount of working capital and the amount of all noncurrent accounts at the beginning of the accounting period in the first column of the working paper.

3 Enter in summary form all transactions which caused increases and decreases in working capital, listing the specific sources and uses of working capital in the lower part of the working paper. Certain transactions which involved only noncurrent accounts (stock dividends, for example) simply are recorded opposite the accounts affected because these are neither sources nor uses of working capital. Exchange transactions (issuance of capital stock in exchange for plant assets, for example) are reported both as financial resources provided and as financial resources applied.

4 Determine that the difference between the financial resources provided and applied is equal to the increase or decrease in the working capital during the accounting period. The fact that the difference between the financial resources provided and applied is equal to the change in working capital does not necessarily prove that the working paper analyses are correct, but it does indicate that all account changes have been analyzed and that no arithmetic errors have been made. An error in classifying a current asset as noncurrent, for example, will not be disclosed.

5 Prepare a formal statement of changes in financial position, showing the financial resources provided and applied during the accounting period, as well as the composition of working capital at the beginning and at the end of the period.

Statement of changes in financial position on a working capital concept

The statement of changes in financial position on a working capital concept for Rose Corporation is presented on page 962. The amounts are taken from the working paper on page 957. Although it would be possible to list individual nonfund adjustments to net income, this generally is not necessary, unless the amounts have some special significance.

Alternative Form Showing Revenue and Expenses An acceptable procedure, which gives the same result, is to begin with total revenue that provided working capital during the period and deduct operating costs and expenses that required the outlay of working capital during the period. This form is illustrated on page 963 for Rose Corporation.

Complete funds flow statement illustrated

ROSE CORPORATION
Statement of Changes in Financial Position (Working Capital Concept)
For Year Ended December 31, Year 5

Financial resources provided

Operations—net income	$ 78,800
Less: Credits (net of charges) not providing working capital (see working paper on page 957 for detail)	1,500
Working capital provided from operations	$ 77,300
Proceeds on condemnation of building (net of income taxes)	182,500
Issuance of capital stock in exchange for equipment	92,800
Total financial resources provided	$352,600

Financial resources applied

Extinguishment of bonds payable	$ 52,500	
Acquisition of land	150,000	
Acquisition of equipment for cash	35,200	
Acquisition of equipment in exchange for capital stock	92,800	
Acquisition of treasury stock	17,500	
Declaration of cash dividends	42,000	
Total financial resources applied		390,000
Decrease in financial resources: working capital		$ (37,400)

	Dec. 31, Year 5	Dec. 31, Year 4	Increase (decrease) in working capital
Composition of working capital			
Current assets:			
Cash	$ 27,100	$ 52,800	$(25,700)
Notes receivable from customers	50,000	30,000	20,000
Accounts receivable (net)	36,900	50,400	(13,500)
Inventories	96,050	57,300	38,750
Short-term prepayments	12,600	9,600	3,000
Total current assets	$222,650	$200,100	
Current liabilities:			
Accounts payable	$ 22,150	$ 31,300	9,150
Accrued liabilities	17,600	16,300	(1,300)
Income taxes payable	42,800	17,000	(25,800)
Dividends payable	42,000	–0–	(42,000)
Total current liabilities	$124,550	$ 64,600	
Working capital	$ 98,100	$135,500	
Decrease in working capital			$(37,400)

Funds statement
showing revenue
and expenses

ROSE CORPORATION
Statement of Changes in Financial Position (Working Capital Concept)
For Year Ended December 31, Year 5

Financial resources provided

Sales.		$313,600
Less: Cost of goods sold.	$158,000	
Operating expenses (other than depreciation) . . .	28,000	
Income taxes expense.	38,300	
Interest expense	12,000	236,300
Working capital provided from operations		$ 77,300
Proceeds on condemnation of building (net of income taxes) . . .		182,500
Issuance of capital stock in exchange for equipment		92,800
Total financial resources provided		$352,600

Financial resources applied

Extinguishment of bonds payable	$ 52,500	
Acquisition of land.	150,000	
Acquisition of equipment for cash	35,200	
Acquisition of equipment in exchange for capital stock . . .	92,800	
Acquisition of treasury stock	17,500	
Declaration of cash dividends.	42,000	
Total financial resources applied		390,000
Decrease in financial resources: working capital		$ (37,400)

Composition of working capital (same as on page 962)

The impact of income taxes on working capital for Year 5 is equal to the income tax expense of $48,300 as reported in the income statement, less $10,000 deferred income taxes, or $38,300. The impact of interest expense on working capital is equal to the total of interest expense of $11,250 reported in the income statement, plus $750 amortization of premium on bonds payable, or $12,000, which is the amount of interest paid in cash during the year.

Statement of changes in financial position on a cash concept

The statement of changes in financial position on a cash concept for Rose Corporation is presented on page 964. The amounts included in this statement are developed in the working paper on page 965. This working paper is an extension of the one prepared on the working capital concept, which appears on page 957.

Funds statement show-ing cash flows

ROSE CORPORATION
Statement of Changes in Financial Position (Cash Concept)
For Year 5

Financial resources provided

Cash provided from operations (see working paper on page 965). . .		$ 47,000
Proceeds on condemnation of building (net of income taxes).		182,500
Issuance of capital stock in exchange for equipment		92,800
Total financial resources provided		$322,300

Financial resources applied

Extinguishment of bonds payable.	$ 52,500	
Acquisition of land	150,000	
Acquisition of equipment for cash	35,200	
Acquisition of equipment in exchange for capital stock . .	92,800	
Acquisition of treasury stock.	17,500	
Total financial resources applied		348,000
Decrease in financial resources: cash		$ (25,700)

Composition of working capital (same as on page 962)

Alternative form of working paper

The working paper for the statement of changes in financial position may be adapted to meet varying needs when the information for solving problems is given in somewhat different form. For example, assuming that only *changes* in account balances for Liz Lock Company during Year 10 are given and that beginning and ending account balances are not available, the working paper for the statement of changes in financial position may take the form illustrated on page 966.

In the Transactions for Year 10 columns, the objective is to *summarize the changes in noncurrent accounts* and to identify the financial resources provided and applied in the process. The credit changes in noncurrent assets ($10,000) and capital stock ($25,000) are explained by entries to record depreciation and the issuance of capital stock. Similarly, the net credit change of $50,000 in retained earnings resulted from net income of $65,000 less cash dividends of $15,000; and the debit change of $5,000 in long-term debt resulted from the extinguishment of long-term debt.

Instead of using a formal working paper to prepare a statement of changes in financial position, some students and instructors prefer to use T accounts, one for working capital and one for each noncurrent account. Such an approach may be more efficient, particularly for solving relatively simple problems. In practice, a working paper generally is used, because it provides a more complete record for permanent files.

ROSE CORPORATION
Working Paper for Statement of Changes in Financial Position (Cash Concept)
For Year Ended December 31, Year 5

	Balances, Dec. 31, Year 4	Transactions for Year 5		Balances, Dec. 31, Year 5
		Debit	Credit	
Cash	52,800		(x) 25,700	27,100
Notes receivable from customers . . .	30,000	(5) 20,000		50,000
Accounts receivable (net).	50,400		(2) 13,500	36,900
Inventories.	57,300	(6) 38,750		96,050
Short-term prepayments.	9,600	(7) 3,000		12,600
Totals	200,100			222,650
Accounts payable.	31,300	(8) 9,150		22,150
Accrued liabilities	16,300		(3) 1,300	17,600
Income taxes payable	17,000		(4) 25,800	42,800
Dividends payable	-0-		(9) 42,000	42,000
All noncurrent accounts (see p. 957) .	135,500	(1) 37,400		98,100
Totals	200,100	108,300	108,300	222,650
Financial resources provided				
Operations—working capital (see p. 957		(1) 77,300		
Add: Decrease in accts. rec. (net). .		(2) 13,500		
Increase in accrued liabilities .		(3) 1,300		
Increase in income taxes pay..		(4) 25,800		
Less: Increase in notes receivable from customers.			(5) 20,000	Cash provided from opera- tions, $47,000
Increase in inventories.			(6) 38,750	
Increase in short-term pre- payments			(7) 3,000	
Decrease in accounts payable			(8) 9,150	
Proceeds on condemnation of bldg.		(1) 182,500		
Issuance of capital stock in ex- change for equipment		(1) 92,800		
Financial resources applied				
Extinguishment of bonds payable . .			(1) 52,500	
Acquisition of land.			(1) 150,000	
Acquisition of equipment for cash .			(1) 35,200	
Acquisition of equipment in ex- change for capital stock			(1) 92,800	
Acquisition of treasury stock.			(1) 17,500	
Declaration of cash dividends		(9) 42,000	(1) 42,000	
Total financial resources pro- vided and applied		435,200	460,900	
Decrease in cash		(x) 25,700		
Totals		460,900	460,900	

Explanations of transactions for Year 5

(1) All financial resources provided and applied from working paper for statement of changes in financial position on working capital concept (see page 957) which involve cash or exchange transactions.

(2) through (8) Analysis of changes in all current accounts which have an effect on the amount of cash pro- vided from operations.

(9) Elimination of effect of declaration of cash dividends not paid.

(x) Balancing entry—decrease in cash during Year 5.

Working paper format
when only changes in
noncurrent accounts
are available

LIZ LOCK COMPANY

Working Paper for Statement of Changes in Financial Position (Working Capital Concept) For Year 10

	Changes in account balances during Year 10		Transactions for Year 10	
	Debit	Credit	Debit	Credit
Increase in working capital . . .	80,000		(X) 80,000	
Noncurrent assets (net)		10,000		(2) 10,000
Long-term debt	5,000		(4) 5,000	
Capital stock.		25,000		(3) 25,000
Retained earnings		50,000	(5) 15,000	(1) 65,000
Totals.	85,000	85,000	100,000	100,000
Financial resources provided				
Operations — net income . . .			(1) 65,000⎫	
Add: Depreciation expense . .			(2) 10,000⎭	
Issuance of capital stock . . .			(3) 25,000	
Financial resources applied				
Extinguishment of long-term debt				(4) 5,000
Cash dividends				(5) 15,000
Total financial resources provided and applied. . .			100,000	20,000
Increase in working capital . . .				(X) 80,000
Totals.			100,000	100,000

Explanation of transactions for Year 10
(1) Net income for the year, a tentative measure of working capital provided from operations.
(2) Depreciation expense added to net income to obtain working capital provided from operations, $75,000.
(3) Issuance of capital stock for cash, a source of working capital.
(4) Extinguishment of long-term debt, a use of working capital.
(5) Declaration of cash dividends, a use of working capital.
(X) Balancing entry — increase in working capital during Year 10.

REVIEW QUESTIONS

1 What are some meanings that may be given to the term *funds* in the preparation of a statement of changes in financial position?

2 Briefly describe the *all-financial-resources* concept of funds flows, and give some examples of *exchange transactions.*

3 Briefly discuss the uses of a statement of changes in financial position by investors.

4 "Last year, Java Oil Company earned $8 a share on sales of $250 million. Its cash flow for the year, a generous $60 million, represented a high return on equity capital." Comment on the implications of this quotation.

5 What basic information is required to prepare a statement of changes in financial position?

6 In the analysis of working capital flows, business transactions may be classified into three categories: Transactions which affect only current asset or current liability accounts, transactions which affect both current accounts and noncurrent accounts, and transactions which affect only noncurrent accounts. Indicate the effect of each category on working capital.

7 Give an example of each of the following situations, assuming preparation of a statement of changes in financial position on a working capital concept:
a A decrease in a noncurrent asset that *is not* a source of working capital
b A decrease in a noncurrent asset that *is* a source of working capital
c An increase in a noncurrent liability that *is not* a source of working capital
d A decrease in stockholders' equity that *is* a use of working capital
e An increase in stockholders' equity that *is not* a source of working capital
f An increase in a noncurrent asset that *is not* a use of working capital
g A decrease in a noncurrent liability that *is not* a use of working capital

8 The following transaction was recorded during the current year:

Land	35,000	
Buildings	450,000	
Mortgage Note Payable (long-term)		380,000
Short-Term Investments		50,000
Cash		55,000

To record acquisition of land and buildings.

Describe two ways this transaction can be reported in a statement of changes in financial position on a working capital concept. Which way do you prefer?

9 Kral Company has outstanding a $5 million issue of serial bonds. The first series of bonds, in the amount of $500,000, matures in July, Year 10. In preparing a statement of changes in financial position for calendar Year 9, the accountant shows a use of working capital of $500,000 relating to these bonds. Is this correct? Explain.

10 Explain why the accumulation of a discount on a long-term investment in bonds and the amortization of deferred revenue items are deducted from net income to compute working capital provided from operations.

11 How is the extinguishment of bonds reported in a statement of changes in financial position on the working capital concept, assuming that sinking-fund investments are liquidated and the proceeds are used to retire the bonds?

12 What two approaches may be followed to compute working capital provided from operations in the statement of changes in financial position?

13 What useful information might management find in a *cash flow statement* for a fiscal year just ended? Is such a statement helpful to outsiders?

14 Briefly outline the procedure for converting net income from the **accrual basis** to the **cash basis** of accounting.

15 Is **cash flow per share** a better measurement of operating results than earnings per share? Explain.

EXERCISES

Ex. 23-1   Select the best answer for each of the following multiple-choice questions:

1 The working capital provided from operations in Marsha Company's statement of changes in financial position for Year 1 was $8,000,000. For Year 1, depreciation on plant assets was $3,800,000, amortization of goodwill was $100,000, and cash dividends declared on common stock were $2,000,000. Based on the information given above, Marsha's net income for Year 1 was: **a** $2,100,000 **b** $4,100,000 **c** $8,000,000 **d** $11,900,000

2 Selected information from Golnar Company's accounting records for Year 1 is as follows:

Proceeds from issuance of common stock	$8,000,000
Proceeds from issuance of preferred stock	2,000,000
Dividends declared and paid on common stock.	1,000,000
Dividends declared and paid on preferred stock	400,000
Acquisition of treasury stock	300,000
Issuance of common stock to employees (not included above) . .	200,000

Assuming funds are defined as working capital, Golnar's statement of changes in financial position for the year ended December 31, Year 1, would show the following sources and uses of funds, based on the information given above:

	Sources	**Uses**
a	$ 9,900,000	$1,400,000
b	$10,000,000	$1,400,000
c	$10,000,000	$1,900,000
d	$10,200,000	$1,700,000

3 The following information on selected cash transactions for Year 1 has been provided by Purdue Company:

Proceeds from short-term borrowings	$1,200,000
Proceeds from long-term borrowings	4,000,000
Acquisitions of plant assets	3,200,000
Purchases of merchandise	8,000,000
Proceeds from issuance of capital stock	2,000,000
5% stock dividend on capital stock	500,000

What is the increase in working capital for the year ended December 31, Year 1, as a result of the above information? **a** $800,000 **b** $2,000,000 **c** $2,800,000 **d** $4,000,000

4 The net income for the year ended December 31, Year 1, for Omar Company was $2,500,000. Additional information is shown on top of page 969.

Depreciation	*$2,900,000*
Dividends declared and paid on preferred stock	*200,000*
Long-term debt:	
Bond discount amortization	*50,000*
Interest expense	*800,000*
Provision for doubtful accounts on long-term receivables	*250,000*
Amortization of goodwill	*90,000*

What is the working capital provided from operations in the statement of changes in financial position for the year ended December 31, Year 1?
a $5,490,000 **b** $5,540,000 **c** $5,790,000 **d** $5,990,000

5 An analysis of the machinery accounts of Pula Company for Year 1 follows:

	Machinery	Accumulated depreciation	Carrying amount
Balances, Jan. 1	*$1,000,000*	*$400,000*	*$600,000*
Acquisitions of machinery for cash . . .	*500,000*		*500,000*
Depreciation		*250,000*	*(250,000)*
Balances, Dec. 31	*$1,500,000*	*$650,000*	*$850,000*

Assuming **funds** are defined as **working capital,** the information concerning Pula's machinery accounts is shown in Pula's statement of changes in financial position for the year ended December 31, Year 1, as:
a A subtraction from net income of $250,000 and a source of funds of $500,000
b An addition to net income of $250,000 and a use of funds of $500,000
c A source of funds of $250,000
d A use of funds of $500,000

Ex. 23-2 Account balances relating to equipment during Year 8 follow:

	Dec. 31	Jan. 1
Equipment	*$210,000*	*$96,000*
Less: Accumulated depreciation	*38,000*	*30,000*

Equipment with a carrying amount of $10,000 and original cost of $25,000 was sold at a gain of $3,000.
Compute the following for Year 8:
a Working capital provided from sale of equipment
b Working capital used to acquire equipment
c Depreciation expense on equipment which should be added to net income in the computation of working capital provided from operations.

Ex. 23-3 Explain how each of the following transactions is shown in a statement of changes in financial position for Year 10, prepared on a working capital concept:
a Cash dividends of $200,000 were declared on December 11, Year 10, payable on January 14, Year 11.
b A 5% stock dividend was distributed; the market value of the dividend shares, $1,020,000, was transferred from retained earnings to paid-in capital accounts.

c Mining properties valued at $380,000 were acquired on January 3, Year 10, in exchange for bonds payable with a face amount of $400,000. The bonds mature on December 31, Year 19. The straight-line method is used for amortization of bond discount.

d An additional income tax assessment of $98,000 was debited to the Retained Earnings account as a prior period adjustment. The assessment resulted from a material error.

e Oil exploration costs of $200,000 were deferred in Year 9 for financial accounting purposes but were deducted in the computation of taxable income. As a result, the Deferred Income Tax Liability account was credited for $90,000. In Year 10, the deferred oil exploration costs were written off as follows:

Oil Exploration Expenses	110,000	
Deferred Income Tax Liability	90,000	
Deferred Oil Exploration Costs		200,000
To write off deferred oil exploration costs.		

Ex. 23-4 Adams Printing Co. reported net income of $80,400 for Year 5. In the computation of net income, the following items were included:

Compensation expense (value of compensatory stock options)	$ 24,000
Amortization of premium on bonds payable	5,000
Investment loss from 25%-owned company	120,000
Depreciation expense	45,000
Doubtful accounts expense (current accounts receivable)	11,200
Unrealized loss in value of marketable equity securities (current portfolio).	25,000
Amortization of organization costs	3,000
Write-down of obsolete inventories by a debit to cost of goods sold . .	18,000
Income taxes expense, of which $27,000 will be paid in Year 8	70,000
Realized profit on long-term construction contracts	35,000
Extraordinary gain (net of income taxes)	41,500

Compute the amount of working capital provided from operations in Year 5.

Ex. 23-5 From the following data, compute the amount of cash provided from operations during the past year:

	Dec 31	Jan. 1
Accounts receivable	$20,200	$15,200
Accounts payable	15,000	24,000
Accrued liabilities	3,600	1,600
Accumulated depreciation (no plant assets were retired during the year)	32,000	26,000
Inventories	30,000	27,500
Short-term prepayments	2,200	3,000
Net income (accrual basis of accounting)	41,225	

Ex. 23-6   The following data are taken from the latest comparative balance sheet of General Cotton Corporation:

	June 30, Year 2	June 30, Year 1
Cash	$ 20,000	$ 15,000
Marketable equity securities (net of allowance)	40,000	55,000
Accounts receivable (net)	50,000	30,000
Inventories	70,000	60,000
Short-term prepayments	5,000	3,000
Noncurrent assets (net)	242,500	209,000
Notes payable (current)	25,000	40,000
Accounts payable	60,000	30,000
Accrued liabilities	2,500	2,000
Long-term debt and stockholders' equity	340,000	300,000

Prepare the composition of working capital as it would appear in the statement of changes in financial position.

Ex. 23-7   A summary of the financial position for Safford Company at the beginning and end of the current fiscal year is given below:

	Feb. 28, Year 10	Feb. 28, Year 9
Working capital	$ 87,500	$ 96,000
Noncurrent assets:		
Investment in common stock of R Corporation (equity method)	82,500	75,000
Land	60,000	45,000
Buildings	120,000	100,000
Less: Accumulated depreciation	(50,000)	(46,000)
Totals	$300,000	$270,000
Long-term debt & stockholders' equity:		
Notes payable, due in five years	$ 20,000	$ -0-
Capital stock, $1 par	200,000	200,000
Retained earnings	80,000	70,000
Totals	$300,000	$270,000

The net income of $25,000 (after depreciation expense of $4,000) included investment income (equity method) of $7,500 from R Corporation. A cash dividend was declared during the year.

Prepare a statement of changes in financial position on a working capital concept for the current fiscal year, without using a working paper.

Ex. 23-8   The net changes in account balances and the Retained Earnings ledger account for Year 1 of Motown Axle Corporation are given on page 972.

	Net changes during Year 1	
	Debits	**Credits**
Current assets	$ 98,100	
Plant assets (net)	30,000	
Goodwill (amortized over 25 years)		$ 1,500
Current liabilities		68,500
Bonds payable		100,000
Discount on bonds payable	1,900	
Preferred stock, $10 par	100,000	
Common stock, no-par value		50,000
Retained earnings		10,000
Totals	$230,000	$230,000

Retained Earnings

Premium on retirement of		Balance, Jan. 1	60,000
preferred stock	5,000	Net income	80,000
Stock dividend on common			
stock	50,000		
Cash dividends declared	15,000		

Ten-year bonds of $100,000 were issued on July 1 at 98, with proceeds used for the retirement of preferred stock. Land with a cost of $55,000 was sold for $70,000, and a new building was acquired for $95,000 cash. Depreciation expense for the year amounted to $10,000.

Prepare a statement of changes in financial position on a working capital concept for Year 1. A working paper is not required.

Ex. 23-9 Karen Corporation reported net income of $40,000 and declared and paid dividends of $15,000 in Year 2. Balance sheets on December 31, Year 2 and Year 1, follow:

KAREN CORPORATION
Balance Sheets
December 31,

	Year 2	Year 1
Assets		
Cash	$ 82,500	$ 12,500
Accounts receivable (net)	67,500	37,500
Inventories	80,000	100,000
Equipment (net)	380,000	300,000
Total assets	$610,000	$450,000
Liabilities & Stockholders' Equity		
Accounts payable	$ 40,000	$ 25,000
Bonds payable (due in Year 15)	80,000	100,000
Capital stock, no-par value	290,000	150,000
Retained earnings	200,000	175,000
Total liabilities & stockholders' equity	$610,000	$450,000

Equipment was acquired for $750,000 cash, capital stock was issued to the public for cash, and capital stock with a market value of $40,000 was issued for new equipment.

Prepare a statement of changes in financial position on a cash concept for Year 2. Compute the cash provided from operations in a separate working paper; do not include the composition of working capital in the statement.

Ex. 23-10 Comparative balance sheets for Hallett Company on December 31, Year 2, follow:

HALLETT COMPANY

Comparative Balance Sheets

December 31,

	Year 2	Year 1
Assets		
Cash	$ 52,500	$ 65,000
Accounts receivable (net)	100,000	90,000
Inventories	97,500	40,000
Plant assets	260,000	155,000
Less: Accumulated depreciation	(80,000)	(50,000)
Total assets	$430,000	$300,000
Liabilities & Stockholders' Equity		
Accounts payable	$ 70,000	$ 55,000
Capital stock, $10 par	280,000	200,000
Paid-in capital in excess of par	25,000	–0–
Retained earnings	55,000	45,000
Total liabilities & stockholders' equity	$430,000	$300,000

On June 15, Year 2, the company issued 8,000 shares of capital stock in exchange for equipment. There were no retirements of plant assets in Year 2. Dividends of $25,000 were declared and paid to stockholders during Year 2. The allowance for doubtful accounts was reduced by $3,000 during Year 2 as a result of writing off accounts known to be uncollectible, and increased by $5,000 at the end of the year to record doubtful accounts expense. The net income can be derived from the data given.

Prepare a statement of changes in financial position on a working capital concept for Year 2, without using a working paper. Do not include the composition of working capital in the statement.

Ex. 23-11 The financial statements on page 974 were prepared for Software Systems Corporation.

SOFTWARE SYSTEMS CORPORATION
Balance Sheet
January 1, Year 1

Assets

Current assets	$37,000
Equipment	48,000
Less: Accumulated depreciation	(15,000)
Patents	5,000
Total assets	$75,000

Liabilities & Stockholders' Equity

Current liabilities	$12,000
Capital stock, no-par value	27,000
Retained earnings	36,000
Total liabilities & stockholders' equity	$75,000

SOFTWARE SYSTEMS CORPORATION
Statement of Changes in Financial Position
For Year Ended December 31, Year 1

Working capital, Jan. 1, Year 1		$25,000
Working capital provided		
Operations —net income	$24,000	
Add: Depreciation expense	10,000	
Amortization of patents	1,000	
Less: Gain on sale of equipment	(4,000)	
Working capital provided from operations		31,000
Issuance of capital stock		13,000
Sale of equipment		7,000
Total working capital provided		$76,000
Working capital applied		
Dividends declared	$12,000	
Acquisition of land.	14,000	
Acquisition of equipment	30,000	
Total working capital applied		56,000
Working capital, Dec. 31, Year 1.		$20,000

Total assets in the balance sheet on December 31, Year 1, are $110,000. Accumulated depreciation on the equipment sold was $6,000.

Based on the information available from the balance sheet on January 1, Year 1, and the statement of changes in financial position for Year 1, prepare a balance sheet for Software Systems Corporation on December 31, Year 1.

SHORT CASES FOR ANALYSIS AND DECISION

Case 23-1 Dixon Engineering Company is a growing producer of electronic measuring instruments and technical equipment. You have been retained by Dixon to advise it in the preparation of a statement of changes in financial position. For the fiscal year ended October 31, Year 2, you have obtained the following information concerning certain events and transactions of Dixon:

(1) Net income for the fiscal year was $800,000, which included a deduction for an extraordinary loss of $93,000 [see item (5) below].

(2) Depreciation expense of $240,000 was included in the income statement.

(3) Uncollectible accounts receivable of $30,000 were written off against the allowance for doubtful accounts. Also, $37,000 of doubtful accounts expense was included in the determination of net income for the fiscal year, and the same amount was added to the allowance for doubtful accounts.

(4) A gain of $4,700 was realized on the sale of a machine; it originally cost $75,000, of which $25,000 was undepreciated on the date of sale.

(5) On April 1, Year 2, a freak lightning storm caused an uninsured inventories loss of $93,000 ($180,000 loss, less reduction in income taxes of $87,000). This extraordinary loss was included in net income as indicated in (1) above.

(6) On July 3, Year 2, land and building were acquired for $600,000; Dixon gave in payment $100,000 cash, $200,000 market value of its unissued common stock, and a $300,000 mortgage note payable.

(7) On August 3, Year 2, $700,000 face amount of Dixon's 10% convertible debentures were converted to $140,000 par value of its common stock. The bonds originally were issued at face amount.

(8) The board of directors declared a $320,000 cash dividend on October 20, Year 2, payable on November 15, Year 2, to stockholders of record on November 5, Year 2.

Instructions For each of the eight items above, explain whether each item is a source or a use of working capital and explain how it should be disclosed in Dixon's statement of changes in financial position for the fiscal year ended October 31, Year 2. If any item is neither a source nor a use of working capital, explain why it is not and indicate the disclosure, if any, that should be made of the item in Dixon's statement of changes in financial position for the fiscal year ended October 31, Year 2.

Case 23-2 Information concerning the debt and stockholders' equity of Sicily Company for the year ended December 31, Year 5, appears below and on page 976.

Short-term borrowings:

Balance, Dec. 31, Year 4	$ 1,200,000
Proceeds from borrowings in Year 5	1,500,000
Payments made in Year 5.	(1,400,000)
Balance, Dec. 31, Year 5	$ 1,300,000

Current portion of long-term debt:

Balance, Dec. 31, Year 4	$ 5,500,000
Transfers from caption "Long-term debt"	6,000,000
Payments made in Year 5.	(5,500,000)
Balance, Dec. 31, Year 5	$ 6,000,000

(cont.)

Long-term debt:

Balance, Dec. 31, Year 4	$42,500,000
Proceeds from borrowings in Year 5	18,000,000
Transfers to caption "Current portion of long-term debt"	(6,000,000)
Payments made in Year 5	(10,000,000)
Balance, Dec. 31, Year 5	$44,500,000

Stockholders' equity, Dec. 31, Year 4:

Convertible preferred stock, $20 par. Each share convertible into 2 shares of common stock. Authorized 60,000 shares; issued and outstanding 55,000 shares	$ 1,100,000
Common stock, $10 par. Authorized 3 million shares; issued and outstanding 2 million shares	20,000,000
Paid-in capital in excess of par: common stock	4,225,000
Retained earnings	10,650,000
Total stockholders' equity	$35,975,000

During Year 5, 30,000 shares of the convertible preferred stock were converted to common stock. Also during Year 5, 100,000 shares of common stock were issued for cash at $25 a share.

Instructions

a Assuming that *funds* are defined as **working capital,** show how the above information should be shown in Sicily Company's statement of changes in financial position for the year ended December 31, Year 5.

b Explain why each change in the accounts listed above is included in or excluded from the statement of changes in financial position for Year 5. Ignore net income and dividends paid for Year 5.

Case 23-3 The following statement of changes in financial position was improperly prepared by the accountant for Al-Hashim & Co.:

AL-HASHIM & CO.
Statement of Changes in Financial Position
December 31, Year 1

Funds provided

Acquisition of land	$105,000
Cash dividends declared (to be paid on Jan. 21, Year 2)	30,000
Stock dividend distributed	50,000
Acquisition of equipment	15,000
Acquisition of marketable securities as short-term investment	150,000
Total funds provided	$350,000

Funds applied

Net income (including gain of $20,000, net of income taxes)	$120,000
Issuance of note payable —due Year 4	85,000
Depreciation and amortization expense	60,000

(cont.)

Sale of equipment—carrying amount (sold at gain of $20,000, net of income taxes)	$ 10,000
Issuance of capital stock pursuant to stock dividend	50,000
Decrease in working capital	25,000
Total funds applied	$350,000

Albert Wright, the president, is upset because he had hoped to increase the working capital during Year 1 by at least $100,000. Furthermore, he is somewhat confused with the arrangement of the statement and wonders if he should plan to issue additional shares of capital stock early in Year 2 to "replenish working capital."

Instructions

a Identify and discuss the weaknesses in the presentation of the statement of changes in financial position for Al-Hashim & Co. as prepared by the accountant. Your discussion should explain why you consider the items to be weaknesses and suggest the proper treatment of any item improperly presented.

b Prepare a revised statement of changes in financial position and advise the president whether or not Al-Hashim & Co. should issue additional shares of capital stock to replenish working capital.

Case 23-4   The income statement for Kansas Lime Company for Year 3 included the following items:

Net income	$459,500
Deferred income taxes expense	20,000
Depreciation expense	160,000
Accumulation of discount on long-term investment in bonds	1,000
Amortization of discount on bonds payable	1,500
Doubtful accounts expense	7,600
Realized gross profit on installment sales made in Years 1 and 2	62,000
Gain on sale of equipment	102,000
Interest revenue	4,800
Expenses for Year 3 which will be paid in Year 4	12,000
Amortization of deferred investment tax credit	4,000
Compensation expense—value of compensatory stock option contracts	15,000
Investment income on investment in Q Co. common stock (equity method of accounting)	5,000

Instructions

a Determine the amount of working capital provided from operations, assuming that the effects of nonoperating transactions on working capital are reported separately.

b Briefly explain the effect on working capital of each item above.

Case 23-5   The statement of changes in financial position for Economy Travel Corporation is shown on page 978.

ECONOMY TRAVEL CORPORATION
Statement of Changes in Financial Position
For Year Ended March 31, Year 10
(in thousands of dollars)

Financial resources provided

Operations—income before gain on sale of aircraft	$ 3,770	(1)
Add: Charges against income not involving working capital:		
Depreciation	11,380	(2)
Deferred federal income tax, amortization of investment tax credit, and deferred debt expense	1,400	(3)
Net loss of unconsolidated subsidiaries	450	(4)
Working capital provided from operations	$ 17,000	(5)
Gain on sale of aircraft, including $1 million of deferred federal income tax	2,100	(6)
Addition to long-term debt	40,000	(7)
Sale of common stock	5,800	(8)
Disposal of aircraft—carrying amount	1,800	(9)
Increase in current portion of contracts receivable on aircraft leases	1,200	(10)
Total financial resources provided	$ 67,900	

Financial resources applied

Dividends on common stock	$ 610	(11)
Addition to long-term contracts receivable, excluding aircraft reclassifications.	3,205	(12)
Investment of funds held for purchase of aircraft	4,785	(13)
Additions to flight, other equipment, and deposits on purchase contracts	62,100	(14)
Long-term debt refinanced	12,000	(15)
Provision for current portion of long-term debt .	8,500	(16)
Long-term advances to unconsolidated subsidiaries	2,250	(17)
Total financial resources applied	93,450	
Increase (decrease) in working capital	$(25,550)	(18)
Working capital, end of year	$ 12,600	(19)

Instructions Briefly explain each item numbered (1) through (19) and comment on the propriety of the format of the statement and the terminology used by Economy Travel Corporation.

PROBLEMS

23-1 Comparative balance sheets for Omega Gear Corporation are presented below:

OMEGA GEAR CORPORATION
Balance Sheets
December 31,

	Year 4	Year 3
Assets		
Current assets	$ 230,600	$ 152,000
Equipment	740,000	600,000
Less: Accumulated depreciation	(218,000)	(210,000)
Goodwill (net)	240,000	250,000
Total assets	$ 992,600	$ 792,000
Liabilities & Stockholders' Equity		
Current liabilities	$ 180,000	$ 80,000
Bonds payable (due Dec. 31, Year 8)	200,000	300,000
Less: Discount on bonds payable	(6,400)	(12,000)
Capital stock, no-par	675,000	550,000
Retained earnings (deficit)	(56,000)	(126,000)
Total liabilities & stockholders' equity	$ 992,600	$ 792,000

Additional information

(1) During Year 4, equipment was sold at its carrying amount of $38,000, and new equipment was acquired for $75,000 cash.
(2) On January 2, Year 4, bonds in the face amount of $100,000 were extinguished at 101. Discount on bonds payable is amortized by the straight-line method.
(3) The Retained Earnings account was affected only by the net income or loss for Year 4.
(4) Capital stock was exchanged for new equipment with a current fair value of $125,000.

Instructions Prepare a statement of changes in financial position for the year ended December 31, Year 4, on a working capital concept, without using a working paper.

23-2 Comparative income statements and balance sheets for the latest two years for Rio Blanco Company are presented below and on page 980.

RIO BLANCO COMPANY
Income Statements
For Years Ended December 31,

	Year 5	Year 4
Net sales (including service charges)	$3,250,000	$2,000,000
Cost of goods sold	2,500,000	1,600,000
Gross profit on sales	$ 750,000	$ 400,000
Expenses (including income taxes expense)	540,000	260,000
Net income	$ 210,000	$ 140,000

RIO BLANCO COMPANY
Balance Sheets
December 31,

	Year 5	Year 4
Assets		
Current assets:		
Cash	$ 125,000	$100,000
Short-term investments	40,000	–0–
Accounts receivable (net)	420,000	290,000
Inventories	330,000	210,000
Short-term prepayments	50,000	25,000
Total current assets	$ 965,000	$625,000
Plant assets	565,000	300,000
Less: Accumulated depreciation	(55,000)	(25,000)
Total assets	$1,475,000	$900,000
Liabilities & Stockholders' Equity		
Current liabilities:		
Accounts payable	$ 265,000	$220,000
Accrued liabilities	70,000	65,000
Dividends payable	35,000	–0–
Total current liabilities	$ 370,000	$285,000
Note payable due in Year 8	250,000	–0–
Total liabilities	$ 620,000	$285,000
Stockholders' equity:		
Common stock, no-par	600,000	450,000
Retained earnings	255,000	165,000
Total liabilities & stockholders' equity	$1,475,000	$900,000

Additional information

(1) The only entries to the Retained Earnings account were for net income and declaration of cash dividends.

(2) No plant assets or common stock were retired during Year 5.

(3) All sales and purchases of merchandise are made on credit. All accounts receivable and accounts payable relate to merchandise transactions. Cash discounts are not allowed to customers, but a service charge is added to an account for late payment. Accounts payable are recorded net of cash discounts, and always are paid within the discount period. The Allowance for Doubtful Accounts at the end of Year 5 was the same as at the end of Year 4; no receivables were written off in Year 5.

(4) The proceeds from the note payable were used to finance a new store building. Common stock was issued to provide additional working capital.

Instructions

a Compute the following for Year 5:

    (1) Cash receipts on accounts receivable

    (2) Cash payments on accounts payable

    (3) Cash payments for expenses (including income taxes expense)

    (4) Cash receipts which were not provided from operations

    (5) Cash payments which were not reflected in cash provided from operations

b Prepare a statement of changes in financial position for Year 5 on a cash concept, showing a single amount for cash provided from operations.

c Prepare a statement of changes in financial position for Year 5 on a working capital concept. Do not include the composition of working capital in the statement.

23-3 The changes in account balances of the single proprietorship owned by Ray Nishiyama for the fiscal year ended July 31, Year 10, are given below:

	Increase (decrease)*
Cash	$30,100
Accounts receivable	(8,000)
Allowance for doubtful accounts	(200)
Inventories	(13,000)
Equipment	28,400
Accumulated depreciation	10,000
Accounts payable	(5,000)
Accrued liabilities	400
Ray Nishiyama, capital	32,300

The parentheses denote a decrease in the debit or credit balance normal for a given account.

Accounts receivable of $1,000 were written off as uncollectible. Equipment costing $7,500 was sold for $2,000, resulting in a loss of $1,600. Net income, including the loss on sale of equipment, amounted to $62,300. The balance of the change in the owner's capital account represents drawings for the year.

Instructions

a Prepare a statement of changes in financial position for Ray Nishiyama on a working capital concept for the year ended July 31, Year 10, without using a working paper. The statement should include the composition of working capital.

b Prepare a statement of changes in financial position on a cash concept for the year ended July 31, Year 10, without using a working paper. Do not include the composition of working capital in the statement.

23-4 The following net changes in account balances were obtained from the accounting records of Minoru Morimoto & Co. for the year ended December 31, Year 5:

MINORU MORIMOTO & CO.
Net Changes in Account Balances
For Year Ended December 31, Year 5

	Debit	Credit
Cash	$ 25,550	
Accounts receivable	20,000	
Allowance for doubtful accounts		$ 2,500
Inventories	35,050	
Equipment	150,000	
Accumulated depreciation		65,000
Goodwill (net)		10,000
Accounts payable		25,000
		(cont.)

Income taxes payable		$ 15,000
Bonds payable, due Jan. 2, Year 25		150,000
Premium on bonds payable		9,500
Preferred stock, $100 par	$240,000	
Common stock, no-par		105,000
Retained earnings		88,600
Totals	$470,600	$470,600

A summary of the activity in the Retained Earnings account during Year 5 follows:

Balance, Jan. 1, Year 5		$3,300,000
Add: Net income	$402,500	
Refund received on Year 3 income taxes (caused by error)	12,500	415,000
Subtotal		$3,715,000
Less: Cash dividends	$210,000	
5% stock dividend.	105,000	
Retirement premium on preferred stock	11,400	326,400
Balance, Dec. 31, Year 5		$3,388,600

Accounts receivable of $20,000 were written off as uncollectible in Year 5. Equipment costing $200,000, which was 80% depreciated, was sold at carrying amount, and new equipment was acquired. The bonds were issued on January 2, Year 5, for $160,000. The semiannual bond interest checks were mailed on December 31, Year 5. Premium on bonds payable is amortized by the straight-line method. The change in the Goodwill account resulted from amortization.

Instructions Prepare a statement of changes in financial position (working capital concept) for Year 5. A working paper is not required. If you use a working paper, the form illustrated on page 966 is appropriate for this problem. The composition of working capital should be included as a part of the statement.

23-5 Comparative account balance at the close of Year 2 and Year 1 for Bozo Corporation are shown below:

BOZO CORPORATION
Comparative Account Balances
December 31,

Debits	Year 2	Year 1
Cash	$ 44,220	$ 35,800
Receivables (net)	40,400	24,000
Inventories	37,600	36,800
Short-term prepayments	4,180	4,400
Land	69,000	19,000
Buildings	276,000	250,000
Equipment	381,600	360,000
Patents	32,000	40,000
Total debits	$885,000	$770,000

(cont.)

Credits

	Year 2	Year 1
Accumulated depreciation of buildings	$ 92,000	$ 80,000
Accumulated depreciation of equipment	238,000	220,000
Accounts payable	64,000	30,000
Accrued liabilities	20,000	10,000
Long-term debt, due in Year 10	65,000	95,000
Common stock, $25 par	230,000	200,000
Paid-in capital in excess of par	85,000	40,000
Retained earnings	91,000	95,000
Total credits	$885,000	$770,000

Early in Year 2, the board of directors of the company approved a transfer of $25,000 from retained earnings to record a 5% stock dividend. In addition, cash dividends of $44,000 were declared and paid. Common stock valued at $50,000 was issued in exchange for land. There were no disposals of buildings or equipment during Year 2, and no new expenditures were made for patents. Net income for Year 2 was $65,000. A premium of $1,200 was paid on the early extinguishment of long-term debt.

Instructions

a Prepare a statement of changes in financial position for the year ended December 31, Year 2, on a working capital concept, without using a working paper. Include the composition of working capital in the statement.

b Prepare a working paper to restate the net income for Year 2 from the accrual basis to the cash basis of accounting.

c Prepare a statement of changes in financial position for the year ended December 31, Year 2, on a cash concept, using the information generated in parts *a* and *b* above. Do not include the composition of working capital in the statement.

23-6 The comparative balance sheets of Cherry Corporation are presented below and on page 984.

CHERRY CORPORATION

Comparative Balance Sheets

December 31,

Assets	Year 6	Year 5	Changes
Current assets:			
Cash	$ 450,000	$ 287,000	$163,000
Notes receivable	45,000	50,000	(5,000)
Accounts receivable (net of allowance			
for doubtful accounts)	479,200	380,000	99,200
Inventories	460,000	298,000	162,000
Total current assets	$1,434,200	$1,015,000	$419,200
Investments:			
Common stock of Roy Co. (3%). . . .	–0–	39,000	(39,000)
Common stock of Zuber Co. (90%). .	246,300	–0–	246,300
Plant assets	455,000	381,000	74,000
Less: Accumulated depreciation	(193,000)	(144,000)	(49,000)
Patents (net)	26,000	19,000	7,000
Total assets	$1,968,500	$1,310,000	$658,500

(cont.)

Liabilities & Shareholders' Equity

Current liabilities:			
Dividends payable	$ 181,000	$ –0–	$181,000
Accounts payable	156,000	40,800	115,200
Accrued liabilities	92,000	84,000	8,000
Total current liabilities	$ 429,000	$ 124,800	$304,200
Shareholders' equity:			
Preferred stock, $2 par	60,000	53,000	7,000
Paid-in capital in excess of par —preferred	6,000	2,500	3,500
Common stock, $10 par	752,000	700,000	52,000
Paid-in capital in excess of par —common	20,000	9,600	10,400
Retained earnings appropriated for contingencies	85,000	–0–	85,000
Retained earnings (unappropriated) .	616,500	420,100	196,400
Total liabilities & shareholders' equity.	$1,968,500	$1,310,000	$658,500

Additional information

(1) For the year ended December 31, Year 6, Cherry reported net income of $496,000.

(2) Uncollectible accounts receivable of $4,000 were written off against the allowance for doubtful accounts.

(3) Cherry's investment in the common stock of Roy Co. was made in Year 2 and represented a 3% interest in the outstanding common stock of Roy Co. During Year 6, Cherry sold this investment for $26,000.

(4) On January 9, Year 6, Cherry acquired 90% (45,000 shares) of the outstanding $10 par common stock of Zuber Co. in a business combination appropriately accounted for as a purchase. To consummate this transaction, Cherry paid $72,000 cash and issued 3,500 shares of its preferred stock and 2,400 shares of its common stock. The consideration paid was equal to the underlying carrying amount of the assets acquired. The market price of Cherry's preferred stock on the date of the transaction was $3 a share, and the market price of its common stock was $12 a share.

    Zuber Co. is considered to be an unrelated business and not compatible with Cherry's operations. Therefore, consolidated financial statements for the two companies are not required. For the year ended December 31, Year 6, Zuber Co. reported net income of $150,000.

(5) During Year 6, a plant asset that was acquired in Year 1 at a cost of $22,000 was sold as scrap for $3,200. At the date of sale, this plant asset had a carrying amount of $4,400.

    In addition, Cherry acquired new plant assets at a cost of $81,000. The remaining increase in plant assets resulted from major repairs that were accounted for properly as capital expenditures.

(6) Amortization of patents for Year 6 was $3,000. A new patent was acquired for cash.

(7) On January 2, Year 6, Cherry declared and issued a 4% stock dividend on its common stock. The market price of the common stock on that date was $12 a share. The market price of the common stock was not affected by the dividend distribution. On December 31, Year 6, cash dividends of $145,000 on the common stock and $36,000 on the preferred stock were declared.

(8) On December 27, Year 6, an appropriation of retained earnings to cover a possible loss of $85,000 arising from a lawsuit was authorized by Cherry's board of directors.

Instructions Prepare a statement of changes in financial position on the working capital concept for the year ended December 31, Year 6. Do not include the composition of working capital in the statement. A working paper is not required.

23-7 The management of Ausman Corporation, concerned over a decrease in working capital, has provided you with the following comparative analysis of changes in account balances between December 31, Year 6, and December 31, Year 7:

AUSMAN CORPORATION
Analysis of Changes in Account Balances
December 31,

	Year 7	Year 6	Increase (decrease)
Cash	$ 145,000	$ 186,000	$ (41,000)
Accounts receivable	253,000	273,000	(20,000)
Inventories	483,000	538,000	(55,000)
Securities held for plant expansion . .	150,000	–0–	150,000
Machinery and equipment	927,000	647,000	280,000
Lease improvements (net)	29,000	38,000	(9,000)
Patents (net)	27,800	30,000	(2,200)
Totals	$2,014,800	$1,712,000	$302,800
Allowance for doubtful accounts	$ 14,000	$ 17,000	$ (3,000)
Accumulated depreciation	416,000	372,000	44,000
Accounts payable	232,800	105,000	127,800
Cash dividends payable	40,000	–0–	40,000
Current portion of 10% serial bonds payable	50,000	50,000	–0–
10% serial bonds payable	250,000	300,000	(50,000)
Preferred stock, $100 par	90,000	100,000	(10,000)
Common stock, $5 par	500,000	500,000	–0–
Retained earnings	422,000	268,000	154,000
Totals	$2,014,800	$1,712,000	$302,800

Additional information During Year 7 the following transactions occurred:
(1) New machinery and equipment were acquired for $386,000. In addition, certain obsolete machinery with a carrying amount of $61,000 was sold for $48,000. No other entries were recorded in Machinery and Equipment or related accounts, other than the provision for depreciation.
(2) Legal costs of $2,000 were paid in a successful defense of a patent; amortization of patents amounted to $4,200.
(3) Preferred stock was acquired at 110 and retired. The premium paid was debited to the Retained Earnings account.

(4) A comparative analysis of retained earnings for the latest two years is presented below:

	Year 7	Year 6
Balances, Jan. 1	$268,000	$131,000
Net income	195,000	172,000
Subtotals	$463,000	$303,000
Cash dividends declared	(40,000)	(35,000)
Premium on retirement of preferred stock	(1,000)	–0–
Balances, Dec. 31	$422,000	$268,000

Instructions
a Prepare a statement of changes in financial position, including the composition of working capital, for the year ended December 31, Year 7. The statement should be prepared on the working capital concept. A working paper is not required. Give supporting computations.
b Prepare a statement of changes in financial position on the cash concept. You need not use a working paper or include the composition of working capital in the statement.

23-8   The analysis below showing net changes in balance sheet accounts on December 31, Year 10, compared with December 31, Year 9, was prepared from the accounting records of Leeann Company. The statement of changes in financial position for the year ended December 31, Year 10, has not yet been prepared.

LEEANN COMPANY
Net Changes in Balance Sheet Accounts
For Year Ended December 31, Year 10

	Net increase (decrease)
Assets	
Cash	$ 61,110
Accounts receivable (net)	76,000
Inventories	37,000
Short-term prepayments	1,000
Plant assets (net)	164,000
Total assets.	$339,110
Liabilities	
Notes payable to banks (current)	$ (15,000)
Accounts payable	(55,500)
Accrued liabilities	33,000
Bonds payable (long-term)	(28,000)
Unamortized bond discount (an increase in net liabilities as a result of amortization)	1,200
Total liabilities	$ (64,300)
	(cont.)

Stockholders' equity

Preferred stock, $50 par	*$100,000*
Common stock, $10 par	*500,000*
Paid-in capital in excess of par: common stock	*200,000*
Appropriation of retained earnings	*30,000*
Retained earnings (unappropriated)	*(426,590)*
Total stockholders' equity	*$403,410*
Total liabilities & stockholders' equity	*$339,110*

Additional information

(1) The net income for the year ended December 31, Year 10, was $183,410. There were no extraordinary items.

(2) During the year ended December 31, Year 10, uncollectible accounts receivable of $24,200 were written off.

(3) A comparison of plant assets at the end of each year follows:

	December 31, Year 10	December 31, Year 9	Net increase (decrease)
Plant assets (at cost)	$670,500	$510,000	$160,500
Less: Accumulated depreciation	224,500	228,000	(3,500)
Plant assets (net)	$446,000	$282,000	$164,000

During Year 10, machinery was acquired at a cost of $45,000. In addition, machinery with a current fair value of $100,000 was acquired in exchange for preferred stock on December 30. Machinery that was acquired in Year 3 at a cost of $48,000 was sold for $13,600. At the date of sale, the machinery had a carrying amount of $4,200. The remaining increase in plant assets resulted from the acquisition of land.

(4) The bonds payable mature at the rate of $28,000 a year. Bond discount is amortized by the straight-line method.

(5) In January, Year 10, the company issued an additional 10,000 shares of its common stock at $14 a share on the exercise of outstanding stock options held by officers. In May, Year 10, the company declared and issued a 5% stock dividend on its common stock when the market price of the common stock was $14 a share. During the year, a cash dividend was declared and paid on the common stock. On December 31, Year 10, there were 840,000 shares of common stock outstanding.

(6) The appropriation of retained earnings for possible future inventory price decline was provided by a debit to retained earnings, in anticipation of an expected future drop in the market prices of inventories.

Instructions

a Prepare a statement of changes in financial position (including the composition of working capital) for the year ended December 31, Year 10. The statement should be prepared on the working capital concept. A working paper may be used but is not required.

b Adjust the working capital provided from operations (computed in *a*) to a cash flow basis, and prepare a statement of changes in financial position on the cash concept. Do not include the composition of working capital in the statement.

23-9 Banner Corporation has prepared its financial statements for the year ended December 31, Year 3, and for the three months ended March 31, Year 4. You have been asked to prepare a statement of changes in financial position on a working capital concept for the three months ended March 31, Year 4. The company's financial statements are presented below and on page 989.

BANNER CORPORATION
Income Statement
For Three Months Ended March 31, Year 4

Revenue:		
Sales		$245,207
Investment income from 30%-owned company (equity method) . . .		5,880
Gain on sale of land		10,700
Total revenue		$261,787
Costs and expenses:		
Cost of goods sold	$138,407	
General and administrative expenses	22,010	
Depreciation expense	1,250	
Interest expense	1,150	
Income taxes expense	34,952	
Total costs and expenses		197,769
Net income		$ 64,018

BANNER CORPORATION
Balance Sheets

	Mar. 31, Year 4	Dec. 31, Year 3
Assets		
Current assets:		
Cash.	$ 87,400	$ 25,300
Short-term investments	7,300	16,500
Accounts receivable (net)	49,320	24,320
Inventories	48,590	31,090
Total current assets	$192,610	$ 97,210
Investment in 30%-owned company (equity method). .	67,100	61,220
Land	18,700	40,000
Building	250,000	250,000
Equipment	81,500	–0–
Accumulated depreciation of building and equipment . .	(16,250)	(15,000)
Other assets	15,100	15,100
Total assets	$608,760	$448,530

(cont.)

Liabilities & Stockholders' Equity

Current liabilities:

Accounts payable	$ 17,330	$ 21,220
Dividends payable	8,000	–0–
Income taxes payable	34,616	–0–
Total current liabilities	$ 59,946	$ 21,220
Bonds payable	115,000	50,000
Discount on bonds payable	(2,150)	(2,300)
Deferred income tax liability	846	510
Other liabilities	186,000	186,000
Convertible preferred stock, $2 par	–0–	30,000
Common stock, $1 par	110,000	80,000
Retained earnings	139,118	83,100
Total liabilities & stockholders' equity	$608,760	$448,530

You previously have satisfied yourself as to correctness of the amounts presented.

Your discussion with the company's controller and a review of the accounting records have revealed the following information.

(1) On January 8, Year 4, the company sold short-term investments for cash at their carrying amount. These investments had been held for less than one year.

(2) The company's preferred stock is convertible to common stock at a rate of one share of preferred for two shares of common. The preferred stock was converted to common stock in January, Year 4.

(3) On January 17, Year 4, land was sold for $32,000 cash. (Ignore the effect of income taxes on the gain on sale of the land.

(4) On March 25, Year 4, the company acquired equipment for cash.

(5) On March 29, Year 4, bonds payable were issued at face amount for cash. Discount on the bonds payable is amortized by the straight-line method.

(6) The investment in the 30%-owned company included an amount attributable to goodwill of $3,220 on December 31, Year 3. Goodwill is being amortized at an annual rate of $480.

(7) Dividends of $8,000 were declared on the preferred and common stock on March 20, Year 4, payable on April 28, Year 4.

Instructions

a Prepare a statement of changes in financial position, including any supporting computations needed, on the working capital concept for the three months ended March 31, Year 4.

b Prepare a working paper to convert the income statement for the three months ended March 31, Year 4, to a cash basis. Assume that the proceeds on the sale of land are reported separately.

c Using the data in parts **a** and **b**, prepare a statement of changes in financial position on the cash concept for the three months ended March 31, Year 4. You need not include the composition of working capital in the statement.

23-10 Balance sheet accounts for Paradise Orchid Company on December 31, Year 2 and Year 1, are shown on page 990.

PARADISE ORCHID COMPANY
Balance Sheet Accounts
December 31,

	Year 2	Year 1
Cash	$ 76,000	$ 170,000
Short-term investments	–0–	30,000
Accounts receivable (net of allowances of $20,000 and		
$8,000 for Year 2 and Year 1, respectively)	435,000	260,000
Inventories	493,000	400,000
Long-term investments (at cost)	520,000	610,000
Equipment (net of accumulated depreciation)	1,953,000	1,700,000
Discount on mortgage bonds payable	16,000	25,000
Totals	$3,493,000	$3,195,000
Bank overdraft	$ 5,000	$ –0–
Notes payable to banks (current)	350,000	40,000
Accounts payable	315,000	290,000
Mortgage bonds payable	800,000	1,000,000
Preferred stock, $100 par, each share convertible to		
three shares of common stock.	250,000	300,000
Common stock, $5 par	542,500	500,000
Paid-in capital in excess of par	655,500	340,000
Retained earnings	575,000	725,000
Totals	$3,493,000	$3,195,000

An analysis of changes in account balances disclosed the following:

(1) Uncollectible accounts amounting to $11,299 were written off in Year 2.
(2) Long-term investments were sold at a gain of $80,000. Short-term investments, however, were sold at a loss of $2,110. (Include the loss on sale of the short-term investments in working capital provided from operations because they were acquired with temporarily idle cash.)
(3) Mortgage bonds mature on December 31, Year 6. On July 1, Year 2, bonds of $200,000 were extinguished at 102. Discount on mortgage bonds is amortized by the straight-line method.
(4) Additional shares of common stock were issued during the year at $44 a share, and 1,500 shares were issued as a result of conversion of preferred stock.
(5) Equipment, cost $60,000, was sold at its carrying amount of $30,000. Depreciation expense of $120,000 was recorded during the year. Additional equipment was acquired for cash.
(6) Net loss for Year 2 (including nonoperating gains and losses) amounted to $110,000.
(7) Cash dividends declared and paid during the year amounted to $40,000.

Instructions
a Prepare an analysis of changes in working capital during Year 2.
b Prepare a statement of changes in financial position for Year 2 which explains the reasons for the change in working capital. Use of a working paper is recommended; if a working paper is not used, supporting computations should be presented. Do not include the composition of working capital in the statement because it has already been prepared in part a.
c Prepare a statement of changes in financial position for Year 2 on the cash concept. Do not include the composition of working capital in the statement.

24 ANALYSIS OF FINANCIAL STATEMENTS

Many groups outside the business enterprise—creditors, investors, regulatory agencies, financial analysts, labor union leaders—are interested in its financial affairs. Management also is interested in the results and relationships reported in financial statements. Outsiders do not have access to the detailed data available to management and must rely on published information in making decisions. In this chapter we shall consider the analysis of financial statements as a basis for decision making by outsiders.

Management makes operating and financial decisions based on a wide variety of reports which are generated by the enterprise's own information system or which are available from other sources. Management's use of financial information has been mentioned in preceding chapters. More sophisticated analyses of profit-volume relationships, make-or-buy decisions, differential costs, financial forecasts, product line profitability, gross profits, distribution costs, and rates of return on investments usually are covered in cost and management accounting courses and for that reason are not discussed in this chapter.

Sources of financial information available to outsiders

The first step in financial analysis is to obtain as much factual information as possible. The major sources of financial information for publicly owned corporations are described in the following sections.

Published Reports   Corporations whose stock is publicly owned issue annual and quarterly reports. Annual reports generally contain comparative financial statements and the accompanying notes, supplementary financial information, and comments by management on the year's operations and prospects for the future. Annual reports are made available to the public as well as to stockholders.

Securities and Exchange Commission (SEC)   Publicly owned corporations are required to file annual reports with the SEC. These reports *(Form 10-K)* are particularly valuable sources of financial information because the SEC prescribes a standard format and terminology and because they typically contain more detailed information than reports to stockholders. Publicly owned corporations generally indicate in their annual reports to stockholders that a copy of **Form 10-K** as filed with the Securities and Exchange Commission may be obtained free of charge by writing to the corporation. A quarterly report filed with the SEC **(Form 10-Q)** also is a valuable source of information.

Credit and Investment Advisory Services Organizations such as Moody's Investors Service and Standard & Poor's Corporation compile financial information for investors in annual volumes and periodic supplements. A wide variety of data on enterprises, particularly small and medium-sized enterprises, is published by such organizations as Dun & Bradstreet, Inc., and Robert Morris Associates. Many trade associations collect and publish financial ratios for enterprises in various industries. Major brokerage firms and investment advisory services compile financial information about publicly owned companies and make it available to their customers. In addition, most brokerage firms maintain a staff of analysts who study business conditions and review published financial statements; visit plants and talk with executives to get information on new products, industry trends, and management changes; and interpret all this information for investors.

Audit Reports When an independent CPA firm performs an audit, its report is addressed to the board of directors, and frequently to the stockholders, of the audited company. The CPA firm's opinion on financial statements is included in annual reports. Frequently, the audit report consists only of the opinion; however, in auditing smaller clients, the CPA firm may prepare a **long-form report** which contains detailed financial information and comments. Banks and other lending institutions often rely on long-form audit reports for financial information about business enterprises applying for loans.

What is financial analysis?

Knowing what to look for and how to interpret it is the essence of the art of financial analysis. Financial analysis is a process of **selection, relation, and evaluation.** The first step is to select from the total information available about a business enterprise the information relevant to the decision under consideration. The second step is to arrange the information in a way that will bring out significant relationships. The final step is to study these relationships and interpret the results.

Financial statements themselves are organized summaries of detailed information, and are thus a form of analysis. The types of financial statements accountants prepare, the way they arrange items in the statements, and their standards of disclosure are influenced by a desire to provide information in convenient and useful form. In using financial statements, analysts focus their attention on key amounts and relationships, then extend their investigation to find out why the conditions revealed by the financial statements exist.

Procedure of analysis

Financial analysis is not primarily a matter of making computations. The important part of the analytical process begins when the computational task is finished. However, there are some analytical procedures that are useful in highlighting important relationships and reducing masses of detail into convenient numerical form so that the essential facts can be grasped quickly.

Ratios Ratios may be expressed as percentages, as fractions, or as a stated comparison between two numbers. For example, we might describe the relationship between $120 million of sales and $24 million of operating income as: (1) operating income is 20% of sales; (2) operating income is $\frac{1}{5}$ of sales; (3) the ratio of sales to operating income is 5 to 1; (4) for every dollar of sales the company earned 20 cents in operating income. Each of these ratios describes the relationship between sales and operating income. The computation of a ratio does not add any information not already inherent in the numbers under study. A useful ratio can be computed only when a significant relationship exists between two numbers; a ratio of two unrelated numbers is meaningless.

Component Percentages: Common-Size Financial Statements The ratio of one number in a financial statement to the total that includes that number is called a **component percentage.** Reducing data to component percentages helps the analyst to visualize both the relative importance of the numbers in the financial statements and the changes from period to period.

Financial statements expressed in component percentages are sometimes called **common-size financial statements.** Two examples, one for Company A and one for Companies A and B, are presented below and on page 994.

Each item in the income statement is reported as a percentage of net sales

COMPANY A
Common-Size Income Statements
For Years Ended December 31,

	Year 2	Year 1
Net sales	100.0%	100.0%
Cost of goods sold	63.2	66.4
Gross profit on sales	36.8%	33.6%
Operating expenses	23.2	24.2
Operating income	13.6%	9.4%
Income taxes expense	5.0	3.2
Net income	8.6%	6.2%

Items in the balance
sheet are reported
as a percentage
of total assets

COMPANIES A AND B
Common-Size Balance Sheets
December 31, Year 1

	Company A	Company B
Assets		
Current assets	56.4%	43.2%
Plant assets (net)	38.7	50.1
Other assets	4.9	6.7
Total assets	100.0%	100.0%
Liabilities & Stockholders' Equity		
Current liabilities	36.2%	20.5%
Long-term liabilities	24.0	12.6
Total liabilities	60.2%	33.1%
Stockholders' equity	39.8	66.9
Total liabilities & stockholders' equity	100.0%	100.0%

In the first example for Company A, reducing the operating data to component percentages helps the analyst to see the major factors that brought about an increase in the rate of earnings per dollar of sales. In the second example, component percentages highlight the difference in the asset and capital structures of Companies A and B. Company A has a larger proportion of debt and a relatively larger amount of current assets; Company B is financed to a larger degree by use of owners' capital and has a relatively larger investment in plant assets.

When information is reduced to simple terms, there may be some loss of clarity or completeness, but there may be some gains. Component percentages emphasize relative size rather than absolute amounts. For example, if Company A has managed to increase its net income from 6.2 to 8.6% of sales only by cutting sales volume in half, there is no hint of this in the common-size income statements. Similarly, the common-size balance sheets will not reveal that Company A may be ten times as large as Company B.

Changes over Time The analytical information that can be gleaned from the financial statements of only one year is limited. We have seen in previous chapters the difficulty of measuring income and financial position accurately. Furthermore, a company's experience in a given year may not be typical. Investigating performance over a reasonable number of years is therefore a useful form of financial analysis.

Most corporate annual reports now include a 5- or 10-year summary of important financial data. The amounts on page 995, for example, are taken from the annual report of Inca Corporation.[1] We can see at a glance that the sales, net income, earnings per share, and cash dividends per share of Inca Corporation are growing steadily.

Example of a 5-year summary

INCA CORPORATION
Sales, Net Income, and Dividends
For Years 1 through 5

	Year 5	Year 4	Year 3	Year 2	Year 1
Sales (millions)	$4,248	$3,573	$3,239	$2,863	$2,591
Net income (millions)	526	477	431	364	305
Earnings per share (dollars). .	9.66	9.03	8.20	6.96	5.84
Cash dividends per share (dollars).	4.30	4.00	3.17	2.27	1.60

There are a number of ways this five-year record can be presented to facilitate analysis. In the summary below relating to sales and net income, the dollar increase each year over the previous year, the percentage increase over the previous year, and the **trend percentage** in relation to the first year in the series are shown for Inca Corporation:

Summary of increases and trend percentages for sales and net income

INCA CORPORATION
Analysis of Changes
For Years 1 through 5

Year	Dollar increase over previous year (in millions of dollars)		Percentage increase over previous year		Trend percentage in relation to Year 1	
	Sales	Net income	Sales	Net income	Sales	Net income
1					100.0%	100.0%
2	$272	$59	10.5%	19.3%	110.5	119.3
3	376	67	13.1	18.4	125.0	141.3
4	334	46	10.3	10.7	137.9	156.4
5	675	49	18.9	10.3	163.9	172.5

Each of these computations points up the change in sales and net income over the five-year period in a slightly different way. If the analyst is primarily interested in absolute change, the dollar changes tell the story. The percentage of increase or decrease year by year expresses

---

[1] When financial data for a number of years are reported, common practice is to report the *most recent* data in the first column and the older data in succeeding columns to the right. We shall follow this practice in this chapter.

growth in relation to the prior year's performance. Trend percentages (computed by dividing the amount for each year by the amount for the base year) reveal a total growth of 63.9% in sales volume and an increase of 72.5% in net income over a period of four years.

A great deal of importance has been placed in recent years on the **compound growth** rates in earnings. Those companies whose earnings increase at a rate substantially above the average rate for other companies are referred to as **growth companies.** The compound growth rate in net income for Inca Corporation during the Years 2 through 5, for example, is the simple average of the percentage increases in net income over the previous year. Therefore, 19.3 + 18.4 + 10.7 + 10.3, or 58.7 ÷ 4 years, gives a compound growth rate in net income of approximately 14.7%. The compound growth rate also can be estimated from compound interest tables by first determining the increase in net income for a period of years (72.5% in four years for Inca Corporation) and then determining the interest rate that would result in a compound amount of 1 of 1.725 over the four-year period.[2]

Analytical objectives

The outcome of business decisions (to buy or sell a company's securities or to extend or refuse to extend credit, for example) naturally depends on future events. Financial statements are essentially a record of the past. Outsiders, therefore, study financial statements as evidence of past performance which may be useful in making forecasts of future performance. The management of a company is responsible for earning as large a return as possible on the resources invested in the company, consistent with the objectives of maintaining a sound financial condition, meeting social responsibilities, and doing business in accordance with high ethical standards. Insofar as the attainment of these objectives can be measured quantitatively (and quantitative information usually is only a part of the basis for any business decision), financial statements provide useful information.

In looking at past performance and present position, the financial analyst seeks answers to two primary questions: (1) What is the company's earnings performance, and (2) is the company in sound financial condition? We can examine the process of analysis within the framework of these two questions.

---

[2] Net income for Year 5 is approximately 173% of Year 1 net income, or 1.73 in terms of a decimal value. Compound interest tables show that 1 would accumulate to 1.69 in four years at 14%, or to 1.81 in four years at 16%. Because 1.73 is $\frac{4}{12}$ between 1.69 and 1.81, the interpolated compound growth rate is 14% + $\frac{4}{12}$ of 2%, or approximately 14.7%.

ANALYSIS OF EARNINGS PERFORMANCE

Unfortunately, an outside analyst usually does not have access to many of the important details that lie behind reported net income. Most published income statements are highly condensed, and the outsider must be satisfied with a general review of the relationship between revenue, cost of goods sold, total operating expenses, and net income. This requires a careful analysis of gross profit percentages and **operating expense ratios** (total operating expenses divided by net sales) over a period of years. Also, the analyst will look at any items of nonoperating revenue and expense and extraordinary items in order to forecast the likely normal earning power of a company.

Net income and accounting practices

The point has been made throughout this book that the amount of net income reported in a given accounting period can be affected by the accounting practices followed. These practices are selected by management; the independent auditor simply informs users that the financial statements were prepared "in conformity with generally accepted accounting principles applied on a basis consistent with that of the preceding year." Unfortunately, a wide variety of accounting principles is considered "generally accepted," and analysts first must determine the accounting practices and principles used and then evaluate their impact on reported net income. In other words, analysts are concerned with the **quality of reported earnings.**

In recent years significant progress has been made in reducing areas of differences in financial accounting and reporting, and additional steps are contemplated by authoritative bodies. The required inclusion in annual reports of a description of the accounting policies used in the preparation of financial statements was an important development.[3] The accounting policies for depreciation, inventories, leases, pension plans, unconsolidated subsidiaries, business combinations, and income taxes, for example, are especially significant to the analyst. In addition, the notes to the financial statements provide useful information on these and other financial accounting and reporting matters.

Trend in earnings

The analysis of earnings always should cover several periods, not only because of the difficulty of measuring income year by year but also because it is important to know how a company performs in periods of prosperity and adversity. Net income may be satisfactory in one year

---

[3] *APB Opinion No. 22,* "Disclosure of Accounting Policies," AICPA (New York: 1972).

and shrink to nothing in the following year, because of unfavorable business conditions.

One of the first things an analyst looks for is the trend of revenue (sales) over a period of years. A rising trend of revenue usually is a sign of an expanding company. Obviously, the revenue trend is not the whole story, because a growth in revenue is not always accompanied by a corresponding increase in net income. The ideal situation is to find a company maintaining a constant or increasing *rate* of net income on a rapidly growing revenue.

The pattern of revenue and net income throughout the business cycle is also an important factor. There is obviously greater risk in investing in or lending to a company whose net income varies widely with changes in business conditions, than in a company able to show *stability* of earnings throughout all phases of the business cycle. A company that must cut back its operations severely during recessions inevitably suffers in terms of such factors as effective product planning and employee morale, and may find it difficult to cover fixed expenses. Furthermore, earnings tend to sag faster than revenue because some expenses are fixed. Investors are interested in identifying a *cyclical* company, not only because the risk of investment is higher, but also because the timing of their investment will depend on the company's performance in relation to cyclical trends. The shifts to *defensive stocks* (stocks of companies that perform well in all phases of the business cycle) when a recession is in the offing and to stocks of cyclical companies at the first sign of an economic upturn is a well-known investment strategy.

Return on investment

Business executives invest capital with the objective of earning a satisfactory rate of return. The rate of return depends on numerous factors, including the nature of competition and the risks inherent in the industry. Management often is evaluated in terms of the rate of return it is able to earn on invested capital. Although outsiders cannot determine the rate of return on the investment for particular divisions or segments of a business enterprise, they can make some overall estimates of the rate. This rate can serve as a valuable index in evaluating the relative standing of a particular company and the effectiveness of its management.

The rate of return on investment for any period is determined by dividing "income" by average investment. The appropriate income amount to be used depends on the related concept of investment. This is illustrated at the top of page 999.

In each case net income excludes any extraordinary items, and the investment is computed as an average for the period. Ratio *1* is a measure of the earnings (after interest and income taxes) that relate to the

Three different rates of return

	Appropriate income amount	Concept of investment (*in all cases an average for the period covered by the income amount*)
1 *Return on total assets:*		
	Net income	÷ total assets
2 *Return on total stockholders' equity:*		
	Net income	÷ total stockholders' equity
3 *Return on common stockholders' equity:*		
	Net income applicable to common stock	÷ common stockholders' equity

total economic resources employed by the company. It is possible to add interest expense to net income in order to compute an approximation of earnings before payment of interest to creditors but after income taxes. Some analysts prefer to compute return on total assets *before interest and income taxes,* in which case a ratio of operating income to total assets is used. If total assets include some unproductive assets, bond sinking funds, or long-term investments, these assets and the related earnings generated by these assets are excluded from rate of return computations.

Rates of return computed on page 1000 are based on these data

BARKER COMPANY
Data for Analysis
(in millions of dollars)

Income statement data			Balance sheet data			
	Year 2	Year 1		Year 2	Year 1	Year 0
Sales.	$130	$ 95	Current assets . . .	$19	$20	$18
Other revenue . . .	10	5	Noncurrent assets .	61	60	56
Total revenue . .	$140	$100	Total assets . . .	$80	$80	$74
Cost of goods sold.	$ 95	$ 65				
Operating						
expenses	26	20	Current liabilities. .	$ 6	$10	$ 9
Interest expense .	1	1	Long-term debt . .	19	20	21
Income taxes			Preferred stock . .	16	16	16
expense.	9	7	Common stock-			
Total expenses. .	$131	$ 93	holders' equity .	39	34	28
Net income.	$ 9	$ 7	Total liabilities &			
Preferred stock			stockholders'			
dividends	1	1	equity.	$80	$80	$74
Available for						
common stock. .	$ 8	$ 6				

Ratios *2* and *3* are computed from the viewpoint of stockholders, and the approach used depends on whether the analyst is interested in the rate of return on total stockholders' equity or on common stockholders' equity. The data for Barker Company on page 999 (given in millions of dollars) are used to compute these ratios.

The rates of return described in the outline on page 999 are computed below for Barker Company (all dollar amounts are stated in millions):

Computation of rates of return

Measurement	Computation	
	Year 2	Year 1
1 Return on total assets . .	$\dfrac{\$9}{\frac{1}{2}(\$80 + \$80)} = \dfrac{\$9}{\$80} = 11.2\%$	$\dfrac{\$7}{\frac{1}{2}(\$80 + \$74)} = \dfrac{\$7}{\$77} = 9.1\%$
2 Return on total stock-holders' equity	$\dfrac{\$9}{\frac{1}{2}(\$55 + \$50)} = \dfrac{\$9}{\$52.5} = 17.1\%$	$\dfrac{\$7}{\frac{1}{2}(\$50 + \$44)} = \dfrac{\$7}{\$47} = 14.9\%$
3 Return on common stockholders' equity	$\dfrac{\$8}{\frac{1}{2}(\$39 + \$34)} = \dfrac{\$8}{\$36.5} = 21.9\%$	$\dfrac{\$6}{\frac{1}{2}(\$34 + \$28)} = \dfrac{\$6}{\$31} = 19.4\%$

Interpreting Return on Investment Each of the measures of return on investment for Barker Company shows an improved performance in the second year. If we look at the underlying factors—the revenue generated per dollar of investment (or **asset turnover rate**) and the net income per dollar of revenue—we can obtain some additional insight:

Asset turnover rate × percentage earned on total revenue equals . . .

	Year 2	Year 1
Revenue generated per dollar of assets:		
$\dfrac{\text{Total revenue}}{\text{Average investment (total assets)}}$	$\dfrac{\$140}{\$80} = \$1.75$	$\dfrac{\$100}{\$77} = \$1.30$
Net income per dollar of revenue:		
$\dfrac{\text{Net income}}{\text{Total revenue}}$	$\dfrac{\$9}{\$140} = 6.4\%$	$\dfrac{\$7}{\$100} = 7.0\%$

Although Barker Company earned a smaller margin of income per dollar of total revenue in the second year, it was able to improve its volume of revenue per dollar of investment from $1.30 to $1.75. This ratio can be viewed as the number of times total assets are turned over and can be used to verify the rates of return on total assets as follows:

<table>
<tr><td>. . . rate of return on
total assets</td><td>Year 2: $1.75 × 6.4% = 11.2 cents per dollar of assets, or 11.2%
Year 1: $1.30 × 7.0% = 9.1 cents per dollar of assets, or 9.1%</td></tr>
</table>

What we have done here is simply multiply the rate earned on revenue by the asset turnover rate to measure the earnings rate on assets. This concept is really a truism: If a profit of 3%, for example, can be earned on sales, and $10 of sales is generated by each $1 of assets, then the rate earned on assets would be 10 × 3%, or 30%.

Trading on the Equity When a business enterprise borrows money for long-term purposes, it is ***trading on the equity,*** or ***using leverage.*** The results from trading on the equity can be favorable or unfavorable to common stockholders. If the rate earned before interest and income taxes on total assets is higher than the interest rate paid for the use of money, the common stockholders will gain; if the interest rate is higher than the earnings rate on assets, then a loss arises from trading on the equity. Issuance of preferred stock produces similar results but is more "expensive" to the common stockholders, because dividends on preferred stock are not deductible in the computation of taxable income.

The fact that the return on common stockholders' equity for Barker Company is higher than the return on total assets is significant. The company is successfully trading on the equity; that is, the total of interest on bonds and dividends on preferred stock is less than the earnings on capital raised through these ***senior securities.*** The company has about $20 million in long-term debt at an interest cost of about 5% before income taxes and $2\frac{1}{2}$% after income taxes, and it has $16 million in preferred stock paying dividends of approximately 6.3% ($1 ÷ $16). The company earned 11.2% after income taxes on its total assets during Year 2. Therefore, the funds raised through the issuance of senior securities earned considerably more than the fixed interest and dividends. This excess accrues to the common stockholders, resulting in a 21.9% rate earned on common stockholders' equity in Year 2 and 19.4% in Year 1.

Earnings, dividends, and equity (book value) per share

Because stockholders think in terms of the number of shares they own or plan to buy or sell, reducing corporate financial information to per-share terms puts it in a useful perspective for stockholders. Perhaps the most commonly used statistics relating to common stocks are ***earnings*** (or ***loss***) ***per share*** and ***dividends per share.*** These appear widely in financial press releases, prospectuses, proxy materials, and reports to stockholders.

Comparative earnings per share data, supported by complete financial statements, are useful in evaluating the performance of a company from the common stockholders' point of view. There is little doubt that earnings (or loss) per share is a highly significant summary amount but it has some serious limitations, and there are dangers in focusing too much attention on it.

The manner of computing and reporting of earnings per share has been a major concern not only of the accounting profession but also of the SEC and the major stock exchanges. The technical aspects of computing and reporting **primary** and **fully diluted** earnings per share are illustrated in Chapter 18.

Dividends on capital stock represent historical facts and should be reported at amounts actually paid, except in cases following stock splits or large stock dividends. In such cases, "the presentation of dividends per share should be in terms of the current equivalent number of shares outstanding at the time of the dividend, so that the earnings and dividends per share will be reported on a comparable basis. When dividends per share are presented on other than a historical basis, the basis of presentation should be disclosed."[4]

Price-Earnings Ratio and Dividend Yield　Investors in corporate securities are more interested in earnings and dividends in relation to the **market price** of their shares than in relation to the equity (book value) of their shares, because market price measures the amount of money they forego at any given time by a decision to continue owning the stock. To illustrate, suppose that Jane Adams owns one share of common stock in a company that currently earns $5 a share and pays a dividend of $2 a share. The equity (book value) is $40 a share and the current market price is $50. The fact that the company is earning a return of $12\frac{1}{2}\%$ on stockholders' equity ($5 ÷ $40) is of secondary interest to Adams, because she gives up the use of $50 by the decision to own this share. Thus, Adams views this investment as one producing an **earnings yield** of 10% ($5 ÷ $50) and a **dividend yield** of only 4% ($2 ÷ $50). In investment circles the earnings yield usually is expressed in reverse as a **price-earnings ratio**[5] of 10 to 1 ($50 ÷ $5).

Intelligent investors monitor the relationships among earnings, dividends, and the market prices of common stock and seek to evaluate such relationships by analyzing the financial data available to them. The table on page 1003 shows these relationships for three companies.

---

[4] *APB Opinion No. 9,* "Reporting the Results of Operations," AICPA (New York: 1966), p. 126.

[5] The price-earnings ratios generally are determined using the primary earnings per share for the latest 12 months, excluding extraordinary items. The price-earnings ratios for stocks traded on the New York and American Stock Exchanges are reported in most daily newspapers, along with the annual price range, the daily high and low prices, the closing price, and the net price change from the previous day's closing price.

	Company C	Company D	Company E
Earnings per share	$1.00	$2.50	$5.00
Dividends per share.	$0.60	$2.00	$2.00
Market price per share during the year:			
High	$7	$50	$110
Low	$3	$35	$ 96
Ending	$5	$40	$100
Price-earnings ratio at year-end.	5–1	16–1	20–1
Dividend yield on market price at year-end.	12%	5%	2%

This divergence in price-earnings and yield ratios (an even wider spread often exists among listed common stocks) suggests that investors assess the risk and future prospects of these three investments in quite different terms. Company C, for example, may be a marginal producer in its industry, with highly volatile earnings performance and low growth prospects. As a result, its common stock sells at a low price-earnings ratio and yields 12%. The common stock of Company D sells at a much higher multiple of earnings and yields 5%. In contrast, Company E appears to be a "growth company"; the price-earnings ratio for its common stock is 20 to 1 and the yield is only 2% because only 40% of its net income is distributed to stockholders.

An investor who tries to determine whether the market price of a common stock is reasonable must consider a variety of factors. All, however, relate to an estimate of the ultimate return on investment; this return depends on the dividends received during the time the stock is held and the price obtained when the stock is sold, both of which are difficult to project with any degree of precision.

Earnings and Fixed Charges A company which finances its operations through long-term debt or preferred stock is committed to pay a fixed return to the holders of these securities. The commitment on long-term debt is stronger than on preferred stock, because in the latter case the obligation is only that preferred dividends will be paid before any dividends on common stock are declared. A company that **passes** a preferred dividend has impaired its financial reputation to some degree, but a company that cannot pay interest on its debt is in serious financial trouble.

Bondholders and preferred stockholders have learned from experience that the relationships between earnings and fixed charges are a good measure of the safety of their investment. The data at the top of page 1004 are used to illustrate two ratios that measure these relationships.

	Company F	Company G
Operating income.	$600,000	$900,000
Less: Interest on long-term debt.	200,000	100,000
Income before income taxes	$400,000	$800,000
Less: Income taxes expense	200,000	400,000
Net income.	$200,000	$400,000
Less: Preferred dividends	50,000	200,000
Net income available to common stockholders	$150,000	$200,000

Times interest earned   The times interest earned ratio may be computed in two ways as shown below:

	Company F	Company G
Method 1: Times interest earned before income taxes:		
(a) Operating income	$600,000	$900,000
(b) Interest charges	$200,000	$100,000
Times interest earned (a ÷ b)	3 times	9 times
Method 2: Times interest earned after income taxes:		
Net income	$200,000	$400,000
(a) Add: Interest charges	200,000	100,000
(b) Income before interest charges.	$400,000	$500,000
Times interest earned (b ÷ a)	2 times	5 times

Because interest expense is deductible in arriving at taxable income, logic would seem to be on the side of method 1. Business executives and investors are strongly conditioned to an after-tax view of corporate affairs, however, which may explain why method 2 generally is used in practice. The after-tax computation always results in a more conservative measurement for coverage of interest charges.

Times preferred dividends earned   The computation of the number of times preferred dividends are earned may also be made in two ways, as illustrated below and on page 1005.

	Company F	Company G
Method 1: Net income to preferred dividends:		
(a) Net income	$200,000	$400,000
(b) Preferred dividend requirement.	$ 50,000	$200,000
Times preferred dividends earned (a ÷ b).	4 times	2 times

These ratios make it appear that preferred dividends of Company F are better protected by earnings than its bond interest; yet bond interest obviously has a prior claim. To overcome this objection, the test of preferred dividend safety most often used is the **number of times combined interest charges and preferred dividends are earned.** This is illustrated for Companies F and G below:

	Company F	Company G
Method 2: Times interest charges and preferred dividends are earned:		
Interest charges	$200,000	$100,000
Preferred dividend requirement	50,000	200,000
(a) Total interest and dividend requirements	$250,000	$300,000
(b) Net income (after taxes) plus interest charges . . .	$400,000	$500,000
Number of times interest charges and preferred dividends are earned (b ÷ a)	1.6 times	1.7 times

No, based on this computation!

"Times-earned" ratios are of interest not only to creditors and preferred stockholders but also to common stockholders. Holders of common stock know that a company which has to omit either interest or preferred dividends will suffer financial embarrassment at the very least; furthermore, they are concerned about a sufficiency of earnings and cash to allow for common dividends. There is little mystery in interpreting times-earned ratios—the higher the ratio the more favorable for bondholders and preferred stockholders. The more difficult question is: How high should the ratios be to satisfy these two groups without being detrimental to the common stockholders? In general, the answer to this question depends on the stability of past and potential earnings over the business cycle; if earnings are stable, lower times-earned ratios can be viewed as satisfactory.

In the analysis of financial statements, the coverage of fixed charges logically should be expanded to include **all** fixed obligations of the reporting company. For example, a company must make regular payments on long-term leases, property taxes, and other fixed commitments, in addition to interest on debt, before dividends can be declared.[6] The ability of a company to generate sufficient revenue over

---

[6] In the computation of the ratio of earnings to fixed charges, some companies have in the past deducted earnings on investments (interest and dividends earned) and gains on retirement of debt from the fixed charges. In *Accounting Series Release No. 119* the Securities and Exchange Commission stated:

The propriety of reducing fixed charges by amounts representing interest or investment income or gains on retirement of debt has been considered in the light of the purposes for which ratios of earnings to fixed charges are used and the Commission has determined that the reduction of fixed charges by the amount of either actual or imputed

variable expenses to cover fixed charges is one of the most important considerations to the analyst.

Equity (Book Value) per Share The term *equity* (or *book value*) often is used in negotiations for the sale of a going business. In closely held corporations, it is not unusual for one stockholder to have a contractual right to acquire the capital stock of other stockholders at a price equal to the equity per share of the stock. Computation of equity per share generally is based on going-concern value, not on the assumption of business liquidation. *Equity per share is the amount of net assets applicable to each share of outstanding capital stock.* When a corporation has only one class of capital stock, equity per share is computed by dividing the total stockholders' equity by the number of shares of capital stock outstanding, as illustrated below:

Equity (book value) per share—one class of capital stock

$$\frac{\text{Total stockholders' equity}}{\text{Number of shares outstanding}} = \frac{\$2,500,000}{100,000} = \$25 \text{ equity per share}$$

If a corporation has treasury stock, the debit balance in the Treasury Stock account is deducted to determine the total stockholders' equity, and the number of shares of capital stock outstanding does not include the treasury stock.

Equity per share is used to some extent as a guide for investors, but usually with recognition that other measurements, such as earnings per share, are more important determinants of market prices for common stocks. The equity per share as traditionally computed may be far different from the per-share *current fair value* of net assets. Even though common stocks often sell at prices far above or far below the equity per share, some investors feel that the equity per share should be considered, along with other information, in making investment decisions.

The concept of "equity per share" is more meaningful and more widely used for common stock than for preferred stock; however, if a corporation has both types of capital stock outstanding, the total equity of the preferred stock must be determined as a preliminary step in the computation of the equity per share of the common stock, as illustrated in the example at the top of page 1007.

---

interest or investment income or debt retirement gains for the purpose of computing fixed charge ratios results in incorrect ratios and is therefore inappropriate. Accordingly, such reductions will no longer be deemed acceptable in registration statements or reports filed with the Commission.

Equity (book value) per share—two classes of capital stock

Equity (book value) per share of common stock —two classes of capital stock outstanding:	
Total stockholders' equity (net of treasury stock)............	$9,280,000
Less: Amount applicable to preferred stock: 10,000 shares, 10% preferred stock, $100 par, callable at $108	1,080,000
Equity applicable to common stock, consisting of 1,000,000 shares outstanding (not including treasury stock)	$8,200,000
Equity (book value) per share of common stock, $8,200,000 ÷ 1,000,000 shares	$ 8.20

The equity of the preferred stock in this example is $108 a share. In the computation of the equity of the preferred stock, consideration must be given to any **dividends in arrears** and other contractual limitations on the equity of preferred stockholders in the net assets of the corporation. On a going-concern basis, is it (1) par or stated value, (2) call price, or (3) liquidation price that is most significant in measuring the equity of the preferred stock? Nearly all preferred stocks issued in recent years contain a call provision; this call price usually is the maximum claim to net assets imposed by the preferred stock contract. Although there may be no immediate prospect that the preferred stock will be called, the call price probably is more significant from the viewpoint of the going concern than is the liquidation price. The authors, therefore, favor using the call price of the preferred stock as the most appropriate measure of the equity applicable to preferred stock.

Significant changes in the equity per share of common stock may result from transactions such as conversions of bonds payable or preferred stock to common stock, issuances of additional shares of common stock, business combinations, and quasi-reorganizations. Some examples of events which increase or decrease the equity per share of common stock are listed below:

Increases in equity per share Net income, reverse splits, issuance of additional common stock at prices above the present equity per share, acquisition of common stock at prices below the present equity per share, and retirement of preferred stock at prices below the present equity per share of the preferred stock.

Decreases in equity per share: Net loss, cash dividends (including any accumulated dividends on preferred stock), stock dividends, stock splits, issuance of additional common stock at prices below the present equity per share, acquisition of common stock at prices above the present equity per share, and retirement of preferred stock at prices above the present equity per share of the preferred stock.

ANALYSIS OF FINANCIAL STRENGTH

A strong earnings record usually accompanies a strong financial position. Furthermore, an unsatisfactory financial position looks much less unfavorable in the face of a good earnings record; a company with proved earning power usually can work out its financial problems. A good earnings record, however, is not the whole story. A company's ability to meet its obligations, to cope with adversity, to shift resources to meet changing conditions—in short, its financial strength—is an important factor to continuing survival and growth. In seeking evidence of financial strength, analysts look first at the relationship between assets and liabilities. They ask questions such as: Will the company be able to meets its debts as they fall due? Has it the resources to meet current commitments and future demands for cash necessary to conduct its business successfully?

Ability to meet short-term obligations

A company's short-term financial strength (or *liquidity*) is dependent on two primary factors: its working capital position and the speed with which it generates liquid assets. We shall use the financial information for Company H on page 1009 as a basis for discussion of these factors.

Working Capital Position The amount by which current assets exceed current liabilities is known as the *working capital* of a business enterprise. Changes in the amount of working capital from period to period are significant, because the amount of working capital is a useful indicator of short-term debt-paying ability.

In addition to the dollar amount of working capital, two analytical indices of current position often are computed. The *current ratio* (current assets divided by current liabilities) helps put the amount of working capital in perspective by showing the relationship between current resources and short-term debt. The *quick ratio* (sometimes called the *acid-test ratio*) focuses on immediate liquidity. Inventories and short-term prepayments, the least liquid assets in the current asset category, are excluded in the computation of the quick ratio. Quick assets consist of cash, short-term investments, and receivables; and the quick ratio is computed by dividing quick assets by current liabilities. The current position of Company H is summarized at the top of page 1010.

Each of the three measurements presented on page 1010 contributes something to the whole picture. The company has maintained its working capital at about $500,000 during the three-year period. However, its relative short-term liquidity has worsened, as indicated by the steady decline in the current ratio from 2.1 to 1.4 and in the quick ratio from 1.0 to 0.5 during the three-year period. This is a picture of a company that may

Data used to analyze working capital position

COMPANY H
Selected Financial Data
For Years 1 through 3
(in thousands of dollars)

	Year 3	Year 2	Year 1
Current assets:			
Cash	$ 50	$ 80	$ 60
Short-term investments	–0–	50	150
Receivables (net).	500	400	300
Inventories (fifo cost)	1,100	700	500
Short-term prepayments	70	60	50
Total current assets.	$1,720	$1,290	$1,060
Current liabilities:			
Notes payable	$ 120	$ 100	$ –0–
Accounts payable	680	330	170
Accrued liabilities	220	170	140
Current portion of long-term debt.	180	200	200
Total current liabilities	$1,200	$ 800	$ 510
Net sales.	$3,500	$3,000	$2,600
Cost of goods sold	(2,600)	(2,000)	(1,900)
Operating expenses	(600)	(500)	(400)
Interest on long-term debt	(48)	(49)	(50)
Income before income taxes	$ 252	$ 451	$ 250
Income taxes expense.	122	231	125
Net income	$ 130	$ 220	$ 125

be heading into financial difficulty, unless these trends can be reversed. The increase in accounts payable from $170,000 to $680,000 during the last two years suggests that payments to creditors may be falling behind schedule. Thus, the analysis has brought to light a potential trouble spot in the company's financial position. On the other hand, if the large increase in accounts payable is the result of large current expenditures for research and product development, or for inventories in anticipation of a sharp increase in sales, then the trend can be evaluated in a different light.

COMPANY H

Analysis of Current Position

For Years 1 through 3

(in thousands of dollars)

	Year 3	Year 2	Year 1
(a) Current assets.	$1,720	$1,290	$1,060
(b) Current liabilities	1,200	800	510
Working capital (a − b)	$ 520	$ 490	$ 550
Current ratio (a ÷ b).	1.4	1.6	2.1
(c) Total quick assets (cash, short-term investments,			
and receivables)	$ 550	$ 530	$ 510
Quick ratio (c ÷ b)	0.5	0.7	1.0

Need for Working Capital A business enterprise generates working capital through a series of events called the ***operating cycle.*** The operating cycle refers to the process of investing in inventories, converting these through sale to receivables, and transforming receivables by collection to cash, which in turn is used to pay current debts incurred in operations and to replace inventories. The average length of time necessary to complete this cycle is important in determining an enterprise's working capital needs. An enterprise with a short operating cycle can manage comfortably on a relatively small amount of working capital and with relatively low quick and current ratios. A long operating cycle requires a larger margin of current assets and higher quick and current ratios unless the credit terms of suppliers can be extended accordingly. The average length of the operating cycle can be estimated by adding the number of days' sales in average inventories to the average age of receivables.

Inventories Turnover The total cost of all goods that have been moved out of inventories during the year is represented by the cost of goods sold amount in the income statement. Therefore, the ratio of cost of goods sold to the average inventories during any period is a measure of the number of times that inventories turn over on the average and must be replaced. The higher this turnover, the shorter the average time between investment in inventories and the sale transaction.

Average inventories should be determined by averaging monthly or quarterly inventory amounts. This information usually is not available to external analysts, however, and therefore only an average of the inventories at the beginning and end of the year is ordinarily feasible. Because many companies adopt a fiscal year that ends when inventories are at a minimum, inventories turnover computed in this manner may appear larger than it really is.

Dividing the annual cost of goods sold by average inventories produces a "times per year" turnover rate. Turnover may be expressed in days by dividing 365 by the number of turnovers per year.[7] An additional useful measure is the **number of days' sales in the ending inventories,** computed by multiplying 365 days by the fraction of which the ending inventories is the numerator and cost of goods sold is the denominator. The three-year analysis of inventories for Company H appears below (dollar amounts are in thousands):

Inventories turnover
and days' sales in
inventories

COMPANY H
Analysis of Inventories
For Years 1 through 3
(in thousands of dollars)

	Year 3	Year 2	Year 1
(a) Cost of goods sold	$2,600	$2,000	$1,900
Inventories at beginning of year	$ 700	$ 500	$ 540*
Inventories at end of year . . .	1,100	700	500
(b) Average inventories	$ 900	$ 600	$ 520
(c) Turnover per year (a ÷ b) . . .	2.9 times	3.3 times	3.7 times
Number of days' sales in **average** inventories (365 ÷ c) . .	126 days	111 days	99 days
Number of days' sales in **ending** inventories	154 days†	128 days	96 days

* Assumed
† 365 × $1,100/$2,600 = 154

These computations show that inventories turnover has slowed during the three-year period from a little over three months to about four months, and that there are enough inventories on hand at the end of Year 3 to meet sales requirements at current levels for approximately five months (154 days).

For a manufacturing enterprise, the overall inventories turnover can be estimated by dividing the cost of goods sold by the sum of the three inventories: material, goods in process, and finished goods. A more precise computation would involve three separate turnover rates: (1) cost of goods sold divided by average finished goods inventory; (2) cost of goods manufactured divided by average goods in process inventory; and (3) material used divided by average material inventory.

[7] A year is sometimes viewed as consisting of 300 business days in the computation of the number of days of sales in inventories or receivables.

It should be pointed out that the foregoing computations would be misleading if current cost of inventories were substantially higher than historical cost. In such cases, alternative measurements should be used to analyze inventories.

Receivables Turnover The turnover of accounts receivable may be computed in a manner comparable to that just described for inventories. Unless a business enterprise has a large amount of cash sales, sales for any period represent the flow of claims to the receivable category. When the sales total is divided by the average balance of receivables during the period, the result is a rough indication of the average length of time necessary to convert receivables to cash. Ideally, only credit sales should be included in the sales amount, and an average monthly balance of **gross** receivables should be used. However, these refinements may not be possible in external analysis, and a less exact computation may serve the purpose of indicating favorable or unfavorable trends. The reasonableness of the ending balance in receivables can be evaluated by computing the **number of days' sales in ending receivables.** The receivables of Company H are analyzed below (dollar amounts are in thousands):

Receivables turnover and days' sales in receivables

COMPANY H

Analysis of Receivables

For Years 1 through 3

(in thousands of dollars)

	Year 3	Year 2	Year 1
(a) Net sales	$3,500	$3,000	$2,600
Receivables at beginning of year.	$ 400	$ 300	$ 280*
Receivables at end of year . .	500	400	300
(b) Average receivables	$ 450	$ 350	$ 290
(c) Receivables turnover (a ÷ b).	7.8 times	8.6 times	9.0 times
Number of days' sales in **average** receivables (365 ÷ c) .	47 days	42 days	41 days
Number of days' sales in **ending** receivables	52 days†	49 days	42 days

* Assumed

† 365 × $500/$3,500 = 52

It is evident that, barring a change in credit terms, collections have slowed down over the three-year period. The trend is unfavorable; interpretation of the absolute amounts depends on the credit terms and policies of the company.

Length of Operating Cycle By adding the average days' sales in inventories and in receivables for Company H, we can obtain a rough estimate of the average length of the operating cycle as follows:

Length of operating
cycle for Company H

	Year 3	Year 2	Year 1
Average days to dispose of inventories	126	111	99
Average days to collect receivables	47	42	41
Average days in operating cycle	173	153	140

The operating cycle of Company H has increased by more than a full month (33 days) from Year 1 to Year 3. If this has happened inadvertently, it may explain the unfavorable trend in the current and quick ratios. If the change is the result of deliberate company policy, it indicates the need for a larger amount of working capital to finance current operations.

Number of Days' Operations to Cover Negative Working Capital When current liabilities exceed current assets, management may wish to estimate the length of time it would take to eliminate the negative working capital as a result of generating liquid assets from operations. For example, assume that the current liabilities of Linda Corporation on March 31 exceed its current assets by $20,000. Assume further that the company's operations are relatively stable over a calendar year and normally generate working capital as follows:

Working capital
provided from
operations . . .

Net income.	$ 75,000
Add: Depreciation and other expenses which do not require the use of working capital	45,000
Working capital normally provided from operations over 12-month period	$120,000

From the foregoing information we can estimate that the negative working capital of $20,000 will be covered in approximately two months:

. . . will cover the
working capital deficit
in two months

$$\frac{\$20{,}000 \text{ (negative working capital)}}{\$120{,}000 \text{ (annual working capital provided from operations)}} \times 365 \text{ days} = 61 \text{ days}$$

Interpreting the analysis of liquidity

The following factors should be considered in interpreting the liquidity of a company as shown by the analytical procedures just described:

1 Creditors tend to adopt the view that the higher the current and quick ratios and the shorter the operating cycle, the better. From the viewpoint of company performance, there are upper limits. It is possible for a company to accumulate working capital in excess of the amount that can be employed profitably. Thus, excessive current and quick ratios are unfavorable indicators. Similarly, an unusually high rate of inventories turnover may indicate that a company is losing business by failing to maintain adequate inventories to serve customers' needs. A rapid turnover of receivables may indicate overly severe credit policies that hold revenue below levels that could be achieved by granting more liberal credit terms.

2 Because creditors and other outsiders place considerable emphasis on working capital position as evidence of short-run solvency, there is a temptation for managers to take steps just before the financial statements are prepared to make the working capital relationships appear better than they are. This process is called **window dressing.** By postponing purchases, allowing inventories to fall below normal levels, using all available cash to pay current liabilities, and pressing collections on accounts receivable, a company can artificially improve its current and quick ratios, as well as its inventories and receivables turnover rates. Decreases in receivable and inventories balances will raise turnover rates. Any equal decrease in both current assets and current liabilities will improve a current ratio that already is higher than 1 to 1.

3 Even when no deliberate attempt has been made to present an artificially good picture, the working capital position shown on year-end financial statements is probably more favorable than at any other time of the year. This is particularly true when a company has adopted a **natural business year** that ends during an ebb in the seasonal swing of business activity. At times of peak activity, receivables, inventories, and current liabilities tend to be at higher levels. There are, of course, many reasons why a natural business year is desirable, and accountants generally encourage companies to adopt such an accounting period.

Analysis of capital structure

The way in which a business enterprise meets its financing needs, as reflected in its **capital structure,** is an important factor in assessing its financial strength. The most common approach for this purpose is to restate the major elements of the equity side of the balance sheet to component percentages of total assets, as shown at the top of page 1015.

Debt and Equity Ratios Analysts often condense the essence of the capital structure of a company into any one of three ratios. The **debt ratio** is the ratio of total liabilities to total assets; the **equity ratio** is the ratio of stockholders' equity to total assets; the **debt to equity ratio** is the ratio of total liabilities to stockholders' equity. Any one of these three ratios tells the essential story about the debt-equity relationship for a company.

Financial analysts compute other ratios to aid them in evaluating capital structure. For example, the ratio of total plant assets to stockhold-

Three ways to measure relationship between debt and equity

Component percentages		Debt and equity ratios	
Total assets	100%	Debt ratio.	28%
Sources of financing:		Equity ratio.	72%
Current liabilities	10%	Debt to equity ratio (28 ÷ 72) . .	39%
Long-term debt	18%		
Total liabilities	28%		
Preferred stock 9%			
Common stockholders' equity 63%	72%		
Total liabilities & stockholders' equity	100%		

ers' equity sometimes is used as a test of the adequacy of equity capital. If the investment in plant assets is high relative to stockholders' equity, this indicates that a company has borrowed heavily to invest in nonliquid assets, which may lead to difficulties should earnings not prove satisfactory.

Evaluating capital structure

What factors should be considered in evaluating the capital structure of a company? The answer to this question depends on the concerns of creditors and stockholders.

Creditors' View Creditors are primarily concerned with the safety of their capital. They view a relatively low debt ratio as a favorable factor because it indicates a substantial cushion of protection against a shrinkage in asset values. Because ultimate repayment of debt will come from either new borrowing or internal cash flow, all creditors are interested in long-run financial strength and a healthy earnings record. The debt ratio and the times-interest-earned ratio are the prime indicators of financial strength from the creditors' viewpoint.

As pointed out in Chapter 20, the use of long-term leases as a method of financing has increased substantially in recent years. Most long-term leases are substitutes for other forms of long-term borrowing and are capitalized in the balance sheets of lessees.

Stockholders' View Present or prospective stockholders are concerned with the company's ability to meet its long-term obligations, because failure to pay interest charges or meet maturities of debt is a serious matter affecting adversely both the credit standing of the company and the position of stockholders. A very low debt ratio, or the absence of long-term debt, is not necessarily to the stockholders' advantage. To the extent that a company can earn a return in excess of the interest rate paid on long-term obligations, its stockholders gain from the leverage factor inherent in a fixed commitment. However, this gain may be more than offset by the increased risks and costs of the various restrictive covenants included in the debt contract by the lender, which may limit management's freedom of action.

It has been argued that the existence of long-term debt or other senior securities increases the risk borne by owners of the common stock and causes the stock to sell at a lower price-earnings ratio. In a well-managed and profitable company, it is doubtful whether a reasonable amount of debt increases the common shareholders' risk sufficiently to be reflected in the price-earnings ratio. If the amount of long-term debt is excessive and earnings are not growing, it is likely that the advantage of increased trading on the equity will be offset by the dampening effect of the large debt on the price of common stock.

Capacity for additional investment and growth in earnings

A business enterprise seldom is able to maintain a stable position over a long period of time; it either changes and grows, or stagnates and dies. A healthy company must be able to finance the development of new products as the old ones lose their profit potential, and to move in new directions as demand and technology change. An important element of financial strength is the ability to generate additional cash when needed.

In part, this means the ability to borrow or to obtain new capital from owners. Another major source of investment capital is earnings retained for use in business operations. Most enterprises typically generate more working capital each period than the amount of net income (see Chapter 23). The amount of working capital provided from operations, less dividend and sinking fund requirements, offers a rough indicator of the internally generated funds available to expand the level of operations (build plant capacity, develop new products, markets, etc.) or to retire long-term debt.

Standards for comparison in analysis

When analysts have computed the significant dollar and percentage changes and ratios and have reduced the mass of financial data to digestible form, they need some criteria as a guide in evaluating these findings and in making business and investment decisions. Three possibilities are discussed in the following sections.

Past Record of the Company A comparison of analytical data over time (sometimes called *horizontal analysis,* in contrast to *vertical analysis,* which deals with single-year financial statements) may reveal trends in performance and position that will aid in determining progress or lack of progress and may help in assessing future prospects. Many companies present trends in sales, earnings, and other data in graphic form. As a basis for forecasting, the projecting of past trends into the future has serious limitations, because changes may reverse direction at any time. However, knowing that the trend is favorable or unfavorable leads to further inquiry as to the underlying reasons.

Another limitation of horizontal analysis is that the past does not afford a basis for comparison with similarly situated companies. For example, if the sales of a company have increased 10%, but industry sales have increased 50%, the 10% increase may appear to be favorable, but the company's sales performance in its industry is very poor.

Comparison with Competitors or Industry as a Whole Perhaps the best way to put a company's performance in perspective is to compare its position and operating results with those of competitors. For example, a study by Dun & Bradstreet, Inc., of the financial statements of drug companies for a recent year showed the following:

Example of financial statistics for an industry

	Current ratio	Net profits on net sales	Return on owners' investment	Total debt to owners' equity	Net sales to inventories (times)
Upper quartile . .	3.5	11.3%	20.4%	35.8%	9.1
Median.	2.6	6.8	15.4	43.5	6.3
Lower quartile . .	1.8	2.9	5.5	63.6	4.6

On the basis of this kind of information, an analyst examining the financial statements of a drug company obtains some idea of the position of the company in relation to others in the industry. Note that Dun & Bradstreet, Inc., apparently computes "inventories turnover" by dividing net sales by the amount of average inventories. Although this procedure often is used by financial analysts as a matter of convenience, it does not measure "turnover," but simply relates the average level of inventory (at cost) to the sales volume for the year (at selling prices).

One of the difficulties in making comparisons among business enterprises is that some enterprises that appear to be in the same industry are not in fact comparable. Industries often are difficult to define. For example, many corporations have diversified their activities by moving into new fields or acquiring other enterprises whose business activities are not closely related, with the result that corporations falling roughly within the same industry are no longer comparable in many respects. When ***diversified enterprises*** report industry segment sales and profitability figures, it is much easier to analyze their financial statements.

In **FASB Statement No. 14,** the Financial Accounting Standards Board established standards for disclosure of information about the reporting company's operations in different industries, its foreign operations and export sales, and its major customers.[8] This **Statement** also required that a company operating predominantly or exclusively in a single industry identify that industry. The information to be reported for each significant industry segment includes: revenue, profitability, identifiable assets, and other related disclosures such as depreciation and capital expenditures. A **significant industry segment** is one which: (1) includes 10% or more of the combined identifiable assets of the company; or (2) generates 10% or more of the company's revenue; or (3) generates 10% or more of the company's operating income or loss. The purpose of disclosure of segment information is to assist users of financial statements to analyze and understand the company's past performance and future prospects.[9] (See **Note 23** on pages 166–168 for International Harvester Company.) A complete discussion of segment reporting appears in **Modern Advanced Accounting** of this series.

Comparison with Independent Statistical Measures It often is used to relate certain financial indexes for a business enterprise to statistical measures. For example, a comparison of the trend of sales or net income with an **index of industrial production** may show whether an enterprise is growing more slowly or faster than the economy. Similarly, indexes may be developed for sales and net income, for example, comparing the performance of a single enterprise to the industry performance index during the same period. Price indexes may be used to deflate sales in dollars to determine whether the growth in sales is a growth in physical volume or the result of inflation. It also may be possible to relate financial data to physical measures of production or output. For example, in the analysis of railroad companies, such statistics as the average freight haul in miles per ton, or the average revenue per ton-mile, give a useful basis for comparing the operating performance of different railroad companies.

Inflation and analysis of financial statements

Financial statements prepared in terms of historical costs do not reflect fully the economic resources or the **real** income (in terms of purchasing power) of a business enterprise. Financial analysts must attempt to evaluate the impact of inflation on the financial position and results of operations of the enterprise they are evaluating. They should raise questions such as: How much of the income can be attributed to price increases? Are expenses (such as depreciation) understated in terms of current

---

[8] *FASB Statement No. 14,* "Financial Reporting for Segments of a Business Enterprise," FASB (Stamford: 1976), p. 1.
[9] Ibid., p. 2.

price levels? Is the company gaining or losing from inflation because of the composition of its assets and the amount of its liabilities? Financial statements adjusted for inflation are illustrated in Chapter 25.

Summary of ratios and other analytical measurements

The more widely used ratios and other measurements discussed in this chapter and their significance are summarized on pages 1020–1021.

The relevance of any of the foregoing measurements depends on the direction of its trend and on its relationship to some predetermined standard. The information available in financial statements can be of great value in appraising the financial position, in forecasting the earning power, and in making other predictive judgments about a company. Relationships among reported data can be extremely informative. However, we must remember that financial statements have limitations and that qualitative factors may be far more important than "cold figures." For example, factors such as the following cannot be ignored by analysts in forecasting the likely earnings performance of a company: (1) Source of markets for its products and services; (2) growth potential for its products and services; (3) market share in its industry; (4) patent protection, if any, for its major products; (5) sensitivity of its earnings to economic fluctuations; and (6) effect of technological and environmental changes on its business activities.

Analysts should keep in mind that although the balance sheet is a statement of assets and claims against these assets, most assets are stated at historical cost, and not all elements of value are included in the balance sheet (for example, capable management, good credit standing, potential new products, internally developed goodwill, and the appreciation in the value of assets, especially natural resources). Furthermore, the **quality of the reported assets** must be carefully evaluated. The income statement, on the other hand, is a product of matching historical costs with realized revenue and covers only a brief period of a company's life. Consequently, the income statement does not necessarily measure the **improvement in the company's economic wealth.** The dangers of attaching too much significance either to the balance sheet or to the income statement should be clearly recognized by those undertaking a serious analysis of financial statements.

REVIEW QUESTIONS

1 Describe four sources from which an outsider might obtain financial information about a business enterprise.

2 Explain what is meant by the following terms:
   a Trend percentage   *d* Capital structure
   b Common-size statements   *e* Growth companies
   c Trading on the equity   *f* Price-earnings ratio

Summary of ratios and other analytical measurements

Ratio or other measurement	Method of computation	What it shows
1 Return on total assets	$$\frac{\text{Net income} + \text{interest expense}}{\text{Average investment in assets}}$$	Productivity of assets
2 Return on common stockholders' equity	$$\frac{\text{Net income} - \text{preferred dividends}}{\text{Average common stockholders' equity}}$$	Earning power on residual owners' equity
3 Earnings per share	$$\frac{\text{Net income} - \text{preferred dividends}}{\text{Average number of shares of common stock outstanding}}$$	Amount earned on each share of common stock
4 Price-earnings ratio	$$\frac{\text{Market price per share}}{\text{Earnings per share}}$$	Whether price of stock is in line with earnings
5 Dividend yield	$$\frac{\text{Dividend per share}}{\text{Market price per share}}$$	Return to stockholders based on current price of stock
6 Number of times interest earned (before income taxes)	$$\frac{\text{Operating income}}{\text{Annual interest expense}}$$	Coverage of interest charges (particularly on long-term debt)
7 Times preferred dividends earned	$$\frac{\text{Net income}}{\text{Annual preferred dividends}}$$	Adequacy of earnings to pay preferred dividends
8 Equity (book value) per share of common stock	$$\frac{\text{Common stockholders' equity}}{\text{Number of shares of common stock outstanding}}$$	Amount of net assets behind each share of common stock
9 Current ratio	$$\frac{\text{Current assets}}{\text{Current liabilities}}$$	Short-run debt-paying ability
10 Quick (acid-test) ratio	$$\frac{\text{Quick assets}}{\text{Current liabilities}}$$	Short-term liquidity
11 Inventories turnover	$$\frac{\text{Cost of goods sold}}{\text{Average inventories}}$$	Ability to control investment in inventories
12 Receivables turnover	$$\frac{\text{Net sales on credit}}{\text{Average receivables}}$$	Possible excessive receivables; effectiveness of collections

(cont.)

13 Debt ratio	$\dfrac{\text{Total liabilities}}{\text{Total assets}}$	*Extent of borrowing and trading on the equity (leverage)*
14 Equity ratio	$\dfrac{\text{Total stockholders' equity}}{\text{Total assets}}$	*Protection to creditors and extent of trading on the equity (leverage)*
15 Debt to equity ratio	$\dfrac{\text{Total debt}}{\text{Total stockholders' equity}}$	*Relationship between borrowed capital and owners' capital*

3 a Discuss some inherent limitations of single-year financial statements for purposes of analysis and interpretation.
  b To what extent are these limitations overcome by the use of comparative financial statements?
  c In what ways can a 10-year summary of financial data be misleading?

4 Describe the effect of each of the transactions listed below on the indicated ratios. Will the ratio increase, decrease, or remain unchanged?

Transactions	*Ratios*
a Purchase of merchandise for cash	**a** Current ratio of 2 to 1
b Payment of accounts payable	**b** Quick ratio of 0.6 to 1
c Accounts receivable written off against Allowance for Doubtful Accounts	**c** Average age of accounts receivable of 60 days
d Declaration of cash dividend on preferred stock	**d** Equity ratio of 60%
e Distribution of a 10% stock dividend	**e** Loss per share of common stock, $1.20
f Conversion of long-term debt to common stock	**f** Return on total long-term capital
g Change from fifo to lifo during period of rising prices	**g** Inventories turnover

5 The following ratios have been used at times by financial analysts. Explain what each ratio indicates, and why it is (or is not) significant.
  a Ratio of plant assets to long-term debt
  b Ratio of net sales to working capital (working capital turnover)
  c Ratio of current liabilities to inventories
  d Ratio of total operating expenses to current liabilities
  e Ratio of plant assets to stockholders' equity
  f Ratio of long-term debt to working capital
  g Ratio of net sales to stockholders' equity
  h Ratio of net income to current assets

6 In analyzing the position and performance of a business enterprise, it is necessary to have some standards or criteria for comparison. Suggest several standards that may be employed.

7 An estimate of inventories turnover sometimes is made by dividing net sales by average inventories. Evaluate this method of computing inventories turnover.

8 What special steps are required to compute the equity (book value) per share of common stock in each of the following cases:
  a Both preferred stock and common stock are outstanding
  b Treasury stock has been acquired.

9 The equity (book value) of 100,000 shares of common stock is $40 a share. Indicate the effect of each of the following four transactions on the equity per share:
  a Issuance of additional shares at $10 pursuant to stock option contract
  b Issuance of additional shares at $60 through rights offering
  c Acquisition of treasury stock at $75 a share
  d Conversion of bonds at 20 shares for every $1,000 bond

10 Two companies have the same amount of working capital. The current debt-paying ability of one company is much weaker than the other. Explain how this could occur.

11 Explain how you would determine the ability of a business enterprise to meet payments on long-term debt or to finance replacements of plant assets, assuming that you had available financial statements for the last five years.

12 If you were asked to choose three analytical computations (ratios, percentages, etc.) that would be most useful in appraising the financial statements of a corporation from the viewpoint of the following parties, which computations would you make, and why do you feel these are of prime importance?
  a Short-term creditor
  b Long-term creditor
  c Prospective investor in the corporation's preferred stock
  d Prospective investor in the corporation's common stock

13 In response to a request that its **profit margins on different products** be disclosed, the management of Dibble Company responded, "Public disclosure would cause us to suffer at the hands of our principal competitors, particularly in regard to one product which accounts for 90% of our sales." In what ways could the disclosure of this information possibly be detrimental to Dibble Company?

14 The following comments by an oil company executive are derived from an article in a financial journal:

> In seeking textbook ratios between current assets and current liabilities, some companies may be going overboard on building up cash. These ratios may not mean much any more. In the old days, when these ratios were established, credit facilities weren't so readily available as they are today. There are elements of liquidity that don't show up on the balance sheet, such as a contractual line of bank credit, which may be just as solid as a savings account. But to some extent, we're stuck with archaic ratios that the investment community likes to see.

Evaluate the comments made by the oil company executive.

15 In *FASB Statement No. 14,* "Financial Reporting for Segments of a Business Enterprise," the FASB established standards for disclosure of information about the reporting enterprise's operations in different industries, its foreign operations and export sales, and its major customers. Define a *significant industry segment* and indicate the type of information that is reported for each such segment.

EXERCISES

Ex. 24-1   Mark Palmer, Inc., has the following capital structure (in millions): 10% bonds, $12.5; 11% preferred stock, $30.0; common stock (paid-in capital and retained earnings), $50.0. Income before interest and income taxes at 40% for the current year was $15 million.
   Compute the amount of earnings available for common stock.

Ex. 24-2   Seacrest Corporation reported earnings per share last year of $4.50 on 100,000 shares of capital stock outstanding during the entire year. On April 1 of the current year, the company declared a 50% stock dividend, and on October 1 it issued 60,000 shares of capital stock for cash. Net income for the current year was $528,000.
   Compute the increase or decrease in earnings per share over last year.

Ex. 24-3   A partial list of trend and common-size percentages for Golden Arc Company for Years 1 and 2 is shown below:

	Year 2	Year 1
Trend percentages:		
Sales (net)	120%	100%
Cost of goods sold	?	100
Gross profit on sales	?	100
Operating expenses and income taxes expense	?	100
Net income	?	100
Common-size percentages:		
Sales (net)	100%	100%
Cost of goods sold	?	?
Gross profit on sales	45%	?%
Operating expenses and income taxes expense	27.5	30
Net income	?%	10%

a Compute the missing trend and common-size percentages.
b If the net income in Year 1 amounted to $10,000, compute the net income for Year 2.

Ex. 24-4   Information for Miklovik Company is presented below and at the top of page 1024.

	Year 2	Year 1
Cash	$ 20,000	$ 30,000
Accounts receivable	60,000	40,000
Less: Allowance for doubtful accounts	(5,000)	(4,000)
Inventories	45,000	35,000
Plant assets (net)	240,000	189,000
Totals	$360,000	$290,000

(cont.)

Accounts payable	$ 50,000	$ 40,000
12% bonds payable	100,000	100,000
Capital stock, $5 par	130,000	100,000
Retained earnings	80,000	50,000
Totals	$360,000	$290,000
Sales (all on credit)	$180,000	$120,000
Cost of goods sold	100,000	70,000
Gross profit on sales	$ 80,000	$ 50,000
Operating expenses and income taxes expense	50,000	30,000
Net income	$ 30,000	$ 20,000

Compute each of the following for Year 2:

a Quick (acid-test) ratio.
b Number of days' sales in gross accounts receivable at year-end. Assume a 365-day year.
c Inventories turnover.
d Equity (book value) per share of capital stock at year-end.
e Number of days' sales in inventories at year-end. Assume a 365-day year.

Ex. 24-5 The information below (in thousands of dollars) for three companies is presented to you at the end of Year 10:

	Ace Company	Bye Company	Coe Company
Total assets	$140,000	$140,000	$140,000
Current liabilities.	$ 20,000	$ 50,000	$ 20,000
10% bonds payable, due in Year 15.	40,000		
12% bonds payable, due in Year 20.		10,000	
10% bonds payable, due in Year 22.			80,000
Stockholders' equity	80,000	80,000	40,000
Total liabilities & stockholders' equity . .	$140,000	$140,000	$140,000
Net income	$ 14,000	$ 12,600	$ 9,800

Compute the following for each company:

a Number of times interest was earned (before income taxes). Assume income tax rate is 50%.
b Rate earned on ending stockholders' equity.
c Rate earned on total assets at end of year (before interest expense and income taxes of 50%).

Ex. 24-6 The comparative balance sheets and other financial information for Pickett & Company, a retail enterprise, are presented on page 1025. Dollar amounts are in thousands.

PICKETT & COMPANY
Comparative Balance Sheets
December 31,
(*in thousands of dollars*)

Assets	Year 2	Year 1
Cash	$ 7,000	$ 4,000
Short-term investments	2,000	4,000
Accounts receivable (net)	13,000	9,000
Inventories	9,000	7,000
Plant assets (net)	69,000	66,000
Total assets	$100,000	$90,000

Liabilities & Stockholders' Equity		
Current liabilities	$ 14,000	$16,000
Bonds payable, due in Year 15	24,000	20,000
Common stock, $10 par	30,000	30,000
Retained earnings	32,000	24,000
Total liabilities & stockholders' equity	$100,000	$90,000

Sales for Year 2 were $100 million, and cost of goods sold amounted to $58 million. Other items from the income statement for Year 2 are: Interest expense, $2 million; income taxes expense, $10 million; and net income, $12 million.

Show how you would compute the following ratios (or measurements) for Year 2 by determining the appropriate dollar or other amounts to be used in computing each item. For example: debt ratio, $38,000 ÷ $100,000.
a Current ratio
b Quick (acid-test) ratio
c Times interest earned (before income taxes)
d Rate of gross profit on sales
e Earnings per share

Ex. 24-7 The following common-size income statements are available for Sigma Corporation for the two years ended December 31, Year 5 and Year 4:

	Year 5	Year 4
Sales	100%	100%
Cost of goods sold	55	70
Gross profit on sales	45%	30%
Operating expenses (including income taxes expense)	20	18
Net income	25%	12%

The trend percentages for sales are as follows:

Year 5	130%
Year 4	100%

Compute the trend percentage for gross profit on sales for Year 5.

Ex. 24-8 Sylvester Corporation has total stockholders' equity of $35,500,000, including $10,750,000 of paid-in capital in excess of par and retained earnings. The capital stock included in stockholders' equity follows:

10% preferred stock, $50 par, callable at $53 per share; 200,000
    shares issued and outstanding (no dividends are in arrears) $10,000,000

Common stock, $10 par, 5,000,000 shares authorized; 1,550,000
    shares issued; 1,500,000 shares outstanding (50,000 shares, cost
    $750,000, in treasury)   15,500,000

    Compute the equity (book value) per share of common stock.

SHORT CASES FOR ANALYSIS AND DECISION

Case 24-1 Shown below and on page 1027 are the financial statements issued by Majestic Company for its fiscal year ended October 31, Year 8:

MAJESTIC COMPANY
Balance Sheet
October 31, Year 8

Assets

Cash	$ 15,000
Accounts receivable (net)	150,000
Inventories	120,000
Total current assets	$285,000
Land	125,000
Trademark (**Note 3**).	250,000
Total assets	$660,000

Liabilities & Stockholders' Equity

Accounts payable		$ 80,000
Accrued liabilities		20,000
Deferred income tax liability (**Note 4**).		80,000
Common stock, $1 par (**Note 5**)	$100,000	
Paid-in capital in excess of par	180,000	
Retained earnings	200,000	480,000
Total liabilities & stockholders' equity		$660,000

MAJESTIC COMPANY
Income Statement
For Year Ended October 31, Year 8

Sales	$1,000,000
Cost of goods sold	750,000
Gross profit on sales	$ 250,000

(cont.)

Expenses:

Doubtful accounts expense	$ 7,000	
Insurance	13,000	
Lease expenses **(Note 1)**	40,000	
Repairs and maintenance	30,000	
Pensions **(Note 2)**	12,000	
Salaries	60,000	$ 162,000
Earnings before income taxes		$ 88,000
Income taxes expense		28,740
Net income		$ 59,260
Earnings per share		$ 0.5926

MAJESTIC COMPANY

Statement of Retained Earnings

For Year Ended October 31, Year 8

Retained earnings, Nov. 1, Year 7	$150,000
Add: Extraordinary gain (net of income tax effect)	25,000
Net income	59,260
Subtotal	$234,260
Less: Dividends ($0.3426 per share)	34,260
Retained earnings, Oct. 31, Year 8	$200,000

Note 1—Long-Term Lease Under the terms of a five-year noncancelable lease for buildings and equipment, the company is obligated to make annual rental payments of $40,000 in each of the next four fiscal years. At the conclusion of the lease term, the company has an option to purchase the leased assets for $20,000 (a bargain purchase option) or renewing the lease for another five-year term at an annual rental of $5,000.

Note 2—Pension Plan Substantially all employees are covered by the company's pension plan. Pension expense is equal to the total of pension benefits paid to retired employees during the year.

Note 3—Trademark The company's trademark was purchased from Apex Corporation on January 2, Year 6, for $250,000.

Note 4—Deferred Income Tax Liability The entire balance in the Deferred Income Tax Liability account arose from tax-exempt municipal bonds that were held during the previous fiscal year, giving rise to a difference between taxable income and reported net income for the fiscal year ended October 31, Year 7. The deferred income tax liability amount was computed on the basis of expected tax rates in future years.

Note 5—Warrants On January 2, Year 7, one common stock warrant was issued to stockholders of record for each common share owned. An additional share of common stock is to be issued on exercise of 10 stock warrants and receipt of an amount equal to par value. For the six months ended October 31, Year 8, the average market price for the company's common stock was $5 a share, and no warrants were exercised.

Note 6—Contingency On October 31, Year 8, the company was contingently liable for product warranties in an amount estimated to aggregate $75,000. This contingency was not recorded.

Instructions Review the preceding financial statements and the related notes. Identify any inclusions or exclusions from them that are in violation of generally accepted accounting principles, and indicate corrective action to be taken. Do not comment as to format or style. Respond in the following order:

Balance Sheet
Income Statement
Statement of Retained Earnings
Notes
General

Case 24-2 Brass Cam Corporation needs additional capital for plant expansion. The board of directors is considering obtaining the funds by issuring additional short-term notes, long-term bonds, preferred stock, or common stock.

Instructions

a What primary factors should the board of directors consider in selecting the best method of financing plant expansion?

b One member of the board of directors suggests that the corporation should maximize trading on the equity, that is, using stockholders' equity as a basis for borrowing additional funds at a lower rate of interest than the expected earnings from the use of the borrowed funds.

(1) Explain how trading on the equity affects earnings per share of common stock.

(2) Explain how a change in income tax rates affects trading on the equity.

(3) Under what circumstances should a corporation seek to trade on the equity to a substantial degree?

c Two specific proposals under consideration by the board of directors are to issue 14% subordinated income bonds, or to issue 14% cumulative, nonparticipating, nonvoting preferred stock, callable at par. In discussing the impact of the two proposals on the debt-to-equity ratio, one member of the board of directors stated that the resulting debt to equity ratio would be the same under either alternative because the income bonds and preferred stock should be included in the same balance sheet classification. What are the arguments (1) for and (2) against inclusion of the subordinated income bonds and the preferred stock in the same balance sheet classification?

Case 24-3 The following information is extracted from reports to stockholders of three large corporations:

(1) Revenue has increased steadily for the past few years and last year rose 10% over that for the previous year to a record $1.6 billion. Earnings from operations rose 19% to $134.2 million, or $3.95 per common share after preferred dividends. Union's profits have grown steadily for the last five years. They have also exceeded industry growth. Our 19% increase compares with 12% for the gas industry and 9% for all industries. (Union Gas Company)

(2) Income reinvested in the business, which also is to the benefit of stockholders, was $130.1 million, or $2.40 per common share. (New Steel Corporation)

(3) The information below relates to Gulf Company (dollar amounts are in millions):

	Year 3	Year 2	Year 1
Gross revenue.	$133	$ 99	$70
Net income	$ 28	$ 18	$12
Working capital	$ 34	$ 52	$87
Current ratio.	2 to 1	5 to 1	10 to 1
Plant assets (net).	$275	$145	$92

Instructions

a Do you think that the information regarding the company's growth compared to industry growth as presented by Union Gas Company is useful to stockholders? Are there any possibilities that such information can be misleading?

b Comment on the information taken from the annual report of New Steel Corporation in view of the following additional facts for the latest year:

(1) Earnings amounted to $4.60 per share compared to an average of $6.59 per share 8 to 10 years ago.

(2) The rate earned on stockholders' equity amounted to less than 8%.

(3) The balance sheet included over $1.28 billion of short-term investments and over $268 million in cash.

c As a stockholder, would you be concerned over the decrease in the current ratio for Gulf Company? Explain carefully.

Case 24-4   As the consultant to the president of Spring Corporation, you are asked to compute some key ratios based on the information in the comparative financial statements. These key ratios will be used by the president to convince creditors that the corporation is solvent and to support the use of going-concern valuation procedures in the financial statements. The president wishes to save time by concentrating on only these key ratios.

The data requested and the computations taken from the financial statements follow:

	This Year	Last Year
Current ratio	2.5:1	2.0:1
Quick (acid-test) ratio	0.7:1	1.2:1
Plant assets to stockholders' equity	2.6:1	2.3:1
Sales to stockholders' equity	2.5:1	2.8:1
Net income	Up 30%	Down 10%
Earnings per common share	$3.12	$2.40
Equity (book value) per common share	Up 5%	Up 8%

Instructions

a The president asks that you prepare a list of brief comments stating how each of these items supports the solvency and going-concern potential of the company. These comments are to be used to support the presentation of data to creditors. You are to prepare the comments as requested, giving the implications and the limitations of each item separately and then the collective inference one may draw from them about the corporation's solvency and going-concern potential.

b Having done as the president requested in part **a**, prepare a brief listing of additional ratio-analysis-type data for the president which you think the creditors are going to ask for to supplement the data provided in part **a**. Explain why you think the additional data will be helpful to creditors in evaluating the solvency of Spring Corporation.

c What warnings should you offer creditors about the limitations of using ratio analysis to evaluate the solvency and the going-concern valuations of assets?

Case 24-5   Betty Simpson, executive vice president of Donald Corporation, was having lunch with three students who were being considered for a position as her assistant. The vice president pointed out that quite a few of her clients were active in acquiring other companies and that "the person who will be hired should be able to make effective overall analyses of the financial strength and operating results of companies that are for sale." In order to get a better line on the business and financial acumen of the three students, she posed the following question to them:

Suppose that I called one of you at 10 P.M. one evening and asked you to fly to Houston the next morning to investigate the operations and financial position of Agnew Corporation, which is for sale at a price of $5 million. I would like to have a preliminary report by phone before 5 P.M. on that same day and a final report within a week. Arrangements have been made for you to visit the corporate offices of Agnew Corporation. What approach would you take in preparing these reports?

The three students then proceeded to summarize their approach to this hypothetical assignment.

Instructions Assuming that you are one of the three students being considered for the position as assistant to the executive vice president, write a brief report summarizing the areas you would evaluate and the approach you would take in preparing the preliminary and the final reports.

Case 24-6 The complete set of financial statements for Andriana Corporation are shown below and on page 1031.

ANDRIANA CORPORATION
Balance Sheet
August 31, Year 6

Assets

Current assets:

Cash		$ 80,000
Accounts receivable (net)		110,000
Inventories		130,000
Total current assets		$ 320,000

Other assets:

Investments in real estate (current fair value)	$1,508,000	
Investment in Chica Co., at cost (Note 2)	160,000	
Plant assets (net)	4,000,000	
Goodwill (Note 3)	250,000	
Discount on bonds payable	42,000	
Total other assets		5,960,000
Total assets		$6,280,000

Liabilities & Stockholders' Equity

Current liabilities:

Accounts payable		$ 140,000
Income taxes payable		320,000
Stock dividend payable		120,000
Total current liabilities		$ 580,000

Other liabilities:

Payable to Reed Co. (Note 4)	$ 300,000	
Liability under employee pension plan	450,000	
Bonds payable (including portion due within one year)	1,000,000	
Deferred income taxes liability	58,000	
Total other liabilities		1,808,000
Total liabilities		$2,388,000

(cont.)

Stockholders' equity:

Common stock	$1,000,000	
Paid-in capital in excess of par	142,000	
Unappropriated retained earnings.	2,750,000	
Total stockholders' equity		$3,892,000
Total liabilities & stockholders' equity.		$6,280,000

ANDRIANA CORPORATION
Statement of Income and Retained Earnings
For Year Ended August 31, Year 6

Sales		$3,500,000
Less: Returns and allowances		35,000
Net sales		$3,465,000
Less: Cost of goods sold		1,039,000
Gross profit on sales		$2,426,000
Less:		
Selling expenses	$1,000,000	
General and administrative expenses (Note 1)	1,079,000	2,079,000
Operating earnings		$ 347,000
Other revenue:		
Purchases discounts	$ 10,000	
Gain on increased value of investments in real estate . . .	100,000	
Gain on sale of treasury stock	200,000	
Correction of error in last year's income statement	90,000	400,000
Ordinary earnings		$ 747,000
Add: Extraordinary item —gain on sale of plant assets		53,000
Income before income taxes		$ 800,000
Less: Income taxes expense		380,000
Net income		$ 420,000
Add: Beginning retained earnings		2,750,000
Subtotal		$3,170,000
Less:		
Dividends (12% stock dividend declared but not issued) .	$ 120,000	
Contingency (Note 4)	300,000	420,000
Ending unappropriated retained earnings		$2,750,000

Notes to financial statements
(1) Depreciation expense is included in general and administrative expenses. During the fiscal year, the company changed from the straight-line method of depreciation to the sum-of-the-years'-digits method.

(2) The company owns 40% of the outstanding common stock of Chica Co. Because the ownership is less than 50%, consolidated financial statements with Chica Co. cannot be presented.

(3) As per federal income tax laws, goodwill is not amortized. The goodwill was acquired in Year 3.

(4) The amount payable to Reed Co. is contingent upon the outcome of a lawsuit which is currently pending. The amount of loss, if any, is not expected to exceed $300,000.

Instructions Identify and explain the deficiencies in the presentation of Andriana's financial statements. If an item appears in both financial statements, identify the deficiencies for each financial statement separately. There are no arithmetical errors in the statements. Organize your answer as follows:

a Deficiencies in the statement of income and retained earnings.

b Deficiencies in the balance sheet.

c General comments.

PROBLEMS

24-1 The major stockholders of Colgate Corporation are concerned over the corporation's current financial position and return on investment. They request your assistance in analyzing the following financial statements:

COLGATE CORPORATION
Statement of Working Capital Deficit
December 31, Year 2

Current liabilities		$223,050
Less: Curent assets:		
Cash.	$ 5,973	
Accounts receivable (net)	70,952	
Inventories	113,125	190,050
Working capital deficit		$ 33,000

COLGATE CORPORATION
Income Statement
For Year Ended December 31, Year 2

Sales	$760,200
Cost of goods sold	452,500
Gross profit on sales	$307,700
Selling and general expenses, including $27,980 depreciation expense	155,660
Income before income taxes	$152,040
Income taxes expense	76,020
Net income	$ 76,020

Assets other than current assets consisted of plant assets with a carrying amount of $443,450 on December 31, Year 2.

Instructions Assuming that Colgate Corporation operates 365 days a year, compute the following (show computations):

a Number of days' sales uncollected on December 31, Year 2.

b Inventories turnover. Assume that the average amount of inventories approximates the year-end balance.

c Number of days' operations required to cover the working capital deficit.

d Rate of return on total assets as a product of asset turnover and the net income ratio (sometimes called profit margin).

24-2 The comparative balance sheets for Auburn Corporation for Year 2 and Year 1 are given on page 1033.

AUBURN CORPORATION
Comparative Balance Sheets
December 31,

	Year 2	Year 1
Assets		
Cash	$ 18,000	$ 12,000
Short-term investments (at cost, which is less than market		
value)	6,000	12,000
Accounts receivable	42,000	30,000
Less: Allowance for doubtful accounts	(12,000)	(6,000)
Inventories	27,000	21,000
Plant assets	270,000	261,000
Less: Accumulated depreciation	(69,000)	(60,000)
Total assets	$282,000	$270,000
Liabilities & Stockholders' Equity		
Accounts payable	$ 12,000	$ 15,000
Accrued liabilities	9,000	3,000
8% long-term note payable, due in Year 12	60,000	60,000
Preferred stock	15,000	30,000
Common stock, $10 par	30,000	30,000
Paid-in capital in excess of par	90,000	90,000
Retained earnings	66,000	42,000
Total liabilities & stockholders' equity	$282,000	$270,000

All sales were made on credit and amounted to $450,000 in Year 2. Gross profit on sales was 40% of sales, and net income was 10% of sales. Income taxes expense was 40% of income before income taxes.

Instructions Compute the following for Year 2:
a Return (before income taxes and interest) on total assets at end of Year 2
b Receivables turnover
c Inventories turnover
d Current ratio
e Quick ratio
f Times interest earned (before income taxes)

24-3 Selected statistics for Elwood Crystal, Inc., for the most recent three years appear below:

	Year 3	Year 2	Year 1
Gross profit percentage.	36%	33⅓%	30%
Inventories turnover	20 times	25 times	14 times
Average inventories	$ 19,200	$18,000	$35,000
Average accounts receivable.	$100,000	$84,375	$43,750
Income tax rate.	40%	30%	20%
Net income as percentage of sales	12%	7%	6%
Maximum credit period allowed to customers	60 days	60 days	30 days

Instructions

a Prepare income statements in comparative form for the three years.

b Comment on the trend in sales volume, the gross profit percentage, and the net income percentage.

c Compute the receivables turnover rates and comment on the trend in view of the changing credit terms. All sales are made on credit.

24-4 You have been assigned by the acquisitions committee of a diversified company to examine a potential acquisition, Salubrious Tan Products, Inc. This company is a merchandiser which appears to be available because of the death of its founder and principal stockholder. Recent financial statements of Salubrious are shown below:

SALUBRIOUS TAN PRODUCTS, INC.

Income Statements

For Years Ended January 31,

	Year 3	Year 2
Sales	$3,000,000	$2,600,000
Less: Costs and expenses:		
Cost of goods sold	$2,256,000	$2,002,000
Wages	350,000	271,000
Supplies	43,600	34,600
Depreciation	100,000	75,000
Interest	22,400	22,400
Loss on write-off of plant assets	75,000	105,000
Total costs and expenses	$2,847,000	$2,510,000
Income before income taxes	$ 153,000	$ 90,000
Income taxes expense	68,000	40,000
Net income	$ 85,000	$ 50,000
Earnings per share	$ 3.08	$ 1.81

SALUBRIOUS TAN PRODUCTS, INC.

Balance Sheets

January 31,

	Year 3	Year 2	Year 1
Assets			
Cash	$ 130,000	$ 120,000	$ 100,000
Accounts receivable (net)	430,000	370,000	300,000
Inventories	400,000	400,000	200,000
Plant assets	900,000	800,000	700,000
Less: Accumulated depreciation	(325,000)	(250,000)	(200,000)
Total assets	$1,535,000	$1,440,000	$1,100,000

(cont.)

	Year 3	Year 2	Year 1
Liabilities & Stockholders' Equity			
Accounts payable	$ 300,000	$ 260,000	$ 220,000
8% notes payable, due Jan. 31, Year 11	280,000	280,000	–0–
Common stock, $25 par	690,000	690,000	690,000
Retained earnings	265,000	210,000	190,000
Total liabilities & stockholders' equity	$1,535,000	$1,440,000	$1,100,000

SALUBRIOUS TAN PRODUCTS, INC.
Statements of Changes in Financial Position (Working Capital Concept)
For Years Ended January 31,

	Year 3	Year 2
Financial resources provided:		
Net income	$ 85,000	$ 50,000
Add: Depreciation	100,000	75,000
Loss on write-off of plant assets.	75,000	105,000
Notes payable	–0–	280,000
Total financial resources provided	$260,000	$510,000
Financial resources applied:		
Plant assets acquired	$200,000	$230,000
Dividends paid	30,000	30,000
Total financial resources applied	$230,000	$260,000
Increase in financial resources (working capital)	$ 30,000	$250,000

Instructions
a Compute the inventories turnover rates for Year 2 and for Year 3.
b Compute the current ratio at the end of Year 3.
c Compute the rate of return on average stockholders' equity for Year 3.
d Summarize the cash flow for Year 3 by revising the statement of changes in financial position to explain the changes in cash position instead of working capital. Prepare a separate analysis to determine the cash provided from operations.
e Comment on the operating results of Salubrious Tan Products, Inc., for Year 3.

24-5   Lobo Company has asked for a line of trade credit from Ball Company. It is estimated that sales to Lobo by Ball will amount to $2,000,000 each year. Ball is a wholesaler that sells nationally, and Lobo is a retail chain operator that has a number of stores in Nebraska. Ball has had a gross profit of approximately 60% in recent years and expects to have a similar gross profit on sales to Lobo. The sales to Lobo will be approximately 15% of Ball's present sales volume. Recent financial statements of Lobo are presented on pages 1036 and 1037.

LOBO COMPANY
Income Statements
For Years Ended December 31,
(in thousands of dollars)

	Year 10	Year 9	Year 8
Net sales	$24,900	$24,500	$24,200
Cost of goods sold	18,000	17,200	16,900
Gross profit on sales	$ 6,900	$ 7,300	$ 7,300
Selling expenses	$ 4,600	$ 4,400	$ 4,300
Administrative expenses	2,700	2,400	2,300
Total expenses	$ 7,300	$ 6,800	$ 6,600
Income (loss) before income taxes expense or credit	$ (400)	$ 500	$ 700
Income taxes expense (credit)	(200)	200	300
Net income (loss)	$ (200)	$ 300	$ 400

LOBO COMPANY
Balance Sheets
December 31,
(in thousands of dollars)

	Year 10	Year 9	Year 8
Assets			
Current assets:			
Cash	$ 1,600	$ 1,800	$ 2,600
Short-term investments (at cost)	–0–	200	400
Accounts and notes receivable (net)	8,500	8,500	8,000
Inventories	2,800	3,200	2,800
Short-term prepayments	600	600	700
Total current assets	$13,500	$14,300	$14,500
Plant assets (net)	5,900	5,400	4,300
Total assets	$19,400	$19,700	$18,800
Liabilities & Stockholders' Equity			
Current liabilities:			
Notes payable	$ 4,200	$ 3,700	$ 3,200
Accounts payable	4,100	3,700	2,800
Accrued liabilities	1,000	1,100	900
Total current liabilities	$ 9,300	$ 8,500	$ 6,900
Long-term debt, 8% ($1 million retired on Dec. 31 each year)	1,000	2,000	3,000
Total liabilities	$10,300	$10,500	$ 9,900
Stockholders' equity	9,100	9,200	8,900
Total liabilities & stockholders' equity	$19,400	$19,700	$18,800

LOBO COMPANY
Statements of Changes in Financial Position
For Years Ended December 31,
(in thousands of dollars)

	Year 10	Year 9	Year 8
Sources of working capital			
Net income (loss)	$(200)	$ 300	$ 400
Add: Depreciation	500	500	400
From operations	$ 300	$ 800	$ 800
Sale of building	–0–	–0–	200
Reissuance of treasury stock	100	100	–0–
Total sources of working capital.	$ 400	$ 900	$1,000
Uses of working capital			
Acquisition of plant assets	$ 1,000	$ 1,600	$1,200
Dividends declared	–0–	100	100
Retirement of long-term debt	1,000	1,000	–0–
Total uses of working capital	$ 2,000	$ 2,700	$1,300
Increase (decrease) in working capital	$(1,600)	$(1,800)	$ (300)

Instructions

a Compute the following ratios for Year 10:
  (1) Rate of return on average total assets (before interest on long-term debt and income taxes)
  (2) Acid-test ratio
  (3) Rate of return on sales
  (4) Current ratio
  (5) Inventories turnover

b As part of the analysis to determine whether or not Ball Company should extend credit to Lobo Company, assume that the ratios below were computed from Lobo's financial statements. For each ratio indicate whether it is a favorable, unfavorable, or neutral statistic in the decision to grant credit to Lobo. Briefly explain your choice for each ratio.

	Year 10	Year 9	Year 8
(1) Rate of return on total assets . . .	(0.87)%	1.12%	1.96%
(2) Rate of return on sales	(0.69)%	0.99%	1.69%
(3) Acid-test ratio	1.19 to 1	1.36 to 1	1.73 to 1
(4) Current ratio	1.67 to 1	1.92 to 1	2.39 to 1
(5) Inventories turnover (times)	4.52	4.32	4.41
(6) Equity relationships:			
Current liabilities	48.0%	43.0%	36.0%
Long-term liabilities	5.0	10.5	16.0
Stockholders' equity	47.0	46.5	48.0
Totals	100.0%	100.0%	100.0%
(7) Asset relationships:			
Current assets	69.5%	72.5%	77.0%
Plant assets	30.5	27.5	23.0
Totals	100.0%	100.0%	100.0%

c Would you grant credit to Lobo Company? Support your answer with facts given in the problem.

d What additional information, if any, would you want before making a final decision?

24-6 Selected information taken from the financial statements for Amalgamated Pipe Corporation for the past four years is shown below:

	Year 10	Year 9	Year 8	Year 7
Net sales	$800,000	$642,000	$624,000	$580,000
Cost of goods sold	560,000	417,300	411,840	400,200
Gross profit on sales	240,000	224,700	212,160	179,800
Net income	56,000	25,680	30,000	34,500
Inventories (fifo basis)	80,000	125,000	82,400	102,000
Accounts receivable	88,000	45,000	50,000	40,000
Industry sales index (Year 7 = 100)	115	112	110	100

All sales are made on credit terms of 2/10, n/30. Use a 365-day year in your computations.

Instructions
a For each of the four years, compute the following and present in tabular form:
  (1) Gross profit as percentage of sales
  (2) Net income as percentage of sales
  (3) Expenses (including income taxes) as percentage of sales
  (4) Number of days' sales in ending inventories (nearest day)
  (5) Number of days' sales in ending accounts receivable (nearest day)
  (6) Index of company's sales to industry sales
b Briefly comment on the trend in each item (1) through (6) in part **a.**

24-7 The stock of Tuborg Clay Company is listed on the New York Stock Exchange. The market price of its common stock was quoted at $19\frac{3}{4}$ a share on December 31, Year 5 and Year 4. The company's balance sheets on December 31, Year 5 and Year 4, and the statements of income and retained earnings for the years then ended, are presented on pages 1039 and 1040.

TUBORG CLAY COMPANY
Balance Sheets
December 31,
(in thousands of dollars)

	Year 5	Year 4
Assets		
Current assets:		
Cash	$ 3,500	$ 3,600
Short-term investments (at cost, which approximates		
market)	13,000	11,000
Accounts receivable (net)	105,000	95,000
Inventories (at lower of cost or market)	126,000	154,000
Short-term prepayments.	2,500	2,400
Total current assets	$250,000	$266,000
Investments (at equity).	2,000	3,000
Plant assets (net)	311,000	308,000
Goodwill and patents (net)	6,000	6,500
Other assets	21,000	24,500
Total assets	$590,000	$608,000

Liabilities & Stockholders' Equity

	Year 5	Year 4
Current liabilities:		
Notes payable	$ 5,000	$ 15,000
Accounts payable	38,000	48,000
Accrued liabilities	24,500	27,000
Income taxes payable	1,000	1,000
Payments due within one year on long-term debt	6,500	7,000
Total current liabilities	$ 75,000	$ 98,000
Long-term debt	169,000	180,000
Deferred income tax liability.	74,000	67,000
Other liabilities	9,000	8,000
Total liabilities	$327,000	$353,000
Stockholders' equity:		
10% cumulative preferred stock, $100 par and call price;		
authorized 50,000 shares; issued and outstanding		
40,000 shares	$ 4,000	$ 4,000
Common stock, $1 par; authorized 20,000,000 shares; is-		
sued and outstanding 10,000,000 shares	10,000	10,000
Paid-in capital in excess of par	107,000	107,000
Retained earnings	142,000	134,000
Total stockholders' equity	$263,000	$255,000
Total liabilities & stockholders' equity	$590,000	$608,000

TUBORG CLAY COMPANY
Statements of Income and Retained Earnings
For Years Ended December 31,
(in thousands of dollars)

	Year 5	Year 4
Net sales	$600,000	$500,000
Costs and expenses:		
Cost of goods sold	$490,000	$400,000
Selling, general, and administrative expenses	66,000	60,000
Other	7,000	6,000
Total costs and expenses	$563,000	$466,000
Income before income taxes	$ 37,000	$ 34,000
Income taxes expense	16,800	15,800
Net income	$ 20,200	$ 18,200
Retained earnings, beginning of year	134,000	126,200
Dividends on common stock	(11,800)	(10,000)
Dividends on preferred stock	(400)	(400)
Retained earnings, end of year	$142,000	$134,000

Instructions Based on the above information, compute items **a** through **h** for Year 5 (show supporting computations):

a Current ratio
b Quick (acid-test) ratio
c Number of days' sales in average net accounts receivable, assuming a business year consists of 365 days and all sales are on credit
d Inventories turnover rate
e Equity (book value) per share of common stock
f Earnings per share of common stock
g Price-earnings ratio on common stock
h Dividend payout ratio (for preferred and common stock combined)

24-8 The income statement, balance sheet, and additional information for Charles Steel & Company are shown below and on page 1041.

CHARLES STEEL & COMPANY
Income Statement
For Year Ended December 31, Year 1

Net sales	$1,500,000
Cost of goods sold	900,000
Gross profit on sales	$ 600,000
Expenses (including bond interest expense)	498,000
Income before income taxes	$ 102,000
Income taxes expense	37,000
Net income	$ 65,000

CHARLES STEEL & COMPANY
Balance Sheet
December 31, Year 1
Assets

Cash	$ 174,000
Accounts receivable (net)	566,000
Inventories	320,000
Plant assets (net)	740,000
Patents (net)	26,000
Other intangible assets (net)	14,000
Total assets	$1,840,000

Liabilities & Stockholders' Equity

Accounts payable	$ 194,000
Income taxes payable	32,000
Miscellaneous liabilities	38,000
10% bonds payable, due Year 18	300,000
7% cumulative, nonparticipating preferred stock, $100 par, callable at	
$110	200,000
Common stock, no-par, 50,000 shares authorized, issued, and out-	
standing	400,000
Retained earnings	720,000
Treasury stock, 400 shares of preferred stock	(44,000)
Total liabilities & stockholders' equity	$1,840,000

Additional information There are no preferred dividends in arrears, and the balances in the Accounts Receivable and Inventories accounts are unchanged from January 1, Year 1. There were no changes in the Bonds Payable, Preferred Stock, or Common Stock accounts during Year 1. All sales are made on credit.

Instructions From the foregoing information, compute the following to the nearest tenth:
a The current ratio on December 31, Year 1.
b The number of times bond interest was earned during Year 1, using the theoretically preferable method.
c The number of days' sales in inventories at the end of Year 1. Use calendar days rather than working days.
d The average number of days in the operating cycle during Year 1.
e The equity (book value) per share of common stock on December 31, Year 1.
f The rate of return for Year 1, based on the year-end common stockholders' equity.
g The debt ratio, with debt defined as total liabilities, on December 31, Year 1.
h The equity ratio on December 31, Year 1.

24-9   Ratio analysis often is applied to test the reasonableness of the relationships among current financial data against those of prior-year financial data. Given prior financial relationships and a few key amounts, a CPA can prepare estimates of current financial data to test the reasonableness of data furnished by a client.

Southern Wholesaling Corporation has in recent prior years maintained the following relationships among the data in its financial statements:

(1) Gross profit rate on net sales	*40%*
(2) Net income rate on net sales	*10%*
(3) Rate of selling expenses to net sales	*15%*
(4) Receivables turnover	*8 per year*
(5) Inventories turnover	*6 per year*
(6) Quick (acid-test) ratio	*2 to 1*
(7) Current ratio	*3 to 1*
(8) Quick-asset composition —8% cash, 32% short-term	
investments, 60% accounts receivable	
(9) Assets turnover	*2 per year*
(10) Ratio of total assets to intangible assets	*20 to 1*
(11) Ratio of accumulated depreciation to cost of plant assets . . .	*1 to 3*
(12) Ratio of accounts receivable to accounts payable	*1.5 to 1*
(13) Ratio of working capital to stockholders' equity	*1 to 1.6*
(14) Ratio of total debt to stockholders' equity	*1 to 2*

The corporation had a net income of $120,000 for Year 15, after income taxes at the rate of 50%, which resulted in earnings of $2.60 per share of common stock. Additional information includes the following:

(1) Capital stock authorized, issued (all in Year 2), and outstanding:
  Preferred, 6% cumulative, nonparticipating, $50 par, issued at 10% above par
  Common, $5 par, issued at 10% above par
(2) Market price of common stock on December 31, Year 15, was $31.25 a share.
(3) Preferred dividends paid in Year 15, $3,000.
(4) Times interest earned in Year 15, 16 times (after interest and income taxes).
(5) The amounts of the following were the same on December 31, Year 15, as on January 1, Year 15; inventories, accounts receivable, 10% bonds payable— due Year 27, and total stockholders' equity.
(6) All purchases and sales were on credit.

Instructions
a Prepare the condensed (1) income statement, and (2) balance sheet for the year ended December 31, Year 15, presenting the amounts you would expect to appear in Southern Wholesaling Corporation's financial statements. Captions appearing in the balance sheet are: Current Assets, Plant Assets, Intangible Assets, Current Liabilities, Long-term Liabilities, and Stockholders' Equity. In addition to the accounts given in the problem, you should include accounts for Short-term Prepayments, Accrued Liabilities, and Administrative Expenses. Show supporting computations.
b Compute the following for Year 15 (show computations): (1) Rate of return on stockholders' equity, (2) price-earnings ratio for common stock, (3) dividends paid per share of common stock, and (4) dividends paid per share of preferred stock.

25 ACCOUNTING FOR INFLATION

One of the primary purposes of financial statements is to provide information for decision making. Decision makers such as investors, creditors, and management realize that financial statements prepared under generally accepted accounting principles may not reflect current economic realities. As a result, it has been suggested that financial statements would be more useful if historical costs were adjusted for the changing value of the dollar, or if historical costs were abandoned entirely and replaced with current fair values or with current costs.

In this chapter we describe some conceptual issues that are faced by accountants and users of financial statements when changes in the general price level or changes in the current costs of assets are incorporated into the accounting model. The final section of this chapter includes a discussion of *FASB Statement No. 33,* "Financial Reporting and Changing Prices," which requires disclosure of *constant-dollar* and *current-cost* information by some large publicly owned corporations.

FINANCIAL STATEMENTS RESTATED FOR CHANGES IN THE GENERAL PRICE LEVEL

Needed: A stable measurement unit

We have seen in preceding chapters that money is the common denominator used in the preparation of financial statements. The dollar, or any other monetary unit, represents a unit of value; it measures the amount of purchasing power available to obtain goods and services. Implicit in the use of money as a measuring unit is the assumption that the dollar is a stable unit of value, just as the mile is a stable unit of distance and an acre is a stable unit of area. But unlike the mile and the acre, the dollar is not a stable measurement unit.

For many years the prices of goods and services in the United States economy have been rising. When the general price level rises, the value of money decreases. The *general price level* is the weighted average of the prices of goods and services in the economy and is measured by an *index* with a base year assigned a value of 100. The reciprocal of the general price-level index represents the *purchasing power* of the dollar. Thus, if Year 1 = 100 and Year 5 = 125, the current (Year 5) purchasing power of the dollar amounts to only 80% (100 ÷ 125 = 0.80) of the base-year dollar; in other words, prices have risen 25%, and purchasing power has decreased by 20%. The most common measurements of the general

1043

price level are: **Consumer Price Index, Producer Price Index,** and **Gross National Product Implicit Price Deflator.** The FASB selected the Consumer Price Index for All Urban Consumers (CPI-U) for the computation of information on a constant-dollar basis.[1] Based on this index, the purchasing power of the dollar at the end of 1980 was less than one-half of its purchasing power at the end of 1972.

Despite the steady erosion in the purchasing power of the dollar in the United States for nearly 50 years, accountants have continued to assume that the value of the dollar is stable. Income tax laws also ignore changes in the purchasing power of the dollar. This unrealistic assumption is one of the reasons why traditional financial statements are considered by many users to be potentially misleading. Consequently, proposals have been made to restate the **historical-cost/nominal-dollar** financial statements to **constant dollars** by use of an appropriate general price-level index.

Historical costs versus current fair value

Even if the historical-cost/nominal-dollar financial statements were restated to reflect the changing value of the dollar, the resulting statements would still be presented in terms of historical costs and would not reflect the current fair values of assets. For example, a tract of land that cost $1 million would be restated at $1.5 million if the general price level had risen by 50%. However, the current fair value of the land might be $5 million because the price of land had risen more than the general price level. Historical cost reflects the fair value of an asset on the date of acquisition; but a significant change in the fair value of the asset after acquisition tends to make historical cost irrelevant for decision-making purposes. As a result, many users of financial statements have argued that **current fair values** of assets should replace historical costs as a valuation basis used in the preparation of financial statements.

Effects of inflation on financial statements

As stated earlier, the United States economy has experienced persistent inflation (increase in the general level of prices) for many years. Stated another way, the value of the dollar has been falling. How does inflation affect the measurement of income and the presentation of financial position for a business enterprise? Suppose that Wasatch Company acquired a building for $1 million early in Year 1 when the general price-level index was 100. The building has an estimated economic life of 20 years and has been depreciated at the rate of $50,000 a year. Assume that the general price-level index at the end of Year 5 is 200; thus, the cost of the building in end-of-Year 5 dollars is $2 million. **The higher constant-dollar cost of the building is attributed entirely to the decrease**

[1] *FASB Statement No. 33,* "Financial Reporting and Changing Prices," FASB (Stamford: 1979), p. 14.

in the purchasing power of the dollar; a doubling in the general price-level index means that a dollar at the end of Year 5 can buy only half as much as in Year 1. Financial statements prepared in accordance with generally accepted accounting principles at the end of Year 5 would include the following information relating to the building:

Data from historical-cost/nominal-dollar financial statements

WASATCH COMPANY
Data from Historical-Cost/Nominal-Dollar Financial Statements
For Year 5

Balance sheet		Income statement	
Building	$1,000,000	Depreciation expense. . .	$50,000
Less: Accumulated deprecia-tion.	250,000		
Carrying amount of building .	$ 750,000		

Is this a meaningful portrayal of economic facts? Clearly it is not. Giving effect to the 50% reduction in the purchasing power of the dollar (100% increase in the general price-level index), the information would be presented more meaningfully as follows:

Data from historical-cost/constant-dollar financial statements

WASATCH COMPANY
Data from Historical-Cost/Constant-Dollar Financial Statements
For Year 5

Balance sheet		Income statement	
Building	$2,000,000	Depreciation expense . .	$100,000
Less: Accumulated deprecia-tion.	500,000		
Carrying amount of building .	$1,500,000		

Both presentations are stated in terms of historical cost; however, in the latter the historical cost is adjusted to reflect the current general price-level index. The increase of $750,000 in the carrying amount of the building would be reflected in the stockholders' equity section of the balance sheet. When financial statements are not adjusted for changes in the general price-level index, carrying amounts of depreciable assets and depreciation expense may be significantly misstated; similarly, inventories, cost of goods sold, other nonmonetary assets, and various other expenses also may be misstated. When the effects of changes in the general price-level index are ignored, net income is measured by matching costs and revenue expressed in *nominal dollars* having *different purchasing power.*

Income Measurement and Maintenance of Capital   Suppose you buy 1,000 pounds of sugar for $400 when the general price level is 100 and sell the sugar for $430 when the general price level reaches 110. How much profit did you make on the transaction? By comparing your cost of $400 with the proceeds of $430, you conclude that you earned a profit of $30. However, in arriving at this result, you are using different types of dollars. It would be more logical to say that your investment of $400 is now equivalent to $440 in terms of current dollars and that you actually lost $10 on the transaction because you cannot buy for $430 now what you could have bought for $400 when you made the investment. In other words, you failed to recover your investment and thus suffered an economic loss (loss in purchasing power) of $10 on the transaction.

To illustrate this point with another example, suppose that a business enterprise acquired land in Year 1 for $100,000 and sold it for $200,000 in Year 11. If the general price-level index doubled during that 10-year period, thus cutting the value of money in half, the enterprise is not "better off" from an economic standpoint as a result of these two transactions; the $200,000 received for the land in Year 11 is equal to the $100,000 invested in Year 1. In terms of the dollar as a measuring unit, however, accountants would record a gain of $100,000 ($200,000 − $100,000) in Year 11 under historical-cost/nominal-dollar accounting. Thus, by combining the Year 1 and Year 11 transactions in dollar terms, accountants conclude that the enterprise is "better off" (by reporting a gain) if it recovers more than the original **number of dollars** invested in the land.

Failure to consider the changing value of money in the preparation of financial statements in a period of inflation means that what is reported as income may be in part, a recovery of capital. The amount of **original capital invested in the business enterprise would not be maintained,** and taxable income, income taxes expense, and net income may be overstated. Taxable income may be overstated because depreciation expense is not large enough to offset the inflation in the prices of plant assets. This characteristic of traditional financial statements is perhaps the major argument in favor of **constant-dollar** accounting. However, failure to recognize the effect of price-level changes during a period of inflation does not necessarily result in an overstatement of net income, because there may be an offsetting purchasing power gain from borrowing. This point is explained in the following section.

Monetary Items and Purchasing Power Gains and Losses   In discussions of the changing value of the dollar, balance sheet accounts are classified either as monetary or as nonmonetary items. Cash, certificates of deposit, notes receivable, accounts receivable, investments in nonconvertible bonds that will be held to maturity, and most liabilities are examples of **monetary items** because they represent current buying power or legal obligations to pay a fixed number of dollars. All other balance sheet accounts (inventories, investments in common stocks, plant assets, intangible assets, and stockholders' equity accounts) are examples of **nonmonetary items.**

Changes in the general price level give rise to gains and losses (known as **purchasing power gains and losses**) as a result of an enterprise's holding monetary items. The ownership of cash or claims to cash in the form of notes and accounts receivable result in a loss of purchasing power when the general price level is rising; in contrast, a policy of borrowing during a period when the general price level is rising results in a gain of purchasing power because the monetary liabilities can be paid with cheaper dollars. We can summarize this point as follows: When the general price level is rising, it is advantageous to be in a **negative monetary position,** that is, to hold an excess of monetary liabilities over monetary assets; a **positive monetary position** (excess of monetary assets over monetary liabilities) results in a loss of purchasing power when the general price level is rising. To illustrate, assume the following balance sheets (in millions of dollars) for two business enterprises:

	X Company	Y Company
Cash and receivables	$600	$100
Inventories and plant assets (net)	300	800
Total assets	$900	$900
Liabilities (current and long-term)	$200	$650
Stockholders' equity	700	250
Total liabilities & stockholders' equity	$900	$900

Comparative balance sheets: historical-cost/nominal-dollar accounting

If the general price-level index had increased by 10% (from 120 to 132, for example) since the two enterprises acquired the nonmonetary assets (inventories and plant assets) and incurred the liabilities, the balance sheets restated to constant dollars would be as shown below:

	X Company	Y Company
Cash and receivables	$600	$100
Inventories and plant assets (net)	330 ($300 × 1.1)	880 ($800 × 1.1)
Total assets	$930	$980
Liabilities (current and long-term)	$200	$650
Stockholders' equity	770 ($700 × 1.1)	275 ($250 × 1.1)
Purchasing power gain or (loss)	(40)*	55†
Total liabilities & stockholders' equity .	$930	$980

Comparative balance sheets: historical-cost/constant-dollar accounting

* Loss from holding cash and receivables, $60 ($600 × 0.10 = $60), reduced by the gain from borrowing, $20 ($200 × 0.10 = $20) = $40. X Company has a positive monetary position.
† Gain from borrowing, $65 ($650 × 0.10 = $65), reduced by the loss from holding cash and receivables, $10 ($100 × 0.10 = $10) = $55. Y Company has a negative monetary position.

The nonmonetary items (inventories, plant assets, and stockholders' equity) are restated to constant dollars by use of a **conversion factor** of 1.1 (132 ÷ 120 = 1.1).[2] Stated another way, the current general price-level index is equal to 110% of the index at the date when inventories and plant assets were acquired. Monetary items are not restated because these items are stated in terms of constant dollars.

To illustrate the fundamental effects of inflation on the two enterprises we used a somewhat static and oversimplified example; we assumed that all assets and liabilities remained unchanged while the general price-level index was rising by 10%. The effects of general price-level changes on revenue and expenses are illustrated in a subsequent section of this chapter.

FAIR-VALUE ACCOUNTING

Significance of changes of value

The restatement of historical-cost/nominal-dollar financial statements for price-level changes is an effort to recognize the fact that the value of the dollar is not stable. Such financial statements require no other departures from generally accepted accounting principles. Some accountants believe that an additional departure is needed to add relevance and usefulness to financial statements. In their view, historical costs and completed transactions should be replaced by **fair-value accounting.** They argue that financial statements showing current fair values of assets and the changes in such values convey a more meaningful picture of the financial position and earning power of a business enterprise.

To illustrate, suppose that an enterprise acquired land for $100,000 and erected a factory building for $600,000. The building is being depreciated over a 30-year life with no residual value, or $20,000 a year. During the first 10 years the fair values of the land and building increased substantially. At the end of the 10-year period (during which the general price level remained stable), it was apparent that the land and building were worth considerably more than their carrying amounts. As a result, the financial statements for the enterprise in the eleventh year showed: (1) Assets that were substantially below current fair value; (2) net income that was overstated because the full economic cost of using the building was not reflected in annual depreciation expense; and (3) rates of return on assets and stockholders' equity that were overstated, be-

---

[2] The adjustment of financial statements for changes in the general price-level index generally is facilitated by computing the relationship between the current index and the base-year index as a **conversion factor** in decimal form. For example, a current index of 126.9 and a base-year (or date-of-transaction) index of 90 gives a conversion factor of 1.41 (126.9 ÷ 90 = 1.41).

cause what essentially was capital recovery in terms of current prices was being reported as a part of net income.

Assuming that at the beginning of the eleventh year the current fair value of the land was $180,000 and the current fair value of the building was $1,000,000 (cost if new of $1,500,000 less depreciation on such cost to date of $500,000), the appraisal **might** be recorded as follows:

Possible journal entry to record current fair values of plant assets

Land—Appraisal Increase	*80,000*	
Building—Appraisal Increase	*900,000*	
Accumulated Depreciation—Appraisal Increase		*300,000*
Appraisal Capital		*680,000*
To record appraisal of land and building to current fair value.		

The annual depreciation expense on the building would be $50,000 ($1,500,000 ÷ 30 years = $50,000) to reflect the current cost of building services being consumed. The balance sheet would show land and building at amounts approximating current fair value, and net income would represent the amount by which the enterprise was "better off" after recovering the current fair value of the remaining building services over the next 20 years (assuming that no further value changes occurred during that period).

Relationship between constant-dollar accounting and fair-value accounting

The use of fair-value accounting does not mean that changes in the general price level would be ignored. Constant-dollar accounting and fair-value accounting are complementary responses to different measurement problems. The two approaches are not mutually exclusive alternatives. Dealing with one is not a substitute for dealing with the other, and either or both approaches may be adopted in a set of financial statements. Restatement of financial statements for general price-level changes does not attempt to deal with specific price changes, and fair-value accounting does not deal specifically with inflation. The different alternatives that may be followed in the preparation of financial statements are:

1 Historical cost/nominal dollars
2 Historical cost/constant dollars
3 Current fair value, without separate identification of the effects of general price-level changes
4 Current fair value, with th effects of general price-level changes shown separately

Financial statements adjusted for changes in the general price level are based on historical costs; however, the unit of measurement (the dollar) is adjusted to reflect changes in its general purchasing power. In contrast, fair-value accounting is a departure from historical cost because the current fair values for assets are derived from appraisals that reflect both changes in the general price level and changes in the relative price levels of specific goods. Thus, fair-value accounting represents a clear break from historical cost for a particular business enterprise. For example, if M Company and N Company bought identical assets at different dates and price levels, historical-cost/constant-dollar accounting would give different adjusted values for the assets of each enterprise. However, fair-value accounting would give the **same value** for the assets of both enterprises because fair-value accounting is not concerned with historical costs.

If changes in the general price level **are not** incorporated in fair-value financial statements, the difference between historical costs and current fair values of assets is referred to as an **unrealized holding gain or loss;** the unrealized holding gain or loss, net of the tax effect, is reported as a separate item in the income statement. If changes in the general price level **are** incorporated in fair-value financial statements, the unrealized holding gain or loss (difference between historical costs and current fair values of assets) consists of (1) a net purchasing power gain or loss, and (2) the net gain or loss resulting from changes in the relative values of specific assets. These two distinct types of net gains or losses are reported separately in the income statement.

Use of current fair values in the preparation of financial statements

Proposals to incorporate current fair values in accounting measurements are not entirely of recent origin. For example, fair values are used in the application of the lower-of-cost-or-market rule to the valuation of inventories and marketable securities, and assets may be written down to current fair value in a quasi-reorganization. In such cases the use of current fair values results in a reduction in the carrying amounts of assets **below** cost (or carrying amount in terms of historical cost). However, current fair values also are used when such values exceed historical cost. For example, marketable securities held by mutual funds and inventories of certain metals and agricultural products frequently are reported at current fair (or market) value.

Estimates of current fair value

Thus far, we have mentioned the possibility of replacing historical costs of assets with current fair values without specifying how these values might be determined. The concept of current fair value most widely referred to in legal proceedings is "an exchange price that a willing and well-informed buyer and an equally willing and well-informed seller would reach through negotiation." This should not be confused with *market value,* which is the price obtainable currently for any asset. No single method of estimating current fair value is entirely satisfactory; therefore, in order to be able to evaluate intelligently the arguments for and against fair-value accounting, it may be helpful to identify some of the methods used to estimate current fair value.

Capitalization of Net Cash Inflows   In theory, the ideal way to estimate the current fair value or *economic value* of an asset is to compute the present discounted amount of the probable future net cash inflows expected to result from the use of the asset. This is known as *direct valuation.* A limitation of the direct valuation approach is that estimates of future net cash inflows are likely to be highly subjective. More importantly, the earnings and cash inflows of a business enterprise are a joint product of all its resources, and it is virtually impossible to identify clearly the contribution to earnings and cash inflows of a particular asset. The concept of direct valuation, although somewhat impractical for the valuation of specific assets, is useful for appraising the merits of two *indirect valuation* methods discussed below.

Exit Values   The *current exit value* of an asset is the amount that could be realized from its current sale; the *expected exit value* of an asset is the nondiscounted amount of cash to which the asset is expected to be converted in the course of operations. Exit values may be viewed as fair values only for assets that are in fact offered for sale, and as minimum values for assets that are continued in use. However, in many cases the fair values of assets may be materially above exit values. Exit values are related to, but are not identical to, market values because exit values may imply an urgent need to sell. Although reasonable estimates of exit values can be made for certain assets such as investments in marketable securities and inventories, estimates of exit values for special-purpose equipment and intangible assets, for example, may be quite difficult to obtain.

Current Cost   The *current cost* of an asset is the estimated cost of acquiring a *new* and substantially *equivalent* asset at current prices, adjusted for estimated depreciation since acquisition and for any operating advantages or disadvantages of the asset.[3] Current cost can be approximated by applying an appropriate *specific-price index* to the historical cost of assets, particularly plant assets. Specific-price indexes are available for broad categories of plant assets. The application of specific-price indexes to determine current cost of plant assets is illustrated on top of page 1052.

---

[3] *FASB Statement No. 33,* pp. 48–49.

Assets	Historical cost	Specific-price indexes at date of acquisition	Current specific-price indexes	Conversion factor	Current cost
Building	$200,000	100	125	1.25 (125/100)	$250,000
Less: Accumulated depreciation . . .	60,000	100	125	1.25 (125/100)	75,000
Carrying amount of building	$140,000				$175,000
Land	400,000	120	168	1.40 (168/120)	560,000

The building was acquired for $200,000 when the specific-price index for building construction in this industry was 100. Because the index now stands at 125, the historical cost of the building is restated to a current cost of $250,000 ($200,000 × 1.25 = $250,000); accumulated depreciation similarly is adjusted. The specific-price index of land costs in the geographic area where the land is located increased from 120 to 168 since the land was acquired; therefore, the historical cost of the land, $400,000, is multiplied by 1.40 (168 ÷ 120 = 1.40) to compute the current cost of $560,000.

This brief discussion should serve to point out that much sharper asset valuation techniques must be developed before fair-value accounting becomes a practical alternative for the preparation of financial statements.

THE FASB'S APPROACH TO ACCOUNTING FOR INFLATION

In *FASB Statement No. 33,* "Financial Reporting and Changing Prices," the FASB adopted components of both constant-dollar accounting and current-cost accounting as *supplementary information* to be included by large publicly owned corporations in their annual reports, together with conventional financial statements. Corporations are subject to the requirements of *FASB Statement No. 33* if they have total assets exceeding $1 billion, or if inventories and net plant assets total more than $125 million. The *minimum* disclosure requirements for the supplementary information were summarized as follows:[4]

A An enterprise is required to disclose (as supplementary information):
  1 Information on income from continuing operations for the current fiscal year on a historical-cost/constant-dollar basis
  2 The purchasing power gain or loss on net monetary items for the current fiscal year
  3 Information on income from continuing operations for the current fiscal year on a current-cost basis

[4] Ibid., pp. 11–14.

4 The current-cost amounts of inventories and plant assets at the end of the current fiscal year

5 Increases or decreases for the current fiscal year in the current-cost amounts of inventories and plant assets, net of inflation

B An enterprise shall disclose, in notes to the supplementary information:

1 The principal types of information used to calculate the current cost of inventories, plant assets, cost of goods sold, and depreciation, depletion, and amortization expense

2 Any differences between (1) the depreciation methods, estimates of economic lives, and residual values of assets used for calculations of historical-cost/constant-dollar depreciation and current-cost depreciation, and (2) the methods and estimates used for calculations of depreciation in the primary financial statements

3 The exclusion from the computations of supplementary information of any adjustments to or allocations of the amount of income taxes expense in the primary financial statements

C An enterprise is required to disclose the following information for each of its five most recent fiscal years:

1 Net sales and other operating revenue

2 Historical-cost/constant-dollar information

    a Income from continuing operations

    b Income per share of common stock from continuing operations

    c Net assets at fiscal year-end

3 Current-cost information

    a Income from continuing operations

    b Income per share of common stock from continuing operations

    c Net assets at fiscal year-end

    d Increases or decreases in the current cost amounts of inventories and plant assets, net of inflation

4 Other information

    a Purchasing power gain or loss on net monetary items

    b Cash dividends declared per share of common stock

    c Market price per share of common stock at fiscal year-end

All enterprises shall report, in a note to the five-year summary, the average level or the end-of-year level (whichever is used for the measurement of income from continuing operations) of the Consumer Price Index for each year included in the summary.

If an enterprise chooses to state net assets, in the five-year summary, at amounts computed from comprehensive financial statements prepared on a historical-cost/constant-dollar basis or on a current-cost/constant-dollar basis, that fact shall be disclosed in a note to the five-year summary.

Enterprises shall provide, in their financial reports, explanations of the information disclosed in accordance with **FASB Statement No. 33** and discussions of its significance in the circumstances of the enterprise.

The FASB provided the additional information outlined below to explain the minimum disclosure requirements for constant-dollar and current-cost data:[5]

1 **Income from continuing operations** is income after applicable income taxes but excluding the results of discontinued operations, extraordinary items, and the cumulative effects of accounting changes. If none of the foregoing is present for a business enterprise, income from continuing operations is identical to net income.

[5] Ibid., pp. 9, 11, 12, 14, 17, 20–22.

2 The purchasing power gain or loss on net monetary items and the increase or decrease in current-cost amounts are excluded from income from continuing operations.

3 Current-cost information need not be disclosed if it is not materially different from constant-dollar information. The reason for omission of current-cost information must be disclosed in notes to the supplementary information.

4 Information relating to income from continuing operations may be presented either in the format of a conventional income statement or in a reconciliation format that discloses adjustments to income from continuing operations in the historical-cost/nominal-dollar income statement.

5 The *average* Consumer Price Index for All Urban Consumers is used by business enterprises that present only the minimum constant-dollar data for a fiscal year. If an enterprise presents comprehensive financial statements on a constant-dollar basis, either the *average* or the *end-of-year* CPI-U may be used.

6 An enterprise that presents only the minimum data required by *FASB Statement No. 33* need not restate any financial statement amounts other than inventories, plant assets, cost of goods sold, and depreciation, depletion, and amortization expense.

7 If the historical-cost/constant-dollar amounts or the current-cost amounts of inventories and plant assets exceed the recoverable amounts of those assets, all data required by *FASB Statement No. 33* must be presented on the basis of the lower recoverable amounts. *Recoverable amount for an asset expected to be sold* is its net realizable value (expected sales proceeds less costs of completion and disposal). *Recoverable amount for an asset continuing in use* is its value in use (net present value of future cash inflows, including ultimate proceeds on disposal). Thus, *value in use* is synonymous with *direct valuation* (see page 1051).

8 Current cost of inventories, plant assets, cost of goods sold, and depreciation, depletion, and amortization expense may be determined by one of the following methods:

    a Indexation by use of either externally or internally developed specific-price indexes

    b Direct pricing by use of current invoice prices; vendors' price lists, quotations, or estimates; or standard manufacturing costs that reflect current costs

Illustration of historical-cost/constant-dollar accounting

Data for Illustration A relatively simple set of financial statements for Baker Company illustrates the application of the constant-dollar provisions of *FASB Statement No. 33.* Baker Company was organized on December 31, Year 4, as a result of a business combination of several separate business enterprises that had operated as partnerships and single proprietorships. All assets were recorded by Baker Company at current fair values on December 31, Year 4. The Consumer Price Indexes for All Urban Consumers (CPI-U) and the related conversion factors for Year 5 are presented at the top of page 1055.

Indexes and conversion factors for Year 5

	CPI-U	Conversion factor to restate to end-of-Year 5 dollars
End of Year 4 (and beginning of Year 5)	150.0	1.092*
Average for Year 5 (also on July 1)	157.5	1.040†
End of Year 5	163.8	1.000

* 163.8 ÷ 150.0 = 1.092
† 163.8 ÷ 157.5 = 1.040

The comparative historical-cost/nominal-dollar balance sheets at the end of Year 4 and Year 5 for Baker Company are shown below:

BAKER COMPANY
Comparative Balance Sheets (Historical-Cost/Nominal-Dollar Basis)
End of Year 4 and Year 5

	End of Year 4	End of Year 5
Assets		
Monetary assets (cash and receivables)	$200,000	$260,000
Inventories (fifo method)	150,000 (1)	130,000 (2)
Land	40,000	40,000
Equipment.	210,000	270,000
Less: Accumulated depreciation.	(–0–)	(24,000)
Total assets	$600,000	$676,000
Liabilities & Stockholders' Equity		
Current liabilities	$ 80,000	$ 90,000
Long-term liabilities	100,000	116,000
Capital stock, $10 par	140,000	140,000
Paid-in capital in excess of par	280,000	280,000
Retained earnings	–0–	50,000
Total liabilities & stockholders' equity	$600,000	$676,000

(1) Recoverable amount $190,000
(2) Recoverable amount $170,000

The historical-cost/nominal-dollar statement of income and retained earnings for Baker Company for Year 5 (the first year of operations) is shown on top of page 1056.

BAKER COMPANY

Statement of Income and Retained Earnings

(Historical-Cost/Nominal-Dollar Basis)

For Year 5 (the first year of operations)

Sales (14,000 units).		$800,000
Cost of goods sold:		
Beginning inventories (fifo method) (3,750 units)	$150,000	
Purchases.	500,000	
Cost of goods available for sale	$650,000	
Less: Ending inventories (fifo method) (3,000 units).	130,000	
Cost of goods sold		520,000
Gross profit on sales.		$280,000
Operating expenses (excluding depreciation).	$ 96,000	
Depreciation expense	24,000	120,000
Income before income taxes		$160,000
Income taxes expense.		70,000
Net income		$ 90,000
Less: Dividends.		40,000
Retained earnings, end of Year 5		$ 50,000

Equipment costing $60,000 was acquired on July 1, Year 5, when the CPI-U stood at 157.5. Historical-cost/nominal-dollar depreciation expense for Year 5 was computed as follows:

Computation of historical-cost/nominal-dollar depreciation expense for Year 5

$210,000 × 10%.	$21,000
$60,000 × 5% (one-half of year)	3,000
Total depreciation expense for Year 5	$24,000

Sales, purchases, and operating expenses (excluding depreciation) took place evenly throughout the year. Inventories are priced on a first-in, first-out basis; goods in ending inventories were acquired evenly during the year. The dividend of $40,000 was paid near the end of Year 5.

The management of Baker Company elected to present the historical-cost/constant-dollar supplementary information required by **FASB Statement No. 33** on a **comprehensive financial statement basis,** and to use the end-of-Year 5 CPI-U in the determination of the constant-dollar amounts.

Exhibit 1—Working Paper to Restate Statement of Income and Retained Earnings A working paper to restate the statement of income and retained earnings for Year 5, in terms of end-of-Year 5 constant dollars, is presented in Exhibit 1 below:

Exhibit 1

BAKER COMPANY

Restatement of Statement of Income and Retained Earnings

to Historical-Cost/Constant-Dollar Basis

For Year 5 (the first year of operations)

	Historical-cost/ nominal-dollar basis	Conversion factors	Historical-cost/ constant-dollar basis
Sales	$800,000	1.040 (A)	$832,000
Cost of goods sold:			
Beginning inventories (fifo method) . .	$150,000	1.092 (B)	$163,800
Purchases.	500,000	1.040 (A)	520,000
Cost of goods available for sale.	$650,000		$683,800
Less: Ending inventories (fifo method) .	130,000	1.040 (A)	135,200
Cost of goods sold	$520,000		$548,600
Gross profit on sales.	$280,000		$283,400
Less: Operating expenses (excluding depreciation).	(96,000)	1.040 (A)	(99,840)
Depreciation expense	(24,000)	(C)	(26,052)
Income before income taxes.	$160,000		$157,508
Income taxes expense.	70,000	1.040 (A)	72,800
Income from continuing operations. . . .	$ 90,000		$ 84,708
Less: Purchasing power loss.		(Exhibit 2)*	(4,800)
Dividends.	(40,000)	1.000 (D)	(40,000)
Retained earnings, end of Year 5	$ 50,000		$ 39,908

(A) *Price index at the end of Year 5 (163.8), divided by the average price index during Year 5 (157.5) = 1.040.*

(B) *Price index at the end of Year 5 (163.8), divided by the price index at the end of Year 4 (150.0) when inventories were acquired = 1.092.*

(C) *Depreciation expense is restated to end-of-Year 5 constant dollars as follows:*

On equipment acquired at end of Year 4: $21,000 × 1.092	*$22,932*
On equipment acquired on July 1, Year 5: $3,000 × 1.040	*3,120*
Total depreciation expense for Year 5	*$26,052*

(D) *Dividends were paid near the end of Year 5, and therefore are stated in terms of constant dollars at the end of Year 5.*

* *See p. 1060.*

A brief explanation of the procedures followed to restate the statement of income and retained earnings follows:

Sales Generally, sales of a business enterprise are assumed to have been made at a uniform rate. Therefore, the amount of Baker's sales for Year 5 ($800,000) is stated in terms of the average price index for the year. To restate sales in terms of end-of-Year 5 constant dollars, a conversion factor of 1.040 is used. This factor is computed by dividing the end-of-Year 5 price index of 163.8 by 157.5, the average price index for Year 5.

Beginning inventories   The goods comprising the beginning inventories were acquired when the price index was 150.0. The amount of the beginning inventories is restated by use of a conversion factor of 1.092, the end-of-Year 5 price index of 163.8 divided by 150.0, the index at the time the inventories were acquired. Recoverable amount of $190,000 (see page 1055) exceeds the $163,800 historical-cost/constant-dollar amount.

Purchases   Purchases also are assumed to have taken place at a uniform rate during Year 5. Consequently, the restatement is accomplished by multiplying by a conversion factor of 1.040, the end-of-Year 5 price index of 163.8 divided by 157.5, the average price index during Year 5.

Ending inventories   Because inventories are priced on a first-in, first-out basis, it is assumed that the goods in the ending inventories were acquired at the average price index for Year 5. Thus, ending inventories are restated to constant dollars by use of the average price index conversion factor of 1.040 (the same conversion factor used to restate purchases). Recoverable amount of $170,000 (see page 1055) exceeds the $135,200 historical-cost/constant-dollar amount computed for ending inventories.

Operating expenses (excluding depreciation)   In our example we have assumed that operating expenses were incurred evenly throughout the year; therefore, operating expenses are restated to constant dollars by application of the average price index conversion factor of 1.040.

Depreciation expense   Depreciation expense in the accounting records consists of two amounts: (1) depreciation of $21,000 on equipment acquired on December 31, Year 4, when the price index was 150.0, and (2) depreciation of $3,000 on equipment acquired on July 1, Year 5, when the price index was 157.5. Therefore, depreciation expense is restated to constant dollars as follows:

Computation of historical-cost/constant-dollar depreciation expense for Year 5	$21,000 × 1.092 (163.8 ÷ 150.0) $22,932
	$3,000 × 1.040 (163.8 ÷ 157.5) 3,120
	Total depreciation expense for Year 5, as restated to constant dollars. $26,052

Income taxes expense   Income taxes accrue throughout the year as revenue and expenses are recorded. Because sales and expenses accrued evenly throughout the year, income taxes expense is adjusted to end-of-Year 5 constant dollars by multiplying the actual income taxes expense of $70,000 by the average price-index conversion factor of 1.040. Income taxes expense in the historical-cost/constant-dollar income statement is based on the income taxes expense as reported in the historical-cost/nominal-dollar income statement and is not computed in direct relationship to the amount of income before income taxes reported in the historical-cost/constant-dollar income statement.

Purchasing power loss   Any gain or loss resulting from the ownership of monetary assets or from borrowing activities is computed in a separate working paper and is added to or subtracted from income from continuing operations. The determination of the purchasing power loss of $4,800 for Year 5 appears in Exhibit 2 on page 1060.

Dividends   Because dividends were paid near the end of Year 5, the amount of dividends paid is stated in terms of constant dollars and requires no restatement. (If dividends had been paid on July 1, Year 5, for example, the amount of dividends would be restated by use of a conversion factor of 1.040.)

Exhibit 1 shows that Baker Company earned income from continuing operations of $84,708 in constant dollars, rather than $90,000 reported in the nominal-dollar income statement. The difference of $5,292 is caused by two major factors: (1) an increase in the cost of goods acquired at the end of Year 4 and sold in Year 5, and (2) an increase in depreciation expense because of an increase in the price index since the equipment was acquired. In addition, Baker incurred a $4,800 purchasing power loss as a result of holding an excess of monetary assets over liabilities during a period when the price index was going up. As a result of the foregoing items, the retained earnings amount appears in the constant-dollar balance sheet (see Exhibit 3 on page 1061) at $39,908 ($50,000 − $5,292 − $4,800 = $39,908).

Exhibit 2—Working Paper for Computation of Purchasing Power Loss   The purchasing power loss of $4,800 that appears in the statement of income and retained earnings on a historical-cost/constant-dollar basis is presented in Exhibit 2 on page 1060.

In the preparation of Exhibit 2, transactions (such as sales) that caused an increase in monetary assets during Year 5 are added to the amount of net monetary items at the beginning of the year; transactions that caused an increase in monetary liabilities or a decrease in monetary assets are deducted. Included under deductions are purchases, operating expenses (excluding depreciation), income taxes expense, dividends, and the acquisition of equipment. Depreciation expense is not included in Exhibit 2 because it is a nonmonetary expense. The amount of net monetary items at the beginning of Year 5 (restated to end-of-Year 5 constant dollars), plus sources and less uses of net monetary assets (restated to end-of-Year 5 constant dollars) gives $58,800 as the amount of net monetary items that *should be* on hand if there were no purchasing power gain or loss. Because net monetary items at the end of Year 5 amount to $54,000, the purchasing power loss is $4,800 ($58,800 − $54,000 = $4,800).

Exhibit 2

BAKER COMPANY

Computation of Purchasing Power Loss

For Year 5 (the first year of operations)

	Historical-cost/ nominal-dollar basis		Conversion factors	Historical-cost/ constant-dollar basis
Net monetary items, beginning of Year 5:				
Monetary assets (cash and receivables).	$200,000			
Current liabilities.	(80,000)			
Long-term liabilities	(100,000)	$ 20,000	1.092 (A)	$ 21,840
Add: Sources of net monetary items during Year 5:				
Sales		800,000	1.040 (B)	832,000
Subtotal		$820,000		$853,840
Less: Uses of net monetary items during Year 5:				
Purchases.	$500,000		1.040 (B)	$520,000
Operating expenses (excluding depreciation).	96,000		1.040 (B)	99,840
Income taxes expense	70,000		1.040 (B)	72,800
Dividends	40,000		1.000 (C)	40,000
Acquisition of equipment.	60,000		1.040 (D)	62,400
Total uses.		766,000		$795,040
Net monetary items as restated at the end of Year 5 if there were no purchasing power gain or loss ($853,840 − $795,040)				$ 58,800
Net monetary items on hand at the end of Year 5:				
Monetary assets (cash and receivables).	$260,000			
Current liabilities.	(90,000)			
Long-term liabilities	(116,000)	$ 54,000		54,000
Purchasing power loss for Year 5 .				$ 4,800

(A) The amount of net monetary items at the beginning of Year 5 is rolled forward by multiplying $20,000 by the conversion factor of 1.092, which is the ratio of the end-of-Year 5 price index to the price index at the beginning of Year 5 (163.8 ÷ 150.0 = 1.092).

(B) Sales, purchases, operating expenses, and income taxes expense are restated in the same manner as in Exhibit 1, that is, by use of a conversion factor for the average price index for Year 5 (163.8 ÷ 157.5 = 1.040).

(C) Dividends were paid near the end of Year 5 and therefore are stated in terms of constant dollars.

(D) Equipment was acquired on July 1, Year 5, when the price index was 157.5; this amount is restated by multiplying the cost of $60,000 by 1.040 (163.8 ÷ 157.5 = 1.040).

Exhibit 3—Working Paper to Restate Comparative Balance Sheets A working paper to restate the comparative balance sheets, in terms of end-of-Year 5 constant dollars, is given as Exhibit 3 below. Note that the balance sheet amounts in constant dollars at the end of Year 4 are ***rolled for-***

Exhibit 3

BAKER COMPANY

Restatement of Comparative Balance Sheets to Historical-Cost/Constant-Dollar Basis

End of Year 4 and Year 5

	End of Year 4			End of Year 5		
	Historical-cost/nominal-dollar basis*	Conversion factors	Historical-cost/constant-dollar basis (end of Year 5)	Historical-cost/nominal-dollar basis	Conversion factors	Historical-cost/constant-dollar basis (end of Year 5)
Assets						
Monetary assets (cash and receivables)....	$200,000	1.092 (A)	$218,400	$260,000	(B)	$260,000
Inventories (fifo method)........	150,000	1.092	163,800	130,000	1.040 (E)	135,200
Land............	40,000	1.092	43,680	40,000	1.092 (A)	43,680
Equipment	210,000	1.092	229,320	270,000	(C)	291,720
Less: Accumulated depreciation	(–0–)		(–0–)	(24,000)	(D)	(26,052)
Total assets	$600,000		$655,200	$676,000		$704,548
Liabilities & Stockholders' Equity						
Current liabilities ...	$ 80,000	1.092	$ 87,360	$ 90,000	(B)	$ 90,000
Long-term liabilities..	100,000	1.092	109,200	116,000	(B)	116,000
Capital stock, $10 par.	140,000	1.092	152,880	140,000	1.092 (A)	152,880
Paid-in capital in excess of par	280,000	1.092	305,760	280,000	1.092 (A)	305,760
Retained earnings ...	–0–		–0–	50,000	(Exhibit 1)†	39,908
Total liabilities & stockholders' equity	$600,000		$655,200	$676,000		$704,548

(A) *Price index at the end of Year 5 (163.8), divided by the price index at the end of Year 4 (150.0)=1.092.*

(B) *Monetary items at the end of Year 5 are not adjusted because these are stated in terms of end-of-Year 5 constant dollars.*

(C) *Equipment is adjusted for the increase in the price index as follows:*

Acquired at the end of Year 4: $210,000 × 1.092	$229,320
Acquired on July 1, Year 5: $60,000 × 1.040 (163.8 ÷ 157.5)	62,400
Total equipment as restated	$291,720

(D) *Accumulated depreciation is adjusted for the increase in the price index as follows:*

On equipment acquired at the end of Year 4: $21,000 × 1.092	$ 22,932
On equipment acquired on July 1, Year 5: $3,000 × 1.040	3,120
Total accumulated depreciation as restated	$ 26,052

(E) *Price index at the end of Year 5 (163.8), divided by the average price index during Year 5 (157.5)=1.040.*

* *Also end-of-Year 4 **constant dollars,** because Baker Company was organized on December 31, Year 4.*

† See p. 1057.

ward, in order to reflect end-of-Year constant 5 dollars, by multiplying each amount by 1.092 (163.8 ÷ 150.0 = 1.092). This rolling forward of the balance sheet amounts is necessary so that the balance sheet at the end of Year 4 can be compared meaningfully with the restated balance sheet at the end of Year 5. Thus, balance sheet amounts on both dates are stated in terms of end-of-Year 5 constant dollars.

The restatement of the balance sheet accounts at the end of Year 5 is explained in the following paragraphs.

Monetary items   Monetary assets (cash and receivables) and liabilities are stated in terms of end-of-Year 5 constant dollars and require no restatement.

Inventories   Inventories at the end of Year 5 are priced by the first-in, first-out method. Goods comprising the ending inventories were acquired evenly throughout Year 5 and therefore are restated by use of a conversion factor of 1.040, the price index at the end of Year 5, 163.8, divided by the average price index during Year 5, 157.5. This is consistent with the restatement of ending inventories in Exhibit 1 on page 1057.

If inventories were priced on a last-in, first-out basis, the ending inventories in this illustration would consist entirely of the cost layer on hand at the beginning of Year 5 and would be restated by application of a conversion factor of 1.092 (163.8 ÷ 150.0 = 1.092).

Land   Because land was acquired at the end of Year 4 when the price index was 150.0, it is restated to $43,680 by multiplying the cost of $40,000 by 1.092 (163.8 ÷ 150.0 = 1.092).

Equipment and accumulated depreciation   Equipment costing $210,000 was acquired at the end of Year 4 when the price index was 150.0, and equipment costing $60,000 was acquired on July 1, Year 5, when the price index was 157.5. One possible approach to the restatement of equipment and accumulated depreciation accounts at the end of Year 5 is presented below:

Equipment			Accumulated Depreciation		
Historical-cost/ nominal-dollar	Conversion factors	Historical-cost/ constant-dollar	Historical-cost/ nominal dollar	Conversion factors	Historical-cost/ constant-dollar
$210,000	1.092 (163.8 ÷ 150.0)	$229,320	$21,000	1.092	$22,932
60,000	1.040 (163.8 ÷ 157.5)	62,400	3,000	1.040	3,120
$270,000		$291,720	$24,000		$26,052

The carrying amount of the equipment at the end of Year 5 is $246,000 ($270,000 − $24,000 = $246,000) in terms of historical-cost/ nominal dollars, and $265,668 ($291,720 − $26,052 = $265,668) in terms of historical-cost/constant dollars. (If the equipment were sold for $250,000 at the beginning of Year 6, a gain of $4,000 would result in terms of historical-cost/nominal dollars, and a loss of $15,668 would result when historical-cost/constant-dollar accounting was applied.)

Capital stock and paid-in capital in excess of par   Paid-in capital accounts are carried in the accounting records at amounts invested by stockholders. These amounts should be restated to current dollars by multiplying each amount by a fraction (conversion factor) in which the current price index is the numerator and the price index at the time the paid-in capital was invested by stockholders is the denominator. Therefore, the conversion factor used to restate the paid-in capital accounts is 1.092 (163.8 ÷ 150.0 = 1.092).

Retained earnings   The balance of $39,908 in retained earnings was determined in Exhibit 1 on page 1057.

If the foregoing steps have been applied accurately, the total of assets at the end of Year 5, as restated, should equal the restated total of liabilities and stockholders' equity, that is, $704,548.

Similar procedures would be followed in subsequent years to adjust financial statements for changes in the Consumer Price Index for All Urban Consumers. For example, if comparative financial statements were presented at the end of Year 6, the amounts appearing in the statements for Year 5, as restated in terms of end-of-Year 5 constant dollars, would be rolled forward to end-of-Year 6 constant dollars.

Illustration of current-cost accounting

The Baker Company example is continued in this section to illustrate the current-cost provisions of **FASB Statement No. 33.** Because of the complexities of the computations, Baker's management elected to present only the **minimum** current-cost supplementary information required by **FASB Statement No. 33,** as summarized on pages 1052–1053.

Inventories   The December 31, Year 4, inventories had been assigned current fair values on that date; thus, they are considered to be stated at current cost. By reference to applicable invoices and vendors' price lists, Baker Company developed a current cost of $144,000 for inventories on December 31, Year 5. Baker also computed recoverable amounts (net realizable value) of the beginning and ending inventories as follows: December 31, Year 4, $190,000; December 31, Year 5, $170,000. Because recoverable amounts of both the beginning and the ending inventories exceeded current-cost amounts, the latter amounts are used for the supplementary information required by **FASB Statement No. 33.**

Cost of goods sold   The average current cost of Baker Company's cost of goods sold for Year 5 is $616,000 as computed in Exhibit 4 on page 1064.

The computation is based on the average current cost per unit of Baker's beginning and ending inventories for Year 5.

Exhibit 4

BAKER COMPANY

Computation of Average Current Cost of Goods Sold

For Year 5

Inventories, Dec. 31, Year 4:

Current cost..	$150,000
Number of units (page 1056)................................	3,750
Average unit current cost ($150,000 ÷ 3,750)...............	$ 40

Inventories, Dec. 31, Year 5:

Current cost..	$144,000
Number of units (page 1056)................................	3,000
Average unit current cost ($144,000 ÷ 3,000)...............	$ 48

Average of current cost of inventories on Dec. 31, Year 4, and Dec. 31,

Year 5 [($40 + $48) ÷ 2]...................................	$ 44
Number of units sold during Year 5 (page 1056).............	14,000
Average current cost of goods sold (14,000 × $44)..........	$616,000

Plant assets   Baker Company's plant assets were stated at current fair values on December 31, Year 4; those accounts (land, $40,000, and equipment, $210,000, or a total of $250,000) are considered to be their current costs on that date. By reference to appropriate specific-price indexes, Baker computed current cost of plant assets on December 31, Year 5, as shown in Exhibit 5 on page 1065.

By the use of appropriate present-value techniques for measuring *value in use,* Baker determined the recoverable amounts for plant assets on December 31, Year 4 and Year 5, to be in excess of current costs. Therefore, current-cost amounts are used for the supplementary information presented on page 1068.

Accumulated depreciation and depreciation expense   There was no accumulated depreciation of plant assets on December 31, Year 4, the date the assets were acquired by Baker Company. The current cost of accumulated depreciation of equipment on December 31, Year 5, is $38,100 as computed in Exhibit 6 on page 1065.

The current cost of Baker's depreciation expense for Year 5 could be stated at $38,100, the same amount as the current cost of Baker's accumulated depreciation on December 31, Year 5. However, **FASB Statement No. 33** suggests that the current cost of depreciation, depletion, and amortization expense may be computed by reference to *average* current cost of the related assets.[6] That technique is illustrated in Ex-

---

[6] Ibid., p. 117

Exhibit 5

BAKER COMPANY

Computation of Current Cost of Plant Assets

End of Year 5

Plant assets	Carrying amount	Conversion factors	Current cost Dec. 31, Year 5
Land.	$ 40,000	1.400 (A)	$ 56,000
Equipment:			
Dec. 31, Year 4, acquisition	$210,000	1.600 (B)	$336,000
July 1, Year 5, acquisition	60,000	1.500 (C)	90,000
Total equipment	$270,000		$426,000
Total plant assets.	$310,000		$482,000

(A) The specific-price index for the land at the end of Year 5 (154), divided by the specific-price index for the land at the end of Year 4 (110) = 1.400.

(B) The specific-price index for the equipment at the end of Year 5 (176), divided by the specific-price index for the equipment at the end of Year 4 (110) = 1.600.

(C) The specific-price index for the equipment at the end of Year 5 (180), divided by the specific price index on July 1, Year 5 (120) = 1.500.

Exhibit 6

BAKER COMPANY

Computation of Current Cost of Accumulated Depreciation of Equipment

End of Year 5

Date acquired	Current cost, Dec. 31, Year 5 (from Exhibit 5)	% depreciated, Dec. 31, Year 5 (p. 1056)	Current cost of accumulated depreciation, Dec. 31, Year 5
Dec. 31, Year 4	$336,000	10%	$33,600
July 1, Year 5	90,000	5	4,500
Totals	$426,000		$38,100

hibit 7 on page 1066, and the average current cost of depreciation expense of $38,100 is used in the presentation of Baker's supplementary information on page 1068. Note that the acquisition dates of the equipment are disregarded when the current cost of depreciation expense is based on the average current cost of the equipment.

Increase or decrease in current cost of inventories, net of inflation   The increase in the current cost of Baker Company's inventories, net of inflation, during Year 5 is computed in Exhibit 8 on page 1066.

In Exhibit 8, current-cost data for inventories, purchases, and cost of goods sold are restated from nominal dollars to **average** (not end-of-year) Year 5 dollars by the use of appropriate conversion factors. The

Exhibit 7

BAKER COMPANY

Computation of Average Current Cost of Depreciation Expense

For Year 5

Current cost of equipment:

Dec. 31, Year 4 (see page 1055)	$210,000
Dec. 31, Year 5 (from Exhibit 5)	426,000
Average current cost for Year 5 [($210,000 + $426,000) ÷ 2]	318,000
Average current cost of depreciation expense for Year 5 ($318,000 × 0.10)	$ 31,800

resultant current-cost/constant-dollar increase in inventories during Year 5 is subtracted from the related current-cost/nominal-dollar amount; the difference represents the amount of the increase in current cost of inventories that is attributable to changes in the general price level and is referred to as the **inflation component.**

Exhibit 8

BAKER COMPANY

Computation of Increase in Current Cost of Inventories, Net of Inflation

For Year 5

	Current-cost/ nominal-dollars	Conversion factors	Current-cost/ average Year 5 dollars
Inventories, Dec. 31, Year 5	$144,000	0.962 (A)	$138,528
Less: Inventories, Dec. 31, Year 4	$150,000	1.050 (B)	$157,500
Add: Purchases (page 1056).	500,000	1.000 (C)	500,000
Subtotal.	$650,000		$657,500
Less: Cost of goods sold (Exhibit 4)	616,000	1.000 (C)	616,000
Net.	$ 34,000		$ 41,500
Increase in current cost of inventories . .	$110,000		$ 97,028
	97,028		
Inflation component	$ 12,972		

(A) The average Consumer Price Index during Year 5 (157.5), divided by the Consumer Price Index at the end of Year 5 (163.8) = 0.962.

(B) The average Consumer Price Index during Year 5 (157.5), divided by the Consumer Price Index at the end of Year 4 (150) = 1.050.

(C) Assumed to be in average Year 5 dollars.

Increase or decrease in current cost of net plant assets, net of inflation The increase in the current cost of Baker's net plant assets, net of inflation, during Year 5 is computed in Exhibit 9 below. The computational techniques in Exhibit 9 are comparable to those in Exhibit 8. It should be noted that *depreciation expense,* at average current cost, rather than the *increase in accumulated depreciation,* is included in the Exhibit 9 computations.

Exhibit 9

BAKER COMPANY
Computation of Increase in Current Cost of Net Plant Assets, Net of Inflation
For Year 5

	Current- cost/ nominal- dollars	Conversion factors	Current- cost/ average Year 5 dollars
Net plant assets, Dec. 31, Year 5. . . .	$443,900 (A)	0.962 (B)	$427,032
Less: Net plant assets, Dec. 31, Year 4	$250,000	1.050 (C)	$262,500
Add: Additions.	60,000	1.000 (D)	60,000
Subtotal	$310,000		$322,500
Less: Depreciation expense (Exhibit 7)	31,800	1.000 (D)	31,800
Net	$278,200		$290,700
Increase in current cost of plant assets	$165,700		$136,332
	136,332		
Inflation component	$ 29,368		

(A) $482,000 current cost of plant assets (Exhibit 5), less $38,100 current cost of accumulated depreciation (Exhibit 6) = $443,900.
(B) The average Consumer Price Index during Year 5 (157.5), divided by the Consumer Price Index at the end of Year 5 (163.8) = 0.962.
(C) The average Consumer Price Index during Year 5 (157.5), divided by the Consumer Price Index at the end of Year 4 (150) = 1.050.
(D) Assumed to be in average Year 5 dollars.

Presentation of supplementary information required by *FASB Statement No. 33*

In this section, we illustrate only the supplementary information required by *FASB Statement No. 33.* Our Baker Company illustration is that of a small company, technically not subject to the disclosure requirements of *FASB Statement No. 33.* However, the required disclosures can be illustrated more easily with a small company than with a large company having complex financial statements. Baker's statement of income from continuing operations adjusted for changing prices appears on page 1068.

BAKER COMPANY

Statement of Income from Continuing Operations Adjusted for Changing Prices

For Year 5

	As reported in primary financial statements (Exhibit 1)	Adjusted for general inflation (Exhibit 1)	Adjusted for changes in specific prices (current costs)
Sales	$800,000	$832,000	$800,000
Cost of goods sold	$520,000	$548,600	$616,000 (Exh. 4)
Operating expenses (excluding depreciation)	96,000	99,840	96,000
Depreciation expense	24,000	26,052	31,800 (Exh. 7)
Income taxes expense	70,000	72,800	70,000
Total costs and expenses	$710,000	$747,292	$813,800
Income (loss) from continuing operations .	$ 90,000	84,708	$ (13,800)
Loss from decline in purchasing power of net amounts owned (Exhibit 2)		$ 4,800	$ 4,800
Increase in specific prices (current cost) of inventories and plant assets held during the year (p. 1069)			$275,700*
Effect of increase in general price level (p. 1069)			42,340
Excess of increase in specific prices over increase in the general price level (p. 1069).			$233,360

* On December 31, Year 5, the current cost of inventories was $144,000 (Exhibit 4), and the current cost of plant assets, net of accumulated depreciation, was $443,900 (Exhibit 9).

The following features of Baker Company's statement of income from continuing operations adjusted for changing prices should be stressed:

1 The statement is in the form of a conventional income statement. An alternative form permitted by *FASB Statement No. 33* is a reconciliation of income from continuing operations in the historical-cost/nominal-dollar income statement to a constant-dollar and a current-cost basis.

2 Because Baker Company chose to present historical-cost/constant-dollar supplementary information on a **comprehensive basis** (see p. 1056), **every** item in the "Adjusted for general inflation" section is restated. In contrast, only cost of goods sold and depreciation expense are restated in the "Adjusted for changes in specific prices" section, because Baker elected to present only the **minimum** current-cost data required by *FASB Statement No. 33.* (see p. 1063).

3 Both the loss from decline in purchasing power and the increase in specific prices of inventories and plant assets are excluded from the computation of income from continuing operations, as required by *FASB Statement No. 33.*

4 The amounts for the increases in specific prices of inventories and plant assets are computed on page 1069.

An example of disclosures required by *FASB Statement No. 33* appears in **Note 25** of the Appendix at the end of Chapter 4 (pages 170–172) for International Harvester Company.

Increases in specific prices of inventories and plant assets

	Increase in specific prices	Effect of increase in general price level	Excess of increase in specific prices other increases in general price level
Inventories (Exhibit 8)	$110,000	$12,972	$ 97,028
Net plant assets (Exhibit 9)	165,700	29,368	136,332
Totals	$275,700	$42,340	$233,360

Appraisal of *FASB Statement No. 33*

In *FASB Statement No. 33,* the FASB took a compromise position between two opposing views on accounting for inflation. One view, favored by the FASB itself in an earlier exposure draft of a proposed Statement, is that historical-cost/constant-dollar financial statements are the most meaningful indicators of the effects of inflation on a business enterprise. Proponents of this view argue that constant-dollar data are more reliable than current-cost data, because constant-dollar amounts are computed with a uniform measure—the Consumer Price Index for All Urban Consumers.

Another view, favored at one time by the SEC, is that constant-dollar data are not as meaningful as current-cost data because of shortcomings of general price-level indexes such as the Consumer Price Index for All Urban Consumers. Such indexes are misleading, the critics claim, because of their assumption of a "mix" of goods and services in the computation of the indexes. Supporters of current-cost measures of inflation argue that current-cost amounts of the resources of a business enterprise provide more relevant data for decision makers than do constant-dollar data.

In issuing *FASB Statement No. 33,* the FASB acknowledged that it represented a first step in the search for the most meaningful presentation of the effects of inflation on a business enterprise. The FASB is committed to a periodic review of *FASB Statement No. 33* and to revision of it as future conditions warrant.

SEC position on accounting for inflation

In *Accounting Series Release No. 271,* the SEC supported the disclosure requirements of *FASB Statement No. 33* by repealing its requirement for the reporting of *replacement-cost* data (similar to current-cost data) in annual reports by certain large corporations. In addition, the SEC established an experimental form of accounting for oil- and gas-producing enterprises, known as *reserve recognition accounting* (or RRA). Under this accounting method, the present value of proved oil and gas reserves was included in supplementary information to the producers' financial statements at the time of discovery of the reserves. The SEC cautioned that reserve recognition accounting was not a form of fair-value accounting but was a method of measuring a producer's success or lack of success in finding proved oil and gas reserves.

Under reserve recognition accounting, the **value** of of an oil and gas producer's proved reserves was recognized as an asset, and the **value** of additions to proved reserves was included in revenue when the additions occurred. In contrast, under historical-cost/nominal-dollar accounting, oil and gas producers recorded only leasehold acquisitions and certain exploration and development costs as assets, and recognized only the proceeds from sales of oil and gas reserves as revenue.

In less than three years, the SEC abandoned the RRA experiment and left to the FASB the development of comprehensive disclosure standards for oil and gas producers.

REVIEW QUESTIONS

1 What evidence can you offer in support of the assertion that "the dollar is not a stable unit of value?"

2 List three indexes of the general price level in the United States. Which index was selected by the FASB as a measure of the general movement in prices?

3 Evaluate the following quotation: "If historical-cost/nominal-dollar financial statements were restated to reflect the changing value of the dollar, assets would be stated at current fair value and net income would not be determined by matching realized revenue with expired costs."

4 Explain how the use of generally accepted accounting principles may result in reporting as a part of net income what is in reality a recovery of capital.

5 Explain each of the following:
 a Monetary items
 b Positive monetary position
 c Negative monetary position
 d Purchasing power gains and losses

6 What is meant by the expression **conversion factor?** Compute the conversion factor for land if the general price-level index was 80 on the date the land was acquired and is 144 today.

7 To what extent have current fair values been used by accountants in the preparation of financial statements?

8 What is a **holding gain or loss?** How is it measured?

9 The basic method of valuation used in accounting for plant assets is historical cost (nominal dollars) less depreciation. At various times during their economic life it is possible to estimate the current fair value of such assets by use of one of the following methods:
 a Capitalization of net cash inflows (or direct valuation)

b Exit values (both current and expected)
c Current cost
　　Explain the meaning of the term **current fair value** and define each of the three methods of estimating current fair value listed above.

10 Evaluate the following quotation: "Accounting is no more than the recording and reporting of transactions. Recognition of the current fair values of assets in the financial statements is neither feasible nor useful; besides, it lacks objectivity."

11 List the minimum supplementary information disclosure requirements of **FASB Statement No. 33,** "Financial Reporting and Changing Prices," in the annual reports of large publicly owned corporations.

12 Define **income from continuing operations** as used in **FASB Statement No. 33.**

13 What are the two methods for presentation of constant-dollar and current-cost income from continuing operations authorized by **FASB Statement No. 33?**

14 May a business enterprise elect to use either the average or the end-of-year Consumer Price Index for All Urban Consumers to compute the constant-dollar information required by **FASB Statement No. 33?** Explain.

15 Define **recoverable amount** as used in **FASB Statement No. 33.**

16 Explain how income taxes expense is computed for historical-cost/constant-dollar supplementary information.

17 Explain how historical-cost/constant-dollar balance sheet data of a prior year are **rolled forward** for a comparative balance sheet.

18 The recoverable amount of Wight Company's land on March 31, Year 6, is $1,482,000. Current cost of the land on that date is $1,843,000. How do these facts affect the preparation of current-cost supplementary information for Wight's annual report for the year ended March 31, Year 6? Explain.

19 What was **reserve recognition accounting** as developed by the SEC?

EXERCISES

Ex. 25-1　Select the best answer for each of the following multiple-choice questions:

1 Which of the following is not a method of determining the current fair value of an asset?
a Current cost
b Exit value
c Restatement of cost for changes in general price level
d Net present value of expected future cash inflows

2 Which of the following methods of reporting attempts to eliminate the effect of the changing value of the dollar?
a Discounted net present value of future cash inflows
b Historical cost restated for changes in the general price level
c Current cost
d Exit value

3 Which of the following asset valuation methods is not a violation of the cost principle?
a Net present value of future cash inflows
b Current cost
c Exit value
d Constant-dollar restatement

4 In current fair value financial statements:
a Purchasing power gains or losses are recognized on net monetary items
b Amounts always are stated in common purchasing power units of measurement
c All balance sheet items are different in amount from what they would be in a historical-cost/nominal-dollar balance sheet
d Holding gains are recognized

5 Financial statements that are expressed under the assumption of a stable monetary unit are:
a Historical-cost/constant-dollar financial statements
b Historical-cost/nominal-dollar financial statements
c Current-cost financial statements
d Current fair value financial statements

6 In accordance with **FASB Statement No. 33,** the Consumer Price Index for All Urban Consumers is used to compute information on a:
a Historical-cost basis
b Current-cost basis
c Nominal-dollar basis
d Constant-dollar basis

Ex. 25-2 Ullman Company was formed on January 2, Year 7. Selected balances from the historical-cost/nominal-dollar balance sheet on December 31, Year 7, were as follows:

Cash	$60,000
Short-term investments, stocks (acquired on Jan. 2, Year 7)	70,000
Short-term investments, bonds, (acquired on Jan. 2, Year 7, and held for	
speculation)	80,000
Long-term note receivable	90,000

The Consumer Price Index for All Urban Consumers was 100 on December 31, Year 6 (and January 2, Year 7), and 110 on December 31, Year 7.
Compute the amounts at which the foregoing items would be presented in a historical-cost/constant-dollar balance sheet. Show computations.

Ex. 25-3 Funakoshi, Inc., paid $1,200,000 in December, Year 6, for certain items of its inventory. In December, Year 7, one half of the items were sold for $1,000,000 when the current fair value of the original items was $1,400,000.
Compute the amount to be shown as the total gain resulting from the above facts in a current fair value income statement for Year 7. Show computations and disregard income taxes.

Ex. 25-4 Carstairs, Inc., was formed on January 2, Year 3, when common stock of $200,000 was issued for cash of $50,000 and land with a current fair value of $150,000. Carstairs did not begin operations until Year 4, and no transactions occurred in Year 3, except the issuance of the common stock. The Consumer Price Index for All Urban Consumers was 100 on December 31, Year 2, and 110 on December 31, Year 3.
Compute the purchasing power gain or loss to be included in a historical-cost/constant-dollar income statement for Carstairs, Inc., for Year 3.

Ex. 25-5 Douglas Corporation acquired a machine for $1,000,000 in Year 4 when the specific-price index was 180. The applicable specific-price index was 190 at the end of Year 5 and 200 at the end of Year 6. Depreciation expense on a historical-cost/nominal-dollar basis was $100,000 a year.

Compute Douglas Corporation's average current cost of depreciation expense for Year 6, in accordance with the provisions of **FASB Statement No. 33.** Show supporting computations to the nearest dollar.

Ex. 25-6 Wickham Corporation acquired a machine in Year 7 when the average Consumer Price Index for All Urban Consumers was 200. The average index was 210 for Year 8, and 220 for Year 9. Wickham prepares supplementary constant-dollar information. Historical-cost/nominal-depreciation on this machine is $200,000 a year, based on cost of $1,600,000 and no residual value.

Compute the amount of depreciation expense for Wickham's historical-cost/constant-dollar supplementary information for Year 9.

Ex. 25-7 For each independent situation below, compute the purchasing power gain or loss, assuming that assets and liabilities remained unchanged during the entire accounting period. The Consumer Price Index for All Urban Consumers rose by 7% during the period:

a *Monetary assets*	$120,000
Monetary liabilities	60,000
b *Monetary assets*	$260,000
Current monetary liabilities	100,000
Long-term monetary liabilities	300,000
c *Cash*	$ 40,000
Short-term investments in common stocks	200,000
Notes receivable	90,000
Accounts receivable	60,000
Inventories	100,000
Plant assets (net of accumulated depreciation)	600,000
Monetary liabilities	475,000
Stockholders' equity	625,000

Ex. 25-8 From the following year-end Consumer Price Indexes for All Urban Consumers, compute the conversion factors to restate the historical-cost/nominal-dollar financial statements for Year 1, Year 2, and Year 3 in terms of end-of-Year 4 constant dollars:

Year 1	90
Year 2	104
Year 3	120
Year 4	126

Ex. 25-9 Antonio Company acquired a machine on December 31, Year 7, for $100,000. The machine is being depreciated on the straight-line basis with no residual value and a five-year economic life. There was a rise in current cost of the machine of 10% during Year 8 and of 10% during Year 9 (based on the December 31, Year 8, current cost).

Compute accumulated depreciation on a current-cost basis for inclusion in Antonio Company's supplementary current-cost information for Year 9.

Ex. 25-10 Benson Company was formed and began operations in Year 1. The company adopted the lifo method of inventory pricing and has consistently used this method. At the end of Year 15, the composition of the inventory and the average Consumer Price Index for All Urban Consumers in the year of purchase were as follows:

Purchased in Year 1 (index = 90)	$380,000
Year 3 layer (index = 100)	20,000
Year 10 layer (index = 120)	15,000
Year 15 layer (index = 135)	35,000
Total inventory at lifo cost, as shown in historical-cost/nominal-dollar	
balance sheet on Dec. 31, Year 15	$450,000

Prepare a working paper to restate the inventory on December 31, Year 15, to reflect changes in the average Consumer Price Index for All Urban Consumers.

Ex. 25-11 Valuation to reflect constant dollars, as opposed to current cost, yields differing amounts for a business enterprise's financial statements. Several transactions concerning one asset of Keystone Corporation, a calendar-year enterprise, are summarized below:

Year 4 Acquired land for $400,000 cash on December 31; current cost at year-end was $400,000.
Year 5 Held this land all year; current cost at year-end was $520,000.
Year 6 Sold this land for $680,000 on October 31.

The average Consumer Price Index for All Urban Consumers for each year was as follows:

Year 4	100
Year 5	110
Year 6	120

On your working paper, duplicate the format below and complete the information required based on the transactions described above. Assume that holding gains and losses are included in current-cost data.

	Historical-cost/ constant-dollars	Current-cost
Valuation of land in balance sheet:		
Dec. 31, Year 4	$	$
Dec. 31, Year 5		
Gain in income statement:		
Year 4	$	$
Year 5		
Year 6		
Totals	$	$

SHORT CASES FOR ANALYSIS AND DECISION

Case 25-1 Advocates of fair-value accounting propose several methods for determining the valuation of assets to approximate current fair values. Two of the methods proposed are current cost and present value of future cash inflows.

Instructions   Describe each of the two methods cited on page 1074 and discuss the advantages and disadvantages of the various procedures used to determine the valuation for each method.

Case 25-2   Jean Daily, the controller of Exeter Company, is discussing a comment you made in the course of presenting your audit report.

". . . and frankly," Daily continued, "I agree that we, too, are responsible for finding ways to produce more relevant financial statements that are as reliable as the ones we now produce.

"For example, suppose we acquired an item of inventory for $400 when the general price-level index was 110. And, later, the item was sold for $750 when the general price-level index was 121 and the current cost was $540. We could calculate and report a 'holding gain' of $100."

Instructions

a Explain to what extent and how current costs already are used under generally accepted accounting principles to value inventories.

b Show how Daily computed the holding gain of $100.

Case 25-3   Valuation of assets is an important topic in accounting theory. Suggested valuation methods include the following:

Historical-cost/nominal-dollars
Historical-cost/constant-dollars
Discounted-cash-inflows
Market price (current selling prices)
Current cost (current purchase prices)

Instructions

a Why is the valuation of assets a significant issue?

b Explain the basic theory underlying each of the valuation methods listed above. Do not discuss advantages and disadvantages of each method.

Case 25-4   A common objective of accountants is to prepare useful financial statements. To attain this objective many accountants maintain that the financial statements must be adjusted for changes in the general price level. Other accountants believe that financial statements should continue to be prepared on the basis of unadjusted historical cost.

Instructions

a List arguments for adjusting financial statements for changes in the general price level.

b List arguments for preparing financial statements only on the basis of unadjusted historical cost.

c In their discussions about accounting for changes in the general price level and the methods of measuring them, uninformed individuals frequently have failed to distinguish between adjustments for changes in the price levels of specific goods and services and adjustments for changes in the purchasing power of the dollar. What is the distinction? Discuss.

Case 25-5   Financial statements are tools for the communication of quantifiable economic information to users as one of the factors for a variety of management and investment decisions. To fullfill this function, accounting data should be quantfiable and relevant for the kinds of decisions to be made. They should be reliable and free from bias. Many accountants believe that for some purposes current cost is a more useful measure than historical cost and recommend that dual financial statements be prepared showing both historical costs and current costs.

Instructions

a Discuss the ways in which historical costs and current costs conform to the standards of reliability and freedom from bias.

b Describe briefly how the current cost of the following assets might be determined.
(1) Inventories
(2) Investments in marketable securities
(3) Equipment
(4) Natural resources

PROBLEMS

25-1 Select the best answer for each of the following multiple-choice questions relating to historical-cost/constant-dollar accounting:

1 Klug Company reported sales of $2,000,000 in Year 3 and $3,000,000 in Year 4. Sales were made evenly throughout each year. The general price-level index during Year 2 remained constant at 100, and at the end of Year 3 and Year 4 it was 102 and 104, respectively. What should Klug report as sales for Year 4 in terms of end-of-Year 4 dollars?
   a $3,000,000   **b** $3,029,126   **c** $3,058,821   **d** $3,120,000

2 On January 2, Year 5, March Corporation mortgaged one of its properties as collateral for a $1,000,000, 15%, five-year loan. During Year 5, the general price level increased evenly, resulting in a 5% increase for the year.
  In a historical-cost/constant-dollar balance sheet at the end of Year 5, at which amount should March report its mortgage note payable?
   a $950,000   **b** $1,000,000   **c** $1,025,000   **d** $1,050,000

3 If land were purchased in Year 10 for $150,000 when the general price-level index was 100 and sold at the end of Year 19 for $240,000 when the index was 170, the historical-cost/constant-dollar income statement for Year 19 shows:
  a A purchasing power gain of $105,000 and a loss on sale of land of $15,000
  b A gain on sale of land of $90,000
  c A purchasing power loss of $15,000
  d A loss on sale of land of $15,000
  e None of the above

4 A business enterprise was formed on January 2, Year 2. Selected account balances from the historical-cost/nominal-dollar balance sheet at December 31, Year 2, were:

Accounts receivable . . . . $ 70,000
Accounts payable 60,000
Long-term debt 110,000
Common stock 100,000

At what amounts should these selected account balances be shown in a historical-cost/constant-dollar balance sheet on December 31, Year 2, if the general price-level index was 100 on December 31, Year 1, and 110 on December 31, Year 2?

	Accounts receivable	Accounts payable	Long-term debt	Common stock
a	$70,000	$60,000	$110,000	$100,000
b	$70,000	$60,000	$110,000	$110,000
c	$70,000	$60,000	$121,000	$110,000
d	$77,000	$66,000	$121,000	$110,000

5 If the base year is Year 1 (when the general price-level index was 100) and land is acquired for $50,000 in Year 5 when the general price-level index is 108.5, the cost of the land restated to Year 1 dollars (rounded to the nearest whole dollar) is:

a $54,250   **b** $50,000   **c** $46,083   **d** $45,750   **e** Some other amount

6 Assume the same facts as in question **5** above. The cost of the land restated to December 31, Year 10, dollars when the general price-level index is 119.2 (rounded to the nearest dollar) is:

a $59,600   **b** $54,931   **c** $46,083   **d** $45,512   **e** Some other amount

7 If land were acquired at a cost of $120,000 in January of Year 13 when the general price-level index was 120 and sold in December of Year 19 when the index was 150, the selling price that results in no gain or loss in historical-cost/constant-dollar financial statements is:

a $180,000   **b** $144,000   **c** $120,000   **d** $150,000   **e** Some other amount

The following information is applicable to questions **8** through **10**:

Equipment acquired for $120,000 on January 2, Year 1, when the general price-level index was 100, was sold on December 31, Year 3, at a price of $85,000. The equipment originally had an economic life of six years, with no residual value, and was depreciated on a straight-line basis. The general price-level index at the end of Year 1 was 120, at the end of Year 2 was 150, and at the end of Year 3 was 175.

8 In historical-cost/constant-dollar comparative financial statements at the end of Year 2, the Year 1 financial statements show equipment (net of accumulated depreciation) at:

a $150,000   **b** $125,000   **c** $100,000   **d** $80,000   **e** Some other amount

9 The historical-cost/constant-dollar financial statements at the end of Year 2 include depreciation expense of:

a $35,000   **b** $30,000   **c** $25,000   **d** $20,000   **e** Some other amount

10 The historical-cost/constant-dollar income statement at the end of Year 3 includes:

a A gain of $35,000   **d** A loss of $20,000
b A gain of $25,000   **e** Some other amount
c No gain or loss

25-2 Meyer Company elected to disclose the minimum current-cost data required by **FASB Statement No. 33.** Meyer sells a single product, which it values at fifo cost in historical-cost/nominal-dollar financial statements. Meyer's perpetual inventory records showed the following information for Year 6:

	Units	Amount
Balance, Dec. 31, Year 5	10,000	$ 60,000
Add: Purchases during Year 6	510,000	4,472,000
Subtotals	520,000	$4,532,000
Less: Sales during Year 6	502,000	4,391,600
Balance, Dec. 31, Year 6	18,000	$ 140,400

Unit price quotations of the three vendors from which Meyer purchases the produce were as follows:

Dec. 31, Year 5	$6.80, $6.80, $7.00
Dec. 31, Year 6	$8.10, $8.30, $8.35

Meyer generally purchases from the vendor quoting the lowest unit cost.

Meyer's selling expenses generally amount to 10% of net sales. Expected unit selling prices of Meyer's product were as follows:

Dec. 31, Year 5 .... $10.40
Dec. 31, Year 6 .... 12.60

Instructions Prepare a working paper to compute Meyer Company's average current cost of goods sold for Year 6, and the current cost of its inventory on December 31, Year 6.

25-3 The latest historical-cost/nominal-dollar income statement for Rossi Corporation is given below:

ROSSI CORPORATION
Income Statement (Historical-Cost/Nominal-Dollar Basis)
For Year Ended December 31, Year 4

Sales (net)		$700,000
Cost of goods sold:		
Inventories, Jan. 1 (lifo method)	$ 80,000	
Purchases (net)	450,000	
Cost of goods available for sale	$530,000	
Less: Inventories, Dec. 31 (lifo method)	95,000	435,000
Gross profit on sales		$265,000
Operating expenses:		
Selling (reducing net monetary assets)	$ 30,000	
General and administrative (reducing net monetary assets) ..	25,000	
Depreciation	35,000	90,000
Income before income taxes		$175,000
Income taxes expense.........................		70,000
Net income		$105,000

All items in the income statement were recorded at a fairly uniform rate throughout Year 4. Beginning inventories and depreciable assets were acquired when the Consumer Price Index for All Urban Consumers was 125. The lifo layer of $15,000 added to inventories during Year 4 consists of goods acquired throughout the year. Changes in the Consumer Price Index for All Urban Consumers during Year 4 are summarized below:

Beginning of Year 4 (conversion factor = 1.200) 150
Average for Year 4 (conversion factor = 1.078) 167
End of Year 4 (conversion factor = 1.000)..................... 180

Instructions Prepare a working paper to restate the income statement to historical-cost/constant-dollars at the **end** of Year 4. Assume that the purchasing power loss as a result of holding net monetary assets during the year was $10,460.

25-4 Hwang Company was organized and began operations on June 1, Year 1, and adopted a fiscal year ending May 31. Hwang rented land and a building under an operating lease on June 1, Year 1. Hwang's equipment acquisitions and related specific-price indexes, during the year ended May 31, Year 2, were as follows:

	Cost	Specific price index
June 1, Year 1.	$ 48,000	120
Dec. 1, Year 1.	39,000	130
Mar. 1, Year 2.	30,000	150
Total	$117,000	

Hwang depreciates equipment to the nearest month by the straight-line method over a 10-year economic life with no residual value.

The specific-price index for Hwang's equipment on May 31, Year 2, was 160. Hwang computed value in use for its equipment as follows:

June 1, Year 1	$ 70,000
May 31, Year 2	155,000

Instructions Prepare a working paper to compute the current cost of Hwang Company's equipment and related accumulated depreciation on May 31, Year 2, and the average current cost of its depreciation expense for the year ended May 31, Year 2. Use fractions for conversion factors and round computations to the nearest dollar.

25-5 The historical-cost/nominal-dollar income statement for Craddock Company for the year ended December 31, Year 2, its first year of operations, follows:

CRADDOCK COMPANY
Income Statement
For Year Ended December 31, Year 2

Sales		$900,000
Cost of goods sold		690,000
Gross profit on sales		$210,000
Expenses:		
Depreciation	$ 15,000	
Other (including interest expense and income taxes		
expense)	120,000	135,000
Net income		$ 75,000

Sales generally averaged $75,000 a month during Year 2, and expenses (including income taxes) were incurred at a relatively even rate throughout Year 2. Both cost of goods sold and the ending inventory consist of a representative sample of goods purchased during Year 2.

Historical-cost/nominal-dollar comparative balance sheets on December 31, Year 1, and on December 31, Year 2, are given on page 1080.

CRADDOCK COMPANY

Comparative Balance Sheets

December 31, Year 1 and Year 2

	Dec. 31, Year 1	Dec. 31, Year 2
Assets		
Monetary assets	$127,500	$ 22,500
Investment in common stock of Louis Company	–0–	100,000
Inventories (lifo method)	–0–	160,000
Land	60,000	60,000
Building (net)	150,000	144,000
Equipment (net)	112,500	103,500
Total assets	$450,000	$590,000
Liabilities & Stockholders' Equity		
Current liabilities	$ 25,000	$135,000
Long-term notes payable	175,000	150,000
Capital stock, $5 par	200,000	200,000
Paid-in capital in excess of par	50,000	50,000
Retained earnings	–0–	55,000
Total liabilities & stockholders' equity	$450,000	$590,000

On April 30, Year 2, Craddock invested $100,000 in the common stock of Louis Company. Also on April 30, Year 2, Craddock declared a dividend of $20,000.

The changes in the Consumer Price Index for All Urban Consumers during Year 2 are summarized below:

	CPI-U	Conversion factor to restate to end-of-Year 2 dollars
Dec. 31, Year 1	1.10	1.100
Apr. 30, Year 2	1.12	1.080
July 1, Year 2, (also the average for the year)	1.15	1.052
Dec. 31, Year 2	1.21	1.000

Instructions

a Prepare a working paper to restate the income statement for Year 2 to a historical-cost/constant-dollar basis using end-of-Year 2 dollars. Compute any purchasing power gain or loss in a supporting schedule (Schedule A).

b Prepare a working paper to restate the balance sheets on December 31, Year 1 and Year 2, to a historical-cost/constant-dollar basis. (Use the form illustrated on page 1061.)

c "Prove" the amount of retained earnings needed in part **b** to balance total assets (as restated) with total liabilities and stockholders' equity (as restated) by preparing a separate statement of retained earnings for Year 2 on a historical-cost/constant-dollar basis.

25-6 Selected current cost data for Wyoming Corporation's inventories and net plant assets during Year 8 are presented on top of page 1081.

	Inventories	Net plant assets
Balances, Dec. 31, Year 7	$120,000	$1,240,000
Purchases or additions	870,000	70,000
Cost of goods sold or depreciation expense	920,000	120,000
Balances, Dec. 31, Year 8	180,000	1,650,000

Relevant Consumer Price Indexes for All Urban Consumers were as follows:

Dec. 31, Year 7	120
Average for Year 8	140
Dec. 31, Year 8	150

Instructions Prepare working papers to compute the following (assume that the current cost of merchandise purchases, costs of goods sold, additions to plant assets, and depreciation expense are stated in average Year 8 dollars):

a Increase in current cost of inventories, net of inflation measured in average Year 8 dollars.

b Increase in current cost of net plant assets, net of inflation, measured in average Year 8 dollars.

25-7 Kojack Company was organized at the end of Year 9. The company's management has decided to supplement its Year 12 historical-cost/nominal-dollar financial statements with historical-cost/constant-dollar financial statements. The following general ledger trial balance (historical-cost/nominal-dollar basis) and additional information are available:

KOJACK COMPANY
Trial Balance
December 31, Year 12

	Debit	Credit
Cash and accounts receivable (net)	$ 540,000	
Short-term investments (common stocks)	500,000	
Inventories	440,000	
Equipment	650,000	
Accumulated depreciation		$ 164,000
Accounts payable		400,000
15% bonds payable, due in Year 30		500,000
Common stock, $10 par		1,000,000
Retained earnings, Dec. 31, Year 11	46,000	
Sales		1,900,000
Cost of goods sold	1,508,000	
Depreciation expense	65,000	
Other operating expenses, interest expense, and income taxes expense.	215,000	
Totals	$3,964,000	$3,964,000

Additional information

(1) Monetary assets (cash and accounts receivable) exceeded monetary liabilities (accounts payable and bonds payable) by $445,000 on December 31, Year

11. The amounts of monetary items are fixed in terms of numbers of dollars regardless of changes in specific prices or in the Consumer Price Index for All Urban Consumers.

(2) Purchases ($1,840,000 in Year 12) and sales were made at a relatively uniform rate throughout Year 12.

(3) Depreciation expense was computed by the straight-line method, with a full year's depreciation taken in the year of acquisition and none in the year of retirement. The depreciation rate is 10%, and no residual value of plant assets is anticipated. Acquisitions and retirements of plant assets have been made fairly evenly over each year, and the retirements in Year 12 consisted of assets acquired during Year 10. An analysis of the Equipment account follows:

Year	Beginning balance	Acquisitions	Retirements	Ending balance
10	$ –0–	$550,000	$ –0–	$550,000
11	550,000	10,000	–0–	560,000
12	560,000	150,000	60,000	650,000

(4) The 15% bonds payable were issued in Year 10, and the short-term investments were acquired at regular intervals during Year 12. Other operating expenses and interest expense are assumed to have been incurred evenly throughout Year 12.

(5) Assume that Consumer Price Indexes for All Urban Consumers (Year 4 = 100) were as follows:

Annual averages	CPI-U	Conversion factors*
Year 9	113.9	1.128
Year 10	116.8	1.100
Year 11	121.8	1.055
Year 12	126.7	1.014

Quarterly averages		CPI-U	Conversion factors*
Year 11	4th	123.5	1.040
Year 12	1st	124.9	1.029
	2d	126.1	1.019
	3d	127.3	1.009
	4th	128.5	1.000

* Average index for 4th quarter of Year 12 (128.5) divided by the index for any preceding period. For example, the conversion factor for Year 9 is 1.128 (128.5 ÷ 113.9 = 1.128).

Instructions

a Prepare a working paper to restate the Equipment account balance on December 31, Year 12, from historical-cost/nominal-dollars to historical-cost/constant-dollars.

b Prepare a working paper to analyze in historical-cost/nominal-dollars the Accumulated Depreciation account for Year 12.

c Prepare a working paper to analyze in historical-cost/constant-dollars the Accumulated Depreciation account for Year 12.

d Prepare a working paper to compute Kojack Company's purchasing power gain or loss on its net holdings of monetary items for Year 12 (ignore income taxes). The working paper should give consideration to appropriate items on (or related to) the balance sheet and the income statement.

25-8 Ponderosa Corporation was organized on December 31, Year 4, and issued 100,000 shares of $1 par capital stock for $500,000. On January 2, Year 5, Ponderosa completed the following transaction:

Land	80,000	
Buildings	200,000	
Equipment	150,000	
Cash		300,000
Long-Term Notes Payable		130,000

To record acquisition of assets valued at current fair value in exchange for cash and long-term notes payable.

The changes in the Consumer Price Index for All Urban Consumers during Year 5 are summarized below:

	CPI-U	Conversion factor to restate to end-of-Year 5 dollars
Dec. 31, Year 4 (also for beginning of Year 5) . .	100	1.232
July 1, Year 5 (also the average for Year 5)	110	1.120
Sept. 30, Year 5	115.5	1.067
Dec. 31, Year 5	123.2	1.000

On September 30, Year 5, Ponderosa paid a cash dividend of 50 cents a share and issued 10,000 additional shares of capital stock at $8 a share.

The balance sheet on December 31, Year 5, and the income statement for Year 5, on a historical-cost/nominal-dollar basis, are as follows:

PONDEROSA CORPORATION
Balance Sheet
December 31, Year 5

Assets		Liabilities & Stockholders' Equity	
Monetary assets	$390,000	Current liabilities	$110,000
Inventories	100,000	Long-term notes payable . .	130,000
Land	80,000	Capital stock, $1 par	110,000
Buildings(net)	192,000	Additional paid-in capital . .	470,000
Equipment (net)	138,000	Retained earnings	80,000
		Total liabilities & stock-	
Total assets	$900,000	holders' equity	$900,000

PONDEROSA CORPORATION
Income Statement
For Year Ended December 31, Year 5

Sales		$1,260,000
Cost of goods sold		920,000
Gross profit on sales		$ 340,000
Expenses:		
Depreciation	$ 20,000	
Other (including interest expense and income taxes expense)	190,000	210,000
Net income		$ 130,000

Sales amounted to approximately $105,000 a month, and expenses accrued at the rate of $17,500 a month. Both the cost of goods sold and the ending inventories consist of a representative cross section of merchandise purchased throughout Year 5. All liabilities are monetary in nature.

Instructions
a Prepare a working paper to restate the statement of income and retained earnings for Year 5 to a historical-cost/constant-dollar basis. Compute the purchasing power gain or loss in a supporting schedule.
b Prepare a working paper to restate the December 31, Year 5, balance sheet to a historical-cost/constant-dollar basis.

APPENDIX: COMPOUND INTEREST TABLES

Table 1 Future Amount of 1 at Compound Interest Due in n Periods: $a_{\overline{n}|i} = (1 + i)^n$

n \ i	½%	1%	1½%	2%	2½%	3%
1	1.005000	1.010000	1.015000	1.020000	1.025000	1.030000
2	1.010025	1.020100	1.030225	1.040400	1.050625	1.060900
3	1.015075	1.030301	1.045678	1.061208	1.076891	1.092727
4	1.020151	1.040604	1.061364	1.082432	1.103813	1.125509
5	1.025251	1.051010	1.077284	1.104081	1.131408	1.159274
6	1.030378	1.061520	1.093443	1.126162	1.159693	1.194052
7	1.035529	1.072135	1.109845	1.148686	1.188686	1.229874
8	1.040707	1.082857	1.126493	1.171659	1.218403	1.266770
9	1.045911	1.093685	1.143390	1.195093	1.248863	1.304773
10	1.051140	1.104622	1.160541	1.218994	1.280085	1.343916
11	1.056396	1.115668	1.177949	1.243374	1.312087	1.384234
12	1.061678	1.126825	1.195618	1.268242	1.344889	1.425761
13	1.066986	1.138093	1.213552	1.293607	1.378511	1.468534
14	1.072321	1.149474	1.231756	1.319479	1.412974	1.512590
15	1.077683	1.160969	1.250232	1.345868	1.448298	1.557967
16	1.083071	1.172579	1.268986	1.372786	1.484506	1.604706
17	1.088487	1.184304	1.288020	1.400241	1.521618	1.652848
18	1.093929	1.196147	1.307341	1.428246	1.559659	1.702433
19	1.099399	1.208109	1.326951	1.456811	1.598650	1.753506
20	1.104896	1.220190	1.346855	1.485947	1.638616	1.806111
21	1.110420	1.232392	1.367058	1.515666	1.679582	1.860295
22	1.115972	1.244716	1.387564	1.545980	1.721571	1.916103
23	1.121552	1.257163	1.408377	1.576899	1.764611	1.973587
24	1.127160	1.269735	1.429503	1.608437	1.808726	2.032794
25	1.132796	1.282432	1.450945	1.640606	1.853944	2.093778
26	1.138460	1.295256	1.472710	1.673418	1.900293	2.156591
27	1.144152	1.308209	1.494800	1.706886	1.947800	2.221289
28	1.149873	1.321291	1.517222	1.741024	1.996495	2.287928
29	1.155622	1.334504	1.539981	1.775845	2.046407	2.356566
30	1.161400	1.347849	1.563080	1.811362	2.097568	2.427262
31	1.167207	1.361327	1.586526	1.847589	2.150007	2.500080
32	1.173043	1.374941	1.610324	1.884541	2.203757	2.575083
33	1.178908	1.388690	1.634479	1.922231	2.258851	2.652335
34	1.184803	1.402577	1.658996	1.960676	2.315322	2.731905
35	1.190727	1.416603	1.683881	1.999890	2.373205	2.813862
36	1.196681	1.430769	1.709140	2.039887	2.432535	2.898278
37	1.202664	1.445076	1.734777	2.080685	2.493349	2.985227
38	1.208677	1.459527	1.760798	2.122299	2.555682	3.074783
39	1.214721	1.474123	1.787210	2.164745	2.619574	3.167027
40	1.220794	1.488864	1.814018	2.208040	2.685064	3.262038
41	1.226898	1.503752	1.841229	2.252200	2.752190	3.359899
42	1.233033	1.518790	1.868847	2.297244	2.820995	3.460696
43	1.239198	1.533978	1.896880	2.343189	2.891520	3.564517
44	1.245394	1.549318	1.925333	2.390053	2.963808	3.671452
45	1.251621	1.564811	1.954213	2.437854	3.037903	3.781596
46	1.257879	1.580459	1.983526	2.486611	3.113851	3.895044
47	1.264168	1.596263	2.013279	2.536344	3.191697	4.011895
48	1.270489	1.612226	2.043478	2.587070	3.271490	4.132252
49	1.276842	1.628348	2.074130	2.638812	3.353277	4.256219
50	1.283226	1.644632	2.105242	2.691588	3.437109	4.383906

TABLE 1

1087

Table 1 Future Amount of 1 (*continued*)

n \ i	3½%	4%	4½%	5%	5½%	6%
1	1.035000	1.040000	1.045000	1.050000	1.055000	1.060000
2	1.071225	1.081600	1.092025	1.102500	1.113025	1.123600
3	1.108718	1.124864	1.141166	1.157625	1.174241	1.191016
4	1.147523	1.169859	1.192519	1.215506	1.238825	1.262477
5	1.187686	1.216653	1.246182	1.276282	1.306960	1.338226
6	1.229255	1.265319	1.302260	1.340096	1.378843	1.418519
7	1.272279	1.315932	1.360862	1.407100	1.454679	1.503630
8	1.316809	1.368569	1.422101	1.477455	1.534687	1.593848
9	1.362897	1.423312	1.486095	1.551328	1.619094	1.689479
10	1.410599	1.480244	1.552969	1.628895	1.708144	1.790848
11	1.459970	1.539454	1.622853	1.710339	1.802092	1.898299
12	1.511069	1.601032	1.695881	1.795856	1.901207	2.012196
13	1.563956	1.665074	1.772196	1.885649	2.005774	2.132928
14	1.618695	1.731676	1.851945	1.979932	2.116091	2.260904
15	1.675349	1.800944	1.935282	2.078928	2.232476	2.396558
16	1.733986	1.872981	2.022370	2.182875	2.355263	2.540352
17	1.794676	1.947901	2.113377	2.292018	2.484802	2.692773
18	1.857489	2.025817	2.208479	2.406619	2.621466	2.854339
19	1.922501	2.106849	2.307860	2.526950	2.765647	3.025600
20	1.989789	2.191123	2.411714	2.653298	2.917757	3.207135
21	2.059431	2.278768	2.520241	2.785963	3.078234	3.399564
22	2.131512	2.369919	2.633652	2.925261	3.247537	3.603537
23	2.206114	2.464716	2.752166	3.071524	3.426152	3.819750
24	2.283328	2.563304	2.876014	3.225100	3.614590	4.048935
25	2.363245	2.665836	3.005434	3.386355	3.813392	4.291871
26	2.445959	2.772470	3.140679	3.555673	4.023129	4.549383
27	2.531567	2.883369	3.282010	3.733456	4.244401	4.822346
28	2.620172	2.998703	3.429700	3.920129	4.477843	5.111687
29	2.711878	3.118651	3.584036	4.116136	4.724124	5.418388
30	2.806794	3.243398	3.745318	4.321942	4.983951	5.743491
31	2.905031	3.373133	3.913857	4.538039	5.258069	6.088101
32	3.006708	3.508059	4.089981	4.764941	5.547262	6.453387
33	3.111942	3.648381	4.274030	5.003189	5.852362	6.840590
34	3.220860	3.794316	4.466362	5.253348	6.174242	7.251025
35	3.333590	3.946089	4.667348	5.516015	6.513825	7.686087
36	3.450266	4.103933	4.877378	5.791816	6.872085	8.147252
37	3.571025	4.268090	5.096860	6.081407	7.250050	8.636087
38	3.696011	4.438813	5.326219	6.385477	7.648803	9.154252
39	3.825372	4.616366	5.565899	6.704751	8.069487	9.703507
40	3.959260	4.801021	5.816365	7.039989	8.513309	10.285718
41	4.097834	4.993061	6.078101	7.391988	8.981541	10.902861
42	4.241258	5.192784	6.351615	7.761588	9.475526	11.557033
43	4.389702	5.400495	6.637438	8.149667	9.996679	12.250455
44	4.543342	5.616515	6.936123	8.557150	10.546497	12.985482
45	4.702359	5.841176	7.248248	8.985008	11.126554	13.764611
46	4.866941	6.074823	7.574420	9.434258	11.738515	14.590487
47	5.037284	6.317816	7.915268	9.905971	12.384133	15.465917
48	5.213589	6.570528	8.271456	10.401270	13.065260	16.393872
49	5.396065	6.833349	8.643671	10.921333	13.783849	17.377504
50	5.584927	7.106683	9.032636	11.467400	14.541961	18.420154

Table 1   Future Amount of 1 (*continued*)

n \ i	7%	8%	9%	10%	12%	15%
1	1.070000	1.080000	1.090000	1.100000	1.120000	1.150000
2	1.144900	1.166400	1.188100	1.210000	1.254400	1.322500
3	1.225043	1.259712	1.295029	1.331000	1.404928	1.520875
4	1.310796	1.360489	1.411582	1.464100	1.573519	1.749006
5	1.402552	1.469328	1.538624	1.610510	1.762342	2.011357
6	1.500730	1.586874	1.677100	1.771561	1.973823	2.313061
7	1.605781	1.713824	1.828039	1.948717	2.210681	2.660020
8	1.718186	1.850930	1.992563	2.143589	2.475963	3.059023
9	1.838459	1.999005	2.171893	2.357948	2.773079	3.517876
10	1.967151	2.158925	2.367364	2.593742	3.105848	4.045558
11	2.104852	2.331639	2.580426	2.853117	3.478550	4.652391
12	2.252192	2.518170	2.812665	3.138428	3.895976	5.350250
13	2.409845	2.719624	3.065805	3.452271	4.363493	6.152788
14	2.578534	2.937194	3.341727	3.797498	4.887112	7.075706
15	2.759032	3.172169	3.642482	4.177248	5.473566	8.137062
16	2.952164	3.425943	3.970306	4.594973	6.130394	9.357621
17	3.158815	3.700018	4.327633	5.054470	6.866041	10.761264
18	3.379932	3.996019	4.717120	5.559917	7.689966	12.375454
19	3.616528	4.315701	5.141661	6.115909	8.612762	14.231772
20	3.869684	4.660957	5.604411	6.727500	9.646293	16.366537
21	4.140562	5.033834	6.108808	7.400250	10.803848	18.821518
22	4.430402	5.436540	6.658600	8.140275	12.100310	21.644746
23	4.740530	5.871464	7.257874	8.954302	13.552347	24.891458
24	5.072367	6.341181	7.911083	9.849733	15.178629	28.625176
25	5.427433	6.848475	8.623081	10.834706	17.000064	32.918953
26	5.807353	7.396353	9.399158	11.918177	19.040072	37.856796
27	6.213868	7.988061	10.245082	13.109994	21.324881	43.535315
28	6.648838	8.627106	11.167140	14.420994	23.883866	50.065612
29	7.114257	9.317275	12.172182	15.863093	26.749930	57.575454
30	7.612255	10.062657	13.267678	17.449402	29.959922	66.211772
31	8.145113	10.867669	14.461770	19.194342	33.555113	76.143538
32	8.715271	11.737083	15.763329	21.113777	37.581726	87.565068
33	9.325340	12.676050	17.182028	23.225154	42.091533	100.699829
34	9.978114	13.690134	18.728411	25.547670	47.142517	115.804803
35	10.676581	14.785344	20.413968	28.102437	52.799620	133.175523
36	11.423942	15.968172	22.251225	30.912681	59.135574	153.151852
37	12.223618	17.245626	24.253835	34.003949	66.231843	176.124630
38	13.079271	18.625276	26.436680	37.404343	74.179664	202.543324
39	13.994820	20.115298	28.815982	41.144778	83.081224	232.924823
40	14.974458	21.724521	31.409420	45.259256	93.050970	267.863546
41	16.022670	23.462483	34.236268	49.785181	104.217087	308.043078
42	17.144257	25.339482	37.317532	54.763699	116.723137	354.249540
43	18.344355	27.366640	40.676110	60.240069	130.729914	407.386971
44	19.628460	29.555972	44.336960	66.264076	146.417503	468.495017
45	21.002452	31.920449	48.327286	72.890484	163.987604	538.769269
46	22.472623	34.474085	52.676742	80.179532	183.666116	619.584659
47	24.045707	37.232012	57.417649	88.197485	205.706050	712.522358
48	25.728907	40.210573	62.585237	97.017234	230.390776	819.400712
49	27.529930	43.427419	68.217908	106.718957	258.037669	942.310819
50	29.457025	46.901613	74.357520	117.390853	289.002190	1083.657442

TABLE 2

1089

Table 2 Present Value of 1 at Compound Interest Due in n Periods: $p_{\overline{n}|i} = \dfrac{1}{(1 + i)^n}$

n	$\frac{1}{2}\%$	1%	$1\frac{1}{2}\%$	2%	$2\frac{1}{2}\%$	3%
1	0.995025	0.990099	0.985222	0.980392	0.975610	0.970874
2	0.990075	0.980296	0.970662	0.961169	0.951814	0.942596
3	0.985149	0.970590	0.956317	0.942322	0.928599	0.915142
4	0.980248	0.960980	0.942184	0.923845	0.905951	0.888487
5	0.975371	0.951466	0.928260	0.905731	0.883854	0.862609
6	0.970518	0.942045	0.914542	0.887971	0.862297	0.837484
7	0.965690	0.932718	0.901027	0.870560	0.841265	0.813092
8	0.960885	0.923483	0.887711	0.853490	0.820747	0.789409
9	0.956105	0.914340	0.874592	0.836755	0.800728	0.766417
10	0.951348	0.905287	0.861667	0.820348	0.781198	0.744094
11	0.946615	0.896324	0.848933	0.804263	0.762145	0.722421
12	0.941905	0.887449	0.836387	0.788493	0.743556	0.701380
13	0.937219	0.878663	0.824027	0.773033	0.725420	0.680951
14	0.932556	0.869963	0.811849	0.757875	0.707727	0.661118
15	0.927917	0.861349	0.799852	0.743015	0.690466	0.641862
16	0.923300	0.852821	0.788031	0.728446	0.673625	0.623167
17	0.918707	0.844377	0.776385	0.714163	0.657195	0.605016
18	0.914136	0.836017	0.764912	0.700159	0.641166	0.587395
19	0.909588	0.827740	0.753607	0.686431	0.625528	0.570286
20	0.905063	0.819544	0.742470	0.672971	0.610271	0.553676
21	0.900560	0.811430	0.731498	0.659776	0.595386	0.537549
22	0.896080	0.803396	0.720688	0.646839	0.580865	0.521893
23	0.891622	0.795442	0.710037	0.634156	0.566697	0.506692
24	0.887186	0.787566	0.699544	0.621721	0.552875	0.491934
25	0.882772	0.779768	0.689206	0.609531	0.539391	0.477606
26	0.878380	0.772048	0.679021	0.597579	0.526235	0.463695
27	0.874010	0.764404	0.668986	0.585862	0.513400	0.450189
28	0.869662	0.756836	0.659099	0.574375	0.500878	0.437077
29	0.865335	0.749342	0.649359	0.563112	0.488661	0.424346
30	0.861030	0.741923	0.639762	0.552071	0.476743	0.411987
31	0.856746	0.734577	0.630308	0.541246	0.465115	0.399987
32	0.852484	0.727304	0.620993	0.530633	0.453771	0.388337
33	0.848242	0.720103	0.611816	0.520229	0.442703	0.377026
34	0.844022	0.712973	0.602774	0.510028	0.431905	0.366045
35	0.839823	0.705914	0.593866	0.500028	0.421371	0.355383
36	0.835645	0.698925	0.585090	0.490223	0.411094	0.345032
37	0.831487	0.692005	0.576443	0.480611	0.401067	0.334983
38	0.827351	0.685153	0.567924	0.471187	0.391285	0.325226
39	0.823235	0.678370	0.559531	0.461948	0.381741	0.315754
40	0.819139	0.671653	0.551262	0.452890	0.372431	0.306557
41	0.815064	0.665003	0.543116	0.444010	0.363347	0.297628
42	0.811009	0.658419	0.535089	0.435304	0.354485	0.288959
43	0.806974	0.651900	0.527182	0.426769	0.345839	0.280543
44	0.802959	0.645445	0.519391	0.418401	0.337404	0.272372
45	0.798964	0.639055	0.511715	0.410197	0.329174	0.264439
46	0.794989	0.632728	0.504153	0.402154	0.321146	0.256737
47	0.791034	0.626463	0.496702	0.394268	0.313313	0.249259
48	0.787098	0.620260	0.489362	0.386538	0.305671	0.241999
49	0.783183	0.614119	0.482130	0.378958	0.298216	0.234950
50	0.779286	0.608039	0.475005	0.371528	0.290942	0.228107

Table 2   Present Value of 1 (*continued*)

n	$3\frac{1}{2}\%$	4%	$4\frac{1}{2}\%$	5%	$5\frac{1}{2}\%$	6%
1	0.966184	0.961538	0.956938	0.952381	0.947867	0.943396
2	0.933511	0.924556	0.915730	0.907029	0.898452	0.889996
3	0.901943	0.888996	0.876297	0.863838	0.851614	0.839619
4	0.871442	0.854804	0.838561	0.822702	0.807217	0.792094
5	0.841973	0.821927	0.802451	0.783526	0.765134	0.747258
6	0.813501	0.790315	0.767896	0.746215	0.725246	0.704961
7	0.785991	0.759918	0.734828	0.710681	0.687437	0.665057
8	0.759412	0.730690	0.703185	0.676839	0.651599	0.627412
9	0.733731	0.702587	0.672904	0.644609	0.617629	0.591898
10	0.708919	0.675564	0.643928	0.613913	0.585431	0.558395
11	0.684946	0.649581	0.616199	0.584679	0.554911	0.526788
12	0.661783	0.624597	0.589664	0.556837	0.525982	0.496969
13	0.639404	0.600574	0.564272	0.530321	0.498561	0.468839
14	0.617782	0.577475	0.539973	0.505068	0.472569	0.442301
15	0.596891	0.555265	0.516720	0.481017	0.447933	0.417265
16	0.576706	0.533908	0.494469	0.458112	0.424581	0.393646
17	0.557204	0.513373	0.473176	0.436297	0.402447	0.371364
18	0.538361	0.493628	0.452800	0.415521	0.381466	0.350344
19	0.520156	0.474642	0.433302	0.395734	0.361579	0.330513
20	0.502566	0.456387	0.414643	0.376889	0.342729	0.311805
21	0.485571	0.438834	0.396787	0.358942	0.324862	0.294155
22	0.469151	0.421955	0.379701	0.341850	0.307926	0.277505
23	0.453286	0.405726	0.363350	0.325571	0.291873	0.261797
24	0.437957	0.390121	0.347703	0.310068	0.276657	0.246979
25	0.423147	0.375117	0.332731	0.295303	0.262234	0.232999
26	0.408838	0.360689	0.318402	0.281241	0.248563	0.219810
27	0.395012	0.346817	0.304691	0.267848	0.235605	0.207368
28	0.381654	0.333477	0.291571	0.255094	0.223322	0.195630
29	0.368748	0.320651	0.279015	0.242946	0.211679	0.184557
30	0.356278	0.308319	0.267000	0.231377	0.200644	0.174110
31	0.344230	0.296460	0.255502	0.220359	0.190184	0.164255
32	0.332590	0.285058	0.244500	0.209866	0.180269	0.154957
33	0.321343	0.274094	0.233971	0.199873	0.170871	0.146186
34	0.310476	0.263552	0.223896	0.190355	0.161963	0.137912
35	0.299977	0.253415	0.214254	0.181290	0.153520	0.130105
36	0.289833	0.243669	0.205028	0.172657	0.145516	0.122741
37	0.280032	0.234297	0.196199	0.164436	0.137930	0.115793
38	0.270562	0.225285	0.187750	0.156605	0.130739	0.109239
39	0.261413	0.216621	0.179665	0.149148	0.123924	0.103056
40	0.252572	0.208289	0.171929	0.142046	0.117463	0.097222
41	0.244031	0.200278	0.164525	0.135282	0.111339	0.091719
42	0.235779	0.192575	0.157440	0.128840	0.105535	0.086527
43	0.227806	0.185168	0.150661	0.122704	0.100033	0.081630
44	0.220102	0.178046	0.144173	0.116861	0.094818	0.077009
45	0.212659	0.171198	0.137964	0.111297	0.089875	0.072650
46	0.205468	0.164614	0.132023	0.105997	0.085190	0.068538
47	0.198520	0.158283	0.126338	0.100949	0.080748	0.064658
48	0.191806	0.152195	0.120898	0.096142	0.076539	0.060998
49	0.185320	0.146341	0.115692	0.091564	0.072549	0.057546
50	0.179053	0.140713	0.110710	0.087204	0.068767	0.054288

TABLE 2

1091

Table 2   Present Value of 1 (*continued*)

n \ i	7%	8%	9%	10%	12%	15%
1	0.934580	0.925926	0.917431	0.909091	0.892857	0.869565
2	0.873439	0.857339	0.841680	0.826446	0.797194	0.756144
3	0.816298	0.793832	0.772183	0.751315	0.711780	0.657516
4	0.762895	0.735030	0.708425	0.683013	0.635518	0.571753
5	0.712986	0.680583	0.649931	0.620921	0.567427	0.497177
6	0.666342	0.630170	0.596267	0.564474	0.506631	0.432328
7	0.622750	0.583490	0.547034	0.513158	0.452349	0.375937
8	0.582009	0.540269	0.501866	0.466507	0.403883	0.326902
9	0.543934	0.500249	0.460428	0.424098	0.360610	0.284262
10	0.508349	0.463193	0.422411	0.385543	0.321973	0.247185
11	0.475093	0.428883	0.387533	0.350494	0.287476	0.214943
12	0.444012	0.397114	0.355535	0.318631	0.256675	0.186907
13	0.414964	0.367698	0.326179	0.289664	0.229174	0.162528
14	0.387817	0.340461	0.299246	0.263331	0.204620	0.141329
15	0.362446	0.315242	0.274538	0.239392	0.182696	0.122894
16	0.338735	0.291890	0.251870	0.217629	0.163122	0.106865
17	0.316574	0.270269	0.231073	0.197845	0.145644	0.092926
18	0.295864	0.250249	0.211994	0.179859	0.130040	0.080805
19	0.276508	0.231712	0.194490	0.163508	0.116107	0.070265
20	0.258419	0.214548	0.178431	0.148644	0.103667	0.061100
21	0.241513	0.198656	0.163698	0.135131	0.092560	0.053131
22	0.225713	0.183941	0.150182	0.122846	0.082643	0.046201
23	0.210947	0.170315	0.137781	0.111678	0.073788	0.040174
24	0.197147	0.157699	0.126405	0.101526	0.065882	0.034934
25	0.184249	0.146018	0.115968	0.092296	0.058823	0.030378
26	0.172195	0.135202	0.106393	0.083905	0.052521	0.026415
27	0.160930	0.125187	0.097608	0.076278	0.046894	0.022970
28	0.150402	0.115914	0.089548	0.069343	0.041869	0.019974
29	0.140563	0.107328	0.082155	0.063039	0.037383	0.017369
30	0.131367	0.099377	0.075371	0.057309	0.033378	0.015103
31	0.122773	0.092016	0.069148	0.052099	0.029802	0.013133
32	0.114741	0.085200	0.063438	0.047362	0.026609	0.011420
33	0.107235	0.078889	0.058200	0.043057	0.023758	0.009931
34	0.100219	0.073045	0.053395	0.039143	0.021212	0.008635
35	0.093663	0.067635	0.048986	0.035584	0.018940	0.007509
36	0.087535	0.062625	0.044941	0.032349	0.016910	0.006529
37	0.081809	0.057986	0.041231	0.029408	0.015098	0.005678
38	0.076457	0.053690	0.037826	0.026735	0.013481	0.004937
39	0.071455	0.049713	0.034703	0.024304	0.012036	0.004293
40	0.066780	0.046031	0.031838	0.022095	0.010747	0.003733
41	0.062412	0.042621	0.029209	0.020086	0.009595	0.003246
42	0.058329	0.039464	0.026797	0.018260	0.008567	0.002823
43	0.054513	0.036541	0.024584	0.016600	0.007649	0.002455
44	0.050946	0.033834	0.022555	0.015091	0.006830	0.002134
45	0.047613	0.031328	0.020692	0.013719	0.006098	0.001856
46	0.044499	0.029007	0.018984	0.012472	0.005445	0.001614
47	0.041587	0.026859	0.017416	0.011338	0.004861	0.001403
48	0.038867	0.024869	0.015978	0.010307	0.004340	0.001220
49	0.036324	0.023027	0.014659	0.009370	0.003875	0.001061
50	0.033948	0.021321	0.013449	0.008519	0.003460	0.000923

Table 3 **Future Amount of Ordinary Annuity of 1 per Period:** $A_{\overline{n}|i} = \dfrac{(1+i)^n - 1}{i}$

n	½%	1%	1½%	2%	2½%	3%
1	1.000000	1.000000	1.000000	1.000000	1.000000	1.000000
2	2.005000	2.010000	2.015000	2.020000	2.025000	2.030000
3	3.015025	3.030100	3.045225	3.060400	3.075625	3.090900
4	4.030100	4.060401	4.090903	4.121608	4.152516	4.183627
5	5.050251	5.101005	5.152267	5.204040	5.256329	5.309136
6	6.075502	6.152015	6.229551	6.308121	6.387737	6.468410
7	7.105879	7.213535	7.322994	7.434283	7.547430	7.662462
8	8.141409	8.285671	8.432839	8.582969	8.736116	8.892336
9	9.182116	9.368527	9.559332	9.754628	9.954519	10.159106
10	10.228026	10.462213	10.702722	10.949721	11.203382	11.463879
11	11.279167	11.566835	11.863262	12.168715	12.483466	12.807796
12	12.335562	12.682503	13.041211	13.412090	13.795553	14.192030
13	13.397240	13.809328	14.236830	14.680332	15.140442	15.617790
14	14.464226	14.947421	15.450382	15.973938	16.518953	17.086324
15	15.536548	16.096896	16.682138	17.293417	17.931927	18.598914
16	16.614230	17.257864	17.932370	18.639285	19.380225	20.156881
17	17.697301	18.430443	19.201355	20.012071	20.864730	21.761588
18	18.785788	19.614748	20.489376	21.412312	22.386349	23.414435
19	19.879717	20.810895	21.796716	22.840559	23.946007	25.116868
20	20.979115	22.019004	23.123667	24.297370	25.544658	26.870374
21	22.084011	23.239194	24.470522	25.783317	27.183274	28.676486
22	23.194431	24.471586	25.837580	27.298984	28.862856	30.536780
23	24.310403	25.716302	27.225144	28.844963	30.584427	32.452884
24	25.431955	26.973465	28.633521	30.421862	32.349038	34.426470
25	26.559115	28.243200	30.063024	32.030300	34.157764	36.459264
26	27.691911	29.525632	31.513969	33.670906	36.011708	38.553042
27	28.830370	30.820888	32.986679	35.344324	37.912001	40.709634
28	29.974522	32.129097	34.481479	37.051210	39.859801	42.930923
29	31.124395	33.450388	35.998701	38.792235	41.856296	45.218850
30	32.280017	34.784892	37.538681	40.568079	43.902703	47.575416
31	33.441417	36.132740	39.101762	42.379441	46.000271	50.002678
32	34.608624	37.494068	40.688288	44.227030	48.150278	52.502759
33	35.781667	38.869009	42.298612	46.111570	50.354034	55.077841
34	36.960575	40.257699	43.933092	48.033802	52.612885	57.730177
35	38.145378	41.660276	45.592088	49.994478	54.928207	60.462082
36	39.336105	43.076878	47.275969	51.994367	57.301413	63.275944
37	40.532785	44.507647	48.985109	54.034255	59.733948	66.174223
38	41.735449	45.952724	50.719885	56.114940	62.227297	69.159449
39	42.944127	47.412251	52.480684	58.237238	64.782979	72.234233
40	44.158847	48.886373	54.267894	60.401983	67.402554	75.401260
41	45.379642	50.375237	56.081912	62.610023	70.087617	78.663298
42	46.606540	51.878989	57.923141	64.862223	72.839808	82.023196
43	47.839572	53.397779	59.791988	67.159468	75.660803	85.483892
44	49.078770	54.931757	61.688868	69.502657	78.552323	89.048409
45	50.324164	56.481075	63.614201	71.892710	81.516131	92.719861
46	51.575785	58.045885	65.568414	74.330564	84.554034	96.501457
47	52.833664	59.626344	67.551940	76.817176	87.667885	100.396501
48	54.097832	61.222608	69.565219	79.353519	90.859582	104.408396
49	55.368321	62.834834	71.608698	81.940590	94.131072	108.540648
50	56.645163	64.463182	73.682828	84.579401	97.484349	112.796867

TABLE 3

1093

Table 3 Future Amount of Ordinary Annuity of 1 (*continued*)

n \ i	3½%	4%	4½%	5%	5½%	6%
1	1.000000	1.000000	1.000000	1.000000	1.000000	1.000000
2	2.035000	2.040000	2.045000	2.050000	2.055000	2.060000
3	3.106225	3.121600	3.137025	3.152500	3.168025	3.183600
4	4.214943	4.246464	4.278191	4.310125	4.342266	4.374616
5	5.362466	5.416323	5.470710	5.525631	5.581091	5.637093
6	6.550152	6.632975	6.716892	6.801913	6.888051	6.975319
7	7.779408	7.898294	8.019152	8.142008	8.266894	8.393838
8	9.051687	9.214226	9.380014	9.549109	9.721573	9.897468
9	10.368496	10.582795	10.802114	11.026564	11.256260	11.491316
10	11.731393	12.006107	12.288209	12.577893	12.875354	13.180795
11	13.141992	13.486351	13.841179	14.206787	14.583498	14.971643
12	14.601962	15.025805	15.464032	15.917127	16.385591	16.869941
13	16.113030	16.626838	17.159913	17.712983	18.286798	18.882138
14	17.676986	18.291911	18.932109	19.598632	20.292572	21.015066
15	19.295681	20.023588	20.784054	21.578564	22.408664	23.275970
16	20.971030	21.824531	22.719337	23.657492	24.641140	25.672528
17	22.705016	23.697512	24.741707	25.840366	26.996403	28.212880
18	24.499691	25.645413	26.855084	28.132385	29.481205	30.905653
19	26.357181	27.671229	29.063562	30.539004	32.102671	33.759992
20	28.279682	29.778079	31.371423	33.065954	34.868318	36.785591
21	30.269471	31.969202	33.783137	35.719252	37.786076	39.992727
22	32.328902	34.247970	36.303378	38.505214	40.864310	43.392290
23	34.460414	36.617889	38.937030	41.430475	44.111847	46.995828
24	36.666528	39.082604	41.689196	44.501999	47.537998	50.815577
25	38.949857	41.645908	44.565210	47.727099	51.152588	54.864512
26	41.313102	44.311745	47.570645	51.113454	54.965981	59.156383
27	43.759060	47.084214	50.711324	54.669126	58.989109	63.705766
28	46.290627	49.967583	53.993333	58.402583	63.233510	68.528112
29	48.910799	52.966286	57.423033	62.322712	67.711354	73.629798
30	51.622677	56.084938	61.007070	66.438848	72.435478	79.058186
31	54.429471	59.328335	64.752388	70.760790	77.419429	84.801677
32	57.334502	62.701469	68.666245	75.298829	82.677498	90.889778
33	60.341210	66.209527	72.756226	80.063771	88.224760	97.343165
34	63.453152	69.857909	77.030256	85.066959	94.077122	104.183755
35	66.674013	73.652225	81.496618	90.320307	100.251364	111.434780
36	70.007603	77.598314	86.163966	95.836323	106.765189	119.120867
37	73.457869	81.702246	91.041344	101.628139	113.637274	127.268119
38	77.028895	85.970336	96.138205	107.709546	120.887324	135.904206
39	80.724906	90.409150	101.464424	114.095023	128.536127	145.058458
40	84.550278	95.025516	107.030323	120.799774	136.605614	154.761966
41	88.509537	99.826536	112.846688	127.839763	145.118923	165.047684
42	92.607371	104.819598	118.924789	135.231751	154.100464	175.950545
43	96.848629	110.012382	125.276404	142.993339	163.575989	187.507577
44	101.238331	115.412877	131.913842	151.143006	173.572669	199.758032
45	105.781673	121.029392	138.849965	159.700156	184.119165	212.743514
46	110.484031	126.870568	146.098214	168.685164	195.245719	226.508125
47	115.350973	132.945390	153.672633	178.119422	206.984234	241.098612
48	120.388257	139.263206	161.587902	188.025393	219.368367	256.564529
49	125.601846	145.833734	169.859357	198.426663	232.433627	272.958401
50	130.997910	152.667084	178.503028	209.347996	246.217476	290.335905

Table 3   Future Amount of Ordinary Annuity of 1 (*continued*)

n \ i	7%	8%	9%	10%	12%	15%
1	1.000000	1.000000	1.000000	1.000000	1.000000	1.000000
2	2.070000	2.080000	2.090000	2.100000	2.120000	2.150000
3	3.214900	3.246400	3.278100	3.310000	3.374400	3.472500
4	4.439943	4.506112	4.573129	4.641000	4.779328	4.993375
5	5.750740	5.866601	5.984711	6.105100	6.352847	6.742381
6	7.153291	7.335929	7.523335	7.715610	8.115189	8.753738
7	8.654021	8.922803	9.200435	9.487171	10.089012	11.066799
8	10.259803	10.636628	11.028474	11.435888	12.299693	13.726819
9	11.977989	12.487558	13.021036	13.579477	14.775656	16.785842
10	13.816448	14.486562	15.192930	15.937425	17.548735	20.303718
11	15.783599	16.645487	17.560293	18.531167	20.654583	24.349276
12	17.888451	18.977126	20.140720	21.384284	24.133133	29.001667
13	20.140643	21.495297	22.953385	24.522712	28.029109	34.351917
14	22.550488	24.214920	26.019189	27.974983	32.392602	40.504705
15	25.129022	27.152114	29.360916	31.772482	37.279715	47.580411
16	27.888054	30.324283	33.003399	35.949730	42.753280	55.717472
17	30.840217	33.750226	36.973705	40.544703	48.883674	65.075093
18	33.999033	37.450244	41.301338	45.599173	55.749715	75.836357
19	37.378965	41.446263	46.018458	51.159090	63.439681	88.211811
20	40.995492	45.761964	51.160120	57.274999	72.052442	102.443583
21	44.865177	50.422921	56.764530	64.002499	81.698736	118.810120
22	49.005739	55.456755	62.873338	71.402749	92.502584	137.631638
23	53.436141	60.893296	69.531939	79.543024	104.602894	159.276384
24	58.176671	66.764759	76.789813	88.497327	118.155241	184.167841
25	63.249038	73.105940	84.700896	98.347059	133.333870	212.793017
26	68.676470	79.954415	93.323977	109.181765	150.333934	245.711970
27	74.483823	87.350768	102.723135	121.099942	169.374007	283.568766
28	80.697691	95.338830	112.968217	134.209936	190.698887	327.104080
29	87.346529	103.965936	124.135356	148.630930	214.582754	377.169693
30	94.460786	113.283211	136.307539	164.494023	241.332684	434.745146
31	102.073041	123.345868	149.575217	181.943425	271.292606	500.956918
32	110.218154	134.213537	164.036987	201.137767	304.847719	577.100456
33	118.933425	145.950620	179.800315	222.251544	342.429446	644.665525
34	128.258765	158.626670	196.982344	245.476699	384.520979	765.365353
35	138.236878	172.316804	215.710755	271.024368	431.663496	881.170156
36	148.913460	187.102148	236.124723	299.126805	484.463116	1014.345680
37	160.337402	203.070320	258.375948	330.039486	543.598690	1167.497532
38	172.561020	220.315945	282.629783	364.043434	609.830533	1343.622161
39	185.640292	238.941221	309.066463	401.447778	684.010197	1546.165485
40	199.635112	259.056519	337.882445	442.592556	767.091420	1779.090308
41	214.609570	280.781040	369.291865	487.851811	860.142391	2046.953854
42	230.632240	304.243523	403.528133	537.636992	964.359478	2354.996933
43	247.776497	329.583005	440.845665	592.400692	1081.082615	2709.246473
44	266.120851	356.949646	481.521775	652.640761	1211.812529	3116.633443
45	285.749311	386.505617	525.858734	718.904837	1358.230032	3585.128460
46	306.751763	418.426067	574.186021	791.795321	1522.217636	4123.897729
47	329.224386	452.900152	626.862762	871.974853	1705.883752	4743.482388
48	353.270093	490.132164	684.280411	960.172338	1911.589803	5466.004746
49	378.999000	530.342737	746.865648	1057.189572	2141.980579	6275.405458
50	406.528929	573.770156	815.083556	1163.908529	2400.018249	7217.716277

TABLE 4

1095

Table 4   Present Value of Ordinary Annuity of 1 per Period: $P_{\overline{n}|i} = \dfrac{1 - \dfrac{1}{(1 + i)^n}}{i}$

n \ i	½%	1%	1½%	2%	2½%	3%
1	0.995025	0.990099	0.985222	0.980392	0.975610	0.970874
2	1.985099	1.970395	1.955883	1.941561	1.927424	1.913470
3	2.970248	2.940985	2.912200	2.883883	2.856024	2.828611
4	3.950496	3.901966	3.854385	3.807729	3.761974	3.717098
5	4.925866	4.853431	4.782645	4.713460	4.645829	4.579707
6	5.896384	5.795476	5.697187	5.601431	5.508125	5.417191
7	6.862074	6.728195	6.598214	6.471991	6.349391	6.230283
8	7.822959	7.651678	7.485925	7.325481	7.170137	7.019692
9	8.779064	8.566018	8.360517	8.162237	7.970866	7.786109
10	9.730412	9.471305	9.222185	8.982585	8.752064	8.530203
11	10.677027	10.367628	10.071118	9.786848	9.514209	9.252624
12	11.618932	11.255077	10.907505	10.575341	10.257765	9.954004
13	12.556151	12.133740	11.731532	11.348374	10.983185	10.634955
14	13.488708	13.003703	12.543382	12.106249	11.690912	11.296073
15	14.416625	13.865053	13.343233	12.849264	12.381378	11.937935
16	15.339925	14.717874	14.131264	13.577709	13.055003	12.561102
17	16.258632	15.562251	14.907649	14.291872	13.712198	13.166118
18	17.172768	16.398269	15.672561	14.992031	14.353364	13.753513
19	18.082356	17.226009	16.426168	15.678462	14.978891	14.323799
20	18.987419	18.045553	17.168639	16.351433	15.589162	14.877475
21	19.887979	18.856983	17.900137	17.011209	16.184549	15.415024
22	20.784059	19.660379	18.620824	17.658048	16.765413	15.936917
23	21.675681	20.455821	19.330861	18.292204	17.332110	16.443608
24	22.562866	21.243387	20.030405	18.913926	17.884986	16.935542
25	23.445638	22.023156	20.719611	19.523456	18.424376	17.413148
26	24.324018	22.795204	21.398632	20.121036	18.950611	17.876842
27	25.198028	23.559608	22.067617	20.706898	19.464011	18.327031
28	26.067689	24.316443	22.726717	21.281272	19.964889	18.764108
29	26.933024	25.065785	23.376076	21.844385	20.453550	19.188455
30	27.794054	25.807708	24.015838	22.396456	20.930293	19.600441
31	28.650800	26.542285	24.646146	22.937702	21.395407	20.000428
32	29.503284	27.269589	25.267139	23.468335	21.849178	20.388766
33	30.351526	27.989693	25.878954	23.988564	22.291881	20.765792
34	31.195548	28.702666	26.481728	24.498592	22.723786	21.131837
35	32.035371	29.408580	27.075595	24.998619	23.145157	21.487220
36	32.871016	30.107505	27.660684	25.488842	23.556251	21.832253
37	33.702504	30.799510	28.237127	25.969453	23.957318	22.167235
38	34.529854	31.484663	28.805052	26.440641	24.348603	22.492462
39	35.353089	32.163033	29.364583	26.902589	24.730344	22.808215
40	36.172228	32.834686	29.915845	27.355479	25.102775	23.114772
41	36.987291	33.499689	30.458961	27.799489	25.466122	23.412400
42	37.798300	34.158108	30.994050	28.234794	25.820607	23.701359
43	38.605274	34.810008	31.521232	28.661562	26.166446	23.981902
44	39.408232	35.455454	32.040622	29.079963	26.503849	24.254274
45	40.207196	36.094508	32.552337	29.490160	26.833024	24.518713
46	41.002185	36.727236	33.056490	29.892314	27.154170	24.775449
47	41.793219	37.353699	33.553192	30.286582	27.467483	25.024708
48	42.580318	37.973959	34.042554	30.673120	27.773154	25.266707
49	43.363500	38.588079	34.524683	31.052078	28.071369	25.501657
50	44.142786	39.196118	34.999688	31.423606	28.362312	25.729764

Table 4   Present Value of Ordinary Annuity of 1 (*continued*)

n \ i	3¹⁄₂%	4%	4¹⁄₂%	5%	5¹⁄₂%	6%
1	0.966184	0.961538	0.956938	0.952381	0.947867	0.943396
2	1.899694	1.886095	1.872668	1.859410	1.846320	1.833393
3	2.801637	2.775091	2.748964	2.723248	2.697933	2.673012
4	3.673079	3.629895	3.587526	3.545951	3.505150	3.465106
5	4.515052	4.451822	4.389977	4.329477	4.270284	4.212364
6	5.328553	5.242137	5.157872	5.075692	4.995530	4.917324
7	6.114544	6.002055	5.892701	5.786373	5.682967	5.582381
8	6.873956	6.732745	6.595886	6.463213	6.334566	6.209794
9	7.607687	7.435332	7.268791	7.107822	6.952195	6.801692
10	8.316605	8.110896	7.912718	7.721735	7.537626	7.360087
11	9.001551	8.760477	8.528917	8.306414	8.092536	7.886875
12	9.663334	9.385074	9.118581	8.863252	8.618518	8.383844
13	10.302738	9.985648	9.682852	9.393573	9.117079	8.852683
14	10.920520	10.563123	10.222825	9.898641	9.589648	9.294984
15	11.517411	11.118387	10.739546	10.379658	10.037581	9.712249
16	12.094117	11.652296	11.234015	10.837770	10.462162	10.105895
17	12.651321	12.165669	11.707191	11.274066	10.864609	10.477260
18	13.189682	12.659297	12.159992	11.689587	11.246074	10.827603
19	13.709837	13.133939	12.593294	12.085321	11.607654	11.158116
20	14.212403	13.590326	13.007936	12.462210	11.950382	11.469921
21	14.697974	14.029160	13.404724	12.821153	12.275244	11.764077
22	15.167125	14.451115	13.784425	13.163003	12.583170	12.041582
23	15.620410	14.856842	14.147775	13.488574	12.875042	12.303379
24	16.058368	15.246963	14.495478	13.798642	13.151699	12.550358
25	16.481515	15.622080	14.828209	14.093945	13.413933	12.783356
26	16.890352	15.982769	15.146611	14.375185	13.662495	13.003166
27	17.285365	16.329586	15.451303	14.643034	13.898100	13.210534
28	17.667019	16.663063	15.742874	14.898127	14.121422	13.406164
29	18.035767	16.983715	16.021889	15.141074	14.333101	13.590721
30	18.392045	17.292033	16.288889	15.372451	14.533745	13.764831
31	18.736276	17.588494	16.544391	15.592811	14.723929	13.929086
32	19.068865	17.873552	16.788891	15.802677	14.904198	14.084043
33	19.390208	18.147646	17.022862	16.002549	15.075069	14.230230
34	19.700684	18.411198	17.246758	16.192904	15.237033	14.368141
35	20.000661	18.664613	17.461012	16.374194	15.390552	14.498246
36	20.290494	18.908282	17.666041	16.546852	15.536068	14.620987
37	20.570525	19.142579	17.862240	16.711287	15.673999	14.736780
38	20.841087	19.367864	18.049990	16.867893	15.804738	14.846019
39	21.102500	19.584485	18.229656	17.017041	15.928662	14.949075
40	21.355072	19.792774	18.401584	17.159086	16.046125	15.046297
41	21.599104	19.993052	18.566109	17.294368	16.157464	15.138016
42	21.834883	20.185627	18.723550	17.423208	16.262999	15.224543
43	22.062689	20.370795	18.874210	17.545912	16.363032	15.306173
44	22.282791	20.548841	19.018383	17.662773	16.457851	15.383182
45	22.495450	20.720040	19.156347	17.774070	16.547726	15.455832
46	22.700918	20.884654	19.288371	17.880067	16.632915	15.524370
47	22.899438	21.042936	19.414709	17.981016	16.713664	15.589028
48	23.091244	21.195131	19.535607	18.077158	16.790203	15.650027
49	23.276565	21.341472	19.651298	18.168722	16.862751	15.707572
50	23.455618	21.482185	19.762008	18.255925	16.931518	15.761861

TABLE 4

Table 4 Present Value of Ordinary Annuity of 1 (continued)

n \ i	7%	8%	9%	10%	12%	15%
1	0.934579	0.925926	0.917431	0.909091	0.892857	0.869565
2	1.808018	1.783265	1.759111	1.735537	1.690051	1.625709
3	2.624316	2.577097	2.531295	2.486852	2.401831	2.283225
4	3.387211	3.312127	3.239720	3.169865	3.037349	2.854978
5	4.100197	3.992710	3.889651	3.790787	3.604776	3.352155
6	4.766540	4.622880	4.485919	4.355261	4.111407	3.784483
7	5.389289	5.206370	5.032953	4.868419	4.563757	4.160420
8	5.971299	5.746639	5.534819	5.334926	4.967640	4.487322
9	6.515232	6.246888	5.995247	5.759024	5.328250	4.771584
10	7.023582	6.710081	6.417658	6.144567	5.650223	5.018769
11	7.498674	7.138964	6.805191	6.495061	5.937699	5.233712
12	7.942686	7.536078	7.160725	6.813692	6.194374	5.420619
13	8.357651	7.903776	7.486904	7.103356	6.423548	5.583147
14	8.745468	8.244237	7.786150	7.366687	6.628168	5.724476
15	9.107914	8.559479	8.060688	7.606080	6.810864	5.847370
16	9.446649	8.851369	8.312558	7.823709	6.973986	5.954235
17	9.763223	9.121638	8.543631	8.021553	7.119630	6.047161
18	10.059087	9.371887	8.755625	8.201412	7.249670	6.127966
19	10.335595	9.603599	8.950115	8.364920	7.365777	6.198231
20	10.594014	9.818147	9.128546	8.513564	7.469444	6.259331
21	10.835527	10.016803	9.292244	8.648694	7.562003	6.312462
22	11.061241	10.200744	9.442425	8.771540	7.644646	6.358663
23	11.272187	10.371059	9.580207	8.883218	7.718434	6.398837
24	11.469334	10.528758	9.706612	8.984744	7.784316	6.433771
25	11.653583	10.674776	9.822580	9.077040	7.843139	6.464149
26	11.825779	10.809978	9.928972	9.160945	7.895660	6.490564
27	11.986709	10.935165	10.026580	9.237223	7.942554	6.513534
28	12.137111	11.051078	10.116128	9.306567	7.984423	6.533508
29	12.277674	11.158406	10.198283	9.369606	8.021806	6.550877
30	12.409041	11.257783	10.273654	9.426914	8.055184	6.565980
31	12.531814	11.349799	10.342802	9.479013	8.084986	6.579113
32	12.646555	11.434999	10.406240	9.526376	8.111594	6.590533
33	12.753790	11.513888	10.464441	9.569432	8.135352	6.600463
34	12.854009	11.586934	10.517835	9.608575	8.156564	6.609099
35	12.947672	11.654568	10.566821	9.644159	8.175504	6.616607
36	13.035208	11.717193	10.611763	9.676508	8.192414	6.623137
37	13.117017	11.775179	10.652993	9.705917	8.207513	6.628815
38	13.193473	11.828869	10.690820	9.732651	8.220993	6.633752
39	13.264928	11.878582	10.725523	9.756956	8.233030	6.638045
40	13.331709	11.924613	10.757360	9.779051	8.243777	6.641778
41	13.394120	11.967235	10.786569	9.799137	8.253372	6.645025
42	13.452449	12.006699	10.813366	9.817397	8.261939	6.647848
43	13.506962	12.043240	10.837950	9.833998	8.269589	6.650302
44	13.557908	12.077074	10.860505	9.849089	8.276418	6.652437
45	13.605522	12.108402	10.881197	9.862808	8.282516	6.654293
46	13.650020	12.137409	10.900181	9.875280	8.287961	6.655907
47	13.691608	12.164267	10.917597	9.886618	8.292822	6.657310
48	13.730474	12.189136	10.933575	9.896926	8.297163	6.658531
49	13.766799	12.212163	10.948234	9.906296	8.301038	6.659592
50	13.800746	12.233485	10.961683	9.914814	8.304498	6.660515

INDEX

Continued from inside front cover

10-7 Total current liabilities, $314,900.

10-8 *a* Royalty paid in third quarter, $31,000.

10-9 *a* Estimated liability, $455,000.

10-11 Corrected retained earnings, $178,950; total assets, $392,150.

11-1 *a* Balance in Land account, $1,500,000; balance in Buildings account, $970,000.

11-2 *a* Loss, $3,400; *b* Loss, $300; *d* Amount recoverable, $36,450.

11-3 *a* Recoverable on Policy A, $297,000; recoverable on Policy B, $78,400.

11-6 *a* Discount on note payable, $14,510.

11-7 *a* Land, $351,400; building, $535,700.

11-8 (1) Gain, $7,000; (4) Gain, $120,000; (6) No gain or loss.

11-9 *a* Gain, $82,905; *c* Debit to Building account, $61,645.

11-10 *a* Loss, $66,000; *b* Total recovered, $111,500; *c* Net gain, $12,500.

11-11 *a* Loss, $57,600; *b* Amount of claim, $55,800; *c* Total loss, $5,950.

12-1 Depreciation for Year 5: *c* $2,025; *d* $900; *e* $933.

12-3 *a* $66,000; b Depreciation for Year 2: (3) $23,760; (4) $14,400.

12-4 *a* Machinery and equipment on Dec. 31, Year 9, $1,106,000; *b* Loss on scrapping of machine, $7,550.

12-5 *a* Depreciation for Year 5, $9,370; *b* Loss on disposal, $5,630.

12-6 *a* Land, $49,000; building, $168,000; *b* Depr. for Year 3: (2) $13,986; (3) $14,600.

12-8 *a* EPS, $5.30; *b* Variable costs of production, $2.15.

12-9 *b* 20%.

12-10 (a) $66,440; (c) 50 years; (m) $30,600.

13-1 Intangible assets, $1,650,000; related expenses for Year 8, $640,000.

13-2 *a* Marie, $1,800,000; Chor, $900,000; *c* Total value of: Marie, $1,932,000; Chor, $1,369,200.

13-3 *a* $69,000; *b* R & D expense, $37,500.

13-4 *b* Amort. for first 40 weeks, $4,200 per telecast.

13-5 *b* Total intangible assets, $33,560.

13-6 *a* $13,000; *c* $71,475; *d* $32,359.

13-7 *a* Prior period adjustment (debit) $186,410.

13-8 *a* (1) $94,700; (4) $81,800.

14-1 Amort. of goodwill for Year 8, $22,500.

14-2 *a* Bal. in account, $3,050,000; *b* Total income, $309,000.

14-3 *a* Bal. in account on Dec. 31, $266,560; *b* Gain on sale of rights, $1,050.

14-4 *a* Unrealized loss: Year 1, $42,000; Year 2, $27,000 (credit).

14-6 *a* Goodwill, $120,000.

14-7 *a* Amount paid for bonds, $450,909; *b* Carrying amount at end of Year 2 (interest method), $455,743.

14-8 *a* Goodwill, $950,000; *d* Loss, $182,875.

14-9 *a* Gain: (1) $565; (2) $528; (3) $525; *b* Total cost of 4,740 shares, $135,185.

14-10 *a* Fund balance at end of Year 3, $96,143; *b* Decrease in net income for Year 3, $1,460.

14-11 *b* Total investments on Dec. 31, $624,775.

15-1 *a* $975,815

15-2 *c* Gain, $34,400.

15-3 *a* $937,688; *b* (3) Bond interest expense, $46,979.

15-4 *a* $2,448,800; *b* Loss, $297,600; *c* Deferred bond issue costs, $35,200.

15-7 *c* Credit to Paid-in Capital in Excess of Par, $554,480.

15-8 *a* Interest expense for Year 5, $39,200; *b* Gain, $2,000.

15-9 *a* $3,898,485.

15-10 *c* Credit to Paid-in Capital in Excess of Par, $1,896,280; *d* Loss, $4,600; *e* Loss, $277,760.

16-1 Amount available for common dividends, $180,000.

16-2 *b* Total stockholders' equity, $6,180,000.

16-3 *b* Total stockholders' equity, $4,520,870.

16-4 *b* Total stockholders' equity, $1,130,744.

16-5 *b* RE on Apr. 30, Year 6, $2,218,500; total stockholders' equity, $6,073,500.

16-6 *b* RE on June 30, Year 2, $13,743,200; *c* Total stockholders' equity, $17,430,700.

16-7 Total stockholders' equity, $1,850,000.

16-8 *a* $25.75; *b* $5.25; *d* Total stockholders' equity, $10,064,200.

16-10 *b* Common stock, $1,042,600; RE, $4,772,400.

17-2 *b* Total stockholders' equity, $78,329,600.

17-4 *b* Total stockholders' equity, $77,175,000.

17-8 Compensation expense: Year 6, $40,000; Year 7, $120,000; Year 8, $20,000; Year 9, $300,000.

18-1 *b* Total stockholders' equity, $7,468,000.

18-3 *c* RE on Dec. 31, Year 5, $1,379,340.

18-4 Paid-in capital in excess of par, $108,090,000; RE, $54,782,500.

18-5 EPS: Year 1, $1.36; Year 5, $2.17.

18-6 Paid-in capital in excess of par, $5,545,000; RE, $360,000.

18-7 *b* Primary EPS: Year 4, $11.50; Year 5, $9.50; Fully diluted EPS: Year 4, $9.60; Year 5, $8.00.

18-8 *a* Net income (corrected) $4,725,000; *b* (1) $7.78; (2) $5.02.

18-9 *b* (1) 9,500,000; (2) 10,500,000; *c* (1) $5.11; (2) $4.72.

18-10 *b* Total stockholders' equity, $5,100,000.

19-1 Pension expense: Year 4, $25,600; Year 5, $20,876.